Java Server Programming

Java EE7 (J2EE 1.7)

Black Book™

Authored by:

DT Editorial Services

Published by:

dreamtech PRESS

ISBN: 978-93-5119-417-0

Reprint: 2016

Printed at: *Durga Printo Graphics, Delhi*

Contents at a Glance

Bonus Chapters Available with the Book

Table of Contents

Bonus Chapters Available with the Book

Introduction

Congratulations on buying the *Java Server Programming Java EE 7 (J2EE 1.7) Black Book book*! This book endorses our continued commitment towards delivering quality IT books based on intensive research on the requirements of our readers. The book is the result of rich implementation of instructional acumen and technical precision of the authors and editors at Dreamtech Press; and promises to offer an affluent solution to students and IT professionals who want to outshine in the Java EE 7 domain. This book further extends our philosophy to present comprehensive and easily understandable reference material on emerging technologies. The book has been written considering the diverse audience of Java EE 7, and promises an exceptional learning experience by presenting relevant, appropriate, and real-life examples. In addition, the book also includes code snippets and executable applications to demonstrate the implementation of various concepts related to Java EE 7.

We've designed this book to grow with you, providing the reference material you need as you move towards software proficiency.

Java EE is no ordinary programming language. It inspires devotion, passion, exaltation, and eccentricity—not to mention exasperation and frustration. We hope that what Java EE has to offer will prove as irresistible to you as it has to so many other programmers.

Many companies are using Java EE to build applications that have more and more to do with cross-platform reliability. We've seen many major corporations making the gradual shift from C++ to Java to Java EE for in-house programming. Java EE's influence is spreading, and there's no sign of stopping it. With each new version, there's more power and depth to work with.

If you are passionate about working with programming challenges, you'll develop a taste for Java EE programming, because what you can do with this language is amazing. You'll see what we mean in page after page of this book.

The Audience

You must be wondering about the aims and objectives behind the release of Java EE 7 edition. This has been released focusing on the developer or IT manager working with server-side and Web-based enterprise Java applications. Therefore, *Java Server Programming Java EE 7 (J2EE 1.7) Black Book* serves you as an excellent guide in true sense—introducing the fast-changing world of today's Java Enterprise Edition (Java EE) APIs and various programming techniques related to it. The release of this book also offers one of the best available resources on the current version of the Java language used in enterprise development.

This book is equally beneficial for people who want to learn Java EE from scratch, or who are already involved in developing applications in Java EE 7. Therefore, *Java Server Programming Java EE 7 (J2EE 1.7) Black Book, Platinum Edition* serves as an excellent guide in true sense—introducing the fast-changing world of Java EE and various programming techniques related to it.

About this Book

Java Server Programming Java EE 7 (J2EE 1.7) Black Book provides a greater emphasis on reference aspects, and the presentation is expanded to reflect the demand for information beyond the description of language features and their immediate use.

The range of topics and coverage offered by this book is a superior mix of APIs; though some readers might quibble with the ordering of topics here, (it is hard to see why JDBC and Servlet begin the tour of Java EE). We know that Java EE 7 is the latest version of Java Platform, Enterprise Edition, which is several years old, and its APIs have grown by leaps and bounds. To cover the older material, the authors have been careful while highlighting what's new and improved. At each juncture, they have done a fine job of listing relevant APIs; because of which the book makes an excellent reference for everyday programming.

This book promises to increase your productivity by its exact presentation of Web and EJB deployment (using freeware Java deployment tools) and the Glassfish server Version 4.0, which is used for deploying components. The full tour of deployment descriptor options for Servlets and EJBs, as provided in the book, will also be appreciated by the working Java developers.

The ways to design truly scalable and maintainable enterprise systems with Java, combined with JSPs, Servlets, and EJBs, has been presented excellently in the book. This book also provides a discussion on software patterns (such as the Front Controller pattern), illustrated with real code. You can be the master of this important emerging technology with the help of the coverage of custom tag libraries; in addition to the evolving JSP Standard Tag Library (JSTL) from Sun and Apache.

This book promises to be an almost indispensable resource for any enterprise Java developer, due to its extensive coverage of today's rich and complex Java EE 7 platform, and practical focus on real-world design and deployment. Therefore, it will serve as both a reference and tutorial to the latest in high-end Java for your next large-scale project.

This book mainly covers the following:

- Java EE container architecture and runtime services related to it
- Web component development with Servlets 3.1 and JavaServer Pages 2.3
- Comprehensive coverage about business logic components with EJB 3.2, all inclusive of session bean and JPA
- SOA architecture, which works with Web services covering SOAP and WSDL.
- Struts 2, Spring 4.0, Java Server Faces 2.2, Hibernate 4.3, and Seam framework.
- Packaging, deploying, and running all Web and Enterprise applications on Glassfish Server Version 4.0.
- The People Management System project, which helps in handling HR operations for large organizations.

There are hundreds of topics covered in this book, and each of them is explained by applications showing how it works. This book is divided into separate and easily accessible topics, each addressing a different programming issue. The following are just a few of those topics:

- EJB 3.2
- JDBC 4.0
- Web containers
- Servlets 3.1
- JSP 2.3
- JSTL
- Struts 2

- JSF 2.2
- Web services
- XML
- JMX
- JavaMail
- JCA 1.7
- Spring 4.0
- Seam
- Hibernate 4.3

The Web tier technology chapters cover the components used in developing the presentation layer of a Java EE or stand-alone Web application:

- Java Servlet
- JavaServer Pages (JSP)
- JavaServer Pages Standard Tag Library (JSTL)
- JavaServer Faces
- Web application internationalization and localization

The Enterprise JavaBeans (EJB) technology chapters cover the components used to develop the Business logic of a Java EE application:

- Session beans
- Entity beans
- Message-driven beans
- JPA
- Hibernate

The platform services chapters cover the system services used by all the Java EE component technologies:

- Transactions
- Resource connections
- Security
- Java Message Service

Our sole intent has been to provide a book with a depth sufficient to make more than one reading rewarding to most programmers. Enjoy reading!

How to Use This Book

In this book, most of the code is tested with the Java Standard Edition 6 and 7 SDK, and the Glassfish server Version 4 providing support for the Java EE 7 platform. In few chapters, such as Hibernate, Seam, and Spring, you need some additional APIs to develop and run the applications.

Conventions

We have used standard conventions throughout this book. This section helps you get acquainted with these conventions to ensure a superior learning experience.

Listing 4.1 provides a sample web.xml file, which maps to a single servlet named FirstServlet (save this file in the `\FirstApp\WEB-INF` folder):

Listing 4.1: Displaying the Code for the web.xml File

```
<?xml version="1.0" encoding="UTF-8"?>

<web-app version="3.1" xmlns="http://xmlns.jcp.org/xml/ns/javaee"
xmlns:xsi="http://www.w3.org/2001/XMLSchema-instance"
xsi:schemaLocation="http://xmlns.jcp.org/xml/ns/javaee
   http://xmlns.jcp.org/xml/ns/javaee/web-app_3_1.xsd">

   <servlet>
         <servlet-name>FirstServlet</servlet-name>
         <servlet-class>FirstServlet</servlet-class>
   </servlet>
   <servlet-mapping>
         <servlet-name>FirstServlet</servlet-name>
         <url-pattern>/FirstServlet</url-pattern>
   </servlet-mapping>
   <session-config>
         <session-timeout>
               30
         </session-timeout>
   </session-config>
</web-app>
```

The reserved words, properties, methods, events, classes, interfaces, namespaces (used in the code snippets), exceptions, etc. are shown distinctly using a different font within the text.

Each figure has a caption to help you understand the figure better.

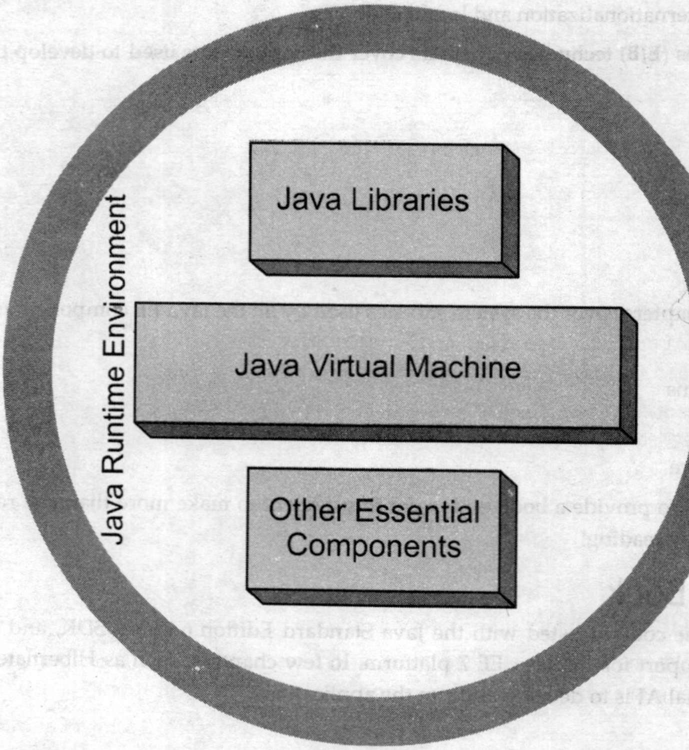

Figure 1.1: Displaying the Components of Java Runtime Environment

Notes are represented in the following format:

NOTE

It is recommended that the interface be as generic as possible to avoid changes at a later stage. As you know, all objects communicate with the interface and not the object itself; therefore, changes in the object and not the interface make the process relatively simple and quick.

The tables are numbered and are placed just below their references in the chapters, as shown below:

Table 2.1: Differences between the GET and POST Methods

Parameter	GET	POST
Transmission of request parameters	Transmits the request parameters in the form of a query string that is appended to the request URL.	Transmits the request parameters within the body of the request.
URL size	Limits you to a maximum of 256 characters in the URL, excluding the number of characters in the actual path.	Does not limit the size of the URL for submitting name/value pairs, as they are transferred in the header and not in the URL.
Purpose	Allows you to retrieve data.	Allows you to retrieve, save, or update data. It also allows you to order a product or send e-mail messages.
Caching ability	Considers the request as cacheable.	Does not consider the request to be cacheable.
Type of resource	Allows a user to access the static resources, such as HTML documents.	Allows a user to transfer the information according to the request made by the client. The POST method is used to transfer large and complex information to the server.

Other Resources

Java EE 7 comes with an immense amount of documentation—hundreds of books worth referring to. The documentations are hosted online, and you can access them using a Web browser. Of course, there are plenty of Web pages out there on Java EE 7. Here are a few:

- Oracle's Java EE 7 tutorial, http://docs.oracle.com/javaee/7/tutorial/doc/ Hibernate, http://hibernate.org/search/documentation/getting-started/
- Seam, http://docs.jboss.org/seam/snapshot/en-US/html/tutorial.html
- Spring framework, http://spring.io/guides/tutorials/web/4/

The code provided in the book will work on a single machine, provided it is networked (that is, it can access `http://localhost` through the local browser).

The Black Book Philosophy

"Complexity kills. It sucks the life out of developers, it makes products difficult to plan, build and test, it introduces security challenges, and it causes end-user and administrator frustration."

Ray Ozzie - Chief Software Architect at Microsoft Corporation

Whichever language or platform you might be learning or working on, being a prolific programmer and administrator, you are bound to face challenges, complications, complexities, and frustrations. We at Dreamtech Press realize this veracity seamlessly and ensure that our Black Book series comes as an accomplished and dexterous solution to these complexities. The unique structure of Black Books ensures that complex topics are chunked into appropriate sections and presented in a more comprehensible manner, employing diagrams, code, and real-life examples for further simplicity. In addition, Black Books ensure a learning path replete with adequate practice avenues of the concepts learned by means of code examples, listings, and executable programs and applications. Each Black Book is designed to grow with its readers, providing all the guidance and reference material they need as they move toward software proficiency. In summation, the Black Book philosophy extends beyond simple pedagogy and seeks to decipher the practical challenges imbibed in the professional roles of its readers, whether students or professionals – that is why we call it "Comprehensive Problem Solver"!

1

Java EE 7: An Overview

Java Enterprise Edition 7 (Java EE 7) is the latest Java platform to develop enterprise applications. Enterprise applications are applications that connect different business departments of an organization, such as Human Resource and Marketing, by using various types of user interfaces. In other words, enterprise applications are software applications that help an organization to manage its business activities. Enterprise applications can be accessed by the end users or partners of the organization through the Internet, intranet, or private networks.

The advancements in communication technology and the Internet have opened a whole new world of opportunities for business organizations. Moreover, with the growth of e-commerce, data has become a valuable asset for an organization. This change in the business environment and the increased importance of data has led to an information-based economy, which has forced many organizations to think for a solution for the smooth functioning of the most basic business practices. As a consequence, the need to simplify and restructure the implementation of business practices was felt, which in turn led to the development of Java EE.

Java EE is provided to Java programmers in the form of an integrated software package that supports a distributed computing architecture, provides definitions to package distributed components, and deploys these components. Java EE is targeted at large-scale business systems. The applications developed by using Java EE are partitioned into functional pieces, which help an organization to ensure scalability and easy maintenance of the applications. Java EE facilitates software deployment by providing standard interfaces and services. Interfaces define how various software modules interconnect with each other, and standard services define how different software modules communicate with each other in an application.

This book introduces you to the most sought after Java platform, i.e., Java EE 7. It explores the Java EE 7 platform, providing an in-depth view of its capabilities, and also introduces you to a wide range of Java EE 7 technologies. Moreover, it highlights the features and functionalities introduced in Java EE 7, which have changed the way enterprise application components are developed and configured in an enterprise application.

This chapter is divided into various sections that provide an overview of Java and Java EE 7. Section A, *Introducing Java*, deals with the history and evolution of Java and discusses the Java platform. Section B, *Enterprise Architecture*, discusses the types of enterprise architectures based on which an enterprise application is created. Section C, *Introducing the Java EE 7 Platform*, discusses Java EE 7, its features, and the various types of Java EE applications that can be developed. The next section, Section D, *Introducing the Servers for Java EE Applications*, discusses various Web and application servers used to deploy and execute Web and enterprise applications. The last section, Section E, *Snapshot of Java EE 7 Related Technologies*, provides an outline of Java EE 7 related technologies described in the book.

Section A: Introducing Java

Java is a platform-independent programming language used to create secure and robust applications that may run on a single computer or may be distributed among servers and clients over a network. Java features such as platform-independency and portability ensure that while developing Java EE enterprise applications, you do not face the problems related to hardware, network, and the operating system.

Now, let's trace the evolution of Java.

Evolution of Java

Before the advent of Java, C was an extremely popular language among programmers. It seemed to be the perfect programming language, combining the best elements of both low-level and high-level languages into a single programming language.

However, similar to the other programming languages, C too had its limitations. As programs written in C grew longer, they became more unwieldy and difficult to use. The reason for this was that there was no easy way to break a long C program into multiple self-contained compartments. This meant that the code in the first line of the program could interfere with the code in the last line, and the programmer had to keep the whole code in mind while writing the program.

Object Oriented Programming (OOP) provided a solution to the problem. With OOP, it is possible to break down long programs into semi-autonomous units. In other words, OOP introduced the motto of *divide and conquer*. That is, you could divide a program into easily conceptualized units, which could be combined to present the solution of a larger problem. Let's understand this with an example. Suppose you have a complex system to preserve food at low temperature, for which you perform various operations manually, such as monitoring the temperature of the food by using a thermometer. When the temperature reaches a certain high point, you start the compressor to circulate the coolant, and then start a fan to blow air over the cooling vanes. This system represents one way of preserving your food. However, there is another way as well: You can connect all these operations into an easily conceptualized unit and make them automatic, similar to a refrigerator. The larger process of preserving food is broken down into smaller processes, each of which is implemented independently. These smaller processes are:

- Monitoring the temperature of the food
- Starting the compressor when the temp reaches a specific point
- Starting a fan to blow air over the cooling vanes

When all these smaller processes are combined as one large process, you arrive at the actual solution of a refrigerator. Apart from breaking down a larger process into smaller processes, you should also note that the internal processing are hidden from your view, and all you have to do is put the food in the refrigerator and take it out when it has to be consumed. In other words, OOP also provides the abstraction feature to hide the complexity of a program or an application from its users.

Objects in OOP work similar to the small processes: they hide the programming details from the rest of the program and reduce the interdependencies that spring up in a long C program. They do this by setting up a well-defined and controllable interface that handles the connection between each object and the rest of the code. To understand the concept better, let's take an example. Suppose you have an object called *Screen,* which contains the details to handle all interactions with the screen. You can use this object in different ways depending on the purpose of using the object (in this case, the screen display). After creating the object, you can simply use the screen object instead of providing the code to handle the screen.

When the OOP feature was added to the C language, the language was renamed as C++. C++ allows programmers to deal with long programs and object oriented code. Apart from this, several other problems were solved as well. For example, supporting objects makes it easier for software manufacturers to provide a user a lot of prewritten, ready-to-use code. To create an object, you use a *class,* which serves as an object's type, similar to a variable referring to the variable type. Support for classes in the C++ language allows software manufacturers to include huge readymade class libraries that users can use to create objects easily. One of the most popular libraries of C++ classes is the Microsoft Foundation Class (MFC) library, which comes with Microsoft Visual C++.

When you write a Windows program in C, you need several pages of solid code just to display a blank window. However, by using a class in the MFC library, you can create the window of your choice easily, by creating an object of the window. The object already has built-in functionalities of the type of window you want to create, so all it takes to create the window is one line of code—the line where you create the new window object by using the selected class.

You can also use an MFC class as a *base class* for your classes, and add the functionality that you want to those classes, by using a process called *inheritance* in OOP. For example, suppose you want your window to display a menu bar. You can do this by *deriving* your own class from a plain MFC window and adding a menu bar to the class. In this way, you can build your own class just by adding a few lines of code to implement the classes that have already been created by Microsoft programmers. (You learn about OOP in depth in this book).

The introduction of class libraries and the concept of using objects were welcomed by Microsoft programmers, and C++ rapidly gained popularity. It seemed as though the perfect programming language had arrived. However, the programming environment itself was about to undergo a great change with the popularization of a new programming environment—the Internet. With the advent of the Internet, Java gained more popularity.

The first version of Java appeared in 1991, and was written in 18 months at Sun Microsystems. Java was not originally created as an Internet programming language. In fact, it was not even called *Java* but *Oak* in those days, and was used internally at Sun Microsystems.

Starting with Java

Before you start working with Java, you must get familiar with the underlying concepts of Java as a programming language. Java refers to a combination of the following four aspects:

- Java programming language
- Java Runtime Environment (JRE)
- Java Virtual Machine (JVM)
- Java platform

Let's discuss these in detail in the following sections.

Java Programming Language

Java programming language is an object oriented language. Its syntax is similar to the C++ language, but provides some advanced features, such as static typing of objects and a rigid system of exceptions, which require every method in the call stack to handle exceptions. Java fulfils the following primary objectives of an OOP language:

- Uses the object oriented methodology
- Allows the same program to be executed on multiple operating systems
- Contains built-in support to use computer networks
- Executes code securely from remote sources

Java is generally considered to be the most popular programming language today. It is also a widely used standard in enterprise programming.

Java Runtime Environment

JRE is also known as Java Runtime Environment, and is included in the Java Development Kit (JDK), which is a set of programming tools required to develop Java applications. JRE consists of Java libraries, JVM, and other components that are required to run Java applications, as shown in Figure 1.1:

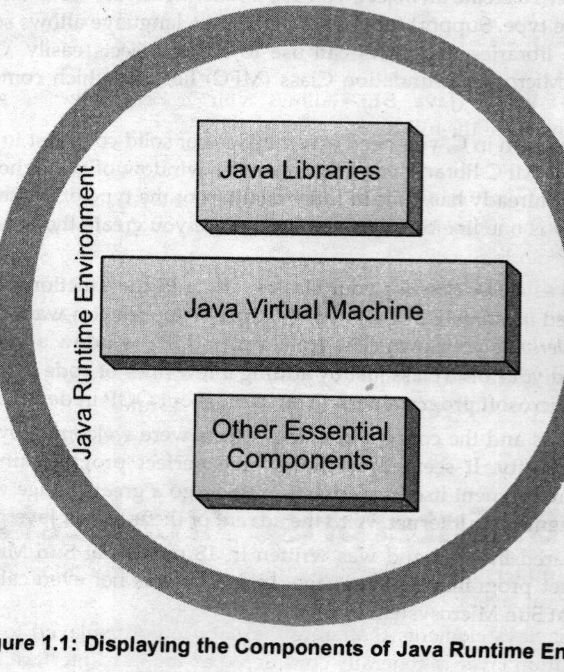

Figure 1.1: Displaying the Components of Java Runtime Environment

Java Virtual Machine

Java itself is implemented as JVM, which is the application that executes the Java program. In other words, a JVM installed on a computer allows you to run Java programs. Therefore, Java programs do not need to be self-sufficient and do not need all the machine-level code that runs on the computer. Instead, a Java program is first *compiled* and then translated into `bytecodes`. Then, JVM reads and interprets these bytecodes to run the program. You should note that when you run a Java applet on a Web page, you are actually running a bytecode file.

JVM ensures that Java programs include less code, because all the machine-level code to run the program is already on the target computer and does not need to be downloaded. To host Java on computers, Sun Microsystems only had to redefine JVM. As programs are stored in bytecode files, the programs can run on any computer that has an installed JVM.

Since Java programs are *interpreted* by JVM, that is, executed bytecode by bytecode, interpretation can be a slow process. It was mainly for this reason that Java 2 introduced the Just In Time (JIT) compiler, which is built into JVM. The JIT compiler reads the bytecodes in sections and compiles them interactively into machine language (that is, the whole Java program is not compiled at once because Java performs runtime checks on various sections of the code). In simple terms, this means that Java programs will run faster with the new JIT compiler.

Using bytecodes also ensures that Java programs are very compact, which makes them ideal to run over the Internet. Running such programs with JVM rather than downloading full programs has another advantage, i.e., security.

Java Platform

A platform in a computer system used to run applications created by using a programming language. For example, Sun Microsystems has provided the Java platform to run or execute Java programs or applications .In addition, Sun Microsystems provides JDK, which is used to build Web or enterprise applications in Java. For each platform, different JDKs are provided to build the required application. For example, an enterprise application in Java is developed by using Java EE SDK and is deployed as well as executed on the Java EE platform.

Over the years, the Java platform has evolved into three major editions, each addressing a distinct set of programming needs. These editions are:

- **Java Platform, Standard Edition (Java SE)**—Allows you to develop desktop and console-based applications. This edition consists of the following:
  - A runtime environment
  - A set of Application Programming Interfaces (APIs) to build a wide variety of applications comprising standalone applications, which can run on various platforms, such as Microsoft Windows, Linux, and Solaris
- **Java Platform, Enterprise Edition (Java EE)**—Allows you to build enterprise applications by using the convenient component-based approach of Java EE. In other words, various components, such as Web and EJB, help a Java developer to develop an enterprise application.
- **Java Platform, Micro Edition (Java ME)**—Enables you to build Java applications for micro-devices, which include handheld devices such as mobile phones, PDAs, and other similar devices with limited display and memory support.

Let's now explore enterprise architecture.

Section B: Enterprise Architecture

Enterprise architecture helps in understanding the structure of an enterprise application and can be broken down into three fundamental logical layers:

- **The presentation layer**—Displays elements that store the data to be displayed to users and collects data from the users. The presentation layer is generally considered as the user interface, which includes the part of the software that creates the controls required to design an interface for a user and validates the actions of the user.

- **The business logic layer**—Helps an application to work with and handle the processing of business logic. The logic of the application is implemented on the business layer.
- **The data storage and access layer**—Helps business applications to read and store data.

It is important to get acquainted with the concept of n-tier architecture whenever you design an enterprise application. You may be aware of the client/server system, which is based on the 2-tier architecture and has a clear separation between the data and the business logic. Apart from the two-tier architecture, the 3-tier architecture also provides separate layers for the presentation logic, the business logic, and the database. Thoug these architectural styles are quite common in current organizations, it is worth noting that they have emerged due to the advent of cheaper hardware platforms for clients, servers, and networking technologies.

Let's discuss these enterprise architecture types in detail in the following sections.

Exploring Enterprise Architecture Types

Java developers select a suitable enterprise architecture type for an application according to their and the application's requirements. Suppose you want to create an application in which the presentation layer needs to implement the business logic as well. In such a case, you can select the single-tier architecture.

You can design enterprise architecture in many ways; however, in this section, we discuss the following types of enterprise architectures:

- The single-tier architecture
- The 2-tier architecture
- The 3-tier architecture
- The n-tier architecture

Let's now discuss these different types of architectures in the following sections.

The Single-Tier Architecture

A single-tier architecture consists of the presentation logic, the business rules, and the data access layers—in a single computing architecture. Figure 1.2 shows the single-tier architecture:

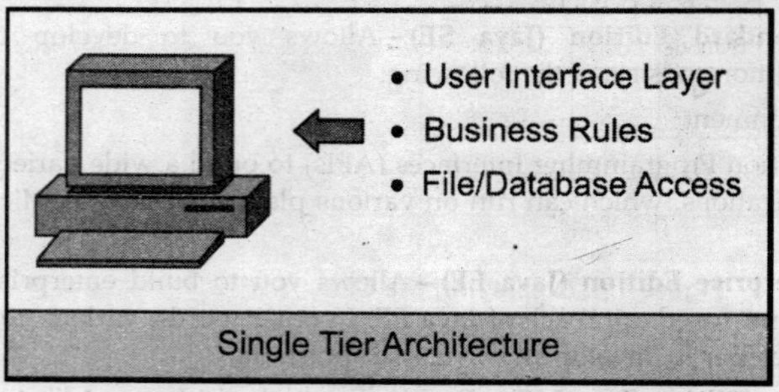

Figure 1.2: Displaying the Single-Tier Architecture

Applications created on the single-tier architecture are relatively easy to manage and implement data consistency, as data is stored at a single location. The only problem is that such applications cannot be scaled up to handle multiple users, and they do not provide an easy means of sharing data across an organization.

The 2-Tier Architecture

The 2-tier architecture separates the data access layer and the business logic layer. This type of architecture is generally data driven; with the application existing entirely on the local machine and the database deployed at a specific and secure location in an organization. This type of architecture is the traditional method of enterprise development. In a 2-tier application, the processing load is entrusted to the client, while the server simply controls the traffic between the application and the data access layers, as shown in Figure 1.3:

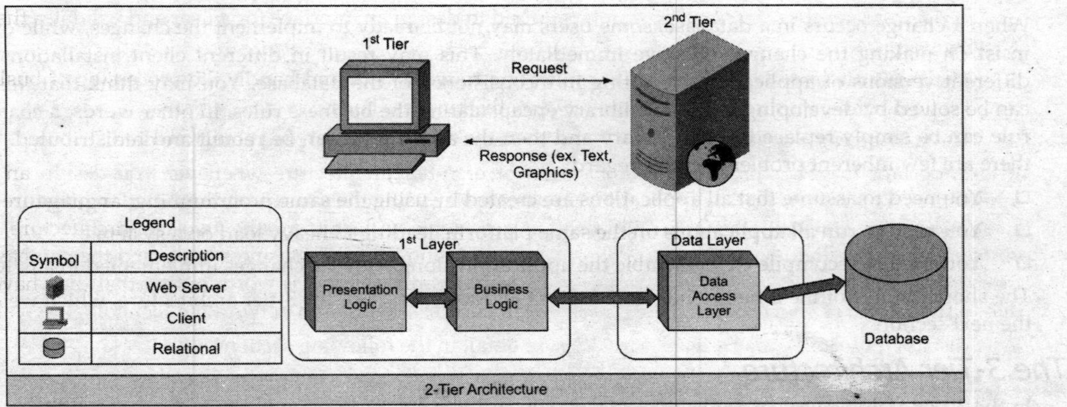

Figure 1.3: Displaying the 2-Tier Architecture

The main objective of the 2-tier architecture is to centralize the data so that multiple users can access a common database at a given time. Due to centralization of data, the load of executing an application is shared with the central database server. The 2-tier architecture is usually referred to as client/server, where a client communicates with a server, as shown in Figure 1.4:

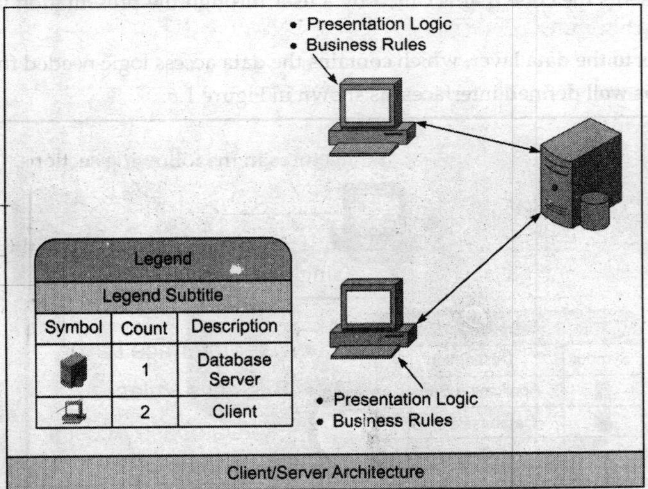

Figure 1.4: Displaying the Client/Server Architecture

The client and server communication in 2-tier architecture is established by providing implementations for the user interface, business logic, and data access layers. Figure 1.5 shows the layers of the 2-tier architecture:

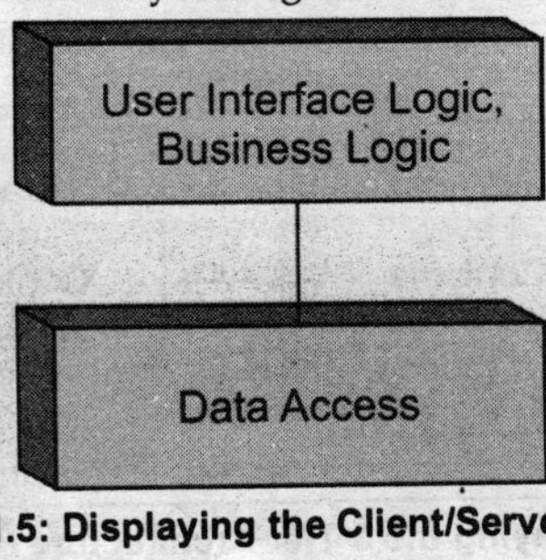

Figure 1.5: Displaying the Client/Server Layers

When a change occurs in a database, some users may not be ready to implement the changes, while others may insist on making the changes effective immediately. This may result in different client installations by using different versions of applications, resulting in inconsistency of the database. You may think that this problem can be solved by developing a reusable library encapsulating the business rules. In other words, a change in any rule can be simply replaced in that library and then the application can be rebuilt and redistributed. However, there are few inherent problems in this regard:

- You need to assume that all applications are created by using the same programming language
- You need to run all applications on the same platform, leading to heavy load on a system
- You need to recompile or reassemble the application along with the changes implemented in a new library

The shortcomings of the 2-tier architecture led to the development of the 3-tier architecture, which we discuss in the next section.

The 3-Tier Architecture

In the 3-tier architecture, an application is virtually split into three separate logical layers. The 3-tier architecture has the following layers:

- **First tier**—Refers to the presentation layer, which consists of a Graphical User Interface (GUI) to interact with a user.
- **Middle tier**—Refers to the business layer, which consists of the business logic for an application. The middle tier represents the code that is called by a user through the presentation layer to retrieve data from the data layer.
- **Third tier**—Refers to the data layer, which contains the data access logic needed for the application.

Each of these layers has well defined interfaces, as shown in Figure 1.6:

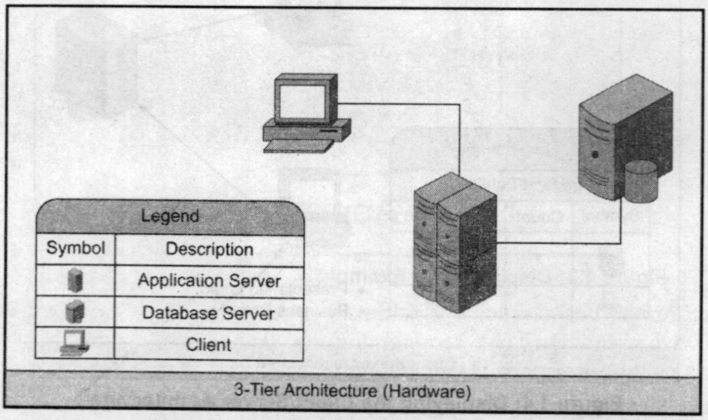

Figure 1.6: Displaying the 3-Tier Architecture (Hardware View)

Figure 1.7 shows the software view of the 3-tier architecture:

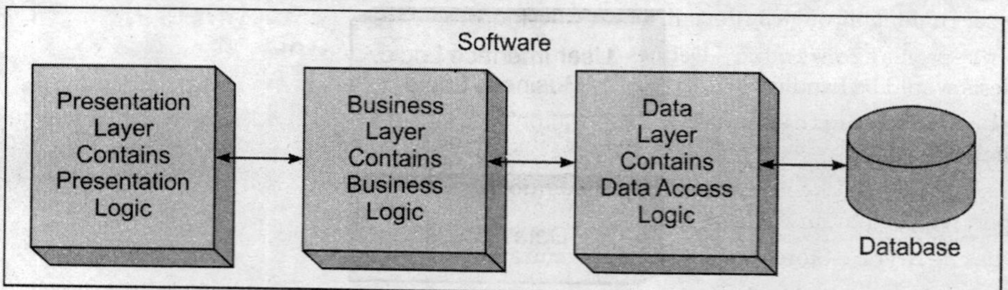

Figure 1.7: Displaying the 3-Tier Architecture (Software View)

As the business logic and the user interface are at different layers, it adds a lot of flexibility when designing an application in the 3-tier architecture, as compared to the 2-tier architecture. By using the 3-tier architecture, multiple user interfaces can be built and deployed without changing the application logic, provided this architecture defines a clear interface to the presentation layer.

The n-Tier Architecture

As the name suggests, there can be numerous layers in the n-tier architecture. Figure 1.8 shows an example of an n-tier architecture, which is formed by combining the 3-tier architecture with the 2-tier architecture:

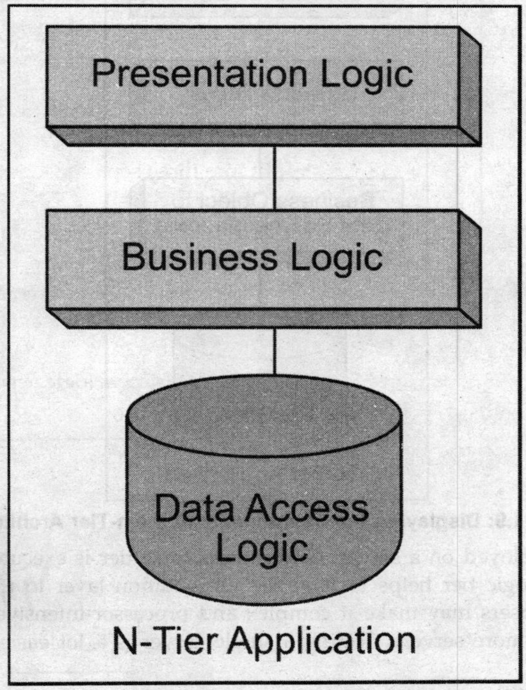

Figure 1.8: Displaying an Example of the n-Tier Architecture

In the n-tier architecture, the business logic is retrieved from the presentation layer. For example, a desktop application serves as a presentation layer representing the user interface, which can communicate with the business logic tier. It is no longer responsible for enforcing business rules or accessing databases.

The n-tier architecture supports various types of configurations to define the application layer. The n-tier architecture can be virtually distributed into the following components:

- **The user interface**—Refers to the interface between a user and a database. The interface may be a Web browser running through a firewall, a heavy desktop application, or even a wireless device.
- **The** `presentation logic`—Defines what will be displayed on the user interface and how a user's requests would be handled.
- **The** `business logic`—Models an application's business logic or rules, often by interacting with the application data.
- `Infrastructure services`—Provide additional functionalities, such as messaging and transactional support required by an application.
- **The** `data layer`—Stores the data of an organization.

Figure 1.9 shows the n-tier architecture:

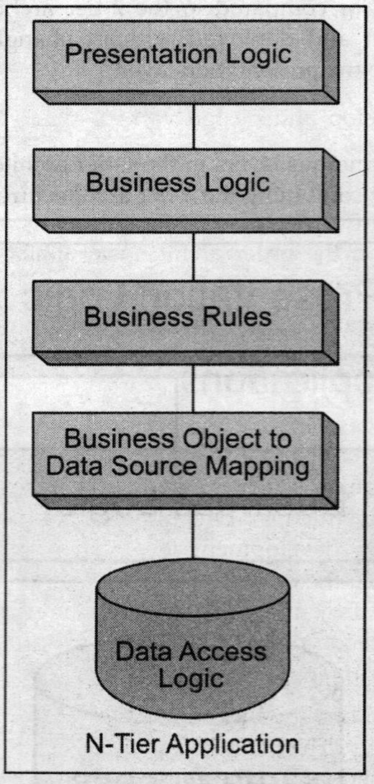

Figure 1.9: Displaying the Components of the n-Tier Architecture

In an application that is deployed on a server, the business logic tier is executed on the server instead of the workstation. The business logic tier helps to bind the presentation layer to the data layer. Accessing of the business logic by multiple users may make it complex and processor-intensive. When this happens, you can scale up the server or add more servers. Scaling a single server is a lot easier and cheaper than upgrading everyone's systems.

Applications based on the n-tier architecture can be employed by using the `Model-View-Controller (MVC) model`. In this model, the application/business logic (Controller) controls the flow of information between a database and a user interface. Therefore, the application design is based on three functional components: Model, View, and Controller, all interacting with each other.

To convert an n-tier application into an enterprise application, you need to extend the middle-tier by allowing multiple application objects that help to create an enterprise application. Each of these application objects must have an interface that allows communication within the application objects. Consequently, with enterprise architecture, you can have multiple applications that use a common set of components across an organization to perform a desired task. This enhances the standardization of business practices by creating a single set of business functions for the organization to access. In addition, in case business rules are changed or updated, changes are required to be made in one business object only. Changes are required in the interface and subsequent objects that access the interface in rare cases only.

NOTE

It is recommended that the interface be as generic as possible to avoid changes at a later stage. As you know, all objects communicate with the interface and not the object itself; therefore, changes in the object and not the interface make the process relatively simple and quick.

The n-tier architecture has the following advantages:

- **Improved maintainability**—Allows you to create applications that are easy to maintain

- **Consistency**—Allows you to develop enterprise applications consistent in terms of component designing and their association with the layer in the architecture where they are providing functionality
- **Interoperability**—Allows you to develop highly interoperable applications, which means that you can implement components in different layers to support different technologies and platforms
- **Flexibility**—Allows you to develop and design various types of components for different layers with flexibility
- **Scalability**—Allows you to add new components without affecting the performance of an existing application, which in turn make applications more scalable

The Java EE 6 architecture is based on the n-tier architecture, which makes it very easy to build enterprise applications based on two, three, or more application layers.

Enterprise applications should meet certain objectives, which we discuss in the next section.

Objectives of Enterprise Applications

Enterprise applications are developed based on various types of architectures described earlier. These enterprise applications should also meet certain objectives. For example, to maintain a competitive edge in the market in terms of technology and infrastructure, an organization needs to adopt new technologies to help manage business in an efficient and cost-effective manner. One place where these shifts in business practices have been felt most deeply is at the application development level. The funding and time allocated to application development is shrinking sharply, while the demand for developing solutions to complex business processes is increasing. The whole IT revolution is driven by the rapidly changing technological and economical landscape, which has created many new challenges for today's enterprise application developers.

The following objectives need to be taken into account while developing enterprise-based solutions:

- Ensuring that robust solutions and high-quality code are provided in an enterprise application so that it can perform the desired tasks efficiently. The main objective of considering robustness as a desired objective in an enterprise application is that users expect the application to be reliable and bug-free.
- Ensuring that scalability and performance is according to the expectations of the users of an enterprise application. It is expected that an enterprise application should provide sufficient scalability; i.e., the capability of an application to hold increased load with the specified resources. The scalability feature is an important consideration for Internet applications, as it is difficult to forecast the number of users and their behavior at any given time. The Java EE infrastructure helps you to meet the scalability objective. You should ensure that enterprise applications are designed so that their operations are efficiently performed in a cluster. In other words, meeting the scalability objective in enterprise applications typically requires deploying multiple server instances in a cluster. Clustering is a complex task that requires sophisticated application server functionality.
- Ensuring that object oriented design principles are implemented in an enterprise application. You know that good object oriented design practice is promoted with the use of design patterns, which serve as persistent solutions to common programming problems. Design patterns are technology and language independent. At present, a separate and distinct industry has evolved from where you can select numerous Java EE patterns.
- Avoiding complexity by finding the simplest way possible to avoid problems. While developing an enterprise application, avoid excessive complexity as this may create problems in executing the application's architecture. Sometimes, the availability of large number of components may tempt a designer to over-engineer Java EE solutions in an application, which may lead to great complexity and addition of irrelevant business requirements. However, remember that complexity only leads to additional cost throughout the software development life cycle, which can result in various problems. On the other hand, a thorough analysis should also be made while developing an enterprise application to ensure that the application does not have a naïve and simplistic view of the requirements.
- Ensuring that clear responsibility of each component is maintained in an enterprise application. While developing an enterprise application, you should ensure that maintenance is not hindered by tightly coupled components. Maintenance is the most expensive and crucial phase of the software development life

cycle process; therefore, you must consider the maintainability of software applications while designing enterprise application.

- Considering the implications of design decisions with the view to simplify the testing of an enterprise application. The main reason for simplifying the testing process of the enterprise application is because testing is an essential activity throughout the software life cycle.
- Ensuring that an enterprise application fits into an organization's long-term strategy, resulting in the promotion of reusability of the applications. Promoting reusability of applications also ensures that duplication of code is minimized (within and across various projects). Note that code reusability results from good object oriented design practice.

Depending on an enterprise application's business requirements, you may also need to meet the following objectives:

- Ensuring that an enterprise application provides support for multiple client types, such as Web applications and standalone Java GUIs, by using Swing and Java applets in an enterprise application. However, such support is often unnecessary, as Web browsers are being widely used nowadays, even for applications intended for use within an organization (ease of deployment is one of the major reasons for this support).
- Ensuring that an enterprise application is portable. The following concerns need to be considered while designing an enterprise application:
  - The extent of portability between resources, such as the databases used by an enterprise application
  - The extent of portability between application servers

None of the preceding objectives are especially new for enterprise developers; however, achieving them comprehensively and economically has always been crucial. A variety of technologies are available to address some of the preceding listed objectives.

Let's now discuss how these objectives are satisfied with the introduction of the Java EE platform, which is used to develop the Java enterprise applications.

Section C: Introducing the Java EE 7 Platform

Java EE 7 is the latest version of the Java platform used to develop robust, scalable, distributive, and secure enterprise level applications. The earlier versions of Java Platform for the enterprise applications were Java 2 Platform, Enterprise Edition (J2EE), followed by specific versions, such as J2EE 1.4. The term J2EE was renamed to Java EE in version 5. Therefore, the new version of this platform has been termed Java EE 7 (formally J2EE 1.7). The previous versions of Java Platform for the enterprise applications are still referred to as J2EE 1.3, J2EE 1.4, Java EE 5, and Java EE 6.

NOTE

Hereafter in this book, we use Java EE instead of J2EE.

J2EE 1.4 is a powerful platform; however, you may still find it difficult to start an application with the help of this platform. At times, even small enterprise applications need a lot of code, which needs to be reduced. You can reuse the code of an application in another application, which reduces time and effort. In addition, you can encapsulate the complexity of code by providing a set of APIs to the programmers. Therefore, the main objective of Java EE is to provide Java programmers a set of classes and interfaces that reduce development time and application complexity, thereby improving the performance of the application.

Java EE can also be defined as an extension to J2EE, and is capable of meeting the requirements of different users in an organization, such as customers, suppliers, and employees, by providing various functionalities and services. For example, Java EE focuses on making the development of enterprise applications easier by supporting annotations and `Plain Old Java Objects (POJOs)`, reducing the need of `Deployment Descriptors`, enhancing Web services, and supporting technologies, such as `Asynchronous JavaScript and XML (AJAX)`. In J2EE 1.4, programmers need to create Extensible Markup Language (XML) Deployment Descriptors to provide action mappings and execution flow to applications. However, with advances in the different versions of Java EE, the creation of XML Deployment Descriptors has become optional. Programmers can now use Java annotations in source files, which allow the Java EE application server to configure a Web or enterprise component at deployment or runtime. The annotations are used to embed program data that needs to be provided in a Deployment Descriptor.

Let's now explore the features and functionalities of the Java EE platform.

Exploring the Features of the Java EE Platform

So far, we have discussed the need of enterprise programming and briefly introduced the latest Java platform for enterprise development. There are several potential paths that you can take to implement enterprise solutions. Among these, there are two common paths, one being driven by Microsoft, with its new .NET suite, and the second offered by Sun Microsystems. You may know about the acquisition contract between Oracle and Sun Microsystems; therefore, Oracle is reviewing the product roadmap of Sun Microsystems. Apart from Microsoft and Sun, there are a host of other players in the field of enterprise solutions as well, such as BEA and International Business Machine (IBM). Although users have such a wide variety of choices, Java EE continues to be a popular choice with them. To understand the reasons for such popularity, let's look at some features of the Java EE platform. These include the following:

- Platform independence
- Managed objects
- Reusability
- Modularity
- Simplified Enterprise JavaBeans (EJB)
- Enhanced Web services
- Support for Web 2.0

Now, let's discuss these features in detail.

Platform Independence

Platform independence is perhaps the most important feature of Java EE. Today, a wide range of information is available in different formats, which is spread across multiple platforms. Therefore, it is essential to adopt a programming language that can function equally well across multiple platforms. For this purpose, Java EE is used in organizations as it is a platform-independent programming language.

Managed Objects

Java EE provides a managed environment for its components. Moreover, Java EE applications are container-centric. These two properties are very critical for building server-side applications, since they allow Java EE components to use the infrastructure services provided by Java EE servers.

Another important property of Java EE applications is the ease by which you can modify and control the behavior of the applications without changing their code. Initially, these properties may appear cumbersome; however, if you consider a large-scale application with numerous components interacting with each other to execute complex business processes, these properties are necessary to maintain such applications.

Reusability

Reusability of code is an important aspect of programming, especially when developing and maintaining multiple, complex applications. Reusability is also important when you need to develop applications that require frequent updates. One method to achieve reusability is to segregate an application into individual components. Another method is to use the concept of object orientation to encapsulate shared functionalities. Java uses both the methods because it is an object oriented language and provides the mechanism for code reusability.

Modularity

When you develop a complete server-side application, the program can become large and complex. As a best practice, you must break the application into various modules, with each module responsible for performing a specific task. This also makes the application much easier to maintain. Java EE provides the property to modularize an application by breaking it down into different tiers associated with individual tasks. These modules further interact with each other to execute the business logic.

Easier Development

Java EE has simplified the way in which components are created and configured. With the use of annotations, you need to write less code in Java EE applications, which further reduces the need for a Deployment Descriptor.

Simplified EJB

The use of POJOs has simplified EJB programming. To store the data of EJBs persistently in a database, a new persistence API has also been introduced in Java EE. In EJB 3, we do not need to create Remote and Home objects for the enterprise beans, and the use of Deployment Descriptors has also been reduced by the use of annotations and dependency injection. For more information about EJB, refer to *Chapter 13, Working with EJB 3.2*.

Enhanced Web Services

Java EE includes the latest Web service APIs that provide a simplified and enhanced approach to design, develop, test, and deploy Web services. For more information about Web Services, refer to *Chapter 19, Implementing SOA using Java Web Services*.

Support for Web 2.0

Web 2.0 is mainly associated with Web applications that allow you to share information, provide user-centered design, and interoperability on World Wide Web. Java EE allows you to develop applications supporting Web 2.0 with the help of technologies such as JavaServer Faces (JSF), JSP Standard Tag Library (JSTL), and AJAX. For more information about JSTL and JSF, refer to *Chapter 9, Implementing JavaServer Pages Standard Tag Library* 1.2 and *Chapter 11, Working with JavaServer Faces 2.2*.

Now that you have a brief knowledge about the general features of the Java EE platform, let's explore the new features introduced in the Java EE 7 platform.

Exploring the New Features of the Java EE 7 Platform

The Java EE 7 platform provides an environment for building enterprise applications by using a distributed multi-tiered application model. The Java EE 7 platform provides the following features:

- **Profiles and configurations**—Serve as a subset of the features of the Java EE 7 platform. Web Profile is introduced as a subset of the Java EE 7 platform, which includes the technologies used by Web application developers such as Glassfish Server 4.0. However, the enterprise technologies that would not be used by Web developers are not provided in the Web Profile. With the evolution of the Java EE 7 platform, the technologies that can be considered for pruning are identified. Pruning a technology refers to the process of adding the technology as an optional component in the Java EE platform instead of a required component. Java EE 7 now comes with an updated Web Profile with the inclusion of JAX-RS 2.0 to provide enhanced support for development of more robust web applications.
- **Enhanced extensibility on a Web tier**—Enables the use of third-party frameworks by self-registering. In other words, you can easily include and configure a third-party framework in a Web application by registering the framework with the Java EE platform. Earlier, Web developers used the third-party frameworks in their applications by registering them with the third-party vendors. They also needed to add or edit XML Deployment Descriptors. This was a tedious task; therefore, the Java EE 7 platform provides an enhanced approach to configure and register these frameworks. Apart from this, an improved context dependency injection helps in binding the Web tier with the transaction tier.
- **Use of annotations**—Allows you to use annotations to define Web components, such as servlets and servlet filters. In addition, the annotations used for dependency injection have been standardized, resulting in the addition of more portability to injectable classes across frameworks. Moreover, the requirements considered while packaging a Java EE application have been simplified as Java EE 7 allows you to directly add an enterprise bean to a Web ARchive (WAR) file. In other words, in Java EE 7, you do not need to create a Java ARchive (JAR) file while packaging an enterprise bean in an Enterprise ARchive (EAR) file.
- **Enhanced support for Web services**—Introduces the new versions of various technologies, such as Java Servlet 3.1, EJB 3.2, and Java API for RESTful Web services (JAX-RS 2.0). You learn more about the new features of each of these technologies in their related chapters in this book.

- **Enhanced support for development of dynamic scalable web applications**—Enables the development of robust dynamic Web applications by introducing support for HTML 5 features. The introduction of WebSockets helps in reducing the response time for bidirectional communication with the server while the support for JSON simplifies parsing of data at the client side. Apart from this, the JMS 2.0 API has been simplified to prune the process of developing messaging applications.
- **Enhancements to meet industry standards for enterprise applications**—Involves features such as improved security configuration, resource definition metadata, and database schema definition to incorporate cloud enhancements. Apart from this, support for batch processing has also been incorporated in Java EE 7. Improved and standardized concurrency APIs provide additional support to develop applications based on parallel processing.

After briefly discussing the new features of the Java EE 7 platform, let's explore the Java EE 7 platform in detail.

Exploring the Java EE 7 Platform

The Java EE 7 platform uses a distributed multi-tiered application model to develop enterprise applications. It provides a runtime infrastructure to manage and host applications. All runtime applications are located in the Java EE application server. Apart from the runtime infrastructure, a set of Java APIs are also provided by the Java EE 7 platform to build Java EE 7 applications. These APIs describe the programming model for Java EE applications.

Let's discuss the runtime infrastructure and Java EE 7 APIs in detail in the following sections.

The Runtime Infrastructure

The runtime infrastructure component includes numerous services to manage enterprise applications. The Java EE architecture provides a uniform way to access platform-level services through its runtime environment. These services include messaging, security, and distributed transactions management. Therefore, you can develop Java EE 7 applications that implement complex database transactions or even Java applets across a network.

The Java EE 7 APIs

In enterprise services, you need server access to run distributed applications. These enterprise services include transaction processing, multithreading, and database access. The Java EE architecture unifies access to such services in its enterprise service APIs. A Java EE 7 application can access these APIs through containers, such as Web and EJB.

Java Platform, Standard Edition (Java SE) SDK, provides core APIs to write Java EE components and development tools, and JVM. Java EE SDK uses some of the core APIs of Java SE SDK to provide a runtime environment to the Java EE application. The following are the noteworthy Java EE 7 APIs:

- Java Servlet 3.1
- JavaServer Pages (JSP) 2.3
- JavaServer Pages Standard Tag Library (JSTL) 1.2
- JavaServer Faces (JSF) 2.2
- Enterprise JavaBeans (EJB) 3.2
- Java Persistent API (JPA) 2.1
- Java Messaging API 2.0
- Java Transaction API (JTA) 1.2
- JavaMail 1.5
- Java EE Connector Architecture (JCA) 1.7
- Java API for RESTful Web Services (JAX-RS) 2.0
- Java API for XML Registries (JAXR) 1.0
- Java API for WebSocket 1.0
- Java API for JSON Processing (JSON-P) 1.0

Apart from the preceding Java EE 7 APIs, a few APIs of Java SE 7 are also used in developing Java EE 7 applications. The following is a list of the noteworthy Java EE 7 APIs included in Java SE 7:

- Java Database Connectivity API 4.0
- Java Naming Directory Interface (JNDI)
- JavaBeans Activation Framework (JAF) 1.1
- Java API for XML Processing (JAXP) 1.3
- Simple Object Access Protocol (SOAP) with Attachments API for Java
- Java API for XML Web Services (JAX-WS) 2.2
- Java Architecture for XML Binding (JAXB) 2.2
- Java Authentication and Authorization Services (JAAS)

Let's discuss each of the Java EE 7 APIs as well as the Java SE 7 APIs that are included in Java EE 7.

Java Servlet 3.1

The Java Servlet technology allows you to create HyperText Transfer Protocol (HTTP)-specific servlets, which extend the capabilities of the servers hosting applications. The servlets are accessed with the help of the request-response programming model. A new version of the Java Servlet technology is introduced in the Java EE 7 platform, i.e., Java Servlet 3.1, which has the following features:

- Provides asynchronous support; i.e., the ability to receive or send data to a client without blocking the data
- Provides the use of annotations for Web components instead of using Deployment Descriptors
- Provides support for Web framework pluggability, which simplifies the task of plugging different Web frameworks in a Web application, depending on the needs of a developer
- Provides enhancements to existing Servlet 2.5 APIs
- Provides support for non-blocking IO with introduction of new listeners and interface in the NIO API
- Provides support for a protocol upgrade such as HTTP

JavaServer Pages 2.3

The JSP technology lets you integrate Java code with Hypertext Markup Language (HTML) in a text-based document. A JSP page is a text-based document that contains:

- Static template data that can be represented in a text-based format, such as HTML, Wireless Markup Language (WML), or XML
- JSP elements that can be used to display dynamic content on a Web page

JavaServer Pages Standard Tag Library 1.2

JSTL 1.2 provides a set of standard tags that can be used in a JSP page by embedding Java code. JSTL includes various tags to control the flow of execution of an application, to support internationalization, and to access a database by using Structured Query Language (SQL). An application using JSTL tags can be deployed on any JSP container that supports the tags.

JavaServer Faces 2.2

JSF provides a component-based API that is used to build robust and rich user interfaces for Web applications. The components in JSF can be easily integrated to create a server-side user interface and can be developed in conjunction with Java Servlet and JSP. The JSF technology also simplifies the task of connecting user interface components to application data sources. In addition, this technology allows client-generated events to connect to event handlers on a server.

Initially, problems were faced in managing user interfaces and in developing business logic. However, the use of the JSF components has solved these problems. In JSF, you can utilize a user interface component along with the relevant renderer to produce presentation code for various devices. This implies that if a client's device changes, you only need to configure your system in such a manner that it uses the same renderer for the new client. You do not need to change the JSF code even if there is a change in the client's device. JavaServer Faces 2.2 has been enhanced with new features which include support for HTML 5 friendly markup, faces flows, and resource library contracts. For more information about JSF refer to *Chapter 11, Working with JavaServer Faces 2.2.*

Enterprise JavaBeans 3.2

EJB 3.2 is a component-based architecture used to develop, deploy, and manage reliable enterprise applications in production environments. An enterprise bean is a server-side piece of code with fields as well as methods to define the modules of the business logic.

An enterprise bean can be considered as a building block that can be used alone or with other enterprise beans to execute the business logic on the Java EE server conforming to the EJB architecture. Java EE provides all infrastructure services to EJB, such as Java Database Connectivity (JDBC), Java Naming Directory Interface (JNDI), Java Message Service (JMS), and Java Transaction APIs (JTA). The latest version of EJB in Java EE 7 is EJB 3.2. Compared to its previous version, EJB 3.1, the programming of EJB components has been made simpler in EJB 3.2. New features that have been incorporated in version 3.2 include support for developing asynchronous local session beans and use of non-persistent timers in EJB Lite. For more information about EJB 3.2, refer to *Chapter 13, Working with EJB 3.2.*

Java Persistent API 2.1

JPA is an API used to manage persistence and object relational mapping in the Java EE and Java SE environments. Java EE 7 introduces JPA 2.1, which incorporates new features, such as additional functionalities for object relational mapping and support for query language and validations. For more information about JPA, refer to *Chapter 14, Implementing Entities and Java Persistence API 2.1.*

Java Message Service API 2.0

Java EE application components can create, send, receive, and read messages by using the JMS API 2.0. The JMS API provides a common set of programming strategies and messaging concepts, which improves the productivity of programmers. JMS API 2.0 in Java EE 7 provides support for concurrent consumption of messages and distributed transactions. The term distributed transaction implies that a database establishes connections to Enterprise Information System (EIS) with the help of the Java EE connector architecture. Apart from this, the API includes the JMSContext object with combined features of a Connection and a Session; and a new interface AutoCloseable.

Java Transaction API 1.2

JTA is used to manage distributed transactions. JTA 1.2 specifies a standard Java interface for a transaction manager to interact with the resource manager, the application server, and with transactional applications. By default, the Java EE 7 architecture provides auto commit, which is used to manage commits and rollbacks of transactions. JTA also allows you to separate an entire transaction based on the database operations performed by an application.

JavaMail 1.5

Sometimes you may need to develop an enterprise application used to send e-mail notifications. You can develop such applications by using the JavaMail API provided by the Java EE platform. The JavaMail API provides a JavaMail service provider, which allows application components to send e-mail messages. The JavaMail API has the following two parts:

- **An application-level interface**—Allows application components to send e-mail messages from Microsoft Outlook or other mail clients
- **A service provider interface**—Helps application components to send e-mails messages from Gmail, Yahoo and other e-mail service providers

Java EE Connector Architecture 1.7

JCA is used to create resource adapters that help Java EE application components to interact with the resource manager of Enterprise Information Systems (EIS). Generally, JCA is used by Java EE tool vendors and system integrators to plug resource adapters to a Java EE product. There is a different resource adapter for each type of database or EIS, since a resource adapter is specific to its resource manager.

Java API for RESTful Web Services 2.0

The Java EE 7 platform provides a Java API to develop Web services based on the Representational State Transfer (REST) architectural style. A JAX-RS application is a Web application comprising classes and libraries that are packaged in a (WAR file. JAX-RS is introduced as an API in the Java EE 7 platform with new interfaces, classes and annotations and allows creation of Web client endpoints as annotated Plain Old Java Objects (POJOs).

Java API for XML Registries 1.0

The Java EE platform provides JAXR, which supports XML Registry and Repository standards and allows an application to access business as well as general purpose registries on the Internet.

Moreover, businesses can share information by using JAXR. XML-based groups on the Internet have developed schemas for particular kinds of XML documents, which can be used in business transactions. For example, two organizations may agree to use schemas for standard purchase and sales order forms. In this case, JAXR would facilitate both parties to access the order forms that are stored as schemas in a standard business registry.

Java API for WebSocket 1.0

The Java EE 7 platform includes the WebSocket API to support two-way communication among peers over single TCP connection. The endpoints are implemented as annotated Plain Old Java Objects (POJOs).

Java API for JSON Processing (JSON-P) 1.0

The Java EE 7 platform includes the JSON-P API to support parsing, transforming, and querying JSON data.

Java Database Connectivity API 4.0

The JDBC API helps to execute SQL commands from Java programs. You can use the JDBC API with enterprise beans, servlets, JSPs, and Java classes to interact with a database. The JDBC API contains application-level interfaces and service provider interfaces. Application-level interfaces are used by application components to access the database, while service provider interfaces help to associate the JDBC driver with the Java EE platform.

Java Naming Directory Interface

JNDI provides the functionality naming and directory services for various objects or resources available in the Java EE container. It provides the methods to perform standard directory operations, such as associating attributes with objects and searching for the objects in a Java EE application. Using JNDI, a Java EE application can store and retrieve any type of named Java objects.

JavaBeans Activation Framework 1.1

JAF is a standard extension to the Java platform providing standard services to identify the type of any arbitrary information, encapsulate access to the information, identify the operations available on it, and instantiate appropriate JavaBean components to perform these operations.

Java API for XML Processing 1.3

You can parse, transform, and validate an application with the help of JAXP. In addition, JAXP allows an application to query XML documents. This API is independent of XML processor implementation. JAXP is now a part of Java SE after the release of Java SE 7.

SOAP with Attachments API for Java

SAAJ is a low-level API used by SOAP handlers in JAX-WS to access SOAP messages. It enables you to develop and use messages that conform to the SOAP 1.1 and SOAP 1.2 specifications. The SAAJ API can be used to write SOAP messaging applications directly without using JAX-RPC or JAX-WS.

Java API for XML Web Services 2.2

The JAX-WS specification helps to create Web service endpoints and enables client components to access Web services. It also describes the deployment information of Web services and clients. The JAX-WS specification supports Web services that use JAXB. The JAXB API is used to bind XML data to Java objects.

Java Architecture for XML Binding 2.2

JAXB helps to bind an XML schema with a Java object in a simple and easy way. It helps in marshalling a Java content tree into XML instance documents, and vice versa. You can also create XML schema from Java objects by using JAXB, and use JAXB independently and with JAX-WS-based services where it is used to bind data for Web service messages.

Java Authentication and Authorization Services

JAAS is a Java-based standard Pluggable Authentication Module (PAM) framework that helps you to implement the authentication and authorization functionalities for one or multiple users in an application. This framework extends the Java platform security architecture to support user-based authorization. You should note that the JAAS framework has now been integrated with Java SE.

After getting a brief overview of the APIs of the Java EE 6 platform, let's now explore the Java EE 6 architecture.

Exploring the Architecture of Java EE 7

The architecture of Java EE 7 is based on the multi-tier distributed application model, in which the application logic is segregated into various application components. A Java EE 7 application contains these application components, which are installed on different machines based on the number of tiers in the Java EE environment.

Java EE applications can be 3-tier or 4-tier (as shown in Figure 1.10), but they are generally considered to be 3-tier as they are located over three different locations: the client machine, the Java EE server, and the database server. This implies that the application logic is divided at different machines, such as client, Java EE server, and database or legacy at the backend. Figure 1.10 shows the Java EE application model comprising both distributed and multi-tiered architectures:

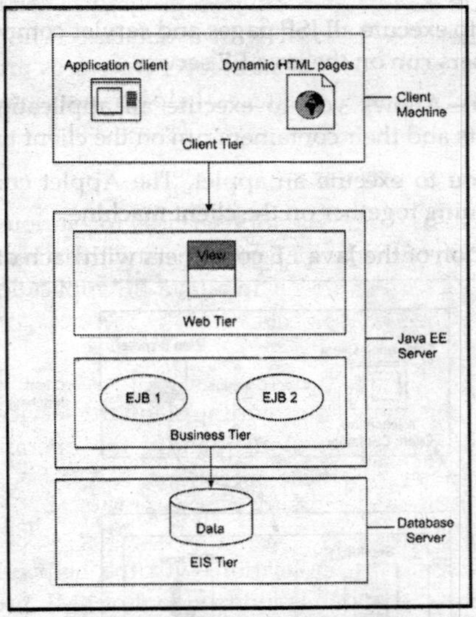

Figure 1.10: Displaying the Java EE Application Model

The 3-tier architecture and applications, shown in Figure 1.10, extend the standard 2-tier architecture.

You can see in Figure 1.10 that the middle tier that is represented by the Java EE server, has been divided into two tiers, the Web tier and the Business tier.

Let's now learn about the containers in Java EE 7.

Describing Java EE 7 Containers

Java EE applications are comparatively easy to write due to the architecture of Java EE, which is component-based and platform-independent. The Java EE server provides various services in the form of containers for every component type. You do not have to develop these services by yourself; and are therefore, free to concentrate on solving the problems related to the implementation of the business logic. Containers are a central theme in the Java EE architecture. The Web and business components are placed in the container of an application server. These components can access the Java EE 7 infrastructure service with the help of well-defined interfaces.

A Java EE container acts as a runtime interface between the application components and the low-level platform-specific functionality that support the components. Java EE containers provide deployment, management, and execution support for application components. A feature of the Java EE platform is its support for declarative programming. Many low-level details, such as persistence, security, and multithreading issues, are declaratively specified in Deployment Descriptor. Java EE containers provide services as well as an execution environment for the components to be deployed on the server.

Different application components are installed in their respective containers during deployment; these containers act as interfaces between the components and the low-level platform-specific functionality that support the components.

Let's now discuss Java EE 7 container types and their architecture.

Container Types

During the deployment of a Java EE application, the components of the application are installed in the Java EE containers available in the Java EE server. The Java EE server is used to execute the application, which contains EJB and Web components. Java EE containers can be categorized as follows:

- **EJB container**—Allows you to execute all enterprise beans for a Java EE application. Enterprise beans and their containers run on the Java EE server.
- **Web container**—Allows you to execute all JSP pages and servlet components for a Java EE application. Web components and their containers run on the Java EE server.
- **Application client container**—Allows you to execute all application client components for a Java EE application. Application clients and their containers run on the client machine.
- **Applet container**—Allows you to execute an applet. The Applet container is a combination of the Web browser and Java Plug-in running together on the client machine.

Figure 1.11 shows the communication of the Java EE containers with each other:

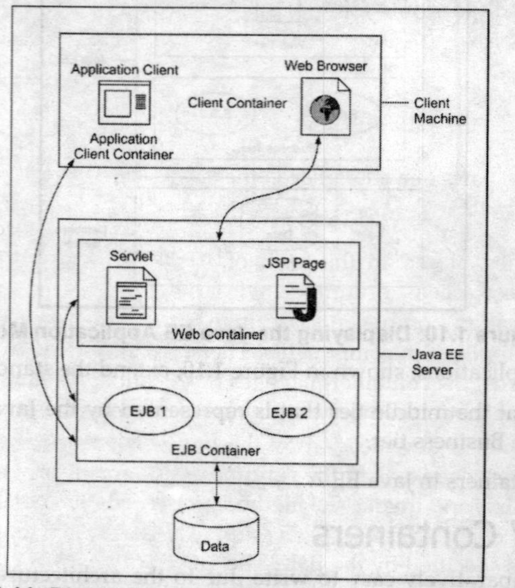

Figure 1.11: Displaying Java EE Components and Containers

Figure 1.11 shows the flow of communication among various the Java EE components and containers. For example, an application client located in the application client container can communicate with the EJB container to access the EJB resource.

Java EE 7 Container Architecture

You must be aware by now that a container is an interface between a component and low-level platform functionality that supports the component. The architecture of a Java EE container includes different components, such as JSP, servlets, and EJBs. An archive file is used to package these components, which also includes different Deployment Descriptors.

Figure 1.12 shows the architecture of a Java EE container:

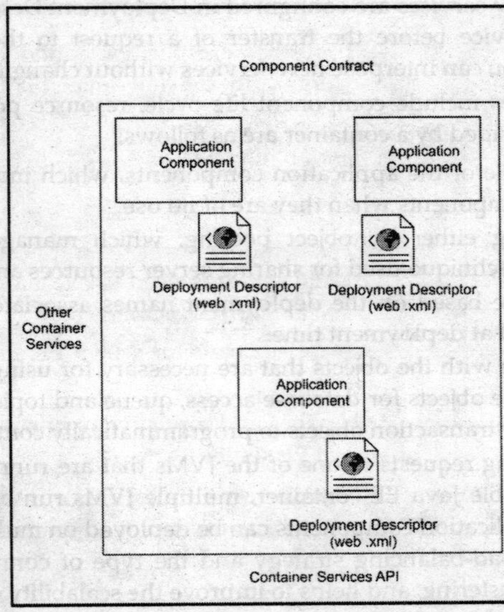

Figure 1.12: Displaying the Java EE Container Architecture

The Java EE container itself is divided into four parts:

- Component contract
- Container service APIs
- Declarative services
- Other container services

Let's now briefly explain these parts of a container in the following sections.

Component Contract

Component contracts are rules, stored in the form of APIs, which application components must extend or implement. A Java EE container acts as a runtime environment to manage application components. At runtime, the instances of these application components are invoked within the JVM of the container. The container manages the life cycle of the application components. Therefore, they have to abide by certain contracts specified by the container. In other words, the container manages the location, instantiation, pooling, initialization, service invocation, and removal of application components by using the component contracts.

For example, suppose an applet is downloaded by the browser and instantiated and initialized in JVM of the browser. In other words, the applet exists in the runtime environment provided by JVM of the browser. As the container has to create, initialize, and invoke the methods on application components, they have to implement or extend certain Java interfaces or classes. Let's suppose that a Java applet is required to extend the `java.applet.Applet` class specified by the JDK. The `init()`, `start()`, `stop()`, and `destroy()` methods control the life cycle of the applet and are present only in the `java.applet.Applet` class. If the applet does not extend this class, JVM cannot call these methods.

Container Services APIs

The container provides APIs and protocols that all application components need to use by extending or implementing them. This is how you can use service APIs, such as JDBC, JTS, JNDI, and JMS, in the container. All these APIs specified in the Java EE platform are provided as a view by the container.

Declarative Services

The Java EE architecture allows you to use Deployment Descriptors to declare application components. These Deployment Descriptors provide services to application components and simplify application programming by allowing components and applications to be customized at packaging and deployment time. In addition, the components can use the required resources during the packaging and deploying of the application. Various elements used to customize Java EE 7 services are configured in Deployment Descriptor, which allows a Java EE container to interpose the new service before the transfer of a request to the application component. The advantage of this approach is that you can interpose new services without changing the application component.

Examples of other container services include component life cycle, resource pooling, garbage collection, and clustering. The runtime services provided by a container are as follows:

- Managing the complete life cycle of the application components, which includes creation and pooling, or destroying of the application components when they are of no use.
- Implementing resource pooling either by object pooling, which manages short lived objects, or by connection pooling, which is a technique used for sharing server resources among clients.
- Populating the JNDI namespace based on the deployment names associated with EJB components. This information is typically supplied at deployment time.
- Populating the JNDI namespace with the objects that are necessary for using container service APIs. Some of the objects include data source objects for database access, queue and topic connection factories to obtain connections to the JMS, and user transaction objects to programmatically control transactions.
- Distributing the load of incoming requests to one of the JVMs that are running on various machines. You should note that in a distributable Java EE container, multiple JVMs run on one or more host machines. Consequently, in this setup, application components can be deployed on multiple JVMs. The distribution of load depends on the type of load-balancing strategy and the type of component in use. The process of distributing load is known as clustering, and helps to improve the scalability of applications.

Let's now understand the process of developing a Java EE 7 application.

Developing Java EE 7 Applications

The development of Java EE 7 applications is governed by various Java EE specifications. In addition, before discussing the development of Java EE 7 applications, you need to know about the Java EE technologies, such as JAX-RS 2.0, Java Servlet 3.1, and JSTL 1.2. These Java EE 7 technologies can be categorized as follows:

- Web services technologies:
  - Enterprise Web Services 1.3
  - Java API for RESTful Services (JAX-RS) 2.0
  - Java API for XML-based Web Services (JAX-WS) 2.2
  - Java API for XML-based RPC 1.1
  - Java Architecture for XML Binding (JAXB) 2.2
  - Java APIs for XML Messaging 1.3
  - Java API for XML Registries (JAXR) 1.0
  - Web Services Metadata for Java Platform
- Web application technologies:
  - Java Servlet 3.1
  - JavaServer Pages 2.3
  - JavaServer Faces 2.2

- JavaServer Pages Standard Tag Library 1.2
- Enterprise application technologies:
  - Context and Dependency Injection for Java (Web Beans 1.1)
  - Dependency Injection for Java 1.0
  - Bean Validation 1.1
  - Enterprise JavaBeans 3.2
  - Java EE Connector Architecture 1.7
  - Common Annotations for Java Platform 1.1
  - Java Message Service API 2.0
  - Java Persistence API 2.1
  - Java Transaction API 1.2
  - JavaMail 1.5
- Management and security technologies:
  - Java Authentication Service Provider Interface for Containers
  - Java EE Application Deployment 1.2
  - Java EE Management 1.1
  - Java Authorization Contract for Containers 1.3
- Java EE related specifications in Java SE:
  - Java API for XML Processing (JAXP) 1.3
  - Java Database Connectivity 4.0
  - Java Management Extensions (JMX) 2.0
  - JavaBeans Activation Framework (JAF) 1.1
  - Streaming API for XML (StAX) 1.0

In the following sections, we explore the possible architectures of Java EE 7 applications, look at some guidelines regarding application development and deployment roles, and finally, describe the application development process in detail.

Probable Java EE Application Architectures

Before moving ahead to discuss the development of Java EE applications, let's briefly review some architectures that you can use to develop Java EE 7 applications. For example, you can use Applet to create a user interface, JSP to implement business logic, and a database as backend to store the user data. In other words, this section helps you to learn how different technologies can be used to build the architecture of various Java EE applications. The following are the various combinations of Java EE application architecture:

- **Applet client with JSP and database**—Represents the Java EE application architecture in which the Java applet resides at the presentation tier (client end) and communicates with the business tier. The business logic is implemented on JSP pages, and JDBC is used at the data access tier, as shown in Figure 1.13:

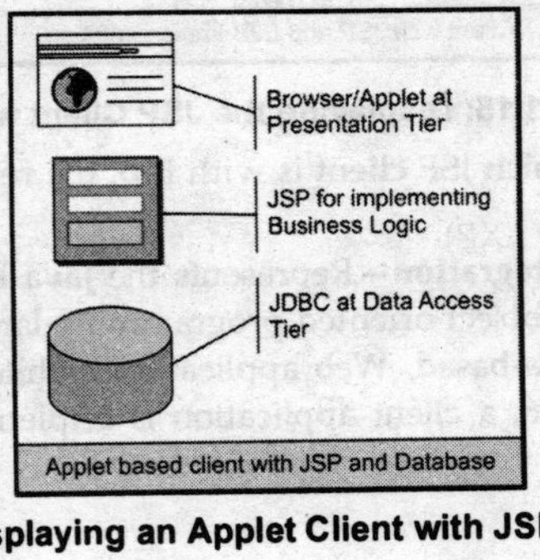

Figure 1.13: Displaying an Applet Client with JSP and Database

The Java applet provides an interactive and dynamic user interface within a Web page and accesses additional content from JSPs. In addition, JSPs access data from a database by using the JDBC API.

- **Application client with EJB** – Represents the Java EE application architecture in which an application client comprises the presentation tier, which communicates with the EJBs residing at the business tier. Figure 1.14 shows the Java EE application architecture in which the application client is used with EJB:

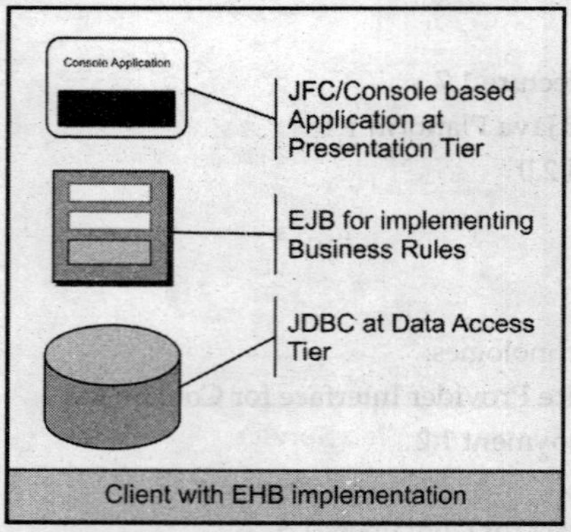

Figure 1.14: Displaying an Application Client with EJB

As shown in Figure 1.14, the business logic is implemented with the help of EJBs that run on separate machines.

- **JSP client with EJB** – Represents the Java EE application architecture in which JSP works on the Web tier to communicate with the business tier in response to a client's requests. Figure 1.15 shows the Java EE application architecture in which JSP is at the client end and business logic is implemented by EJBs:

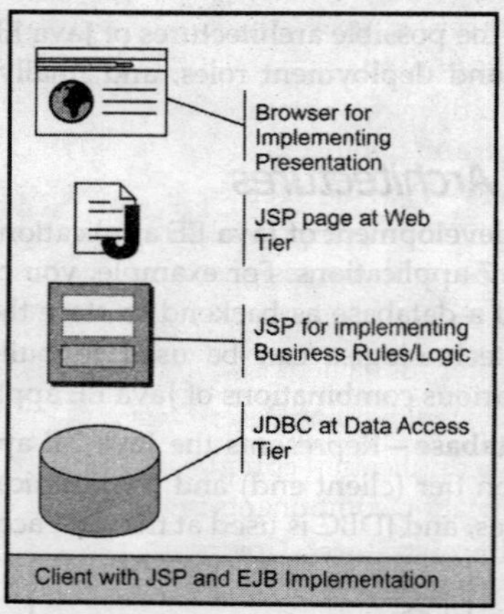

Figure 1.15: Displaying the JSP Client with EJB

In the Java EE architecture in which JSP client is with EJB, the response is generated as a Web page and is sent to the client's Web browser.

- **Web services for application integration** – Represents the Java EE application architecture in which Web components are implemented in object oriented programming languages other than Java, such as C#. Note that even though Java EE is Java-based, Web application architecture is not limited to Java components only. For example, in Figure 1.16, a client application is implemented in C# to access data from a Web service implemented in Java:

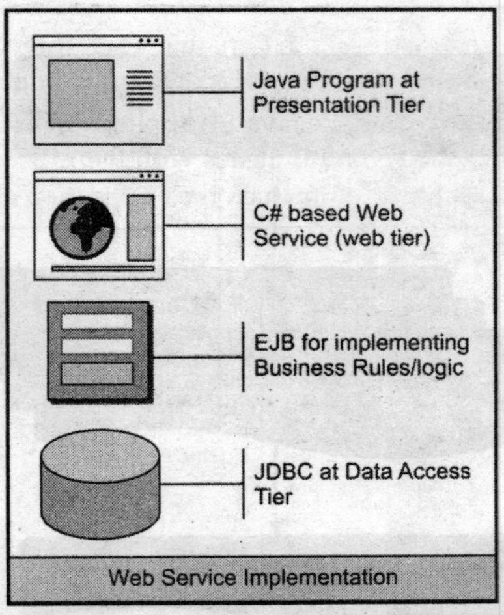

Figure 1.16: Displaying Web Services for Application Integration

After exploring different Java EE application architectures, let's now describe the role of different people in developing a Java EE application.

Application Development and Deployment Roles

Different people play different roles in the development of a Java EE application. These roles are defined according to the Java EE specification. The reusable modules of the application help to divide the development and deployment processes of the application into distinct roles, which are as follows:

- **Java EE product providers**—Design and provide the Java EE platform, APIs, and other features in the Java EE specification. Product providers are the third party vendors that provide the operating system, the database system, the application server, or Web server. These products implement the Java EE platform according to the Java EE 7 specification.
- **Tool providers**—Provide tools to develop, assemble, and deploy Java EE applications, which are used by component providers, assemblers, and deployers.
- **Application component providers**—Provide Web components, EJBs, applets, or application clients for use in Java EE applications. The application component providers design the HTML documents and develop Web or EJB components. The people who are assigned this role can perform the following tasks:
  - Write and compile the source code
  - Specify a Deployment Descriptor for a client
  - Bundle the compiled files and Deployment Descriptor for application deployment
- **Application assemblers**—Receive application components from component providers, specify Deployment Descriptor, and package the application components into a Java EE application.
- **Application deployers and administrators**—Configure as well as deploy Java EE 7 applications and manage the environment on which the Java EE 7 applications run. The duties of an application deployer include setting transaction controls and security attributes, and specifying connections to databases.

Let's now move ahead and explore the application development process.

Application Development Process

The Java EE specification describes the application development process in certain predefined steps, as shown in Figure 1.17:

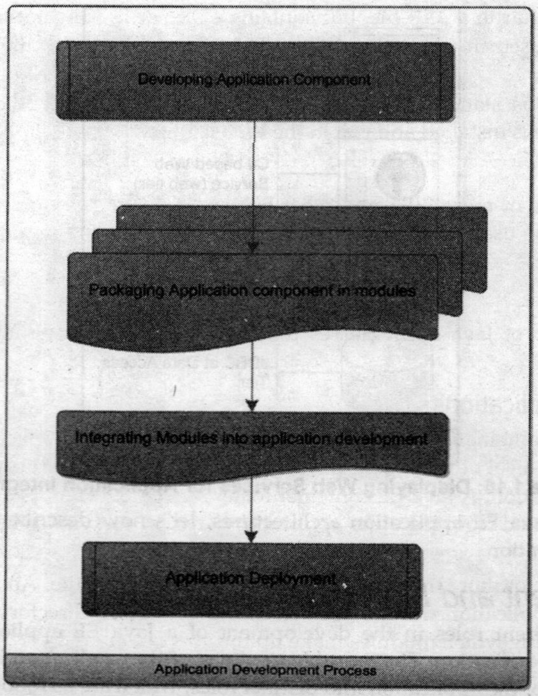

Figure 1.17: Displaying Java EE Application Development Process

As Figure 1.17 shows, you first need to model the business rules in the form of application components and then package the application components into modules. The multiple modules are then integrated into Java EE applications, and, finally, the packaged application is deployed and installed on the Java EE platform application server(s).

Let's now understand the preceding steps in detail.

Developing the Application Component

In Java EE, the development process involves dividing the entire application into modules, and modules into application components. This ensures efficient resource utilization as well as ease in the development of the application. After all the components have been developed, they are integrated to make a module. These modules are further integrated to create the final application. The development of different components, such as servlets, JSPs, and EJBs, has been described in more detail in the respective chapters of this book.

Packaging Application Components into Modules

Application components of the same type are packaged into a module. A Deployment Descriptor describes the structure of each module. You can have three different types of modules in an application:

- The Web module
- The EJB module
- The Client module

The Web Module

A Web module represents a Web application. Assembling servlets, JSP files, and static content such as HTML pages into a single deployable unit creates a Web module. A Web module contains the following components:

- One or more servlets, JSP files, and HTML files
- A Deployment Descriptor, stored in an (XML) file

- A WAR file that is similar to a `JAR` file, but contains a `WEB-INF` directory. The `web.xml` file configures the Web components used in the Web module. This file also specifies the runtime behavior of the Web components.

Web modules are created as standalone applications, or combined with other modules to create Java EE applications. A Web module is installed and run in the Web container of an Application server.

The EJB Module

An EJB module contains one or more EJBs, and other helper classes and resources. Extensive use of annotations in EJB 3.0 has eliminated the use of Deployment Descriptors, which were required earlier when working with previous versions of Java EE.

The Client Module

A client module is a group of Java client classes that can be directly accessed by a client. These classes are packaged into JAR files.

Packaging Modules into Applications

A Java EE application is a combination of one or more EJB JAR files, Web application `WAR` files, and application client `JAR` files. The highest level of packaging (EAR-based packaging) is performed when one or more modules are packaged into an application. A Java EE container loads each application by using a different class-loader so that each application is isolated from the other applications. This allows multiple Java EE applications to coexist within one Java EE container.

In a Java EE application, one or more modules are composed into an `EAR` file. An EAR file is similar to a JAR file, except that it contains an application.xml file (located in the `META-INF` directory). The `application.xml` file provides a means of specifying which modules make up the application.

A sample composition of modules is shown in Figure 1.18:

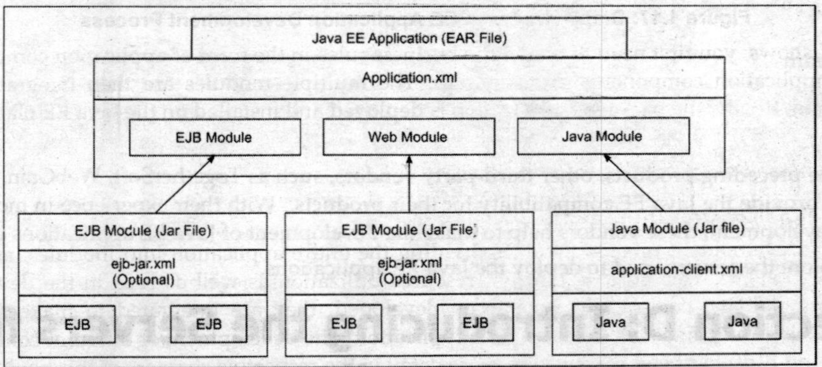

Figure 1.18: Displaying the Composition of Modules into Applications

You can package a Java EE application into the EAR file by using the JAR command. In other words, you should package all the files in the EAR file that can be deployed on the Java EE application server. Any Java EE application package should contain Java EE modules and the application Deployment Descriptor.

Deploying the Application

When you deploy a Java EE application, you install and configure the packaged modules onto a Java EE platform. The steps involved in deploying a Java EE application are as follows:

- **Installing the application**—Allows you to copy EAR files on the application server. During the deployment of the EAR file on the application server, additional implementation classes are generated with the help of a container, and finally the application is installed on the server.
- **Configuring the application**—Allows you to customize applications with application server-specific information.

Let's now discuss a few compatible products for the Java EE platform.

Listing the Compatible Products for the Java EE Platform

Every Java EE technology must have an associated compatibility test suite (CTS), which verifies that a product correctly implements the standards required for delivering secure, robust, and scalable applications. For example, a servlet container must use HTTP posted form variables provided by the `HttpServletRequest` object, which is passed to the servlet. The test for this condition would be to post variables to a servlet and verify that the servlet receives all the variables with the correct values.

Sun Microsystems requires every technology that supports the Java EE platform and its specifications to pass the corresponding test suite. The tests also verify correct interoperation of the Java EE technologies, as specified by the Java EE specification.

Some of the products compatible with the Java EE platform are as follows:

- Allaire
- ATG
- Bea Systems
- Borland
- Computer Associates
- Fujitsu
- Hitachi
- HP
- IBM
- IONA
- iPlanet
- Macromedia
- NEC
- Oracle
- Pramati
- SilverStream
- Sybase
- Talarian
- Trifork

Apart from the preceding products, other third-party vendors, such as TogetherSoft, WebGain, and Borland, are committed to provide the Java EE compatibility for their products. With their experience in modeling and rapid application development, these vendors help to make the development of Java EE applications easy and quick.

Let's now explore the servers used to deploy the Java EE applications.

Section D: Introducing the Servers for Java EE Applications

Depending on the application type, a developer can select the appropriate server for an application. For example, if the developer wants to deploy a Web application, the Tomcat server or the glassfish application server can be used. This section introduces the servers that can be used for Web or enterprise Java applications, which are of two types:

- Web servers
- Application servers

Note that the selection of a server depends on the type of application. A Web application is deployed on a Web server; however, an enterprise application is deployed on an application server.

Let's now briefly discuss these servers in the following sections.

Introducing Web Servers

A Web server is a computer or virtual machine used to run Web applications. The main purpose of the Web server is to provide Web pages to clients. In the case of Web servers, a client uses a Web browser to make an HTTP request for a specific resource. You can deploy and run Java Web applications on the Tomcat server, which is an open source Web server introduced by Apache. The latest version of the Tomcat server is Tomcat 6.0. You can download the Tomcat server from the Tomcat website or using the http://tomcat.apache.org/ link, and install it on your computer. However, before installing the Tomcat server, you must ensure that Java is also installed on the computer. By default, the Tomcat server uses port 8080 to run Web applications. After installing Tomcat, you can start or stop the Tomcat server by using its Windows service installed on your computer.

Introducing Application Servers

An application server is a server program that provides the business logic for an application. In other words, the application server provides a GUI to run three-tier applications. The application server acts similar to an extended virtual machine used to run applications and handle database transactions. In Java Platform, the term application server sometimes refers to the Java EE platform. The following are some noteworthy application servers used to deploy Java EE applications:

- The WebLogic application server
- The WebSphere application server
- The JBoss application server
- The Glassfish Application server

NOTE

In this book, we use the Glassfish Application server to run both Web and enterprise applications.

Let's explore each of these application servers in detail.

The WebLogic Application Server

The WebLogic application server, owned by Oracle (originally BEA Systems), serves as the server software application that runs on the middle tier. It is the leading online transaction processing platform used to connect various users in a distributed computing environment. The WebLogic application server is based on the Java EE platform and includes connectors so that a client can interoperate with various server applications and EJB components. The WebLogic application server provides the functionality of resource pooling and connection sharing to developers.

The WebSphere Application Server

The WebSphere application server, owned by IBM, is built by using open standards, such as Java EE, XML, and Web Services. It works with various Web servers, such as Apache HTTP Server, Netscape Enterprise Server, and Microsoft Internet Information Services. The latest WebSphere application server, version 7, has the following features:

- Provides flexible management capabilities for various WebSphere application server-based editions
- Offers the facility of managing application artifacts, irrespective of the packaging and programming models
- Simplifies the process of updating the configurations of an application with the help of a property file

The JBoss Application Server

The JBoss application server, owned by JBoss, is an open source Java EE-based application server. It allows you to package, deploy, and run various Java EE applications developed by using Java EE related technologies, such as EJB, JSP, JSF, and Hibernate. JBoss AS 5.1 is the latest version of the JBoss application server and can operate as a Java EE 7 application server.

The Glassfish Application Server

The Glassfish application server is a platform for server-side applications and Web services. It is developed as the Glassfish open source project and is also known as Sun Java System Application Server. Glassfish application server version 4 is used to package, deploy, and run Java EE 7 applications.

The server used to run applications in this book is Glassfish Server 4.0. Therefore, ensure that the Glassfish server 4.0 is installed on your computer before running the applications of this book. The process of downloading and installing Glassfish server 4.0 is discussed in *Appendix B, Installing Java EE 7 SDK*.

This ends the discussion on the servers used to package, deploy, and run Java EE 7 applications. Let's now briefly explore all the Java EE 7 related technologies that has been discussed in the succeeding chapters of this book.

Section E: Snapshot of Java EE Related Technologies

Java EE is a set of coordinated technologies that reduces the complexity of developing, deploying, and managing multi-tier, server-centric enterprise applications. These technologies help to build stable and secure Web and enterprise applications. This book discusses the following Java EE related technologies, which are used to create, deploy, and manage enterprise applications:

- Java Database Connectivity
- Java Servlet
- JSP
- JavaServer Faces
- JavaMail
- Enterprise JavaBeans
- Hibernate
- Seam
- Java Connector Architecture
- Web Services
- Struts
- Spring
- JAAS
- AJAX

Now let's discuss each of these technologies in detail.

Java Database Connectivity

The JDBC technology helps establish connections between Java applications and databases such Oracle, MySQL, and MS SQL Server 2005. Many Web or enterprise applications need to interact with databases to store client-specific information. The JDBC technology provides the JDBC API, which is implemented in Java-based applications to enable the applications to access data from databases.

For example, large organizations have numerous chunks of employee and client information. These organizations need to store the information in a database so that the information can be managed, processed, and used efficiently. Web or enterprise applications need to interact with backend databases to retrieve and manipulate data. This led to the evolution of JDBC, which provides the JDBC API to enable Java-based applications to connect to databases.

Chapter 3, Working with JDBC 4.0, discusses JDBC 4.0 and the JDBC API with the help of various examples, ensuring better comprehension of the various classes, interfaces, and methods of the API.

Java Servlet

Java Servlet, a Java platform technology, provides a component-based, platform-independent approach to create Web applications. While developing Web or enterprise applications, a servlet uses the JDBC API to access databases. Java EE provides Servlet 3.1 with new features, such as annotations, to develop a servlet class. *Chapter 4, Working with Servlets 3.1*, describes the Servlet API and the Servlet context.

In a Web application, client details such as logging information need to be maintained across multiple Web pages to implement session handling. Earlier, other mechanisms, such as URL rewriting, hidden form fields, and cookies, were used for session handling. Java Servlet provides an API to implement the session handling mechanism to retain a client's state.. *Chapter 5, Handling Sessions in Servlets 3.1*, elucidates the advantages and disadvantages of various session handling mechanisms provided by Java Servlet.

JavaServer Pages

The JSP technology is an extension of the Java Servlet technology, and has been created to support embedding of Java code in HTML pages. JSP makes it easier to combine static content with dynamic content, ensuring an easy approach to build Web applications. JSP enables you to embed Java code in an HTML page by using scriptlets. The focus of Java EE 7 has been to simplify the development of Web or enterprise applications by using Java annotations. JSP 2.3 extends this impetus of Java and allows the use of annotations for dependency injection on JSP tag handlers and context listeners.

Chapter 8, Implementing JSP Tag Extensions, elaborates on various topics related to JSP, such as classic and simple JSP tag handlers and the Tag Extension API. The chapter also includes examples and applications to provide you a better understanding of implementing classic and simple tag handlers.

JavaServer Faces

While developing a Web application, a developer designs a UI to interact with clients, develops the business logic to process data, and implements navigation rules to be followed when a client accesses the application. Before the introduction of JSF, programmers had to manually provide the code to define common tasks such as validating user inputs and converting user input strings into Java objects to build Web applications. Consequently, this diverted the attention of the programmers from the business logic of the applications. However, JSF has helped simplify the complexity of code for programmers and enabled them to handle these tasks easily through its APIs and tags. In addition, JSF also helps programmers to design rich UIs with its components. As a consequence, the programmers are now able to concentrate on developing and implementing the business logic, which is an essential part of any application.

Chapter 11, Working with JavaServer Faces 2.2 shows you how to create the standard UI components by using the JSF core and HTML tags.

JavaMail

JavaMail is introduced to implement the functionality of sending and receiving mails in an enterprise application. JavaMail provides the JavaMail API, which contains the classes and interfaces required to develop mail and messaging applications. The JavaMail API provides a platform and protocol-independent framework to send and receive mails. *Chapter 12, Understanding JavaMail 1.5*, discusses JavaMail 1.5 and also shows you how to create an application to send and receive mails. This application also helps you to understand the implementation of various classes and interfaces of the JavaMail API.

Enterprise JavaBeans

Initially, Java programmers used JavaBeans to implement the business logic while developing an enterprise application. JavaBeans help to create UI components, but do not provide services such as transaction management and security, which are required to develop robust and secure enterprise applications. This led to the evolution of EJB, which extends Java components and provides services that help in enterprise application development.

However, EJB has proved to be a complex technology for programmers, as they need to create the Home and Remote interfaces. In EJB 3, programmers do not need to create the Remote interfaces. In addition, EJB 3 also introduces Java Persistence, a standard API used to manage persistence and Object Relational Mapping (ORM). *Chapter 14, Implementing Entities and Java Persistence API 2.1*, discusses the Java Persistence API and Java Persistence Query Language (JPQL), which has simplified the task of creating Java queries.

Hibernate

Hibernate is an open source framework that enables a developer to work easily with relational databases in an enterprise application. In addition to the Java Persistence API, Hibernate provides the feature of mapping Java classes to database classes. Hibernate also generates Hibernate Query Language (HQL) calls, which automate the process of handling result sets. Hibernate can be used in both standalone Java applications and Java EE applications using Java Servlet and EJB. *Chapter 15, Implementing Java Persistence Using Hibernate 4.3*, describes the Hibernate API used to generate HQL queries. The chapter also includes an application to demonstrate the implementation of Hibernate 4.3.

Seam

Seam is a framework that integrates the JSF and EJB technologies. JSF helps to create UI components of an enterprise application. However, creating UI components by using JSF requires large volumes of coding. Due to this, programmers have to focus more on the presentation layer of an enterprise application, when they should be focusing on the business logic. Using Seam allows a developer to focus on the business logic of the application.

Chapter 16, Implementing JBoss Seam, discusses the Seam context and components, and provides an application to demonstrate the implementation of Seam.

Java EE Connector Architecture

As more and more businesses adopt e-business strategies, integration with existing enterprise information systems (EISs) is becoming the key to success. Organizations with successful e-businesses need to integrate their existing EISs with new Web applications. They also need to extend the reach of their EISs to support business-to-business (B2B) transactions.

Java Connector Architecture (JCA) defines the standard to integrate different EISs. Before JCA was defined, no specification for the Java platform addressed the problem of providing a standard architecture for integrating heterogeneous EISs. Most EIS vendors and application server vendors used non-standard vendor-specific architectures to provide connectivity between application servers and EISs. With the advent of JCA, businesses can now look forward to easy and simplified integration of their EISs to implement B2B transactions. *Chapter 17, Java EE Connector Architecture 1.7*, discusses JCA, EIS resources, and EIS services in detail.

Web Services

As a result of major IT developments over the last few years, most people and companies now use broadband connections to connect to the Internet. The applications implementing Web services were introduced to simplify the process of accessing the resources on the Internet.

The applications that implement Web services are simple applications that run on a Web browser. These applications are built based on Web browser standards and can generally be accessed by any browser on any platform. Web services are composed of modularized services that can be registered, searched, and called over the Internet. Web services generally use SOAP to transfer data over the Internet.

Chapter 19, *Implementing SOA using Java Web Services*, discusses the Web Service specifications of Java EE 7, such as JAXB, JAX-WS, and JAXR.

Struts

The tasks of creating the model, view, and controllers of a Web application have been simplified by the evolution of the Struts framework. Struts provide various tags, which have simplified the implementation of the view component. Instead of providing code to implement the functionality of a view, Struts provides various tags. You can use these tags to simplify the implementation of various functionalities, such as validation.

Chapter 20, Working with Struts 2, describes the Struts 2 API, and demonstrates how to create a simple login application by using the Struts 2 API.

Spring

JavaBeans, which were used to implement business logic, did not provide services such as state and transaction management. Therefore, EJB was introduced to solve these problems with the help of EJB containers. The EJB container provides state management and transaction services during runtime. However, programmers find it difficult to create enterprise applications by using EJB as they have to create the Home and Remote interfaces. Moreover, running EJB-based enterprise applications are increasingly difficult for Java programmers. Therefore, Spring was introduced to simplify the task of the programmers. Spring, an open source application development framework, is a collection of sub-frameworks, also called layers, such as Spring AOP, Spring ORM, Spring Web Flow, and Spring Web Model View Controller.

Chapter 21, Working with Spring 4.0, discusses Spring in detail and includes an application developed by using the Spring Web MVC framework.

JAAS

Java EE provides JAAS to implement security in Web and enterprise applications. Security refers to the process of implementing authentication and authorization to access the Web resources of an application. Security can be implemented programmatically or declaratively, as discussed in *Chapter 22, Securing Java EE 7 Applications*. The chapter includes various applications to reveal the implementation of programmatic, form-based, and declarative security.

AJAX

Earlier, while accessing a Web page, clients had to wait for a long time after refreshing a page or clicking a button. While refreshing a Web page, the browser first sends the request to the Web server, which then performs the required operations. After this, the response is provided to the browser. While performing these operations, the client cannot do anything other than waiting for the response to be provided by the server. However, now, all this has changed. AJAX, with the help of JavaScript, provides asynchronous client and server interaction. The AJAX engine handles a client's request instead of sending the request to the server. Moreover, clients can perform other tasks while a request is being processed, since AJAX enables asynchronous client and server communication. Appendix A, *AJAX,* discusses the AJAX architecture and expains in detail how AJAX handles client requests by using the AJAX engine.

Let's now recap the main points of the chapter in a short summary.

Summary

The chapter has been divided into five sections: A, B, C, D, and E. Section A has discussed the evolution of Java from other programming languages such as C and C++. It has introduced Java as a programming language, a platform, and a virtual machine used to compile Java applications. Section B has discussed the different types of enterprise architectures; i.e., single tier, 2-tier, 3-tier, and n-tier architecture, based on which enterprise applications are created. It has also discussed the objectives of an enterprise application. Section C has primarily focused on Java EE 7 and discussed its features, APIs, architecture, and containers. This section has also discussed the compatible products for the Java EE platform and provided various types of architectures for developing an enterprise application. Section D has described Web and application servers used to run Web and Java EE applications, respectively. Section E has provided an overview of Java EE related technologies that are covered in the book and the need for each technology.

The next chapter explains about Web applications in Java EE 7.

Quick Revise

Q1. What is Java?

Ans. Java is a platform-independent programming language used to create secure and robust applications that may run on a single computer or may be distributed among servers and clients over a network.

Q2. What is Java EE application?

Ans. A Java EE application is a collection of Java EE modules. These modules can be Web components or enterprise components. The Web components can be servlets and JSPs and enterprise components can be EJBs, connectors, and other application clients. All these Java EE modules are combined to form an integrated enterprise application. A single archive file with a .ear extension is created to package a Java EE application.

Q3. Define a servlet.

Ans. A servlet is a simple Java program, which is executed on the server to generate dynamic content by using the Java technology. The dynamic content is normally an HTML document, and may also be an XML document as well. A servlet is capable of maintaining a state of a user in a session-based application. A Web container in a Web server is responsible for the life cycle management of a servlet.

Q4. What is a 3-tier architecture?

Ans. A 3-tier architecture is basically a client/server architecture in which the user interface, business logic, and data handling code are developed and maintained as independent modules. These three tiers are named the Presentation tier (user interface), the Application tier (business logic), and the Data tier (data access and storage).

Q5. What is an EJB?

Ans. EJB refers to Enterprise JavaBean, a distributed application component model. Applications created with EJB are highly scalable, transactional, and secure. An EJB is maintained throughout its life cycle by the EJB container.

Q6. Name the technologies included in the Java EE platform.

Ans. The key technologies that make the Java EE platform are Java Servlet, JSP, EJB, JCA, JMX, JAXR, JMS, JNDI, JTA, JDBC, the Deployment API, and J2EE Authorization Contract for Containers.

Q7. Differentiate between Java, Standard Edition, Java, Enterprise Edition, and Java Micro Edition.

Ans. The three Java editions can be differentiated as follows:

- Java, Standard Edition is a set of APIs used to develop a variety of applications, including standalone applications, applets, and client applications
- Java, Enterprise Edition is used to develop server-side applications with a component-based approach
- Java, Micro Edition is used to build applications for micro devices, such as mobile phones

Q8. A messaging standard that allows Java EE application components to create, send, and receive messages is ....

A. JMS **B. JAAS** **C. JDBC** **D. JNDI**

Ans. The correct option is A

Q9. List the three modules of an enterprise application developed by using Java EE 6.

Ans: The three modules of an enterprise application are as follows:

- The Web module
- The EJB module
- The Client module

Q10. Explain the two tasks involved in deploying an application.

Ans. The two tasks involved in deploying an application are as follows:

- **Installing the application:** Refers to the process in which EAR files are copied on the application server, additional implementation classes are generated with the help of the container, and finally the application is installed on the server
- **Configuring the application**: Refers to the process in which the application is customized with application server-specific information.

2

Web Applications and Java EE 7

If you need an information on:

A Web application is a collection of multiple Web components that interact with each other to execute specific business logic. You can use Web browsers to access Web applications over a network, such as the Internet or intranet. Web applications perform various operations, such as accepting input data and dynamically generating one or more Web documents as responses. The Web documents generated as responses are displayed to a user in standard formats, such as `Hypertext Markup Language (HTML)`, which are supported by common Web browsers.

In the Java EE platform, Web components such as Java Servlet or JavaServer Pages (JSPs) provide dynamic capabilities for a Web server. Servlets are Java classes that dynamically process requests and generate the desired responses. JSP pages are text-based documents that are executed as servlets and are used for creating static content. Web components process requests and perform other required operations by the help of a runtime platform known as a Web container. The Web components access various services, such as request dispatching and security, with the help of a Web container. For example, when a Web component is accessed by a user, the authenticity of the user is identified with the help of the Web container. In addition, the request sent by a user is controlled by the Web container.

While deploying an application on the Web container, you need to configure its various aspects, such as resource to a url-pattern, initialization parameters, and session details. The configuration information is maintained in an `Extensible Markup Language` (XML) file, called Web application `Deployment Descriptor`. However, in the `Java EE 7 platform`, the use of annotations has minimized the task of providing configuration information in Deployment Descriptors.

This chapter introduces Web components, Web modules, and Web containers. As Web applications mostly use `Hyper Text Transfer Protocol (HTTP)` for data transfer, the chapter also provides a detailed knowledge about HTTP request and response. Further, a detailed description of the Web application is provided, including its benefits, components, and structure. Towards the end, the chapter discusses various Web application models and also explores the Model, View, and Controller components.

Let's start our discussion by exploring the role of HTTP in transferring information on the Internet.

Exploring the HTTP Protocol

`HTTP` is a stateless, application-level communication protocol used to transfer information on the Internet. The main aim of `HTTP` is to send and receive user information over a network. As an application-level protocol, `HTTP` also defines the types of requests that clients can send to a server and the responses that the server sends back to the clients. Each request has a `Uniform Resource Locator (URL)`, which is a string that identifies a Web component or a static object, such as an `HTML` page or an image file. Therefore, most of the Java EE Web clients use `HTTP` to browse a URL and communicate over a network. If the communication between the client and server in a Web application is HTTP-based, the Web server converts the HTTP client request to an HTTP request object. Next, the HTTP request object is delivered to the Web component that is identified by the request `URL`. Further, the Web component sends the `HTTP` response object, which is then converted into the `HTTP` response by the application server and finally sent to the client.

In this section, let's explore the working of HTTP and the concepts related to it, such as HTTP requests and responses.

Processing HTTP Requests

Let's try to understand the underlying nature of `HTTP` requests and working of the `HTTP` protocol over a network with the help of an example. Consider a scenario where a user wants to visit a URL, say `www.google.com/intl/en/privacy.html`. Now, the process of sending the request and retrieving the response from the specified URL would be as follows:

- The user makes a request for the specific URL
- The Web browser establishes a connection with the `www.google.com` server by locating its IP address from a DNS server
- The Web browser then sends a request to the server to retrieve the `/intl/en/privacy.html` file

- The server responds with the information about the requested `HTML` page and the contents of the `privacy.html` file

This process of sending a request and receiving a response from the server is known as transaction. An `HTTP` session, i.e. the process of maintaining the client's state, remains open till a single transaction is completed. After the transaction is completed, the session is automatically closed. For example, if you want to access the http://www.google.com URL, the HTTP session would remain open until the server is connected to the requested `URL` to access the requested Web page.

Let's use the telnet command line interface to remotely access the `www.google.com` server. By default, telnet connects on server port 23.

NOTE

Telnet is a network protocol used on the Internet to establish a connection with remote servers. In Windows 7, by default, the Telnet Client Windows feature is disabled. You first need to enable the Telnet Client Windows feature from the Windows Features dialog box, which is displayed by accessing the Turn Windows features on or off option from Control Panel. Next, type telnet in the Search programs and files text box of the Start menu to access the Telnet Client console.

The following command establishes a connection with the www.google.com server by using Telnet Client console :

```
open www.google.com 80
```

Telnet, a client-server protocol, looks up the IP address of `www.google.com` and connects to it on server port 80. The console establishes a connection with the server and the relevant message is displayed, as shown in Figure 2.1:

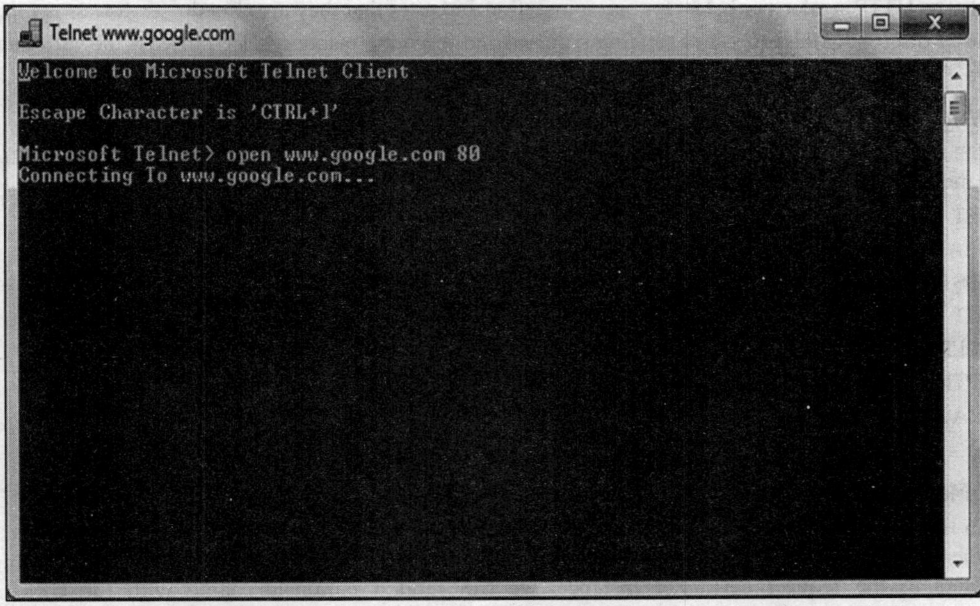

Figure 2.1: Displaying the Connection with the google.com Server

After the connection is established, press the ENTER key until the cursor reaches to a blank space.

Now, you can make a request to access the `/intl/en/privacy.html` file. The following command shows the use of the `HTTP GET` method to access the requested page:

```
GET /intl/en/privacy.html HTTP/1.1
```

After this request has been sent to the server, the server replies by sending a response header along with the resource requested.

Figure 2.2 shows the output that is echoed to the console after a short duration:

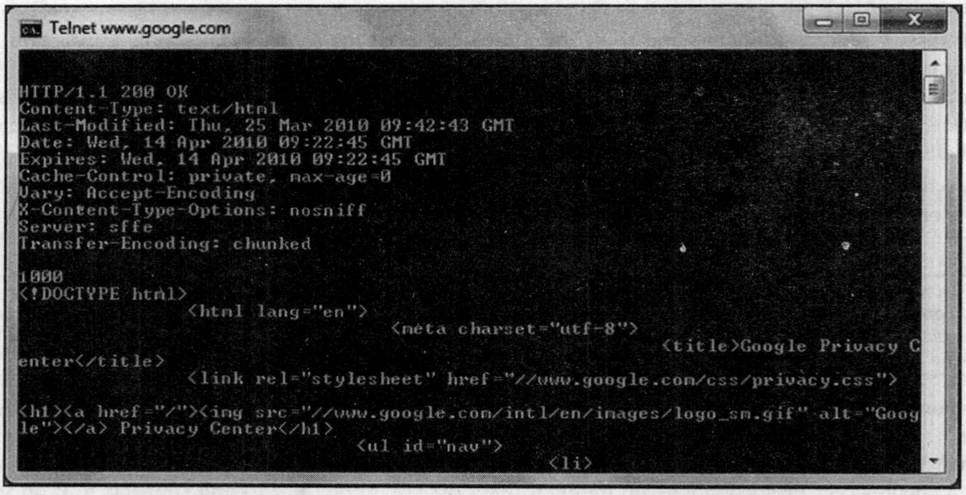

Figure 2.2: Displaying the Output of the Request Made

In Figure 2.2, the code provided after Transfer-Encoding: chunked is written in HTML, so that you can recognize the text. The HTTP sessions only last for one transaction and after that they are closed.

Now, after discussing the process of sending requests and receiving responses, let's discuss the various methods of HTTP requests in detail.

Describing HTTP Requests

An `HTTP` request is a class consisting of `HTTP` style requests, request lines, request methods, request `URL`, header fields, and body content. `HTTP` 1.1 defines the following request methods to be used with user requests:

- GET
- HEAD
- POST
- PUT
- DELETE
- OPTIONS
- TRACE

Now let's discuss each of these in detail.

The **GET** Method

You can use the GET method to access the static resources, such as HTML documents and images. Apart from the static resources, the GET method also allows you to retrieve the dynamic information by using query parameters in the request URL. For instance, we can send a parameter name with the URL, such as `http://www.domain.com?name=Tim`. In this example, Tim is the dynamic information sent by including the `name` parameter in the request URL. The Web server can then access this dynamic information through the `name` parameter.

The GET method contains a Request-URI, which is used to retrieve information from the request. URI stands for Uniform Resource Identifier. If the Request-URI refers to the data-producing process, the produced data is sent as an entity in the response. However, if the Request-URI refers to the source text of the process, the text is returned as the output. The usage of the `GET` methods can be changed according to the request made by the user. If the user request includes the If-Modified-Since, If-Unmodified-Since, If-Match, If-None-Match, or If-Range header fields, the `GET` method is converted to a conditional `GET` method, in which case the conditional header fields are defined. The desired entity is transferred to the client only if the condition specified in the conditional header field is fulfilled. You should note that the conditional `GET` method allows cached entities to be refreshed, resulting in the reduction of unnecessary network usage.

If the `GET` method associated with a request contains the range header field, it is called a partial `GET` method. If the required data already exists with the client, it is not transferred by the partial `GET` method, which leads to the reduction of network usage. In this type of method, only a part of the entity is transferred; therefore, the name partial GET method.

The **HEAD** Method

Sometimes, a client might only need to view the header of a response (`Content-Type or Content-Length`). In such cases, the client can use the `HEAD` request method to retrieve the header. The `HEAD` method is similar to the `GET` method, except that the server does return a message body in response to the HEAD method.

The HEAD request method can be used to retrieve the meta information of the entity requested by the user. The meta information in the HEAD request method must be identical to the information sent in the response to a `GET` request. Sometimes, the response to a `HEAD` request is cacheable. It indicates that the information contained in the response may be used to update a previously cached entity from that resource. In case of any modifications, if the new field value indicates that the cached entity differs from the current entity, the cached entity needs to be updated.

Based on the type of the request, the client application specifies the resource that is required as a part of the request. To understand this concept better, consider a scenario where a user provides the `http://www.oracle.com/technetwork/java/index.html` URL in the address bar of a Web browser. The Web browser sends the `GET` request to the `oracle.com` Web server to locate the `index.html` resource. You should note that a URI should specify a resource name in the HTTP lexicon. In other words, apart from the domain name in URL, a specific resource name should also be provided. For example, in our case, URL is `http://www.oracle.com/technetwork/java/index.html`, which contains index.html as the resource name and oracle.com as the Web server. The `index.html` file is located at the /technetwork/java location of the Web server serving the `oracle.com` domain.

The **POST** Method

The POST method is generally used in cases where a large amount of information needs to be sent to a Web server. This method allows you to access dynamic resources and provides the following functionalities:

- Defines annotations of existing resources
- Posts a message to a mailing list or newsgroup
- Defines a block of data, such as the result of submitting a form, to a data-handling process
- Extends a database through an append operation

The function of the `POST` method is dependent on the `Request-URI`. The posted entity is a part of that `URI` in the same way as a file is a part of a directory containing it or a news article is a part of a newsgroup to which it is posted.

The 200 (OK) or 204 (No Content) response status is generated if the response provided by the POST method does not contain the resource identified by a URI. If the resource that is requested by a user is created on the origin server, the 201 (Created) response status is provided. The `201` (Created) response contains a new resource describing the request status and a location header.

A `POST` request allows the encapsulation of multi-part messages into the request body. For example, you can use `POST` requests to upload text or binary files from the server. `POST` requests can also be used in applets to send serializable Java objects, or even raw bytes, to the Web server. In addition, `POST` requests offer a wider choice compared to `GET` requests in terms of the contents of a request.

Table 2.1 lists the differences between the GET and POST requests:

Table 2.1: Differences between the GET and POST Methods

Parameter	GET	POST
Transmission of request parameters	Transmits the request parameters in the form of a query string that is appended to the request URL.	Transmits the request parameters within the body of the request.
URL size	Limits you to a maximum of 256 characters in the URL, excluding the number of characters in the actual path.	Does not limit the size of the URL for submitting name/value pairs, as they are transferred in the header and not in the URL.
Purpose	Allows you to retrieve data.	Allows you to retrieve, save, or update data. It also allows you to order a product or send e-mail messages.
Caching ability	Considers the request as cacheable.	Does not consider the request to be cacheable.
Type of resource	Allows a user to access the static resources, such as HTML documents.	Allows a user to transfer the information according to the request made by the client. The POST method is used to transfer large and complex information to the server.

The **PUT** Method

The PUT method allows you to store an entity in the specified `Request-URI`. You should note that if the Request-URI in the URL does not reference the name of an existing resource, the Web server creates the resource with the specified name. Apart from creating a new resource, if any modification is done to an existing resource, the 200 (OK) or 204 (No Content) response codes are generated. These response codes depict that the modification in the existing resource is done successfully. If a new resource is created on the request of a user, the 201(Created) response code is generated, informing the user about the successful creation of the resource. However, if either the new resource is not created properly or the modifications are not done appropriately in the existing resource, the corresponding response codes are generated, reflecting the nature of the problem.

Various `URIs` can identify a single resource. For example, a resource might have a `URI` for identifying all logged in users, which is separate from the `URI` identifying each login user. In this case, a `PUT` request on a general `URI` may result in various other `URIs` that are being defined by Web server.

The **DELETE** Method

You can delete a resource, if it is no longer needed, by using the DELETE method. While deleting a resource, you should provide the name of the resource to be deleted in the Request-URI. You should note that if the response contains the status of deletion of a resource, the 200 (OK) response code is generated, depicting that the resource has been successfully deleted. If the response is `202` (Accepted), it specifies that the resource has not yet been deleted. Similarly, if the response code is `204` (No Content), it specifies that the resource has been deleted but the response does not include an entity. Responses to the `DELETE` method are not cacheable. This method permanently deletes the files from the cache as well.

The **OPTIONS** Method

The OPTIONS method requests the information related to various communication options available on request and response. You should note that the responses to the `OPTIONS` method are not cacheable. The capabilities of a Web server and the options or requirements related to a resource can be determined with the help of the OPTIONS method. If an entity body is included in the `OPTIONS` method, the media type should be provided by the Content-Type field.

If an asterisk (*) is the `Request-URI`, the `OPTIONS` method is applied generally to the server instead of being applied to a specific resource. As the communication options of a server mainly depend on the requested resource, the `*` request is useful as a `ping` or `no-op` type of method. It only allows the client to test the capabilities of the server; for example, the * request can be used to test a proxy for HTTP/1.1 compliance. If the Request-URI does not contain an asterisk, the OPTIONS method applies only to the options that are available while communicating with that resource.

The **TRACE** Method

The TRACE method is used to invoke a remote application layer associated with a request message. A TRACE request must not include an entity. A client uses the TRACE method to diagnose or test the input received at the other end of the request chain.

The value in the header field of the TRACE method acts as a trace of the request chain. For the client's benefit, the Max-Forwards header field limits the length of the request chain, which is useful for testing a chain of proxies forwarding messages in an infinite loop.

Describing the HTTP Responses

When an HTTP request is received by a server, the status of the response is displayed with some meta information about the response. This meta information constitutes the part of the response header. The server also sends the content that corresponds to the resource specified in the request, except for the case of the HEAD request. The following code snippet provides the meta information about the response:

```
Response = Status-Line                    ;
           *(( general-header             ;
           | response-header              ;
           | entity-header ) CRLF) ;
           CRLF
           [ message-body ]               ;
```

The response that is to be displayed to the user contains a status line. A status line is generally the first line of the response header. The status line provides the information related to protocol versions, as well as the status codes, depending upon the responses. The response-header field allows the Web server to pass additional information of the response to the client. These headers inform the server about further access to the resources requested by the Request-URI.

If a client sends a request to a URL, for example http://www.oracle.com/technetwork/java/index.html, the browser receives the content from the index.html files as a part of the request. The content header of the response include the Content-Type, Date, and Expires fields. These fields are used to set time-related data in a Web application. For example, the Expires header field of a page can be set to the date specified in the Date header field to indicate the browsers that they should not cache the page.

To indicate the type of content in request and response bodies, the response header fields use Multipurpose Internet Mail Extensions (MIME). MIME types include text/html and image/gif content types. In these content types, the first part of the header indicates the type of data, such as text and image, while the second part indicates the standard extension, such as html for text and gif for image. MIME is used to facilitate the exchange of different kinds of data files. At the beginning of each transmission, HTTP servers use MIME headers. Then, the information in MIME headers is used by the browsers to decide how to parse and render the content. MIME header is also used by browsers while transmitting data in the request body and deciding the type of data being sent. For example, the default MIME type is application/x-www-form-urlencoded, which is used for encoding in POST requests.

Let's now explore Web applications.

Introducing Web Applications

A Web application is a server-side application that contains Web components (servlets and JSP pages), HTML/XML documents, and other resources in a directory structure or archived format, known as a Web Archive (WAR) file. A Web application is generally located at a central server, which provides services to various clients. In a Web server, the Web components can be conveniently distributed as Java Archive (JAR) files with the .war extension.

Web applications are of the following two types:

- **Presentation-oriented**—Generates dynamic content and Web pages by using various markup languages, such as `HTML and XML`. A presentation-oriented application generally serves as a client for the service-oriented Web applications.
- **Service-oriented**—Implements a Web service and is invoked by presentation-oriented Web applications.

Figure 2.3 shows the interaction between a Web client and a database:

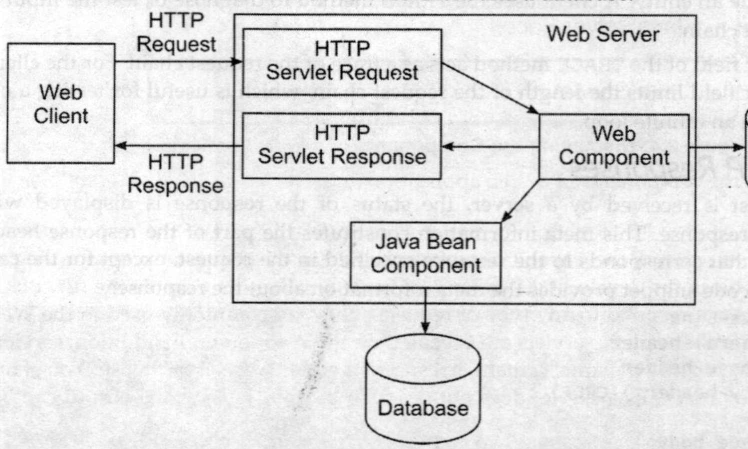

Figure 2.3: Displaying Request Processing in a Web Application

Figure 2.3 depicts that:

- A Web server converts the request into an HttpServletRequest object.
- The HttpServletRequest object is sent to a Web component to establish a communication with JavaBeans components or a database for generating the dynamic content.
- The HttpServletResponse object is generated by the Web component to retrieve the data from the database. Finally, the HttpServletResponse object displays the data to the client as the response generated by the Web server.

The development of Web application requires the following support:

- **A programming model and an API support**—Specify how to develop applications.
- **Server-side runtime support**—Includes support for applicable network services, and a runtime for executing the applications.
- **Deployment support**—Includes support for installing the application on the server. It also deploys the configuration details of the application components, such as specifying initialization parameters and specifying any database.

Let's now explore the components of a Web application.

Describing Components of a Web Application

A Web application consists of Web components, such as Java Servlet and JSPs. Earlier, Web-based applications used to face maintenance problems, which were solved by using the Model/View/Controller (MVC) paradigm for building user interfaces.

An application based on the MVC paradigm contains three components, Model, View, and Controller. A View is created by using JSP and the logic to manage requests is implemented in servlets, which serve as Controller. Moreover, the existing business rules in an application are referred to as Model.

With the introduction of Java Servlet and JSP technologies, the new technologies have also been introduced to build interactive Web applications.

Figure 2.4 shows the components of a Web application:

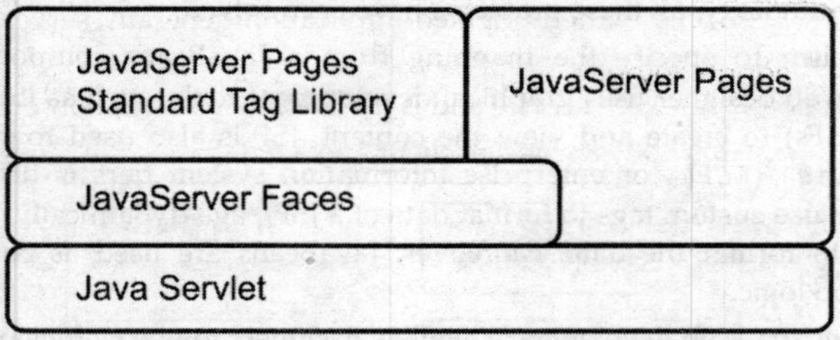

Figure 2.4: Displaying the Components of a Web Application

Now, let's discuss about the components of a Web application in detail.

Java Servlet

A Java Servlet is used to extend the capabilities of servers in a client-server programming model and is considered the building block for developing Web applications. Java Servlet extends the functionality of a Web server. Although servlets can respond to any type of requests, they are commonly used in the Web applications hosted by Web servers. Unlike applets, servlets are executed on the Web server. In addition, servlets are portable platforms that are used to provide dynamic content, irrespective of the Web server in use. You should note that a browser-based application that calls a servlet does not need support for Java, as the output can be of any other type, such as HTML or XML.

Servlets are based on Java. This feature allows servlets to function on any platform that has a `Java Virtual Machine (JVM)` and a Web server that supports servlets. In a general Web application, if we make any change in the code of a servlet, it is necessary to recompile and redeploy that servlet so that the change is reflected in the application. Servlets can communicate directly with existing enterprise resources by using generic APIs, such as `Java Database Connectivity (JDBC)`. As a result, you can simply and quickly develop the applications. In addition, developers can use servlets to extend the functionalities of a Web application similar to any Java application. For example, a Controller servlet can be extended to become a secure Controller. The functionalities of the original Controller can also be retained along with new security features.

The performance of servlets is better as compared to the Common Gateway Interface (CGI) scripts. This is because a CGI script needs to be loaded in various processes for every request. On the other hand, a servlet, once loaded in the memory, can be run multiple times on a single lightweight thread. Apart from this advantage, servlets can also maintain or pool various connections to databases, resulting in less time consumption to process requests. Servlets can also directly access the parameters passed with the HTTP request because these parameters are considered as objects. However, in CGI-based applications, a form posts the parameters that are converted into environment properties to be used in programs.

JavaServer Pages

JSP pages are used to create static content in the form of text-based documents. Apart from the static content, you can provide the dynamic content in the JSP pages. The JSP technology provides a rapid approach of developing Web pages and allows you to reuse the code based on the component-based architecture.

Let's look at how the JSP technology was introduced. You should note that both Java Servlet and JSP technologies have been introduced to achieve specific tasks. The Java Servlet technology was developed to serve as a mechanism to:

- Accept the client's requests from the Web browsers
- Get the enterprise data from the application tier or databases
- Perform application logic on the data
- Format the data for presentation in the browser

Initially, the Web designers could not preview the look and feel of an `HTML` page until runtime. It was also very difficult to locate the appropriate sections of code in a servlet when data or its display format changed. In addition, if the code of a servlet was modified, Web designers had to recompile and reload the servlets into the Web server, provided that the presentation and business logic were implemented in a single servlet. With the introduction of the JSP technology, all these problems have been solved.

JSP provides a mechanism to specify the mapping from a JavaBeans component to the `HTML` (or `XML`) presentation format. A Web designer uses graphical development tools, such as JSP standard tag library (JSTL) and JavaServer Faces (JSFs) to create and view the content. JSF is also used to specify where data from the `Enterprise JavaBeans (EJB)` or enterprise information system tiers is displayed. Nowadays, the JSP technology allows you to use custom tags to format data of a JSP page dynamically; whereas, earlier you need to provide the Java code to format the data. Moreover, JavaBeans are used as components in a JSP page to implement the application logic.

The JSP technology allows the Web developers as well as designers to work efficiently and effectively. The Web designers can use the JavaBeans components or custom tags (provided by Web developers) to design user interfaces. Similarly, the main role of Web developers is to implement the logic in the application; therefore, the knowledge of designing the user interface is not required.

JSTL and JSF

As explained in the previous subsection, the JSP technology is used to develop simple Web pages to provide dynamically generated content. Two more components, JSTL and JSF, can be used in a JSP page to simplify the code provided in a JSP page. JSTL is a set of libraries used by JSP for implementing JSTL tags; whereas, the JSF technology is a framework to build user interfaces for Web applications.

JSF, with a well-defined programming model, enables developers to quickly and easily build Web applications by using reusable `User Interface (UI)` components in a page. JSF allows the Web applications to manage all the complexities of creating a UI on the server.

When a client sends a request to access a Web component, the component is processed in the server to generate the desired output for the client's request. The servlets used in the application are capable of handling complex logic processing, navigation paths between screens, and enterprise data.

You can reduce Java code within JSP pages by using custom tags and JavaBeans components in a Web application.

Web components of a JSF application are of the following types:

- **Presentation components**—Generates the HTML or XML response. A JSP page, JSF page, or servlet can be a presentation component. You should note that in a JSP page, the reusable custom tags or presentation logic can be implemented.
- **Front components**—Handles or converts the HTTP request into a form of an application.

The basic mechanism of using the presentation and front components is illustrated in Figure 2.5:

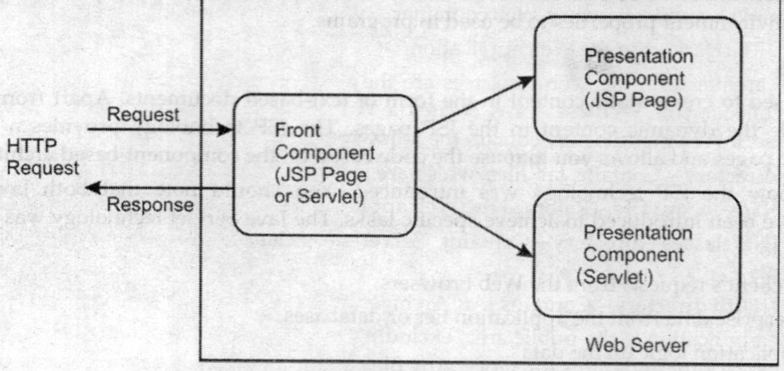

Figure 2.5: Displaying Roles of Web Components

As shown in Figure 2.5, firstly the front component accepts a request from a user. Next, the front component identifies the appropriate presentation component to forward the request. Further, the request is processed and the response is returned to the front Controller. Finally, the response is forwarded to the user.

Apart from the presentation and front components, `Deployment Descriptor` is an important part of `Java EE` Web applications, as it helps in configuring the Web components. The following are the reasons of defining Deployment Descriptor:

- **Initializing parameters for servlets and Web applications**—Allow you to reduce the amount of coding required to define initializing parameters within the Web applications. For example, if a servlet requires access to a database, you can provide the login and password to access the database in Deployment Descriptor. In addition, you can configure the servlets and its initialization parameters used in a Web application in Deployment Descriptor.
- **Servlet/JSP definitions**—Include the name of the servlet or JSP, the class of the servlet or JSP, and the description of the servlet, which is optional. Each servlet/precompiled JSP used in a Web application should be defined in Deployment Descriptor.
- **Servlet/JSP mappings**—Provide information that is used by Web containers to map incoming requests to servlets and JSPs.
- **Specifying MIME types**—Allow you to specify the MIME types for each Web application in Deployment Descriptor.
- **Security**—Allows you to manage access control for an application by using Deployment Descriptor, for example, authentication and authorization details for users.

Let's now explore the structure or modules of Web applications.

Describing Structure /Modules of Web Applications

As we have learned earlier, a Web application comprises static resource, such as files, images, Web components, helper classes, and libraries. The Web container enhances the capabilities of Web components and makes them easier to develop. In addition, the Web container provides the services, such as security and transaction management, for the Web components.

You should note that the process of creating, packaging, deploying, and running a Web application varies from the traditional standalone Java classes. The process to create, deploy, and execute a Web application can be summarized in the following steps:

- Develop the code for the Web component
- Develop Deployment Descriptor for a Web application
- Compile the Web components, along with the helper classes that are referenced by the components
- Package the Web application into a deployable unit
- Deploy the Web application on a Web container
- Access a URL referencing the Web application

In the Java EE architecture, the Web resources are the Web components as well as files containing static Web content. The collection of Web resources creates a Web module, which is the smallest deployable unit. In addition to these, a Web module may contain the following files:

- **A public directory**—Contains tag files, which are implementations of tag libraries
- **A WEB-INF/web.xml file**—Refers to the Web application Deployment Descriptor
- **A WEB-INF/classes directory**—Contains Server-side classes—servlets, utility classes, and JavaBeans components
- **A WEB-INF/lib directory**—Contains JAR Archives of libraries called by Server-side classes

The root of the application is the public area, excluding the `WEB-INF` directory. All the HTML files used in the application must be kept under this directory. Any files under the public area can be used by the Web container. The application specific subdirectories, such as package directories, can be created under the `/WEB-INF/classes` location.

The Web application modules can be deployed and packaged in two ways:

- As an unpacked file structure
- As a JAR file, known as a WAR file

The use and composition of a WAR file is different from a JAR file. The WAR file is created by using a .war extension and can be deployed into any Web container that conforms to the Java Servlet specification.

You should note that a runtime `Deployment Descriptor`, web.xml, is included in the WAR file, and needs to be deployed on the application server. The web.xml file is located in the /WEB-INF folder of the application directory.

Figure 2.6 shows the common directory structure that has been followed throughout the book:

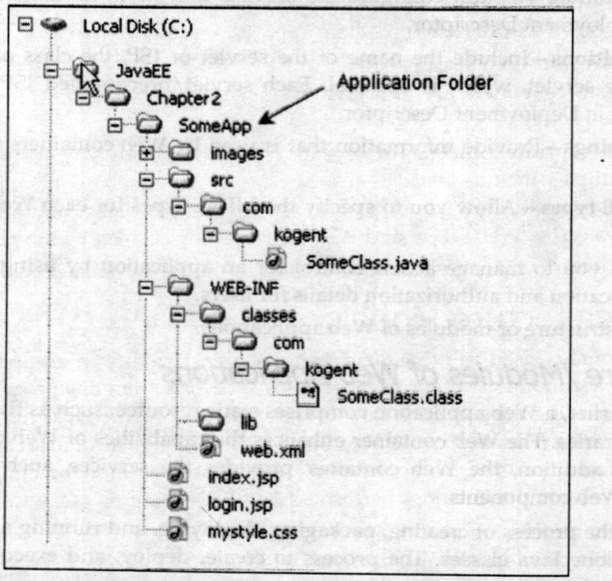

Figure 2.6: Displaying the Directory Structure of a Web Application

Figure 2.6 shows the structure of the Web application to be deployed in the Web container. The directory structure, defined in Figure 2.6, is considered as common directory structure throughout the book. To follow the structure, you need to create a folder named Java EE under any public area. Next, you need to create the folders on the basis of chapter numbers that contain chapter-specific applications.

In Figure 2.6, SomeApp is the application folder in which all the files of the application are placed. The SomeApp folder also contains some other folders, such as images, src and WEB-INF. The images folder stores all the image files that are used in the application. The src folder stores all the Java files used in the application. The WEB-INF folder is used to store the web.xml file, along with two sub-folders, classes and lib. The `classes` folder is used to store the .class files; whereas, the lib folder is used to store the executable JAR files required in the application. All the JSP and HTML pages are stored in the root directory of an application. All the Java source files in the application are defined under a common package named com.kogent.

After understanding the directory structure of the Java EE applications, let's learn about the Web container, which serves as an interface to deploy Web applications.

Describing Web Containers

A Web container refers to the platform that holds the Web components and provides platform-specific functionality to these components. To execute a Web component, you need to assemble it in the Web module and deploy it in the Web container. Alternatively, a Web container serves as a runtime environment for a Web application. The Web application runs within a Web container of a Web server. In addition, a Web container is used to provide Web components associated with the Web application.

Few Web servers may also be used to provide additional services, such as security, concurrency, transaction, and secondary storage. The EJB container is used to provide these additional services. A Web server does not need to be located on the same machine as the EJB server. Java EE application components use the protocols and methods available in the container to access the functionality provided by the server.

The Java EE application server supports the following types of Web containers:

- **Web containers in a Java EE application server**—Refer to the built-in Web containers in Java EE supported application servers, such as BEA's WebLogic server, Borland's Inprise application server, Netscape's iPlanet application server, and IBM's WebSphere application servers.
- **Web containers built into Web servers**—Refer to Web containers that are integrated with the Web server. Few examples of such containers are Sun Java System Web Server from Sun Microsystems and Jakarta Tomcat from Apache project.
- **Web container in a separate runtime**—Refers to Web servers and Web containers that are configured separately. The examples include Apache and Microsoft IIS, which require a separate Java runtime to actually run the servlets and Web server plug-in to integrate the Java runtime with the Web server. The communication between the Web server and Web container is managed by the plug-in.

Let's now learn about the various Web architecture models, such as Model-1 and Model-2 architectures.

Exploring Web Architecture Models

Earlier, different programmers used to implement the same functionality in an application in different ways. Therefore, the logic and execution flow of an application used to vary from one programmer to another. This led to the problem of understanding the execution flow of the application, which was resolved with the introduction of development models. These models provide a standard way of flow control in an application and describe the technologies used in different parts of the application. A development model facilitates the design process by separating the code according to the functions performed by different parts of an application.

Two types of development models are used for Web applications in Java. These models are classified based on different approaches used to develop Web applications, which are:

- Model-1 architecture
- Model-2 architecture

Let's learn about these models in detail.

Describing the Model-1 Architecture

The Model-1 architecture (Figure 2.7) was the first development model used to develop Web applications. This model uses JSP to design applications, which is responsible for all the activities and functionalities provided by the application. Applications using the Model-1 architecture contain a number of JSP pages, with each page providing different functionality and view to different users.

Figure 2.7 shows the Model-1 architecture:

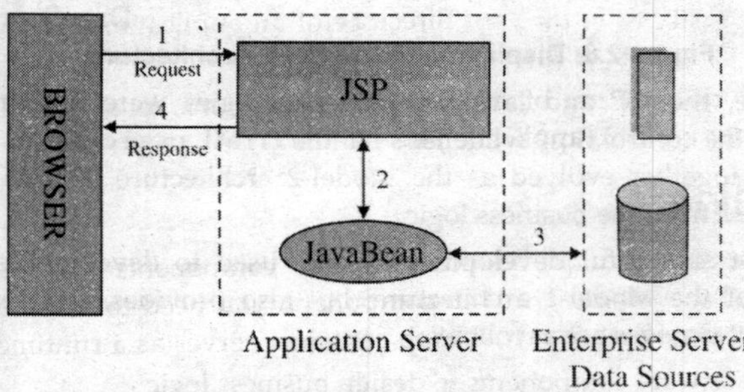

Figure 2.7: Displaying the Model-1 Architecture

In the Model-1 architecture (Figure 2.7), Web applications are developed by mixing the business and presentation logic. In this model, JSP pages receive HTTP requests, which are then transferred to the data layer by JavaBeans. After the requests are serviced, JSPs send HTTP responses back to the client. A JSP page not only contains display elements, but also retrieves HTTP parameters, calls the business logic, and handles the HTTP session.

The Model-1 architecture is page-centric and only suitable for small Web applications. Web applications implementing this type of architecture contain a series of JSP pages, where a user needs to navigate from one page to another. Consequently, the Model 1 architecture is not suitable for large Web applications because of these and some other limitations.

Despite its simple structure and easy to learn features, the Model-1 architecture was not successful for designing large projects because this model architecture:

- Leads to inflexibility and difficulty in maintaining applications. A single change in one page may cause changes in other pages, leading to unexpected results.
- Involves the developer at both the page development and the business logic implementation stages. There is no provision for the division of labor between the page designer and the business logic developer.
- Increases the complexity of a program with the increase in the size of the JSP page; therefore, it is difficult to trace the flow of control and debug the program.
- Increases the effort required for maintaining JSP pages in an application.

Let's now understand the second type of architecture, that is, Model-2.

Describing the Model-2 Architecture

The drawbacks in the Model-1 architecture led to the introduction of a new model, called Model-2. The Model-2 architecture was targeted at overcoming the drawbacks of Model-1 and helping developers to design more powerful Web applications. As it came after the advent of Model-1, it was named Model-2 to recognize it as a part of the Model-1 series.

Figure 2.8 shows the Model-2 architecture:

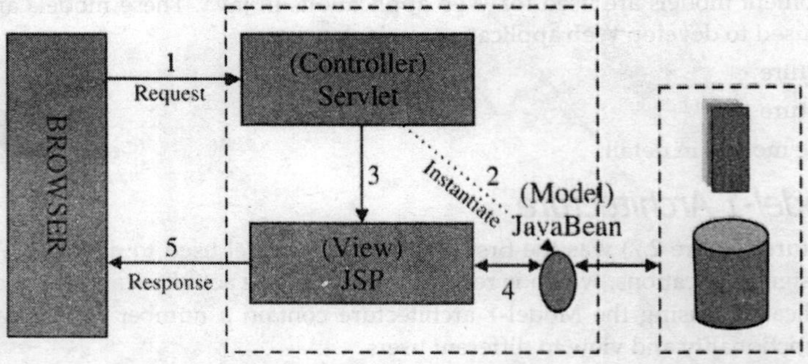

Figure 2.8: Displaying the Model-2 Architecture.

In the Model-2 architecture, the JSP and Java Servlet technologies were used together to develop a Web application. Servlets handle the control flow while JSPs handle HTML page creation. In due course, the approach of using JSPs and servlets together evolved as the Model-2 architecture. In this type of design model, the presentation logic is separated from the business logic.

So far, Model-2 is the most successful development model used to develop Web applications. It not only overcomes the limitations of the Model-1 architecture, but also provides new features that have their own advantages. Some of these advantages are as follows:

- Allows use of reusable software components to design business logic
- Offers great flexibility to the presentation logic, which can be modified without affecting the business logic

- Allows each software component to perform a different task, making it easy to design an application by simply embedding these components in the application

The Model-2 architecture resembles the classical MVC architecture. Let's now discuss the MVC architecture in detail next.

Exploring the MVC Architecture

Today, a Web application may need to interact with different types of clients having different types of user interfaces. A Web application may need to represent an HTML view to a client, a Wireless Markup Language (WML) view to a wireless client, and an XML view to some other type of client.

When a Web application needs to support only one type of client with one type of interface, it is a good idea to combine client-specific data and business logic with the interface-specific logic. However, if this type of approach is used for Web applications that require interaction with multiple types of clients, it would require different applications to support each type of client. This leads to the repetition of non-interface specific code in the interface-specific code, which further leads to increased effort in designing, debugging, and maintaining Web applications.

The solution to this problem is to use the MVC architecture while designing Web applications. The idea behind the MVC architecture is to separate the core business model functionality of the Web application from the presentation and control logic of the interface-specific application. With this arrangement, it is possible to have multiple views of the same data model of the Web application. Under MVC architecture, data (Model) and user interface (View) are separated from each other so that any change in the user interfaces does not affect the data in the database, and vice versa.

A Web application can ensure a coherent interaction with users by allowing the three components of MVC--Model, View, and Controller--to communicate with each other. .

Figure 2.9 shows the interaction among the various MVC components:

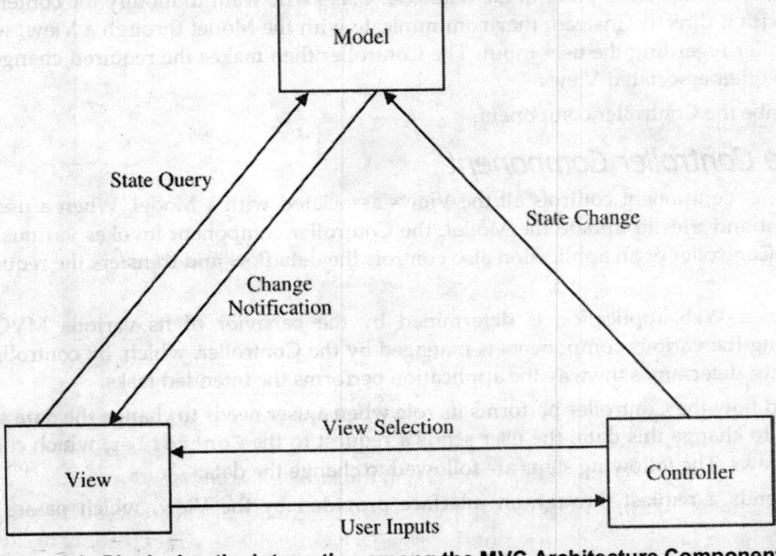

Figure 2.9: Displaying the Interaction among the MVC Architecture Components

Figure 2.9 shows that View retrieves the data of an application by using the query methods of the Model. In addition, whenever a user sends a request, it passes through the `Controller`. Then, the Controller intercepts the request from the View and passes it to the Model for appropriate action. MVC architecture allows separation of the business logic, data, and the presentation logic. In addition, Controller, which is a servlet, stores all the business logic. A View, normally a JSP page, contains all the code for presentation. A Model is implemented by using a pure Java or bean class. The different components in the application, such as Controller, Model, and View, are reusable and make applications highly scalable.

Let's learn more about each of the components of the MVC architecture next.

Describing the Model Component

The Model component displays the data on which an application is based. In a Web application, JavaBeans hold the data needed by a Web application to process user queries. Events sent to Web Controller serves the basis for all modifications to the data. The Model component represents the data and the business logic of the application, and is not associated with the presentation logic of the application. The Model component does not provide the specification for data access logic. It performs its interfacing with other components by using a set of public methods.

An application may have many states that need to be stored somewhere. These states are encapsulated by the Model component of the application. All the functionalities and features of the application are provided by the Model component. The application behaves according to the business logic of the application, implemented by the Model component. Any change in the state of the `Model` component state is notified immediately; and this change is reflected in all Views.

Describing the View Component

A View provides the Graphical User Interface (GUI) for Model. A user interacts with the application through View, which displays the information based on Model and allows the user to alter data. A Model can have multiple Views. The information provided by a Model has different meanings for different users and is interpreted by them in different ways. A View is responsible for displaying the information to users in a form that is understandable to them.

Model manages the database, the content of which can be changed and updated frequently. Any change in the database must be reflected to the user as soon as possible. Therefore, a `View` communicates with a Model to get information, if any change takes place in the database. Users who want to modify the content of a Model do not communicate with it directly. Instead, they communicate with the Model through a View, which communicates with the Controller regarding the user input. The Controller then makes the required changes in the Model and also notifies the other associated Views.

Let's now describe the Controller component.

Describing the Controller Component

The `Controller` component controls all the Views associated with a Model. When a user interacts with the View component and tries to update the Model, the Controller component invokes various methods to update the Model. The Controller of an application also controls the data flow and transfers the requests between Model and View.

The behavior of a Web application is determined by the behavior of its various MVC components. The interaction among the various components is managed by the Controller, which, by controlling the flow among these components, determines the way the application performs the intended tasks.

Let's understand how the Controller performs its role when a user needs to change the data stored in a Model. If the user wishes to change this data, the user sends a request to the `Controller`, which consults the Model to update all the Views. The following steps are followed to change the data:

1. The user sends a request through an interface provided by the View, which passes the request to the Controller.
2. The Controller receives the input request.
3. The Controller processes the request according to the Controller logic, and if access to the Model is not required, the process moves to step 5.
4. The Model is accessed and modified, if required. It then needs to notify all the associated Views regarding the modification.
5. The View presents a user interface according to the modified or original Model, as the case may be.

6. The View remains idle after the current interaction and waits for the next interaction to begin.

This process is repeated again for every new request.

Let's now summarize the concepts described in the chapter.

Summary

The chapter has discussed various methods of HTTP request, such as GET, POST, PUT, and DELETE. In addition, you have also learned about the meta information displayed to a user in the form of HTTP response. Further, various Web components of a Web application, such as JSP and servlets have been described. Moreover, the chapter has explored the different types of Web containers. Towards the end, you have learned about various Web application models and the MVC architecture that is used nowadays to develop a Web application.

The next chapter explains how Web applications can access data from relational databases using JDBC.

Quick Revise

Q1. The two Web components are ……………………… .

A. Servlets and web.xml | **B. JSP and web.xml**

C. JSP and servlets | **D. Servlets and Tag Libraries**

Ans. C

Q2. What is used to map an incoming request to Java Servlet/JSP?

A. `web.xml` | **B. JSP page**

C. URL pattern | **D. Servlets**

Ans. A

Q3. HTTP is a communication ……… used to transfer information on the Internet.

A. protocol | **B. component**

C. resource | **D. request**

Ans. A

Q4. Which of the following status code is displayed to represent the non-existence of a resource on the Web server?

A. 404 | **B. 401**

C. 500 | **D. 503**

Ans. A

Q5. Which of the following components provides services such as security, concurrency, and life-cycle management of the Web components in a Web application?

A. Web container | **B. Web application**

C. JSP | **D. Servlets**

Ans. A

Q6. What is a Web container?

Ans. A container that manages the execution of JSP pages and servlets is known as a Web container. It serves as a runtime environment for a Web application.

Q7. What is `web.xml`?

Ans. The web.xml file is a Deployment Descriptor, which stores the configurations details of a Web application. The configuration detail includes details of all the servlets and filters, and the URL mapping for each of them.

Q8. Define JSTL.

Ans. JSTL is a set of tag libraries that help us in embedding logic into a JSP page without inserting any Java code in the page.

Q9. Explain HTTP.

Ans. HTTP is a stateless application-level communication protocol. It is a request–response protocol; i.e. an HTTP client requests for a particular service from the HTTP server and the server generates a response for that client.

Q10. Explain the MVC architecture.

Ans. The MVC architecture allows the separation of business logic, data, and presentation logic. In this architecture, the Controller, which is a Java Servlet, stores all the business logic. The View, normally a JSP page, contains all the code for presentation. The Model, or the data part, is implemented by using pure Java or bean classes. The different objects in the application, such as Model, View, and Controller, are reusable and make Web applications highly scalable.

3

Working with JDBC 4.0

Enterprise applications that are created using the Java EE technology need to interact with databases to store application-specific information. For example, search engines use databases to store information about the Web pages and job portals use databases to store information about the candidates and employers who access the Web sites to search and advertise jobs on the Internet. Interacting with database requires database connectivity, which can be achieved by using the Open Database Connectivity (ODBC) driver. This driver is used with Java Database Connectivity (JDBC) to interact with various types of databases, such as `Oracle`, `MS Access`, My SQL, and `SQL Server`. JDBC is an Application Programming Interface (API), which is used in Java programming to interact with databases. JDBC works with different database drivers to connect to different databases.

This chapter focuses on JDBC, which is used to provide database connectivity to enterprise applications. In this chapter, you first learn about JDBC drivers as well as the features of JDBC 3.0 and 4.0 versions. You also learn about the JDBC APIs that provide various classes and interfaces to develop a JDBC application. Next, the use of java.sql and javax.sql pacakages in JDBC implmentation is described in detail. Towards the end, you learn to work with transactions in the JDBC application.

Introducing JDBC

JDBC™ is a specification from Sun Microsystems that provides a standard abstraction (API / protocol) for Java applications to communicate with different databases. It is used to write programs required to access databases. JDBC, along with the database driver, is capable of accessing databases and spreadsheets. JDBC can also be defined as a platform-independent interface between a relational database and the Java programming language. The enterprise data stored in a relational database can be accessed with the help of JDBC APIs. The JDBC API allows Java programs to execute SQL statements and retrieve results. The classes and interfaces of JDBC allow a Java application to send requests made by users to the specified Database Management System (DBMS). Instead of allowing the drivers to target a specific database, the users can specify the name of the database used to retrieve the data.

The following are the characteristics of JDBC:

- Supports a wide level of portability.
- Provides Java interfaces that are compatible with Java applications. These providers are also responsible for providing the driver services.
- Provides higher level APIs for application programmers. The JDBC API specification is used as an interface for the application and DBMS.
- Provides JDBC API for Java applications. The JDBC call to a Java application is made by the SQL statements. These statements are responsible for the entire communication of the application with the database. The user can send any type of SQL queries as requests to a database.

Components of JDBC

JDBC has four main components through which it can communicate with a database. These components are as follows:

- **The JDBC API**—Provides various methods and interfaces for easy and effective communication with the databases. It also provides a standard to connect a database to a client application. The application-specific user processes the SQL commands according to his need and retrieves the result in the ResultSet object. The JDBC API provides two main packages, `java.sql`, and `javax.sql`, `to` interact with databases. These packages contain the Java SE and Java EE platforms, which conform to the write once. run anywhere (WORA) capabilities of Java.
- **The JDBC DriverManager**—Loads database-specific drivers in an application to establish a connection with the database. It is also used to select the most appropriate database-specific driver from the previously loaded drivers when a new connection to the database is established. In addition, it is used to make database-specific calls to the database to process the user requests.
- **The JDBC test suite**—Evaluates the JDBC driver for its compatibility with Java EE. The JDBC test suite is used to test the operations being performed by JDBC drivers.

- **The JDBC-ODBC bridge**—Connects database drivers to the database. This bridge translates JDBC method calls to ODBC function calls, and is used to implement JDBC for any database for which an ODBC driver is available. The bridge for an application can be availed by importing the `sun.jdbc.odbc` package, which contains a native library to access the ODBC features.

JDBC Specification

With the emergence of JDBC 4.0, various changes, such as support for Binary Large Object (BLOB) and Character Large Object (CLOB) have been introduced in JDBC API.

The specifications that are available in different versions of JDBC are as follows:

- **JDBC 1.0**—Provides basic functionality of JDBC.
- **JDBC 2.0**—Provides JDBC API in two sections, the JDBC 2.0 Core API and the JDBC 2.0 Optional Package API.
- **JDBC 3.0**—Provides classes and interfaces in two Java packages, java.sql and javax.sql. JDBC 3.0 is a combination of JDBC 2.1 core API and the JDBC 2.0 Optional Package API. The JDBC 3.0 specification provides performance optimization features and improves the features of connection pooling and statement.
- **JDBC 4.0**—Provides the following advance features:
    - Auto loading of the Driver interface
    - Connection management
    - `ROWID` data type support
    - Annotation in SQL queries
    - National Character Set Conversion Support
    - Enhancement to exception handling
    - Enhanced support for large objects
- **JDBC 4.1**—It is a part of Java EE 7.

The complete implementation of JDBC 4.0 is released with Java EE 6 and can also be used with Java EE 5 and Java EE 7.

JDBC Architecture

A JDBC driver is required to process the SQL requests and generate results. JDBC API provides classes and interfaces to handle database-specific calls from users. Some of the important classes and interfaces defined in JDBC API are as follows:

- DriverManager
- Driver
- Connection
- Statement
- PreparedStatement
- CallableStatement
- ResultSet
- DatabaseMetaData
- ResultSetMetaData
- SqlData
- Blob
- Clob

The `DriverManager` in the JDBC API plays an important role in the JDBC architecture. It uses some database-specific drivers to effectively connect enterprise applications to databases.

Figure 3.1 demonstrates the simple JDBC architecture:

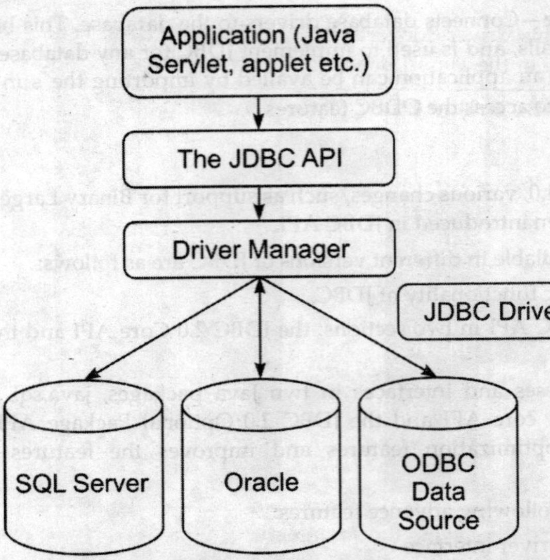

Figure 3.1: Displaying the Architecture of JDBC

As shown in Figure 3.1, the Java application that needs to communicate with a database has to be programmed using JDBC API. The JDBC driver (third-party vendor implementation) supporting data source, such as Oracle, and SQL Server, has to be added in the Java application for JDBC support, which can be done dynamically at run time. The dynamic plugging of the JDBC drivers ensures that the Java application is vendor independent. In other words, if you want to communicate with any data source through JDBC, you need a JDBC driver that intelligently communicates with the respective data source.

Some of the available drivers are pure Java drivers and are portable for all the environments; whereas, others are partial Java drivers and require some libraries to communicate with the database. You need to understand the architectures of all the four types of drivers to decide which driver to use to communicate with the data source.

Let's now learn about the JDBC drivers in detail.

Exploring JDBC Drivers

The different types of drivers available in JDBC are listed in Table 3.1:

Table 3.1: Types of JDBC Drivers

JDBC Driver Types	Description
Type-1 Driver	Refers to the Bridge Driver (JDBC-ODBC bridge)
Type-2 Driver	Refers to a Partly Java and Partly Native code driver (Native-API Partly Java driver)
Type-3 Driver	Refers to a pure Java driver that uses a middleware driver to connect to a database (Pure Java Driver for Database Middleware)
Type-4 Driver	Refers to a Pure Java driver (Pure), which is directly connected to a database

Now let's discuss each of these drivers in detail.

Describing the Type-1 Driver

The Type-1 driver acts as a bridge between JDBC and other database connectivity mechanisms, such as ODBC. An example of this type of driver is the Sun JDBC-ODBC bridge driver, which provides access to the database through the ODBC drivers. This driver also helps the Java programmers to use JDBC and develop Java applications to communicate with existing data sources. This driver is included in the Java 2 SDK within the `sun.jdbc.odbc` package. This driver converts JDBC calls into ODBC calls and redirects the request to the ODBC driver. The architecture of the Type-1 driver is shown in Figure 3.2:

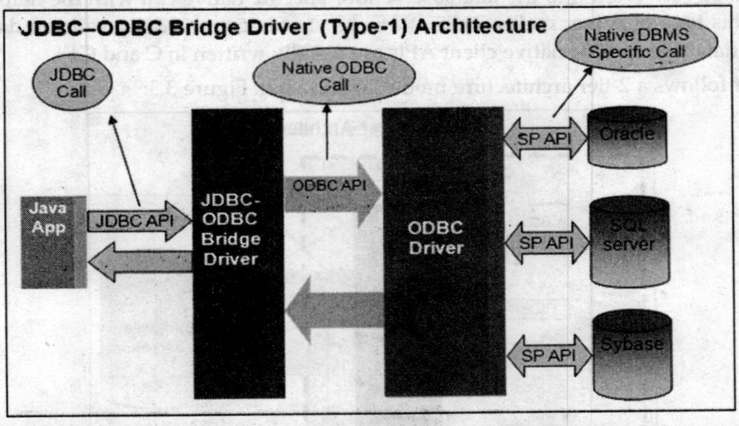

Figure 3.2: Displaying the Architecture of the JDBC Type-1 Driver

Figure 3.2 shows the architecture of the system that uses the JDBC-ODBC bridge driver to communicate with the respective database. In Figure 3.2, SP API refers to the APIs used to make a Native DBMS specific call. Figure 3.2 shows the following steps that are involved in establishing connection between a Java application and data source through the Type-1 driver:

1. The Java application makes the JDBC call to the JDBC-ODBC bridge driver to access a data source.
2. The JDBC-ODBC bridge driver resolves the JDBC call and makes an equivalent ODBC call to the ODBC driver.
3. The ODBC driver completes the request and sends responses to the JDBC-ODBC bridge driver.
4. The JDBC-ODBC bridge driver converts the response into JDBC standards and displays the result to the requesting Java application.

The Type-1 driver is generally used in the development and testing phases of Java applications.

Advantages of the Type-1 Driver

Some advantages of the Type-1 driver are as follows:

- Represents single driver implementation to interact with different data stores
- Allows us to communicate with all the databases supported by the ODBC driver
- Represents a vendor independent driver

Disadvantages of the Type-1 Driver

Some disadvantages of the Type-1 driver are as follows:

- Decreases the execution speed due to a large number of translations
- Depends on the ODBC driver; and therefore, Java applications also become indirectly dependent on ODBC drivers
- Requires the ODBC binary code or ODBC client library that must be installed on every client
- Uses `Java Native Interface (JNI)` to make ODBC calls

The preceding disadvantages make the Type-1 driver unsuitable for production environment and should be used only in case where no other driver is available. The Type-1 driver is also not recommended when Java applications are required with auto-installation applications, such as applets.

Describing the Type-2 Driver (Native API Driver)

The JDBC call can be converted into the database vendor specific native call with the help of the Type-2 driver. In other words, this type of driver makes `Java Native Interface (JNI)` calls on database specific native client API. These database specific native client APIs are usually written in C and C++.

The Type-2 driver follows a 2-tier architecture model, as shown in Figure 3.3:

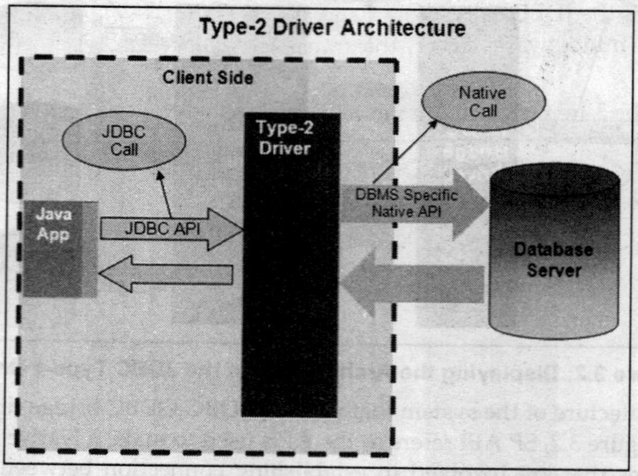

Figure 3.3: Displaying the Architecture of the JDBC Type-2 Driver

As shown in Figure 3.3, the Java application that needs to communicate with the database is programmed using JDBC API. These JDBC calls (programs written by using JDBC API) are converted into database specific native calls in the client machine and the request is then dispatched to the database specific native libraries. These native libraries present in the client are intelligent enough to send the request to the database server by using native protocol.

This type of driver is implemented for a specific database and usually delivered by a DBMS vendor. However, it is not mandatory that Type-2 drivers have to be implemented by DBMS vendors only. An example of Type-2 driver is the WebLogic driver implemented by BEA WebLogic. Type-2 drivers can be used with server-side applications. It is not recommended to use Type-2 drivers with client-side applications, since the database specific native libraries should be installed on the client machines.

Advantages of the Type-2 Driver

Some advantages of the Type-2 driver are as follows:

- Helps to access the data faster as compared to other types of drivers
- Contains additional features provided by the specific database vendor, which are also supported by the JDBC specification

Disadvantages of the Type-2 Driver

Some disadvantages of the Type-2 driver are as follows:

- Requires native libraries to be installed on client machines, since the conversion from JDBC calls to database specific native calls is done on client machines
- Executes the database specific native functions on the client JVM, implying that any bug in the Type-2 driver might crash the JVM
- Increases the cost of the application in case it is run on different platforms

Examples of the Type-2 Driver

Some examples of the Type-2 driver are as follows:

- **OCI (`Oracle` Call Interface) Driver**—Communicates with the `Oracle` database server. This driver converts JDBC calls into `Oracle` native library calls.

- **WebLogic OCI Driver for** `Oracle`—Makes JNI calls to WebLogic library functions. The WebLogic OCI driver for Oracle is similar to the Oracle OCI driver.
- **Type-2 Driver for Sybase**—Converts JDBC calls into Sybase dblib or ctlib calls, which are native libraries to connect to Sybase.

Describing the Type-3 Driver (Java to Network Protocol/All Java Driver)

The Type-3 driver translates the JDBC calls into a database server independent and middleware server-specific calls. With the help of the middleware server, the translated JDBC calls are further translated into database server specific calls.

The Type-3 drivers follow the 3-tier architecture model, as shown in Figure 3.4:

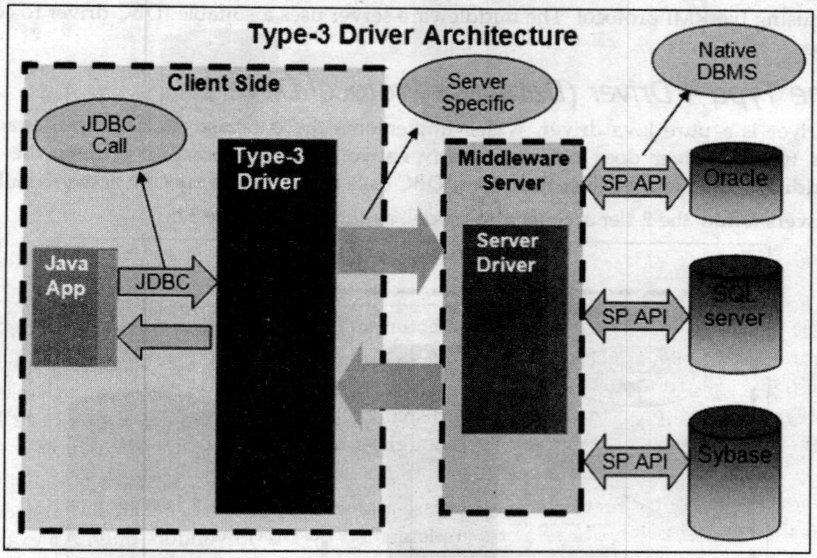

Figure 3.4: Displaying the Architecture of the JDBC Type-3 Driver

As shown in Figure 3.4, a JDBC Type-3 driver listens for JDBC calls from the Java application and translates them into middleware server specific calls. After that, the driver communicates with the middleware server over a socket. The middleware server converts these calls into database specific calls. These types of drivers are also known as *net-protocol fully Java technology-enabled* or *net-protocol* drivers.

The middleware server can be added in an application with some additional functionality, such as pool management, performance improvement, and connection availability. These functionalities make the Type-3 driver architecture more useful in enterprise applications. Type-3 driver is recommended to be used with applets, since this type of driver is auto downloadable.

Advantages of the Type-3 Drivers

Some advantages of the Type-3 driver are as follows:

- Serves as an all Java driver and is auto downloadable.
- Does not require any native library to be installed on the client machine.
- Ensures database independency, because a single driver provides accessibility to different types of databases.
- Does not provide the database details, such as username, password, and database server location, to the client. These details are automatically configured in the middleware server.
- Provides the facility to switch over from one database to another without changing the client-side driver classes. Switching of databases can be implemented by changing the configurations of the middleware server.

Disadvantage of the Type-3 Driver

The main disadvantage of the Type-3 driver is that it performs the tasks slowly due to the increased number of network calls as compared to Type–2 drivers. In addition, the Type-3 driver is also costlier as compared to other drivers.

Examples of the Type-3 Drivers

Some examples of the Type-3 driver are as follows:

- **IDS Driver**—Listens for JDBC calls and converts them into IDS Server specific network calls. The Type-3 driver communicates over a socket to IDS Server, which acts as a middleware server.
- **WebLogic RMI Driver**—Listens for JDBC calls and sends the requests from the client to the middleware server by using the RMI protocol. The middleware server uses a suitable JDBC driver to communicate with a database.

Describing the Type-4 Driver (Database Protocol Driver)

The Type-4 driver is a pure Java driver, which implements the database protocol to interact directly with a database. This type of driver does not require any native database library to retrieve the records from the database. In addition, the Type-4 driver translates JDBC calls into database specific network calls.

The Type-4 drivers follow the 2-tier architecture model, as shown in Figure 3.5:

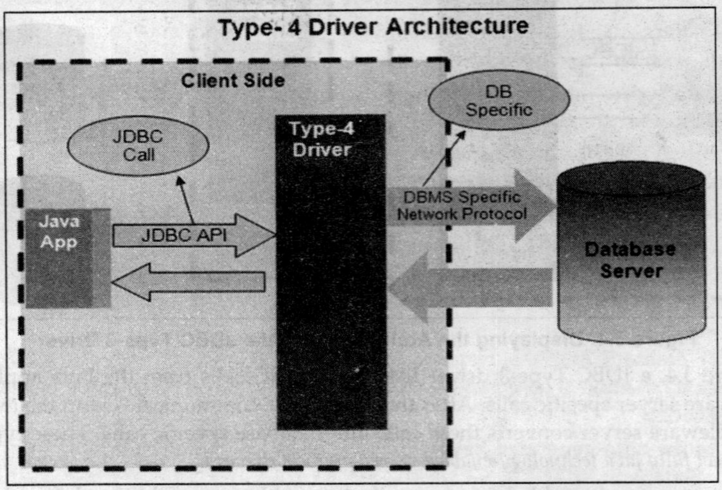

Figure 3.5: Displaying the Architecture of the JDBC Type-4 Driver

As shown in Figure 3.5, the Type-4 driver prepares a DBMS specific network message and then communicates with database server over a socket. This type of driver is lightweight and generally known as a thin driver. The Type-4 driver uses database specific proprietary protocols for communication. Generally, this type of driver is implemented by DBMS vendors, since the protocols used are proprietary.

You can use the Type-4 driver when you want an auto downloadable option for the client-side applications. In addition, it can be used with server-side applications.

Advantages of the Type-4 Driver

Some advantages of the Type-4 driver are as follows:

- Serves as a pure Java driver and is auto downloadable
- Does not require any native library to be installed on the client machine
- Uses database server specific protocol
- Does not require a middleware server

Disadvantage of the Type-4 Driver

The main disadvantage of the Type-4 driver is that it uses database specific proprietary protocol and is DBMS vendor dependent.

Examples of the Type-4 Driver

Some examples of the Type-4 driver are:

- Thin Driver for `Oracle` from `Oracle` Corporation
- WebLogic and MSSQLServer4 for MS SQL Server from BEA Systems

Exploring the Features of JDBC

JDBC 3.0 specification provides several features and procedures that can be used by Java database programmers. The core packages, along with the additional features, are present in the JDBC 3.0 version. Let's explore these features in detail next.

Additional Features of JDBC 3.0

The features introduced in JDBC 3.0 are as follows:

- **The JDBC metadata API**—Includes the instance of the `ParameterMetaData` interface to describe the parameter properties and their types used in the `PreparedStatement` interface.
- **Named parameters**—Updates the `CallableStatement` object so that users can access the parameters by using the names rather than the indexes of the parameters.
- **Changes to data types**—Include several new and modified data types. Few data type changes made in the JDBC 3.0 specification are:
  - **Large objects (BLOB, CLOB, and REF)**—Allow you to update the BLOB, CLOB, and REF type values in a database. Two new data types, BOOLEAN and DATALINK, have been introduced in JDBC 3.0.
  - **ResultSet values**—Updates the values of the ResultSet and ARRAY types available.
  - **New data types**—Include two new data types, java.sql.Types.DATALINK and java.sql.Types.BOOLEAN. These data types update the SQL data types with the same name. The DATALINK data type is capable of accessing the external resources; whereas, the BOOLEAN data type is equivalent to the BIT type. The value of the DATALINK data type is accessed by using the getURL() method, and the respective value of the boolean data type is accessed by using the getBoolean() method. These two methods take an instance of the ResultSet interface associated with the application.
  - **Access to the auto-generated keys**—Helps access the values of the auto-generated keys. You need to specify Statement.RETURN_GENERATED_KEYS or Statement.NO_GENERATED_KEYS in the execute() method to access the values of the auto-generated keys. The values for the auto-generated keys can be accessed in ResultSet. The ResultSet contains the values for the auto-generated keys and the getGeneratedKeys() instance method is used to access the values of the auto-generated keys.
- **Connector relationship**—Maintains the connection between JDBC and (Java EE). The connector architecture provides a set of connectors through which the enterprise applications connect to JDBC. This connection provides a resource adapter, which is used to connect JDBC to remote systems. The JDBC API provides three main service providers to define the connector architecture, which are as follows:
  - `ConnectionPoolDataSource`—Refers to an interface provided by the JDBC API. The ConnectionPoolDataSource interface is used to connect the applications to JDBC DataSource and back-end systems.
  - `XADataSource`—Refers to a feature of JDBC 2.0 API Optional Package. XADataSource provides transactional support to enterprise applications for accessing the resources.
  - Security Management: Maintains the security mechanism for enterprise applications.
- **`ResultSet` functionality**—Requires the programmer to close all the connections and results manually in JDBC programming. JDBC 3.0 supports the functionality of cursor holdability to ensure that the Connection

and ResultSet objects are closed. You need to maintain the following two constants to maintain the `ResultSet` holdability within an application:

- **HOLD_CURSOR_OVER_COMMIT**—Ensures that `ResultSet` objects are open till a commit operation is performed
- **CLOSE_CURSOR_AT_COMMIT**—Ensures that `ResultSet` objects are closed after a commit operation is performed

- **Returning multiple results**—Refers to a feature of the JDBC 3.0 specification to provide the Statement interface, which can access multiple results simultaneously. The Statement interface includes a new method in JDBC API to access multiple results. The new method added to the JDBC API is an overloaded form of the `getMoreResults()` method. It includes an integer flag that is used to specify the behavior of `ResultSets`. The flags included in the JDBC API are as follows:
  - **CLOSE_ALL_RESULTS**—Closes all the previously opened Resultsets by calling the getMoreResults() method
  - **CLOSE_CURRENT_RESULT**—Closes the current ResultSet object by calling the getMoreResults() method
  - **KEEP_CURRENT_RESULT**—Retains the current ResultSet object by using the getMoreResults() method
- **Connection pooling**—Allows you to maximize the performance of enterprise applications in the JDBC 3.0 specification.

Table 3.2 describes the properties of connection pooling:

Table 3.2: Properties of Connection Pooling

Property Name	Description
maxStatements	Specifies the maximum number of statements that the connection pool can keep open
initialPoolSize	Specifies the number of physical connections that the pool should keep open while being initialized
minPoolSize	Specifies the minimum number of physical connections that can remain in the pool while it is being initialized
maxPoolSize	Specifies the maximum number of physical connections that can remain in the pool while it is being initialized
maxIdleTime	Specifies the time duration within which an unused pool should remain open prior to the closing of the connection
propertyCycle	Specifies the time interval, in seconds, that a pool should wait for the property policy

- **PreparedStatement pooling**—Allows you to compile the commonly used SQL statements to improve the performance of the statement. The `PreparedStatement` pooling is needed to increase the lifetime of the `PreparedStatement` object. The concept of the `PreparedStatement` pooling comes from the connection pooling mechanism.
- **Using Savepoints**—Add the most exciting features to JDBC 3.0 specifications. Transactions in a database ensure that the persisted data remains in a consistent state. However, sometimes the data of a current transaction might be rolled back. A Savepoint is an intermediate point within a transaction at which a transaction may be rolled back.

Now, let's discuss about the new features that have been added to JDBC 4.0.

New Features in JDBC 4.0

Many new and advanced functionalities were introduced in JDBC 4.0. JDBC 4.0 includes the enhanced features of JDBC, which are mentioned as follows:

- **Auto loading of the JDBC driver class**—Provides auto loading of the JDBC drivers instead of loading them explicitly. In the previous versions of JDBC, you had to use the `Class.forName()` method to load the driver in a database. In JDBC 4.0, when the `getConnection()` method is called in an application, the `DriverManager` object automatically loads a driver in the database.
- **Connection management enhancement**—Allows the database programmers to establish a new connection by specifying the host name and an available port number. This can be done by using a set of parameters to maintain a standard connection. Connection management enhancement also adds some methods to the pre-existing interfaces, such as `Connection` and `Statement`.
- **Support for RowId**—Adds the `RowId` interface to the JDBC 4.0 specification to provide support for the `ROWID` data type. `RowId` is useful in tables where multiple columns do not have a unique identifier.
- **`Dataset` implementation of SQL using annotations**—Introduces the concept of annotation while using SQL, which ultimately results in fewer lines of code. The annotations are used along with the queries. The query results can be bound to the Java classes to speed up the processing of the query output. The JDBC 4.0 specification provides the following two main annotations:
  - **The SELECT annotation**—Retrieves query specific data from a database. You can use the SELECT annotation in a SELECT query within a Java class. The attributes of the SELECT annotation are described in Table 3.3:

Table 3.3: Attributes of the SELECT Annotation

Name	Type	Description
sql	String	Specifies a simple SQL SELECT query.
value	String	Represents the value specified for the sql attribute.
tableName	String	Specifies the name of the table created in a database.
readOnly, connected, scrollable	boolean	Indicates whether DataSet is ReadOnly or Updatable. It also indicates whether or not DataSet is connected to a back-end database. In addition, it indicates whether or not it is scrollable when the query is used in a connection.
allColumnsMapped	boolean	Indicates whether or not the column names used in the annotations are mapped to the corresponding fields in DataSet.

  - **The UPDATE annotation**—Updates the queries used in database tables. The `UPDATE` annotation must include the SQL annotation type to update the fields of a table.
- **SQL exception handling enhancements**—Introduces certain enhancements to the `SQLException` class, which are as follows:
  - **New exception subclasses**—Provide new classes as enhancement to SQLException. The new classes that are added to the `SQLException` exception class include SQL non-transient exception and SQL transient exception. The SQL non-transient exception class is called when an already performed JDBC operation fails to run, unless the cause of the `SQLException` exception is corrected. On the other hand, the SQL transient exception class is called when a previously failed JDBC operation succeeds after retry.
  - **Casual relationships**—Support the Java SE chained exception mechanism by the `SQLException` class (also known as Casual facility). It allows handling multiple SQL exceptions raised in the JDBC operation.
  - **Support for the for-each loop**—Implements the chain of exceptions in a chain of groups by the `SQLException` class. The `for-each` loop is used to iterate on these groups.
  - **SQL XML support**—Introduces the concept of `XML` support in SQL DataStore. Some additional APIs have been added to JDBC 4.0 to provide this support.

Describing JDBC APIs

JDBC API is a part of the JDBC specification and provides a standard abstraction to use JDBC drivers. The JDBC API provides classes and interfaces that are used by Java applications to communicate to databases. The JDBC driver communicates with a relational database for any requests made by a Java application by using the JDBC API. The JDBC driver not only processes the SQL commands, but also sends back the result of processing of these SQL commands. In addition, the JDBC API can be used to access the required data from all the database types, such as SQL Server, Sybase, and Oracle. A programmer does not need to write different programs to access the data from the database. The JDBC API satisfies the *write once, run anywhere* behavior of Java. Therefore, JDBC is used largely to access data from various data sources.

The JDBC API is based upon the X/Open Call Level Interface (CLI) specification and SQL standard statements. This is also the basic standard for ODBC.

The JDBC 4.0 API specification is used to process and access data sources by using Java. The API includes drivers to be installed to access the different data sources. The API is used with SQL statements to read and write data from any data source in a tabular format. This facility to access data from the database is available through the group of `javax.sql.RowSet` interfaces. JDBC 4.0 API is mainly divided into the following two packages:

- java.sql
- javax.sql

The JDBC 4.0 API includes both the java.sql package, called as the JDBC core API, and the javax.sql package, called as the JDBC Optional Package API..Now, let's discuss them in detail.

*The **java.sql** Package*

The `java.sql` package is also known as the JDBC core API. This package includes the interfaces and classes to perform JDBC core operations, such as creating and executing SQL queries. The `java.sql` package consists of the interfaces and classes that need to be implemented in an application to access a database. The developer uses these classes and interfaces to access the database in an application. The classes and interfaces in the `java.sql` package can be classified into the following categories based on different operations:

- Connection management
- Database access
- Data types
- Database metadata
- Exceptions and warnings

Let's discuss these categories in detail.

Connection Management

The connection management category contains the classes and interfaces used to establish a connection with a database.

Table 3.4 describes the classes and interfaces of the connection management category:

Table 3.4: Classes and Interfaces of Connection Management

Class/Interface	Description
java.sql.Connection interface	Creates a connection with a specific database. You can use SQL statements to retrieve the desired results within the context of a connection.
java.sql.Driver interface	Creates and registers an instance of a driver with the DriverManager object.
java.sql.DriverManager class	Provides the functionality to manage database drivers.
java.sql.DriverPropertyInfo class	Retrieves the properties required to obtain a connection.
java.sql.SQLPermission class	Sets up logging stream with DriverManager object.

Database Access

SQL queries are executed to access the application-specific data after a connection is established with a database. The interfaces listed in Table 3.5 allow you to send SQL statements to the database for execution and read the results from the respective database:

Table 3.5: Interfaces of the Database Access Category

Interface	Description
java.sql.CallableStatement	Executes stored procedures.
java.sql.PreparedStatement	Allows the programmer to create parameterized SQL statements.
java.sql.ResultSet	Abstracts the results of executing the `SELECT` statements. This interface provides methods to access the results row-by-row.
java.sql.Statement	Executes SQL statements over the underlying connection and access the results.
java.sql.Savepoint	Specifies a `Savepoint` in a transaction.

The java.sql.PreparedStatement and java.sql.CallableStatement interfaces extend the java.sql.Statement interface.

Data Types

In the JDBC API, various interfaces and classes are defined to hold the specific types of data to be stored in a database. For example, to store the BLOB type values, the Blob interface is declared in the java.sql package. Table 3.6 describes the classes and interfaces of various data types in the `java.sql` package:

Table 3.6: Classes and Interfaces for Data Types in the java.sql Package

Class/Interface	Description
java.sql.Array interface	Provides mapping for `ARRAY` of a collection.
java.sql.Blob interface	Provides mapping for the `BLOB SQL type.`
java.sql.Clob interface	Provides mapping for the `CLOB` SQL type.
java.sql.Date class	Provides mapping for the SQL type `DATE`. Although, the `java.util.Date` class provides a general-purpose representation of date, the `java.sql.Date` class is preferable for representing dates in database-centric applications, as the type maps directly to SQL `DATE` type. Note that the `java.sql.Date` class extends the `java.util.Date` class.
java.sql.NClob interface	Provides mapping of the Java language and the `National Character Large Object` types. The NClob interface allows you to store the values of the character string up to the maximum length.
java.sql.Ref interface	Provides mapping for SQL type `REF`.
java.sql.RowId interface	Provides mapping for Java with the SQL `ROWID` value.
java.sql.Struct interface	Provides mapping for the SQL structured types.
java.sql.SQLXML interface	Provides mapping for the SQL XML types available in the JDBC API.
java.sql.Time class	Provides mapping for the SQL type `TIME`, and extends the `java.util.Date` class.
java.sql.Timestamp class	Provides mapping for the SQL type TIMESTAMP and extends the `java.util.Date` class.
java.sql.Types class	Holds a set of constant integers, each corresponding to a SQL type.

In addition to the data types mentioned in Table 3.6, the JDBC API provides certain user-defined data types (UDT) available in JDBC API. The UDTs available in the java.sql package are listed in Table 3.7:

Table 3.7: Interfaces for UDT in the java.sql Package

Interface	Description
java.sql.SQLData	Provides a mapping between the SQL UDTs and a specific class in Java.
java.sql.SQLInput	Provides methods to read the UDT attributes from a specific input stream. The input stream contains a stream of values depicting the instance of the SQL structured or SQL distinct type.
java.sql.SQLOutput	Writes the attributes of the output stream back to the database.

JDBC API also provides some default data types that are associated with a database. The default types include the `DISTINCT` and `DATALINK` types. The `DISTINCT` data type maps to the base type to which the base type value is mapped. For example, a `DISTINCT` value based on a `SQL NUMERIC` type maps to a `java.math.BigDecimal` type. A `DATALINK` type always represents a `java.net.URL` object of the URL class defined in the `java.net package.`

Database Metadata

The metadata interface is used to retrieve information about the database used in an application. JDBC API provides certain interfaces to access the information about the database used in the application. These metadata interfaces are described in Table 3.8:

Table 3.8: Classes and Interfaces of Database MetaData

Class/Interface	Description
java.sql.DatabaseMetaData	This interface provides the comprehensive information about the database.
java.sql.ParameterMetaData	The object of this interface is used to retrieve information about the types and properties for each parameter provided in a `PreparedStatement` object
java.sql.ResultSetMetaData	The object of this interface is used to fetch the information about the types and properties of the columns specified in a `ResultSet` object

Exceptions and Warnings

JDBC API provides classes and interfaces to handle the unwanted exceptions raised in an application. The API also provides classes to handle warnings related to an application.

Table 3.9 describes the classes for exception handling:

Table 3.9: Classes for Exception Handling

Classes	Description
java.sql.BatchUpdateException	Updates batches.
java.sql.DataTruncation	Identifies data truncation errors. Note that data types do not always match between Java and SQL.
java.sql.SQLException	Represents all JDBC-related exception conditions. This exception also embeds all driver and database-level exceptions and error codes.
java.sql.SQLWarning	Represents database access warnings. Instead of catching the SQLWarning exception, you can use the appropriate methods on `java.sql.Connection`, `java.sql.Statement`, and `java.sql.ResultSet` objects to access the warnings.

Let's now briefly discuss the JDBC extension APIs (`javax.sql`) available in JDBC API.

The *javax.sql* Package

The `javax.sql` package is also called as the JDBC extension API, and provides classes and interfaces to access server-side data sources and process Java programs. The JDBC extension package supplements the javax.sql package, and provides the following support:

- DataSource
- Connection and statement pooling
- Distributed transaction
- Rowsets

DataSource

The javax.sql.DataSource interface represents the data sources related to the Java application.

Table 3.10 describes the interfaces of the `DataSource` interface provided by the `javax.sql` package:

Table 3.10: Interfaces for DataSource

Interface	Description
javax.sql.DataSource	Represents the `DataSource` interface used in an application
javax.sql.CommonDataSource	Provides the methods that are common between the DataSource, `XADataSource` and `ConnectionPoolDataSource` interfaces

Connection and Statement Pooling

The connections made by using the `DataSource` objects are implemented on the middle-tier connection pool. As a result, the functionality to create new database connections is improved. The classes and interfaces available for connection pooling in the `javax.sql` package are listed in Table 3.11:

Table 3.11: Classes and Interfaces for Connection Pooling

Class/Interface	Description
javax.sql.ConnectionPoolDataSource interface	Provides a factory for the `PooledConnection` objects.
javax.sql.PooledConnection interface	Provides an object to manage connection pools.
javax.sql.ConnectionEvent class	Provides an Event object, which offers information about the occurrence of an event.
javax.sql.ConnectionEventListener interface	Provides objects used to register the events generated by the `PooledConnection` object.
javax.sql.StatementEvent class	Represents the `StatementEvent` interface associated with the events that occur in the `PooledConnection` interface. The `StatementEvent` interface is then sent to the `StatementEventListeners` instance, which is registered with the instance of the `PooledConnection` interface.
javax.sql.StatementEventListener interface	Provides an object that registers the event with an instance of `PooledConnection` interface.

Distributed Transaction

The distributed transaction mechanism allows an application to use the data sources on multiple servers in a single transaction. JDBC API provides certain classes and interfaces to handle distributed transactions over the middle-tier architecture, as listed in Table 3.12:

Table 3.12: Classes and Interfaces for Distributed Transaction

Class/Interface	Description
javax.sql.XAConnection	Provides the object that supports distributed transaction over middle-tier architecture
javax.sql.XADataSource	Provides a factory for the `XAConnection` objects

Rowsets Object

A `RowSet` object is used to retrieve data in a network. In addition, the `RowSet` object is able to transmit data over a network. JDBC API provides the `RowSet` interface, with its numerous classes and interfaces, to work with tabular data, as described in Table 3.13:

Table 3.13: Classes and Interfaces for RowSet

Class/Interface	Description
javax.sql.RowSetListener interface	Receives notification from the `RowSet` object on the occurrence of an event
javax.sql.RowSetEvent class	Provides the Event object, which is generated on the occurrence of an event on the `RowSet` object
javax.sql.RowSetMetaData interface	Contains information about the columns specified in a RowSet object
javax.sql.RowSetReader interface	Populates the disconnected RowSet object with rows of data
javax.sql.RowSetWriter interface	Implements the `RowSetWriter object, which is also called RowSet` writer
javax.sql.RowSet interface	Adds support to the JDBC API for the JavaBeans™ component model

Exploring Major Classes and Interfaces

You have already learned about the classes and interfaces of the `java.sql` and `javax.sql` packages. Among these classes and interfaces discussed in the preceding sections, some noteworthy classes and interfaces play an important role in providing JDBC implementations in a Java application, which we explore in this section. You can establish a database connection by using the classes and interfaces of JDBC, such as DriverManager and Driver. These classes and interfaces allow you to load a driver, create a connection, and retrieve or update data in a database.

Let's explore the following major classes and interfaces in detail:

- The DriverManager class
- The Driver interface
- The Connection interface
- The Statement interface

The DriverManager Class

DriverManager is a non-abstract class in JDBC API. It contains only one constructor, which is declared private to imply that this class cannot be inherited or initialized directly. All the methods and properties of this class are declared as static. The DriverManager class performs the following main responsibilities:

- Maintains a list of DriverInfo objects, where each DriverInfo object holds one driver implementation class object and its name
- Prepares a connection using the driver implementation that accepts the given JDBC URL

Table 3.14 describes the methods of the DriverManager class:

Table 3.14: Methods of the DriverManager Class

Method	Description
static void deregisterDriver(Driver driver)	Drops a driver from the list of drivers maintained by the DriverManager class.
static Connection getConnection(String url)	Establishes a connection of a driver with a database. The DriverManager class selects a driver from the list of drivers and creates the connection.
static Connection getConnection(String url, Properties info)	Establishes a connection of a driver with a database on the basis of the URL and info passed as parameters. URL is used to load the selected driver for a database. The info parameter provides information about the string/value tags used in the connection.
static Connection getConnection(String url, String username, String password)	Establishes a connection of a driver with a database. The DriverManager class selects a driver from the list of drivers and creates the connection. Along with URL, it takes two more parameters, username and password. The username parameter specifies the user for which the connection is being made, and the password parameter represents the password of the user.
static Driver getDriver(String url)	Locates the requested driver in the DriverManager class. The url parameter specifies the URL of the requested driver.
static Enumeration getDrivers()	Accesses a list of drivers present in a database.
static int getLoginTimeout()	Specifies the maximum time a driver needs to wait to log on to a database.
static PrintStream getLogStream()	Returns the logging or tracing PrintStream object.
static PrintWriter getLogWriter()	Returns the log writer.
static void println(String message)	Prints a message used in a log stream.
static void registerDriver(Driver driver)	Registers a requested driver with the DriverManager class.
static void setLoginTimeout(int seconds)	Sets the maximum time that a driver needs to wait while attempting to connect to a database.
static void setLogStream(PrintStream out)	Sets the logging or tracing PrintStream object.
static void setLogWriter(PrintWriter out)	Sets the logging or tracing PrintWriter object.

The Driver Interface

The `Driver` interface is used to create Connection objects that provide an entry point for database connectivity. Generally, all drivers provide the `DriverManager` class that implements the `Driver` interface and helps to load the driver in a JDBC application. The drivers are loaded for any given connection request with the help of the `DriverManager` class. After the Driver interface is loaded, its instance is created and registered with the DriverManager class.

Table 3.15 describes all the methods provided in the Driver interface:

Table 3.15: Methods of the Driver Interface

Methods	Description
boolean acceptsURL(String url)	Checks whether or not the specified URL format is acceptable by the driver
connection connect(String url, Properties info)	Establishes the connection with the database by using the given URL

Table 3.15: Methods of the Driver Interface	
Methods	**Description**
int getMajorVersion()	Accesses the major version number of the driver
int getMinorVersion()	Retrieves the minor version number of the driver
DriverPropertyInfo[] getPropertyInfo(String url, Properties info)	Retrieves the properties of the driver on the basis of the given URL
boolean jdbcCompliant()	Reports whether the current driver is a genuine JDBC Compliant^{TM} driver
Logger getParentLogger()	Returns the parent Logger of all the Loggers used by this driver

The Connection Interface

The `Connection` interface is a standard type that defines an abstraction to access the session established with a database server. JDBC driver provider must implement the `Connection` interface. The `Connection` type of object (an instance of the class that implements the `Connection` interface) represents the session established with the data store.

The `Connection` interface provides methods to handle the `Connection` object.

Table 3.16 describes the methods present in the Connection interface:

Table 3.16: Methods of the Connection Interface	
Methods	**Description**
void clearWarnings()	Clears all the warnings for a Connection object. This method throws the SQLException exception when an error occurs.
void close()	Closes a connection and releases the Connection object associated with the connected database. It also releases the JDBC resources associated with the connection.
void commit()	Commits the changes made in the previous commit/rollback and releases any database locks held by the current Connection object.
Statement createStatement()	Creates the Statement object to send SQL statements to the specified database. This method takes no argument; therefore, it can be executed by using the Statement object.
Statement createStatement(int resultSetType, int resultSetConcurrency)	Creates a Statement object, which is used to load the SQL statements to the specified database. The ResultSet object generated by this Statement object is of the mentioned type and concurrency.
Statement createStatement (int resultSetType, int resultSetConcurrency, int resultSetHoldability)	Creates an object with the mentioned type, concurrency, and holdability.
boolean getAutoCommit()	Retrieves the auto-commit mode for the current Connection object.
String getCatalog()	Gets the name of the current catalog used in the current Connection object.
int getHoldability()	Gets the current holdability of the ResultSet object created by using a Connection object.
DatabaseMetaData getMetaData()	Gets the DatabaseMetaData object containing the metadata information. You should ensure that the database must be connected with a Connection object.

Table 3.16: Methods of the Connection Interface

Methods	Description
int getTransactionIsolation()	Provides the transaction isolation level of the Connection object related to a database.
Map getTypeMap()	Gets a map object related to a Connection object.
SQLWarning getWarnings()	Retrieves any warning associated with a Connection object.
boolean isClosed()	Specifies whether or not a database Connection object is closed.
boolean isReadOnly()	Specifies whether or not a Connection object is read-only.
String nativeSQL(String sql)	Allows you to convert the SQL statements passed to the Connection object into the systems native SQL grammar.
CallableStatement prepareCall(String sql)	Creates a CallableStatement object to call database stored procedures.
CallableStatement prepareCall(String sql, int resultSetType, int resultSetConcurrency)	Creates a CallableStatement object that generates the ResultSet object of the specified type and concurrency.
CallableStatement prepareCall(String sql, int resultSetType, int resultSetConcurrency, int resultSetHoldability)	Creates a CallableStatement object that generates the ResultSet object of the specified type, concurrency, and holdability.
PreparedStatement prepareStatement(String sql)	Creates a PreparedStatement object to send the SQL statements over a connection.
PreparedStatement prepareStatement(String sql, int autoGeneratedKeys)	Creates a PreparedStatement object that retrieves auto-generated keys.
PreparedStatement prepareStatement(String sql, int[] columnIndexes)	Creates a PreparedStatement object that retrieves auto-generated keys by using a given array.
PreparedStatement prepareStatement(String sql, int resultSetType, int resultSetConcurrency)	Generates a PreparedStatement object that generates the ResultSet object with the given type and concurrency.
PreparedStatement prepareStatement(String sql, int resultSetType, int resultSetConcurrency, int resultSetHoldability)	Generates a PreparedStatement object that generates the ResultSet object with the given type, concurrency, and holdability.
PreparedStatement prepareStatement(String sql, String[] columnNames)	Creates a PreparedStatement object that retrieves the auto-generated keys. The columnNames parameter of PreparedStatement is an array containing the names of the columns that contain the auto-generated keys in the target table.
void releaseSavepoint(Savepoint savepoint)	Releases the savepoint associated with the Connection object of the current transaction.
void rollback ()	Rolls back all the transactions and releases any database locks that are currently done by the Connection object.
void rollback(Savepoint savepoint)	Rollbacks all the changes made by the Connection object after a savepoint object is created.
void setAutoCommit(boolean autoCommit)	Sets the current transaction to the connections auto-commit mode.
void setCatalog(String catalog)	Sets the given catalog name for current Connection object's

Table 3.16: Methods of the Connection Interface

Methods	Description
	database.
void setHoldability(int holdability)	Changes the holdability of the current Connection object.
void setReadOnly(boolean readOnly)	Sets the connection to the read-only mode to optimize the specified database.
Savepoint setSavepoint()	Creates an unnamed savepoint in the current transaction and returns the savepoint associated with the previous transactions.
Savepoint setSavepoint(String name)	Creates a savepoint with the name specified in the current transaction. It returns the new Savepoint object.
void setTransactionIsolation(int level)	Checks the transaction isolation level of the specified Connection object.
void setTypeMap(Map map)	Installs the TypeMap object as the current type map for the current connection.
Array createArrayOf(String typeName, Object[] elements)	Refers to a Factory method used to create Array objects.
Blob createBlob()	Creates an object implementing the Blob interface.
Clob createClob()	Creates an object implementing the Clob interface.
NClob createNClob()	Creates an object implementing the NClob interface.
SQLXML createSQLXML()	Creates an object implementing the SQLXML interface.
Struct createStruct(String typeName, Object[] attributes)	Refers to the factory method that creates Struct objects

The `Connection` interface also provides certain fields that can be used to handle connection transactions. Table 3.17 describes the fields available in the `Connection` interface:

Table 3.17: Fields of the Connection Interface

Fields	Description
static int TRANSACTION_NONE	Refers to a constant representing that transactions are not supported.
static int TRANSACTION_READ_COMMITTED	Prevents a transaction from reading a row with uncommitted changes. It is only used to read non-repeatable rows in a table.
static int TRANSACTION_READ_UNCOMMITTED	Indicates that non-repeatable and phantom reads are allowed in a transaction. It allows a row to be changed during a transaction. The changed row can be read by other transactions before the changes in the row are committed.
static int TRANSACTION_REPEATABLE_READ	Prevents non-repeatable reads and simultaneous transactions in a single row.
static int TRANSACTION_SERIALIZABLE	Prevents reading non-repeatable rows in a table.

Let's now learn about the Statement interface.

The Statement Interface

The `Statement` interface defines a standard abstraction to execute the SQL statements requested by a user and return the results by using the ResultSet object. The Statement object contains a single ResultSet object at a time. It is possible that the data reading done with the help of one ResultSet object is interleaved with the reading done by the other. In such a case, each ResultSet object must be generated by different `Statement` objects. The `execute()` method of all the statements implicitly closes the current ResultSet object (if it is open) of a statement. The Statement interface provides specific methods to execute and retrieve the results from a database. The PreparedStatement interface provides the methods to deal with the `IN` parameters; whereas, the `CallableStatement` interface provides methods to deal with the `IN` and `OUT` parameters.

The `Statement` interface also provides certain methods that are used with a database. These methods are described in Table 3.18:

Table 3.18: Methods of the Statement Interface

Methods	Description
void addBatch(String sql)	Adds the SQL commands to the existing list of commands for the Statement object. These commands are executed in a batch by calling the executeBatch() method.
void abort(Executor executor)	Terminates an open connection with the database.
void cancel()	Cancels the statement, if the data sources do not support the statement.
void clearBatch()	Clears all the commands listed in the batch of the Statement interface.
void clearWarnings()	Clears the warnings that are generated on the Statement object. You should note that after the execution of the clearWarnings() method, the `getWarnings()` method returns null, provided a new warning is not generated for this Statement object.
void close()	Closes the Statement object. Therefore, it releases its control from the database and connection.
boolean execute(String sql)	Executes the SQL commands that may return multiple result sets along with one or more update counts.
boolean execute(String sql, int autoGeneratedKeys)	Executes the SQL commands that may return multiple result sets along with one or more update counts. It also indicates whether a driver or the auto-generated keys are available for the retrieval.
boolean execute(String sql, int[] columnIndexes)	Executes the SQL commands that may return multiple result sets along with one or more update counts. It also indicates the driver about the availability of the auto-generated keys in an array. The array contains the list of the indexes and the tables containing the auto-generated keys.
boolean execute(String sql, String[] columnNames)	Executes the SQL commands that may return multiple result sets along with one or more update counts. It also indicates the driver about the availability of the auto-generated keys in an array. The array contains the name of the columns in the target table that contains the auto-generated keys.
int[] executeBatch()	Executes the SQL commands in a batch. The method returns the update count as an integer greater or equal to 0 after the successful execution of the batch statements. The integer array is used to represent the array of the SQL commands listed in the batch.
ResultSet executeQuery(String sql)	Executes a SQL command and returns a single ResultSet object.
int executeUpdate(String sql)	Executes the SQL Data Definition Language (DDL) statements, such as `INSERT`, `UPDATE`, and `DELETE`.
int executeUpdate(String sql, int autoGeneratedKeys)	Executes the SQL statements and notifies the driver about the availability of the auto-generated keys. The auto-generated keys are helpful to retrieve data from the database.
int executeUpdate(String sql, int[] columnIndexes)	Executes the SQL statements on the basis of the SQL query and column index passed as an argument. This method also notifies the driver about the availability of the auto-generated keys. The auto-generated keys are

Table 3.18: Methods of the Statement Interface

Methods	Description
	helpful to retrieve data from the database. The array index of the auto-generated keys indicates the indexes and tables that contain the auto-generated keys.
int executeUpdate(String sql, String[] columnNames)	Executes the SQL statements and notifies the driver about the availability of the auto-generated keys. These keys are responsible for data retrieval from the database. The array index of the auto-generated keys indicates the columns of the target table that contains the auto-generated keys.
Connection getConnection()	Retrives an object of Connection type, which is used to maintain the connection of a Java application with a database.
int getFetchDirection()	Retrieves the direction of the rows from the database tables that are generated from the ResultSet object. The fetch direction for a Statement object can be set with the help of the `setFetchDirection()` method. If the fetch direction is not set, the fetch direction is implementation specific.
int getFetchSize()	Gets the number of rows of default fetch size from the current ResultSet object.
ResultSet getGeneratedKeys()	Gets the auto-generated keys created by executing the Statement object.
int getMaxFieldSize()	Gets the maximum number of bytes that can be returned for the column values.
int getMaxRows()	Provides the maximum number of rows in a ResultSet produced by the Statement object.
boolean getMoreResults()	Navigates to the next result in the ResultSet object. It is also used to close the currently opened result set.
int getMoreResults(int current)	Navigates to the next result in the object of the statement. It deals with the ResultSet object by using the instructions specified in the given flag.
int getQueryTimeout()	Provides the number of seconds the driver has to wait to execute the statements.
ResultSet getResultSet()	Gets the current ResultSet object generated by the Statement object.
int getResultSetConcurrency()	Gets the concurrency of the ResultSet object generated by the Statement object.
int getResultSetHoldability()	Gets the holdability of the ResultSet object generated by the Statement object.
int getResultSetType()	Retrieves the result set type for the ResultSet object.
int getUpdateCount()	Retrieves the current result set as an update count. The value returned by this method is either a positive or negative value, indicating the number of records that have been updated in a result set.
SQLWarning getWarnings()	Gets the warnings generated on the Statement object.
void setCursorName(String name)	Sets the cursor name to the given string. The cursor name is used by the Statement objects to execute this method.
void setEscapeProcessing(boolean enable)	Sets the escape processing on or off.
void setFetchDirection(int direction)	Sets the direction for the driver to process the rows in the ResultSet object.
void setFetchSize(int rows)	Sets the number of rows that should be fetched from the database.

Table 3.18: Methods of the Statement Interface

Methods	Description
void setMaxFieldSize(int max)	Sets the maximum number of bytes for the ResultSet object to store binary values.
void setMaxRows(int max)	Sets the maximum number of rows that a ResultSet can contain.
void setQueryTimeout(int seconds)	Sets the number of seconds a driver needs to wait for executing the Statement object.

The Statement interface also comprises few fields. Table 3.19 describes the fields available in the Statement interface:

Table 3.19: Fields of Statement Interface

Fields	Description
static int CLOSE_ALL_RESULTS	Closes all the open ResultSet objects. All the ResultSet objects should be closed before calling the getMoreResults() method.
static int CLOSE_CURRENT_RESULT	Indicates that the current ResultSet object connected with the specified database must be closed before calling the getMoreResults() method.
static int EXECUTE_FAILED	Indicates the occurrence of errors while executing a batch statement.
static int KEEP_CURRENT_RESULT	Indicates that the current ResultSet object should not be closed before calling the getMoreResults() method.
static int NO_GENERATED_KEYS	Indicates that the generated keys should not be made available for retrieval.
static int RETURN_GENERATED_KEYS	Indicates that the generated keys should be made available for retrieval.
static int SUCCESS_NO_INFO	Indicates that a batch statement has been executed successfully.

Table 3.19 shows all the required fields in the Statement interface. These are used by a database to communicate with an application.

The `Statement` object is created after the connection to the specified database is made. This object is created by using the `createStatement()` method of the `Connection` interface, as shown in the following code snippet:

```
Connection con = DriverManager.getConnection (url, "username", "password");
Statement stmt = con.createStatement();
```

Now let's discuss how the java.sql package is used to implement database connectivity in an application.

Exploring JDBC Processes with the java.sql Package

The java.sql package is used by a Java application to communicate with a database. The JDBC application-specific code should be written within an application that has to communicate with the database. There are some basic steps to use JDBC in a Java application. Let's now discuss the basic steps involved in using JDBC in an application. The following heads help you to understand how JDBC implementations are provided in a Java application by using the `java.sql` package:

- Basic JDBC steps
- Simple JDBC application
- PreparedStatement interface
- CallableStatement interface
- ResultSets
- Batch updates

- Advance data types

Now, let's discuss each of them in detail.

Understanding Basic JDBC Steps

To establish a connection with a database and retrieve the desired results, you need to perform various steps. For example, you need to register a driver with the DriverManager object, obtain a connection, and execute SQL queries.

Figure 3.6 shows the basic steps involved in using JDBC to write a database program in Java:

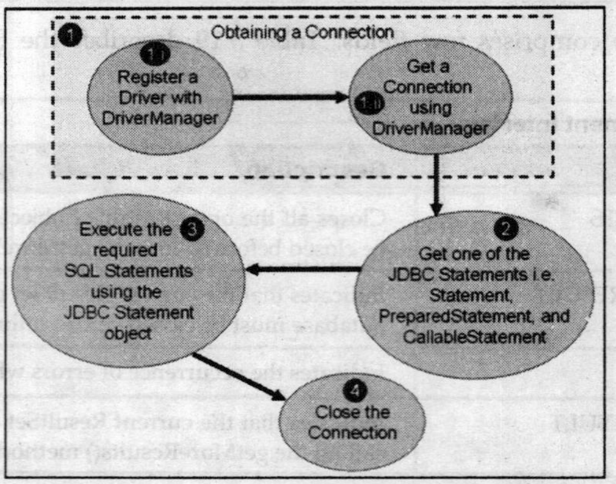

Figure 3.6: Showing Basic Steps to use JDBC

Figure 3.6 shows the following broad steps that need to be performed to implement JDBC in Java application:

1. Obtaining a connection
2. Creating a JDBC Statement object
3. Executing SQL statements
4. Closing the connection

Let's discuss each of them in detail.

Obtaining a Connection

To obtain an object of the Connection interface, you need to first register a driver with the DriverManager class by invoking the registerDriver() method, setting the System property, or invoking the `Class.forName()` method. Then, the connection is obtained by using the `java.sql.DriverManager` class.

You need to perform the following steps to obtain a connection using the DriverManager class:

1. Register a Driver object with DriverManager
2. Establish a connection using DriverManager

Now, let's discuss each of these steps in detail.

Registering a Driver object with DriverManager

Registering a driver with the DriverManager class makes the registered driver available to the `DriverManager` class, so that the `DriverManager` object can use it to establish a connection with the database. When a driver is registered with the `DriverManager` class, it creates the `DriverInfo` object to maintain the driver details and stores these details in a class variable of the java.util.Vector type.

You can register the driver by using any one of the following three approaches:

- Invoke the `registerDriver()` method, which is a static method declared in the DriverManager class. The java.sql.Driver type of object is passed as an argument to the `registerDriver()` method. The following code snippet shows how to register the `Driver` object with DriverManager:

```
DriverManager.registerDriver (new sun.jdbc.odbc.JdbcOdbcDriver());
```

- Invoke the Class.forName (<driver class name>) method, which is used to load the driver class explicitly. According to the JDBC specifications, a static code block should be provided in every JDBC driver implementation class. This code block passes the object of the driver implementation class through the `registerDriver()` method. The following code snippet shows how to register the `Driver` object with `DriverManager` by using the `Class.forName()` method:

```
Class.forName ("sun.jdbc.odbc.JdbcOdbcDriver");
Where the sun.jdbc.odbc.JdbcOdbcDriver class contains the following code:
public class JdbcOdbcDriver extends … {
static { DriverManager.registerDriver (new sun.jdbc.odbc.JdbcOdbcDriver()); }
}
```

In the preceding code snippet, observe that the result is similar to using the `registerDriver()` method.

NOTE

It is recommended to call the newInstance() method on the Class object, which is returned by the Class.forName() method as some of the JVMs do not call the static initializers until an instance of the class is created.

- Set the `System` property, where the name of the property is jdbc.drivers. The value of the `System` property can be mapped to one or more driver implementation class names, where ':' character is used as a delimiter.

The following code snippet shows registering the driver with the DriverManager class:

```
System.setProperty ("jdbc.drivers", "sun.jdbc.odbc.JdbcOdbcDriver");
Use the above method in our application, or while executing the application using a Java
command, we can set System properties using the –D option of java command, example:
java –Djdbc.drivers=sun.jdbc.odbc.JdbcOdbcDriver MyJdbcEx1
```

Note that in the JDBC 4.0 specifications, the `getConnection()` method of the DriverManager class has been enhanced to support the Java Standard Edition Service Provider mechanism. With this feature, the JDBC 4.0 Driver must include the META-INF/services/java.sql.Driver file. Therefore, when using JDBC 4.0 driver, you do not need to perform this step; that is, explicitly registering a Driver with DriverManager.

Establishing a Connection using DriverManager

You can now establish connection with a database after registering the driver with the DriverManager class. To create a connection, invoke any one of the following methods of the DriverManager class:

- getConnection (String url)
- getConnection (String url, String username, String password)
- getConnection (String url, Properties info)

In the preceding methods, <url> is a JDBC URL, which represents a unique name used to identify the driver and obtain the connection. The JDBC URL even contains additional information, such as username and password, required to establish the connection. The syntax of the JDBC URL is as follows:

```
jdbc: <sub protocol> : <info>
```

In the preceding syntax:

- **Jdbc**—Represents the protocol in the JDBC URL
- **<sub protocol>**—Specifies the vendor specific name of the driver used to create the connection
- **<info>**—Takes additional information required to establish the connection, such as the database name and port number, which vary from one driver to another

The following code snippet shows some JDBC URLs:

```
For Type-1 driver, i.e. JDBC-ODBC Bridge Driver, the JDBC URL is:
jdbc: odbc: SuchitaDSN.
For Oracle Type-2 driver:
String dbName = "kogent";
String oracleURL = "jdbc:oracle:oci8:@" + dbName;

//oracleURL = "jdbc:oracle:oci8:@kogent"

For Oracle Type-4 driver:
String host = "192.168.1.123";
```

```
String DSNName = "XE";
int port = 1521;
String oracleURL = "jdbc:oracle:thin:@" + host + ":" + port + ":" + DSNName;
//oracleURL = "jdbc:oracle:thin:@192.168.1.123:1521:XE"
```

When the getConnection() method is invoked, it checks if any one of the drivers registered with the DriverManager class recognizes the given JDBC URL. If a driver accepts the URL, that driver is used by DriverManager to establish the connection with the DBMS located by the given JDBC URL. Consequently, if no driver accepts the URL, the DriverManager class throws the java.sql.SQLException exception to the application.

Creating a JDBC Statement Object

You can execute the SQL statements only after creating the JDBC Statement object. The utility objects available to execute SQL statements are `Statement`, `PreparedStatement`, and `CallableStatement`.

Invoke the `createStatement()` method on the current `Connection` object to create the Statement object. The following code snippet shows how to create the Statement object using the `createStatement()` method:

```
Statement stmt = con.createStatement();
```

Executing SQL Statements

After the Statement object is created, it can be used to execute the SQL statements by using the execute(), executeUpdate(), or executeQuery() methods. The executeQuery() method is only used in the SELECT statement. For other database operations, such as INSERT, UPDATE, and DELETE, the executeUpdate() method is used to execute statements. The following code snippet shows how to execute a SQL statement:

```
//Using executeQuery()
String query = "SELECT col1, col2, col3 FROM table_name";
ResultSet results = stmt.executeQuery(query);
//Using executeUpdate()
String query= "INSERT INTO table_name VALUES (value1, value2, …, value n)";
int count = stmt.executeUpdate(query);
```

If the statement produces a ResultSet object after executing the SQL statements, the ResultSet instance is used to retrieve the result. The next() method is invoked on the ResultSet object to navigate through a row at a time. The following code snippet shows the use of the ResultSet object within a connection:

```
while(results.next())
{
   System.out.println(results.getString(1) + " " +
   results.getString(2) + " " +
   results.getString(3));
}
```

Closing the Connection

You need to close the connection and release the session after executing all the required SQL statements and obtaining the corresponding results. This can be done by calling the close() method of the Connection interface. The following code snippet shows how to close a connection:

```
con.close();
```

Now let's create a simple application to implement JDBC APIs.

Creating a Simple JDBC Application

Let's now learn to create a simple JDBC application that inserts a record in a database table. In our case, we are inserting the record of a student in the *students* table of the Oracle data source. To insert the details of a student, you first need to establish a connection with the database and then execute the INSERT statement.

Figure 3.7 displays how to use JDBC to obtain a connection and communicate with the database:

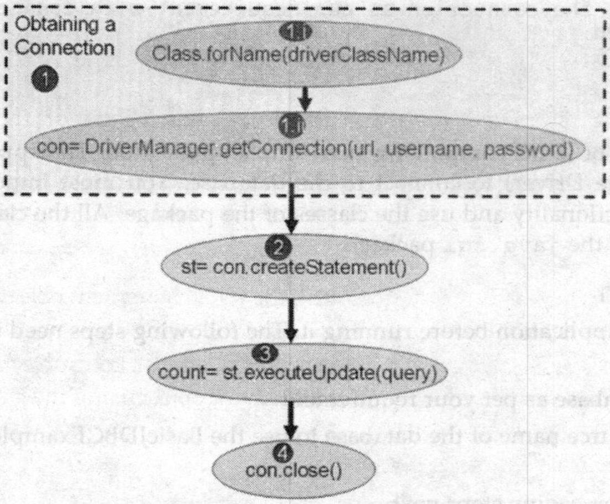

Figure 3.7: Creating and Using Connection

The steps shown in Figure 3.7 describe how to get a connection and execute the SQL statements. The following are the basic steps to use JDBC to connect to the data store and execute a simple SQL query:

1. Obtain the connection
2. Get the utility objects, such as `Statement`, `PreparedStatement`, and `CallableStatement`, to execute SQL statements
3. Execute the required SQL statements
4. Close the connection

Now, let's try to understand the concept better by creating a simple application, BasicJDBCExample. In this application, let's cerate the JDBCExample1.java file, which demonstrates the basic steps to access a database using JDBC.

Listing 3.1 shows the code for the JDBCExample1.java file:

Listing 3.1: Showing the JDBCExample1.java File

```
package com.kogent.jdbc;

import java.sql.*;
public class JDBCExample1 {
  public static void main(String args[])
  throws SQLException, ClassNotFoundException {

        String driverClassName="sun.jdbc.odbc.JdbcOdbcDriver";
        String url="jdbc:odbc:XE";
        String username="scott";
        String password="tiger";

        String query = "INSERT INTO students VALUES (101, \'Kumar\')";

        //Load driver class
        Class.forName (driverClassName);

        // obtain a connection
        Connection con=DriverManager. getConnection
        (url, username, password);

        // Obtain a Statement
        Statement st=con. createStatement();
        //Execute the Query
        int count=st. executeUpdate (query);
        System.out.println ("Number of rows effected by this query = "+count);
```

```
            // Closing the connection as our requirement with connection is
            //completed
            con.close();
    }//main
}//class
```

Listing 3.1 shows the uses of JDBC components in a simple application. The application uses the JDBC Type-1 driver (JDBC-ODBC Bridge Driver) to connect to the database. You must import the `java.sql` package to provide the basic SQL functionality and use the classes of the package. All the classes and methods used by the application are wrapped in the `java.sql` package.

Configuring the Application

You need to configure an application before running it. The following steps need to be performed to configure a JDBC application:

1. Create a table in a database as per your requirement
2. Configure the data source name of the database to use the BasicJDBCExample application to connect to the database

Let's learn to perform the preceding steps next.

Creating a Table

The BasicJDBCExample application uses a table named students. The students table can be created by using the `CREATE` TABLE statement. The following code snippet shows how to create the students table in a database:

```
CREATE TABLE <table name> (
   <column_name1> <type>,
   <counmn_name2> <type>,
   ...
   ...
   <column_namen> <type>);
Example:

CREATE TABLE students (
   stdId NUMBER(3),
stdName VARCHAR2(30));
```

Creating a Data Source Name

The code of the JDBCExample1.java file uses the Type-1 (JDBC-ODBC Bridge Driver) Type-1 driver to connect to the database, which requires a Data Source Name (DSN) to connect to the database.

Perform the following steps to create a DSN in Windows 7:

1. Select Start→Control Panel→System and Security→Administrative Tools→Data Sources (ODBC). The ODBC Data Source Administrator dialog box appears, as shown in Figure 3.8:

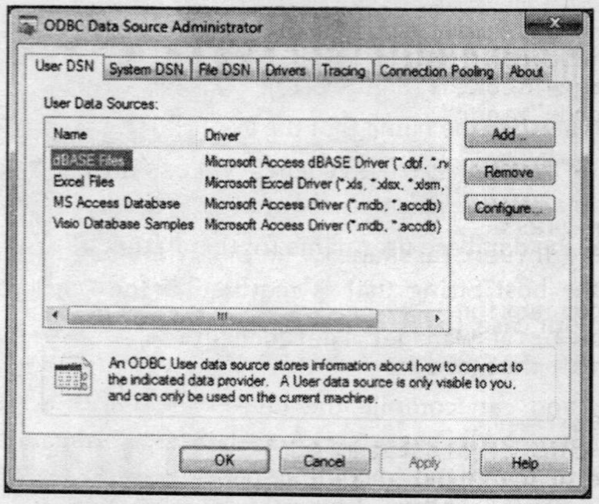

Figure 3.8: Displaying the ODBC Data Source Administrator Screen

2. Click the `Add` button to add the data source to which the driver is to be connected. The Create New Data Source dialog box appears, as shown in Figure 3.9:

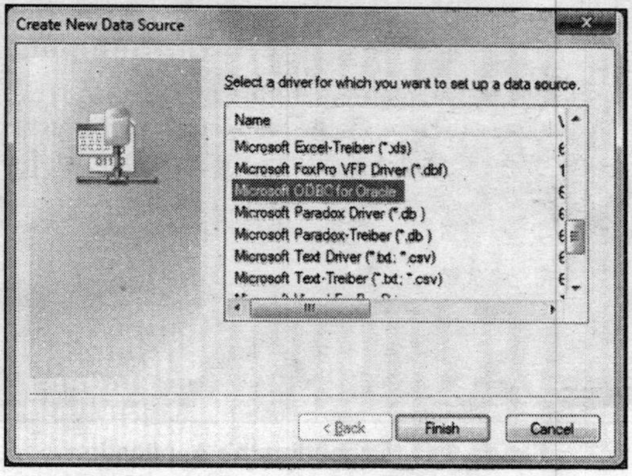

Figure 3.9: Creating a New Data Source

3. Select the required driver. In our case, we have selected `Microsoft ODBC for Oracle`, as we want to connect to the Oracle database.
4. Click the `Finish` button (Figure 3.9) to open the `Microsoft ODBC for Oracle Setup` dialog box, as shown in Figure 3.10:

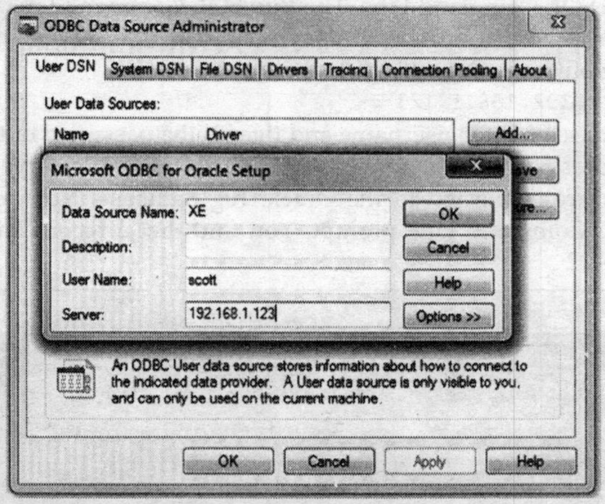

Figure 3.10: Displaying the Microsoft ODBC for Oracle Setup Dialog Box

5. Enter the details in the following fields (Figure 3.10):
   - **Data Source Name**—Specifies the name that the application uses within the JDBC URL. In our case, we have specified XE as the Data Source Name.
   - **Description**—Specifies a brief description about the DSN. This field is optional.
   - **User Name**—Specifies the database user name (optional). In our case, the user name is scott.
   - **Server**—Represents the host String that is required if the oracle database server is installed on a different computer. In our case, the IP of the server is 192.168.1.123.
6. Click the OK button to create the DSN.

   After creating the DSN, you can compile the Java source file by using Command Prompt. To open Command Prompt, select Start→All Programs→Accessories→Command Prompt. Command Prompt opens, where you can execute javac command to compile the source file and java command to run the .class file. Figure 3.11 shows the compilation and execution of the JDBCExample1.java file:

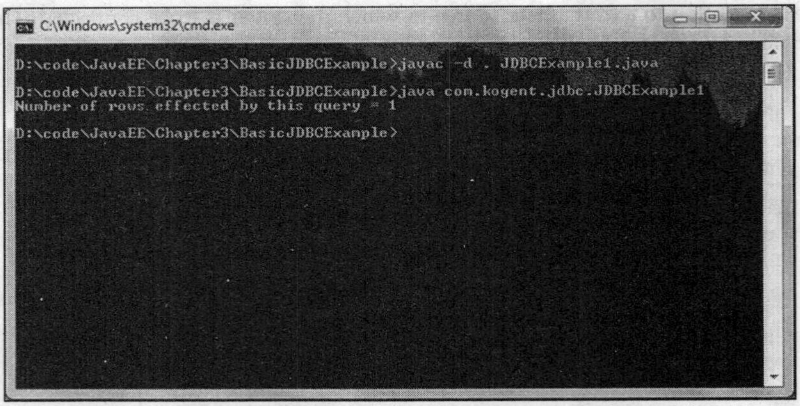

Figure 3.11: Executing the Application

After executing the JDBCExample1 class, a record is inserted in the students table of the Oracle database. You can verify the updation of the record by opening the Run SQL Command Line window and connecting to the Oracle server.

You should ensure that the Oracle Client is installed on your system. In our case, we are using Oracle 10g Client edition. You can open the Run SQL Command Line window by selecting Start→All Programs→Oracle Client 10g Express Edition→Run SQL Command Line. The Run SQL Command Line window opens. Now, you should enter the username and password to log on to the Oracle database server. In our case, we have executed the following command to log on to the Oracle 10g database:

```
connect scott/tiger@192.168.1.123
```

In the preceding command, scott is the username and tiger is the password of the Oracle 10g server. In addition, 192.168.1.123 is the IP address of the machine on which the Oracle 10g server is installed. After executing the preceding command, you are connected to the Oracle 10g database. Now, enter the **select * from students;** command at the Run SQL Command Line prompt. You find that a record has been inserted into the students table, as shown in Figure 3.12:

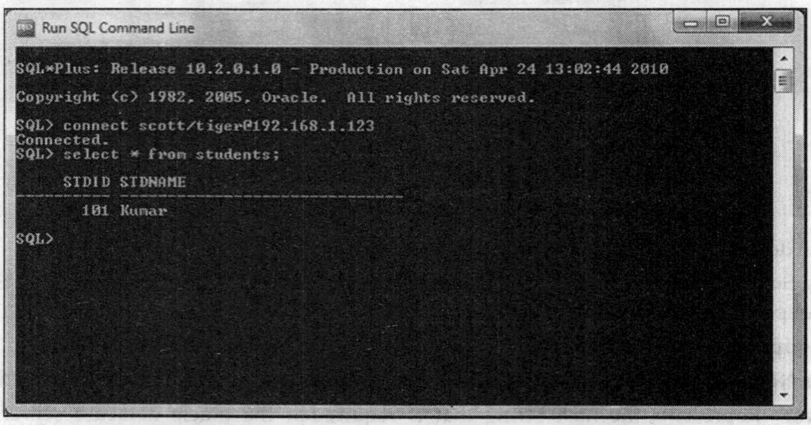

Figure 3.12: Showing Records from the students Table in Run SQL Command Line

Now let's discuss the PreparedStatement interface in detail.

Working with the PreparedStatement Interface

The PreparedStatement interface, which extends the Statement interface, can be used to represent a precompiled query, which can be executed multiple times. Let's now first understand the difference between the execution process of a Statement object and the PreparedStatement object to exeute a SQL query.

Next, you learn about the setXXX() methods and the advantages as well as disadvantages of the PreparedStatement interface. You also learn how to implement the PreparedStatement interface to execute the SQL query.

Comparing the Execution Control of the Statement and PreparedStatement Objects

When a Statement object is used to execute a query (that is, calling any one of the execute methods), the query is processed as follows:

1. The executeXXX() method is invoked on the Statement object by passing the SQL statement as parameter.
2. The Statement object submits the SQL statement to the database.
3. The database compiles the given SQL statement.
4. An execution plan is prepared by the database to execute the SQL statements.
5. The execution plan for the compiled SQL statement is then executed. Now, if the SQL statement is a data retrieval statement, such as the SELECT statement, the database caches the results of the SQL statement in the buffer.
6. The results are sent to the Statement object.
7. Finally, the response is sent to the Java application in the form of ResultSet.

Figure 3.13 displays the entire execution flow of the Statement object:

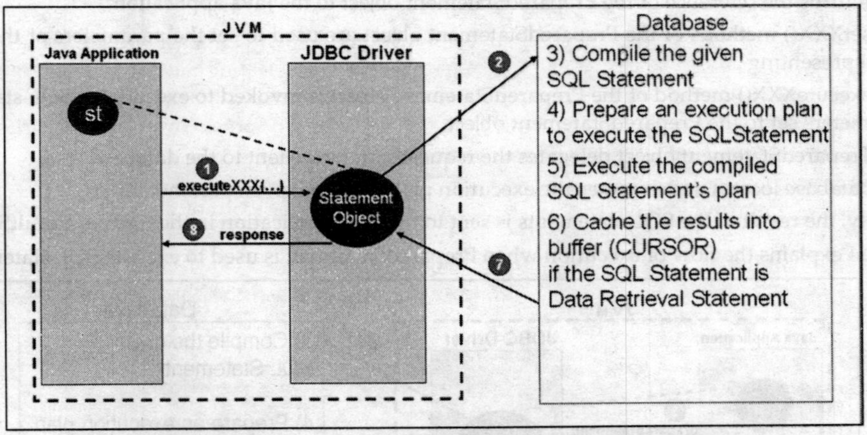

Figure 3.13: Displaying the Process Flow of the Statement Object

In Figure 3.13, the st element represents the Statement object reference. Compilation of a query includes syntax checking, name validation, and pseudo code generation. After a query is validated, the query optimizer prepares for the execution of the query and then returns what it considers to be the best alternative. The SQL statement needs to be executed each time it is requested.

It is not necessary to compile the SQL statement and prepare execution plan to execute a statement multiple times. DBMSs are designed to store the execution plans and execute them multiple times, if required. Consequently, the processing time of the DBMS is optimized. These stored execution plans of the SQL statements are known as pre-compiled SQL statements. DBMS intelligently maintains the compiled queries and provides a unique identity for the prepared execution plan, which the client uses to execute the same query next time. JDBC specifications support the use of this feature provided by DBMS. The PreparedStatement interface is designed specifically to support this feature.

PreparedStatements are pre-compiled; therefore, their execution is much faster as compared to the Statement objects included in an application. PreparedStatement extends the Statement interface; therefore, it inherits all the properties of the Statement interface. The execute methods do not take any parameter while using the PreparedStatement object.

You should keep in mind the following points while using the PreparedStatement interface:

- A PreparedStatement object must be associated with one connection.
- A PreparedStatement object represents the execution plan of a query, which is passed as parameter while creating the PreparedStatement object.
- After the connection on which the PreparedStatement object was created is closed, PreparedStatement is implicitly closed.
- When a PreparedStatement object is used to execute a query (that is, calling any one of the execute methods), the query is processed as follows:
  - The prepareStatement() method of the Connection object is used to get the object of the PreparedStatement interface
  - The Connection object submits the given SQL statement to the database
  - The database compiles the given SQL statement
  - An execution plan is prepared by the database to execute the SQL statements
  - The database stores the execution plan with a unique ID and returns the identity to the Connection object
- The Connection object prepares a PreparedStatement object, initializes it with the execution plan identity, and returns the reference of the PreparedStatement object to the Java application.
- The setXXX() methods of the PreparedStatement object are used to set the parameters of the SQL statement it is representing .
- The executeXXX() method of the PreparedStatement object is invoked to execute the SQL statement with the parameters set to the PreparedStatement object
- The PreparedStatement object delegates the request sent by a client to the database
- The database locates and executes the execution plan with the given parameters
- Finally, the result of the SQL statements is sent to the Java application in the form of ResultSet

Figure 3.14 explains the flow of execution when PreparedStatement is used to execute SQL statements:

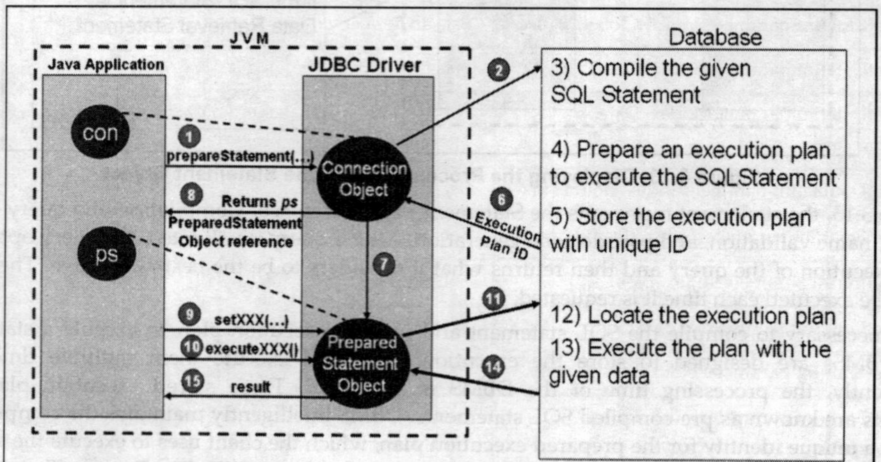

Figure 3.14: Showing Steps Involved in Using the PreparedStatement Object

In Figure 3.14, the con and ps elements represent the references of the Connection and PreparedStatement objects, respectively.

Describing the setXXX() Methods of the PreparedStatement Interface

You need to set the value of each placeholder ('?') parameter that is used inside the query string before executing a PreparedStatement object. The values for these placeholder parameters are provided at runtime to the SQL queries used within the PreparedStatement object. The values of this parameter can be set by using `setXXX()` methods.

Table 3.20 describes the setXXX() methods of the PreparedStatement interface:

Table 3.20: Methods Available in the PreparedStatement Interface

Method	Description
void setArray(int i, Array x)	Sets the values of parameters to the given array object
void setAsciiStream(int parameterIndex, InputStream x, int length)	Sets the values of the PreparedStatement parameter according to the given input stream, specified in the method
void setBigDecimal(int parameterIndex, BigDecimal x)	Sets the values of the parameter by using the values specified in the `java.math.BigDecimal` value
void setBinaryStream(int parameterIndex, InputStream x, int length)	Sets the binary values for the parameters used in the PreparedStatement object
void setBlob(int parameterIndex, Blob x)	Sets an integer value to the specified Blob object
void setBoolean(int parameterIndex, boolean x)	Sets the boolean values for the parameters used in the PreparedStatement object
void setByte(int parameterIndex, byte x)	Sets the byte values for the parameters used in the PreparedStatement object
void setBytes(int parameterIndex, byte[] x)	Sets the byte values in an array for the parameters used in the PreparedStatement object
void setCharacterStream(int parameterIndex, Reader reader, int length)	Sets the character values for the PreparedStatement parameters and also specifies the length of the characters
void setClob(int parameterIndex, Clob x)	Sets an integer value to the specified Clob object
void setDate(int parameterIndex, Date x)	Sets the PreparedStatement parameter with a `java.sql.Date` value
void setDate(int parameterIndex, Date x, Calendar cal)	Sets the PreparedStatement parameter with a `java.sql.Date` value and also uses the Calendar object to set the value of the parameter
void setDouble(int parameterIndex, double x)	Sets the value of the parameter to the `Java` double value
void setFloat(int parameterIndex, float x)	Sets the value of the parameter to the `Java` float value
void setInt(int parameterIndex, int x)	Sets the value of the parameter to the `Java` int value
void setLong(int parameterIndex, long x)	Sets the value of the parameter to the `Java` long value
void setNull(int parameterIndex, int sqlType)	Sets the NULL values for the parameters of the specified sqlType
void setNull(int parameterIndex, int sqlType, String typeName)	Sets the NULL values for the parameters of the specified sqlType and typeName
void setObject(int parameterIndex, Object x)	Sets the value of the parameter by using the given object value
void setObject(int parameterIndex, Object x, int targetSqlType)	Sets the value of the parameter by using the given object value
void setObject(int parameterIndex, Object x, int targetSqlType, int scaleOrLength)	Sets the value of the parameter by using the given object value

Table 3.20: Methods Available in the PreparedStatement Interface

Method	Description
void setRef(int parameterIndex, Ref x)	Sets the values of the parameters to the REF (<structured-type>) value
void setShort(int parameterIndex, short x)	Sets the value of the parameter to the Java short value
void setString(int parameterIndex, String x)	Sets the value of the parameter to the Java String value
void setTime(int parameterIndex, Time x)	Sets the value of the parameter to the java.sql.Time value
void setTime(int parameterIndex, Time x, Calendar cal)	Sets the value of the parameter to the java.sql.Time value by using the Calendar object
void setTimestamp(int parameterIndex, Timestamp x)	Sets the value of the parameter to the java.sql.Timestamp value
void setTimestamp(int parameterIndex, Timestamp x, Calendar cal)	Sets the value of the parameter to the java.sql.Timestamp value by using the calendar object
void setURL(int parameterIndex, URL x)	Sets the value of the parameter to the java.net.URL value

Advantages and Disadvantages of Using a PreparedStatement Object

The advantages of using a PreparedStatement object are as follows:

- Improves the performance of an application as compared to the Statement object that executes the same query multiple times. The PreparedStatement object performs the execution of queries faster by avoiding the compilation of queries multiple times.
- Inserts or updates the SQL99 data type columns, such as BLOB and CLOB with the help of setXXX() methods.
- Provides a programmatic approach to set the values. In other words, the value of each paramater provided in a SQL query is passed separately by using the PreparedStatement object, unlike the Statement object.

The main disadvantage of PreparedStatement is that it can represent only one SQL statement at a time, i.e. you cannot execute more than one statement by a single PreparedStatement.

Using the PreparedStatement Interface

The following are some of the situations when you should use PreparedStatement in a JDBC application:

- When a single query is being executed multiple times
- When a query consists of numberous parameters and complex types (SQL99 types)

PreparedStatement is used to increase the efficiency and reduce the execution time of a query. An instance of PreparedStatement must be created to execute a precompiled SQL statement. Follow these broad-level steps to use the PreparedStatement interface:

1. Create a PreparedStatement object
2. Provide the values of the PreparedStatement parameters
3. Execute the SQL statements

Let's discuss each of these steps in detail.

Creating a PreparedStatement Object

The prepareStatement(String) method of the Connection object is used to create the PreparedStatement object. The `Connection` object is used to access the `PreparedStatement` object, where the query supplied in the `prepareStatement()` method can contain zero or more question ma.ks ('?', known as parameters). The values of question mark parameters can be set after the query is compiled.

The following code snippet shows how to create the PreparedStatement object in a connection:

```
Class.forName("oracle.jdbc.driver.OracleDriver");
Connection con= DriverManager.getConnection (url, "user", "password");
String query="insert into mytable values (?,?,?)";
//Step1: Get PreparedStatement object
PreparedStatement ps=con.prepareStatement (query);
```

In the preceding code snippet, `con` object of the Connection interface is used to call the `prepareStatement()` method to obtain the `PreparedStatement` object. In the preceding code snippet, `ps` is the PreparedStatement object created by using the `con` object.

Providing the Values of the PreparedStatement Parameters

You need to set the values of the question mark placeholders after creating the `PreparedStatement` object. The values of the question marks can be set by using the `setXXX()` methods. For example, if the question mark indicates the value of an integer data type, you can use the setInt() method for the particular parameter. If you have a parameter of the `Java` String, you can call the setString() method to set the value of the parameter. Note that these values should be set before prepared statements are executed.

In PreparedStatement, there is a `setXXX()` method for each data type declared in `Java`. The `setXXX()` method takes two arguments. The first argument indicates the parameter index and the second argument indicates the value of the parameter. Note that the parameter index starts from 1.

The following code snippet shows how to set the values of the question mark parameter:

```
//Step2: setting values for the parameters
ps.setString(1,"abc1");
ps.setInt(2,38);
ps.setDouble(3,158.75);
```

Executing the SQL Statements

You can execute the precompiled SQL statements by using the execute(), executeUpdate(), or executeQuery() methods of the PreparedStatement interface. The result of these methods is same as that of the respective methods in the Statement interface.

The following code snippet shows how to execute the SQL statements:

```
ps.setString(1,"abc1");
ps.setInt(2,38);
ps.setDouble(3,158.75);
//Step3: Executing the SQL statements
int n = ps.executeUpdate(); // n is the number of rows or tables
that are being updated
```

Listing 3.2 demonstrates the use of PreparedStatement in an application named PreparedStatement, which contains the PreparedStatementEx1.`java file`. In Listing 3.2, the PreparedStatement object is used to execute the INSERT statement:

Listing 3.2: Showing the code for the PreparedStatementEx1.`java` File

```
package com.kogent.jdbc;
import java.sql.*;
/**
 * @author Suchita
 */
public class PreparedStatementEx1 {
  public static void main(String s[]) throws Exception {
        Class.forName("oracle.jdbc.driver.OracleDriver").newInstance();
        Connection con= DriverManager.getConnection (
        "jdbc:oracle:thin:@192.168.1.123:1521:XE","scott","tiger");
        String query="INSERT INTO mytable VALUES (?,?,?)";
        //Step1: Get PreparedStatement
        PreparedStatement ps=con.prepareStatement (query);
        //Step2: set parameters
        ps.setString(1,"abc1");
        ps.setInt(2,38);
        ps.setDouble(3,158.75);
        //Step3: execute the query
        int i=ps.executeUpdate();
        System.out.println("record inserted count:"+i);
        //To execute the query once again
        ps.setString(1,"abc2");
```

```
            ps.setInt(2,39);
            ps.setDouble(3,158.75);
            i=ps.executeUpdate();
            System.out.println("query executed for the second time count: "+i);
            con.close();
      }//main
   }//class
```

Listing 3.2 uses the PreparedStatement object along with the Connection object. The setXXX() methods are used to set the values of the arguments. The preceding listing sets the values of the integer, string, and double data types. The executeUpdate() method used in Listing 3.2 retrieves the number of rows affected by executing the SQL statement.

The output of Listing 3.2 is shown in Figure 3.15:

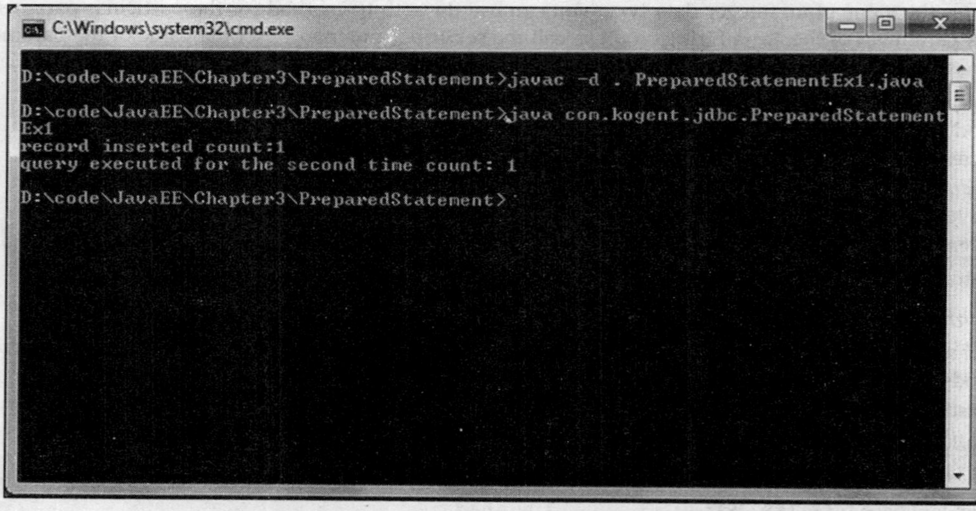

Figure 3.15: Displaying the Output of the PreparedStatement Ex1.java File

After learning about the PreparedStatement interface, let's now proceed to learn about the CallableStatement interface.

Working with the CallableStatement Interface

The CallableStatement interface extends the `PreparedStatement` interface and also provides support for both input as well as output parameters. The CallableStatement interface provides a standard abstraction for all the data sources to call stored procedures and functions, irrespective of the vendor of the data source. This interface is used to access, invoke, and retrieve the results of SQL stored procedures, functions, and cursors. Stored procedures let you write queries that are quick to run and easy to invoke. It is often easier to update an application by altering or making a few changes in the stored procedures. Functions are similar to procedures; however, the major difference between a function and procedure is that a function always returns a scalar value. You can also use cursors with CallableStatement to retrieve a ResultSet from a database.

Let's now demonstrate the use of CallableStatement with stored procedures, functions, and cursors.

Describing Stored Procedures

A stored procedure is a subroutine used by applications to access data from a database. Stored procedures are callead by using the CallableStatement interface in `Java`. The procedures called by the CallableStatement object are the database programs that contain the database interface. A stored procedure has the following properties:

- Contains input, output, or both these parameters
- Returns a value through the OUT parameter after executing the SQL statements
- Returns multiple ResultSet objects when required

Stored procedures are generally a group of SQL statements that allows you to make a single call to a database. The SQL statements in a stored procedure are executed statically for better performance. A stored procedure encapsulates the values of the following types of parameters:

- **IN**—Refers to the parameter whose value cannot be overwritten and referenced by a stored procedure
- **OUT**—Refers to the parameter whose value can be overwritten; however, cannot be referenced by a stored procedure
- **IN OUT**—Refers to the parameter whose value can be overwritten and referenced by the stored procedure

The following code snippet shows how to create or replace a stored procedure:

```
CREATE or [REPLACE] PROCEDURE procedure_name
   [(parameter [, parameter])]
   IS
   [Declarations] BEGIN
        executables
        [EXCEPTION exceptions]
   END [procedure_name];
```

Using the CallableStatement Interface

In Java, the CallableStatement interface is used to call the stored procedures and functions. Therefore, the stored procedure can be called by using an object of the `CallableStatement` interface. The broad-level steps to use the CallableStatement interface in an application are:

1. Creating the CallableStatement object
2. Setting the values of the parameters
3. Registering the OUT parameters type
4. Executing the procedure or function
5. Retrieving the parameter values

Let's discuss these in details:

Creating the CallableStatement Object

The first step to use the CallableStatement interface is to create the CallableStatement object. The CallableStatement object can be created by invoking the prepareCall (String) method of the Connection object. The syntax to call the prepareCall() method in an application is:

```
// calling the prepareCall method with parameters.
CallableStatement cs= con.prepareCall ("{call procedure_name(?, ?, ...)}");

cs= con.prepareCall ("{call procedure_name}");// with no parameter
```

Setting the Values of the Parameters

You need to set the values of the IN and IN OUT type parameters in the stored procedure after creating the CallableStatement object. The values of these parameters can be set by calling the setXXX() method of the CallableStatement interface. The setXXX() method is used to pass the values to the IN, OUT, and IN OUT parameters. The values for a parameter can be set by using the following syntax:

```
cs.setXXX (int index, XXX value);
```

Registering the OUT Parameters Type

The OUT or IN OUT parameter used in a procedure represented by `CallableStatement` must be registered to collect the values of the parameters after the stored procedure is executed. You can register the parameters by invoking the registerOutParameter() method of the CallableStatement interface. This method defines the type of parameter used in the CallableStatement interface. The parameters can be registered by using the following syntax:

```
cs.registerOutParameter (int index, int type);
```

Executing the Procedure or Function

After registering the `OUT` parameter type, you need to execute the procedure. The `execute()` method of the `CallableStatement` interface is used to execute the procedure and does not take any argument.

Retrieving the Parameter Values

You need to retrieve the OUT or IN OUT type parameter values of the stored procedure after executing the stored procedure. You can use the `getXXX()` method of the CallableStatement interface to retrieve the parameter values of the procedure.

After you have retrieved the results, repeat the steps if you want to execute the same procedure again with different parameter values. After performing all tasks associated with the database connection, it is a good practice to invoke the `close()` method on the CallableStatement object.

An Example of Using the CallableStatement Interface

As learned earlier, you can use the CallableStatement interface to execute a stored procedure with the IN and OUT parameters. In this section, you first learn to implement the CallableStatement interface to execute a stored procedure that accepts the IN parameters. In other words, we create the createAccount stored procedure that needs IN parameters for execution, which are provided by using the CallableStatement interface in an application.

Later, the CallableStatement interface is used with the OUT parameter. In other words, the `getBalance()` stored procedure is created, which provides the balance of an account holder as the output to the application invoking the stored procedure.

Executing a Stored Procedure with the IN Parameter

Let's now create an application named CallableStatement to call a stored procedure using the CallableStatement interface. First, create two tables called bank and personal_details by using SQL queries, as shown in the following code snippet:

```
CREATE TABLE bank (
   Accno NUMBER,
   Name VARCHAR2(20),
   Bal NUMBER(10,2),
   Acctype NUMBER
);
CREATE TABLE personal_details (
   Accno NUMBER,
   address VARCHAR2(20),
   phno NUMBER
);
```

In addition, create a procedure named `createAccount()` to insert data into database tables. The following code snippet shows the SQL query to create the createAccount() procedure:

```
CREATE or REPLACE PROCEDURE createAccount (accnumber NUMBER, actype NUMBER,
acname VARCHAR2, amt NUMBER, addr VARCHAR2, phno NUMBER) is
BEGIN
INSERT INTO bank VALUES (accnumber, acname, amt, actype);
INSERT INTO personal_details VALUES ( accnumber, addr, phno);
END;
/
```

In the preceding code snippet, the values in the bank and personal_details tables are inserted by using the createAccount() procedure.

Figure 3.16 shows the output of executing the preceding code snippets at the Run SQL Command Line window:

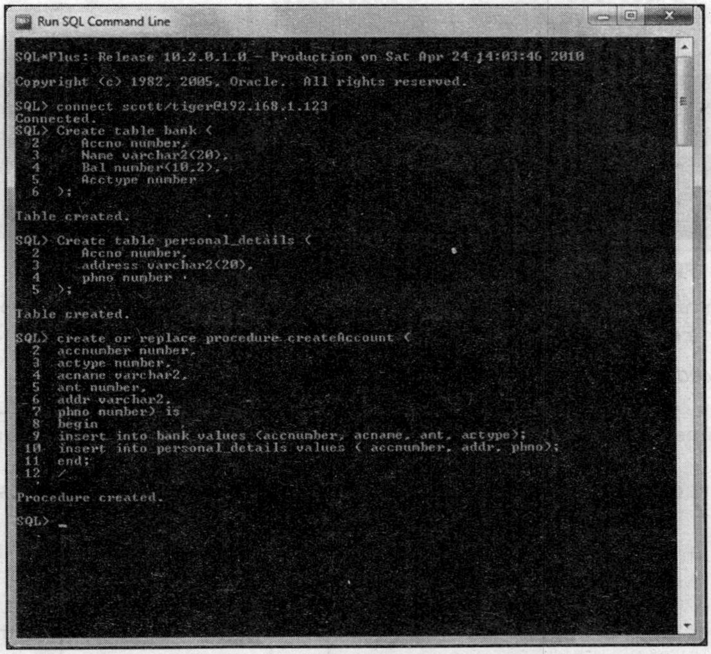

Figure 3.16: Showing the Creation of Table and Stored Procedure

The tables and procedures created in the Oracle 10g database, as shown in Figure 3.16, are used in Listing 3.3 to call the createAccount() stored procedure by using CallableStatement. Listing 3.3 shows the use of the IN parameter to work with CallableStatement:

Listing 3.3: Showing the Code for the CallableStatementEx1.java File

```
package com.kogent.jdbc;
import java.sql.*;
/**
 * @author Suchita
 */
public class CallableStatementEx1 {
  public static void main(String s[]) throws Exception {
       Class.forName("oracle.jdbc.driver.OracleDriver").newInstance();
       Connection con=DriverManager.getConnection(
       "jdbc:oracle:thin:@192.168.1.123:1521:XE","scott","tiger");
       // Get CallableStatement
       CallableStatement cs= con.prepareCall ("{call
       createAccount (?,?,?,?,?,?)}");
       // set IN parameters
       cs.setInt(1, 103);
       cs.setInt(2, 9);
       cs.setString(3, "Neeraj");
       cs.setDouble(4, 10000);
       cs.setString(5, "Delhi");
       cs.setInt(6, 123456789);
       // register OUT parameters
       //In this procedure example we don't have OUT parameters
       //executing the stored procedure
       cs.execute();
       System.out.println("Account Created");
       con.close();
  }//main
}//class
```

The output of Listing 3.3 is shown in Figure 3.17:

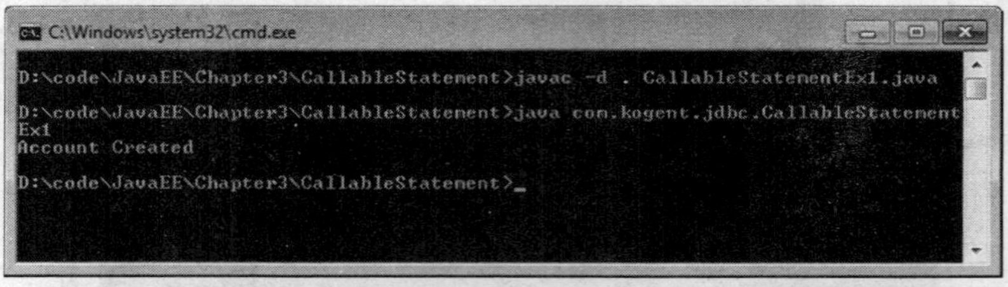

Figure 3.17: Showing the Output of CallableStatementEx1.java File

If CallableStatement uses the OUT parameter to work with the stored procedure, you need to register the OUT parameter using the `registerOutParameter()` method of the CallableStatement interface.

Executing a Stored Procedure with the OUT Parameter

In this section, let's create an application that calls a stored procedure named `getBalance()` by using the CallableStatement interface. First, create a procedure named `getBalance()`, as shown in the following code snippet:

```
CREATE OR REPLACE PROCEDURE getBalance (acno NUMBER, amt OUT NUMBER) IS
BEGIN

SELECT bal INTO amt FROM bank WHERE accno=acno;
END;
/
```

In the preceding code snippet, the OUT parameter is used to hold the value (amount) retrieved by executing the SQL query.

Figure 3.18 shows the `getBalance()` procedure created by using the Run SQL Command Line window:

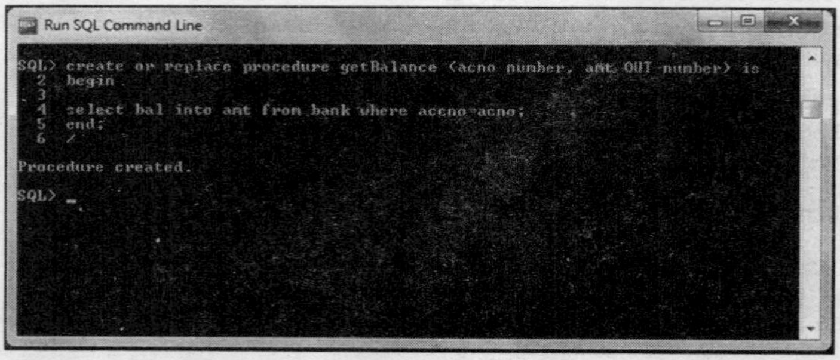

Figure 3.18: Creating a Procedure by Using the OUT Parameter

Let's now create another .java file, CallableStatementEx2.`Java, in the` CallableStatement application to execute the `getBalance()` stored procedure with the OUT parameter by using the CallableStatement interface. Listing 3.4 shows the use of the OUT parameter with the stored procedure:

Listing 3.4: Showing the Code for the `CallableStatementEx2.Java` File

```
package com.kogent.jdbc;
import java.sql.*;
/**
 * @author Suchita
 */
public class CallableStatementEx2 {
public static void main(String s[]) throws Exception {

        Class.forName("oracle.jdbc.driver.OracleDriver").newInstance();
        Connection con=DriverManager.getConnection(
        "jdbc:oracle:thin:@192.168.1.123:1521:XE","scott","tiger");

        CallableStatement cs= con.prepareCall("{call getBalance(?,?)}");
```

```
            cs.setInt(1, Integer.parseInt(s[0]));
            cs.registerOutParameter(2, Types.DOUBLE);
            cs.execute();

            System.out.println("Balance : "+ cs.getDouble(2));
            con.close();
    }//main
}//class
```

Figure 3.19 displays the output of Listing 3.4:

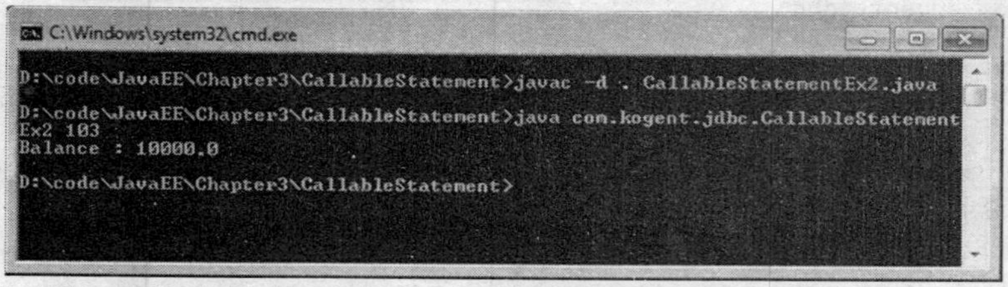

Figure 3.19: Showing the Output of CallableStatementEx2.java File

In the next subsection, let's discuss how to call functions using CallableStatement interface.

Calling Functions using CallableStatements

Most of the databases provide support for the numeric, string, time, date, system, and conversion functions. These functions are used in SQL statements to return scalar values stored in a database. The scalar functions supported by a DBMS must also be supported by the database drivers used in the application. The user can access these functions by calling the metadata methods.

Table 3.21 describes the scalar function types supported by Oracle:

Table 3.21: Scalar Functions and their Uses

Function Type	Use
Numeric Functions	Operate on numeric data types, such as round(), trunc()
Character Functions	Operate on the string data types, such as concat(), lower(), and length()
Time & Date Functions	Access all the time and date related information from a database
System functions	Retrieve the information about the DBMSs used in an application
Conversion Functions	Convert the data type of a given value into the required type

In addition to these pre-defined functions, DBMS has a feature to create user-defined functions. User-defined functions can be used within Data Manipulation Language (DML) queries; however, it is not recommended to use DML queries within a function. The user-defined functions can be used in the following situations:

- In the column names of a SELECT statement
- In the WHERE clause as a condition
- In the value clause of an INSERT statement
- In the SET clause of an UPDATE statement

The following syntax shows how to create a user-defined function:

```
CREATE [OR REPLACE] FUNCTION function_name [(parameter [, parameter])]
RETURN return_datatype
IS/AS
[Declaration_section]
BEGIN
   executable_section
   [EXCEPTION exception_section]
END [function_name];
```

The procedure to call a function in an application is the same as that of procedures. The syntax to invoke a function in JDBC (String argument of the prepareCall() method) is as follows:

```
{call ?:=function_name(?, ?, ...)} // with String parameters

{call ?:=function_name}// with no parameter
```

Listing 3.5 shows the use of a user-defined function in CallableStatament application by using CallableStatement interface:

Listing 3.5: Showing the Code for the CallableStatementEx3.java File

```
package com.kogent.jdbc;

import java.sql.*;
import java.util.*;
/**
 * @author Suchita
 */
public class CallableStatementEx3 {
public static void main(String s[]) throws Exception {

        Class.forName("oracle.jdbc.driver.OracleDriver").newInstance();
        Connection con=DriverManager.getConnection(
        "jdbc:oracle:thin:@192.168.1.123:1521:XE","scott","tiger");
        CallableStatement cs=con.prepareCall ("{call ?:=getBalanceF(?)}");
        cs.registerOutParameter (1, Types.DOUBLE);
        cs.setInt(2,Integer.parseInt(s[0]));
        cs.execute();
        System.out.println(cs.getDouble(1));
        con.close();
  }//main
}//class
```

Listing 3.5 executes a user-defined function, `getBalanceF()`, by using the CallableStatement object, which is used to access the function from the `Oracle` database. The desired output of the function is then displayed to the user.

Figure 3.20 shows the creation of the `getBalanceF()` function in the Oracle database:

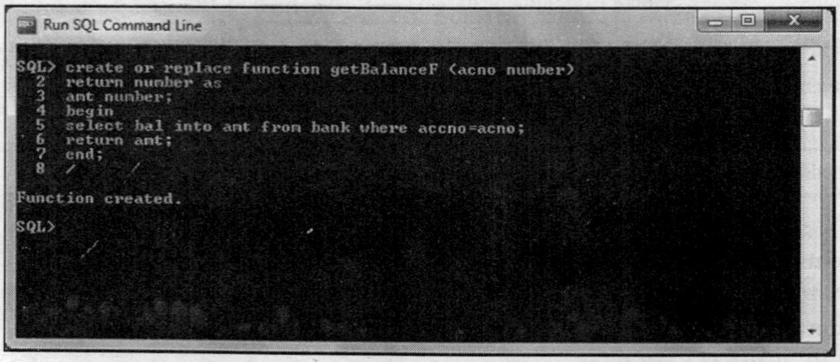

Figure 3.20: Creating a User-Defined Function

Figure 3.21 displays the output of CallableStatementEx3.java file:

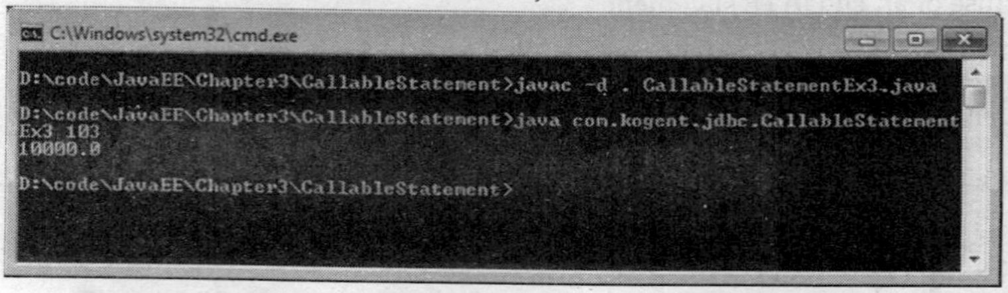

Figure 3.21: Showing Output of CallableStatementEx3.java File

All the features discussed so far are used to retrieve a single record from a database. You can use a cursor to retrieve a ResultSet containing multiple records from the database. Let's discuss about the use of cursors in CallableStatements to retrieve the ResultSet object.

Using Cursors in CallableStatements

A cursor allows you to iterate through the rows in a ResultSet. In other words, a cursor defines the run time execution environment for a query. You can open the cursor to execute the queries in that environment and read the output of the query from the cursor.

The syntax to create a cursor is shown in the following code snippet:

```
CREATE OR REPLACE PACKAGE package_name AS
TYPE type_name IS REF CURSOR;
END;
/
```

Cursors are used to retrieve ResultSet from a database through CallableStatement. Listing 3.6 shows the use of cursors to get the ResultSet object to access multiple records from a database:

Listing 3.6: Showing the Code for the CallableStatementEx4.`java File`

```
package com.kogent.jdbc;
import java.sql.*;
import java.util.*;
public class CallableStatementEx4 {
   public static void main(String s[]) throws Exception {
         Class.forName("oracle.jdbc.driver.OracleDriver").newInstance();
         Connection con=DriverManager.getConnection(
         "jdbc:oracle:thin:@192.168.1.123:1521:XE","scott","tiger");
         CallableStatement cs=
         con.prepareCall("{call ?:=getAccountDetails(?)}");
         cs.registerOutParameter(1, oracle.jdbc.OracleTypes.CURSOR);
         cs.setInt(2,Integer.parseInt(s[0]));
         cs.execute();
         ResultSet rs=(ResultSet) cs.getObject(1);
         while (rs.next()){
                System.out.print(rs.getInt(1)+"\t");
                System.out.print(rs.getString(2)+"\t");
                System.out.println(rs.getDouble(3));
         }//while
         con.close();
   }//main
}//class
```

Listing 3.6 uses the cursors and functions in the Oracle 10g database to access the ResultSet object representing all the accounts of the given account_type.

Figure 3.22 displays the creation of the cursor and functions associated with Listing 3.6:

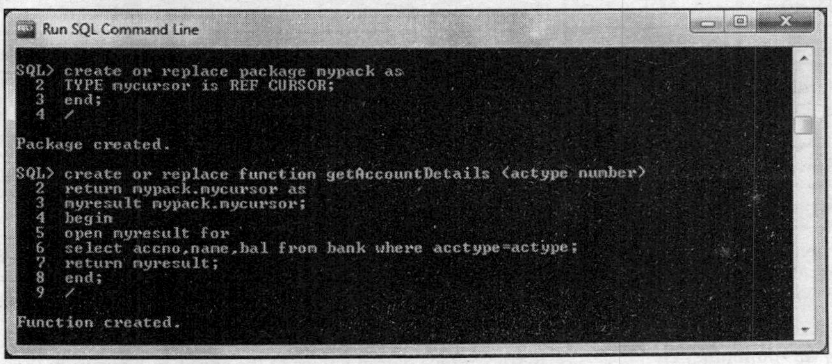

Figure 3.22: Creating a Cursor and Functions

Figure 3.23 shows the output of the CallableStatementEx4 class created in Listing 3.6:

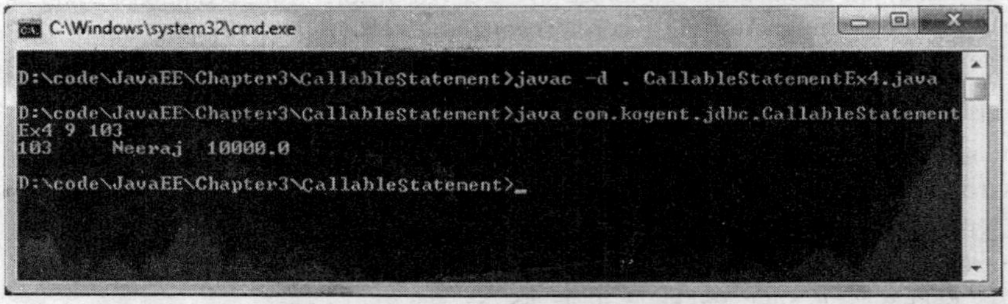

Figure 3.23: Showing the Output of the CallableStatementEx4.java File

Working with ResultSet

A ResultSet is an interface provided in the `java.sql` package, and is used to represent data retrieved from a database in a tabular format. It implies that a ResultSet object is a table of data returned by executing a SQL query. A ResultSet object encapsulates the resultant tabular data obtained when a query is executed. A ResultSet object holds zero or more objects, where each of the objects represents one row that may span over one or more table columns. You can obtain a ResultSet object by using the executeQuery() or getResultSet() method of a Statement object. Some of the important points related to a ResultSet object are as follows:

- Resultsets follow the iterate pattern.
- A ResultSet object is associated with a statement within a connection.
- You can obtain any number of ResultSet objects using one Statement object; however, only one ResultSet object can be opened at a time. When you try to open a ResultSet object using a Statement object that is already associated with an opened ResultSet object, the existing ResultSet object is implicitly closed.
- ResultSet object is automatically closed when its associated Statement object is closed.

Describing the Methods of ResultSet Interface

The `java.sql.ResultSet` interface provides certain methods to work with `ResultSet` objects. The methods available in the ResultSet interface are used to move the cursor throughout the result set and read the data.

Table 3.22 describes some of the most commonly used methods in the ResultSet interface:

Table 3.22: Methods of the java.sql.ResultSet Interface

Methods	Description
boolean absolute(int row)	Moves the cursor to the specified row in the ResultSet object.
void afterLast()	Places the cursor just after the last row in the ResultSet object.
void beforeFirst()	Places the cursor before the first row in the ResultSet object.
void cancelRowUpdates()	Cancels all the changes made to the rows in the ResultSet object.
void clearWarnings()	Clears all warning messages on a ResultSet object.
void close()	Closes the ResultSet object and releases all the JDBC resources connected to it.
void deleteRow()	Deletes the specified row from the ResultSet object and the database.
boolean first()	Moves the cursor to the first row in the ResultSet. object.
Array getArray(int columnIndex)	Retrieves the value of the specified column from the ResultSet object.
InputStream getAsciiStream(int columnIndex)	Retrieves a specified column in the current row as a stream of ASCII characters.
Date getDate(int columnIndex)	Retrieves the column values of the specified types from the current row. The type can be any of the `Java` predefined data types, such as int, long, byte, character, string, double, or large object types.

Table 3.22: Methods of the java.sql.ResultSet Interface	
Methods	**Description**
Date getDate(String columnLabel)	Retrieves the specified column from the current row in the ResultSet object. The object retrieved is of the `java.sql.Date` type in the `Java` programming language.
Date getDate(String columnName, Calendar cal)	Retrieves the specified column from the current row in the ResultSet object. The object retrieved is of the `java.sql.Date` type.
int getFetchDirection()	Specifies the direction (forward or reverse) in which the ResultSet object retrieves the row from a database.
int getFetchSize()	Retrieves the size of the associated ResultSet object.
ResultSetMetaData getMetaData()	Retrieves the number, type, and properties of the ResultSet object.
Object getObject(int columnIndex)	Retrieves a specified column in the current row as an object in the `Java` programming language on the basis of the column index value passed as a parameter.
Object getObject(int columnIndex, Map <String, Class<?>>map)	Retrieves a specified column as an object on the basis of the column number and Map instance passed as parameters.
Object getObject(String columnLabel)	Retrieves a specified column in the current row as an object on the basis of the column name passed as a parameter.
Object getObject(String columnLabel, Map<String,Class<?>> map)	Retrieves a specified column in the current row as an object on the basis of the column name and Map instance passed as parameters.
int getRow()	Retrieves the current row number associated with the ResultSet object.
Statement getStatement()	Retrieves the Statement object associated with the ResultSet object.
Time getTime(int columnIndex)	Retrieves the column values as a `java.sql.Time` object on the basis of column index passed as an integer parameter.
Time getTime(int columnIndex, Calendar cal)	Retrieves the column values as a `java.sql.Time` object on the basis of column index as well as the cal object of the Calender class passed as parameters.
Time getTime(String columnName)	Retrieves the column values as a `java.sql.Time` object on the basis of column name passed as a String value.
Time getTime(String columnName, Calendar cal)	Retrieves the column values as a `java.sql.Time` object on the basis of String value of column name as well Calender object cal as parameters.
Timestamp getTimestamp(int columnIndex)	Retrieves the column values as a `java.sql.Timestamp` object on the basis of the column index passed as a parameter.
Timestamp getTimestamp(int columnIndex, Calendar cal)	Retrieves the column values as a `java.sql.Timestamp` object on the basis of the column index and the cal object of the Calendar class passed as parameters.
Timestamp getTimestamp(String columnName)	Retrieves the column values as a `java.sql.Timestamp` object on the basis of the column name passed as a parameter.
Timestamp getTimestamp(String columnName, Calendar cal)	Retrieves the column values as a `java.sql.Timestamp` object on the basis of the column name and the cal object of the Calendar class passed as arguments.
int getType()	Retrieves the type of the ResultSet object used in a connection.
SQLWarning getWarnings()	Retrieves the warning reported on the ResultSet object.
void insertRow()	Inserts the specified row and content into the ResultSet object and database.

Table 3.22: Methods of the java.sql.ResultSet Interface

Methods	Description
boolean isAfterLast()	Specifies whether the cursor of the ResultSet object is at the end of the last row.
boolean isBeforeFirst()	Specifies whether the cursor is before the first row in the ResultSet object or not.
boolean isFirst()	Specifies whether the cursor is on the first row or not.
boolean isLast()	Detects whether the cursor is on the last row of the ResultSet object or not.
boolean last()	Moves the cursor to the last row in this ResultSet object.
void moveToCurrentRow()	Moves the cursor to the current row in the ResultSet object.
void moveToInsertRow()	Moves the cursor to the inserted row in the ResultSet object.
boolean next()	Moves the cursor forward one row. The method returns true if the cursor is positioned on a row and false if the cursor is positioned after the last row.
boolean previous()	Moves the cursor backward one row. The method returns true if the cursor is positioned on a row and false if the cursor is positioned before the first row.
void refreshRow()	Refreshes the current row associated with the ResultSet object with the recent updates.
boolean relative(int rows)	Moves the cursor to a relative number of rows or columns specified in the method.
boolean rowDeleted()	Retrieves whether the row has already been deleted or not.
boolean rowInserted()	Determines whether the current row has an insertion or not.
boolean rowUpdated()	Retrieves whether the current row has been updated or not.
void setFetchDirection(int direction)	Sets the direction of the ResultSet object.
void setFetchSize(int rows)	Sets the size of the ResultSet object.
void updateArray(int columnIndex, Array x)	Updates the column in the ResultSet object with a `java.sql.Array` value.
void updateXXX()	Updates the column values of the current row of the specified type. The type can be any of the `Java` predefined data types, such as int, long, byte, character, string, double, and the large object types.
void updateRow()	Updates the current row with new content.
boolean wasNull()	Reports whether the last column has a SQL null value or not.
void updateNull(String columnName)	Updates a specific column with a NULL value.
void updateObject(int columnIndex, Object x)	Updates the specific column with an Object value.
void updateTime(int columnIndex, Time x)	Updates the time value with a `java.sql.Time` value.
void updateTimestamp(int columnIndex, Timestamp x)	Updates the time value with a `java.sql.Timestamp` value.
int getConcurrency()	Retrieves the concurrency mode of the ResultSet object.
String getCursorName()	Retrieves the SQL cursor name used by the ResultSet object.

Using ResultSet

After obtaining a ResultSet object, you can use a result set to read the data (ResultSet content) encapsulated in it. Figure 3.24 shows the process flow involved in getting ResultSet from the Statement object and reading the data from the ResultSet object. The st and rs parameters represent the Statement and ResultSet object references, respectively.

Figure 3.24 shows the ResultSet operations:

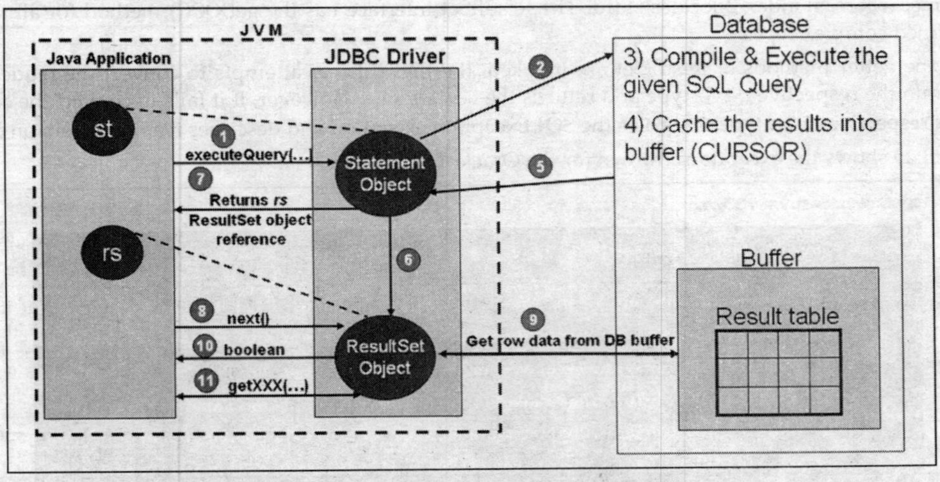

Figure 3.24: Explaining the ResultSet Operations

Note that for every next() method invoked, the JDBC driver may not necessarily get the data row from the database buffer. This means that after every step 8, shown in Figure 3.24, there may not always be a step 9. Instead, the JDBC driver can get multiple rows of data at a time and buffer it on the client side. The buffering of data on the client size depends on the fetch size set for the ResultSet object. The fetch size of a result set can be set by using the setFetchSize (int) method of ResultSet object.

You can retrieve data from a ResultSet object in two simple steps:

- Move the cursor position to the required row
- Read the column data using the getXXX() methods

Let's discuss these steps in detail.

Moving the Cursor Position

While obtaining data from a ResultSet object, the cursor is initially placed before the first row, i.e. beforeFirst(). You can use the next() method of result set to move the cursor position to the next record in the result set. When the cursor is moved to the next record, it returns a boolean value indicating whether or not any record is available in the result set. The next() method returns true if it successfully positions the cursor on the next row; otherwise, it returns false.

NOTE

JDBC 2.0 also introduces some other methods in ResultSet to move the cursor position, provided the ResultSet is of the scrollable type. The ResultSet generated is forward by default; therefore, you can iterate through it only in the forward direction from the first to the last row.

Reading the Column Values

After moving the cursor to the respective row, you can use the getter methods of ResultSet to retrieve the data from the row where the cursor is positioned. Getter methods of ResultSet are overloaded, that means, there are two getter methods for each of the JDBC type. One of these two methods takes column index of type `int` as an input, where column index starts with 1; and the other method takes column name of the String type. You should note that the column names that are passed to getter methods are not case sensitive. If the same column is present more than once in a select list, the first instance of the column is to be returned.

Note that the column index supplied to the getXXX() methods is the index that starts with 1, where the index numbers are given based on the resulted tabular data, and not on the source table that is queried.

For example, suppose a table of students contains two columns, stdId, and stdName. Now, if you obtain a ResultSet for the `select stdName, stdId from the students` query, the column index 1 locates the stdName; whereas, index 2 locates stdId. The ResultSet interface has the getXXX() method for all the basic and predefined complex types.

When the getter methods of ResultSet are invoked, the JDBC driver attempts to convert the requested column value into the respective `Java` type and returns the `Java` value. However, if it fails to convert the column value into its respective `Java` type, it throws the SQLException exception and describes it as a conversion error.

Figure 3.25 shows the exceptions thrown for the Oracle Thin driver:

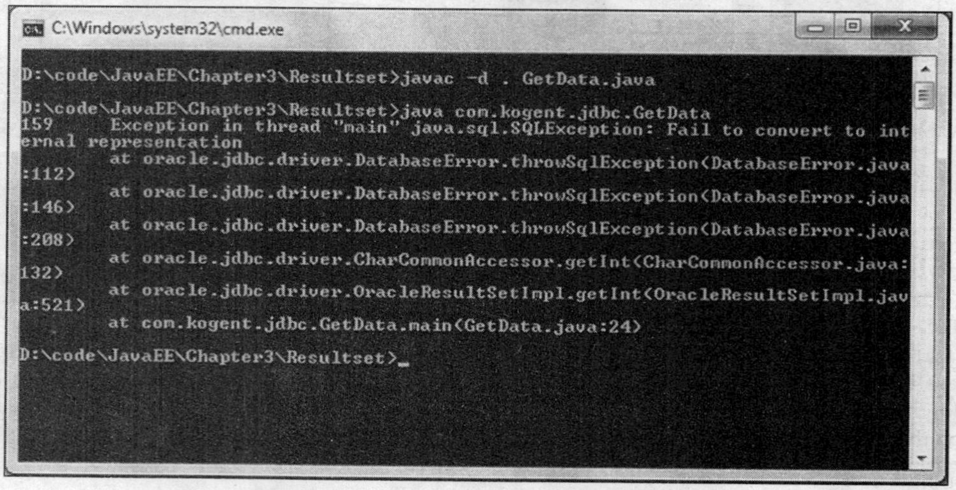

Figure 3.25: Showing an Example of SQLException

Figure 3.25 shows the error message when the JDBC driver fails to convert the SQL type to the `Java` type. In our case, we have created the GetData.java file in which the column value is of String type and we have used getInt() method to retrieve the colum value. The allowable mappings for the various SQL types to `Java` types under the JDBC specification are described in Table 3.23:

Table 3.23: JDBC and Java Data Types

JDBC Type	Java Type
CHAR	String
VARCHAR	String
LONGVARCHAR	String
NUMERIC	`java.math.BigDecimal`
DECIMAL	`java.math.BigDecimal`
BIT	boolean
BOOLEAN	boolean
TINYINT	byte
SMALLINT	short

Table 3.23: JDBC and Java Data Types

JDBC Type	Java Type
INTEGER	int

In Java, the value of a column can be retrieved in the form of an object in a ResultSet by using the getObject() method.

The getObject() method of ResultSet uses the conversions as described in Table 3.24:

Table 3.24: Showing the Conversion of JDBC to Java Object Type

JDBC Type	Java Object Type
CHAR	String
VARCHAR	String
LONGVARCHAR	String
NUMERIC	java.math.BigDecimal
DECIMAL	java.math.BigDecimal
BIT	boolean
BOOLEAN	boolean
TINYINT	Integer
SMALLINT	Integer
INTEGER	Integer
BIGINT	Long
REAL	Float
FLOAT	Double
DOUBLE	Double
BINARY	byte[]
VARBINARY	byte[]
LONGVARBINARY	byte[]
DATE	java.sql.Date
TIME	java.sql.Time
TIMESTAMP	java.sql.Timestamp
DISTINCT	Object type of underlying Type
CLOB	java.sql.Clob
BLOB	java.sql.Blob
ARRAY	java.sql.Array
STRUCT	java.sql.Struct or java.sql.SQLData
REF	java.sql.Ref
DATALINK	java.net.URL
JAVA_OBJECT	Underlying Java class
ROWID	java.sql.RowId

Table 3.24: Showing the Conversion of JDBC to Java Object Type	
JDBC Type	**Java Object Type**
NCHAR	String
NVARCHAR	String
LONGNVARCHAR	String

Let's now look at some examples of using ResultSet.

Retrieving All the Rows in a Table

As already explained, you can retrieve rows from a table by using the ResultSet object. Let's now understand how you can retrieve all the rows of the `mytable` table. A row in the mytable table can store data of different types, such as a string, integer, and floating-point number.

Let's now create an application named ResultSet, which contains the GetAllRows.`java` file. Listing 3.7 shows how you can retrieve all the rows from the mytable table:

Listing 3.7: Showing the Code for the GetAllRows.`java File`

```
package com.kogent.jdbc;
import java.sql.*;
/**
 * @author Suchita
 */
public class GetAllRows {

   public static void main(String args[])throws
   SQLException, ClassNotFoundException {

         //Get Connection
         Connection con=prepareConnection();

         // Obtain a Statement
         Statement st=con.createStatement();
         String query = "select * from mytable";

         //Execute the Query
         ResultSet rs=st.executeQuery (query);

         System.out.println ("COL1\tCOL2\tCOL3");
   while (rs.next()){
         System.out.print (rs.getString ("COL1") + "\t");
         System.out.print (rs.getInt ("COL2") + "\t");
         System.out.println (rs.getInt("COL3"));
         }//while
         con.close();
   }//main
   public static Connection prepareConnection()
         throws SQLException,
         ClassNotFoundException  {

         String driverClassName="oracle.jdbc.driver.OracleDriver";
         String url="jdbc:oracle:thin:@192.168.1.123:1521:XE";
         String username="scott";
         String password="tiger";

         //Load driver class
         Class.forName (driverClassName);

         // Obtain a connection
         return DriverManager. getConnection (url, username, password);
   }//prepareConnection
}//class
```

In Listing 3.7, the `next()` method is used to move the cursor position in the forward direction. The application throws an exception if the user tries to move the cursor in the backward direction from the relative position of the cursor.

NOTE

The column names used with the getXXX() methods of ResultSet object are not the actual table column names; instead, they are the column names of the table that would be created as a ResultSet. For instance, if you use a query to select col1 as c1, col2 as c2, and col3 as c3 from the mytable table, the column names that you need to use in these getXXX() methods are c1, c2 and c3 and not col1, col2 and col3.

In Listing 3.7, we have obtained the data by using column names. However, we can also obtain the data by using column numbers. Use the following code snippet in place of the code with column names (as shown in Listing 3.7) to obtain the data using column numbers:

```
while (rs.next()) {
   System.out.print (rs.getString (1) + "\t");
   System.out.print (rs.getInt (2) + "\t");
   System.out.println (rs.getDouble (3));
}//while
```

NOTE

Using the column index form of the getXXX() methods is more efficient than the column name form, because the driver does not have to deal with the extra steps of parsing the column name, finding it in the select list, and then turning it into a number.

Compiling and running the application shown in Listing 3.7 gives the output, as shown in Figure 3.26:

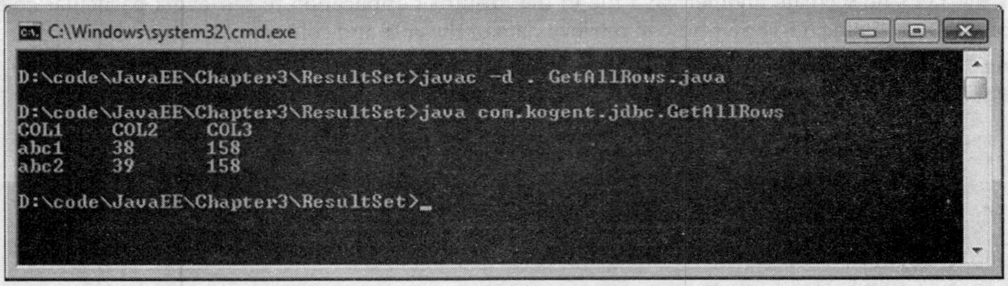

Figure 3.26: Showing the Output of the GetAllRows.java File

If we try to read the column values (without calling the `next()` method on `ResultSet`) obtained after executing the query, an exception is raised, as shown in Figure 3.27:

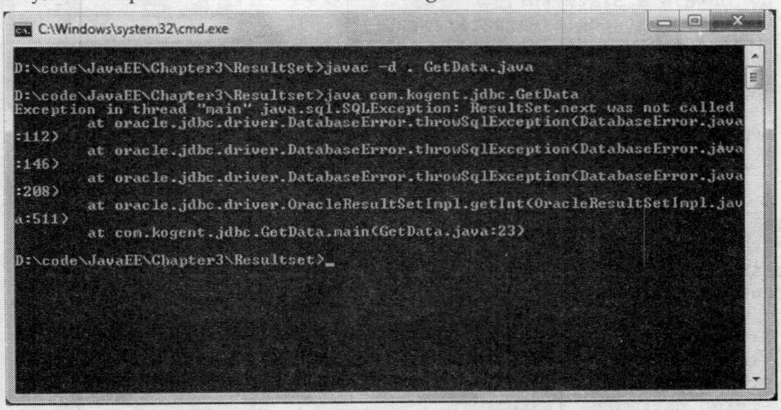

Figure 3.27: Showing the Output Without Calling the next() Method

We have created the GetData.java file in which the next() method on the ResultSet instance is not invoked; therefore, the SQLException exception is generated, as shown in Figure 3.27. If you see an exception as shown in

Figure 3.27, it implies that you have attempted to read the data from the ResultSet immediately after obtaining it, without first calling the next() method. Note that even if you retrieve only one record (that is, one row), you still need to call the next row before reading column values. In such a case, the `rs.next()` method is used.

If you attempt to retrieve/read the column values even after the last record, the SQLException exception is raised. For example, if in Listing 3.7, you try to call the getXXX() method after the while loop, an exception is raised as shown in Figure 3.28:

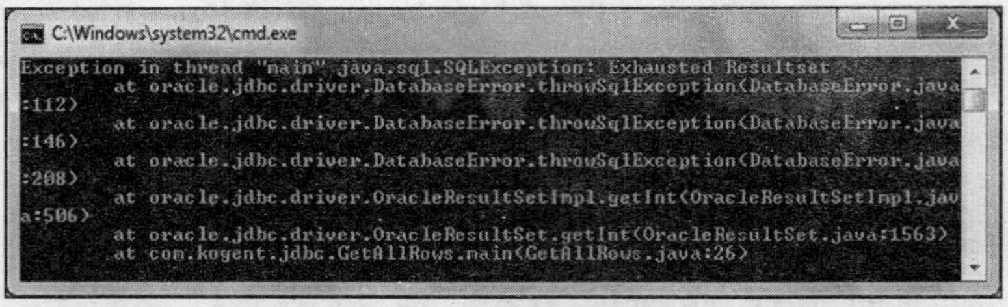

Figure 3.28: Showing the Output of GetAllRows.java Accessing ResultSet after Last Record

Therefore, if the SQLException exception is raised, you must check the control of your application to ensure that it does not read the data when the position of the ResultSet cursor is after the last record.

Retrieving a Particular Column Using ResultSet

Apart from retrieving all the columns from a table, you can also retrieve data of a particular column from the ResultSet. Let's now create another .java file in the ResultSet application to retrieve a particular column from a database table. Listing 3.8 shows how to retrieve data of the col1 and col2 columns from the `mytable` table:

Listing 3.8: Showing the Code for the GetData.`java File`

```
package com.kogent.jdbc;

import java.sql.*;
/**
* @author Suchita
*/
public class GetData {
public static void main(String args[])throws SQLException,
ClassNotFoundException {
        //Get Connection
        Connection con=prepareConnection();

        // Obtain a Statement
        Statement st=con.createStatement();
        String query = "select col3, col1 from mytable";
                          //Execute the Query
        ResultSet rs=st.executeQuery(query);

        while (rs.next()){
                System.out.print (rs.getInt(1)+ "\t");
                System.out.println (rs.getString(2));
        }//while
 }//main

 public static Connection prepareConnection()throws
 SQLException, ClassNotFoundException  {

        String driverClassName="oracle.jdbc.driver.OracleDriver";
        String url="jdbc:oracle:thin:@192.168.1.123:1521:XE";
        String username="scott";
        String password="tiger";

        //Load driver class
        Class.forName(driverClassName);
```

```
            // Obtain a connection
            return DriverManager.getConnection(url,username,password);
        }//prepareConnection
    }//class
```

In Listing 3.8, the SELECT statement is used to retrieve the data of the col1 and col3 columns from the mytable table, and the `next()` method is used to move the cursor position in the forward direction.

The output of Listing 3.8 is shown in Figure 3.29:

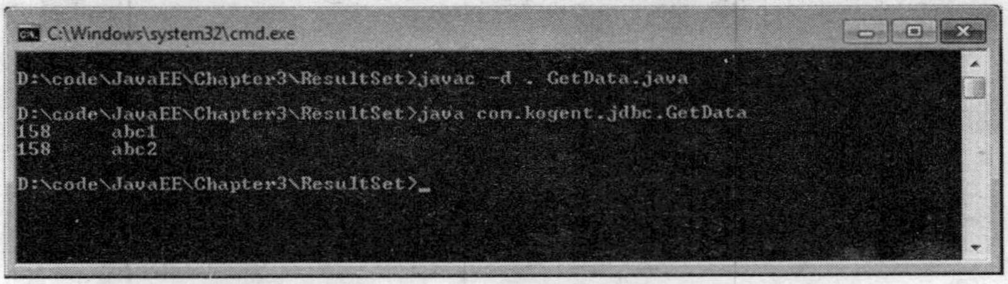

Figure 3.29: Showing the Output of GetData

You can change the query in Listing 3.8, as shown in the following code snippet:

```
    query = "select col3, col1 from mytable";
      to
    query = "select col3 as c3, col1 as c1 from mytable";
```

Now, in the getXXX() methods of ResultSet, you pass c1 and c3 instead of col1 and col3, respectively, as shown in the following code snippet:

```
    System.out.print (rs.getString("c3") + "\t");
    System.out.println (rs.getInt("c1"));
```

The following code snippet shows the internal implementation of column name version of the getXXX() method in a ResultSet:

```
    public String getString(String s){
      int index=findColumn(s);
      return getString(index);
    }
```

In the preceding code snippet, the findColumn(s) method of ResultSet object returns the index number of the first found column, where the column name matches with the specified string column name.

The following are the possible exceptions that might be raised while executing this application:

- ClassNotFoundException, as shown in Listing 3.8.
- SQLException, if the column names used in the SQL query are not correct, as shown in Figure 3.30:

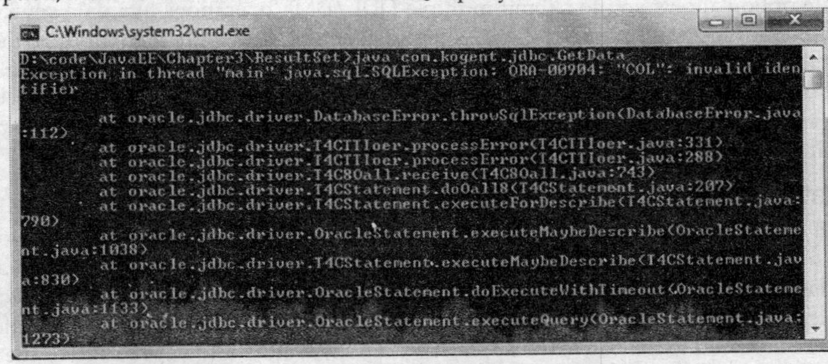

Figure 3.30: Showing the SQLException when Column Name is Incorrect

In this case, verify that the column names used in the query are correct.

- The SQLException exception can be raised if the column types used with the getXXX() methods of ResultSet are incorrect.

Figure 3.31 shows the SQLException exception that is raised while executing the GetData class, in which the value of a field is not internally converted into int:

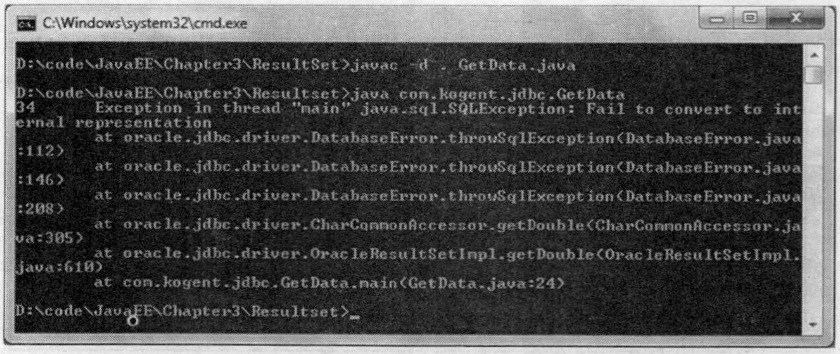

Figure 3.31: Showing the SQLException with Incorrect getXXX() Method

If the exception shown in Figure 3.31 is raised, you should check the column names used with the getXXX() methods of ResultSet. Note that the preceding two exceptions are different, and to programmatically differentiate these exceptions and write supplementary code snippets, you need to depend on the SQL State and Error Code, which are vendor dependent. For example, if you observe the exception message shown in Figure 3.30, you find the exception message as ORA-00904. In this exception message, 00904 represents the error code. You use the getErrorCode() method of SQLException to obtain only the exception (error) code in an application.

- Instead of using column names with the getXXX() methods of ResultSet, you can use column index. However, if improper column index is used, you can encounter the same exception as shown in Figure 3.31. In this case, verify that the column indexes used with the getXXX() methods are correct.

You can use the preceding example to create a query for particular rows. In this case, you need to change the query, as shown in the following code snippet:

```
String query= "select * from mytable where COL1='abc1'";
   Or
String query= "select * from mytable where COL2=36";
   Or
String query= "select * from mytable where COL2>=36";
```

Working with Batch Updates

The batch update option allows you to submit multiple DDL/DML operations to a data source to process data simultaneously. Submitting multiple DDL/DML queries together, rather than submitting them individually, improves the performance of the query execution time. The `Statement`, `PreparedStatement`, and `CallableStatement` objects can be used to submit batch updates. It implies that the `Statement`, `PreparedStatement`, and `CallableStatement` objects are capable of keeping track of batches to be processed so that all the batches can be submitted together for processing.

Using Batch Updates with the Statement Object

Using the batch updates option with the `Statement` object allows you to submit a set of heterogeneous DDL/DML commands as a single unit (batch) to the underlying data source. When the Statement object is created using the `createStatement()` method of the Connection interface, it is associated with an empty batch. An application can use the addBatch (String) method to add a statement to the batch. After all the statements have been added to the batch, the application can invoke the `executeBatch()` method, if the batch needs to be submitted for processing. However, if the application does not submit the batch, it can invoke the `clearBatch()` method on the `Statement` object to remove all the statements.

Describing the Batch Update Methods

The following methods have been added in the Statement interface to support batch update:

- **addBatch (String)**—Adds one SQL statement to a batch. Only DDL and DML commands that return a simple update count can be added to the batch.
- **int [] executeBatch()**—Submits a batch to the underlying data source. When the batch is submitted to the data source, the statements in a batch are executed in the sequence in which they have been added to the batch.
- **clearBatch()**—Clears the batch before submitting it for processing.If the batch is executed successfully, the executeBatch() method returns an array of integer whose length is equal to the number of statements in the batch, and each element in the batch represents the respective statements update count. If the value of any element in this array is equal to Statement.SUCCESS_NO_INFO, it indicates that the statement has been executed successfully but the number of rows affected is unknown. In case a statement in a batch fails to be executed and produces a result set, further processing of the batch depends on the JDBC driver. In this case, the JDBC driver may still continue executing the batch or may terminate it. However, in most cases, the JDBC driver terminates the batch processing. Irrespective of the fact that the driver is implemented or not, if the batch fails to execute, the executeBatch() method throws BatchUpdateException. After the executeBatch() method is executed, the JDBC driver resets the batch.
- **The java.sql.BatchUpdateException**—Refers to an exception that is raised if the batch fails to execute. It is a subclass of `java.sql.SQLException`, which uses the `getUpdateCounts()` method of the current object and returns the `int` array, whose value can be:
  - **Less than the size of the batch**—Denotes that the driver has terminated the batch after the first failure of the execution of a query. Therefore, if the length of an array is n, it means that the first n statements in the batch have been executed successfully.
  - **Equal to the size of the batch**—Denotes that the driver has continued the batch execution process even after the batch has failed to execute. In this case, the value of each element in the array specifies the update count. If the array value pertains to the statement that has failed to execute, the array value becomes equal to the `Statement.EXECUTE_FAILED` field.

Example of Using Batch Updates with the Statement Object

Let's now look at an example of using batch updates with the `Statement` object. Let's create an application, called BatchUpdate, containing the `BatchUpdateEx1.java` file, which is used to perform batch updates. Listing 3.9 shows the code for the `BatchUpdateEx1.java` file:

Listing 3.9: Showing the Code for the BatchUpdateEx1.java File

```
package com.kogent.jdbc;
import java.sql.*;
import java.util.*;
import java.io.*;
/**
 * @author Suchita
 */
public class BatchUpdateEx1 {
  public static void main(String s[]) throws Exception {
  Driver d= (Driver) (Class.forName("oracle.jdbc.driver.OracleDriver").newInstance());
       Properties p=new Properties();
       p.put("user","scott");
       p.put("password","tiger");
       Connection con=d.connect("jdbc:oracle:thin:@192.168.1.123:1521:XE",p);
       Statement st=con.createStatement();
       //statement1
       st.addBatch("insert into emp(empno,sal,deptno) values("+s[0]+",1000,10)");
       //statement2
       st.addBatch("update emp set sal=2000 where empno="+s[0]);
       //statement3
              st.addBatch("insert into emp(empno,sal,deptno) values(202,1000,10)");
       //statement4
```

```
            st.addBatch("insert into emp(empno,sal,deptno) values(203,1000,10)");
        try {
            int[] counts=st.executeBatch();
            System.out.println("Batch Executed Successfully");
            for (int i=0;i<counts.length;i++){
            System.out.println("Number of records effected by statement"+(i+1)+":
            "+counts[i]);
            }//for
        }//try
        catch(BatchUpdateException e){
            System.out.println("Batch terminated with an abnormal condition");
            int[] counts=e.getUpdateCounts();
            System.out.println("Batch terminated at statement"+ (counts.length+1));
            for (int i=0;i<counts.length;i++) {
            System.out.println("Number of records effected by the statement"+
            (i+1)+": "+counts[i]);
            }//for
        }//catch
        con.close();
    }//main
}//class
```

Listing 3.9 demonstrates how to perform batch updates using the `Statement` object. It also shows that the SQL statements added to the batch are executed in the order in which they have been added to the batch. In addition, it shows how to get update counts by using `BatchUpadateException`.

Figure 3.32 shows the output of Listing 3.9:

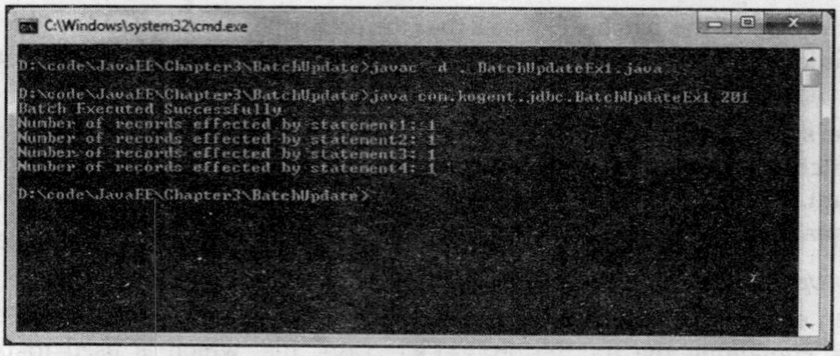

Figure 3.32: Showing the Output of the BatchUpdateEx1.java File

Figure 3.32 shows the successful execution of the batch used in Listing 3.9. You can run the preceding example again with argument value 203 to understand how the `BatchUpdateException` exception functions, as shown in Figure 3.33:

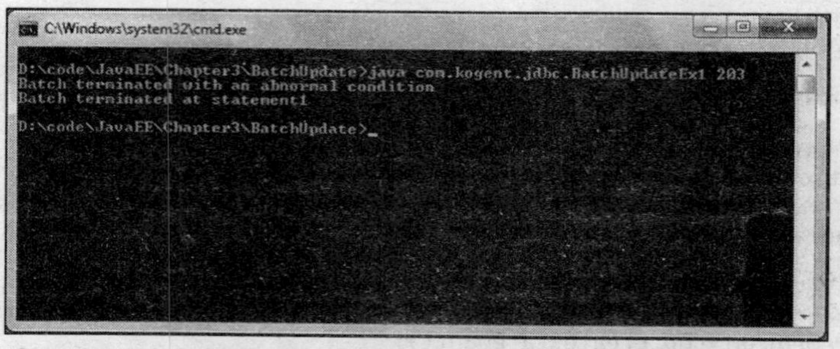

Figure 3.33: Showing the Output of the BatchUpdateEx1.java File with a Different Parameter

In Figure 3.33, a message specifying the termination of the batch execution is displayed as you try to insert a record with `empno` 203, which already exists (empno column of emp table is set with primary key constraint) in the database.

After learning to use batch updates with the `Statement` object, let's now learn how to implement batch updates using the `PreparedStatement` object.

Using Batch Updates with the PreparedStatement Object

Using the batch updates feature with the `PreparedStatement` object is a bit different as compared to the Statement object. You can relate various input parameter values to a PreparedStatement object by using batch updates. The `PreparedStatement` interface provides various methods to support batch updates:

- **addBatch()** – Adds a set of input parameter values to a batch
- **int [] executeBatch()** – Executes a batch of statements in the specified data source
- **clearBatch()** – Clears the batch before submitting it for execution

Let's create an application, called BatchUpdate, to understand the concept better. In this application, you need to create the `BatchUpdateEx2.java` file, which is used to perform batch updates by using the `PreparedStatement` object.

Listing 3.10 shows the code for the `BatchUpdateEx2.javafile:`

Listing 3.10: Showing the Code for the BatchUpdateEx2.java File

```
package com.kogent.jdbc;
import java.sql.*;
import java.util.*;
import java.io.*;
/**
 * @author Suchita
 */
public class BatchUpdateEx2 {
  public static void main(String s[]) throws Exception {
Driver d= (Driver) (Class.forName("oracle.jdbc.driver.OracleDriver").newInstance());
        Properties p=new Properties();
        p.put("user","scott");
        p.put("password","tiger");
        Connection con=d.connect("jdbc:oracle:thin:@192.168.1.123:1521:XE",p);
        PreparedStatement ps= con.prepareStatement("insert into emp(empno,sal,deptno)
        values(?,?,?)");
        ps.setInt(1,301);
        ps.setDouble(2,1000);
        ps.setInt(3,10);
        ps.addBatch();

        ps.setInt(1,302);
        ps.setDouble(2,2000);
        ps.setInt(3,10);
        ps.addBatch();
        try {
                int counts[]= ps.executeBatch();
                System.out.println("Batch Executed Successfully");
                for (int i=0;i<counts.length;i++){
                System.out.println("Number of records effected by statement"+(i+1)+":
                "+counts[i]);
                }//for
        }//try
        catch(BatchUpdateException e){
                System.out.println("Batch terminated with an abnormal condition");
                int[] counts=e.getUpdateCounts();
                System.out.println("Batch terminated at statement"+ (counts.length+1));
                for (int i=0;i<counts.length;i++) {
                System.out.println("Number of records effected by the statement"+
                (i+1)+":"+counts[i]);
                }//for
        }//catch
        con.close();
  }//main
}//class
```

The example shown in Listing 3.10 demonstrates how to perform batch updates using `PreparedStatement` and how to get update counts from `BatchUpadateException`. It also shows that the SQL statements added to the batch are executed in the order in which they have been added.

Figure 3.34 shows the output of Listing 3.10:

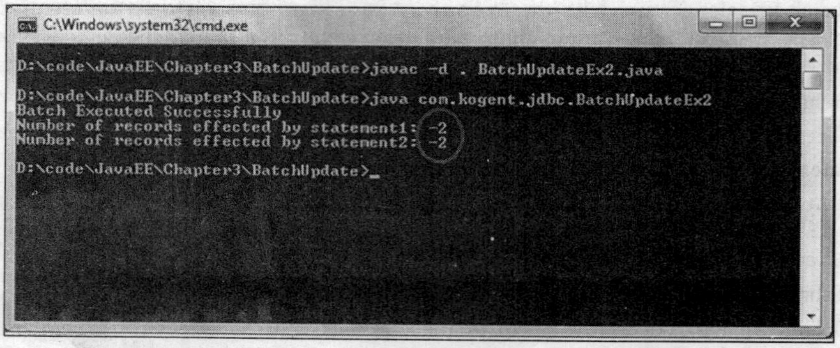

Figure 3.34: Showing the Output of BatchUpdateEx2.java

When you execute Listing 3.10, SQL statements specified in the batch are executed and the emp table is modified. Figure 3.35 shows the content of the emp table after the batch updates have been performed:

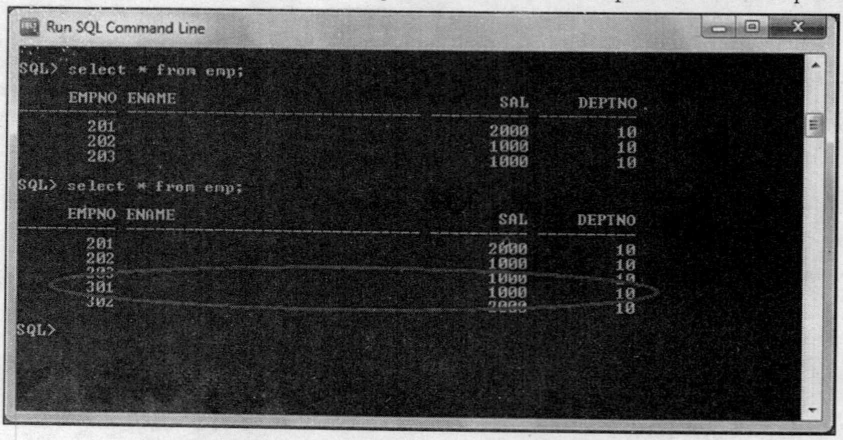

Figure 3.35: Showing the Content of the emp Table

NOTE

In Figure 3.34, update counts are shown as -2; whereas, the records are inserted successfully (Figure 3.35). In such cases, the update count value is equal to Statement.SUCCESS_NO_INFO, which indicates that the statement has been executed successfully but the number of rows affected is unknown.

Describing SQL99 Data Types

SQL-I999 specifies the SQL-I999 object model that adds UDTs to SQL. There are two types of UDTs: distinct and structured. A distinct type is based on a built-in data type, such as integer and a structured type has an internal structure, such as address that might contain the details of street, state, and postal code attributes.

The data types available in SQL-I999 types are as follows:

- BLOB data type
- CLOB data type
- STRUCT data type

- ARRAY data type
- REF data type

All these types are packaged in the `java.sql` package, which provides the classes and interfaces to hold these objects. Let's describe these UDTs available in SQL-1999 types in detail.

Describing the BLOB Data Type

A BLOB is a built-in data type used to store binary large objects, such as images, audios, or multimedia clips, as column values in a database table. The java.sql package provides the `Blob` interface to represent BLOB values. BLOB values can be implemented by using the SQL locator. This locator indicates that a Blob object contains a pointer to point to SQL BLOB values in a database. Blob objects provide logical pointers to the binary large objects rather than copies of the objects. Most of the databases process only one data page into the memory at a time; i.e., the whole BLOB does not need to be processed and stored in memory just to access the first few bytes of the Blob object. The lifetime of the Blob object is based on the lifetime of a transaction as well as the database in use.

The Blob interface provides various methods to store and retrieve BLOB values in an application.

Table 3.25 describes the methods provided by the Blob interface:

Table 3.25: Methods of the Blob Interface

Method	Description
InputStream getBinaryStream()	Retrieves the BLOB value, stored by the Blob object, as a stream.
byte[] getBytes(long pos, int length)	Retrieves all or some portion of the BLOB values stored by the Blob object.
long length()	Returns the number of bytes of the BLOB values taken by the Blob object.
long position(Blob pattern, long start)	Returns the byte position of the BLOB value designated by the Blob object.
long position(byte[] pattern, long start)	Returns the position of the BLOB value in an array of bytes designated by the Blob object.
OutputStream setBinaryStream(long pos)	Retrieves the stream used to write the BLOB value.
int setBytes(long pos, byte[] bytes)	Writes the BLOB value in an array of bytes designated by the Blob object, starting at position `pos`, and returns the number of bytes written. The position and the number of bytes to be written must be specified in this method.
int setBytes(long pos, byte[] bytes, int offset, int len)	Sets all or part of the specified `byte` array to the `BLOB value` designated by the `Blob object` and returns the number of bytes written to the `BLOB value`.
void truncate(long len)	Truncates the BLOB value represented by the Blob object.

Now let's use these methods to store BLOB values into the database. The following heading describes the following tasks:

- Store BLOB values into the database
- Read BLOB values

Now, let's discuss each of them in detail.

Storing BLOB values

The Blob interface of JDBC does not provide any database-independent mechanism to construct a Blob instance; and therefore, you need to either write your own implementation or depend on the implementation of the driver vendor. If you are working with a previous version of JDBC 4.0, you can use the setBinaryStream (...) method of the PreparedStatement and CallableStatement interfaces to construct a Blob instance as an InputStream of the specified length. The constructed Blob instance is passed as parameter to the `setBlob()` method of the the `PreparedStatement` and `CallableStatement` interfaces to store BLOB data in the database. Let's create an application called `Blob` to understand the concept better. This application contains a Java file named `InsertBlobEx.java`, which is used to store BLOB values, as shown in Listing 3.11:

Listing 3.11: Showing the Code for the InsertBlobEx.java File

```
package com.kogent.jdbc;
import java.sql.*;
import java.util.*;
import java.io.*;
/**
* @author Suchita
*/
public class InsertBlobEx
{
   public static void main(String s[]) throws Exception
   {
         Driver d= (Driver) (Class.forName(
         "oracle.jdbc.driver.OracleDriver").newInstance());
         Properties p=new Properties();
         p.put("user","scott");
         p.put("password","tiger");
         Connection con=d.connect("jdbc:oracle:thin:@192.168.1.123:1521:XE",p);
         PreparedStatement ps= con.prepareStatement(
         "insert into personaldetails(empno,photo) values(?,?)");
         ps.setInt(1,Integer.parseInt(s[0]));
         File f=new File("MyImg101.gif");
         FileInputStream fis= new FileInputStream(f);
         ps.setBinaryStream(2,fis, (int)f.length());
         int i=ps.executeUpdate();
         System.out.println("Record inserted successfully , count : "+i);
         con.close();
   }//main
}//class
```

You should create the personaldetails table before executing the code shown in Listing 3.11. The following code snippet shows the command used to create the personaldetails table in the Oracle database:

```
create table personaldetails(empno number, photo BLOB);
```

When you execute the code given in Listing 3.11, an image is inserted into the Oracle database. The image value is stored into the database by using the `setBinaryStream()` method of the PreparedStatement interface. Figure 3.36 shows the output of the InsertBlobEx class:

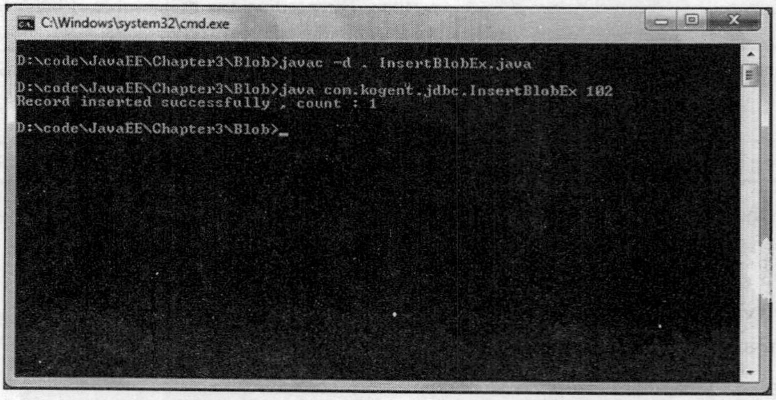

Figure 3.36: Displaying the Output of the InsertBlobEx Class

In the earlier versions of JDBC 4.0, the Blob interface did not provide any database-independent mechanism to construct the Blob instance; therefore, to solve this problem, JDBC 4.0 APIs provide a `createBlob()` method in the `java.sql.Connection` interface. The createBlob() method allows to create a `Blob object` to which the bytes can be set and passed as a parameter into the `setBlob()` method of the PreparedStatement and CallableStatement interfaces.

The following code snippet creates a Blob object, b, in JDBC 4.0:

```
Connection con= ... //obtain the connection
Blob b=con.createBlob(); //creates an empty Blob (Blob object with no bytes)
b.setBytes(1, data); //here data is a byte[]
Now, the above created Blob object can be used with setBlob() method
```

After learning how to store the value of a Blob object in a database using the `getBinaryStream()` method, let's now learn how to retrieve the value of the Blob object from a database.

Reading a BLOB value

You can retrieve a BLOB value from a database by using the Blob object. Let's create a .java (`ReadBlobEx.java`) file in the Blob application to read BLOB values to understand the concept better. Listing 3.12 shows the code of the `ReadBlobEx.java` file:

Listing 3.12: Showing the `ReadBlobEx.java File`

```
package com.kogent.jdbc;
import java.sql.*;
import java.util.*;
import java.io.*;
/**
 * @author Suchita
 */
public class ReadBlobEx {
  public static void main(String s[]) throws Exception {

        Driver d= (Driver) (Class.forName(
        "oracle.jdbc.driver.OracleDriver").newInstance());

        Properties p=new Properties();
        p.put("user","scott");
        p.put("password","tiger");

        Connection con=d.connect(
        "jdbc:oracle:thin:@192.168.1.123:1521:XE",p);
        Statement st=con.createStatement();
        ResultSet rs=st.executeQuery( "select * from personaldetails");

        while (rs.next()) {

                int empno=rs.getInt(1);
                InputStream is=rs.getBinaryStream(2);

                FileOutputStream fos=new FileOutputStream("MyImg"+empno+".gif");
                int i=is.read();

                while (i!=-1){
                        fos.write(i);
                        i=is.read();
                }//while
        }//while
        System.out.println("Image's retrived");
        con.close();
  }//main
}//class
```

Listing 3.12 uses the `getBinaryStream()` method provided by the Blob interface to retrieve BLOB values (the inserted image in this case). Figure 3.37 shows the output of the ReadBlobEx class:

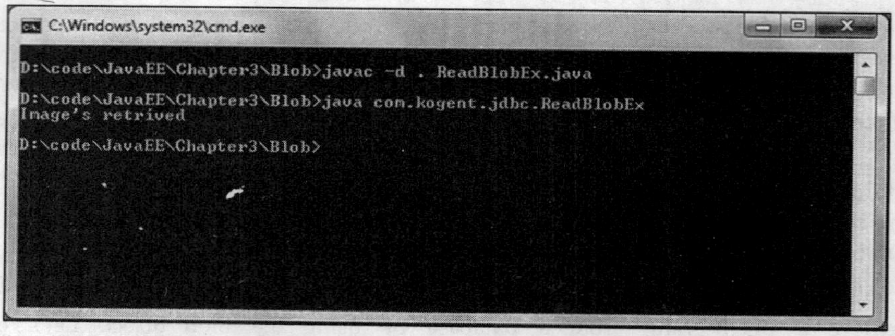

Figure 3.37: Displaying the Output of the ReadBlobEx Class

Describing the CLOB Data Type

CLOB is a built-in data type used to store large amount of textual data. It can also be refered as a collection of data stored as a single entity in a DBMS. CLOB stores the values of large character objects as a column value of a row in a database. The java.sql package provides the `Clob` interface to represent the CLOB values. A Clob object contains a SQL locator to point to the CLOB data in a database. Similar to the Blob object, the lifetime of the Clob object is based on the lifetime of a transaction and the database in use.

The Clob interface provides various methods to store and retrieve CLOB values in a database, as described in Table 3.26:

Table 3.26: Methods of the Clob Interface

Method	Description
InputStream getAsciiStream()	Retrieves a CLOB value designated by the Clob object as well as data stream.
Reader getCharacterStream()	Retrieves the CLOB value as the `java.io.Reader` object.
String getSubString(long pos, int length)	Retrieves a copy of the substring specified in the method. The CLOB value must be designated by the Clob object.
long length()	Retrieves the number of characters from the CLOB value designated by the Clob object.
long position(Clob searchstr, long start)	Retrieves the position of the character from the CLOB value by starting from the value of the start parameter.
long position(String searchstr, long start)	Retrieves the character position in the CLOB value where the searchstr String appears. The searchstr String represents the String to be searched in the CLOB value.
OutputStream setAsciiStream(long pos)	Retrieves the stream to be written into the CLOB value. The starting position of the stream must be specified by the pos parameter of the method. In addition, the CLOB value must be designated by the Clob object.
Writer setCharacterStream(long pos)	Retrieves the stream used to write the CLOB value, starting from the position specified by the pos parameter of the method.
int setString(long pos, String str)	Writes the specified string, passed as the str parameter, into the CLOB value at the specified position, pos.
int setString(long pos, String str, int offset, int len)	Writes the specified string of the len length into the CLOB value, starting from a specified position.
void truncate(long len)	Truncates the CLOB value for length of len characters, associated with the Clob object.

The `java.sql.Clob` interface provides a logical pointer to the character large object rather than a copy of the large object. Let's now discuss how to retrieve CLOB values from a database and how to store these values in the database.

Now let's understand them in detail.

Storing CLOB Values

Similar to the Blob interface, the Clob interface provides no database-independent mechanism to construct the Clob instance, so you need to either write your own implementation or depend on the implementation of the vendor. If you are working with a previous version of JDBC 4.0, you can use the setCharacterStream(…) method of the PreparedStatement and CallableStatement interfaces to construct a Clob instance as a ReaderObject of specified length. You can store the CLOB data in a database by passing the `Clob` instance as a parameter to the `setClob()` method of the `PreparedStatement` and `CallableStatement` interfaces.

Let's create an application called Clob to understand the concept better. This application contains the `InsertEmployeeProfile.java` file to store `CLOB` values. Listing 3.13 shows the code for the InsertEmployeeProfile.java file:

Listing 3.13: Showing the Code for the InsertEmployeeProfile.java File

```
package com.kogent.jdbc;
import java.sql.*;
import java.util.*;
import java.io.*;
/**
 * @author Suchita
 */
public class InsertEmployeeProfile {
   public static void main(String s[]) throws Exception {
         Driver d= (Driver) (Class.forName(
         "oracle.jdbc.driver.OracleDriver").newInstance());
         Properties p=new Properties();
         p.put("user","scott");
         p.put("password","tiger");
         Connection con=d.connect("jdbc:oracle:thin:@192.168.1.123:1521:XE",p);
         PreparedStatement ps= con.prepareStatement(
         "insert into empprofiles values(?,?)");
         ps.setInt(1,Integer.parseInt(s[0]));
         File f=new File(s[1]);
         FileReader fr= new FileReader(f);
         ps.setCharacterStream(2,fr, (int)f.length());
         int i=ps.executeUpdate();
         System.out.println("Record inserted successfully , count : "+i);
         con.close();
   }//main
}//class
```

The user needs to create a table (empprofiles), which contains the employee profile to store the employee details into the database by using the CLOB value. In other words, to execute Listing 3.13, you first need to create the empprofiles table in the Oracle database, as shown in the following code snippet:

```
create table empprofiles (
empno number,
profile CLOB );
```

Listing 3.13 shows how to store a CLOB value into the database by using the `setCharacterStream()` method provided by the `PreparedStatement` interface. We are storing a word document in the Oracle database. The document contains all the details of a particular employee.

Figure 3.38 shows the output of the InsertEmployeeProfile class:

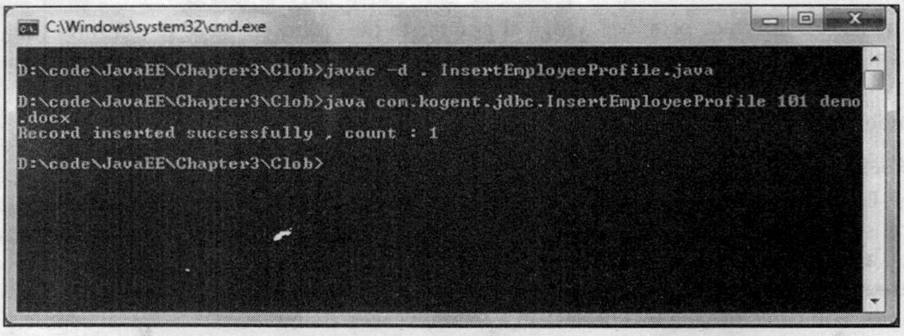

Figure 3.38: Displaying the Output of the InsertEmployeeProfile Class

The JDBC 4.0 APIs provide the `createClob()` method in `java.sql.Connection interface`. The createClob() method allows you to create an empty Clob object. The byte data to the empty Clob object can be added or set by invoking the setString() or other relevant methods depending on the type of the byte data that you want to add to the object. The following code snippet shows how to create a `Clob` object:

```
Connection con= ... //obtain the connection
Clob b=con.createClob(); //creates an empty Clob (Clob object with no bytes)
b.setString(1, data); //where data is a String
Now, the above created Clob object can be used with setClob() method
```

After learning how to store CLOB values into a database by using the `getCharacterStream()` method, let's learn to retrieve CLOB values from the database.

Reading CLOB Values

The Clob interface provides the `getClob()` method to access the CLOB values stored in a database. You can also retrieve CLOB values from a database by using the Clob object.

Let's create the `GetEmployeeProfile.java` file in the Clob application to retrieve CLOB values. Listing 3.14 shows the code for the `GetEmployeeProfile.java` file:

Listing 3.14: Showing the Code for the GetEmployeeProfile.java File

```
package com.kogent.jdbc;

import java.sql.*;
import java.util.*;
import java.io.*;
/**
 * @author Suchita
 */
public class GetEmployeeProfile {
  public static void main(String s[]) throws Exception {
        Driver d= (Driver) (Class.forName(
        "oracle.jdbc.driver.OracleDriver").newInstance());
        Properties p=new Properties();
        p.put("user","scott");
        p.put("password","tiger");
        Connection con=d.connect("jdbc:oracle:thin:@192.168.1.123:1521:XE",p);
        Statement st=con.createStatement();
        ResultSet rs=st.executeQuery(
        "select profile from empprofiles where empno="+s[0]);
        while (rs.next()) {
                Reader r=rs.getCharacterStream(1);
                FileWriter fw=new FileWriter("ProfileOf"+s[0]+".doc");
                int i=r.read();
                while (i!=-1){
                        fw.write(i);
                        i=r.read();
                }//while
        }//while
        System.out.println("Profile retrieved");
```

```
        con.close();
    }//main
}//class
```

Listing 3.14 is used to access the details of the employee by using the `getCharacterStream()` method of the ResultSet interface.

Figure 3.39 shows the output of the GetEmployeeProfile class:

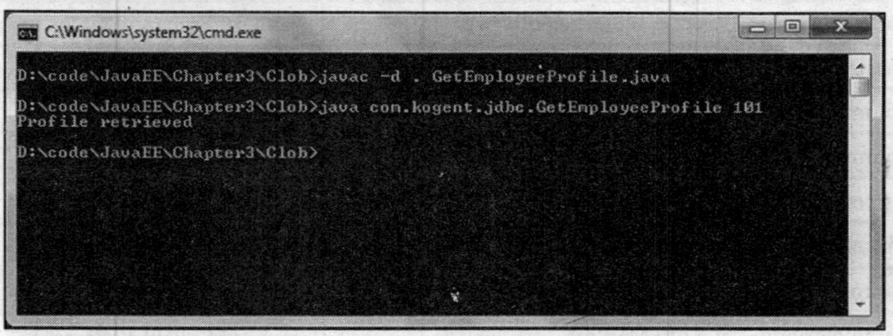

Figure 3.39: Displaying the Output of the GetEmployeeProfile Class

NOTE

The Blob and Clob objects can persist even after the transaction in which they are created is complete. Moreover, these objects may persist for a long time in case of lengthy transactions. This results in shortage of resources for the application using these objects. To overcome this problem, JDBC 4.0 provides the free() method of java.sql.Blob and java.sql.Clob, which you can use to release the Blob and Clob objects when they are not required by the application.

Describing the STRUCT (OBJECT) Data Type

Most of the databases now enable you to create STRUCT data types (also known as structured type), which are used to define complex data types. This is required in case you want to create a UDT in a database. For example, you might need to create a UDT to represent the address of an employee in a single column. The following code snippet shows the syntax to create a structured type in a database:

```
create type <name> as OBJECT (<variable name> <type>, ...);
```

After creating a structured type, you can reference it to create the required UDT. The following code snippet shows the example of creating a UDT:

```
CREATE TYPE empaddress AS OBJECT (
    flatno NUMBER,
    street VARCHAR2(20),
    city VARCHAR2(15),
    state VARCHAR2(10),
    pincode NUMBER
);
```

The preceding code snippet creates a structured type named empaddress, which can store the values of the flatno and pincode fields of type NUMBER, and the street, city, and state fields of type VARCHAR2. It also shows how to create a table with the empaddress type column and insert record into that table.

After learning to create a structured type, let's now learn how to store and retrieve the values of structured types. JDBC provides two approaches to store and retrieve the values of structured types:

- A UDT in Java to represent the database object type
- The java.sql.Struct interface

Let's learn about these in detail next.

Using User-Defined Object Types in Java to Represent Database Object Types

JDBC specification includes support for UDT by providing various methods in the PreparedStatement, CallableStatement, and ResultSet interfaces of JDBC API.

Table 3.27 shows the methods to support UDT:

Table 3.27: Methods Supporting UDT along with their Interfaces

Method	Interface
setObject (int parameterindex, Object o)	java.sql.PreparedStatement
setObject (int parameterindex, Object o, int targetSqltype)	java.sql.PreparedStatement
setObject (int parameterindex, Object o, int targetSqltype, int scale)	java.sql.PreparedStatement
getObject (int columnindex)	java.sql.ResultSet
getObject (int columnindex, java.util.Map m)	java.sql.ResultSet
getObject (String columnName)	java.sql.ResultSet
getObject (String columnName, java.util.Map m)	java.sql.ResultSet
getObject (int parameterindex)	java.sql.CallableStatement
getObject (int parameterindex, java.util.Map m)	java.sql.CallableStatement
getObject (String parameterName)	java.sql.CallableStatement
getObject (String parameterName, java.util.Map m)	java.sql.CallableStatement

In a JDBC application, UDTs must conform to the following rules:

- They should be declared as public non-abstract classes.
- They should be subtypes of the `java.sql.SQLData` interface. The `java.sql.SQLData` interface declares the following methods:
  - **String getSQLTypeName()**—Returns the fully qualified name of the SQL UDT represented by the Struct object. This method is called by the JDBC driver to retrieve the name of the UDT instance, which is mapped to this instance of the `java.sql.SQLData interface`.
  - **void readSQL (SQLInput stream, String typeName)**—Populates the current Struct object with data read from a database. This method generally reads each statement of the SQL type from the given input stream. This is done by calling a method of the SQLInput interface to read the data in the order they appear in the SQL definition of the type. It then assigns the data to appropriate fields of the Struct object. The JDBC driver initializes the input stream with a type map before calling this method, which is used by the appropriate `SQLInput` reader method on the stream.
  - **void writeSQL (SQLOutput stream)**—Writes the current object to the specified SQLOutput stream, which converts it back to its SQL value in the data source. The implementation of the method generally writes each element of the SQL type to the given output stream. This is done by calling a method of the SQLOutput interface to write each item in the order they appear in the SQL definition of the type.
- They should have a no argument constructor.

Let's create an application called `SQLDataInterface` to understand the concept better. In this application, you need to create the EmployeeAddress.java file, which is used to implement the `SQLData` interface to represent the empaddress type created in the preceding code snippet.

Listing 3.15 shows the code of the EmployeeAddess.java file:

Listing 3.15: Showing the Code for the EmployeeAddress.java File

```
package com.kogent.jdbc;

import java.sql.*;
/**
 * @author Suchita
 */
public class EmployeeAddress implements SQLData {
  public EmployeeAddress(){}
  public void writeSQL(SQLOutput so) throws SQLException {
```

```
        so.writeInt(fno);
        so.writeString(street);
        so.writeString(city);
        so.writeString(state);
        so.writeInt(pin);
    }//writeSQL
    public void readSQL(SQLInput si, String name) throws SQLException{
        fno=si.readInt();
        street=si.readString();
        city=si.readString();
        state=si.readString();
        pin=si.readInt();
        typename=name;
    }//readSQL
    public String getSQLTypeName()
    {return typename;}
        public void setFlatno(int i){fno=i;}
    public void setStreet(String s){street=s;}
    public void setCity(String s){city=s;}
    public void setState(String s){state=s;}
    public void setPin(int i){pin=i;}
    public void setTypeName(String s){typename=s;}
    public int getFlatno(){return fno;}
    public String getStreet(){return street;}
    public String getCity(){return city;}
    public String getState(){return state;}
    public int getPin(){return pin;}
    String street,city,state, typename;
    int fno,pin;
}//class
```

Listing 3.15 shows the JDBC UDT to represent the empaddress type that holds the values of the flatno, street, city, state, and pin fields.

Implementing the ***java.sql.Struct*** *Interface*

Now, let's understand the STRUCT data type by creating an application called EmployeeAddress. In this application, you need to create a .java (InsertPersonalDetails.java) file that stores an `EmployeeAddress` object in the Oracle database. You can copy the EmployeeAddress.java file in the EmployeeAddress application directory. You need to perform the following steps to implement the EmployeeAddress application:

- Create an object type named empaddress and a database table named personaldetails in the `Oracle` database
- Create a java file `InsertPersonalDetails.java`, which inserts the object of the `EmployeeAddress` class in the `Oracle` database

Let's start creating an object type and a database table. Figure 3.40 shows the SQL commands to create the `empaddress` object type and `personaldetails` table in the `Oracle` database using the Run SQL Command Line prompt of Oracle:

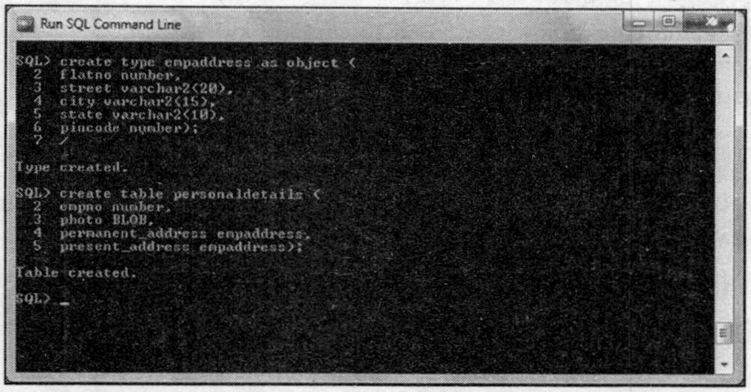

Figure 3.40: Creating Tables using Run SQL Command Line

After creating the object type and table, you need to create a java file, `InsertPersonalDetails.java`, which inserts the object of the `EmployeeAddress` class into the Oracle database. The `InsertPersonalDetails.java` file is shown in Listing 3.16:

Listing 3.16: Showing the Code for the InsertPersonalDetails.java File

```
package com.kogent.jdbc;

import java.sql.*;
import java.util.*;
import java.io.*;
/**
 * @author Suchita
 */
public class InsertPersonalDetails {

  public static void main(String s[]) throws Exception {

        Driver d= (Driver) (Class.forName(
        "oracle.jdbc.driver.OracleDriver").newInstance());

        Properties p=new Properties();
        p.put("user","scott");
        p.put("password","tiger");
        Connection con=d.connect("jdbc:oracle:thin:@192.168.1.123:1521:XE",p);
        PreparedStatement ps= con.prepareStatement(
        "insert into personaldetails(empno,photo,permanent_address) values(?,?,?)");
        /*
        Here we consider Present Address is same as Permanent Address, so we want to
        insert null in place of Present Address
        */
        ps.setInt(1,7934);
        File f=new File("MyImage.gif");
        FileInputStream fis= new FileInputStream(f);
        ps.setBinaryStream(2,fis, (int)f.length());

        EmployeeAddress addr=new EmployeeAddress();
        addr.setFlatno(106);
        addr.setCity("Hyd");
        addr.setStreet("SRN");
        addr.setPin(5000049);
        addr.setState("AP");
        addr.setTypeName("EMPADDRESS");
        ps.setObject(3,addr);
        int i=ps.executeUpdate();
        System.out.println("Personal Details of employee 7934 inserted successfully");
        con.close();
  }//main
}//class
```

Listing 3.16 uses the `setObject()` method of the PreparedStatement interface to store the `EmployeeAddress` object into the Oracle database.

After creating all the required files, let's execute the `InsertPersonalDetails.java` file, as shown in Figure 3.41:

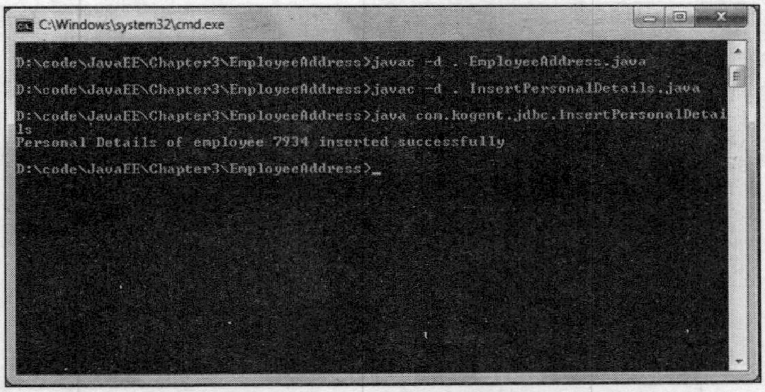

Figure 3.41: Showing the Output of the InsertPersonalDetails.java File

Figure 3.41 shows the output of Listing 3.16, which inserts a record into the personaldetails table.

NOTE

To update the OBJECT type, you can use the same setObject() method as used in Listing 3.16.

Let's now learn how to retrieve the object type value by creating the `GetEmployeeAddress.java` file in the EmployeeAddress application. Listing 3.17 shows the code of `GetEmployeeAddress.java` file:

Listing 3.17: Showing the Code for the GetEmployeeAddress.java File

```
package com.kogent.jdbc;
import java.sql.*;
import java.util.*;
import java.io.*;
/**
 * @author Suchita
 */
public class GetEmployeeAddress {
   public static void main(String s[]) throws Exception {
          Driver d= (Driver) (Class.forName(
          "oracle.jdbc.driver.OracleDriver").newInstance());
          Properties p=new Properties();
          p.put("user","scott");
          p.put("password","tiger");
          Connection con=d.connect("jdbc:oracle:thin:@192.168.1.123:1521:XE",p);
          Statement st=con.createStatement();
          ResultSet rs=st.executeQuery(
          "select permanent_address from personaldetails where empno="+s[0]);
          if (rs.next()){
                  HashMap map=new HashMap();
                  map.put("EMPADDRESS", EmployeeAddress.class);
                  EmployeeAddress addr=(EmployeeAddress)rs.getObject(1,map);
                  System.out.println("Employee Found Address:");
                  System.out.println("Flatno : "+addr.getFlatno());
                  System.out.println("Street : "+ addr.getStreet());
                  System.out.println("Pin    : "+addr.getPin());
          }//if
          con.close();
   }//main
}//class
```

Listing 3.17 shows the code to retrieve the object type value from the Oracle database and represent it as the EmployeeAddress type of object in Java.

Figure 3.42 shows the output of Listing 3.17:

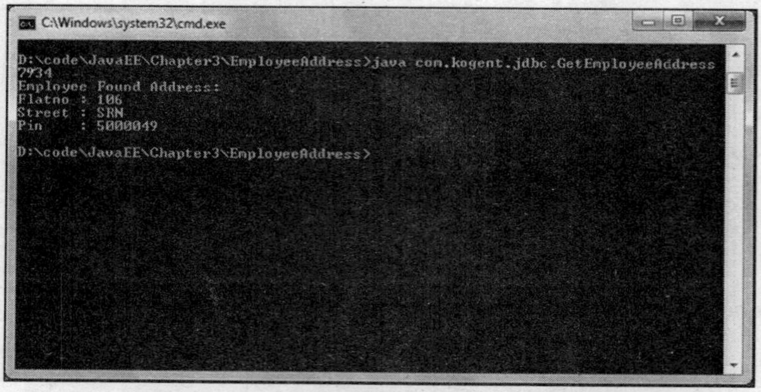

Figure 3.42: Showing the Output of the GetEmployeeAddress.java File

Figure 3.42 shows the output of Listing 3.17 that retrieves the object type value from the Oracle database by using the EmployeeAddress type.

In addition to UDTs, JDBC includes a built-in type, `java.sql.Struct`, which represents the SQL structured type. A `Struct` object contains values for each attribute associated with the `Struct` data type. By default, an instance of Struct is valid until the application has a reference of its instance. The `Struct` interface provides certain methods to work with the Struct objects.

Table 3.28 describes the methods of the `Struct` interface:

Table 3.28: Methods of the Struct Interface

Method	Description
Object[] getAttributes()	Retrieves the structured type attributes and ordered values. Struct values are represented by the `Struct` object.
Object[] getAttributes(Map map)	Retrieves the structured type attributes and ordered values in an array. Struct values are represented by the `Struct` object.
String getSQLTypeName()	Retrieves the SQL type name and SQL type of the SQL Structured type associated with the Struct object.

The Struct types can be used with JDBC programs to communicate with a database. Let's now create an application named Struct, which contains the GetEmployeeAddressUsingStruct.java file to show the use of STRUCT UDTs. Listing 3.18 shows the code of GetEmployeeAddressUsingStruct.java file:

Listing 3.18: Showing the Code for the GetEmployeeAddressUsingStruct.java File

```
package com.kogent.jdbc;

import java.sql.*;
import java.util.*;
import java.io.*;
/**
 * @author Suchita
 */
public class GetEmployeeAddressUsingStruct {

  public static void main(String s[]) throws Exception {

        Driver d= (Driver) (Class.forName(
        "oracle.jdbc.driver.OracleDriver").newInstance());
        Properties p=new Properties();
        p.put("user","scott");
        p.put("password","tiger");
        Connection con=d.connect("jdbc:oracle:thin:@192.168.1.123:1521:XE",p);
        Statement st=con.createStatement();
        ResultSet rs=st.executeQuery(
```

```
            "select permanent_address from personaldetails where empno="+s[0]);

            if (rs.next()){
                  System.out.println("Employee Found: Address");
                  Struct struct=(Struct)rs.getObject(1);
                  Object addr[]=struct.getAttributes();
                  System.out.println("Flatno  : "+addr[0]);
                  System.out.println("Street  : "+ addr[1]);
                  System.out.println("Pin     : "+addr[4]);
            }//if
            con.close();
      }//main
  }//class
```

The output of Listing 3.18, in which we have used the STRUCT UDT, is shown in Figure 3.43:

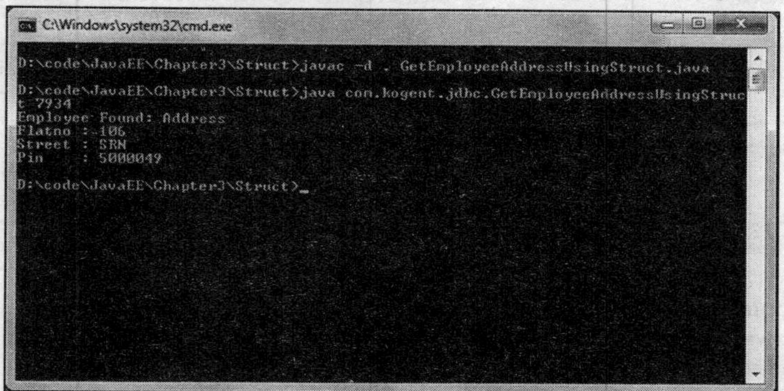

Figure 3.43: Showing the Output of the GetEmployeeAddressUsingStruct.java File

Describing the ARRAY Data Type

Array, one of the SQL99 data types, offers you the facility to include an ordered list of values within a column. The `java.sql` package provides a `java.sql.ARRAY` interface to store the values of the array types. The array object can be implemented by using a SQL locator, which indicates that the array object contains a logical pointer to locate the array value in a database. Since array objects contain UDTs, you need to create a custom mapping between the Class object for the class implementing the SQLData interface and the UDTs. You need to perform the following steps to create a custom mapping:

- Create a class that implements the SQLData interface. The methods of the SQLData interface are used by the data type that need custom mapping.
- Define a Map type that contains the SQL types for UDTs and the classes that implement the SQLData interface.

The Array interface provides some methods to create custom mapping between the classes and UDTs. These methods are described in Table 3.29:

Table 3.29: Methods of the Array Interface

Method	Description
Object getArray()	Retrieves the content of the Array object. Array values must be designated by the Array objects.
Object getArray(long index, int count)	Retrieves a portion of the array value specified by the index. The array value must be designated by the Array object.
Object getArray(long index, int count, Map map)	Retrieves a portion of the array value specified by the index. It also specifies the number of elements that you can access. The array value must be designated by the Array object.

Table 3.29: Methods of the Array Interface

Method	Description
Object getArray(Map map)	Retrieves the content of the SQL array value. The array value is designated by the Array object.
int getBaseType()	Retrieves the JDBC elements present in an array. The array value must be designated by the Array object.
String getBaseTypeName()	Retrieves the name of the SQL elements in an array. The array value must be designated by the Array object.
ResultSet getResultSet()	Retrieves the SQL ResultSet elements present in an array. The array value must be designated by the Array object.
ResultSet getResultSet(long index, int count)	Retrieves the sub array elements, starting at the index of the array. The array value must be designated by the Array object.
ResultSet getResultSet(long index, int count, Map map)	Retrieves the sub array elements, starting at the index of the array. The sub array also contains a count of the elements. The array value must be designated by the Array object.
ResultSet getResultSet(Map map)	Retrieves the SQL array elements stored in the specified Map instance.

The Array type contains more than one value of the same data type. The syntax to create an array type in the database is as follows:

```
create Type <type name> as VARRAY(<length>) of <type>
```

To insert a record by using the Statement interface, you do not need to use the `java.sql.Array` interface. Instead, you can execute the preceding query by using the `executeUpdate()` method. You can use the `setArray()` method of the PreparedStatement interface to bind an array object as a parameter to a statement. However, in earlier versions of JDBC, the Array interface did not provide any database-independent mechanism to construct an array instance. In such cases, you need to either write your own implementation or depend on the implementation of the driver vendor.

Let's now create an application named Arrays. The application contains the InsertEmpPassportDetails.java file, which uses the SQL ARRAY type with the PreparedStatement object. Listing 3.19 shows the code of the InsertEmpPassportDetails.java file:

Listing 3.19: Showing the Code for the InsertEmpPassportDetails.java File

```
package com.kogent.jdbc;

import java.sql.*;
import java.util.*;
import oracle.sql.*;
/**
 * @author Suchita
 */

public class InsertEmpPassportDetails {
  public static void main(String s[]) throws Exception {
        Driver d= (Driver) (Class.forName(
        "oracle.jdbc.driver.OracleDriver").newInstance());
        Properties p=new Properties();
        p.put("user","scott");
        p.put("password","tiger");

        Connection con=d.connect(
```

```
        "jdbc:oracle:thin:@192.168.1.123:1521:XE",p);

        PreparedStatement ps=con.prepareStatement(
        "INSERT INTO emppassportDetails VALUES(?,?,?)");

        ps.setInt(1,7934);
        ps.setString(2,"12345A134");

        String s1[]={"v1","v2","v3","v4","v5"};

        ArrayDescriptor ad=ArrayDescriptor.createDescriptor("VISA_NOS",con);
        ARRAY a=new ARRAY(ad,con,s1);

        ps.setArray(3,a);
        int i=ps.executeUpdate();
        System.out.println("Row Inserted, count : "+i);
        con.close();
    }//main
}//class
```

Listing 3.19 uses the SQL Array types to insert the array values into an array. To insert the array values in the array, you need to create the Array type in the database, so that the values inserted from the application through the Array type can be stored in the array. The Array type for the Arrays application is the emppassportDetails table with the columns. The following code snippet shows how to create the emppassportDetails table:

```
create table emppassportDetails (
empno number, passportno varchar2(10),
visas_taken visa_nos);
insert into emppassportDetails values(7934, '12345A123',
  visa_nos('v1','v2','v3','v4','v5'));
```

The ARRAY type can be created at the Run SQL Command Line prompt, and then can be used by the user to insert data into the emppassportDetails table.

Figure 3.44 shows the output of the Array type at the Run SQL Command Line prompt:

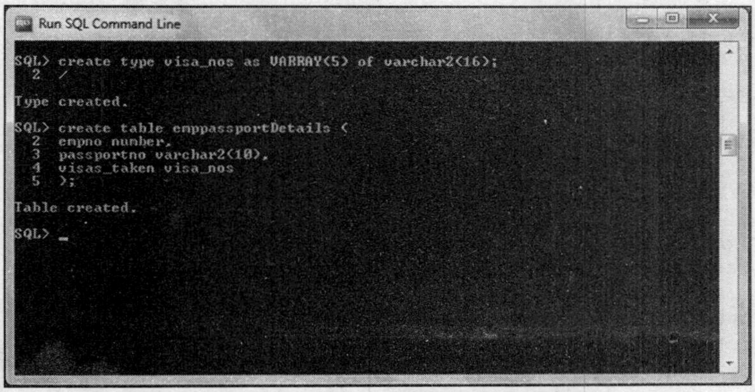

Figure 3.44: Creating an ARRAY Type in Oracle

Figure 3.44 shows the Array type created in the Oracle database. This type is used by the `InsertEmpPassportDetails`.java file to store the data into the database. The table (emppassportDetails) contains the array types to store multiple data of the same type in a column. The column values inserted through Listing 3.19 are stored in one of the columns in the table (emppassportDetails).

Figure 3.45 shows the output of Listing 3.19 (`InsertEmpPassportDetails.java`) using the ARRAY types:

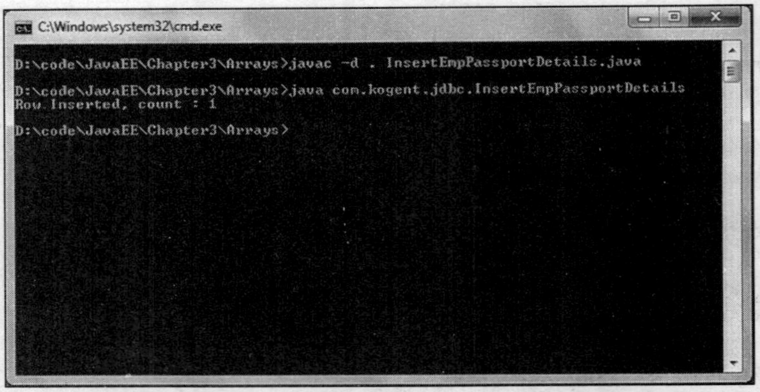

Figure 3.45: Showing the Output of the InsertEmpPassportDetails.java File

In Listing 3.19, we have used the implementation for Array given by Oracle, which works only with the Oracle JDBC driver; consequently making the application a vendor-dependent application. JDBC 4.0 solves this problem by introducing the `createArrayOf()` method in `java.sql.Connection object`. The `createArrayOf()` method of `java.sql.Connection object` allows you to create vendor-independent `java.sql.Array` type of object with the given element type and value, as shown in the following code snippet:

```
PreparedStatement ps=con.prepareStatement("insert into emppassportDetails values(?,?,?)");
   ps.setInt(1,7934);
   ps.setString(2,"12345A134");
   String s1[]={"v1","v2","v3","v4","v5"};
   Array a=con.createArrayOf("VARCHAR", s1);
ps.setArray(3,a);
```

We can also retrieve the Array type value from a database using JDBC. Let's now create the GetEmpPassportDetails.java file in the Arrays application. Listing 3.20 shows how to read the ARRAY type value from the database using JDBC:

Listing 3.20: Showing the Code for the GetEmpPassportDetails.java File

```
package com.kogent.jdbc;
import java.sql.*;
import java.util.*;
/**
 * @author Suchita
 */
public class GetEmpPassportDetails
{
   public static void main(String s[]) throws Exception
   {
         Driver d= (Driver) (Class.forName(
         "oracle.jdbc.driver.OracleDriver").newInstance());

         Properties p=new Properties();
         p.put("user","scott");
         p.put("password","tiger");

         Connection con=d.connect(
         "jdbc:oracle:thin:@192.168.1.123:1521:XE",p);

         Statement st=con.createStatement();

         ResultSet rs=st.executeQuery("select passportno, visas_taken from
         emppassportDetails where empno="+s[0]);

         if (rs.next())
```

```
            {
                    System.out.println(
                    "\nEmployee Found, His Passport Details are:\n");
                    System.out.println("PassportNo:"+rs.getString(1)+"\n");
                    System.out.print("Visa's Taken are :\n\t");

                    Array a=rs.getArray(2);
                    ResultSet rs1=a.getResultSet();
                    /*
                    The ResultSet produced here to represent Array value has 2 columns where
                    1st column represents the element index 2nd column represents the values
                    */
                    boolean flag=rs1.next();
                    while(flag) {
                            System.out.print(rs1.getString(2));
                            flag=rs1.next();
                            if (flag)
                            System.out.print(",");
                    }//while
            }//if
            else
                    System.out.println("Employee not Found");
            System.out.println();
            con.close();
        }//main
    }//class
```

The example shown in Listing 3.20 reads the Array type value from the Oracle database.

Figure 3.46 shows the output of Listing 3.20:

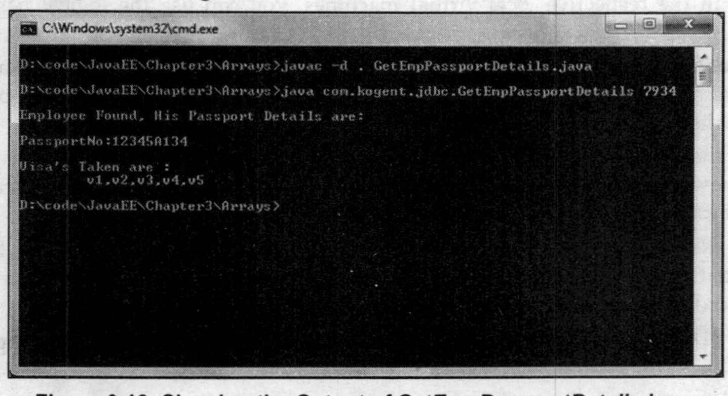

Figure 3.46: Showing the Output of GetEmpPassportDetails.java

In the output shown in Figure 3.46, data is selected from the Oracle database. In Listing 3.20, the data is searched based on the specified employee number. In case the specified employee number is not found in the Oracle database, the *Employee not Found* message is displayed.

Note that the Array objects remain valid for at least the duration of the transaction in which they are created. This results in the shortage of resources in case of lengthy transactions. You can use the `free()` method of `java.sql.Array` interface in JDBC 4.0 to release the array resources.

Describing the REF Data Type

The `java.sql.Ref` interface represents the REF type values, which are instances of the structured type. Each `REF` value contains a unique identifier, which points to the `Ref` object. The values are stored either as a column value in a table or as an attribute value in the structured type. Since the `REF` value is a logical pointer to a SQL structured type, a `Ref` object is also used as a logical pointer to the REF values. `Ref` objects are stored in the database by using the methods of the `PreparedStatement`interface.

Table 3.30 describes the methods of the `Ref` interface:

Table 3.30: Methods of the Ref Interface

Method	Description
String getBaseTypeName()	Returns the name of the SQL structured type referenced by the SQL Ref object
Object getObject()	Retrieves the SQL ref object, which references the SQL structured type
Object getObject(Map map)	Retrieves the SQL structured type and maps the Java type given by the map specified as an argument
void setObject(Object value)	Sets the values of the SQL structured type, which is the reference of Ref object

After learning how to implement the classes and interfaces of the `java.sql` package, let's discuss the implementation of the `javax.sql` package.

Exploring JDBC Processes with the **javax.sql** Package

The `javax.sql` package, available in the JDBC API, is also known as the JDBC extension package. The javax.sql package is used to develop the client/server sided applications and provide server sided extension facilities, such as connection pooling and RowSet implementation. In addition, it uses the XA enabled connections for distributed transactions. The javax.sql package provides the following implementations that are used in building server-side applications:

- **JNDI-based lookup to access databases via logical names**—Allows you to access database resources by using logical names assigned to these resources. In other words, instead of allowing each client to load the driver classes in the respective local virtual machines, you can use the logical names assigned to each resource.
- **Connection pooling**—Serves as an intermediate layer provided by the javax.sql package to handle multiple connections. In this case, the responsibility for connection pooling is shifted from Application developers to the driver and the application server vendors.
- **Distributed transaction**—Provides support to handle multiple transactions in the Java EE environment by using the framework provided by the javax.sql package. With this framework, you can enable the support for distributed transactions with minimal configuration.
- **The RowSet**—Refers to a JavaBeans compliant object that hides resultsets. The RowSet retrieves and accesses the data stored in a database. A RowSet may be connected when the JDBC connection is established and disconnected when the JDBC connection session ends up.

To understand the JDBC process with the javax.sql packages, let's explore the following broad-level steps in detail:

- Using DataSource to make a connection
- Implementing Connection pooling
- Using RowSet objects
- Using transactions

Using DataSource to Make a Connection

With the help of the classes and interfaces provided by the `javax.sql` package, such as DataSource and DriverManager you can establish as well as manage connection with a data source. However, the `DataSource` mechanism is only preferred because it has many advantages over the `DriverManager` mechanism. The `DataSource` interface provides the following advantages, when used to make a connection:

- The developers need not provide code to implement a driver class.

- If the properties of a data source or driver changes, instead of modifying the application code, you can simply make the appropriate changes in the configurations of the data source.
- The connections established by using the DataSource object have the pooling and distributed transactions capabilities. This object also allows the Web container to communicate with the middle-tier infrastructure. However, the connections established with the help of DriverManager do not have the capabilities of connection pooling or distributed transaction.

`DataSource` implementations are provided by the driver vendor. A particular `DataSource` object represents a particular physical data source, and each connection created by `DataSource` is a connection to that physical data source.

The Java Naming and Directory Interface (JNDI) naming service is used to provide a logical name for the DataSource to make a connection. This naming service uses the Java Naming and Directory Interface™ (JNDI) API. The DataSource object can be used to retrieve the logical name associated with the underlying database. The application can then use the `DataSource` object to create the connection to the physical data source it represents.

The DataSource object helps in maintaining connection pooling; therefore, it can be used to work with the middle-tier infrastructure. Moreover, a `DataSource` object can also be implemented to work with the middle-tier infrastructure so that the connections it produces can be used for distributed transactions without any special coding.

Exploring Connection Pooling

Connection pooling means that the connection is reused rather than created each time it is requested. A connection pool facilitates reusability of database connections and maintains a memory cache of connections. The connection pooling module lies at the top layer of the standard JDBC driver product.

This practice of using connection pooling in server-side application is performed in the background. In addition, it does not affect the procedure by which an application is coded. Instead of using the DriverManager class, a DataSource object (an object implementing DataSource interface) is used by an application to obtain a connection from the connection pool. A `DataSource` object is registered with a JNDI naming service. After the DataSource object is registered, it can be automatically retrieved by using the JNDI naming service. The following code snippet shows the creation of the DataSource object in a connection pool:

```
Context contxt = new InitialContext();
DataSource ds = (DataSource) contxt.lookup("jdbc/SequeLink");
```

In the preceding code snippet, if the `DataSource` object provides connection pooling, the concerned application automatically benefits from the connection reuse. This can be achieved without any code manipulation. The reused connections from the pool perform tasks similar to the newly created physical connections. When all the required tasks are performed by the application, the connection is explicitly closed. The following code snippet shows the procedure to close the database connection:

```
Connection dbcon = ds.getConnection("scott", "tiger");
// Do some database activities using the connection...
dbcon.close();
```

In the preceding code snippet, the closing event of a pooled connection signals the pooling module to place the connection back in the connection pool for future reuse.

Traditional Connection Pooling

A general framework has been provided by the JDBC API to provide the support for traditional connection pooling. In traditional connection pooling, third-party vendors provide `classes` that support the connection pooling mechanism. In this way, the implementation of the specific caching or pooling algorithms can be done by third-party vendors or users. The JDBC 4.0 API uses the ConnectionEvent class and provides various interfaces to create connection pool. To provide connection pooling in a server-sided application, the DataSource must implement following interfaces:

- **ConnectionPoolDataSource**—Specifies the data source that is being used in a connection pool. The ConnectionPoolDataSource interface also acts as a factoy for the pooled Connection objects.
- **PooledConnection**—Refers to an object that manages the hierarchy for connection pool.

- **ConnectionEventListener**—Refers to an object that handles the events generated by a PooledConnection object.
- **JDBCDriverVendorDataSource**—Refers to a class that implements the standard `ConnectionPoolDataSource` interface. This `interface` provides `hooks`, which can be used by the third-party vendors to implement pooling as a layer on top of their JDBC drivers. Moreover, in this case, the `ConnectionPoolDataSource` interface acts as a `factory` that creates `PooledConnection` objects.
- **JDBCDriverVendorPooledConnection**—Requires a JDBC driver vendor with a class that implements the standard `PooledConnection` interface to implement the connection pooling mechanism. The third-party vendors implement pooling on JDBC drivers with the help of this interface. In such cases, a PooledConnection object acts as a factory of the Connection objects. A `PooledConnection` object is the physical connection to the database, while the `Connection` object created by the `PooledConnection` object is simply a handle to the `PooledConnection` object.
- **PoolingVendorDataSource**—Requires a third-party vendor to provide a class which implements the `DataSource` interface to implement the connection pooling mechanism in a server-sided application. This interface is the entry point that allows interaction with their pooling module. The `ConnectionPoolDataSource` object creates `PooledConnection` objects as per the need.
- **PoolingVendorConnectionCache**—Specifies that to define the `PoolingVendorConnectionCache class`, the JDBC 4.0 API does not provide the interfaces, which are to be used between the `DataSource` object and the connection cache. Usually, a connection cache module contains one or multiple classes. Figure 3.47 shows the `PoolingVendorConnectionCache` class, which is used as a simple way to convey this concept. The connection cache module must contain a class that implements the ConnectionEventListener interface. Whenever the connection is closed or a connection error occurs, the PoolingVendorConnectionCache interface receives ConnectionEvent objects from PooledConnection objects. Moreover, when a connection closes on a `PooledConnection` object, the connection cache module returns the `PooledConnection` object to the cache, as shown in Figure 3.47:

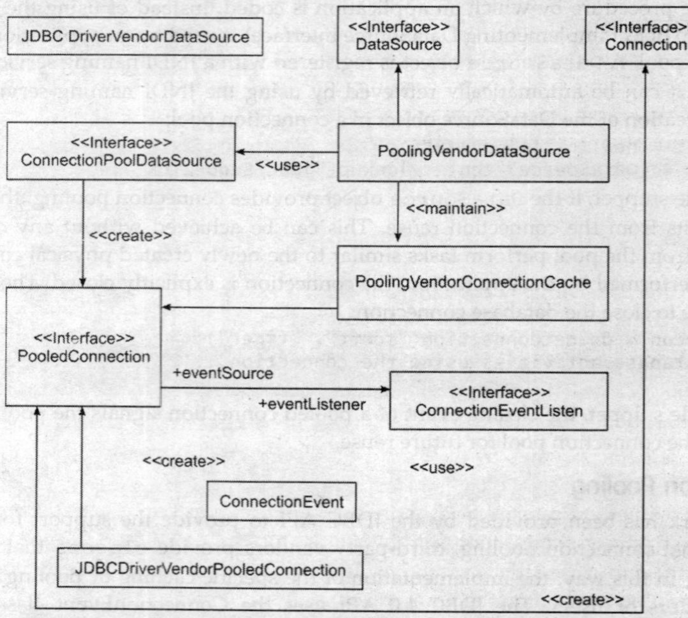

Figure 3.47: Showing the JDBC Connection Pooling Architecture

Connection Pooling with the **javax.sql** Package

You can also implement the connection pooling mechanism in an application by using the `javax.sql` package. The `javax.sql` package provides a transparent meaning of connection pooling. This approach enables the

Application server and the database driver to handle connection pooling internally. It is also important to remember that as long as you use DataSource objects to get connections, connection pooling will automatically be enabled after you configure the Java EE application server.

You should note that the change in the additional connection pool is maintained by the Application server with the coordination of the JDBC driver. In other words, there is no additional programming requirement for JDBC client applications. Instead, the administrator of the Java EE server is required to configure a connection pool on the Application server. The syntax and the names of classes used to configure the connection pool are implementation dependent. However, with a JDBC 4.0 compliant Application server and database driver, the server administrator typically specifies the following:

- A class implementing the javax.sql.ConnectionPoolDataSource interface
- A class implementing the java.sql.Driver interface
- The size of the pool (minimum and maximum sizes)
- Connection time out
- The authentication parameters, such as loginid and password

The javax.sql package provides interfaces and classes to configure the Java EE server to enable connection pooling; therefore, the client application does not implement or access these interfaces directly. The javax.sql package specifies three interfaces and one class to implement connection pooling. The interfaces and class for connection pooling provided by the javax.sql package are:

- The javax.sql.ConnectionPoolDataSource interface
- The javax.sql.PooledConnection interface
- The javax.sql.ConnectionEventListener interface
- The javax.sql.ConnectionEvent class

Let's discuss these interface and classes used for connection pooling in the javax.sql package.

The javax.sql.ConnectionPoolDataSource Interface

The javax.sql.ConnectionPoolDataSource interface is similar to the javax.sql.DataSource interface. However, instead of returning java.sql.Connection objects, the javax.sql.ConnectionPoolDataSource interface returns the javax.sql.PoolConnection objects. The following code snippet lists the methods that return javax.sql.PooledConnection objects:

```
public javax.sql.PooledConnection getPooledConnection()
   throws java.sql.SQLException
   public javax.sql.PooledConnection
   getPooledConnection (String user, String password)
   throws java.sql.SQLException
```

As shown in the preceding code snippet, both the getPooledConnection() and getPooledConnection(String user, String password) methods return the javax.sql.PooledConnection objects.

The javax.sql.PooledConnection Interface

When connection pooling is enabled, objects implementing the javax.sql.PooledConnection interface hold a physical database connection. This interface is a factory of javax.sql.Connection objects.

The following are the methods provided by the PooledConnection interface:

```
public javax.sql.Connection getConnection() throws java.sql.SQLException
```

The getConnection() method returns a java.sql.Connection object. The returned Connection object, in turn, is a proxy for the physical connection held by the javax.sql.PooledConnection object. You need to invoke the close() method to close the connection with the database. The following code snippet shows the implementation of the close() method on the PooledConnection object:

```
public void close() throws java.sql.SQLException
```

As shown in the preceding code snippet, the close() method throws the SQLException exception, if any exception occurs during the closing of the connection with the database.

The javax.sql.ConnectionEventListener Interface

The connection pooling components implement the `ConnectionEventListener` interface. The connection pooling components are mainly provided by the driver vendor or other software vendors. The JDBC driver notifies the `ConnectionEventListener` object, which registers a pooled connection when an application finishes execution. The notification of the event occurs after the application calls the close method on the `PooledConnection` object. The `ConnectionEventListener` interface is also notified when the connection is established. The JDBC driver also notifies the listener, before the driver throws the SQLException exception, but the PooledConnection object is already in use. There are two different methods, `connectionClosed()` and `connectionErrorOccured()`, containing the `ConnectionEventListener` interface. The following code snippet represents the `connectionClosed()` method in the `ConnectionEventListener` interface:

```
public void connectionClosed(ConnectionEvent event)
```

When the application calls the `close()` method, the connectionClosed() method is invoked. In this case, the connection pool marks the connection for reuse, as given in the following code snippet:

```
public void connectionErrorOccured(ConnectionEvent event)
```

When fatal connection errors occur, only the connectionErrorOccured (ConnectionEvent event) method is invoked. In this case, the connection pool may close the `connection` on this event and remove it from the pool.

The javax.sql.ConnectionEvent Class

The `javax.sql.ConnectionEvent` class represents connection-related events and provides information about them. The `ConnectionEvent` objects are generated when the application closes the pooled connection and the listeners are notified. This event handling is similar to the event handling in Abstract Window Toolkit (AWT) events. It is decided by the connection pool whether or not to add the connection event listeners to the pooled connection and when connection events oocur, the connection listeners are notified.

Implemention of Connection Pooling

The application server implements the mechanism of connection pooling by implementing the `ConnectionPoolDataSource class`. First, you need to instantiate the `ConnectionPoolDataSource` class, set its properties, and then bind the class to a name in JNDI context.

The following code snippet shows how to implement the `ConnectionPoolDataSource` class:

```
com.application.server.ConnPoolDataSource cds = new
   com.application.server.ConnPoolDataSource();
cds.setDatabaseName("myDB");
cds.setServerName("myServer");
Context contxt = new InitialContext();
contxt.bind("jdbc/pooled", cds);
```

The preceding code snippet shows a data source that is created in JNDI. The user can access this data source name to establish a connection. The data source returns a connection.

The data source, which is to be set with a connection, must provide the following properties:

- **InitialPoolSize**—Specifies the number of connections that the connection pool can maintain during a session.
- **minPoolSize**—Indicates the minimum number of connections to be maintained in the pool. The 0 value indicates that connections will be created when required.
- **maxPoolSize**—Indicates the maximum number of connections the pool should entertain. The 0 value indicates that there is no limit.
- **maxIdleTime**—Indicates the idle time of connections in a pool. It is represented in seconds.

Using RowSet Objects

The `javax.sql.RowSet` object is a set of rows from the `ResultSet` object, or some other data source, such as a file or spreadsheet, represented in tabular form. All `RowSet` objects inherit the `ResultSet` interface and can be used as `JavaBeans` components in a visual Bean development environment. A RowSet is created and configured at design time and executed at run-time. The inbuilt JavaBeans properties enable the RowSet object to be configured and connected to the JDBC DataSource. A group of setter methods is used to pass input parameters to the command property of the RowSet object. The value assigned to the command property is generally the SQL query, which is used to retrieve the data from the database. All RowSet objects have properties that are defined as getter and setter methods in the implementation classes. The BaseRowSet abstract class helps to set and get the required properties in JDBC RowSet implementations. All the RowSet reference implementations inherit this class; and therefore, have access to the methods of the BaseRowSet class.

As you know that the connection can be obtained in two different ways, either by using the DriverManager mechanism or by using DataSource object. In both these ways, you need to set the username and password properties. In case of DriverManager, you need to set the url and in case of the DataSource object, you need to set the data source name property. You should note that the default value for the `type` property is `ResultSet.TYPE_SCROLL_INSENSITIVE`, and for the `concurrency` property is `ResultSet.CONCUR_UPDATABLE`. If you are working with a driver or database that does not offer scrollable and updatable `ResultSet` objects, you can use a `RowSet` object populated with the same data as a `ResultSet` object; thereby, making the `ResultSet` object scrollable and updatable.

A listener for a `RowSet` object is a component that is to be notified whenever a change or called event occurs in the RowSet object. Due to any of the following changes, the `RowSet` interface generates an event that is handled by the listeners:

- A cursor movement
- The update, insertion, or deletion of a row
- A change in the entire RowSet content

The listeners must be registered with the RowSet class to receive notifications from a particular `RowSet`. Therefore, all listeners must implement the `RowSetListener` interface. A listener for a `RowSet` object implements the following methods defned in the `RowSetListener` interface corresponding to the three events discussed in the preceding list:

- **cursorMoved**—Includes the actions that a listener should perform when the cursor in the RowSet object moves
- **rowChanged**—Specifies the actions that a listener should perform when one or more column values in a row are updated, a new row is inserted, or an existing row is deleted
- **rowSetChanged**—Specifies the actions that the listener should perform when the entire RowSet object is populated with new data

Depending on the implementation of an application, the JDBC `RowSet` objects are categorized as:

- Connected RowSet objects
- Disconnected RowSet objects
- JdbcRowSet objects
- CachedRowSet objects
- WebRowSet objects
- FilteredRowSet object
- JoinRowSet objects

Let's explore these in detail next.

Connected **RowSet** Objects

A connected RowSet object creates a connection to a database, by using JDBC driver, and maintains that connection throughout its lifetime. `JdbcRowSet` is one of the standard `connected RowSet` implementations. The `JdbcRowSet` object is connected to a database, which makes it similar to the `ResultSet` object. In addition, the `JdbcRowSet` object is often used as a wrapper to make a nonscrollable and read-only `ResultSet` object scrollable and updatable.

Disconnected **RowSet** Objects

A disconnected `RowSet` object makes a connection to a data source only to read data from the `ResultSet` object or write the data back to the data source. After reading or writing data to its data source, the `RowSet` object disconnects from the data source. As a disconnected RowSet object does not connect to its data source; thereby, the object performs the task of reading and writing data independently. The disconnected RowSet objects are serializable as well as lightweight compared to a JdbcRowSet or ResultSet object. Due to this reason, the disconnected RowSet objects are efficient for thin clients.

Figure 3.48 shows the CachedRowSet interface, which defines the capabilities available to the disconnected RowSet object:

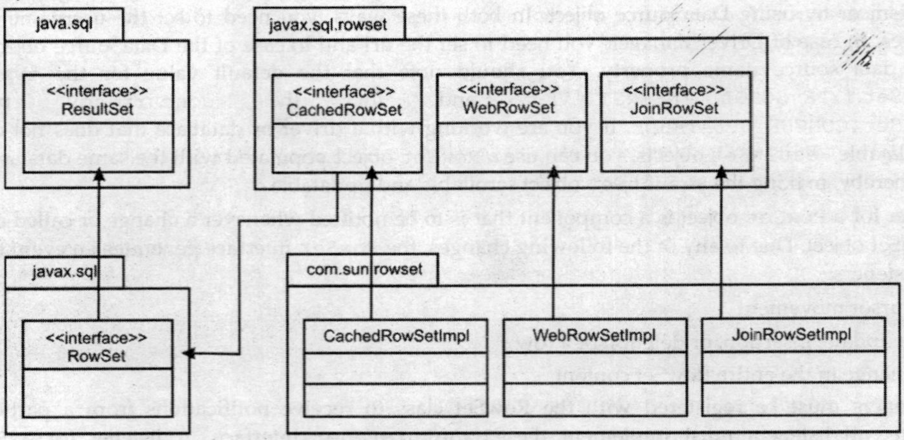

Figure 3.48: Displaying the RowSet Inheritance Hierarchy

JdbcRowSet Objects

The `JdbcRowSet` object is simply a wrapper around the `ResultSet` object and always maintains a connection to its data source, similar to a `ResultSet` object. The main difference between a `JdbcRowSet` and `ResultSet` object is that a `JdbcRowSet` object has a set of properties and also participates in the `JavaBeans` event model. The use of the `JdbcRowSet` object makes it a `JavaBeans` component. A `JdbcRowSet` object can be used this way because it is effectively a wrapper for the driver that has obtained its connection to the database. Another benefit of using the JdbcRowSet object is that it makes a ResultSet object as scrollable and updatable. All `RowSet` objects are scrollable and updatable by default. For example, a `JdbcRowSet` object populated with the `ResultSet` data is also scrollable and updatable.

The `JdbcRowSetImpl` is used as a default constructor to create new instances of the JdbcRowSet objects. A new instance is initialized with default values in the `BaseRowSet` class, which can be set with new values when required. The commands and properties needed to establish a connection are set, and after which the `execute()` method is invoked. The new instance does not work until the `execute()` method is called.

The following code snippet creates a new `JdbcRowSetImpl` object, sets the command and connection properties, sets the placeholder parameter, and then invokes the `execute()` method:

```
JdbcRowSetImpl jrs = new JdbcRowSetImpl();
jrs.setCommand("SELECT * FROM TITLES WHERE TYPE = ?");
jrs.setURL("jdbc:myDriver:myAttribute");
jrs.setUsername("cervantes");
jrs.setPassword("sancho");
jrs.setString(1, "BIOGRAPHY");
jrs.execute();
```

The preceding code snippet performs the following tasks:

- Establishes a connection between the RowSet and the database
- Creates a `PreparedStatement` object to make a program more interactive and sets its placeholder parameters
- Executes the statement provided in the setCommand() method to create a ResultSet object

CachedRowSet Objects

The CachedRowSet object inherits the JdbcRowSet class, in addition to its own capabilities and additional features. This object caches its rows in memory; therefore, it does not need to always connect to its data source. Usually, the CachedRowSet object retrieves rows from a ResultSet object but it can also contain rows from files in tabular formats, such as spreadsheets. The CachedRowSet object is a disconnected RowSet and connects with the data source only when it is reading the data to populate the rows or when it is updating changes in the underlying data source. You can perform the following functions with a CachedRowSet object:

- Create a CachedRowSet object
- Set the properties of the CachedRowSet object
- Fill a CachedRowSet object
- Read data from the CachedRowSet object
- Retrieve the RowSetMetaData object
- Update a CachedRowSet object

Let's discuss each of these in detail.

*Creating a **CachedRowSet** Object*

The default implementation for the CachedRowSet object creates a CachedRowSet object. The default constructor is used to create the new instance. The following code snippet shows how to create a new instance of the CachedRowSet object:

```
CachedRowSetImpl crs=new CachedRowSetImpl();
```

In the preceding code snippet, the properties of the CachedRowSet object are set to the default properties of the BaseRowSet object. In addition, the CachedRowSet object has one synchronization provider object RIOptimisticProvider of the SyncProvider type. The classes and interfaces for synchorization provider implementation are provided by the javax.sql.rowset.spi package. The RowSetReader is used by the RIOptimisticProvider objects to read data into the CachedRowSet object, as this RowSet object does not contain any established connection to the database. This RowSetReader object obtains a connection by using the values set either for username, password, and JDBC URL; or for the data source name. The RIOptimisticProvider provider also provides the RowSetWriter object to synchronize any changes made to the rows of the CachedRowSet object while it was disconnected from the underlying data source. If you are not using the RowSetWriter object, the SyncProvider objects are retrieved from the SyncFactory class. The following code snippet is used to get the list of synchronization providers in a CachedRowSet object:

```
java.util.Enumeration Providers=SyncFactory.getRegisteredProviders();
```

The method mentioned in the preceding code snippet returns the list of providers to specify a particular SyncProvider object that the CachedRowset object can use. The following code snippet shows how to create the instance of the CachedRowSet object by providing a specific SyncProvider object:

```
CachedRowSetImpl crs2=new
CachedRowSetImpl("com.fred.providers.HighAvailbilityProvider");
```

The value for the synchronization parameter can be set using the setSynchProvider() method of CachedRowSet:

```
crs.setSyncProvider("com.fred.providers.HighAvailbilityProvider");
```

Setting the Properties of the CachedRowSet Object

All RowSet objects have common properties, therefore, the properties for the CachedRowSet objects are to be set by using the setter methods available in the RowSet interface. The following code snippet shows how to set the values for the CachedRowSet objects:

```
//basic parameters required to set for establishing a connection with Database
crs.setUsername("user");
crs.setPassword("password");
crs.setUrl("jdbc:mySubprotocol:mySubname");
crs.setCommand("select * from survey");
```

In the preceding code snippet, the setCommand() method is used to set the command property, which is a query that produces the ResultSet object. You can read data into a RowSet object from a ResultSet object.

Filling a CachedRowSet Object

To populate data from ResultSet object to RowSet object, you only have to call the `execute()` method on the `CachedRowSet` object, as shown in the following code snippet:

```
//populate data into rowset object from ResultSet object
crs.execute();
```

In the preceding code snippet, when the `execute()` method is called, the reader of the disconnected RowSet object works behind the scene. The `execute()` method is provided by the default `SyncProvider` object, `RIOptimisticProvider`. Then, the RowSetReader object gets a connection to the database either by using the JDBC URL or the data source. Next, the reader object executes the query that is to be set for the command property. The result of the query is saved in the ResultSet object, which is in turn provided to the CachedRowSet object.

Reading Data from CachedRowSet Object

Data is read from a `CachedRowSet` object by using getter methods inherited from the `ResultSet` interface. The following code snippet illustrates how the rows of the crs `CachedRowSet` object are iterated and the column values of each row are read:

```
while(crs.next())
{
   String name=crs.getString("NAME");
   int id=crs.getInt("ID");
   Clob comment=crs.getClob("COM");
   short dept = crs.getClob("DEPT");
   System.out.println(name+" "+id+" "+comment+" "+dept);
}
```

Retrieving RowSetMetaData Object

The user can retrieve the information about columns in the `CachedRowSet` object by using the `RowSetMetaData` object. The `getMetaData()` method of the `ResultSet` interface returns a `ResultSetMetaData` object, which is further casted to the `RowSetMetaData` object. Finally, the object is assigned to the rsmd variable. The following code snippet shows how to retrieve information in the CachedRowSet object:

```
RowSetMetaData rsmd=(RowSetMetaData)crs.getMetaData();
int count=rsmd.getColumnCount();
int type=rsmd.getColumnType(2);
```

Updating a CachedRowSet Object

Updating a `CachedRowSet` object is similar to updating a `ResultSet` object. When the `CachedRowSet` object is disconnected from data source, the updates in the `CachedRowSet` are performed; however, the results of updates are not finally written to data source. To write the results of updates, a connection with the data source has to be established. Therefore, after invoking the `updateRow()` or `insertRow()` method, another method, `acceptChanges()`, is called on the `CachedRowSet` object to write the update results on the database. During the invocation of the acceptChanges() method, the `RowSetWriterImpl` object is called on the `CachedRowSet` object internally, which establishes the connection with the data source and also updates the changes in the data source.

The following code snippet shows the steps to update the `CachedRowSet` object:

```
//update 3rd and 4th column of current row
crs.updateShort(3, 58);
crs.updateInt(4, 150000);
crs.updateRow();
crs.acceptChanges();

//Build a new row ,inserts into crs and finally inserts into datasource
crs.moveToInsertRow();
crs.updateString("Name", "Shakespeare");
crs.updateInt("ID", 10098347);
crs.updateShort("Age", 58);
crs.updateInt("Sal", 150000);
```

```
crs.insertRow();
crs.moveToCurrentRow();
crs.acceptChanges();
```

In the preceding code snippet, a connection is established corresponding to each call of the `acceptChanges()` method, which is called after calling the `updateRow()` and `insertRow()` methods to change or insert multiple rows. The advantages of using the `CachedRowSet` objects are as follows:

- Obtains a connection to a data source and execute a query
- Reads the data from the resulting ResultSet object and populates itself with that data
- Manipulates data and make changes to data while it is disconnected
- Reconnects to the data source to write the changes back to it
- Checks and resolves the conflicts with the data source

The JDBC API does not need to be implemented for using the `CachedRowSet` objects. The CachedRowSet object is serializable, which is the main reason to use a CachedRowSet object to pass data between different components of an application. Working on a network environment, a CachedRowSet object can be used to send the result of query that is executed by Enterprise JavaBeans.

WebRowSet Objects

A `WebRowSet` object has all the capabilities of a `CachedRowSet` object and is used to read and write the database query results into an `XML` file. Enterprises on different locations and platforms can communicate through `XML; therefore, the XML` language has become the standard for Web services communication. As a consequence, a `WebRowSet` object solves a real problem by making it easy for Web services developers to write the Web service programs to send and receive data from a database in the form of an `XML` document.

*Creating and Populating a **WebRowSet** Object*

The new instance of the WebRowSet object can be created by using the reference of the WebRowSetImpl class. The following code snippet shows the code to create an instance of the WebRowSet object:

```
WebRowSet wrs = new WebRowSetImpl();
wrs.populate(rs);
```

In the preceding code snippet, `wrs` has no data; however, it has the default properties of a `BaseRowSet` object. Its `SyncProvider` object is first set to the `RIOptimisticProvider` implementation, which is the default configuration for all disconnected RowSet objects. You can set various properties, such as URL, username, password for the WebRowSet object, as shown in the following code snippet:

```
wrs.setCommand("SELECT col1,col2 from emp");
wrs.setURL("jdbc:mySubprotocol:myDatabase");
wrs.setUsername("myUsername");
wrs.setPassword("myPassword");
wrs.execute();
```

The preceding code snippet sets the properties for the WebRowSet object.

Writing and Reading the WebRowSet Object to XML Document

The WebRowSet object can be used to read and write the data into an XML document. The readXml() method is used to read the data from the XML document; whereas, the the `writeXml()` method allows you to write data in the XML document.

The uses of the `writeXml()` and `readXml()` methods are described as follows:

- **Using the writeXml() method**—Writes the invoked WebRowSet object as an XML document that represents the current state of object. The method writes the XML document to the stream that is passed to it. The stream can be an OutputStream object, such as a FileOutputStream object, if the user wants to write in binary format; or a Writer object, such as a FileWriter object, if the user wants to write in characters.

The following code snippet writes the wrs WebRowSet object as an XML document to the FileOutputStream object fileOutputStream:

```
java.io.FileOutputStream fileOutputStream = new  java.io.FileOutputStream("emp.xml");
wrs.writeXml(fileOutputStream);
```

The FileWriter object is used to write the character data to an XML file, as shown in the following code snippet:

```
java.io.FileWriter fileWriter = new java.io.FileWriter("emp.xml");
wrs.writeXml(fileWriter);
```

Two variations of the writeXml() method, fileOutputStream and fileWriter, are used for the WebRowSet object with the content of a ResultSet object before writing it to a stream, as shown in the following code snippet:

```
priceList.writeXml(rs, fileOutputStream);
priceList.writeXml(rs, fileWriter);
```

- **Using the readXml() method**—Parses an XML document to construct the WebRowSet object. Similar to writing, an XML document, which is to be read, is represented by the FileInputStream or FileWriter object and is passed to the readXml() method.

The following code snippet explains how to read from XML document into a WebRowSet object:

```
java.io.FileInputStream fileInputStream = new java.io.FileInputStream("emp.xml");
wrs.readXml(fileInputStream);
```

The FileReader object is used to read the XML character data to a WebRowSet object, as shown in the following code snippet:

```
java.io.FileReader fileReader = new java.io.FileReader("emp.xml");
wrs.readXml(fileReader);
```

Using the WebRowSet Object in XMLFormat

The WebRowSet object contains data; and the properties and metadata about the columns. The WebRowSet XML schema is an XML document that defines the content of an XML document. It also defines the format in which the document must be presented. This schema is used by both the sender and recipient because it tells the sender how to write the XML document and the receiver how to parse the XML document. The XML document representing a WebRowSet object includes the following three types of information:

- **Properties of WebRowSet object**—Refer to standard synchronization provider properties, including general RowSet properties. A WebRowSet object is created and populated from a table having two rows and five columns from a data source. The standard writeXml() method describes the internal properties of the WebRowSet object.

The following code snippet shows the use of the writeXml() method to describe the internal properties:

```
<properties>
   <command>select col, col2 from test_table</command>
   <concurrency>1</concurrency>
   <datasource/>
   <escape-processing>true</escape-processing>
   <fetch-direction>0</fetch-direction>
   <fetch-size>0</fetch-size>
   <isolation-level>1</isolation-level>
   <key-columns/>
   <map/>
   <max-field-size>0</max-field-size>
   <max-rows>0</max-rows>
   <query-timeout>0</query-timeout>
   <read-only>false</read-only>
   <rowset-type>TRANSACTION_READ_UNCOMMITED</rowset-type>
   <show-deleted>false</show-deleted>
   <table-name/>
   <url>jdbc:thin:oracle</url>
   <sync-provider>
   <sync-provider-name>.com.rowset.provider.RIOptimisticProvider</sync-provider-name>
        <sync-provider-vendor>Sun Microsystems</sync-provider-vendor>
        <sync-provider-version>1.0</sync-provider-name>
        <sync-provider-grade>LOW</sync-provider-grade>
        <data-source-lock>NONE</data-source-lock>
   </sync-provider>
</properties>
```

- **Metadata**—Describes the metadata associated with the tabular structure used by a WebRowSet object. Metadata is similar to the java.sql.ResultSet interface. The WebRowSet object is also used to retrieve the metadata information about the ResultSet interface.

The following code snippet shows the columns that are described between the column definition tags:

```
<metadata>
  <column-count>2</column-count>
  <column-definition>
        <column-index>1</column-index>
        <auto-increment>false</auto-increment>
        <case-sensitive>true</case-sensitive>
        <currency>false</currency>
        <nullable>1</nullable>
        <signed>false</signed>
        <searchable>true</searchable>
        <column-display-size>10</column-display-size>
        <column-label>COL1</column-label>
        <column-name>COL1</column-name>
        <schema-name/>
        <column-precision>10</column-precision>
        <column-scale>0</column-scale>
        <table-name/>
        <catalog-name/>
        <column-type>1</column-type>
        <column-type-name>CHAR</column-type-name>
  </column-definition>
  <column-definition>
        <column-index>2</column-index>
        <auto-increment>false</auto-increment>
        <case-sensitive>false</case-sensitive>
        <currency>false</currency>
        <nullable>1</nullable>
        <signed>true</signed>
        <searchable>true</searchable>
        <column-display-size>39</column-display-size>
        <column-label>COL2</column-label>
        <column-name>COL2</column-name>
        <schema-name/>
        <column-precision>38</column-precision>
        <column-scale>0</column-scale>
        <table-name/>
        <catalog-name/>
        <column-type>3</column-type>
        <column-type-name>NUMBER</column-type-name>
  </column-definition>
</metadata>
```

- **Data**—Describes the data available in a database before the changes are made due to the synchronization of the WebRowSet object. This helps to evaluate the changes between the original and current data. A WebRowSet object contains the ability to synchronize the changes in its data back to the data source. The WebRowSet object provides a table structure and the CurrentRow tag is used to map each row of table. A columnValue tag can contain either the stringData or binaryData tag, depending on its SQL type. You should note that the BLOB and CLOB data types use binaryData tag. They describe a WebRowSet object that has not undergone any changes since its instantiation.

The following code snippet shows the content of the WebRowSet object:

```
<data>
  <currentRow>
        <columnValue>
               firstrow
        </columnValue>
        <columnValue>
               1
        </columnValue>
  </currentRow>
  <currentRow>
        <columnValue>
               secondrow
```

```
            </columnValue>
            <columnValue>
                    2
            </columnValue>
      </currentRow>
      <currentRow>
            <columnValue>
                    thirdrow
            </columnValue>
            <columnValue>
                    3
            </columnValue>
      </currentRow>
      <currentRow>
            <columnValue>
                    fourthrow
            </columnValue>
            <columnValue>
                    4
            </columnValue>
      </currentRow>
    </data>
```

Implementing Changes in a Database by Using WebRowSet Objects

Different operations can be performed on the WebRowSet object to update it. You can update the WebRowSet object by deleting, inserting, and updating an existing row, which are explained as follows:

- **Deleting a row**—Removes the row from a WebRowSet object. To delete a row, move the cursor to the desired row and invoke the deleteRow method.

The following code snippet shows the deletion of a row, in which the wrs WebRowSet object is used to delete the third row:

```
    <data>
      <currentRow>
            <columnValue>
                    firstrow
            </columnValue>
            <columnValue>
                    1
            </columnValue>
      </currentRow>
      <currentRow>
            <columnValue>
                    secondrow
            </columnValue>
            <columnValue>
                    2
            </columnValue>
      </currentRow>
      <deleteRow>
            <columnValue>
                    thirdrow
            </columnValue>
            <columnValue>
                    3
            </columnValue>
      </deleteRow>
      <currentRow>
            <columnValue>
                    fourthrow
            </columnValue>
            <columnValue>
                    4
            </columnValue>
      </currentRow>
    </data>
```

In the preceding code snippet, the `XML` description marks third row as the `deleteRow` and deletes the row from the `WebRowSet` object.

- **Inserting a row**—Refers to the addition of a new row into the WebRowSet object. To insert a new row, move the cursor to the row where the row insertion is to be performed, then call the update methods to insert values into the row, and finally insert that row into ResultSet and database. The following code snippet is used to insert a new row into the WebRowSet object:

```
wrs.moveToInsertRow();
wrs.updateString(1, "fifththrow");
wrs.updateString(2, "5");
wrs.insertRow();
wrs.acceptChanges();
```

The insertion to the WebRowSet object can be performed in the XML file.

The following code snippet shows the XML format insertion to the WebRowSet object:

```
<data>
  <currentRow>
        <columnValue>
                firstrow
        </columnValue>
        <columnValue>
                1
        </columnValue>
  </currentRow>
  <currentRow>
        <columnValue>
                secondrow
        </columnValue>
        <columnValue>
                2
        </columnValue>
  </currentRow>

  <currentRow>
        <columnValue>
                newthirdrow
        </columnValue>
        <columnValue>
                III
        </columnValue>
  </currentRow>
  <insertRow>
        <columnValue>
                fifthrow
        </columnValue>
        <columnValue>
                5
        </columnValue>
        <updateValue>
                V
        </updateValue>
  </insertRow>
  <currentRow>
        <columnValue>
                fourthrow
        </columnValue>
        <columnValue>
                4
        </columnValue>
  </currentRow>
</data>
```

- **Updating an existing row**—Creates a specific XML file that holds both the updated value and the value that is replaced. The value that is replaced becomes the original value, and the new value becomes the current value. The following code snippet shows how to move the cursor to a specific row, perform some modifications, and also update the row when the execution of the wrs object is completed:

```
wrs.absolute(5);
wrs.updateString(1, "new4thRow");
wrs.updateString(2, "IV");
wrs.updateRow();
```

The `modifyRow` tag is used to update the `WebRowSet` object in an XML document. Both the original as well as updated values are associated within the tags for original row values tracking.

The following code snippet shows the process to update the WebRowSet object in a `XML` document:

```
<data>
  <currentRow>
        <columnValue>
                firstrow
        </columnValue>
        <columnValue>
                1
        </columnValue>
  </currentRow>
  <currentRow>
        <columnValue>
                secondrow
        </columnValue>
        <columnValue>
                2
        </columnValue>
  </currentRow>
  <currentRow>
        <columnValue>
                newthirdrow
        </columnValue>
        <columnValue>
                III
        </columnValue>
  </currentRow>
  <currentRow>
        <columnValue>
                fifthrow
        </columnValue>
        <columnValue>
                5
        </columnValue>
  </currentRow>
  <modifyRow>
        <columnValue>
                fourthrow
        </columnValue>
        <updateValue>
                new4thRow
        </updateValue>
        <columnValue>
                4
        </columnValue>
        <updateValue>
                IV
        </updateValue>
  </modifyRow>
</data>
```

FilteredRowSet Objects

A `FilteredRowSet` object allows the user to limit the number of rows that are visible in a `RowSet` object so that the user can work only with the relevant data. The user can also apply more than one filter to `FilteredRowSet` in one application to work with different sets of rows and columns each time. The filters inherit a `WebRowSet` object, which inherits the `CachedRowSet` object. Therefore, a WebRowSet object has the capabilities of both the `FilteredRowSet and CachedRowSet` objects. In case of `JdbcRowSet`, filtering is done by using query language, because it is always connected to a data source. The `FilteredRowSet` object provides a method to filter data without executing a query on the data source, which in turn avoids having connection with the data source and sending queries to it.

Creating a Filter

A filter is created by using the `javax.sql.rowset.Predicate` interface. Each application that wishes to apply a filter must implement the `Predicate` interface. The `FilteredRowSet` object enforces filter constraints in two directions, i.e., either column number or column name.

The following code snippet shows the simple implementation of the Predicate interface:

```
import javax.sql.rowset.*;
public class Filter1 implements Predicate
{
   private int lo;
   private int hi;
   private String colName;
   private int colNumber;
   public Filter1(int lo, int hi, int colNumber)
   {
          this.lo = lo;
          this.hi = hi;
          this.colNumber = colNumber;
   }
   public Filter1(int lo, int hi, String colName){
          this.lo = lo;
          this.hi = hi;
          this.colName = colName;
   }
   public boolean evaluate(RowSet rowset) {
          CachedRowSet crs = (CachedRowSet)rowset;
          if (rowset.getInt(colNumber) >= lo &&
          (rowset.getInt(colNumber) <= hi)) {
                 return true;
          }else { return false; }
   }
}
```

Using FilteredRowSet Object

The `FilteredRowSet` object can be used with the `ResultSet` object to populate the `RowSet` object. The following code snippet shows the use of the `ResultSet` object to populate the `RowSet` object:

```
FilteredRowSet frs = new FilteredRowSetImpl();
   frs.populate(rs);
   Range name = new Range("50", "100", "EMP_ID");
   frs.setFilter(name);
   frs.next() // only IDs from 50 to 100 will be returned.
```

In general, the `Predicate` object is initialized with the following features:

- The lower limit of the range within which the values of a column number or column name must lie.
- The upper limit of the range within which the values of a column number or column name must lie.
- The column name or number of the value, which must lie within the range of values set by the upper and lower limits. Note that the range of values is inclusive, meaning that a value at the boundary is included in the range.

Updating a FilteredRowSet Object

The `Predicate` interface can be applied on the `FilteredRowSet` object in a bi-directional manner. Any effort to update the `FilteredRowSet` object that violates the set criteria throws the `SQLException exception`. The range criteria for the FilteredRowSet object can be changed by applying a new Predicate object to the instance of the FilteredRowSet object. After changing the criteria of FilteredRowSet, all the updates should be done according to the new criteria set. Updating the FilteredRowSet object is same as updating the CachedRowSet object.

JoinRowSet Objects

The `JoinRowSet` interface encapsulates the related data from `RowSet` objects that form a `SQL JOIN` relationship. The Joinable interface provides the methods to set, read, and unset a match column. In addition, the Joinable interface should be implemented by all the RowSet objects. The column matching process is the basis of the SQL JOIN operation. The match column may be set by using the appropriate version of the JointRowSet interface's addRowSet() method. The main purpose of the `JoinRowSet` interface is to establish a `SQL JOIN` between disconnected `RowSet` objects, because they do not connect to data source to make `SQL JOIN`. A RowSet object can become a part of SQL JOIN relation by adding the RowSet object with JoinRowSet object, because the connected JdbcRowSet object extends the Joinable interface. The `Joinable` interface is not added in the `JoinRowSet` object because it is always connected with the data source and can perform `SQL JOIN` by using `SQL` query.

Exploring the Methods Used in the Joinable Interface

The `Joinable` interface has methods to specify a common column, based on which `SQL JOIN` is made. However, it does not have the facility to add two `RowSet` objects into one, which is provided by the `JoinRowSet` interface. You can set the JoinRowSet constants in the setJoinType() method to define the type of the join. The following SQL `JOIN` constant types can be set on the `setJoinType()` method:

- CROSS_JOIN
- FULL_JOIN
- INNER_JOIN
- LEFT_OUTER_JOIN
- RIGHT_OUTER_JOIN

NOTE

If no join type is provided, the INNER_JOIN join is set on the setJoinType() method, as the default value.

*Using a **JoinRowSet** Object to form a **JOIN***

To form the basis of the JOIN relation, you first need to add the RowSet object to the JoinRowSet object. You should note that when the JoinRowSet object is created, it is empty. Therefore, you should define the column in which each RowSet object is to be added to the JoinRowSet object. The RowSet object contains a match column, and the value in each match column should be comparable to the values in the other match column. A match column can be set by using the following methods:

- Matching a column by using the setMatchColumn() method of the Joinable interface before a RowSet object is added to a JoinRowSet object. The `RowSet` object must implement the `Joinable` interface to use this method. After setting the match column value, the value can be reset by using the `setMatchColumn()` method at any time.
- Adding a column name or number, or an array of column names or numbers by invoking the addRowSet() method. A match column parameter is passed as an argument in four of the five addRowSet() methods.

The following code snippet adds two `CachedRowSet` objects to a `JoinRowSet` object. For simplicity, no `SQL JOIN` type is set, so the default `JOIN` type, which is `INNER_JOIN`, is established.

The following code snippet shows the implementation of the JoinRowSet object:

```
JoinRowSet jrs = new JoinRowSetImpl();
ResultSet rs1 = stmt.executeQuery("SELECT * FROM EMPLOYEES");
CachedRowSet empl = new CachedRowSetImpl();
empl.populate(rs1);
empl.setMatchColumn(1);
jrs.addRowSet(empl);
ResultSet rs2 = stmt.executeQuery("SELECT * FROM ESSP_BONUS_PLAN");
CachedRowSet bonus = new CachedRowSetImpl();
bonus.populate(rs2);
bonus.setMatchColumn(1); // EMP_ID is the first column
jrs.addRowSet(bonus);
```

In the preceding code snippet, the EMPLOYEES table, whose match column is set to the first column EMP_ID is first added to the JoinRowSet object jrs. Then, the ESSP_BONUS_PLAN table with the same match column EMP_ID is added. The rows in the ESSP_BONUS_PLAN table are added to jrs, only if the EMP_ID value ESSP_BONUS_PLAN matches with an EMP_ID value in EMPLOYEE table. In broad terms, everyone in the bonus plan is an employee so all the rows in the ESSP_BONUS_PLAN table are added to the JoinRowSet object. The jrs is an inner JOIN of the two RowSet objects based on the EMP_ID columns. A program can traverse or modify a RowSet object by using RowSet methods, as shown in the following code snippet:

```
jrs.first();
int employeeID = jrs.getInt(1);
String employeeName = jrs.getString(2);
```

The following code snippet adds an additional CachedRowSet object. In this case, the match column (EMP_ID) is set when the CachedRowSet object is added to the JoinRowSet object, as shown in the following code snippet:

```
ResultSet rs3 = stmt.executeQuery("SELECT * FROM SITE");
CachedRowSet site = new CachedRowSetImpl();
site.populate(rs3);
jrs.addRowSet(site, 1);
```

The JoinRowSet object jrs now contains values from all three tables.

Working with Transactions

The DBMSs manage the databases over multiple environments where numerous users are working. There may be chances of data loss over multiple environments and the users. Therefore, to overcome such problems, the DBMS provides a mechanism to maintain data integrity within the DBMS. Transactions are used to ensure data integrity when multiple users access and modify data in a DBMS. A database transaction includes the interaction between the databases and users. Transactions are required to ensure data integrity, correct application semantics, and a consistent view of data during concurrent access. In general, DBMS provides the feature of Atomicity, Consistency, Isolation, and Durability for each transaction in a database. These properties are collectively called the ACID (Atomicity, Consistency, Isolation, and Durability) properties.

Let's know about the ACID properties.

ACID Properties

The ACID properties are maintained by the transaction manager of DBMS to retain the integrity of the data over the database. Let's describe the ACID properties for the transaction mechanism.

Atomicity

The guarantee of either all or none of the tasks of a transaction to be performed is defined as atomicity. This property provides an ability to save (commit) or cancel (rollback) the transaction at any point, and controls all the statements of a transaction.

Consistency

The Consistency property guarantees that the data remains in a legal state when the transaction begins and ends, implying that if the data used in the transaction is consistent before starting the transaction, it remains consistent even after the end of the transaction. If the data satisfies the integrity constraints of that type, it is known as consistent data or data in legal state.

For example, if an integrity constraint specifies that the age should not be a character and should be a positive value, a transaction is aborted during its execution if this rule is violated.

Isolation

The isolation is the ability of the transaction to isolate or hide the data used by it from other transactions until the transaction ends. The isolation is done by preparing locks on the data. The following set of problems may occur when the user performs concurrent operations on the data:

- **Dirty Read**—Specifies that a transaction tries to read data from a row that has been modified but yet to be committed by other transactions.

- **Non-repeatable Read**—Occurs when the read lock is not acquired while performing the SELECT operation. For example, if you have selected data under the T1 transaction, and meanwhile if the same is being updated by some other transaction, say T2, then the T1 transaction reads two versions of data. This type of data read is considered as non-repeatable read. It can be avoided by preparing a read lock by transaction T1 on the data that is has selected.
- **Phantom Read**—Specifies the situation when the collection of rows, returned by the execution of two identical queries, are different. This can happen when range locks are not acquired while executing the SELECT query. Consider an example, where in a transaction T1, you have executed query Q1 and got some results (say 10 rows). It is possible that during transaction T1, another transaction T2 has made some changes due to which the execution of the query Q1 within T1 now results in different number of rows (say 11 rows). This problem is referred as phantom read problem, which happens if some other transaction inserts a new record that is being used by an already running transaction.

Durability

The durability property guarantees that the user has been notified of the successful transaction, which can persist all the statements in the transaction or leave the complete transaction unsaved. This property specifies that after successful execution of the transaction, the system guarantees the updation of data in the database even if the computer crashes after the execution of the transaction.

Types of Transactions

A database transaction is used to provide data integrity and security to the database. All the JDBC specific drivers are required to provide transaction support for all the database operations. The database operations can include concurrent access of data from a data source. These transaction mechanisms are used to provide a secure way to access the data over multiple environments. The transaction mechanism is categorized into three different types, which are as follows:

- **Local transaction**—Specifies a transaction whose statements are executed on a single transactional resource through one resource object (that is, through one session). This type of transaction is based on only local networks connected to the data source object. The local transactions are easier to use in a local network. These transactions are not supported for the transactions in multiple networks on a distributed system.
- **Distributed transaction**—Specifies a transaction whose statements are executed on one or more transactional resources through multiple resource objects. In case of a distributed transaction, the transaction manager is responsible for all the database specific operations. It must support all the ACID properties of the transaction mechanism. A distributed transaction must be synchronized and available at different locations.
- **Nested transaction**—Specifies a transaction that occurs within the reference of another transaction. It must also satisfy the ACID properties. The changes made by a nested transaction are not visible to the existing or host transaction. The changes occurred in the nested transaction can be notified to the host transaction after they have been committed. This satisfies the Isolation property of the transaction mechanism.

Transaction Management

Transaction management in the database operation is necessary to maintain the integrity and security of data from unauthorized access. The resource manager in a transaction management system can manage local transactions because all the statements in it are associated with a single session. You need a transaction manager to manage the transactional resource objects required to execute a SQL statement. The JDBC API includes the support for transaction semantics associated with single Connection (Local Transaction) and support to participate in transactions involving multiple resource objects (Distributed Transaction). JDBC API allows you to perform the following operations to execute a transaction containing multiple resource objects:

- **Setting the Auto Commit attribute**—Allows you to specify when to end a transaction. Executing a transaction is either dependent on a JDBC driver or the underlying data source. JDBC API does not have any method to start the transaction explicitly. New transaction generally starts when you execute a SQL statement, such as calling the execute, executeUpdate, or executeQuery methods that require a transaction.

The Auto Commit attribute of connection can be set by using the `setAutoCommit` (boolean) method of connection, and calling this method with the true argument enables auto commit. On the other hand, calling the `setAutoCommit` (boolean) method of connection with the false argument disables auto commit. Moreover, JDBC driver provider decides the default argument for the Auto Commit attribute, but in general, it is set to true. If Auto Commit is enabled, JDBC driver commits the transaction as soon as each individual SQL statement is complete. The point at which a statement is considered complete depends on the type of SQL statement as well as what the application does after executing it. For DML (`Insert`, `Update`, `Delete`) and DDL statements, the statement is complete as soon as its execution completes. The following code snippet is used to set the Auto Commit mode before creating a new transaction:

```
// Assume con is a Connection object
con.setAutoCommit(false);
```

If Auto Commit is disabled, the transaction must be explicitly ended by using the commit or rollback method. You can successfully end a transaction and save all the statements present in it by invoking the `commit()` method. However, invoking the rollback() method makes the transaction unsuccessful, implying that none of the statements in the transaction are saved. You can disable the auto commit option if you want to group multiple statements into a single transaction and then decide to save or not to save the statements at the end of the transaction.

- **Setting the isolation levels**—Notify the visible data within a transaction. There are four isolation levels used in transaction management, which are as follows:
  - **READ UNCOMMITED**—Notifies the occurrence of dirty, non-repeatable, and phantom reads.
  - **READ COMMITED**—Notifies the occurrence of non-repeatable and phantom reads.
  - **REPEATABLE READ**—Notifies the occurrence of only phantom reads.
  - **SERIALIZABLE**—Specifies that all transactions occur in a completely isolated fashion. Dirty, non-repeatable, and phantom reads cannot occur at this isolation level.

  The isolation level in a transaction can be specified by using the Connection object passed by the connection. The default isolation level is always specified by the underlying data source. Sometimes, the user needs to specify the isolation level explicitly. The JDBC API provides the `setTransactionIsolation(int)` method to set the transaction isolation for a transaction. Similarly, the getTransactionIsolation() method is used by the user to retrieve the transaction isolation associated with a connection. If a driver used in a connection does not support the isolation level, the method throws a SQLException.
- **Savepoints**—Set points within a transaction. A Savepoint specifies a mark up to which the user can roll back without affecting the rest of the changes of a transaction. The DatabaseMetaData interface available in JDBC API provides the methods to support the Savepoint within a transaction. The JDBC API provides the setSavepoint(String) method of the Connection interface to set a Savepoint in a transaction. The transaction can be rolled back up to the Savepoint by using the rollback (savepoint) method of the Connection interface. The following code snippet shows how to set a Savepoint and rollback mechanism in a database:

```
Statement s = conn.createStatement();
int rows = s.executeUpdate("INSERT INTO TABLE1 (COLUMN1) VALUES " + "('FIRST')");
// set Savepoint
Savepoint sp = conn.setSavepoint("SAVEPOINT_1");
rows = s.executeUpdate("INSERT INTO TABLE1 (COLUMN1) " +
"VALUES ('SECOND')");
...
conn.rollback(sp);
...
conn.commit();
```

The preceding code snippet shows how to insert a record into a table in a database, and set a Savepoint, sp, in the database. The INSERT statement is successfully updated in the database. In the second insertion operation, the transaction is rolled back to the sp Savepoint. Therefore, this transaction is cancelled and the changes made to the database by the second INSERT statement are undone due to the calling of the rollback. You should note that the first INSERT statement is committed even after the rollback of the second INSERT statement.

The savepoints created during a transaction need to be released after the completion of the database transaction. The `releaseSavepoint()` method of the Connection interface can be called to release the savepoints. In other words, the releaseSavepoint() method removes the specified Savepoint from the current transaction. After a `Savepoint` has been released, the attempts to reference the current transaction in a rollback operation causes a `SQLException` to be thrown.

To understand the concept better, let's create an application called TranMGT. In this application, you need to create a .java (TransferAmount.java) file, which is used to perform transaction management. The code for the `TransferAmount.java file` is shown in Listing 3.21:

Listing 3.21: Showing the Code for the TransferAmount.java File

```
package com.kogent.jdbc;
import java.sql.*;
import java.util.*;
import java.io.*;
/**
 * @author Suchita
 */
public class TransferAmount {
  public static void main(String s[]) throws Exception {
        Driver d= (Driver) (Class.forName(
        "oracle.jdbc.driver.OracleDriver").newInstance());
        Properties p=new Properties();
        p.put("user","scott");
        p.put("password","tiger");
        Connection con=d.connect("jdbc:oracle:thin:@192.168.1.123:1521:XE",p);
        con.setAutoCommit(false);
        String srcaccno=s[0];
        String destaccno=s[1];
        PreparedStatement ps= con.prepareStatement(
        "update bank set bal=bal+? where accno=?");
        ps.setInt(1,500);
        ps.setString(2,destaccno);
        int i=ps.executeUpdate();
        ps.setInt(1,-500);
        ps.setString(2,srcaccno);
        int j=ps.executeUpdate();
        if (i==1&&j==1){
                con.commit();
                System.out.println("Amount transfered");
                con.close();
                return;
        }
        con.rollback();
        System.out.println("Cannot transfer the amount");
        con.close();
  }//main
}//class
```

The application shown in Listing 3.21 is used to transfer money from one account to another in a transaction. A table, bank, must be created before executing Listing 3.21, as shown in the following code snippet:

```
Create table bank (accno varchar2(20), bal number (10, 2));
Insert into bank values ('101', 10000);
Insert into bank values ('102', 10000);
```

The bank table is created at the Run SQL Command Line prompt to execute the `TransferAmount.java` application. The data in the bank table is used by the application to transfer the amount, and the output of this table is shown in Figure 3.49:

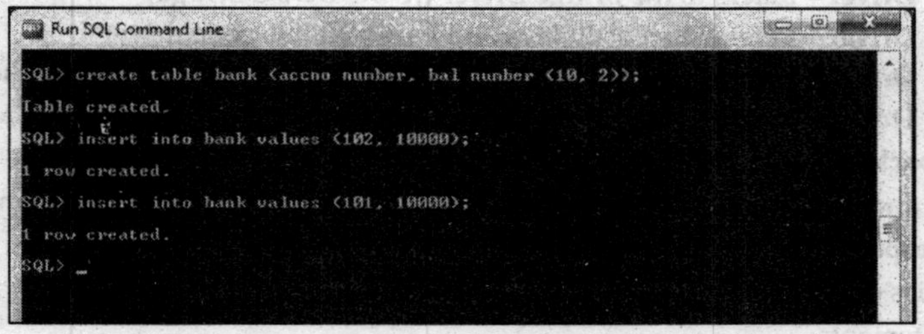

Figure 3.49: Creating a Table and Inserting Data

Figure 3.49 shows the creation of the required table (bank) for the application shown in Listing 3.21. The application uses the content of the table and performs the transaction. It uses the common SQL queries to update the database and also shows the transaction management by using the savepoints and rollbacks. Figure 3.50 shows the output of the TransferAmount class:

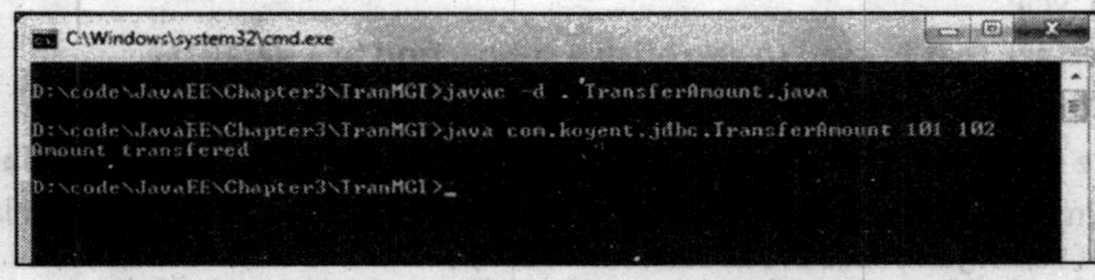

Figure 3.50: Showing the Output of TransferAmount.java

Figure 3.50 shows the output of the application created in Listing 3.21 by using the transaction properties. The application initially sets the auto-commit mode as it starts a new transaction in the given data source. Then, the required transactions update the records in the database. The transaction is committed after the updation process is complete. However, if an error occurs, the transaction can be rolled back to undo the changes made to the database.

Summary

In this chapter, you have learned about JDBC and its basic architecture. The chapter has further explored various JDBC drivers that help an application to establish connection with a database. Next, the chapter has discussed about the new features of JDBC 4.0 and advanced topics, such as ResultSet, Updateable, and Scrollable ResultSet, batch update, advanced data types, and RowSet. Further, you have learned how to develop the client-server applications by using the `java.sql` and `javax.sql` packages of JDBC API. Finally, you have learned to manage and work with transactions in JDBC applications.

In the next chapter, you learn about Servlets 3.1.

Quick Revise

Q1. What is JDBC?

Ans. JDBC is a specification from Sun Microsystems that provides a standard abstraction (API / Protocol) for Java applications to communicate with different databases.

Q2. What are the components of JDBC?

Ans. The components of JDBC are as follows:

- The JDBC API
- The JDBC DriverManager
- The JDBC Test Suite
- The JDBC-ODBC Bridge

Q3. Explain the different types of JDBC drivers.

Ans. The different types of JDBC drivers are as follows:

- **Type-1 Driver**—Refers to the Bridge Driver (JDBC-ODBC Bridge)
- **Type-2 Driver**—Refers to a Partly Java and Partly Native code driver
- **Type-3 Driver**—Refers to a pure Java driver that uses a Middleware Driver to connect to a database
- **Type-4 Driver**—Refers to a Pure Java driver, which is directly connected to a database

Q4. Name the packages that are used to implement JDBC in an application.

Ans. The java.sql and javax.sql packages are used to implement JDBC in an application.

Q5. State the properties of connection pooling.

Ans. The properties of connection pooling are as follows:

- maxStatements
- initialPoolSize
- minPoolSize
- maxPoolSize
- maxIdleTime
- propertyCycle

Q6. Name the interface that is used to establish a connection to a database.

Ans. The java.sql.Connection interface is used to obtain a connection to a database.

Q7. Write the code statements used to register the Driver object with the DriverManager class.

Ans. The code statements used to register the Driver object with the DriverManager class are as follows:

```
Class.forName ("sun.jdbc.odbc.JdbcOdbcDriver");
Where the sun.jdbc.odbc.JdbcOdbcDriver class contains the following code:
public class JdbcOdbcDriver extends … {
static { DriverManager.registerDriver (new sun.jdbc.odbc.JdbcOdbcDriver()); }
}
```

Q8. List the different types of RowSet objects.

Ans. The different types of RowSet objects are as follows:

- Connected RowSet objects
- Disconnected RowSet objects
- JdbcRowSet objects
- CachedRowSet objects
- WebRowSet objects
- FilteredRowSet object
- JoinRowSet objects

Q9. Name the interfaces and classes of the javax.sql package that are used for connection pooling.

Ans. The interfaces and classes of the javax.sql package used for connection pooling are as follows:

- The javax.sql.ConnectionPoolDataSource interface
- The javax.sql.PooledConnection interface
- The javax.sql.ConnectionEventListener interface
- The javax.sql.ConnectionEvent class

Q10. List the different advanced data types.

Ans. The different advanced data types are as follows:

- BLOB data type
- Character Large Object (CLOB) data type
- STRUCT data type
- ARRAY data type
- REF data type

4

Working with Servlets 3.1

The Java Servlet technology provides a simple, vendor-independent mechanism to extend the functionality of a Web server. This technology provides high level, component-based, platform-independent, and server-independent standards to develop Web applications in Java. The Java Servlet technology is similar to other scripting languages, such as Common Gateway Interface (CGI) scripts, JavaScript (on the client-side), and Hypertext Preprocessor (PHP). However, servlets are more acceptable since they overcome the limitations of CGI, such as low performance and scalability.

A servlet is a simple Java class, which is dynamically loaded on a Web server and thereby enhances the functionality of the Web server. Servlets are secure and portable as they run on Java Virtual Machine (JVM) embedded with the Web server and cannot operate outside the domain of the Web server. In other words, servlets are objects that generate dynamic content after processing requests that originate from a Web browser. They are Java components that are used to create dynamic Web applications. Servlets can run on any Java-enabled platform and are usually designed to process HyperText Transfer Protocol (HTTP) requests, such as GET, and POST.

The chapter first explores the general features of Java Servlet, after which you learn about the features of the latest version of Java Servlet, i.e., 3.1. Next, the chapter explains the classes and packages of the Servlet Application Programming Interface (API) used to develop Web applications. You also learn about the life cycle of a servlet and configuring a servlet in the web.xml file. In addition, you learn to create a sample servlet in two ways, by mapping it in the web.xml file and by using annotations. Moreover, the chapter also provides a walkthrough to the noteworthy interfaces of the `javax.servlet` and `javax.servlet.http` packages. Toward the end of the chapter, you learn about request delegation, request scope and servlet collaboration.

We begin the chapter by first exploring the features of Java Servlet.

Exploring the Features of Java Servlet

Java Servlet provides various key features, such as security, performance, as well as the request and response model. Servlets are considered as a request and response model in which requests are sent by users and their appropriate responses are generated by a Web server. In addition, a key feature of a servlet is that you can create multiple instances of a servlet with different data and each servlet can be configured with different names. A Java Servlet also provides support for the security policy used to control accessibility permissions, such as a user accessing a resource. In addition, scripting languages can be used in servlets to dynamically modify or generate Hypertext Markup Language (HTML) pages. Apart from this, servlets also support various HTTP methods, such as GET and POST, which are used to redirect requests and responses.

Now, let's learn about these features in detail.

Servlet – A Request and Response Model

Servlets are based on the programming model that accepts requests and generates responses accordingly. A developer extends the GenericServlet or HttpServlet class to create a servlet. The `service()` method in a servlet is defined to handle requests and responses. The following code snippet defines the service() method for the `MyServletApplication` servlet class:

```
import javax.servlet.*;
public class MyServletApplication extends GenericServlet {
  public void service (ServletRequest   request, ServletResponse  response)
  throws ServletException, IOException
  {
       ...
  }
  ...
}
```

The `service()` method is provided with request and response parameters. These parameters encapsulate the data sent by a client, which provides access to the parameters and allows servlets to generate responses. Servlets normally use an input stream to retrieve most of their parameters, and an output stream is used to send responses. The following code snippet shows how the request parameter is used to invoke the `getInputStream()` method:

```
ServletInputStream    input = request.getInputStream();
```

```
ServletOutputStream   output = response.getOutputStream();
```

In the preceding code snippet, instances of the input and output streams are created, which may be used to read or write data.

Servlet and Environment State

Servlets are similar to any other Java objects and have instance-specific data. This implies that servlets are also independent applications that run within the server environment and do not require any additional classes (which are required by some alternative server extension APIs).

When servlets are initialized, they have access to some servlet-specific configuration data. This enables the initialization of different instances of the same servlet-class with different data, and their management as differently named servlets. The data, provided with each servlet instance at the time of its initialization, also includes some information about the persistent state of an instance. The `ServletContext` object provides the ability to servlets to interact with other servlets in a Web application.

Next, let's discuss the different modes in which a servlet can be used.

Usage Modes

Servlets can be used in various modes. However, these modes are not supported by all server environments. At the core of a request–response protocol, the basic modes in which servlets can be used are as follows:

- Servlets can be chained together into filter chains by the servers
- Servlets can support protocols, such as HTTP
- Servlets serve as a complete, efficient, and portable replacement for CGI-based extensions in HTTP-based applications
- Servlets can be used with HTML to dynamically generate some parts of a Web document in HTTP-based applications

Now, let's discuss the life cycle of a servlet.

Servlet Life Cycle

When a server loads a servlet, the `init()` method of the servlet is executed. The servlet initialization process is completed before any client request is addressed or before the servlet is destroyed. The server calls the init() method once, when the server loads the servlet, and does not call the method again unless the server reloads the servlet. A server cannot reload a servlet after the servlet is destroyed. After initialization, the servlet handles client requests and generates responses. Finally, the `destroy()` method is invoked, to destroy the servlet.

Let's discuss various possible sources from where a servlet is loaded. Moreover, you also explore different situations in which a servlet is loaded.

Possible Sources of Servlets

When a client requests for a servlet, the server maps the request of the client and loads the servlet. The server administrator can specify the mapping of client requests to servlets in the following ways:

- Mapping client requests to a particular servlet, for example, client requests made to a specific database.
- Mapping client requests to the servlets found in an administered servlets directory. This servlet directory may be shared among different servers that share the processing load for the clients of a website.
- Configuring some servers to automatically invoke servlets that filter the output of other servlets. For example, a particular type of output generated by a servlet may invoke other servlets to carry out post processing, probably to perform format conversions.
- Invoking the specific servlets without administrative intervention by properly authorized clients.

Figure 4.1 displays the various sources of servlets:

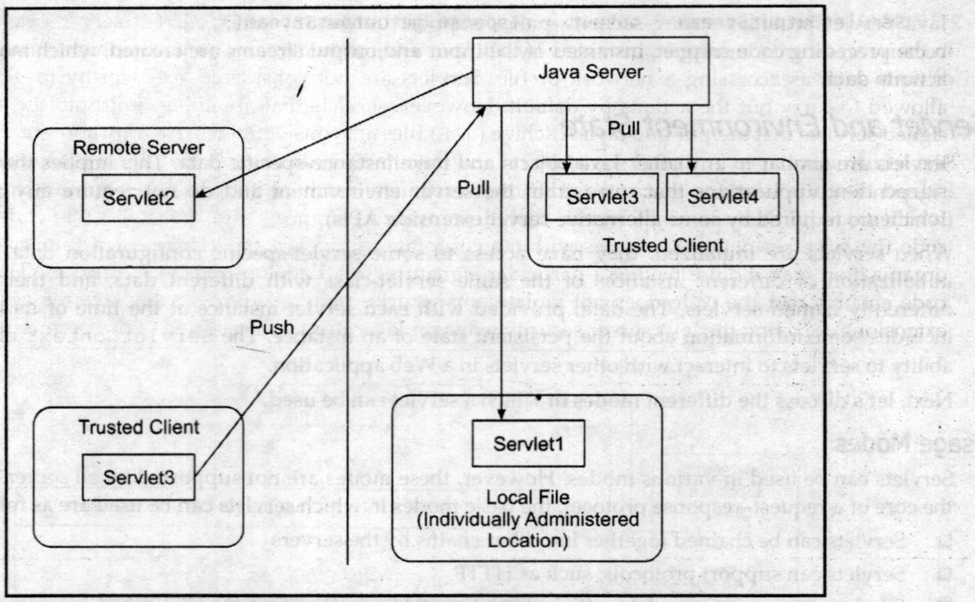

Figure 4.1: Displaying the Possible Sources of Loading a Servlet

Figure 4.1 shows the various possible sources of servlets, which can be as follows:

- Individually administered locations
- Directory of servlets that are shared between servers
- Authorized clients

After having a brief understanding about life cycle of a servlet and exploring its possible sources, let's describe the primary methods of a servlet, which are init(), service(), and destroy().

Primary Servlet Methods

The following are the methods used in the life cycle of a loaded servlet:

- `init()`–Refers to the method that an application server uses to load and initialize a servlet. The `init()` method is typically used to create or load objects that will be used by the servlet to handle client requests. The application server calls the `init()` method to provide a new servlet with the information related to its context.
- `service()`–Helps servlets to handle client requests. Servlets handle many requests after initialization. One `service()` method call is generated by each client request. These requests may be concurrent. This enables servlets to coordinate activities among multiple clients. To share data between requests, the class-static state may be used.
- `destroy()`–Terminates an executing servlet. Servlets process client requests until they are explicitly terminated by the Web server by calling the `destroy()` method. When a servlet is destroyed, it becomes eligible for garbage collection.

Security Features

Servlets have access to information about their clients. Peer identities can be determined reliably when servlets are used with secure protocols, such as Secure Sockets Layer (SSL). Servlets that rely on HTTP also have access to HTTP-specific authentication data.

Servlets have various advantages of Java. For example, as in Java, memory access violations and strong typing violations are also not possible with servlets. Due to these advantages, faulty servlets do not crash servers, which is common in most C language server extension environments.

Java Servlet provides strong security policy support unlike any other current server extension API. This is because a security manager, provided by all Java environments, can be used to control the permissions for actions such as accessing a network or file. Servlets are not considered trustworthy in general and are not allowed to carry out the actions by default. However, servlets that are either built into the server, or digitally signed servlets that are put into Java ARchive (`JAR`) files are considered trustworthy and granted permissions by the security manager. A digital signature on any executable code ensures that the organization that created and signed the code takes the guarantee of its trustworthiness. Such digital signatures cannot support answerability for the code by themselves. However, they do provide assurance about the use of that code. For example, all code that accesses network services within a corporate Intranet of the Management Information System (MIS) organization may require having a particular signature, to access those network services. The signature on the code ensures that the code does not violate any security policy. Figure 4.2 displays the approaches to server extensions depicting the Java server security manager layer used by servlets to verify permissions:

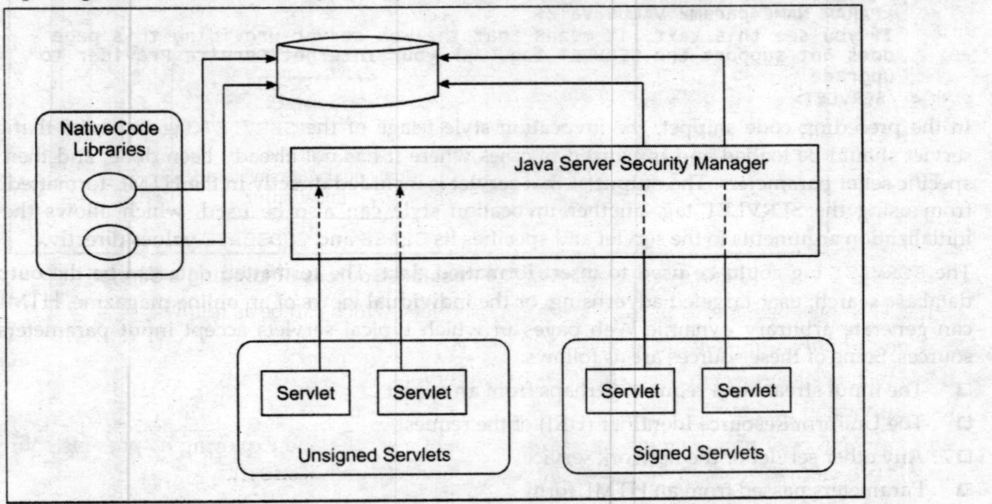

Figure 4.2: Showing the Activities of Signed and Unsigned Servlets

Figure 4.2 compares two approaches to server extensions:

- Activities of servlets in the case of signed servlets, which are monitored at fine granularity by the Java security manager
- Activities of native code extensions in the case of unsigned servlets, which are never monitored

In both cases, the host operating system usually provides very coarse-grained protection.

In languages such as C or scripting languages, extension APIs cannot support fine-grained access controls, even if they do allow digital signatures for their code. This explains that Pure Java™ extensions are fundamentally more secure than current competitive solutions including, in particular ActiveX of Microsoft.

There are some immediate commercial applications for such improved security technologies. At present, it is not possible for most Internet Service Providers (ISPs) to accept server extensions from their clients. The reason is that the ISPs do not have proper methods to protect themselves or their clients from the attacks building on extensions, which use native C code or CGI facilities. However, it has been observed that extensions built with pure Java Servlet can prevent modification of data. Along with the use of digitally signed code, ISPs can ensure that they safely extend their Web servers with the servlets provided by their customers.

HTML-Aware Servlets

It has been observed that many servlets directly generate HTML formatted text, because it is easy to do so with standard internationalized Java formatted output classes, such as `java.io.PrintWriter`. To dynamically modify HTML pages or generate HTML pages, you do not have to use scripting languages.

You can also use other approaches to generate Java HTML formatted text. For example, some multi-language sites that serve pages in multiple languages, such as English and Japanese, usually maintain language-specific libraries of localized HTML template files. These sites also display the localized HTML templates by using localized message catalogs. Other sites may also have developed HTML generation packages. These packages are particularly well accustomed to other specific needs for dynamic Web page generation, for example, the ones that are closely integrated with other application toolsets.

Servlets may also be invoked by Web servers that provide complete servlet support, to help in preprocessing Web pages by using the server-side include functionality. This kind of preprocessing can be indicated to Web servers by a special HTML syntax. The following code snippet shows the syntax that is used in HTML files to indicate preprocessing of Web pages:

```
<SERVLET NAME=ServletClassName>
   <PARAM NAME=param1 VALUE=val1>
   <PARAM NAME=param2 VALUE=val2>
   If you see this text, it means that the Web server providing this page
   does not support the SERVLET tag. Ask your Internet Service Provider to
   upgrade!
< /SERVLET>
```

In the preceding code snippet, the invocation style usage of the `SERVLET` tag indicates that a preconfigured servlet should be loaded and initialized in cases where it has not already been done, and then invoked with a specific set of parameters. The output of that servlet is included directly in the HTML-formatted response. Apart from using the SERVLET tag, another invocation style can also be used, which allows the passing of the initialization arguments to the servlet and specifies its `CLASS` and `CODEBASE` values directly.

The `SERVLET` tag could be used to insert formatted data. The formatted data can be the output of a Web or database search, user-targeted advertising, or the individual views of an online magazine. HTML-aware servlets can generate arbitrary dynamic Web pages in which typical servlets accept input parameters from different sources. Some of these sources are as follows:

- The input stream of a request, perhaps from an applet
- The Uniform Resource Identifier (URI) of the request
- Any other servlet or the network service
- Parameters passed from an HTML form

The input parameters are used to generate HTML-formatted responses. A servlet often checks with one or more databases, or other data with which the servlet is configured, to decide the exact data that is to be returned with the response.

HTTP-Specific Servlets

HTTP-specific servlets are those servlets that are used with the HTTP protocol. These servlets can support any HTTP method, such as `GET`, `POST`, and `HEAD`; redirect requests to other locations; and send HTTP-specific error messages. They can also have access to the parameters passed through standard HTML forms. HTTP-specific servlets include the HTTP method to be executed and the Uniform Resource Identifier (URI), which describes the destination of the request. The following code snippet shows some of the methods used in HTTP-specific servlets:

```
String method = request.getMethod();        // e.g. POST
String uri = request.getRequestURI();
String name = request.getParameter("name");

String phone = request.getParameter ("phone");
String card = request.getParameter ("creditcard");
```

In HTTP-specific servlets, request and response data is always provided in the Multipurpose Internet Mail Extensions (MIME) format. This implies that the servlet first specifies the data type and then writes the encoded data. This allows servlets to refer the data format regarding arbitrary sources of input data, and then return the data in the appropriate form for the particular request. Examples of request and response data formats are HTML, graphics formats, such as `Joint Photographic Experts Group (JPEG)` or `Moving Picture Experts Group (MPEG)`, and data formats that are used by some applications.

In most applications, HTTP servlets are considered better than CGI programs in terms of performance, flexibility, portability, and security. Therefore, rather than using CGI or a C language plug-in, write your next server extension by using the Java Servlet API.

Performance Features

Let's discuss the performance feature of servlets. One of the most prominent performance features of Java Servlets is that a new process need not be created for every new request received. In most environments, several servlets run in parallel to the server within the same process. This is a big advantage. When you use servlets in such environments with HTTP, performance is assumed to be much better than what it would be if the CGI or Fast-CGI approach was used.

Figure 4.3 displays the different approaches to depict the functionality and performance of a servlet:

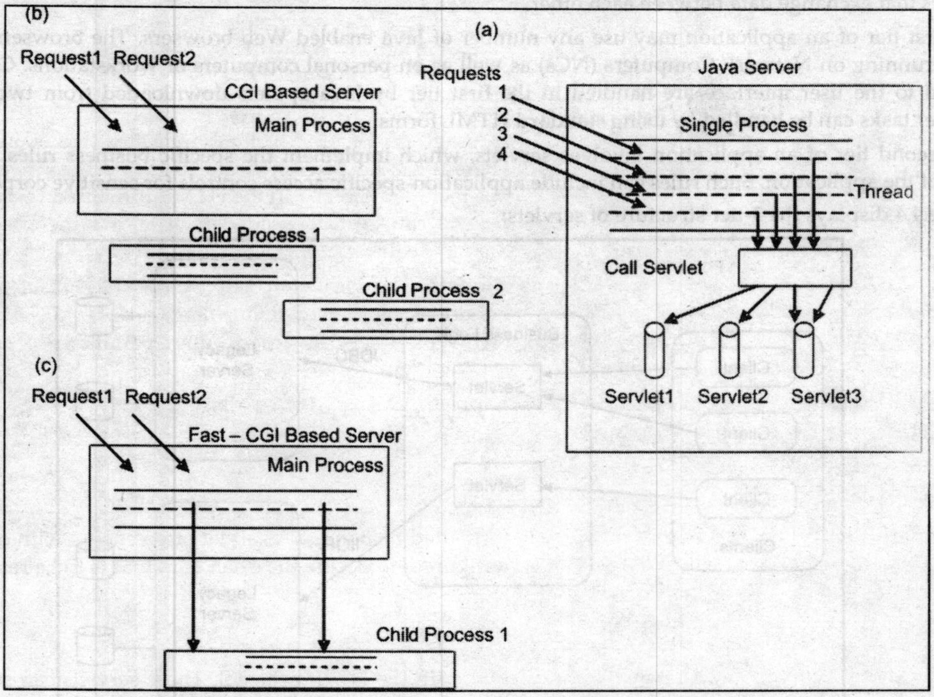

Figure 4.3: Showing Different Servlet Functional Approaches

Figure 4.3 compares the following three server extension approaches:

- The servlet approach, which allows embedding to be supported inside a server, as shown by section (a) of Figure 4.3
- The CGI approach, which involves creating a new child process with every new request, as shown by section (b) of Figure 4.3
- The Fast-CGI approach, which involves creating one child process for multiple requests, as shown by section (c) of Figure 4.3

The difference between these approaches is that the servlet approach require only lightweight thread context switches, whereas Fast-CGI involves heavyweight process context switching on each request, and regular CGI requires even heavier weight process start-up and initialization code on each request. After a servlet is initialized, it can address requests from multiple clients in most environments. This spreads the cost of initialization over many methods. It also enables all client requests made to a service to share data and communication resources as well as use system caches effectively.

Java Servlet can take the advantage of additional processors, with multiple implementations of JVM. The Java Virtual Machine (JVM) enables you to scale applications from entry-level servers to the mainframe class multiprocessors. This also helps to provide better throughput and timely response to clients. Pure Java programs are platform-independent; therefore, they can run on any operating system. In other words, you can select any operating system that best addresses your requirements for any given application. The implementation of Java Servlet is beneficial for many large Web-based applications that use Java and other Internet technologies.

3-Tier Applications

Using Java Servlet helps a user to opt for 3-tier applications. Many organizations require you to use multi-tier applications. Many clients and single server models are giving way to a single application, which includes many servers that exchange data between each other.

The first tier of an application may use any number of Java enabled Web browsers. The browsers can include those running on Network Computers (NCs) as well as on personal computers or workstations. Complex tasks related to the user interface are handled in the first tier by Java applets downloaded from two-tier servers. Simpler tasks can be handled by using standard HTML forms.

The second tier of an application involves servlets, which implement the specific business rules and business logic of the application. Such rules can include application-specific access controls for sensitive corporate data.

Figure 4.4 displays the 3-tier structure of servlets:

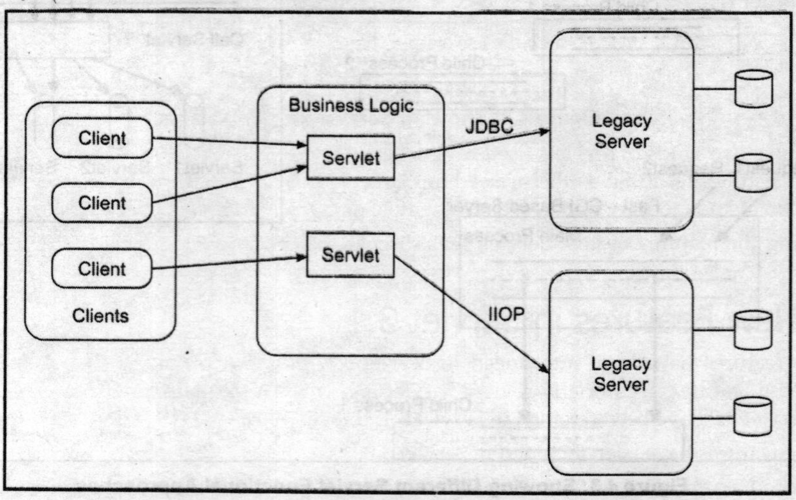

Figure 4.4: Showing 3-Tier Structure of Servlets

Figure 4.4 shows how servlets can be used to connect the second tier of an application to the first tier. A variety of client technologies may be used to connect to other tiers.

The third tier of an application involves data repositories. This tier can be accessed by using relational database interfaces such as Java Database Connectivity (JDBC), or other interfaces supported by legacy data, for example, Remote Procedure Call (RPC)-like protocols such as Open Network Computing (ONC) RPC, Distributed Computing Environment (DCE) RPC, and Common Object Request Broker Architecture (COBRA)/Internet Inter-Orb Protocol (IIOP).

Web Publishing System

Many organizations have large collections of data. They have to manage and publish the data, which is usually flexible and tends to change. For example, an organization may maintain a collection of both historical and real-time weather data that needs to be presented in easily understood formats in the form of a response to the current application.

In this case, you can use a Web publishing system that provides sites to access historical and real-time weather data from a database. In other words, the required data can be accessed from the database by using JDBC. The weather data (including temperature, wind, rainfall, a frame of image data, or a stream of MPEG data) is sent by a Java equipped remote recording station to a site receiving the data. The servlet processing the data at the collecting site may selectively store the data. For example, it may store data of a specific time period, such as the last two weeks, or it may discard some data immediately.

The collecting sites may receive queries from other sites, such as individual browsers or other collecting sites, to return data in a specific format. In that case, servlets process the saved data and return the response of the query in the appropriate format, such as a Web page with current data and historical tables and graphs, to a user. Some servlets can also perform administrative tasks, such as archiving and deleting data, or pulling data from staging areas, as part of an automated data distribution system.

Figure 4.5 shows communication between two servlets:

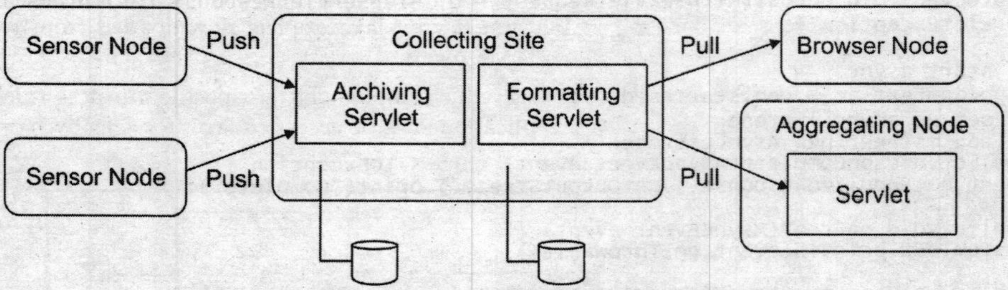

Figure 4.5: Showing Servlet Communication

Figure 4.5 shows two kinds of servlets used by a collecting site. One is used by the remote sensor nodes to push data to the collecting site, and the other is used by clients to pull data from the collecting site in a specific format. Such clients can include tertiary nodes, which assemble data from multiple collecting sites.

After exploring the features of Java Servlet, let's discuss the new enhancements that have been introduced in Servlet 3.0.

Exploring New Features in Servlet 3.1

Various new features have been introduced in Servlet 3.1, the new version of Java Servlet. However, before discussing these features, let's briefly review Servlet 3.0, which was the previous version of Java Servlet. The features of Servlet 3.0 have been retained in Servlet 3.1; therefore, let's first discuss the features of Servlet 3.0.

The following features have been included in Servlet 3.0:

- Introduction of annotations as an enhanced feature. When you use annotations to create servlets, using Deployment Descriptor in the form of the web.xml file to map the servlet is optional. Developers can directly mark a servlet by using annotations. However, if Deployment Descriptor is also used, it overrides the configuration information provided by using annotations. Some of the annotations introduced in Servlet 3.0 are as follows:
  - **@WebServlet annotation**—Marks the annotated class as a servlet
  - **@WebInitParam annotation**—Specifies the init parameters to be passes to the servlet.
  - **@WebListener annotation**—Marks the annotated class as a listener
- Introduction of Web fragments to implement the concept of modularization of the web.xml file. A Web fragment can be assumed as a segment of the web.xml file. This implies that one or more Web fragments constitute a web.xml file. All configuration information specified in the web.xml file can also be specified in the web-fragment.xml file. When multiple web-fragment.xml files exist for a Web application, the order of their execution can be decided by specifying absolute or relative ordering.
- Introduction of the concept of asynchronous processing, which is implemented by setting the `asyncSupported` attribute of the @WebServlet or @WebFilter annotation. The asyncSupported attribute

takes a Boolean value, which should be set to true to obtain asynchronous processing. In asynchronous processing, a servlet does not have to wait for a response from the request made for a resource, such as database.

All the listed features of Servlet 3.0 have been retained in Servlet 3.1; now let us discuss the features of Servlet 3.1.

The following features have been included in Servlet 3.1:

- **Support for non-blocking IO** – The new release of Servlet 3.1 allows non-blocking processing with the help of ReadListener and WriteListener. It should be noted that non-blocking IO can only be used in async mode or the upgrade mode. The async mode can be set in a servlet using the @WebServlet annotation. The following code snippet shows how to enable async in the servlet:

```
// enable async in the servlet
@WebServlet(urlPatterns="/test", asyncSupported=true)
public class TestServlet extends HttpServlet {
protected void doPost(HttpServletRequest req, HttpServletResponse res)throws IOException,
ServletException {

// start async
AsyncContext ac = req.startAsync();
// set up async listener
ac.addListener(new AsyncListener() {
public void onComplete(AsyncEvent event) throws IOException {
event.getSuppliedResponse().getOutputStream().print("Complete");
}
public void onError(AsyncEvent event) {
System.out.println(event.getThrowable());
}
public void onStartAsync(AsyncEvent event) {
}
public void onTimeout(AsyncEvent event) {
System.out.println("my asyncListener.onTimeout");
}
});

// set up ReadListener to read data for processing
ServletInputStream input = req.getInputStream();
ReadListener readListener = new ReadListenerImpl(input, res, ac);
input.setReadListener(readListener);
   }
}
```

In the preceding code, the @WebServlet annotation is used to enable async in the servlet. Next, async is started and async listener is set. Then, ReadListener is set up to read data for processing.

The read operation needs to be delegated to the ReadListenerImpl interface. The code of the ReadListenerImpl interface is as follows:

```
class ReadListenerImpl implements ReadListener {
private ServletInputStream input = null;
private HttpServletResponse res = null;
private AsyncContext ac = null;

// store the processed data to be sent back to client later
private Queue queue = new LinkedBlockingQueue();

ReadListenerImpl(ServletInputStream in, HttpServletResponse r,
     AsyncContext c) {
  input = in;
  res = r;
  ac = c;
}

public void onDataAvailable() throws IOException {
  StringBuilder sb = new StringBuilder();
  int len = -1;
  byte b[] = new byte[1024];

  // We need to check input#isReady before reading data.
```

```
        // The ReadListener will be invoked again when
        // the input#isReady is changed from false to true

        while (input.isReady() && (len = input.read(b)) != -1) {
            String data = new String(b, 0, len);
            sb.append(data);
        }
        queue.add(sb.toString());
    }

    public void onAllDataRead() throws IOException {
        // now all data are read, set up a WriteListener to write
        ServletOutputStream output = res.getOutputStream();
        WriteListener writeListener = new WriteListenerImpl(output, queue, ac);
        output.setWriteListener(writeListener);
    }

    public void onError(final Throwable t) {
        ac.complete();
        t.printStackTrace();
    }
}
```

In the preceding code, the data is read in non-blocking mode. After calling the setReadListener() method, the onDataAvailable() method is invoked immediately to check whether there is data to read. Otherwise, it will be invoked after the data is being ready.

After reading all the data, the onAllDataRead() method of the ReadListenerImpl interface sets up a WriteListenerImpl for writing data in a non-blocking mode. The code of the WriteListenerImpl interface is as follows:

```
    class WriteListenerImpl implements WriteListener {
    private ServletOutputStream output = null;
    private Queue queue = null;
    private AsyncContext ac = null;

    WriteListenerImpl(ServletOutputStream sos, Queue q, AsyncContext c) {
        output = sos;
        queue = q;
        ac = c;
    }

    public void onWritePossible() throws IOException {
        // write while there is data and is ready to write
        while (queue.peek() != null && output.isReady()) {
            String data = queue.poll();
            output.print(data);
        }
        // complete the async process when there is no more data to write
        if (queue.peek() == null) {
            ac.complete();
        }
    }

    public void onError(final Throwable t) {
        ac.complete();
        t.printStackTrace();
    }
}
```

- **HTTP protocol upgrade mechanism**—Specifies an upgrade mechanism that allows transition of HTTP from 1.1 to some other, incompatible protocol. The capabilities and nature of the communication entirely depends on the newly chosen protocol. Only after accepting the newly upgraded protocol by a client and server, the message exchange takes place between them with the help of chosen new protocol. The protocol upgrade is decided by using the Servlet.service() method. To achieve this, you need to add a new method HttpServletRequest.upgrade() and two new interfaces: javax.servlet.http.HttpUpgradeHandler and javax.servlet.http.WebConnection. Web Socket is an example of protocol upgrade.
- **Security enhancement features**—Servlets 3.1 API improves the reliability and integrity of servlet-based applications by applying the following:

- **Run-as security roles to init and destroy methods**—Specify that security roles are defined for a particular application, which can be mapped to a servlet by annotating the servlet class with @RunAs. In Servlet 3.1, if a security role is bound to a servlet, the call made from that servlet to an Enterprise Java Bean (EJB) will be executed under the permission set of the role, which is bounded by the @RunAs.
- **Session fixation attack defense**—A Web hacker through sessions can obtain security IDs used by websites for authentication purposes. In fact, the hacker can have full permissions to hack an account, this is called as session fixation attacks. In Servlet 3.1, the session fixation attack can be secured by changing the session ID once a user has successfully authenticated to the application. The session ID can be changed by calling the new HttpServletRequest.changeSessionId() method after the session has already been created. For this purpose the newly introduced HttpSessionIdListener interface can be used to implement listener classes that are responsible for changing a session identifier.

- **Miscellaneous features**—There are various types new features are also added in Servlet 3.1. For example, the ServletResponse.reset() method clears the data that exists in the buffer, status code, or headers. The ServletResponse.setCharacterEncoding() method sets the character encoding (MIME charset) of the response, which has to be sent to a client. Moreover, relative protocol URL can be specified in HttpServletResponse.sendRedirect() method, so that it allows a URL to be specified without a scheme. For example, instead of specifying "http://somehost.com/abc/example.jsp" as a redirect address you can specify, "//somehost.com/abc/example.jsp". In this case the scheme of the corresponding request will be used.

After discussing the new features and enhancements of Servlet 3.1, let's now explore the Servlet API.

Exploring the Servlet API

The Servlet API is a part of the Java Servlet specification designed by the Java Community Process (JCP). This API is supported by all servlet containers, such as Tomcat and WebLogic. The Servlet API contains classes and interfaces that define a standard contract between a servlet class and Servlet container. These classes and interfaces are available in the following two packages of the Servlet API:

- javax.servlet
- javax.servlet.http

Let's learn about these packages in detail in the following sections.

Describing the javax.servlet Package

The `javax.servlet` package contains some interfaces and classes that allow a servlet to access the basic services provided by a Servlet container. The Servlet container provides the implementation of the classes and interfaces packaged under the `javax.servlet` package.

The central abstraction of the Servlet API is the `Servlet` interface. The two classes in the Servlet API that implement the `Servlet` interface are `GenericServlet` and `HttpServlet`. Generally, developers implement the `HttpServlet` interface to create their servlets for Web applications that employ the HTTP protocol.

The basic `Servlet` interface defines a `service()` method to handle client requests,. This method is called for each request that is routed to an instance of a servlet by the Servlet container.

The contract between a Web application and a Web container is provided by the `javax.servlet` package. This allows Servlet container vendors to focus on developing the container in the manner most suited to their requirements (or those of their customers), as long as the package provides the specified implementations of the interfaces used in a servlet. The package provides a standard library to process client requests and develop servlet-based applications, from a developer's perspective.

The Servlet interface that defines the core structure of a servlet is provided in the `javax.servlet` package, which is the basis for all servlet implementations. However, for most servlet implementations, the subclass from a defined implementation of this interface provides the basis for a Web application.

The various interfaces and classes, such as ServletConfig and ServletContext, provide the additional services to a developer. An example of such a service is the Servlet container that provides a servlet with access to a client request through a standard interface. The `javax.servlet` package, therefore, provides the basis to develop a cross-platform, cross-servlet container Web application, and allows programmers to focus on developing a Web application.

Developers sometimes also use the `javax.servlet.http` package. Additionally, you need the `javax.servlet` package to build servlet implementations that use a non-HTTP protocol. For example, you can extend classes from the `javax.servlet` package to implement a Simple Mail Transfer Protocol (SMTP) servlet that provides an e-mail service to clients.

Let's now discuss the interfaces, classes, and exception classes of the `javax.servlet` package.

Explaining the Interfaces and Classes of the javax.servlet Package

The `javax.servlet` package comprises fourteen interfaces. While building an application, a programmer can implement seven interfaces, such as Servlet, and ServletRequestListener. A Servlet container provides the implementation for the following seven interfaces:

- ServletConfig
- ServletContext
- ServletRequest
- ServletResponse
- RequestDispatcher
- FilterChain
- FilterConfig

The Servlet container must provide an object for the preceding interfaces to a servlet. The `getServletContext()` method is probably the most important method of the `ServletConfig` Interface. This method returns the `ServletContext` object, which communicates with the Servlet container when you want to perform some action, such as writing to a log file or dispatching requests. There is only one `ServletContext` object for a Web application per JVM. This object is initialized when the Web application starts and is destroyed only when the Web application shuts down. One useful application of the `ServletContext` object is as a persistence mechanism. A programmer may store attributes in the `ServletContext` interface so that they are available throughout the execution of an application and not just for the duration of a request for a resource.

The Servlet container provides the classes that implement the `ServletRequest` and `ServletResponse` interfaces. These classes provide client request information to a servlet and the object used to send a response to the client.

An object defined by the `RequestDispatcher` interface manages client requests by directing them to an appropriate resource on the server.

The `FilterChain`, `FilterConfig`, and `Filter` interfaces are used to implement the filtering functionality in an application. You can also combine the interfaces into chains, implying that you can chain them such that before being processed by a container, the request is filtered through each filter defined in the application. The response goes down the chain in reverse.

A programmer building a Web application implements the following seven interfaces:

- Servlet
- ServletRequestListener
- ServletRequestAttributeListener
- ServletContextListener
- ServletContextAttributeListener
- SingleThreadModel
- Filter

The preceding interfaces are defined so that a Servlet container can invoke the methods defined in the interfaces. Therefore, the Servlet container needs to know only the methods defined in the interfaces. The details of the implementation of the methods are provided by the developers.

The event classes used to notify the changes made to the `ServletContext` object and its attributes are `ServetContextEvent` and `ServletContextAttributeEvent`, respectively.

Initially, the system creates a single instance of a servlet. If a new request is received while the previous one is being processed, a new thread is created for each new user request, with multiple threads running concurrently. This implies that the `doGet()` and `doPost()` methods need to carefully synchronize the access to fields and other shared data because, multiple executing threads may access the data simultaneously. You can implement the `SingleThreadModel` interface in a servlet, if you want to prevent this multithreaded access, as shown by the following code snippet:

```
public class YourServlet extends HttpServlet implements SingleThreadModel
{
   ...
}
```

If you implement the SingleThreadModel interface, the system ensures that a single instance of a servlet is never accessed by more than one request thread. This is implemented by queuing all the requests and passing them one by one to a single servlet instance. However, the server can create a pool of multiple instances, with each addressing one request at a time. This implies that there is no need to worry about simultaneous access to regular fields (instance variables) of a servlet. However, access to class variables (static fields) or shared data stored outside the servlet still needs to be synchronized.

Synchronous and frequent access to servlets can significantly hurt performance (latency). The server remains idle instead of handling pending requests, when a servlet waits for Input/Output (I/O). Therefore, think twice before using the `SingleThreadModel` approach.

NOTE

The SingleThreadModel interface has been deprecated as of Java Servlet API 2.4, with no direct replacement

Two classes, `ServletRequestEvent` and `ServletRequestAttributeEvent`, are used to indicate the life cycle events and attribute events for a `ServletRequest` object. The `ServletContext` object of a Web application is the source of the event.

To read or send binary data to or from a client, the `ServletInputStream` and `ServletOutputStream` classes provide input and output streams, respectively.

Useful implementations of the `ServletRequest` and `ServletResponse` interfaces are provided by the wrapper classes `ServletRequestWrapper` and `ServletResponseWrapper`, respectively. These implementations can be subclassed to allow programmers to adapt or enhance the functionality of the wrapped object for their own Web application. This can be done to implement a basic protocol agreed between a client and a server or to transparently adapt the requests or responses to a particular format that the Web application requires.

Explaining the Exception Classes of the **javax.servlet** Package

The following two exceptions are present in the `javax.servlet` package:

- ServletException
- UnavailableException

Generally, the `ServletException` exception is thrown by a servlet to indicate a problem with a user request. The problem may be in processing a request or sending of a response.

Whenever the `ServletException` exception is thrown to a Servlet container, an application loses control of the request being processed. It is the responsibility of the Servlet container to clean up the request and return a response to a client. Instead of sending a response, the Servlet container may also return an error page to the client indicating a server problem, depending on implementation and configuration of the container.

A `ServletException` exception should be thrown only as a last resort. The preferred approach to deal with an insuperable problem is to handle the problem and then return the type of the problem to the client.

An application throws the `UnavailableException` exception when a requested resource is not available. The resource can be a servlet, a filter, or any other configuration details required by the servlet to process requests, such as a database, a domain name server, or another servlet.

Exploring the javax.servlet.http Package

The `javax.servlet.http` package contains some interfaces and classes that enhance the basic functionality of a servlet to support HTTP-specific features, such as request and response headers, different request methods, and cookies.

As discussed earlier, there are two classes (`GenericServlet` and `HttpServlet`) in the Servlet API, which implement the `Servlet` interface. `HttpServlet` is an abstract class that extends the `GenericServlet` base class and provides a framework to handle the HTTP protocol. The following section discusses the classes and interfaces of the `javax.servlet.http` package.

Explaining the Interfaces of the javax.servlet.http Package

The `javax.servlet.http` package comprises the following eight interfaces:

- HttpServletRequest
- HttpServletResponse
- HttpSession
- HttpSessionBindingListener
- HttpSessionContext
- HttpSessionActivationListener
- HttpSessionAttributeListener
- HttpSessionListener

The `HttpServletRequest` interface retrieves data from a client to a servlet for use in the `HttpServlet.service()` method. This interface allows the `service()` method to access the HTTP protocol specified header information. The `HttpServletResponse` interface allows the `service()` method of a servlet to manipulate the HTTP protocol specified header information. This interface also returns the data to its client. The `HttpSession` interface is used to maintain a session between an HTTP client and the HTTP server. This session is used to maintain the state and user identity across multiple connections or requests during a given period.

The `HttpSessionContext` interface provides a group of the HttpSessions objects associated with a single session. The getSessionContext() method is used by a servlet to get the `HttpSessionContext` object. The `HttpSessionContext` interface also provides various methods to servlets to list the IDs or retrieve a session based on the ID. The `HttpSessionActivationListener` interface notifies a Web container about the activation or passivation of a session object. The `HttpSessionAttribute` interface is implemented to receive the notifications of changes in the attribute lists of sessions within a Web application. The `HttpSessionListener` interface notifies the changes made in the active sessions in a Web application.

NOTE

The HttpSessionContext interface has been deprecated as of Java™ Servlet API 2.1 for security reasons, with no replacement.

The `HttpSessionBindingListener` interface has the `valueBound()` and `valueUnbound()` methods to notify a listener that it is being bound to a session or unbound from a session.

Next, we discuss the classes of the javax.servlet.http package.

Explaining the Classes of the javax.servlet.http Package

Apart from the interfaces, the `javax.servlet.http` package also has various classes, which are as follows:

- Cookie
- HttpServlet
- HttpServletRequestWrapper

- HttpServletResponseWrapper
- HttpSessionBindingEvent
- HttpSessionEvent
- HttpUtils

HttpServlet is an abstract class that simplifies the writing of HTTP servlets. As HttpServlet is an abstract class, servlet programmers must override at least one of the following methods: doGet(), doPost(), doPut(), doDelete() and getServletInfo(). The HttpServletRequestWrapper class provides a convenient implementation of the HttpServletRequest interface to adapt a request to a servlet. Similarly, the HttpServletResponseWrapper class provides a convenient implementation of the HttpServletResponse interface to adapt the response from a servlet. The HttpSessionBindingEvent class communicates to the HttpSessionBindingListener object regarding bounding to or unbounding from the HttpSession value. The HttpSessionEvent class represents event notifications for changes in a session within a Web application. As already discussed, the HttpSession interface maintains a session and manages the session with the help of the Cookie class. The HttpUtils class is a collection of static utility methods useful to HTTP servlets.

After learning about the Servlet API, let's discuss the servlet life cycle next.

Explaining the Servlet Life Cycle

Servlets follow a life cycle that governs the multithreaded environment in which the servlets run. It also provides a clear perception about some of the mechanisms available to a developer to share server-side resources.

The primary reason why servlets and JavaServer Pages (JSP) outperform traditional CGI is the servlet life cycle. Servlets follow a three-phase life cycle, namely initialization, service, and destruction. This three-phase life cycle is opposed to the single-phase life cycle. Of the three phases, the initialization and destruction phases are performed only once while the service phase is carried out many times.

The first phase of the servlet life cycle is initialization. It represents the creation and initialization of the resources the servlet may need in response to service requests. All servlets must implement the javax.servlet.Servlet interface, which defines the init() method that corresponds to the initialization phase of a servlet life cycle. As soon as a servlet is loaded in a container, the init() method is invoked before servicing any requests.

The second phase of a servlet life cycle is the service phase. This phase of the servlet life cycle represents all the interactions carried out along with the requests that are handled by the servlet until it is destroyed. The service phase of the servlet life cycle corresponds to the service() method of the Servlet interface. The service() method of a servlet is invoked once for every request. Then, its sole responsibility is to generate the response to that request.

The service() method takes two object parameters, javax.servlet.ServletRequest and javax.servlet.ServletResponse. These two objects represent a request for dynamic resource from a client and a response sent by a servlet to the client, respectively. A servlet is usually multithreaded. This implies that a single instance of a servlet is loaded by a servlet container at a given instance, by default. The initialization of the servlet is done only once, and after that, each request is handled concurrently by threads executing the service() method of the servlet.

The destruction phase is the third and final phase of the servlet life cycle. This phase represents the termination of the servlet execution and its removal from the container. The destruction phase corresponds to the destroy() method of the Servlet interface. The container calls the destroy() method when a servlet is to be removed from the container.

The invocation of the destroy() method enables the servlet to terminate gracefully and clean up any resources held or created by it during execution. To efficiently manage application resources, a servlet should properly use all the three phases of its life cycle. A servlet loads all the required resources during the initialization phase, which may be needed to service client requests. The resources are used during the service phase and then can be given up in the destruction phase.

We have discussed the three events or phases that form the life cycle of a servlet. However, there are many more methods that need to be considered by a Web developer. HTTP is primarily used to access content on the Internet. Though a basic servlet does not know anything about HTTP, a special implementation of the servlet, namely `javax.servlet.http.HttpServlet` has been specifically designed for this purpose.

When the Servlet container creates a servlet for the first time, the container invokes the `init()` method of the servlet. After this, each user request results in the creation of a thread, which calls the `service()` method of the respective instance. Though the servlet in question can implement a special interface, (`SingleThreadModel`), which stipulates that not only a single thread is permitted to run at a time, but also multiple concurrent requests can be made. The `service()` method then calls the `doGet()`, `doPost()`, or any other `doXXX()` method. However, the calling of the doXXX() method depends on the type of HTTP request received. Finally, when the server decides to unload a servlet, it first calls the servlet's `destroy()` method.

Let's now discuss the various methods used in the life cycle of the servlet.

The *init()* Method

As mentioned earlier, the `init()` method is called when a servlet is created for the first time. It is not called again for other user requests. Therefore, the `init()` method is used only for one-time initializations. A servlet is normally created when a user invokes a URL corresponding to the servlet, for the first time; however, the servlet is loaded on the server when a Servlet container maps the user request to the servlet. The following code snippet shows the `init()` method definition:

```
public void init() throws ServletException
{
   // Initialization code...
}
```

Reading server-specific initialization parameters is one of the most common tasks that the `init()` method performs. For example, a servlet might need to know various information details, such as database settings, password files, server-specific performance parameters, hit count files, or serialized cookie data from previous requests.

When you need to read the initialization parameters, you have to first obtain a `ServletConfig` object by using the `getServletConfig()` method, and then call the `getInitParameter()` method on the result. The following code snippet shows how to obtain a `ServletConfig` object:

```
public void init() throws ServletException
{
   ServletConfig config = getServletConfig();
   String param1 = config.getInitParameter("parameter1");
}
```

In the preceding code snippet, notice that the `init()` method uses the `getServletConfig()` method to obtain a reference to the `ServletConfig` object. The object has a `getInitParameter()` method, which can be used to look up the initialization parameters associated with the servlet. Similar to the `getParameter()` method used in the `init()` method of applets, both the input (i.e., the name of the parameter) and the output (i.e., the parameter value) are nothing but Strings.

You can read the initialization parameters by calling the `getInitParameter()` method of the `ServletConfig` object. However, setting up these initialization parameters is the job of the `web.xml` file, which is called Deployment Descriptor, which we discuss in the *Understanding Servlet Configuration* section of this chapter.

The *service()* Method

Each time a server receives a request for a servlet, the server spawns a new thread and calls for the `service()` method. It is possible that the server spawns a new thread by reusing an idle thread from a thread pool. The `service()` method verifies the HTTP request type (`GET`, `POST`, `PUT`, `DELETE`) and accordingly calls the `doGet()`, `doPost()`, `doPut()`, `doDelete()` methods. A normal request for a URL or a request from an HTML form that has no `METHOD` specified results in a `GET` request. Apart from the GET request, an HTML form can also specify POST as the request method type. The following code snippet explains the implementation of the POST method:

```
<html>
<form name="greetForm" method="post">
```

Now, if you have a servlet that needs to handle both POST and GET requests identically, you may be tempted to override the service() method directly rather than implementing both the doGet() and doPost() methods. However, remember, this is not a good idea. Instead, just you can use the doPost() method to call the doGet() method (or vice versa), as shown in the following code snippet:

```
@Override
public void doGet(HttpServletRequest request, HttpServletResponse response)
  throws ServletException, IOException
{
  // Servlet code
}
@Override
public void doPost(HttpServletRequest request, HttpServletResponse response)
  throws ServletException, IOException
{
  doGet(request, response);
}
```

In the preceding code snippet, the @Override annotation is used. Though this approach takes a couple of extra lines of code, it has several advantages over the approach of directly overriding of the service() method. One advantage is that you can add support for other HTTP request methods later by adding the doPut(), doTrace() methods in a subclass. Another advantage of using this approach is that you can add support to retrieve the date on which modifications on data have been made by adding the getLastModified() method. However, overriding the service() method eliminates this option because the getLastModified() method is invoked by the default service() method. Finally, as an added advantage, you can get automatic support for the HEAD, OPTION, and TRACE requests.

NOTE

If a servlet needs to handle both GET and POST identically, the doPost() method should call the doGet() method or vice versa. Remember, you should not override the service()method directly.

During the entire request and response process, most of the time, you only care about the GET or POST requests. Therefore, you override either the doGet() method or the doPost() method or both. However, if required, you can also override the following methods depending upon the request types:

- The doDelete() method for DELETE requests
- The doPut() method for PUT requests
- The doOptions() method for OPTIONS requests
- The doTrace() method for TRACE requests

Remember, however, that you have automatic support for OPTIONS and TRACE.

The doHead() method is not provided in versions 2.1 and 2.2 of the Servlet API, because in those versions the system answers HEAD requests automatically by using the status line and header settings of the doGet() method. However, the doHead() method is included in version 2.3 to enable the generation of responses to HEAD requests.

The destroy() Method

The destroy () method runs only once during the lifetime of a servlet, and signals the end of the servlet instance. A Servlet container holds a servlet instance till the servlet is active or its destroy() method is called. The following code snippet shows the method signature of the destroy() method:

```
public void destroy ()
```

As soon as the destroy() method is activated, the Servlet container releases the servlet instance.

NOTE

It is not recommended to implement the finalize() method in the servlet object; instead, provide the code for the finalization tasks of an application in the destroy() method.

After learning about the life cycle of a servlet, let's understand servlet configuration.

Understanding Servlet Configuration

You may sometimes need to provide initial configuration information for a servlet. The configuration information for the servlet may include a `String` or a set of `String` values, listed in the `web.xml` file as initialization parameters required during the initialization of the servlet. Due to this functionality, servlets are allowed to have initial parameters specified outside of the compiled code and changed without requiring recompiling of the servlet. Each servlet has an object associated with it, called `ServletConfig`. This object is created by the container and implements the `javax.servlet.ServletConfig` interface. The `ServletConfig` object contains the initialization parameter and you can retrieve the reference of the `ServletConfig` object by invoking the `getServletConfig()` method. The following code snippet shows the method provided by the `ServletConfig` object to access an initialization parameter:

```
getInitParameter(String name)
```

The `getInitParameter()` method returns a `String` object that contains the value of the named initialization parameter or null, if the parameter does not exist. The following code snippet shows the getInitParameterNames() method of the ServletConfig object:

```
getInitParameterNames()
```

The `getInitParameterNames()` method returns the names of the initialization parameters of a servlet as an enumeration of `String` objects. An empty enumeration is returned by the method if the servlet has no initialization parameters.

A servlet can define initial parameters by using the `init-param`, `param-name`, and `param-value` elements in the `web.xml file`. Each `init-param` element defines one initial parameter. This initial parameter must contain a parameter name and value specified by the `param-name` and `param-value` child elements, respectively. A servlet may have as many initial parameters as needed. However, note that initial parameter information for a specific servlet should be specified within the `<servlet>` element for that particular servlet.

A servlet can be configured with the help of the `web.xml` file, which lies in the `WEB-INF` directory of a Web application. This file controls many behavioral aspects of the servlet and JSP. Many servers provide graphical interfaces that allow you to specify initialization parameters and control various behavioral aspects of servlets and JSP pages.

These graphical interfaces are server-specific. However, these interfaces also use the `web.xml` file, which is completely portable. The `web.xml` file contains an XML header, a `DOCTYPE` declaration, and a `web-app` element. To specify initialization parameters, the `web-app` element must contain a `<servlet>` element with three subelements, which are as follows:

- servlet-name
- servlet-class
- init-param

The <servlet-name> element specifies the name that helps you to access the servlet. The <servlet-class> element specifies the fully qualified (that is, the package name is included with the servlet class name) class name of the servlet, and the `init-param` element specifies names and values for parameter initialization.

Several changes have been introduced since the Servlet 2.5 specification to the web.xml file format to make its use more convenient. For example, in the previous versions of Java Servlet, only one servlet could be bound to a filter at a time, as shown in the following code snippet:

```
<filter-mapping>
   <filter-name>MyFilter</filter-name>
   <servlet-name>MyServlet</servlet-name>
</filter-mapping>
```

In the preceding code snippet, the MyServlet servlet is mapped to the MyFilter filter; however, in Servlet 3.0, you can bind all servlets at once by using an asterisk. The asterisk is used in the <servlet-name> element to represent all servlets. The following code snippet shows you how to bind all servlets to the MyFilter filter at once:

```
<filter-mapping>
   <filter-name>MyFilter</filter-name>
   <servlet-name>*</servlet-name>
</filter-mapping>
```

Apart from this, Servlet 3.0 provides support for configuring multiple patterns for a filter. In the earlier versions of Java Servlet, you could use the <filter-mapping> element with just one <url-pattern>element, whereas Servlet 3.0 supports multiple <url-pattern> elements. Consider the following example in which multiple <url-pattern> elements have been provided for the MyServlet servlet:

```
<servlet-mapping>
   <servlet-name>MyServlet</servlet-name>
   <url-pattern>/servlet/*<url-pattern>

   <url-pattern>/servlet/*<url-pattern>
</servlet-mapping>
```

Listing 4.1 provides a sample web.xml file, which maps to a single servlet class named FirstServlet:

Listing 4.1: Displaying the Code for the web.xml File

```
<?xml version="1.0" encoding="UTF-8"?>

<web-app version="3.1" xmlns="http://xmlns.jcp.org/xml/ns/javaee"
xmlns:xsi="http://www.w3.org/2001/XMLSchema-instance"
xsi:schemaLocation="http://xmlns.jcp.org/xml/ns/javaee
   http://xmlns.jcp.org/xml/ns/javaee/web-app_3_1.xsd">

   <servlet>
         <servlet-name>FirstServlet</servlet-name>
         <servlet-class>FirstServlet</servlet-class>
   </servlet>
   <servlet-mapping>
         <servlet-name>FirstServlet</servlet-name>
         <url-pattern>/FirstServlet</url-pattern>
   </servlet-mapping>
   <session-config>
         <session-timeout>
               30
         </session-timeout>
   </session-config>
</web-app>
```

In Listing 4.1, the `web.xml` file contains an XML header, a `DOCTYPE` declaration, and a `web-app` element. The `<servlet-name>` element contains the name of the servlet and `<servlet-class>` contains the fully qualified class name of the servlet. The `<servlet-mapping>` element contains two subelements, `<servlet-name>` and `<url-pattern>`. The `<servlet-name>` element contains the name of the servlet as provided in the `<servlet>` element.

Now, let's learn how to create a servlet.

Creating a Sample Servlet

Let's create a simple servlet in the FirstApp application, which handles HTTP request and sets the value of the `name` attribute at the initialization of the servlet, which is displayed on the browser. Moreover, the value of the init-param, `greeting`, is set in the web.xml file. Listing 4.2 provides the code for `FirstServlet` (save the FirstServlet.java file in the `\FirstApp\src\com\kogent` folder):

Listing 4.2: Showing the Code for the FirstServlet.java File

```
package com.kogent;
import java.io.*;
import javax.servlet.*;
import javax.servlet.http.*;
public class FirstServlet extends HttpServlet
{
   @Override
   public void init(ServletConfig config) throws ServletException
```

```
        {
                super.init(config);
                config.getServletContext().setAttribute("name", "Charu Verma");
        }
        @Override
        public void doGet(HttpServletRequest request, HttpServletResponse response) throws
        IOException, ServletException
        {
                response.setContentType("text/html");
                PrintWriter printwrite = response.getWriter();
                printwrite.println("<html>");
                printwrite.println("<head>");
                String greet;
                String name;
                greet = getServletConfig().getInitParameter("greeting");
                name=getServletContext().getAttribute("name").toString();
                printwrite.println("<title>"+greet+"</title>");
                printwrite.println("</head>");
                printwrite.println("<body>");
                printwrite.println("<h1>"+greet+"</h1>");
                printwrite.println("<h2>"+name+"</h2>");
                printwrite.println("</body>");
                printwrite.println("</html>");
        }
    }
```

The FirstServlet servlet class handles the HttpRequest object and so the object is extended with the HttpServlet class. The FirstServlet servlet class overrides the init() and doGet() methods. The value for the `name` attribute is set in the init() method. The doGet() method retrieves the value of the `greeting` initializing parameter, which will be set in the web.xml file. The doGet() method also displays the value of the `name` attribute.

In Listing 4.2, the `getServletContext()` method of the `ServletConfig` object calls the setAttribute() method, to set the value and the `getAttribute()` method to retrieve the value of the `name` attribute. The `getInitParameter()` method is used to retrieve the value of init-param, which will be set in the web.xml file (Listing 4.3).

Create a `JavaEE` folder in the C: drive for the applications that you create in all the chapters of this book.

Now, let's define directory structure for the FirstApp application to store the `FirstServlet` servlet class, configure the servlet in the web.xml file, and then package, deploy, and run the `FirstApp` application.

Exploring Directory Structure

The root directory for all the applications in this book is JavaEE, which is created in the C: drive. The `chapter4` folder is created under this root directory, JavaEE.

Figure 4.6 shows the directory structure of the FirstApp Web application:

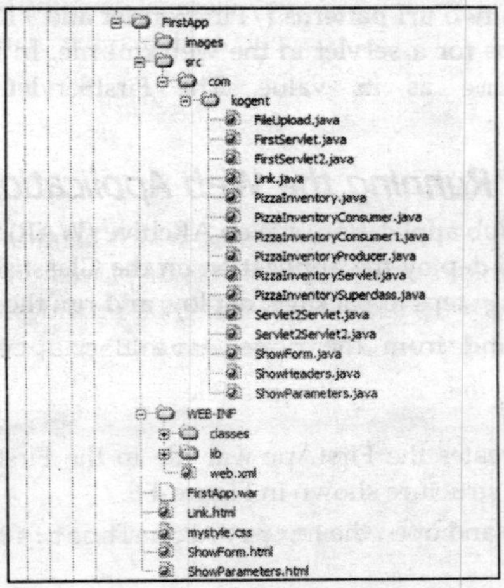

Figure 4.6: Displaying the Directory Structure of the FirstApp Application

In Figure 4.6, FirstApp is the name of the created application. Run the following command from the `C:\JavaEE\chapter4\FirstApp\src\com\kogent` location to compile the FirstServlet servlet:

```
javac -d C:\JavaEE\chapter4\FirstApp\WEB-INF\classes FirstServlet.java
```

The preceding command compiles the `FirstServlet.java` file and creates the `com.kogent` package that contains the class file of `FirstServlet`. The `com.kogent` package is created under the `classes` folder (Figure 4.6).

Configuring the Servlet

Configuration implies mapping a servlet and providing the initialization parameter values for it. Servlet configuration for any Web application is done in the web.xml file. Listing 4.3 shows how to configure the `FirstServlet` servlet (save the web.xml file in the `\FirstApp\WEB-INF` folder):

Listing 4.3: Showing the Code for the web.xml File

```
<?xml version="1.0" encoding="UTF-8"?>

<web-app version="3.1" xmlns="http://xmlns.jcp/org/xml/ns/javaee"

xmlns:xsi="http://www.w3.org/2001/XMLSchema-instance"

xsi:schemaLocation="http:// xmlns.jcp/org/xml/ns/javaee

http:// xmlns.jcp/org/xml/ns/javaee/web-app_3_1.xsd">

  <servlet>
        <servlet-name>FirstServlet</servlet-name>
        <servlet-class>com.kogent.FirstServlet</servlet-class>
        <init-param>
              <param-name>greeting</param-name>
              <param-value>Welcome</param-value>
        </init-param>
  </servlet>
  <servlet-mapping>
        <servlet-name>FirstServlet</servlet-name>
        <url-pattern>/FirstServlet</url-pattern>
        <url-pattern>/FServlet</url-pattern>
  </servlet-mapping>
  <session-config>
        <session-timeout>30</session-timeout>
  </session-config>
</web-app>
```

The web.xml file is saved under the WEB-INF folder of the FirstApp application (Figure 4.6). In Listing 4.3, the FirstServlet servlet is mapped to two url-patterns (/FirstServlet and /FServlet). From Servlet 3.0 onwards, you can provide multiple url patterns for a servlet in the web.xml file. In Listing 4.3, the `greeting` initialization parameter is provided `Welcome` as its value. The FirstServlet servlet class is configured to the com.kogent.FirstServlet class.

Packaging, Deploying and Running the Web Application

Before deploying the FirstApp Web application, a Web ARchive (WAR) file is created to package the entire Web application. Further, you need to deploy the application on the Glassfish Server 4.0 and finally you can run the application. Perform the following steps to package, deploy, and run the FirstApp application.

1. Run the following command from the `code\JavaEE\chapter4\FirstApp` location to create the FirstApp.war file:

   ```
   jar -cvf FirstApp.war .
   ```

   The preceding command creates the FirstApp.war file in the FirstApp folder (Figure 4.6). The WAR file contains the entire directory structure shown in Figure 4.6.
2. Start the Glassfish Server 4.0 and open the `http://localhost:4848/` URL. The Login window appears.

3. Enter `admin` as the user name and `adminadmin` as the password. After logging to the Web application, the Index page of the application is displayed.
4. Select the `Applications` option in the directory tree on the left side of the index page, to deploy the `FirstApp` WAR file, as shown in Figure 4.7:

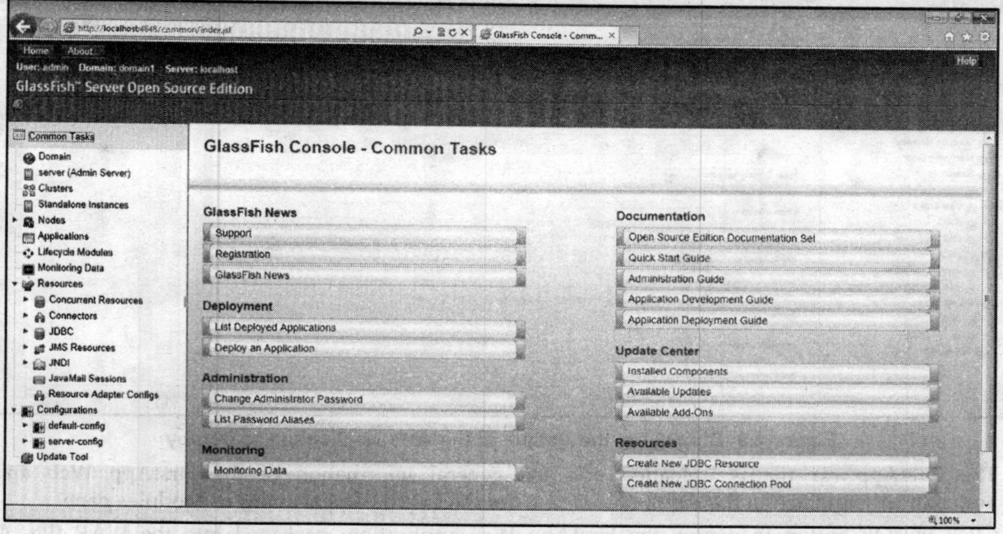

Figure 4.7: Displaying the Admin Console of the Glassfish Server 4.0

After selecting the `Applications` option, the Applications pane is displayed (Figure 4.8).

5. Click the `Deploy` button, as shown in Figure 4.8:

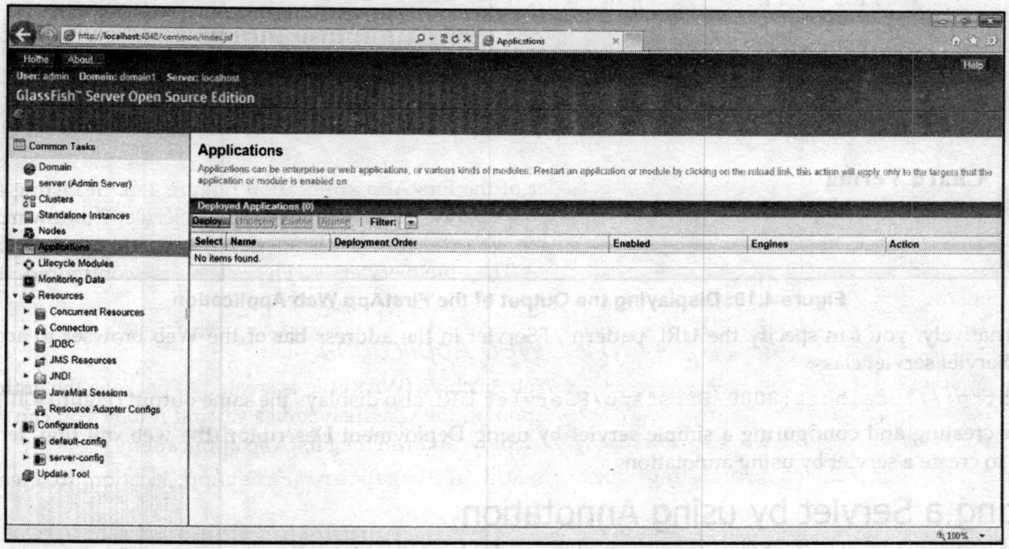

Figure 4.8: Displaying the Applications Window

The Deploy Applications or Modules pane is displayed (Figure 4.9).

6. Click the Browse button and locate the FirstApp.war file. The location for the FirstApp.war file to be deployed is shown in Figure 4.9:

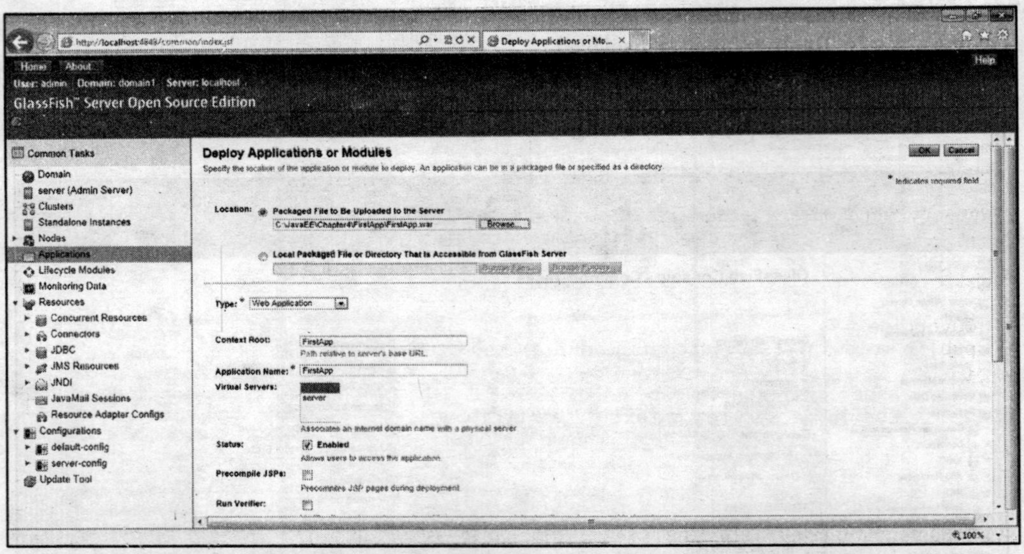

Figure 4.9: Displaying the Details of the Web Application to Deploy

The FirstApp.war file is uploaded and the general information of the FirstApp Web application automatically updated in the required text boxes of the Deploy Applications or Modules pane.

7. Click the Ok button to deploy the FirstApp Web application, packaged into the WAR file. After the application is deployed, you need to run the application to display the output.
8. Open the `http://localhost:8080/FirstApp/FirstServlet` URL. Figure 4.10 displays the output of the FirstApp Web application:

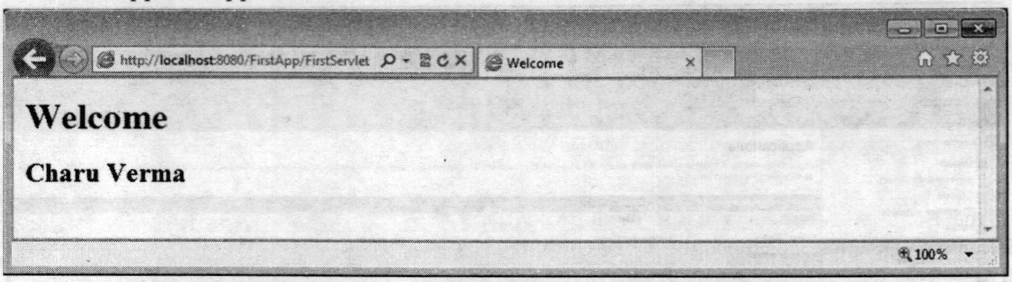

Figure 4.10: Displaying the Output of the FirstApp Web Application

Alternatively, you can specify the URL pattern /FServlet in the address bar of the Web browser to access the FirstServlet servlet class.

The `http://localhost:8080/FirstApp/FServlet` URL also displays the same output (Figure 4.10).

After creating and configuring a simple servlet by using Deployment Descriptor (the web.xml file), let's learn how to create a servlet by using annotations.

Creating a Servlet by using Annotation

Instead of using Deployment Descriptor, a servlet can also be created by using annotations. This is a new feature, introduced in the Servlet 3.0 API, greatly simplifies the creation of a servlet. You need to import two packages, namely `javax.sevlet.http.annotation` and `javax.servlet.http.annotation.jaxrs`, to create a servlet by using annotations. Let's discuss how you can re-create the `FirstServlet` servlet class by using annotations. Listing 4.4 shows the modified code for the FirstServlet `servlet`, saved as the `FirstServlet2.java` file (save the FirstServlet2.java file in the `\FirstApp\src\com\kogent` folder):

Listing 4.4: Displaying the Code for the FirstServlet2.java File

```
package com.kogent;

import java.io.*;
import javax.servlet.*;
import javax.servlet.http.*;
import javax.servlet.annotation.WebServlet;
import javax.servlet.annotation.*;

@WebServlet(name="FirstServlet2", urlPatterns="/FirstServlet2",
        initParams={@WebInitParam(name="greeting",value="welcome") })

public class FirstServlet2 extends HttpServlet
{
  @Override
  public void init(ServletConfig config) throws ServletException
  {
        super.init(config);
        config.getServletContext().setAttribute
                                ("name", "Charu Verma");
  }

        @Override
  public void doGet(HttpServletRequest request, HttpServletResponse response)
        throws IOException, ServletException
  {
        response.setContentType("text/html");
        PrintWriter printwrite = response.getWriter();
        printwrite.println("<html>");
        printwrite.println("<head>");
        String greet;
        String name;
        greet = getServletConfig().getInitParameter("greeting");
        name = getServletContext().getAttribute("name").toString();
        printwrite.println("<title>"+greet+"</title>");
        printwrite.println("</head>");
        printwrite.println("<body>");
        printwrite.println("<h1>"+greet+"</h1>");
        printwrite.println("<h2>"+name+"</h2>");
        printwrite.println("</body>");
        printwrite.println("</html>");
  }
}
```

Save the `FirstServlet2.java` file in the `src\com\kogent` folder (Figure 4.6) and compile the file to generate the .class file. This time, you are not required to provide a mapping for the `FirstServlet2` servlet in the `web.xml` file. Just re-create the FirstApp.war file, deploy the new WAR file, and open the URL http://localhost:8080/FirstApp/FirstServlet2. The same output is displayed that was generated for the FirstServlet servlet class (Figure 4.10).

After learning to create a servlet by using annotations, let's briefly discuss the ServletConfig and ServletContext objects in the next section.

Working with ServletConfig and ServletContext Objects

ServletContext objects help to provide context information in a Servlet container. A `ServletContext` object is used to communicate with the Servlet container while `ServletConfig`, which is a servlet configuration object, is passed to the servlet by the container when the servlet is initialized. A `ServletConfig` object contains a `ServletContext` object, which specifies the parameters for a particular servlet while the `ServletContext` object specifies the parameters for an entire Web application. The `ServletContext` object parameters are available to all the other servlets in that application.

The following code snippet sets an attribute named `name` with the value `Charu Verma`:

```
public void init(ServletConfig config) throws ServletException
```

```
{
   super.init(config);
   config.getServletContext().setAttribute("name", "Charu Verma");
}
```

In the preceding code snippet, the call to the super.init(config) method ensures that the `GenericServlet` class receives a reference to the `ServletConfig` object. The implementation of the `GenericServlet` class maintains a reference to the `ServletConfig` object and requires the invocation of the `super.init(config)` method in subclasses.

In the preceding code snippet, `config` is the instance of `ServletConfig` passed as an argument to the `init()` method. The `setAttribute()` method is used to set the value of the `name` attribute. The value of this attribute is accessed with the help of the getAttribute() method. This attribute is available for all the servlets in the Web application and can be accessed in any servlet.

Now let's learn to work with the `HttpServletRequest` and `HttpServletResponse` interfaces.

Working with the HttpServletRequest and HttpServletResponse Interfaces

We discussed earlier in this chapter that the most common HTTP requests are the `GET` and the `POST` methods. You must implement these methods to handle different types of requests. The servlet container recognizes the type of HTTP request made and passes the request to the correct servlet method. Accordingly, you do not override the `service()` methods as you do for Servlets that extend the `GenericServlet class`; rather, you override the appropriate request methods.

Let's now learn about the `HttpServletRequest` and `HttpServletResponse` interfaces in detail in the following sections.

Using the HttpServletRequest Interface

An `HttpServletRequest` object always represents a client's HTTP request. `HttpServletRequest` is an interface and a subtype of the `ServletRequest` interface. The Web container provider implements this interface to encapsulate all HTTP-based request information, including headers and request methods.

All properties, such as request parameters and attributes of the `ServletRequest` interface are also accessible through the `HttpServletRequest` interface.

Let's learn about the implementation of the HttpServletRequest interface under the following subheads:

- The role of form data
- Form data and parameters
- Headers
- File uploads

The Role of Form Data

You can understand the role of Form Data better by considering a real-life scenario. When you use a search engine, visit an online bookstore, track stocks on the Internet, or ask a Web-based site for quotes on plane tickets, you may have seen funny-looking URLs such as `http://host/path?user=John+Smith&origin=lon&dest=par`. The part of the URL after the question mark (i.e., `user=John+Smith&origin=lon&dest=par`) is known as Form Data (or query data). This is the most common way by which a server-side program gets information from a Web page. For `GET` requests, Form Data can be attached to the end of the URL after a question mark (as in the proceeding example). For `POST` requests, Form Data can be sent to the server separately.

CGI programming involves a tedious traditional approach of extracting the needed information from Form Data. First, you have to read the data one way for `GET` requests (in traditional CGI, this is usually through the `QUERY_STRING` environment variable) and in a different way for `POST` requests (by reading the standard input in traditional CGI). Second, you have to separate the pairs at the ampersands and then separate the parameter names (left of the equal signs) from the parameter values (right of the equal signs). Third, you have the URL-decode values. All the alphanumeric characters are sent unchanged, but spaces are replaced with plus signs and other characters are replaced with `%XX`, where `XX` implies the American Standard Code for Information Interchange (ASCII) or International Organization for Standardization (ISO) Latin-1 value of the character. The process is reversed for the server-side program. For example, if a user enters the values `~jim`, `~robert`, and `~hall` into text fields with the name users in an HTML form, the data is sent as `users=%7Ejim%2C+%7Erobert%2C+and+%7Ehall`, and the original string is reconstituted by the server-side program. Finally, the fourth reason that makes parsing Form Data in CGI programs a tedious process is that values can be omitted (for example `param1=val1&param2=&param3=val3`) or a parameter can have more than one value (for example `param1=val1&param2=val2&param1=val3`). Therefore, special cases need to be applied in your parsing code for these situations.

Form Data and Parameters

One of the important features of servlets is that parsing of a form is handled automatically. You only need to call the `getParameter()` method of the `HttpServletRequest` object with the case-sensitive parameter name as an argument. The `getParameter()` method is used in the same way when data is sent by the `GET` request as when it is sent by the `POST request`. The servlet can identify which request method is used and automatically returns the String value according to the URL-decoded value of the first occurrence of that parameter name. If the parameter exists but has no value, an empty `String` is returned. In addition, if no such parameter exists, null is returned. You should call the `getParameterValues ()` method (which returns an array of Strings) instead of the `getParameters()method` (which returns a single `String`), if the parameter can potentially have more than one value. The return value of the `getParameterValues ()` method is null for parameter names that do not exist. A single element array is returned when only a single value exists for the parameter.

Parameter names are case-sensitive; therefore, for example, `request.getParameter("Param1")` and `request.getParameter("param1")` are not interchangeable.

Finally, for debugging, it is sometimes useful to get a full list of parameters, although most real servlets look for a specific set of parameter names. You can use the `getParameterNames() method` to get the list of parameter names in the form of an enumeration, each entry of which can be cast to a `String` and used in the `getParameter()` or `getParameterValues()` method . You should note that the order in which the parameter names appear within the enumeration is not specified by the `HttpServletRequest` interface.

Let's now discuss the role of request parameters. Perhaps the most commonly used methods of the `HttpServletRequest` object are `getParameter()` and `getParameters()`that involve getting request parameters. Whenever an HTML form is filled and sent to a server, the fields of the form are passed as parameters. This includes any information sent through input fields, selection lists, combo boxes, check boxes, and hidden form fields. However, the form submission excludes file uploads. Any information passed as a query string is also available on the server-side as a request parameter. The `HttpServletRequest` object includes the following methods to access request parameters:

- `getParameter(java.lang.String parameterName)`–Takes a parameter name as a parameter and returns a `String` object representing the corresponding value. This method returns null when it does not find a parameter of the given name.
- `getParameters(java.lang.String parameterName)`–Allows you to get all the parameter values for the same parameter name returned as an array of Strings. The `getParameters()` method is similar to the `getParameter()` method. However, note that the `getParameters()` method should be used when there are multiple parameters with the same name. Often, an HTML form check box or combo box sends multiple values for the same parameter name.
- `getParameterNames()`–Returns the parameter names in the form of an enumeration, which are used in a request. This method can be used with the `getParameter()` and `getParameters()` methods, to obtain a list of names and values of all the parameters included with a request.

Let's now create a servlet that reads and displays all the parameters sent with a request. You can use such a servlet to get a little more familiar with parameters, and to debug HTML forms by seeing the information being sent. Listing 4.5 provides the code for such a servlet (save the ShowParameters.java file in the `\FirstApp\src\com\kogent` folder):

Listing 4.5: Displaying the Code for the ShowParameters.java File

```
package com.kogent;

import java.util.*;
import java.io.*;
import javax.servlet.*;
import javax.servlet.http.*;

public class ShowParameters extends HttpServlet
{

    public void doGet(HttpServletRequest request, HttpServletResponse
    response) throws IOException, ServletException
    {
            response.setContentType("text/html");
            PrintWriter out = response.getWriter();
            out.println("<html>");
            out.println("<head>");
            out.println("<title>Request HTTP Parameters Sent</title>");
            out.println("</head>");
            out.println("<body>");
            out.println("<p>Parameters sent with request:</p>");
            Enumeration enm = request.getParameterNames();

            while (enm.hasMoreElements())
            {
                    String pName = (String) enm.nextElement();
                    String[] pValues = request.getParameterValues(pName);
                    out.print("<b>"+pName + "</b>: ");
                    for (int i=0;i<pValues.length;i++)
                    {
                            out.print(pValues[i]);
                    }
                    out.print("<br>");
            }

            out.println("</body>");
            out.println("</html>");
    }
    public void doPost(HttpServletRequest request, HttpServletResponse
    response) throws IOException, ServletException
    {
            doGet(request, response);
    }
}
```

Save the ShowParameters.java file in the src\com\kogent folder (Figure 4.6) and compile and deploy the `ShowParameters` servlet in the FirstApp Web application with a mapping to the `/ShowParameters` path. Now, create a few simple HTML forms and use the servlet to see the parameters being sent. In Listing 4.6, `ShowParameters.html` provides a sample HTML form (save the ShowParameters.html file in the \FirstApp folder):

Listing 4.6: Showing the Code for the ShowParameters.html File

```
<html>
<head>
   <title>Example HTML Form</title>
</head>
<body>

   <p>To debug a HTML form set its 'action' attribute to reference the
   ShowParameters Servlet.</p>
   <form action="ShowParameters" method="post">
           Name: <input type="text" name="name"><br>
           Password: <input type="password" name="password"><br>
           Select Box:
```

```
                <select name="selectbox">
                <option value="option1">Option 1</option>
                <option value="option2">Option 2</option>
                <option value="option3">Option 3</option>
            </select><br>
            Importance:
            <input type="radio" name="importance" value="very">Very,
            <input type="radio" name="importance" value="normal">Normal,
            <input type="radio" name="importance" value="not">Not<br>
            Comment: <br>
            <textarea name="textarea" cols="40" rows="5"></textarea><br>
            <input value="Submit" type="submit">
        </form>
    </body>
    </html>
```

Save the `ShowParameters.html` file in the base directory of the FirstApp Web application and deploy the new WAR file. After deploying the file, browse the following URL:

http://localhost:8080/FirstApp/ShowParameters.html

The ShowParameters.html page is displayed, as shown in Figure 4.11:

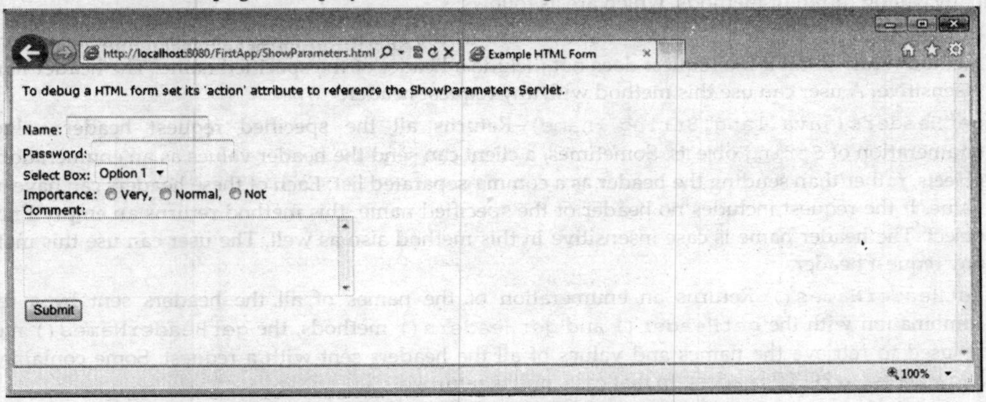

Figure 4.11: Displaying the ShowParameters Page

After entering the relevant details in the HTML form (Figure 4.11), the parameters are sent to the `ShowParameters` servlet. The parameters sent from the ShowParameters.html page are displayed by the ShowParameters Servlet, as shown in Figure 4.12:

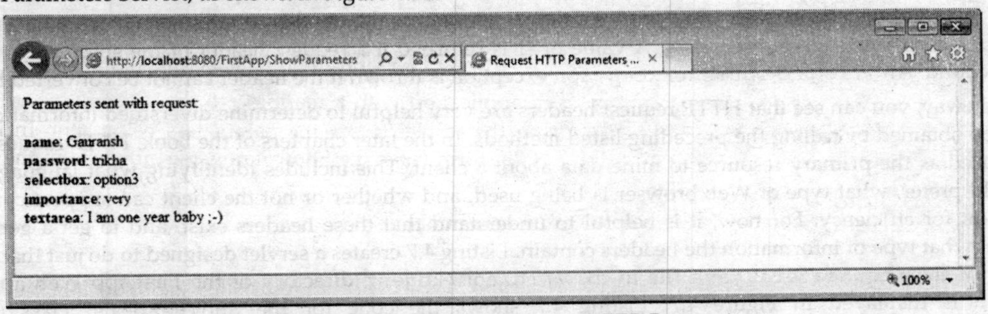

Figure 4.12: Displaying the Request HTTP Parameters

On the server-side, each piece of information received from an HTML form is referenced by the same name as defined in the HTML form and is linked to the value that a user has entered for the respective field. The `ShowParameters` servlet calls the `getParameterNames()` method to retrieve a list of all the parameter names and subsequently calls the `getParameters()` method to retrieve the matching value or set of values for each name. The following code snippet shows the implementation of the `getParameterNames()` method:

```
Enumeration enm = request.getParameterNames();
while (enm.hasMoreElements())
{
   String pName = (String) enm.nextElement();
   String[] pValues = request.getParameterValues(pName);
   out.print("<b>"+pName + "</b>: ");
   for (int i=0;i<pValues.length;i++) { out.print(pValues[i]);}
   out.print("<br>");
}
```

A servlet can fetch information from HTML clients by using parameters. The `ShowParameters` servlet only takes the parameters from the HTML page and displays them back to a client. However, normally, these parameter values are combined and processed with other code to generate responses. Later on in the book, you learn to use this functionality with servlets and JSP to interact with clients, including sending e-mail messages and user authentication.

<h3>HTTP Headers

HTTP headers are set by a client to give information to a server about software that the client is using and how the client wants a server to send back the requested information. HTTP request headers can be accessed from a servlet by calling different methods, which are as follows:

- `getHeader(java.lang.String name)`—Returns the specified request header value as a `String`. This method returns null if the request does not include a header of the specified name. The header name is case insensitive. A user can use this method with any request header.
- `getHeaders(java.lang.String name)`—Returns all the specified request header values as an enumeration of `String` objects. Sometimes, a client can send the header values as an enumeration of String objects, rather than sending the header as a comma-separated list. Each of these headers can have a different value. If the request includes no header of the specified name, this method returns an empty Enumeration object. The header name is case insensitive in this method also as well. The user can use this method with any request header.
- `getHeaderNames()`—Returns an enumeration of the names of all the headers sent by a request. In combination with the `getHeader()` and `getHeaders()` methods, the `getHeaderNames()` method can be used to retrieve the names and values of all the headers sent with a request. Some containers do not allow access to HTTP headers. In that case, null is returned.
- `getIntHeader(java.lang.String name)`—Returns the value of the specified request header as an int type. A value of -1 is returned by this method if the request does not contain a header of the specified name. A `NumberFormatException` exception is thrown if the header cannot be converted to an integer.
- `getDateHeader(java.lang.String name)`—Returns the specified request header value as a long value representing a `Date` object. The returned date is counted as the number of milliseconds since the epoch. The header name is case insensitive. A value of -1 is returned if a request header of the specified name is not found. An `IllegalArgumentException` exception is thrown if the header cannot be converted to a date.

In this way, you can see that HTTP request headers are very helpful to determine diversified information, which can be obtained by calling the preceding listed methods. In the later chapters of the book, HTTP request headers are used as the primary resource to mine data about a client. This includes identifying what language a client would prefer, what type of Web browser is being used, and whether or not the client can support compressed content for efficiency. For now, it is helpful to understand that these headers exist, and to get a general idea about what type of information the headers contain. Listing 4.7 creates a servlet designed to do just that. Save the code of the `ShowHeaders.java` file in the `/src/com/kogent` directory of the FirstApp Web application, which is displayed in Figure 4.7. Listing 4.7 shows the code for the `ShowHeaders` class (save the ShowHeaders.java file in the \FirstApp\src\com\kogent folder):

Listing 4.7: Displaying the Code for the ShowHeaders.java File

```
package com.kogent;
import java.util.*;
import java.io.*;
import javax.servlet.*;
import javax.servlet.http.*;
```

```
public class ShowHeaders extends HttpServlet
{
    public void doGet(HttpServletRequest request, HttpServletResponse
    response) throws IOException, ServletException
    {
            response.setContentType("text/html");
            PrintWriter out = response.getWriter();
            out.println("<html>");
            out.println("<head>");
            out.println("<title>Request's HTTP Headers</title>");
            out.println("</head>");
            out.println("<body>");
            out.println("<p>HTTP headers sent by your client:</p>");
            Enumeration enm = request.getHeaderNames();
            while (enm.hasMoreElements())
            {
                    String headerName = (String) enm.nextElement();
                    String headerValue = request.getHeader(headerName);
                    out.print("<b>"+headerName + "</b>: ");
                    out.println(headerValue + "<br>");
            }
            out.println("</body>");
            out.println("</html>");
    }
}
```

Compile the ShowHeaders servlet class and configure the servlet to the `/ShowHeaders` path in the web.xml file. The following code snippet provides the configuration of the ShowHeaders servlet class in the web.xml file:

```
...
<servlet>
   <servlet-name>ShowHeaders</servlet-name>
   <servlet-class>com.kogent.ShowHeaders</servlet-class>
</servlet>
<servlet-mapping>
   <servlet-name>ShowHeaders</servlet-name>
   <url-pattern>/ShowHeaders</url-pattern>
</servlet-mapping>
```

Deploy the FirstApp Web application and after reloading the Web application, browse to `http://localhost:8080/FirstApp/ShowHeaders` to view a listing of all the HTTP headers sent by your browser. Figure 4.13 shows the details of the HTTP headers:

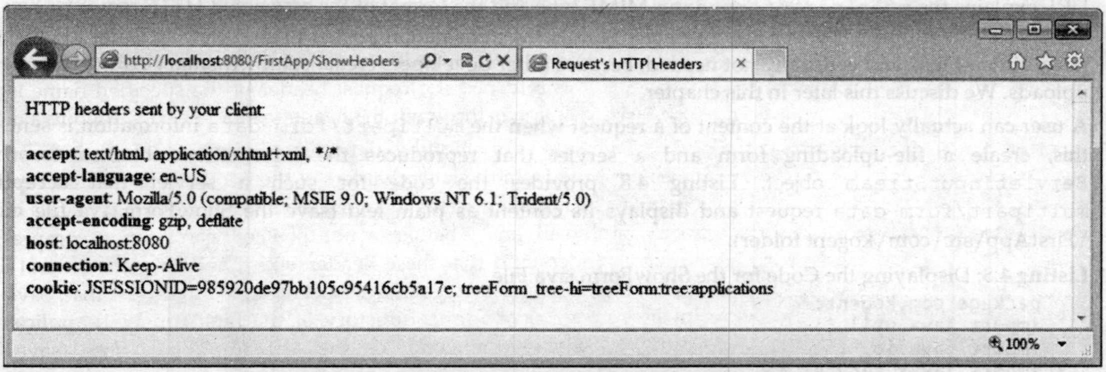

Figure 4.13: Displaying the Request's HTTP Headers

Listing 4.7 is a good example to illustrate how headers are normally sent by a Web browser. They are self-descriptive and can therefore be understood easily. You can probably imagine how these headers can be used to infer browser and internationalization information. Table 4.1 lists some of the most relevant request headers:

Table 4.1: Various Request Headers

Request header	Description
`Accept`	Specifies certain media types that can be accepted for a response. Accept headers can be used to specify that the request is limited to a set of desired media types.
`Accept-Charset`	Indicates the character sets that can be accepted for a response. This header accepts clients that can understand comprehensive or special-purpose character sets. Due to this, the server can represent responses in those character sets. All user agents can accept the ISO-8859-1 character set.
Referer (sic)	Allows a client to state the address (URI) of the resource from which the Request URI was obtained.
`Accept-Language`	Restricts the set of natural languages that are preferred as a response to a request. Otherwise, this header is similar to the Accept header.
`Host`	Specifies the Internet host and port number of a requested resource, as obtained from the original URL given by a user or referring resource. This header is mandatory for HTTP 1.1.
`User-Agent`	Contains information about the user agent (or browser) making a request. This header is used for statistical purposes, to trace violations of protocol, and to automatically recognize user agents.

File Uploads

File uploads are simple for HTML developers but difficult for server-side developers. Usually, discussions on Servlets and HTML forms conveniently skip the topic of file uploads. However, a servlet developer must have a good understanding of HTML form file uploads. For example, consider a situation where a client needs to upload something besides a simple string of text, such as a picture. In this case, using the `getParameter()` method will not work because it produces unpredictable results. Therefore, to read the picture uploaded the Servlet API provides the MIME type.

There are two primary MIME types for form information, `application/x-www-form-urlencoded` and `multipart/form-data`. In the MIME type `application/x-www-form-urlencoded`, the results in the Servlet API automatically parse out name and value pairs. The information is then available by invoking `HttpServletRequest.getParameter()` or any of the other related methods as described earlier. The second MIME type, `multipart/form-data`, is usually considered difficult, because the Servlet API does not provide any support for it. The information is left as it is and you are responsible for parsing the request body by using either the `getInputStream()` or `getReader()` method.

The Request For Comments (RFC) 1867 memo provided at the `http://www.ietf.org/rfc/rfc1867.txt` URL explains the `multipart/form-data` MIME type and the format of the associated HTTP requests. You can determine how to properly and appropriately handle the information posted to a servlet, by using RFC. This is not a difficult task and is usually not needed, because other developers create complementary APIs to handle file uploads. We discuss this later in this chapter.

A user can actually look at the content of a request when the `multipart/form-data` information is sent. For this, create a file-uploading form and a servlet that reproduces the information obtained from the `ServletInputStream` object. Listing 4.8 provides the code for such a servlet that accepts a `multipart/form-data` request and displays its content as plain text (save the ShowForm.java file in the \FirstApp\src\com\kogent folder):

Listing 4.8: Displaying the Code for the ShowForm.java File

```
package com.kogent;
import java.util.*;
import java.io.*;
import javax.servlet.*;
import javax.servlet.http.*;

public class ShowForm extends HttpServlet
{
   public void doPost(HttpServletRequest request, HttpServletResponse
   response) throws IOException, ServletException {
         response.setContentType("text/plain");
```

```
            PrintWriter out = response.getWriter();

            ServletInputStream sis = request.getInputStream();
            for (int i = sis.read(); i != -1; i = sis.read()) {
                    out.print((char)i);
            }
    }
    public void doGet(HttpServletRequest request, HttpServletResponse
    response) throws IOException, ServletException {
                    doPost(request, response);
    }
}
```

Save the preceding code as `ShowForm.java` in the `/src/com/kogent` directory of the FirstApp Web application. Configure the ShowForm servlet to `/ShowForm` in the web.xml file by using the following code snippet:

```
...
<servlet>
   <servlet-name>ShowForm</servlet-name>
   <servlet-class>com.kogent.ShowForm</servlet-class>
</servlet>
<servlet-mapping>
   <servlet-name>ShowForm</servlet-name>
   <url-pattern>/ShowForm</url-pattern>
</servlet-mapping>
```

Now, any information posted by any form can be viewed by directing the request to `http://localhost:8080/FirstApp/ShowForm`. You can run the `ShowForm` servlet only after creating an HTML form used to upload a file. Listing 4.9 provides the code to create an HTML page (save the ShowForm.html file in the \FirstApp folder):

Listing 4.9: Displaying the Code for the ShowForm.html File

```
<html>
   <head>
         <title>Example HTML Form</title>
                  </head>
   <body>
         <p>The ShowForm Servlet will display the content posted by an HTML
         form. Try it out by choosing a file (smaller size is preferred) to
         reference the ShowForms Servlet.</p>
         <form action="ShowForm" method="post"
                  enctype="multipart/form-data">
                  Name: <input type="text" name="name"><br>
                  File: <input type="file" name="file"><br>
                  <input value="Submit" type="submit">
         </form>
   </body>
</html>
```

Save the code shown in Listing 4.9 as `ShowForm.html` in the base directory of the FirstApp Web application and browse the `http://localhost:8080/FirstApp/ShowForm.html` URL. A small HTML form with two inputs, a name and a file to upload is displayed, as shown in Figure 4.14:

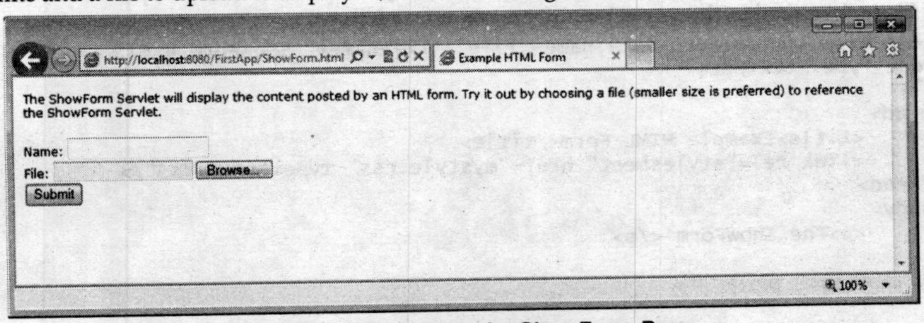

Figure 4.14: Displaying the ShowForm Page

Enter appropriate values for the `Name` and `File` fields in the form (Figure 4.14). In this case, a small file is preferred because its content is going to be displayed by the `ShowForm` Servlet. A good candidate for a file to be uploaded is `ShowForm.html`. After entering the values, click the `Submit` button to show the content of the uploaded file. For example, using `ShowForm.html` as the file displays a form similar to the one shown in Figure 4.15:

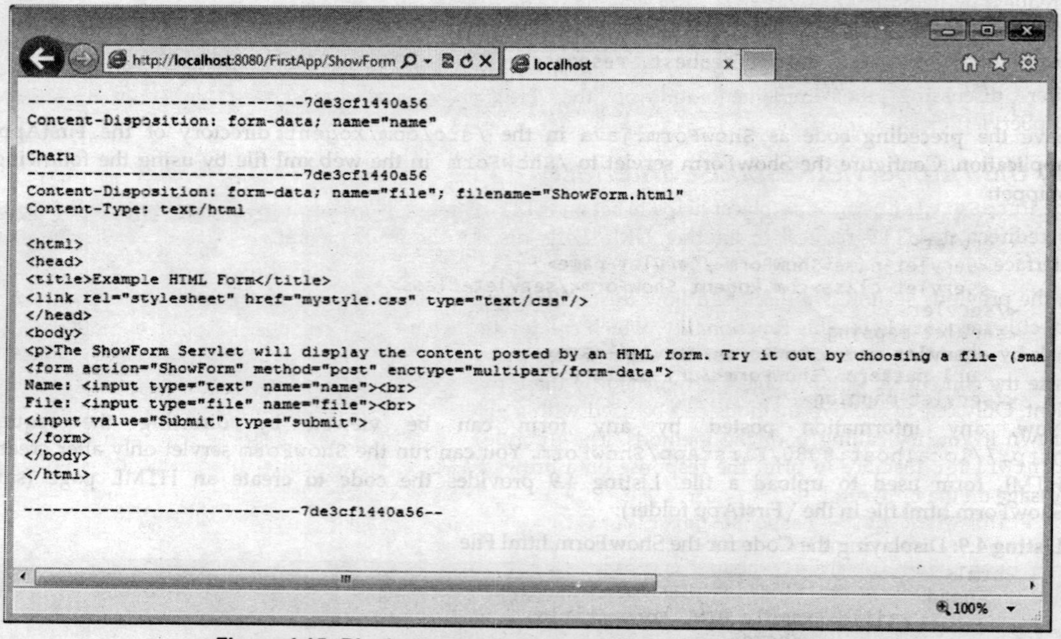

Figure 4.15: Displaying the Output of the ShowForm.html File

The following line is displayed in Figure 4.15 depicting the unique token for the start portion of the multipart of the uploaded file:

```
-----------------------------7de3cf1440a56 .
```

The preceding line declares the start of the multipart section and concludes at the ending token, which is identical to the start but has -- appended to it. Between the starting and ending tokens are sections of data (possibly nested multiparts) with headers used to describe the content. For example, the Content-Disposition header is displayed as follows:

```
Content-Disposition: form-data; name="name"

Charu
```

The Content-Disposition header defines the information as part of the form and is identified by the name "name". The value of `name` is the content that follows it. By default, the MIME type of `name` is text/plain. The uploaded file is described in the second multipart, shown as follows:

```
Content-Disposition:form-data;name="file"; filename=" ShowForm.html"
Content-Type: text/html
<html>
  <head>
       <title>Example HTML Form</title>
       <link rel="stylesheet" href="mystyle.css" type="text/css"/>
  </head>
  <body>
       <p>The ShowForm </p>
. . .
. . .
```

In the preceding code snippet, the Content-Disposition header specifies the form field name to be filled, which corresponds to the field name listed in the HTML form, and describes Content-Type as text/html, as it is not text/plain. The output after the Content-Type header includes code of the `ShowForm.html file`.

So far, you have learned how the `HttpServletRequest` object is used to retrieve HTML form parameters from a request by using the `getParameter()` method. The `HttpServletRequest` object is also used to retrieve HTTP request header information, upload a file by using the `getInputStream()` method, and display the content of the uploaded file by using the `getWriter()` method of the `HttpServletResponse` object.

After discussing the implementation of the HttpServletRequest interface, let's learn about the HttpServletResponse interface.

Using the HttpServletResponse Interface

The `HttpServletResponse` object helps to set an HTTP response header, set the content type of the response, or redirect an HTTP request to another URL. Let's discuss the implementation of the HttpServletResponse interface.

In the previous section, we discussed how to send information back to a client. The `HttpServletResponse` object is responsible for this functionality, which creates an empty HTTP response. Custom content can be sent back by obtaining an output stream by using either the `getWriter()` or `getOutputStream()` method to write the content. A suitable object is returned by these two methods to send either text or binary content to a client. Only one of the two methods can be used with a given `HttpServletResponse` object. An exception is thrown if you try calling both the methods. The `HttpServletResponse` object is also used to provide an `PrintWriter` instance to print the response on a browser. The following code snippet displays the welcome message on the browser:

```
PrintWriter out = response.getWriter();
        out.println("<html>");
        out.println("<head>");
        out.println("<title>Welcome Message</title>");
        out.println("</head>");
        out.println("<body>");
        out.println("<p>Welcome to the Users</p>");
```

In the preceding code snippet, the `getWriter()` method is used to get an output stream to send the HTML markup. When you use an instance of the `PrintWriter` object, you need to provide a `String` object and call the `print()`, `println()`, or `write()` method.

In this section, you learn about the implementation of the HttpServletResponse interface under the following headings:

- Response header
- Response redirection
- Response redirection translation issues
- Auto-refresh/wait pages

Response Header

The `HttpServletResponse` object is used to manipulate the HTTP headers of a response and to send the content back to a client. HTTP response headers inform a client the type and amount of content being sent, and the type of server sending the content.

The `HttpServletResponse` object includes the following methods to manipulate HTTP response headers:

- `addHeader(java.lang.String name, java.lang.String value)`—Adds a response header having the given name and value. This method can be used to create response headers with multiple values.
- `containsHeader(java.lang.String name)`—Returns a `Boolean` value that indicates whether the named response header is already been set or not.
- `setHeader(java.lang.String name, java.lang.String value)`—Sets the name and value of a response header as specified in the arguments. The previous value is overwritten, if the header is already

set. The `containsHeader()` method can be used to test whether a header is already present or not, before setting its value.

- `setIntHeader(java.lang.String name, int value)`–Sets the name and integer values for a response header, as specified in the arguments. The previous value is overwritten, if the header is already set. The `containsHeader()` method can be used to test whether a header is already present or not, before setting its value.
- `setDateHeader(java.lang.String name, long date)`–Sets the given name and date values for a response header. The date is provided in terms of milliseconds since the epoch. The previous value is overwritten with the new value, if the header is already set.
- `addIntHeader(java.lang.String name, int value)`–Adds a response header having the name and integer values, as specified in the arguments. Response headers can be assigned multiple values when created by using this method.
- `addDateHeader(java.lang.String name, long date)`–Adds a response header having the name and date values, as specified in the arguments. The previous response header values are not overwritten and response headers can have multiple values.

Table 4.2 provides a description of the HTTP response header fields and their values:

Table 4.2: Response Header Fields and their Values

Header Field	Header Value
`Age`	Represents the estimated time since the last response generated from the server. The value of this header field is usually a positive integer.
`Content-Length`	Indicates the size of the message body, in decimal number of octets (8-bit bytes), sent to a recipient.
`Content-Type`	Refers to the MIME type corresponding to the content of an HTTP response. A browser can use this value to determine whether the content is rendered internally or launched to be rendered by an external application.
`Date`	Represents the date and time at which a message originated.
`Location`	Specifies the location of a new resource in case HTTP response codes redirect a client to such a resource. The location is specified as an absolute address.
`Pragma`	Specifies the implementation-specific directives that may be applied to any recipient along the request-response chain. *No-cache,* which indicates that a resource should not be cached, is the most commonly used value.
`Retry-After`	Indicates the tentative duration for which a service is unavailable to a requesting client. It is used with a 503 (Service Unavailable) response. A date can be returned as a value of this field. The value can also be an integer representing the number of seconds (in decimals) after the time of the response.
`Server`	Represents information about the server that generated the current response, as a String value.

Response Redirection

In this section, the response code of HTTP and its different functions have been discussed. The `setStatus()` method of an `HttpServletResponse` object can be used to send any HTTP response code to a client. The servlet sends back a status code 200, OK if everything works smoothly. A status code of 302 is sent by the servlet displaying the Resource Temporarily Moved message, which informs a client that the resource they were looking for is not at the requested URL, but can be found at the URL specified by the Location header in the HTTP response. The 302 response code is very helpful because almost every Web browser automatically follows the new link without informing the user. This allows a servlet to take the request of a user and forward it to any other resource on the Internet.

The 302 response code has excellent uses besides its intended purpose. The reason for this is that the 302 response code has a very common implementation. Most websites often track the users who visit their sites to get an idea about their interests so that they can send information related to their interests. The technique for tracking website users requires the extracting of the referrer header of an HTTP request. This can be done easily by keeping track of the information sent by a site. The problem originates because the link on a site that directs to an external resource also sends a request back to the originating site from where it was sent. To solve the problem, a clever trick can be used that relies on the HTTP 302 response code. In this trick, rather than providing direct links to external resources, all links can be encoded in such a way that they all lead to the same servlet on your site, but at the same time, the real link can be included as a parameter. After that, link tracking can be implemented by providing the intended link through a servlet. In addition, a 302 status code is sent back to the client along with the real link to visit.

HTTP-aware sites commonly use a servlet to track links. The HTTP 302 response code is used very often because it provides the `sendRedirect()` method in the `HttpServletResponse` object. The `sendRedirect()` method takes one parameter, a `String`, representing the new URL, and automatically sets the HTTP 302 status code with appropriate headers. Using the `sendRedirect()` method and the `java.util.Hashtable` class, it is easy to create a servlet to track the links used. Let's create a servlet, named Link, to understand the use of the `sendRedirect()` method. Listing 4.10 shows the code for the `Link.java` file (save the Link.java file in the \FirstApp\src\com\kogent folder):

Listing 4.10: Displaying the Code for the Link.java File

```
package com.kogent;
import java.util.*;
import java.io.*;
import javax.servlet.*;
import javax.servlet.http.*;

public class Link extends HttpServlet
{
   static private Hashtable links = new Hashtable();

   String stamp;
   public Link()
   {
        stamp = new Date().toString();
   }

   public void doGet(HttpServletRequest request, HttpServletResponse
   response) throws IOException, ServletException
   {
        String lnk = request.getParameter("link");
        if (lnk != null && !lnk.equals(""))
        {
                synchronized (links)
                {
                        Integer count = (Integer) links.get(lnk);
                        if (count == null)
                        {
                                links.put(lnk, new Integer(1));
                        }
                        else
                        {
                                links.put(lnk, new
                                Integer(1+count.intValue()));
                        }
                }
                response.sendRedirect(lnk);
        }
        else
        {
                response.setContentType("text/html");
                PrintWriter out = response.getWriter();
                request.getSession();
                out.println("<html>");
                out.println("<head>");
                out.println("<title>Links Tracker Servlet</title>");
                out.println("</head>");
```

```
                        out.println("<body>");
                        out.println("<p>Links Tracked Since");
                        out.println(stamp+":</p>");
                        if (links.size() != 0) {
                              Enumeration enm = links.keys();
                              while (enm.hasMoreElements())
                              {
                                    String key = (String)enm.nextElement();
                                    int count =
                                    ((Integer)links.get(key)).intValue();
                                    out.println(key+" : "+count+" visits<br>");
                              }
                        }
                        else {
                              out.println("No links have been tracked!<br>");
                        }
                        out.println("</body>");
                        out.println("</html>");
                  }
            }
            public void doPost(HttpServletRequest request, HttpServletResponse
            response) throws IOException, ServletException {
                  doGet(request, response);
            }
      }
```

Some links used by the `Link` servlet class are needed to complement the `Link` servlet. The links can be encoded properly to redirect a user to any resource. Encoding the links only requires passing the real link as a link parameter in a query `String`. The code given in Listing 4.11 is that of a simple HTML page that includes a few properly encoded links. Save the HTML code provided in Listing 4.11 as `Link.html` in the base directory of the FirstApp Web application. Listing 4.11 shows the code for the `Link.html` file (save the Link.html file in the \FirstApp folder):

Listing 4.11: Displaying the Code for the Link.html File

```
   <html>

      <head>
            <title>Some Links Tracked by the Link Servlet</title>
                  </head>
      <body>
            Some good links for Servlets and JSP. Each link is directed through
            the Link Servlet. Click on a few and visit the
      <a href="Link">Link Servlet</a>.
            <ul>
                  <li><a href="Link?link=http://www.java.sun.com">
                  Java Product Site</a></li>
                  <li><a href="Link?link=http://www.javaplanet.com">
                  Java Planet</a></li>
                  <li><a href="Link?link=http://java.sun.com">
                  Sun Microsystems</a></li>
            </ul>
      </body>

   </html>
```

After creating the new FirstApp.war file and deploying the FirstApp Web application, browse the `http://localhost:8080/FirstApp/Link.html` URL. The Link.html page that comprises multiple links is displayed as shown in Figure 4.16 :

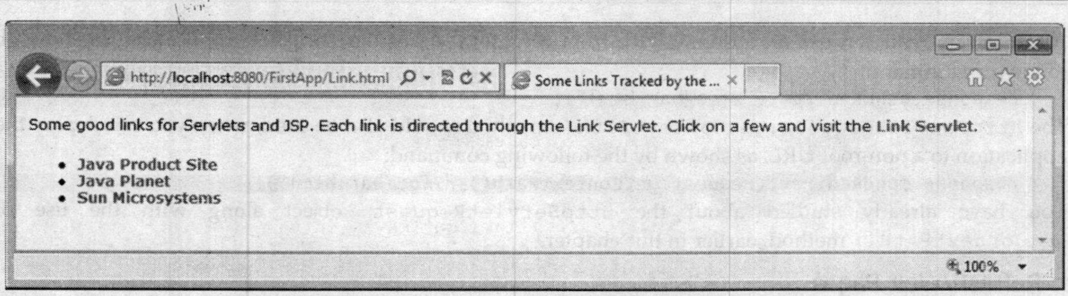

Figure 4.16: Displaying the Link.html Page

Each link on the Link.html page is directed through the Link servlet, which in turn redirects a browser to visit the correct link. Before each redirection, the `Link` servlet logs the number of times the link has been visited by keying the link URL to an Integer object in a hashtable. You can browse the `http://localhost:8080/FirstApp/Link URL`, to view information about the links visited. The results are same as of the last reloading of the `Link` servlet. This servlet does not log the information for long-term use.

After clicking each link on the Link.html page multiple times, click the `Link Servlet` link. You are redirected to the `Link` servlet, as shown in Figure 4.17:

Figure 4.17: Displaying the Link Servlet

Now, let's discuss the concerns related to response redirection translation.

Response Redirection Translation Issues

Response redirection is tool that intimates a user about the resource to which a response is to be redirected. It works with any implementation of the Servlet API. However, there is a specific bug that arises while using relative response redirection. Consider the following command, which is used to redirect response:

```
response.sendRedirect("../foo/bar.html");
```

The preceding command works perfectly when used in some servlets but not in others. The problem comes from using the relative back `../` to traverse back a directory. A JSP page can use this command correctly; (you have to assume that the browser translates the URL correctly) but the JSP page can use it only if the requested URL is combined with the correct path and ends on an appropriate resource. For instance, if `http://localhost:8080/foo/bar.html` is a valid URL, then `http://localhost:8080/foo/../foo/bar.html.` should also be valid. However, `http://localhost:8080/foo/foo/../foo/bar.html` will not reach the same resource.

This might seem an irrelevant problem. However, request dispatching that we introduce in the next section makes it clear why this is an issue. Request dispatching allows requests to be forwarded on the server-side, which means that the requested URL does not change, but the server-side resource that handles the request can be changed. Relative redirections are not always safe; using `../` can be bad. The solution is to either use absolute redirections or a complete URL, as shown by the following command:

```
response.sendRedirect("http://localhost/foo/bar.html");
```

Alternatively, you can use an absolute URL from the root, "/", of the foo Web application, as shown by the following command:

```
response.sendRedirect("/foo/bar.html");
```

The HttpServletRequest.getContextPath() method should also be used, when you can deploy the Web application to a non-root URL, as shown by the following command:

```
response.sendRedirect(request.getContextPath()+"/foo/bar.html");
```

You have already studied about the HttpServletRequest object along with the use of the getContextPath() method, earlier in this chapter.

Auto-Refresh/Wait Pages

The other useful response header technique is to send a wait page or a page that auto-refreshes to a new page after a given time period to a user. This tactic is helpful in cases when there is a possibility of getting a response which might take an uncontrollable time to generate or for cases where you want to ensure a brief pause in a response. In this case, the entire mechanism involves setting the refresh response header. The header can be set by using the following command:

```
response.setHeader("Refresh", "time; URL=url" );
```

In the preceding command, time is replaced with the amount of seconds the page should wait, and url is replaced with the URL that the page should eventually load. For instance, if you want to load the http://localhost/foo.html URL after waiting for 10 seconds, the header is set by using the following command:

```
response.setHeader("Refresh", "10; URL=http://localhost:8080/foo.html");
```

The technique of sending a page that auto-refreshes is very helpful because it allows a proper message to be conveyed to clients until their requests are being processed. For example, a simple your-request-is-being-processed-page, which automatically refreshes to display the results of the response after a few seconds, can be displayed to the client. Alternatively, the client has to wait until a request is completely processed, before sending back any content. The alternative approach is used in most of the cases. However, this approach requires the client browser to wait for the response. Due to this, sometimes the client may assume that the request may result as timed-out, and may make a time-consuming request twice.

Another practical use for a wait page is to slow down a request. This is done by a developer to get better and more relevant information. For example, a wait page that displays either an advertisement or legal information before redirecting a user to the desired page.

NOTE

In some situations, the Refresh response header can prove to be helpful. Sometimes it can be considered as the de facto standard; however, it is not a standard HTTP 1.1 header.

Now, let's learn how to delegate a request to a resource and discuss request scopes.

Exploring Request Delegation and Request Scope

Request delegation refers to the request of a single client passing through many servlets or other resources in a Web application. The entire process is performed entirely on the server-side, unlike response redirection. Request delegation does not require any action from a client or extra information sent between the client and the server. Request delegation is available through the javax.servlet.RequestDispatcher object, which can be obtained by calling any of the following methods of the ServletRequest object:

- getRequestDispatcher(java.lang.String path)—Returns the RequestDispatcher object for the path provided as an argument. The path value must start from the base directory / and can direct to any resource in a Web application.
- getNamedDispatcher(java.lang.String name)—Returns the RequestDispatcher object for the named servlet. The servlet-name elements of the web.xml file define the valid names.

The following two methods are provided by a RequestDispatcher object to include different resources and to forward a request to a different resource:

- forward(javax.servlet.ServletRequest,javax.servlet.ServletResponse)–Delegates a request and response to the resource of the RequestDispatcher object. A call to the forward() method may be used only if no content is previously sent to a client. After the completion of the processing of the forward() method, no further data can be sent to the client.
- include(javax.servlet.ServletRequest,javax.servlet.ServletResponse)–Works similar to the forward() method, but has some restrictions. Any number of resources can be included by a servlet by using the include() method; however, the resource cannot set headers or commit a response.

While a request delegation is often used to break a large servlet into smaller and more relevant parts, a simple case involves separating a common HTML header that is being shared by all the pages of a website. The include() method of the RequestDispacher object provides a convenient method to include the header in any other servlet that needs the header. In the case of request delegation, any future changes to the header are automatically reflected on all the servlets. A much more elegant solution to this problem is provided by JSPs. In practice, a servlet request delegation is usually used to break large servlets into smaller and relevant parts.

In addition to this, simple server-side components include request delegations, which are a key part of server-side Java implementations of popular design patterns. As far as Java Servlet and JSP are concerned, design patterns are commonly agreed-upon methods to build Web applications that are robust in functionality and easily maintainable.

You may already know that there are well-defined scopes for variables in Java. Local variables are declared inside methods and are by default only available inside the scope of that method. Instance variables, declared in a class but outside a method or Constructor, are available to all methods in a Java class. There are many other possible scopes as well. These scopes help to keep track of objects and to allow JVM to accurately carry out garbage-collection of the memory. Apart from the various Java variable scopes, such as local and global, the servlets also provide some new scopes. The request scope is introduced by a request delegation.

The request scope and the other scopes are not officially marked by the Servlet specification. A set of methods defined by the servlet specification in the javax.servlet package allow you to bind objects to and retrieve objects from various containers (that are themselves objects) . As an object bound in this manner is referenced by the container it is bound to, the bound object is not destroyed until the reference is removed. Therefore, bound objects are in the same scope as the container they are bound to. For example, the HttpServletRequest object is bound to a container and includes the methods of the HttpServletRequest interface. The methods of the HttpServletRequest object can be used to bind, access, and remove objects to and from the request scope that is shared by all servlets to which a request is delegated. This is an important concept and can easily be shown in the Servlet2Servlet class, created in Listing 4.12.

A request scope can be defined as a method in which an object is passed between two or more servlets with the assurance that the object goes out of scope (that is, it will be garbage-collected) after the last servlet has performed its task. In later chapters, more examples of this concept are provided. Let's first create the Servlet2Servlet servlet that passes an object to another servlet, Servlet2Servlet2. Listing 4.12 provides the code for the Servlet2Servlet.java file (save the Servlet2Servlet.java file in the \FirstApp\src\com\kogent folder):

Listing 4.12: Displaying the Code for the Servlet2Servlet.java File

```
package com.kogent;
import java.io.*;
import javax.servlet.*;
import javax.servlet.http.*;

public class Servlet2Servlet extends HttpServlet
{
  public void doGet(HttpServletRequest request, HttpServletResponse
  response) throws IOException, ServletException
  {
        response.setContentType("text/html");
        String param = request.getParameter("value");

        if(param != null && !param.equals(""))
        {
```

```
                request.setAttribute("value", param);
                RequestDispatcher rd =
        request.getRequestDispatcher("/Servlet2Servlet2");
                rd.forward(request, response);
                return;
        }

        PrintWriter out = response.getWriter();
        out.println("<html>");
        out.println("<head>");
        out.println("<title>Servlet #1</title>");
        out.println("</head>");
        out.println("<body>");
        out.println("<h1>A form from Servlet #1</h1>");
        out.println("<form>");
        out.println("Enter a value to send to Servlet #2.");
        out.println("<input name=\"value\"><br>");
        out.print("<input type=\"submit\" ");
        out.println("value=\"Send to Servlet #2\">");
        out.println("</form>");
        out.println("</body>");
        out.println("</html>");
    }
}
```

Compile the Servlet2Servlet servlet and map it to the `/Servlet2Servlet` URL pattern in the web.xml file by using the following code snippet:

```
...
<servlet>
  <servlet-name>Servlet2Servlet</servlet-name>
  <servlet-class>com.kogent.Servlet2Servlet</servlet-class>
</servlet>

<servlet-mapping>
  <servlet-name>Servlet2Servlet</servlet-name>
  <url-pattern>/Servlet2Servlet</url-pattern>
</servlet-mapping>
```

Listing 4.13 shows the code for the `Servlet2Servlet2.java` file (save the `Servlet2Servlet2.java` file in the \FirstApp\src\com\kogent folder):

Listing 4.13: Displaying the Code for the Servlet2Servlet2.java File

```
package com.kogent;

import java.io.*;
import javax.servlet.*;
import javax.servlet.http.*;

public class Servlet2Servlet2 extends HttpServlet
{

  public void doGet(HttpServletRequest request, HttpServletResponse
  response) throws IOException, ServletException
  {
        response.setContentType("text/html");
        PrintWriter out = response.getWriter();
        out.println("<html>");
        out.println("<head>");
        out.println("<title>Servlet #2</title>");
        out.println("</head>");
        out.println("<body>");
        out.println("<h1>Servlet #2</h1>");
        String value = (String)request.getAttribute("value");
        if(value != null && !value.equals(""))
        {
                out.print("Servlet #1 passed a String object via ");
                out.print("request scope. The value of the String is: ");
```

```
                out.println("<b>"+value+"</b>.");
        }

        else
        {
                out.println("No value passed!");
        }
        out.println("</body>");
        out.println("</html>");
    }
}
```

Now, save the code given in Listing 4.13, with the name `Servlet2Servlet2.java` in the `/src/com/kogent` directory of the `FirstApp` Web application. In addition, compile the Servlet2Servlet2 servlet and map it to the `/Servlet2Servlet2` URL pattern in the web.xml file, as provided in the following code snippet:

```
...
<servlet>
   <servlet-name>Servlet2Servlet2</servlet-name>
   <servlet-class>com.kogent.Servlet2Servlet2</servlet-class>
</servlet>
<servlet-mapping>
   <servlet-name>Servlet2Servlet2</servlet-name>
   <url-pattern>/Servlet2Servlet2</url-pattern>
</servlet-mapping>
```

Redeploy the FirstApp Web application and the application is ready for execution. Next, browse the `http://localhost:8080/FirstApp/Servlet2Servlet` URL. Figure 4.18 shows the servlet response that appears similar to a simple HTML form asking you to enter a value to pass to the second servlet:

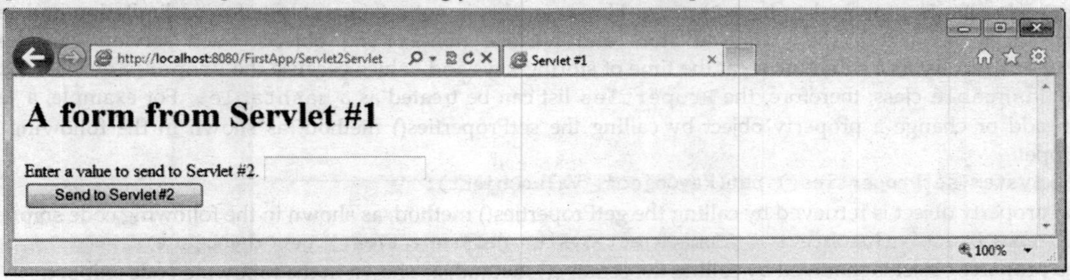

Figure 4.18: Displaying the Output of the `Servlet2Servlet` Servlet

Type a value in the `Enter a value to send to Servlet#2` text box to send to the second servlet. In our case, we have entered the value, Charu. Now, click the `Send to Servlet #2` button. The second servlet appears, as shown in Figure 4.19:

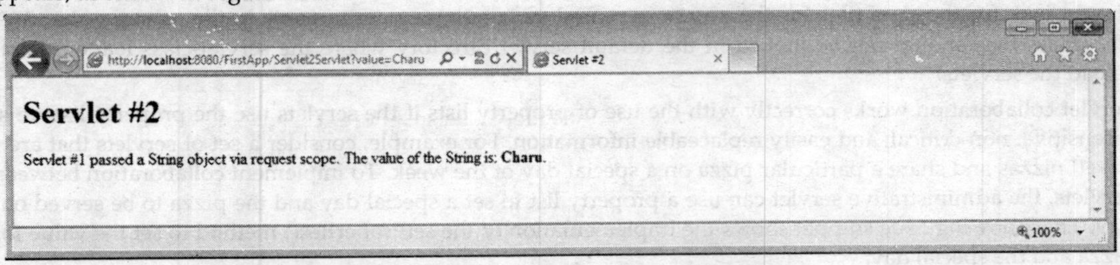

Figure 4.19: Displaying Servlet 2 in Progress

The preceding example demonstrates how the value of one servlet is passed to the other servlet. After discussing the concept of request delegation and request scope, let's now learn how to share information among servlets by using the servlet collaboration technique.

Implementing Servlet Collaboration

Servlet sometimes cooperate with each other by sharing information. This sort of cooperation is known as servlet collaboration. The collaborating servlets can pass the shared information between each other through method invocations; however, to do this, each servlet is required to know about the servlets with which it is collaborating. This adds unnecessary burden on the server. Several other techniques can be used to carry out for servlet collaboration. Let's discuss these techniques in the following sections.

Collaboration through the System Properties List

A simple way for servlets in collaboration to share information is by using Java's system-wide `Properties` list. The `Properties` list is found in the `java.lang.System` class and holds standard system properties, such as `java.version` and `path.separator` as well as application-specific properties. Servlets can use the Properties list to hold the information they need to share. A servlet can add or change a property by using the setProperties() method, as shown in the following code snippet:

```
System.setProperties().put("key", "value");
```

The concerned servlet, or some other servlet running in the same JVM, can later get the value of the property by calling the `getProperties()` method, as shown in the following code snippet:

```
String value = System.getProperty("key");
```

The property can also be removed, by calling the remove() method, as shown in the following code snippet:

```
System.getProperties().remove("key");
```

Generally, you should include a prefix while defining the key for a property, which contains the name of the servlet's package and the name of the collaboration group, for example, `com.kogent.Servlet.ShoppingCart`. The `Properties` class is `String`-based, which implies that each key and value is supposed to be a `String`. However, this is not a commonly enforced limitation and can be ignored by servlets if they want to store and retrieve non-`String` objects. Such servlets can use the `Properties` list as a `hashtable` at the time of storing keys and values because the `Properties` class extends the `Hashtable` class; therefore, the `Properties` list can be treated as a `hashtable`. For example, a servlet can add or change a property object by calling the setProperties() method, as shown in the following code snippet:

```
System.setProperties().put(keyObject, valueObject);
```

The property object is retrieved by calling the getProperties() method, as shown in the following code snippet:

```
SomeObject valueObject = (SomeObject)System.getProperties().get(keyObject);
```

The property object is removed by calling the remove() method, as shown in the following code snippet:

```
System.getProperties().remove(keyObject);
```

Due to the misuse of the `Properties` list, the `getProperty()`, `list()` and `save()` methods of the `Properties` class throw the `ClassCastException` exception and it is also assumed that each key and value is of the `String` type. Due to this reason, you should use some other technique for Servlet collaboration. JVM should look for the class files for the `keyObject` and `valueObject` arguments in the server's `CLASSPATH`. The class files should not be looked in the default servlet directory where the servlet-class loaders load and reload the servlets.

Servlet collaboration works correctly with the use of property lists if the servlets use the property lists to share insensitive, non-critical, and easily replaceable information. For example, consider a set of servlets that are used to sell pizzas and share a particular pizza on a special day of the week. To implement collaboration between the servlets, the administrative servlet can use a property list to set a special day and the pizza to be served on that day. The following code snippet shows the implementation of the setProperties() method to set the value for the pizza and the special day:

```
System.setProperties().put("com.kogent.ServingPizza.special.pizza", "Cheese pizza");
System.setProperties().put("com.kogent.ServingPizza.special.day", new Date());
```

Now, every other servlet on the server is able to access the `special` properties and display it with the code shown in the following code snippet:

```
String pizza = System.getProperty("com.kogent.ServingPizza.special.pizza");
Date day = (Date)System.getProperties().get("com.kogent.ServingPizza.special.day");
DateFormat df = DateFormat.getDateInstance(DateFormat.SHORT);
```

```
String today = df.format(day);
prnwriter.println("Our pizza special today (" + today + ") is: " + pizza);
```

In the preceding code snippet, the System.getProperty() method is used to retrieve the value of the com.kogent.ServingPizza.special.pizza key.

Collaboration through a Shared Object

Sharing information through a shared object is another way for servlets to collaborate with one another. A shared object can hold a pool of shared information and make it available to each servlet as required. In a sense, the system `Properties` list is a special case example of a shared object. To manipulate an object's data, the shared object often incorporates some business logic or rules. By incorporating a rule that the shared object's data be available only through well-defined methods, the rule protects the shared object's data. The rule helps to protect data integrity and triggers events so that they can handle certain conditions. Moreover, various data manipulations can be abstracted into a single method invocation. This capability is not available in the case of the `Properties` list. The garbage collector is an important aspect of collaborating through a shared object. If at any time a loaded servlet does not reference the object, then the servlet can reclaim it. Therefore, every servlet that uses a shared object must save a reference to the object to keep the garbage collector at bay.

Let's consider the previous example in which we used servlets to sell pizzas. Collaboration between servlets to maintain a shared inventory of ingredients can be implemented through a shared object. For this, you first need to create a shared `PizzaInventory` class. The `PizzaInventory` class is defined to maintain the ingredient count and display the count through public methods. An example of the `PizzaInventory` class is shown in Listing 4.14. Notice that this class is a singleton (a class that has just one instance). This makes it easy for every servlet sharing the class to maintain a reference to the same instance.

Now, let's discuss the shared inventory class. Listing 4.14 shows the code for PizzaInventory.java (save the PizzaInventory.java file in the \FirstApp\src\com\kogent folder):

Listing 4.14: Displaying the Code for the PizzaInventory.java File

```
package com.kogent;

public class PizzaInventory
{
  // Protect the constructor, so no other class can call it
  private PizzaInventory() { }

  // Create the only instance, save it to a private static variable
  private static PizzaInventory instance = new PizzaInventory();

  // Make the static instance publicly available
  public static PizzaInventory getInstance() { return instance; }

  // How many servings of each item do we have?
  private int cheese = 0;
  private int wheatflour = 0;
  private int beans = 0;
  private int capsicum = 0;

  // Add to the inventory
  public void addCheese(int added) { cheese += added };
  public void addWheatflour(int added) { wheatflour += added };
  public void addBeans(int added) { beans += added };
  public void addCapsicum(int added) { capsicum += added };

  // Called when it is time to make a pizza.
  // Returns true if there are enough ingredients to make the pizza,
  // false if not. Decrements the ingredient count when there are enough.
  Synchronized public boolean makePizza()
  {
        // Pizza requires one serving of each item
        if (cheese > 0 && wheatflour > 0 && beans > 0 && capsicum > 0)
        {
              Cheese--; wheatflour--; beans--; capsicum--;
```

```
                return true;             // can make the pizza
            }
            else
            {
                // could order more ingredients
                return false;            // cannot make the pizza
            }
        }
    }
```

Save the PizzaInventory.java file in the src\com\kogent directory of the FirstApp Web application. PizzaInventory maintains an inventory count for four pizza ingredients: `cheese`, `wheatflour`, `beans`, and `capsicum`. The PizzaInventory class holds the count of the ingredients with the private instance variables. Information of the count should be kept in an external database to maintain a record of the quantity of ingredients used to produce pizzas. Each ingredient's inventory count is increased by using the `addCheese()`, `addWheatflour()`, `addBeans()`, and `addCapsicum()` methods. These methods may be called from a servlet accessed by the ingredient prepared in the day.

In the `makePizza()` method, the value of the inventory counts are decreased together. The role of this method is to check whether or not there are enough ingredients to make a full pizza. If there is, then the method decreases the ingredient count and returns `true`. However, if the ingredients are insufficient, then the `makePizza()` method returns `false` (in an improved version, the method may choose to order more ingredients). The `makePizza()` method may be called by a servlet selling pizzas over the Internet, and perhaps also by a servlet communicating with the check-out cash register. Remember that, similar to all the other non-servlet-class files, the class file for `PizzaInventory` is placed somewhere in the server's `CLASSPATH` (such as `server_root/classes`). Listing 4.15 shows you how a servlet adds ingredients to the inventory.

Let's now create a servlet to add some ingredients to a shared inventory. Listing 4.15 shows the code for the `PizzaInventoryProducer.java` file (save the `PizzaInventoryProducer.java` file in the \FirstApp\src\com\kogent folder):

Listing 4.15: Displaying the Code for the PizzaInventoryProducer.java File

```
package com.kogent;
import java.io.*;
import java.util.*;
import javax.servlet.*;
import javax.servlet.http.*;
import com.kogent.* ;

public class PizzaInventoryProducer extends HttpServlet
{
  // Get (and keep) a reference to the shared PizzaInventory instance

  PizzaInventory inventory = PizzaInventory.getInstance();

  public void doGet(HttpServletRequest req, HttpServletResponse res)
  throws ServletExcveption, IOException
  {
        res.setContentType("text/html");
        PrintWriter prnwriter = res.getWriter();

        prnwriter.println("<HTML>");
        prnwriter.println("<HEAD><TITLE>Pizza Inventory Producer
                             </TITLE></HEAD>");

        // Produce random amount of each item
        Random random = new Random();

        int cheese = Math.abs(random.nextInt() % 10);
        int wheatflour = Math.abs(random.nextInt() % 10);
        int bean = Math.abs(random.nextInt() % 10);
        int capsicum = Math.abs(random.nextInt() % 10);

        // Add the item sto the inventory
```

```
            inventory.addCheese(cheese);
            inventory.addWheatflour(wheatflour);
            inventory.addBeans(beans);
            inventory.addCapsicum(capsicum);

            // Print the production results
            prnwriter.println("<BODY>");
            prnwriter.println("<H1>Added ingredients:</H1>");
            prnwriter.println("<PRE>");
            prnwriter.println("cheese: " + cheese);
            prnwriter.println("wheatflour: " + wheatflour);
            prnwriter.println("beans: " + beans);
            prnwriter.println("capsicum: " + capsicum);
            prnwriter.println("</PRE>");
            prnwriter.println("</BODY></HTML>");
      }
   }
```

Save the PizzaInventoryProducer.java file in the src\com\kogent directory of the FirstApp Web application and compile the PizzaInventory and PizzaInventoryProducer servlets. The following code snippet is used to map the PizzaInventoryProducer servlet to the /PizzaInventoryProducer by using the <url-pattern> element in the web.xml file:

```
...
<servlet>
   <servlet-name>PizzaInventoryProducer</servlet-name>
   <servlet-class>com.kogent.PizzaInventoryProducer </servlet-class>
</servlet>

<servlet-mapping>
   <servlet-name>PizzaInventoryProducer</servlet-name>
   <url-pattern>/PizzaInventoryProducer</url-pattern>
</servlet-mapping>
```

Create a new FirstApp.war file and redeploy the FirstApp Web application. Now, browse the `http://localhost:8080/FirstApp/PizzaInventoryProducer` URL to see the output.

A random amount of each ingredient (somewhere between zero to nine servings) is produced and added to the inventory, whenever the `PizzaInventoryProducer` servlet is accessed. Figure 4.20 shows the result of executing the PizzaInventoryProducer servlet:

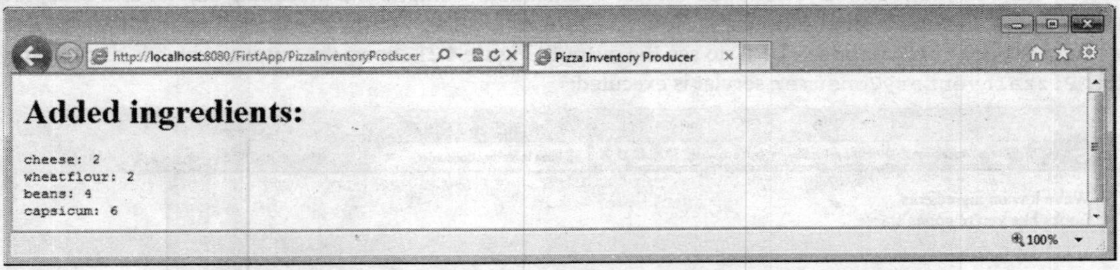

Figure 4.20: Displaying the Output of the PizzaInventoryProducer Servlet

The `PizzaInventoryProducer` servlet plays the important role of maintains a reference to the shared `PizzaInventory` instance. This implies that the `PizzaInventory` instance cannot be reclaimed by the garbage collector until the servlet is loaded.

Now, let's create a servlet that calls the `makePizza()` method, informing the inventory that it wants to make a pizza. The `PizzaInventoryConsumer`.java file provides the code for the servlet. Save the `PizzaInventoryConsumer`.java file in the `src\com\kogent` directory of the `FirstApp` Web application. Listing 4.16 shows the code for the `PizzaInventoryConsumer`.java file (save the `PizzaInventoryConsumer`.java file in the \FirstApp\src\com\kogent folder):

Listing 4.16: Displaying the Code for the PizzaInventoryConsumer.java File

```
   package com.kogent ;
```

```
import java.io.*;
import javax.servlet.*;
import javax.servlet.http.*;
import com.kogent.* ;

Public class PizzaInventoryConsumer extends HttpServlet
{
  // Get (and keep) a reference to the shared PizzaInventory instance
  private PizzaInventory inventory = new PizzaInventory.getInstance();

  public void doGet(HttpServletRequest req, HttpServletResponse res)
  throws ServletException, IOException
  {
        res.setContentType(“text/html”);
        PrintWriter prnwriter = res.getWriter();

        prnwriter.println(“<HTML>”);
        prnwriter.println(“<HEAD><TITLE>Pizza Inventory Consumer
                          </TITLE></HEAD>”);

        prnwriter.println(“<BODY><BIG>”);

        if(inventory.makePizza())
        {
               prnwriter.println(“Your pizza will be ready
                                   in a few minutes.”);
        }
        else
        {
               prnwriter.println(“We’re low on ingredients.<BR>”);
               prnwriter.println(“Looks like you’re gonna starve.”);
        }
        prnwriter.println(“</BIG></BODY></HTML>”);
  }
}
```

The `PizzaInventoryConsumer` servlet does not need to decrease the ingredients count by itself. It maintains a reference to the `PizzaInventory` instance. This implies that the `PizzaInventory` instance can be referenced even if the `PizzaInventoryProducer` servlet is unloaded. Compile the preceding servlet and redeploy the `FirstApp` Web application. Now, browse the `http://localhost:8080/FirstApp/PizzaInventoryConsumer` URL to see the output. Figure 4.21 shows the output, which is displayed when the `PizzaInventoryConsumer` servlet is executed:

Figure 4.21: Displaying the Output of the PizzaInventoryConsumer Servlet

You can also make a servlet act as a shared object. There is an added advantage of using a shared servlet. Sharing allows a servlet to maintain its state by using its `init()` and `destroy()` methods. In addition, each time a shared servlet is accessed, the servlet can print its current state. Let's re-create the PizzaInventory servlet to implement the concept of sharing a servlet.

Listing 4.17 shows the code for the re-created `PizzaInventoryServlet.java` file (save the `PizzaInventoryServlet.java` file in the \FirstApp\src\com\kogent folder):

Listing 4.17: Displaying the Code for the PizzaInventoryServlet.java File

```
package com.kogent;

import java.io.*;
import javax.servlet.*;
import javax.servlet.http.*;


public class PizzaInventoryServlet extends HttpServlet
{

   // How many "servings" of each item do we have?
   private int cheese = 0;
   private int wheatflour = 0;
   private int beans = 0;
   private int capsicum = 0;

   // Add to the inventory as more servings are prepared.
   public void addCheese(int added) { cheese += added; }
   public void addWheatflour(int added) { wheatflour += added; }
   public void addBeans(int added) { beans += added; }
   public void addCapsicum(int added) { capsicum += added; }

   // Called when it is time to make a pizza.
   // Returns true if there are enough ingredients to make the pizza,
   // false if not. Decrements the ingredient count when there are enough.
   synchronized public boolean makePizza()
   {
                 // Pizza requires one serving of each item
                 if (cheese > 0 && wheatflour > 0 && beans > 0 && capsicum > 0)
         {
                        cheese--; wheatflour--; beans--; capsicum--;
                        return true;  // can make the pizza
                 }
                 else
         {
                        // Could order more ingredients
                        return false;  // cannot make the pizza
                 }
   }

   // Display the current inventory count.
   public void doGet(HttpServletRequest req, HttpServletResponse res)
   throws ServletException, IOException
   {
                 res.setContentType("text/html");
                 PrintWriter prnwriter = res.getWriter();

                 prnwriter.println("<HTML><HEAD><TITLE>Current
                          Ingredients</TITLE></HEAD>");
                 prnwriter.println("<BODY>");
                 prnwriter.println("<TABLE BORDER=1>");
                 prnwriter.println("<TR><TH COLSPAN=2> Current ingredients:</TH>
                          </TR>");
                 prnwriter.println("<TR><TD>Cheese:</TD><TD>" + cheese + "</TD>
                          </TR>");
                 prnwriter.println("<TR><TD>Wheatflour:</TD><TD>" + wheatflour +
                         "</TD></TR>");
                 prnwriter.println("<TR><TD>Beans:</TD><TD>" + beans + "</TD></TR>");
                 prnwriter.println("<TR><TD>Capsicum:</TD><TD>" + capsicum +
                         "</TD></TR>");
                 prnwriter.println("</TABLE>");
                 prnwriter.println("</BODY></HTML>");
   }

   // Load the stored inventory count
```

```
public void init(ServletConfig config) throws ServletException
{
            super.init(config);
            loadState();
}

public void loadState()
{
            // Try to load the counts
            FileInputStream file = null;
            try
     {
            file = new
              FileInputStream("PizzaInventoryServlet.state");
            DataInputStream in = new DataInputStream(file);
            cheese = in.readInt();
            wheatflour = in.readInt();
                  beans = in.readInt();
            capsicum = in.readInt();
            file.close();
            return;
            }
            catch (IOException ignored)
     {
            // Problem during read
            }
            finally
     {
            try
            {
                  if (file != null) file.close();
            }
            catch (IOException ignored) { }
            }
}

public void destroy()
{
            saveState();
}

public void saveState()
{
            // Try to save the counts
            FileOutputStream file = null;
            try
     {
            file = new
              FileOutputStream("PizzaInventoryServlet.state");
            DataOutputStream prnwriter = new DataOutputStream(file);

            prnwriter.writeInt(cheese);
            prnwriter.writeInt(wheatflour);
            prnwriter.writeInt(beans);
            prnwriter.writeInt(capsicum);
            return;
            }
            catch (IOException ignored)
     {
```

```
                    // Problem during write
                    }
                    finally
               {
                    try
                    {
                         if (file != null) file.close();
                    }
                    catch (IOException ignored) { }
                    }
          }
     }
```

Now, save the PizzaInventoryServlet.java file in the src\com\kogent directory of the FirstApp Web application. Then, redeploy the FirstApp Web application and view the output by accessing the http://localhost:8080/FirstApp/PizzaInventoryServlet URL. The PizzaInventoryServlet servlet is no longer a singleton but a normal HTTP servlet, which defines an init() method that loads its state as well as a destroy() method that saves its state. Figure 4.22 shows the output of the PizzaInventoryServlet servlet:

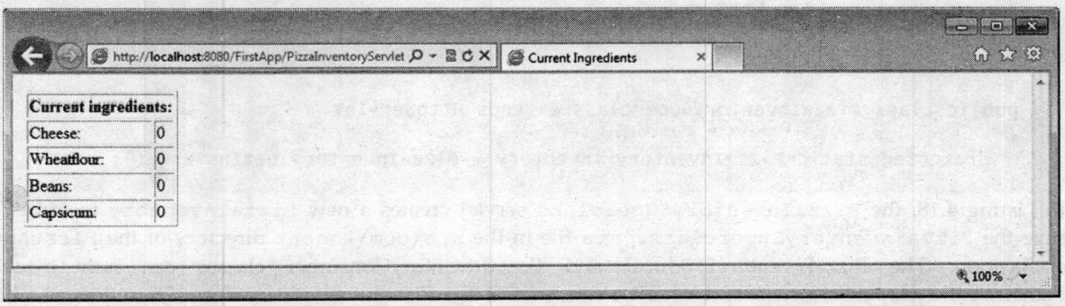

Figure 4.22: Displaying the Output from PizzaInventoryServlet, Showing its State

Remember that even as a servlet, the PizzaInventoryServlet.class file should remain in the server's standard CLASSPATH. This is required to keep the PizzaInventoryServlet servlet from being reloaded. Both the PizzaInventoryProducer and PizzaInventoryConsumer classes can get a reference to the PizzaInventoryServlet servlet. The following code snippet shows how to reuse the PizzaInventoryServlet servlet:

```
// Get the inventory Servlet instance if we haven't before
if (inventory == null)
{
   inventory = ( PizzaInventoryServlet)
               ServletUtils.getServlet("PizzaInventoryServlet",
               req, getServletContext());

   // If the load was unsuccessful, throw an exception
   if (inventory == null)
   {
        throw new ServletException
        ("Could not locate PizzaInventoryServlet");
   }
}
```

In the preceding code snippet, instead of calling PizzaInventory.getInstance() method, the producer and consumer classes can ask the PizzaInventoryServlet instance from the server.

Collaboration through Inheritance

Collaborating through inheritance is perhaps the easiest technique of servlet collaboration. In the inheritance technique, each servlet requiring collaboration can extend the same class and opt for inheriting the same shared information. This simplifies the code of the collaborating servlets and allows only the proper subclasses to access the shared information. Moreover, the common superclass can hold a reference to the shared information or hold the shared information itself.

In the following sections, you learn to collaborate with servlets through inheritance in two ways, by inheriting a shared reference and by inheriting the shared information.

Inheriting a Shared Reference

In case of inheriting a shared reference, a common superclass can hold any number of references to shared business objects, which are easily made available to its subclasses. Such a superclass is shown in Listing 4.18, which we can use for our `PizzaInventory` example.

Listing 4.18 shows the code for `PizzaInventorySuperclass.java` (save the `PizzaInventorySuperclass.java` file in the \FirstApp\src\com\kogent folder):

Listing 4.18: Displaying the Code for the PizzaInventorySuperclass.java File

```
package com.kogent;

import javax.servlet.*;
import javax.servlet.http.*;
import com.kogent.* ;


public class PizzaInventorySuperclass extends HttpServlet
{
  protected static PizzaInventory inventory = PizzaInventory.getInstance();
}
```

In Listing 4.18, the `PizzaInventorySuperclass` servlet creates a new `PizzaInventory` instance. Now, save the `PizzaInventorySuperclass.java` file in the `src\com\kogent` directory of the `FirstApp` Web application. The PizzaInventoryProducer and PizzaInventoryConsumer classes can now extend the PizzaInventorySuperclass class and inherit a reference to the PizzaInventory instance. To understand how the PizzaInventoryProducer class can extend and inherit the reference to the PizzaInventory instance, the code for the PizzaInventoryConsumer servlet is revised in Listing 4.19.

Listing 4.19 shows the revised code for `PizzaInventoryConsumer.java` (save the `PizzaInventoryConsumer.java` file in the \FirstApp\src\com\kogent folder):

Listing 4.19: Displaying the Code for the PizzaInventoryConsumer.java File

```
package com.kogent ;

import java.io.*;
import javax.servlet.*;
import javax.servlet.http.*;

public class PizzaInventoryConsumer extends PizzaInventorySuperclass
{
  public void doGet(HttpServletRequest req, HttpServletResponse res)
        throws ServletException, IOException
  {
              res.setContentType("text/html");
              PrintWriter prnwriter = res.getWriter();

              prnwriter.println("<HTML>");
              prnwriter.println("<HEAD><TITLE>Pizza Inventory Consumer
                          </TITLE></HEAD>");

              prnwriter.println("<BODY><BIG>");

              if (inventory.makePizza())
        {
```

```
                prnwriter.println("Your pizza will be ready in a
                                        few minutes.");
            }
            else
            {
                        prnwriter.println("We're low on ingredients.<BR>");
                        prnwriter.println("Looks like you're gonna starve.");
                }

                prnwriter.println("</BIG></BODY></HTML>");
        }
    }
```

The `PizzaInventory` class does not have to be a singleton anymore. The reason is that subclasses naturally inherit the same instance. The class file for the `PizzaInventorySuperclass` class should be put in the server's `CLASSPATH`. This is required to keep the `PizzaInventorySuperclass` class from being reloaded.

Inheriting Shared Information

Apart from allowing servlets to hold shared references, you can also inherit the shared information. For this, you can use a common superclass to hold the shared information by itself and optionally make it available through inherited business logic methods.

The following code snippet shows how the `PizzaInventorySuperclass` class holds its own shared information:

```
    public class PizzaInventorySuperclass extends
            HttpServlet {
        // How many "servings" of each item do we have?
        private static int cheese = 0;
        private static int wheatflour = 0;
        private static int beans = 0;
        private static int capsicum = 0;

        // Add to the inventory as more servings are prepared.
        protected static void addCheese(int added) { cheese += added; }
        protected static void addWheatflour(int added) { wheatflour
                                                          += added; }
        protected static void addBeans(int added) { beans += added; }
        protected static void addCapsicum(int added) { capsicum
                                                         += added; }

        // Called when it is time to make a pizza.
        // Returns true if there are enough ingredients to make the pizza,
        // false if not. Decrements the ingredient count when there are enough.
        synchronized static protected boolean makePizza()     {
            // ...etc...
        }
        // ...The rest matches PizzaInventoryServlet...
```

Now, let's discuss the difference between the `PizzaInventorySuperclass` and `PizzaInventoryServlet` servlets to analyze what changes are required to inherit the shared information in a servlet. There are only two differences between the two servlets, which are as follows:

- All the variables and methods of the `PizzaInventorySuperclass` servlet are static, which is not the case with the `PizzaInventoryServlet` class. This guarantees that only one inventory is maintained for all the subclasses.
- All the methods of the `PizzaInventorySuperclass` servlet are protected. This implies that the methods will be available only to the subclasses.

With this, we come to the end of the chapter. Let's now recap the main points of the chapter in a short summary.

Summary

This chapter has discussed the latest version of the Java Servlet API, version 3.1. you have first explored the general features of a Java Servlet, after which the features of Servlet 3.1 have been discussed. The chapter has then explained the classes and packages of the Servlet API that are used to develop Web applications. You have also learned about the life cycle of a servlet and configuring a servlet in the web.xml file. Apart from this, you have learned to create a sample servlet, first by mapping it in the web.xml file and then by using annotations. The chapter has also listed the noteworthy interfaces of the Servlets. At the end of the chapter, you have learned about request delegation, request scope and servlet collaboration.

The next chapter discusses to implement the session handling in Servlets 3.1.

Quick Revise

Q1. The two arguments passed to the `forward()` method of the `RequestDispatcher` class are objects of the ………………………………………………………. classes.

A. HttpServletRequest and HttpServletResponse **B. HttpServletResponse and PrintWriter**

C. ServletContext and ServletConfig **D. HttpServletRequest and ServletContext**

Ans. The correct option is A.

Q2. To get an object of the `PrintWriter` class, we use the `getWriter()` method of the ………………………. class.

A. HttpServletRequest **B. HttpServletResponse**

C. SessionContext **D. HttpSession**

Ans. The correct option is B.

Q3. A life cycle method of a servlet is ………………………………… .

A. init() **B. service()**

C. `destroy()` **D. Above All**

Ans. The correct option is D.

Q4. We can get an object of the `RequestDispatcher` class by using the `getRequestDispatcher()` method on the ……………………………. class.

A. ServletRequest **B. ServletContext**

C. Both A and B **D. None**

Ans. The correct option is C.

Q5. Initialization parameters can be fetched by using the …………………………… method.

A. getAttribute() **B. getParameter()**

C. getInitParameter() **D. getServletContext()**

Ans. The correct option is C.

Q6. The number of `ServletContext` objects present for an application is ………………………… .

A. 2 **B. 1**

C. Not fixed **D. Each for a Servlet**

Ans. The correct option is B.

Q7. `HttpServlet` extends ………………………… .

A. The javax.servlet.GenericServlet class **B. The javax.servlet.http.GenericServlet class**

C. The javax.servlet.http.HttpServletRequest interface **D. The javax.servlet.ServletInputStream class**

Ans. The correct option is A.

Q8. The method used to fetch the value of an object in the request scope is ……………………………….

A. getAttribute() **B. getParameter()**

C. getInitParameter() **D. None**

Ans. The correct option is A.

Q9. What is a servlet?

Ans. A servlet is a simple Java class working on the request-response model. Various interfaces and classes to handle common HTTP-specific services are defined in the Java Servlet API. Each servlet implements the Servlet interface by providing implementation of the life cycle methods, init(), ser ice(), and destroy().

Q10. Differentiate between the ServletContext and ServletConfig objects.

Ans. A `ServletContext` object is used to communicate with a Servlet container while `ServletConfig`, which is a Servlet configuration object, is passed to the servlet by a container when the servlet is initialized. A `ServletContext` object is contained within a `ServletConfig` object.

Q11. What is the difference between the `getRequestDispatcher()` methods of the `ServletRequest` and `ServletContext interfaces`?

Ans. Both `getRequestDispatcher()` methods take a String parameter, which is a path to the location where a user's request would be forwarded. The `getRequestDispatcher()` method of the ServletRequest interface can accept both types of paths, i.e. the relative path from the requesting servlet and the path relative to the context root. However, the `getRequestDispatcher()` method of the `ServletContext` interface cannot accept the relative path.

Q12. Define the `init()` method of a servlet.

Ans. The `init()` method of the HttpServlet class is called before a servlet handles the first request and is used to initialize the servlet. This `init()` method also saves the `ServletConfig` object by using the super.`init()` method and stores the initialization details of a servlet. This method is called once only.

Q13. How is the `GET` method different from the `Post` method?

Ans. In the case of the GET method, all data submitted with an HTML form is attached with a URL. This method is faster and easier to use than the POST method but not as secure, and the upper limit of the URL length limits the amount of data transferred. The Post method, on the other hand, puts name/value combinations inside the HTTP request body and is therefore more secure. In addition, there is no limit for the amount of data that can be sent in this method.

Q14. Which of the following interfaces support non-blocking IO in Servlets 3.1?

A. ReadListener

B. WriteListener

C. ReadListenerImpl

D. WriteListenerImpl

Ans. The correct options are A and B.

Q15. Which annotation is used to enable async in the servlet?

A. @WebServlet

B. @WebFilter

C. @WebInitParam

D. @WebListener

Ans. The correct option is A.

Q16. What is HTTP protocol upgrade mechanism in Servlet 3.1?

Ans. The HTTP protocol upgrade mechanism allows transition from HTTP 1.1 to some other incompatible version of protocol. The capabilities and nature of the communication entirely depends on the newly chosen protocol. Only after accepting the newly upgraded protocol by a client and server, the message exchange takes place between them with the help of chosen new protocol. The protocol upgrade is decided by using the Servlet.service() method. To achieve this, you need to add a new method HttpServletRequest.upgrade() and two new interfaces: javax.servlet.http.HttpUpgradeHandler and javax.servlet.http.WebConnection. Web Socket is an example of protocol upgrade.

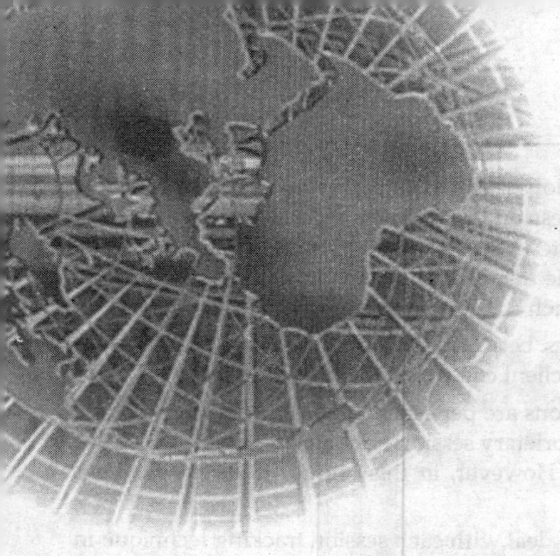

5

Handling Sessions in Servlets 3.1

A HyperText Transfer Protocol (HTTP) session stores the information of activities performed by users, such as requesting and accessing resources over a network. An HTTP session helps a servlet to keep track of the activities of a user. The process of keeping a track of a client's state in servlets is termed as session handling, which is also known as session tracking. The process of tracking the details of a session in servlets is similar to other session tracking mechanisms used in previous technologies, such as Common Gateway Interface (CGI).

Servlets provide convenient ways to synchronize multiple sessions between a client and server. As a result, servlets are able to maintain the session state on the server until the client completes the browsing session.

Some common and widely-used techniques to maintain HTTP sessions are persistent cookies, Uniform Resource Locator (URL) rewriting, and hidden form fields. There are few proprietary session tracking strategies, which are vendor dependent that persist state to a disk and/or a database. However, in this regard, there are no clear winners; with pros and cons to each technique.

To implement session tracking in servlets, you need not required to deal with each session tracking technique in your Web applications. Instead, you can use an Application Programming Interface (API), which selects the most appropriate HTTP session technique based on the capabilities of the client and server. The API used for HTTP session technique provides abstract details, such as whether the browser has cookies enabled or the server supports URL rewriting. In addition, to maintain HTTP sessions with servlet session tracking, API provides various possible implementations, such as cookies and URL rewriting.

Firstly, the chapter introduces you to session and how client's state is traced within a session. Further, different session tracking techniques, such as hidden form fields, cookies, and URL rewriting are explored in detail. Later, the chapter explores the session handling API for servlets, which helps overcome the disadvantages of the traditional session tracking techniques. Then, a simple login application is developed to demonstrate the session handling process. Towards the end, a servlet class is developed to show how to change session ID in Servlets 3.1.

Let's start the chapter with an introduction about a session.

Describing a Session

A session can be defined as a collection of HTTP requests shared between a client and Web server over a period of time. While creating a session, you require setting its lifetime, which is set to thirty minutes by default. After the set lifetime expires, the session is destroyed and all its resources are returned back to the servlet engine. The succeeding subsections discuss about the life-cycle of a session and focus on how to create and destroy sessions. Prior moving ahead towards the discussion on session life-cycle, let's first discuss about session tracking and its mechanisms.

Introducing Session Tracking

Session tracking is a process of gathering the user information from Web pages, which can be used in an application. Let's cite an example, a shopping cart application can be taken as the most common example of session tracking. In the shopping cart application, a client accesses the server several times from the same browser and visits several Web pages. After browsing the Web pages, the client decides to purchase some of the items offered by the Web site for sale and clicks the BUY ITEM button. In this case, if a stateless server-side object serves each transaction, and the client's side does not provide any identification on each request; it would not be possible to maintain a filled shopping cart over several HTTP requests from the client. If the user visits a Web page multiple times and selects different items to be added to the shopping cart in each visit, the stateless nature of HTTP might not relate each visit to the same session. Therefore, even writing a stateless transaction data to persistent storage would not be a solution in this regard.

Therefore, session tracking involves identifying the user sessions by related ID numbers and tying the requests to their sessions by using the said ID number. Cookies and URL rewriting are the typical mechanisms for session tracking. Depending upon the Servlet specification, session tracking is implemented through HTTP session objects by the servlet container in the application server. These HTTP session objects are instances of a class and implement the `javax.servlet.http.HttpSession` interface. The getSession() method of the HttpSession interface is used to create the HTTP session object and the stateful client interaction.

The question may arise about the scope of the HTTP session object. Will it be limited to single request or multiple requests or across users? The scope of the HTTP session object is limited to the single client. It is important to note that you cannot use session objects to share the data between different applications and different clients of the same application. There is only one HTTP session object for each client in each application.

After having a brief overview about session tracking, let's discuss about the various mechanisms that can be used to implement session tracking in servlets.

Exploring the Session Tracking Mechanisms

To track the session details for a specific user to maintain the session, you need to implement a mechanism in your Web application. You can implement the following session tracking mechanisms to track the session details:

- Cookies
- Hidden form fields
- URL rewriting
- Secure Socket Layer (SSL) sessions

Let's discuss these in detail.

Using Cookies

While working with session tracking, numerous approaches have been adapted to add a degree of statefulness to the HTTP protocol. Among these approaches, the most widely accepted one is the use of cookies. A cookie is used to transmit an identifier between a server and a client. The transmitting of an identifier is in conjunction with stateful servlets, which can maintain session objects. These session objects are simply the dictionaries that store values (Java objects) together with their associated keys (Java Strings). The following steps describe the usage of cookies:

- After creating a session, the server (container) sends a cookie (as a response from stateful servlet) with a session identifier back to the client. Some other useful information, such as username and password, is also sent with the cookie (all less than 4 KB). The cookie, named `JSESSIONID`, is sent by the container as a response in the HTTP response header.
- Then, whenever any subsequent request is received from the same Web client session (assuming the client supports cookies), the cookie is sent back by the client to the server as part of the request. In this case, the cookie value is used by the server to look for the session state information to be passed to the servlet.
- Finally, with subsequent responses, the container sends the updated cookie back to the client.

As the container handles the process of sending a cookie, the servlet code is not required while using cookies. A Web browser automatically handles the process of sending cookies back to the server unless the user disables cookies.

The cookie is used by the container to maintain a session. Cookies can be retrieved by a servlet by using the `getCookies()` method of the `HttpServletRequest` object. The cookie attributes can be examined by the servlet using the accessor methods of the `javax.servlet.http.Cookie` objects.

The servlet container sends a cookie to the client. Upon each HTTP request, the cookie is returned back to the server. This way, the session id indicated by the cookie is associated with the request. You should note that you can use HTTP cookies to store information about a session and for each subsequent connection the current session can be looked up and then information about that session is extracted from a location on the server machine. For example, in the following code snippet, the code to retrieve the session information is provided that can be implemented in a servlet:

```
String sesID = makeUniqueString();
Hashtable sesInfo = new Hashtable();
Hashtable hashtab = findTableStoringSessions();
hashtab.put(sesID, sesInfo);
Cookie sesCookie = new Cookie("JSESSIONID", sesID);
sesCookie.setPath("/");
response.addCookie(sesCookie);
```

The preceding code snippet requests the server, which uses the `hashtab` hash table to associate a session ID of the `JSESSIONID` cookie with the `sesInfo` hash table of data associated with that particular session. A cookie is the most widely used approach for session handling. The servlet's session tracking API handles sessions and performs the following tasks:

- Extracting the cookie that stores other cookie's session identifier
- Setting an appropriate expiration time for the cookie
- Associating hash tables with each request
- Generating a unique session identifier

Now, let's discuss the Cookies API as it would help you to understand about the classes and interfaces used for session tracking.

In Java Servlet `API, Cookie` is a class of the `javax.servlet.http` package, which abstracts the notion of a cookie. You can implement session tracking using cookies with the help of the addCookie() and getCookies() methods. These methods are provided by the `javax.servlet.http.HttpServletRequest` and `javax.servlet.http.HttpServletResponse` interfaces and are used to add cookies to HTTP responses and to retrieve the cookies from HTTP requests, respectively. A cookie is abstracted by the `Cookie` class. The following code snippet shows a constructor that instantiates a cookie instance with the given name and value:

```
public Cookie(String name, String value)
```

The Cookie class provides various methods, such as getValue() and setValue(),which simplify working with cookies. For all the cookie parameters, the Cookie class provides `getter` and `setter` methods. The following code snippet shows the implementation of some of the methods of the Cookie class:

```
public String getValue()
public void setValue(String newvalue)
```

The `getter` and `setter` methods can be used to access or set the value of a cookie. Similarly, there exist other methods that can be used to access or change other parameters; such as path and header of a cookie. The following code snippet shows the implementation of the addCookie() method provided by the `javax.servlet.http.HttpServletResponse` interface to set cookies:

```
public void addCookie(Cookie cookie)
```

To set multiple cookies, you can call this method as many times as you want. The following code snippet shows the implementation of the getCookies() method provided by the `javax.servlet.http.HttpServletRequest` interface to extract all cookies contained in the HTTP request:

```
public Cookie[] getCookies()
```

Now, you can create your servlet to track the activities of a user using cookies by providing the code for the following actions:

- Check if there is a cookie contained in the incoming request
- Create a cookie and send it with the response, if there is no cookie in the incoming request
- Display the value of the cookies, if there is a cookie in the incoming request

Let's create a new Web application, HandleSession, to implement session tracking using cookies. This application follows the same directory structure as discussed in *Chapter 2, Web Applications and Java EE 7*.Let's now create the `CookieServlet` servlet class (in the HandleSession application) to show how to work with a cookie. Listing 5.1 shows the code of the `CookieServlet.java` file (save the `CookieServlet.java` file in the \HandleSession\src\com\kogent folder):

Listing 5.1: Showing the Source Code of the CookieServlet Servlet Class

```
package com.kogent;

import java.io.*;
import java.util.Random;
import javax.servlet.http.*;
import javax.servlet.ServletException;

public class CookieServlet extends HttpServlet
{
   protected void doGet(HttpServletRequest request, HttpServletResponse
```

```
        response) throws ServletException, IOException
        {
                Cookie[] coki = request.getCookies();
                Cookie tokenCookie = null;
                if(coki !=null)
                {
                        for(int i=0; i<coki.length; i++)
                        {
                                if (coki[i].getName().equals("token"))
                                {
                                        tokenCookie = coki[i];
                                        break;
                                }
                        }
                }

                response.setContentType("text/html");
                PrintWriter prnwriter = response.getWriter();
                prnwriter.println("<html><head><title>Extracting the token
                        cookie</title></head><body");
                prnwriter.println("style=\"font-family:arial;font-size:12pt\">");

                String resetParam = request.getParameter("resetParam");
                if(tokenCookie==null || (resetParam != null &&
                        resetParam.equals("yes")))
                {
                        Random rnd = new Random();
                        long cookieid = rnd.nextLong();
                        prnwriter.println("<p>Welcome. A new token " + cookieid + "is
                                now established</p>");
                        tokenCookie = new Cookie("token",
                                Long.toString(cookieid));
                        tokenCookie.setComment("A cookie named token to identity
                                user");
                        tokenCookie.setMaxAge(-1);
                        tokenCookie.setPath("/HandleSession/CookieServlet");
                        response.addCookie(tokenCookie);
                }
                else
                {
                        prnwriter.println("Welcome back.. Your token is " +
                                tokenCookie.getValue() + ".</p>");
                }

                String requestURLSame = request.getRequestURL().toString();
                String requestURLNew = request.getRequestURL() + "?resetParam=yes";

                prnwriter.println("<p>Click <a href=" + requestURLSame +" > here
                        </a>again to continue browsing with the "+ " same
                        identity.</p>");
                prnwriter.println("<p>Otherwise, click <a href = " + requestURLNew +
                        "> here</a> to start browsing with a new identity. </p>");
                prnwriter.println("</body></html>");
                prnwriter.close();
        }
    }
}
```

In Listing 5.1, the CookieServlet servlet class first retrieves all the cookies that are contained in the request object. In case the cookies are present, the CookieServlet servlet class locates the cookie named `token`. If the servlet class does not find a cookie with the name `token`, then the Web container, on the CookieServlet servlet class request, creates a cookie called `token` and adds it to the response. A random number for the cookie is created by the servlet class. The servlet class creates a cookie with the help of the parameters, as shown in the following code snippet:

```
Name : token
Value :  A random number
Comment : A cookie named tokens to identify user
Max-Age : -1 (The value of -1 indicates that the cookie will be discarded when the
```

```
         Browserexits)
  Path : /HandleSession/CookieServlet(This path enables the browser to send the
         cookie to only those requests   under
         http://localhost:8080/HandleSession/CookieServlet
```

If you are deploying this application on a remote machine (server) and accessing it from another machine (client), you need to set the domain name to be that of the server name; by default, it is localhost. Compile the CookieServlet.java file using the following command from the C:\JavaEE\Chapter5\HandleSession\src\com\kogent location:

```
javac -d C:\JavaEE\chapter5\HandleSession\WEB-INF\classes CookieServlet.java
```

The execution of the preceding command would compile the CookieServlet servlet class and store the .class file along with package directory under the WEB-INF\classes directory of the HandleSession application.

Now, let's create the web.xml file to configure and map the CookieServlet servlet class to the /CookieServlet url pattern. Listing 5.2 shows the code of the web.xml file (save the web.xml file in WEB-INF folder of the HandleSession application):

Listing 5.2: Configuring the CookieServlet Servlet Class

```
  <?xml version="1.0" encoding="UTF-8"?>
  <web-app version="3.1" xmlns="http://xmlns.jcp.org/xml/ns/javaee"
xmlns:xsi="http://www.w3.org/2001/XMLSchema-instance"
xsi:schemaLocation="http://xmlns.jcp.org/xml/ns/javaee http://xmlns.jcp.org/xml/ns/javaee/web-app_3_1.xsd">
  <servlet>
    <servlet-name>CookieServlet</servlet-name>
    <servlet-class>com.kogent.CookieServlet</servlet-class>
  </servlet>
  <servlet-mapping>
    <servlet-name>CookieServlet</servlet-name>
    <url-pattern>/CookieServlet</url-pattern>
  </servlet-mapping>
  </web-app>
```

Save the code of Listing 5.2 as the web.xml file under the WEB-INF directory of the HandleSession Web application. Now, package the Web application into HandleSession.war, as discussed in *Chapter 4, Working with Servlets 3.1*, and deploy it on the Glassfish Server 4.0. Now, run the servlet in a browser by browsing the `http://localhost:8080/HandleSession/CookieServlet URL`. Figure 5.1 displays the output of `CookieServlet.java`, showing the new token value for the newly created cookie named *token*:

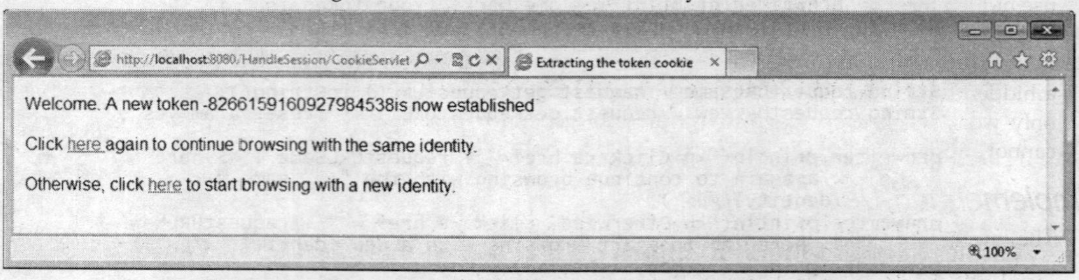

Figure 5.1: Displaying the Output of CookieServlet Servlet Class

In Figure 5.1, there are two hyperlinks. Click the first hyperlink to browse through the same identity of the cookie. However, to browse with the new identity, click the second hyperlink. When you click the second hyperlink, a new identity is created, with the new cookie value and it is displayed on the browser. After clicking the second hyperlink, the resetParam parameter is set to yes, as shown in the address bar in Figure 5.2:

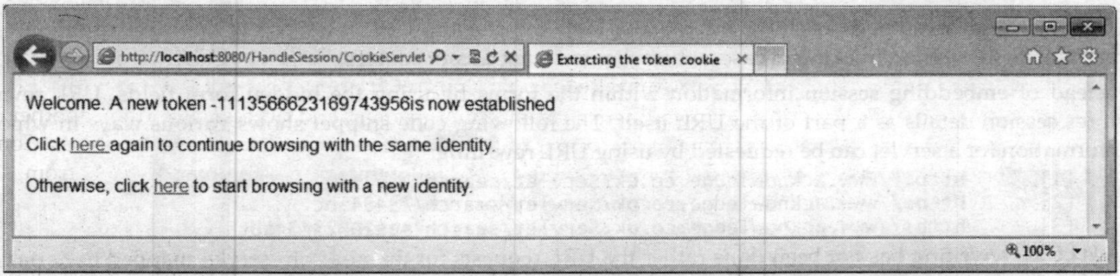

Figure 5.2: Browsing CookieServlet with New Token Value

Figure 5.2 displays the new token value. Now, to continue with the same token value, as shown in Figure 5.2, click the first hyperlink. After clicking the first hyperlink, the same request URL is retrieved and the browser displays the `Welcome back` message, as shown in Figure 5.3:

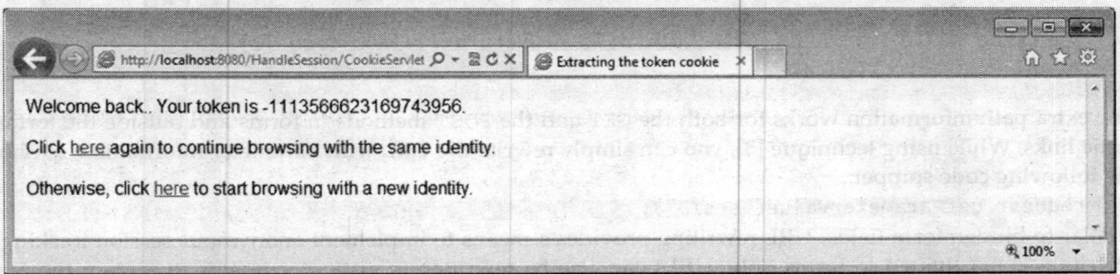

Figure 5.3: Browsing CookieServlet with the Same Identity

After discussing how to use cookies, let's now discuss another approach used for session tracking, the hidden form fields.

Using Hidden Form Fields

The hidden form fields are the fields in a Hypertext Markup Language (HTML) or JavaServer Pages (JSP) form that are not shown to the user and used to store information about a session. You can use the following syntax to use hidden form fields in an HTML page:

```
<INPUT TYPE="HIDDEN" NAME="session" VALUE="...">
```

In the preceding syntax, the `hidden` value is assigned to the `type` attribute, which implies that the input field is a hidden form field. However, using hidden form fields has a major disadvantage, that is, hidden form fields only work when every page is dynamically generated by a form submission. Therefore, hidden form fields cannot support general session tracking and can only support tracking within a specific series of operations.

Implementing URL Rewriting

The mechanism of URL rewriting is similar to that of cookies. The URL rewriting mechanism uses the `encodeURL()` method of the response object to encode the session ID into the URL path of a request. The following code snippet shows an example of URL rewriting in which the name of the path parameter is `jsessionid`:

```
http://host:port/myapp/index.html?jsessionid=6789
```

The server uses the value of the rewritten URL to find the session state information, and to pass the information to the servlet. This is similar to the functionality of cookies. Although, cookies are typically enabled; however, to ensure session tracking using URL rewriting, the `encodeURL()` method is used in the servlets. In addition, the `encodeRedirectURL()` method is used in servlets to redirect to a resource.

According to the Servlet specification, if cookies are enabled, then any call to the `encodeURL()` and `encodeRedirectURL()` methods does not result in any action. In case the cookies are disabled, the servlet can call the `encodeURL()` method of the response object to append a session ID to the URL path for each request. Alternatively, the `encodeRedirectURL()` method is used to redirect a Web page to a resource. As a result,

URL rewriting helps in associating the request with the session. URL rewriting is the most commonly used mechanism for session tracking in cases when clients do not accept cookies.

Instead of embedding session information within the forms by using the hidden form fields, URL rewriting stores session details as a part of the URL itself. The following code snippet shows various ways in which the information for a servlet can be requested by using URL rewriting:

```
[1]     http://www.acknowledge.co.uk/Servlet/search
[2]     http://www.acknowledge.co.uk/Servlet/search/23434abc
[3]     http://www.acknowledge.co.uk/Servlet/search?sesID=23434abc
```

In [1],URL rewriting has not been done rather the URL requests for the `search` servlet mapped to `/search` in web.xml. In [2], URL has been rewritten at the server to add extra path information. This extra information is embedded in the pages returned to the client. The following code snippet shows how to retrieve the extra path information, provided in [2]:

```
public void doGet(HttpServletRequest request, HttpServletResponse response)
{
   ...
   String sesID = request.getPathInfo(); // return 2343abc from [2]
   ...
}
```

The extra path information works for both the `GET` and the `POST` methods in forms and outside the forms with static links. While using technique [3], you can simply rewrite the URL with parameter information, as shown in the following code snippet:

```
request.getParameterValue("sesID");
```

Similar to hidden form fields, URL rewriting provides a means to implement anonymous session tracking. URL rewriting is not limited to forms only. URLs can also be rewritten in static documents to contain the required session information. However, URL rewriting suffers from a disadvantage that the URLs must be dynamically generated and most importantly, the chain of HTML page generation cannot be broken. Therefore, URL rewriting is a tedious and error-prone process.

The mechanism of URL rewriting can be better understood by creating a servlet. Let's create the `TokenServlet` servlet class, which performs the following tasks:

- Checks whether or not the client sends a token with its request
- Creates a new token, if no token has been sent by the client

In addition, the TokenServlet servlet class provides two hyperlinks—one that includes the token and other does not.

Listing 5.3 shows the code of the `TokenServlet.java` file (save the `TokenServlet.java` file in the \HandleSession\src\com\kogent folder):

Listing 5.3: Implementing the URL Rewriting Mechanism

```
package com.kogent;

import java.io.*;
import java.util.Random;
import javax.servlet.http.*;
import javax.servlet.ServletException;

public class TokenServlet extends HttpServlet
{
  protected void doGet(HttpServletRequest request, HttpServletResponse
  response) throws ServletException, IOException
  {
          String tokensID = request.getParameter("tokens");
          response.setContentType("text/html");
          PrintWriter prnwriter = response.getWriter();
          prnwriter.println("<html><head><title>Tokens</title></head><body");
          prnwriter.println("style=\"font-family:verdana;font-size:10pt\">");
          if(tokensID==null)
          {
                  Random rnd = new Random();
```

```
                tokensID = Long.toString(rnd.nextLong());
                prnwriter.println("<p>Welcome. A new token " + tokensID + "
                is now established</p>");
        }
        else
        {
                prnwriter.println("Welcome back.. Your token is " + tokensID
                + ".</p>");
        }

        String requestURLSame = request.getRequestURL().toString()+"?tokens=
        " + tokensID;
        String requestURLNew = request.getRequestURL().toString();

        prnwriter.println("<p>Click <a href=" + requestURLSame +" > here
        </a> again to continue browsing with the same identity.</p>");
        prnwriter.println("<p>Click <a href=" + requestURLNew +" > here </a>
        to continue browsing with a new identity.</p>");
        prnwriter.println("</body></html>");
        prnwriter.close();
    }
}
```

Save the code of Listing 5.3 as the `TokenServlet.java` file in the `src\com\kogent` directory of the `HandleSession` Web application. When you click the `here` hyperlink in the `TokenServlet` servlet class, the URL path is retrieved using the getRequestURL() method and the URL is rewritten with the parameter information. Compile the TokenServlet servlet class and configure it in the web.xml file, created in Listing 5.2 for the HandleSession Web application. The following code snippet shows how to configure and map the TokenServlet servlet class to the /TokenServlet url pattern:

```
<servlet>
   <servlet-name>TokenServlet</servlet-name>
   <servlet-class>com.kogent.TokenServlet</servlet-class>
</servlet>
<servlet-mapping>
   <servlet-name>TokenServlet</servlet-name>
   <url-pattern>/TokenServlet</url-pattern>
</servlet-mapping>
```

You can run the `TokenServlet` servlet class only after packaging the resources of the HandleSession Web application in the `HandleSession.war` file. Then, you need to redeploy the Web application on the Glassfish Server 4.0 and navigate the `http://localhost:8080/HandleSession/TokenServlet` URL. After navigating this URL, you can notice that the query parameter, `tokens`, is not included in the initial request. The servlet not only creates a new token but also generates two links. A query string is included in one link, which is passed as a query parameter in the request. Therefore, the servlet can recognize the user from this parameter and display the `Welcome back` message. This allows the user to continue browsing with the same identity. Another link, that does not include the query parameter, is also generated by the servlet. This link allows the user to continue browsing with a new identity, every time the link is clicked. Figure 5.4 shows the output of the `TokenServlet` servlet class when `it` is executed for the first time:

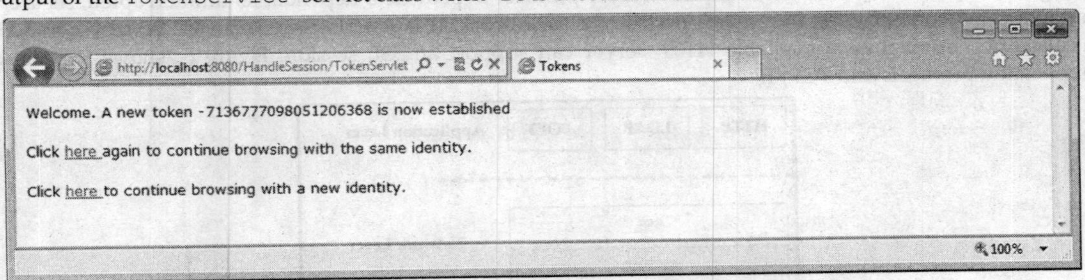

Figure 5.4: Displaying the Output of TokenServlet Servlet Class

After clicking the first link shown in Figure 5.4, the address bar of the browser (Figure 5.5) shows rewritten URL including the `tokens parameter` in the request. The `tokens` parameter added in the URL contains the new token identity based on the user's requests. Figure 5.5 shows the output when the first link is clicked:

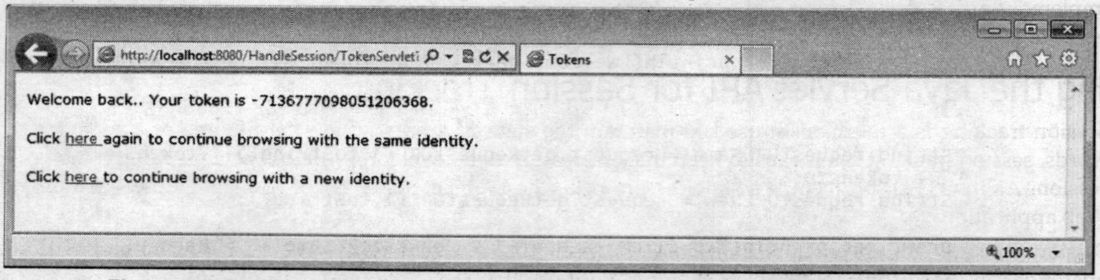

Figure 5.5: Displaying the Output of TokenServlet Servlet Class Using URL Rewriting

Clicking the second link allows the user to continue browsing with a new identity. Figure 5.6 shows the output when the second link is clicked:

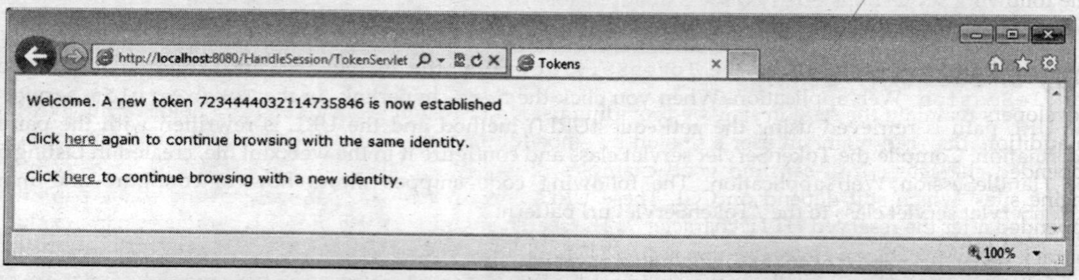

Figure 5.6: Displaying the Output of Browsing the TokenServlet Servlet Class with a New Identity

Although, the URL rewriting mechanism can solve the problem of session tracking, it has two main limitations:

- It is not a secure session tracking mechanism as the token or session id is visible in the URL during a session
- It can only be used with servlets or other dynamic pages as the links in static pages are hardcoded and cannot change dynamically for every user

You can use cookies as a session tracking mechanism to overcome the preceding problems of the URL rewriting mechanism.

Using Secure Socket Layer

SSL is used to protect the data during transmission that covers all network services. This layer uses Transmission Control Protocol (TCP)/Internet Protocol (IP) to support typical application tasks that require communication between clients and servers. It is an encryption technology that runs on top of TCP/IP and below application level protocols, such as HTTP. SSL ensures the security of data transported and routed through HTTP. SSL is designed to utilize TCP as a communication layer protocol to provide a dependable, uninterrupted, secure, and authenticated connection between two points over a network. It is used mostly in an HTTP server and client applications. Almost each available HTTP server can support an SSL session. Figure 5.7shows SSL between application protocols and TCP/IP:

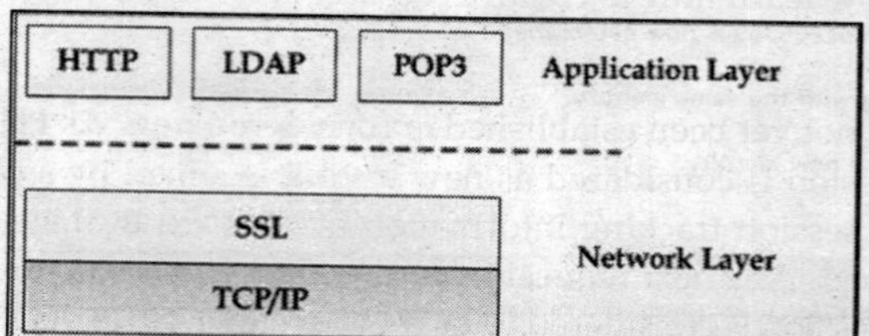

Figure 5.7: Displaying SSL between Application Protocols and TCP/IP

Apart from the cookies, hidden form fields, URL rewriting, and SSL mechanisms, the session details of a user can also be tracked by using Java Servlet API. The `HttpSession` interface in Java Servlet API also helps in implementing session tracking. Let's discuss the `HttpSession` interface in the next section and learn how to use it to implement session tracking.

Using the Java Servlet API for Session Tracking

Session tracking is a mechanism used to maintain the state of a user within the lifetime of a session. In other words, session tracking is a means to keep track of session data, which represents the data being transferred in a session. As the HTTP protocol is a stateless protocol, the Web container needs to manage the session data in a Web application.

Session tracking is used when session data of a user might be required by a Web server to complete specific operations in the current session. For example, suppose you are shopping on an online book store. You access the online book store Web site and add items to the shopping cart. When you proceed for checkout, then due to session tracking the server would be known that the user who added items to the shopping cart is logging out. The following subsections briefly discuss about history of session tracking and provide a description about how to create and track a session.

History of Session Tracking

Developers maintain the session state by providing user information into hidden form fields on an HTML page. In addition, they can maintain user's session by embedding the user activities into URLs with a long String of appended characters. You can find good examples of embedding user activities into URLs mostly in search engine sites, which still depend on CGI. These URLs contain the URL parameter name/value pairs that are appended after the reserved HTTP character ?. The search engine sites use the URL parameter name/value pairs to track the user choices. However, appending URL parameters can result in a very long URL that needs to be carefully parsed and managed by the CGI script. The URL parameter name/value pairs cannot be passed through URL from session to session. Once the control over the URL is lost, that is once the user leaves one of the pages, the user information is lost forever.

Later, browser cookies were introduced by Netscape, which can be used by each server to store user related information on the client side. However, one of the drawbacks of using cookies is that cookies are not fully supported by some browsers and most browsers limit the amount of data that can be stored with a cookie.

To overcome the shortcomings faced while using cookies and to maintain the user session, the HTTP Servlet specification was introduced. The HTTP Servlet specification protects the code from the complexities of tracking sessions. Servlets may use the HttpSession object to track the input provided by the user over the span of a single session as well as to share the session details with other servlets.

Session Creation and Tracking

An instance of a class that implements the `javax.servlet.http.HttpSession` interface represents each client session in the standard Servlet API. The servlets can use the `HttpSession` object to set or get the information about the session which must be of the application-level scope. A servlet can retrieve or create the `HttpSession` object for the user by calling the `getSession()` method. The `getSession()` method accepts a `boolean` argument that specifies whether to create a new session object for the client if no session already exists within the application. Let's now learn how to create a session.

Creating a Session

A prospective session that has not yet been established is considered `new`. As HTTP protocol is request-response based; therefore, the HTTP session is considered as new until it is joined by a client. The client is considered to have joined the session when session tracking information is returned to the server indicating that the session has been successfully established. Any next request from the client is not recognized as a part of the session until the client joins the session. A session is considered to be `new`, in either of the following cases:

- The client does not have knowledge about the session
- The client opts for not joining the session

In both the cases, the servlet container could not correlate a request with the previous request by any means. Therefore, a servlet developer must design the application in such a manner that it could handle a situation where a client has not yet joined a session or will not join a session.

As explained earlier, the servlet container uses the HTTP session objects that implement the `javax.servlet.http.HttpSession` interface to track and manage the user sessions. The `HttpSession` interface contains public methods, such as setAttribute() and getAttribute(), to set as well as get the session information, respectively. The following code snippet shows the implementation of the `setAttribute()` method of the `HttpSession` interface:

```
void setAttribute(String name, Object value)
```

The `setAttribute()` method binds the specified object under the specified name, to the session. The following code snippet shows the implementation of the `getAttribute()` method of the `HttpSession` interface:

```
Object getAttribute(String name)
```

The `getAttribute()` method retrieves the object that is attached to the session with the specified name. A `null` value is returned if there is no match. According to the configuration of a servlet as well as the servlet container, sessions may automatically expire after the specified time or the servlet may invalidate the session explicitly. The following methods can be used by servlets to manage the session life-cycle specified by the `HttpSession` interface:

- `void invalidate()` – Invalidates the session instantly and unbinds any bound objects from the session.
- `void setMaxInactiveInterval(int interval)` – Sets a session timeout interval as an integer value in seconds. Timeout cannot be indicated by a negative value. A value of 0 results in immediate timeout.
- `boolean isNew()` – Returns `true` if a new session is created within the request that creates a new session; otherwise, it returns `false`.
- `long getCreationTime()` – Returns the time of creation of the session object. The time is measured in milliseconds and is calculated since midnight, January 1, 1970.
- `long getLastAccessedTime()` – Returns the time associated with the most recent request made by the client during the session. The time is measured in milliseconds and is calculated since midnight, January 1, 1970. Session creation time is returned by the method if the client session has not yet been accessed.

Let's create a servlet to understand the implementation of the HTTP session object. Listing 5.4 provides the code of the `MySessionServlet` servlet class, which creates the `HttpSession` object and prints the data held by the request and session objects (save the `MySessionServlet.java` file in the \HandleSession\src\com\kogent folder):

Listing 5.4: Showing the Code of the MySessionServlet.java File

```
package com.kogent ;

import java.io.*;
import javax.servlet.*;
import javax.servlet.http.*;
import java.util.Date;

public class MySessionServlet extends HttpServlet
{

  public void doGet (HttpServletRequest req, HttpServletResponse res)
  throws ServletException, IOException
  {
        // Retrieve the session object for the current user session.
        // A new session is created if a session object has not been
        // created previously.
        HttpSession sessionObj = req.getSession(true);

        // Create and update the variable that holds a count indicating
        // the number of times the page has been visited during the current
```

```
// user session.
Integer count = (Integer) sessionObj.getAttribute("count");

if (count == null)
{
        count = new Integer(1);
}
else
{
        count = new Integer(count.intValue() + 1);
}

// Save the updated count value to the current user session
sessionObj.setAttribute("count", count);


// Displaying the output to the user
res.setContentType("text/html");
PrintWriter prnwriter = res.getWriter();

prnwriter.println("<head><title> " + "Displaying the Details of
Current User Session" + "</title></head><body>");
prnwriter.println("<h1>Displaying the Details of Current User
Session</h1>");
prnwriter.println("<h2><I>You have visited this page</I><b><font
color=\"blue\">" + count + "</font></b><I> times.</I></h2><p>");

prnwriter.println("<BR>");


// Displaying the request related information from the request
// object
prnwriter.println("<Table ALIGN=CENTER Border=\"1\"
BorderColor=\"Red\">");
prnwriter.println("<TH COLSPAN=2 ALIGN=CENTER>Summary of Request
Data</TH>");

prnwriter.println("<TR><TD WIDTH=\"50%\" ALIGN=LEFT
VALIGN=CENTER>");
prnwriter.println("Session ID in Request Object");
prnwriter.println("</TD>");
prnwriter.println("<TD WIDTH=\"50%\">");
prnwriter.println(req.getRequestedSessionId());
prnwriter.println("</TD></TR>");

prnwriter.println("<TR><TD WIDTH=\"50%\" ALIGN=LEFT
VALIGN=CENTER>");
prnwriter.println("Is Session ID in Request from a Cookie");
prnwriter.println("</TD>");
prnwriter.println("<TD WIDTH=\"50%\">");
prnwriter.println(req.isRequestedSessionIdFromCookie());
prnwriter.println("</TD></TR>");

prnwriter.println("<TR><TD WIDTH=\"50%\" ALIGN=LEFT
VALIGN=CENTER>");
prnwriter.println("Is Session ID in Request from the URL");
```

```
prnwriter.println("</TD>");
prnwriter.println("<TD WIDTH=\"50%\">");
prnwriter.println(req.isRequestedSessionIdFromURL());
prnwriter.println("</TD></TR>");

prnwriter.println("<TR><TD WIDTH=\"50%\" ALIGN=LEFT
VALIGN=CENTER>");
prnwriter.println("Is Requested Session ID Valid");
prnwriter.println("</TD>");
prnwriter.println("<TD WIDTH=\"50%\">");
prnwriter.println(req.isRequestedSessionIdValid());
prnwriter.println("</TD></TR>");

prnwriter.println("</Table>");

prnwriter.println("<BR><BR>");

// Displaying the session related information from the session
// object
prnwriter.println("<Table ALIGN=CENTER Border=\"1\"
BorderColor=\"Red\">");
prnwriter.println("<TH COLSPAN=2 ALIGN=CENTER>Summary of Session
Data</TH>");

prnwriter.println("<TR><TD WIDTH=\"50%\" ALIGN=LEFT
VALIGN=CENTER>");
prnwriter.println("Is it a New Session");
prnwriter.println("</TD>");
prnwriter.println("<TD WIDTH=\"50%\">");
prnwriter.println(sessionObj.isNew());
prnwriter.println("</TD></TR>");

prnwriter.println("<TR><TD WIDTH=\"50%\" ALIGN=LEFT
VALIGN=CENTER>");
prnwriter.println("Session ID");
prnwriter.println("</TD>");
prnwriter.println("<TD WIDTH=\"50%\">");
prnwriter.println(sessionObj.getId());
prnwriter.println("</TD></TR>");

prnwriter.println("<TR><TD WIDTH=\"50%\" ALIGN=LEFT
VALIGN=CENTER>");
prnwriter.println("Session Creation Time");
prnwriter.println("</TD>");
prnwriter.println("<TD WIDTH=\"50%\">");
prnwriter.println(new Date(sessionObj.getCreationTime()));
prnwriter.println("</TD></TR>");

prnwriter.println("<TR><TD WIDTH=\"50%\" ALIGN=LEFT
VALIGN=CENTER>");
prnwriter.println("Time at which Session was Last Accessed");
prnwriter.println("</TD>");
prnwriter.println("<TD WIDTH=\"50%\">");
prnwriter.println(new Date(sessionObj.getLastAccessedTime()));
prnwriter.println("</TD></TR>");
prnwriter.println("</Table>");
```

```
            prnwriter.println("<BR><BR>");

            // User can reaccess the servlet using this hyperlink to see
            // Session Tracking in action. Clicking the hyperlink refreshes
            // the page and increment the session variable count by one every
            // time it is clicked.
            String url = req.getRequestURL().toString();
            prnwriter.println(" Click <a href=" + url + "> here </a> to reload
            the servlet and see session tracking in action. <br>");

        prnwriter.println("</body>");
            prnwriter.close();
        }
    }
```

Save `MySessionServlet` in the `src\com\kogent` directory of the `HandleSession` Web application. Now, configure and map the `MySessionServlet` servlet class to the /MySessionServlet url pattern in the `web.xml` file and then create `HandleSession.war`. Redeploy the `HandleSession` Web application on the `Glassfish` Server 4.0 and browse the URL `http://localhost:8080/HandleSession/MySessionServlet` to see the output of the `MySessionServlet` servlet class.

Figure 5.8 shows the output of the `MySessionServlet` servlet class, displaying the results of the accessor methods on the request and session objects as well as listing request and session data:

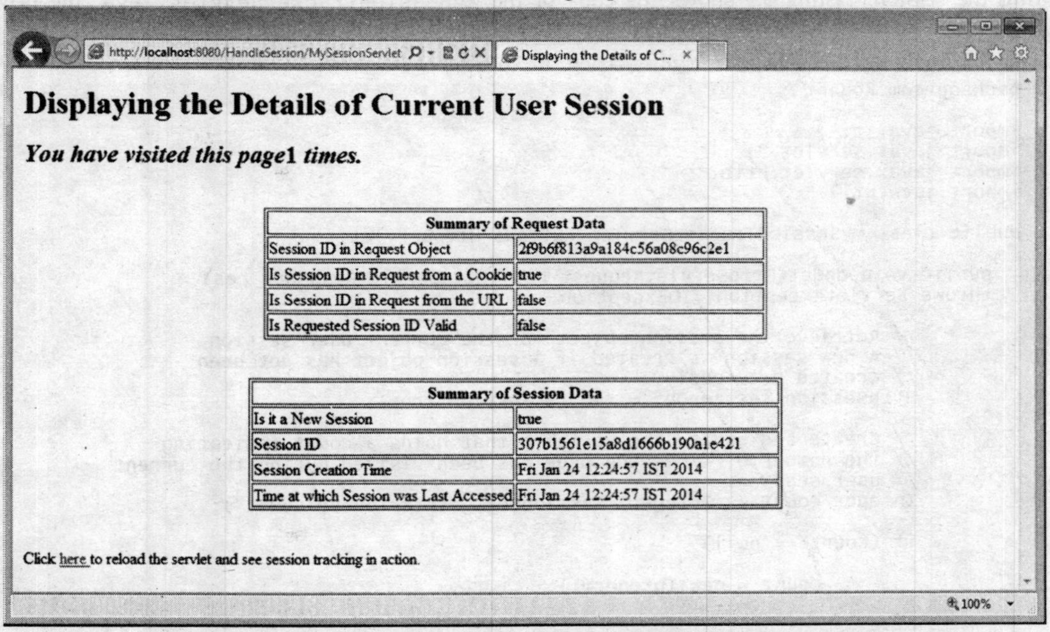

Figure 5.8: Displaying the Output of MySessionServlet Servlet Class

In Figure 5.8, if a user clicks the `here` link and the cookies are enabled in the browser settings, then the request and session data get changed. In such a case, change the Web browser settings, for example, disable cookies and click the `here link` that causes URL rewriting.

Tracking a Session Using Servlet API

The Servlet API provides various methods and classes, such as getSession() and HttpSession that are particularly designed to handle session tracking.

The session tracking API, which is the part of the Servlet API and provides session tracking functionality, can be used in any Web server that supports servlets. However, the level of support depends on the server.

For example, session objects can be written to Java Web Server even if the server disk memory fills up or the server shuts down. However, to take advantage of this option; the items that are placed in the session are required to implement the `Serializable` interface.

Exploring Session Tracking Basics

In session tracking, the user identity is linked with the `javax.servlet.http.HttpSession` object that can be used by the servlets to store or retrieve information about that user. Any set of arbitrary Java objects can be saved in a session object. For example, to store the user's shopping cart content in a database, a user's current HttpSession instance is retrieved by using the `getSession()` method of the `HttpServletRequest` interface, as shown in the following code snippet:

```
public HttpSession HttpServletRequest.getSession(boolean create)
```

The current session that is associated with the user who makes the request, is returned by the `getSession()` method. If the `createBoolean` variable has a value `true`, the `getSession()` method creates the session; otherwise, the method returns null. The `getSession()` method must be called at least once before writing any output to the response to ensure that the session is maintained properly.

Let's create another servlet class, MySessionTrackerServlet, to have a better understanding of the concept of session tracking. The MySessionTrackerServlet servlet class fetches and prints all the attributes associated with the current user session along with a count for the number of times the servlet has been visited by the user during the session. Listing 5.5 shows the code of the `MySessionTrackerServlet.java` file (save the `MySessionTrackerServlet.java` file in the \HandleSession\src\com\kogent folder):

Listing 5.5: Showing the Code of the `MySessionTrackerServlet.java File`

```
package com.kogent ;

import java.io.*;
import javax.servlet.*;
import javax.servlet.http.*;
import java.util.*;

public class MySessionTrackerServlet extends HttpServlet
{
   public void doGet(HttpServletRequest req, HttpServletResponse res)
   throws ServletException, IOException
   {
         // Retrieve the session object for the current user session.
         // A new session is created if a session object has not been
         // created previously.
         HttpSession sessionObj = req.getSession(true);

         // Create and update the variable that holds a count indicating
         // the number of times the page has been visited during the current
         // user session.
         Integer count = (Integer) sessionObj.getAttribute("Count");

         if (count == null)
         {
               count = new Integer(1);
         }
         else
         {
         count = new Integer(count.intValue() + 1);
         }
         // Save the updated count value to the current user session
         sessionObj.setAttribute("Count", count);
         // Add some more attributes to the current user session
         sessionObj.setAttribute("UserName", "Pallavi");
         sessionObj.setAttribute("UserID", sessionObj.getId());
         sessionObj.setAttribute("MyFavouriteColor", "Red");
         // Displaying the output to the user
         res.setContentType("text/html");
         PrintWriter prnwriter = res.getWriter();
```

```
        prnwriter.println("<HTML><HEAD><TITLE>My Session Tracker
        Servlet</TITLE></HEAD>");
        prnwriter.println("<BODY><H1>Demonstrating Session Tracking</H1>");

        // Display the hit cnt for this page for the current user
        prnwriter.println("You have visited this page <b><font
        color=\"blue\">" + count + ((count.intValue()==1)?"</font></b>
        time." : "</font></b> times."));
        prnwriter.println("<P>");

        prnwriter.println("<H2><I>Displaying Session Data</I></H2>");
        prnwriter.println("<Table Border=\"1\" BorderColor=\"Blue\">");

        Enumeration names = sessionObj.getAttributeNames();
        while(names.hasMoreElements())
        {
                String name = (String) names.nextElement();
                prnwriter.println("<TR><TD WIDTH=\"50%\" ALIGN=LEFT
                VALIGN=CENTER><I>");
                prnwriter.println(name);
                prnwriter.println("</I></TD><TD>");
                prnwriter.println(sessionObj.getAttribute(name));
                prnwriter.println("</TD></TR>");
        }
        prnwriter.println("</TABLE>");
        prnwriter.println("</BODY></HTML>");
    }
}
```

The `MySessionTrackerServlet` servlet class tracks the number of times the client accesses it. When the client accesses the `MySessionTrackerServlet` servlet class for the first time, the new session is created and each time the client accesses it, the value of `count` variable is incremented by one and the browser displays the number of times the client has accessed the servlet. The other variables related to the current client session are also displayed by the servlet.

Save the `MySessionTrackerServlet` servlet class in the `src\com\kogent` directory of the `HandleSession` Web application. Configure the `MySessionTrackerServlet` servlet class in the `web.xml` file. Then, compile the `MySessionTrackerServlet` servlet class, package the `HandleSession` application, and redeploy the Web application on the `Glassfish` Server 4.0. Browse the `http://localhost:8080/HandleSession/MySessionTrackerServlet` URL to view the output, as shown in Figure 5.9:

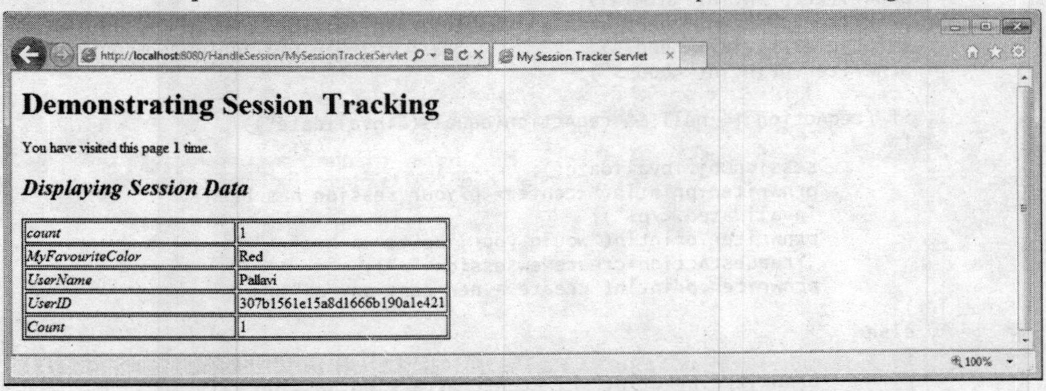

Figure 5.9: Displaying the Output of the MySessionTrackerServlet Servlet Class

The `MySessionTrackerServlet` servlet class first retrieves the `HttpSession` object linked with the current client session. The `getSession()` method, with a `Boolean` value of `true` as an argument, creates a session if it does not exist for the user. The servlet then fetches and sets the value of the `Integer` object `count`, which is bound to the current user session with a name `Count`. The servlet initializes the `Count` variable, if it is previously `null`. Otherwise, the servlet increments the value of the `Count` variable by one and resets it for the user session. The servlet also fetches the values of other variables associated with the current user session.

Finally, the servlet displays the value for the `count` variable and all the name/value pairs for the variables associated with the current user session.

Demonstrating Session Life-Cycle with Cookies

Let's now explore the life-cycle of `HttpSession` objects, by creating a servlet class, Track`SessionLifeCycle`. The servlet examines certain session attributes and provides link to invalidate the existing session. We will also examine the behavior of the servlet in the absence of cookies, and then discuss the ways to generate Web pages that work as desired, irrespective of whether cookies are accepted by the client browser or not.

The Track`SessionLifeCycle` servlet class generates a page that displays session object data including session ID, creation time of the session object, last accessed time, and max inactive interval for the session. The Track`SessionLifeCycle` servlet class also provides links to reload the page and invalidate the current user session. Listing 5.6 shows the code of the `TrackSessionLifeCycle.java` file (save the Track`SessionLifeCycle.java` file in the \HandleSession\src\com\kogent folder):

Listing 5.6: Displaying the Code of the Track`SessionLifeCycle Servlet` Class

```
package com.kogent ;

import javax.servlet.*;
import javax.servlet.http.*;
import java.io.*;
import java.util.*;

public class TrackSessionLifeCycle extends HttpServlet
{
  protected void doGet (HttpServletRequest req, HttpServletResponse res)
  throws ServletException, IOException
  {
        String url = "/HandleSession/TrackSessionLifeCycle";
        String reqAction = req.getParameter("requestAction");

        HttpSession sessionObj = req.getSession();

        res.setContentType("text/html");
        PrintWriter prnwriter = res.getWriter();
        prnwriter.println("<html>");
        prnwriter.println("<head><title>Demonstrating Session
        LifeCycle</title></head>");
        prnwriter.println("<body>");

        if (reqAction != null && reqAction.equals("invalidate"))
        {
               sessionObj.invalidate();
               prnwriter.println("<center><p>Your session has been
               invalidated.</p>");
               prnwriter.println("Would you like to <a href=\"" + url +
               "?requestAction=createNewSession\">");
               prnwriter.println("create a new session</a>");
        }
        else
        {
               prnwriter.println("<h1><center>Tracking Session Life
               Cycle</center></h1>");
               prnwriter.println("<br><Table ALIGN=CENTER Border=\"1\"
               BorderColor=\"Blue\">");

               prnwriter.println("<TR><TD WIDTH=\"50%\" ALIGN=LEFT><I>");
               prnwriter.println("Session Status");
               prnwriter.println("</I></TD><TD>");
               if (sessionObj.isNew())
               {
```

```
                    prnwriter.println("New Session");
                }
                else
                {
                    prnwriter.println("Old Session");
                }
                prnwriter.println("</TD></TR>");

                prnwriter.println("<TR><TD WIDTH=\"50%\" ALIGN=LEFT><I>");
                prnwriter.println("Session ID:");
                prnwriter.println("</I></TD><TD>");
                prnwriter.println(sessionObj.getId());
                prnwriter.println("</TD></TR>");

                prnwriter.println("<TR><TD WIDTH=\"50%\" ALIGN=LEFT><I>");
                prnwriter.println("Creation Time:");
                prnwriter.println("</I></TD><TD>");
                prnwriter.println(new Date(sessionObj.getCreationTime()));
                prnwriter.println("</TD></TR>");

                prnwriter.println("<TR><TD WIDTH=\"50%\" ALIGN=LEFT><I>");
                prnwriter.println("Last Accessed Time:");
                prnwriter.println("</I></TD><TD>");
                prnwriter.println(new
                Date(sessionObj.getLastAccessedTime()));
                prnwriter.println("</TD></TR>");

                prnwriter.println("<TR><TD WIDTH=\"50%\" ALIGN=LEFT><I>");
                prnwriter.println("Maximum Inactive Interval
                (seconds):");
                prnwriter.println("</I></TD><TD>");
                prnwriter.println(sessionObj.getMaxInactiveInterval());
                prnwriter.println("</TD></TR>");

                prnwriter.println("</TABLE>");
                prnwriter.println("<br><br><center><a href =\"" + url +
                "?requestAction=invalidate\">");
                prnwriter.println("Invalidate the session</a>");
                prnwriter.println("<br><center><a href =\"" + url + "\">");
                prnwriter.println("Reload this page</a>");
            }
            prnwriter.println("</body></html>");
            prnwriter.close();
        }
    }
```

Save the code of Listing 5.6 as the `TrackSessionLifeCycle.java` file in the `src\com\kogent` directory of the `HandleSession` application. Configure the `TrackSessionLifeCycle servlet` class in the `web.xml` file and map it to the/`TrackSessionLifeCycle` url pattern. After configuring, compile the `TrackSessionLifeCycle` servlet class, package the application into `HandleSession.war`, and redeploy the HandleSession application. To run the servlet, browse `http://localhost:8080/HandleSession/TrackSessionLifeCycle`.

Figure 5.10 displaysthe output of `TrackSessionLifeCycle` showing the new session, since the user is accessing this page for the first time:

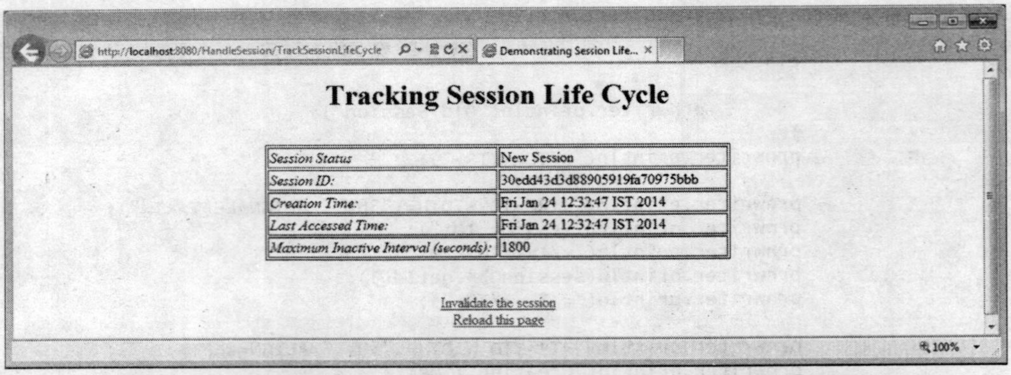

Figure 5.10: Displaying the Output of TrackSessionLifeCycle Servlet Class

The else block of the if…else block provided in Listing 5.6 is executed when the servlet is invoked without any parameters and performs the following steps:

- Calls the `isNew()` method to check for the status of the session that whether it is new or old.
- Calls the `getSession()` method on the `HttpSession` object with the `true` Boolean value passed as an argument.
- Calls the `getId()` method to get the session ID.
- Calls the`getCreationTime()` method to get the creation time of the session. When this method returns the creation time as milliseconds since January 1, 1970 00:00:00 GMT, the returned value needs to be converted into a `Date` object by using the new constructor.
- Calls the`getLastAccessedTime()` method to get the time the session was last accessed.
- Calls the `getMaxInactiveInterval()` method to get the current max-inactive setting.

After printing the details, such as sessionID, creation time of the session, last accessed time of the session, the servlet generates two links, one to invalidate the session and the other to reload the page. The first link has query string as request Action=invalidate that is appended to the URL. When you click the `Invalidate the session`link, the `if` block of the `doGet()` method is executed. However, the second link simply points to the same page. Ensure that cookies are enabled in your browser configuration so that cookies can be stored on your system. Figure 5.11displays the browser's output, when the `Invalidate the session` link is clicked:

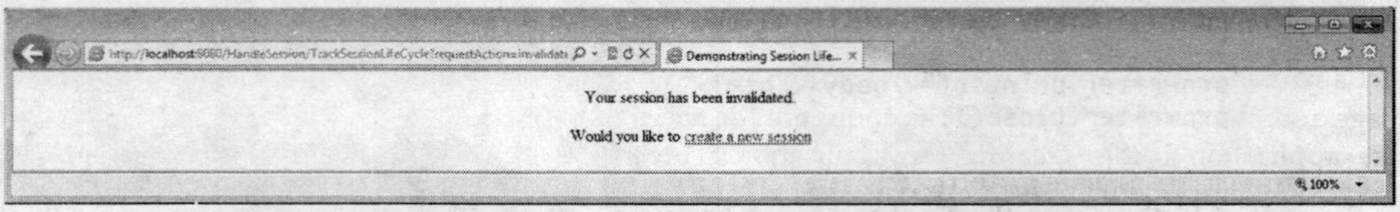

Figure 5.11: Displaying a Message Depicting the Expiration of a Session

Now, when you click the `create a new session` link, a new session is created, as shown in Figure 5.12:

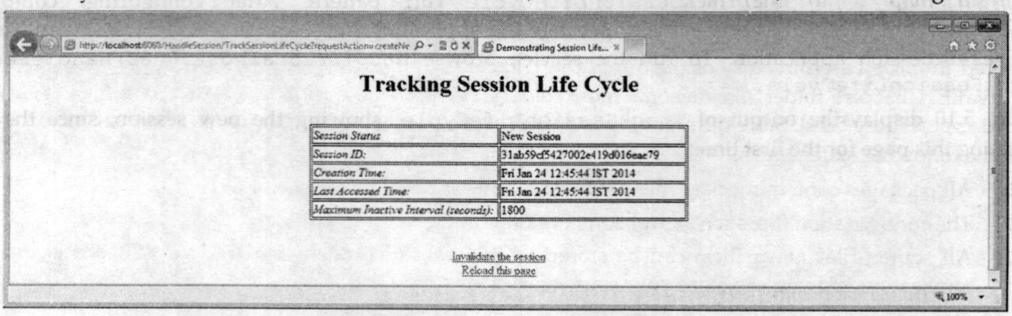

Figure 5.12: Creating a new session

Now, let's see what happens if the code in the `else` block is executed again. Click the `Reload this page` link. You find that the session status displays that the session is old. Figure 5.13 displays the output when the`Reload this page` link is clicked:

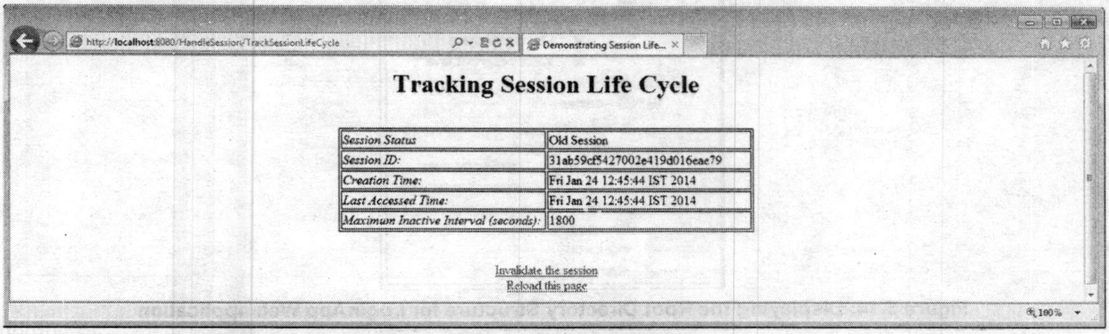

Figure 5.13: Reloading the Old Session

You may notice in Figure 5.13 that the session ID and the session creation time are same as they were before reloading the page, as shown in Figure 5.12. Therefore, every time you click the `Reload this page` link, only the last accessed time changes and not the session ID and the session creation time.

This illustrates how simple it is to create and keep track of sessions. Now, let's see what happens if you click the `Invalidate the session` link. As this URL has a query parameter `action=invalidate`, the `if` block of the `doGet()` method will be executed to invalidate the created session.

Now, click the `Create a new session` link. The resulting page should be similar to Figure 5.12. Examine the `if` block of the code of Listing 5.6. This part of the `TrackSessionLifeCycle` servlet class gets the session from the request, calls the `invalidate()` method, and generates a new link back to the previous page.

Now let's create a login application using Session Tracking API. In this application, a user logs on with the username and password and after logging into the application, the user browses the session details. Finally, the user logs out and the session is terminated.

Creating Login Application using Session Tracking

Let's create the login Web application, in which the user logs on with the username and password, and then creates a session. Till the session is active, the user can browse the session details; however, once the user logs out, the session becomes invalid.

Let's name the Web application as `LoginApp` to demonstrate session tracking. This application has an HTML page and two servlets. These will be configured in the web.xml file. You should know the directory structure of the application before creating the application. Therefore, let's first discuss the directory structure of the `LoginApp` application. The directory structure of the LoginApp Web application would make it easy to understand where to save the Java, HTML, and configuration files.

Exploring the Directory Structure of Login Application

The `servlets`, `HTML` pages, and the `Cascading Style Sheet (CSS)` files of the LoginApp application are stored under a base directory of the application. Create a folder for your application say, `LoginApp`, in the C:\JavaEE\Chapter5 folder. Create some more folders, such as `WEB-INF`, `WEB-INF\classes`, `WEB-INF\lib`, `and src`(Figure 5.14). Store different types of files at the proper location in the directory structure, as described in the following statements:

- All packages containing class files are stored in the WEB-INF\classes folder.
- The configuration file, such as web.xml, is stored in the WEB-INF folder.
- All source files (.java files) can be stored in the src\com\kogent folder. This folder is optional in your application and you can store your source files at any other location.

Figure 5.14 displays the directory structure of the LoginApp application:

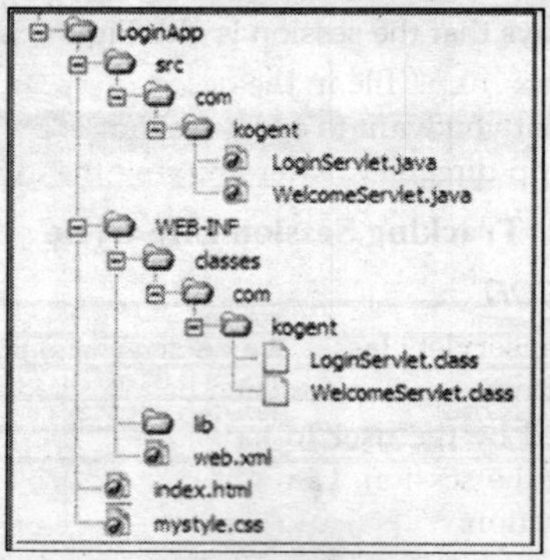

Figure 5.14: Displaying the Root Directory Structure for LoginApp Web application

As shown in Figure 5.14, `LoginApp` is the root folder containing the `WEB-INF` folder, `src` folder, and `index.html` file. The `WEB-INF` folder has two folders, `classes` and `lib`, and a file `web.xml`. As discussed earlier, the package containing `LoginServlet` and `WelcomeServlet` class files is stored at the WEB-INF\classes location under the `LoginApp` directory. The `src\com\kogent` is the optional folder containing source files (`LoginServlet.java` and `WelcomeServlet.java`). The configuration file, `web.xml`, is stored in the WEB-INF folder.

Building the Front-End

The `HTML` page acts as a front-end of the `LoginApp` Web application. The `index.html` page displays a login page for the users. On the basis of the user details entered in index.html, a session is maintained. The user details include the username and password. Listing 5.7 shows the code of the `index.html` file in the `C:\JavaEE\Chapter5\LoginApp` location:

Listing 5.7: Showing the Code of the Front-End

```
<!DOCTYPE html>
<HTML>
  <HEAD>
        <TITLE>Login Application</TITLE>
  </HEAD>
<BODY>
  <FORM METHOD="POST" ACTION="LoginServlet">
  <H1>Login Application using Session Tracking</H1>
  <TABLE ALIGN=CENTER BORDER="0" >
  <TR>
  <TD VALIGN=TOP ALIGN=RIGHT>
        <B>User ID:</B>
  </TD>
  <TD VALIGN=TOP>
  <B><INPUT NAME="username" TYPE="TEXT" MAXLENGTH= "20" SIZE = "20"></B>
  </TD>
  </TR>
  <TR>
  <TD VALIGN=TOP ALIGN=RIGHT>
  <B>Password:</B>
  </TD>
  <TD VALIGN=TOP>
  <B><INPUT NAME="password" TYPE="Password" MAXLENGTH="20" SIZE = "20"></B>
  </TD>
  </TR>
  <TR><TD VALIGN=CENTER>
  <B><INPUT VALUE = "Log In" TYPE= "SUBMIT"></B>
  </TD>
  </TR>
  </TABLE>
```

```
    </FORM>
  </BODY>
  </HTML>
```

Save the code of Listing 5.7 as the `index.html` file in the base `LoginApp` directory and link the `mystyle.css` stylesheet to `index.html`. The style that you want to apply to your HTML page can be stored in the mystyle.css file, which is saved in the base LoginApp directory. After entering the login details, the `LoginServlet` servlet class is requested.

Creating and Managing a Session

In the `LoginApp` Web application, two servlet classes are created, `LoginServlet` and `WelcomeServlet`. The `LoginServlet` servlet class creates a new session for each user and retrieves the data from index.html. Based on the username and password entered by the user in index.html, the LoginServlet servlet class sets two new attributes, username and password, in the session. Listing 5.8 provides the code of the LoginServlet.java file at the `LoginApp\src\com\kogent` location:

Listing 5.8: Setting the Values of the username and password Attributes

```
package com.kogent;
import javax.servlet.http.*;
import java.io.*;
public class LoginServlet extends HttpServlet
{
  public void doPost(HttpServletRequest request,HttpServletResponse response)
  {
        try {
                String username = request.getParameter("username");
                String password = request.getParameter("password");
                HttpSession session = request.getSession(true);
                PrintWriter writer = response.getWriter();
                if (session.isNew() != true)
                {
                        writer.println("<h1>Session is Active</h1>");
                        writer.println("<p><a href=\"index.html\">HomePage" + "</a> and 
                        return to login page");
                }
                else
                {
                        session.setAttribute("username", username);
                        session.setAttribute("password", password);
                        response.setContentType("text/html");
                        writer.println("<html><body style=\"font-
                        family:verdana;font-size:10pt\">");
                        writer.println("<h1>Login Application using Session 
                        Tracking</h1>");
                        writer.println("<p>Thank you, " + username + ".<p> You are now 
                        logged in");
                        String newURL = response.encodeURL("WelcomeServlet");
                        writer.println("Click <a href=\"" + newURL + "\">here</a> for 
                        another servlet");
                        writer.println("</body></html>");
                        writer.close();
                }
        }
        catch (Exception e)
        {
                e.printStackTrace();
        }
  }
}
```

The LoginServlet servlet class checks whether the session is new or not. If the session is not new, the user is prompted to go to the homepage as a session already exists. However, if the session is new, the HTML page is designed, which provides a link to the user to browse and the request is forwarded to `WelcomeServlet`. The

WelcomeServlet servlet class displays the session details of the logged in user. Listing 5.9 provides the code of WelcomeServlet (save the WelcomeServlet.java file in the \HandleSession\src\com\kogent folder):

Listing 5.9: Showing the Code of the WelcomeServlet Servlet Class

```
package com.kogent;
import javax.servlet.http.*;
import java.io.*;
import java.util.*;
public class WelcomeServlet extends HttpServlet
{
   public void doGet(HttpServletRequest request,HttpServletResponse response)
   {
          HttpSession session = request.getSession();
          try {
                   PrintWriter writer = response.getWriter();
                   if (session == null || session.isNew())
                   {
                            writer.println("You are not logged in");
                   }
                   else
                   {
                            response.setContentType("text/html");
                            writer.println("<html><body style=\"font-
                            family:verdana;font-size:10pt\">");
                            writer.println("<h1>Login Application using Session
                            Tracking</h1>");
                            writer.println("<p>Thank you, you are already logged in");
                            writer.println("<p>Here is the data in your session");
                            Enumeration names = session.getAttributeNames();
                            while (names.hasMoreElements())
                            {
                                     String name = (String) names.nextElement();
                                     Object value = session.getAttribute(name);
                                     writer.println("<p>name=" + name + " value=" + value);
                            }
                   }
                   session.invalidate();
                   writer.println("<p><a href=\"index.html\">Logout" + "</a> and return to
                   login page");
                   writer.println("</body></html>");
                   writer.close();
          }
          catch (Exception e)
          {
                   e.printStackTrace();
          }
   }
}
```

When the request is forwarded to the WelcomeServlet servlet class, the servlet retrieves the session and checks whether the session is new or not. If the session is new, the logout message is displayed to the user. However, if the same session continues, the session details of the logged in user are displayed on the browser.

The getAttribute() method is used to retrieve the values of username and password attributes. The getAttributeNames() method is used to retrieve the values of the attributes that are set during the user session. In the following code snippet, the while loop is used to retrieve the attribute name and its value, which is displayed on the browser:

```
Enumeration names = session.getAttributeNames();
while (names.hasMoreElements())
{
   String name = (String) names.nextElement();
   Object value = session.getAttribute(name);
   writer.println("<p>name=" + name + " value=" + value);
}
```

After displaying the session details, the session is explicitly terminated using the invalidate() method. The user can end up the session by clicking the logout link.

The LoginApp Web application created a session for the user who had logged in with the username and password. After logging into the application, the user browses to get the session details. During the session, username and password have been set as the attributes in the user session, and the values of these attributes are retrieved by the WelcomeServlet servlet class and are displayed on the browser.

Now, compile the two servlets from the src\com\kogent directory by using the following command:

```
javac -d C:\JavaEE\chapter5\LoginApp\WEB-INF\classes *.java
```

The execution of the preceding command creates the package directory under the WEB-INF\classes folder. Prior to packaging, deploying, and running the LoginApp Web application, these servlets need to be configured in web.xml.

Configuring the Login Application

To configure the LoginApp application, the configuration file used is web.xml, which maps the URL path, forwarded by index.html to the LoginServlet servlet class and also defines the url pattern for the WelcomeServlet servlet class. Listing 5.10 shows the code of the web.xml file, located in the WEB-INF folder of the LoginApp application (save the web.xml file in the \HandleSession\WEB-INF folder):

Listing 5.10: Configuring the Servlets and HTML Page of the LoginApp Application

```
<?xml version="1.0" encoding="UTF-8"?>

<web-app version="3.1" xmlns="http://xmlns.jcp.org/xml/ns/javaee"
xmlns:xsi="http://www.w3.org/2001/XMLSchema-instance"
xsi:schemaLocation="http://xmlns.jcp.org/xml/ns/javaee http://xmlns.jcp.org/xml/ns/javaee/web-app_3_1.xsd">

<servlet>
  <servlet-name>LoginServlet</servlet-name>
  <servlet-class>com.kogent.LoginServlet</servlet-class>
</servlet>
<servlet-mapping>
  <servlet-name>LoginServlet</servlet-name>
  <url-pattern>/LoginServlet</url-pattern>
</servlet-mapping>
<servlet>
  <servlet-name>WelcomeServlet</servlet-name>
  <servlet-class>com.kogent.WelcomeServlet</servlet-class>
</servlet>
<servlet-mapping>
  <servlet-name>WelcomeServlet</servlet-name>
  <url-pattern>/WelcomeServlet</url-pattern>
</servlet-mapping>
<session-config>
  <session-timeout>30</session-timeout>
</session-config>
<welcome-file-list>
  <welcome-file>index.html</welcome-file>
</welcome-file-list>
</web-app>
```

In Listing 5.10, web.xml configures the LoginServlet and WelcomeServlet servlet classes and also provides the url pattern for these servlets. The full package structure has been provided for each servlet class, as shown in Figure 5.14.Moreover, the session timeout has also been set to 30 minutes and the welcome file which will be displayed when the LoginApp Web application runs, is index.html.

Now, before running the LoginApp Web application, it is packaged in the WAR file (LoginApp.war) by using the following command:

```
jar -cvf LoginApp.war .
```

The preceding command creates the LoginApp.war file containing all the files of the LoginApp directory.

Running the Login Application

After packaging the `LoginApp` Web application, start the Glassfish Server 4.0 and deploy `LoginApp.war`. Now, browse `http://localhost:8080/LoginApp` to see the output of the LoginApp application. Figure 5.15 displays the output of index.html, which serve as the Login page:

Figure 5.15: Displaying the Output of index.html

In Figure 5.15, enter the User ID and Password and click the `Log In` button. In our case, we have entered Charu in the User ID text box and `gunnu` as password in the Password text box. Then, click the Log In button to forward the request to the `LoginServlet` servlet class. The `LoginServlet` servlet class creates a new session for the user Charu and displays a welcome message, as shown in Figure5.16:

Figure 5.16: Displaying the Output of the LoginServlet Servlet Class

The `LoginServlet` servlet class creates a session for the logged in user. To view the session details and value of the attributes set in the session, the user can click the `here` link shown in Figure 5.16. After clicking the link, the request is sent to `WelcomeServlet` and the session details are displayed, as shown in Figure 5.17:

Figure 5.17: Displaying the Output of the WelcomeServlet Servlet Class

By clicking the `Logout` link, shown in Figure 5.17, the user can explicitly end the session and return to index.html.

Therefore, the `LoginApp` application maintains a session for the user who logs in with the username and password. Based on the username and password, the `username` and `password` attributes are set in the session and till the user is in the same session, the session details can be viewed. After logging out, the session is explicitly terminated and the user is no longer in the session and anew session is created for the new user.

This ends up the discussion about session tracking. Let's now learn about how to handle session ID.

Handling Session ID

In Servlet 3.1, HttpSessionIdListener interface is newly introduced to provide security in session handling. It is used to implement listener classes that are responsible to change a session identity. To change a session ID, the changeSessionId() method of the HttpSessionIdListener interface is invoked after a session has been created.

It should be noted that a website hacker can obtain security ID that is used by a website for authentication purpose. It is also possible that a security ID can grant such permissions to the hacker that is related to one's personal belonging. This type of security concerns are solved by the HttpSessionIdListener interface.

The inheritance diagram of the javax.servlet.http.HttpSessionIdListener interface is shown in Figure 5.18:

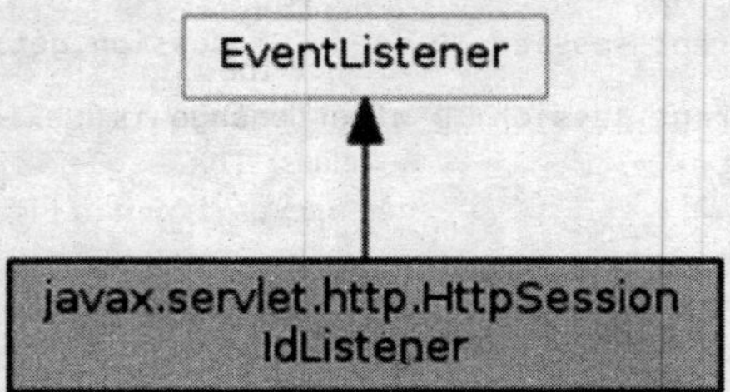

Figure 5.18: Inheritance Diagram of HttpSessionIdListener

The following APIs accepts listener classes to implement the HttpSessionIdListener interface:

- addListener (String className)
- <T extends EventListener> void addListener (T t)
- void addListener (Class <? extends EventListener> listenerClass)
- <T extends EventListener> void createListener(Class<T> clazz)
- @WebListener

The HttpSessionIdListener interface has a method, named void sessionIdChanged (HttpSessionEvent se, String oldSessionId). Whenever a session ID change takes place, a notification is sent. Let's create a servlet class, ChangingSessionID. In this servlet class, a session ID is displayed two times. First time, the servlet class displays session ID before invoking the changeSessionId() method and second time it displays session ID after invoking the changeSessionId() method

Listing 5.11 shows the code of the `ChangingSessionID.java` file (save the `ChangingSessionID.java` file in the \HandleSession\src\com\kogent folder):

Listing 5.11: Displaying the Code of the ChangingSessionID `Servlet` Class

```
package com.kogent ;

import java.io.*;
import javax.servlet.*;
import javax.servlet.http.*;
import java.util.Date;

public class ChangingSessionID extends HttpServlet
{
```

```
    public void doGet (HttpServletRequest req, HttpServletResponse res)
            throws ServletException, IOException
    {
                res.setContentType("text/html;charset=UTF-8");
            PrintWriter out = res.getWriter();
            HttpSession session = req.getSession();

    try
    {
    out.println("<!DOCTYPE html>");

    out.println("<html>");

    out.println("<head>");

    out.println("<title>Servlet SessionIdTest</title>");

    out.println("</head>");

    out.println("<body>");

    out.println("<h1>Servlet SessionIdTest at " + req.getContextPath() + "</h1>");

    out.println("<p>The current session ID is : " + session.getId());
    req.changeSessionId();
    out.println("<p>The current session ID after change is : " + session.getId());

    out.println("</body>");

    out.println("</html>");


    }
       finally
       {
       out.close();
       }

    }

    }
```

Save the code of Listing 5.11 as the ChangingSessionID.java file in the src\com\kogent directory of the HandleSession Web application. Compile the ChangingSessionID servlet class and configure it in the web.xml file, created in Listing 5.2 for the HandleSession Web application. The following code snippet shows how to configure and map the ChangingSessionID servlet class to the /ChangingSessionID url pattern:

```
    <servlet>
         <servlet-name>ChangingSessionID</servlet-name>
         <servlet-class>com.kogent.ChangingSessionID</servlet-class>
       </servlet>

       <servlet-mapping>
    <servlet-name>ChangingSessionID</servlet-name>
    <url-pattern>/ChangingSessionID</url-pattern>
       </servlet-mapping>
```

You can run the ChangingSessionID servlet class only after packaging the resources of the HandleSession Web application in the HandleSession.war file. Then, you need to redeploy the Web application on the Glassfish Server 4.0 and navigate the http://localhost:8080/HandleSession/ChangingSessionID URL. Figure 5.19 displays the output of ChangingSessionID servlet:

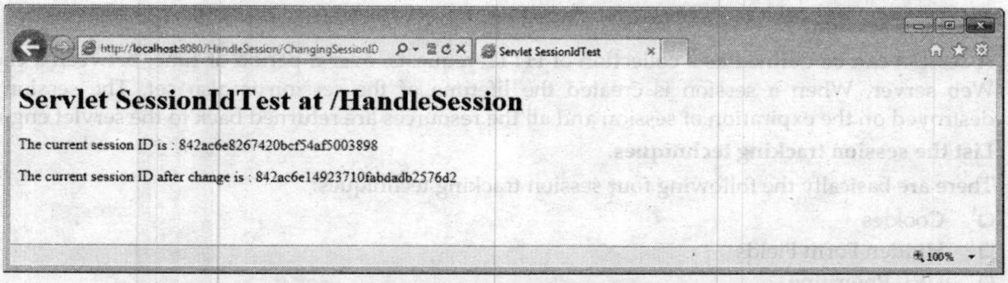

Figure 5.19: Displaying the Output of the ChangingSessionID Servlet Class

Let's briefly summarize all the concepts that have been covered so far in this chapter before moving to the next chapter.

Summary

This chapter has described the implementation of session handling in servlets. Session handling can be done by using many mechanisms, such as Cookies, URL-Rewriting, hidden form fields, and SSL. Apart from this, the session tracking API is also used to handle sessions in servlets. The `javax.servlet.http.HttpSession` interface helps in maintaining the client's session. The various methods, such as `setAttribute()` and `getAttribute()` used to set or retrieve the value of an attribute in a session are discussed in the chapter. The `LoginApp` Web application has been designed in this chapter, which demonstrates the session tracking of the user logged in by using the `HttpSession` interface. The various other servlets created in the chapter explain URL-Rewriting and working with Cookies. At the end, a servlet class is created to show how to perform change in session ID in Servlets 3.1

The next chapter discusses how to handle events and implement wrappers in Servlets 3.1.

Quick Revise

Q1. If cookies are disabled on client-side, the alternate session mechanism that can be used is ……………………… .

A. Either Cookies or URL rewriting
B. URL rewriting
C. Cookies and URL rewriting
D. None

Ans. B

Q2. The interface that defines the `getSession()` method is ……………………………… .

A. HttpServletRequest
B. ServletRequest
C. ServletResponse
D. HttpServletResponse

Ans. A

Q3. The ……………………… method of `HttpServletRequest` returns null if a session does not exist.

A. getSession()
B. getSession(true)
C. getSession(false)
D. getNewSession()

Ans. C

Q4. The ……………………………… method on the session object is used to remove a set attribute.

A. removeAllValues()
B. removeAttribute("attributeName")
C. removeAttributes()
D. removeAllAttributes()

Ans. B

Q5. Which statement is false:

A. URL rewriting can be used to track a session
B. SSL has a built in mechanism to obtain the data to define a session
C. The name of session tracking cookies must be `JSESSIONID`
D. There is no restriction for name of the cookie tracking the session

Ans. D

Q6. What is a session?

Ans. A session can be defined as a collection of HTTP requests, over a period of time, between a client and a Web server. When a session is created the lifetime of the session is also set. The session object is destroyed on the expiration of session and all the resources are returned back to the servlet engine.

Q7. List the session tracking techniques.

Ans. There are basically the following four session tracking techniques:

- Cookies
- Hidden Form Fields
- URL Rewriting
- Secure Socket Layer (SSL) sessions

Q8. How cookies are used to track a session?

Ans. Using cookies is the simplest and easiest way to track a session. A unique session id (stored in the form of a cookie) is sent by the server to the client as a part of the response and the same session id saved with the client is sent to the server as a part of the request which helps the server to recognize the unique client session.

Q9. List the methods of the HttpSession interface which help a servlet to manage session life-cycle.

Ans. The HttpSession interface provides the following methods to manage session life-cycle:

- Invalidate()
- setMaxInactiveInterval(int interval)
- isNew()
- getCreationTime()
- getLastAccessedTime()

Q10. Cookie is a class of the .... package.

Ans. javax.servlet.http

Q11. Enlist the APIs that accept listener classes to implement the HttpSessionIdListener interface.

Ans. The following APIs accepts listener classes to implement the HttpSessionIdListener interface:

- addListener (String className)
- <T extends EventListener> void addListener (T t)
- void addListener (Class <? extends EventListener> listenerClass)
- <T extends EventListener> void createListener(Class<T> clazz)
- @WebListener

6

Implementing Event Handling and Wrappers in Servlets 3.1

The concept of event handling allows you to handle the events related to the life cycle of a servlet or session. When an event occurs in a Web application, a relevant listener is notified about the occurrence of the event and the relevant task is performed. To have a better understanding of event handling, let's consider an example. When a client request is received by a Web container, firstly the container maps the request with an appropriate servlet. After the servlet is identified, the Web container loads the servlet class and creates an instance of the servlet. The servlet is then initialized by calling the init() method. After calling the init() method, the service() method passes the request and response objects to the Web container. The Web container invokes the destroy() method to remove the servlet, if the servlet is not required. Now, as you can see that in this example, various events, such as initializing a servlet, servicing a request, and destroying the servlet are occurring. These events can be handled by using event handling. To implement the event handling process in this example, you need to create a listener class that is notified by the container about these events.

Apart from handling the events as described in the preceding example, event handling can also be used to handle session level events, such as adding or removing an attribute from a session. In case of life cycle events of a servlet, a context listener is created and notified about the initialization and destruction of a ServletContext or the addition and deletion of an attribute from the ServletContext. Similarly, a session listener notifies a class when a session is initialized or destroyed, or when an attribute is added or removed from a session.

Java Servlet also allows you to use wrappers to modify the request and response objects. In other words, with the help of wrappers you can add the additional information, such as value of an attribute that is used in a session to the request sent by a user.

This chapter introduces events and explains the process of event handling. The chapter also describes different types of servlet and session level events. Next, you create an onlineshop application to implement the process of handling events. In addition, the chapter also discusses about wrapper classes that are used to modify the request and response data before pre or post operations.

Introducing Events

An event refers to a set of actions that may occur while an application is running. It could also be defined as a set of actions, such as clicking a button or pressing a key, performed by a user. The following list shows some of the events that may occur during the life cycle of a servlet:

- Initializing servlets
- Adding, removing, or replacing attributes in ServletContext
- Creating, activating, passivating, or invalidating a session
- Adding, removing, or replacing attributes in a servlet session
- Destroying servlets

Now, let's discuss how these events can be handled in servlets.

Introducing Event Handling

In Java, events are generated by objects. When an event is fired, a specific method of an object (to be notified) is called. This specific method is then notified about the event and the event object is passed as a parameter to that method. These methods are known as event handlers. However, in servlets, the listener objects are created to listen to events that may occur during the life cycle of a servlet. The event handling can be implemented by using the pre-defined interfaces, which help developers to deal with the `ServletContext` interface and the `HttpSession interface`. A developer can use multiple listeners based on the type of events in a single Web application. These listeners are called event listeners.

The event listeners are Java classes that are notified about the life cycle events of a servlet whenever an event occurs. Apart from the life cycle events, such as creating or destroying the servlets, the event listeners are also notified about the modification of attributes in the `ServletContext` or `HttpSession` object.

A developer creates an event listener class to implement the appropriate listener interface and register it in the `web.xml file`. In Servlet 3.1, it is not mandatory to configure the event listener class; instead, you can simply annotate the listener class. Using annotations, you can declare a listener class as a Web component and can invoke it in a servlet. The servlet container creates an object of the event listener class while deploying an application. The object is then invoked by the servlet container at runtime.

Earlier, you need to set the shared resources by using the `<context-param>` tag of the web.xml file and then access them by using the `getInitParameter()` method of the `ServletContext` object. However, while setting the shared resources by using the `<context-param>` tag, the developer is not aware of the sequence in which the resources of an application are accessed. Due to this, the developer was not able to provide the code to perform the appropriate task on the occurrence of an event. The solution to this problem is to give major control to only one servlet, which can listen to the application life cycle events. Event listeners are introduced to notify the listener (servlet) about the occurrence of an event.

Let's now explore the different types of servlet events and event listeners.

Working with the Types of Servlet Events

The events that can occur during the life cycle of a servlet can be grouped into various categories on the basis of their level of occurrence. The following is the list of various levels of servlet events:

- **Request level events**—Refer to the events related to the client's information to a servlet. There are two event listeners, `ServletRequestListener` and `ServletRequestAttributeListener`, to handle request level events. The `ServletRequestListener` interface is implemented to get notifications about the incoming and outgoing requests' scope in a Web component. The `ServletRequestAttributeListener` interface is implemented to get notifications about the changes made in the request attribute.
- **Servlet context level events**—Refer to the application level events. The `ServletContextListener` interface is implemented to notify the initialization or destruction of the servlet in the `ServletContext` interface. The class implementing the `ServletContextAttributeListener` interface is notified about the changes made to the attributes of the `ServletContext` object.
- **Servlet session level events**—Refer to the events that are used to maintain the session of a client. The `HttpSessionListener` and `HttpSessionActivationListener` interfaces are implemented to notify the creation, invalidation, activation, passivation, and timeout events of the `HttpSession` interface. The `HttpSessionAttributeListener` interface can be implemented to notify the changes in the attributes of a session and the class implementing the `HttpSessionBindingListener` interface is notified when a servlet is bound to or unbound from a session.

Let's now discuss the preceding levels of servlet events in detail in the following subsections.

Implementing the Servlet Context Level Events

A `ServletContext` object is created and associated with a Web application at the time of its deployment. This object stores all the information about the servlets associated with the Web application. The developer can create a database connection when the `ServletContext` object is created, and may close the connection when the `ServletContext` object is destroyed. To handle the events associated with the creation and destruction of the `ServletContext` object, you need to create a listener that implements the `ServletContextListener` interface. This interface helps to notify the listener about the occurrence of the following events:

- Creation of the ServletContext and its availability to service the first request
- Termination of the ServletContext

The `ServletContextAttributeListener` interface helps to notify a listener about any changes or modifications made to the attributes of the ServletContext object.

The `ServletContextAttributeListener` event listener notifies about the following three events:

- Adding a new attribute to the context
- Replacing an existing attribute in the context
- Removing an attribute from the context

The ServletContextListener and ServletContextAttributeListener interfaces have various methods that are invoked by the object of the event listener that implements either of these interfaces to notify about the ServletContext events.

Explaining Servlet Context Life Cycle Event Handling

The events in a servlet life cycle can be monitored and handled by defining an object of a listener. Then, the listener's object invokes an appropriate method based upon the occurrence of the servlet life cycle events. This process is used to handle the servlet context life cycle events.

Let's now discuss about the various methods of the listener interfaces, ServletContextListener and ServletContextAttributeListener and then define a listener class.

Describing the ServletContextListener Interface

The ServletContextListener interface receives notifications about the changes in the ServletContext object of the Web application. To receive notification events, the listener class implements the ServletContextListener interface, which must be configured in the Deployment Descriptor of the Web application. The ServletContextListener interface extends the EventListener class.

Table 6.1 describes the methods provided by the ServletContextListener interface:

Table 6.1: Noteworthy Methods of the ServletContextListener Interface

Methods	Description
void contextInitialized (ServletContextEvent sce)	Notifies that the initialization process for the Web application is going to start. During the notification process, a notification about context initialization is sent to all ServletContextListener prior to initializing any filter or servlet in the Web application.
void contextDestroyed (ServletContextEvent sce)	Notifies that the ServletContext object is going to shut down. All servlets and filters should be destroyed prior to the notification about the ServletContext object destruction.

Describing the ServletContextAttributeListener Interface

The ServletContextAttributeListener interface allows us to monitor the changes made to the attribute events of a ServletContext. The ServletContext attribute events are as follows:

- Adding an attribute
- Replacing an attribute
- Removing an attribute

Implementing the ServletContextAttributeListener interface enables a user to receive notifications whenever the attribute list on the ServletContext object of a Web application changes. Note that to receive notification events, the implementation class must be configured in the Deployment Descriptor of a Web application.

Table 6.2 describes the methods provided by the ServletContextAttributeListener interface:

Table 6.2: Noteworthy Methods of the ServletContextAttributeListener Interface

Methods	Description
void attributeAdded (ServletContextAttributeEvent scab)	Notifies about the addition of a new attribute in the ServletContext object. It is called just after the addition of the attribute.
void attributeRemoved (ServletContextAttributeEvent scab)	Notifies about the removal of an existing attribute from the ServletContext object. It is called just after the removal of the attribute.
void attributeReplaced ServletContextAttributeEvent scab)	Notifies about the replacement of an attribute in the ServletContext object. It is called just after the replacement of an attribute.

Let's learn how to handle events for servlet context by creating a Web application named events.

Handling Events for ServletContext

In this section, let's implement the event handling mechanism in ServletContext by creating a Web application called events. In this application, the `ServletContextListener` object notifies about the creation and destruction of the ServletContext object. In addition, the `ServletContextAttributeListener` object notifies about adding, replacing, or removing an attribute from the servlet context.

Implementing the ServletContextListener Interface

You need to create a listener class that implements the `ServletContextListener` interface and a simple servlet to display a message. The listener class is notified about the initialization and destruction of ServletContext in the events Web application. This listener class implements the `ServletContextListener` interface.

Listing 6.1 provides the code for the `ContextListener` class (save the `ContextListener.java` file in the `\events\src\com\kogent\listeners` folder):

Listing 6.1: Showing the Implementation of the ServletContextListener Interface

```
package com.kogent.listeners;
import javax.servlet.ServletContext;
import javax.servlet.ServletContextEvent;
import javax.servlet.ServletContextListener;
import javax.swing.*;
public class ContextListener implements ServletContextListener
{
   private ServletContext cont=null;
   public void contextInitialized(ServletContextEvent evt)
   {
         this.cont = evt.getServletContext();
         System.out.println("Context intialized........!!!!!");
         JOptionPane.showMessageDialog(null,"Context intialized.........!!!!!");
   }
   public void contextDestroyed(ServletContextEvent evt)
   {
         System.out.println("Context destroyed.........!!!!!");
         JOptionPane.showMessageDialog(null,"Context destroyed.........!!:!!");
         this.cont=null;
   }
}
```

In Listing 6.1, the `ContextListener` class is notified about the initialization of ServletContext before a servlet is initialized in the events Web application. A dialog box appears displaying the message that the servlet context of the Web application has been initialized, when the contextInitialized() method receives the notification about initialization. The following code snippet demonstrates how to map the `ContextListener` class in the `web.xml` file:

```
<listener>
   <listener-class>com.kogent.listeners.ContextListener</listener-class>
</listener>
```

Let's create a simple servlet, `DemoServlet`, to display a hello message to all users.

Listing 6.2 provides the code for the `DemoServlet` servlet (save the `DemoServlet.java` file in the `\events\src\com\kogent\servlets` folder):

Listing 6.2: Implementing Event Handling in the `DemoServlet` Servlet

```
package com.kogent.servlets;
import java.io.*;
import javax.servlet.*;
import javax.servlet.http.*;
public class DemoServlet extends HttpServlet
{

   @Override
   protected void doGet(HttpServletRequest request, HttpServletResponse response) throws
   ServletException, IOException
   {
```

```
            PrintWriter pw = response.getWriter();
            response.setContentType("text/html");
            pw.println("<html><head></head><body>");
            pw.println("Hello World: This Servlet has been initialized");
            pw.println("</body></html>");
      }
   }
```

Now, configure the `DemoServlet` servlet in the `web.xml file`. The listener class and the servlet class are mapped in the `web.xml` file.

Listing 6.3 shows the code for the web.xml file (save the web.xml file in the `\events\WEB-INF` folder):

Listing 6.3: Displaying the Code for the web.xml File

```
<?xml version="1.0" encoding="UTF-8"?>
<web-app version="3.1" xmlns="http://xmlns.jcp.org/xml/ns/javaee"
xmlns:xsi="http://www.w3.org/2001/XMLSchema-instance"
xsi:schemaLocation="http://xmlns.jcp.org/xml/ns/javaee
http://xmlns.jcp.org/xml/ns/javaee/web-app_3_1.xsd">

<listener>
  <listener-class>com.kogent.listeners.ContextListener</listener-class>
</listener>

<servlet>
  <servlet-name>DemoServlet</servlet-name>
  <servlet-class>com.kogent.servlets.DemoServlet</servlet-class>
</servlet>

<servlet-mapping>
  <servlet-name>DemoServlet</servlet-name>
  <url-pattern>/DemoServlet</url-pattern>
</servlet-mapping>

<session-config>
  <session-timeout>30</session-timeout>
</session-config>

<welcome-file-list>
  <welcome-file>DemoServlet</welcome-file>
</welcome-file-list>
</web-app>
```

In Listing 6.3, the `DemoServlet` servlet is displayed as a welcome page to the users. According to Servlet 3.1 specification, Glassfish Server 4.0 servlets can also be specified as a welcome file. Now, compile the `ContextListener` listener class and `DemoServlet` servlet class, and generate the `events.war file`, which is deployed on the `Glassfish Server 4.0`. When the `events.war file` is deployed on the `Glassfish Server 4.0`, the `Message` box appears, as shown in Figure 6.1:

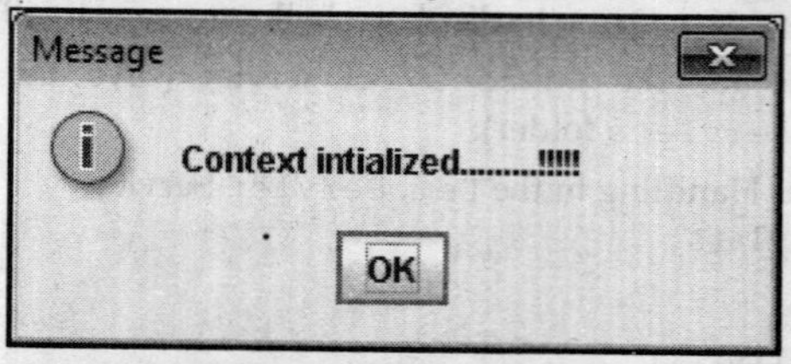

Figure 6.1: Displaying a Message after the Web Application is Deployed

After initializing the `ServletContext` of the `events` Web application, the welcome message can be displayed by browsing the `http://localhost:8080/events URL`.

NOTE

URL stands for Uniform Resource Locator.

When the `events` Web application is undeployed, the `contextDestroyed()` method of the `ContextListener` class is invoked and the `Message` dialog box appears, as shown in Figure 6.2:

Figure 6.2: Displaying a Message after the Web Application is Undeployed

Similar to the notification of initialization and destruction of a ServletContext, the notifications with respect to the modifications made in attributes of `ServletContext` are provided with the help of the `attributeAdded()`, `attributeRemoved()`, and `attributeReplaced()` methods of the `ServletContextAttributeListener` interface.

Implementing the ServletContextAttributeListener Interface

The `ServletContextAttribListener` class implements the `ServletContextAttributeListener` interface and its methods are notified depending upon the event generated.

Listing 6.4 provides the code for the `ServletContextAttribListener` class (save the `ServletContextAttribListener.java` file in the `\events\src\com\kogent\listeners` folder):

Listing 6.4: Implementing the ServletContextAttributeListener Interface in the ServletContextAttribListener Class

```
package com.kogent.listeners;

import javax.servlet.ServletContextAttributeEvent;
import javax.servlet.ServletContextAttributeListener;
import javax.swing.*;

public class ServletContextAttribListener
implements ServletContextAttributeListener {

   //This method is invoked when an attribute
   //is added to the ServletContext object
   public void attributeAdded (ServletContextAttributeEvent scae)
   {
        JOptionPane.showMessageDialog(null,"Attribute Added!!!!!");
   }

   //This method is invoked when an attribute
   //is removed from the ServletContext object
   public void attributeRemoved (ServletContextAttributeEvent scae)
   {
        JOptionPane.showMessageDialog(null,"Attribute Removed!!!!!");
   }

   //This method is invoked when an attribute
   //is replaced in the ServletContext object
   public void attributeReplaced (ServletContextAttributeEvent scae)
   {
        JOptionPane.showMessageDialog(null,"Attribute Replaced!!!!!");
   }
}
```

In Listing 6.4, the `ServletContextAttribListener` class is a simple Java class, which is notified when the attributes from the `ServletContext` object are added, replaced, or removed. The relevant method of this class is invoked depending upon the event fired.

The following code snippet shows the mapping to be added to the web.xml file (Listing 6.3) for the ServletContextAttribListener class:

```
<listener>
<listener-class>com.kogent.listeners.ServletContextAttribListener</listener-class>
</listener>
```

Now, let's create a HyperText Markup Language (HTML) page that forwards the request to servlets when a form is submitted. The servlets then detect the type of action, such as adding, removing, or replacing the attributes, and notify to the ServletContextAttribListener class.

Listing 6.5 provides the code for the servletcontextattrib.html file (save the servletcontextattrib.html file in the \events folder):

Listing 6.5: Showing the Code for the ServletContextAttrib.html File

```
<!DOCTYPE html>
<html>
  <head>
        <title>Working With Attributes Of the ServletContext Object</title>
        </head>
  <body>
        <h1>Demonstrating Servlet Context Attribute Listener </h1>
        <form name="theForm" action="./servletcontextattrib" method="POST">
        <table width="75%">
                <tr><td rowspan="3">Select an Action</td>
                        <td><input type="radio" name="action" value="add">
                        Add Attribute To ServletContext</td>
                </tr>
                <tr>
                        <td><input type="radio" name="action" value="remove">
                        Remove Attribute From ServletContext</td>
                </tr>
                <tr>
                <td><input type="radio" name="action" value="replace">
                        Replace Attribute In ServletContext</td>
                </tr>
                <tr><td>Enter Servlet Context Attribute Name</td>
                        <td><input type="text" name="name" value=""></td>
                </tr>
                <tr><td>Enter Servlet Context Attribute Value</td>
                        <td><input type="text" name="value" value=""></td>
                </tr>
                <tr><td colspan="2" align="center">
                        <input type="submit" name="btnSubmit" value="Submit">
                        </td>
                </tr>
        </table>
        </form>
  </body>
</html>
```

In Listing 6.5, an HTML page is designed. This HTML page has three radio buttons for three different actions. There are two text boxes as well, which hold the name of the attribute and its value. Depending upon the action selected in the HTML page, the respective method of the ServletContextAttribListener class is called. When the ServletContextAttrib.html form is submitted, the request is forwarded to the ServletContextAttrib servlet, which is mapped to the /servletcontextattrib URL pattern in the web.xml file.

Listing 6.6 provides the code for the ServletContextAttrib servlet (save the ServletContextAttrib.java file in the \events\src\com\kogent\servlets folder):

Listing 6.6: Showing the Code for the ServletContextAttrib.java File

```
package com.kogent.servlets;
import java.io.*;
import javax.servlet.*;
import javax.servlet.http.*;
```

```
public class ServletContextAttrib extends HttpServlet
{
   public void service(HttpServletRequest request,
   HttpServletResponse response)
   throws IOException, ServletException
   {
         response.setContentType("text/html");
         ServletOutputStream out = response.getOutputStream();
         out.print("<html>");
         out.print("<head>");
         out.print("<title>ServletContext Attributes</title>");
         out.print("</head>");
         out.print("<body>");
         ServletContext context = getServletContext();
         String action = request.getParameter("action");
         String name = request.getParameter("name");
         String value = request.getParameter("value");

         if (action == null) {}
         else {
                  if (action.equals("add"))
                  {
                           String test = (String) context.getAttribute(name);
                           if (test == null)
                           {
                                    context.setAttribute(name, value);
                           out.print("Added Attribute To ServletContext object");
                           } else {
                           context.setAttribute(name, value);
                           out.print("Replaced Attribute in ServletContext");
                           }
                  }

                  else if (action.equals("remove"))
                  {
                           String test = (String) context.getAttribute(name);
                           if (test == null) {
                           out.print("Attribute does not exist");
                           } else {
                           context.removeAttribute(name);
                           out.print("Removed Attribute From ServletContext");
                           }
                  }

                  else
                  {
                           String test = (String) context.getAttribute(name);
                           if (test == null)
                           {
                                    context.setAttribute(name, value);
                                    out.print("Added Attribute To ServletContext object");
                           } else {
                           context.setAttribute(name, value);
                           out.print("Replaced Attribute in ServletContext");
                           }
                  }
         }

         out.print("<center> <br /> <br />");
         out.print("<a href='./servletcontextattrib.html'>");
         out.print("Back To Home Page");
         out.print("</a>");
         out.print("</center>");
         out.print("</body>");
```

```
            out.print("</html>");
        }
    }
```

In Listing 6.6, `ServletContextAttrib` is a servlet class that responds to the request sent by the `servletcontextattrib.html` form. The `ServletContextAttrib` class retrieves the data, such as the name of the attribute, the value of the attribute, and the action to be performed. Depending upon the following actions selected by a user, the relevant method is invoked to perform a task:

- **The add action**—Allows the servlet container to invoke the attributeAdded() method to add a new attribute (provided by the user) to the ServletContext
- **The remove action**—Allows the servlet container to invoke the attributeRemoved() method to remove the attribute selected by the user from the ServletContext
- **The replace action**—Allows the servlet container to invoke the attributeReplaced() method to replace the old value of an attribute with a new value

Compile both the `ServletContextAttribListener` and `ServletContextAttrib` classes. After compiling these classes, map the `ServletContextAttrib` servlet class in the web.xml file (Listing 6.3). The following code snippet shows the mapping for the `ServletContextAttrib` servlet:

```
<servlet>
  <servlet-name>ServletContextAttrib</servlet-name>
  <servlet-class>com.kogent.servlets.ServletContextAttrib</servlet-class>
</servlet>
  <servlet-mapping>
  <servlet-name>ServletContextAttrib</servlet-name>
  <url-pattern>/servletcontextattrib</url-pattern>
</servlet-mapping>
```

Now, create a new `events.war` file to be deployed on the `Glassfish Server 4.0`. After deploying the `Web ARchive` (WAR) file, browse the `http://localhost:8080/events/servletcontextattrib.html` URL.

Figure 6.3 displays the `output of the servletcontextattrib HTML` page when the attribute name and value are entered in the relevant text boxes, and the `Add Attribute To ServletContext` radio button is selected:

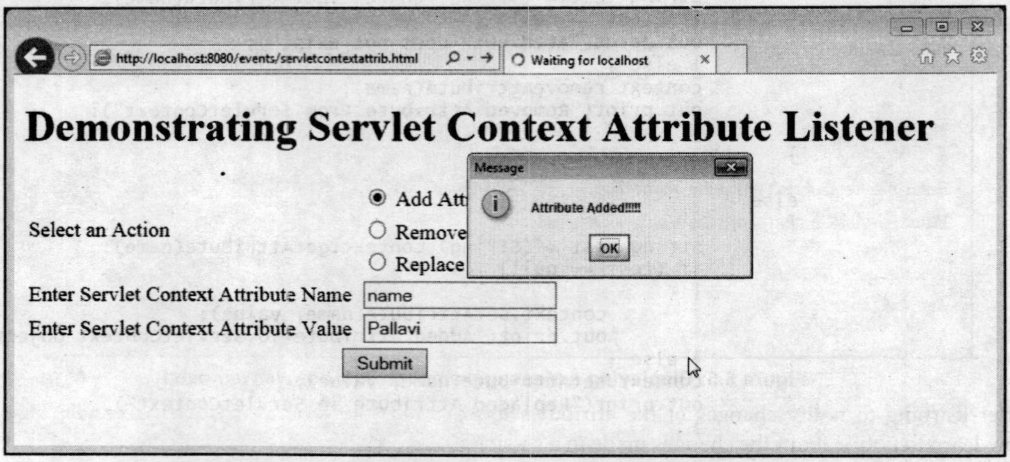

Figure 6.3: Displaying a Message when a New Attribute is Added

In Figure 6.3, when the user clicks the `Submit` button, a message box appears with the `Attribute Added!!!!` message.

You can also replace the value of an attribute with a new value by selecting the `Replace Attribute In ServletContext` radio button in the `servletcontextattrib HTML` page and clicking the `Submit` button. The attribute value is replaced.

Figure 6.4 displays a message box after the `ServletContextAttribListener` class is notified about the replacement of the attribute value:

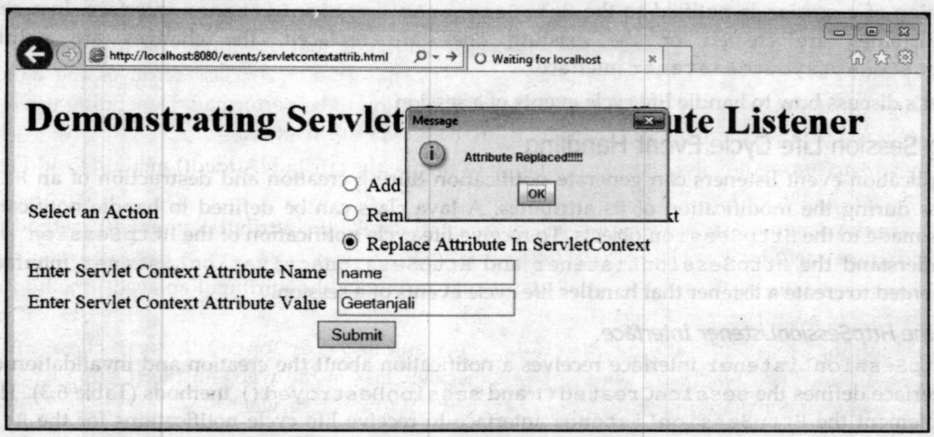

Figure 6.4: Displaying a Message when an Attribute is Replaced

In Figure 6.4, the value of the `name` attribute is replaced with `Geetanjali` and the `attributeReplaced()` method of the `ServletContextAttribListener` class is invoked.

You can also remove an attribute, when no longer required. In the `servletcontextattrib HTML` page, you can remove the `name` attribute by specifying its name and value, selecting the `Remove Attribute From ServletContext` radio button, and clicking the `Submit` button.

Figure 6.5 displays the message that appears when the name attribute is removed from the servlet context:

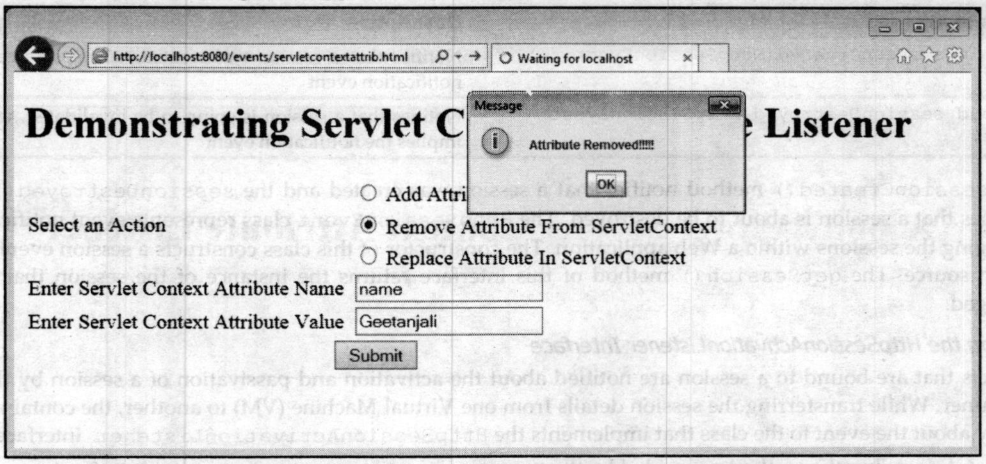

Figure 6.5: Displaying a Message when an Attribute is Removed

After learning to notify changes of the attributes to `ServletContextAttributeListener` interface, let's now learn to notify about the changes made in a session.

Implementing the Servlet Session Level Events

The session level events refer to maintaining the state of a user or a client session. In a session, a class is notified about the servlet session level events during the occurrence of any of the following events:

- Creating a session
- Adding, removing, or replacing the attributes of a session
- Destroying a session

When any of these events occur, the appropriate interface is notified about the event. The `HttpSessionListener` interface is notified about the creation and destruction of a session. The activation or passivation of a session is notified to the `HttpSessionActivationListener` interface. In a session, when new attributes are created or the existing ones are replaced, the changes are notified in the `HttpSessionAttributeListener` interface.

Now, let's discuss how to handle life cycle events of a session.

Explaining Session Life Cycle Event Handling

The application event listeners can generate notification during creation and destruction of an `HttpSession` object or during the modification of its attributes. A Java class can be defined to handle notifications for the changes made to the `HttpSession` objects. To receive life cycle notification of the `HttpSession object`, let's first understand the `HttpSessionListener` and `HttpSessionActivationListener` interfaces that are implemented to create a listener that handles life cycle events of a session.

Describing the HttpSessionListener Interface

The `HttpSessionListener` interface receives a notification about the creation and invalidation of a session. This interface defines the `sessionCreated()` and `sessionDestroyed()` methods (Table 6.3). The Java class can implement the `HttpSessionListener` interface to receive life cycle notifications for the `HttpSession` interface.

Implementations of the `HttpSessionListener` interface provide the notification of changes made in the active sessions in a Web application. You need to provide the configuration details about the implementation class in Deployment Descriptor for the Web application so that the application can be notified about the occurrence of events.

Table 6.3 describes the methods provided by the `HttpSessionListener` interface:

Table 6.3: Noteworthy Methods of the HttpSessionListener Interface

Methods	Description
`void sessionCreated(HttpSessionEvent se)`	Notifies that a session was created, where `se` implies the notification event
`void sessionDestroyed(HttpSessionEvent se)`	Notifies that a session is going to be invalidated, where `se` implies the notification event

The `sessionCreated()` method notifies that a session was created and the `sessionDestroyed()` method notifies that a session is about to be destroyed. The `HttpSessionEvent` class represents event notifications for changing the sessions within a Web application. The constructor of this class constructs a session event from the given source. The `getSession()` method of this interface returns the instance of the session that has been changed.

Describing the HttpSessionActivationListener Interface

Objects that are bound to a session are notified about the activation and passivation of a session by the servlet container. While transferring the session details from one Virtual Machine (VM) to another, the container should notify about the event to the class that implements the `HttpSessionActivationListener` interface.

Table 6.4 describes the methods provided by the `HttpSessionActivationListener` interface:

Table 6.4: Noteworthy Methods of the HttpSessionActivationListener Interface

Methods	Description
`void sessionDidActivate(HttpSessionEvent se)`	Notifies about the activation of a session
`void sessionWillPassivate(HttpSessionEvent se)`	Notifies about the passivation of a session

Similar to context attributes, the changes in session attributes are notified to the `HttpSessionAttributeListener` interface.

Handling Events for Session Attribute

The changes in the attributes of a session can be notified by implementing the `HttpSessionAttributeListener` interface. The classes whose instances are added or removed by a session also implement the `HttpSessionBindingListener` interface, apart from the `HttpSessionAttributeListener` interface. In addition, you also learn about the `HttpSessionBindingEvent` class used to bound or unbound an object from a session.

Let's now discuss the `HttpSessionAttributeListener` interface in detail.

Describing the HttpSessionAttributeListener Interface

The HttpSessionAttributeListener interface can be implemented to get notifications about the changes made to the attribute lists of sessions within a Web application.

Table 6.5 describes the methods provided by the `HttpSessionAttributeListener` interface:

Table 6.5: Noteworthy Methods of the `HttpSessionAttributeListener` Interface

Methods	Description
`void attributeAdded (HttpSessionBindingEvent se)`	Notifies about the addition of an attribute to a session. This method is invoked after the addition of an attribute.
`void attributeRemoved (HttpSessionBindingEvent se)`	Notifies about the removal of an attribute from a session. This method is invoked after the removal of an attribute.
`void attributeReplaced (HttpSessionBindingEvent se)`	Notifies about the replacement of an attribute in a session. This method is invoked after an attribute is replaced.

The `attributeAdded()`, `attributeRemoved()`, and `attributeReplaced()` methods notify about addition, removal, and replacement of an attribute, respectively from the session. These methods are also present in the `ServletContextAttributeListener` interface, as discussed previously. However, in the `HttpSessionAttributeListener` interface, these methods are notified about the changes made in the attributes of a session.

In addition to these interfaces, the `HttpSessionBindingEvent` class is an important class in listening session events. Now, let's discuss the `HttpSessionBindingEvent` class.

Describing the HttpSessionBindingEvent Class

Whenever an object is bound to or unbound from a session, the object that implements the `HttpSessionBindingListener interface` is notified about the event by the `HttpSessionBindingEvent` class. The `HttpSessionBindingEvent` class also notifies the `HttpSessionAttributeListener` interface that is configured in the Deployment Descriptor about bounding, unbounding, or replacing an attribute in a session. A session binds an object by calling the `HttpSession.setAttribute()` method, and unbinds it by calling the `HttpSession.removeAttribute()` method. The following constructors are present in the `HttpSessionBindingEvent` class:

- **Two Arguments Constructor** – Creates an event that notifies an object about its bounding or unbounding from a session. An object needs to implement the `HttpSessionBindingListener` interface to receive an event. The following code snippet shows the two argument constructor of the `HttpSessionBindingEvent` class:

  ```
  public HttpSessionBindingEvent(HttpSession session, String name)
  ```

  The arguments passed in the preceding code snippet are as follows:

  - **session** – Represents the session to which an object bounds or unbounds
  - **name** – Represents the name with which an object bounds or unbounds

- **Three Arguments Constructor** – Creates an event that notifies an object about its bounding or unbounding from a session. The object requires to implement the `HttpSessionBindingListener` interface to receive an event.

The following code snippet shows the three argument constructors of the `HttpSessionBindingEvent` class:

```
public HttpSessionBindingEvent(HttpSession session, String name, Object value)
```

The arguments passed in the preceding code snippet are as follows:

- **session** – Represents the session to which an object bounds or unbounds
- **name** – Represents the name with which an object bounds or unbounds
- **value** – Represents the value with which an object bounds or unbounds

Table 6.6 describes the methods provided by the `HttpSessionBindingEvent` class to retrieve the value of the bound attribute:

Table 6.6: Noteworthy Methods of the HttpSessionBindingEvent Class

Syntax	Description
`HttpSession getSession()`	Retrieves the session object. It overrides the `getSession()` method in the `HttpSessionEvent` class.
`String getName()`	Retrieves the name with which an attribute bounds or unbounds from a session. A `String` that specifies the name with which the attribute bounds or unbounds from the session is returned by the method.
`Object getValue()`	Retrieves the value of an added, removed, or replaced attribute. The returned value represents the value of an added attribute if the attribute was added (or bound). The returned value represents the value of the attribute that is either removed or unbound from a session. If the attribute was replaced, the returned value represents the old value of the attribute.

After learning about the interfaces and classes that help in session life cycle event handling, let's create the `SessionListener` class in the `events` Web application. The `SessionListener` class implements the `HttpSessionListener` and `HttpSessionAttributeListener` interfaces so that it is notified about the session level events.

Implementing the HttpSessionListener and HttpSessionAttributeListener Interfaces

In this subsection, let's create a simple Java class that implements the `HttpSessionListener` interface so that when the attributes of the session are changed, the `SessionListener` class is notified.

Listing 6.7 provides the code for the `SessionListener` class (save the `SessionListener.java` file in the `\events\src\com\kogent\listeners` folder):

Listing 6.7: Implementing the HttpSessionAttributeListener Interface in the SessionListener Class

```
package com.kogent.listeners;

import javax.servlet.http.*;
import javax.servlet.*;
import javax.swing.*;
import javax.servlet.http.HttpSessionAttributeListener;
import javax.servlet.http.HttpSessionBindingEvent;

public class SessionListener implements HttpSessionListener,
HttpSessionAttributeListener
{
  public void sessionCreated(HttpSessionEvent hse)
  {
       JOptionPane.showMessageDialog(null, "Session Created!!!!");
  }

  public void sessionDestroyed(HttpSessionEvent hse)
  {
       JOptionPane.showMessageDialog(null, "Session Destroyed!!!!");
  }

  public void attributeAdded(HttpSessionBindingEvent event)
  {
  JOptionPane.showMessageDialog(null,"Attribute Added:" +
  event.getName() + "', '" + event.getValue());
  }
```

```
    public void attributeRemoved(HttpSessionBindingEvent event) {
    JOptionPane.showMessageDialog(null,"Attribute Removed" + event.getName() + "', '" +
    event.getValue());
    }

    public void attributeReplaced(HttpSessionBindingEvent event) {
    JOptionPane.showMessageDialog(null,"Attribute Replaced" + event.getName() + "', '" +
    event.getValue());
    }
}
```

SessionListener is a simple Java class that implements the HttpSessionListener and HttpSessionAttributeListener interfaces. When the HttpSession object is created, the SessionListener class is notified about the creation of the session and a Message box is displayed. When the attributes of this session change, then the SessionListener class is notified about the change and the respective message will be displayed. Similar to other listeners, the SessionListener class is also mapped in the web.xml file (Listing 6.3).

The following code snippet shows the mapping for the `SessionListener` class:

```
<web-app>
.......
   <listener>
         <listener-class>com.kogent.listeners.SessionListener
         </listener-class>
   </listener>
......
</web-app>
```

Now, let's create two servlet classes, SessionCreateServlet and SessionDestroyServlet to create and destroy a session, respectively. The `SessionCreateServlet` class creates a session and when the `HttpSession` object is created, the `SessionListener` class is notified that a session has been created.

Listing 6.8 provides the code for the `SessionCreateServlet` servlet (save the `SessionCreateServlet.java` file in the `\events\src\com\kogent\servlets` folder):

Listing 6.8: Showing the Code for the SessionCreateServlet.java File

```
package com.kogent.servlets;
import java.io.*;
import java.util.Date;
import javax.servlet.*;
import javax.servlet.http.*;
public class SessionCreateServlet extends HttpServlet
{
   @Override
   public void doGet (HttpServletRequest req, HttpServletResponse res)
   throws ServletException, IOException
   {
         // Get the session object.
         HttpSession session = req.getSession(true);

         // Set content type for the response.
         res.setContentType("text/html");

         // Then write the data of the response.
         PrintWriter out = res.getWriter();
         out.println("<html><body>");
         out.println("<a href=\"/events/mysessiondestroy\">Destroy Session</a>");
         out.println("<h2>Session Created</h2>");
         out.println("<h3>Session Data:</h3>");
         out.println("New Session: " + session.isNew());
         out.println("<br>Session ID: " + session.getId());
         out.println("<br>Creation Time: " + new Date(session.getCreationTime()));
         session.setAttribute("User", "kogent");
         out.println("</body></html>");
   }
}
```

In Listing 6.8, a new attribute is set by using the `setAttribute()` method of the `HttpSession` object. The `SessionCreateServlet` class also displays the ID and the time of the session. However, when the user clicks the `Destroy Session` link, the request is forwarded to the servlet mapped to the `/mysessiondestroy` `url-pattern`. Now, create the `SessionDestroyServlet` servlet class which invalidates the session and removes the `User` attribute from the session.

Listing 6.9 provides the code for the `SessionDestroyServlet` servlet class (save the `SessionDestroyServlet.java` file in the `\events\src\com\kogent\servlets` folder):

Listing 6.9: Showing the Code for the SessionDestroyServlet.java File

```
package com.kogent.servlets;
import java.io.*;
import javax.servlet.*;
import javax.servlet.http.*;
public class SessionDestroyServlet extends HttpServlet
{
  @Override
  public void doGet (HttpServletRequest req, HttpServletResponse res)
  throws ServletException, IOException {
        // Get the session object and remove the attribute from the session.
        HttpSession session = req.getSession(true);
        session.removeAttribute("User");

        // Invalidate the session.
        session.invalidate();

        // Set content type for response.
        res.setContentType("text/html");

        // Then write the data of the response.
        PrintWriter out = res.getWriter();
        out.println("<html><body>");
        out.println("<a href=\"/events/index.html\">Reload Welcome Page</a>");
        out.println("<h2>Session Destroyed</h2>");
        out.println("</body></html>");
        out.close();
  }
}
```

In Listing 6.9, the `SessionDestroyServlet` servlet class retrieves the session by using the `getSession()` method and destroys the session by invoking the `invalidate()` method on the `HttpSession` object.

Let's create the `index.html file`, which is a simple HTML form used to pass a request to the `SessionCreateServlet` servlet to create a new session.

Listing 6.10 provides the code for the `index.html file` (save the `index.html` file in the `\events` folder):

Listing 6.10: Showing the Code for the index.html File

```
<!DOCTYPE html>
<html>
        <head>
        <title>Example Demonstrating Session Event Handling</title>
        </head>
  <body>
        <h2>Session Event Listener</h2>
        <p>
        This example demonstrates the use of a session event listener.
        </p>
        <p>
        <a href="/events/mysessioncreate">Create New Session</a><br><br>
        </p>
        <p>
Click the <b>Create New Session</b> link above to start a new session.<br>
        </p>
  </body>
</html>
```

After creating the listener and the relevant servlets, configure these servlets in the web.xml file (Listing 6.3). The following code snippet shows how to map the `SessionCreateServlet` and `SessionDestroyServlet` classes:

```
<servlet>
……..
   <servlet-name>sessioncreate</servlet-name>
         <servlet-class>com.kogent.servlets.SessionCreateServlet
         </servlet-class>
   </servlet>

   <servlet-mapping>
         <servlet-name>sessioncreate</servlet-name>
         <url-pattern>/mysessioncreate</url-pattern>
   </servlet-mapping>

   <servlet>
         <servlet-name>sessiondestroy</servlet-name>
         <servlet-class>com.kogent.servlets.SessionDestroyServlet</servlet-class>
   </servlet>

   <servlet-mapping>
         <servlet-name>sessiondestroy</servlet-name>
         <url-pattern>/mysessiondestroy</url-pattern>
   </servlet-mapping>
……..
</servlet>
```

The preceding code snippet maps the `SessionCreateServlet` to `/mysessioncreate` and `SessionDestroyServlet` to `/mysessiondestroy` url-pattern. Now, compile all the Java source files, create a new WAR file for the `events` Web application, and deploy the `events.war` file on Glassfish Server 4.0. After deploying the `events.war file`, browse the URL `http://localhost:8080/events/index.html`.

Figure 6.6 displays the `index` page of the `events` Web application:

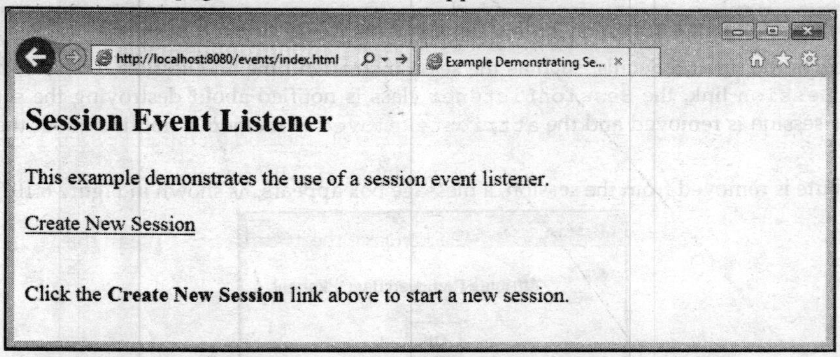

Figure 6.6: Displaying the index Page of the events Web Application

If the user clicks the `Create New Session` link, as shown in Figure 6.6, a new `HttpSession` object is created. The `SessionListener` class is notified about the creation of the new session and a Message box appears, as shown in Figure 6.7:

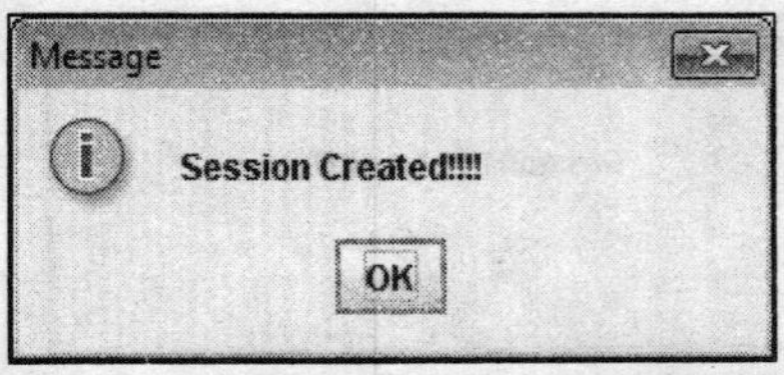

Figure 6.7: Displaying the Session Created Message

After receiving the notification that a session has been created, a new attribute called `User` is created. The `SessionListener` class is also notified about the creation of the User attribute in the current session. A message box appears with the information about the newly created attribute, as shown in Figure 6.8:

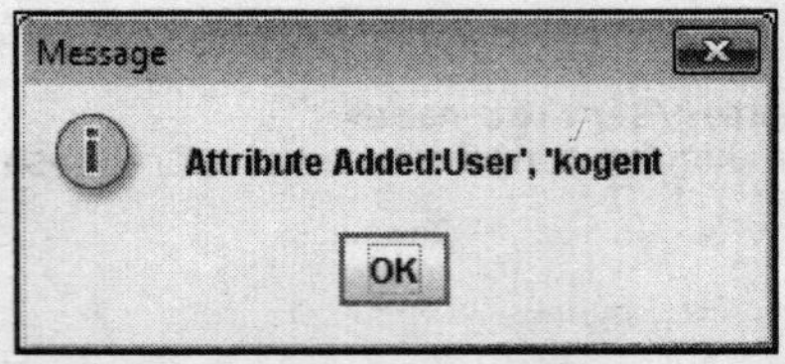

Figure 6.8: Displaying the Attribute Created Message

After the `attributeAdded()` method of the `SessionListener` class is notified about adding the `User` attribute, the `SessionCreateServlet` class writes the session ID and the creation time on the browser, as shown in Figure 6.9:

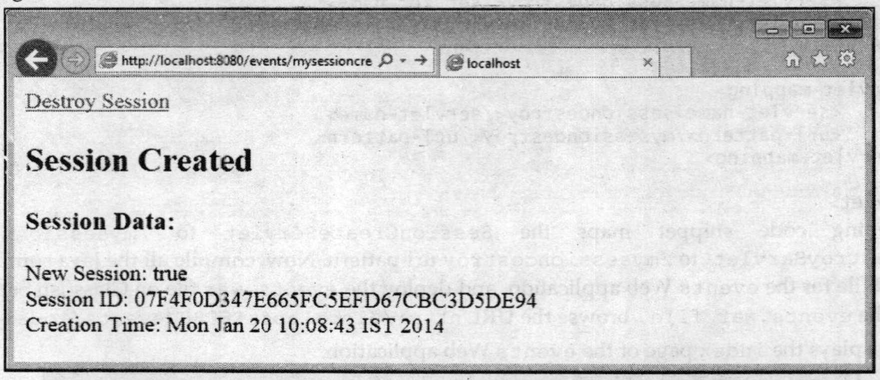

Figure 6.9: Displaying the Details of the Newly Created Session

Figure 6.9 displays the session details, such as the session creation time and session ID. Now, if the user clicks the `Destroy Session` link, the `SessionListener` class is notified about destroying the servlet. The `User` attribute of this session is removed and the `attributeRemoved()` method is notified about the removal of the attribute.

When the attribute is removed from the session, a message box appears, as shown in Figure 6.10:

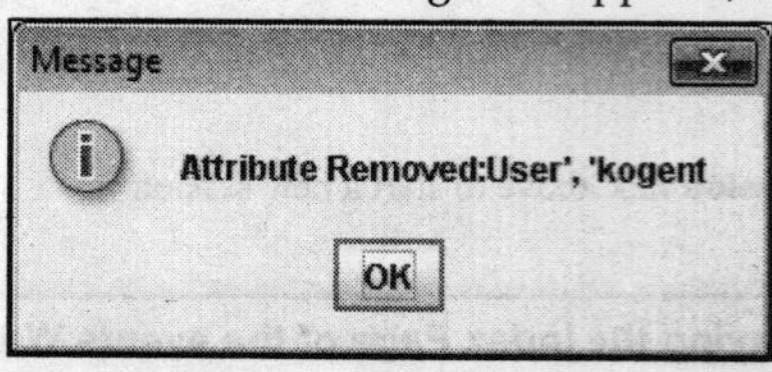

Figure 6.10: Displaying the Attribute Removed Message Box

After removing the attribute, a message about the invalidation of the session is displayed, as shown in Figure 6.11:

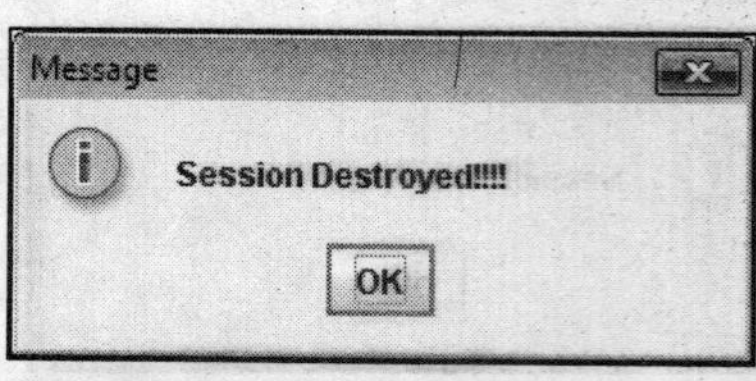

Figure 6.11: Displaying the Session Destroyed Message Box

After learning about listeners and how to implement them, let's create an online shopping application.

Developing the onlineshop Web Application

You should have noticed that when you shop products online, you can add and remove the products from your shopping cart. In this section, you learn to create a sample online shop application named `onlineshop` using listeners. In this application, you create an `onlineshop` directory according to the directory structure discussed in `Chapter 2, Web Applications and Java EE` 7 of this book. Then, you create the `products.txt` file that contains the details of the available products separated by the | symbol and save the file at `\onlineshop\WEB-INF` location.

Listing 6.11 provides the details of the available products:

Listing 6.11: Showing the Data for the products.txt File

```
P001|EJB In Simple Steps|14.95
P002|Java EE 7|12.95
P003|Struts Black Book|14.95
P004|C# Project Book|13.95
```

Let's now learn how to create different JavaBeans for the onlineshop Web application.

Creating the JavaBeans for the onlineshop Web Application

Now, create a JavaBean named `Product` to set and get the data of various products. Listing 6.12 provides the code for `Product` JavaBean (save the `Product.java` file in the `\onlineshop\src\com\kogent\business` folder):

Listing 6.12: Showing the Code for the `Product.java` File

```
package com.kogent.business;

import java.io.Serializable;
import java.text.NumberFormat;

public class Product implements Serializable
{
  private String code;
  private String description;
  private double price;

  public Product() {
        code = "";
        description = "";
        price = 0;
  }

  public void setCode(String code)
  {
        this.code = code;
  }

  public String getCode()
  {
        return code;
  }

  public void setDescription(String description)
  {
        this.description = description;
  }

  public String getDescription()
  {
        return description;
  }

  public void setPrice(double price)
  {
```

```
            this.price = price;
      }

      public double getPrice()
      {
            return price;
      }

      public String getPriceCurrencyFormat()
      {
            NumberFormat currency = NumberFormat.getCurrencyInstance();
            return currency.format(price);
      }
}
```

Listing 6.12 uses set and get methods to set and retrieve the description, code, and price of each product. The `Product` JavaBean helps in displaying all the available products. When the user picks a single product to add in his cart then the `LineItem` JavaBean sets and gets the details of that product.

Listing 6.13 provides the code for the `LineItem` JavaBean (save the `LineItem.java` file in the `\onlineshop\src\com\kogent\business` folder):

Listing 6.13: Showing the Code for the `LineItem.java File`

```
package com.kogent.business;

import java.io.Serializable;
import java.text.NumberFormat;

public class LineItem implements Serializable
{
   private Product product;
   private int quantity;

   public LineItem() {}

   public void setProduct(Product p)
   {
         product = p;
   }

   public Product getProduct()
   {
         return product;
   }

   public void setQuantity(int quantity)
   {
         this.quantity = quantity;
   }
   public int getQuantity()
   {
         return quantity;
   }

   public double getTotal()
   {
         double total = product.getPrice() * quantity;
         return total;
   }

   public String getTotalCurrencyFormat()
   {
         NumberFormat currency = NumberFormat.getCurrencyInstance();
         return currency.format(this.getTotal());
   }
}
```

In Listing 6.13, the product details of the selected item are set or get through the instance of the `Product` JavaBean (Listing 6.12). The `LineItem class` also calculates the total amount based on the price and quantity of that product. The total amount is then converted into a specified currency format.

Listing 6.14 provides the code for the `Cart` class to add items into or remove items from the cart (save the `Cart.java` file in the `\onlineshop\src\com\kogent\business` folder):

Listing 6.14: Showing the Code for the `Cart.java File`

```
package com.kogent.business;

import java.io.Serializable;
import java.util.ArrayList;

public class Cart implements Serializable
{
   private ArrayList<LineItem> items;

   public Cart()
   {
         items = new ArrayList<LineItem>();
   }

   public ArrayList<LineItem> getItems()
   {
         return items;
   }

   public int getCount()
   {
         return items.size();
   }

   public void addItem(LineItem item)
   {
         String code = item.getProduct().getCode();
         int quantity = item.getQuantity();
         for (int i = 0; i < items.size(); i++)
         {
               LineItem lineItem = items.get(i);
               if (lineItem.getProduct().getCode().equals(code))
               {
                     lineItem.setQuantity(quantity);
                     return;
               }
         }
         items.add(item);
   }
   public void removeItem(LineItem item)
   {
         String code = item.getProduct().getCode();
         for (int i = 0; i < items.size(); i++)
         {
               LineItem lineItem = items.get(i);
               if (lineItem.getProduct().getCode().equals(code))
               {
                     items.remove(i);
                     return;
               }
         }
   }
}
```

As you can see in Listing 6.14, the `addItem()` method is used to add the items selected by the user to the shopping cart and the `removeItem()` method is used to remove the selected item from the shopping cart. Now, compile the Java files created in Listing 6.12, 6.13, and 6.14 to create the `com.kogent.business` package. You also need a Java class to retrieve the product details from a file. Let's create a simple Java class, ProductIO that reads the data from the products.txt file.

Listing 6.15 shows the code for the ProductIO class (save the ProductIO.java file in the \onlineshop\src\com\kogent\data folder):

Listing 6.15: Showing the Code for the ProductIO.java File

```
package com.kogent.data;

import java.io.*;
import java.util.*;
import com.kogent.business.*;

public class ProductIO
{
   public static Product getProduct(String code, String filepath)
   {
         try
         {
               File file = new File(filepath);
               BufferedReader in =
               new BufferedReader(
               new FileReader(file));

               String line = in.readLine();
               while (line != null)
               {
                     StringTokenizer t = new StringTokenizer(line, "|");
                     String productCode = t.nextToken();
                     if (code.equalsIgnoreCase(productCode))
                     {
                           String description = t.nextToken();
                           double price =
                           Double.parseDouble(t.nextToken());
                           Product p = new Product();
                           p.setCode(code);
                           p.setDescription(description);
                           p.setPrice(price);
                           in.close();
                           return p;
                     }
                     line = in.readLine();
               }
               in.close();
               return null;
         }
         catch(IOException e)
         {
               e.printStackTrace();
               return null;
         }
   }
   public static ArrayList<Product> getProducts(String filepath)
   {
         ArrayList<Product> products = new ArrayList<Product>();
         File file = new File(filepath);
         try
         {
               BufferedReader in =
```

```
                    new BufferedReader(
                    new FileReader(file));

                    String line = in.readLine();
                    while (line != null)
                    {
                            StringTokenizer t = new StringTokenizer(line, "|");
                            String code = t.nextToken();
                            String description = t.nextToken();
                            String priceAsString = t.nextToken();
                            double price = Double.parseDouble(priceAsString);
                            Product p = new Product();
                            p.setCode(code);
                            p.setDescription(description);
                            p.setPrice(price);
                            String codes = p.getCode();
                            products.add(p);
                            line = in.readLine();
                    }
                    in.close();
                    return products;
            }
            catch(IOException e)
            {
                    e.printStackTrace();
                    return null;
            }
    }
}
```

In Listing 6.15, the `getProducts()` method loads a file from the specified file path and reads the `products.txt` file. All details of the products are then set in the `ProductIO` class by using the `set` property of the `Product` JavaBean. You should note that when the ServletContext is initialized, the `getProducts()` `method` is invoked through the `CartContextListener` listener class.

After the initialization of the ServletContext, the `CartContextListener` listener class sets the attributes required for the application.

Let's now learn to create the `CartContextListener` listener class.

Creating the CartContextListener Class

The `CartContextListener` listener class is notified about the initialization of the context and then the `contextInitialized()` method is invoked. The `CartContextListener` listener class implements the `ServletContextListener` interface.

Listing 6.16 provides the code for the `CartContextListener` listener class (save the CartContextListener.java file in the `\onlineshop\src\com\kogent\listeners` folder):

Listing 6.16: Showing the Code for the CartContextListener.java File

```
package com.kogent.listeners;

import javax.servlet.*;
import java.util.*;
import com.kogent.business.*;
import com.kogent.data.*;

public class CartContextListener implements ServletContextListener
{
   public void contextInitialized(ServletContextEvent event)
   {
        ServletContext sc = event.getServletContext();
```

```
    // initialize the customer service email address that's used
    //  throughout the web site
            String custServEmail = sc.getInitParameter("custServEmail");
            sc.setAttribute("custServEmail", custServEmail);

            // initialize the current year that's used in the copyright notice
            GregorianCalendar currentDate = new GregorianCalendar();
            int currentYear = currentDate.get(Calendar.YEAR);
            sc.setAttribute("currentYear", currentYear);

            // initialize the path for the products text file
            String productsPath = sc.getRealPath("WEB-INF/products.txt");
            sc.setAttribute("productsPath", productsPath);

            // initialize the list of products
            ArrayList<Product> products = new ArrayList<Product>();
            products = ProductIO.getProducts(productsPath);
            sc.setAttribute("products", products);
    }

    public void contextDestroyed(ServletContextEvent event)
    {
    }
}
```

In Listing 6.16, when the context is initialized, the `com.kogent.listeners.CartContextListener` listener class is notified about the initialization of the context. The `CartContextListener` listener class sets the `custServEmail` attribute to the `context-param` value specified in the `web.xml` file and the `currentYear` attribute to the current date. Moreover, the `CartContextListener` class sets the `productsPath` attribute to `WEB-INF\products.txt`. The `getProducts()` method of the `ProductIO` class is invoked to return an `ArrayList`, which is set to the `products` attribute.

At the time of initializing a ServletContext, four attributes are created, `custServEmail`, `currentYear`, `productsPath`, and `products`. These attributes can be used as and when required. Now, map the `CartContextListener` listener class and provide the `context-param` value in the `web.xml` file.

Listing 6.17 provides the code to configure the listener and servlet classes in the `web.xml` file (save the web.xml file in the `\onlineshop\WEB-INF` folder):

Listing 6.17: Showing the Code for the Configuration of Listener and Servlet Classes

```
<?xml version="1.0" encoding="UTF-8"?>
<web-app version="3.1" xmlns="http://xmlns.jcp.org/xml/ns/javaee"
xmlns:xsi="http://www.w3.org/2001/XMLSchema-instance"
xsi:schemaLocation="http://xmlns.jcp.org/xml/ns/javaee
http://xmlns.jcp.org/xml/ns/javaee/web-app_3_1.xsd">

<context-param>
        <param-name>custServEmail</param-name>
        <param-value>pallavi.sharma@kogentindia.com</param-value>
</context-param>

<listener>
   <listener-class>com.kogent.listeners.CartContextListener</listener-class>
</listener>

<servlet>
   <servlet-name>Welcome</servlet-name>
   <servlet-class>com.kogent.servlets.Welcome</servlet-class>
</servlet>
<servlet-mapping>
   <servlet-name>Welcome</servlet-name>
   <url-pattern>/Welcome</url-pattern>
</servlet-mapping>

<servlet>
```

```
    <servlet-name>CartServlet</servlet-name>
    <servlet-class>com.kogent.servlets.CartServlet</servlet-class>
  </servlet>
  <servlet-mapping>
    <servlet-name>CartServlet</servlet-name>
    <url-pattern>/cart</url-pattern>
  </servlet-mapping>

  <servlet>
    <servlet-name>CartNxtServlet</servlet-name>
    <servlet-class>com.kogent.servlets.CartNxtServlet</servlet-class>
  </servlet>
  <servlet-mapping>
          <servlet-name>CartNxtServlet</servlet-name>
          <url-pattern>/CartNxtServlet</url-pattern>
  </servlet-mapping>

  <servlet>
    <servlet-name>Checkout</servlet-name>
    <servlet-class>com.kogent.servlets.Checkout</servlet-class>
  </servlet>
  <servlet-mapping>
    <servlet-name>Checkout</servlet-name>
    <url-pattern>/Checkout</url-pattern>
  </servlet-mapping>

  <welcome-file-list>
    <welcome-file>
         Welcome
    </welcome-file>
  </welcome-file-list>
  </web-app>
```

Listing 6.17 defines `custServEmail` as a context parameter that is assigned a value. The `com.kogent.listeners.CartContextListener` class is also specified as the listener class in Deployment Descriptor. Now, let's design the front end of the onlineshop Web application.

Building the Front-End of the onlineshop Web Application

The front-end of the onlineshop application displays the products available to add in the shopping cart. In the `onlineshop` Web application, you create servlets, such as `Welcome`, `CartServlet`, `CartNxtServlet`, and `Checkout`. Let's first create the `Welcome` servlet that displays the details of all products by retrieving the value of the *`products`* attribute. The *`products`* attribute returns the `ArrayList` in which the description and price of each product is displayed on the browser.

Listing 6.18 shows the code for the `Welcome` servlet class (save the `Welcome.java` file in the `\onlineshop\src\com\kogent\servlets` folder):

Listing 6.18: Showing the Code for the `Welcome.java` File

```
package com.kogent.servlets;

import java.io.*;
import javax.servlet.*;
import java.util.*;
import javax.servlet.http.*;
import com.kogent.business.Product;
import com.kogent.data.*;

public class Welcome extends HttpServlet
{

protected void processRequest(HttpServletRequest request, HttpServletResponse response)
  throws ServletException, IOException
  {
       int i = 0;
```

```
        String pass =null;
        ServletContext ctx =getServletContext();
        response.setContentType("text/html;charset=UTF-8");

        PrintWriter out = response.getWriter();
        out.println("<html><head><title>Online Shop</title></head><body>");
        out.println("<h1>The onlineshop Application</h1>");
        out.println("<table cellpadding=5 border=1><tr valign=bottom><td
        align=left><b>Description</b></td><td align=left><b>Price</b></td><td
        align=left></td></tr>");
        ArrayList<Product> products = new ArrayList<Product>();
        products = (ArrayList<Product>) ctx.getAttribute("products");
        for(i=0; i<products.size(); i++)
        {
        out.println("<tr valign=top>");
        out.println("<td>" + products.get(i).getDescription() + "</td>");
        out.println("<td>" + products.get(i).getPriceCurrencyFormat() + "</td>");
                pass = products.get(i).getCode();
        out.println("<td><a href=./cart?productCode=" + pass + ">Add To
        Cart</a></td></tr>");
        }
        out.println("</table><br/>");
        out.println("<b> Email ID" + ctx.getAttribute("custServEmail") + "<br/> </b>");
        out.println("</body></html>");
        out.close();
    }

    @Override
    protected void doGet(HttpServletRequest request, HttpServletResponse response) throws
    ServletException, IOException
    {
        processRequest(request, response);
    }

    @Override
    protected void doPost(HttpServletRequest request, HttpServletResponse response) throws
    ServletException, IOException
    {
        processRequest(request, response);
    }

    @Override
    public String getServletInfo()
    {
        return "Short description";
    }
    // </editor-fold>
}
```

Listing 6.18 creates a `Welcome` servlet that retrieves the servlet context and the value of the `products` attribute. The detail of each product is displayed in the table format and the `Add To Cart` link is also created for each product, which would add the product in the shopping cart of the user. On clicking the `Add To Cart` link, the `productCode` parameter is also passed to the `CartServlet servlet class`. The `productCode` parameter contains the code for the product selected by the user to add in the shopping cart. The `getAttribute()` method also retrieves the value of the `custServEmail` attribute defined during the initialization of context.

First, you need to compile all the required JavaBeans and servlet classes of the onlineshop application and deploy the application on the Glassfish Server 4.0. Next, you can access the http://localhost:8080/onlineshop URL to display the first page of the application, i.e., Welcome servlet.

Figure 6.12 displays the `Welcome` servlet:

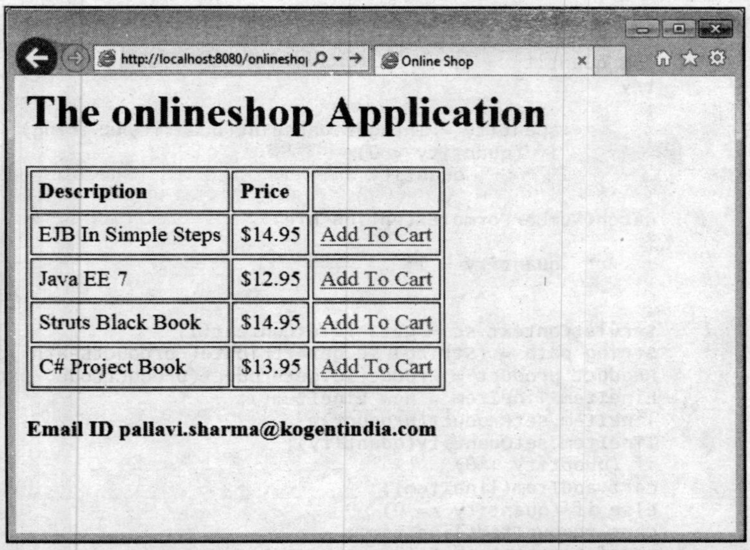

Figure 6.12: Displaying the Products Available in the onlineshop Application

Figure 6.12 displays the products available in the onlineshop Web application. The description and price of each product is displayed and the user can add the specified product by clicking the link available for each product. When a user clicks the `Add To Cart` link, the request is forwarded to the `Cart` Servlet, which creates an `HttpSession` for the user and retrieves the value of the `productCode` parameter sent by the `Welcome` Servlet.

Based on the `productCode`, the details of that product is retrieved by calling the `getProduct()` method of the `ProductIO` class. After that the value for the new attribute named `cart` is set and the request is dispatched to the `CartNxtServlet` servlet class.

Listing 6.19 provides the code for the `CartServlet servlet (save the CartServlet.java file in the \onlineshop\src\com\kogent\servlets` folder):

Listing 6.19: Showing the Code for the `CartServlet.java File`

```
package com.kogent.servlets;

import java.io.*;
import javax.servlet.*;
import javax.servlet.http.*;
import com.kogent.business.*;
import com.kogent.data.*;

public class CartServlet extends HttpServlet
{
protected void processRequest(HttpServletRequest request, HttpServletResponse response)
  throws ServletException, IOException
  {
        String productCode = request.getParameter("productCode");
        String quantityAsString = request.getParameter("quantity");
        HttpSession session = request.getSession();

        synchronized(session)
        {
                Cart cart = (Cart) session.getAttribute("cart");
                if (cart == null)
                {
                        cart = new Cart();
                        session.setAttribute("cart", cart);
                }
```

```
                //if the user enters a negative or invalid quantity,
                //the quantity is automatically reset to 1.
                int quantity = 1;
                try
                {
                        quantity = Integer.parseInt(quantityAsString);
                        if (quantity < 0)
                                quantity = 1;
                }
                catch(NumberFormatException nfe)
                {
                        quantity = 1;
                }

                ServletContext sc = getServletContext();
                String path = (String) sc.getAttribute("productsPath");
                Product product = ProductIO.getProduct(productCode, path);
                LineItem lineItem = new LineItem();
                lineItem.setProduct(product);
                lineItem.setQuantity(quantity);
                if (quantity > 0)
                cart.addItem(lineItem);
                else if (quantity <= 0)
                cart.removeItem(lineItem);
                session.setAttribute("cart", cart);
                String url = "/CartNxtServlet";
                RequestDispatcher dispatcher =
                getServletContext().getRequestDispatcher(url);
                dispatcher.forward(request, response);
        }
    }
    @Override
    protected void doGet(HttpServletRequest request, HttpServletResponse response) throws
    ServletException, IOException
    {
        processRequest(request, response);
    }

    @Override
    protected void doPost(HttpServletRequest request, HttpServletResponse response) throws
        ServletException, IOException
    {
        processRequest(request, response);
    }

    @Override
    public String getServletInfo()
    {
        return "Short description";
    }
    // </editor-fold>
}
```

In Listing 6.19, the `CartServlet` servlet is created. The `CartServlet` servlet creates a new `HttpSession` for new users or maintains the session for the existing users. The `CartServlet` servlet receives the client's request from the `Welcome` servlet and retrieves the value of the `productCode` parameter passed with the request. After setting the new attribute `cart`, the `CartServlet` servlet forwards the request to the `CartNxtServlet` servlet class.

However, if the value of the quantity variable is less than or equal to zero, the `removeItem()` method of the `com.kogent.business.Cart` class is invoked; however, if the quantity is greater than zero, the `addItem()` method is called. The `RequestDispacher` class is used to forward the request to the `CartNxtServlet servlet class`.

Listing 6.20 provides the code for `CartNxtServlet` (save the CartNxtServlet.java file in the `\onlineshop\src\com\kogent\servlets` folder):

Listing 6.20: Showing the Code for the CartNxtServlet.java File

```
package com.kogent.servlets;
import java.io.*;
import javax.servlet.*;
import javax.servlet.http.*;
import com.kogent.business.*;
import java.util.*;
public class CartNxtServlet extends HttpServlet
{
protected void processRequest(HttpServletRequest request, HttpServletResponse response)
  throws ServletException, IOException
  {
        HttpSession session =request.getSession();
        response.setContentType("text/html;charset=UTF-8");
        PrintWriter out = response.getWriter();
        out.println("<html><head><title>Online Shop</title></head><body>");
        out.println("<h1>Items in Shopping Cart </h1>");
        Cart carts = (Cart) session.getAttribute("cart");
        ArrayList<LineItem> items = new ArrayList<LineItem>();
        items=  carts.getItems();
        out.println("<table border=1
        cellpadding=5><tr><th>Quantity</th><th>Description</th><th>Price</th><th>Amount
        </th></tr>");
        for ( int i =0; i<items.size(); i++) {
        out.println("<tr valign=top><td><form action=./cart method=post><input
        type=hidden name=productCode value=" + items.get(i).getProduct().getCode() +
        ">");
        out.println("<input type=text size=2 name=quantity value=" +
        items.get(i).getQuantity()+ ">");
        out.println("<input type=submit name=updateButton value=Update></form></td>");
        out.println("<td>" + items.get(i).getProduct().getDescription() + "</td>");
        out.println("<td>" + items.get(i).getProduct().getPrice() + "</td>");
        out.println("<td>" + items.get(i).getTotalCurrencyFormat() + "</td>");
        out.println("<td><form action=./cart method=post><input type=hidden
        name=productCode value=" + items.get(i).getProduct().getCode() + ">");
        out.println("<input type=hidden name=quantity value=0><input type=submit
        value=RemoveItem></form></td></tr>");
        }
        out.println("</table>");
        out.println("<br><form action=./Welcome method=post><input type=submit
        name=continue value=ContinueShopping></form>");
        out.println("<br><form action=./Checkout method=post><input type=submit
        name=Logoff value=Checkout></form>");
        out.println("</body></html>");
        out.close();
  }
  @Override
  protected void doGet(HttpServletRequest request, HttpServletResponse response) throws
  ServletException, IOException
  {
        processRequest(request, response);
  }
  @Override
  protected void doPost(HttpServletRequest request, HttpServletResponse response) throws
  ServletException, IOException
  {
        processRequest(request, response);
  }
  @Override
  public String getServletInfo() {
        return "Short description";
  }
}
```

The code in Listing 6.20 creates the `CartNxtServlet` servlet class, which contains the details of the products added by the user in the shopping cart. The quantity of each product can be updated by the user by clicking the `Update` button. The amount of the items is also updated based on the price and the quantity of the products selected. The various hidden form fields are used in the `CartNxtServlet` servlet class to send the product ID and quantity (selected by the user) `as` hidden values with the client's request. If the user wishes to remove any item from his cart, the `RemoveItem` button can be clicked. The `CartServlet` servlet class then invokes the `removeItem()` method as the quantity parameter contains the value, zero.

The various items that you can shop are shown in Figure 6.12, you click the Add To Cart link to add the item in the shopping cart. Once you have clicked the link, the items that are available in your shopping cart are displayed. If you want to further shop for more items, click the ContinueShopping button. In our case, we have added three items in the shopping cart, as shown in Figure 6.13:

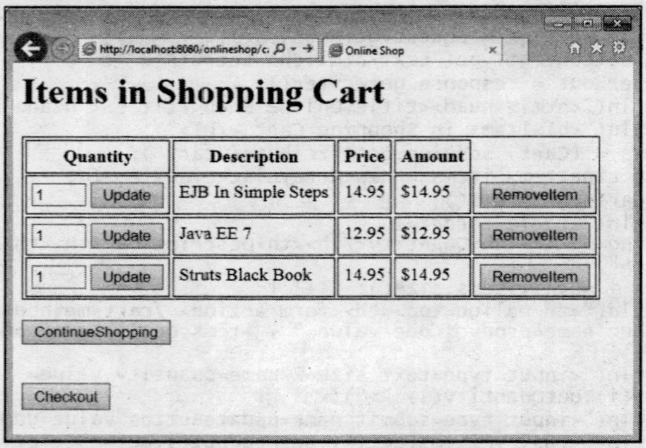

Figure 6.13: Displaying Items in the Online Shopping Cart

If you want to select more items, you can click the `ContinueShopping` button that again forwards the request to the `Welcome` servlet. Figure 6.13 displays the shopping cart of the user who has added three products in his cart. Once the user clicks the `Checkout` button, the request is forwarded to the `Checkout` servlet and the session is terminated. The `Checkout` servlet invalidates the session and prompts the user to close the browser window to end the shopping.

Listing 6.21 provides the code for the `Checkout` servlet (save the `Checkout.java` file in the `\onlineshop\src\com\kogent\servlets` folder):

Listing 6.21: Showing the Code for the `Checkout.java File`

```
package com.kogent.servlets;
import java.io.*;
import javax.servlet.*;
import javax.servlet.http.*;
public class Checkout extends HttpServlet
{
   protected void processRequest(HttpServletRequest request, HttpServletResponse response)
   throws ServletException, IOException
{
        response.setContentType("text/html;charset=UTF-8");
        PrintWriter out = response.getWriter();
        out.println("<html><head><title>Online Shop</title></head><body>");
        out.println("<h1>The onlineshop Application</h1>");
        HttpSession session = request.getSession();
        session.invalidate();
        out.println("Click close to terminate the online shopping");
        out.close();
   }

   @Override
```

```
    protected void doGet(HttpServletRequest request, HttpServletResponse response) throws
    ServletException, IOException
  {
        processRequest(request, response);
    }

    @Override
  protected void doPost(HttpServletRequest request, HttpServletResponse response) throws
    ServletException, IOException
  {
        processRequest(request, response);
    }

    @Override
    public String getServletInfo()
    {
        return "Short description";
    }
    // </editor-fold>
  }
```

The servlets created in Listing 6.18, 6.19, 6.20, and 6.21 are provided under the com.kogent.servlets package. Compile all the servlets. Prior to the creation of the WAR file, it is essential to map all these servlets in the web.xml file. After mapping all the servlets, create the onlineshop.war file and deploy this Web application on the Glassfish Server 4.0. Browse the http://localhost:8080/onlineshop URL to run the application.

Let's now learn about wrappers in the next section.

Introducing Wrappers

One of the features in Java Servlet 3.1 specification is the request and response wrappers. Wrappers are sandwiched between servlet classes and servlet containers and can easily handle the servlet environment by wrapping the servlet's APIs. The core objects of the servlet API are ServletRequest as well as ServletResponse and the core Hypertext Transfer Protocol (HTTP) specific objects are HttpServletRequest and HttpServletResponse. These core objects of a servlet cannot be used directly; therefore, wrappers are used to wrap these objects. This section introduces wrapper API and helps you to understand how the interaction with servlets is performed by using wrapper classes.

Let's first discuss about the need of wrappers in detail.

Exploring the Need for Wrappers

Wrappers allow you to add additional functionalities to the request and response object given by the servlet container. Wrappers allow you to change the data of a user's request as well as add some additional information to that request before sending the data to a servlet or a (JavaServer Pages) JSP page. In addition, wrappers help you to perform some pre/post operations for the calls made on the request or response objects. Moreover, with the help of wrappers, you can change the functionality of the predefined methods on request and response objects with their new APIs. To override a functionality of a predefined method, wrapper objects passed as arguments to calling servlet should be the same as request and response objects of the called servlet.

The following are some situations in which wrappers can be used:

- Making response object capable to provide output in the form of DOM objects on client
- Checking the content type while setting it in response
- Caching the output printed to the client and then flushing it after the entire response is generated

Filters can also use wrappers to wrap a request or response so that it can change the behavior of the request or response to perform some filtering tasks.

Exploring the Types of Wrapper Classes

The Java Servlet API 3.1 provides the following four wrapper classes:

- javax.servlet.ServletRequestWrapper

- javax.servlet.ServletResponseWrapper
- javax.servlet.http.HttpServletRequestWrapper
- javax.servlet.http.HttpServletResponseWrapper

These classes implement Decorator Pattern, which is a core design pattern that is used to add additional functionality to a particular object. All these four classes are public non-abstract classes provided with one constructor that takes an argument of their respective wrapped type. The `ServletRequestWrapper` class accepts `ServletRequest` as an argument and the `ServletResponseWrapper` class accepts `ServletResponse` as an argument.

Explaining the ServletRequestWrapper Class

The `ServletRequestWrapper` class implements the `ServletRequest` interface. This class is further extended by Web developers to call their overridden methods.

Table 6.7 describes some of the commonly-used methods of the `ServletRequestWrapper` class:

Table 6.7: Noteworthy Methods of the ServletRequestWrapper Class

Method	Default Behavior
getRequest()	Returns the wrapped request object
getAttribute()	Calls the getAttribute() request method on the wrapped request object
getParameter()	Calls the getParameter() request method on the wrapped request object
getParameterValues()	Calls the getParameterValues() request method on the wrapped request object
getRequestDispatcher()	Calls the getRequestDispatcher() request method on the wrapped request object
removeAtrribute()	Calls the getRequestDispatcher() request method on the wrapped request object
setAttribute()	Calls the setAttribute() request method on the wrapped request object

Explaining the ServletResponseWrapper Class

The `ServletResponseWrapper` class implements the `ServletResponse` interface. This class is further extended by Web developers to define their overridden methods.

Table 6.8 describes some of the commonly-used methods of the `ServletResponseWrapper` class:

Table 6.8: Noteworthy Methods of the ServletResponseWrapper Class

Method	Default Behavior
getBufferSize()	Calls the getBufferSize() response method on wrapped response object
getResponse()	Returns the wrapped ServletResponse object
getWriter()	Calls the getWriter() response method on the wrapped response object
setContentLength()	Calls the setContentLength() response method on the wrapped response object
setContentType()	Calls the setContentType() response method on the wrapped response object

Explaining the HttpServletRequestWrapper Class

The `HttpServletRequestWrapper` class implements the `HttpServletRequest` interface. This class is further extended by Web developers to define their overridden methods.

Table 6.9 describes some of the commonly-used methods of the `HttpServletRequestWrapper` class:

Table 6.9: Noteworthy Methods of the HttpServletRequestWrapper Class

Method	Default Behavior
getCookies()	Calls the getCookies() request method on the wrapped request object
getHeaders()	Calls the getHeaders() request method on the wrapped request object
getMethod()	Calls the getMethod() request method on the wrapped request object
getPathInfo()	Calls the getPathInfo() request method on the wrapped request object

Table 6.9: Noteworthy Methods of the HttpServletRequestWrapper Class	
Method	**Default Behavior**
getSession()	Calls the getSession() request method on the wrapped request object
getRequestURI()	Calls the getRequestURI() request method on the wrapped request object

Explaining the HttpServletResponseWrapper Class

The `HttpServletResponseWrapper` class implements the `HttpServletResponse` interface. This class is further extended by Web developers to define their overridden methods.

Table 6.10 describes some of the commonly-used methods of the `HttpServletResponseWrapper` class:

Table 6.10: Noteworthy Methods of the HttpServletResponseWrapper Class	
Method	**Default Behavior**
addCookie()	Calls the addCookie() response method on the wrapped response object
encodeRedirectURL()	Calls the encodeRedirectURL() response method on the wrapped response object
encodeURL()	Calls the encodeURL() response method on the wrapped response object
sendRedirect()	Calls the sendRedirect() response method on the wrapped response object
setHeader()	Calls the setHeader() response method on the wrapped response object

Working with Wrappers

In this section, let's discuss the use of wrappers by creating a Web application, named `wrapper`. When a user accesses the `wrapper` Web application, the request parameter is not sent in the request Uniform Resource Identifier (URI); therefore, the `getParameter()` method must return null. Instead of returning null as the value of the parameter, you can customize a servlet to return the `None` string with the help of a wrapper. The `wrapper` Web application also checks whether or not the content type set for the response object is a supported type.

Let's now create the required files for the `wrapper` Web application.

Creating the Home HTML Page

The `Home HTML` page consists of a form that has two buttons to send the request with and without wrappers. The user can submit the request by clicking any of these two buttons. One of the buttons sends the request to the `WrapperTestServlet` servlet, which processes the request using wrappers. The other button sends the request to the `TestServlet` servlet, which processes the request without using wrappers.

Listing 6.22 shows the code for the `Home.html` file (save the file in the \wrapper folder):

Listing 6.22: Showing the Code for the Home HTML Page

```
<html>
   <body>
         <form method=post action="WrapperTestServlet">
               <input type="submit" value="Send Request using
               Wrappers"/><BR><BR>
         </form>
         <form method=post action="TestServlet">
               <input type="submit"  value="Send Request without using
               Wrappers"/>
         </form>
   </body>
</html>
```

Listing 6.22 shows that the request from the Home HTML page is sent to the WrapperTestServlet class. Let's now create the `WrapperTestServlet` class to retrieve the value of the parameter passed along with the user's request.

Creating the WrapperTestServlet.java File

The `WrapperTestServlet` class retrieves the request parameter that is not sent by the user and then prints the value of the request parameter using the out.println () method. The WrapperTestServlet class uses wrappers and calls the overridden methods, namely getParameter() and setContentType(), of the request and response objects, respectively.

Listing 6.23 shows the code for the WrapperTestServlet.java file (save the WrapperTestServlet.java file in the \wrapper\src\com\kogent\servlet folder):

Listing 6.23: Showing the Code for the WrapperTestServlet.java File

```
package com.kogent.servlet;

import javax.servlet.*;
import java.io.*;
import com.kogent.mywrappers.*;

public class WrapperTestServlet extends GenericServlet
{
  public void service (ServletRequest req, ServletResponse res)
  throws ServletException, IOException
  {
        MyRequestWrapper mreq = new MyRequestWrapper(req);
        MyResponseWrapper mres = new MyResponseWrapper(res);

        String testparam=mreq.getParameter("myparam");
        mres.setContentType ("text/xml");

        //These methods is invoked just to test
        //whether the wrapper functionality is working or not
        PrintWriter out=res.getWriter ();
        out.println ("<html><body><b>");
        out.println ("Parameter value is "+ testparam);
        out.println ("</b></body></html>");
  }//service
}//class
```

In Listing 6.23, the instances of the `MyRequestWrapper` and `MyResponseWrappper` classes are created to modify the current request and response objects.

Let's now learn to create the TestServlet.java file.

Creating the TestServlet.java File

The `TestServlet` class retrieves the request parameter that is not sent by the user and then prints the value of this parameter using the `out.println()` method. Listing 6.24 shows the code for the `TestServlet.java` file (save the `TestServlet.java` file in the `\wrapper\src\com\kogent\servlet` folder):

Listing 6.24: Showing the Code for the TestServlet.java File

```
package com.kogent.servlet;

import javax.servlet.*;
import java.io.*;

public class TestServlet extends GenericServlet
{
  public void service (ServletRequest req, ServletResponse res)
  throws ServletException, IOException
  {
        String testparam=req.getParameter("myparam");
        res.setContentType ("text/xml");

        //These methods is invoked just to test
        //whether the wrapper functionality is working or not
        PrintWriter out=res.getWriter ();
        out.println ("<html><body><b>");
        out.println ("Parameter value is "+ testparam);
        out.println ("</b></body></html>");
  }//service
}//class
```

In Listing 6.24, the value of the `myparam` attribute is retrieved and displayed.

Let's now learn to create the MyRequestWrapper.java file.

Creating the MyRequestWrapper.java File

The `MyRequestWrapper` class extends the `ServletRequestWrapper` class to get the permission to override its methods. The `MyRequestWrapper` class overrides the `getParameter ()` method of the `ServletRequestWrapper` class. The `getParameter()` method of the `MyRequestWrapper` class first calls the `getParameter ()` method of the `ServletRequestWrapper` super class, which returns the value of the `myparam` attribute and assigns it to string `s1`. If request parameter or s1 is found to be null, it sets `s1` to `None` String and displays it to the user. In this way, the `getParameter ()` method of the `ServletRequestWrapper` class is overridden; otherwise, this method returns the null value.

Listing 6.25 shows the code for the `MyRequestWrapper.java` file (save the `MyRequestWrapper.java` file in the `\wrapper\src\com\kogent\mywrappers` folder):

Listing 6.25: Showing the Code for the MyRequestWrapper.java File

```
package com.kogent.mywrappers;

import javax.servlet.*;

public class MyRequestWrapper extends ServletRequestWrapper
{
    public MyRequestWrapper (ServletRequest req)
    {
            super(req);
    }

    public String getParameter(String s)
    {
            String s1=super.getParameter(s);
            if(s1==null)
                    s1="None";
            return s1;
    }//getParameter
}//class
```

Let's now create the MyResponseWrapper.java file.

Creating the MyResponseWrapper.java File

The `MyResponseWrapper` class extends the `ServletResponseWrapper` class to get the permission to override the methods of the `ServletResponseWrapper` class. This class overrides the `setContentType()` method of the `ServletRequestWrapper` class. The `setContentType()` method of the `MyResponseWrapper` class sets the content type of response to `text/html` using the `setContentType()` method of the `ServletResponseWrapper` super class.

Listing 6.26 provides the code for the `MyResponseWrapper.java` file (save the file in the `\wrapper\src\com\kogent\mywrappers` folder):

Listing 6.26: Showing the Code for the MyResponseWrapper.java File

```
package com.kogent.mywrappers;

import javax.servlet.*;

public class MyResponseWrapper extends ServletResponseWrapper
{
    public MyResponseWrapper (ServletResponse res)
    {
            super(res);
    }

    public void setContentType(String s)
    {
            if (!s.equals("text/html"))
                    s="text/html";
            /*
```

```
        Here we consider that our application is designed intelligent
        to provide only html response content
        If we want different types also to be allowed then we need
        to check accordingly
      */

      super.setContentType(s);
   }//setContentType
}//class
```

Creating the web.xml File

The `web.xml` file provides the mapping for the `TestServlet` servlet with the `/testSer` URI.

Listing 6.27 provides the code for the `web.xml` file (save the web.xml file in the `\wrapper\WEB-INF` folder):

Listing 6.27: Showing the Code for the web.xml File

```
<?xml version="1.0" encoding="UTF-8"?>

<web-app version="3.1" xmlns="http://xmlns.jcp.org/xml/ns/javaee"
xmlns:xsi=http://www.w3.org/2001/XMLSchema-instance
xsi:schemaLocation="http://xmlns.jcp.org/xml/ns/javaee
http://xmlns.jcp.org/xml/ns/javaee/web-app_3_1.xsd">

   <servlet>
         <servlet-name>WrapperTestServlet</servlet-name>
         <servlet-class>com.kogent.servlet.WrapperTestServlet</servlet-class>
   </servlet>

   <servlet-mapping>
         <servlet-name>WrapperTestServlet</servlet-name>
         <url-pattern>/WrapperTestServlet</url-pattern>
   </servlet-mapping>

   <servlet>
         <servlet-name>TestServlet</servlet-name>
         <servlet-class>com.kogent.servlet.TestServlet</servlet-class>
   </servlet>

   <servlet-mapping>
         <servlet-name>TestServlet</servlet-name>
         <url-pattern>/TestServlet</url-pattern>
   </servlet-mapping>

</web-app>
```

After creating the web.xml file, let's now learn to package, deploy, and run the wrapper Web application.

Packaging, Deploying, and Running the wrapper Web Application

To package the wrapper Web application, you first need to compile all the .java files so that the .class files are generated in the `classes` directory of the Web application. Next, create the `wrapper.war` file and deploy the `wrapper` Web application on the Glassfish Server 4.0. Now, browse the `http://localhost:8080/wrapper/Home.html` URL to run the application.

Figure 6.14 shows the output of the `wrapper` Web application:

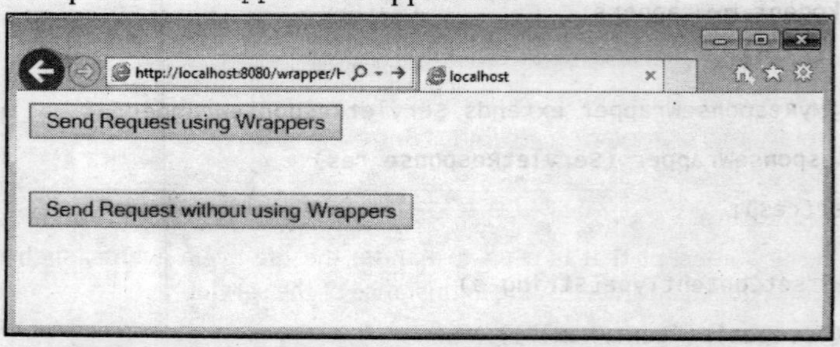

Figure 6.14: Showing the Output of the Home HTML Page

In Figure 6.14, when you click the `Send Request using Wrappers` button, the client request is forwarded to the `WrapperTestServlet` servlet.

Figure 6.15 shows the output of the `WrapperTestServlet` servlet:

Figure 6.15: Displaying the Output when Send Request using Wrappers Button is Clicked

When you click the Send Request without using Wrappers button, the client request is forwarded to the TestServlet servlet.

Figure 6.16 shows the output on clicking the Send Request without using Wrappers button:

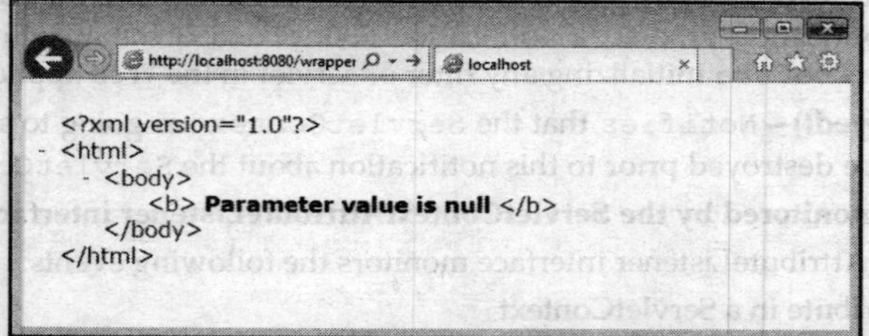

Figure 6.16: Displaying the Output when Send Request without using Wrappers Button is Clicked

This completes the discussion about wrappers. Let's now quickly summarize the topics covered in the chapter.

Summary

This chapter has described about events and event handling process. In addition, you have learned about servlet and session level events that can occur in a Web application and how listeners are notified about an event. Next, you learn to implement the event handling process by creating an onlineshop Web application. The chapter discussed the concept of wrappers and how to implement them in Java Servlet 3.1.

After understanding about event handling and wrappers in servlets, let's learn about JSP and its role in Web applications in the next chapter.

Quick Revise

Q1. List the events that can occur during the life cycle of a servlet.

Ans. The following events can occur during the life cycle of a servlet:

- ❑ Initializing servlets
- ❑ Adding, removing, or replacing attributes in ServletContext
- ❑ Creating, activating, passivating, or invalidating a session
- ❑ Adding, removing, or replacing attributes in servlet session
- ❑ Destroying servlets

Q2. What is event handling?

Ans. Event handling is a concept that is used to handle the life cycle events, such as initializing a servlet, servicing a client request, and destroying an instance of the servlet.

Q3. What are the various levels of servlet events?

Ans. The various levels of servlet events are as follows:

- ❑ Request level events
- ❑ Servlet context level events
- ❑ Servlet session events

Q4. List the listener interfaces used to handle servlet context life cycle events.

Ans. The servlet context life cycle events can be handled by using the following interfaces:

- ❑ ServletContextListener
- ❑ ServletContextAttributeListener

Q5. List the listener interfaces used to handle servlet session level events.

Ans. The following listener interfaces are used for handling servlet session events:

- ❑ HttpSessionListener
- ❑ HttpSessionActivationListener
- ❑ HttpSessionAttributeListener

Q6. Explain the methods defined in the ServletContextListener interface.

Ans. The methods of the ServletContextListener interface are as follows:

- ❑ **contextInitialized()** – Notifies that the initialization process for the Web application is going to start. During the notification process, a notification about context initialization is sent to all the servlet context listeners `before` initializing any filter or servlet in the Web application.
- ❑ **contextDestroyed()** – `Notifies` that the `ServletContext` is going to shut down. All servlets and filters should be destroyed prior to this notification about the `ServletContext` destruction.

Q7. Which events are monitored by the ServletContextAttributeListener interface?

Ans. The ServletContextAttributeListener interface monitors the following events:

- ❑ Adding an attribute in a ServletContext
- ❑ Replacing an attribute in a ServletContext
- ❑ Removing an attribute from a ServletContext

Q8. Explain the methods of the ServletContextAttributeListener interface.

Ans. The methods of the ServletContextAttributeListener interface are as follows:

- ❑ **attributeAdded()** – `Notifies` about the addition of a new attribute to the `ServletContext`. It is called just after the addition of the attribute.
- ❑ **attributeRemoved()** – `Notifies` about the removal of an existing attribute from the `ServletContext`. It is called just after the removal of the attribute.
- ❑ **attributeReplaced()** – `Notifies` about the replacement of an attribute on the `ServletContext`. It is called just after the replacement of an attribute.

Q9. List the various servlet session level events that can occur during a session.

Ans. The various servlet session level events that can occur during a session are as follows:

- ❑ Creating a session
- ❑ Destroying a session
- ❑ Adding, removing, or replacing the attributes of a session

Q10. Explain the methods of the HttpSessionBindingEvent class.

Ans. The methods of the HttpSessionBindingEvent class are as follows:

- ❑ **getSession()** – Retrieves the session object. It overrides the getSession() method of the HttpSessionEvent class.
- ❑ **getName()** – Retrieves the name with which an attribute is bound to or unbound from the session.
- ❑ **getValue()** – Retrieves the value of an added, removed, or replaced attribute.

7

Java Server Pages 2.3 and Expression Language 3.0

JSP stands for Java Server Pages, which is a Java-based technology developed to simplify the development of dynamic Web pages. JSP pages provide a means of separating the presentation logic from the business logic and help to directly embed Java code in static Hyper Text Markup Language (HTML) pages. The presentation logic is provided by HTML tags and the business logic for dynamic content is handled by JSP tags. JSP is a server-side technology and JSP pages are processed on a Web server in the JSP Servlet engine. When a client requests for a JSP page, the JSP Servlet engine first processes the requested page to generate the HTML code for dynamic content, then compiles the page into a servlet, and then executes the resulting servlet to generate an output to the client.

Sometimes JSP programmers need to fetch application data stored in JavaBeans components, which is accomplished with the help of using the Expression Language (EL). EL is introduced in JSP 2.0, and in JSP 2.1, EL of JSP 2.0 and JSF 1.1 are combined to form a single unified EL (EL 2.1). The latest release of EL is EL 3.0. This release adds a variety of features that enable EL to be used as a stand-alone tool.

This chapter begins by providing an introduction to the JSP technology. The chapter also discusses the advantages of JSP over Java Servlet and explores the different architectures of JSP pages. Apart from this, the chapter explains the life cycle of a JSP page and also explores the various JSP basic tags, implicit objects, and action tags. Then, the chapter explore about EL 3.0. Towards the end, you learn about JSP implicit objects within EL expressions, and how to use custom tag library with EL functions.

So let's start the chapter with a brief overview about the JSP technology.

Introducing JSP Technology

JSP is a Java-based Web application development technology and serves as an advancement of the Java Servlet technology. Before the introduction of JSP pages, servlets were used by Java programmers to provide dynamic content to clients. In case of servlets, both the processing of requests and the generation of responses were handled by a single servlet class. Servlets usually contain HTML code embedded in Java code. Therefore, programmers who created servlets needed a thorough knowledge of Java programming and basic knowledge about HTML programming. In addition, servlets do not separate the presentation logic from the business logic in an application.

JSP greatly simplifies the process of creating dynamic Web pages. In JSP, the Java code is embedded within the HTML code to provide dynamic content to a client. There is a clear separation between the presentation logic, which is provided by HTML tags and the business logic, which is handled by embedded Java code. This separation allows you to divide the tasks of providing code for presentation and business logic in an application between designers and programmers having different skills. This implies that, in case of JSP, designers can implement the presentation logic code and the user interface in HTML, and Java programmers can later add the code for dynamic content to implement the business logic. As far as their execution is concerned, JSP pages provide all the benefits of servlets. Apart from this, JSP pages are easier to write than servlets. JSP pages are translated to a servlet during compilation, and the response is sent to a client by generating dynamic content in the form of the servlet.

Various versions of JSP have been released since the development of the JSP specification. The latest version of JSP is version 2.3. JSP 2.3 is a maintenance release of JSP specification. There are no major changes in this release except that ER specification is not a part of JSP specification. JSP 2.3 supports and depends on EL 3.0.

Listing Advantages of JSP over Java Servlet

JSP offers various advantages over Java Servlet. It provides a better server-side scripting support as compared to Java Servlet. Java programmers can create servlets easily, but handling Java code is always a tough job for Web page designers. As stated earlier, a JSP page has HTML code, and some Java code embedded with the HTML code. This makes creating a Web page easy as the basic designing of the page is done by using the HTML code. You can use the Java code to add dynamic content to the page. The Java code is embedded by using different JSP constructs. The following are some reasons to prefer JSP over Java Servlet:

- Allows you to place static code and components symmetrically in a Web page. These static Web pages are designed by Web designers by using HTML code. Designing static Web pages by using servlets requires a good knowledge of Java, but Web designers may not be comfortable with Java programming constructs. In addition, while using servlets, you have to enclose HTML code in the `out.println()` method, which disables all Integrated Development Environment (IDE) support for generating HTML content. Therefore, using JSP is always easier than using servlets for the same HTML output.

- Facilitates automatic recompilation of a JSP page by a Web container for any update in the code; whereas, you need to recompile your servlet for every single change in the source code of the servlet.
- Allows you to access a JSP page directly as a simple HTML page; whereas, servlets cannot be accessed directly and have to be first mapped in the web.xml file.
- Allows you to create a JSP page by using a simple HTML template and the JSP page is automatically handled by the JSP container. However, in servlets you need to provide the Java code to generate dynamic HTML pages.

These advantages of JSP make it a popular technology to use in the presentation logic of any Web application. After discussing the advantages of JSP over Java Servlet, let's explore the various architectures of a JSP page in the next section.

Exploring the Architecture of a JSP Page

According to JSP specifications, there are two approaches to build Web applications. These approaches are known as the JSP Model 1 and JSP Model 2 architectures, respectively. Let's discuss these models in detail in the following sections.

The JSP Model I Architecture

In the JSP Model I architecture, a Web browser directly accesses JSP pages of a Web container. These JSP pages interact with JavaBeans in an application. When a client sends a request from a JSP page, the response (i.e., a JSP page or servlet) is sent back to the client depending on which hyperlinks are selected or which request parameters are invoked by the client request. If the generated response requires accessing a database, the JSP page uses a JavaBean, which retrieves the required data from the database. Figure 7.1 shows the architecture of JSP Model I:

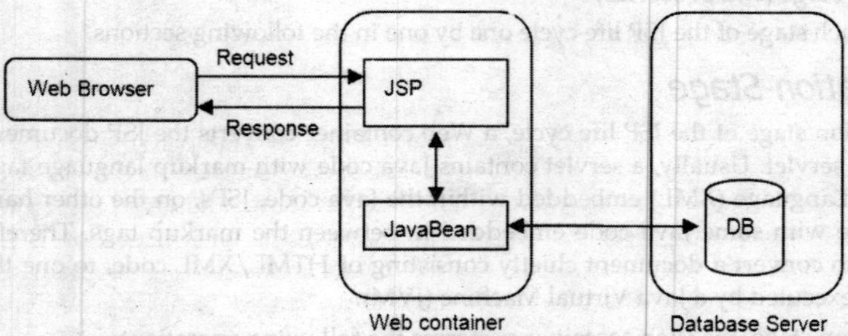

Figure 7.1: Showing the JSP Model I Architecture

Let's now discuss the JSP Model II architecture.

The JSP Model II Architecture

In the JSP Model II architecture, servlets are used by a Web browser to communicate with a JSP page. The servlets are positioned between the Web browser and the JSP pages, and they act as a controller to dispatch requests to the next requested JSP page based on the requested Uniform Resource Locator (URL) and input parameters. The servlet also creates JavaBean instances, if they are required by the JSP page to store data. The Controller servlet then decides which JSP page to forward to as a response, based on the client request. A JavaBean invokes the database server if data is needed from the server. Figure 7.2 shows the architecture of JSP Model II:

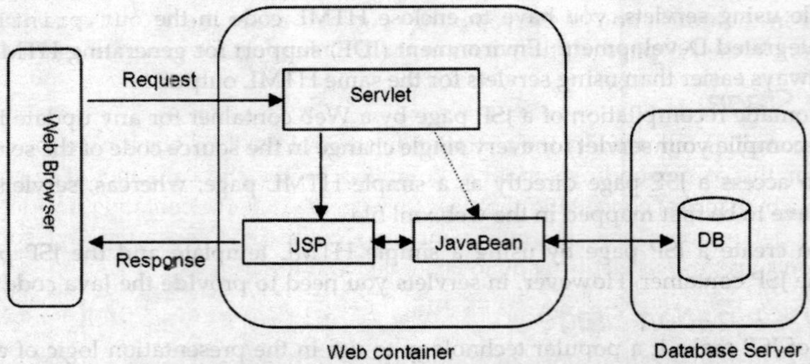

Figure 7.2: Showing the JSP Model II Architecture

Now that you are familiar with JSP architecture, let's discuss the life cycle of a JSP page in the next section.

Describing the Life Cycle of a JSP Page

A JSP page is not executed directly. It follows a well-defined process that first involves the translation of the JSP page into its corresponding servlet and then the compilation of the source file of the servlet into a class file. The resulting translated servlet is then loaded into memory and initialized, similar to any other servlet. Every time a JSP page is requested, its corresponding servlet is executed. Therefore, most of the stages of the JSP life cycle are similar to that of a servlet. The major stages of the life cycle of a JSP are as follows:

- The page translation stage
- The compilation stage
- The loading & initialization stage
- The request handling stage
- The destroying stage (end of service)

Let's now discuss each stage of the JSP life cycle one by one in the following sections.

The Page Translation Stage

In the page translation stage of the JSP life cycle, a Web container converts the JSP document into an equivalent Java code, that is, a servlet. Usually, a servlet contains Java code with markup language tags, such as HTML or Extensible Markup Language (XML) embedded within the Java code. JSPs, on the other hand, consist primarily of markup language with some Java code embedded in between the markup tags. Therefore, the objective of page translation is to convert a document chiefly consisting of HTML/XML code, to one that has more of Java code, which can be executed by a Java Virtual Machine (JVM).

In the page translation stage, the Web container performs the following operations:

- Locates the requested JSP page
- Validates the syntactic correctness of the JSP page
- Interprets the standard JSP directives, actions, and custom actions used in the JSP page
- Writes the source code of the equivalent servlet for the JSP page

After a JSP page is translated into a servlet, all the requests for that JSP page are served by its corresponding servlet class. This servlet class works similar to any other simple servlet. The translation of JSP is done automatically by the Web server. JSP page translation occurs only when necessary, that is, at some point before the page has to serve its first request. This process is also performed when the JSP source code is updated and the page is redeployed. A Web container can decide when the translation should occur. The two possible instances where a translation can occur are as follows:

- When a first-time user requests a JSP page.
- When a JSP page is loaded into a Web container. This is also called JSP pre-compilation.

If there is any error in the translation of the page, the container raises the 500 (internal server error) exception and if a change occurs in the JSP page, all the stages of the JSP life cycle are executed again.

The Compilation Stage

The page translation stage is followed by the compilation stage of the JSP life cycle. In the compilation stage, the Java source code for the corresponding servlet is compiled by the JSP container. The container converts the source code into Java byte (class) code. After the class file is generated, the container decides to either discard the code or retain it for debugging. Generally, most containers discard the generated Java source code by default. After the compilation stage, the servlet is ready to be loaded and initialized.

The Loading & Initialization Stage

During the loading and initialization stage of the JSP life cycle, the JSP container loads and instantiates the servlet that has been generated and compiled in the translation and compilation stages, respectively. The JSP container, as part of the loading and initialization process, performs the following operations:

- **Loading**—Loads the servlet generated during the translation and compilation stages. Normal Java class loading options are used to load the servlet. The loading process is terminated if the Web container fails to load the servlet class.
- **Instantiation**—Creates an instance of a servlet class. To create a new instance of the generated servlet, the JSP container uses the no-argument constructor. The JSP translator (part of the JSP container) is responsible for including a no-argument constructor in the servlet generated after the translation of the JSP page.
- **Initialization**—Initializes the instantiated object after successful instantiation of the JSP equivalent servlet object. As per the servlet's life cycle, the container initializes the object by invoking the `init (ServletConfig)` method. This method is implemented by the container by calling the `jspInit()` method. This indicates that the `jspInit()` method acts as the `init(ServletConfig)` method of the servlet.

If the loading and initialization stage is performed successfully, the Web container activates the servlet object and makes it available and ready to handle client requests.

NOTE

A JSP page equivalent servlet instance put into service by a container may not handle any request in its lifetime.

The next stage in the JSP life cycle is the request handling stage.

The Request Handling Stage

During the request handling stage of the JSP life cycle, only those objects of a JSP equivalent servlet that are initialized successfully are used by the Web container to handle client requests. The container performs the following operations in the request handling stage:

- Creates the `ServletRequest` and `ServletResponse` objects. If a client uses the HTTP protocol to make a request, the container creates the `HttpServletRequest` and `HttpServletResponse` objects, where the request object corresponds to the client request. In other words, the request data and client information can be retrieved by a servlet by using the request object. The response object can be used by the servlet to generate the response to a client.
- Passes the request and response objects created in the preceding step to the servlet object to invoke the `service()` method. In the case of a JSP equivalent servlet, the container invokes the `_jspService()` method.

Let's now look at the final stage of the JSP life cycle, that is, the destroying stage.

The Destroying Stage

If a servlet container decides to destroy a servlet instance of a JSP page, the container needs to end the services provided by the instance. The servlet container performs the following operations to destroy the servlet instance:

- Allows all the currently running threads in the service() method of the servlet instance to complete their operations. Meanwhile, the servlet container makes the servlet instance unavailable for new requests.
- Allows the servlet container to invoke the `destroy()` method on the servlet instance, after the current threads have completed their operations on the `service()` method. The `destroy()` method leads to the invocation of the `jspDestroy()` method.
- Releases all the references of the servlet instance and renders them for garbage collection, after the `destroy()` method is processed. In addition, the servlet's life cycle is complete after the invocation of the destroy() method.

  With this, we complete our discussion on the JSP life cycle. There are various basic tags and implicit objects that constitute the JSP technology. Let's explore them in the next section.

Working with JSP Basic Tags and Implicit Objects

A JSP page consists of various elements or tags, such as scripting elements, implicit objects, and directives. Scripting elements, such as declaration tags, expression tags, and scriptlet tags, help to declare variables and object references in a JSP page. Scripting elements help to generate and display dynamic content. Directives are used in a JSP page to include the content of a static or dynamic file within another file. Directives are also used to import Java files within JSP pages.

The Java Servlet API includes various interfaces that provide useful and suitable abstractions to Java programmers. Some examples of these interfaces are `HttpServletRequest`, `HttpServletResponse`, and `HttpSession`. These abstractions encapsulate an object's implementation. For example, the `HttpServletRequest` interface represents an HTTP request sent from a client along with elements, such as headers and form parameters, as well as provides convenient methods, such as `getParameter()` and `getHeader()`, to extract relevant data from the request. JSP implicit objects provide a convenient way to access the interfaces and objects of the servlet API without writing additional code.

Let's now discuss in detail the basic tags and implicit objects that constitute a JSP page, in the following sections.

Exploring Scripting Tags

JSP scripting tags, also called JSP scripting elements, allow you to add Java coding statements into a JSP page. The Java code incorporated by using scripting elements is translated and generated by the JSP translator while translating the page into a servlet. In most cases, Java is the scripting language used to build a JSP page; however, other supported languages can also be used, depending on the language supported by a Web container.

Let's now learn about the classification of the scripting elements and the use of these elements.

Classifying the Scripting Tags

The JSP scripting tags are categorized into the following three types of tags:

- Scriptlet
- Declarative
- Expression

The Scriptlet Tag

Scriptlet tags allow you to write the script code (or the Java code) to implement the `_jspService()` method functionality. The JSP translator translates the statements of this tag into the `_jspService ()` method of the servlet generated for a JSP page. You can use a scriptlet tag to perform the following tasks:

- Declaring variables that you can use later in a JSP page. In other words, you can declare variables and write valid expressions within the scriptlet tags.
- Using any of the JSP implicit objects or any other object declared with a `<jsp:useBean>` element.

Note that if the script code is not valid, an exception is thrown at the compilation stage of the JSP life cycle.

You can include multiple scriptlet tags in a single JSP document. The following code snippet shows the traditional JSP syntax to use a scriptlet tag:

```
<%
   script code (allows multiple statements)
%>
```

The following code snippet shows the XML-based syntax for a scriptlet tag:

```
<jsp:scriptlet>
   script code (allows multiple statements)
</jsp:scriptlet>
```

Let's now look at an example that illustrates the use the scriptlet tag. The following code snippet shows the syntax to use a scriptlet tag in a JSP page:

```
<html>
<body>
<%
   for (int i=0;i<5;i++)
   {
        out.println(i);
   }
%>
</body>
</html>
```

In the preceding code snippet, the for loop of Java is used in a JSP page between the scriptlet tags to print numbers 1 to 5 in five lines. The following code snippet shows the equivalent servlet code for this JSP page, as generated by the JSP container:

```
   public void _jspService(HttpServletRequest request, HttpServletResponse
   response) throws ServletException, IOException
   {
   ...
   out.write("<html><body>");
   for (int i=0;i<5;i++) {
        out.print(i);
   }
   out.write("</body></html>");
   ...
```

The Declarative Tag

The declarative tag allows you to write the script code you need to provide in the generated servlet class, outside the `_jspService()` method. This tag allows you to declare instance and class variables and implement class methods, such as `jspInit()` and `jspDestroy()`. The following code snippet shows the syntax of the declarative tag:

```
<%!
   script code (allows multiple statements)
%>
```

The following code snippet shows the XML-based syntax for the declarative tag:

```
<jsp:declaration>
   script code (allows multiple statements)
</jsp:declaration>
```

The following code snippet shows an example illustrating the use of the declarative tag:

```
<%!
int a,b;
int fun(int a)
{
   return a;
}
%>
<%a=1;%>
<%b=fun(a);%>
<%out.println(b);%>
```

In the preceding code snippet, two integer variables, a and b, and the fun() method are defined by using the declarative tag. A value of 1 is then assigned to variable a, which is passed as an argument to the fun() method. This method processes the argument and stores the result in variable b. Finally, the value received by variable b is displayed on the browser.

The Expression Tag

An expression tag allows you to write a Java expression, which is then resolved and the resultant value is displayed. The expression tag places the given Java expression in the out.print() method during the translation stage of the JSP life cycle. Consequently, the output of the Java expression is displayed with the output of the JSP page.

An expression tag also provides a simple and convenient way to access script (i.e., Java) variables. The following code snippet shows the syntax of the expression tag:

```
<%=
   script code (allows only one expression)
%>
```

The following code snippet shows the XML-based syntax for the expression tag:

```
<jsp:expression>
   script code (allows only one expression)
</jsp:expression>
```

Let's now look at an example to use the expression tag. The following code snippet shows the syntax to use an expression tag in a JSP page:

```
<%! int count; %>
<html>
<body>
<% count++; %>
This page is requested by <%=count%> number of users till now.
</body>
</html>
```

The preceding code snippet can be embedded on a JSP page to count the number of requests received for the specific page. Each time a new user accesses the JSP page on the browser, the value of the count variable is incremented by 1, and displayed on the browser. For example, when a user accesses the JSP page for the first time, the count variable is declared and initialized at 0 (by default). The expression written in the scriptlet tag (<%count++%>) increments the value of the count variable by one and prints this value on a Web page. Now, when another user accesses this page, the value of the count variable is incremented by 1 and the browser displays the result as 2.

Consider the following points when using expression tags:

- Do not end an expression with; because the expression given in this tag is placed within the out.print() method.
- You can resolve an expression given in the expression tag to any type, such as int, float, double, Boolean, String, or Object, but not to void.

Writing any code violating these rules raises a translation stage error. In addition, nested scripting tags are not allowed in expression tags. This means that a scripting tag cannot have another type of scripting tag. For example, consider the following code snippet:

```
<%
for (int i=0;i<5; i++)
{
   <%=i%>    //out.println(+i);
}
%>
```

In the preceding code snippet, the expression tag (<%= %>) is nested within the scriptlet tag (<% %>), which would raise a translation error.

Let's now learn how to use scripting tags in a Web application.

Using the JSP Scripting Tags

In this section, we create a Web application to learn the use of JSP scripting tags, such as declarative, expression, and scriptlets. The use of scripting tags varies from simple to complex Web applications. In simple Web applications, servlets and JSP scripting tags are used with JavaBeans to build Web applications. However, in complex applications, scripting tags are used with custom tags and other Model-View-Controller (MVC) frameworks, such as Struts and JSF. In this section, we create a simple Web application by using scripting tags.

Let's create the `ScriptingElements` Web application containing the `ScriptingTags` JSP page, which uses page directives to import the `java.util` package, and specify the scripting language as Java. In the declaration tag, three integer variables--`count`, `a`, and `b`--are declared. The `fun()` method accepts a parameter, `a`, and returns an integer value after multiplying the value of `a` with 10. The value returned by the `fun()` method is stored in the `b` variable. The `count` variable is used to keep track of the number of times the Web page is accessed. Listing 7.1 shows the code for the `ScriptingTags` JSP page (save the `ScriptingTags.jsp` file in the `\ScriptingElements` folder):

Listing 7.1: Showing the Code of the ScriptingTags.jsp File

```
<%@ page import ="java.util.*" language="java" %>
<html>
<body>
  <center><h1>Using Scripting Elements</h1></center>
  <%! int count,a,b;
      int fun(int a)
      {
        return 10*a;
      }
  %>
  <%
      a=1;
      count++;
      for (int i=0;i<5;i++)
      {
        out.println("Value of i in iteration
        no."+i+":  <b>"+i+"</b><br/>");
      }
      b=fun(a);
      out.println("Value returned by fun():  <b>"+b+"</b><br/>");
  %>
  This page is requested by <b><%=count%></b> number of times on date
  <b><%=new Date()%></b>.
</body>
</html>
```

You do not need to map the JSP page in the `web.xml` file; however, an empty `web.xml` file must exist at the appropriate place in the root directory. The following code snippet shows the code to create an empty `web.xml` configuration file:

```
<web-app/>
```

Store the `ScriptingTags.jsp` and `web.xml` files in the `ScriptingElements` directory according to the standard directory structure of a Web application. Figure 7.3 shows the directory structure of the `ScriptingElements` Web application:

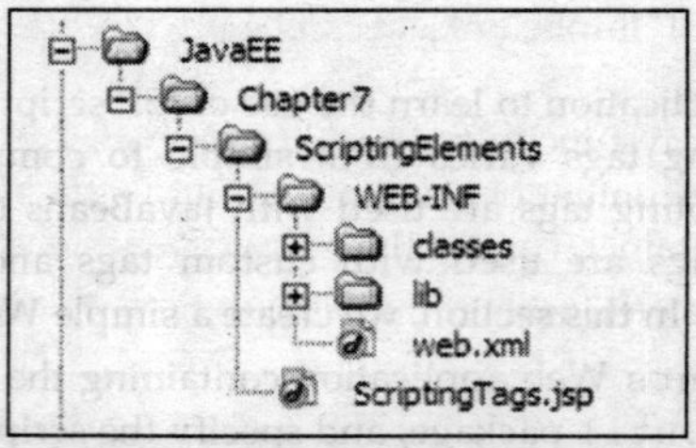

Figure 7.3: Displaying the Directory Structure of the ScriptingElements Web Application

Now, package the ScriptingElements application into the .war file that can be deployed on the `GlassFish 4.0` application server. Next, deploy the `ScriptingElements.war` file on the server, after starting the server. Browse the `ScriptingElements` Web application by using the `http://localhost:8080/ScriptingElements/ScriptingTags.jsp` URL. Figure 7.4 shows the output of the `ScriptingTags JSP` page as displayed in the Web browser:

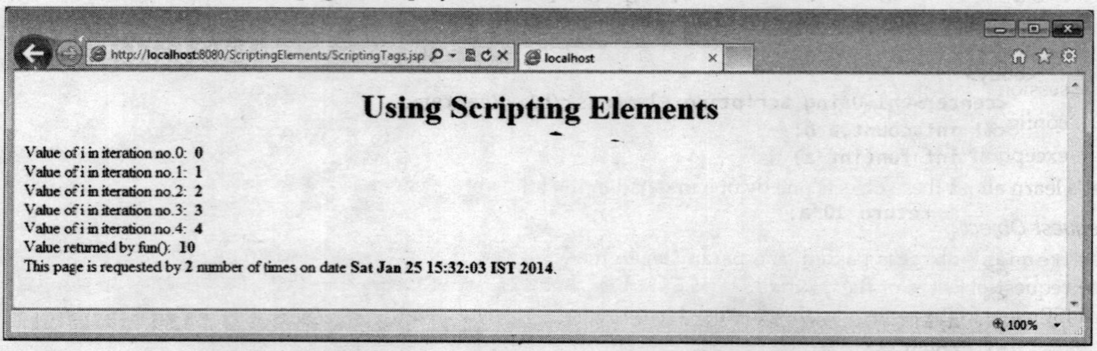

Figure 7.4: Showing the Output of the ScriptingTags JSP Page

Figure 7.4 shows the use of JSP scripting tags in the `ScriptingTags` JSP page. The scripting tags are used to iterate the values of the a and b variables. Figure 7.4 also shows the number of times a user has requested the specific Web page.

Apart from scripting elements, you can also use predefined objects, known as implicit objects, in a JSP page. Let's now understand how to implement implicit objects.

Exploring Implicit Objects

JSP implicit objects are used in a JSP page to make the page dynamic. Java objects within scripting elements can be used to create and access the dynamic content. JSP implicit objects are predefined objects that are accessible to all JSP pages. These objects are called implicit objects because you do not need to instantiate these objects. JSP implicit objects are automatically instantiated by the JSP container while writing the script content in the scriptlet and expression tags. JSP specification standardizes some object reference names, which are available for every JSP page so that any vendor-implemented translators have to take the responsibility of initializing these objects in the `_jspService()` method.

Listing the Features of Implicit Objects

A JSP implicit object has the following features:

- Helps Java developers to access the services and resources provided by a JSP container.
- Helps you to generate the dynamic content of Web pages.
- Does not allow you to declare a JSP implicit object explicitly because they are automatically instantiated by the JSP container.
- Allows you to use a JSP implicit object without importing them into your JSP page. This implies that a user only needs to use a reference variable associated with a given object as a JSP implicit object is declared

automatically. In other words, a JSP implicit object can be directly used to call the methods associated with them.

- Helps Java developers in many ways, including handling HTML parameters, sending a request to a Web component, and incorporating the content of a component into a JSP page. A JSP implicit object can also be used to log data through a JSP container, control the output stream, and handle exceptions more efficiently.

Let's now discuss the implicit objects as well as their implementation.

Explaining Types of Implicit Objects

When a JSP page is translated, the nine most commonly used JSP implicit objects are initialized by the JSP Servlet engine in the `_jspService()` method. These JSP implicit objects are listed as follows:

- request
- response
- out
- page
- pageContext
- application
- session
- config
- exception

Let's learn about these objects one by one in detail in the following sections.

The request Object

The `request` object is passed as a parameter to the `_jspService()` method when a client request is made. The request object is of the `javax.servlet.http.HttpServletRequest` type. You can use request objects in a JSP page in the same way they are used in servlets.

The response Object

The `response` object is used to carry the response of a client request after the `_jspService()` method is executed. This object is of the `javax.servlet.http.HttpServletResponse` type.

The out Object

The `out` implicit object provides access to the output stream of a servlet. This object is a subtype of the `javax.servlet.jsp.JspWriter` class. The `out` object can be used directly in JSP scriptlets to display text data on a browser, as JSP expressions are automatically placed in the output stream. In other words, the `out` object is used to write text data in the output stream.

The page Object

The `page` object refers to a servlet of the JSP page processing a current request. It also works as an instance of the generated servlet in a JSP page. This object is of the `java.lang.Object` type and therefore is rarely used in a JSP page. In addition, you cannot directly use this object to call servlet methods.

The pageContext Object

The `pageContext` object represents the context of the current JSP page. It provides a single API to manage different scoped attributes. This object is of the `javax.servlet.jsp.PageContext` type.

The application Object

The `application` object refers to the entire environment of a Web application to which a JSP page belongs. This object is of the `javax.servlet.ServletContext` type.

The session Object

The `session` object helps to access session data and is of the `HttpSession` type. It is declared if the value of the session attribute in a page directive is true. If we explicitly specify the session attribute to false, the JSP

Servlet engine does not declare this object. In such a case, if you try to access the session object, an error is generated.

The config Object

The `config` object specifies the configuration of the parameters passed to a JSP page. This object is of the `javax.servlet.ServletConfig` type. To show the use of the `config` object within a JSP page, you need to associate a servlet with a JSP file by using the `<jsp-file>` element. After associating a servlet, all the initialization parameters for the named servlet are made available to the JSP page by the `ServletConfig` object.

The exception Object

The `exception` object is of the `java.lang.Throwable` type and is only available for JSP pages that act as the error handlers for other pages. This object is only available to the JSP error pages that have the `isErrorPage` attribute set to `true` within the `page` directive.

All the objects discussed so far are available only within scriptlet and expression tags. These objects should not be used in the declaration tag. However, you can use the `getServletConfig()` method if you want to get the `ServletConfig` type of the reference of an object in a declaration tag while implementing the `jspInit()` or `jspDestroy()` method. In addition, you can use the `getServletContext()` method of the `ServletConfig` type to get the `ServletContext` object.

Using Implicit Objects

Let's now learn to use implicit objects in a JSP page to create a dynamic Web page. In this section, we develop a simple Web application, `ImplicitObjects`, by using implicit objects, such as `request`, `session`, and `pageContext`. This Web application performs three tasks: it overrides the `jspInit()` method to perform initializations, it uses the initialization parameter to implement an object of the `ServletConfig` interface, and it accesses a JSP document placed in a private folder.

The `ImplicitObjects` Web application contains the following pages:

- The Home HTML page: Represents the index page of the Web application
- The request JSP page: Displays the welcome message
- The pageContext JSP page: Shows the use of the pageContext implicit object
- The other JSP page: Shows the use of other implicit objects such as `page`, `session`, `out`, `application` and `config`.

The `Home HTML` page of the `ImplicitObjects` Web application consists of a simple form with a text field, `Name`, and a button, `Invoke JSP`. Listing 7.2 shows the code for the `Home HTML` page (save the `Home.html` file in the `\ImplicitObjects` folder):

Listing 7.2: Showing the Code for the Home.html File

```
<html>
   <body>
         <form action="request.jsp">
               Name : <input type="text" name="name">
               <input type="submit" value="Invoke JSP"/>
         </form>
   </body>
</html>
```

When a user clicks the `Invoke JSP` button on the `Home HTML` page, the `request` JSP page is displayed. This page displays a greeting message followed by the user name entered on the `Home HTML` page. After you submit the Home HTML page, request details, such as type of request, its Uniform Resource Identifier (URI), and request protocol, are displayed in tabular form. These request details are retrieved by using the methods of the `request` JSP implicit object, such as `getMethod()`, `getRequestURI()`, `getProtocol()`, and `getHeader()`. Listing 7.3 shows the code for the `request JSP` page (save the `request.jsp` file in the `\ImplicitObjects` folder):

Listing 7.3: Showing the Code for the request.jsp File

```
<html>
  <head>
        <title>
        Using Implicit Objects
        </title>
  </head>
  <body>

  Hello, <b><%=request.getParameter("name")%></b><br/><br/>
  Your request details are <br/><br/>
  <table border="1">
  <tr><th>Name</th><th>Value</th></tr>
  <tr><td>request method</td>
  <td><%= request.getMethod() %></td></tr>
  <tr><td>request URI</td>
  <td><%= request.getRequestURI() %></td></tr>
  <tr><td>request protocol</td>
  <td><%= request.getProtocol() %></td></tr>
  <tr><td>browser</td>
  <td><%= request.getHeader("user-agent") %></td></tr>
  </table>
  <%
        if (session.getAttribute("sessionVar")==null)
        {
                session.setAttribute("sessionVar",new Integer(0));
        }
  %>

  <table>
        <tr><th align=left>Would you like to see use of remaining
                imlplicit objects?</th></tr>
        <tr>
        <form name=form1 action="pageContext.jsp" method="post">
        <td><input type="radio" name="other" value="Yes">Yes</td>
        <td><input type="radio" name="other" value="No" > No</td></tr>
        <tr><td><input type="submit" value="Submit"></td></tr>
        </form>
  </table>
  </body>
</html>
```

After clicking the `submit` button displayed on the `request JSP` page, the control is transferred to the `pageContext JSP` page. This page uses the `pageContext` implicit object to forward a request to the `other` JSP page. Listing 7.4 shows the code for the `pageContext.jsp` file (save the `pageContext.jsp` file in the `\ImplicitObjects` folder):

Listing 7.4: Showing the Code for the pageContext.jsp File

```
<HTML>
  <HEAD>
  <TITLE> Intermediate </TITLE>
  </HEAD>

  <BODY>
  <%
        if("Yes".equals(request.getParameter("other")))
        {
                pageContext.forward("other");
        }
```

```
    %>
    </BODY>
</HTML>
```

The other JSP page shows the use of the page, session, out, config, and application implicit objects. This page overrides the jspInit() method, which retrieves the other initialization parameter of the other JSP page from the web.xml file. The same initialization parameter value is fetched by calling the getInitParmeter method of the config implicit object, config.getInitParameter("count"). In the other JSP page, we use the page implicit object's log method to log the message, anothermessage (((HttpServlet)page).log("anothermessage");). The implicit object, session, invokes the getAttribute() method to get the value of the sessionVar attribute, which shows the number of active sessions in the request JSP page. The implicit object, application, is used to retrieve the value of the context parameter, param1, set in web.xml. We use the application.getInitParameter("param1") method to retrieve the value of the param1 parameter in the other JSP page. Listing 7.5 shows the code for the other.jsp file (located in the \ImplicitObjects\WEB-INF\jsppages folder):

Listing 7.5: Showing the Code for the other.jsp File

```
<html>
<body>
  <%!int count;
        public void jspInit()
        {
               ServletConfig sc=getServletConfig();
               count = Integer.parseInt(sc.getInitParameter("count"));
               System.out.println("In jspInit");

        }
  %>

  <%
        out.println("<H1>Using page, session, out, config, and application
        Implicit Objects</H1>");
  %>

  Count value without using config implicit object: <b> <%=count%></b> <br/>
  <%
        this.log("log message");
        ((HttpServlet)page).log("anothermessage");
        ServletContext ct = config.getServletContext();
        out.println("Value of sessionVar is:"+"  <b>"+
        session.getAttribute("sessionVar")+"</b><br/>");
        out.println("Server name and version using config implicit
        object:"+"  <b>"+ct.getServerInfo()+"</b><br/>");
        out.println("Value of context parameter param1 obtained using
        application implicit object:"+"  <b>"+
        application.getInitParameter("param1")+"</b><br/>");
        out.println("Count value retrieved using config implicit object:" +
        "  <b>"+config.getInitParameter("count")+"</b>");
  %>
</body>
</html>
```

The web.xml file initializes an application level parameter, param1, with the value param1. In the ImplicitObjects Web application, we configure the other JSP page in web.xml. Although it is not mandatory to declare a JSP page in web.xml, we do it for the following reasons:

- The initialization parameter count for the other JSP page is configured in web.xml.
- The other JSP page is placed in a private folder (jsppages) to avoid direct access to the page.

The other JSP page is configured by using the <jsp-file> nested tag of the <servlet> tag. The servlet name specified in the <servlet-name> tag is myjsp, which is mapped to the URI to access this page.

The other JSP page is placed in the WEB-INF/jsppages folder. Listing 7.6 shows the code for the web.xml file (save the web.xml file in the \ImplicitObjects\WEB-INF folder):

Listing 7.6: Showing the Code for the web.xml File

```
<?xml version="1.0" encoding="UTF-8"?>
<web-app version="3.1"
  xmlns="http://xmlns.jcp.org/xml/ns/javaee"
  xmlns:xsi="http://www.w3.org/2001/XMLSchema-instance"
  xsi:schemaLocation="http://xmlns.jcp.org/xml/ns/javaee
  http://xmlns.jcp.org/xml/ns/javaee/web-app_3_1.xsd">

  <context-param>
        <param-name>param1</param-name>
        <param-value>param1</param-value>
  </context-param>

  <servlet>
        <servlet-name>myjsp</servlet-name>
        <jsp-file>/WEB-INF/jsppages/other.jsp</jsp-file>
        <init-param>
              <param-name>count</param-name>
              <param-value>10</param-value>
        </init-param>
  </servlet>
  <servlet-mapping>
        <servlet-name>myjsp</servlet-name>
        <url-pattern>/other</url-pattern>
  </servlet-mapping>

</web-app>
```

To run the ImplicitObjects Web application effectively, you need to make a new folder, say ImplicitObjects, and place the files of the Web application in it, such as Home.html, pageContext.jsp, other.jsp, and web.xml, as shown in Figure 7.5:

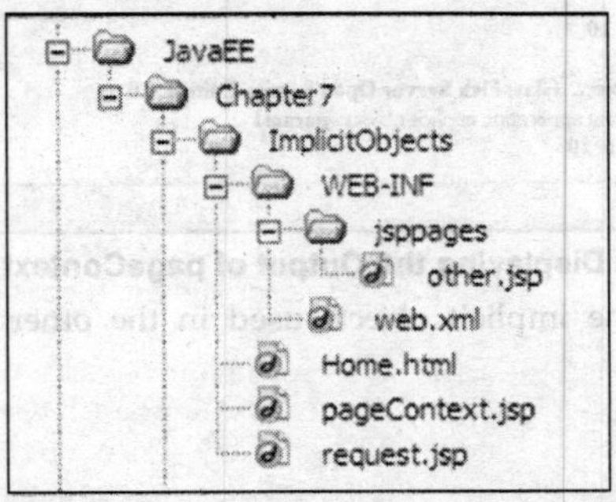

Figure 7.5: Showing the Directory Structure for ImplicitObjects Web Application

Now, package the ImplicitObjects application into the .war file and deploy the ImplicitObjects.war file on the GlassFish 4.0 application server. Next, start the Glassfish server and browse the ImplicitObjects application by using the http://localhost:8080/ImplicitObjects/Home.html URL. Figure 7.6 displays the Home page of the ImplicitObjects application:

Figure 7.6: Displaying the Output of the Home HTML Page

When a user clicks the `Invoke JSP` button, the `request JSP` page is displayed, as shown in Figure 7.7:

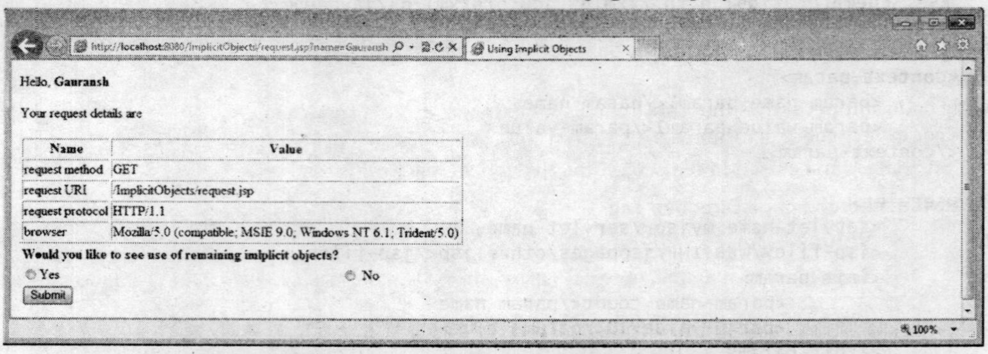

Figure 7.7: Displaying the Result of Processing the request JSP Page

Figure 7.7 shows all request details, such as request type, request URI, browser request details, and request protocols, in the form of a table.

When a user selects the `Yes` radio button and clicks the `Submit` button, the `pageContext JSP` page is displayed, as shown in Figure 7.8:

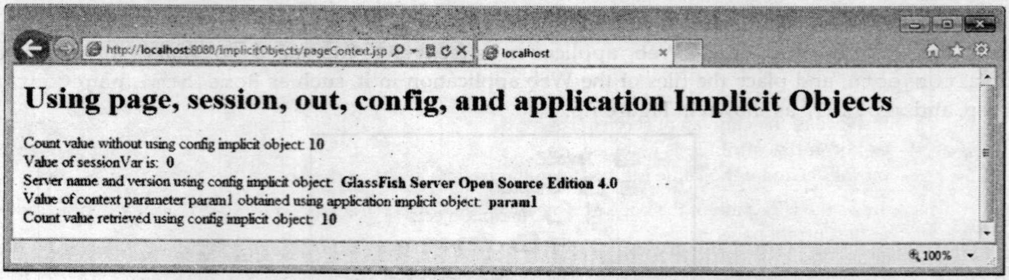

Figure 7.8: Displaying the Output of pageContext JSP Page

Figure 7.8 shows the values of the implicit objects used in the other JSP page in the `ImplicitObjects` application.

Let's now learn about directive tags.

Exploring Directive Tags

Directive tags provide directions that are used by the JSP translator during the translation stage of the JSP life cycle. These tags are used to set global values, such as class declarations, methods to be implemented, and output content type. The following sections discuss the various types of directive tags and how they are used in a JSP page.

Explaining the Types of Directive Tags

According to JSP specification, there are three standard directive tags available with all JSP-compliant containers. These directive tags are as follows:

- page
- include
- taglib

Let's discuss each of these directives in detail.

The page Directive Tag

The `page` directive tag holds the instructions that are used by a JSP translator during the translation stage of the JSP life cycle. These instructions affect different properties associated with the whole JSP page. The `page` directive can be used multiple times in a JSP page, and when used on any part of the JSP page automatically applies to the entire page. However, it is considered a good programming practice to use the `page` directive at the starting of the JSP page. The syntax of the `page` directive tag is as follows:

```
<%@page attributes %>
```

The following code snippet shows the XML-based syntax for the page directive tag:

```
<jsp:directive.page attributes/>
```

A total of 11 attributes can be used in the `page` directive tag, as listed in Table 7.1:

Table 7.1: Attributes of the page Directive Tag

Attribute	Value
Language	Takes the type of scripting language to be used in scripting tags, as a value. The default value is Java.
Import	Takes a comma separated list of Java classes as a value.
extends	Takes a complete qualified class name of the class that is extended by the equivalent servlet class written by the translator of the current JSP page.
buffer	Takes the buffer size in kilobytes. The values of this attribute are none, 8 kb, 16 kb, 32 kb, and 64 kb. The default value is 8 kb.
autoFlush	Specifies whether or not to automatically flush the output when the buffer is full. If a `true` value is given to this attribute, it automatically flushes the buffer as soon as the buffer is full. If this attribute is assigned a `false` value, an exception is generated when the buffer overflows. The default value of this attribute is true.
isThreadSafe	Takes `true` or `false` as its value; the default value is `true`. This attribute specifies whether a JSP page is thread-safe or not. In other words, the `isThreadSafe` attribute specifies whether the instance of the equivalent servlet class of the JSP page is capable of handling simultaneous requests or not. If this attribute is assigned a `false` value, only one thread can use the service provided by one object and if the value is `true`, simultaneous requests can be handled by the JSP page.
errorPage	Takes the URL path of the page to which a request is to be redirected when an exception is generated in the current page.
isErrorPage	Takes either `true` or `false` as its value; the default value is `false`. This attribute specifies whether the current page is an error page or not. If this attribute is assigned a `true` value, an additional implicit object, `exception`, also becomes available for the current JSP page.
contentType	Takes the response content Multipurpose Internet Mail Extensions (MIME) type, and optionally, character encoding. The default value is `text/html`.
Session	Takes `true` or `false` as a value, which indicates whether a session is required or not; the default value is `true`. If this attribute is assigned a `false` value, the JSP page cannot use the implicit object, `session`.
Info	Takes a String, which can be retrieved by using the `getServletInfo()` method.
pageEncoding	Specifies the encoding type to be used by a Web container to compile a JSP page. Examples of encoding types are ISO-8859-1 and UTF-8.

As stated earlier, a JSP page can contain any number of page directive tags. However, except for the import tag, none of the other tags are allowed to be specified more than once.

The include Directive Tag

The `include` directive tag is used to combine the content of two or more files during the translation stage of the JSP life cycle. This directive appends the text of the included file to a JSP page, without any processing or modification. The included file can be static or dynamic. If the included file is dynamic, its JSP elements are first translated before being included in the JSP page. In other words, the included file is translated into a page. However, if any changes are made in the included page after the page is translated, the changes are not reflected in the page until the JSP page is translated once again. The syntax of the `include` directive tag is as follows:

```
<%@include file="file path" %>
```

The following code snippet shows the XML-based syntax for the `include` directive tag:

```
<jsp:directive.include file=" file path  "/>
```

The following code snippet shows an example of using the `include` directive tag to merge the `Test.jsp` and `Test1.html` files:

```
<%@include file="/Test.jsp" %>
<%@include file="/Test1.html" %>
```

Note that if any changes are made to the included page, the behavior of the `include` directive tag with respect to the recompilation of the page depends on a Web container. This means that if any changes are made in the included page, some containers recognize and apply the changes to the JSP page, while others do not.

The taglib Directive Tag

The `taglib` directive tag is used to declare a custom tag library in a JSP page so that the tags related to that custom tag library can be used in the same JSP page. The following code snippet shows the syntax of the `taglib` directive:

```
<%@taglib uri="URI" prefix="unique_prefix" %>
```

Any special XML equivalent element for the `taglib` directive tag is not available as the declaration of a custom tag library is done by using the XML namespace syntax.

After discussing the syntax of the various directive tags, let's learn to use these tags in a JSP page.

Using JSP Directive Tags

JSP directives are used in a JSP page to add functionality to the page. Let's create a Web application called `directiveTags` by using JSP directives. The `directiveTags` application contains the following pages:

- `The Login HTML page`—Accepts user details and redirects a user to the required JSP page
- `The LoginProcess JSP page`—Allows you to connect to a database to process a user request
- `The MyError JSP page`—Represents a JSP page that is called when an error or exception is raised

The Oracle database is used to access the `userdetails` table in the `directiveTags` application. Therefore, you need to create the `userdetails` table to work with the application before creating the required JSP pages. The following code snippet shows the code to create the `userdetails` table and insert data in the table, for the `directiveTags` application:

```
create table userdetails(uname varchar2(15), pass varchar2(10));
insert into userdetails values('Charu', 1234567);
```

Let's now create the required pages for the application. Listing 7.7 shows the code for the `Login.html` file, which is the home page of the `directiveTags` application (located in the `\directiveTags` folder):

Listing 7.7: Showing the Code for the Login.html File

```
<html>
<body>
   <pre>
   <form action="LoginProcess.jsp">
          <b>User Name</b> : <input type="text" name="uname"/>
          <b>Password</b>  : <input type="password" name="pass"/>
          <input type="submit" value="LogIN"/>
   </form>
   </pre>
</body>
```

```
</html>
```

The `Login HTML` page allows a user to enter a user name and password, which are stored in a database. After entering the user name and password, the `LoginProcess JSP` page is called to handle the request. Listing 7.8 shows the code for the `LoginProcess.jsp` file (save the LoginProcess.jsp file in the \directiveTags folder):

Listing 7.8: Showing the Code for the LoginProcess.jsp File

```
<%@page import="java.sql.*" errorPage="/MyError.jsp"%>
<html>
<body>
  <%
  Connection con=null;
  String uname=request.getParameter("uname");
  String pass=request.getParameter("pass");
  try
  {
          Class.forName("oracle.jdbc.driver.OracleDriver");
          con=DriverManager.getConnection(
                  "jdbc:oracle:thin:@192.168.1.123:1521:XE","scott","tiger");
          Statement st=con.createStatement();
          ResultSet rs=st.executeQuery(
                  "select * from userdetails where
                  uname = \'" + uname + "\' and
                  pass = " + pass );
          if (!rs.next())
          {
  %>
  User details given for user name : <%=request.getParameter("uname")%> and
  password : <%=request.getParameter("pass")%> are not valid <br/>
  Try again <%@include file="Login.html"%>
 </body>
 </html>
  <%
                  return;
          }//if
  }//try
  finally
  {
          try
          {
                  con.close();
          }
          catch(Exception e){}
  }//finally
  %>

  This is a Home Page <br/>
  Welcome, <%=uname%>
 </body>
 </html>
```

The `LoginProcess JSP` page shows the use of the JSP page directive, which imports the `java.sql` package to the `LoginProcess` JSP page. The `java.sql` package helps the `LoginProcess` JSP page to access the `userdetails` table in the Oracle database that stores user information. After a user submits a request, the `LoginProcess JSP` page is used to generate the appropriate response for each request made.

The `LoginProcess JSP` page also includes another JSP page, named `MyError`, which is used to handle any exception that may occur in the `LoginProcess JSP` page. In other words, any exception in the `LoginProcess JSP` page is forwarded to the `MyError JSP` page. Listing 7.9 shows the code for the `MyError.jsp` file (save the MyError.jsp file in the \directiveTags folder):

Listing 7.9: Showing the Code for the MyError.jsp File

```
<%@page isErrorPage="true"%>
<html>
<body>
  An exception is raised while processing the request: <br/>
  <b>Exception : </b> <br/>
      <%=exception.getMessage()%>
</body>
</html>
```

All the files created in the `directiveTags` application need to be placed properly as shown in Figure 7.9. As the application imports the `java.sql` package, you need to include a `Java ARchive (JAR)` file (depending on the database used in an application) in the `lib` directory of the application, which is used to access a database within a JSP page. In our case, we have included the `classes12.jar` file in the `lib` directory as we are using the Oracle database for the `directiveTags` application. Figure 7.9 shows the directory structure of the `directiveTags` application:

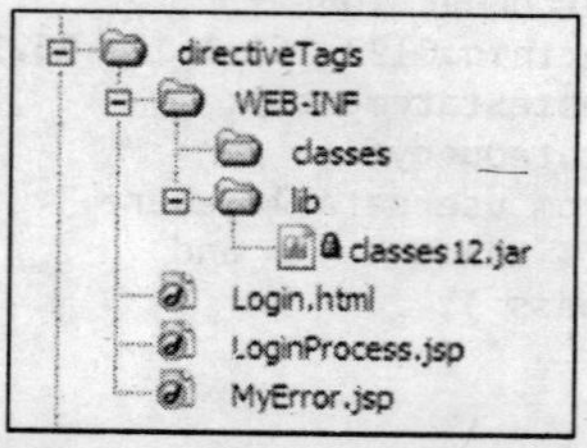

Figure 7.9: Displaying the Directory Structure for the directiveTags Web Application

Deploy the `directiveTags` application on the `Glassfish` application server. Next, start the `Glassfish` server and browse the `directiveTags` application by using the `http://localhost:8080/directiveTags/Login.html` URL. Figure 7.10 shows the output of the `Login HTML` page:

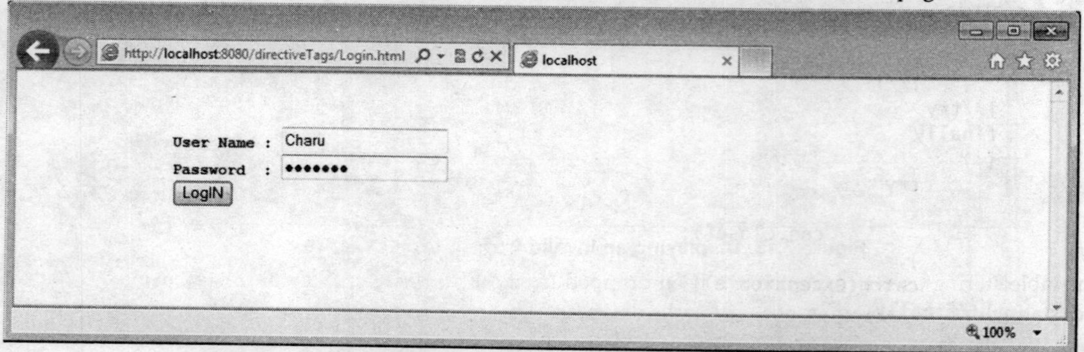

Figure 7.10: Displaying the Output of the Login HTML Page

Enter the user name and password on the `Login HTML` page and click the LogIN button. The JSP Servlet engine checks for the availability of the user name and the password in the Oracle database. If the entries are valid, you are directed to the `LoginProcess JSP` page, shown in Figure 7.11:

Figure 7.11: Displaying the Output of the LoginProcess JSP Page for a Valid Login

Figure 7.11 shows the output for a successful login in the `Login HTML` page. The database is called each time a user enters values in the user name and password fields. If the entries are not available in the database, the user is redirected to another page, shown in Figure 7.12:

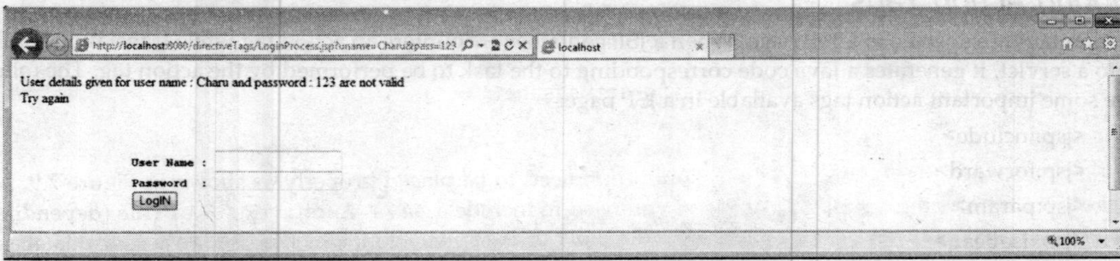

Figure 7.12: Displaying the Output of the LoginProcess JSP Page for an Invalid Login

Now, to test the functionality of the `isErrorPage` element used in the `MyError.jsp` file, delete the `userdetails` table from the Oracle database. The following code snippet shows the syntax for deleting a table from the database:

```
drop table userdetails;
```

When you run the command shown in the preceding code snippet, the `userdetails` table is removed from the database. Now, if you make a request to the `LoginProcess JSP` page by clicking the `LogIN` button, an `SQLException` exception is raised in the page and the request is forwarded to the `MyError JSP` page, as shown in Figure 7.13:

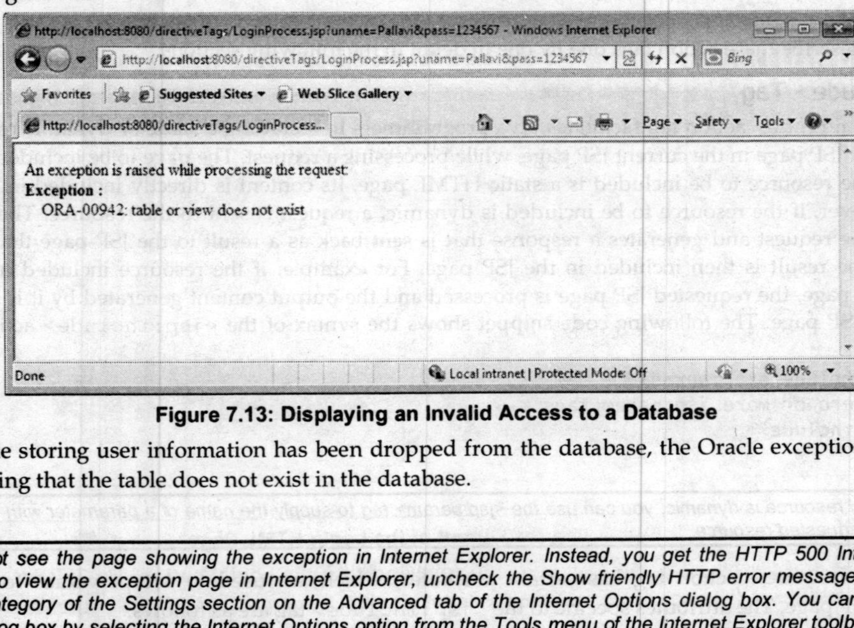

Figure 7.13: Displaying an Invalid Access to a Database

As the table storing user information has been dropped from the database, the Oracle exception `ORA-00942` is raised, stating that the table does not exist in the database.

NOTE

You may not see the page showing the exception in Internet Explorer. Instead, you get the HTTP 500 Internal Server Error message. To view the exception page in Internet Explorer, uncheck the Show friendly HTTP error messages check box in the Browsing category of the Settings section on the Advanced tab of the Internet Options dialog box. You can open the Internet Options dialog box by selecting the Internet Options option from the Tools menu of the Internet Explorer toolbar.

This completes our discussion on basic tags and implicit objects of JSP. Some action tags are also available in JSP. These tags help Java programmers to perform some basic actions in JSP pages. Let's learn to work with these action tags in the next section.

Working with Action Tags in JSP

Action tags were first introduced in JSP 1.1, and additional tags were added in the later specifications. Action tags allow Java programmers to include some basic actions, such as inserting the resources of other pages, forwarding a request to another page, creating or locating JavaBean instances, and setting and retrieving JavaBean properties, in JSP pages. Let's discuss the JSP action tags and learn to declare a JavaBean in a JSP page.

Exploring Action Tags

Action tags are specific to a JSP page. When a JSP container encounters an action tag while translating a JSP page into a servlet, it generates a Java code corresponding to the task to be performed by the action tag. The following are some important action tags available in a JSP page:

- <jsp:include>
- <jsp:forward>
- <jsp:param>
- <jsp:useBean>
- <jsp:setProperty>
- <jsp:getProperty>
- <jsp:plugin>
- <jsp:params>
- <jsp:fallback>
- <jsp:attribute>
- <jsp:body>
- <jsp:element>
- <jsp:text>

Now, let's describe these action tags one by one in detail in the following sections.

The <jsp:include> Tag

The `<jsp:include>` action tag facilitates Java programmers in including a static or dynamic resource, such as an HTML or JSP page in the current JSP page, while processing a request. The page to be included is specified by a URL. If the resource to be included is a static HTML page, its content is directly included in the current JSP page. However, if the resource to be included is dynamic, a request is sent to the resource. Then, the resource processes the request and generates a response that is sent back as a result to the JSP page that requested the resource. The result is then included in the JSP page. For example, if the resource included in a JSP page is another JSP page, the requested JSP page is processed and the output content generated by it is included in the requesting JSP page. The following code snippet shows the syntax of the `<jsp:include>` action tag in a JSP page:

```
<jsp:include attributes>
<!-- Zero or more jsp:param tags -->
</jsp:include>
```

NOTE

If the included resource is dynamic, you can use the <jsp:param> tag to supply the name of a parameter with its corresponding value to the requested resource.

The `<jsp:include>` action tag has certain attributes, which are used to accept values for the specified requested JSP page. The attributes specific to the `<jsp:include>` tag are as follows:

- **The page attribute**—Takes a relative URL, which specifies the location of the resource to be included in the JSP page. This attribute allows Java programmers to provide an expression that evaluates to a String representing the relative URL that specifies the resource. The relative URL can be specified directly or as an expression within a page attribute. The following syntax shows how to use the page attribute in a JSP page:
  - <jsp:include page="/Header.html"/>
  - <jsp:include page="<%=mypath%>"/>

  The relative URL cannot take a protocol name, port number, or domain name. It starts with the / (forward slash) character, specifying that the URL is taken relative to the context path.

- **The flush attribute** — Takes either the `true` or `false` value, to indicate whether the buffer needs to be flushed or not before including a resource. If the `true` value is assigned to this attribute, the buffer is flushed before including the resource. The attribute takes `false` as its default value. After the action specified in the `<jsp:include>` tag is completed, the JSP container continues to process the rest of the JSP page.

You may remember that we talked about the `include` directive tag under The Include Directive heading of this chapter. Though both the `<jsp:include>` action tag and the include directive tag are used to include content into a JSP page, they are very different from one another.

The `include` directive tag incorporates the content of a specified page in a generated servlet page while translating a JSP page during the translation phase. In general, the `include` directive tag is used to include files, such as HTML, JSP, XML, or a simple .txt file, into a JSP page statically. The `file` attribute, which is used to refer to the file to be included, is the only mandatory attribute available in the `include` directive tag. The following code snippet shows the use of the JSP `include` directive tag in a JSP page:

```
%@include file="test.jsp"
```

In the preceding code snippet, `test.jsp` is the file to be included in the current JSP page. The content of the `test JSP` page is incorporated in the current JSP page during the translation stage. You cannot use an expression to specify the URL path to include the resource in the JSP page while using the `include` directive tag.

The `<jsp:include>` action tag is used to incorporate the response generated by executing the specified JSP page or servlet. The response is included during the processing of a request, when a request for the page is received from a user. In other words, the specified JSP page is included in the request handling phase of the included JSP page life cycle. The following code snippet shows the use of the `<jsp:include>` action tag in a JSP page:

```
<jsp:include page= "test.jsp">
```

In the preceding code snippet, the output of the `test.jsp` file is included in the current JSP page. The respective logic for `include` is written in the equivalent servlet generated for the JSP page.

Unlike the `include` directive tag, the `<jsp:include>` action tag accepts expressions. This implies that, with the `<jsp:include>` action tag, you can decide the page to include at runtime, which is not possible with the `include` directive tag.

The <jsp:forward> Tag

The `<jsp:forward>` tag forwards a JSP request to another resource, which can be either static or dynamic. If the request is forwarded to a dynamic resource, a `<jsp:param>` tag can be used to pass a name and value of a parameter to a resource. We use the `page` directive with the value of the `buffer` parameter set to `none`, to specify that the output of the JSP page should not be buffered.

When the output stream is not buffered and some output is written to it, a `<jsp:forward>` action throws a `java.IllegalStatexception` exception. The `<jsp:forward>` action in a JSP page works similar to the `forward()` method of the `RequestDispatcher` interface. The following code snippet shows the use of the `<jsp:forward>` action tag in a JSP page:

```
<jsp:forward attributes>
<!-- Zero or more jsp:param tags -->
</jsp:forward>
```

The `<jsp:forward>` action takes a `page` attribute to specify the page to which the current request is to be forwarded. The page attribute takes a relative URL to locate a resource. This allows Java programmers to provide an expression, which results in a String value representing the relative URL to locate the resource. You can specify the relative URL directly or by using an expression. The following snippet shows the use of the `page` attribute in the `<jsp:forward>` action tag in a JSP page:

```
<jsp:forward page="/Header.html"/>
<jsp:forward page="<%=mypath%>"/>
```

The URL specified in the page attribute cannot have a protocol name, port number, or domain name. If the URL starts with the / character, the URL is taken to be relative to the context path; if it does not, the URL is taken to be relative to the JSP page. After the forward action is complete, the JSP container does not continue processing the rest of the JSP page.

The <jsp:param> Tag

The `<jsp:param>` tag allows Java programmers to pass a name and value of a parameter to a dynamic resource, while including it in a JSP page or forwarding a request from a JSP page to another JSP page. The `<jsp:param>` tag is also used to pass parameters to an applet configured in the JSP page by using the `<jsp:plugin>` tag. The following code snippet shows the syntax to use the `<jsp:param>` tag in a JSP page:

```
<jsp:param attributes />
```

You can use more than one `<jsp:param>` tag if you want to pass more than one parameter. The `<jsp:param>` action tag contains two attributes, `name` and `value`, which are discussed as follows:

- **name**—Specifies the name of the parameter and takes a case-sensitive String literal as its value. The parameter name should be unique. A different name should be used for each parameter.
- **value**—Specifies the value of the parameter. It takes either a case-sensitive String literal or an expression that is evaluated in the request handling stage of the JSP life cycle.

The following code snippet shows the use of the JSP `param` and `include` actions in a JSP page, along with the attributes of the `<jsp:param>` action tag:

```
<jsp:include page="/MyPage2.jsp">
<jsp:param name="uname" value="User1"/>
<jsp:param name="user_type" value="admin"/>
</jsp:include>
```

The <jsp:useBean>Tag

To separate the business logic from the presentation logic, it is often a good idea to encapsulate the business logic in a Java object (a JavaBean), and then instantiate and use this Java object within a JSP page. The `<jsp:useBean>`, `<jsp:setProperty>`, and `<jsp:getProperty>` tags help in this task.

The `<jsp:useBean>` action tag is used to instantiate a JavaBean or locate an existing JavaBean instance, and assign it to a variable name (or id). The object's lifetime can also be specified by providing a value, such as application scope, to the `scope` attribute. The `<jsp:useBean>` action tag ensures that the object having the specified `id`, and which lies in the appropriate specified `scope`, is available. The object can then be referenced by using its associated id within the JSP page, depending on the scope of the JavaBean. The following code snippet shows the syntax of the `<jsp:useBean>` action tag:

```
<jsp:useBean attributes>
<!-optional body content-->
</jsp:useBean>
```

The `<jsp:useBean>` action tag has certain attributes that add extra characteristics to it. For example, the `scope` attribute of the `<jsp:useBean>` action tag makes a JavaBean instance available in different scopes. Some attributes specific to the `<jsp:useBean>` tag are as follows:

- **id**—Represents the name assigned to a JavaBean, which is later used as a variable to access the JavaBean. The `id` attribute is used to locate an existing JavaBean instance in the appropriate scope specified in the `<jsp:useBean>` action tag. This attribute is case sensitive and must follow the naming conventions used to define Java variables.
- **scope**—Represents the scope in which a JavaBean instance has to be located or created. The value of `scope` for the JavaBean instance can be `page`, `request`, `session`, or `application`. The default scope is `page`. The various scope values can be defined as follows:
- **page scope**—Indicates that a JavaBean can be used where the `<jsp:useBean>` action tag is used within a JSP page, until a response is sent back to a client or a request is forwarded to another resource.
- **request scope**—Indicates that a JavaBean can be used from any JSP page, which processes the same request until a response is sent to a client by the JSP page.
- **session scope**—Indicates that a JavaBean can be used from any JSP page invoked in the same session as the JSP page that created the JavaBean. The JavaBean instance exists throughout the entire session, and can be

accessed by any page sharing the session. The page directive must have a `true` value for the `session` attribute in the JSP page by which the JavaBean is created.

- **application scope**—Indicates that a JavaBean can be used from any JSP page in the same application as the JSP page that created the JavaBean. This JavaBean exists throughout the session of a Web application, and can be accessed by any page in the application.
- **class**—Takes the qualified class name to create a JavaBean instance if the JavaBean instance is not found in the given scope. The class specified by the class name assigned to the `class` attribute should not be an abstract class and should have a no-argument constructor. The JSP container calls the no-argument constructor to create a JavaBean instance by using the `new` keyword.

NOTE

The class attribute does not allow expressions. This implies that the class name cannot be given dynamically and should be explicitly entered while coding a JSP page.

- **beanName**—Takes a qualified class name or an expression of a JavaBean. A JSP container uses the `instantiate` method defined in the `java.beans.Beans` class to instantiate the JavaBean. While instantiating the JavaBean, the `instantiate()` method of the `java.beans.Beans` class first verifies whether the specified name represents the serialized template or not. If the serialized template is found, the `instantiate` method reads it by using a class loader to instantiate the JavaBean. The serialized form is located in the file with the name `packagename.classname.ser`. If the specified name does not represent a serialized template, the instantiate method uses the no-argument constructor to create an instance.

NOTE

You can use either the class attribute or the beanName attribute in a <jsp:useBean> tag; both attributes cannot be used together in a <jsp:useBean> tag as they refer to the same values.

- **type**—Takes a qualified class or interface name, which can be the class name given in the `class` or `beanName` attribute or the super type of a class. This attribute is also used with or without `class` or `beanName`. When the `type` attribute is used with the `class` or `beanName` attribute, the reference of a JavaBean located or created is stored in a reference variable of the type as specified by the `type` attribute. The variable name will be as specified in the `id` attribute. When the `type` attribute is used without the `class` or `beanName` attribute, the JSP container only tries to locate the JavaBean but does not instantiate the JavaBean. If the JavaBean is not found, the JSP container throws the `InstantiationException` exception.

The <jsp:setProperty> Tag

The `<jsp:setProperty>` action tag sets the value of a property by using the setter methods of a JavaBean. Before using the `<jsp:setProperty>` action tag, the JavaBean must be instantiated. In addition, the `name` attribute of the JavaBean must be the same as the reference variable name of the JavaBean instance. The JavaBean can also be instantiated by using the `<jsp:useBean>` action tag as explained earlier. While using the `<jsp:useBean>` action tag, the `name` attribute of the `<jsp:setProperty>` action tag must be the same as the `id` attribute of the `<jsp:useBean>` action tag. These attributes are used to ensure co-ordination between the `<jsp:useBean>` and `<jsp:setProperty>` action tags as both these tags work together. The following code snippet shows the syntax of the `<jsp:setProperty>` tag:

```
<jsp:setProperty attributes/>
```

The <jsp:setProperty> tag contains various attributes, which are described as follows:

- **name**—Takes the name of an existing JavaBean as a reference variable to invoke a setter method. The value of this attribute must match the value of the `id` attribute of the `<jsp:useBean>` tag to set the properties of a bean. Consequently, you should declare the `<jsp:useBean>` tag before the `<jsp:setProperty>` tag in a JSP page.
- **property**—Takes the name of the property to be set, and specifies the setter method to be invoked. This attribute is used in two different ways. One is to use an asterisk (`*`) with the value of the `property` attribute. Doing this matches all the properties of a JavaBean with the request parameter names. However,

if you want to match any specific property of the JavaBean, you need to specify the value of the `property` attribute with the property name rather than use *. The following code snippet shows the syntax to use the `property` attribute with * and with a specific property name:

```
// Syntax to use property attribute with '*'

<jsp:setProperty name="name of reference variable" property="*" />

// Syntax to use property attribute with specific value

<jsp:setProperty name="name of reference variable" property="property name" />
```

When you use asterisk `(*)` with the property attribute, the value and param attributes are not applicable. However, when you specify a specific property name for the property attribute, the value and param attributes are `applicable`.

The values sent for a request parameter from a client to a server are always of type `String`. These values must be converted into JavaBean property types. If a property has the `PropertyEditor` class, as indicated in the JavaBeans specification, the `setAsText(String)` method is used to convert the value of the request parameter from String to a JavaBean compatible data type. If the `setAsText(String)` method fails to convert the type, an `IllegalArgumentException` exception is thrown by the method.

- **value**—Takes the value that has to be set to the specified JavaBean property. This attribute accepts the value as the `String` type or as an expression that is evaluated at runtime. If the value is not of the `String` type, the value is converted to a JavaBean compatible data type.

NOTE

*The value attribute should not be used if the property attribute is set to *, because * refers to all properties and we cannot set all the properties by using one value.*

The following code snippet shows the syntax to use the `<jsp:setProperty>` tag with the `value` attribute:

```
<jsp:setProperty name="name of reference variable"
   property="property name" value=" Property value as String "/>
```

Or

```
<jsp:setProperty name="name of reference variable" property="property name"
   value=" <%= Property value as expression %> "/>
```

- **param**—Specifies the request parameter name whose value is to be assigned to a JavaBean property. When setting JavaBean properties from request parameters, it is not always necessary for the JavaBean to have the same property names as the request parameters. If the `param` value is not specified, it is assumed that the request parameter and the JavaBean property have the same names.

NOTE

*The param attribute must also not be used when the property of a JavaBean is set to *, because * refers to all properties and we cannot set requested parameters for all properties by using one value.*

The following code snippet shows the syntax to use the param property:

```
<jsp:setProperty name="reference variable name" property="property name"
    param="request parameter name"/>
```

The following code snippet shows the syntax to set all the properties in a JavaBean while setting the JavaBean properties from the request object:

```
<jsp:setProperty name="abcbean" property="*"/>
```

The following code snippet shows the syntax to set a specific property in a JavaBean while setting the JavaBean properties from the request object:

```
<jsp:setProperty name="abcbean" property="uname" param="uname"/>
```

When setting a JavaBean property to a value, you should specify the value attribute as either a String or an expression that is evaluated at runtime, as shown by the syntax in the following code snippet:

```
<jsp:setProperty name="abcbean" property="uname" value="<%=uname%>"/>
```

The <jsp:getProperty> Tag

The `<jsp:getProperty>` action tag retrieves the value of a property by using the getter methods of a JavaBean and writes the value to the current JspWriter. The following code snippet shows the syntax to use the `<jsp:getProperty>` action tag:

```
<jsp:getProperty attributes/>
```

The `<jsp:getProperty>` action tag takes two attributes, `name` and `property`, which are described as follows:

- **name**—Takes the reference variable name on which you want to invoke the getter method. If a JavaBean is instantiated by using the `<jsp:useBean>` action tag, the value assigned to the `name` attribute should match the `id` attribute value of the `<jsp:useBean>` action tag. This implies that the `<jsp:useBean>` action tag must appear before the `<jsp: setProperty>` tag in a JSP page.
- **property**—Takes the value of a JavaBean property and invokes the getter method of the property. This attribute takes the name of the property as an argument. For example, if the `getUname` method needs to be called, the property attribute takes the value `uname`, as shown in the following code snippet:

```
<jsp:getProperty name="mybean" property="uname"/>
```

In the preceding code snippet, the `<jsp:getProperty>` tag gets the value of the `uname` property, by using the `mybean` instance, and includes this value into the output.

NOTE

The <jsp:getProperty> tag is not designed to access Enterprise JavaBeans (EJB) and indexed properties.

The <jsp:plugin> Tag

The `<jsp:plugin>` action tag provides support for including a Java applet or JavaBean in a client Web browser, by using a built-in or downloaded Java plug-in. In the request handling stage of the JSP life cycle, the `<jsp:plugin>` action tag is substituted by either the `<object>` or `<embed>` tag, depending on the browser version. In general, the attributes of the `<jsp:plugin>` action tag perform the following operations:

- Specify whether the component added in the <object> tag is a JavaBean or an applet
- Locate the code that needs to be run
- Position an object in the browser window
- Specify a URL from which the plug-in software is to be download
- Pass parameter names and values to an object

The following code snippet shows the syntax to use the `<jsp:plugin>` action tag in a JSP page:

```
<jsp:plugin attributes>
<!-optionally one jsp:params and or one jsp:fallback tag can be used -->
</jsp:plugin>
```

The `<jsp:plugin>` tag takes some predefined attributes, which are described as follows:

- **type**—Specifies the type of object that needs to be presented to the browser. The object can be an applet or a JavaBean.
- **code**—Takes the qualified class name of the object that has to be presented.
- **codebase**—Takes the base URL where the specified class can be located. This is an optional attribute.
- **name**—Specifies the name of the instance of a JavaBean or an applet, which helps it to be invoked by the same JSP page to communicate with one another.
- **archive**—Specifies a comma-separated list representing pathnames. A pathname is used to locate archive files, which are preloaded with a class loader that is present in the directory named codebase. Archive files distinctively improve the performance of an applet and are loaded securely, frequently over a network. The `archive` attribute of the `<jsp:plugin>` tag is similar to the `archive` attribute of the HTML applet tag.
- **width**—Specifies the initial width, in pixels, for the image shown by an applet or a JavaBean.
- **height**—Specifies the initial height, in pixels, for the image shown by an applet or a JavaBean.
- **align**—Specifies the position of an applet. The values the `align` attribute can take are `bottom`, `top`, `middle`, `left`, or `right`. The default value is `bottom`.

- **hspace**—Specifies the amount of horizontal space, in pixels, that should be assigned to the left and right side of an applet or a JavaBean displayed by the browser. The value assigned to the `hspace` attribute must be a nonzero number.
- **vspace**—Specifies the amount of vertical space, in pixels, that should be assigned to the bottom and top of an applet or a JavaBean. The value assigned to the `vspace` attribute must be a nonzero number.
- **jreversion**—Specifies the version of Java Runtime Environment (JRE) as required by the corresponding applet or JavaBean. The default value is 1.2.
- **nspluginurl**—Specifies the URL from which a client can download the JRE plug-in as required for Netscape Navigator. The value of this attribute is the complete URL specifying a protocol name, port number (this is optional), and domain name.
- **iepluginurl**—Specifies the URL from which a client can download the JRE plug-in as required for Internet Explorer. The value of this attribute is the complete URL specifying a protocol name, port number (optional), and domain name.

The <jsp:params> Tag

The `<jsp:params>` action tag sends the parameters that you want to pass to an applet or a JavaBean. The following code snippet shows the syntax to use the `<jsp:params>` action tag in a JSP page:

```
<jsp:params>
<!- one or more jsp:param tags-->
</jsp:params>
```

To specify more than one parameter value, you can use more than one `<jsp:params>` action tag within a `<jsp:params>` tag.

The <jsp:fallback> Tag

The `<jsp:fallback>` action tag allows you to specify a text message that is displayed if the required plug-in cannot run. This action tag must be used as a child tag with the `<jsp:plugin>` action tag. If the plug-in runs and the applet or JavaBean cannot run, the plug-in generally displays a popup window clarifying the error to the user. The following code snippet shows the syntax to use the `<jsp:fallback>` action tag in a JSP page:

```
<jsp:fallback>
Text message that has to be displayed if the plugin cannot be started
</jsp:fallback>
```

The <jsp:attribute>Tag

The `<jsp:attribute>` action tag is used to specify the value of a standard or custom action attribute. For example, you can use the `<jsp:attribute>` tag to set the attributes of the `<jsp:setProperty>` attribute, as shown in the following code snippet:

```
<jsp:setProperty name="mybean">
   <jsp:attribute name="property">uname</jsp:attribute>
   <jsp:attribute name="value">
         <jsp:expression>uname</jsp:expression>
   </jsp:attribute>
</jsp:setProperty>
```

The `<jsp:attribute>` tag accepts the `name` and `trim` attributes, where `name` specifies the attribute name that you want to set, and `trim` takes `true` or `false`, indicating whether the whitespace coming at the beginning and the end of the `<jsp:attribute>` tag should be discarded or not. By default, the heading and trailing whitespaces are discarded; consequently, the default value of the trim attribute is `true`.

NOTE

The JSP container discards the heading and trailing whitespaces at transaction time and not at the request handling phase. For example, if you use an expression tag in the body part of an attribute action tag, and the expression tag produces a value with heading and trailing whitespaces, these whitespaces are not discarded by the JSP container. In the preceding code snippet, if the uname variable contains leading and trailing whitespaces, then the container does not eliminate the whitespaces.

If the body of the `<jsp:attribute>` tag is empty, you can specify its value by " ".

The <jsp:body> Tag

The <jsp:body> action tag is used to specify the content (or body) of a standard or custom action tag. Generally, the body content of a standard or custom action invocation is implicitly defined as the body of that tag. However, if one or more <jsp:attribute> tags appear in the body of the tag, the body of a standard or custom action can be defined explicitly by using the <jsp:body> tag. The <jsp:body> tag is required if the standard action or custom tag has multiple <jsp:attribute> tags.

You can use the <jsp:body> tag to specify the content for the body of JSP actions tags, except for some action tags such as <jsp:body>, <jsp:attribute>, <jsp:scriptlet>, <jsp:expression>, and <jsp:declaration>.

A tag is said to have an empty body if one or more <jsp:attribute> tags appear in the body of a tag invocation with no or empty <jsp:body> tags. The following code snippet shows the use of the <jsp:body> tag:

```
<jsp:useBean id="mybean">
   <jsp:attribute name="class" trim="true">
         com.kogent.MyBean
   </jsp:attribute>
   <jsp:attribute name="scope">session</jsp:attribute>
   <jsp:body>
         <jsp:setProperty name="mybean" property="*"/>
   </jsp:body>
</jsp:useBean>
```

The <jsp:element> Tag

The <jsp:element> action tag is used to dynamically define the value of the tag of an XML element. This action tag allows you to create an XML tag with a given name. The content of the <jsp:element> tag is a template for the attributes and child nodes of the XML tag you want to create. The <jsp:element> action tag can be used in JSP pages and tag files. The following code snippet shows the syntax of the element tag:

```
<jsp:element name="name">
   jsp:attribute*
   jsp:body?
</jsp:element>
```

In the preceding syntax, the name attribute of the element tag specifies the name of the XML element it has to create. You can also give an expression as the name of the XML element. The <jsp:element> tag can be an empty tag or can contain one <jsp:body> or multiple <jsp:attribute> attributes, with or without the <jsp:body> tag. The following code snippet shows the use of the name attribute with the element action tag:

```
<jsp:element name="mytag"/>
```

The <jsp:element> shown in the preceding code snippet creates an empty tag with the name, mytag.

The following code snippet shows another example of using the <jsp:element> tag with the <jsp:attribute> tag:

```
<jsp:element name="mytag">
   <jsp:attribute name="myatt">Myval</jsp:attribute>
</jsp:element>
```

The <jsp:element> tag shown in the preceding code snippet creates an empty element, named mytag, with the myatt=Myval attribute.

The following code snippet shows the use of <jsp:tag> to create a tag with attribute and body content:

```
<jsp:tag name="mytag">
   <jsp:attribute name="myatt">Myval</jsp:attribute>
   <jsp:body>Hello</jsp:body>
</jsp:tag>
```

The preceding code snippet creates the tag named mytag with an attribute, myatt=Myval, and body text content as Hello.

The <jsp:text> Tag

A `<jsp:text>` tag is used to enclose template data in an XML tag. The text tag can be used in a JSP page or tag file. The content of a `<jsp:text>` tag is passed to the implicit object, `out`. A `<jsp:text>` tag has no attributes and can appear at any place where template data appears. The following code snippet shows the syntax to use the `<jsp:text>` tag:

```
<jsp:text> template data </jsp:text>
```

In the preceding code snippet, template data text is used within the `<jsp:text>` tag. Instead of text, you can also use expressions within the `<jsp:text>` tag.

After discussing the syntax of various action tags, let's now learn how to declare a JavaBean in a JSP page.

Declaring a Bean in a JSP Page

Let's create the `useBeanEx` Web application to learn how to create a JavaBean and declare it in a JSP page. Before declaring a JavaBean in a JSP page, you must create the JavaBean. Therefore, we create a JavaBean called `RegForm`, which is used to set and get attributes, such as user name and e-mail address, of a user.

The following broad-level steps need to be performed to declare a JavaBean in a JSP page:

1. Create a JavaBean
2. Declare the JavaBean in a JSP page by using the `<jsp:useBean>` tag
3. Access the properties of the JavaBean
4. Generate dynamic content
5. Deploy and run the `useBeanEx` application

Let's now learn to implement the steps one by one in the following sections.

Creating a JavaBean

In this section, we create a JavaBean called `RegForm`. Listing 7.10 shows the code for the `RegForm` JavaBean (save the RegForm.java file in the \RegForm\src\com\kogent folder):

Listing 7.10: Showing the Code for the RegForm.java File

```
package com.kogent;

public class RegForm implements java.io.Serializable
{
   private String uname, pass, repass, email, fn, ln, address;

   public void setUserName(String s){uname=s;}
   public void setPassword(String s){pass=s;}
   public void setRePassword(String s){repass=s;}
   public void setEmail(String s){email=s;}
   public void setFirstName(String s){fn=s;}
   public void setLastName(String s){ln=s;}
   public void setAddress(String s){address=s;}

   public String getUserName(){return uname;}
   public String getPassword(){return pass;}
   public String getRePassword(){return repass;}
   public String getEmail(){return email;}
   public String getFirstName(){return fn;}
   public String getLastName(){return ln;}
   public String getAddress(){return address;}
}//class
```

Declaring a JavaBean in a JSP Page

After creating the JavaBean, you can declare it in a JSP page by using the `<jsp:useBean>` tag. For this, you have to create a JSP page. Listing 7.11 shows the code for a JSP page named RegProcess, in which we declare the JavaBean created in Listing 7.10 (save the RegProcess.jsp file in the \RegForm folder):

Listing 7.11: Showing the Code for the RegProcess.jsp File

```
<%@page errorPage="Registration.html"%>
<html>
<body>

<jsp:useBean id="regform">
  <jsp:attribute name="class" trim="true">com.kogent.RegForm</jsp:attribute>
  <jsp:attribute name="scope">session</jsp:attribute>
  <jsp:body>
       <jsp:setProperty name="regform" property="*"/>
  </jsp:body>
</jsp:useBean>

<form action="RegProcessFinal.jsp"><pre> <b>
First Name  : <input type="text" name="first_name"/>
Last Name   : <input type="text" name="last_name"/>
Address     : <input type="text" name="address"/>

<input type="submit" value="Register"/>
</b></pre></form>
</body>
</html>
```

In Listing 7.11, the `<jsp:useBean>` action tag creates an instance of a JavaBean class according to the attributes specified in the JSP page. The following is a brief description of the attributes of the `<jsp:useBean>` action tag:

- `id`—Specifies the name of the JavaBean that you want to declare
- `class`—Specifies name of the JavaBean class, which helps the JSP container to search the JavaBean class and create its instance.
- `scope`—Specifies the scope of the JavaBean

The preceding attributes help the JSP container to create an instance of the JavaBean class. The `<jsp:useBean>` action tag has some more attributes along with the attributes that are used in the `RegProcess` `JSP` page.

Accessing JavaBean Properties

You can verify the properties of a JavaBean, such as password, e-mail, and firstName, by using the `<jsp:getProperty>` action tag. This action tag uses the name and property tags to read the JavaBean properties. Let's create the `ViewRegistrationDetails.jsp file` to show the use of the `<jsp:getProperty>` action tag to read JavaBean properties. Listing 7.12 shows the code for the ViewRegistrationDetails JSP page (save the ViewRegistrationDetails.jsp file in the \RegForm folder):

Listing 7.12: Showing the Code for the ViewRegistrationDetails.jsp File

```
<jsp:useBean id="regform" type="com.kogent.RegForm" scope="session"/>
<%@page errorPage="Registration.html"%>
<html>
  <body> <pre>

  <b>User Name   :</b> <jsp:getProperty name="regform" property="userName"/>

  <b>Password    :</b> <jsp:getProperty property="password" name="regform"/>

  <b>Email ID    :</b> <jsp:getProperty name="regform" property="email"/>

  <b>First Name  :</b> <jsp:getProperty name="regform" property="firstName"/>

  <b>last Name   :</b> <jsp:getProperty name="regform" property="lastName"/>
```

```
    <b>Address      :</b> <jsp:getProperty name="regform" property="address"/>

    </pre>
    <form method=post action="javascript:alert('The remaining process is
          under development');">
    <input type="submit" value="Register"/>
    </form>
    </body>
  </html>
```

Before reading JavaBean properties, the JSP container needs to locate the instance of the JavaBean class you create. After the JSP container locates the instance of the JavaBean class, the container starts reading the JavaBean properties by using the `<jsp:getProperty>` tag. Listing 7.12 shows the attributes used with the `<jsp:getProperty>` tag. The `name` attribute specifies the name of the JavaBean class to the JSP container and the `property` attribute specifies the JavaBean properties that have to be read.

Generating Dynamic Content within a JSP Page

The next step is to create an HTML page, named `Registration`, to retrieve the required data from users to set the properties of the `RegForm` JavaBean. The `Registration.html` file contains a button called `Register`. When a user clicks this button after providing the required user details, the user is directed to the `RegProcess JSP` page to set the properties of the `RegForm` JavaBean, based on the details entered by the user. In other words, we use the `Registration HTML` page to generate dynamic content in the `RegProcess JSP` page. Listing 7.13 shows the code for the Registration HTML page (save the Registration.html file in the \RegForm folder):

Listing 7.13: Showing the Code for the Registration HTML Page

```
<html>
<body>
   <pre>
   <form action="RegProcess.jsp">
          <pre><b>
          UserName    : <input type="text" name="userName"/>
          Password    : <input type="password" name="password"/>
          RePassword : <input type="password" name="rePassword"/>
          EMail ID    : <input type="text" name="email"/>
          <input type="submit" value="Register"/>
          </b></pre>
   </form>
   </pre>
</body>
</html>
```

In Listing 7.13, the `param` names such as `userName`, `password`, and `rePassword` are the same as the property names in the RegForm JavaBean. However, other `param` names, such as `first_name` and `last_name`, are different from the property names, such as `firstName` and `lastName`. Therefore, the `RegProcess` JSP page is created to set these properties in the `RegForm` JavaBean.

Using the `RegProcess` JSP page, you can declare a JavaBean in JSP. This page also collects more information about the user in the `RegForm` JavaBean in addition to what is collected by using the `Registration.html` page. A `Register` button is provided in the `RegProcess` JSP page. When you click this button after entering the required user information, you are directed to the `RegProcessFinal` JSP page. Listing 7.14 provides the code for the `RegProcessFinal` JSP page (save the RegProcessFinal file in the \RegForm folder):

Listing 7.14: Showing the Code for the RegProcessFinal JSP Page

```
<%@page errorPage="Registration.html"%>

<jsp:useBean id="regform" class="com.kogent.RegForm" scope="session"/>

<jsp:setProperty name="regform" property="firstName" param="first_name"/>
```

```
<jsp:setProperty name="regform" property="lastName" param="last_name"/>
<jsp:setProperty name="regform" property="address"/>

<html>
<body>
   <pre>
   Your registration details are valid,
   <a href="ViewRegistrationDetails.jsp">Click</a> to view Registration
           Details and confirm.
   </pre>
</body>
</html>
```

NOTE

Before using the <jsp:setProperty> or <jsp:getProperty> tag in a JSP page, you must declare a JavaBean in that JSP page by using the <jsp:useBean> tag.

Deploying and Running the Application

You must place the pages and other resources of the `useBeanEx` application as per the correct directory structure, as shown in Figure 7.14:

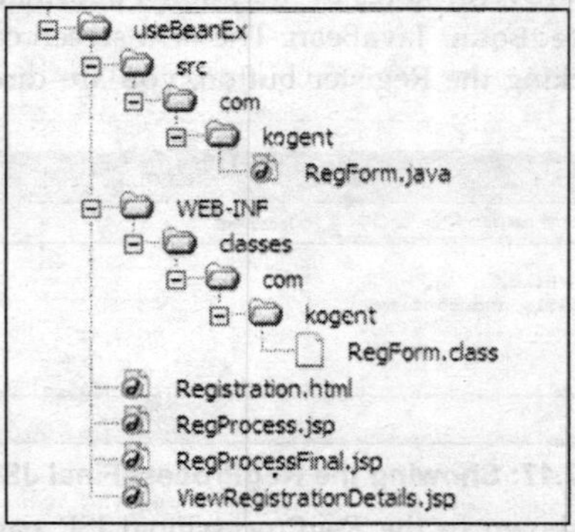

Figure 7.14: Showing the Directory Structure for the useBeanEx Application

NOTE

It is optional to include Deployment Descriptor (web.xml), containing an empty </web-app> tag in the WEB-INF directory of the useBeanEx application.

Create the Web ARchive (WAR) file for the application and then deploy the `useBeanEx` application on the GlassFish 4.0 application server. Next, browse the `useBeanEx` application by using the `http://localhost:8080/userBeanEx/Registration.html` URL and enter the details shown in Figure 7.15:

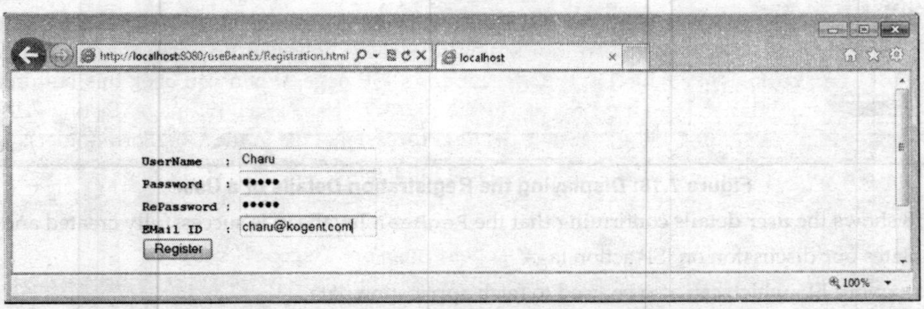

Figure 7.15: Showing the Output of the Registration HTML Page

Click the `Register` button to continue with the registration process. In this application, the user name, password, and e-mail id are stored in the `RegBean` JavaBean by using the `<jsp:useBean>` and `<jsp:setProperty>` tags. In addition, the `RegBean` instance is set in the `session` scope. After entering the details and clicking the `Register` button (Figure 7.15), the `RegProcess` JSP page appears, where users are required to provide more information about themselves, as shown in Figure 7.16:

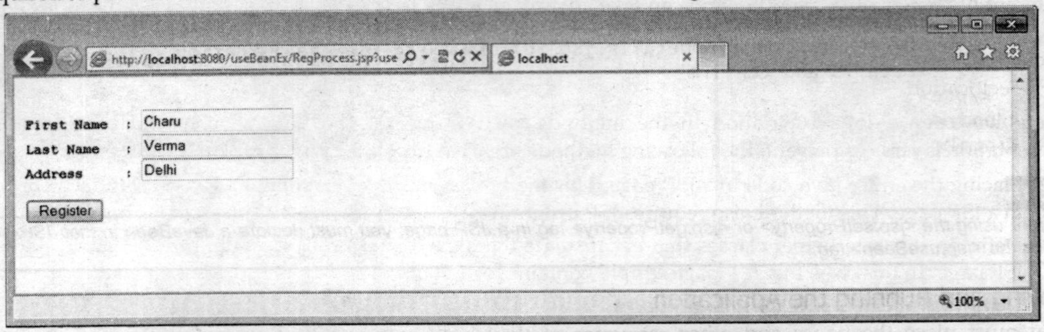

Figure 7.16: Showing the Registration Process Window

Clicking the `Register` button (Figure 7.16) stores the additional information, which includes the first name, last name, and address values, in the `RegBean` JavaBean. The next screen confirms the validity of the registration details provided by you. After clicking the Register button, you are directed to the `RegProcessFinal JSP` page, as shown in Figure 7.17:

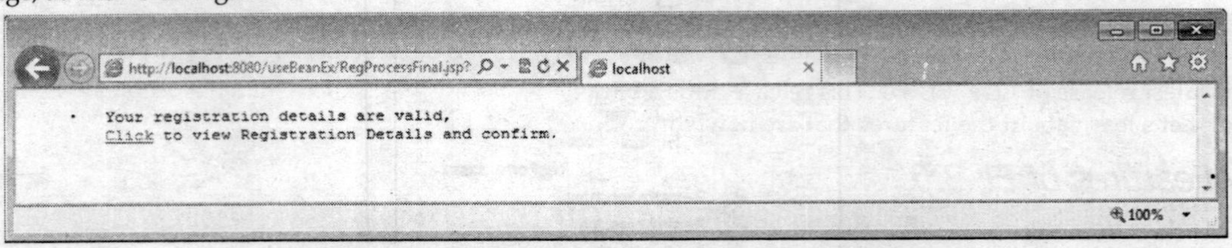

Figure 7.17: Showing the RegProcessFinal JSP Page

Click the hyperlink (Figure 7.17) shown in the RegProcessFinal JSP page to display all the details you have entered, as shown in Figure 7.18:

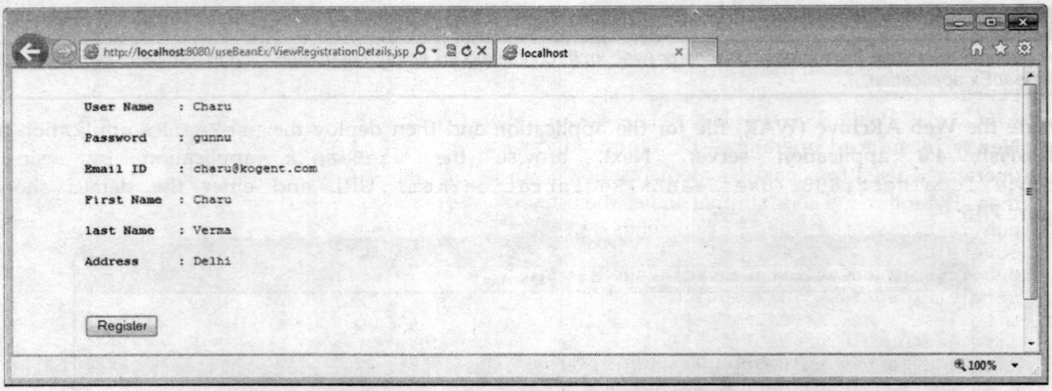

Figure 7.18: Displaying the Registration Details of a User

Figure 7.18 shows the user details confirming that the `RegBean` JavaBean is successfully created and set.

This completes our discussion on JSP action tags.

Let's now explore EL, which can also be used to fetch application data.

Exploring EL

EL is a language that allows JSP programmers to fetch application data stored in JavaBeans components. It is a new feature introduced in JSP 2.0, and in JSP 2.1, EL of JSP 2.0 and JSF 1.1 are combined to form a single unified EL (EL 2.1). The languages have been combined so that JSP programmers do not have to worry about the different life cycles of JSP and JSF and can take advantage of the new mechanisms that JSF applications use. The EL specification was previously defined in the JSP 2.1 specification. It now has its own independent specification document, which states that EL is generally applicable to a variety of technologies and is not dependent on the JSP specification.

There has been a lot of variation in the methods used to embed the Java code or the business logic in presentation layers. At present, the following methods are used to call the Java code from a JSP page:

- Placing the entire Java code in a JSP page. This method is useful when small Java code is to be incorporated in a JSP page. This method also requires JSP programmers to be familiar with the Java technology.
- Defining separate helper classes that encapsulate the entire Java code and calling these helper classes in a JSP page. In this case, the `JSP` page simply contains few blocks of code to use the helper classes.
- Using JavaBeans and JSP page action tags, such as `<jsp:useBean>`, `<jsp:getProperty>`, and `<jsp:setProperty>`, to call the Java code.
- Using JSP EL, which uses short notations to access and display object properties.
- Creating tag handler classes to embed the Java code. These classes are invoked by using custom tags, which are similar to XML tags.

The incorporation of EL to the JSP technology has helped reduce the use of `scriptlets` in JSP pages. EL expressions cannot be used in JSP `scriptlets`, `expressions`, or `declaration` elements. On the other hand, EL expressions provide short hand notations to retrieve, present, and manipulate Web application data.

The latest release of EL is EL 3.0. This release adds a variety of features that enable EL to be used as a stand-alone tool. Let's learn about the features that are newly introduced in EL 3.0.

New Features of EL 3.0

EL 3.0 is the latest release of EL. Now, it has independent specification. A variety of features are added to this release. These features are as follows:

- **Standalone environment**—The EL API enables Java EE developers to invoke ad-hoc Java EL. They need to create an instance of the newly introduced ELProcessor class. This class provides a method, named eval() with a string parameter, which represents the script to be evaluated. This method returns the result that can be used as a variable in the scope of the Java application. The following code snippet shows the use of the ELProcessor class and the eval() method:

```
ELProcessor el = new ELProcessor();
assert ((Integer)el.eval("x = [1, 2, 3]; x[0]")) == 1;
```

- **Newly introduced operators**—EL 3.0 introduces various new operators. For example, the semi-colon (;) operator is used to separate statements. Some other operators are count, sum, forEach, reduce, filter, and map. The following code snippet shows the use of these operators:

```
public class ELTestServlet extends HttpServlet {
@Override
public void doGet(HttpServletRequest req, HttpServletResponse res) throws
ServletException, IOException {
List list = new ArrayList<>();
list.add(Double.valueOf(1.5));
list.add(Double.valueOf(2.4));
list.add(Double.valueOf(3.7));

ELProcessor elp = new ELProcessor();
elp.defineBean("data", list);
Object message = (Double)elp.eval(
"n = data.stream().count(); s = data.stream().sum(); sq = data.stream().map(i ->
i*i).sum(); Math.sqrt(sq/n - Math.pow(s/n, 2))");
res.getWriter().println(message);
```

```
message = (Double)elp.eval(
"n = 0; s = 0; sq = 0; data.stream().forEach(d -> (n = n + 1; s = s + d; sq = sq + d*d));
Math.sqrt(sq/n - Math.pow(s/n, 2))");
res.getWriter().println(message);
message = (Double)elp.eval(
"n = 0; s = 0; sq = data.stream().reduce(0, (a, i) -> (n = n + 1; s = s + i; a + i*i));
Math.sqrt(sq/n - Math.pow(s/n, 2))");
res.getWriter().println(message);
}
}
```

Moreover, the assignment operator (=) is introduced, which is used for changing values; and the string concatenation operator (+) is used to join two strings.

- **Static field and method reference**—EL 3.0 allows the use of static field or static method of a class. The syntax of using the static field and method reference is:

```
classname.field
```

For example,

```
Boolean.TRUE
```

It should be noted that only the public static fields and methods of a class can be referenced, and static fields cannot be modified. You also need to import the package whose classes members are need to be referenced, except the java.lang.* package. This is because, the java.lang.* package is the default package that does not required to be import explicitly.

- **Lambda expressions**—EL 3.0 enables Java EE developers to write lambda expressions. A lambda expression (->) is a value expression with parameters. An example of lambda expression is as follows:

```
ELProcessor el = new ELProcessor();
assert ((Integer)(el.eval("((a,b) -> a+b)(3, 6)"))) == 9;
```

- **Use of T construct**—EL 3.0 supports static references by using the T construct (Type). For example, the java.* and javax.* packages are available by default, but you can modify them using T construct, as shown here:

```
${T(java.util.Calendar).JULY}
${T(java.util.Calendar).getInstance()}
```

Similarly, you can call constructors as a static method without a name. However, if you need to call the default constructor of Calendar class, you can use T construct as shown here:

```
${T(java.util.Calendar).()}
```

- **Handling collections**—EL 3.0 provides support for collection objects. It allows you to construct sets, lists, and maps dynamically. For example, the java.lang.util.Set<Object> code constructs a set.

EL also provides a set of operations that can be applied on collections. These operations are carried out by invoking methods. It should be noted that as the methods that support the collection operations do not exist in Java SE 7; therefore, they are implemented in the Expression Language with ELResolvers.

Let's now understand the basic syntax of using EL and discuss the various types of EL expressions. You also learn about the different types of tag attributes as well as resolve EL expressions. Apart from this, you learn to work with EL operators and EL objects.

Understanding the Basic Syntax of using EL

EL expressions are enclosed between the `${` and `}` characters. The most general example of an EL expression is `${object.data}`. The `object` in the preceding expression can be any Java object representing different scopes, such as `request`, and `session`. The use of EL expressions greatly reduces the quantity of code written for a task. JSP EL has the following features:

- Deferred expressions, which can be assessed at various stages of a page's life cycle
- Method expressions, which call the methods to carry out event handling, validation, and other functions for JSF User Interface (UI) components
- Value expressions, which can set and get the data of external objects
- A flexible mechanism, which allows customization of variable and property resolution to evaluate an `EL` expression
- Expressions to carry out arithmetic calculations

Classifying EL Expressions

EL expressions can be categorized into the following types:

- ❑ Immediate and deferred expressions
- ❑ Value expressions
- ❑ Method expressions

Let's learn about these in detail in the following sections.

Immediate and Deferred Expressions

Two constructs are used to represent EL expressions, `${expr}` and `#{expr}`. In a JSP page, `${expr}` is used for expressions that need to be evaluated immediately and `#{expr}` is used for expressions that are evaluated at a later time. Therefore, an EL expression that uses the `${expr}` syntax is called an immediate expression, and the EL expression that uses the `#{expr}` syntax is called a deferred expression.

In immediate expressions, the JSP container processes the expression and provides the corresponding response immediately at the time of request handling. Deferred expressions are also introduced in the JSF technology. In deferred expressions, the evaluation of the expressions is deferred due to multiple phases in the JSF life cycle. All operations, such as component data validation and event handling, need to be performed in a specific order. Therefore, the evaluation of a deferred expression is postponed to an appropriate time.

Immediate expressions may be used in template text or as values of the attributes of a JSP tag that takes a runtime value. Such expressions can only read but cannot set the value of a property. The following code snippet is an example of a JSP tag using an immediate expression:

```
<fmt:formatNumber value="${sessionScope.cart.sum}"/>
```

In the preceding code snippet, the `${ sessionScope.cart.sum }` expression retrieves the value of the `sum` property from the JavaBean named `cart`. The `sum` property specifies the total price of all constituent items in the cart.

In deferred expressions, JSF Controller evaluates the expression in different phases of the JSF life cycle, based on the component in which the expression is used. The following code snippet shows an example of a JSF HTML tag that uses a deferred expression:

```
<h:inputText id="name" value="#{employee.name}" />
```

In the preceding code snippet, when the JSF page containing the `<h:inputText>` tag is requested, JSF implementation evaluates the `#{employee.name}` expression in the Render Response phase of the JSF page life cycle. After submitting this page, JSF assesses this expression in more than one phase of its life cycle, during which operations such as retrieving the value of the `#{employee.name}` expression from the previous page, validating the expression, and setting the value of the expression to the name property of the managed JavaBean are performed. This means that deferred expressions are `lvalue` expressions, that is, expressions that can read or write data on a JavaBean. The `#{employee.name}` expression acts as an `rvalue` expression, which only reads data during the initial request and acts as the `lvalue` expression during postback.

Value Expressions

Value expressions are used to refer to objects such as `JavaBeans`, collections, enumerations, and implicit objects, and their properties. An object is referred to by using the value expression containing the name of the object. Suppose the `${employee}` expression is used in a JSP page, where `employee` refers to the name of a JavaBean. When the Web container comes across the `${employee}` expression, it invokes the `PageContext.findAttribibue (String)` method internally, which searches for the employee JavaBean in the request, session, and application scopes. If the employee JavaBean does not exist, a null value is returned.

To refer to an enum constant by using value expression, a String literal is used. The following code snippet shows the syntax for an enumeration declaration:

```
public enum PlayCardSuite {hearts, spades, diamonds, clubs}
```

The following code snippet shows the syntax to access a constant defined by the `PlayCardSuite` enumeration by using EL:

```
${PlayCardSuite.spades}
```

The expression shown in the preceding code snippet is an example of a value expression, which is used to refer to the eum constant of the `PlayCardSuite` enumeration.

Now let's discuss the syntax of value expressions to access the properties and elements of a collection in a JavaBean. For this, we use the (.) and ([ ]) operators. For example, the `name` property of the `employee` JavaBean can be referred to by using either the `${employee.name}` or `${employee["name"]}` expression. Double or single quotes can be used to represent a String literal. To access a specific element of a collection, such as a list or an array inside a JavaBean, the [ ] notation having an int value is used. For example, `${employee.phonenos[1]}` accesses the second phone number of the `phonenos` array.

Value expressions are of two types, `rvalue` and `lvalue`. An `rvalue` expression can only read data, and not write data. On the other hand, the `lvalue` expression can read as well as write data. Examples of `rvalue` expressions are `${"hello"}`, `${employee.age+20}`, and `${false}`. EL supports all types of literals in Java, such as Boolean, integer, floating point, and String.

Value expressions may be embedded in static text or as a value of a tag attribute that can take an expression. The following code snippet shows how to embed a value expression in static text:

```
<prefix:tag>
  some text ${expr} some text
</prefix:tag>
```

In the preceding code snippet, the `${expr}` expression is embedded within a text String. If the body of the <prefix:tag> tag is dependent on another tag, then the embedded expression is not evaluated.

Method Expressions

Method expressions are used to call public methods, which return a value or object. Such expressions are usually deferred expressions. JSF HTML tags represent UI components on a JSF page. These tags use method expressions to call functions that perform operations such as validating a UI component or handling the events generated on a UI component. The following code snippet shows the use of method expressions in a JSF page:

```
<h:form>
  <h:inputText
        id="email"
        value="#{employee.email}"
        validator="#{employee.validateEmail}"/>
  <h:commandButton
  id="submit"
  action="#{customer.submit}" />
</h:form>
```

The various elements shown in the preceding code snippet can be briefly described as follows:

- The `inputText` tag—Shows the `UIInput` component in the form of a text field on a Web page
- The `validator` attribute—Calls the `validateEmail` method of the employee JavaBean
- The `action` attribute of the `commandButton` tag—Calls the `submit` method, which carries out processing after submitting the Web page
- The `validateEmail` method—Refers to the method that is called during the validation phase of the JSP life cycle
- The `submit` method—Refers to the method that is called during the invoke application phase of the JSP life cycle

The TLD (Tag Library Descriptor) file is used to define the signatures of methods referenced by the attributes used in the preceding code snippet.

You are now familiar with the classification of EL expressions. Let's now discuss tag attribute types, such as static, dynamic, and deferred-method.

Describing Tag Attribute Types

Resolving EL expressions depends on the type of tag attribute defined in TLD. For custom tags, you need to specify the type of expression accepted by the custom tag. There are four categories of attribute types that define how an EL expression is evaluated. These attribute type categories are as follows:

- **Static attribute**—Refers to the attribute where the value of the `rtexprvalue` element is assigned as `false` and can be of any type, such as `int`, `String`, and `com.Example.Order`. A static attribute produces a translation error if an expression is passed to the attribute.
- **Dynamic attribute**—Refers to the attributes where the `rtexprvalue` element is assigned the `true` value and can be of any type, such as `int`, `String`, and `com.Example.Order`. Whenever an expression is provided to a dynamic attribute that is not deferred-value or deferred-method, the expression is parsed with the type similar to the attribute type, and the expression is resolved immediately.
- **Deferred-value attribute**—Refers to the attribute of the `javax.el.ValueExpression` type.
- **Deferred-method attribute**—Refers to the attribute of the `javax.el.MethodExpression` type. If an attribute is declared as deferred-value or deferred-method in TLD, the attribute must be of type `ValueExpression` or `MethodExpression`. The JSP container parses the expression but does not evaluate it. The result of parsing the expression is passed to the Tag handler attribute.

Resolving EL Expressions

Resolving an EL expression involves searching of the components of the EL expression, which are separated by the dot (.) operator. EL expressions are resolved from left to right. The unified EL API includes some classes and implementations to resolve EL expressions. Table 7.2 lists commonly used classes of the unified EL API:

Table 7.2: Commonly Used Classes of the EL API

Class	Description
ValueExpression	Represents a value expression.
MethodExpression	Represents a method expression.
ELResolver	Defines object resolution rules to resolve EL expressions.
ELContext	Stores the state of an EL resolution. The object of the ELContext class provides access to other objects, such as `JspContext`, to resolve EL expressions.

Several implementations of the `ELResolver` class are available to resolve an EL expression referring to a specific object or its property. The classes shown in Table 7.2 are used to build custom EL resolvers.

If the EL expression is a value expression, it can be resolved as follows:

1. A value expression is parsed and a `ValueExpression` object is generated, when a JSP page containing the EL value expression is requested for the first time.
2. The `getValue()` method of the `ValueExpression` object is called.
3. The `getValue()` method also calls the `getValue()` method of the suitable resolver.
4. The `setvalue()` method is called if the expression is of `lvalue` type.

If the EL expression is a method expression, it can be resolved as follows:

1. The `BeanELResolver` object is created, which searches the object that has the definition of the method referred in this expression.
2. The `MethodExpression` object is created to represent the method expression.
3. The `getMethodInfo()` method is invoked, which calls the `getValue()` method of the `BeanELResolver` object that resolves the expression.

After resolving an EL expression, if the `propertyResolved` flag of the `ELContext` object is set to true, the resolver is detached from the EL expression.

Many standard implementations of EL resolver classes exist in the EL API. For example, to resolve the `${employee.name}` expression, a standard `BeanELResolver` object is used, which first resolves or searches for the `employee` JavaBean and then resolves a specific property name. Table 7.3 lists all the standard EL resolver classes:

Table 7.3: Standard EL Resolver Classes

Class	Description
ArrayELResolver	Performs property resolution on arrays
BeanELResolver	Performs property resolution on JavaBeans
ListELResolver	Performs property resolution on objects of the List class
MapELResolver	Performs property resolution on objects of the Map class
ResourceBundleELResolver	Performs property resolution on the objects of the I.esourceBundle class

The following are few EL expressions with their descriptions:

- **${arr[2]}** – Returns the value of the element at position 2 of an array named arr
- **${employee.name}** – Returns the value of the name property of the employee JavaBean
- **${list1[4]}** – Returns the value of fourth element of the list1 list
- **${map1.key1}** – Returns the value of the key1 key in the map1 map
- **${RB1.key1}** – Returns the message corresponding to the key1 key in the resource bundle named RB1

If you do not have an EL resolver implementation to handle your EL expression, you need to create a custom EL resolver and register it with the corresponding JSP application. A `CompositeELResolver` instance holds references to all standard and custom resolvers. This instance is iterated to check whether or not the current resolver can resolve the specified EL expression.

JSP provides two more resolvers, which refer to implicit objects. These are `ImplicitObjectResolver` and `ScopedAttributeResolver`. Consider the expression `${sessionScope.map}`. When a JSP container encounters this expression, it first resolves the implicit object `sessionScope` and then uses `MapELResolver` to resolve the map attribute as map represents an instance of the Map class. The `ScopedAttributeResolver` object resolves an object stored in one of the scopes, such as page, request, session, and application. For example, in the case of the `${employee}` expression, the `ScopedAttributeResolver` object searches for the employee JavaBean in all the scopes. If the value is not found, the object returns a null value.

Describing EL Operators

EL operators are introduced in the unified EL API so that Java programmers can perform arithmetic calculations. Now, you can create EL expressions that perform arithmetic operations by using the operators of EL.

Let's now discuss the various types of EL operators.

Exploring the Types of EL Operators

EL provides support for any type of arithmetic, relational, or logical operations. EL operators can be categorized as follows:

- Arithmetic operators
- Relational and logical operators
- The empty operator
- String concatenation operator
- Conditional operator
- Assignment operator
- Semicolon operator

Let's discuss these operators in detail.

Arithmetic Operators

All types of arithmetic operators (+,-, /,*, or %) are used in EL expressions. The % operator is used to divide the two integer values and return their reminder. Div and mod are alternative names of the division (/) and modulus (%) operators, respectively. The minus (-) operator is used as a unary operator to work with negative numbers. EL also supports floating point numbers, which are fractional numbers.

Relational and Logical Operators

EL provides a set of relational and logical operators that are used in many programming languages. All relational and logical operators can be denoted by using symbols or short text forms. Table 7.4 lists the relational operators used in EL:

Table 7.4: Relational Operators in EL

Operator Symbol	Short Text Form	Description
>	gt	Greater than
>=	ge	Greater than or equal to
<	lt	Less than
<=	le	Less than or equal to
==	eq	Equal to
!=	ne	Not equal to

In case any operand of the operators is a character, EL changes the character data into a numerical value.

The Empty Operator

The empty operator is a prefix operator, which means it takes one operand on its right side. This operator is used to check for empty values, which differ according to the data type of the operand. Table 7.5 lists the empty values for different data types:

Table 7.5: Empty Values for Different Data Types

Data Type	Empty Value
String	""
Identifier	Null
Array	No elements
Map	No elements
List	No elements

String Concatenation Operator

The += operator is used to combine two strings. It results out a string.

Conditional Operator

The ?: operator is a conditional operator that takes three parameters. For example, in the A?B:C expression, it evaluates A and B or C is come out as its output result.

Assignment Operator

The = is called as assignment operator. It assigns right hand side expression value to its left hand side expression.

Semicolon Operator

The ; operator is used to separate two statements.

Let's now learn about the precedence order of EL operators.

Precedence Order of EL Operators

Parentheses can override precedence of most but not all operators; Examples of operators whose precedence is not affected with the use of parenthesis are [ ] and ;. Table 7.6 shows a list of EL operators with their precedence in decreasing order:

Table 7.6: Order of Precedence of EL Operators

Order	Operator
1	[] .

Table 7.6: Order of Precedence of EL Operators

Order	Operator
2	()
3	Unary operators such as -, !, and empty
4	* / %
5	+ -
6	+=
7	< > <= >= lt gt le ge
8	== != eq ne
9	&&
10	||
11	? :
12	->
13	=
14	;

Let's now learn to use EL operators.

Using EL Operators

Now, let's put all the EL operators in use by creating the Operators application. Listing 7.15 demonstrates several EL expressions using arithmetic, relational, logical, and empty operators (save the operators.jsp file in the \Operators folder):

Listing 7.15: Showing the Code for the operators.jsp File

```
<html>
   <head>
         <title>Using EL Operators</title>
   </head>
   <body>
         <h2>Using EL Operators</h2>
         <h3>Arithmetic Expressions</h3>
         <b>You Score in IELTS is ${1 + 2 * 4 - 6 / 2}.</b><br/>
         <b>Today temperature of Delhi is ${-4 - 8} degree celsius.</b><br/>
         <b>Is 3/4 equals to 0.75 ? ${(3/4 == 0.75)? "Yes"  :  "No"}</b><br/>
         <b>Mathematical Constant PI has value ${22/7} </b><br/>
         <b>GDP of India is  ${20 div 2}.</b><br/>
         <b>I have ${2003 mod 8} mobiles.</b><br/>
         <b>I have ${2003 % 8} mobiles.</b><br/>
         <h3>Logical Operators </h3>
         <b>This Logical and EL expression \${(1&lt;2) && (4&lt;3)} is ${(1<2) &&
         (4<3)}</b><br/>
         <b>This Logical or EL expression \${(1&lt;2) || (4&lt;3)} is
         ${(1<2) || (4<3)}</b><br/>
         <b>This Logical not EL expression \${!(1&lt;2)} is ${!(1<2)} </b><br/>

         <h3>Comparison Operators </h3>
         <b>Is 4 > 3 ?  ${4 > 3}</b><br/>
         <b>Is "a" > "b"? ${"a" > "b"}</b><br/>
         <b>Is 4 >= 3 ${4 >= 3}</b><br/>
         <b>Is 4 <= 3 ${4 < 3}</b><br/>
         <b>Is 4 == 4? ${4 == 4}</b><br/>
         <h3>empty Operator</h3>
         <b>empty "" ${empty ""}</b><br/>
         <b>empty "string" ${empty "string"}</b><br/>
         <b>empty null ${empty null}</b>
   </body>
</html>
```

Listing 7.15 shows you the use of the addition, subtraction, division, and modulus operators in EL expressions, under the heading `Arithmetic Expressions`. The conditional operator (?:) is also used in the line `<b> Is 3/4 equals to 0.75? ${(3/4 == 0.75)? "Yes": "No"} </b><br/>`. Under the second heading, namely `Logical Operators`, you learn how to perform some logical expressions, by using the &&, | |, and ! operators. If you want to print an EL expression as it is, you need to prefix it with backslash (/). Apart from this, you also learn to perform comparisons by using the <, <=, >, >=, and == relational operators, under the heading `Comparison Operators`. An empty prefix operator is also used on a blank String and null value.

Package the Operators application into the Operators.war file and then, deploy the `Operators.war` file on the GlassFish 4.0 application server. Now, open the Internet Explorer browser and type the URL `http://localhost:8080/Operators/operators.jsp` to view the output of the `operators JSP` page, as shown in Figure 7.19:

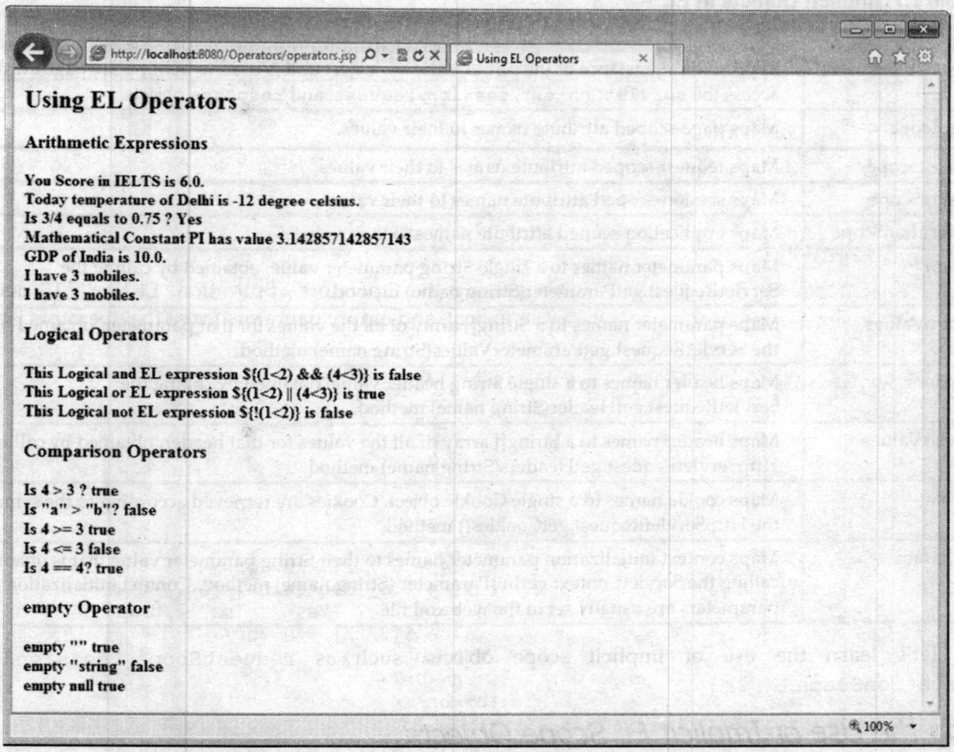

Figure 7.19: Displaying the Output of operators JSP Page

In Figure 7.19, all arithmetic numbers under the `Arithmetic Expressions` heading are displayed by using arithmetic EL expressions and all false and true results are displayed by using relational and logical operators. You have to scroll down to see the results after using the empty operator on various types of Strings.

After learning about EL 3.0, let's now learn how to use JSP implicit objects within EL expressions.

Using JSP Implicit Objects within EL Expressions

JSP programmers can directly use implicit objects in an EL expression. They do not need to write extra code to use these objects. Some of these objects allow access to variables in particular JSP scopes. The implicit scope objects used in EL are `pageScope`, `requestScope`, `sessionScope`, and `applicationScope`. All these scope objects map the scope attribute names to their values, respectively.

You can also access HTTP request parameters by using the implicit objects `param` and `paramValues`. Request header information can be retrieved by using the `header` and `headerValues` implicit objects. The `param` and `header` objects map the parameter and header names to a `String`. The `paramValues` and `headerValues` objects map the parameter and header names of all the values for that parameter or header to a `String[]` array. In the earlier versions of Java Servlet, the `ServletRequest.getParameter(String name)` and `ServletRequest.getHeader(String name)` methods were used to map the parameter and header names to a String. Similarly, the `ServletRequest.getParameterValues(String name)` and `HttpServletRequest.getHeaders(String)` methods were used to map parameter and header names of all values for that parameter or header to a `String[]` array.

The role of `initParam` is to provide access to context initialization parameters. The implicit object `pageContext` provides access to all properties of a context of a JSP page, such as the `ServletContext` and `HttpSession` objects and their properties.

Table 7.7 provides a brief description of the implicit objects in EL:

Table 7.7: Implicit Objects in EL

Object Name	Description
pageContext	Represents an instance of the `pageContext` object and is used to manipulate page attributes and access the `servletContext`, `session`, `request`, and `response` objects.
pageScope	Maps page-scoped attribute names to their values.
requestScope	Maps request-scoped attribute names to their values.
sessionScope	Maps session-scoped attribute names to their values.
applicationScope	Maps application-scoped attribute names to their values.
param	Maps parameter names to a single String parameter value, obtained by calling the ServletRequest.getParameter(String name) method.
paramValues	Maps parameter names to a String[] array of all the values for that parameter, obtained by calling the ServletRequest.getParameterValues(String name) method.
Header	Maps header names to a single String header value, obtained by calling the ServletRequest.getHeader(String name) method.
headerValues	Maps header names to a String[] array of all the values for that header, obtained by calling the HttpServletRequest.getHeaders(String name) method.
cookie	Maps cookie names to a single Cookie object. Cookies are retrieved according to the semantics of the HttpServletRequest.getCookies() method.
initParam	Maps context initialization parameter names to their String parameter value that is obtained by calling the ServletContext.getInitParameter (String name) method. Context initialization parameters are usually set in the web.xml file.

Now, let's learn the use of implicit scope objects, such as `requestScope`, `sessionScope`, and `applicationScope`.

Showing the Use of Implicit EL Scope Objects

The example shown in this section illustrates how to access scoped variables in a JSP EL. The process of accessing scoped variables starts from the servlet, which is configured in the web.xml file to handle a request. The servlet performs the business logic on the data sent with the request and sets the output data in different scopes, such as request, session, or application. The servlet sets the output data in the request, session or application scope by invoking the `setAttribute()` method on the `HttpServletRequest`, `HttpSession`, or `ServletContext` object, respectively and then forwards the control to the JSP page to display the output data by using the `RequestDispatcher.forward()`or `HttpServletResponse.sendRedirect()` method. There is another scope, called PageContext, which stores page scoped variables or objects used on a JSP or servlet page. Therefore, this scope is not shared by servlets and JSPs.

Now, let's see how scoped variables are accessed in EL. To access and display a scoped variable on a browser, EL requires expressions such as ${name}, where name is a scoped variable. When an EL supporting container encounters this expression, it searches for the name variable in the specified order: `PageContext`, `HttpServletRequest`, `HttpSession`, and `ServletContext`. If it gets the name variable, it calls the `toString()` method on the variable value and provides the output.

If you use the `<%=pageContext.findAttribute("name")%>` syntax to access the name variable, the search is only limited to the page scope. However, to search a resource in all scopes, you can use the following syntax of the `<jsp:useBean>` tag:

```
<jsp:useBean id="name" type="package.class" scope=" ">
```

To use the preceding syntax, you should have information about the scope of the servlet and the qualified path of the JavaBean class.

Let's create the `ImplicitObjects2` Web application containing a servlet, which sets attributes or variables in different scopes, and a JSP page, which accesses these variables by using the EL syntax. Listing 7.16 shows the code for the `SetscopedVariables.java` file, which sets the value of the `attribute1` attribute (located in the `\ImplicitObjects2\src\com\kogent\` folder):

Listing 7.16: Showing the Code for the SetScopeVariables.java File

```
import java.io.*;
import javax.servlet.*;
import javax.servlet.http.*;
public class SetScopeVariables extends HttpServlet
{
  public void doGet(HttpServletRequest req, HttpServletResponse res)
  throws ServletException, IOException
  {
        req.setAttribute("attribute1", "First Value");
        HttpSession session = req.getSession();
        session.setAttribute("attribute2", "Second Value");
        ServletContext application = getServletContext();
        application.setAttribute("attribute3",new java.util.Date());
        req.setAttribute("repeated", "Request");
        session.setAttribute("repeated", "Session");
        application.setAttribute("repeated", "ServletContext");
        RequestDispatcher dispatcher =
        req.getRequestDispatcher("GetScopeVariables.jsp");
        dispatcher.forward(req, res);
  }
}
```

In Listing 7.16, we set the attribute1, attribute2, and attribute3 attributes to First Value, Second Value, and current date and time Strings, respectively. The attribute1, attribute2, and attribute3 attributes are set in the request, session, and application scope, respectively. There is another attribute, called repeated, which is set in all the three scopes. Finally, the servlet transfers the control to the GetScopedVariables JSP page.

In Listing 7.17, the values of the attribute1, attribute2, attribute3 attributes are accessed, irrespective of the scopes where these attributes are stored. The code to access these attributes is provided in Listing 7.17. Apart from this, Listing 7.17 also contains some code statements that restrict the search of a particular attribute in a particular scope, such as sessionScope.attribute1. Listing 7.17 shows the use of some implicit objects (save the GetScopeVariables.jsp file in the \ImplicitObjects2 folder):

Listing 7.17: Showing the Code for the GetScopeVariables.jsp File

```
<HTML>
<HEAD>
  <TITLE>Accessing Scoped Variables</TITLE>
</HEAD>
<BODY>
  <TABLE BORDER=2 ALIGN="CENTER">
  <TR><TH>
  Accessing Scoped Variables
  </TABLE>
  <P>
  <UL>
  <LI><B>Accessing attribute1 directly:</B> ${attribute1}
```

```
    <LI><B>Accessing attribute1 using requestScope implicit object:</B>
    ${requestScope.attribute1}
    <LI><B>Checking whether attribute1 is present in session scope using
    sessionScope implict object:</B>${sessionScope.attribute1}

    <LI><B>Accessing attribute2 directly:</B> ${attribute2}
    <LI><B>Checking whether attribute2 is present in application scope using
    applicationScope implict object:</B> ${applicationScope.attribute2}

    <LI><B>Accessing attribute3 directly:</B> ${attribute3}

    <LI><B>Accessing repeated attribute directly:</B> ${repeated}
    <LI><B>Checking repeated attribute only in application scope using
    applicationScope implicit object:</B> ${applicationScope.repeated}
    </UL>
  </BODY>
  </HTML>
```

Deploy the `ImplicitObjects2` application on GlassFish 4.0 application server. To execute the example, open Internet Explorer and type the URL http://localhost:8080/ImplicitObjects2/SetScopeVariables. Figure 7.20 shows the output of executing the SetScopeVariables servlet:

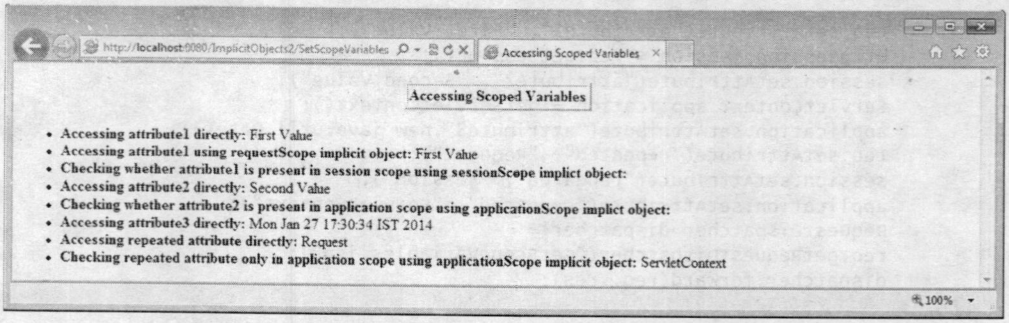

Figure 7.20: Accessing Attributes by using Scoped Variables

In Figure 7.20, you can see that no value is displayed in the third and fifth lines because the JSP container is not able to find attribute1 and attribute2, respectively in the application scope. This is another advantage of EL: it does not generate a NullPointerException exception or return null value if it is unable to find an attribute in a particular scope. It only displays an empty String as the output.

After learning how to use implicit scope EL objects, let's now discuss the implementation of the paramValues and pageContext implicit EL objects.

Showing the Use of Implicit EL Objects

In the example shown in this section, a user is asked to enter some information and then retrieve and display the information along with other information, such as the server name, `JSESSIONID`.

The `index HTML` page is a simple HTML form that contains the `email` text box, three check boxes, and a `Submit` button. When a user submits this form, the control is transferred to the `impobjects2 JSP` page. Listing 7.18 shows the code for the `index.html` file (save the index.html file in the \ImplicitObjects2 folder):

Listing 7.18: Showing the Code for the index.html File

```
<html>
  <head>
        <title>Index Page</title>
  </head>
  <body>
        <form action="impobjects2.jsp" method="get">
        <table BORDER=2 ALIGN="CENTER">
```

```
        <TR><Th>
                Using Implicit Objects
        </th></TR>
        </table>
        <table>
                <tr><td colspan=2><h3>Pet Shopping Cart</h3></td></tr>
                <tr><td>
                        Your Email Id :<input type="text"
                        name=email size="30"/>
                </td></tr>
                <tr><td>
                        What type of pets do you have?
                </td></tr>
                <tr><td>
                        cat <input type="checkbox" name="pettype"
                        value="cat" />
                </td></tr>
                <tr><td>
                        dog <input type="checkbox" name="pettype"
                        value="dog" />
                </td></tr>
                <tr><td>
                        rabbit <input type="checkbox"
                        name="pettype" value="rabbit"/>
                </td></tr>
        </table>
        <table>
                <tr><td>
                        <input type=submit value="Submit">
                </td></tr>
        </table>
        </form>
    </body>
</html>
```

In Listing 7.19, the `impobjects2 JSP` page displays the e-mail id of the user by using the `param` implicit object. The `<c:forEach>` tag of the JSTL core library is used in the `impobjects2 JSP` page. The `<c:forEach>` tag iterates over the collection represented by the `paramValues` implicit object, assigns each value to the `pet` variable, and prints the values stored in the `pet` variable. You need to map the index.html file as the welcome page in the web.xml file. Listing 7.19 shows the code for the `impobject2.jsp` file (save the impobject2.jsp file in the \ImplicitObjects2 folder):

Listing 7.19: Showing the Code for the impobject2.jsp File

```
<%@ taglib prefix="c" uri="http://java.sun.com/jsp/jstl/core" %>
<HTML>
   <HEAD>
        <TITLE>Using Implicit Objects</TITLE>
   </HEAD>
   <BODY>
        <TABLE BORDER=2 ALIGN="CENTER">
        <TR><TH>
                Using Implicit Objects
        </TH></TR>
        </TABLE>
        <P><UL>
                <LI><B>Your Email ID is :</B> ${param.email}
                <Li><B>You have selected pets:</B>
                        <c:forEach var="pet" items="${paramValues.pettype}">
                          ${pet}  
```

```
                    </c:forEach>
                <LI><B>User-Agent Header:</B> ${header["User-Agent"]}
                <LI><B>JSESSIONID Cookie Value:</B>
                    ${cookie.JSESSIONID.value}
                <LI><B>Server:</B> ${pageContext.servletContext.serverInfo}
        </UL>
    </BODY>
</HTML>
```

In Listing 7.19, the JSTL core library is included to use its `<c:forEach>` tag. The `{header["User-Agent"]}` expression displays the browser associated with the user agent header. The implicit object `cookie` is used to retrieve the value of `JSESSIONID`, which is a large String consisting of alphabets and numbers. Finally, the `pageContext` object is used to fetch the server name, which processes the `index HTML` page and displays the results.

Store the `index.html` and `implobject2.jsp` files in the `ImplicitObjects2` directory according to the standard directory structure of Web applications. To use the JSTL core library, you must place the `jstl.jar` file in the `lib` folder under the `WEB-INF` folder of the `ImplicitObjects2` directory. Now, redeploy the `ImplicitObjects2` application on the GlassFish 4.0 application server. Next, open the Internet Explorer browser and type the URL `http://localhost:8080/ImplicitObjects2/`. The output of the `index HTML` page is displayed, as shown in Figure 7.21:

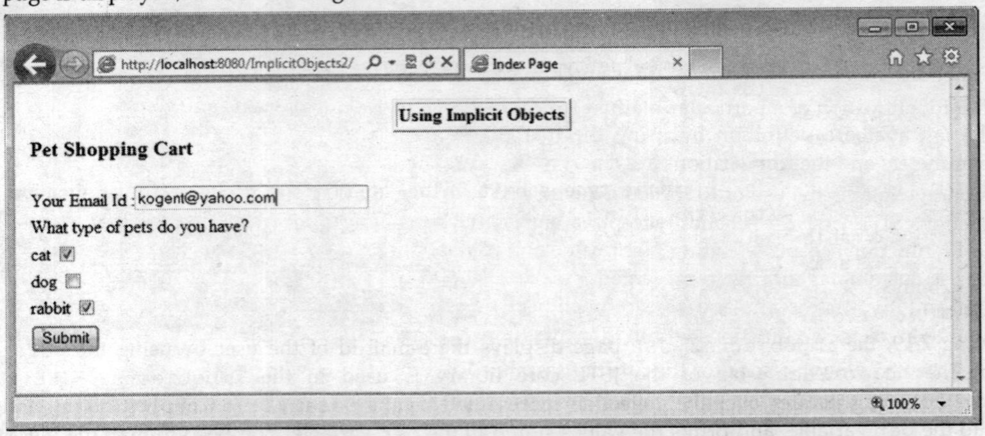

Figure 7.21: Displaying the Output of the index HTML Page

In Figure 7.21, the user enters `kogent@yahoo.com` as the e-mail id and then selects the check boxes corresponding to `cat` and `rabbit`. After clicking the `Submit` button, the request is redirected to the impobject2 JSP page and the submitted details are displayed, as shown in Figure 7.22:

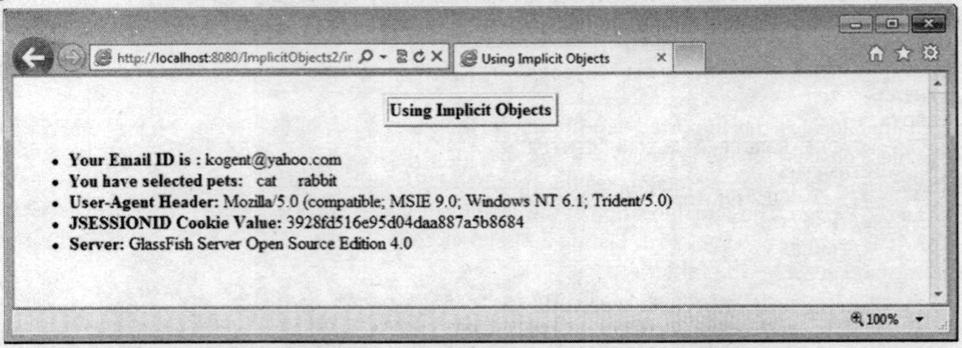

Figure 7.22: Displaying the User Details by using Implicit Objects

Figure 7.22 displays the e-mail id and the selected check boxes values, the compatible browser type, JSESSIONID, and the name of the server with version, in the form of a bulleted list.

You are now familiar with using expressions in EL. Now, let's explore how to use custom tag library with EL functions.

Using Custom Tag Library with EL Functions

Sometimes, Java programmers may need to change the format of data or manipulate the data before it is displayed on a Web page. A custom tag library can be used for this purpose; however, EL provides no such built-in library. Therefore, Java programmers need to define their own methods. The prefix assigned to a function tag library is used to access EL functions. In other words, EL has the concept of qualified functiohs. EL functions are public static methods in Java classes, which are mapped in TLD.

As far as a tag library is concerned, each tag library may include zero or more static functions that are listed in the TLD file. Moreover, the name given to a function in the TLD file is exposed to EL. A public static method in the specified public class implements the functions. You have to be very careful about naming a function in a tag library, since the name of the function must be unique in the library. If the function is not declared correctly, or if there are multiple functions bearing the same name, an error is generated during translation time.

We have already covered method expressions, which appear similar but are not identical to EL functions. The differences between function expressions and method expressions are as follows:

- Functions are static methods that return single values but method expressions use non-static public methods.
- Functions are recognized during translation time but methods are recognized dynamically at runtime.
- The identification of a particular method is provided in a method expression and that method is invoked in the tag attribute definition by using the method expression. On the other hand, in functions, function parameters and their invocations are a part of EL expressions.

This section explains the use of EL functions with a Web application, ELFunctions. This application uses two EL functions. The first EL function accepts a signed integer value and returns its absolute value, while the second EL function accepts a floating point value and rounds it into an integer value. The functions JSP page includes a custom tag library represented by the URI http://www.kogentindia.com/el-functions-taglib, and invokes the abs and round functions by using the XML namespaces notation, such as f:abs( ). Listing 7.20 invokes two functions within EL expressions (save the functions.jsp file in the \ELFunctions folder):

Listing 7.20: Showing the Code for the functions.jsp File

```
<%@ taglib prefix="f" uri="http://www.kogentindia.com/el-functions-taglib" %>
<html>
<head>
  <title>Using EL Functions</title>
</head>
<body>
  <h1>Using EL Functions </h1>
  The absolute value of \${num} is ${f:abs(-300)}.<br/>
  The rounded value of \${calc} is ${f:round(6.666666666666667)}.<br/>
</body>
</html>
```

A JSP container locates the imported tag library in the web.xml file of the ELFunctions application. The web.xml file consists of the <taglib> tag having two nested tags, <taglib-uri> and <taglib-location>. The <taglib-uri> tag takes the specified URI in the uri attribute of the taglib directive in the functions JSP page. The actual location of the TLD file is specified in the <taglib-location> tag, which is /WEB-INF/function-taglib.tld. Listing 7.21 shows code for the web.xml file (save the index.html file in the \ELFunctions\WEB-INF folder):

Listing 7.21: Showing the Code for the web.xml File

```
<?xml version="1.0" encoding="UTF-8"?>
<web-app version="3.1"
```

```
    xmlns="http://xmlns.jcp.org/xml/ns/javaee"
    xmlns:xsi="http://www.w3.org/2001/XMLSchema-instance"
    xsi:schemaLocation="http://xmlns.jcp.org/xml/ns/javaee
    http://xmlns.jcp.org/xml/ns/javaee/web-app_3_1.xsd">

    <taglib>
        <taglib-uri>
            http://www.kogentindia.com/el-functions-taglib
        </taglib-uri>
        <taglib-location>
            /WEB-INF/function-taglib.tld
        </taglib-location>
    </taglib>

</web-app>
```

EL function definitions are contained within another TLD file. The `function-taglib.tld` file maps the function calls in the `functions.jsp` file to the `<function>` tags. The Java class implementing the function, which in this case is `java.lang.Math` for both the `abs` and `round` functions, is specified in the `<function-class>` tag. These functions signatures are specified in the `<function-signature>` tag. Listing 7.22 provides function definitions of the functions used in Listing 7.20 (save the function-taglib.tld file in the `\ELFunctions\WEB-INF` folder):

Listing 7.22: Showing the Code for the function-taglib.tld File

```
<?xml version="1.0" encoding="UTF-8" ?>
<taglib version="2.1" xmlns="http://xmlns.jcp.org/xml/ns/javaee"
xmlns:xsi="http://www.w3.org/2001/XMLSchema-instance"
xsi:schemaLocation="http://xmlns.jcp.org/xml/ns/javaee/web-jsptaglibrary_2_1.xsd">

  <description>A taglib to define some EL accessible functions.</description>
  <tlib-version>2.1</tlib-version>
  <short-name>ELFunctionTaglib</short-name>
  <uri>/ELFunctionTagLibrary</uri>

  <function>
        <name>abs</name>
        <function-class>java.lang.Math</function-class>
        <function-signature>int abs( int )</function-signature>
  </function>

  <function>
        <name>round</name>
        <function-class>java.lang.Math</function-class>
        <function-signature>int round( double )</function-signature>
  </function>

</taglib>
```

Deploy the `ELFunctions` application on the Glassfish application server. Next, open Internet Explorer and type the URL http://localhost:8080/ELFunctions/functions.jsp. The functions JSP page is displayed, as shown in Figure 7.23:

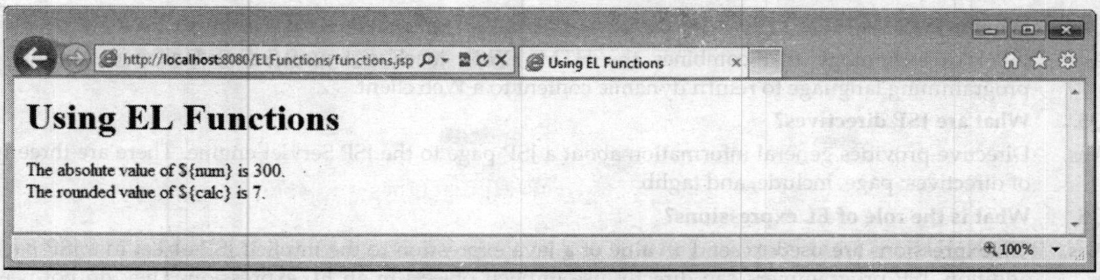

Figure 7.23: Displaying the output of EL Functions

Figure 7.23 displays the absolute value of the signed integer, i.e., 300. The second expression rounds 6.6666666667 to 7. In the `ELFunctions` application, the absolute value of the signed integer is returned by method evaluation but a null value is returned if the return type of the Java method is void.

If an exception is thrown during method evaluation, the exception must be wrapped in an `ELException` exception. This is because EL uses the `ELException` exception for any exception that may occur during parsing or expression evaluation.

With this, we come to the end of the chapter. Let's now recap the main points of the chapter in a short summary.

Summary

The chapter has provided an introduction to the JSP 2.3 technology. It has discussed the advantages of the JSP technology over Java Servlet technology. You have also learned about the different architectures of JSP pages. In addition, the chapter has explained the life cycle of a JSP page, and explored various basic tags, implicit objects, and action tags used in JSP. Then, you have learned about EL and various features added in its new release 3.0. Finally, you have learned about JSP implicit objects within EL expressions, and how to use custom tag library with EL functions.

The next chapter discusses the implementation of the various JSP tag extensions.

Quick Revise

Q1. Which of the following are the JSP life cycle methods?

A. jspInit()

B. jspService(ServletRequest, ServletResponse)

C. jspDestroy()

D. jspService(HttpServletRequest, HttpServletResponse)

Ans. The correct options are A, C, and D.

Q2. Which of the following uses of the `<jsp:useBean>` tag for a JSP page that uses the `java.sun.com.MyBean` JavaBean component are correct?

A. <jsp:useBean id="java.sun.com.MyBean" scope="page"/>

B. <jsp:useBean id="MyBean" class="java.sun.com.MyBean"/>

C. <jsp:useBean id="MyBean" type="java.lang.String" scope="page"/>

D. <jsp:useBean id="MyBean" beanName="java.sun.com.MyBean" scope="page">

Ans. The correct options are B and C.

Q3. Use ………………………… when resources require dynamic data or change frequently.

A. <jsp:insert>

B. <jsp:include>

C. <jsp:directive.include>

D. <%@ include %>

Ans. The correct option is B.

Q4. What is JSP?

Ans. JSP is a technology that combines the HTML/XML markup languages and elements of the Java programming language to return dynamic content to a Web client.

Q5. What are JSP directives?

Ans. Directive provides general information about a JSP page to the JSP Servlet engine. There are three types of directives: page, include, and taglib.

Q6. What is the role of EL expressions?

Ans. EL expressions are used to send a value of a Java expression to the implicit JSP object in a JSP page. In addition, JSP programmers can directly use implicit objects in an EL expression. They do not need to write extra code to use these objects. Some of these objects allow access to variables in particular JSP scopes.

Q7. What are predefined variables or implicit objects?

Ans. To simplify code in JSP expressions and scriptlets, we use nine automatically defined variables, sometimes called implicit objects. These variables are request, response, out, session, application, config, exception, pageContext, and page.

Q8. What are JSP actions?

Ans. Actions are commands given to a JSP Servlet engine. They direct the engine to perform certain tasks during the execution of a page. The following are some examples of action tags that are used in a JSP page to define JSP actions:

- <jsp:include>
- <jsp:forward>
- <jsp:useBean>
- <jsp:setProperty>
- <jsp:getProperty>
- <jsp:plugin>

Q9. Which of the following symbol is called as conditional operator?

A. >

B. [ ]

C. ?:

D. &&

Ans. The correct option is C.

Q10. Which of the following symbol is called as lambda?

A. ||

B. [ ]

C. +

D. ->

Ans. The correct option is D.

8

Implementing JSP Tag Extensions

JavaServer Pages (JSP) allows you to create and use tag extensions or custom tags in a Web page. The custom tags are defined as the user-defined tags that are present in JSP tag libraries (JSTL). These tags reduce the use of scripting elements in a JSP page. Whenever you want to use the JSP scripting elements, such as JSP expressions, scriptlets, and declaration, you need to provide Java code within these elements. The process of importing Java code in a JSP page combines the business logic of an application with the scripting elements used in a JSP page. This reduces the capabilities of the presentation layer of the application. In addition, the use of Java code along with JSP elements in a JSP page leads to the difficulty in debugging and maintaining the JSP page. To overcome these problems, JSP custom tags are used, as they eliminate the need of using or importing Java code in JSP pages.

Tag extensions or custom tags allow you to create new and reusable tags that are defined in separate Java classes. These tag extensions play an important role in separating presentation layer from the business logic layer. After creating custom tags, you can use them in any JSP page with the help of their tag libraries. These tag libraries help in easy maintenance and debugging of JSP pages. Apart from tag extensions, JavaBeans are also used to separate business logic from presentation logic in a JSP page. The use of JavaBeans in a JSP page has a limitation that only three JSP standard tags, `<jsp:useBean>`, <jsp:`getProperty`>, and <jsp:`setProperty`> can be used to interact with JavaBeans. The JSP standard tags bind the instances of the scoped variables and then get or set those instances for the properties of JavaBeans.

JSP provides custom tags as extension mechanism to create new user-defined tags without the need of writing a Java code in a JSP page. Custom tags are defined in Java classes called tag handlers and are declared in a tag library with a unique name and a tag handler is used to process these tags.

This chapter begins with a discussion on the elements of tag extensions. Next, the classes and interfaces provided by the tag extension Application Programming Interface (API) are explored in detail. You also learn how to create applications of the simple and classic tag handlers. Further, the chapter explores about the JSP fragments that can be used in a JSP page. Towards the end, the chapter discusses another feature known as tag file, which allows you to create custom tags using the JSP syntax.

Exploring the Elements of Tag Extensions

A tag library provides the capability to define new and customized tags. Tag libraries can be imported into a JSP page by using the taglib directive. You can find the details of a tag library, such as name of the tags, classes to which the tags are mapped, and validator class in the Tag Library Descriptor (TLD) file. You should note that depending upon the context in which they are used, tag extensions and custom tags have been used interchangeably in this chapter.

The following are the major features of custom tags:

- **Reusability**—Allows you to reuse the custom tags in multiple JSP pages
- **Readability**—Makes the page cleaner, shorter, and readable by removing the complex Java code from the JSP page
- **Maintainability**—Specifies that an application can be modified and debugged during its lifetime by using custom tags
- **Portability**— Specifies that custom tag libraries are portable and not dependent on specific JSP containers

The custom tags are used in a `JSP` page to increase its performance and productivity. These tags generally refer to the custom actions developed by users and contain the following basic elements:

- The `TLD` file
- The tag handler
- The `taglib` directive

Let's now discuss these elements along with their usage in a JSP page.

The TLD File

The TLD file is an Extensible Markup Language (XML) document describing a tag library, which serves as a container of custom tags. These custom tags are used to encapsulate the functionalities to be provided within a JSP page. TLD is used by a JSP container to interpret the pages that include the `taglib` directives. The documentation of the tag library and version information of the JSP container for individual tags is also provided in the TLD file. This file may contain the name of the `TagLibraryValidator` class to validate a JSP page that conforms to a set of constraints defined in a tag library. Each action in a tag library is described by giving its name, the class of its tag handler, information on any scripting variables created by the action, and information on attributes of the action. Scripting variable information can be given directly in TLD or through a `TagExtraInfo` class. The TLD file is used by JSP Engine tools without instantiating objects or loader classes. In JSP, the format of the TLD file is represented in XML schema, which provides a more extensible TLD that can be used as a single source document.

The taglib Directive

As discussed earlier, the taglib directive is used in a JSP page to implement the functionality of a custom tag. To set a custom tag in a JSP page, you need to provide the Uniform Resource Identifier (URI) of the tag library and a prefix for the tag library.

The following code snippet shows how to specify a TLD in a JSP page:

```
<%@ taglib prefix="p" uri="Mytld.tld" %>
```

In the preceding code snippet, the custom tags, located in the Mytld.`tld` file, can be accessed by using the p prefix. The `taglib` directive used in a JSP page provides the following features:

- Declares that a tag library is used
- Identifies the location of the tag library with the help of the uri attribute
- Associates a tag prefix with the usage of actions in the library

The JSP container maps the uri attribute used in the `taglib` directive in the following two steps:

1. Resolves the value of the uri attribute into a TLD file resource path
2. Derives the TLD object from the TLD resource path

If the JSP container cannot locate a TLD resource path for a given URI, a fatal translation error, such as cannot load the class, may occur.

The Tag Handler

A tag handler is a Java class where a custom tag is defined. The JSP container invokes the tag handler object to evaluate a custom tag during the execution of a JSP page. You can define tag handlers for custom tags either by implementing interfaces or by extending an abstract base class from the `javax.servlet.jsp.tagext` package. The various tag handler interfaces included in JSP specifications are `Tag`, `BodyTag`, `IterationTag`, and `SimpleTag`. In addition, the JSP technology defines two types of tag handlers: classic tag handler and simple tag handler. The classic tag handlers are based on the original tag development methodology, which is used if the scripting elements are required in attribute-values pair or the tag body. On the other hand, simple tag handlers are used to evaluate custom tags that do not use scripting elements in attribute values or the tag body.

Let's now discuss the interfaces and abstract classes to create tag handlers by exploring the tag extension API.

Exploring the Tag Extension API

The tag extension API provides the `javax.servlet.jsp.tagext` package containing various classes and interfaces used to handle custom tags in a JSP page. The Tag interface works as a protocol between the tag handler and the implementation classes used in the JSP page. Tag extensions are similar to HTML/XML tags that are embedded in a JSP page.

NOTE

HTML stands for Hypertext Markup Language.

Some of the terms associated with the implementation of a tag extension are as follows:

- **Tag name** – Refers to a unique name that is a combination of prefix and suffix, separated by a colon. For example, in the <jsp:forward /> tag, jsp is a prefix and forward is a suffix.

- **Attributes**—Refers to a value that is assigned to an attribute of a tag. For example, the <jsp:forward/> tag has only one attribute, `page`. You should note that the use of attributes is optional.
- **Nesting**—Refers to a process in which a tag is used within another tag. For example, the <jsp:param /> tag is used within the <jsp:include /> and <jsp:forward /> tags. A tag that encloses the other tag within itself is called the parent tag and the tag that is enclosed inside the parent tag is called the child tag.
- **Body content**—Refers to the content, such as expressions and scriptlets that is provided between the start and end of a tag.

After having a brief knowledge about tag extensions and understanding their role in a JSP page, let's discuss the interfaces and classes provided in the tag extension API.

The Tag Extension Interfaces

The tag extension API provides a number of interfaces, within the javax.servlet.jsp.tagext package, to implement custom tags in a JSP page. These interfaces are used to provide interaction between the JSP engine and tag handler.

The following is the list of the tag extension interfaces defined in JSP 2.3:

- The `Tag` interface
- The `JspTag` interface
- The `IterationTag` interface
- The `BodyTag` interface
- The `DynamicAttributes` interface
- The `SimpleTag` interface
- The `TryCatchFinally` interface
- The `JspIdConsumer` interface

The `JspIdConsumer` interface is introduced in the JSP 2.1 version of the Java EE 6 platform.

The Tag Interface

The `Tag` interface defines the basic protocol between a tag handler and a JSP page. The classic tag handlers are built by using the `Tag` interface. The `Tag` interface provides various methods, such as `doStartTag()` and `doEndTag()` that are invoked in the tag handler by the JSP engine during the start and end of a tag. The `doStartTag()` method is invoked by the JSP engine while encountering the start of a tag in a JSP page. The value returned by the doStartTag() method indicates whether the body should be skipped or evaluated within a JSP page. The `doEndTag()` method is invoked by the JSP engine while encountering the end of a tag in a JSP page. The value returned by the `doEndTag()` method indicates whether or not the rest of the page should continue to be evaluated. The `doEndTag()` method is not executed in case an exception arises while evaluating the body content of a tag.

Table 8.1 describes various methods of the `Tag` interface:

Table 8.1: Describing the Methods of the Tag Interface

Method	Description
int doStartTag()	Processes the start tag of a custom tag in the tag handler class. This method is invoked by the JSP engine in the tag handler class. The `doStartTag()` method is executed once the properties of the `pageContext` attribute are set. The doStartTag() method returns either the `Tag.EVAL_BODY_INCLUDE` field to evaluate the body of the custom tag or the `SKIP_BODY` field to skip the evaluation of the custom tag. If an error occurs during the processing of the start tag, the `JspException` exception is thrown.
int doEndTag()	Processes the end tag of a custom tag in the tag handler class. This method is invoked by the JSP engine in the tag handler class. The doEndTag() method is invoked after the processing of the `doStartTag()` method is complete. The body of the custom tag may or may not be evaluated, depending on the value returned by the `doStartTag()` method. If the `doStartTag()` method returns the `EVAL_PAGE` field, the rest of the page continues

Table 8.1: Describing the Methods of the Tag Interface

Method	Description
	to be evaluated. However, if the method returns the `SKIP_PAGE` field, the rest of the page is not evaluated, the request is completed, and the `doEndTag()` method of enclosing tag is not invoked. If this request is forwarded or included from another page (or servlet), only the evaluation of the current page is stopped. If an error occurs while processing the end tag, the `JspException` exception is thrown.
void setParent(Tag t)	Sets the nearest enclosing tag handler for custom tag in a JSP page.
Tag getParent()	Returns the immediate super class or ancestor class of the current class. This method is used in the nested structure of a tag handler.
void release()	Releases any acquired resources.

Apart from methods, the Tag interface also provides fields, as described in Table 8.2:

Table 8.2: Describing the Fields of the Tag Interface

Field	Description
`EVAL_BODY_INCLUDE`	Evaluates the body of a custom tag when this field is returned as a value for the `doStartTag()` method
`EVAL_PAGE`	Continues the evaluation of the rest of the JSP page when this field is returned as a value for the `doEndTag()` method
`SKIP_BODY`	Skips the body evaluation of the custom tag when this field is returned as a value for the `doStartTag()` and `doAfterBody()` methods
`SKIP_PAGE`	Skips the evaluation of the rest of the JSP page when this field is returned as a value for the `doEndTag()` method

The JspTag Interface

The `JspTag` interface serves as a base interface for the `Tag` and `SimpleTag` interfaces. This interface is mainly used for organizational and type-safety purposes. The `BodyTag`, `IterationTag`, `SimpleTag`, and `Tag` interfaces are the sub-interfaces of the `JspTag` interface.

The IterationTag Interface

The `IterationTag` interface is used to build tag handlers that repeatedly re-evaluate the body of a custom tag. The `IterationTag` interface extends the `Tag` interface. In other words, the `IterationTag` interface acquires all the methods of the Tag interface. Apart from the methods of the `Tag` interface, the `IterationTag` interface also provides the `doAfterBody()` method, which is invoked to determine whether or not to re-evaluate the body of the custom tag. The `doAfterBody()` method is invoked only after the body of the custom tag is evaluated.

Table 8.3 describes the method of the `IterationTag` interface:

Table 8.3: Describing the Method of the IterationTag Interface

Method	Description
int doAfterBody()	Determines whether or not to re-evaluate the body of a custom tag. If the body content of the custom tag is re-evaluated, the `doAfterBody()` method returns the `EVAL_BODY_AGAIN`; otherwise, the `SKIP_BODY` is returned. If an error occurs while processing the `doAfterBody()` method, the JspException exception is thrown.

Table 8.4 describes the fields of the `IterationTag` interface:

Table 8.4: Describing the Fields of the IterationTag Interface

Field	Description
EVAL_BODY_AGAIN	Re-evaluates the body content of a tag when this field is returned by the `doAfterBody()` method

The BodyTag Interface

The BodyTag interface extends the IterationTag interface and acquires all the methods of the IterationTag interface. The BodyTag interface has some additional methods to evaluate the body content of a custom tag. Implementing the BodyTag interface is similar to the implementation of the IterationTag interface, except that the doStartTag() method can return the SKIP_BODY and EVAL_BODY_INCLUDE or EVAL_BODY_BUFFERED fields.

Table 8.5 describes various methods of the BodyTag interface:

Table 8.5: Describing the Methods of the BodyTag Interface

Method	Description
void doInitBody()	Evaluates the body of a custom tag before initializing it. The doInitBody() method is not invoked for empty tags or for non-empty tags whose doStartTag() method returns the SKIP_BODY or EVAL_BODY_INCLUDE field.
void setBodyContent(BodyContent b)	Sets the body content of the custom tag. The setBodyContent() method is invoked by the JSP engine at every tag invocation. This method is invoked before the invocation of the doInitBody() method. The setBodyContent() method is not invoked for empty tags or for non-empty tags whose doStartTag() method returns the SKIP_BODY or EVAL_BODY_INCLUDE field.

The BodyTag interface provides the EVAL_BODY_BUFFERED field, which requests the creation of a new buffer to evaluate the body of the custom tag. The EVAL_BODY_BUFFERED field is returned as a value from the doStartTag() method only when the tag handler class has implemented the BodyTag interface.

The DynamicAttributes Interface

The DynamicAttributes interface is implemented by a tag handler to provide support for dynamic attributes. A tag handler, which implements the DynamicAttributes interface, also declares its support for dynamic attributes in TLD. The DynamicAttributes interface defines whether or not the tag handler accepts dynamic attributes. The tag handler should implement the DynamicAttributes interface, whenever it accepts the dynamic attributes; otherwise, the container considers it as an invalid tag handler.

Tag handlers implement the DynamicAttributes interface to accept dynamic attributes. The errors occurring at the translation-time are avoided by calling the setDynamicAttribute() method for the dynamic attributes that are not declared in TLD. The DynamicAttributes interface provides a single method, namely, setDynamicAttribute(String uri, String localName, Object value). The setDynamicAttribute() method avoids translation-time errors when a tag is declared to accept dynamic attributes that are passed as arguments and are not declared in TLD. If the tag handler does not accept the given attribute, the JspException exception is thrown. The container must not call the doStartTag() or doTag() methods for the tag.

Let's now discuss the SimpleTag interface of the tag extension API, which is used to build simple tag handlers.

The SimpleTag Interface

The simple tag handlers are created by implementing the SimpleTag interface, which defines the doTag() method to perform the same task as performed by the doStartTag()and doEndTag() methods of the classic tag handlers. The doTag() method is called only once for a given tag and performs various tasks, such as evaluating and iterating the body content of the tag.

Table 8.6 describes the methods of the SimpleTag interface:

Table 8.6: Describing the Methods of the SimpleTag Interface

Method	Description
void doTag()	Handles various tasks, such as evaluating and iterating the body content of a tag. This method throws the JspException exception, if an error occurs while processing the custom tag. The SkipPageException exception is thrown, if the JSP page that (either directly or indirectly)

Table 8.6: Describing the Methods of the SimpleTag Interface

Method	Description
	invoked the custom tag needs to cease evaluation.
`JspTag getParent()`	Returns the parent of the custom tag for collaboration purposes.
`void setJspBody(JspFragment jspBody)`	Provides the body of the custom tag as a `JspFragment` object. The `setJspBody()` method is invoked zero or more times prior to the `doTag()` method. If the `action` element is empty in the current JSP page, this method is not invoked.
`void setJspContext(JspContext pc)`	Provides the simple tag handler with the `JspContext` object.
`void setParent(JspTag parent)`	Sets the parent of the custom tag for collaboration purposes. The `setParent()` method is invoked when the current tag is nested within another tag invocation.

The TryCatchFinally Interface

The `TryCatchFinally` interface is used to handle the exceptions that may occur within the tag handler class. When the JSP container invokes the tag handler methods, such as `doStartTag()` and `doEndTag()`, these methods may throw the `JspException` exception. Therefore, you need to implement the `TryCatchFinally` interface in the tag handler class to handle such exceptions.

Table 8.7 describes the methods of the `TryCatchFinally` interface:

Table 8.7: Describing the Methods of the TryCatchFinally Interface

Method	Description
`void doCatch(Throwable t)`	Gets invoked whenever there an exception arises during the evaluation of the body of the current tag or whenever the `doStartTag()`, `doEndTag()`, `doInitBody()`, and `doAfterBody()` methods are invoked.
`void doFinally()`	Gets invoked after the processing of the `doEndTag()` method is complete. This method can also be invoked if an exception occurs while evaluating the body of the current tag or when the `doStartTag ()`, `doEndTag ()`, `doInitBody ()`, and `doAfterBody ()` methods are invoked.

The JspIdConsumer Interface

The `JspIdConsumer` interface indicates that the JSP container should provide a compiler generated id to a tag handler. The `jspId` attribute of the tag handler is set by the container, which acts as the part of the tag property. Every tag of a JSP page has a unique id that can be used to access the tags of a tag handler. The `jspId` attribute is a String value and is similar to the `<jsp:id>` tag; however, the only difference is that `<jsp:id>` is evaluated at the execution time, while jspId is evaluated at the request time.

The `JspIdConsumer` interface provides a single method, `setJspId(String id)`, which helps in generating a unique identification during the translation process performed by the Web container.

After understanding the interfaces provided by the tag extensions API, let's now explore the tag extension classes.

The Tag Extension Classes

The tag extension API provides a number of classes, within the `javax.servlet.jsp.tagext` package, to implement custom tags. You should note that these classes are abstract in nature and help to establish the interaction between the JSP engine and a tag handler.

The following is the list of the tag extension classes defined in JSP 2.3:

- The `TagSupport` class
- The `BodyContent` class
- The `BodyTagSupport` class
- The `SimpleTagSupport` class

- The TagAdapter class
- The TagLibraryInfo class
- The TagInfo class
- The TagFileInfo class
- The TagAttributeInfo class
- The TagExtraInfo Class
- The PageData class
- The TagLibraryValidator class
- The ValidationMessage class
- The TagData class
- The VariableInfo class
- The TagVariableInfo class
- The FunctionInfo class
- The JspFragment class

Let's now discuss each of these classes in detail.

The TagSupport Class

The TagSupport class is a class that implements the Tag as well as IterationTag interfaces and provides support for all the methods of these interfaces. In addition, the TagSupport class provides a static method, which facilitates coordination among other cooperating tags.

Table 8.8 describes various methods of the TagSupport class:

Table 8.8: Describing the Methods of the TagSupport Class

Method	Description
`int doAfterBody()`	Processes the body content of a tag after the invocation of the doStartTag() method. If an error occurs while processing the doAfterBody() method on the current tag, the JspException exception is thrown.
`int doEndTag()`	Returns the EVAL_PAGE field, by default, on executing the end tag. If an error occurs while processing the end tag, the JspException exception is thrown.
`int doStartTag()`	Returns the SKIP_BODY field after the default execution of the start tag. If an error occurs during the execution of the start tag, the JspException exception is thrown.
`Object getValue(String k)`	Returns the String value associated with the specified key.
`String getId()`	Returns either the values of the id attribute of a custom tag or the null value.
`Enumeration<String> getValues()`	Enumerates through the keys to get the corresponding values.
`Tag findAncestorWithClass(Tag from, Class class)`	Returns the nearest class to the class in which instance is passed as a parameter of the method. The specified class can be used as replacement of the getParent() method of the Tag interface.
`void removeValue(String k)`	Removes the String value associated with the specified key.
`void setId(String id)`	Sets the id attribute for the current tag handler.
`void setPageContext(PageContext pageContext)`	Sets the page context for the current tag handler.

Table 8.9 describes the fields of the TagSupport class:

Table 8.9: Describing the Fields of the TagSupport Class

Field	Description
`id`	Specifies a String value for a tag
`PageContext`	Provides access to all the namespaces and page attributes associated with a JSP page

Let's discuss the BodyContent class of the tag extension API.

The BodyContent Class

The BodyContent class is a subclass of the JspWriter class and encapsulates the evaluation of the body of an action. This class does not contain any actions; instead, contains only the result of invocation of the actions.

The BodyContent class contains several methods to read its contents, convert the content into String, and clear the contents. The buffer size of the BodyContent class is not limited. You should note that the autoFlush property cannot be enabled for this class because no backup stream is available for this class. To create instances of the BodyContent class, you can use either the pushBody() or popBody() method of the PageContext class.

Table 8.10 describes various methods of the BodyContent class:

Table 8.10: Describing the Methods of the BodyContent Class

Method	Description
`Reader getReader()`	Returns the value of the BodyContent object as a Reader object.
`String getString()`	Returns the value of the BodyContent object as a String.
`void writeOut(Writer out)`	Writes the contents of the BodyContent object into a Writer object. If an I/O error occurs while writing the contents of the BodyContent object into the given Writer object, the IOException exception is thrown.
`JspWriter getEnclosingWriter()`	Returns the enclosing JspWriter object.
`void clearBody()`	Clears the body of the buffer without throwing any exceptions.

Let's discuss the BodyTagSupport class of the tag extension API.

The BodyTagSupport Class

The BodyTagSupport class implements the BodyTag interface and acquires all the methods of the BodyTag interface with some additional methods of its own. This class acts as a base class to create tag handlers without defining each method of the BodyTag interface.

Table 8.11 describes the methods of the BodyTagSupport class:

Table 8.11: Describing the Methods of the BodyTagSupport Class

Method	Description
`BodyContent getBodyContent()`	Returns the current BodyContent object.
`int doAfterBody()`	Determines whether or not to re-evaluate the body of a custom tag. When the doAfterBody() method returns the EVAL_BODY_AGAIN field, the body of a custom tag is re-evaluated. In case, it returns the SKIP_BODY field, the body content is not evaluated. If an error occurs while processing the doAfterBody() method, the JspException exception is thrown.
`int doEndTag()`	Processes the end tag and returns the EVAL_PAGE field. If an error occurs while processing the doEndTag() method, the JspException exception is thrown.
`int doStartTag()`	Returns the EVAL_BODY_BUFFERED field after the execution of the start tag. If an error occurs while processing the start tag, the JspException exception is thrown.
`JspWriter getPreviousOut()`	Returns the enclosing JspWriter object from the bodyContent object.
`void doInitBody()`	Prepares to evaluate the body of a custom tag before evaluating the body for the first time. If an error occurs while processing the custom tag, the JspException exception is thrown.
`void release()`	Releases any acquired resources.
`void setBodyContent(BodyContent b)`	Sets the body content of the custom tag.

The `BodyTagSupport` class provides a single field, namely, `bodyContent`, which specifies the body content for the tag handler.

The FunctionInfo Class

The `FunctionInfo` class provides information about a function defined in the tag library. This class is instantiated from the TLD file and is available only at the time of translation of a JSP page.

Table 8.12 describes the methods of the `FunctionInfo` class:

Table 8.12: Describing the Methods of the FunctionInfo Class

Method	Description
`String getFunctionClass()`	Returns the class of a function
`String getFunctionSignature()`	Returns the signature of a function
`String getName()`	Returns the name of a function

The JspFragment Class

The `JspFragment` class encapsulates the JSP code in an object that can be invoked multiple times. This class is generated manually either by the page author or by the TLD file.

NOTE

Page author is responsible for developing the JSP page and decides which directives and actions should be used in the JSP page.

Table 8.13 describes the methods of the `JspFragment` class:

Table 8.13: Describing Methods of the JspFragment Class

Method	Description
`JspContext getJspContext()`	Returns the `JspContext` object that is used by the current `JspFragment` object at the time of invocation of the tag
`void invoke(Writer out)`	Executes the `JspFragment` object and passes all the output to the `Writer` or `JspWriter` object that is obtained from the `getOut()` method of the `JspContext class`

The SimpleTagSupport Class

The `SimpleTagSupport` class implements the `SimpleTag` interface. This class provides the definition for all the implemented methods of the `SimpleTag` interface and eliminates the need to define each method in a simple tag handler.

Table 8.14 describes the methods of the `SimpleTagSupport` class:

Table 8.14: Describing the Methods of the SimpleTagSupport Class

Method	Description
`void doTag()`	Processes a simple tag handler. The `JspException` exception is thrown to indicate that an error has occurred while processing the simple tag handler. The `SkipPageException` exception is thrown, if the JSP page that invoked the custom tag has to cease evaluation. A simple tag handler generated from a tag file must throw this exception if an invoked classic tag handler returns the `SKIP_PAGE` field or the `SkipPageException` exception.
`JspTag findAncestorWithClass(JspTag from, Class class)`	Returns the nearest instance of the class specified as a parameter to the `SimpleTagSupport` class. The `findAncestorWithClass()` method uses the `getParent()` method from the `Tag` or `SimpleTag` interface for coordination among cooperating tags.
`JspFragment getJspBody()`	Returns a fragment that encapsulates the body passed by the container through the `setJspBody()` method.

Table 8.14: Describing the Methods of the SimpleTagSupport Class

Method	Description
`JspContext getJspContext()`	Returns the page context passed by the container through the `setJspContext` object.
`JspTag getParent()`	Returns the parent tag of a simple tag on which the `getParent()` method is called for collaboration purposes.
`void setJspBody(JspFragment jspBody)`	Stores the specified `JspFragment` object that encapsulates the body of the custom tag. The `setJspBody()` method is not called if the body of a simple tag is empty.
`void setJspContext(JspContext pc)`	Stores the provided JSP context in the private `JspContext` field. A sub class can access JspContext through the `getJspContext()` method.
`void setParent(JspTag parent)`	Sets the parent tag of the simple tag for collaboration purposes. The `setParent()` method is invoked when a simple tag is invoked within another tag invocation.

Let's now discuss the `TagAdapter` class.

The TagAdapter Class

The `TagAdapter` class allows collaboration between classic tag handlers and simple tag handlers. The `TagAdapter` class wraps the functionality of a simple tag handler in an object of type, `TagAdapter` class. The wrapped object of a simple tag handler is passed to the `setParent()` method of the `Tag` interface. To retrieve the instance of the `SimpleTag` interface, the classic tag handler needs to invoke the `getAdaptee()` method. The classic tag handlers use the functionality of the wrapped object of simple tag handler with the help of the `Tag` interface. The constructor of the `TagAdapter` class creates a new `TagAdapter` object that wraps the given instance of a simple tag and returns the parent tag when the `getParent()` method is invoked.

Table 8.15 describes the methods of the `TagAdapter` class:

Table 8.15: Describing the Methods of the TagAdapter Class

Method	Description
`JspTag getAdaptee()`	Gets an instance of simple tag handler that is being adapted to the `Tag` interface
`Tag getParent()`	Returns the parent of the simple tag

The tag extension API contains classes that provide translation-time information for processing custom tags in a JSP page. The classes that provide translation-time processing information are `TagLibraryInfo`, `TagInfo`, `TagFileInfo`, `TagAttributeInfo`, TagExtraInfo, and `PageData`.

The TagLibraryInfo Class

The `TagLibraryInfo` class provides translation-time information associated with a `taglib` directive and TLD. Table 8.16 describes the methods of the `TagLibraryInfo` class:

Table 8.16: Describing the Methods of the TagLibraryInfo Class

Method	Description
`FunctionInfo getFunction(String name)`	Returns the information of a specified function by searching all the functions in a tag library. The `getFunction()` method returns null if the specified function does not exist.
`FunctionInfo[] getFunctions()`	Returns an array of all the functions that are defined in a tag library. The `getFunctions()` method returns a zero length array if no functions are defined in the tag library.
`String getInfoString()`	Returns the information (documentation) of TLD as a String value.
`String getPrefixString()`	Returns the name (prefix) of custom action that is assigned in the `taglib` directive.
`String getReliableURN()`	Returns Uniform Resource Name (URN) specified in the uri element of

Table 8.16: Describing the Methods of the TagLibraryInfo Class	
Method	**Description**
	TLD.
String getRequiredVersion()	Determines the required version of the JSP container as a String.
String getShortName()	Returns the prefix as indicated in TLD.
TagInfo getTag(String shortname)	Returns the TagInfo object for the specified tag name by searching through all the tags in a tag library. The getTag() method returns null if the specified tag is not found.
TagFileInfo getTagFile(String shortname)	Returns the TagFileInfo object for the specified tag name by looking through all the tag files in a tag library. The getTagFile() method returns null if the tag with the specified shortname is not found.
TagFileInfo[] getTagFiles()	Returns an array describing the tag files that are defined in a tag library. The getTagFiles() method returns zero length array if the tag library defines no tag files.
TagInfo getTags()	Returns an array describing the tags that are defined in tag library. The getTags() method returns a zero length array if no tags are defined in the tag library.
String getURI()	Returns the String value associated with the uri attribute of the taglib directive for the current library.

Table 8.17 describes the fields of the TagLibraryInfo class:

Table 8.17: Describing the Fields of the TagLibraryInfo Class	
Fields	**Description**
functions	Specifies an array describing the functions that are defined in a tag library
info	Specifies the information (documentation) for the TLD file
jspversion	Specifies the version of the JSP specification in which the tag library is written
prefix	Specifies the prefix assigned to the taglib from the taglib directive
shortname	Specifies the preferred short name (prefix) as indicated in TLD
tagFiles	Returns an array of the TagFileInfo type containing the tag files of a tag library
tags	Returns an array of the TagInfo class that provides the description of tags in the current tag library
tlibversion	Specifies the version of a tag library
uri	Specifies the String value associated with the uri attribute of the taglib directive for the current tag library
urn	Specifies the reliable URN indicated in TLD

The TagInfo Class

The TagInfo class provides information of a specific tag provided in a tag library. The TagInfo class is an instance of TLD.

Table 8.18 describes the methods of the TagInfo class:

Table 8.18: Describing the Methods of the TagInfo Class	
Method	**Description**
TagAttributeInfo[] getAttributes()	Returns an array of tag attributes, which are defined in TLD. The getAttributeInfo() method returns zero length array if the tag has no attributes.
String getBodyContent()	Returns the body content of the tag as a String value.
String getDisplayName()	Returns the short name of the tag.
String getInfoString()	Returns the information of the tag as a String value.

Table 8.18: Describing the Methods of the TagInfo Class

Method	Description
`String getLargeIcon()`	Returns the path to a large icon.
`String getSmallIcon()`	Returns the path to a small icon.
`String getTagClassName()`	Returns the name of the tag handler class for the current tag.
`TagExtraInfo getTagExtraInfo()`	Returns the `TagExtraInfo` instance for extra tag information.
`TagLibraryInfo getTagLibrary()`	Returns the instance of the `TagLibraryInfo` class.
`String getTagName()`	Returns the name of tag.
`TagVariableInfo[] getTagVariableInfos()`	Returns an array of the `TagVariableInfo` objects that are corresponding to the variables specified by this tag; otherwise, returns a zero length array, if no variables are specified.
`VariableInfo[] getVariableInfo(TagData data)`	Returns information on the scripting objects created by the tag at runtime.
`boolean hasDynamicAttributes()`	Specifies whether or not the tag handler supports dynamic attributes. The `hasDynamicAttributes()` method returns true if the tag handler supports dynamic attributes.
`boolean isValid(TagData data)`	Specifies whether or not the instance of the `TagData` class passed as a parameter is valid.
`void setTagExtraInfo(TagExtraInfo tei)`	Sets extra tag information by setting the instance of the `ExtraTagInfo` class.
`void setTagLibrary(TagLibraryInfo tl)`	Sets the `TagLibraryInfo` element as it is dependent on TLD information as well as on specific tag library instance.
`ValidationMessage[] validate(TagData data)`	Performs translation-time validation of the specified `TagData` instance and returns an array of the `ValidationMessage` class. The `validate()` method returns a zero length array if no error occurs while validating the `TagData` instance.

Table 8.19 describes the field of the `TagInfo` class:

Table 8.19: Describing the Fields of the TagInfo Class

Field	Description
`BODY_CONTENT_EMPTY`	Assigns a static constant for the `getBodyContent()` method when the body content is empty
`BODY_CONTENT_JSP`	Assigns a static constant for the `getBodyContent()` method when the body content is in JSP
`BODY_CONTENT_SCRIPTLESS`	Assigns a static constant for the `getBodyContent()` method when the body content is scriptless
`BODY_CONTENT_TAG_DEPENDENT`	Assigns a static constant for the `getBodyContent()` method when the body content is tag dependent

The TagFileInfo Class

The `TagFileInfo` class provides information about a tag file in a tag library. TLD instantiates the `TagFileInfo` class and is available only at translation-time. The following code snippet shows the constructor of the `TagFileInfo` class:

```
TagFileInfo(name, path, TagInfo)
```

The TagFileInfo class should be instantiated only from the tag library code, which is used for parsing a TLD in a JSP page. The following parameters are supplied to the constructor of the TagFileInfo class:

- **name** – Specifies a unique name for a tag
- **path** – Specifies a path to locate the .tag file implementing the `TagFileInfo` class
- **TagInfo** – Specifies the information about a tag

Table 8.20 describes the methods of the TagFileInfo class:

Table 8.20: Describing the Methods of the TagFileInfo Class	
Method	**Description**
`String getName()`	Returns a unique action name of the tag
`String getPath()`	Returns a path to locate the .tag file
`TagInfo getTagInfo()`	Returns a `TagInfo` object containing the information about the tag

The TagAttributeInfo Class

The `TagAttributeInfo` class contains information about tag attributes and this information is available at translation-time. TLD instantiates the `TagAttributeInfo` class, which has ID as its attribute. This ID attribute specifies a String value for a custom tag.

Table 8.21 describes the methods of the `TagAttributeInfo` class:

Table 8.21: Describing the Methods of the TagAttributeInfo Class	
Methods	**Description**
`boolean canBeRequestTime()`	Returns true if an attribute can hold a request-time value.
`TagAttributeInfo getIdAttribute(TagAttributeInfo[] a)`	Returns the `TagAttributeInfo` reference with name `id`. The `getIdAttribute()` method goes through an array of `TagAttributeInfo objects` and searches the specific `id`.
`String getName()`	Returns the name of the attribute.
`String getTypeName()`	Returns the type of attribute as String.
`boolean isFragment()`	Returns true if a tag attribute represents the `JspFragment` class.
`boolean isRequired()`	Returns true if the attribute is required.
`String toString()`	Returns a `String` representation of the current `TagAttributeInfo` object.

The TagExtraInfo Class

The `TagExtraInfo` class provides a mechanism to validate custom tags using tag attributes in TLD. You can use this class to either specify that the tag is defining scripting variables or to perform the translation-time validation of the tag attributes. The JSP translator ensures that the initial value returned by the getTagInfo() method is according to the TagInfo object for the tag being translated.

Table 8.22 describes the methods of the `TagExtraInfo` class:

Table 8.22: Describing the Methods of the TagExtraInfo Class	
Method	**Description**
`TagInfo getTagInfo()`	Returns the `TagInfo` object of the custom tag.
`VariableInfo[] getVariableInfo(TagData data)`	Returns an array of scripting variables defined by the specified tag. The `getVariableInfo()` method returns a zero length array, if no scripting variables are defined.
`boolean isValid(TagData data)`	Returns whether or not the specified `TagData` instance is valid.
`void setTagInfo(TagInfo tagInfo)`	Sets the specified `TagInfo` for the custom tag handler.
`ValidationMessages[] validate(TagData data)`	Returns an array of the `ValidationMessages` object, which is the result of the translation-time validation of attributes. The `validate()` method returns a null object or a zero length array in case of no errors.

The PageData Class

The `PageData` class provides the translation-time information on a JSP page. This information corresponds to the XML view of the JSP page. Objects of the `PageData` class are generated by the JSP translator, when being passed to a `TagLibraryValidator` instance. The `PageData` class provides a single method, i.e.

getInputStream(), which returns an input stream of a JSP page in the form of XML and the Stream encoding is done in UTF-8.

NOTE

UTF stands for Unicode Transformation Format.

The VariableInfo Class

The VariableInfo class determines the type of the scripting variables that are created or modified by a tag at runtime. Values for the scripting variables are assigned from scoped attributes. These scripting variables cannot be of primitive data types. In the object of the VariableInfo class, you can either provide fully qualified class name or short class name. You should ensure that when fully qualified class name is given, the specified class should be provided in the classpath of the Web application. If short class name is given in the VariableInfo objects, it should be in the context of the import directives of a JSP page and the classpath should remain in the Web application.

Table 8.23 describes the methods of the VariableInfo class:

Table 8.23: Describing the Methods of the VariableInfo Class

Method	Description
String getClassName()	Returns the type of the specified scripting variable
boolean getDeclare()	Declares a scripting variable during runtime
int getScope()	Returns the scope of the variable, such as AT_BEGIN, AT_END, or NESTED
String getVarName()	Returns the name of the scripting variable

Table 8.24 describes the fields of the VariableInfo class:

Table 8.24: Describing the Fields of the VariableInfo Class

Field	Description
AT_BEGIN	Specifies the scope information of scripting variable, which is visible after the execution of the start tag.
AT_END	Specifies the scope information of scripting variable, which is visible after the execution of the end tag.
NESTED	Specifies the scope information of scripting variable, which is visible only within the start/end tags.

The TagData Class

The object of the TagData class is used as an argument in the validate(), isValid(), getVariableInfo() methods of the TagExtraInfo class at the translation-time.

Table 8.25 describes the methods of the TagData class:

Table 8.25: Describing the Methods of the TagData Class

Method	Description
Object getAttribute(String attName)	Returns the value associated with an attribute. If a static value is specified with the attribute, then this method returns a different value specified in the tag. If a value is not specified, then this method returns null.
Enumeration<String> getAttributes()	Returns an enumeration of the attributes specified with respect to the TagData class.
String getAttributeString(String attName)	Returns the value of a given attribute.
String getId()	Returns the value of an id attribute of a tag, or null if no such attribute exists.
void setAttribute(String attName, Object value)	Sets the value of an attribute.

The TagData class provides a single field, REQUEST_TIME_VALUE, which specifies a value as a request time expression. The tag extension API provides classes, such as TagLibraryValidator and ValidationMessage to validate a JSP page.

The TagLibraryValidator Class

The TagLibraryValidator class validates a JSP page during the translation-time and performs the validation on the XML representation of the JSP page. This class provides an important method, validate() to validate the page. The JSP engine calls the validate () method while compiling the JSP page using the taglib directive. The validate(String prefix, String uri, PageData page) method contains three parameters, prefix, uri, and page. The first two parameters are used to indicate how a tag library is mapped in the JSP page, while the last parameter is used to represent the XML view of the page being validated. The validate() method returns the list of sources of errors if the page is not valid; otherwise, it returns null in case it is valid.

Table 8.26 describes the methods of the TagLibraryValidator class:

Table 8.26: Describing the Methods of the TagLibraryValidator Class

Method	Description
Map<String, Object> getInitParameters()	Returns the init parameters data as the Map object (key-value pair).
void release()	Releases any data kept by the instance of the TagLibraryValidator class for validation purposes.
void setInitParameters(Map<String, Object> map)	Sets the init parameter as the name-value pair in TLD for the TagLibraryValidator object.
ValidationMessage[] validate(String prefix, String uri, PageData page)	Allows you to validate a JSP page. The validate() method is invoked once for every unique tag library URI in the XML. If a page is valid, then this method returns null; otherwise, it returns an array of the ValidationMessage objects.

The ValidationMessage Class

A validation message is a piece of information that is provided by either the TagLibraryValidator or the TagExtraInfo object. A JSP container supports the <jsp:id> tag for high quality validation errors. This container tracks all the JSP pages passed to it and provides them a unique id, which is similar to the value of the <jsp:id> attribute. Each XML element in the XML view is recognized by this attribute. Then, this attribute can be used by the TagLibraryValidator class in one or more ValidationMessage object's attribute. The JSP container can also use this ValidationMessage object to retrieve information about the location of errors.

Table 8.27 describes the methods of the ValidationMessage class:

Table 8.27: Describing the Methods of the ValidationMessage Class

Method	Description
String getId()	Returns the <jsp:id> attribute. However, if there is no information about the ValidationMessage object, a null value is returned.
String getMessage()	Returns the localized validation message.

Let's now create an application for classic tag handlers in the next section.

Working with Classic Tag Handlers

A classic tag handler is a Java class that implements the Tag, IterationTag, or BodyTag interface. The implementation class instantiates a tag handler object or reuses an existing tag handler object for each action provided in the JSP page. The handler object is responsible for the interaction between the JSP page and additional server-side objects.

Exploring the Life Cycle of Classic Tag Handlers

The life cycle of a classic tag handler begins with the creation of a tag handler instance. Context setting as well as parent setting is also a part of the life cycle process of a tag handler. A classic tag handler goes through the following seven phases in its life-time:

- **Tag handler instance creation**–Refers to a phase in which a JSP engine finds a new tag in the JSP page and creates an instance of the tag handler to handle the tag. This instance is then pooled by the container to be reused whenever the tag needs to be invoked.
- **Context setting**—Refers to a phase in which the tag handler instance is made aware of its execution environment. This is done by passing a reference of the current PageContext method to the tag handler instance through the setPageContext() method.
- **Parent setting**—Refers to the phase in which nesting of classic tags is possible as tag handlers can communicate with each other. For example, a nested tag can ask its parent tag for information; therefore, the setParent() method is invoked and the reference of parent tag is passed to the closest tag handler. In case of the non nested tag handler, a null value is passed to the tag handler.
- **Executing doStartTag() method**—Refers to the phase in which the JSP engine processes the start tag for the instance of tag handler. This method is invoked by the JSP page implementation object. This method returns the following constants to determine whether the tag body should be evaluated or not:
  - **SKIP_BODY**—Indicates the JSP engine to skip the body content of the tag. The SKIP_BODY field is returned in case of an empty tag. The body of the tag is skipped and the doEndTag() method is called to close the tag.
  - EVAL_BODY_INCLUDE—Indicates a constant returned by the doStartTag() method of the tag handler that implements the Tag interface, if the body of a tag needs to be evaluated.
  - EVAL_BODY_TAG—Indicates a constant that is used to evaluate the body content of the tag. This is generally used if the tag implements the BodyTag interface or extends the BodyTagSupport class.
- **Executing doEndTag() method**—Refers to the phase in which the doEndTag() method is invoked to close all the connections made in the JSP page. The tag handler calls this method to complete any server-side work and is also used to write the output in the JspWriter object. The tag handler can directly write the output generated by the pageContext.getOut() to the JspWriter object. The output can also be written to the enclosing writer by using the popBody() method in the pageContext. The following two constants are retrieved from the method to control the flow of evaluation:
  - EVAL_PAGE— Represents the constant that is used to continue the processing of the JSP page.
  - SKIP_PAGE—Represents the constant that is used to force the JSP engine to skip the evaluation of the page.
- **Releasing State**—Refers to the phase in which the release() method is invoked to de-reference all the instances made by the tag handler and also to perform garbage collection.

Implementing Classic Tags

To understand how the classic tag handler is implemented, let's create a tag handler class, a TLD file, and a JSP file. Let's create a Tag class, CustomMessage.java, which extends the BodyTagSupport class that returns a message. The following are the broad-level steps to develop the classicTag application:

- Creating the tag handler for the classicTag application
- Creating TLD for the classicTag application
- Creating the home.html file for the classicTag application
- Creating the JSP file for the classicTag application
- Configuring the web.xml file for the classicTag application
- Defining the directory structure of the classicTag application
- Packaging, running, and deploying the classicTag application

Now, let's discuss each of these steps in detail.

Creating the Tag Handler for the classicTag Application

The tag handler contains the functionality of the tag coded inside it. Listing 8.1 provides the code for tag handler file, `CustomMessage.java` (save the `CustomMessage.java` file in the `\classicTag\src\com\kogent\tags` folder):

Listing 8.1: Showing the Code of the `CustomMessage.java` File

```
package com.kogent.tags;
import javax.servlet.ServletRequest;
import javax.servlet.jsp.tagext.*;

public class CustomMessage extends BodyTagSupport
{
   private static final long serialVersionUID = 1L;
   public void setParamName(String s)
   {
          pname=s;
   }
   public String getParamName()
   {
          return pname;
   }
   public int doStartTag()
   {
          ServletRequest req=pageContext.getRequest();

          String pvalue=req.getParameter(pname);
          if ((pvalue.equals("japan")) || (pvalue.equals("Japan")))
          {
                 return EVAL_BODY_INCLUDE;
          }
          else
          {

                 return SKIP_BODY;
          }
   } //doStartTag//doStartTag
   public int doAfterBody()
   {
          return SKIP_BODY;
   }//doAfterBody

   public int doEndTag()
   {
          return EVAL_PAGE;
   }//doEndTag

   String pname;
}
```

In Listing 8.1, a classic tag handler class (`CustomMessage`) is created by extending the `BodyTagSupport` class to define the behavior of the `CustomMessage` tag, which is an empty tag. The JSP container starts the processing of a custom tag by invoking the `doStartTag()` method of the tag handler class. The `doStartTag()` method returns the `SKIP_BODY` constant to skip the execution of the body of the tag. After the successful execution of the `doStartTag()` method, the `doEndTag()` method is invoked that returns the `EVAL_PAGE` constant to evaluate the rest of the JSP page.

Creating TLD for the classicTag Application

All the custom tags must be declared in TLD. Listing 8.2 shows the declaration of the `CustomMessage` tag in the `CustomTags.tld` file (save the `CustomTags.tld` file in the `\classicTag\WEB-INF` folder):

Listing 8.2: Showing the Code of the `CustomTags.tld` File

```
<?xml version="1.0" ?>
<taglib version="2.1" xmlns="http://xmlns.jcp.org/xml/ns/javaee"
xmlns:xsi="http://www.w3.org/2001/XMLSchema-instance"
xsi:schemaLocation="http://xmlns.jcp.org/xml/ns/javaee/web-jsptaglibrary_2_1.xsd">
   <jsp-version>2.3</jsp-version>
```

```
<tlib-version>1.1</tlib-version>
<short-name>tag</short-name>

<tag>
        <name>check</name>
        <tag-class>com.kogent.tags.CustomMessage</tag-class>
        <body-content>JSP</body-content>

        <attribute>
                <name>paramName</name>
                <required>true</required>
                <rtexprvalue>false</rtexprvalue>
        </attribute>
</tag>
</taglib>
```

In Listing 8.2, a TLD file, `CustomTags.tld`, is created where the classic tag named check is declared. TLD contains a parent tag named `<tag>` containing various child tags, such as `<name >`, <tag-class>, and `<body-content>`. The `<name>` tag is used to specify a name to the tag; whereas, the `<tag-class>` specifies a tag handler class encapsulating the functionality. Lastly, the `<body-content>` tag specifies whether the tag is empty or not. The `<body-content>` has been set to JSP, as the tag used in Listing 8.3 is not empty.

Creating the home.html File for the classicTag Application

The `classicTag` application displays the `home.html` file as the home page, which contains a `check` button. When a user clicks the checks button, the control is sent to the `TestPage.jsp` file, which further processes the client request. Listing 8.3 shows the source code for the `home.html` file (save the `home.html` file in the `\classicTag` folder):

Listing 8.3: Showing the `home.html` File

```
<html>
   <body>
        <form action="TestPage.jsp">
                <b> PREDICT AND WIN!!!!</b>
                <BR/>
                <BR/>
                <p style="color:blue">The country which is known as "land of rising
                sun"</p>
                <input type="text" name="opt"/>
                <input type="submit" value="check"/>
        </form>
   </body>
</html>
```

Let's now create the JSP file for the `classicTag` application.

Creating the JSP File for the classicTag Application

When the JSP container finds a custom tag in the JSP page, it searches for TLD in the `\WEB-INF` folder and executes the custom tag. The JSP file is created to use the custom tag by importing the tag library using the `taglib` directive. The code for the `TestPage.jsp` file is shown in Listing 8.4 (save the `TestPage.jsp` file in the `\classicTag` folder):

Listing 8.4: Showing the `TestPage.jsp` File

```
<%@taglib uri="/WEB-INF/CustomTags.tld" prefix="tag"%>
<html>
   <body>
        <tag:check paramName = "opt">
                <b>congratulations you have won a prize!!!</b>
        </tag:check>
   </body>
</html>
```

In Listing 8.4, the `TestPage.jsp` file imports a tag library using the **`taglib`** directive. It then uses the `<CustomMessage>` tag to access the message associated with the `CustomMessage` tag.

Configuring the web.xml File for the classicTag Application

Configure the `web.xml` file for classic tags and set `home.html` as the welcome file, as shown in Listing 8.5 (save the web.xml file in the `\classicTag\WEB-INF` folder):

Listing 8.5: Showing the `web.xml` File for the `classicTag` Application

```
<?xml version="1.0" encoding="UTF-8"?>
<web-app version="3.1"
   xmlns="http://xmlns.jcp.org/xml/ns/javaee"
   xmlns:xsi="http://www.w3.org/2001/XMLSchema-instance"
   xsi:schemaLocation="http://xmlns.jcp.org/xml/ns/javaee
   http://xmlns.jcp.org/xml/ns/javaee/web-app_3_1.xsd">

   <welcome-file-list>
         <welcome-file>home.html</welcome-file>
   </welcome-file-list>
</web-app>
```

Defining the Directory Structure of the classicTag Application

After the files are created and the application is configured, you need to define the directory structure of the `classicTag` application. Figure 8.1 displays the directory structure of the `classicTag` application:

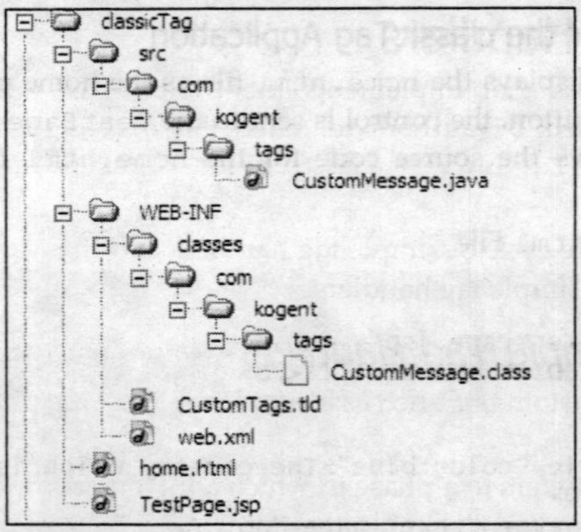

Figure 8.1: Showing the Directory Structure of the classicTag Application

Packaging, Running, and Deploying the classicTag Application

To package the `classicTag` application, you first need to create the `classicTag.war` file. Then, deploy this Web ARchive (WAR) file as a Web application on Glassfish Server 4.0. Browse `http://localhost:8080/classicTag` URL to run the classicTag application, as shown in Figure 8.2:

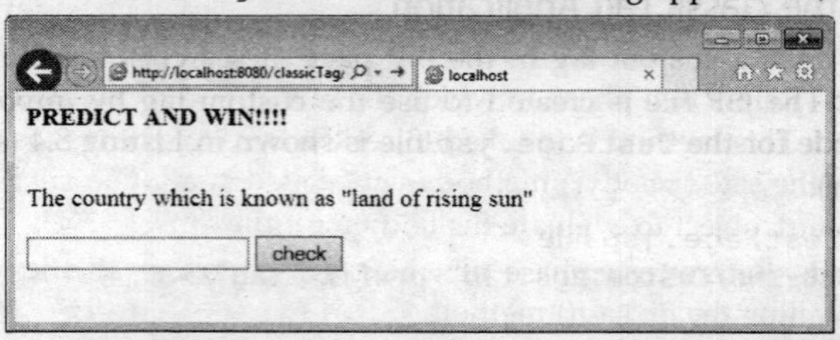

Figure 8.2: Displaying an HTML Page as the Home Page of the classicTag Application

In Figure 8.2, an HTML page that accepts a value from the user is displayed. In our case, we have entered Japan, as shown in Figure 8.3:

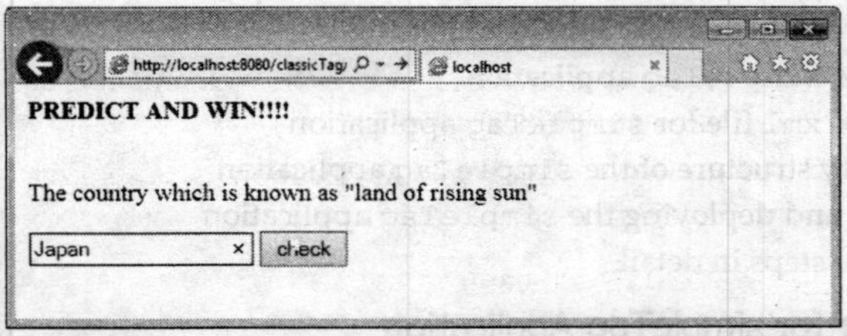

Figure 8.3: Showing the HTML Page when a User Clicks the check Button

If the user enters the correct value, then a message is displayed, as shown in Figure 8.4:

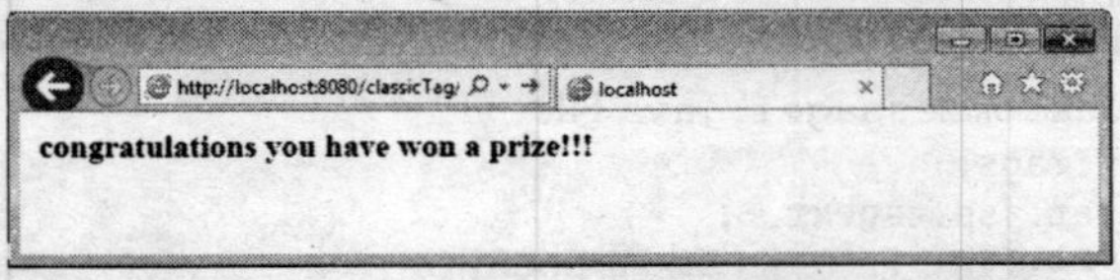

Figure 8.4: Showing an Output when an Answer Entered by a User is Correct

Now, let's create an application on simple tag handlers in the next section.

Working with Simple Tag Handlers

A simple tag handler is a Java class that implements the `SimpleTag` interface and has a no-argument constructor. This class is mainly used by authors to make the use of tags flexible in tag handlers. The `javax.servlet.jsp.tagext.SimpleTagSupport` class provides a default implementation of all the methods in simple tags.

In this section, let's first discuss the life cycle of simple tag handlers and then create the `simpleTag` application demonstrating the implementation of simple tag handlers.

Exploring the Life Cycle of Simple Tag Handlers

When a `JSP` container encounters a custom tag, such as a simple tag in a `JSP` page, it goes through the following phases:

- **Tag handler instance creation**—Refers to a phase in which a JSP engine finds a new tag in the JSP page and creates an instance of the tag handler to handle the tag. Unlike classic tag handlers, this instance of tag handler is never pooled by the container. Therefore, the instantiation of a tag is required, whenever a tag is invoked.
- **Context setting**—Refers to a phase in which the tag handler instance is made aware of its execution environment. This is done by passing the reference of current JspContext to the tag handler instance through the setJspContext() method.
- **Parent setting**—Refers to a phase in which `the setParent()` method is invoked on the tag handler instance.
- **Setting the Body Content**—Refers to a phase in which the set`JspBody`() method is called by the container, if a tag is not empty bodied. This method is invoked to set the body of the tag, as a `JspFragment` object. If a tag is empty in the page, the set`JspBody`() method is not called at all. The tag handler calls the `invoke()` method on the `JspFragment` object to evaluate the body multiple times.
- **Executing doTag() method**—Refers to a phase in which evaluation of all the logic, iteration, and body content of a tag occurs by calling the `doTag`() method.

Implementing Simple Tag Handler

Let's now create an application, simpleTag, to understand the use of simple tags in a `JSP` page. Create a tag handler class, a TLD file, and a JSP file in the `simpleTag` application. The following are the broad-level steps to develop the `simpleTag` application:

- Creating a tag handler for `simpleTag` application

- Creating a TLD file for simpleTag application
- Creating a JSP file for simpleTag application
- Configuring the web.xml file for simpleTag application
- Defining the directory structure of the simpleTag application
- Packaging, running, and deploying the simpleTag application

Let's discuss each of these steps in detail.

Creating the Tag Handler for simpleTag Application

The tag handler for the simpleTag application contains the functionality of the tag coded inside it. The code for the tag handler is provided in the CustomMessage1.java file, as shown in Listing 8.6 (save the CustomMessage1.java file in the \simpleTag\src\com\kogent\tags folder):

Listing 8.6: Showing the CustomMessage1.java File

```
package com.kogent.tags;
import javax.servlet.jsp.tagext.*;
import javax.servlet.jsp.*;
import java.io.*;
import java.util.Date;
public class CustomMessage1 extends SimpleTagSupport {
   public void doTag() throws JspException,IOException {
   JspContext context=getJspContext();
   JspWriter Out=context.getOut();
   Out.println("Welcome!!! You are visting this Web page on "+new Date());
   }
}
```

In Listing 8.6, the doTag() method of the SimpleTagSupport class creates the instance of the JspWriter object to generate a response. The println() method is used to print the message showing the current date and time on the browser. The object of the Date class is supplied as a parameter to the println() method to show the current date and time on the browser.

Creating TLD for the simpleTag Application

You can create a TLD file for the simpleTag application to make an entry of the custom tag. The code for TLD, CustomTags.tld is shown in Listing 8.7 (save the CustomTags.tld file in the /simpleTag/WEB-INF folder):

Listing 8.7: Showing the CustomTags.tld File

```
<?xml version="1.0" ?>
<taglib version="2.1" xmlns="http://xmlns.jcp.org/xml/ns/javaee"
   xmlns:xsi="http://www.w3.org/2001/XMLSchema-instance"
xsi:schemaLocation="http://xmlns.jcp.org/xml/ns/javaee/web-jsptaglibrary_2_1.xsd">
   <jsp-version>2.3</jsp-version>
   <tlib-version>1.1</tlib-version>
   <short-name>tag</short-name>
   <tag>
           <name>CustomMessage1</name>
           <tag-class>com.kogent.tags.CustomMessage1</tag-class>
           <body-content>empty</body-content>
   </tag>
</taglib>
```

In Listing 8.7, a TLD named, CustomTags.tld, is created to reuse the functionality encapsulated in the CustomMessage1.java file. The CustomTags.tld file uses the tag named <tag>, which is the parent tag containing child tags, such as <name>, <tag-class>, and <body-content>. The <name> tag specifies the name of the custom tag. The <tag-class> tag specifies the tag handler class, which holds the functionality of the custom tag and the <body-content> tag that specifies whether or not the custom tag is empty.

The <body-content> tag is set to empty, as the tag used in Listing 8.8 is empty.

Creating the JSP File for the simpleTag Application

The JSP file for the `simpleTag` application is created to use the custom tag by importing the tag library using the `taglib` directive, as shown in Listing 8.8 (save the `test.jsp` file in the `\simpleTag` folder):

Listing 8.8: Showing the `test.jsp` File

```
<%@taglib uri="/WEB-INF/CustomTags.tld" prefix="tag"%>
<!DOCTYPE html>
<html>
   <head>
         </head>
   <body>
         <tag:CustomMessage1/><br>
   </body>
</html>
```

Configuring the web.xml File for the simpleTag Application

Now, configure the `web.xml` file for the `simpleTag` application and set the test.jsp file as the welcome file, as shown in Listing 8.9 (save the web.xml file in the `\simpleTag\WEB-INF` folder):

Listing 8.9: Showing the `web.xml` File for `simpleTag` Application

```
<?xml version="1.0" encoding="UTF-8"?>
<web-app version="3.1"
   xmlns="http://xmlns.jcp.org/xml/ns/javaee"
   xmlns:xsi="http://www.w3.org/2001/XMLSchema-instance"
   xsi:schemaLocation="http://xmlns.jcp.org/xml/ns/javaee
   http://xmlns.jcp.org/xml/ns/javaee/web-app_3_1.xsd">
   <welcome-file-list>
         <welcome-file>test.jsp</welcome-file>
   </welcome-file-list>
</web-app>
```

When the JSP container finds a custom tag in the JSP page, then it searches for the CustomTags.tld file in the WEB-INF directory and executes the tag.

Defining the Directory Structure of the simpleTag Application

After all the files are created and the `simpleTag` application is configured, you need to define the directory structure of the `simpleTag` application. Figure 8.5 displays the directory structure of the `simpleTag` application:

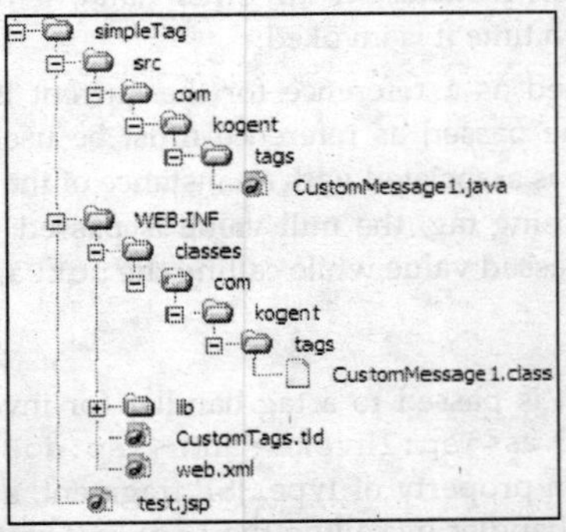

Figure 8.5: Displaying the Directory Structure of the simpleTag Application

Packaging, Running, and Deploying the simpleTag Application

You need to create the `simpleTag.war` file to package the `simpleTag` application and deploy this WAR file as a Web application on the Glassfish Server 4.0. Browse `http://localhost:8080/simpleTag` URL to run the application, as shown in Figure 8.6:

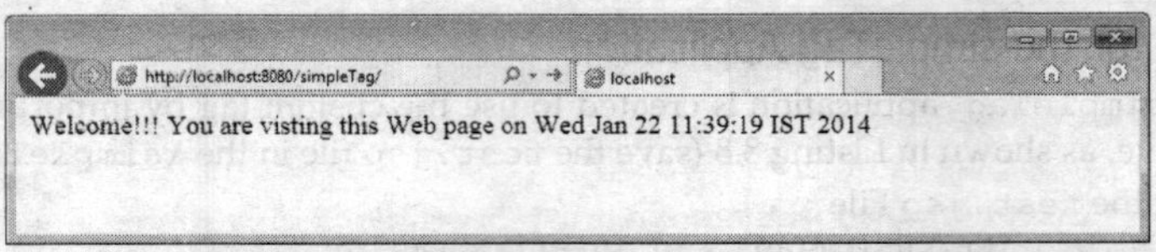

Figure 8.6: Showing a Simple Tag in a JSP Page

In Figure 8.6, the current time is displayed to the user accessing the JSP page with the help of a simple tag, named `CustomMessage1`.java. Now, let's discuss about JSP fragments in the next section.

Working with JSP Fragments

JSP fragments are portions of the JSP code in the `JspFragment` object, which can be invoked multiple times in an application. These fragments are configured either by specifying the `<jsp:attribute>` standard action in a tag file as a `fragment` type or as a body content of a simple tag.

The `JspFragment` instance is associated with the `JspContext` object of the current JSP page before being passed to a tag handler. This instance is also associated with the parent or simple tag instance, as whenever there is any custom action invoked from within a `JSP fragment`, the `setParent()` method can be called with an appropriate value. The `invoke()` method of the `JspFragment` class executes the body of the `JSP fragment` and directs the output to either the `Writer` or the `JspWriter` object returned by the `getOut()` method of the `JspContext` object associated with the fragment. The implementation of these methods might lead to the `JspException` exception, which must be handled by the tag handler itself. The following subsections describe the creation and invocation of a JSP fragment.

Creating a JSP Fragment

JSP fragments are created as an instance of a class that implements the `JspFragment` abstract class. This instance should be configured in such a manner that it produces the contents of the body of the fragment, when invoked. If the fragment specifies the body of a `<jsp:attribute>` action, then the fragment needs to evaluate the body of the `<jsp:attribute>` action each time the fragment is invoked. However, if the fragment defines the body of a simple tag, the behaviour of the fragment changes depending on the body content of the tag, whenever it is invoked. For example, if the body content is dependent on a tag, then the fragment must echo the contents of the body each time it is invoked. On the other hand, if the body content is scriptless, then the fragment must evaluate the body each time it is invoked.

The `JspFragment` instance is passed as a reference for the current JspContext. If the fragment requires to invoke a tag handler, then the value passed as reference must be used while calling the `setJspContext()` method. The `JspFragment` instance is associated with an instance of the tag handler of the nearest enclosing tag invocation. In case there is no enclosing tag, the null value is passed. Whenever the fragment invokes a tag handler, the fragment must use the passed value while calling the `setParent()` method.

Invoking a JSP Fragment

When the JSP fragment is created, it is passed to a tag handler for invocation. JSP fragments can be invoked either by using standard actions, such as`<jsp:invoke>` and `<jsp:doBody>` or by using a tag handler written in Java. The JSP fragment has a bean property of type, JSP fragment, and is passed to the tag handler. These fragments can be invoked in the tag handler by calling the `invoke()` method. The tag handler is responsible for setting the values of all the declared AT_BEGIN and NESTED variables in the calling page or in the JspContext of a tag.

If the <jsp:invoke> or `<jsp:doBody>` actions are used to invoke the JSP fragment, then you should specify a value for the `var` attribute and create the `Writer` object to expose the invocation as a String object. If the value for the `varReader` attribute is specified, a custom `Writer` object is created to expose the result of the invocation of the JSP fragment as a `Reader` object. During the invocation of the JSP fragment object, the JSP container:

- Specifies that before the execution of the fragment body, if a non-null value is assigned to the `Writer` object, the values of `JspContext.getOut()` method and implicit `out` object must be updated to send the output to the `Writer` object. The container must call the pushBody(writer) method on the current

JspContext object. In this method, the instance of the Writer class is passed to the fragment upon invocation, and the body of the fragment is evaluated.

- Specifies that if a classic tag handler is invoked and returns the SKIP_PAGE field as well as throws the SkipPageException exception, the JSP fragment must throw the SkipPageException exception implying that the calling page needs to be skipped for evaluation.
- Specifies that after a fragment is evaluated, an exception is thrown and the value of the JspContext.getOut() method must be restored by calling the popBody() method on the current JspContext object.
- Specifies that if the `<jsp:invoke>` or `<jsp:doBody>` action is used to invoke a fragment and the value for the var or varReader attribute is provided, then a scoped variable with a name similar to the value of the `var` or `varReader` attribute is created (or modified) in the page scope. In addition, this value is set to a `Reader` object that can invoke the fragment automatically.
- Specifies that when the evaluation of a tag is completed, then the tag discards the fragment instance associated with it so that it can be reused by the JSP container.

Exploring the JspFragment Class

The `JspFragment` class encapsulates an object with a portion of the JSP code that can be invoked multiple times in an application. JSP fragments can encapsulate these portions of the JSP code either as a body of a simple tag or as the `<jsp:attribute>` standard action. The `<jsp:attribute>` standard action specifies a fragment attribute. The definition of the JSP fragment contains template text and JSP action elements, and does not contain any scriptlets or scriptlet expressions. The `JspFragment` abstract class is an implementation of container at the translation time and is capable of executing the defined fragment.

A tag handler can invoke the fragment zero or more times or pass the fragment to other tags for the purpose of communicating the values to/from a `JspFragment` object. The tag handlers store/retrieve values from/in the `JspContext` associated with the fragment.

Table 8.28 describes the methods of the `JspFragment` class:

Table 8.28: Describing the Methods of the JspFragment Class

Method	Description
`JspContext getJspContext()`	Returns the `JspContext` object that is bound to the current `JspFragment` instance during invocation
`void invoke(Writer out)`	Executes the fragment and directs all output to the specified `JspWriter object` returned by the `getOut()` method of the `JspContext` class associated with the fragment

Now, let's discuss tag files that allow you to create custom tags by using the JSP syntax.

Working with Tag Files

`Tag` files allow you to build custom tags by using the JSP syntax. These files are translated into Java code automatically by the JSP container similar to the process of producing Java servlets from JSP pages. The tag files hide the complexity of building custom JSP tag libraries.

`Tag` files are imported in JSP pages by using the following syntax:

```
<%@taglib prefix=" " tagdir=" " %>
```

In the preceding syntax, `tagdir` specifies the path of the tag file and `the <prefix:tagFileName>` pattern is used to invoke tag files from JSP pages.

A tag file should have the `.tag` file extension so that it can be recognized by the JSP container. You can store the tag file in the `/WEB-INF/tags` directory of a Web application or in the `/WEB-INF` directory. The syntax used in the tag files is similar to that of the JSP pages. However, there are few differences in the tags used in the tag files and JSP pages. For example, the `<%@taglib%>` directive used in tag files is equivalent to the `<%@page%> directive used` in JSP pages.

Instead of declaring attributes and variables in a separate `.tld` file, the tag files use the `<%@attribute%>` and `<%@variable%>` directives to create attributes and variables. When a JSP page invokes a tag file, the custom tag that may have a body (between the <prefix:tagFileName> and </prefix:tagFileName> tags) is executed by the tag file with the help of the <jsp:doBody> standard action. The following tasks can be performed by using a tag file:

- Handling dynamic attributes in tag files
- Exporting variables from a tag file to a JSP page
- Using attributes to provide names for variables
- Invoking JSP fragments from tag files

Let's discuss these tasks one by one in detail.

Handling Dynamic Attributes in Tag Files

The JSP page invokes a tag file that accepts dynamic attributes by using the <shortname:tagfile> tag. A tag file accepts only declared attributes, by default. To support dynamic attributes, a tag file must use the <%@tag dynamic-attributes="varName"%> expression, which provides the name of the variable that holds all the dynamic attributes in the java.util.Map interface. The tag file iterates over the items of variables with the <c:forEach> action to retrieve the name and value of each attribute with the help of the ${variable.key} and ${variable.value} expressions. The tag file uses the <jsp:element> standard action to generate HTML elements whose names are obtained at runtime.

Exporting Variables from a Tag File to a JSP Page

A tag file exports the scopes of its local variables to the invoking JSP page by using the <%@variable%> directive. As each tag file has its own page scope, the local variables of the invoking page are not accessible in the invoked tag file and vice versa. The JSP page may use tag attributes and global variables to pass parameters to the invoked tag. The JSP container, for each attribute, creates a local variable in the page scope of the tag file that allows you to get an attribute's value by using the ${attributeName} constructs. Therefore, tag attributes act as parameters passed by value, while global variables act as parameters passed by reference.

The name of a variable can be specified in a tag file using <%@variable name-given="..."%>, or in a JSP page. The type of a variable can be indicated with <%@variable variable-class="..."%>.

After declaring a variable in a tag file with the <%@variable%> directive, you have to set its value by using the <c:set> tag. The JSP container creates another variable with the given name in the JSP page, and the second variable is initialized with the value of the corresponding variable from the tag file. Changing the value of the variable from the JSP page does not affect the corresponding variable from the tag file. However, the JSP container, updates the variable from the JSP page depending on the scope attribute from <%@variable%>, which can be either AT_BEGIN, NESTED or AT_END.

If scope is AT_END, the variable from the JSP page is initialized with the value of the tag file variable after the execution of the tag file.

If scope is AT_BEGIN, the variable from the JSP page is updated before the <jsp:doBody> and <jsp:invoke> tags and at the end of the execution of a tag file. If scope is NESTED, the JSP variable is updated only before the <jsp:doBody> and <jsp:invoke> tags with the value of the tag file variable. After the execution of the tag file, in the NESTED case, the JSP variable is restored to the value it had before the invocation of the tag file.

Using Attributes to Provide Names for Variables

Attributes are also used to provide names for variables in a tag file. Let's consider an example of the variableAttr.tag tag file defining a variable whose name is provided by a JSP page (variableAttr.jsp) as the value of a tag attribute (v). The tag file creates a variable by defining an alias (a) using <%@variable name-from-attribute="v" ... alias="a" ...%>.

The variableAttr.tag file sets the value of the variable with <c:set var="a" value="..."/>, outputs the name of the variable with ${v}, and outputs the value of the variable with ${a}. The variableAttr.jsp page invokes the tag file with <demo:variableAttr v="x"/> and works with the variable named x. The JSP container creates the x variable automatically, setting it to the value of a, which is 123.

The code for the variableAttr.tag file is shown in the following code snippet:

```
<%@attribute name="v" required="true" %>
<%@variable name-from-attribute="v"
  variable-class="java.lang.Long"
  alias="a" scope="AT_END" %>
<%@taglib prefix="c" uri="http://java.sun.com/jsp/jstl/core" %>
<c:set var="a" value="${123}"/>
<p> TAG: ${v} = ${a} </p>
```

The code for the variableAttr.jsp file is shown in the following code snippet:

```
<%@taglib prefix="demo" tagdir="/technology/WEB-INF/tags/demo" %>
<demo:variableAttr v="x"/>
<p> JSP: x = ${x} </p>
```

Let's now learn how to invoke JSP fragments from tag files.

Invoking JSP Fragments from Tag Files

The tag files support JspFragment attributes, which are used to invoke JSP fragments. To understand the invocation of JSP fragments, let's create a tag file, `fragmentAttr.tag` and a JSP page, `fragmentAttr.jsp`. The JSP page invokes the `fragmentAttr.tag` tag file with the help of the `<demo:fragmentAttr> tag` that provides two simple attributes (`attr1` and `attr2`) and a fragment attribute (template). All three attributes are declared in the tag file with `<%@attribute%>`. The template attribute is declared as a fragment attribute by using `fragment="true"` along with `<%@attribute%>`.

The tag file declares a nested variable (`data`) with `<%@variable%>`. The value of the variable is set by the tag file with `<c:set>`.

The code of the fragmentAttr.tag file is shown in the following code snippet:

```
<%@attribute name="template" fragment="true" %>
<%@attribute name="attr1" %>
<%@attribute name="attr2" %>
<%@variable name-given="data" scope="NESTED" %>
<%@taglib prefix="c" uri="http://java.sun.com/jsp/jstl/core" %>
<c:set var="data" value="${attr1}"/>
<jsp:invoke fragment="template"/>
<c:set var="data" value="${attr1} - ${attr2}"/>
<jsp:doBody/>
<c:set var="data" value="${attr2}"/>
<jsp:invoke fragment="template"/>
<c:set var="data" value="${attr2} - ${attr1}"/>
<jsp:doBody/>
```

The code of the fragmentAttr.jsp file is shown in the following code snippet:

```
<%@taglib prefix="demo" tagdir="/technology/WEB-INF/tags/demo" %>
<demo:fragmentAttr attr1="value1" attr2="value2">
  <jsp:attribute name="template">
        <p> Template: ${data} </p>
  </jsp:attribute>
  <jsp:body> <p> Body Content: ${data} </p> </jsp:body>
</demo:fragmentAttr>
```

In the preceding code snippet, the `<jsp:attribute>` and `<jsp:body>` standard actions are used to define the two JSP fragments , which are invoked from the tag file with `<jsp:invoke>` and `<jsp:doBody>`, respectively.

Now, let's recapitulate the topics covered in this chapter.

Summary

In this chapter, you have learned about the need and features of JSP tag extensions. Next, you have learned about the elements of JSP tag extensions and tag extension API, including classes and interfaces that are used to create the custom tags. The applications for simple tag handlers and classic tag handlers are also created in the chapter. Next, the chapter has explored the concept of fragments used in a JSP page. Finally, you have learned about tag files that are used to create custom tags using the JSP syntax.

In the next chapter, you learn about JavaServer Pages Standard Tag Library (JSTL), which provides custom tag libraries containing tags for conditional structures, iteration, internationalization, and HTTP manipulation, XML, and SQL statements.

Quick Revise

Q1. **……………………………… is a valid taglib directive.**

A. **<%taglib uri="/stats" prefix="stats"%>**
B. **<%@taglib uri="/stats" prefix="stats"%>**
C. **<%!taglib uri="/stats" prefix="stats"%>**
D. **<%taglib uri="/stats" prefix="stats"%>**
E. **<%@taglib name="/stats" prefix="stats"%>**

Ans. B

Q2. **Which of the following elements are the valid `<taglib>` elements in the `web.xml file`?**

A. **uri**
B. **taglib-uri**
C. **tagliburi**
D. **tag-uri**
E. **taglib-location**

Ans. B, E

Q3. **The………………….. interface is implemented by a tag handler to provide support for dynamic attributes.**

A. **DynamicAttributes**
B. **BodyTag**
C. **IterationTag**
D. **JspTag**

Ans. A

Q4. **Which of the following are valid return types of the `doAfterBody()` method of the Iteration-Tag interface?**

A. **EVAL_BODY_INCLUDE**
B. **`SKIP_BODY`**
C. **EVAL_PAGE**
D. **SKIP_PAGE**

Ans. B

Q5. **The ………………class validates a JSP page during translation-time and performs the validation on the xml representation of the JSP page.**

A. **TagLibraryValidator**
B. **TagData**
C. **FunctionInfo**
D. **TagVariableInfo**

Ans. A

Q6. **Which of the following are the life cycle phases of classic tag handlers?**

A. **Tag handler instance creation**
B. **Context setting**
C. **Executing doEndTag() method**
D. **Parent setting**
E. **All of the above**

Ans. E

Q7. **What is a tag handler?**

Ans. A tag handler is a Java class where a custom tag is defined. The JSP container invokes the tag handler object to evaluate a custom tag during the execution of a JSP page.

Q8. **What is the main difference between classic and simple tag handler?**

Ans. Classic tag handlers are cached and reused by container but simple tag handlers are not cached and reused by the containers.

Q9. **Which method of the simple tag handler is used to process the tag?**

Ans. doTag()

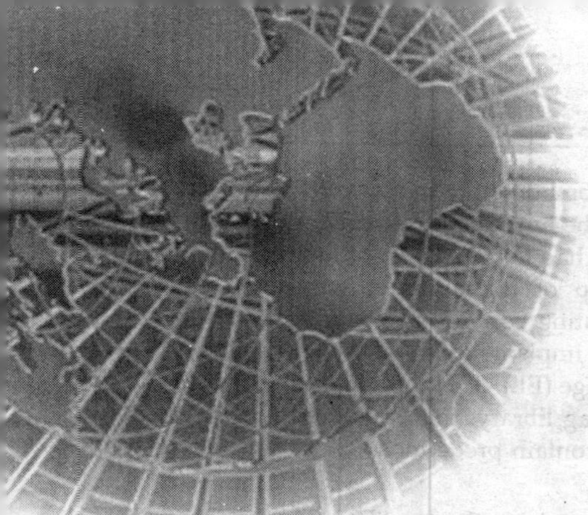

9

Implementing JavaServer Pages Standard Tag Library 1.2

JavaServer Pages Standard Tag Library (JSTL) was introduced as a component of the Java EE platform to enable Web designers to easily create JavaServer Pages (JSP) pages. Before the introduction of JSTL, Web designers had to extensively use scriptlets while creating JSP pages. Moreover, they had to spend a lot of time in coding custom tags. JSTL provides a solution to these problems with the help of tag libraries, which are capable of implementing common tasks, such as performing iteration, evaluating conditions, ensuring database access, processing Extensible Markup Language (XML) documents, and implementing internationalization, in JSP pages. JSTL also provides support for the unified Expression Language (EL). JSTL provides tag libraries such as the core tag library, the XML tag library, the internationalization tag library, the Structured Query Language (SQL) tag library, and the functions tag library. These tag libraries contain predefined sets of tags to use in JSP pages.

This chapter begins by providing an introduction to JSTL. Then it explains the tag libraries available in JSTL, including the core tag library, the XML tag library, the internationalization tag library, and the SQL tag library, and also explains how to implement these tag libraries.

Let's begin by introducing JSTL.

Introducing JSTL

Initially, Web designers used scriptlets in JSP pages to generate dynamic content. This resulted in readability issues and also made it difficult to maintain the JSP page. Custom tags were introduced to overcome the problems faced in using scriptlets. Although custom tags proved to be a better choice than scriptlets, they had certain limitations too. Web designers had to spend a lot of time in coding, packaging, and testing these tags before using them. This meant that Web designers were often left with little time to concentrate on the designing of Web pages.

The introduction of JSTL has helped Web designers overcome the shortcomings of custom tags, by encapsulating the common functionalities that the Web designer may need to develop Web pages. These functionalities included the use of tag libraries, such as core, SQL, and XML. JSTL is introduced particularly for those Web designers who are not well versed with Java programming. JSTL 1.2, introduced in the Java EE 5 platform, aligns with the unified EL. Note that the unified EL helps JavaServer Faces (JSF) to use JSTL tags. The same version of JSTL, i.e., JSTL 1.2, is used in the Java EE 7 platform as well.

Let's now learn about the features of JSTL.

Explaining the Features of JSTL

JSTL aims to provide an easy way to maintain JSP pages. The use of tags defined in JSTL has simplified the task of the designers to create Web pages. They can now simply use a tag related to the task that they need to implement in a JSP page. The main features of JSTL are as follows:

- Provides support for conditional processing and Uniform Resource Locator (URL)-related actions to process URL resources in a JSP page. You can also use the JSTL core tag library that provides iterator tags used to easily iterate through a collection of objects.
- Provides the XML tag library, which helps you to manipulate XML documents and perform actions related to conditional and iteration processing on parsed XML documents.
- Enables Web applications to be accessed globally by providing the internationalization tag library. Internationalization means that an application can be created to adapt to various locales so that people of different regions can access the application in their native languages. The internationalization tag library makes the implementation of localization in an application easy, fast, and effective.
- Enables interaction with relational databases by using various SQL commands. Web applications require databases to store information required for the application, which can be manipulated by using the SQL tag library provided by JSTL.
- Provides a series of functions to perform manipulations, such as checking whether an input String contains the substring specified as a parameter to a function, or returning the number of items in a collection, or the number of characters in a String. These functions can be used in an EL expression and are provided by the functions tag library.

Let's now explore JSTL tag libraries.

Exploring the Tag Libraries in JSTL

A tag library provides a number of predefined actions that bind functionalities to a specific JSP page. JSTL provides tag libraries that include a wide range of actions to perform common tasks. For example, if you want to access data from database, you can use SQL tag library in your application. JSTL is a standard tag library that is composed of five tag libraries. Each of these tag libraries represents separate functional areas and is used with a prefix. Table 9.1 describes the tag libraries available in JSTL:

Table 9.1: Tag Libraries in JSTL, with their Uniform Resource Identifier (URI) and Tag Prefix

Name of the Tag Library	Function	URI	Prefix
Core tag library	Variable support	http://java.sun.com/jsp/jstl/core	c
	Flow control		
	Iterator		
	URL management		
	Miscellaneous		
XML tag library	Core	http://java.sun.com/jsp/jstl/xml	x
	Flow control		
	Transformation		
Internationalization tag library	Locale	http://java.sun.com/jsp/jstl/fmt	fmt
	Message formatting		
	Number and date formatting		
SQL tag library	Database manipulation	http://java.sun.com/jsp/jstl/sql	sql
Functions tag library	Collection length	http://java.sun.com/jsp/jstl/functions	fn
	String manipulation		

After exploring the different tag libraries of JSTL, let's discuss these tag libraries in detail in the following sections.

Working with the Core Tag Library

The core tag library contains tags that are related to variables and flow control support in an application. For example, if you want to set the value of a variable, you can use the `<c:set>` tag of the core tag library. This library also provides a generic way to access URL-based resources. In addition, the core tag library specifies the content that can be included or processed within a JSP page.

Now, let's explore the different tags of the core tag library.

Exploring the Tags in the Core Tag Library

Let's discuss the tags available in the core tag library, based on their functionalities. Table 9.2 categorizes the tags of the core tag library based on their functionalities:

Table 9.2: Tags of the Core Tag Library

Function	Tag
Variable support	remove set
Flow control	choose when otherwise if

Table 9.2: Tags of the Core Tag Library

Function	Tag
Iterator	forEach forTokens
URL management	import param redirect param url param
Miscellaneous	catch

Next, we describe the functions of the core tag library in detail.

Describing the Variable Support Tags

JSTL provides the following tags for variable support in an application:

- The <c:set> tag
- The <c:remove> tag

The <c:set> Tag

The <c:set> tag sets the property and value of an EL variable in a JSP scope (i.e., page, request, session, or application). This tag also creates an EL variable, if the variable does not already exist.

The syntax of the <c:set> tag can be used in the following two ways:

- The <c:set> tag without body
- The <c:set> tag with body

The <c:set> Tag without Body

The following code snippet shows the use of the <c:set> tag without a body to set a value for a variable:

```
<c:set var="bookName" scope="session" value="Black Book:Java EE 7"/>
   <c:out value="${bookName}"/>
```

The preceding code snippet shows a value being set for the bookName variable by using the <c:set> tag. This tag does not contain the body element; however, the value of the bookName variable is set with the help of a value attribute.

The <c:set> Tag with Body

Variables can be set by using the <c:set> tag within the body of another tag, as shown in the following code snippet:

```
<c:set var="bookName">
Black Book:Java EE 7
</c:set>
<c:out value="${bookName}"/>
```

In the preceding code snippet, the value for the bookName variable is set in the body of the <c:set> tag.

The <c:remove> Tag

The <c:remove> tag is used to remove a variable from a scope. The following code snippet shows the use the <c:remove> tag:

```
<c:remove var="bookName" scope="session"/>
```

In the preceding code snippet, the <c:remove> tag removes the bookName variable from the session scope.

Describing the Flow Control Tags

Before the introduction of JSTL, coding conditional constructs by using scriptlets was a difficult task. Later, JSTL provided the following tags in the core tag library to control the flow of execution in a JSP page:

- The <c:if> tag

- The <c:choose> tag
- The <c:when> tag
- The <c:otherwise> tag

You should note that the <c:choose>, <c:when>, and <c:otherwise> tags are dependent on each other on the basis of the condition specified in a JSP page. As the syntax of these tags cannot be explained independently, they are described together under the *The <c:choose>, <c:when>, and <c:otherwise> Tags* section.

Let's discuss these tags in the following sections.

The <c:if> Tag

The <c:if> tag allows conditional execution of actions specified in the body of a tag. The actions executed are based on the conditions that are set according to the value of the `test` attribute. The following code snippet shows the use of the <c:if> tag:

```
<c:if test="${(empty user.userid || empty user.password)}">
  Provide User ID and password
</c:if>
```

In the preceding code snippet, the `Provide User ID and password` message is displayed if the user ID or password property is null.

The <c:choose>, <c:when>, and <c:otherwise> Tags

The <c:choose>, <c:when>, and <c:otherwise> tags work similar to the switch statement used in Java. The `<c:choose>` tag provides context to the `<c:when>` and `<c:otherwise>` tags. The `<c:when>` tag has an attribute named `test` to specify a condition. If the specified condition evaluates to true, the JSP container evaluates the body of the `<c:when>` tag. In such a case, no other <c:when> tags below the <c:choose> tag are evaluated and the flow of execution moves to the line after the closing <c:choose> tag. If none of the <c:when> tags evaluates to true, then the <c:otherwise> tag is evaluated.

The following code snippet shows the use of the <c:choose>, <c:when>, and <c:otherwise> tags to produce text, based on the type category of an employee:

```
<c:choose>
<c:when test="${employee.type == 'part-time'}" >
...
</c:when>
<c:when test="${employee.type == 'full-time'}" >
...
</c:when>
<c:when test="${employee.type == 'permanent'}" >
...
</c:when>
<c:when test="${employee.type == 'on contract'}" >
...
</c:when>
<c:otherwise>
...
</c:otherwise>
</c:choose>
```

In the preceding code snippet, the nested <c:when> tags evaluate the condition based on the employee's category. When the test condition of a nested <c:when> tag is evaluated to true, the body of the <c:when> tag is executed. If none of the test conditions is true, the body of the <c:otherwise> tag is executed.

Exploring Iterator Tags

JSTL provides the <c:forEach> tag to iterate over a collection of objects, such as java.util.Collecton, java.util.Map, java.lang.String, java.util.Iterator, and java.util.Enumeration. The <c:forEach> tag also iterates over an array of the java.lang.Object type and an array of primitive data types.

The `java.util.Iterator` and `java.util.Enumeration` collection objects must be used with utmost caution, as these objects are not resettable. Therefore, they must be used within one iteration tag. If an array of a String object contains a list of comma-separated values, such as January, February, March, April, May, then the

<c:forEach> tag iterates over it as array of the java.lang.String object. The following code snippet demonstrates the implementation of the `<c:forEach>` tag in a JSP page:

```
<table>
        <c:forEach var="name" items="${names}">
        <tr>
        <td>
                Name>:<c:out value="${name}"/>
        </td>
        </tr>
        </c:forEach>
</table>
```

In the preceding code snippet, the <c:forEach> tag iterates over a collection of the name object, which contains a list of names. The value of each name is retrieved and displayed in a table format.

The <c:forEach> tag can also be used to iterate over an array of primitive data types, as shown in the following code snippet:

```
The list of even numbers between 0 to 50:
   <br/>
           <c:forEach var="i" begin="0" end="50" step="2">
           <c:out value="${i}"/>
   <br/>
   </c:forEach>
```

In preceding code snippet, the `<c:forEach>` tag is used to display a list of even numbers between 0 and 50. In this case, the `begin` attribute is used to set the initial value for the `i` variable. On the other hand, the `end` attribute is used to set a value until which the iteration will continue. In the preceding code snippet, the 0 value is assigned to the `begin` attribute and 50 value is assigned to the `end` attribute.

Exploring URL Tags

JSTL provides various URL tags to implement common URL-related actions. Some of these actions include importing resources, redirecting Hypertext Transfer Protocol (HTTP) responses, URL rewriting, and specifying request parameters.

The `<jsp:include>` tag helps to include static and dynamic resources from the same context as that of the current JSP page. This tag cannot access resources that are outside a Web application as a resource conflict may occur if a resource is being accessed by various Web applications. For this reason, JSTL provides the `<c:import>` tag, which is more powerful than the `<jsp:include>` tag and helps to reduce the possibility of resource conflict among various Web applications. The syntax to use the <c:import> tag is as follows:

```
<c:import url = "jsp page">
</c:import>
```

Exploring Miscellaneous Tags

The core tag library provides some other tags, known as miscellaneous tags, which are used to perform various tasks, such as implementing the try and catch block. An important miscellaneous tag is the <c:catch> tag, which helps a JSP page to handle exceptions. Code that can raise exceptions is kept within the body of the <c:catch> tag. This tag can catch exceptions that are subclasses of the java.lang.Throwable class, which includes all Java exceptions.

Instead of handling an exception by using an error page, you can use the <c:catch> tag. This tag prevents the invocation of an error page in case an exception is not handled in a JSP page.

The following code snippet shows the use of the <c:catch> tag:

```
<c:catch var ="catchException">
<% int x = 2/0;%> /--raises exception
</c:catch>
The exception is: ${catchException.message}
```

In the preceding code snippet, an integer is divided by zero, which raises an exception that is caught by the <c:catch> tag.

After having a basic conceptual knowledge of the core tag library, let's learn to use the tags of this library in a Web application.

Using the Core Tag Library in the coreTagApp Application

In this section, let's create a Web application, `coreTagApp`, to demonstrate the use of the core tag library. In the coreTagApp Web application, the core tag library is used to implement the functionality of searching a Java book based on its audience level. Moreover, you can display the details of a Java book with the help of the details JSP page created in the Web application. The broad-level steps to create the `coreTagApp` Web application are as follows:

- Create the JSP pages
- Configure the application
- Define the directory structure of the application
- Package, deploy, and run the application

Now let's perform these steps in the following sections.

Creating the JSP Pages

The coreTagApp application contains the following three JSP pages:

- **The select JSP page**—Helps to search books based on audience level
- **The details JSP page**—Displays the details of the books
- **The menu JSP page**—Provides parameters named option1 and option2, which accept different values based on the condition specified in the details.jsp page.

The select JSP page is the home page of the `coreTagApp` application. This page contains a combo box named `level`, which contains the Beginner, Intermediate, and Advance values. These values represent the audience level, which is used as a parameter to search a Java book. The select JSP page also contains a button, `Submit`, which a user clicks after selecting an audience level. Listing 9.1 provides the code for the select.jsp file (save the select.jsp file in the `\coreTagApp` folder):

Listing 9.1: Showing the Code for the select JSP Page

```
<%@ page language="java" import="java.util.*" pageEncoding="ISO-8859-1"%>
<%@ taglib prefix="c" uri="http://java.sun.com/jsp/jstl/core" %>
<!DOCTYPE html >
<html>
   <head>
          <title>welcome  to the world of Java books......</title>

   </head>
<body>
   <c:set var="message" value="Welcome to JSTL!" scope="session" />
   <h2 align="center"><c:out value="${message}"/></h2>
   <form action="details.jsp" method="post">
   <table align="center">
<tr><td colspan=2 align="center"><h4>welcome to the world of Java books</h4></td></tr>
   <tr><td>A place where you can get information on Java books</td></tr>
   <tr><td> select audience level <select name="level">
          <option>Beginner</option>
          <option>Intermediate</option>
          <option>Advance</option>
   </select>
   </td></tr>
   <tr><td colspan="2"><input type="submit" value="Submit"></td></tr>
   </table>
</form>
</body>
</html>
```

In Listing 9.1, the <c:set> core tag is used to set the value for a variable, called `message`, through an attribute called `value`. The <c:out> tag is used to display the value of the `message` variable by using the `value` attribute. This attribute is assigned the value of the `message` variable used as an expression.

After a user has selected an appropriate audience level and clicked the `Submit` button, the request is forwarded to another JSP page, named `details`. Listing 9.2 shows the code for the details.jsp file (save the details.jsp file in the `\coreTagApp` folder):

Listing 9.2: Showing the Code for the details.jsp File

```
<%@ page language="java" import="java.util.*" pageEncoding="ISO-8859-1"%>
<%@ taglib prefix="c" uri="http://java.sun.com/jsp/jstl/core" %>
<!DOCTYPE html >
<html>
  <head>
        <title>book detail:</title>

  </head>
<body>
  <c:set var="level" value="${param.level}" scope="session" />
  <c:choose>
        <c:when test="${level eq 'Beginner'}">
        <b> Books for beginner level audience are as follows:</b>
        </c:when>
  <c:when test="${level eq 'Intermediate'}">
  <b> Books for intermediate level audience are as follows:</b>
  </c:when>
  <c:when test="${level eq 'Advance'}">
  <b>Books for advance level audience are as follows: </b>
  </c:when>
  <c:otherwise>
  </c:otherwise>
  </c:choose>
  <c:if test="${level eq 'Beginner'}">
        <c:import url="menu.jsp">
        <c:param name="option1" value="EJB 3.2 in Simple steps"/>
        <c:param name="option2" value=" Beginning Java 7"/>
  </c:import>
  </c:if>
  <c:if test="${level eq 'Intermediate'}">
        <c:import url="menu.jsp">
        <c:param name="option1" value="Thinking in Java"/>
        <c:param name="option2" value="Java 7 platform unleashed"/>
        </c:import>
  </c:if>
  <c:if test="${level eq 'Advance'}">
        <c:import url="menu.jsp">
<c:param name="option1" value="Java Server programming Java EE 7:Black Book"/>
<c:param name="option2" value="Java Server programming Java EE 6:Black Book"/>
  </c:import>
  </c:if>
  <c:url value="select.jsp" var="backurl"/>
  <br><br><a href="${backurl}">Back</a>
</body>
</html>
```

In Listing 9.2, the audience level selected in the select JSP page is set in the `level` variable with the help of the <c:set> tag. The `level` variable is checked against a condition specified in the `test` attribute of multiple <c:if> tags. The actions are executed based on the conditions that are set according to the value of the `test` attribute. The <c:import> tags are nested within each of the <c:if> tags to import the menu JSP page. This page contains parameters named `option1` and `option2`, which are provided different values by using multiple <c:param> tags in the details JSP page. The code for the menu.jsp file is shown in Listing 9.3 (save the menu.jsp file in the `\coreTagApp` folder):

Listing 9.3: Showing the Code for the menu.jsp File

```
<html>
<body>
<hr>
  <table align="center" width="300" cellspacing="3" >
```

```
    <tr align="center" bgcolor="#fee9c2" height=20>
          <td>${param.option1}</td>
          <td>${param.option2}</td>
    </tr>
  </table>
  <hr>
  </body>
  </html>
```

Listing 9.3 shows parameters named `option1` and `option2`, which accept different values based on the condition specified in the details JSP page.

Now, after creating the required JSP pages of the `coreTagApp` application, let's configure the application.

Configuring the coreTagApp Application

The `coreTagApp` application is configured by using the web.xml file. Listing 9.4 provides the code for the web.xml file (save the `web.xml` file in the `\coreTagApp\WEB-INF` folder):

Listing 9.4: Showing the Code for the web.xml File for the `coreTagApp` Application

```
<?xml version="1.0" encoding="UTF-8"?>
<web-app version="3.1"
   xmlns="http://xmlns.jcp.org/xml/ns/javaee"
   xmlns:xsi="http://www.w3.org/2001/XMLSchema-instance"
   xsi:schemaLocation="http://xmlns.jcp.org/xml/ns/javaee
   http://xmlns.jcp.org/xml/ns/javaee/web-app_3_1.xsd">
   <welcome-file-list>
   <welcome-file>select.jsp</welcome-file>
   </welcome-file-list>
</web-app>
```

In Listing 9.4, the select JSP page is mapped as the welcome file. Therefore, the select JSP page is displayed as the home page of the `coreTagApp` Web application.

Now, let's define the directory structure of the `coreTagApp` application.

Defining the Directory Structure of the coreTagApp Application

After creating the JSP pages of the `coreTagApp` application and configuring the application, you need to define the directory structure of the application. Figure 9.1 displays the directory structure of the `coreTagApp` application:

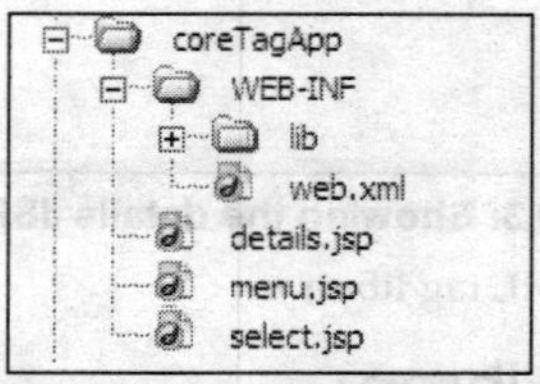

Figure 9.1: Showing the Directory Structure of the coreTagApp Application

Create a directory structure as shown in Figure 9.1, and arrange all the files of the application accordingly. Now, the application is ready to be packaged, deployed, and run.

Packaging, Deploying, and Running the coreTagApp Application

Perform the follow these steps to package, deploy, and run the coreTagApp application:

1. Create the coreTagApp.war file and deploy it on the GlassFish Server 4.0.
2. Run the coreTagApp application by using the `http://localhost:8080/coreTagApp` URL. The `select` home page of the application appears, as shown in Figure 9.2:

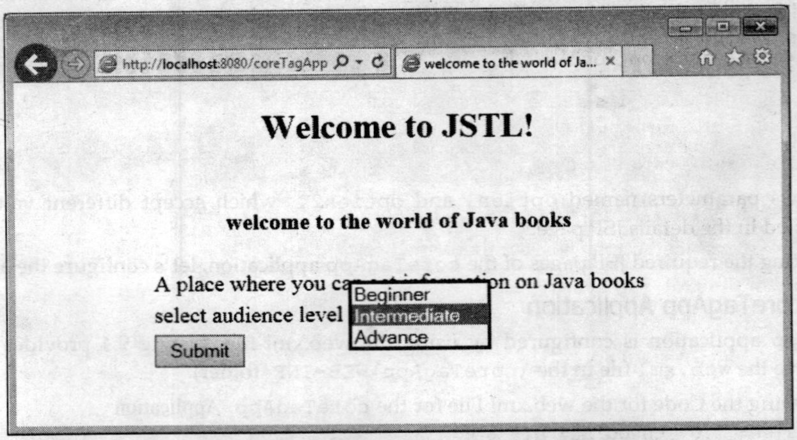

Figure 9.2: Showing the select JSP Page

3. Select the audience level and click the Submit button (Figure 9.2).

The details JSP page appears, which retrieves the value of the `level` parameter by using the param.level expression. This parameter is then used to dynamically retrieve the required books, based on the selected audience level. The `<c:if>` tag is used to evaluate the `level` parameter and set the name of the required books by importing the menu JSP page.

The details JSP page is shown in Figure 9.3:

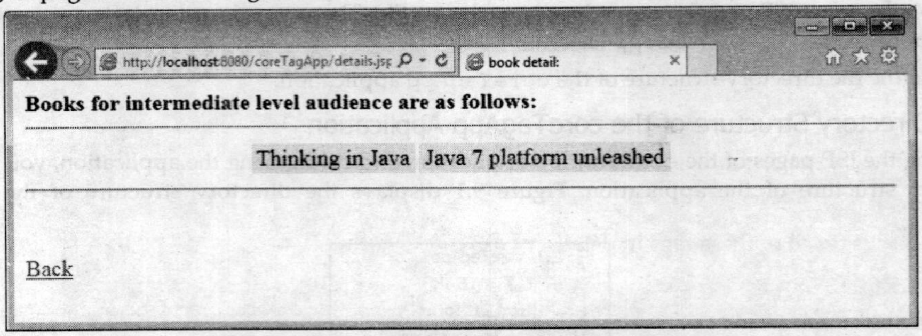

Figure 9.3: Showing the details JSP Page

Let's now move ahead and discuss the XML tag library.

Working with the XML Tag Library

JSTL provides XML tags in a JSP page to manipulate XML documents. XML tags are similar to the tags provided in the core tag library. However, what differentiates XML tags and makes them more powerful than the core library tags is their support for XML Path (XPath) expressions. XPath is a language used to extract specific portions of an XML document to manipulate the data in these portions. In JSTL XML tags, the XPath expressions are assigned to the `select` attribute to select portions of XML data streams. XPath is used as a language for the select attribute only. This implies that the value specified for the `select` attribute is evaluated by using the XPath language, whereas, for all other attributes, the values are evaluated by using the rules associated with JSP EL.

Other than the standard XPath syntax, JSTL XML tags also support scopes, such as $foo, $param, $header, $cookie, $pageScope, $sessionScope, $requestScope, and $applicationScope, to access data of a Web application within an XPath expression.

Some examples of implementation of scopes by using XPath expressions are as follows:

- $sessionScope:profile: Specifies the profile and name of the session-scoped EL variable

- $initParam:mycom.productId: Specifies the String value of the mycom.productId context parameter

The scope named `$sessionScope` of an XPath expression is used to set the session scope of an EL variable named profile. Similarly, `$initParam`, the scope of an XPath expression, initializes the `mycom.productId` context parameter, with a String value.

Let's now learn about the various tags of the XML tag library.

Exploring the Tags of the XML Tag Library

XML tags can be categorized on the basis of their functionalities, as shown in Table 9.3:

Table 9.3: Tags of the XML Tag Library

Function	Tags
Core	out parse set
Flow Control	choose when otherwise forEach if
Transformation	transform param

Now, let's discuss each of the functional categories of the XML tag library.

Describing XML Core Tags

The core XML tags enable you to parse and access XML data efficiently. The XML core tags available in JSTL are as follows:

- The <x:parse> tag
- The<x:out> tag
- The<x:set> tag

Let's now discuss each of these tags in detail.

The <x:parse> Tag

The `<x:parse>` tag is used to parse an XML document and save the result to a variable or the `varDom` attribute. The `varDom` attribute contains a `String` value that is the name of a scoped variable. After the XML document is parsed, it can be used for manipulation by an XPath expression.

The syntax of the `<x:parse>` tag can be used in the following two ways:

- The <x:parse> tag without body
- The <x:parse > tag with body

The <x:parse> Tag without Body

An XML document that you want to parse can be specified with the `xml` attribute of the <x:parse> tag.

The syntax to use the <x:parse> tag without a body to parse an XML document by using the `xml` attribute is as follows:

```
<x:parse xml="XMLDocument"
{var="var" [scope="scope"]|varDom="var" [scopeDom="scope"]}
[systemId="systemId"]
[filter="filter"]/>
```

The following code snippet parses and saves an XML document to the `parsed` variable:

```
<c:import url="book.xml" var="book"/>
<x:parse xml="${book}" var="parsed"/>
```

The <x:parse> Tag with Body

XML documents can also be parsed by placing the XML content directly inside the <x:parse> tag. The syntax to parse an XML document by using the <x:parse> tag with body is as follows:

```
<x:parse
{var="var" [scope="scope"]|varDom="var" [scopeDom="scope"]}
[systemId="systemId"]
[filter="filter"]>
XML Document to parse
</x:parse>
where scope is {page|request|session|application}
```

Table 9.4 describes the attributes of the <x:parse> tag:

Table 9.4: Attributes of the <x:parse> Tag

Name of the Attribute	Type	Description
xml	String, Reader, javax.xml.transform. Source, or an object exported by <x:parse>, <x:set> or <x:transform>	Specifies the source XML document to be parsed. If a source is exported by the <x:set> tag, the source must correspond to a well-formed XML document.
systemId	String	Specifies the system identifier (URI) for parsing an XML document.
filter	org.xml.sax.XMLFilter	Represents the filter to be applied to the source XML document.
var	String	Specifies the name of the scoped variable exported to the parsed XML document.
scope	String	Specifies the scope for the variable containing the parsed XML document.
varDom	String	Specifies the name of the scoped variable that is exported to the parsed XML document. This scoped variable is of the org.w3c.dom.Document type.
scopeDom	String	Specifies the scope for the varDom variable.

After learning the use of the <x:parse> tag, let's discuss the <x:out> tag.

The <x:out> Tag

The <x:out> tag displays an output of an XPath expression. The syntax of the <x:out> tag is as follows:

```
<x:out select="XPathExpression" [escapeXml="{true|false}"]/>
```

In the preceding syntax, the XPath expression is assigned to the select attribute. The result of the evaluation of the expression is written to the current JspWriter object, which is the equivalent of using the <%=...%> JSP expression tag or the <c:out> tag.

After an XML document is parsed and saved to a variable, you can use XPath expressions to extract specific elements from the document. The <x:out> tag is used to access specific elements from the parsed XML document. The following code snippet shows you how to access the title and description elements of a parsed XML document:

```
<x:out select="$parsed/book/title"/>
<x:out select="$parsed/book/description"/>
```

In the preceding code snippet, the <x:out> tag is used to access a subelement, such as title and description of the parent element, book, of the parsed XML document. Table 9.5 describes the attributes of the <x:out> tag:

Table 9.5: Attributes of the <x:out> Tag

Name of the Attribute	Type	Description
escapeXml	String	Specifies a Boolean value used to determine whether or not the characters, such as <, >, and & should be converted into their corresponding character entity code
select	String	Specifies the XPath expression to be evaluated

Let's now discuss the <x:set> tag.

The <x:set> Tag

The <x:set> tag is used to evaluate an XPath expression. The result of the <x:set> tag expression is stored in a scoped variable.

The syntax to use the <x:set> tag is as follows:

```
<x:set select="XPathExpression"
var="varName" [scope="{page|request|session|application}"]/>
```

In the following code snippet, the <x:set> tag is used to set the value of the `title` element of a parsed XML document to the `name` variable:

```
<x:set var="name" select="$parsed/book/title"/>
```

Table 9.6 describes the attributes of the <x:set> tag:

Table 9.6: Attributes of the <x:set> Tag

Name of the Attribute	Type	Description
`scope`	`String`	Specifies the scope for a variable containing the result of an XPath expression
`select`	`String`	Specifies an XPath expression to be evaluated
`var`	`String`	Specifies a name of a scoped variable to hold the result of an XPath expression

This concludes the discussion on XML core tags. Now, let's learn about XML flow control tags.

Describing Flow Control Tags

XML flow control tags control the flow of execution based on the result of XPath expressions. These tags are similar to the core tags of the core tag library, except that they apply to XPath expressions. The XML tag library provides the following flow control tags:

- The <x:if> tag
- The <x:choose> tag
- The <x:when> tag
- The <x:otherwise> tag
- The <x:forEach> tag

Let's discuss these tags one by one.

The <x:if> Tag

The <x:if> tag is used to evaluate the expression provided in the `select` attribute. If the specified expression evaluates to true, the body content of the <x:if> tag will be rendered. The syntax of the <x:if> tag is as follows:

```
<x:if select="PathExpression"
[var="varName"] [scope="{page|request|session|application}"]>
body content
</x:if>
```

Table 9.7 describes the attributes of the <x:if> tag:

Table 9.7: Attributes of the <x:if> Tag

Name of the Attribute	Type	Description
`select`	`String`	Evaluates the test condition that specifies whether or not the body content of the <x:if> tag should be processed.
`var`	`String`	Returns the name of the exported scoped variable after the condition specified in the <x:if> tag is satisfied. This scoped variable is of boolean type.
`scope`	`String`	Specifies the scope for the variable containing the result of an XPath expression.

The <x:choose> Tag

The <x:choose> tag is similar to the <c:choose> tag, which processes the body content of the first <x:when> tag whose test condition evaluates to true. If none of the test conditions of multiple <x:when> tags evaluates to true, the body content of the <x:otherwise> tag is processed, if present. The syntax to use the <x:choose> tag is as follows:

```
<x:choose>
body content (<x:when> and <x:otherwise> subtags)
</x:choose>
```

The <x:when> Tag

The purpose of using the <x:when> tag is similar to the <c:when> tag. However, the implementation of these tags varies. As compared to the <c:when> tag, the <x:when> tag does not support the `test` attribute; instead, it uses the `select` attribute, which specifies an XPath expression to be evaluated. The <x:when> tag is used to provide an alternative option within the <x:choose> tag.

The syntax of the <x:when> tag is as follows:

```
<x:when select="XPathExpression">
body content
</x:when>
```

In the preceding syntax, the value specified in the `select` attribute of the <x:when> tag is an XPath expression. This XPath expression returns a Boolean value. If the first <x:when> tag evaluates to true, the JSP container processes the body content of the <x:when> tag and writes the result to the current JSPWriter object. The <x:when> tag provides a single attribute, `select`, which represents a test condition that should be true to process the body content of the <x:when> tag.

The <x:otherwise> Tag

The <x:otherwise> tag is used optionally as the last alternative within the <x:choose> tag. The syntax to use the <x:otherwise> tag is as follows:

```
<x:otherwise>
. . .. .. . . ..
</x:otherwise>
```

Within the <x:choose> tag, if none of the nested <x:when> test conditions evaluates to true, the body content of the <x:otherwise> tag is evaluated by the JSP container, and the result is written to the current JSPWriter object.

The following code snippet shows the interaction among the <x:choose>, <x:when>, and <x:otherwise> tags:

```
<x:choose>
<x:when select='book/price>400'> This is a meant for advance                    level
  audience</x:when>
<x:when select='book/price<300'> This is a meant for intermediate level audience</x:when>
<x:otherwise>This book is meant for beginner level audience </x:otherwise>
</x:choose>
```

In preceding code snippet, the <x:when> tags nested within <x:choose> tag test the condition on the price tag extracted from book.xml. When the test condition of a nested <x:when> tag is evaluated to be true, then the body of the <x:when> tag is executed. If none of the test condition is true, then the body of the <x:otherwise> tag executes.

The <x:forEach> Tag

The <x:forEach> tag iterates over the result of an XPath expression The syntax of the <x:forEach> tag is as follows:

```
<x:forEach [var="varName"] select="XPathExpression">
body content
</x:forEach>
```

Table 9.8 describes the attributes of the <x:forEach> tag:

Table 9.8: Attributes of the <x:forEach> Tag

Name of the Attribute	Type	Description
`select`	`String`	Represents an XPath expression to be evaluated.

Table 9.8: Attributes of the <x:forEach> Tag

Name of the Attribute	Type	Description
var	String	Provides a name for the exported scoped variable representing the current item of an iteration. The accessibility of this scoped variable is nested and its type depends on the result of the XPath expression of the select attribute.

Next, we learn about transformation tags.

Describing Transformation Tags

The XML transform tags help transform XML documents by using Extensible Stylesheet Language (XSL). The following code snippet shows the use of the <x:transform> tag:

```
<c:import url="http://acme.com/customers" var="xml"/>
<c:import url="/WEB-INF/xslt/customerList.xsl" var="xslt"/>
<x:transform xmlText="${xml}" xsltText="${xslt}"/>
<x:transform source="${xml}" xslt="${xslt}">
</x:transform>
```

In the preceding code snippet, an external document of the XML type (retrieved by an absolute URL) is translated by a local XSLT (context relative path). The result of this translation is written to a JSP page. At times, you may need to use the same XSLT transformation to different source XML documents. To prevent multiple transformations, you can process the transformation XSLT once, and then save the transformer object for successive transformations. JSTL 1.2, which is delivered as a part of the JSP 2.3 specification, allows you to save transformer objects to improve the performance of a JSP page.

The transformations tag category contains the following two tags:

- <x:transform>
- <x:param>

Now, let's discuss each of these tags in detail.

The <x:transform> Tag

The <x:transform> tag applies a transformation to an XML document based on a specified XSLT.

The syntax of the <x:transform> tag can be used in the following two ways:

- The <x:transform> tag without body
- The <x:transform> tag with body
- The <x:transform> tag with body and optional parameters

The <x:transform> Tag without Body

The syntax to use the <x:transform> tag without body content is as follows:

```
<x:transform
xml="XMLDocument" xslt="XSLTStylesheet"
[xmlSystemId="XMLSystemId"] [xsltSystemId="XSLTSystemId"]
[{var="varName" [scope="scopeName"]|result="resultObject"}]/>
```

The <x:transform> Tag with Body

The syntax to use the <x:transform> tag with body content is as follows:

```
<x:transform
xml="XMLDocument" xslt="XSLTStylesheet"
[xmlSystemId="XMLSystemId"] [xsltSystemId="XSLTSystemId"]
[{var="varName" [scope="scopeName"]|result="resultObject"}]>
<x:param> tags </x:param>
</x:transform>
```

The <x:transform> Tag with Body and Optional Parameters

The syntax to use the <x:transform> tag with body and optional transformation parameters is as follows:

```
<x:transform
xslt="XSLTStylesheet"
```

```
xmlSystemId="XMLSystemId" xsltSystemId="XSLTSystemId"
[{var="varName" [scope="scopeName"]|result="resultObject"}]
XML Document to parse
optional <x:param> actions </X:param>
</x:parse>
where scopeName is {page|request|session|application}
```

Table 9.9 describes the attributes of the <x:transform> tag:

Table 9.9: Attributes of the <x:transform> Tag

Name of the Attribute	Type	Description
`result`	`String`	Specifies an object that in turn specifies how the transformation result should be processed.
`scope`	`String`	Specifies the scope for the variable containing the transformed XML document.
`var`	`String`	Specifies the name of the scoped variable that is exported to the parsed XML document. The scoped variable is of the org.w3c.dom.Document type.
`doc`	`String`	Specifies an XML document as the source to be translated (if an XML document is exported by the <x:set> tag, then the <xml:transform> tag should transform the complete XML document).
`docSystem Id`	`String`	Specifies the system identifier (URI) to parse an XML document.
`xslt`	`String`	Specifies a transformation XSLT as a `String`, `Reader`, or Source object.
`xsltSystemId`	`String`	Specifies the system identifier (URI) to parse an XSLT stylesheet.

The result of the transformation of an XML document by using XSLT is not stored in any object by default; rather, it is written directly on to a JSP page. You can store the result of a transformation by the following ways:

- Specifying the `result` attribute of the <x:transform> tag with a value of the `Result` type
- Specifying the `var` and `scope` attributes of the <x:transform> tag with a `Document` object saved in a scoped variable.

Let's now discuss the <x:param> tag.

The <x:param> Tag

The <x:param> tag sets the transformation parameters for the nested action of the <x:transform> tag. The syntax of the <x:param> tag is as follows:

```
<x:param name="name" value="value"/>
Syntax 2: Parameter value specified in the body content
<x:param name="name">
parameter value
</x:param>
```

Table 9.10 describes the attributes of the <x:param> tag:

Table 9.10: Attributes of the <x:param> Tag

Name of the Attribute	Type	Description
`name`	`String`	Specifies the name of the transformation parameter
`value`	`String`	Specifies the value of the transformation parameter

The <x:param> tag must be nested within the <x:transform> tag to set the transformation parameters. The value of the transformation parameter is specified either through the `attribute` value, or through the body content of the <x:transform> tag.

Let's now discuss how to implement the XML tags in a Web application.

Using the XML Tag Library in the XMLTagApp Application

In this section, we create the `XMLTagApp` Web application, to parse, extract, and transform an XML document.

The broad-level steps to create the `XMLTagApp` Web application are as follows:

- Create an XML file
- Create a JSP page
- Configure the application
- Define the directory structure of the application
- Package, deploy, and run the application

Creating the XML file

Let's create an XML file named book.xml to store or maintain the details of the various books in the `XMLTagApp` Web application. The code for the book.xml file is shown in Listing 9.5 (save the book.xml file in the `\XMLTagApp` folder):

Listing 9.5: Showing the Details of the Books in the book.xml File

```
<?xml version="1.0" encoding="UTF-8"?>
<xml-body>
<books>

  <book>
  <title>Java EE Black Book</title>
  <description>The Best Book on Java EE </description>
  <author>Kogent Learning Solutions Inc.</author>
  </book>

  <book>
  <title>Java 7 Black Book</title>
  <description>The Best Book on Java 7</description>
  <author>Kogent Learning Solutions Inc.</author>
  </book>

</books>
</xml-body>
```

In Listing 9.5, the book.xml file is parsed and its elements are extracted in the details JSP page, which is the home page of the `XMLTagApp` Web application.

Creating the details JSP Page

Create a JSP page named details, which parses, extracts, and manipulates the data in the XML file by using XML tags. Listing 9.6 provides the code for the details JSP page (save the details.jsp file in the \XMLTagApp folder):

Listing 9.6: Showing the Code for the details.jsp File

```
<%@ page language="java" import="java.util.*" pageEncoding="ISO-8859-1"%>
<%@ taglib prefix="c" uri="http://java.sun.com/jsp/jstl/core" %>
<%@ taglib prefix="x" uri="http://java.sun.com/jsp/jstl/xml" %>
<!DOCTYPE html>
<html>
  <head>
        <title>My JSP 'details.jsp' starting page</title>
              </head>
<body>
  <c:import url="book.xml" var="book"/>
  <x:parse xml="${book}" var="parsed"/>
  Details on the Books are as follows:
  <table>
  <tr>
  <th>Title of the Book:</th>
  <td width="10%"> </td>
  <th>Description</th>
  <td width="10%"> </td>
```

```
        <th>Author of the Book:</th>
        </tr>
        <x:forEach select="$parsed//book">
        <tr>
        <td colspan><x:out select="title"/></td>
        <td width="10%"> </td>
        <td colspan><x:out select="description"/></td>
        <td width="10%"> </td>
        <td><x:out select="author"/></td>
        </tr>
        </x:forEach>
        </table>
    </body>
    </html>
```

In Listing 9.6, the details JSP page uses the <c:import> tag to import the book.xml file. The page also uses the <x:parse> tag to parse the book.xml file and store the result in a variable called `parsed`. After the XML document is parsed, the details JSP page is used to display the details of each book in a table format by using the <x:forEach> tag.

Configuring the XMLTagApp Application

Let's now configure the `XMLTagApp` Web application in the web.xml file and set the details JSP page in the<welcome-file> tag. The code for web.xml is shown in the Listing 9.7 (save the web.xml file in the \XMLTagApp\WEB-INF folder):

Listing 9.7: Showing the Code for the web.xml File for the XMLTagApp Application

```
<?xml version="1.0" encoding="UTF-8"?>
<web-app version="3.1"
  xmlns="http://xmlns.jcp.org/xml/ns/javaee"
  xmlns:xsi="http://www.w3.org/2001/XMLSchema-instance"
  xsi:schemaLocation="http://xmlns.jcp.org/xml/ns/javaee
  http://xmlns.jcp.org/xml/ns/javaee/web-app_3_1.xsd">
<welcome-file-list>
  <welcome-file> details.jsp </welcome-file>
</welcome-file-list>
</web-app>
```

Defining the Directory Structure of the XMLTagApp Application

Now, after creating the required files for the XMLTagApp Web application, you need to arrange the files in a directory structure, as shown in Figure 9.4:

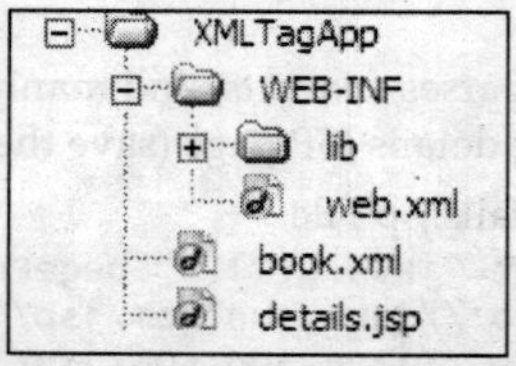

Figure 9.4: Showing the Directory Structure of the XMLTagApp Web Application

Packaging, Deploying, and Running the XMLTagApp Application

Perform the following steps to package, deploy, and run the XMLTagApp Web application:

1. Create the XMLTagApp.war file and deploy it on the Glassfish Server 4.0.
2. Run the XMLTagApp Web application by using the `http://localhost:8080/XMLTagApp` URL. The details JSP page appears, as shown in Figure 9.5:

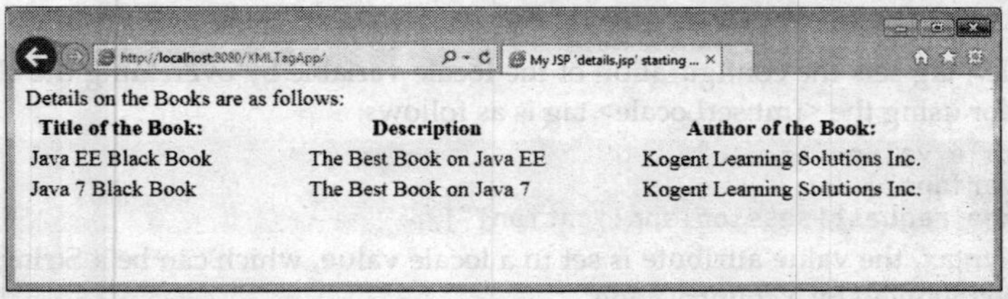

Figure 9.5: Showing the Book Details Extracted from an XML File in a JSP Page

With this, we complete our discussion on XML tags. Apart from covering different aspects of these tags, you have also learned how to implement these tags in a Web application.

Next, we discuss how to work with the internationalization tag library.

Working with the Internationalization Tag Library

The internationalization tags in JSTL are used to set a locale for a Web page, create localized messages, and format as well as parse data elements such as numbers, currencies, dates, and times in a localized or customized manner. Based on the locale of a client, the internationalization tags use a localization context containing a locale and a resource bundle to display the data to the client. The localization context is defined in the following two ways:

- Creating an instance of the LocalizationContext class
- Specifying a String value to the localization context parameter while deploying a Web application

Let's now explore the tags of the internationalization tag library.

Exploring the Tags of the Internationalization Tag Library

The internationalization tag library provides a set of tags that are categorized on the basis of their functionalities. Table 9.11 provides a list of the tags of the internationalization tag library along with their functions:

Table 9.11: Tags of the Internationalization Tag Library Categorized According to their Functions

Function	Tags
Setting a locale	`setLocale` `requestEncoding`

Messaging	`bundle`
	`message`
	`param`
	`setBundle`

Formatting number and date	`formatNumber`
	`formatDate`
	`parseDate`
	`parseNumber`
	`setTimeZone`
	`timeZone`

Let's now explore the tags of the internationalization tag library on the basis of their functions.

Describing the Tags for Setting the Locale

A locale for JSP pages is set by the internationalization tag library. The language and formatting conventions of the locale are used to format the JSP page.

The internationalization tag library provides the following set of tags to set or format the locale in a JSP page:

- The <fmt:setLocale> tag
- The <fmt:requestEncoding> tag

Let's discuss each of these tags in detail.

The <fmt:setLocale> Tag

The <fmt:setLocale> tag sets the configuration of the locale variable by overriding the client-specific locale for a page. The syntax for using the <fmt:setLocale> tag is as follows:

```
<fmt:setLocale value="locale"
[variant="variant"]
[scope="{page|request|session|application}"]/>
```

In the preceding syntax, the value attribute is set to a locale value, which can be a String value, and which must be a language code followed by a country code.

Table 9.12 describes the attributes of the <fmt:setLocale> tag:

Table 9.12: Attributes of the <fmt:setLocale> Tag

Name of the Attribute	Type	Description
scope	String	Returns the scope for a variable that contains the locale configuration information.
value	String or java.util. Locale	Returns a value associated with a locale of the String type, which has two letters as language code (as defined by ISO-39) and must be in lowercase, and two letters as country code (as defined by ISO-3166), which must be in uppercase. There should be a hyphen (-) or (_) underscore between the language code and the country code.
variant	String	Returns a variant that is either browser or vendor specific.

Let's now discuss the <fmt:requestEncoding> tag.

The <fmt:requestEncoding> Tag

The <fmt:requestEncoding> tag is used to set the character encoding of a request. It is used to correctly decode the request parameter values if their encoding is different from that specified by ISO-8859-1.

The <fmt:requestEncoding> tag is needed because most browsers do not follow the HTTP-specification and do not include a Content-Type header in their requests.

The syntax of the <fmt:requestEncoding> tag is as follows:

```
<fmt:requestEncoding [value="charsetName"]/>
```

The <fmt:requestEncoding> tag provides the value attribute to specify the name of the character encoding to be applied while decoding the parameters of a request. This attribute accepts the String type value.

After learning about the tags used to format the locale, let's discuss the messaging tags of JSTL internalization tag library.

Exploring Messaging Tags

JSTL messaging tags are used to display content in a language identified by the locale set for a JSP page. The JSTL internalization tag library supports the following messaging tags:

- The <fmt:setBundle> tag
- The <fmt:bundle> tag
- The <fmt:message> tag

Now let's discuss each of these tags in detail.

The <fmt:setBundle> Tag

The <fmt:setBundle> tag is used to create a I18N localization context. The basename attribute is used to set the name of a resource bundle.

The I18N localization context is stored in the scoped variable defined by using the `var` attribute. If the name of a variable is not specified for the `var` attribute, the 118N localization context is stored in the `javax.servlet.jsp.jstl.fmt.LocalizationContext` configuration variable. This defines the default I18N localization context in the given scope.

The syntax of the <fmt:setBundle> tag is as follows:

```
<fmt:setBundle basename="basename"
```

```
[var="varName"]
[scope="{page|request|session|application}"]/>
```

Table 9.13 describes the attributes of the <fmt:setBundle> tag:

Table 9.13: Attributes of the <fmt:setBundle> Tag

Name of the Attribute	Type	Description
basename	String	Defines a name for the resource bundle. This is the fully qualified resource name of the bundle, which is as same as the fully qualified class name created in an application. You should note that the name specified for the basename attribute is separated from the package name by using a separator (.). In addition, the name does not contain any file type (such as .class or .properties) suffix.
scope	String	Defines the scope of the var attribute or a localization context configuration variable.
var	String	Defines the name of the scoped variable that contains the value of the object type, javax.servlet.jsp.jstl.fmt.LocalizationContext.

Let's now discuss the <fmt:bundle> tag.

The <fmt:bundle> Tag

The <fmt:bundle> tag creates a localization context and loads a resource bundle into this context. The basename attribute is used to specify the name of this resource bundle. The scope of this localized context is limited to the body of the <fmt:bundle> tag.

The syntax of the <fmt:bundle> tag is as follows:

```
<fmt:bundle basename="basename"
[prefix="prefix"]>
body content
</fmt:bundle>
```

Table 9.14 describes the attributes of the <fmt:bundle> tag:

Table 9.14: Attributes of the <fmt:bundle> Tag

Name of the Attribute	Type	Description
basename	String	Identifies a resource bundle to be set as the default bundle, which has been set by using the <fmt:setBundle> tag. This is the fully qualified resource name of the bundle.
prefix	String	Specifies the prefix to be appended to the value of the message key of any nested <fmt:message> action.

Let's now discuss the <fmt:message> tag.

The <fmt:message> Tag

The <fmt:message> tag contains a localized message corresponding to a given key.

The syntax of the <fmt:message> tag can be used in the following there ways:

- The<fmt:message> tag without body
- The <fmt:message> tag with body
- The <fmt:message> tag with message parameters

The <fmt:message> Tag without Body

The message key may be specified by the key attribute of the <fmt:message> tag.

The syntax of the <fmt:message> tag without body content is as follows:

```
<fmt:message key="messageKey"
[bundle="resourceBundle"]
[var="varName"]
[scope="{page|request|session|application}"]/>
```

The <fmt:message> Tag with Body

When the <fmt:message> tag is used with body, the key attribute is not used and the message to be set is provided in the body of the tag.

The syntax of the <fmt:message> tag with body content is as follows:

```
<fmt:message [bundle="resourceBundle"]
[var="varName"]
[scope="{page|request|session|application}"]>
Any Message
</fmt:message>
```

The <fmt:message> Tag with Message Parameters

In the presence of one or more `<fmt:param>` subtags, a localized text message is passed to the `applyPattern()` method, and the values of the `<fmt:param>` tags are collected in an `Object[]` array and passed to the `format()` method. The locale of the `java.text.MessageFormat` class is set to the appropriate localization context locale before the `applyPattern()` method is called.

If the message is compound (message that contains more than one variable) and no `<fmt:param>` subtags are specified, the applyPattern() method is not used. The `<fmt:message>` tag prints the output by using the current `JspWriter` object, unless the `var` attribute is specified, in which case the result is stored in the named JSP attribute.

The syntax of the <fmt:message> with the message parameters specified by using the <fmt:param> tag is as follows:

```
<fmt:message [bundle="resourceBundle"]
[var="varName"]
[scope="{page|request|session|application}"]>
Key
```

```
optional <fmt:param> subtags</fmt:param>
</fmt:message>
```

The <fmt:param> subtag contains a single argument (for parametric replacements) that is passed to a compound message or provides a pattern or format in its parent message tag. The parameter values for the variables of a compound message may be specified by one or more `<fmt:param>` subtags (one for each parameter value). This procedure is known as parametric replacement.

In a compound message or pattern, at least one param tag must be specified for each variable. The following code snippet uses the <fmt:message>, <fmt:param>, and <fmt:formatNumber> tags to display the total number of athletes based on a specified client locale:

```
<fmt:message key="athletesRegistered">
<fmt:param>
<fmt:formatNumber value="${athletesCount}"/>
</fmt:param>
</fmt:message>
```

Depending on the locale, the output of the code snippet could be as follows:

```
french: Il y a 10 582 athletes enregistres.
english: There are 10,582 athletes registered.
```

If the `<fmt:message>` tag is nested inside a `<fmt:bundle>` tag, and the parent `<fmt:bundle>` tag contains a `prefix` attribute, the prefix specified to the `prefix` attribute is appended to a message key. The `<fmt:message>` tag uses a resource bundle of the `I18N` localization context identified to format the message according to the specified client locale.

Table 9.15 describes the attributes of the <fmt:message> tag:

Table 9.15: Attributes of the <fmt:message> Tag

Name of the Attribute	Type	Description
key	String	Specifies the message key used to locate a message
bundle	String	Specifies a localization context in which the message key looks up for a resource bundle

Table 9.15: Attributes of the <fmt:message> Tag		
Name of the Attribute	**Type**	**Description**
var	String	Specifies the name of an exported scoped variable, which stores a localized message
scope	String	Specifies the scope of the variable defined in the var attribute

Next, let's learn about formatting tags.

Describing Formatting Tags

JSTL provides formatting tags to parse and format locale-sensitive numbers and dates in a JSP page. The internationalization tag library provides the following formatting tags:

- The <fmt:formatNumber> tag
- The <fmt:formatDate> tag
- The <fmt:timeZone> tag
- The <fmt:setTimeZone> tag

The <fmt:formatNumber> Tag

The <fmt:formatNumber> tag is used to format a numeric value, such as a number, currency, or percentage, in a locale-sensitive or customized manner. The numeric value may be provided by the value attribute; if the value is not provided, then it is read from the body of the tag. Whether the given value is formatted as a number, currency, or percentage depends on the value of the type attribute.

The syntax of the <fmt:formatNumber> tag is as follows:

```
<fmt:formatNumber value="numericValue"
          [type="{number|currency|percent}"]
          [pattern="customPattern"]
          [currencyCode="currencyCode"]
          [currencySymbol="currencySymbol"]
          [groupingUsed="{true|false}"]
          [maxIntegerDigits="maxIntegerDigits"]
          [minIntegerDigits="minIntegerDigits"]
          [maxFractionDigits="maxFractionDigits"]
          [minFractionDigits="minFractionDigits"]
          [var="varName"]
          [scope="{page|request|session|application}"]/>
```

Table 9.16 describes the attributes of the <fmt:formatNumber> tag:

Table 9.16: Attributes of the <fmt:formatNumber> Tag		
Name of the Attribute	**Type**	**Description**
currencyCode	String	Specifies the currency code (as defined by ISO 4217). The currencyCode attribute is applicable when currencies are to be formatted.
currencySymbol	String	Specifies the symbol of the currency. This attribute is only applicable when currencies need to be formatted (i.e., if type is equal to currency); otherwise, this attribute is ignored.
groupingUsed	String	Specifies whether or not any grouping separators, such as comma and semi colon are contained in the formatted output.
maxFractionDigits	String	Specifies the maximum number of digits in the fractional part of the formatted output.
maxIntegerDigits	String	Specifies the maximum number of digits in the integer part of the formatted output.
minFractionDigits	String	Specifies the minimum number of digits in the fractional part of the formatted output.
minIntegerDigits	String	Specifies minimum number of digits in the integer portion of the formatted output.

Table 9.16: Attributes of the <fmt:formatNumber> Tag

Name of the Attribute	Type	Description
pattern	String	Specifies a custom formatting pattern, which is applied only when numbers are to be formatted. In other words, if the value of the type attribute is either not specified or is equal to number, then the specified pattern is applied. Otherwise, the specified custom pattern is ignored.
scope	String	Specifies the scope of the variable defined in the var attribute.
type	String	Specifies the type to which a value is to be formatted, such as number, currency, or percentage.
value	String or Number	Specifies the numeric value to be formatted.
var	String	Specifies the name of the scoped variable used to store the formatted result in the form of a String.

Let's now discuss the <fmt:formatDate> tag.

The <fmt:formatDate> Tag

The <fmt:formatDate> tag is used to format the date and time that is displayed in a JSP page. This tag depends on the value of the type attribute. You can format the time component, the date component, or both the components of a specified date. The date and time components are formatted by using one of the predefined formatting styles for date (specified by the dateStyle attribute) and time (specified by the timeStyle attribute) of a JSP page's formatting locale.

The syntax of the <fmt:formatDate> tag is:

```
<fmt:formatDate value="date"
[type="{time|date|both}"]
[dateStyle="{default|short|medium|long|full}"]
[timeStyle="{default|short|medium|long|full}"]
[pattern="customPattern"]
[timeZone="timeZone"]
[var="varName"]
[scope="{page|request|session|application}"]/>
```

Web designers may also apply a customized formatting style to time and date by specifying the pattern attribute, in which attributes, such as type, dateStyle, and timeStyle are ignored. The <fmt:formatDate> tag is used to format the current date and time, as shown in the following code snippet:

```
<jsp:useBean id="now" class="java.util.Date" />
<fmt:formatDate value="${now}" />
```

If the date or time is in the form of a String and needs to be formatted, this String object must be parsed into the Date object by using the <fmt:parseDate> tag. The result is provided to the <fmt:formatDate> tag. The following code snippet shows how the <fmt:parseDate > tag is used to parse the date and the <fmt:formatDate> tag is used to format the parsed date:

```
<fmt:parseDate value="4/13/02" var="parsed" />
<fmt:formatDate value="${parsed}" />
```

Table 9.17 describes the attributes of the <fmt:formatDate> tag:

Table 9.17: Attributes of the <fmt:formatDate> Tag

Name of the Attribute	Type	Description
value	String	Specifies the date and the time to be formatted.
type	String	Specifies whether time or date or both time and date need to be formatted.
dateStyle	String	Specifies an already defined formatting style for the date, which follows the semantics specified in the java.text.DateFormat class. The formatting style specified in the dateStyle attribute is applicable only when a date or both date and time need to be formatted. In other words, if the value of the type attribute is either not

Table 9.17: Attributes of the <fmt:formatDate> Tag		
Name of the Attribute	**Type**	**Description**
		specified or is equal to `date`, then the specified formatting style is applied. Otherwise, the specified style is ignored.
`timeStyle`	`String`	Specifies an already defined formatting style for the date that follows the semantics specified in the `java.text.DateFormat` class. The formatting style specified in the dateStyle attribute is applicable only when a time or both date and time need to be formatted. In other words, if the value of the type attribute is either not specified or is equal to `time`, then the specified formatting style is applied. Otherwise, the specified style is ignored.
`pattern`	`String`	Specifies a custom formatting style used to format the date and time.
`timeZone`	`String or java.util.TimeZone`	Specifies the time zone in which to represent the formatted time.
`var`	`String`	Specifies the scoped variable that stores a String value as a result of formatting. By default, the scope of the variable assigned to the `var` attribute is false.

Time information on a page may be tailored to the preferred time zone of a client. This is useful when a server is accessed by different clients in different time zones. If information about the time to be formatted or parsed in a time zone is different from that in the JSP container, the `<fmt:formatDate>` and `<fmt:parseDate>` tags may be nested inside the `<fmt:timeZone>` tag or provided with the `timeZone` attribute. We discuss the <fmt:timeZone> tag in the following section.

The <fmt:timeZone> Tag

The `<fmt:timeZone>` tag specifies the time zone in which time information is to be formatted or parsed. The syntax of the <fmt:timeZone> tag is as follows:

```
<fmt:timeZone value="timeZone">
body content
</fmt:timeZone>
```

In the following code snippet, the current date and time are formatted in the GMT+1:00 time zone:

```
<fmt:timeZone value="GMT+1:00">
  <fmt:formatDate value="${now}" type="both" dateStyle="full"
  timeStyle="full"/>
</fmt:timeZone>
```

The <fmt:timeZone> tag provides a single attribute, value, which is either of the String or TimeZone type. If the time zone is given as a `String` value in the <fmt:timeZone> tag, the value is parsed by using the `getTimeZone()` method.

Now, let's learn about the <fmt:setTimeZone> tag.

The <fmt:setTimeZone> Tag

The `<fmt:setTimeZone>` tag stores the specified time zone in a scoped variable or time zone configuration variable. The syntax of the <fmt:setTimeZone> tag is as follows:

```
<fmt:setTimeZone value="timeZone"
[var="varName"]
[scope="{page|request|session|application}"]/>
```

Table 9.18 describes the attributes of the <fmt:setTimeZone> tag:

Table 9.18: Attributes of the <fmt:setTimeZone> Tag		
Name of the Attribute	**Type**	**Description**
`scope`	`String`	Specifies the scope of the variable assigned to the `var` attribute or time zone configuration variable

Table 9.18: Attributes of the <fmt:setTimeZone> Tag

Name of the Attribute	Type	Description
value	String or java.util.TimeZone	Defines the time zone ID for a region. For example, for America/Los_Angeles, the time zone ID used is GMT-8.
var	String	Defines the name of a scoped variable that stores the time zone as a java.util.TimeZone object.

If the var attribute is not given, the time zone is stored in the timeZone configuration variable, thereby making it as a new default time zone of the given scope. If time zone is defined as a String value, then the time zone is parsed by using the getTimeZone() method.

After exploring the internationalization tags, let's now learn how to use them in a Web application.

Using the Internationalization Tag Library in Web Applications

In this section, we implement the tags of the internationalization tag library. We create two separate Web applications named dateFormatApp and numFormatApp, to demonstrate the use of the <fmt:formatDate> and <fmt:formatNumber> tags, respectively.

Using the <fmt:formatDate> Tag in the dateFormatApp Application

Let's create a Web application named dateFormatApp, which implements the <fmt:formatDate> tag of the internationalization tag library.

The following are the broad-level steps to create the dateFormatApp Web application:

- Create a JSP page
- Configure the Web application
- Define the directory structure of the Web application
- Package, deploy, and run the Web application

Let's now perform these steps in the following sections.

Creating the formatDate JSP Page

The formatDate JSP page is the home page of the dateFormatApp Web application and displays the current date and time of most of the important cities of the world. It also displays the formatted current date and time of these cities. The <fmt:formatDate> tag is used in the formatDate JSP page to format the date in a specified pattern.

Listing 9.8 provides the code of the formatDate JSP page (save the formatDate.jsp file in the \dateFormatApp folder):

Listing 9.8: Showing the Code for the formatDate.jsp File

```
<%@ page language="java" import="java.util.*" pageEncoding="ISO-8859-1"%>
<%@ taglib uri="http://java.sun.com/jsp/jstl/fmt" prefix="fmt" %>
<%@ taglib prefix="c" uri="http://java.sun.com/jsp/jstl/core" %>
<!DOCTYPE html>
<html><head>
        <title>CHECK TIME!!!</title>
        </head>
<body>
  <c:set var="now" value="<%=new java.util.Date()%>" />
  <c:set var="los" value="<%=TimeZone.getTimeZone("America/Los_Angeles")%>" />
  <c:set var="lon" value="<%=TimeZone.getTimeZone("Europe/London")%>" />
  <c:set var="rom" value="<%=TimeZone.getTimeZone("Rome ")%>" />
  <c:set var="pari" value="<%=TimeZone.getTimeZone("Paris")%>" />
  <c:set var="port" value="<%=TimeZone.getTimeZone("Portugal ")%>" />
  <c:set var="ind" value="<%=TimeZone.getTimeZone("IST")%>" />
   <c:set var="syd" value="<%=TimeZone.getTimeZone("Australia/Sydney")%>" />
<b>CURRENT TIME AT SOME OF THE POPULAR CITIES OF THE WORLD!!</b>
<BR/>
```

```
<BR/>
<table border="1" cellpadding="0" cellspacing="0"
  style="border-collapse: collapse" bordercolor="#111111"
  width="63%" id="AutoNumber2">
<tr>
  <td width="51%" colspan="2" bgcolor="yellow">Los Angeles:</td>
  <td width="49%" colspan="2" bgcolor="yellow">
  <fmt:timeZone value="$los}">
  <fmt:formatDate value="${now}" timeZone="${los}"
  type="both" />
  </fmt:timeZone>
  </td>
</tr>
<tr>
  <td width="51%" colspan="2" bgcolor="yellow">London:</td>
  <td width="49%" colspan="2" bgcolor="yellow">
  <fmt:timeZone value="$lon}">
  <fmt:formatDate value="${now}" timeZone="${lon}"
  type="both" />
  </fmt:timeZone>
  </td>
</tr>
<tr>
  <td width="51%" colspan="2" bgcolor="yellow">Rome:</td>
  <td width="49%" colspan="2" bgcolor="yellow">
  <fmt:timeZone value="$rom}">
  <fmt:formatDate value="${now}" timeZone="${rom}"
  type="both" />
  </fmt:timeZone>
  </td>
</tr>
<tr>
  <td width="51%" colspan="2" bgcolor="yellow">Paris:</td>
  <td width="49%" colspan="2" bgcolor="yellow">
  <fmt:timeZone value="$pari}">
  <fmt:formatDate value="${now}" timeZone="${pari}"
  type="both" />
  </fmt:timeZone>
  </td>
</tr>
<tr>
  <td width="51%" colspan="2" bgcolor="yellow">New- Delhi:</td>
  <td width="49%" colspan="2" bgcolor="yellow">
  <fmt:timeZone value="$ind}">
  <fmt:formatDate value="${now}" timeZone="${ind}"
  type="both" />
  </fmt:timeZone>
  </td>
</tr>
<tr>
  <td width="51%" colspan="2" bgcolor="yellow">Sydney:</td>
  <td width="49%"colspan="2" bgcolor="yellow">
  <fmt:timeZone value="$syd}">
  <fmt:formatDate value="${now}" timeZone="${syd}"
  type="both" />
  </fmt:timeZone>
  </td>
</tr>
</table>
<BR>
<BR>
<BR>
```

```
<BR>
<B>FORMATTING DATE USING PATTERN:<B>
<BR>
<BR>
<table border="1" cellpadding="0" cellspacing="0"
style="border-collapse: collapse" bordercolor="#111111"
width="63%" id="AutoNumber2">
<tr>
  <td width="51%" colspan="2" bgcolor="yellow">Los Angeles:</td>
  <td width="49%" colspan="2" bgcolor="yellow">
  <fmt:timeZone value="$los}">
  <fmt:formatDate value="${now}" timeZone="${los}"
  type="both" pattern="dd-MMM-yyyy hh:mm:ss" />
  </fmt:timeZone>
  </td>
</tr>
<tr>
  <td width="51%" colspan="2" bgcolor="yellow">London:</td>
  <td width="49%" colspan="2" bgcolor="yellow">
  <fmt:timeZone value="$lon}">
  <fmt:formatDate value="${now}" timeZone="${lon}"
  type="both" pattern="dd-MMM-yyyy hh:mm:ss"/>
  </fmt:timeZone>
  </td>
</tr>
<tr>
  <td width="51%" colspan="2" bgcolor="yellow">Rome:</td>
  <td width="49%" colspan="2" bgcolor="yellow">
  <fmt:timeZone value="$rom}">
  <fmt:formatDate value="${now}" timeZone="${rom}"
  type="both" pattern="dd-MMM-yyyy hh:mm:ss"/>
  </fmt:timeZone>
  </td>
</tr>
<tr>
  <td width="51%" colspan="2" bgcolor="yellow">Paris:</td>
  <td width="49%" colspan="2" bgcolor="yellow">
  <fmt:timeZone value="$pari}">
  <fmt:formatDate value="${now}" timeZone="${pari}"
  type="both" pattern="dd-MMM-yyyy hh:mm:ss"/>
  </fmt:timeZone>
  </td>
</tr>
<tr>
  <td width="51%" colspan="2" bgcolor="yellow">New- Delhi:</td>
  <td width="49%" colspan="2" bgcolor="yellow">
  <fmt:timeZone value="$ind}">
  <fmt:formatDate value="${now}" timeZone="${ind}"
  type="both" pattern="dd-MMM-yyyy hh:mm:ss" />
  </fmt:timeZone>
  </td>
</tr>
<tr>
  <td width="51%" colspan="2" bgcolor="yellow">Sydney:</td>
  <td width="49%"colspan="2" bgcolor="yellow">
  <fmt:timeZone value="$syd}">
  <fmt:formatDate value="${now}" timeZone="${syd}"
  type="both" pattern="dd-MMM-yyyy hh:mm:ss"/>
  </fmt:timeZone>
  </td>
</tr>
</table>
</body>
</html>
```

In Listing 9.8, the time zones for the selected cities are set in the variables, such as los, rom, and lon. These time zones are retrieved by using the `TimeZone.getTimeZone()` method. The variable assigned to the `timeZone` attribute is then used by the `<fmt:formatDate>` tag to set the time according to the time zone given as a parameter to the `timeZone` attribute.

Configuring the dateFormatApp Application

Let's now configure the `dateFormatApp` application in the web.xml file. Listing 9.9 shows the code for the web.xml file (save the web.xml file in the \dateFormatApp\WEB-INF folder):

Listing 9.9: Showing the web.xml File for the dateFormatApp Application

```
<?xml version="1.0" encoding="UTF-8"?>
<web-app version="3.1"
   xmlns="http://xmlns.jcp.org/xml/ns/javaee"
   xmlns:xsi="http://www.w3.org/2001/XMLSchema-instance"
   xsi:schemaLocation="http://xmlns.jcp.org/xml/ns/javaee
   http://xmlns.jcp.org/xml/ns/javaee/web-app_3_1.xsd">
<welcome-file-list>
   <welcome-file>formatDate.jsp</welcome-file>
</welcome-file-list>
</web-app>
```

In Listing 9.9, the formateDate.jsp file is set as the welcome file.

Now let's understand the directory structure of the `dateFormatApp` Web application.

Defining the Directory Structure of the dateFormatApp Application

You can create a directory structure and arrange the files created for the `dateFormatApp` Web application, as shown in Figure 9.6:

Figure 9.6: Showing the Directory Structure of the dateFormatApp Web Application

Packaging, Deploying, and Running the dateFormatApp Application

Perform the following steps to package, deploy, and run the dateFormatApp Web application:

1. Create the dateFormatApp.war file and deploy it on the Glassfish Server 4.0.
2. Run the Web application by using the `http://localhost:8080/dateFormatApp` URL. The formatDate JSP page is displayed, as shown in Figure 9.7:

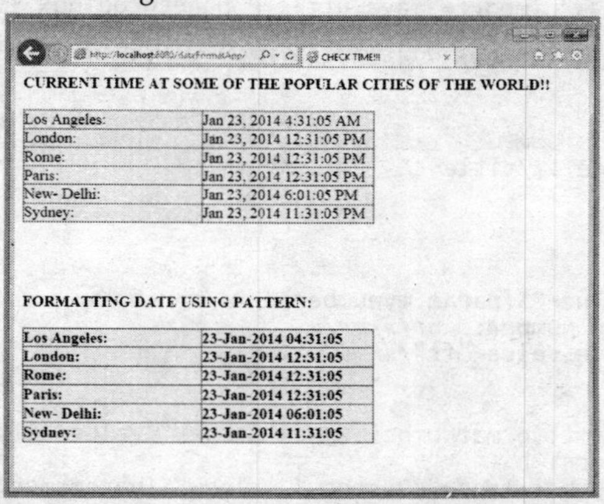

Figure 9.7: Showing the Default and Formatted Current Date and Times

After learning to use the `<fmt:formatDate>` tag in a Web application, let's learn to use the `<fmt:formatNumber>` tag.

Using the <fmt:formatNumber> Tag in the numFormatApp Application

Let's create a Web application named numFormatApp, which uses the <fmt:formatNumber> tag of the internationalization tag library. The home page of the Web application is index.html, which accepts a number from a user. The number is stored in the mynumber parameter that is passed to a JSP page named formatNum. The formatNum.jsp file formats the value of the mynumber parameter by using number format tags.

The following are the broad-level steps to create the numFormatApp Web application:

- Create the JSP and HTML pages
- Configure the Web application
- Define the directory structure of the Web application
- Package, deploy, and run the Web application

Let's now perform these steps in the following sections.

Creating the formatNum JSP and index HTML Pages

The index HTML page is the home page of the numFormatApp application. The code for the index.html file is shown in Listing 9.10 (save the index.html file in the \numFormatApp folder):

Listing 9.10: Showing the index.html File

```
<html>
<head>
   <title>Format a number</title>
</head>
<body>
   <form method=post action="formatNum.jsp">
   <pre>
          <b>Number :  <input type="text" name="mynumber"/>
          <input type="submit" value="Format Number"/>
          </b>
   </pre>
   </form>
</body>
</html>
```

The numFormatApp Web application displays index as the home page, which contains the Format Number button and a text box to accept a number to be formatted. When a user clicks the Format Number button, the control is transferred to the formatNum JSP page. Listing 9.11 shows the code for the formatNum JSP page (save the formatNum.jsp file in the \numFormatApp folder):

Listing 9.11: Showing the Code for the formatNum.jsp File

```
<%@ page language="java" import="java.util.*" pageEncoding="ISO-8859-1"%>
<%@ taglib uri="http://java.sun.com/jsp/jstl/fmt" prefix="fmt" %>
<%@ taglib prefix="c" uri="http://java.sun.com/jsp/jstl/core" %>
<!DOCTYPE html>
<html>
   <head>
          <title>welcome!!</title>

   </head>
   <body>
          My Number:
          <b><c:out value="${param.mynumber}"/></b> <br/>
          Formatting My Number: <br/><br/>
          <fmt:setLocale value="fr"/>
          In FRENCH:
          <pre>
          <b>MY NUM: <fmt:formatNumber type="number" value="${param.mynumber}"/></b>
          Default pattern:<b>
          <fmt:formatNumber type="currency" value="${param.mynumber}"/></b>
          Using pattern (0,00,00.0000):
          <b>
          <fmt:formatNumber type="currency" value="${param.mynumber}"
          pattern="00,0,00.0000"/> </b>
          </pre>
```

```
            <br/>
            In US:
            <fmt:setLocale value="en_US"/>
            <pre>
            <b>MY NUM: <fmt:formatNumber type="number" value="${param.mynumber}"/></b>
            Default pattern:<b>
            <fmt:formatNumber type="currency" value="${param.mynumber}"/></b>
            Using pattern (0,00,00.0000):
            <b>
            <fmt:formatNumber type="currency" value="${param.mynumber}" currencySymbol="$"
            pattern="0,00,00.0000" var="fmt_mynumber"/>
            <c:out value="${fmt_mynumber}"/>
            </b></pre>
            <br/>
      </body>
   </html>
```

Listing 9.11 retrieves the value of the mynumber parameter provided by the user in the home page of the Web application and formats it by using the `<fmt:formatNumber>` tag.

Now, let's configure the `numFormatApp` Web application in the web.xml file.

Configuring the numFormatApp Application

You need to configure the index HTML page of the `numFormatApp` application in the web.xml file. The code for the web.xml file is shown in the Listing 9.12 (save the web.xml file in the `\numFormatApp\WEB-INF` folder):

Listing 9.12: Showing the web.xml File for the `numFormatApp` Application

```
   <?xml version="1.0" encoding="UTF-8"?>
   <web-app version="3.1"
      xmlns="http://xmlns.jcp.org/xml/ns/javaee"
      xmlns:xsi="http://www.w3.org/2001/XMLSchema-instance"
      xsi:schemaLocation="http://xmlns.jcp.org/xml/ns/javaee
      http://xmlns.jcp.org/xml/ns/javaee/web-app_3_1.xsd">
   <welcome-file-list>
      <welcome-file> index.html </welcome-file>
   </welcome-file-list>
   </web-app>
```

In Listing 9.12, the index.html file is mapped as the welcome file in Deployment Descriptor (web.xml).

Defining the Directory Structure of the `numFormatApp Application`

After configuring the `numFormatApp` Web application, you create a directory structure to arrange the files of the application. Figure 9.8 shows the directory structure of the of the `numFormatApp` application:

Figure 9.8: Showing the Directory Structure of the numFormatApp Application

After creating the directory structure of the numFormatApp Web application, we need to package, deploy, and run the application.

Packaging, Deploying, and Running the numFormatApp Application

Perform the following steps to package, deploy and run the `numFormatApp` application:

1. Create the numFormatApp.war file and deploy it on the Glassfish Server 4.0.
2. Run the Web application by using the URL `http://localhost:8080/numFormatApp`. The index HTML page of the Web application appears, as shown in Figure 9.9:

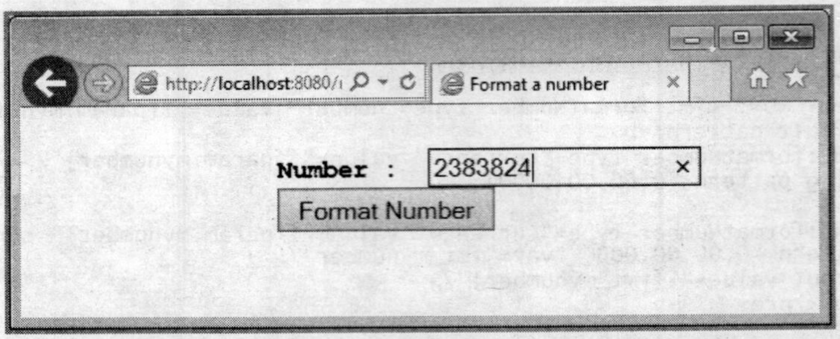

Figure 9.9: Displaying the Home Page of the numFormatApp Application

3. Enter a number in the Number text box in the index HTML page. In our case, we enter 2383824 and click the `Format Number` button. The control is passed to the formatNum JSP page to process the request.

   The formatNum JSP page formats the given number in French and US locale formats, with the default and given pattern, as shown in Figure 9.10:

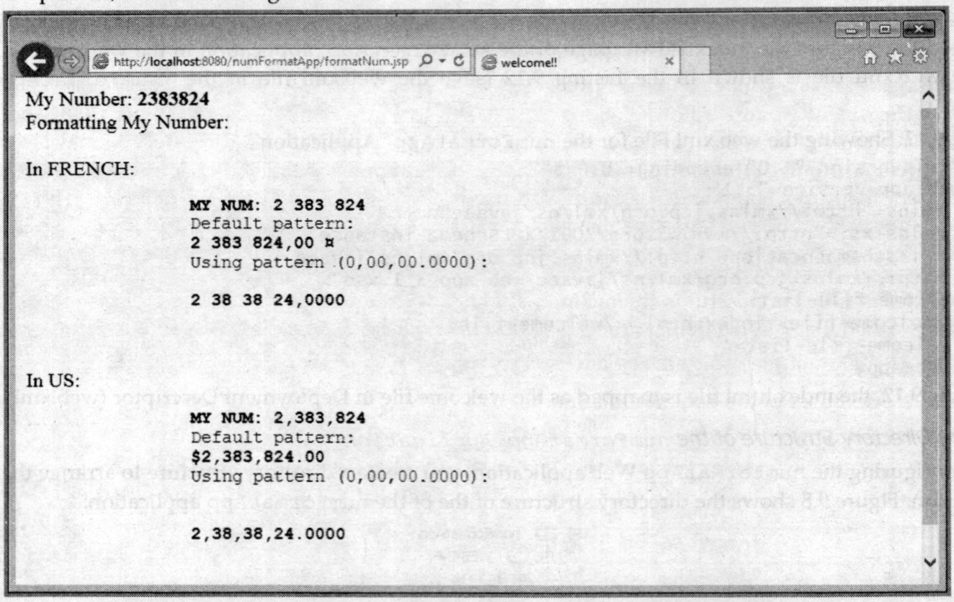

Figure 9.10: Showing a Number Formatted According to Various Locales

Let's now learn about the tags of the SQL tag library.

Working with the SQL Tag Library

The fourth JSTL tag library is the SQL tag library, which provides tags for interacting with relational databases. Interaction with databases is required to perform operations such as specifying data sources, creating queries, and performing updates. Web designers often need these SQL tags to access databases from JSP pages.

The SQL tag library depends on data sources to obtain connections. SQL statements are executed and the results are returned within the context of a connection retrieved from a data source. The data source is explicitly specified by the `dataSource` attribute of the `<sql:setDataSource>` tag.

Let's first explore the tags of the SQL tag library and then learn how to implement them in a Web application.

Exploring Tags of the SQL Tag Library

The tags of the SQL tag library are categorized based on the functionalities specified in Table 9.19:

Table 9.19: Functional Categorization and Associated Tags of the SQL Tag Library

Function	Tags
Getting a database connection	setDataSource
Accessing a database	query dateParam param transaction update

Now, let's discuss these tags under each functional category in detail.

The Tag for Getting a Database Connection

The SQL tag library provides the `<sql:setDataSource>` tag to allows an application to connect to databases. You can use the `<sql:setDataSource>` tag to get instances of a data source by either of the following ways:

- **Using the** `dataSource` **attribute**—Allows you to access a data source associated with a Java Naming and Directory Interfaces (JNDI) name. You can do this by passing the JNDI name as the value of the `dataSource` attribute. The following code snippet shows how to set a data source by setting the value for the `dataSource` attribute:

```
<sql:setDataSource dataSource="<Expression>" var="<Name>" scope="<scope>"/ >
```

- **Using the** `url` **attribute**—Allows you to set the URL for a Java Database Connectivity (JDBC) connection to the url attribute of the `<sql:setDataSource>` tag. Apart from the `url` attribute, you may also need to set the driver attribute, which is optional and specifies a class implementing a database server. If this is required, then user name and password also need to be specified to access a database. The syntax of the `<sql:setDataSource>` tag is as follows:

```
<sql:setDataSource url="<Expression>" driver="<Expression>" user="<Expression>"
   password="<Expression>" var="<Name>" scope="<Scope>"/>
```

JSTL provides tags that are useful in interacting with relational databases with the help of certain tags defined in a tag library called the SQL tag library. Table 9.20 describes the attributes of the <sql:setDataSource> tag:

Table 9.20: Attributes of the <sql:setDataSource> Tag

Table 9.20: Attributes of the <sql:setDataSource> Tag

Name of the Attribute	Type	Description
dataSource	String or javax.sql. DataSource	Specifies a data source. If specified as a `String`, this attribute can either be a relative path to a JNDI resource, or a JDBC parameter, `String`.
driver	String	Specifies the JDBC driver class name.
url	String	Specifies the JDBC URL used to connect to a database.
user	String	Specifies the user credentials on behalf of which a connection to the database is created.
password	String	Specifies a password for the user assigned to the `user` attribute with which the JDBC connection to a data source is established.
var	String	Specifies the name of the exported scoped variable for the specified data source.
scope	String	Specifies the scope of a variable for the specified data source. The `<sql:setDataSource>` tag exports the data source specified (either as a DataSource object or as a String) as a scoped variable.

A data source may be specified by either the `dataSource` attribute (as a `DataSource` object, JNDI relative path, or by providing the details for various JDBC attributes, such as driver, url, user, password.

Tags to Access a Database

The SQL tag library provides various tags that are used to access a database. These tags are as follows:

- The <sql:query> tag
- The <sql:update> tag
- The <sql:transaction> tag
- The <sql:param> tag
- The <sql:dateParam> tag

Now, let's discuss each of these tags in detail.

The <sql:query> Tag

The `<sql:query>` tag is used to query a database.

The syntax of the `<sql:query>` tag can be used in the following ways:

- The <sql:query> tag without body
- The <sql:query> tag with body
- The <sql:query> tag with optional query parameters

The <sql:query> Tag without Body

The syntax to use the <sql:query> tag without body content is as follows:

```
<sql:query sql="sqlQuery"
var="varName" [scope="{page|request|session|application}"]
[dataSource="dataSource"]
[maxRows="maxRows"]
[startRow="startRow"]/>
```

The <sql:query> Tag with Body

The syntax to use the <sql:query> tag with a body to specify query arguments is as follows:

```
<sql:query sql="sqlQuery"
var="varName" [scope="{page|request|session|application}"]
[dataSource="dataSource"]
[maxRows="maxRows"]
[startRow="startRow"]>
<sql:param> actions</sql:param>
</sql:query>
```

The <sql:query> Tag with Optional Query Parameters

The syntax to use <sql:query> tag with a body to specify query and optional query parameters is as follows:

```
<sql:query var="varName"
[scope="{page|request|session|application}"]
[dataSource="dataSource"]
[maxRows="maxRows"]
[startRow="startRow"]>
query
optional <sql:param> actions </sql:param>
</sql:query>
```

Table 9.21 describes the attributes of the <sql:query> tag:

Table 9.21: Attributes of the <sql:query> Tag

Name of the Attribute	Type	Description
dataSource	javax.sql.DataSource or String	Specifies the name of the variable assigned to the dataSource attribute of the <sql:setDataSource> tag, which is associated with the database used to execute a query. The relative path to a JNDI resource or the parameters for the JDBC DriverManager facility is represented by a String value.
maxRows	String	Specifies the maximum number of rows to be included in a query result. If the maximum number of rows is not specified, or set to -1, no limit on the

Table 9.21: Attributes of the <sql:query> Tag

Name of the Attribute	Type	Description
		maximum number of rows is enforced.
scope	String	Specifies the scope of the variable assigned to the var attribute for a query result.
sql	String	Specifies an SQL query statement, such as SELECT, UPDATE, and DELETE in a JSP page.
startRow	String	Specifies that a returned Result object includes the rows starting at the index specified for the startRow attribute. The first row of the original query resultset is at index 0. If the index is not specified, rows are included starting from the first row at index 0.
var	String	Specifies the name of an exported scoped variable for a query result.

The `<sql:query>` tag queries a database and gets back a single resultset containing rows of data. If the query produces no result, an empty `Result` object (of size zero) is returned. The SQL query statement may be specified by the `sql` attribute or from the body content of the `<sql:query>` tag.

A parameter marker (?) can be used in a query statement that represents the parameters of the JDBC PreparedStatement statement. You can provide values for these parameters by using nested parameter tags, such as <sql:param>. The `<sql:query>` tag implements the `SQLExecutionTag` interface, allowing parameter values to be provided by custom parameter actions.

The <sql:update> Tag

The `<sql:update>` tag executes an SQL `INSERT`, `UPDATE`, or `DELETE` statement. In addition, the `<sql:update>` tag can be used to execute SQL Data Definition Language (DDL) statements.

The syntax of the `<sql:update>` tag can be used in the following three ways:

- The <sql:update> tag without body
- The <sql:update> tag with body
- The <sql:update> tag with optional update parameters

The <sql:update> Tag without Body

The syntax of the <sql:update> tag without body content is as follows:

```
<sql:update sql="sqlUpdate"
[dataSource="dataSource"]
[var="varName"] [scope="{page|request|session|application}"]/>
```

The <sql:update> Tag with Body

The syntax to use the <sql:update> tag with a body to specify an update parameter is as follows:

```
<sql:update sql="sqlUpdate"
[dataSource="dataSource"]
[var="varName"] [scope="{page|request|session|application}"]>
<sql:param> actions </sql:param>
</sql:update>
```

The <sql:update> Tag with Optional Update Parameters

The syntax to use the <sql:update> tag to specify an update statement and optional update parameters is as follows:

```
<sql:update [dataSource="dataSource"]
[var="varName"] [scope="{page|request|session|application}"]>
update statement
optional <sql:param> actions</sql:param>
</sql:update>
```

Table 9.22 describes attributes of the <sql:update> tag:

Table 9.22: Attributes of the <sql:update> Tag		
Name of the Attribute	**Type**	**Description**
dataSource	javax.sql.DataSource or String	Specifies the name of the variable assigned to the dataSource attribute of the <sql:setDataSource> tag. The data source associated with the variable is used to execute an update query. The relative path to a JNDI resource or the parameters for the JDBC DriverManager facility is represented by a String value.
scope	String	Specifies the scope of the variable assigned to the var attribute that is used for the result of the update SQL statement.
sql	String	Specifies an update SQL statement in a JSP page.
var	String	Specifies the name of the scoped variable used for the result of a database update. The type of this variable is java.lang.Integer.

The sql attribute or body content of an action represents the SQL update statement. Parameter markers (?) may exist in the update statement, representing JDBC PreparedStatement parameters. Similar to the <sql:query> tag, you can provide parameter values for the <sql:update> tag by using nested parameter actions, such as <sql:param>. The <sql:update> tag also implements the SQLExecutionTag interface.

The connection to a database is obtained in the same manner as described for the <sql:query> tag. The result of the <sql:update> tag is stored in a scoped variable defined by the var attribute, if the attribute has been specified. The result represents the number of rows affected by the update. Zero is returned if no rows are affected by the update statement.

The <sql:transaction> Tag

The <sql:transaction> tag establishes a transaction context for the <sql:query> and <sql:update> subtags.

The syntax of the <sql:transaction> tag is as follows:

```
<sql:transaction [dataSource="dataSource"]
[isolation=isolationLevel]>
<sql:query> and <sql:update> statements
</sql:transaction>
isolationLevel ::= "read_committed"
| "read_uncommitted"
| "repeatable_read"
| "serializable"
```

Table 9.23 describes the attributes of the <sql:transaction> tag:

Table 9.23: Attributes of the <sql:transaction> Tag		
Name of the Attribute	**Type**	**Description**
dataSource	javax.sql.DataSource or String	Specifies the name of the variable assigned to the dataSource attribute of the <sql:setDataSource> tag. The data source associated with the variable is used to execute SQL transactions. The relative path to a JNDI resource or parameters for the JDBC DriverManager facility is represented by a String value.
isolation	String	Specifies the transaction isolation level. If not specified, this attribute represents the isolation level with which the data source is configured.

The <sql:transaction> tag groups nested <sql:query> and <sql:update> tags into a transaction. The transaction isolation levels are the ones defined by the java.sql.Connection interface. The tag handler of the <sql:transaction> tag must perform the following tasks in its life cycle by using the following methods:

- **doCatch()** – Calls the rollback() method of the Connection interface.
- **doEndTag()** – Calls the commit() method of the Connection interface.

- **doFinally()**—Enables the auto-commit mode by calling the setAutoCommit(true) method on the Connection object. The doFinally() method closes a JDBC connection when a transaction isolation level is saved. The connection is restored by using the setTransactionIsolation() method.
- **doStartTag()**—Specifies the transaction isolation level of Database Management System (DBMS). If the isolation level of transaction is set to TRANSACTION_NONE (i.e., transactions are not supported), an exception is thrown, which results in the failure of the transaction. For any other transaction isolation level, the auto-commit mode should be disabled by using the `setAutoCommit (false)` method of the `Connection` class. If the isolation attribute is specified, the current transaction isolation level is saved (and therefore can be restored later) and set to the specified level (by using the setTransactionIsolation() Connection method).

The `Connection` object is obtained and managed similar to the <sql:query> tag, and it can be never obtained from a parent tag. In other words, the <sql:transaction> tag cannot be nested to propagate a connection.

The `<sql:transaction>` tag commits and rollbacks a transaction (if it catches an exception) by calling the JDBC `Connection` `commit()` and `rollback()` methods, respectively. As the `<sql:transaction>` tag body does not support the execution of SQL statements by using the `<sql:update>` tag, the result is unpredictable. The behavior of the `<sql:transaction>` tag is undefined if it is executed in the context of a larger JTA user transaction.

To ensure database integrity, several updates to a database may be grouped into a transaction by nesting multiple `<sql:update>` tags inside a `<sql:transaction>` tag. For example, the following code snippet shows how the `<sql:transaction>` tag is used to transfer money between two accounts in one transaction, by using multiple updates:

```
<sql:transaction dataSource="${dataSource}">
<sql:update>
UPDATE account
SET Balance = Balance - ?
WHERE accountNo = ?
<sql:param value="${transferAmount}"/>
<sql:param value="${accountFrom}"/>
</sql:update>
<sql:update>
UPDATE account
SET Balance = Balance + ?
WHERE accountNo = ?
<sql:param value="${transferAmount}"/>
<sql:param value="${accountTo}"/>
</sql:update>
</sql:transaction>
```

Let's now discuss the <sql:param> tag.

The <sql:param> Tag

The `<sql:param>` tag is used as a subtag (such as `<sql:query>` and `<sql:update>`) of the `SQLExecutionTag` interface that is used to set the values of parameter markers (?) in an SQL statement.

The syntax of the `<sql:param>` tag can be used in either of the following ways:

- The <sql:param> tag without body
- The <sql:param> tag with body

The <sql:param> Tag without Body

The syntax of using the <sql:param> tag without body is as follows:

```
<sql:param value="value"/>
```

The <sql:param> Tag with Body

The sayntax of the <sql:param> tag with body content containing the value of a parameter is as follows:

```
<sql:param>
parameter value
</sql:param>
```

The <sql:param> tag provides a single attribute, `value`, which is used to provide a value to a parameter.

The `<sql:param>` tag substitutes a value for a parameter marker (?) in an SQL statement. Parameters are substituted in the order in which they are specified. The `<sql:param>` tag locates its nearest ancestor, which is an instance of the `SQLExecutionTag` interface, and calls its `addSQLParameter()` method. The specified parameter value is provided to the `addSQLParameter()` method to substitute the value in the parameter marker in the SQL statement.

The <sql:dateParam> Tag

The `<sql:dateParam>` tag is used as a subtag of the `SQLExecutionTag` interface to set the values of parameter markers (?) for values of the `java.util.Date` type.

The syntax of the <sql:dateParam> tag is as follows:

```
<sql:dateParam value="value" type="[timestamp|time|date]"/>
```

Table 9.24 describes the attributes of the <sql:dateParam> tag:

Table 9.24: Attributes of the <sql:dateParam> Tag

Name of the Attribute	Type	Description
value	java.util.Date	Specifies a parameter value for the DATE, TIME, or TIMESTAMP column in a database table.
type	String	Specifies a date, time or timestamp. By default, the timestamp is provided.

The <sql:dateParam> tag converts the specified `Date` object to objects such as `java.sql.Date`, `java.sql.Time`, or `java.sql.Timestamp` with the help of the `value` attribute.

If the specified `Date` object is an instance of the `java.sql.Time`, `java.sql.Date`, or `java.sql.Timestamp` class, the `Date` object is passed directly to a database without any type conversion.

Next, let's learn to use the tags of the SQL tag library in a Web application.

Using the SQL Tag Library in the SqlTagApp Application

In this section, we implement SQL tags with the help of a Web application named `SqlTagApp`.

The following are the broad-level steps to create the `SqlTagApp` Web application:

- Create the JSP page
- Create a book table in the Oracle database
- Configure the Web application
- Define the directory structure of the Web application
- Package, deploy, and run the Web application

Creating the bookDB JSP Page

Let's first create the bookDB.jsp file, which is the home page for the `SqlTagApp` Web application. This page shows the interaction with the Oracle database by using SQL tags, as shown in the code given in Listing 9.13 (save the bookDB.jsp file in the `\SqlTagApp` folder):

Listing 9.13: Showing the Code of the bookDB.jsp File

```
<%@ taglib uri="http://java.sun.com/jstl/core_rt" prefix="c" %>
<%@ taglib uri="http://java.sun.com/jstl/sql_rt" prefix="sql" %>
<sql:setDataSource var="datasource"
  driver="oracle.jdbc.driver.OracleDriver"
  url="jdbc:oracle:thin:@192.168.1.123:1521:XE" user="scott" password="tiger"
  />
<sql:query var="books" dataSource="${datasource}">
  SELECT id, title, price FROM book
</sql:query>
<html>
  <head>
        <title>Accessing Database using JSTL</title>
```

```
    </head>
    <h2> Books Available in the Database</h2>
    <body>
          <table border="1">
          <tr>
          <td>id</td><td>title</td><td>price</td>
          </tr>
          <c:forEach varStatus="status" items="${books.rows}" var="row">
          <tr>
          <td><c:out value="${row.id}" /></td>
          <td><c:out value="${row.title}" /></td>
          <td><c:out value="${row.price}" /></td>
          </tr>
          </c:forEach>
          </table>
    </body>
  </html>
```

In Listing 9.13, a connection to the Oracle database is created by using the `datasource` variable. In addition, the result of the SELECT statement is stored in the `books` variable. The value of a row is stored in the `row` variable and is accessed by using the separator (.) along with the `row` variable, followed by the name of the column. For example, the `row.id` expression is used to retrieve the value of `the` id column.

Creating the book Table in the Oracle Database

The `SqlTagApp` Web application establishes a connection with the book table in the Oracle database. The table structure of the book table is shown in Table 9.25:

Table 9.25: Structure of the book Table

Column Name	Data Type
ID	NUMBER
TITLE	VARCHAR2(30)
PRICE	VARCHAR2(30)

After defining the structure of the book table, let's move to the next step and configure the `SqlTagApp` application.

Configuring the SqlTagApp Application

We now configure the `SqlTagApp` application in the web.xml file. The code for web.xml is shown in Listing 9.14 (save the web.xml file in the `\SqlTagApp\WEB-INF` folder):

Listing 9.14: Showing the web.xml File for the `SqlTagApp` Application

```
<?xml version="1.0" encoding="UTF-8"?>
<web-app version="3.1"
  xmlns="http://xmlns.jcp.org/xml/ns/javaee"
  xmlns:xsi="http://www.w3.org/2001/XMLSchema-instance"
  xsi:schemaLocation="http://xmlns.jcp.org/xml/ns/javaee
  http://xmlns.jcp.org/xml/ns/javaee/web-app_3_1.xsd">
<welcome-file-list>
  <welcome-file>bookDB.jsp</welcome-file>
</welcome-file-list>
</web-app>
```

In Listing 9.14, the bookDB.jsp file is set as the welcome file for the SqlTagApp Web application.

Defining the Directory Structure of the SqlTagApp Application

You can create the directory structure for the `SqlTagApp` application, and arrange all the files of the application, as shown in Figure 9.11:

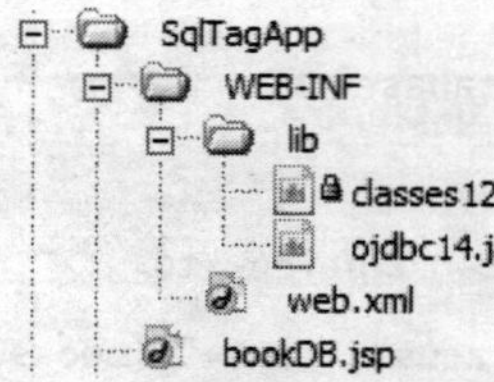

Figure 9.11: Showing the SqlTagApp Directory Structure

Packaging, Deploying, and Running the SqlTagApp Application

Perform the following steps to package, deploy, and run the `SqlTagApp` Web application:

1. Create the SqlTagApp.war file and deploy it on the Glassfish Server 4.0.
2. Access the Web application by using the URL `http://localhost:8080/SqlTagApp`. The first page of the application is `bookDB.jsp`, as shown in Figure 9.12:

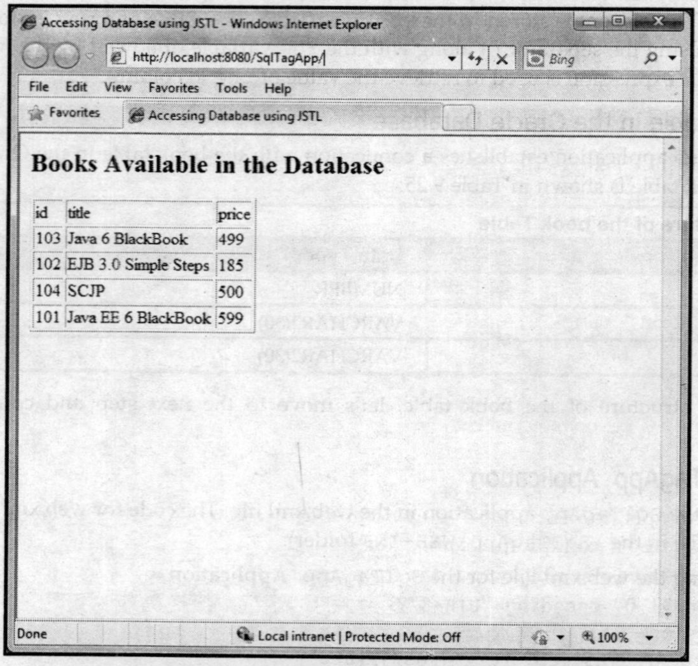

Figure 9.12: Showing the Use of SQL Tags

Let's now discuss the functions tag library.

Working with the Functions Tag Library

The functions tag library contains various functions to support tasks such as calculating the length of a collection or performing String manipulation. Let's learn about the functions available in the functions tag library in detail in the following sections.

Exploring the Functions Available in the Functions Tag Library

The functions tag library provides a set of functions that can be used with EL. The tags of the functions tag library use the `fn` prefix and allow you to perform String manipulations without using Java code within scriptlet tags.

Table 9.26 shows the functions available in the functions tag library according to their category:

Table 9.26: Functions in the Functions Tag Library

Category	Functions
Collection length	`length`

String manipulation	`toUpperCase, toLowerCase`
	`subString, subStringAfter, subStringBefore`
	`trim`
	`replace`
	`indexOf, startsWith, endsWith,`
	`contains, containsIgnoreCase`
	`split, join`
	`escapeXml`

Let's discuss each of these functional categories in detail.

Describing the Collection length Function

The functions tag library provides a single collection length function called `fn:length`. The `fn:length` function can be applied to any collection to return the number of items in a collection. When applied to a String, the `fn:length` function returns the number of characters from the String.

The following code snippet shows the use of the `fn:length` function:

```
<%@ taglib uri="http://java.sun.com/jsp/jstl/core"
prefix="c" %>
<%@ taglib uri="http://java.sun.com/jsp/jstl/functions"
prefix="fn" %>
<html>
<head><title>Hello</title></head>
<input type="text" name="username" size="25">
<input type="submit" value="Submit">
<input type="reset" value="Reset">
</form>
<c:if test="${fn:length(param.username) > 0}" >
<%@include file="response.jsp" %>
</c:if>
</body>
</html>
```

In preceding code snippet, the `fn:length` function returns the value of the parameter named `username`. This value is checked against a condition specified by using the `<c:if>` tag. If the condition evaluates to true, another JSP page named response is included in the current JSP page.

Exploring the String Manipulation Functions

JSTL provides several useful functions, such as escapeXml and indexOf, to perform String manipulation in a JSP page. Table 9.27 shows various JSTL functions supporting String manipulation:

Table 9.27: JSTL Functions for String Manipulation

Function	Description
`escapeXml`	Returns the String values after escaping the characters that can be interpreted by using XML
`indexOf, startsWith, endsWith, contains, and containsIgnoreCase`	Verify whether or not a `String` contains another `String`
`join`	Returns a String from an array that contains values separated by a separator, such as ; or ,

Let's now learn to implement the JSTL function in a Web application.

Using the JSTL Functions in the JSTLFunctionApp Application

Let's now create a Web application named `JSTLFunctionApp` to implement the tags of the functions tag library. The following are the broad-level steps to create the `JSTLFunctionApp` Web application:

- Create the JSP page
- Configure the Web application
- Define the directory structure of the Web application
- Package, deploy, and run the Web application

Creating the index JSP Page

Let's create a JSP page named index, which is a home page of the `JSTLFunctionApp` Web application. The index.jsp file demonstrates various JSTL functions, as shown in the code of Listing 9.15 (save the index.jsp file in the `\JSTLFunctionApp` folder):

Listing 9.15: Showing the Code for the index.jsp File

```
<%@ page language="java" import="java.util.*" pageEncoding="ISO-8859-1"%>
<%@ taglib uri="http://java.sun.com/jsp/jstl/functions" prefix="fn" %>
<%@ taglib uri="http://java.sun.com/jsp/jstl/core" prefix="c" %>
<html>
<head><title>example showing JSTL functions</title></head>
<body>
<h2>Using various JSTL 1.2 functions</h2>
<c:set var="var" value="Example showing usage of JSTL functions"/>
The length of the test String: ${fn:length(var)}<br />
Does the test String contain "JSTL"? ${fn:contains(var,"JSTL")}<br />
Putting the String into upper case using fn:toUpperCase(): ${fn:toUpperCase(var)}<br />
Splitting the String into a String array using fn:split(), and returning the array length:
  ${fn:length(fn:split(var," "))}<br />
</body>
</html>
```

Configuring the JSTLFunctionApp Application

Let's now configure the `JSTLFunctionApp` Web application in the web.xml file and set the index JSP page in the<welcome-file> tag. The code for the web.xml file is shown in Listing 9.16 (save the web.xml file in the `\JSTLFunctionApp\WEB-INF` folder):

Listing 9.16: Showing the Code for the web.xml File for the `JSTLFunctionApp Application`

```
<?xml version="1.0" encoding="UTF-8"?>
<web-app version="3.1"
  xmlns="http://xmlns.jcp.org/xml/ns/javaee"
  xmlns:xsi="http://www.w3.org/2001/XMLSchema-instance"
  xsi:schemaLocation="http://xmlns.jcp.org/xml/ns/javaee
  http://xmlns.jcp.org/xml/ns/javaee/web-app_3_1.xsd">
<welcome-file-list>
  <welcome-file>index.jsp</welcome-file>
</welcome-file-list>
</web-app>
```

Defining the Directory Structure of the JSTLFunctionApp Application

Create a directory structure as shown in Figure 9.13, and arrange the preceding files accordingly:

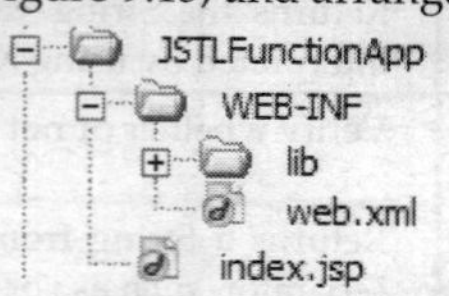

Figure 9.13: Showing the JSTLFunctionApp Directory Structure

Packaging, Deploying, and Running the JSTLFunctionApp Application

Perform the following steps to package, deploy, and run the JSTLFunctionApp application:

1. Create the JSTLFunctionApp.war file and deploy it on the Glassfish Server 4.0.
2. Run the Web application using the URL `http://localhost:8080/JSTLFunctionApp`. The index JSP page of the application is shown in Figure 9.14:

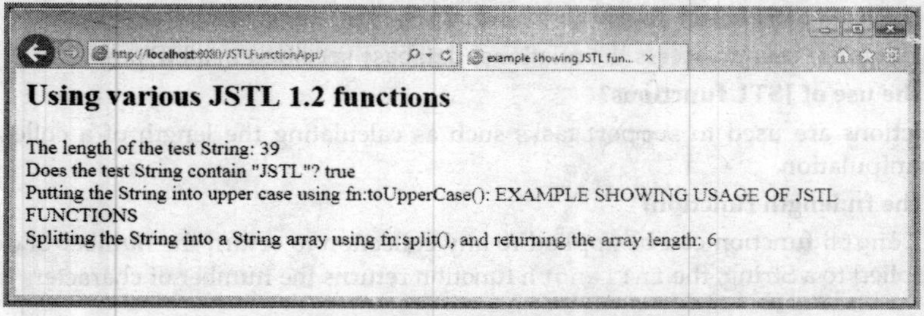

Figure 9.14: Showing the Output of a Test String

Figure 9.14 displays the length of the specified String and converts the text of the String in upper case by using tags of the functions tag library.

Let's now summarize the concepts discussed in the chapter.

Summary

The chapter has provided an introduction to JSTL and discussed its various features in detail. It has also discussed the various tag libraries supported by JSTL, including the core tag library, the XML tag library, the internationalization tag library, the SQL tag library, and the functions tag library. The chapter has also explained the process to create Web applications to demonstrate the use of these tag libraries.

In the next chapter, you will learn about the use of filters in Web applications.

Quick Revise

Q1. What is JSTL?

Ans. JSTL is a collection of tag libraries, which provides commonly needed functionalities, such as performing iteration, conditionals, database access, XML processing, and internationalization, in JSP pages.

Q2. The total number of libraries that JSTL provides is ……………..

A. 4
B. 3
C. 5
D. 6

Ans. The correct option is C.

Q3. What are JSTL core tags used for?

Ans. JSTL core tags are used to perform iteration and conditional processing, and to access URL-based resources.

Q4. How many flow control tags are available in the core tag library?

A. 2
B. 3
C. 4
D. 5

Ans. The correct option is D

Q5. What is the <x:transform> tag used for?

Ans. The <x:transform> tag applies a transformation to an XML document based on a specified XSLT.

Q6. What are JSTL XML tags used for?

Ans. JSTL XML tags are used to parse and transform the data used in a JSP page.

Q7. What are JSTL internationalization tags used for?

Ans. JSTL internationalization tags are used to format data such as dates, numbers, or time specifications in different domains.

Q8. What is the use of JSTL SQL tags?

Ans. JSTL SQL tags are used to access the relational database specified in a JSP page.

Q9. What is the use of JSTL functions?

Ans. JSTL functions are used to support tasks such as calculating the length of a collection or performing String manipulation.

Q10. What is the fn:length function?

Ans. The `fn:length` function can be applied to any collection to return the number of items in a collection. When applied to a String, the `fn:length` function returns the number of characters from the String.

10

Implementing Filters

A filter is a Java class that is called for responding to the requests for resources, such as Java Servlet and JavaServer Pages (JSP). Filters dynamically change the behavior of a resource when a client requests the resource. In other words, the filter mapped to a resource, such as a Uniform Resource Locator (URL) or a servlet, is invoked when the resource is accessed. Filters intercept and process the requests before the requests are forwarded to servlets, and process the responses after the response has been generated by the servlet. Usually, a filter encapsulates and modifies the values of `request`, `response`, or header before or after the execution of the requested target resource. Filters need to be configured in order to serve client requests. Filters can also be put into a chain, where multiple filters can be invoked one after the other. A filter in a chain can either transfer the control to the next filter or redirect the request out of the chain to retrieve the requested resource.

Filters were introduced in Servlet 2.3 specification. The Servlet specification defines APIs for filters ensuring that filters not only run on the application server that you develop it on, but also on any other application servers that follow the Servlet specification.

In this chapter, you learn about filters and their use. Then, you learn to set up a development environment to create, configure, and test applications implementing filters. In addition, the chapter helps you to configure a filter using Deployment Descriptor as well as annotations. Moreover, you also learn how to define initializing parameters for filters. Next, the chapter helps you to manipulate the response using filters. Finally, the chapter discusses the issues raised by using threads with filters.

Exploring the Need of Filters

The need for implementing filters can be understood with the help of few examples. Let's take an example of a Web application that formats the data to be presented to clients in a specific format, say Excel. However, at a later point of time, the clients may require data in some other format, such as Hypertext Markup Language (HTML), Portable Document Format (PDF), or Word. In such a situation, instead of modifying the code every time to change the format of data, a filter can be created to transform data dynamically in the required formats.

Let's consider another example where a developer creates a Web application in which a servlet handles user logins. This implies that when a user submits his credentials, the servlet verifies the credentials against the user information. The servlet also creates a session for the user, so that other components in the application can also use the session details of the user. At a later point of time, the developer might require maintaining a login entry for each user login attempt in the application server's log system. In order to implement this, the developer would need to change the existing code or add additional code to the servlet and redeploy the Web application.

In such a situation, a servlet, besides fulfilling its primary objective that is to accept request and send responses to clients has to also implement additional functionalities. This additional load on the servlet reduces the efficiency of the application. To overcome this problem, filters were introduced that can implement these additional functionalities, such as verifying login credentials and maintaining the server log in a database. One of the most striking features of the filters is that they can be reused in other Web applications as well.

Some of the situations and tasks where filters can be used are as follows:

- Security verification
- Session validation
- Logging operations
- Internationalization
- Triggering resource access events
- Image conversion
- Scaling maps
- Data compression
- Encryption
- Tokenization
- Mime type changing

- Caching and XSL transformations of XML responses
- Debugging

Let's now learn how the filters work in a Web application.

Exploring the Working of Filters

When you send a request for a specific resource or a collection of resources, the request is intercepted by a filter. In order to properly intercept a request, a filter should have access to the HTTP request and response objects. The filter accesses the HTTP request and response objects by accessing the `javax.servlet.ServletRequest` and `javax.servlet.ServletResponse` objects. The filter also needs to access the list of chained filters that can be invoked in a sequence. To access the chained filters, the filter uses the `javax.servlet.FilterChain` object. After completing its work, a filter can call the next chained filter, block the request, throw an exception, or call up the originally requested resource.

After calling up the original resource, the control goes back to the last filter in the chain, which can inspect and modify the response headers and data, handle response, throw an exception, or call the filter before the last filter in the chain. The process carries on in the reverse order up through the filter chain.

Let's now discuss the Filter Application Programming Interface (API) that is used to create filters.

Exploring Filter API

The Filter API includes three interfaces:

- Filter
- FilterConfig
- FilterChain

These interfaces are present in the javax.servlet package. The following sections discuss each of these interfaces in detail.

The Filter Interface

A filter can be created in an application by implementing the `javax.servlet.Filter` interface, which is the basic interface defined in the Servlet API.

The `Filter` interface calls the following methods during the life cycle of a filter:

- **The `init()` method**—Refers to the method that is invoked by the Web container only once when the filter is initialized. The servlet container passes the `FilterConfig` object as a parameter through the `init()` method.
- **The `doFilter()` method**—Refers to the method that is invoked each time a user requests a resource, such as a servlet to which the filter is mapped. When the `doFilter()` method is invoked, the servlet container passes the `ServletRequest`, `ServletResponse`, and `FilterChain` objects. The `FilterChain` object is passed to control **the** next object, if any.
- **The `destroy()` method**—Refers to the method that is invoked when the filter instance is destroyed.

Table 10.1 lists the syntax and working of all the preceding three methods of the `Filter` interface:

Table 10.1: Methods of the Filter Interface

Method	Syntax	Description
init	void init(FilterConfig filterConfig) throws ServletException	Initializes a filter and places it into service. A filter cannot be placed into service by the Web container if either a `ServletException` is thrown by the `init()` method or the method is not invoked within the time period specified by the Web container.
doFilter	void doFilter(ServletRequest request, ServletResponse response, FilterChain chain)throws	Filters a request/response pair, whenever the pair is passed through a filter chain. The method takes an instance of the FilterChain interface as an argument, which helps the filter to forward the request and

Table 10.1: Methods of the Filter Interface		
Method	**Syntax**	**Description**
	IOException, ServletException	response to the next filter in the chain. The doFilter() method encapsulates the actual logic of the filter. For example, this method can be implemented to perform the following tasks: • Examining the request • Carrying out input filtering by wrapping the request object with filter content or headers • Carrying out output filtering by wrapping the response object with filter content or headers • Invoking the next filter in the filter chain by calling the `FilterChain` object (`chain.doFilter()`) or blocking the request by not forwarding the request/response pair to the next filter in the filter chain • Setting the response headers can be done directly after invoking the next filter in the filter chain
destroy	void destroy()	Removes the filter instance indicating that the filter is being moved out of service. This method is invoked only once for all threads within the doFilter() method. Once the destroy() method is called by the Web container, the doFilter() method cannot be called again on this filter instance. The destroy() method enables the filter to give up any resources being held, such as memory, file handles, or threads and ensures the synchronization of any persistent state with the current state of filter in memory.

The FilterConfig Interface

The `FilterConfig` interface is used to store the initialized data. The `init()` method of the `Filter` interface takes a filter configuration object as an argument, which is an instance of the `FilterConfig` interface. The filter receives filter configuration information during initialization from a servlet container through the `FilterConfig` object. The `getFilterName()`, `getInitParameter()`, `getInitParameterNames()`, and `getServletContext()` methods of the `FilterConfig` interface help in retrieving the filter name, initialization parameter values, and the reference to the `ServletContext, respectively.`

Table 10.2 describes the methods available in the `FilterConfig` interface:

Table 10.2: Methods of the FilterConfig Interface		
Method	**Syntax**	**Description**
`getFilterName`	String getFilterName()	Returns the filter name as assigned in Deployment Descriptor.
`getInitParameter`	String getInitParameter(String name)	Returns the named `initialization` parameter value as a `String. A null` value is returned if the parameter is not found. The `name` represents a `String` specifying the name of the `initialization` parameter.
`getInitParameterNames`	Enumeration getInitParameterNames()	Returns an `Enumeration` of `String` objects. The String objects in the Enumeration represent the initialization parameter names for the filter. An empty `Enumeration is returned,` if no initialization parameters are found for the

Table 10.2: Methods of the FilterConfig Interface

Method	Syntax	Description
		filter.
getServletContext	ServletContext getServletContext()	Returns a reference of the ServletContext interface in which a filter is executed. It returns a ServletContext object, used by the filter to interact with the servlet container.

The FilterChain Interface

The FilterChain interface provides a mechanism to invoke a series of filters, which are specified in a filter chain, in an application. The filter chain instance is the instance of the class that implements the FilterChain interface.

The objects of the FilterChain interface are provided by the Web container to invoke the next filter in the chain of filters. In case the invoked filter is the last one in the chain, the target resource is invoked. The FilterChain interface specifies only the doFilter() method, which invokes the next filter or the targeted resource. The following code snippet shows the syntax of the doFilter() method:

```
public void doFilter(ServletRequest request,
ServletResponse response) throws IOException, ServletException
```

In the preceding syntax:

- The request parameter refers to the target resource request that is passed to the next filter in the chain
- The response parameter refers to the filter response that is forwarded to the target resource
- The doFilter() method causes the invocation of the next filter in the chain. The resource at the end of the chain is invoked in case the calling filter is the last chained filter

Let's now learn how to configure a filter.

Configuring a Filter

The web.xml file is used to configure filters to resources, such as servlet, JSP page, or Web application. This configuration helps to process the request and response objects. With the introduction of annotations in Servlet, filters can also be configured using annotations. Prior to the use of annotations, Deployment Descriptor was used for defining configuration and mapping for filters and servlets. The use of annotations eliminates the need of Deployment Descriptor. The mapping and configuration logic can be directly included within the filter class. In this section, you learn to:

- Configure a filter using Deployment Descriptor
- Configure a filter using Annotations

Configuring Filters Using Deployment Descriptor

You can configure filters as part of a Web application by using the application's web.xml Deployment Descriptor, which is located in the WEB-INF directory of the Web application. In Deployment Descriptor, you can declare and map the filter either to specific or multiple URL patterns or to servlets in the Web application. You can declare any number of filters and bind them with a specific pattern to any number of servlets or URL patterns. The <filter> and <filter-mapping> elements are used for configuring filters. The <filter> element must immediately succeed the <context-param> element and precede the <listener> and <servlet> elements in the web.xml file. The <filter> element declares a filter, defines a name for the filter, and specifies the Java class that executes the filter. One or more initialization parameters can also be specified inside the <filter> element by using the <init-param> element.

The following code snippet shows the code for adding a filter declaration in the web.xml file:

```
<filter>
   <filter-name>DemoFilter</filter-name>
   <display-name>demofilter</display-name>
   <description>This is my demo filter</description>
```

```
        <filter-class>com.kogent.DemoFilter</filter-class>
        <init-param>
              <param-name>InitParamName</param-name>
              <param-value>InitParamValue</param-value>
        </init-param>
    </filter>
```

In the preceding code snippet, the `<filter-name>` element specifies the name of the filter and the `<filter-class>` element specifies the Java class that executes the filter. The description and display-name parameters are optional. The <init-param> element specifies the initialization parameters. `InitParamName` is the name of the initialization parameter specified by the <param-name> element and `InitParamValue` is the value of the initialization parameter specified by the <param-value> element. The filter class in a Web application can read the initialization parameters by using the `FilterConfig.getInitParameter()` or `FilterConfig.getInitParameterNames()` method.

The `<filter-mapping>` element defines the filter that is to be executed on the basis of the URL pattern or filter-name specified within the `<filter-mapping>` element. You need to specify the name of the filter and the URL pattern for creating a filter mapping using a URL pattern. The `<filter-mapping>` element must immediately succeed the `<filter>` element(s).

The following code snippet shows how to map a filter to a particular URL pattern:

```
    <filter-mapping>
       <filter-name>DemoFilter</filter-name>
       <url-pattern>/myPattern/*</url-pattern>
    </filter-mapping>
```

In the preceding code snippet, the DemoFilter filter is mapped to the requests containing the /myPattern/ URL pattern. According to Servlet specification, the `<filter-mapping>` element supports multiple url patterns for a filter. The following code snippet shows mapping of a filter to multiple URL patterns:

```
    <filter-mapping>
       <filter-name>DemoFilter</filter-name>
       <url-pattern>/myPattern/*</url-pattern>
       <url-pattern>/myDemoPatterns/*</url-pattern>
    </filter-mapping>
```

In the preceding code snippet, the DemoFilter filter is mapped to the request containing /myPattern/ and /myDemoPatterns/ URL patterns. Therefore, multiple URL patterns can be mapped to a single filter using the `<url-pattern>` element. Similarly, multiple filters can be mapped to a specific URL pattern. The filters can also be mapped to a specific servlet by mapping the filter to the name of the servlet that is registered in the Web application. The following code snippet shows the code for mapping a filter to the name of a servlet:

```
    <filter-mapping>
       <filter-name>DemoFilter</filter-name>
       <servlet-name>DemoServlet</servlet-name>
    </filter-mapping>
```

In the preceding code snippet, the DemoFilter filter is mapped to DemoServlet servlet. You can also map the filter to multiple servlets registered in a Web application, as shown in the following code snippet:

```
    <filter-mapping>
       <filter-name>DemoFilter</filter-name>
       <servlet-name>DemoServlet</servlet-name>
       <servlet-name>MyServlet</servlet-name>
    </filter-mapping>
```

In the preceding code snippet, the DemoFilter filter is mapped to the DemoServlet servlet and the MyServlet servlet. Apart from using Deployment Descriptor, filters can also be configured by using annotations.

Configuring Filters Using Annotations

With the introduction of annotations, the configuration code can be directly included in the code of the filter class. The @WebFilter annotation is used to mark a filter.

The following code snippet shows how a filter can be configured using annotations:

```
    @WebFilter(filterName="DemoFilter", urlPatterns={"/myPattern/*"})
```

In the preceding code snippet, the filterName attribute defines the name of the filter and urlPatterns attribute defines the URL pattern which causes the invocation of the filter.

This completes the discussion about configuring filters. The next section focuses on the implementation of filters.

Creating a Web Application Using Filters

In this section, you learn how to implement and use filters by creating a simple Web application in which a login filter checks the login credentials entered by the user before the request for a servlet is made. Let's now create the FilterApp Web application in which the user logs in with a user name and password. The login credentials entered by the user are verified by a filter. If the user enters correct login credentials then the control is redirected to a servlet which displays a welcome message to the user; otherwise, an error message of invalid user credentials is displayed on the browser.

In *Chapter 5, Handling Sessions in Servlet 3.1*, you have created the `LoginApp` Web application, which contained a servlet to validate user credentials. In the `LoginApp` Web application, a client directly communicated with the `LoginServlet`, which was used for validating the user credentials. In the `FilterApp` Web application, the Web container invokes a filter to validate user credentials when the client requests for a resource. The Web container then invokes the target resource, such as a servlet if the user credentials are correct. A filter is used to ensure that the servlet is used only for handling requests and generating responses, while the validation is taken care of by the filter.

As discussed in the `Configuring a Filter` section of this chapter, filters can be configured by using Deployment Descriptor, as well as annotations. In this section, you learn to create the `FilterApp` Web application using both the ways. First, create the application using Deployment Descriptor to configure filters. Then, recreate the `FilterApp` Web application by using annotations to mark filters.

Using Deployment Descriptor to Configure a Filter

Let's now create the FilterApp Web application by using Deployment Descriptor for configuring filters used in the application. The `FilterApp` Web application includes filters for verifying user credentials, servlets for testing filters, and a home page for submitting user credentials.

Perform the following steps to create and run the FilterApp application:

- Create a generic filter
- Write the code for the first filter
- Creating the home page
- Creating a servlet to test the filter
- Configuring the filter and the servlet
- Running the FilterApp Web application

Creating a Generic Filter

A filter is created by implementing the `Filter` interface. However, instead of implementing the `Filter` interface for every filter that you create, you can create a generic filter for all the filters in a Web application. The generic filter can hold all the needed methods of the `Filter` interface. The other filters can access the methods of a generic filter by implementing the generic filter in an application.

Let's create the `MyGenericFilter` filter for the `FilterApp` Web application. The generic filter implements the `Filter` interface and defines all the necessary methods of the `Filter` interface. Instead of implementing the `Filter` interface, every time while creating a new filter, you can extend this generic filter and can overwrite the required methods. Apart from creating a filter, you also need to configure the filter in the web.xml file.

Listing 10.1 provides the code for the `MyGenericFilter` filter (save the `MyGenericFilter.java` file in the `\FilterApp\src\com\kogent\filter` folder):

Listing 10.1: Showing the Code for the `MyGenericFilter.java` File

```
package com.kogent.filter;
import java.io.*;
import javax.servlet.*;
```

```
import javax.servlet.http.*;
public class MyGenericFilter implements Filter
{
   private FilterConfig filterconf = null;
   public void doFilter(final ServletRequest req, final ServletResponse res,
   FilterChain chain) throws IOException, ServletException
   {
         chain.doFilter(req,res);
   }

   public FilterConfig getFilterConfig()
   {
         return filterconf;
   }

   public void setFilterConfig(final FilterConfig filterconf)
   {
         this.filterconf = filterconf;
   }

   public void init(FilterConfig filterconf)
   {
         this.filterconf = filterconf;
   }

   public void destroy()
   {
         this.filterconf = null;
   }
}
```

In Listing 10.1, the `MyGenericFilter` class implements the `Filter` interface. Each instance of a generic filter has an instance variable that can hold the `FilterConfig` interface object to represent the configuration details of a filter. In the MyGenericFilter class, the filterconf variable holds the instance of the `FilterConfig` interface. As shown in Listing 10.1, the instance of the `FilterChain` interface is passed as an argument to the `doFilter()` method to call the next filter in the filter chain. When the Web container invokes the `doFilter()` method of the MyGenericFilter filter and if there are no more filters available in the chain, the Web container invokes the target resource. The `getFilterConfig()and setFilterConfig()` methods are utility methods that retrieve and set the filter configuration details, respectively. The `init()` method is invoked by the Web container during initialization of a filter. The `destroy()` method is called by the Web container when the current filter instance needs to be removed from service.

Compile your generic filter. After compilation, the `MyGenericFilter.class` file should be located in the `FilterApp\WEB-INF\classes\com\kogent\filter` directory.

Writing Your First Filter

In order to create a filter, you first create a class, `MyFilter`, which is a Java class implementing the `MyGenericFilter` interface. As discussed in the `Filter` interface, the following methods must be implemented while writing a filter:

- public void init(FilterConfig config)
- public void doFilter(ServletRequest request, ServletResponse response, FilterChain chain)
- public void destroy()

The `init()` method is called by the Web container to indicate that the `MyFilter` filter has been placed into service. The `doFilter()` method declared in the `MyFilter` class examines the request, verifies the user credentials, and finally invokes the targeted servlet. The `destroy()` method is invoked when the servlet is taken out of service. The `MyFilter` filter inherits the `init()` and `destroy()` methods from the `MyGenericFilter` Filter and overrides the `doFilter()` method.

Listing 10.2 shows the code for the `MyFilter` class (save the `MyFilter.java` file in the `\FilterApp\src\com\kogent\filter` folder):

Listing 10.2: Showing the Code for `MyFilter.java` File

```
package com.kogent.filter;

import java.io.*;
import javax.servlet.*;
import javax.servlet.http.*;

public class MyFilter extends MyGenericFilter
{
   public void doFilter(ServletRequest req, ServletResponse res,
   FilterChain chain) throws IOException, ServletException
   {
                  String password =
                  ((HttpServletRequest) req).getParameter("password");
                  if(password.equals("mypassword"))
         {
                        String uri = ((HttpServletRequest)req).getRequestURI();
                        chain.doFilter(req, res);
         }
         else
         {
                        res.setContentType("text/html");
                  PrintWriter pw = res.getWriter();
                        pw.println("<html>");
                        pw.println("<head><title>Wrong Password</title></head>");
                        pw.println("<body>");
                        pw.println("<h3>Sorry, the password was incorrect.</h3>");
                        pw.println("</body>");
                        pw.println("</html>");
         }
   }
}
```

In Listing 10.2, the `doFilter()` method retrieves the password entered by the user and checks whether the password entered is `mypassword`. If the password entered is correct, the `MyFilter` filter invokes the targeted servlet; otherwise, an error message is displayed to the user indicating that the user has entered an incorrect password.

Compile the `MyFilter.java` file. After compilation, the class file should be located in the `\FilterApp\WEB-INF\classes\com\kogent\filter` folder.

Creating the Home Page

In the FilterApp application, let's create the `index.html` file used to access a servlet to test the MyFilter filter.

Listing 10.3 shows the code for the index.html file (save the index.html file in the \FilterApp folder):

Listing 10.3: Showing the Code for the index.html File

```
<!DOCTYPE html>
<html>
         <head>
         <title>Login Application Using Filters </title>
         </head>
<body>
         <h1>Login Application Using Filters </h1>
   <form action="/FilterApp/WelcomeServlet">
   <table>
   <tr>
         <td>User Name</td>
         <td>
         <input type="text" name="username"/>
         </td>
   </tr>
   <tr>
         <td>Password</td>
         <td><input type="password" name="password"/>
```

```
            </td>
    </tr>
    <tr>
            <td></td>
            <td><input type="submit" value="Submit"/></td>
    </tr>
    </table>
    </form>
</body>
</html>
```

Let's now learn to create the `WelcomeServlet` servlet, which invokes the `MyFilter` filter during initialization.

Creating a Servlet to Test the Filter

The `WelcomeServlet` servlet receives users' requests and sends the desired responses. When the `WelcomeServlet` servlet is initialized, the `MyFilter` filter is invoked. The `MyFilter` filter verifies the user credentials and then invokes the target servlet, `WelcomeServlet`.

The `WelcomeServlet` servlet displays a welcome message to the user if the password entered is `mypassword`.

Listing 10.4 shows the code for the `WelcomeServlet.java` file (save the `WelcomeServlet.java` file in the `\FilterApp\src\com\kogent\servlets` folder):

Listing 10.4: Showing the Code for `WelcomeServlet.java` File

```
package com.kogent.servlets;
import java.io.*;
import javax.servlet.*;
import javax.servlet.http.*;
import java.util.*;
public class WelcomeServlet extends HttpServlet
{
        @Override
   public void doGet(HttpServletRequest req,HttpServletResponse res)
   throws ServletException, IOException
   {
               res.setContentType("text/html");
               PrintWriter out = res.getWriter();
               String username = req.getParameter("username");
               out.println("<html><body>Welcome:<b>" + username + "<br/><br/>");
               out.println(new Date().toString());
               out.println("</b></body></html>");
   }
}
```

Now, compile the `WelcomeServlet.java` file. After compilation, the .class file should be located in the `\FilterApp\WEB-INF\classes\com\kogent\servlets` folder.

Configuring the Filter and the Servlet

In order to execute the `FilterApp` application, you are required to provide a mapping for the filter in the web.xml file, which is located in the FilterApp\WEB-INF folder. Listing 10.5 provides the code for mapping the `MyFilter` filter (save the `web.xml` file in the `\FilterApp\WEB-INF` folder):

Listing 10.5: Showing the Code for the web.xml File

```
<?xml version="1.0" encoding="UTF-8"?>
<web-app version="3.1" xmlns="http://xmlns.jcp.org/xml/ns/javaee"
  xmlns:xsi="http://www.w3.org/2001/XMLSchema-instance"
  xsi:schemaLocation="http://xmlns.jcp.org/xml/ns/javaee
  http://xmlns.jcp.org/xml/ns/javaee/web-app_3_1.xsd">

  <filter>
        <filter-name>MyFilter</filter-name>
        <filter-class>com.kogent.filter.MyFilter</filter-class>
  </filter>

  <filter-mapping>
        <filter-name>MyFilter</filter-name>
```

```
        <servlet-name>WelcomeServlet</servlet-name>
    </filter-mapping>

    <servlet>
        <servlet-name>WelcomeServlet</servlet-name>
        <servlet-class>com.kogent.servlets.WelcomeServlet</servlet-class>
    </servlet>

    <servlet-mapping>
        <servlet-name>WelcomeServlet</servlet-name>
        <url-pattern>/WelcomeServlet</url-pattern>
    </servlet-mapping>

    <session-config>
        <session-timeout>
        30
        </session-timeout>
    </session-config>

</web-app>
```

In Listing 10.5, the `MyFilter` filter is mapped to the `WelcomeServlet` servlet class.

Let's now discuss the directory structure of the `FilterApp` Web application.

Exploring the Directory Structure of FilterApp Application

All the files for the application are saved under a base directory named as `FilterApp.` Create the `FilterApp` directory under local drive of your computer. Create the remaining required folders as shown in the directory structure displayed in Figure 10.1. Place the respective files accordingly at proper locations in the directory structure as described by the following statements:

- All packages containing class files are placed in FilterApp\WEB-INF\classes folder
- The configuration file, such as web.xml is placed into FilterApp\WEB-INF folder
- All source files (.java files) for filters can be placed in FilterApp\src\com\kogent\filter folder
- All source files (.java files) for servlets can be placed in `FilterApp\src\com\kogent\servlets` folder

Figure 10.1 displays the directory structure of the `FilterApp` application:

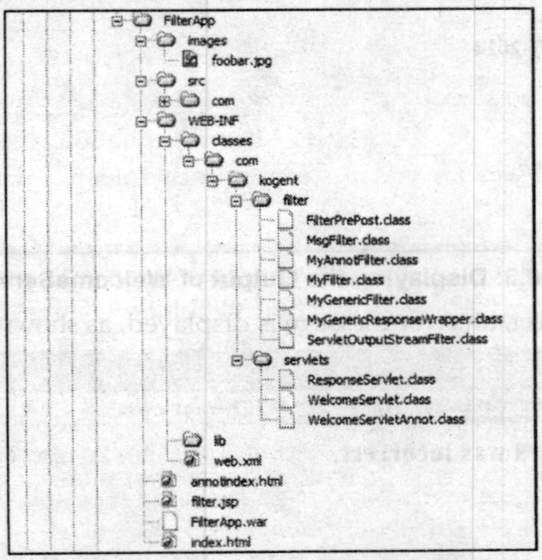

Figure 10.1: Displaying the Root Directory Structure for FilterApp Web Application

As shown in Figure 10.1, `FilterApp` is the root folder containing `WEB-INF` folder, `src` folder, and `index.html` file. The `WEB-INF` folder has two folders, `classes` and `lib`, and a file called `web.xml`. As discussed earlier, the package containing `the` .class files is placed at the WEB-INF\classes location under the `FilterApp` directory. The `src\com\kogent` is the optional folder containing source files. The configuration file, `web.xml`, is placed in the WEB-INF folder.

NOTE

The additional files, such as annotindex.html and filter.jsp as well as other Java source files have been created later in the chapter.

You also need to configure the compiler. Ensure that your compiler has all the necessary Java ARchive (JAR) files in its `CLASSPATH`, and that it can compile all Java files under \FilterApp\WEB-INF\classes directory.

Running the FilterApp Web Application

After creating all the required files, let's package and deploy the `FilterApp` application to test the filter. Now, navigate to the `http://localhost:8080/FilterApp/index.html` URL to view the output of the `FilterApp` application. The browser displays a login page as shown in Figure 10.2, in which the user needs to enter the username and password:

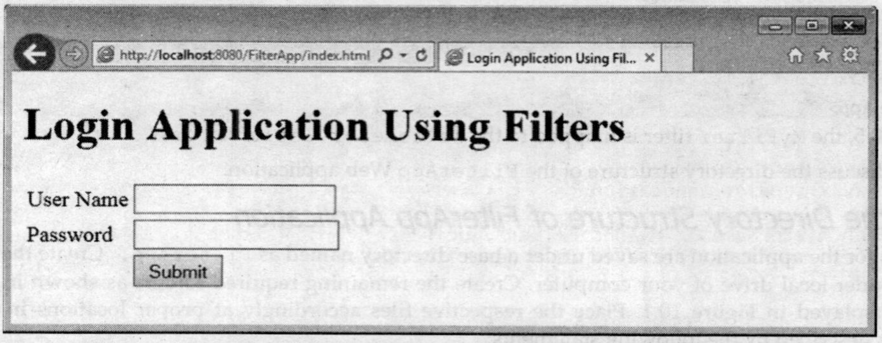

Figure 10.2: Displaying the index.html Page of FilterApp application

If the password entered by the user is `mypassword`, the Web container invokes the `WelcomeServlet` servlet and displays a welcome message to the user, as shown in Figure 10.3:

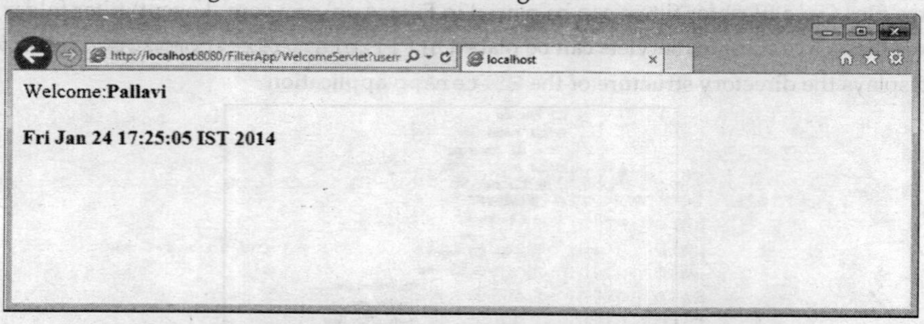

Figure 10.3: Displaying the Output of WelcomeServlet Servlet

In case the password is not correct, an error message is displayed, as shown in Figure 10.4:

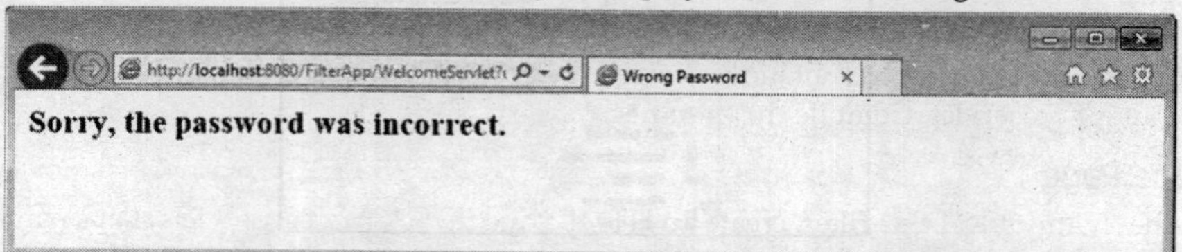

Figure 10.4: Displaying the Output of WelcomeServlet Servlet When Password is Incorrect

In this section, you learned to create a filter using Deployment Descriptor.

Let's now learn to create a filter using annotations.

Using Annotations to Configure a Filter

Starting from Servlet API 3.0, annotations can be used for marking filters rather than making an entry for mapping filters in Deployment Descriptor. Let's recreate the `MyFilter` filter created in the `FilterApp` application using annotations in place of Deployment Descriptor.

Creating a Filter using Annotations

To create a filter using annotations, you need to first create a class, `MyAnnotFilter`, which is a Java class implementing the `MyGenericFilter` class. The `MyAnnotFilter` class is similar in functionality to the `MyFilter` class. The only difference between the two is that `MyAnnotFilter` class also includes the code for annotations.

Listing 10.6 shows the code for the `MyAnnotFilter` class (save the `MyAnnotFilter.java` file in the `\FilterApp\src\com\kogent\filter` folder):

Listing 10.6: Showing the Code for `MyAnnotFilter.java` File

```
package com.kogent.filter;

import java.io.*;
import javax.servlet.*;
import javax.servlet.http.*;
import javax.servlet.annotation.*;

@WebFilter(filterName = "MyAnnotFilter", urlPatterns={"/WelcomeServletAnnot"})
public class MyAnnotFilter extends MyGenericFilter
{

   public void doFilter(ServletRequest req, ServletResponse res,
   FilterChain chain) throws IOException, ServletException
   {
                  String password =
                  ((HttpServletRequest) req).getParameter("password");
                  if(password.equals("mypassword"))
         {
                        String file = ((HttpServletRequest)req).getRequestURI();
                        chain.doFilter(req, res);
         }
         else
         {
                        res.setContentType("text/html");
                  PrintWriter pw = res.getWriter();
                        pw.println("<html>");
                        pw.println("<head><title>Wrong Password</title></head>");
                        pw.println("<body>");
                        pw.println("<h3>Sorry, the password was incorrect.</h3>");
                        pw.println("</body>");
                        pw.println("</html>");
         }
   }
}
```

In Listing 10.6, the `@WebFilter` annotation provides the required mapping between the filter and the `WelcomeServletAnnot` servlet. Compile the `MyAnnotFilter.java` file.

Creating the Home Page

In order to test the `MyAnnotFilter` filter, create an HTML page that can access servlets. Let's name this page as the `annotindex.html`.

Listing 10.7 shows the code for the `annotindex.html` file (save the annotindex.html file in the `\FilterApp` folder):

Listing 10.7: Showing the Code for annotindex.html Page

```
<!DOCTYPE html>
<html>
```

```
            <head>
            <title>Login Application Using Filters </title>
            </head>
    <body>
            <h1>Login Application Using Filters</h1>
       <p>The filters applied in this login application use annotations</p>
       <form action="/FilterApp/WelcomeServletAnnot">
       <table>
       <tr>
            <td>User Name</td>
            <td>
            <input type="text" name="username"/>
            </td>
       </tr>
       <tr>
            <td>Password</td>
            <td><input type="password" name="password"/>
            </td>
       </tr>
       <tr>
            <td></td>
            <td><input type="submit" value="Submit"/></td>
       </tr>
       </table>
       </form>
    </body>
    </html>
```

After creating the `annotindex HTML` page in the root directory, `FilterApp`. Let's now recreate the `WelcomeServlet` servlet and name it `WelcomeServletAnnot`, which invokes the `MyAnnotFilter` filter during initialization.

Creating a Servlet to Test the Filter

The `WelcomeServletAnnot` servlet receives users' requests and sends the desired responses. When `WelcomeServletAnnot` is initialized, the `MyAnnotFilter` filter is invoked, which verifies the user credentials and invokes the target servlet, `WelcomeServletAnnot`. The `WelcomeServletAnnot` servlet displays a welcome message to the user if the password entered is `mypassword`.

Listing 10.8 shows the code for `WelcomeServletAnnot.java` file (save the `WelcomeServletAnnot.java` file in the `\FilterApp\src\com\kogent\servlets` folder):

Listing 10.8: Showing the Code for the `WelcomeServletAnnot.java` File

```
    package com.kogent.servlets;

    import java.io.*;
    import javax.servlet.*;
    import javax.servlet.http.*;
    import java.util.*;

    public class WelcomeServletAnnot extends HttpServlet
    {
            @Override
       public void doGet(HttpServletRequest req,HttpServletResponse res)
       throws ServletException, IOException
       {
                    res.setContentType("text/html");
                    PrintWriter out = res.getWriter();
                    String username = req.getParameter("username");
                    out.println("<html><body>Welcome:<b>" + username + "<br/><br/>");
                    out.println(new Date().toString() + "</b>");
                    out.println("<p> This servlet invokes the filter that uses
                    annotations in place of a deployment descriptor for
                    marking the filter</p>");
                    out.println("</body></html>");
```

```
    }
  }
```

Now, compile the `WelcomeServletAnnot.java` file.

You need to provide the mapping for the `WelcomeServletAnnot` servlet to execute the Web application. Map the `WelcomeServletAnnot` servlet to the `/WelcomeServletAnnot` URL pattern in the web.xml file. The following code snippet shows the mapping for the `WelcomeServletAnnot` servlet:

```
<servlet>
  <servlet-name>
        WelcomeServletAnnot
  </servlet-name>
  <servlet-class>
        com.kogent.servlets.WelcomeServletAnnot
  </servlet-class>
</servlet>
<servlet-mapping>
  <servlet-name>WelcomeServletAnnot</servlet-name>
  <url-pattern>/WelcomeServletAnnot</url-pattern>
</servlet-mapping>
```

Include the mapping shown in the preceding code snippet for the `WelcomeServletAnnot` servlet in the `web.xml` file for the `FilterApp` Web application. Apart from servlets, you also need to configure filters in the web.xml file. However, as we are using annotations, the mapping for the filter is not required to be included in the web.xml file.

To test the `MyAnnotFilter` filter, package and deploy the `FilterApp` application and navigate to the `http://localhost:8080/FilterApp/annotindex.html` URL.

The browser displays a login page as shown in Figure 10.5, in which the user needs to enter the username and password:

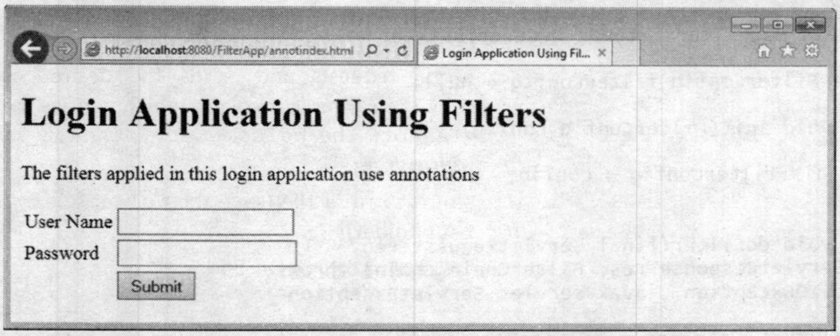

Figure 10.5: Displaying the annotindex.html Page

If the password entered by the user is `mypassword`, the Web container invokes the `WelcomeServletAnnot` servlet and displays a welcome message to the user, as shown in Figure 10.6:

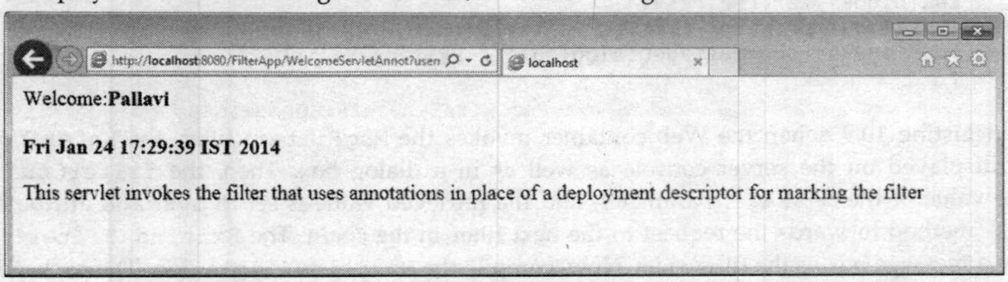

Figure 10.6: Displaying the Output of the WelcomeServletAnnot Servlet

This completes the discussion about creating filters using annotations. As you know, certain parameters can be provided for servlets that are initialized at the time of initialization of servlets. Such parameters are known as initializing parameters and are used to provide certain values to be used in an application. Similar to servlets, you can also provide initializing parameters to filters in the web.xml file. Let's now learn to create filters using initializing parameters in the next section.

Using Initializing Parameter in Filters

In this section, you learn to develop a simple filter that uses an initializing parameter. The name and value of an initializing parameter is specified in Deployment Descriptor. An initializing parameter helps a filter to retrieve a value to be used in that filter. You should note that the initializing parameter is defined during the initialization of the filter.

Let's create a filter, `MsgFilter`, which defines the `message` initializing parameter declared in the web.xml file of the `FilterApp` application. Further, you need to create the filter.jsp file to display the value of the `message` parameter. In order to invoke the `MsgFilter` filter with filter.jsp, you need to map the `MsgFilter` filter to `filter.jsp` in the `web.xml` file. Finally, you can run the `FilterApp` application to test the `MsgFilter` filter.

Creating the MsgFilter Filter

Let's create the `MsgFilter` filter that provides the value of the initializing parameter `message` to the `Request` scope before the target resource is called. Listing 10.9 shows the code for `MsgFilter.java` file (save the MsgFilter.java file in the `\FilterApp\src\com\kogent\filter` folder):

Listing 10.9: Showing the Code for `MsgFilter.java` File

```
package com.kogent.filter;

import javax.servlet.FilterChain;
import javax.servlet.ServletRequest;
import javax.servlet.ServletResponse;
import javax.servlet.FilterConfig;
import javax.swing.JOptionPane;

public class MsgFilter extends MyGenericFilter
{
  private FilterConfig filterConfig = null;

  public void init(FilterConfig config)
        {
        this.filterConfig = config;
        }

  public void doFilter(final ServletRequest req,
  final ServletResponse res, FilterChain chain) throws
  java.io.IOException, javax.servlet.ServletException
  {
        System.out.println("Entering Filter");
        JOptionPane.showMessageDialog(null," Entering Filter!");
        String message=filterConfig.getInitParameter("message");
        req.setAttribute("message",message);
        chain.doFilter(req,res);
        System.out.println("Exiting Filter");
        JOptionPane.showMessageDialog(null," Exiting Filter!");
        }
}
```

As shown in Listing 10.9, when the Web container invokes the `MsgFilter` filter, the `Entering Filter!` message is displayed on the server console as well as in a dialog box. Then, the `filterConfig` instance retrieves the value of the `message` parameter, and the retrieved value is set to `message` attribute. Then, the `doFilter()` method forwards the request to the next filter in the chain. The `Exiting Filter!` message is displayed in a message box as the filter exits. Now, compile the `MsgFilter.java` file. The package containing the class file should be located at the `FilterApp\WEB-INF\classes` folder.

Creating a JSP Page to Test the Filter

Let's now create a JSP page, filter and place it in the root directory of the FilterApp application. This JSP page is used to configure and test the MsgFilter filter.

Listing 10.10 provides the code for the filter.jsp file (save the filter.jsp file in the \FilterApp folder):

Listing 10.10: Showing the Code for the filter.jsp File

```
<html>
  <head>
        <title>Implementing Filters</title>
  </head>
  <body>
        <hr>
        <p><%=request.getAttribute("message")%></p>
        <p>Check your console output!</p>
        <hr>
  </body>
</html>
```

In Listing 10.10, the request implicit object retrieves the value of the message attribute set in the MsgFilter class. The Web container invokes the MsgFilter filter when the filter JSP page requests the message attribute. The MsgFilter class retrieves the value of an initializing parameter and sets the value to the message attribute. Then, the request is sent back to the target resource, filter.jsp, and the value of the message attribute is displayed.

Configuring the Filter

In order to test the MsgFilter filter, you need to configure it first. So, let's now configure the MsgFilter filter and map it to the filter JSP page. The following code snippet shows the mapping for the MsgFilter filter to be added in the web.xml file:

```
<filter>
   <filter-name>messageFilter</filter-name>
   <filter-class>com.kogent.filter.MsgFilter</filter-class>
   <init-param>
        <param-name>message</param-name>
        <param-value>A message to you!</param-value>
   </init-param>
</filter>
<filter-mapping>
   <filter-name>messageFilter</filter-name>
   <url-pattern>/filter.jsp</url-pattern>
</filter-mapping>
```

In the preceding code snippet, messageFilter is the name specified for the MsgFilter filter. The initializing parameter message is initialized with the parameter value A message to you!. When the Web container initializes the MsgFilter filter, the message parameter is initialized with its value and can be accessed by the MsgFilter filter. The MsgFilter filter is mapped to the filter JSP page. The Web container first invokes the filter named messageFilter for any requests for the filter JSP page.

The preceding code snippet shows the filter mapping in the web.xml file. Save the web.xml file after incorporating the necessary changes.

Let's now learn how to test a filter.

Testing a Filter

Let's now test the filter by running the FilterApp application. In order to test the filter, first ensure that the Glassfish Server 4.0 is running. Type the http://localhost:8080/FilterApp/filter.jsp URL in a browser. The result should be a page displaying the message, A message to you! accompanied by the instruction to view the console for any output. The MsgFilter filter is first invoked when the request is forwarded to the filter JSP page, and retrieves the initialization parameter value for setting the message attribute.

Figure 10.7 shows the output when `http://localhost:8080/FilterApp/filter.jsp` URL is entered in the browser:

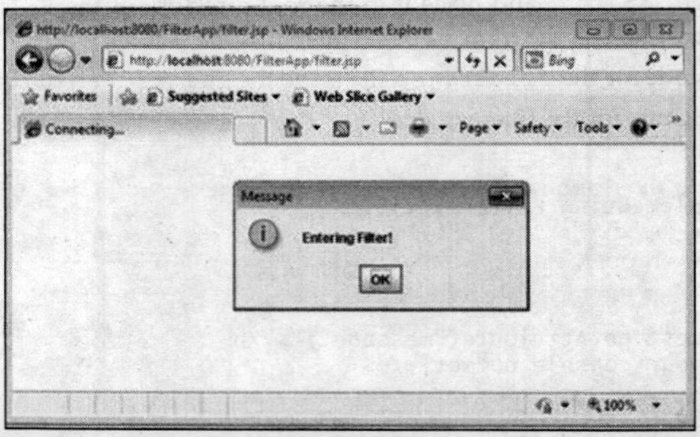

Figure 10.7: Showing the Output Indicating that Filter has Started Processing the Request

As you click the `OK button`, another dialog box is displayed indicating that the `MsgFilter` filter has completed its execution. The `Exiting Filter!` message is displayed, as shown in Figure 10.8:

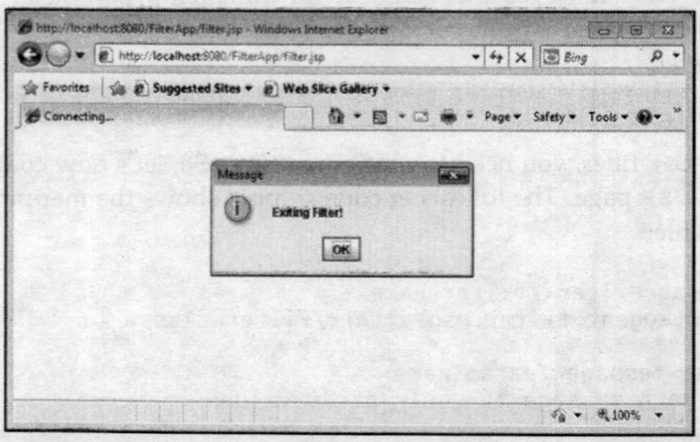

Figure 10.8: Showing the Output Indicating that Filter has Completed Processing the Request

Once the filter completes processing, the request is redirected to the `filter JSP` page. The `filter` JSP page retrieves the value of the `message` attribute and displays it on the browser, as shown in Figure 10.9:

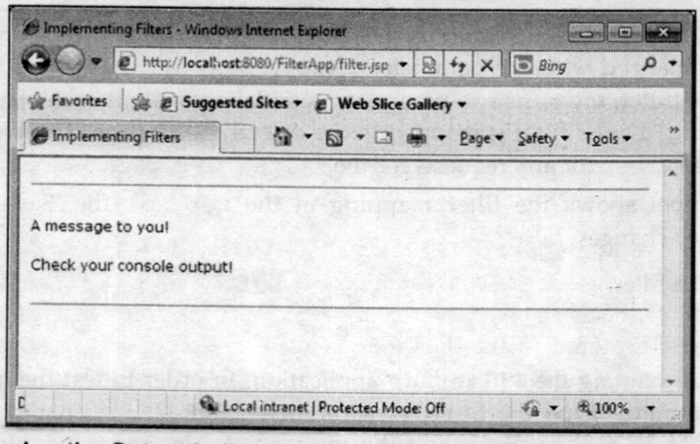

Figure 10.9: Showing the Output Indicating that Filter has Completed Processing the Request

This completes the discussion about creating filters.

Let's now discuss about manipulating responses in the next section.

Manipulating Responses

In this section, you learn to create a filter that can manipulate the responses to a request. In order to do so, you need the HttpServletResponseWrapper class, a custom ServletOutputStream class, and a filter. You also need a JSP page to attach the filter for testing it. You should then configure the filter, and finally test it.

The filter uses the HttpServletResponseWrapper class to wrap the response object before it is sent to the target resource. The HttpServletResponseWrapper object acts as a wrapper for the ServletResponse object. It helps in wrapping the response, so that the response can be modified after being delivered by the target resource.

The HttpServletResponseWrapper class uses a custom ServletOutputStream class that allows you to manipulate the response after the target resource has generated the response. The response generated cannot be modified if the ServletOutputStream has been closed. The ServletOutputStream class manipulates the response.

Creating the ServletOutputStreamFilter Class

Let's now create the ServletOutputStreamFilter class. Listing 10.11 shows the code for ServletOutputStreamFilter class (save the ServletOutputStreamFilter.java file in the \FilterApp\src\com\kogent\filter folder):

Listing 10.11: Showing the Code for the ServletOutputStreamFilter Class

```
package com.kogent.filter;

import java.io.*;
import javax.servlet.*;

public class ServletOutputStreamFilter extends ServletOutputStream
{
        DataOutputStream datastream;

   public ServletOutputStreamFilter(OutputStream out)
        {
        datastream=new DataOutputStream(out);
        }

   public void write(int num) throws IOException
        {
        datastream.write(num);
   }

        @Override
   public void write(byte[] num) throws IOException
        {
        datastream.write(num);
        }

        @Override
   public void write(byte[] num, int of, int ln) throws IOException
        {
        datastream.write(num, of, ln);
        }
}
```

In Listing 10.11, the ServletOutputStreamFilter class extends the ServletOutputStream class. To hold a DataOutputStream that needs to be written on the browser, the datastream instance variable is created. Whenever the constructor of the ServletOutputStreamFilter class is called, the out parameter is cast to a DataOutputStream and is stored in the datastream object. Compile the ServletOutputStreamFilter class. After compilation, the ServletOutputStreamFilter.class file should be located in the \FilterApp\WEB-INF\classes\com\kogent\filter folder.

Now, after creating the ServletOutputStreamFilter class, you are going to create the MyGenericResponseWrapper class, which uses the ServletOutputStreamFilter class.

Creating the MyGenericResponseWrapper Class

To use the ServletOutputStreamFilter class, you need to implement a class that can act as a response object. The instance of the MyGenericResponseWrapper class is sent to the target resource instead of the original response object. You implement some utility methods in the MyGenericResponseWrapper class to retrieve the content type and content length for the content it holds.

Listing 10.12 shows the code for the MyGenericResponseWrapper class (save the MyGenericResponseWrapper.java file in the \FilterApp\src\com\kogent\filter folder):

Listing 10.12: Showing the Code for the MyGenericResponseWrapper Class

```
package com.kogent.filter;

import java.io.*;
import javax.servlet.*;
import javax.servlet.http.*;
public class MyGenericResponseWrapper extends HttpServletResponseWrapper
{
   private ByteArrayOutputStream outstream;
           private int contentLen;
           private String contentTyp;
   public MyGenericResponseWrapper(HttpServletResponse res)
           {
           super(res);
           outstream = new ByteArrayOutputStream();
           }
           @Override
   public ServletOutputStream getOutputStream()
           {
           return new ServletOutputStreamFilter(outstream);
           }
   public byte[] getData()
           {
           return outstream.toByteArray();
           }
   @Override
   public PrintWriter getWriter()
   {
                     return new PrintWriter(getOutputStream(), true);
   }
           @Override
   public void setContentType(String type)
           {
           this.contentTyp = type;
           super.setContentType(type);
           }
   @Override
   public String getContentType()
           {
           return this.contentTyp;
           }

   public int getContentLength()
           {
           return contentLen;
           }
           @Override
   public void setContentLength(int len)
           {
           this.contentLen=len;
           super.setContentLength(len);
           }
}
```

In Listing 10.12, the MyGenericResponseWrapper class extends the HttpServletResponseWrapper class and declares three instance variables: outstream, contentLen, and contentTyp. The outstream variable is an instance of the ByteArrayOutputStream class that holds any content written by the target resource, and the contentLen variable is an int type variable declared to hold the content length. The contentTyp variable is defined to hold the content type. The getOutputStream() method handles the binary content. The method will be used by the target resource when writing its binary response. The getData() method is declared to retrieve the content of the response. The getWriter() method handles the character content. This method is used by the target resource to write the character text response. The setContentType() and getContentType() methods handle the content type. The set and get methods are used to set or retrieve the content type of the response. These methods have been overridden in Listing 10.12 to make sure that the content type values can be obtained later. Similarly, the get and set methods are provided to set or retrieve the content-length of the response. Compile the MyGenericResponseWrapper.java file. After compilation, the MyGenericResponseWrapper.class file should be located in the `\FilterApp\WEB-INF\classes\com\kogent\filter` folder.

Creating the Filter

Let's create a filter that uses the `MyGenericResponseWrapper` class. This filter adds content to the response of the target resource before and after the target is invoked. Listing 10.13 shows the code for the `FilterPrePost` class (save the FilterPrePost.java file in the `\FilterApp\src\com\kogent\filter` folder):

Listing 10.13: Showing the Code for the FilterPrePost.java File

```
package com.kogent.filter;

import java.io.*;
import javax.servlet.*;
import javax.servlet.http.*;

public class FilterPrePost extends MyGenericFilter
{
   public void doFilter(final ServletRequest req, final ServletResponse res,
   FilterChain chain) throws IOException, ServletException
   {
          OutputStream outstream = res.getOutputStream();
          outstream.write("<HR>PRE<HR>".getBytes());

          MyGenericResponseWrapper wrap =
          new MyGenericResponseWrapper((HttpServletResponse) res);
          chain.doFilter(req, wrap);
          outstream.write(wrap.getData());
          outstream.write("<HR>POST<HR>".getBytes());
          outstream.close();
          }
}
```

In Listing 10.13, `FilterPrePost` is a Java class that extends the `MyGenericFilter class`. The instance of the MyGenericResponseWrapper class is created which invokes the parameterized constructor. The instance of the `MyGenericResponseWrapper` class is passed to the next filter in the chain. Then the response received is written to the `ServletOutputStream` class by using the `getData()` wrapper method, which contains the response of the filter that is previously called. Compile the FilterPrePost.java file and place the .class file in the `\FilterApp\WEB-INF\classes\com\kogent\filter` folder.

Creating the Servlet to Test the Filter

Let's now learn to create a servlet to which the FilterPrePost filter is attached. Listing 10.14 shows the code for the ResponseServlet.java file (save the ResponseServlet.java file in the `\FilterApp\src\com\kogent\servlets` folder):

Listing 10.14: Showing the Code for the ResponseServlet.java File

```
package com.kogent.servlets;

import java.io.*;
import java.net.*;
import javax.servlet.*;
import javax.servlet.http.*;

public class ResponseServlet extends HttpServlet
{
        @Override
  protected void doGet(HttpServletRequest req, HttpServletResponse res)
```

```
        throws ServletException, IOException
    {
            res.setContentType("text/html;charset=UTF-8");
        PrintWriter out = res.getWriter();
        out.println("This is a TEST SERVLET");
        out.close();
        }
}
```

In Listing 10.14, the `ResponseServlet` class extends the `HttpServlet` class. The `This is a TEST SERVLET` message is printed to test the filter. Compile the `ResponseServlet.java` file. After compilation, the .class file should be located at the `\FilterApp\WEB-INF\classes\com\kogent\servlets` folder.

Configuring the Filter

In order to configure the filter, you need to provide a mapping in the `web.xml` file. The following code snippet shows the code for mapping the filter:

```
<filter>
   <filter-name>prePost</filter-name>
   <filter-class>com.kogent.filter.FilterPrePost</filter-class>
</filter>
<filter-mapping>
   <filter-name>prePost</filter-name>
   <servlet-name>ResponseServlet</servlet-name>
</filter-mapping>
```

In the preceding code snippet, the `prePost` filter is configured to the `FilterPrePost` class that is defined in the `com.kogent.filter` package. The prePost filter is mapped to the `ResponseServlet` class. The following code snippet shows the mapping for the ResponseServlet servlet class:

```
<servlet>
        <servlet-name>ResponseServlet</servlet-name>
        <servlet-class>com.kogent.servlets.ResponseServlet</servlet-class>
</servlet>
<servlet-mapping>
        <servlet-name>ResponseServlet</servlet-name>
        <url-pattern>/ResponseServlet</url-pattern>
</servlet-mapping>
```

The Web container first invokes the filter named `prePost` for any requests to the `ResponseServlet` class.

Save changes to web.xml. Now after configuring the filter, let's test the filter to see the output.

Testing the FilterPrePost Filter

Let's now test the FilterPrePost filter to see the output. You should ensure that the Glassfish Server 4.0 is running. Now, browse the the `http://localhost:8080/FilterApp/ResponseServlet` URL.

Figure 10.10 displays the output of the `ResponseServlet` class:

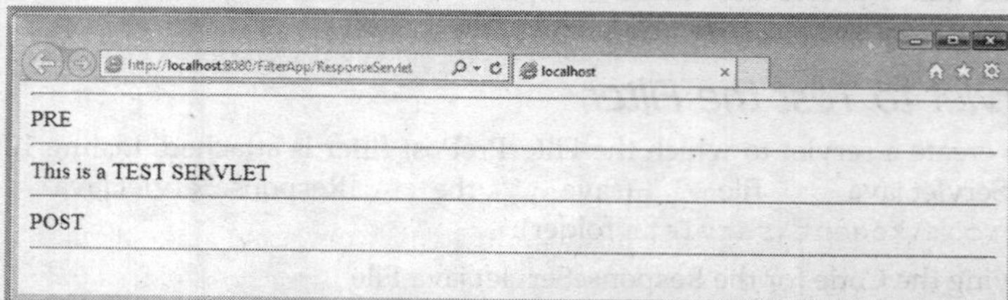

Figure 10.10: Displaying the Output of the ResponseServlet Class

Discussing Issues in Using Threads with Filters

Filters are used in an environment where threads need to collaborate with each other to carry out various functionalities provided by a Web application. All requests are handled by a single instance of the filter class. Therefore, a single instance may be used by more than one request at the same time. Each request will execute methods on the same filter instance in different threads; therefore, developers need to write filters in a threadsafe manner.

Developers, who are not familiar with threads, may make a common mistake of using object variables to store data, which applies only to a single thread. The variables for storing data used in a particular request should be created inside the method, so that each thread will have its own instance. On the other hand, if the variables are created outside the methods, then all threads will share the same instance. The following code snippet shows how to write a threadsafe filter class:

```
public void doFilter(final ServletRequest req, final ServletResponse           res,
   FilterChain chain) throws IOException, ServletException
{
   lHitCount++;
   chain.doFilter(req, res);
   System.out.println("This filter has been hit = " + lHitCount + " times");
}
```

The preceding code snippet shows the doFilter() method of a filter class which is used for counting the number of times the filter class is invoked. The code uses an integer object variable named `lHitCount` for storing the number of hits. The problem arises when two requests for this filter is made to the server at the same time. In this case, both threads may increment the `lHitCount` variable before either thread executes the line that prints the count to the log file. Therefore, both threads print the same value. The increment in `lHitCount` is done when the count value is printed to the log file, as shown by the following code snippet:

```
System.out.println("This filter has been hit = " + (++lHitCount) + " times");
```

However, this may also result in thread issues, as the JVM may not complete the two operations of incrementing and printing at once. The JVM may switch to another thread, which may lead to a thread issue. To avoid threading issues, a thread may be paused for few seconds, while the other thread can perform the operation at the same time. This would not lead to a conflict between the two threads.

In the following code snippet, the sleep() method is used to pause a thread for 5 seconds:

```
public void doFilter(final ServletRequest req, final ServletResponse           res,
   FilterChain chain) throws IOException, ServletException
{
   lHitCount++;
   try
   {
         Thread.sleep(5000);
   }
   catch(InterruptedException e)
   {
         System.out.println("MyException:" + e);
   }
   chain.doFilter(req, resp);
         System.out.println("This filter has been hit = " + lHitCount + "
         times");
   }
```

The preceding code snippet prints the following output on the console of application server:

```
This filter has been hit = 2 times
This filter has been hit = 2 times
```

In addition, data can be shared among multiple threads. If one thread modifies the shared instance while the other thread is retrieving data using that instance, then inappropriate data would be retrieved. This would happen only if the instance being accessed is not threadsafe. So, to avoid such circumstances, threadsafe classes, such as `HashTable`, should be used instead of `HashMap` for sharing data.

Summary

The chapter introduced filters, described their relevance, and demonstrated how filters work in the context of a Web application. You have also learned how to configure filters using Deployment Descriptor as well as annotations. Then, the FilterApp application is developed in which a generic filter is created by using the `Filter` interface. In the `FilterApp` Web application, the MyFilter filter is used to verify the user credentials. Next, the `FilterApp` application is rebuild using annotations to configure filters. Further, you have also learned how to use initializing parameters with filters. Toward the end, the chapter also discussed how filters can manipulate the response of a target resource.

The next chapter discusses JavaServer Faces (JSF), an MVC framework, and creates an application using JSF tags.

Quick Revise

Q1. What is a filter?

Ans. A filter is a Java class that is invoked in response to requests for resources, such as Java Servlet or JavaServer Pages.

Q2. List the interfaces defined in the Filter API.

Ans. The Filter API defines the following three interfaces:

- Filter
- FilterConfig
- FilterChain

Q3. List the methods of the Filter interface.

Ans. The Filter interface provides the following three methods:

- init()
- doFilter()
- destroy()

Q4. Which class is used to manipulate responses in filters?

Ans. The HttpServletResponseWrapper class is a custom class that wraps the response object before it is sent to the target resource.

Q5. When should filters be used?

Ans. Filters are used to perform the following tasks:

- Security verification
- Session validation
- Logging operations
- Internationalization
- Triggering resource access events
- Image conversion
- Scaling maps
- Data compression
- Encryption

Q6. Explain the life cycle of a filter.

Ans. When a target resource is requested, the Web container invokes the init() method of the filter class mapped to that target resource. The init() method initializes the corresponding filter and invokes the doFilter() method. The doFilter() method forwards the request to the next filter in the chain. If the next filter in the chain is the last filter, the target resource is invoked. Finally, the destroy method is invoked to remove the filter instance from memory.

Q7. Which interface should be implemented while creating a filter?

Ans. While creating a filter, the filter class must implement the Filter interface to override the methods of this interface.

Q8. Where do we configure the filters?

Ans. We configure the filters in Deployment Descriptor (web.xml). The web.xml file is used to map a filter to a resource or to a URL pattern.

11

Working with JavaServer Faces 2.2

While developing a Web application, the developer designs a User Interface (UI) to interact with the clients, develops business logic to process data, and implements navigation rules to be followed when the clients access the application. Prior to the introduction of JavaServer Faces (JSF), the developer had to manually write the code to define the common tasks, such as validating user inputs and converting user input strings into specific Java objects to build Web applications. JSF is a Web application framework, which allows a developer to handle Web-based tasks easily with the help of its Application Programming InterfaceAPIs and tags and to design rich user interfaces with its components.

JSF can be defined as a framework that makes Web application development easy by supporting different rich, powerful, and ready-to-use UI components. JSF framework is based on Model-View-Controller (MVC) which is one of the most popular design patterns available for implementing separate layers, such as view, model, and controller to provide greater maintainability of an application.

JSF not only provides simple tags to design a UI component, such as label, text box, list box, but also enables you to perform the following tasks:

- Binding of UI components with some model data
- Handling different events on UI components (such as text change in a text box) on server side
- Validating user inputs and conveying all validation error messages to the client
- Defining navigation rules from one view to another according to the output of business process.

Creating a Web application using JSF is a simple and easy task from the perspective of a Web developer. The standard and powerful features of JSF, such as UI components and use of annotation make it a preferred choice among all available Java technologies used for developing a Web application.

JSF is a product of Java Community Process (JCP), which provides suggestions for new Java application programming interfaces and technology enhancements in the form of Java Specification Requests (JSR). The first specification for the initial release of JSF came as JSR 127. This specification was for both JSF 1.0 and JSF 1.1 versions. The latest version of JSF is JSF 2.2 that has been specified in JSR 344.

You need to download different JARs and TLD files to support the development of JSF-based Web applications for the versions prior to Java EE 5. Later, JSF 1.2 became a part of Java Platform, Enterprise Edition 5 (Java EE 5); therefore, while using Java EE 5 as development platform for your Web application, you can use JSF tags and other APIs, such as `java.util`, `javax.faces` for creating UI components, handling events, input validation, and defining page navigation. In the Java EE 7 platform, the latest version of JSF, JSF 2.2 is introduced with some new features, such as HTML 5 friendly markup, resource library contract, faces flows, and stateless views.

In the chapter you learn about JSF 2.2, its features, architecture, and elements. Then you learn about the JSF request processing life cycle. Next, you learn about JSF tag libraries, UI components, and backing beans. In addition, you learn about the implementation of input validation and type conversion in JSF application. Moreover, how to handle navigation among various JSF pages and implement internationalization in JSF pages is also described in the chapter. Towards the end, a Web application is created by using the JSF framework. In this application, you can add, edit, update, and delete the records of employees of an organization.

Introducing JSF

JSF technology includes a set of APIs, which represent different UI components and helps in managing their states. These APIs further help in handling events on the UI components and validate user inputs through the UI components. JSF framework provides the flexibility of creating simple as well as complex applications as this technology uses the most popular Java server technologies (Servlet and Java Server Page) and does not limit a developer to a specific markup language or client device. The UI component classes bundled with JSF APIs contain logic implementation for various component functionalities and do not have any client-specific presentation logic; therefore, the JSF UI components can be rendered for different client devices. Currently, JSF provides a custom renderer and Java Server Page (JSP) custom tag library for rendering UI components for an HTML client.

JSF is a robust Web application framework that implements an event programming model to handle different events and actions performed by the client on different UI components. To handle each event, a listener should be registered on server side. While developing a Web application, a developer has to write navigation rules inside source code to navigate from one Web page to another. JSF provides a simple way to define navigation rules in a configuration file, and displays different error messages showing the real cause of errors to clients. These messages are generated while validating user inputs against some validation rule and can be displayed on the same page that contains the UI components.

There are different Web application frameworks that implement one or more forms of MVC design pattern. JSF is based on MVC2 pattern and this pattern is based on component type development. In this pattern, the developers have to concenterate only on their respective component. This introduces separate layers, such as model, view, and controller and helps the developer to concentrate on a single type of component by making a Web application easy to maintain. The different categories of UI components, such as model, view, and controller are created for different functionalities, such as use of TextField, DialogBox, SimpleLabel, and ColorChooser and can be used separately.

NOTE

JSF technology is based on the MVC architecture. It is used for separating presentation logic from business logic; therefore, if you have been practicing MVC, then it is very simple to work with JSF.

Explaining the Features of JSF

Java technology provides various frameworks to develop a Web application. Some of these frameworks, such as Struts, are more popular than JSF, but the rich yet simple features of JSF make it one of the preferred choices for designing and managing UI components in a Web application. The following are the various features of JSF:

- Provides an easy-to-use environment that is Integerated Development Environment (IDE) for developing Web applications with JSF UI components. It has extensive tool support from the companies, such as Sun, IBM, and Oracle.
- Facilitates creating complex UI components in a Web page through its own set of tags, which are provided as JSP custom tag library. Designing a UI component is easy with JSF as it is based on MVC design pattern, which clearly separates presentation and business logic.
- Provides a way to manage all UI components in a Web page. Managing UI components includes validation of user input, state of component, page navigation, and event handling.
- Provides extensible architecture, which means that you can add other functionalities over JSF and can easily customize and reuse JSF UI components.
- Supports multiple client devices. There are different renderers to make same UI component to be rendered or displayed for different client devices. Various component classes can be extended to create custom component tag libraries to support a particular type of client.
- Contains components that support internationalization and enable displaying localized messages according to the specified Locale.
- Supports a standard Rapid Application Development (RAD) Java Web application framework, which enables fast development of a powerful application with a set of reusable components.
- Provides the developer with a way to link visual components to the controller or model components without breaking the layering.
- Provides Expression Language (EL) for a JSF page. As JSF pages use JSP tags, it is difficult to embed separate ELs into one JSF page. One of the key concerns of Java EE specification is to keep its different Web tier technologies, such as JSP, JSF, and JSP Standard Tag Library (JSTL) aligned. This alignment resulted in the creation of a Unified EL, which integrates JSP 2.0 EL and JSF 1.1 EL. JSP 2.1 and JSF 1.2 support this Unified EL. In other words, you can use the JSTL tags with JSF components.
- Helps in building Web 2.0 applications that use Asynchronous JavaScript and XML technology (AJAX) and further reduces the complexities involved in creating UI components.
- Allows the configuration of application wide ResourceBundle to EL using <resource-bundle> element in the faces-config.xml file.

In addition to the features mentioned so far, JSF 2.0 has various new features. The previous version, JSF 1.1, was developed to support JSP 1.2; therefore, could not work with new JSP versions, such as JSP 2.1. The new features added in JSF 2.0 are as follows:

- Provides the ViewDeclarationLanguage API that allows developers to integrate the view declaration languages with JSF runtime environment.
- Introduces Facelets as the non-JSP view declaration language. You learn about Facelets in detail in *Appendix I, Working with Facelets*.
- Introduces the composite component feature that simplifies the development of custom components. In JSF 2.0, you can define the composite User Interface (UI) components in the Extensible Markup Language (XML) file using Hyper Text Markup Language (HTML) contents as well as elements from the http://java.sun.com/jsf/composite namespace.
- Provides an integration of JSF with AJAX. Initially many JSF and AJAX integrated frameworks, such as ICEFaces, Ajax4jsf and many more were available; however, these frameworks lead to compatibility issues. The JSF users need to use the third party frameworks to add AJAX functionality in the JSF application; therefore, JSF 2.0 introduced the jsf.ajax.request() method to return the AJAX request to the view component. In addition to this method, the <f:ajax> tag was also used to send AJAX request back to the view component.
- Provides support for notifications of system-related events. In the previous version of JSF, JSF 1.2, the notifications of FacesEvents were provided to FacesListeners and the PhaseEvents notifications were provided to PhaseListeners. Therefore, the notifications of other events, such as system-related events were not provided. JSF 2.1 provides support for the notification of the SystemEvents to SystemEventListeners.
- Allows you to use annotations to define managed beans. In other words, instead of providing the XML configurations for managed beans, you can use annotations.

In addition to the features listed so far, various new features have been introduced in JSF 2.2, the latest version of JSF. The new features added in JSF 2.2 are as follows:

- Supports HTML 5 friendly markup to include new features and tags of HTML 5 in JSF components. This is accomplished with the help of pass-through attributes and pass-through elements. Pass-through attributes help in rendering HTML 5 attributes that are not natively supported by the JSF component. Pass-through attributes can be added to a JSF component by placing them into the namespace http://xmlns.jcp.org/jsf/passthrough and prefixing the attributes as shown in the following code snippet:

```
<html xmlns="http://www.w3.org/1999/xhtml"
xmlns:h="http://xmlns.jcp.org/jsf/html"
xmlns:pt="http://xmlns.jcp.org/jsf/passthrough">
<h:head><title>JSF2.2</title></h:head>
<h:body>
      <h:form id="form">
           <h:inputText id="address" value="#{bean.address}"
          pt:type="address" pt:placeholder="Enter address"/>
      </h:form>
</h:body>
</html>
```

  The preceeding code snippet shows an h:inputText component with two normal and two pass-through attributes. The pass-through attributes can also be added using f:passThroughAttribute and f:passThroughAttributes tag as shown in the following code snippet:

```
<h:inputText id="address" value="#{bean.address}">
          <f:passThroughAttribute name="type" value="address"/>
           <f:passThroughAttribute name="placeholder" value="Enter address"/>
</h:inputText>
```

  Along with pass-through attributes, JSF 2.2 also provides pass-through elements which enable the developers to build the view with HTML elements that can be linked with respective JSF components on the server side. Pass-through elements can be created by defining at least one of their attributes in the namespace http://xmlns.jcp.org/jsf as shown in the following code snippet:

```
<html xmlns="http://www.w3.org/1999/xhtml"
xmlns:jsf="http://xmlns.jcp.org/jsf">
```

```
<head jsf:id="head"><title>JSF2.2</title></head>
<body jsf:id="body">
<form jsf:id="form">
        <input type="text" jsf:id="address"
placeholder="Enter address"
jsf:value="#{bean.address}"/>
<button jsf:action="#{bean.save}">Save</button>
</form>
</body>
</html>
```

Here, JSF adds a component to the tree and links it to the respective element for which an attribute is in the http://xmlns.jcp.org/jsf namespace.

- Introduces Resource Library Contracts to enable facelet templates to be used consistently in a Web application dynamically across its all Web pages. Facelet templates are created with XHTML and CSS and have been the default technology to declare views. Resource Library Contracts allow reusing facelet templates throughout an application in an interchangeale manner to allow a consistent look and feel.
- Introduces faces flows that allow the complete business logic to be encapsulated within a single module along with the respective views having well defined exit and entry points. For example, in order to buy a book from an online store, you need to go through a sequence of pages to accomplish the purchase process. You can have an add to cart page, address verification page, payment detail page, and confirmation page. All these pages along with the related resources can be packaged within a single module that can be reused in other similar applications.
- Support for stateless views to enable creation of views for which no data is stored by the JSF StateManager.

Now, let's explore the architecture of JSF.

Exploring the JSF Architecture

Similar to most of the popular Web application frameworks, JSF implements MVC design pattern. The implementation of MVC design pattern helps to design different components separately, and each of these components implements different type of logic. For example, you can create view component for presentation logic and model component for business logic implementation. A controller is another component, which controls the execution of various model methods and navigates from one view to another in a Web application. In JSF, you have a single front controller, which handles all JSF requests mapped to it. Figure 11.1 shows the MVC design pattern:

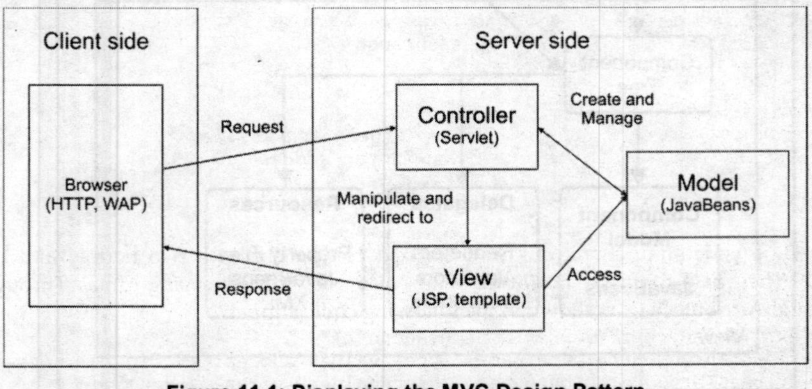

Figure 11.1: Displaying the MVC Design Pattern

The controller part of the JSF architecture consists of a Controller Servlet, that is, `FacesServlet`, a centralized configuration file, faces-config.xml, and a set of event handlers for the Web application. The Front Controller Servlet receives all the requests and manages the request processing life cycle of each request to generate response for the client. In JSF, the FacesServlet is a Servlet that is responsible to manage the request processing life cycle of the Web application and is also used by JSF to design the user interface. Every JSF application contains the `web.xml` file, which specifies a Java Servlet of type `FacesServlet`. The application settings are also configured in FacesServlet through which all requests are channeled. On the basis of the results of component events, the flow of an application's pages is also controlled by the FacesServlet. This process of handling the flow of pages is represented in the FrontController design pattern. The FacesServlet also manages client requests by referencing the page mappings provided in the faces-config.xml configuration file. This configuration file contains a number of JSF configurations that we discuss in the Configuring JSF Application section later in this chapter. Event Listeners respond to component events, which perform some processing and generate an outcome that can be used by `FacesServlet`.

The Model in JSF architecture (Figure 11.2) is a set of server-side JavaBeans that retrieves the values from the model components, such as the database and defines methods on the basis of these values. These JavaBeans may further persist in a database through an underlying persistence layer. This layer may include Java Data Objects, Enterprise JavaBeans, or an Object-Relational Mapping implementation, such as hibernate. The view in JSF architecture comprises stateful UI components.

The UI Components are rendered in different ways according to the type of the client. The view delegates this task to separate the renderers, each taking care of one specific output type, such as HTML or Wireless Markup Language (WML). You can also attach various additional delegates such as validators and converters to specific components. Converters are used to validate and convert the values entered by the user. The client always submits strings as values for input fields that may need to be converted to a numerical data type, if the string values have to be used in a calculation. Validators check if the values delivered by the client are syntactically correct or are according to a specified format. The view also features resources, which may be used for localization of the Web application. Figure 11.2 shows the MVC architecture implemented in JSF:

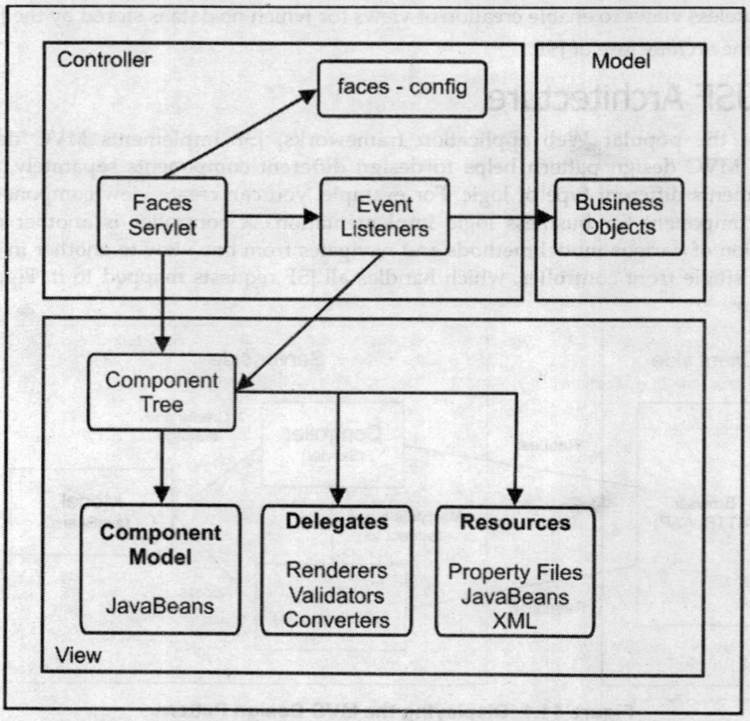

Figure 11.2: Displaying the MVC Architecture of JavaServer Faces

In Figure 11.2, various JSF elements as mapped with MVC architecture. Let's discuss different JSF elements, such as UI components, backing beans, and event listeners in the following section.

Describing JSF Elements

JSF technology has its own set of elements, such as, UI component, renderer, converter, and backing beans which altogether form the JSF framework. These elements provide the core features of JSF technology. In this section, we are talking about various JSF components (elements), such as UI components, validators, and renderers. Let's discuss all the JSF components and explain how they all are related to each other. The following are the elements of JSF:

- UI Component
- Renderer
- Validator
- Backing Beans
- Converter
- Events and Listeners
- Message
- Navigation

UI Component

UI components are the basic reusable components for developing UIs using the JSF framework. The developer can define UI components as stateful objects maintained on server side. The server communicates with the client through these UI components. These components are simple JavaBeans containing properties, methods, and events. The JSF UI components are also called the Web application UI components.

In a Web application, every interaction between a client and a server requires a complete HTTP request-response cycle to generate a message on client side to invalid data input or any other server side error. Each interaction between a client and a server needs to redisplay the request page with an additional error message for previously entered data in input fields. In JSF, no separate logic is required to redisplay the request page with past data values since the JSF UI components can remember their values. The JSF UI components are known as stateful UI components. All UI components are organized as a component tree and are usually displayed as a JSF page. The component tree, also known as view, is the internal presentation of a JSF page. The nested components in the component tree are presented as child components for the component that encloses it. Figure 11.3 shows an internal presentation of a component tree designed for a UI:

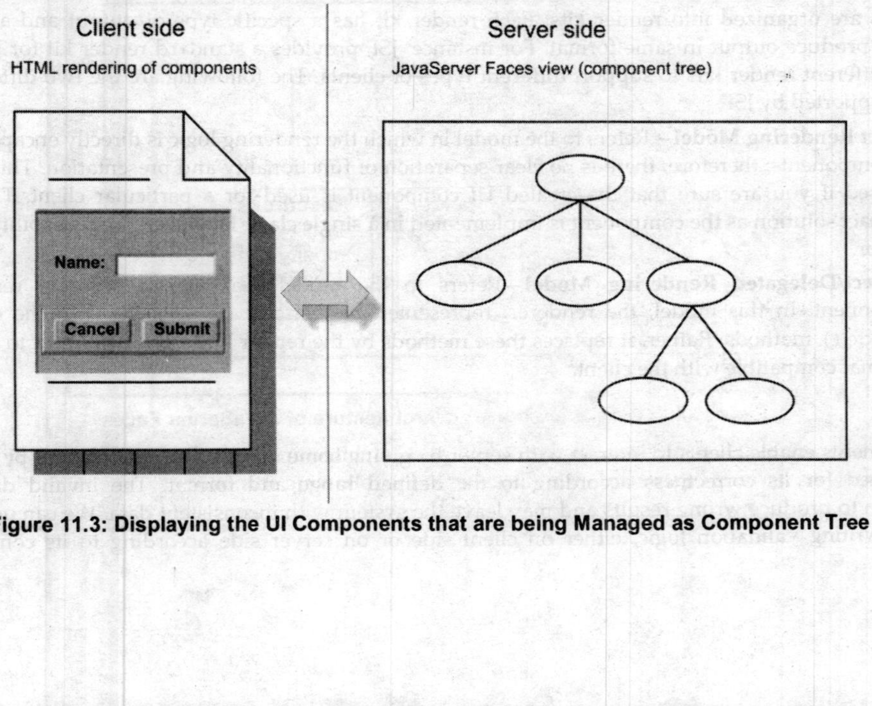

Figure 11.3: Displaying the UI Components that are being Managed as Component Tree

In Figure 11.3, you can see a form with one label, one text field, and a panel with two buttons. The rendering language other than HTML is used to display a form on client side and store the internal representation of the request page. The UI components provide only the functionality and do not involve any presentation logic for displaying the form. The element named renderer is used to ensure how a UI component appears to the user. The separation of UI components from presentation logic provides an easy way to display the responses for different client requests.

Each UI component in a view has its own component identifier. The component identifier can either be provided by the developer or can be generated automatically by JSF implementation at runtime.

To use the JSF UI components, instead of writing any code (HTML, JavaScript, and CSS), you just need to assemble and configure them. JSF provides various standard UI components, such as labels, text boxes, check boxes, radio buttons, panels, and data grids. All the UI components are discussed later in the chapter.

Renderer

Usually, Web applications send a response to the clients Web browser in HTML format. However, the client devices, such as mobile phones or PDAs do not provide the HTML based browser. Some of the formats supported by these handheld devices are WML and Extensive Hyper Text Markup Language (XHTML) basic. Since handheld technology is growing very fast, there arises a need to create a Web application that could respond to other markup languages as well. Earlier, without JSF, we had to incorporate many changes in the Web application to add support for different clients.

JSF introduces renderers, which completely separate the functionality of a component from the presentation logic on the client-side. A Web application does not require many changes in it due to the use of renderers. A JSF UI component is capable of rendering itself, which is known as direct rendering. JSF also supports another type of rendering, called as indirect/delegated rendering, in which a separate class handles the process of rendering. This separate class is known as renderer. A renderer class is responsible for handling the encoding, which is a process of creating the presentation of UI components in some markup language for the given client. The renderers are child components of UI components and used to set and get data from UI components. Let's create a simple HtmlInputText component using the following code snippet:

```
<h:inputText label="Name" id="name" required="true"/>
```

When a component is rendered and the response is created for the HTML client, the following HTML code lines are sent to the client browser, as shown in the following code snippet:

```
<input id="myForm:name" type="text" name="myForm:name" />
```

Renderers are organized into render kits. Each render kit has a specific type of output and all its registered renderers produce output in same format. For instance, JSF provides a standard render kit for HTML 4.0. You can use different render kits to support different types of clients. The following are the two different rendering models supported by JSF:

- **Direct Rendering Model**—Refers to the model in which the rendering logic is directly encapsulated into the UI components; therefore, there is no clear separation of functionality and presentation. This technique can be used if you are sure that the created UI component is used for a particular client. This results in a compact solution as the component is implemented in a single class. However, the reusability of component is poor.
- **Indirect/Delegated Rendering Model**—Refers to the model that uses a separate renderer for the component. In this model, the renderer, represented by `render` class works with the `encode()` and `decode()` methods. Rather, it replaces these methods by the render kit to get the output to be displayed in a format compatible with the client.

Validators

UI components enable clients to interact with server by giving some inputs. The data entered by the client must be validated for its correctness according to the defined range and format. The invalid data may cause application to produce wrong results and may leave the system with inconsistent data. We can use JavaScript or Java for writing validation logic, either on client side or on server side according to its complexity. While working with JSF components, the Java code is not required to validate the input data; instead, JSF can handle the validation of data in the following three different ways:

- Implementing validation inside the UI component
- Using validator method in backing beans
- Using validator classes

The first way of handling validation is at UI component level where the component itself handles simple validation logic, which is specific to it only; therefore, cannot be used by other components. We can also implement validation logic in validator method of the backing bean that helps in validating one or more fields of a form, but again other components cannot use it. The third way to handle validation is to use Validator classes, also known as validators. The validators provide validation for generic cases, such as validating a field for allowed length of string or for an allowed number range.

We can attach validators with the component that needs to be validated for its data; however, more than one validator can be attached with one component. When some validation error is encountered, validators simply add error message in the existing message list. You can see in the following code snippet how a `Length` validator is associated with the `HtmlInputText` component:

```
<h:inputText label="Name" id="name" required="true">
        <f:validateLength minimum="2" maximum="25"/>
</h:inputText>
```

The preceding code snippet shows a text field whose id is name and validates the length of that field.

Backing Beans

JSF architecture follows MVC design pattern and consequently focuses on separating business logic and data from presentation logic. The model part in backing beans contain business logic and data, while the view consists of presentation logic with UI components.

In a JSF application, there are some JavaBean objects, which handle or store data between the business model and UI component at intermediate stage. These JavaBean objects are known as Backing Beans. Backing beans also play the role of a Controller by handling the interaction between the view and the Model. In other words, in JSF, the objects that handle the interaction between view and Model are called backing beans.

Generally, a single backing bean is created for a single view, but you can create a number of backing beans for a single view. Backing bean data model is usually a copy of the application model. All changes in the component model are often propagated back to the application model through the backing beans model.

Backing beans are normal JavaBeans that contain properties and event listener methods for storing and manipulating the user's data. The event listener methods can also manipulate the UI or execute the application logic in the backend. We can associate a UI component with a property of backing bean through EL value binding. We can also bind the method of backing beans with some UI action component (such as button) to process the logic. For example, we can enable the execution of backing bean method when a button is clicked to perform some action. The following code snippet shows the code to bind a UI component with a property of a given backing bean:

```
<h:inputText label="Name" id="name" value="#{student.name}" required="true"/>
```

We can also bind a backing bean instance directly with a component instance. This binding is useful when you want to manipulate a component using a Java code. We can bind a backing bean property with the component instance directly by using the binding property of a component's tag, as shown in the following code snippet:

```
<h:inputText label="Name" id="name" value="#{student.name}"
binding="#{student.inputName}" required="true"/>
```

The model objects are not directly bound to UI components and are manipulated by backing beans. In addition, you do not need to write codes for creation or instantiation of backing beans, because in JSF a declarative mechanism is used for the creation of backing beans. That is you can configure a backing bean in `faces-config.xml` file and define the name of the object, the class to be , and the scope of that object. The beans that are configured also known as `Managed Beans`. Therefore, all backing beans are managed beans. The following code snippet shows the code to configure a backing bean:

```
<managed-bean>
   <managed-bean-name>student</managed-bean-name>
   <managed-bean-class>com.kogent.Student</managed-bean-class>
   <managed-bean-scope>session</managed-bean-scope>
</managed-bean>
```

The preceding code snippet shows the configuration of a backing bean in the faces-config.xml file. Let's now discuss the converters in the next subsection.

Converters

In general, Web applications interact with the client through HTTP request and response. The data from client to server travels as HTTP request parameter, which can be a string only. We can enter only a string through a UI component, whereas in the backing bean or in the model layer the data can be any Java object. This is where we need a `Converter`. A converter is a translator, which can convert a Java object into a string and an input string into some Java object. JSF provides a number of standard converters for common types, such as date and numbers. We can also develop our own custom converters, which further support extendibility from third party.

We can associate a converter with any UI component through simple markup style, as shown in the following code snippet:

```
<h:inputText id="dob" value="#{student.dob}">
   <f:convertDateTime type="date" pattern="dd-MM-yyyy"/>
</h:inputText>
```

The renderers use converters during the process of encoding and decoding. JSF converters also support formatting and localization. For example, we have a DateTime converter to display Date object in different string formats (short and long) according to the client Locale.

Events and Listeners

JSF implements an event driven processing, where events generated on different UI components can be mapped to the execution of a method. A user can interact with the Web application by generating different events on different UI components. For example, a user can generate a click event on a command button or the value change event on some input text box. The JSF event model is based on simple JavaBean's event model. It means that JSF uses JavaBeans to handle events with event objects and event listeners. A UI component can generate one or more types of events, and we can register respective event listener with the component to respond to those events. The event listeners further invoke associated backing bean method to process the appropriate logic. Now, the developers do not need to work on stateless HTTP request/response model directly.

While writing JSF applications, we just need to assign listeners to the UI components for the generated events on these UI components. JSF supports an interesting way to create a simple method in your backing bean and assigns it as event listener to the UI component, as shown in the following code snippet:

```
<h:inputText id="empid" valueChangeListener="#{employee.valueChanged}"/>
```

In the preceding code snippet, the valueChanged() method of employee backing bean has been registered as listener for Value-change event of an HTMLInputText component.

JSF defines four different types of standard events, which are as follows:

- Action events
- Value-change events
- Data model events
- Phase events

In addition to these standard events defined in the JSF framework, this framework's UI components can be customized to support a number of other types of events. Let's discuss the standard JSF events.

Action Events

The UI component, which represents a command, can generate action events. A component that can generate an action event is also known as an action source. For example, HtmlCommandButton is an action source and can trigger an action event. For handling action events, you can associate an action listener with the UI component.

There are two types of action listeners, one that affects navigation, and the other does not. The action listener, which does not affect navigation executes the code, modifies backing bean or application model, and redisplays the current page. On the other hand, the action listener, which affects navigation, executes the logic and returns the output to navigation model to select the next page to be displayed to the client.

The action listener, which affects navigation, checks the output of action method configured with the component responsible for firing the action event. An action method is a backing bean method, which is invoked when an action event is fired. The string returned from the action method is dynamic in nature; therefore, can have different values. The following code snippet shows the code to configure an action method with the HtmlCommandButton component:

```
<h:commandButton type="submit" value="Add Employee" action="#{employee.addNew}"/>
```

The action listener shown in the preceding code snippet is addNew(). The method to be used as action method must return a string according to the logic performed. The `addNew()` method of backing bean, `employee` is shown in the following code snippet:

```
public class Employee {
   ...
   public String addNew() {
         if(...){
                  return "success";
         }
         else{
                  return "error";
         }
   }
}
```

In some cases we can directly put some string as action attribute instead of retrieving a string from an action method. The action listener returns the hard coded (or static) outcome string. The following code snippet shows how you can hard code a string instead of invoking a backing bean method:

```
<h:commandButton type="submit" value="Cancel" action="cancel"/>
```

In the preceding code snippet, the submit type command button is created and string type value is provided for the action attribute.

NOTE

The way an output string maps to another view, has been discussed later in this chapter.

If you do not want to affect navigation by an action event and just need to process some logic, you need to configure an action listener method instead of action method with the component. The action listener method again is a backing bean method, which returns void and takes an ActionEvent object as an argument. The action listener method has the access to action resource component. The following code snippet shows the code to configure an action listener method:

```
<h:commandButton type="submit" value="Update"
actionListener="#{employee.update}"/>
```

The backing bean method, update() must have the structure shown in the following code snippet:

```
public class Employee {
   ...
   public void update(ActionEvent e) {

   }
}
```

Value-change Events

We have different input UI components, such as the text box and text area that are used to take input from the client. Whenever, an end user enters a new value into these components, a value-change event is fired. We have a valueChangeListener attribute to store the reference of the method that handles the value-change event. In the same way as configuring backing bean methods as action event listener, we can set backing bean method as a value-change listener. The following code snippet shows how to set a backing bean's method as `valueChangeListener`:

```
<h:inputText id="rollno" name="rollno"
  valueChangeListener="#{student.processValueChange}"/>
```

In the preceding code snippet, the processValueChange() method of the `student` backing bean takes an object of javax.faces.event.ValueChangeEvent class as argument. The structure of the processValueChange() method is shown in the following code snippet:

```
public class Student {
   ......
   public void processValueChange(ValueChangeEvent e){
        HtmlInputText comp=(HtmlInputText)e.getComponent();
        ... ...
   }
}
```

When a form is submitted with some value changes in the component, the value-change event is fired only after the associated validators validate the new value entered in the input component. Similar to an action listener, we can also register some event listener classes that implement an interface instead of configuring value-change event method.

Data Model Events

The data model events are associated with data-aware UI components. A data-aware component is a component that gives a list of items to be selected. The example of data-aware component is `HtmlDataTable`. This component cycles through rows in a data source and exposes individual rows to child components. The data model event is fired when data-aware components process a row. Data model event is different from other two events discussed earlier as we cannot register DataModelListener with the component itself in JSP, rather it is registered in the Java code.

The data model event is not fired by the data-aware component itself, rather it is fired by an object of javax.faces.model.DataModel. DataModel is an abstraction for different data binding technologies that are used to adapt a variety of data sources, such as arrays, lists, and ResultSets. The object of DataModel allows the registration of DataModelListener to handle DataModelEvent.

Phase Events

Every request in a JSF application has a life cycle, which is a set of six different stages or phases. These phases include getting request-based view, obtaining component values from request parameters, validate user input, update backing bean and model objects, invoking action listener and returning response back to the client. We have discussed all these life-cycle phases later in this chapter.

Each phase has its start point and end-point and a single event is fired when a phase either begins or ends. Both events, the event at start point and the event at end point, are known as phase events. Phase events are not fired by any UI component; rather, they are generated by JSF. Similar to implementing the data model events, we need to implement a Java interface to register an event listener. However, phase events are used internally and you can use them for implementing some specific logic in your application. The listener for a phase event is registered directly with the instance of `javax.faces.lifecycle.LifeCycle`, which represents the entire life cycle of request processing.

Message

Messages are an integral part of the JSF framework. Generally, a message is used to inform the user about different errors that can occur while processing the logic. A message may be associated with some component or it can be an application level message; therefore, we have two categories of messages, application errors (business logic) and user input errors (empty text field, invalid input text). Different validators can add messages to `FacesContext` and also provide different validations. The converters can convert the messages into application or user input errors. In addition to error messages, we can also have informational messages, such as the messages conveying information to the user about successful addition of a new record in the database.

HtmlMessage and HtmlMessages are two components used to display messages. HtmlMessage is used to display a single message associated with a specific component, as shown in the following code snippet:

```
<h:message for="name" style="color:red"/>
```

All messages associated with FacesContext can be displayed at a single location using HtmlMessages component, as shown in the following code snippet:

```
<h:messages style="color:red"/>
```

JSF supports Internationalization; therefore, all messages can be localized to support client Locale. Messages provide an easy way to communicate different errors and other processing details to the user. The standard validators and converter automatically generates an error message if it finds any incorrect data. We can also create messages in our validator method, action method, and action listener methods, as shown in the following code snippet:

```
FacesContext fc=FacesContext.getCurrentInstance();
fc.addMessage(null, new FacesMessage(FacesMessage.SEVERITY_WARN,
"Your Error Message", ""));
```

You can create an object of FacesMessage with its severity level, message summary, and message detail. The created message needs to be added in FacesContext and can be displayed on any page using <h:messages/> tag.

Navigation

A Web application is a collection of Web pages linked together in a particular sequence to solve a particular purpose, such as shopping. The clients need to go through these pages to perform the desired task and the Web developer has to implement this navigation logic. Earlier, the navigation logic was implemented in Servlet or JSP code to dispatch the client's request to an appropriate view. However, if the Web application is small (consisting two or three pages) it is a simple task to dispatch the client's request to an appropriate view ; but it becomes complex to keep track of all the paths when the size of an application (number of Web pages) increases to enterprise level.

JSF provides an efficient yet simple way to configure all navigation rules declaratively in a single location, that is, in faces-config.xml file. You can define a set of navigation rules to navigate from one view to another view, which are used by navigation handler. It is the responsibility of navigation handler to load the JSF page according to the outcome (return value) of action method. For every page, you can define a navigation rule with a number of navigation cases for different outcomes. The example of a navigation rule for a page with two navigation cases is shown in the following code snippet:

```
<navigation-rule>
  <from-view-id>/login.jsp</from-view-id>
  <navigation-case>
       <from-outcome>success</from-outcome>
       <to-view-id>/welcome.jsp</to-view-id>
  </navigation-case>
  <navigation-case>
       <from-outcome>failure</from-outcome>
       <to-view-id>/login.jsp</to-view-id>
  </navigation-case>
</navigation-rule>
```

In the preceding code snippet, a navigation rule is defined for login.jsp page. The two cases are provided for two different outcomes, `success` and `failure`. This approach of defining navigation rules in a centralized configuration file helps you to maintain all logical paths in an application easily.

You have learned about JSF elements, their functionalities, and their integration. All these elements, such as all UI components, management of backing beans, implementation of standard validators and converters, and configuration of navigation rules in a JSF Web application are discussed later in this chapter.

Exploring the JSF Request Processing Life Cycle

The JSF framework processes a request in predefined steps similar to other Web application frameworks. You can also develop a Web application in JSF, without knowing the request processing details. This reduces the efforts in the enhancements of the existing JSF application. While discussing about the phases of the JSF request process life cycle, the request processing details are also explored.

The request-processing life cycle starts as soon as a request is submitted to the JSF controller Servlet and ends when the client receives a response for the request. Following are the six different phases of JSF request processing life cycle and are given in the order they are executed by the JSF framework:

- The Restore View Phase
- The Apply Request Values Phase
- The Process Validations Phase
- The Update Model Values Phase
- The Invoke Application Phase
- The Render Response Phase

The execution of all these phases is not required for a given request. The request processing life cycle can be terminated in any phase by executing `FacesContext.responseComplete()` method, which skips the other phases of the life cycle. For example, when any invalid input is found in the Process Validation Phase, the current page/view is to be redisplayed and some of the phases, such as Invoke Application Phase, may not execute.

These phases altogether make sure that the processing of a request follows a logical path. For example, no application logic is executed before the form is validated for the input data. Further, implementation of these life cycle phases helps a developer in concentrating on business logic instead of form validation and data conversion. The basic idea behind implementing the life cycle is to make sure that before executing any business logic invoked as a consequence of some action, we have a fully populated backing bean with all validated data.

If you want to create custom JSF UI components, you need to concentrate on first and last phases of JSF request processing life cycle. Figure 11.4 represents the JSF request processing life cycle:

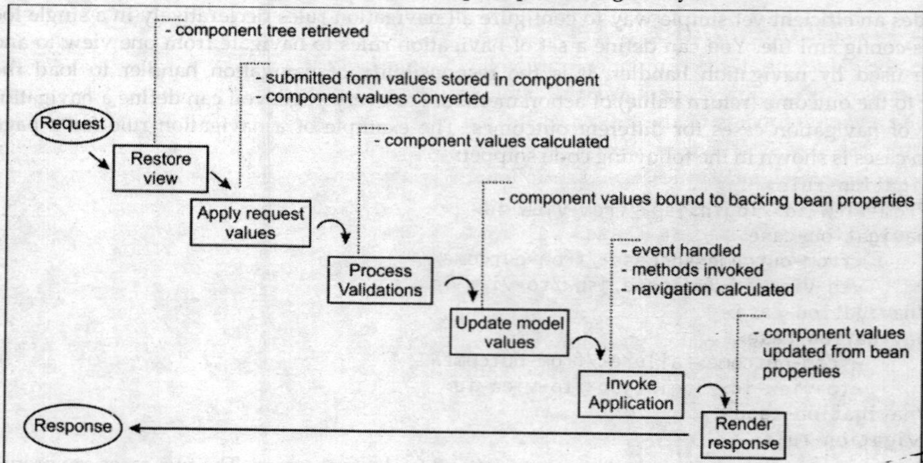

Figure 11.4: Displaying the JSF Request Processing Life Cycle

In a JSF-based application, whenever a request is received by the controller Servlet, an instance of the `javax.faces.context.FacesContext` class is created. The `FacesContext` object contains the state information related to the current JSF request. The `FacesContext` object is accessed and modified in almost all of the request life cycle phases. Let's discuss all six phases of the JSF request processing life cycle with the description of all the functions performed by the framework.

The Restore View Phase

A view can be defined as a collection of components in a request page. All the components in a request page or view are grouped together as a tree; therefore, every view is a tree of components having a unique identification, that is view ID. The JSF controller Servlet finds the view ID from the request, which can be determined by the requested JSP page name. The controller can load the existing view or can create a new view if it does not exist.

The Restore View phase can handle three different views, new view, initial view, and postback. In case of a new view, this phase creates the view of the request page and associates event handlers and validators to the components in the view. This phase also stores the view as root component using setViewRoot() method on `FacesContext` instance. When the JSF page is requested for the first time, the view needs to be loaded for the first time (initial view) and the controller creates an empty view. In case of initial view, the framework directly moves to render the response page.

If the user requests a page accessed earlier (postback), the controller needs to restore the view with the current state of the view. In case of postback, the next phase after Restore View phase is the Apply Request Values phase.

The Apply Request Values Phase

There are a set of JSF UI components that receive the input as request data from the user and then processes it. In the Apply Request Values phase, the JSF implementation iterates the component objects in the component tree and requests every component to decode itself. Decoding is the process in which the framework sets the submitted values for the components based on the request parameters. The component value can be validated in this phase if the immediate property is true for the component. In case of validation error, an error message is added and the render response phase starts. If the immediate property of the component is set to false, then the submitted string values are converted into the desired data type. At the end of this phase, each component stores recent values submitted through current request. After the completion of this phase, the existing events are broadcasted for the associated event listeners.

The action events can fire in this phase but are handled in the invoke application phase. In this phase, they are created and added to the FacesContext instance.

The Process Validations Phase

In this phase, the values of all the components are validated against some validation rules. We can associate a given component with some JSF standard validator or can define our own validators. The validators are registered with the components of the JSF page. In case, the value of a given component is found invalid, a validation error message is added in the FacesContext and the render response phase starts to display the current view with the validation message. The following code snippet shows an HtmlInputText component created with a validator to validate its value for its length:

```
<h:inputText label="Name" id="name" value="#{student.name}" required="true"
  valueChangeListener="#{student.change}">
  <f:validateLength minimum="2" maximum="25"/>
</h:inputText>
```

All the value change events associated with different components are fired and used by the appropriate listener in this phase. If all the submitted values are found valid, the framework enters into the update model values phase of the life cycle.

The Update Model Values Phase

The Process Validation phase ensures that all component values are valid. After validating component values, all values of the backing beans or model objects are updated with the component values to save the state of components so that these values can be used in subsequent requests. Every component can be associated with some backing bean property and the backing bean is updated with the current value of the component. The following code snippet shows the code to associate the `name` property of `student` backing bean with an `HtmlInputText` component:

```
<h:inputText label="Name" id="name" value="#{student.name}" required="true">
</h:inputText>
```

In the preceding code snippet, backing bean properties are associated with a component through a value binding expression, such as `#{sudent.name}`. When these expressions are evaluated, the `FacesServlet` searches for the appropriate backing beans in request, application, or session scope. By the end of this phase, we have all component values set with all validated user inputs and updated backing beans. Now, we are ready to execute our business logic in the invoke application phase.

The Invoke Application Phase

In the previous phases, we have not executed any business logic. We have just updated component model and backing bean model with the current and valid data. In the Apply Request Values phase, we have added all action events in the FacesContext for their handling in invoke application phase. In invoke application phase, the JSF framework broadcasts all the added action events, which are further handled by the registered action event listeners. We can register some backing bean methods as action listeners or action methods. The action method may contain the logic for different operations, such as rendering responses and adding messages. Action methods are also integrated with the navigation model and helps in determining the next view or page to be displayed.

After the completion of all phases and handling of all events by the respective listeners, the framework is ready with the next view for the user.

The Render Response Phase

The Render Response phase is the last phase in the JSF request-processing life cycle. This phase is responsible for sending responses to the client. The state of the view (component tree) is saved in this phase before the response is rendered for the client. The state of the view can be stored on the server side using client session or can be saved on the client side using hidden fields. Saving the state of a view is important, so that it can be restored in the Restore view phase in case of postback. In case of postback, all error messages that are added in Apply Request Values phase, Process Validations phase, or Update Model Values phase are also displayed along with the current state of the components in the view.

JSF framework is not bound to a particular display technology to render the response to the client. We can have different approaches to render the responses. We can use the output of encoding method with the markup code, which is either stored in some template resource or generated by another application for the client. The JSF implementations use a different approach, that is, it uses the output of decoding methods with some dynamic resources such as JSP page.

During Render Response phase, all component values are converted into a string to be displayed. When this phase completes, the Web container sents the response to the client as a response page in browser.

We have discussed all six phases of the JSF request processing life cycle that explain how a JSF request (read it Faces request) is changed into JSF response (read it Faces response). A brief explanation of Faces and Non-Faces request and responses are as follows:

- **Faces Response**—Refers to the Servlet response constructed after the execution of Render Response phase of request processing life cycle.
- **Non-Faces Response**—Refers to the Servlet response, which is not constructed by the execution of Render Response phase, for example a JSP page that does not have JSF components.
- **Faces Request**—Refers to the Servlet request sent from previously generated faces response, for example, a form submitted from a JSF UI component, where request URI recognizes JSF component tree for processing the request.
- **Non-Faces Request**—Refers to the Servlet request sent to an application component, such as Servlet of JSP page, rather than directed to the JSF component tree.

These four request and response types lead to four combinations, which define the request and response scenarios that may occur in a Web application based on JSF. In case of Non-Faces request or Non-Faces response, the JSF request processing life cycle is not followed.

Exploring JSF Tag Libraries

We can design pages in a JSF application by using different JSF UI components. The various UI components can be created easily for the page by using tags defined in the JSF tag library. In addition to laying out different components in the page, designing a page in JSF application includes making provision in the page to use backing beans, validators, converters, and other backend objects associated with the components.

JSF 1.2 provides two different tag libraries, JSF HTML tag library and JSF core tag library. These tag libraries provide tags to create pages in JSF application with a rich set of UI components supporting event handling and input validation. You must include the following standard tag libraries to use JSF UI components in a JSP page:

- **JSF HTML tag library**—Defines the tags that represent general HTML UI components. These HTML components include `HtmlInputText`, `HtmlInputTextarea`, `HtmlForm`, and `HtmlCommandButton`.
- **JSF core tag library**—Defines the tags that perform core actions. This tag library does not depend upon specific render kit.

We can use these tag libraries simply by providing a taglib directive in our JSP page with proper uri and prefix, as shown in the following code snippet:

```
<%@ taglib uri="http://java.sun.com/jsf/html" prefix="h"%>
<%@ taglib uri="http://java.sun.com/jsf/core" prefix="f"%>
```

The code lines in the preceding code snippet must be the first two lines in a JSP page in a JSF based Web application.

Let's discuss all JSF HTML tags and JSF core tags. All these tags have been fully described with their syntax and behavior.

JSF HTML Tags

The JSF HTML tag library provides JSF component tags for all UI components and HTML RenderKit. It means that all the tags discussed for JSF HTML tag library are rendered to some HTML response for the client browser. Each tag in JSF HTML tag library corresponds to a specific class of UI components present in the `javax.faces.component.html` package.

All HTML UI components created using the tags defined in the JSF HTML tag library render to different HTML tags. For example <h:form> tags render to the HTML <form> element. All JSF HTML tags support common HTML tag attributes, such as alt, style, tabindex, and width. In addition, Dyanamic Hyper Text Markup Language (DHTML) event attributes, such as onclick, ondbclick, onmouseover are also supported by JSF HTML tags. All JSF HTML tags have some common attributes, which are listed in Table 11.1:

Table 11.1: Representing the Basic HTML Tag Attributes

Attribute	Description	Component Type
id	Takes a string, which is a component identifier and must be unique within the closest parent component.	UI components
binding	Binds a component with a backing bean property.	
rendered	Takes a boolean value. By default this value is true, which indicates rendering of component. If this value is set to false, it suppresses rendering of component, which means the component is not rendered at all.	
styleClass	Refers to the class name of the Cascading StyleSheet (CSS).	
value	Sets the value of a component. Typically used for value binding.	Input, Output, and Command type of components
valueChangeListener	Binds a method, which can respond to value change events.	Input component
converter	Sets converter class name.	Input and Output components
validator	Sets Validator class or Validator method for a component.	Input component

Table 11.1: Representing the Basic HTML Tag Attributes		
Attribute	**Description**	**Component Type**
required	Takes a boolean value. If the value is true, then it requires a value to be entered in the associated field, otherwise it is not necessary to enter the value in associated field.	Input component

Now, let's discuss various JSF HTML tags and their behavior with examples.

The <h:commandButton> Tag

The `<h:commandButton>` tag is used to create a command button in the JSP page. This represents an HtmlCommandButton component. This tag is rendered to HTML <input> element with a type attribute, `submit` or `reset;` therefore, this tag can be used to create a submit button which when clicked would send the form data to the server and would fire an action event. The most commonly used attributes of the <h:commandButton> tag are shown in Table 11.2:

Table 11.2: Showing the CommonAttributes of <h:commandButton > Tag	
Attribute	**Description**
action	Accepts a string or a method binding expression as its value. The navigation handler determines the JSF page to be loaded next according to the string or the outcome of the action method.
actionListener	Accepts a method binding expression as its value. You should note that the signature of this method must be void methodName(ActionEvent object).
image	Accepts the context relative path of an image as its value, which would be displayed on the button.
immediate	Accepts a boolean value. The default value of this attribute is false, in which the action and action listener methods are invoked at the end of request life cycle.
type	Accepts the type of the rendered input element. This can be set as a button, submit or reset. The default type is submit.
value	Accepts a string as its value, which would be displayed on the button. We can provide string or value expression for the value attribute.

Let's consider the following code snippet that uses the <h:commandButton> tag:

```
<h:commandButton value="Login" action="#{user.login}"/>
<h:commandButton value="Check Availability" actionListener="#{user.check}" />
```

In the preceding code snippet, the first `<h:commandButton>` tag displays the `Login` submit button and binds a `login` method of the `user` backing bean with the button. The method of backing bean (`user`) assigned to the `action` attribute in method binding expression returns a string that determines navigation flow. The second `<h:commandButton>` tag displays the Check Availability (a submit) button and registers an action listener method (`check`) from backing bean (`user`) that performs an operation named Check Availability.

The <h:commandLink> Tag

Normally, we use a button to submit the data of a form or to invoke an action. However, sometimes we may want to perform the same thing using HTML hyperlink. The `<h:commandLink>` tag renders an HTML hyperlink, which is capable of submitting form data and firing some action. It also supports sending of parameters to an action method or action listener method using UIParameter component. Table 11.3 shows the most commonly used attributes of the `<h:commandLink>` tag:

Table 11.3: Showing the CommonAttributes of the <h:commandLink> Tag

Attribute	Description
action	Accepts a string or a method binding expression as its value. The navigation handler determines the JSF page to be loaded next according to the string or the outcome of the action method. The signature of the action method should be String methodName().
actionListener	Accepts a method binding expression as its value. You should note that the signature of the method must be void methodName(ActionEvent object).
charset	Accepts the character encoding of the linked reference as its value.
immediate	Accepts a boolean value. If the value is set to false, the action or action listener methods are invoked in the end of request life cycle. The default value of the `immediate` attribute is false.
type	Accepts the content type of the linked resource as its value. For example, text/html and image/gif.
value	Accepts a string or an expression referencing a value. For example, the label displayed by the link.

Let's consider the following code snippet that uses the <h:commandLink> tag:

```
<h:commandLink action="#{student.delete}" value="Delete">
    <f:setPropertyActionListener target="#{student.roll}" value="#{user.roll}"/>
</h:commandLink>
```

In the preceding code snippet, the `roll` property of the backing bean, `student` is set with the value of roll property of user bean before the action invoke phase, that is, before the `delete()` method of student backing bean is executed. You learn about the <f:setPropertyActionListener> tag in detail later in the *JSF Core Tags* section.

The <h:dataTable> Tag

This tag is used to create an HtmlDataTable component and helps to create a data grid. The HtmlDataTable component automatically populates with data sets. The data grid is a necessary component for any UI framework; therefore, it has been developed as a standard data grid. The `<h:dataTable>` tag renders to an HTML `<table>` element but its rows are automatically created according to the data set stored in the table. The columns of this table can be defined using the UIColumn components. Table 11.4 shows the most commonly used attributes of the <h:dataTable> tag:

Table 11.4: Showing the Common Attributes of <h:dataTable> Tag

Attribute	Description
bgcolor	Specifies the background color for the table.
border	Accepts an integer value as the width of table border.
cellpadding	Accepts an integer value that specifies how much padding exist around table cells.
cellspacing	Specifies spacing between table cells.
columnClasses	Accepts comma-separated list of CSS classes for columns of tables.
first	Accepts the index of the first row shown in the table.
footerClass	Specifies the CSS class for the table footer.
frame	Specifies the values of the sides of the frame surrounding the table. The allowed values are none, above, below, hsides, vsides, lhs, rhs, box, and border.
headerClass	Specifies the CSS class for the table header.
rowClasses	Accepts comma-separated list of CSS classes for rows.

Table 11.4: Showing the Common Attributes of <h:dataTable> Tag

Attribute	Description
rules	Specifies the lines to be drawn between cells. The allowed values are groups, rows, columns, and all.
summary	Sets the summary of the table depicting the purpose as well as structure of the table. The value of the `summary` attribute is mainly used for non-visual feedback such as speech.
var	Accepts a string value, which is created by the data table and used to represent the current item. This value is associated with the `var` attribute.

The following code snippet shows the use of the <h:dataTable> tag:

```
<h:dataTable value="#{applicationScope.students}" var="student" cellspacing="1">
<h:column>

  <f:facet name="header">
       <h:outputText value="Roll No."/>
  </f:facet>
  <h:outputText value="#{student.roll}"/>
  </h:column>

       <h:column>
       <f:facet name="header">
             <h:outputText value="Student Name"/>
       </f:facet>

       <h:outputText value="#{student.name}"/>
  </h:column>
</h:dataTable>
```

In the preceding code snippet, the column component tags represent the UIData and UIColumn components, respectively. We have created columns for standard data grid using the <h:column> element, which represents the UIColumn component. The HtmlDataTable component supports data binding to a set of data objects represented by the DataModel instance. The DataModel instance holds the data model of a component and can be instantiated, saved in a separate context from the component definition, and can be used by different components simultaneously. As the UIData component iterates over the rows of the data represented by the DataModel instance, it also processes the UIColumn component for each row.

The <h:form> Tag

The `<h:form>` tag is used to create an HTML form element on the JSF page. The `<h:form>` contains other required input fields, such as name, age, address, and zip . You should place all the input UI components within the <h:form> tag, because the form is concerned with user input. The HTML form created by this tag behaves as a normal form element, which can be submitted to the server with data to be processed.

We can have more than one `<h:form>` tags in a single page. Only one form, which contains the click command button, is submitted to the server.

While using the `<h:form>` tag, you do not need to provide method and action attributes as they are required in an HTML form element. The default method used to provide method and action attributes in an HTML form element is post and action would be the result obtained from the `getActionURL()` method of ViewHandler for the application. Table 11.5 shows the commonly used attributes of the <h:form> tag:

Table 11.5: Showing the Common Attributes of the <h:form> Tag

Attribute	Description
id	Accepts a string that is a component identifier and must be unique within the closest parent component

Table 11.5: Showing the Common Attributes of the <h:form> Tag	
Atrribute	**Description**
binding	Accepts a value expression, which binds it with some backing bean property
rendered	Accepts a boolean value indicating that whether the component will be rendered or not
styleClass	Sets the style class to be applied when the component is rendered

Let's consider the following code snippet that uses the <h:form> tag:

```
<h:form id="loginForm">
   //Other UI components
</h:form>
```

The <h:form> tag in the preceding code snippet is used to encapsulate UI components into a form named loginForm.

The <h:graphicImage> Tag

The `<h:graphicImage>` tag is used to display images on a Web page. In JSF pages, the HtmlGraphicImage component is created to handle the images embedded in the designed page. The `<h:graphicImage>` tag creates a simple HTML `<img>` element. The src property of `<img>` tag is obtained from the uri property of the `<h:graphicImage>` tag. Table 11.6 shows the most commonly used attributes of the `<h:graphicImage>` tag:

Table 11.6: Showing the Common Attributes of the <h:graphicImage > Tag	
Attribute	**Description**
id	Accepts a string, which is component identifier and must be unique within the closest parent component.
binding	Accepts a value expression, which binds this attribute with a backing bean property.
rendered	Accepts a boolean value indicating whether or not the component will be rendered.
styleClass	Sets the style class to be applied when the component is rendered.
value	Accepts the image file name with full path as its value. This value is rendered as the value for the `src` attribute of the `<img>` element.
alt	Sets some textual description of the image.
height	Sets the height of the image.
style	Specifies the CSS style to be applied.
url	Accepts the context relative path for the resource image. It works as an alias for the `value` attribute.
width	Sets the width of the image.

Let's consider the following code snippet that uses the `<h:graphicImage>` tag:

```
<h:graphicImage value="images/animal.jpg" width="300"/>
```

The `<h:graphicImage>` tag in the preceding code snippet displays a graphic image (animal.jpg) located in images directory.

The <h:inputHidden> Tag

The `<h:inputHidden>` tag is used to create an input element, which is not displayed to the user of the page. Using this tag a hidden field can be added to the page, which need not be displayed on the page, but required to process logic. The `<h:inputHidden>` tag corresponds to the `HtmlInputHidden` component and renders to a simple `<input>` element with its type set to hidden. Table 11.7 shows the most commonly used attributes of the `<h:inputHidden>` tag:

Table 11.7: Showing the Common Attributes of the <h:inputHidden> Tag

Attribute	Description
immediate	Accepts a boolean value. If the value of this attribute is set to true the value of the component is validated immediately in the apply request phase instead of waiting for validation phase.
required	Accepts a boolean value. If the value of this attribute is set to true the user is required to enter some value for this input component.
valueChangeListener	Accepts a method expression to define a listener to handle the value change event for this component

Let's consider the following code snippet that uses the `<h:inputHidden>` tag:

```
<h:inputHidden id="roll" value="#{student.roll}"/>
```

The preceding code snippet shows the use of the <h:inputHidden> tag. When you use this tag inside the <h:form> tag, the value of the roll parameter is sent to the server as a hidden parameter.

The <h:inputSecret> Tag

The `<h:inputSecret>` tag creates an HtmlInputSecret component and renders an HTML `<input>` element with type set as password. The text entered into this secret field cannot be read, as the characters are displayed using asterisk or other character. Table 11.8 shows the most commonly used attributes of the `<h:inputSecret>` tag:

Table 11.8: Showing the Common Attributes of the <h:inputSecret> Tag

Attribute	Description
immediate	Accepts a boolean value. If the value of this attribute is set to true the value of the component is validated immediately in the apply request phase instead of waiting for validation phase.
redisplay	Accepts a boolean value. When the value of the `redisplay` attribute is set to true, the value of input field is redisplayed on reloading the Web page.
required	Accepts a boolean value and setting this value to true ensures that the user is required to enter some value for this input component.
valueChangeListener	Accepts a method expression to define a listener to handle the value change event for this component.

The following code snippet shows the use of the <h:inputSecret> tag:

```
<h:inputSecret redisplay="false" value="#{user.password}"/>
```

The preceding code snippet converts the password entered by a user into encoded form such as ****.

The <h:inputText> Tag

The `<h:inputText>` tag is used to create a single line text box, which is the most common component to take input from the user. The `<h:inputText>` tag corresponds to the `HtmlInputText` class and renders to simple `<input>` element with type, text. As other input UI components, this tag can also be attached with some validator or converter. Table 11.9 shows the most commonly used attributes of the <h:inputText> tag:

Table 11.9: Showing the Common Attributes of the <h:inputText> Tag

Attribute	Description
immediate	Accepts a boolean value. If this value is set to true the value of a component is validated immediately in the apply request phase instead of waiting for validation phase.
required	Accepts a boolean value. If this value is set to true the user is required to enter some value for this input component.
valueChangeListener	Accepts a method expression to define a listener to handle the value change event for this component.

Let's consider the following code snippet that uses the <h:inputText> tag:

```
<h:inputText id="uname" label="User Name" value="#{user.fullName}" required="true"/>
```

In the preceding code snippet, the `HtmlInputText` component has been bound with the `fullName` property of the `user` backing bean with a value expression. Setting all the required attributes to `true` ensures that the user must enter some string in the text field.

The <h:inputTextarea> Tag

The `<h:inputTextarea>` tag is used to create a multiline text input control. This tag corresponds to `Html rich text box` and renders to HTML `<textarea>` element. The `<h:inputTextarea>` tag has the properties to set column (that is width in characters) as well as row (that is height in characters) of text area. Table 11.10 shows the most commonly used attributes of the `<h:inputTextarea>` tag:

Table 11.10: Showing the Common Attributes of the <h:inputTextarea> Tag

Attribute	Description
cols	Sets the number of characters in the text area.
immediate	Accepts the boolean value. This value is set to true to process validation early in the request processing life cycle.
required	Accepts a boolean value. If this value is set to true the user is required to enter some value for this input component.
rows	Sets the number of rows.
valueChangeListener	Accepts a method expression to define a listener to handle the value change event for this component.

Let's consider the following code snippet that uses the `<h:inputTextarea>` tag:

```
<h:inputTextarea id="address" cols="20" rows="3" value="#{student.address}"/>
```

The `HtmlInputTextarea` component in the preceding code snippet creates a multiline text box, which has been bound with the `address` property of the student backing bean.

The <h:message> Tag

The JSF provides a simple way of displaying messages, which have been added to FacesContext by some validator, converter, or some other method for a specific UI component. A message can be displayed using the `<h:message>` tag. The associated UI component can be referred by setting the `for` attribute with the id of that particular component. Table 11.11 shows the most commonly used attributes of the `<h:message>` tag:

Table 11.11: Showing the Common Attributes of the <h:message> Tag

Attribute	Description
for	Specifies the ID of the component whose message is displayed as applicable only to h:message.
errorClass	Applies the specified CSS class to error messages.
errorStyle	Applies the provided CSS style to error messages.
fatalClass	Applies the specified CSS class to fatal messages.
fatalStyle	Applies the provided CSS style to fatal messages.
infoClass	Applies the specified CSS class to information based messages.
infoStyle	Applies the provided CSS style to information based messages.
showDetail	Accepts a boolean value specifing whether or not the message details should be displayed.
showSummary	Accepts a boolean value specifying whether or not the summary part of the message should be displayed. By default, the value of this attribute is false for the <h:message> tag.

Table 11.11: Showing the Common Attributes of the <h:message> Tag	
Attribute	**Description**
tooltip	Accepts a boolean value specifying whether or not the summary message should be displayed in tooltip.
warnClass	Applies the specified CSS class to warning message.
warnStyle	Applies the provided CSS style to warning message.

Let's consider the following code snippet that uses the `<h:message>` tag:

```
<h:message for="uname"></h:message>
or
<h:message for="uname" errorClass="error"/>
```

The first `<h:message>` tag displays an error message for the component named, `uname`. The second tag additionally applies the CSS style class (error) to display same error message in a particular format.

The <h:messages> Tag

There may be a number of messages that can be added during the request processing process. In addition, there can be different application level messages, which are not associated with any particular component. The `<h:messages>` tag is used to display all the messages added into FacesContext at once.

Table 11.12 shows the most commonly used attributes of the <h:messages> tag:

Table 11.12: Showing the Common Attributes of the <h:messages> Tag	
Attribute	**Description**
errorClass	Applies the specified CSS class to the error messages.
errorStyle	Applies the provided CSS style to the error messages.
fatalClass	Applies the specified CSS class to fatal messages.
fatalStyle	Applies the provided CSS style to fatal messages.
globalOnly	Accepts a boolean value specifying whether or not to display only global messages. By default, its value is false.
infoClass	Applies the specified CSS class to information based messages.
infoStyle	Applies the provided CSS style to information based message.
layout	Specifies the layout for a message, which can either be a list or a table. If you do not use this attribute then the layout is displayed in the form of a list.
showDetail	Accepts a boolean value specifying whether the message details should be provided or not. By default this value is false.
showSummary	Accepts a boolean value specifying whether the message summaries should be displayed or not. By default this value is true.
tooltip	Accepts a boolean value specifying whether the message details are rendered in a tooltip or not; if the showDetail and showSummary attributes are true then the tooltip is rendered.
warnClass	Applies the CSS class for warning message
warnStyle	Applies the CSS style for warning message

Let's consider the following code snippet that uses the <h:messages> tag:

```
<h:messages errorClass="error" warnClass="warn"/>
```

The <h:messages> tag in the preceding code snippet displays all error and warning messages in their respective formats.

The <h:outputFormat> Tag

The `<h:outputFormat>` tag works similar to the `<h:outputText>` tag but it also formats the compound messages. The `<h:outputFormat>` tag allows a page author to display the concatenated messages as a message format pattern. This tag is used to display parameterized text. The value attribute of the <h:outputFormat> tag specifies a message format pattern and the substation parameters are specified with the <f:param> tag. The associated parameters should be defined in the same order as they appear in the message format pattern. Table 11.13 shows the most commonly used attribute of the <h:outputFormat> tag:

Table 11.13: Showing the Common Attribute of the <h:outputFormat> Tag

Important Attribute	
escape	Accepts a boolean value. If set to true, escapes <, >, and & characters. The default value of the escape attribute is false.

Let's consider following code snippet to understand the use of the <h:outputFormat> tag.

```
<h:outputFormat id="msg" value="Hello {0}, Your Roll number is {1}.">
    <f:param value="#{student.name}"/>

    <f:param value="#{student.rollno}"/>
</h:outputFormat>
```

The <h:outputFormat> tag in the preceding code snippet displays a command message, which automatically contains the name and roll number of the student.

The <h:outputLabel> Tag

The <h:outputLabel> tag is used to create the HtmlOutputLabel component on a JSF page. The HtmlOutputLabel component is used as a label for a given component. It displays a label for a component, which is associated with the component through the given id. Table 11.14 shows the most commonly used attribute of the <h:outputLabel> tag:

Table 11.14:Showing the Common Attribute of the <h:outputLabel> Tag

Attribute	Description
for	Specifies the ID of the component to be labeled.

Let's consider the following code snippet that uses the <h:outputLabel> tag:

```
<h:outputLabel for="msg">Your Message</h:outputLabel>
<h:inputText id="msg" value="#{user.message}"/>
```

The <h:outputLabel> tag in the preceding code snippet displays the label, `Your Message` before the text field component named msg.

The <h:outputLink> Tag

The <h:outputLink> tag is used to create an HTML anchor on a Web page that helps you to navigate through the current Web page to other locations. Unlike the HtmlCommandLink component, the HtmlOutputLink component does not generate any action event, as the URL is already specified using the value attribute. The <h:outputLink> tag renders to the HTML <a> element, and the href attribute of this anchor element is set with the value set for value attribute of the <h:outputLink> tag. Table 11.15 shows the most commonly used attributes of the <h:outputLink> tag:

Table 11.15: Showing the Common Attributes of the <h:outputLink> Tag

Attribute	Description
Id	Accepts a string, which is component identifier and must be unique within the closest parent component.
binding	Accepts a value expression, which binds this attribute with some backing bean property.
Layout	Accepts the type of layout markup used while rendering the component group. If this attribute is set to block, then the HTML <div> element is produced; otherwise, <span> is produced.

Table 11.15: Showing the Common Attributes of the <h:outputLink> Tag

Attribute	Description
rendered	Accepts boolean value indicating whether or not the component will be rendered.
style	Applies the specified CSS style when the component is rendered.
styleClass	Applies the CSS style class when the component is rendered.
value	Accepts the linked resource name with its path. The value set for the value attribute is set as the value for the href attribute of the rendered HTML anchor tag.

Let's consider the following code snippet that uses the <h:outputLink> tag:

```
<h:outputLink value="login.faces">Login</h:outputLink>
or
<h:outputLink value="login.faces">
   <h:outputText value="Login"/>
</h:outputLink>
```

The <h:outputLink> tag in the preceding code snippet displays a hyperlink (named Login) on a Web page. When a user clicks this hyperlink, request goes to the login.faces page.

The <h:outputText> Tag

The <h:outputText> tag is used to display the single line output string. The string to be displayed can be defined giving JSF expression for value attributes. The <h:outputText> tag corresponds to HtmlOutputText component. Table 11.16 shows the most commonly used attributes of the <h:outputText> tag:

Table 11.16: Showing the Common Attribute of the <h:outputText> Tag

Attribute	Description
escape	Defines whether or not special characters, such as <,>, and & is to be escaped. For escaping these characters the value should be true but by default the value is false.

Let's consider following code snippet that uses the <h:outputText> tag:

```
<h:outputText value="#{user.name}"/>
or
<h:outputText value="Welcome"/>
```

The first <h:outputText> tag in the preceding code snippet reads the value of the name property of (user) backing bean and displays it on browser. The second tag displays the Welcome string (specified in its value attribute) on browser.

The <h:panelGrid> Tag

The <h:panelGrid> tag corresponds to the HtmlPanelGrid component and renders to the HTML <table> element. An entire table can be presented using the <h:panelGrid> tag. You can also define header and footer using the <f:facet> tag, which renders the <thead> and <tfoot> elements. The number of columns can be set by using the columns property of the <h:panelGrid> tag. Table 11.17 shows the most commonly used attributes of the <h:panelGrid> tag:

Table 11.17: Showing the Common Attributes of the <h:panelGrid> Tag

Attribute	Description
bgcolor	Specifies the background color of a table
border	Specifies the width of table border
cellpadding	Specifies the padding space to be provided around the table cells
cellspacing	Specifies the space to be provided between table cells

Table 11.17: Showing the Common Attributes of the <h:panelGrid> Tag	
Attribute	**Description**
columnClasses	Specifies the lists of CSS classes (separated by comma) for columns
columns	Specifies the total number of columns in a table
footerClass	Specify the CSS class for the footer of the table
frame	Specifies the frame surrounding the table that needs to be drawn; valid values for this purpose are: none, above, below, hsides, vsides, lhs, rhs, box, and border
headerClass	Specifies the CSS class for the header of the table
rowClasses	Specifies the lists of CSS classes (separated by comma) for rows
rules	Specifies the lines drawn between cells; valid values are: groups, rows, columns, and all
summary	Provides the purpose and structure of the table, that is basically used for non-visual feedback such as speech

The following code snippet shows the use of the <h:panelGrid> tag:

```
<h:panelGrid id="panel" columns="2" border="1">
   <h:outputLabel for="uid">User ID</h:outputLabel>
   <h:inputText id="uid" value="#{user.userName}"/>
   <h:outputLabel for="pwd">Password</h:outputLabel>
   <h:inputText id="pwd" value="#{user.password}"/>
</h:panelGrid>
```

In the preceding code snippet, a table with two columns and two rows is created by using the <h:panelGrid> tag. The number of rows created depend on the number of other components enclosed in the <h:panelGrid> tag.

The <h:panelGroup> Tag

The <h:panelGroup> tag can encapsulate a set of other components to make a single entity. This tag creates HtmlPanelGroup components that do not render any output, but are used as a place holder. The <h:panelGroup> tag is used to create a blank cell inside a table rendered by the <h:panelGrid> element. Table 11.18 shows the most commonly used attributes of the <h:panelGroup> tag:

Table 11.18: Showing the Common Attributes of the <h:panelGroup> Tag	
Attribute	**Description**
id	Accepts a string, which is a component identifier and must be unique within the closest parent component
binding	Accepts a value expression, which binds this attribute with some backing bean property
layout	Allows you to set the type of layout markup to be used when rendering the component group. If this attribute is set to block, the HTML <div> element is produced; otherwise, <span> is produced
rendered	Accepts a boolean value indicating whether the component should be rendered or not
style	Allows you to set the CSS style to component when the component is rendered
styleClass	Allows you to set the CSS style class to component when the component is rendered

The following code snippet shows the use of the <h:panelGroup> tag:

```
<h:panelGroup id="panel1">
   <h:commandButton value="Login" action="#{user.login}"/>
```

```
        <h:commandButton value="New User" action="#{user.newUser}"/>
    </h:panelGroup>
```

The <h:panelGroup> tag in the preceding code snippet displays the Login and New User buttons as one group.

The <h:selectbooleanCheckbox> Tag

The `<h:selectbooleanCheckbox>` tag is used to create a **HtmlSelectbooleanCheckbox** component, which represents single boolean value. The `<h:selectbooleanCheckbox>` tag renders to an HTML `<input>` element with type checkbox. Table 11.19 shows the most commonly used attributes of the <h:selectbooleanCheckbox> tag:

Table 11.19: showing the Common Attributes of the <h:selectbooleanCheckbox> Tag

Attribute	Description
binding	Accepts a value expression, which binds the value (entered by user) with some backing bean property.
converter	Allows you to set the converter instance registered with the component.
Id	Accepts a string, which is a component identifier and must be unique within the closest parent component.
immediate	Allows you to set the process validation early in the life cycle of JSF, by default it is true.
styleClass	Allows you to set the CSS style class to be applied when the component is rendered.
required	Allows you to set a boolean value to a field and setting it to true ensures that the user is required to enter some value for this input component.
rendered	Accepts a boolean value indicating whether the component should be rendered or not.
validator	Accepts a method expression and represents the validator method to be invoked to validate the current value of the component.
value	Allows you to set the current value of a component. A value expression can be used to bind the current value with a backing bean property.
valueChangeListener	Allows you to set the method expression to define a listener to handle the value change event for this component

The following code snippet shows the use of the <h:selectbooleanCheckbox> tag:

```
    <h:selectbooleanCheckbox value="#{student.status}"/>
```

The preceding code snippet, code is written to display a checkbox, which takes the value of status property of student backing bean.

The <h:selectManyCheckbox> Tag

As the name suggests, the `<h:selectManyCheckbox>` tag renders a group of checkboxes to be selected. This tag corresponds to `HtmlSelectManyCheckbox` component that renders to the HTML `<table>` element and `<input>` elements of type checkbox. The items to be selected can be encapsulated within the `<h:selectManyCheckbox>` tag by using the `<f:selectItem>` or `<f:selectItems>` tag (discussed later in this chapter). Table 11.20 shows the most commonly used attributes of the <h:selectManyCheckbox> tag:

Table 11.20: Showing the Common Attributes of the <h:selectManyCheckbox> Tag

Attribute	Description
binding	Accepts a value expression, which binds the attribute with some backing bean property.
converter	Allows you to set the converter instance registered with the component.

Table 11.20: Showing the Common Attributes of the <h:selectManyCheckbox> Tag

Attribute	Description
disabledClass	Accepts a CSS style class to be applied on disabled options.
enabledClass	Accepts a CSS style class to be applied on enabled options.
id	Accepts a string, which is a component identifier and must be unique within the closest parent component.
immediate	Allows you to set the value of process validation early in the life cycle of JSF. By default this value is true.
layout	Allows you to set the orientation of components for the Web page that needs to be displayed. The allowed values are pageDirection and lineDirection. The default value is lineDirection and its options are rendered horizontally.
styleClass	Allows you to set the CSS style class to be applied when the component is rendered.
required	Allows you to set the boolean value and setting it to true ensures that the user is required to enter some value for this input component.
rendered	Accepts a boolean value indicating whether the component will be rendered or not.
validator	Accepts a method expression and represents the validator method to be invoked to validate the current value of the component.
value	Allows you to set the current value of the component. A value expression can be used to bind the current value with a backing bean property.
valueChangeListener	Allows you to set the method expression to define a listener to handle the value change event for this component.

The following code snippet shows the use of the <h:selectManyCheckbox> tag:

```
<h:selectManyCheckbox id="country" value="#{user.country}">
   <f:selectItem itemLabel="India" itemValue="ind"/>
   <f:selectItem itemLabel="Pakistan" itemValue="pak"/>
   <f:selectItem itemLabel="Sri Lanka" itemValue="srl"/>
</h:selectManyCheckbox>
```

The `<h:selectManyCheckbox>` tag displays a group of checkboxes with id (equals to country). This tag represents each item of a group using the <f:selectItem> tag.

The <h:selectManyListbox> Tag

The `<h:selectManyListbox>` tag corresponds to `HtmlSelectManyListbox` component, which renders to the HTML `<select>` element. All the child components of the `<f:selectItem>` tag are rendered to the HTML `<option>` element. The `<h:selectManyListbox>` tag provides a list box of choices, which allows the selection of multiple options from the list. The size attribute of this tag defines the total number of options that can be displayed at a time. Table 11.21 shows the most commonly used attributes of the `<h:selectManyListbox>` tag:

Table 11.21:Showing the Common Attributes of <h:selectManyListbox> Tag

Attribute	Description
binding	Accepts a value expression, which binds this attribute with some backing bean property.
converter	Allows you to set the converter instance registered with a component
id	Accepts a string, which is a component identifier and must be unique within the closest parent component.

Table 11.21:Showing the Common Attributes of <h:selectManyListbox> Tag

Attribute	Description
immediate	Allows you to set the process validation early in the life cycle of the JSF.
styleClass	Allows you to set the CSS style class to be applied when the component is rendered.
required	Specifies whether a value is required for input component or not, and setting it to true ensures that the user is required to enter some value for this input component.
rendered	Accepts a boolean value indicating whether the component should be rendered or not.
validator	Accepts a method expression and represents the validator method to be invoked to validate the current value of the component.
value	Allows you to set the current value of the component. A value expression can be used to bind the current value with some backing bean property
valueChangeListener	Allows you to set a method expression to define a listener to handle value change event for this component

The following code snippet shows the use of <h:selectManyListbox> tag:

```
<h:selectManyListbox id="country" value="#{user.country}" size="2">
   <f:selectItem itemLabel="India" itemValue="ind"/>
   <f:selectItem itemLabel="Pakistan" itemValue="pak"/>
   <f:selectItem itemLabel="Sri Lanka" itemValue="srl"/>
</h:selectManyListbox>
```

The preceding code snippet uses the <h:selectManyListbox> tag to display a listbox. The `<f:selectItem>` tag is used to specify different options to be selected in this listbox. These options are rendered as the `<option>` element.

The <h:selectManyMenu> Tag

The `<h:selectManyMenu>` tag creates a multiselect menu, which corresponds to the `HtmlSelectManyMenu` component. The `HtmlSelectManyMenu` component is similar to the `HtmlSelectManyListbox` component, except that the number of options displayed using this component is always one. As the `<h:selectManyListbox>` tag, the `<h:selectManyMenu>` tag also renders to the HTML `<select>` element with all child elements rendered to its `<option>` elements. Table 11.22 shows the most commonly used attributes of the `<h:selectManyMenu>` tag:

Table 11.22: Showing the Common Attributes of the <h:selectManyMenu> Tag

Attribute	Description
binding	Accepts a value expression, which binds this attribute with some backing bean property.
converter	Allows you to set the converter instance registered with the component.
id	Accepts a string, which is a component identifier and must be unique within the closest parent component.
immediate	Allows you to set a boolean value to process validation early in the life cycle of the JSF.
styleClass	Allows you to set the CSS style class to be applied when the component is rendered.
required	Specifies whether a value is required for input component or not, and setting it to true ensures that the user is required to enter some value for the input component.

Table 11.22: Showing the Common Attributes of the <h:selectManyMenu> Tag

Attribute	Description
rendered	Accepts a boolean value indicating whether the component should be rendered or not.
validator	Accepts a method expression and represents the validator method to be invoked to validate the current value of the component.
value	Allows you to set the current value of a component. A value expression can be used to bind the current value with some backing bean property.
valueChangeListener	Allows you to set a method expression to define a listener to handle the value change event for the menu component.

The following code snippet shows the use of the `<h:selectManyMenu>` tag:

```
<h:selectManyMenu id="country" value="#{user.country}">
    <f:selectItem itemLabel="India" itemValue="ind"/>
    <f:selectItem itemLabel="Pakistan" itemValue="pak"/>
    <f:selectItem itemLabel="Shri Lanka" itemValue="srl"/>
</h:selectManyMenu>
```

In the preceding code snippet, the <h:selectManyMenu> tag is created, whose id is country and contains three items, India, Pakistan, and Srilanka. This tag can be accessed from request processing page by using its id, country. Let's now discuss the <h:selectOneListbox> tag in the next subsection.

The <h:selectOneListbox> Tag

The `<h:selectOneListbox>` tag corresponds to the `HtmlSelectOneListbox` component and is rendered similar to `HtmlSelectManyListbox` tag. The only difference between these tags is that the `<h:selectOneListbox>` tag does not allow the selection of more than one option from a list box. You can set the size of a list box to set the number of options to be displayed at a time. Table 11.23 shows the most commonly used attributes of the `<h:selectOneListbox>` tag:

Table 11.23: Showing the Common Attributes of the <h:selectOneListbox> Tag

Attribute	Description
binding	Accepts a value expression, which binds this attribute with some backing bean property.
converter	Allows you to set the converter instance registered with the component.
id	Accepts a string, which is a component identifier and its value should be unique within the ancestor component.
immediate	Allows you to set a boolean value that specifies the phase during which the value change event of JSF life cycle would occur.
styleClass	Allows you to set the CSS style class to be applied when a component is rendered.
required	Allows you to set a boolean value and if it is set to true the user is required to enter some value for this input component.
rendered	Accepts a boolean value indicating whether or not the component will be rendered.
validator	Accepts method expression and represents the validator method to be invoked to validate the current value of the component.
value	Allows you to set the current value of a component. A value expression can be used to bind the current value with some backing bean property.

Table 11.23: Showing the Common Attributes of the <h:selectOneListbox> Tag

Attribute	Description
valueChangeListener	Allows you to set a method expression to define a listener to handle the value change event for this component that is listbox.

The following code snippet shows the use of the `<h:selectOneListbox>` tag:

```
<h:selectOneListbox id="country" value="#{user.country}" size="3">
   <f:selectItem itemLabel="France" itemValue="frc"/>
   <f:selectItem itemLabel="America" itemValue="usa"/>
   <f:selectItem itemLabel="Germany" itemValue="grm"/>
   <f:selectItem itemLabel="England" itemValue="eng"/>
</h:selectOneListbox>
```

The preceding code snippet uses the <h:selectOneListbox> tag to display a listbox on browser. In this listbox, you can select only one option out of various options given in it.

The <h:selectOneMenu> Tag

The `<h:selectOneMenu>` tag represents the `HtmlSelectOneMenu` component , which provides a list of options and out of the list of options only one option is allowed to be selected. This tag displays a drop-down list box on browser. Table 11.24 shows the most commonly used attributes of the `<h:selectOneMenu>` tag:

Table 11.24: Showing the Common Attributes of the <h:selectOneMenu> Tag

Attribute	Description
binding	Accepts a value expression, which binds this attribute with some backing bean property.
converter	Allows you to set the converter instance registered with a component.
id	Accepts a string, which is a component identifier and its value should be unique within the ancestor component.
immediate	Allows you to set a boolean value that specifies in which phase of the JSF life-cycle the value change event should occur.
styleClass	Allows you to set the CSS style class to be applied when the component is rendered.
required	Specifies whether a value is required for input component or not, and if the value is set to true the user is required to enter some value for this input component.
rendered	Accepts a boolean value indicating whether the component will be rendered or not.
validator	Accepts a method expression and represents the validator method to be invoked to validate the current value of the component.
value	Allows you to set the current value of the component. A value expression can be used to bind the current value with some backing bean property.
valueChangeListener	Accepts an expression for method binding. This expression represents a method of value change listener. This method is invoked when a new value is set for the menu component.

The following code snippet shows the use of the `<h:selectOneMenu>` tag:

```
<h:selectOneMenu id="country" value="#{user.country}">
   <f:selectItem itemLabel="France" itemValue="frc"/>
   <f:selectItem itemLabel="America" itemValue="usa"/>
   <f:selectItem itemLabel="Germany" itemValue="grm"/>
</h:selectOneMenu>
```

The preceding code snippet uses the `<h:selectOneMenu>` tag to display the drop-down listbox. You can select only one option from this drop-down list box.

The <h:selectOneRadio> Tag

The `<h:selectOneRadio>` tag is rendered similar to the `<h:selectManyCheckbox>` tag. In JSF an HTML `<table>` element is rendered that contains input elements of radio type. The only difference is that from the HTML <table> table element when you select an option then previously selected option will be deselected automatically. The `<h:selectOneRadio>` tag represents the `HtmlSelectOneRadio` component. Table 11.25 shows the most commonly used attributes of the `<h:selectOneRadio>` tag:

Table 11.25: Showing the Common Attributes of the <h:selectOneRadio> Tag

Attribute	Description
binding	Accepts a value expression, which binds this attribute with some backing bean property.
converter	Allows you to set the converter instance registered with a component.
disabledClass	Specifies a CSS style class that should be applied on disabled option.
enabledClass	Specifies a CSS style class that should be applied on enabled option.
id	Accepts a string, which is a component identifier and the value should be unique within the ancestor component.
immediate	Allows you to set a boolean value that specifies the phase of the JSF life-cycle, the value change event should occur.
layout	Allows you to set the orientation of the list of options on the JSF page. The allowed values are pageDirection and lineDirection. The default value is lineDirection and all options are rendered horizontally.
styleClass	Allows you to set the CSS style class to be applied when the component is rendered.
required	Allows you to set a boolean value and if this value is set to true, the user is required to enter some value for this input component.
rendered	Accepts a boolean value that specifies whether the component is rendered or not.
validator	Accepts a method expression and represents the validator method to be invoked to validate the current value of the component.
value	Allows you to set the current value of the component. A value expression can be used to bind the current value with some backing bean property.
valueChangeListener	Allows you to set a method expression to define a listener to handle the value change event for the radio button component.

The following code snippet shows the use of `<h:selectOneRadio>` tag:

```
<h:selectOneRadio id="sex" value="#{student.sex}">
    <f:selectItem itemValue="Male" itemLabel="Male" />
    <f:selectItem itemValue="Female" itemLabel="Female"/>
</h:selectOneRadio>
```

The preceding code snippet uses the `<h:selectOneRadio>` tag to display radio buttons labeled as Male and Female respectively.

The <h:column> Tag

The `<h:column>` tag is used with the `<h:dataTable>` tag to define the columns provided in a data grid. You can set CSS classes for any header and footer generated for the table using the headerClass and footerClass attributes. Table 11.26 shows the most commonly used attributes of the `<h:column>` tag:

Table 11.26: Showing the Common Attributes of the <h:column> Tag	
Attribute	**Description**
binding	Accepts a value expression, which binds this attribute with some backing bean property.
id	Accepts a string, which is a component identifier and the value should be unique within the ancestor component.
rendered	Accepts a boolean value that specifies whether the component is rendered or not.
footerClass	Allows you to set the CSS style class for the footer generated for a column in a table.
headerClass	Allows you to set the CSS style for the header generated for a column in a table.

The following code snippet shows the use of the <h:column> tag:

```
<h:dataTable value="#{school.students}" var="stud">
    <h:column>
        <f:facet name="header">
            <h:outputText value="Roll No."/>
        </f:facet>
        <h:outputText value="#{stud.roll}"/>
    </h:column>
    <h:column>
        <f:facet name="header">
            <h:outputText value="Student Name"/>
        </f:facet>
        <h:outputText value="#{stud.name}"/>
    </h:column>
</h:dataTable>
```

The preceding code snippet uses the `<h:column>` tag inside the <h:dataTable> tag to define two columns named Roll no. and Student Name, respectively. The `<h:column>` tag uses the `<h:facet>` tag, (discussed later in this chapter).

JSF Core Tags

The JSF core Tag library contains tags for different JSF custom actions and these tags do not depend on any particular render kit. The JSF core tags can be categorized according to their usage in an application. For example, core tags support event handling to implement standard JSF validators and converters, and create items and items in a list. Table 11.27 shows various tag types and their respective tags that the JSF core tag library contains:

Table 11.27: Showing the JSF Core Tag Types and Tags under These Types	
Tag types	**Tags**
Event handling tags	f:actionListener
	f:valueChangeListener
Container for form tags	f:view
Component attributes Configuration tag	f:attribute
Data conversion tags	f:converter
	f:convertDateTime
	f:convertNumber
Facet tag	f:facet
Localization tag	f:loadBundle
Parameter substitution tag	f:param

Table 11.27: Showing the JSF Core Tag Types and Tags under These Types

Tag types	Tags
Tags for representing items in a list	f:selectItem
	f:selectItems
Container tag	f:subview
Validator tags	f:validateDoubleRange
	f:validateLength
	f:validateLongRange
	f:validator
Output tag	f:verbatim

The <f:actionListener> Tag

The `<f:actionListener>` tag adds an action listener to a component. It registers an `ActionListener` instance with the closest parent component. However, you can use the actionListener attribute of the component tag, but this tag registers only a single action listener method with the component. The `<f:actionListener>` tag is used to register more than one action listener with a single action event generated. All action listener classes used in JSF must implement the `javax.faces.event.ActionListener` interface. Table 11.28 describes the attributes of `<f:actionListener>` tag:

Table 11.28: Describing the Attributes of the <f:actionListener> Tag

Attribute	Description
type	Accepts a fully qualified name of the class that has implemented the ActionListener interface and defines the processAction() method.
binding	Accepts a value as a binding expression, which evaluates an object. This object should implement javax.faces.event.ActionListener interface.

The following code snippet shows the use of the <f:actionListener> tag:

```
<h:commandButton value="Add Student">
        <f:actionListener type="com.kogent.Listener1" />
        <f:actionListener type="com.kogent.Listener2" />
    </h:commandButton>
```

The preceding code snippet uses the <f:actionListener> tag inside the <h:commandButton> tag to register Listener1 and Listener2 classes with the Add Student button.

The <f:valueChangeListener> Tag

The `<f:valueChangeListener>` tag is used to register a value change listener for the closest parent component. Using this tag, you can register more than one value change listeners with a single component. All listener classes registered using `<f:valueChangeListener>` tag must implement javax.faces.event.ValueChangeListener interface. Table 11.29 lists the most commonly used attributes of the `<f:valueChangeListener>` tag:

Table 11.29: Showing the Common Attributes of the <f:valueChangeListener> Tag

Attribute	Description
type	Takes a fully qualified name of the class that has implemented the ValueChangeListener interface and defines the processValueChange() method.
binding	Accepts a value as a binding expression, which evaluates an object. This object should implement `javax.faces.event.ValueChangeListener` interface.

The following code snippet shows the use of the <f:valueChangeListener> tag:

```
<h:inputText id="rollno" immediate="true" onchange="submit()">
   <f:valueChangeListener type="com.kogent.SomeListener"/>
</h:inputText>
```

The preceding code snippet shows the use of the `<f:valueChangeListener>` tag to register the `SomeListener` class with the value change event that will occur in rollno text field.

The <f:view> Tag

The `<f:view>` tag encloses all other JSF components on a Web page. As you have learned earlier, all the components of a Web page are grouped into a component tree, also known as view. There is a `UIViewRoot` component at the root of every view; otherwise, a view cannot exist. The `<f:view>` tag is used to create the `UIViewRoot` on a Web page; therefore, all components of a JSF page should be enclosed within the `<f:view>` and `</f:view>` tags. Table 11.30 lists the important attributes of the <f:view> tag:

Table 11.30: Showing the Common Attributes of the <f:view> Tag

Attribute	Description
locale	Allows you to set a Locale, which needs to be supported by a Web page. If the expression is given, it must evaluate to `java.util.Locale` or a string that needs to be converted to `Locale`.
renderKitId	Allows you to set the identifier for the RenderKit to be used.
beforePhase	Accepts a method binding expression and binds the expression to a method that is called before every phase except the Restore View phase. The method should take `javax.faces.event.PhaseEvent` object and return void.
afterPhase	Accepts a method binding expression and binds the expression to a method that is called after every phase except the Restore View phase. The method should take the `javax.faces.event.PhaseEvent` object and return void.

The following code snippet shows the use of the `<f:view>` tag:

```
<f:view>
   ...........Other JSF components of the JSF page.........
</f:view>
```

The <f:view> tag may contain other component tags, such as <h:form>, <h:commandButton> and many more. Let's now discuss the <f:attribute> tag in the next subsection.

The <f:attribute> Tag

The `<f:attribute>` tag is used to add an attribute, which is a key/value pair, to the closest parent component. The name attribute takes the name for the nearest parent component and the value attribute takes the value that needs to be set for the component attribute. Table 11.31 shows the most commonly used attributes of the `<f:attribute>` tag:

Table 11.31: Showing the Common Attributes of <f:attribute> Tag

Attribute	Description
Name	Specifies the name of the nearest parent component attribute
Value	Specifies the value of the nearest parent component attribute

The following code snippet shows the use of the <f:attribute> tag:

```
<h:commandButton id="cmd1">
   <f:attribute name="value" value="Add New"></f:attribute>
</h:commandButton>
```

The preceding code snippet uses <f:attribute> tag to add attribute (value) to the HtmlCommandButton component.

The <f:converter> Tag

The `<f:converter>` tag is used to register a converter instance for a component. There are various ways to register converters for a component, such as using the <f:converter> tag. The <f:converter> tag can be nested within a component by specify the name of the class, which implements the javax.faces.convert.Converter interface as a value of the converterId attribute of the <f:converter> tag. Table 11.32 shows the most commonly used attributes of the <f:converter> tag:

Table 11.32: Displaying the Common Attributes of the <f:converter> Tag

Attribute	Description
converterId	Specifies an ID for the Converter class, which is used during the custom conversion.
binding	Accepts a value expression that must evaluate to an object, which implements `javax.faces.convert.Converter` interface.

The following code snippet uses the <f:converter> tag:

```
<h:inputText value="#{student.rollno}" >
   <f:converter converterId="javax.faces.Integer"/>
</h:inputText>
```

In the preceding code snippet, the <f:converter> tag registers a converter instance.

The <f:convertDateTime> Tag

The `<f:convertDateTime>` tag is used to register datetime converter for a component. This represents a standard JSF validator that converts a string into the date object. Table 11.33 shows the most commonly used attributes of the <f:convertDateTime> tag:

Table 11.33: Showing the Common Attributes of the <f:convertDateTime> Tag

Attribute	Description
dateStyle	Allows you to set the predefined formatting style for the date string that needs to be displayed. The dateStyle style is applied only when the `type` attribute is set to either `date` or `both`. The allowed values for the `dateStyle` attribute are default, short, medium, long, and full.
locale	Allows you to set the Locale whose predefined style needs to be used while formatting and parsing.
pattern	Allows you to set custom formatting style as defined in the java.text.SimpleDateFormat class. This attribute defines how the date can be formatted.
timeStyle	Allows you to set the predefined formatting style for the time component of the date string. This is applied only when the type attribute is set to time or both (date or time). The allowed values for the timeStyle attribute are default, short, medium, long, and full.
timeZone	Allows you to set the time zone in which date and time can be formatted. By default it is GMT.
type	Specifies whether only date or date and time needs to be formatted. Its default value is date and it can take either `date` or `both`.
binding	Accepts a value expression, which evaluates to an instance of the javax.faces.convert.DateTimeConverter class.

The following code snippet shows the use of the <f:convertDateTime> tag:

```
<h:inputText id="dateofbirth" value="#{student.birthDate}" required="true">
   <f:convertDateTime type="date" pattern="dd-MM-yyyy"/>
</h:inputText>
```

In the preceding code snippet, the `<f:convertDateTime>` tag registers the date-time converter with the dateofbirth text field component.

The <f:convertNumber> Tag

The `<f:convertNumber>` tag is used to register a `NumberConverter` instance for the closest parent component. You can customize the input component using the `<f:convertNumber>` tag to take the specified number in a specific format type for currency, simple number, and percentage. Table 11.34 shows the commonly used attributes of the <f:convertNumber> tag:

Table 11.34:Showing the Common Attributes of the <f:convertNumber> Tag

Attribute	Description
currencyCode	Allows you to set the currency code as defined in ISO 4217, whenever you need to convert the currency into your desired format.
currencySymbol	Defines the currency symbol to be used.
groupingUsed	Accepts a boolean value, which indicates whether the formatted output contains grouping separators or not.
integerOnly	Accepts a boolean value, which indicates whether parsing and formatting of a value could be done on integer part.
locale	Defines the Locale whose predefined styles for numbers will be used.
maxFractionDigits	Allows you to set the maximum number of digits that needs to be formatted in the output's fractional portion.
maxIntegerDigits	Allows you to set the maximum number of digits that needs to be formatted in the output's integer portion.
minFractionDigits	Allows you to set the minimum number of digits that needs to be formatted in the output's fractional portion.
minIntegerDigits	Allows you to set the minimum number of digits that needs to be formatted in the output's integer portion.
pattern	Defines the custom formatting pattern.
type	Specifies the formatting style of the number. The allowed values are number, currency, and percentage. The default value is number.
binding	Accepts a value expression that evaluates to an instance of javax.faces.convert.NumberConverter class.

The following code snippet uses the <f:convertNumber> tag:

```
<h:inputText value="#{book.price}" >
   <f:convertNumber type="currency" currencySymbol="$"/>
</h:inputText>
```

The preceding code snippet uses the `<f:convertNumber>` tag to register the `NumberConverter` instance with price property of the book backing bean.

The <f:facet> Tag

The `<f:facet>` tag adds facet to a component and identifies a nested component that has a special relationship with its enclosing tag. This tag registers a named facet on the closest parent component. Table 11.35 shows the most commonly used attributes of the `<f:facet>` tag:

Table 11.35: Showing the Common Attribute of the<f:facet> Tag

Attribute	Description
name	Specifies the name of the facet to be created

The following code snippet shows the use of the `<f:facet>` tag:

```
<h:panelGrid id="panel" columns="2" border="1" rules="rows">
   <f:facet name="header">
         <h:outputText>Login Form</h:outputText>
   </f:facet>
   <f:facet name="footer">
         <h:outputText>Some footer Text.</h:outputText>
```

```
        </f:facet>
        <h:outputLabel for="uid">User ID</h:outputLabel>
        <h:inputText id="uid" value="#{user.userName}"/>
        <h:outputLabel for="pwd">Password</h:outputLabel>
        <h:inputText id="pwd" value="#{user.password}"/>
    </h:panelGrid>
```

The preceding code snippet uses the `<f:facet>` tag inside the `<h:panelGrid>` tag to add header and footer to a panel grid, named panel.

The <f:loadBundle> Tag

The `<f:loadBundle>` tag loads the resource bundle and stores it in the request scope. The key/value pairs from the resource bundle are stored as `Map`. You can directly use the name of the variable assigned to resource bundle to access the localized messages in other component tags used in the JSF page. Table 11.36 shows the most commonly used attributes of the `<f:loadBundle>` tag:

Table 11.36: Showing the Common Attributes of the <f:loadBundle> Tag

Attribute	Description
basename	Defines the base name of the resource bundle to be loaded.
var	Specifies the reference name of a request scope attribute, and under that reference name the resource bundle will be exposed as a Map.

The following code snippet uses the `<f:loadBundle>` tag:

```
    <f:loadBundle basename="com.kogent.ApplicationMessages" var="msg"/>
    .... .... ....
            <h:commandLink action="addnew" value="#{msg.addnew}"/>
```

The preceding snippet uses the `<f:loadBundle>` tag to display the text messages written inside the `ApplicationMessages.properties` file on JSF UI components.

The <f:param> Tag

At times, you may need to specify additional parameters for a component. This can be done by using the `UIParameter` component, which is created by using the `<f:param>` tag. The parameters are added to enclosing component using a name/value pair created by the `<f:param>` tag. Table 11.37 shows the most commonly used attributes of the <f:param> tag:

Table 11.37: Showing the Common Attributes of the <f:param> Tag

Attribute	Description
binding	Accepts a value binding expression to link the specified value to the backing bean property and this value is later bound to the component of the UI component created by the current custom action.
id	Defines the component identifier.
name	Defines the name of the parameter to be created.
value	Allows you to set the value of a parameter.

The following code snippet shows the use of the <f:param> tag:

```
    <h:outputLink value="edit.faces">
      <h:outputText value="Edit"/>
      <f:param name="roll" value="#{student.rollno}"/>
    </h:outputLink>
```

The preceding code snippet displays a hyperlink (named Edit) on browser. When the user clicks the hyperlink, roll parameter specified using <f:param> tag is also passed as a parameter to the URL request to edit.faces Web page.

The <f:selectItem> Tag

The `<f:selectItem>` tag is a `UISelectItem` component and provides a single option to select one or more components. The `UISelectItem` component is not displayed by default. Its rendering depends on the enclosing parent component. The `<f:selectItem>` tag element may render to checkbox, radio button, or items in the list box or the drop-down list. Table 11.38 shows the most commonly used attributes of the `<f:selectItem>` tag:

Table 11.38: Showing the Common Attributes of the <f:selectItem> Tag

Attribute	Description
binding	Accepts a value binding expression to a backing bean property bound to the component.
id	Defines the component identifier.
itemDescription	Allows you to provide the description of the selectItem instance.
itemDisabled	Accepts a boolean value indicating whether the option created by this tag will be disabled or not.
itemLabel	Specifies the label that needs to be displayed for the selectItem instance.
itemValue	Allows you to set the value, which needs to be submitted to the server if an option is selected from the `selectItem` instance.
value	Accepts a value binding expression, which points to the SelectItem instance.

The following code snippet shows the use of the `<f:selectItem>` tag:

```
<h:selectOneMenu id="department" value="#{employee.department}" required="true">
  <f:selectItem itemValue="prod" itemLabel="Production"/>
  <f:selectItem itemValue="test" itemLabel="Testing"/>
  <f:selectItem itemValue="sal" itemLabel="Sales"/>
</h:selectOneMenu>
```

The preceding code snippet uses the `<f:selectItem>` tag to represent each option of the `HtmlSelectOneMenu` component.

The <f:selectItems> Tag

The `<f:selectItems>` tag works similar to the `<f:selectItem>` tag, but this tag provides a list of options to select one or more components. The `<f:selectItems>` tag corresponds to the UISelectItems component, which is used to configure multiple choices in one request. Table 11.39 shows the most commonly used attributes of the `<f:selectItems>` tag:

Table 11.39: Showing the Common Attributes of the <f:selectItems> Tag

Attribute	Description
binding	Accepts a value binding expression to a backing bean property bound to the component.
id	Defines the component identifier.
value	Accepts a value binding expression, which points to a List or array of SelectItem instances.

The following code snippet shows the use of the `<f:selectItems>` tag:

```
<h:selectOneRadio id="cities" value="#{student.city}">
  <f:selectItems value="#{citybean.options}"/>
</h:selectOneRadio>
```

In the preceding code snippet, the `<f:selectItems>` tag represents all the cities mentioned as options in the `HtmlSelectOneRadio` component.

Let's create a managed bean named citybean in the faces-config.xml file. The following code snippet shows the code to create the CityBean.java file:

```
package com.kogent;
import java.util.ArrayList;
import java.util.List;
import javax.faces.model.SelectItem;

public class CityBean{
  private List cities;
  public CityBean(){
        cities = new ArrayList();
        SelectItem city = new SelectItem("del", "Delhi");
        cities.add(city);
        city = new SelectItem("fdb", "Faridabad");
        cities.add(city);
        city = new SelectItem("lck", "Lucknow");
        cities.add(city);
  }

  public void setOptions(List cities){
        this.cities =cities ;
  }
  public List getOptions(){
        return this.cities;
  }
}
```

In preceding code snippet, the CityBean class has a getter and setter method corresponding to the <f:selectItems> tag. Let's discuss the <f:subview> tag in next subsection.

The <f:subview> Tag

The `<f:subview>` tag creates a subview of a view. It works as a container for all JSF core and custom components that are used in a nested page included by using the `<jsp:include>` tag or JSTL's `<c:import>` tag. Table 11.40 shows the most commonly used attributes of the <f:subview> tag:

Table 11.40: Showing the Common Attributes of the <f:subview> Tag

Attribute	Description
binding	Accepts a value binding expression to a backing bean property bound to a component
id	Defines component identifier
rendered	Allows you to set a boolean value, that specifies whether a component will be rendered or not

The following code snippet shows the use of the `<f:subview>` tag:

```
<f:subview id="footer">
   <jsp:include page="footer.jsp">
</f:subview>
```

The `<f: subview>` tag represents footer as a subview of a Web page on a browser. Let's discuss the <f:validateDoubleRange> tag in the next subsection.

The <f:validateDoubleRange> Tag

The `<f:validateDoubleRange>` tag is used to register the `DoubleRangeValidator` instance on the input UI component. The `DoubleRangeValidator` validator validates the current value of a component for the given range of specified value. Table 11.41 shows the most commonly used attributes of the `<f:validateDoubleRange>` tag:

Table 11.41: Showing the Common Attributes of the <f:validateDoubleRange> Tag	
Attribute	**Description**
maximum	Sets the maximum value allowed for this component
minimum	Sets the minimum value allowed for this component
binding	Accepts a value expression, which must evaluate to an instance of DoubleRangeValidator

The following code snippet shows the use of the <f:validateDoubleRange> tag:

```
<h:inputText id="num" value="#{bean.number}" required="true">
   <f:validateDoubleRange minimum="2.0" maximum="10.0"/>

</h:inputText>
```

Let's learn about the <f:validateLength> tag.

The <f:validateLength> Tag

The `<f:validateLength>` tag is used to register the `LengthValidator` instance on the input UI component. Using the `<f:validateLength>` tag with an input component specifies the length of the input string. Table 11.42 shows the commonly used attributes of the `<f:validateLength>` tag:

Table 11.42: Showing the Common Attributes of the <f:validateLength> Tag	
Attribute	**Description**
maximum	Sets the maximum length specified for this component
minimum	Sets the minimum length specified for this component
binding	Accepts a value expression, which must evaluate to an instance of LengthValidator

The following code snippet shows the use of the `<f:validateLength>` tag:

```
<h:inputSecret id="pwd" label="Password" value="#{user.password}" required="true">
   <f:validateLength minimum="4" maximum="10"/>

</h:inputSecret>
```

Let's learn about the <f:validateLongRange> tag.

The <f:validateLongRange> Tag

The `<f:validateLongRange>` tag is used to register `LongRangeValidator` on a component. Using the `<f:validateLongRange>` tag with the input component specifies the range of the input value. Table 11.43 shows the commonly used attributes of the `<f:validateLongRange>` tag:

Table 11.43: Showing the Common Attributes of the <f:validateLongRange> Tag	
Attribute	**Description**
maximum	Sets the maximum value specified for this component
minimum	Sets the minimum value specified for this component
binding	Accepts a value expression, which must evaluate to an instance of LongRangeValidator

The following code snippet shows the use of the `<f:validateLongRange>` tag:

```
<h:inputText id="num" value="#{bean.number}">
   <f:validateLongRange maximum="30" minimum="15"/>

</h:inputText>
```

Let's learn about the <f:validator> tag.

The <f:validator> Tag

The `<f:validator>` tag is used to register a custom validator on an input UI component. You need to create a custom validator class implementing the `javax.faces.validator.Validator` interface and configure it in the `faces-config.xml` file, so that the custom validator class can be used by the `<f:validator/>` tag. Table 11.44 shows the commonly used attributes of the `<f:validator>` tag:

Table 11.44: Showing the Common Attributes of the <f:validator> Tag

Attribute	Description
validatorId	Specifies the validator identifier of the Validator class that needs be created and registered on the component.
binding	Accepts a value expression, which must evaluate to an object that implements javax.faces.validator.Validator interface

The following code snippet shows the use of the `<f:validator>` tag:

```
<h:inputText id="email" required="true" value="#{student.email}">
   <f:validator validatorId="MyEmailValidator" />

</h:inputText>
```

The preceding code snippet registers a custom validator class (MyEmailValidator) with a text field component (email). You need to manually create the `MyEmailValidator` class to implement the `javax.faces.validator.Validator` interface. The `MyEmailValidator` class should to be configured in the `faces-config.xml` file using the `validator`, `validator-id`, and `validator-class` elements.

The <f:verbatim> Tag

The `<f:verbatim>` tag is used to create as well as register the `UIOutput` child component on the `UIComponent` parent component. All the components inside the <f:view> tag should be provided in JSF component tree; therefore, the HTML and JSP tags can be nested with <f:verbatim> tag. It solves the problem occurred when a page contains both the JSF elements as well as the HTML elements and you can not control the HTML elements programmatically. You cannot use any JSF components within the `<f:verbatim>` tag. Table 11.45 shows the commonly used attributes of the `<f:verbatim>` tag:

Table 11.45: Showing the Common Attributes of the <f:verbatim> Tag

Attribute	Description
escape	Accepts a boolean value indicating whether the generated markup should be escaped or not. The default value of the `escape` attribute is false.
rendered	Accepts a boolean value indicating whether the component will be rendered or not. The default value of the `rendered` attribute is true.

The following code snippet shows the use of the `<f:verbatim>` tag:

```
<f:verbatim>
   <h3>Some Heading</h3>

</f:verbatim>
```

In the preceding code snippet, the <f:verbatim> tag is used to provide the head in the HTML page. Let's now discuss the <f:phaseListener> tag.

The <f:phaseListener> Tag

The `<f:phaseListener>` tag is used to register a `PhaseListener` instance on the `UIViewRoot` component in which it is enclosed. It registers a phase listener for the current page or view. Table 11.46 shows the most commonly used attributes of the <f:phaseListener> tag:

Table 11.46: Showing the Important Attributes of the <f:phaseListener> Tag	
Attribute	**Description**
type	Accepts a fully qualified name of the phase listener class that needs to be created and registered for the current Web page.
binding	Accepts a value expression that should bind to an object, which implements the javax.faces.event.PhaseListener interface.

The following code snippet shows the use of the `<f:phaseListener>` tag:

```
<f:view>
   <f:phaseListener type = "com.kogent.MyPhaseListener"/>
</f:view>
```

In the preceding code snippet, a phase listener class is used. This class can be created by implementing the `javax.faces.event.PhaseListener` interface. The structure of the `MyPhaseListener` class is shown in the following code snippet:

```
package com.kogent;

import javax.faces.event.PhaseEvent;

import javax.faces.event.PhaseId;

import javax.faces.event.PhaseListener;

public class MyPhaseListener implements PhaseListener

{
   public void beforePhase(PhaseEvent event){

   }
   public void afterPhase(PhaseEvent event){

   }

   public PhaseId getPhaseId(){
         return PhaseId.ANY_PHASE;
   }

}
```

In the preceding code snippet, the methods, such as beforePhase(), afterPhase(), and getPhaseId() of the PhaseListener interface are implemented.

The <f:setPropertyActionListener> Tag

The `<f:setPropertyActionListener>` tag creates a special `ActionListener` instance and registers it with the associated `ActionSource`, such as `HtmlCommandButton`. The <f:setPropertyActionListener> tag is used to create and register the instance of ActionListener, when the instance of this component is created for the first time. Table 11.47 shows the commonly used attributes of the `<f:setPropertyActionListener>` tag:

Table 11.47: Showing the Common Attributes of the <f:setPropertyActionListener> Tag	
Attribute	**Description**
value	Accepts a value expression that is used to store the value of target attribute
target	Accepts a value expression that defines the destination of value attribute

The following code snippet shows the use of the `<f:setPropertyActionListener>` tag:

```
<h:commandLink action="#{student.delete}" value="Delete">
   <f:setPropertyActionListener target="#{student.roll}" value="#{user.roll}"/>

</h:commandLink>
```

In the preceding code snippet, the roll property of the backing bean, student is set with the value of roll property of user bean before the action invoke phase, that is before the `delete()` method of student backing bean is executed.

You have learned about various HTML and Core tags provided by JSF to build UI components on a Web page. Now, let's learn about the JSF standard components.

JSF Standard UI Components

JSF is a UI framework, implying that it not only provides some tags to create and customize UI components on the Web page, but also enables programmers to access these components within the code. Therefore, all the UI components have their corresponding component classes, which can be created and manipulated with the code to provide logical behavior of the components on the Web page. While discussing different HTML and Core JSF tags, the corresponding component classes have been specified, for example HtmlInputText, HtmlInputTextarea, HtmlCommandButton. The JSF standard components are categorized into different goups according to their characteristics as well as super classes. For example, the classes, such as HtmlInputHidden, HtmlInputSecret, HtmlInputText, and HtmlInputTextarea are provided under Input family as they all extend the base class UIInput and are used to take input string from the user. Table 11.48 lists all base component classes with their categories and different HTML subclasses:

Table 11.48: Describing the Base UI Component Classes and their HTML Subclasses

Class	Family	HTML Subclasses	Description
UIComponent			Serves as an abstract class for all components.
UIComponentBase			Serves as an abstract base class with basic implementations of almost all UIComponent methods.
UIColumn	Column		Represents table column, which is used to configure template columns for the parent UIData component.
UICommand	Command	HtmlCommandButton, HtmlCommandLink	Represents the user command,
UIData	Data	HtmlDataTable	Represents a data-aware component that cycles through rows in the underlying data source and exposes individual rows to child components. Requires child UIColumn components,
UIForm	Form	HtmlForm	Represents an input form, which must enclose all input components,
UIGraphic	Image	HtmlGraphicImage	Displays an image based on its URL
UIInput	Input	HtmlInputHidden, HtmlInputSecret, HtmlInputText, HtmlInputTextarea	Accepts input, processes it, and then displays the output.

Table 11.48: Describing the Base UI Component Classes and their HTML Subclasses

Class	Family	HTML Subclasses	Description
UIMessage	Message	HtmlMessage	Displays messages for a specific component.
UIMessages	Messages	HtmlMessages	Displays all messages, component related and/or application-related.
UIOutput	Output	HtmlOutputFormat, HtmlOutputLabel, HtmlOutputLink, HtmlOutputText	Holds a read-only value and displays it to the user.
UIParameter	Parameter		Represents a parameter for a parent component.
UIPanel	Panel	HtmlPanelGrid, HtmlPanelGroup	Groups a set of child components together.
UISelectBoolean	Checkbox	HtmlSelectBooleanCheckbox	Collects and displays a single boolean value.
UISelectItem	SelectItem		Represents a single item or item group. The instance may be nested with UISelectMany or UISelectOne component. This leads to the addition of SelectItem instances to the parent component of option.
UISelectItems	SelectItems		Represents multiple items or item groups. The instance may be nested with UISelectMany or UISelectOne component. This leads to the addition of SelectItem instances to the parent component of option.
UISelectMany	SelectMany	HtmlSelectManyCheckbox, HtmlSelectManyListbox, HtmlSelectManyMenu	Displays a set of items, and allows the user to select zero or any number of items.
UISelectOne	SelectOne	HtmlSelectOneRadio HtmlSelectOneListbox HtmlSelectOneMenu	Displays a set of items, and allows the user to select only one of them.
UIViewRoot	ViewRoot		Represents entire view; contains all components on the Web page.

Figure 11.5 show the class hierarchy of JSF standard components. It shows different UI component classes that have been extended from the `javax.faces.component.UIComponentBase` class, which implements the default behavior of all methods defined by the `javax.faces.component.UIComponent` class. The

UIComponent class is an abstract base class for all UI components in JSF. Figure 11.5 shows the hierarchical representation of the JSF standard components:

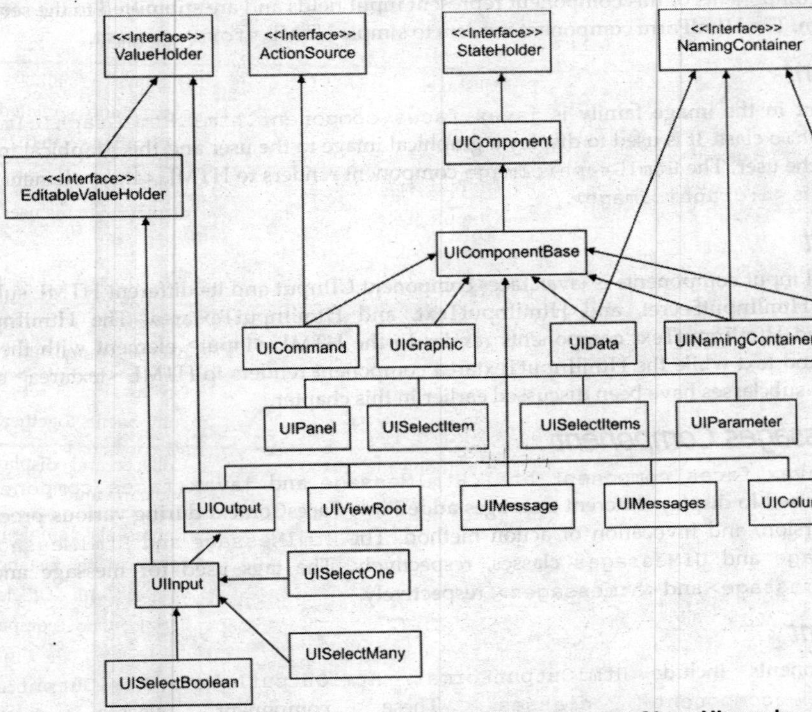

Figure 11.5: Displaying the Base UI Component Class Hierarchy

In Figure 11.5, some of the UI components extend different base classes while some of them implement different interfaces, which provide different behavior to those base classes. For example, the UIInput class extends from the UIOutput class and implements the javax.faces.component package. The EditableValueHolder interface provides additional features supported by editable components. These features are further extended by the subclasses, such as HtmlInputText and HtmlInputTextarea.

Now, let's briefly discuss the various components provided in abstract base class for all UI components (Figure 11.5).

Command Components

We have two command components, HtmlCommandButton, and HtmlCommandLink. These components or classes have been extended from the javax.faces.component.UICommand class and are capable of generating action events, means they behave as action source. The creation of these classes in the JSF page has been discussed earlier while discussing <h:commandButton> and <h:commandLink>.

Data Component

The UIData is a component that supports data binding to a collection of data objects, such as ArrayList and ResultSet. The javax.faces.component.html.HtmlDataTable is the direct subclass of the UIData class. The HtmlDataTable class is used to create a standard data grid with the iteration of different objects in the set of data objects provided in JSF and creates individual rows of the HTML table for each object in the set. The tag used to create the HtmlDataTable component is <h:dataTable>.

Form Component

The javax.faces.component.html.HtmlForm is a subclass of the UIForm class that represents an input form. All the child components of this component represent input fields and are submitted to the server with the submission of a form. The HtmlForm component renders to simple HTML <form> element.

Image Component

The only component in the image family is javax.faces.component.html.HtmlGraphicImage, which extends the UIGraphic class. It is used to display a graphical image to the user and this graphical image cannot be manipulated by the user. The HtmlGraphicImage component renders to HTML <img> element and the tag used for its creation is <h:graphicImage>.

Input Component

The base class for all input components is javax.faces.component.UIInput and its different HTML subclasses are HtmlInputHidden, HtmlInputSecret, and HtmlInputText, and HtmlInputTextarea. The HtmlInputHidden, HtmlInputSecret, and HtmlInputText components render to the HTML <input> element with the typeset as hidden, password, and text while the HtmlInputTextarea component renders to HTML <textarea> component. The tags for all these subclasses have been discussed earlier in this chapter.

Message and Messages Component

The components javax.faces.component.html.HtmlMessage and javax.faces.component.html.HtmlMessages are used to display different messages added into FacesContext during various processes, such as validation, conversion, and invocation of action method. The HtmlMessage and HtmlMessages classes extend the UIMessage and UIMessages classes, respectively. The tags used for message and message components are <h:message> and <h:messages>, respectively.

Output Component

The output components include HtmlOutputFormat, HtmlOutputLabel, HtmlOutputLink, and HtmlOutputText component classes. These component classes extend the javax.faces.component.UIOutput component class. The different tags to create the output components are <h:outputFormat>, <h:outputLabel>, <h:outputLink>, and <h:outputText> and the characteristics of these output components are discussed earlier in the *JSF HTML tags* section. These components hold a read-only value and display it to the user.

Parameter Component

The javax.faces.component.UIParameter component represents a parameter for the parent component. UIParameter extends UIComponentBase base class and does not have any HTML subclass, as it is not rendered in the response. The core JSF tag used to create this component is <f:param>.

Checkbox Component

In the checkbox family of component, the base component class is UISelectBoolean and the only HTML subclass is javax.faces.component.html.HtmlSelectBooleanCheckbox. This component collects and displays single boolean value. The tag used for this component is <h:selectBooleanCheckbox>.

SelectItem and SelectItems Component

The base classes for the SelectItem and SelectItems groups are UISelectItem and UISelectItems, respectively. These classes do not have any HTML subclass, as they do not render themselves. Their rendering behavior is controlled by the parent component. The core JSF tags for these two components are <f:selectItem> and <f:selectItems>, respectively.

SelectMany and SelectOne Component

The base component for the SelectMany and SelectOne components are UISelectMany and UISelectOne respectively. The SelectMany family represents the components that allow users to select zero or more items from the given number of items. The HTML subclasses of the UISelectMany component class include the HtmlSelectManyCheckbox, HtmlSelectManyListbox, and HtmlSelectManyMenu classes.

Similarly, the SelectOne component allows users to select a single option from the given set of choices. The HTML subclass of the UISelectOne component class includes HtmlSelectOneListbox, HtmlSelectOneMenu, and HtmlSelectOneRadio. The tags to create these components have been discussed with their different attributes and examples earlier in the chapter.

ViewRoot Component

The components in a JSF view are organized in a component tree, which is headed by the javax.faces.component.UIViewRoot component at the root. The UIViewRoot is represented by the <f:view> tag. Using the UIViewRoot component, you can set and retrieve the current render kit, Locale for the page, and its viewId property. You can bypass the navigation system and write your own logic for navigation by creating a new instance of UIViewRoot, and calling the setViewRoot() method on the FacesContext object.

You have learned about different UIComponent classes in which you have learned about different component classes that are created and manipulated internally, while using their corresponding tags provided by JSF to place these components in JSF view. Though the methods and properties of these component classes have not been discussed in this chapter, as they are out of scope of this book, but you can use the standard naming conventions to interact and manipulate these components in your code.

Working with Backing Beans

Backing bean is a simple JavaBean that stores data at an intermediate stage and facilitates interaction between the view and model layer. A backing bean is used with a set of properties to map each property to the value of some component in a view or to the component itself. In addition to the get and set methods for these properties, the backing bean can have various methods to support event handling and validation of the data before the application logic is executed or model layer is interacted for database operations. These backing beans are created and managed automatically by JSF, which is configured by the developer in the faces-config.xml file; therefore, the backing beans are also known as Managed beans. Note that all backing beans should be managed but all managed beans are not supposed to be backing beans. Let's learn to develop a backing bean to use with a given view. The following code snippet shows code for a JSF page with different components:

```
<%@ page language="java" pageEncoding="ISO-8859-1"%>
<%@ taglib uri="http://java.sun.com/jsf/html" prefix="h"%>
<%@ taglib uri="http://java.sun.com/jsf/core" prefix="f"%>
<html>
  <head>
        <title>Welcome</title>
        <link rel="stylesheet" href="mystyle.css" type="text/css" />
  </head>
  <body>
        <f:view>
              <h:form id="studentForm">
                    <h:outputText id="message" value="Welcome, Guest!"
                    binding="#{student.outputText}"/>
                    <h:panelGrid id="panel" columns="2" border="1">
                    <h:outputText value="Roll No." />
                    <h:inputText id="rollno" value="#{student.rollno}" />
                    <h:outputText value="Name" />
                    <h:inputText label="Name" id="name" value="#{student.name}" />
                    <h:commandButton id="button1"
                    actionListener="#{student.showMessage}"
                    value="Show Message"/>
                    <h:commandButton id="button2"
```

```
                    action="#{student.showDetail}" value="Show Detail"/>
                    </h:panelGrid>
                </h:form>
            </f:view>
    </body>
</html>
```

In preceding code snippet, we have created an HtmlForm component with different child components, such as HtmlInputText and HtmlCommandButton. The values of two input field components, rollno and name are bound to two different properties of student backing bean.

In preceding code snippet, we have bound an `HtmlOutputText` component (with id message) with another property, `outputText`, of student backing bean. You can bind a backing bean property with the value of a component by using the value expression for the value attribute; however to bind the value with a component, you can use value expression for binding attribute of the component.

The following code snippet shows the structure of student backing bean with its three properties along with get and set methods:

```
package com.kogent;

import javax.faces.component.html.HtmlOutputText;
import javax.faces.event.ActionEvent;

public class Student {
  private String rollno;
  private String name;

  private HtmlOutputText outputText;

  public String getName() {
        return name;
  }
  public void setName(String name) {
        this.name = name;
  }
  public String getRollno() {
        return rollno;
  }
  public void setRollno(String rollno) {
        this.rollno = rollno;
  }
  public HtmlOutputText getOutputText() {
        return outputText;
  }

  public void setOutputText(HtmlOutputText outputText) {
        this.outputText = outputText;
  }

  public void showMessage(ActionEvent event){
        //Some application logic..
        outputText.setValue("Welcome "+this.name);
  }

  public String showDetail(){
        //Some application logic..
        return "success";
  }
}
```

In preceding code snippet, the backing bean class is `com.kogent.Student` and we are referring it with the name `student` in the JSF page, which is a reference name for the `Student` bean when managed in the `faces-config.xml` file. All the three properties of student backing bean are automatically populated during the Apply Request Values phase. The binding of a component with backing bean property makes the component accessible in the backing bean to be manipulated logically.

Using the Backing Bean Method as an Event Handler

A backing bean can have various methods that can be used as event listeners. We can handle two types of events through backing bean methods, which are action events and value change events.

A backing bean can be used as action listener. The action listeners are of two types, one that affects navigation and other does not.

The backing bean method, which can be used as an action listener and does not affect navigation must have a signature `void methodName(ActionEvent event)`. The `void showMessage(ActionEvent event)` method that has been created in the Student class does not affect navigation and the current view is redisplayed, as given in the following code snippet:

```
public void showMessage(ActionEvent event){
   //Some application logic..
   outputText.setValue("Welcome "+this.name);
}
```

The methods, such as methodName(ActionEvent event) and showMessage(ActionEvent event) are commonly referred as action listener methods and are registered with the action resources, such as `HtmlCommandButton`, using its `actionListener` attribute, as given in the following code snippet:

```
<h:commandButton id="button"
actionListener="#{student.showMessage}" value="Submit"/>
```

Further, there are other types of backing bean methods, which can be registered with action resources and are used by some default action listener affecting navigation from one view to another. Such backing bean methods are known as action methods and can be associated with the action resource component using its action attribute, as shown in the following code snippet:

```
<h:commandButton id="button2"
action="#{student.showDetail}" value="Show Detail"/>
```

The signature of an action method must be `String methodName()`. The string returned by the action method, which is an outcome of some application logic execution is further used by navigation system to decide the next view to be displayed. The following code snippet shows the implementation of the `showDetail()` method created in the `Student` class:

```
public String showDetail(){
   //Some application Logic
   return "success";
}
```

In addition, you can also register a backing bean method as value change event listener; therefore, the signature of a registered method must be `void methodName(ValueChangeEvent event)`. This method will be fired with a value change event only when there is a change in the value of the associated component. You can register a value change listener with different input components such as `HtmlInputText` and `HtmlInputTextarea` by giving a method expression for their `valueChangeListener` attribute, as shown in the following code snippet:

```
<h:inputText id="rollno" value="#{student.rollno}"
valueChangeListener="#{student.rollChanged}"/>
```

In the preceding code snippet, we have registered a backing bean method `rollChanged()` as `ValueChangeEvent` listener. This method is invoked before the invocation of any action method or action listener method. The following code snippet shows the code that add the backing bean method, `rollChanged()` to the `Student` class as a `ValueChangeEvent` listener:

```
public void rollChanged(ValueChangeEvent event){
   HtmlInputText component=(HtmlInputText)event.getComponent();
```

```
        if(((String)event.getNewValue()).length()!=3)
        component.setStyle("color:red");
        else
        component.setStyle("color:black");
    }
```

Let's learn to use backing bean as validator.

Using Backing Bean Method as Validator

We have different standard validators provided by the JSF framework. These validators can be used to validate the values of different input components submitted by the user. However, JSF provides another way to validate the input components, that is, by using a backing bean method as a validator method. A backing bean method having signature, `void methodName(FacesContext, UIComponent, Object)` can be registered as a validator with an input component. the following code snippet shows an example of validator method created in backing bean:

```
public void validateRollNo(FacesContext facesContext, UIComponent uiComponent,
    Object value) throws ValidatorException{
    //Some Logic to validate value
    HtmlInputText htmlInputText = (HtmlInputText) uiComponent;
    FacesMessage facesMessage = new FacesMessage(htmlInputText.getLabel()+
    ": Some Validation Error");
    throw new ValidatorException(facesMessage);
}
```

In the preceding code snippet, the `validateRollNo()` method simply executes a logic to validate the given value; and if the value is invalid, this method creates an instance of the `FacesMessage` class and throws `ValidatorException`, which stops further execution of the JSF life cycle phases and the current page is redisplayed with some error message using the `<h:messages/>` tag element.

Managing Backing Beans

The backing beans need to be created and initialized automatically using the Managed Bean Creation facility. This facility allows the declaration of different beans with their initialization in a central location, i.e., at the JSF configuration file. You can also define the scope of a bean, such as request, session, or application. All managed beans can be accessed using JSF EL. You can configure a managed bean with the `<managed-bean>` element, as shown in the following code snippet:

```
<managed-bean>
   <managed-bean-name>student</managed-bean-name>
   <managed-bean-class>com.kogent.Student</managed-bean-class>
   <managed-bean-scope>request</managed-bean-scope>
</managed-bean>
```

While declaring a managed bean, you need to specify its name, class, and scope. The `<managed-bean-name>` element defines the reference name, which can be used in JSF EL to access a bean. You can also initialize simple properties while declaring managed beans by using the `<managed-property>` element, as shown in the following code snippet:

```
<managed-bean>
   <managed-bean-name>student</managed-bean-name>
   <managed-bean-class>com.kogent.Student</managed-bean-class>
   <managed-bean-scope>request</managed-bean-scope>
   <managed-property>
         <property-name>name</property-name>
         <value>Prakash</value>
   </managed-property>
</managed-bean>
```

In addition to simple bean properties, you can also initialize `List` or `Map` type of properties using `<list-entries>` and `<map-entries>` respectively. For example, a bean having a List type property can be initialized as `cities` and `Map` type of property as Locales, as shown in the following code snippet:

```
<managed-bean>
   <managed-bean-name>citybean</managed-bean-name>
   <managed-bean-class>com.kogent.CityBean</managed-bean-class>
   <managed-bean-scope>application</managed-bean-scope>
   <managed-property>

         <property-name>cities</property-name>
         <list-entries>
               <value>Delhi</value>
               <value>Pune</value>
               <value>Mumbai</value>
         </list-entries>
   </managed-property>
   <managed-property>
         <property-name>locales</property-name>
         <map-entries>

               <map-entry>
                     <key>en</key>
                     <value>English</value>
               </map-entry>
               <map-entry>
                     <key>fr</key>
                     <value>French</value>
               </map-entry>
         </map-entries>
   </managed-property>
</managed-bean>
```

You can also declare `ArrayList` and Maps as managed beans by setting `<managed-bean-class>` as `java.util.ArrayList` or `java.util.HashMap`, as shown in the following code snippet:

```
<managed-bean>
   <managed-bean-name>cities</managed-bean-name>
   <managed-bean-class>java.util.ArrayList</managed-bean-class>
   <managed-bean-scope>application</managed-bean-scope>
   <list-entries>
         <value>Delhi</value>
         <value>Mumbai</value>
         <value>Kolkata</value>
   </list-entries>
</managed-bean>
```

You can also refer to one managed bean while setting the property of another managed bean using a value binding expression.

JSF Input Validation

In a Web application, the user input validation is required before executing any application logic. The invalid data submitted by the user may cause unexpected errors and may lead to inconsistency; therefore, a framework is preferred. A framework supports user input validation in a way that it does not affect other application logic development. JSF framework can validate user submitted data in the Process Validation phase, which comes before the Update Model Values phase and Invoke Application phase; this reduces the risk of updating model layer with any invalid data input. JSF being a UI framework equips all input component classes and corresponding tags to handle the validation of values. JSF provides following two basic ways to apply validation on the components that are used for taking inputs:

- Using validator method in backing bean
- Using validators

Using Validator Method

You have learned to create a validator method in a backing bean and associating it with input component using a method expression for its validator attribute. The signature of the validator method must be `void methodName(FacesContext, UIComponent, Object) throws ValidatorException`. You can use a `validator` attribute, `validateEmail()` of backing bean, `student`, with an input component, as shown in the following code snippet:

```
<h:inputText id="email" value="#{student.email}" size="30"
validator="#{student.validateEmail}" />
```

You can define the `validateEmail()` method in the backing bean class, as shown in the following code snippet:

```
public void validateEmail(FacesContext facesContext, UIComponent uiComponent,
Object value) throws ValidatorException
{
  //Logic to validate value for being a valid email id.
}
```

You can create a number of validator methods in a backing bean. The only disadvantage of defining a validator method in a backing bean is that you can bind only one validator method with a component in a Web page. This also makes backing bean more complex.

Using Validators

Another way to validate the value of an input component is to associate the value with custom validators class, which implements the `javax.faces.validator.Validator` interface. JSF provides its own set of validators, known as standard JSF validators. You can also create your own validator classes. The validators can be associated with a component in following two ways:

- Using the custom tag of validator inside the component tag.

The following code snippet shows an example of using the custom tag of validator to associate a specific validator with an input component:

```
<h:inputText id="uid" label="User ID" value="#{user.userName}">
  <f:validateLength minimum="4" maximum="10"/>
</h:inputText>
```

The preceding code snippet uses the <f:validateLength> custom tag of validator.

- Using the `<f:validator>` tag inside the component tag. The following code snippet shows the use of the `<f:validator>` tag:

```
<h:inputText id="uid" label="User ID" value="#{user.userName}" >
  <f:validator validatorId="someID"/>
</h:inputText>
```

The preceding code snippet uses the <f:validator> element with the identifier of validator.

The validators, which do not have customized tags, can be implemented by using the `<f:validator>` tag.

You can associate single input components with multiple validators, which is not possible when a validator method is used.

Let's discuss the two types of validators, standard JSF validators and custom validators.

Standard JSF Validators

JSF provides various standard validators to support some common validation rules, such as validating string for length, validating input value whether it falls under the given range or not. There is a set of three standard JSF validators, which are listed in Table 11.49:

Table 11.49: Showing the Standard JSF Validators

Validator Class	Validator's Custom Tag	Properties
LengthValidator	<f:validateLength>	maximum, minimum
DoubleRangeValidator	<f:validateDoubleRange>	maximum, minimum
LongRangeValidator	<f:validateLongRange>	maximum, minimum

These validators can be used with their custom tags.

We have already described these standard validator tags in detail while discussing JSF Core Tags earlier in this chapter.

Custom Validators

If the standard validators do not satisfy the validation criteria that you want to apply for a component, you can create custom validators. For example, JSF do not provide any validator to validate the email id of a user. In such cases, JSF allows you to create custom validator classes. You can create a validator class by implementing the `javax.faces.validator.Validator` interface and defining its only method , `validate()`.The following code snippet shows the code to create custom validator class:

```
package com.kogent.validator;

import javax.faces.application.FacesMessage;
import javax.faces.component.UIComponent;
import javax.faces.component.html.HtmlInputText;
import javax.faces.context.FacesContext;
import javax.faces.validator.Validator;
import javax.faces.validator.ValidatorException;
public class MyValidator implements Validator {
    public void validate(FacesContext facesContext, UIComponent uiComponent,
    Object value) throws ValidatorException {

            boolean valid=true;
            //Some logic to validate the value.
            .. .. ..
            .. .. ..
            if (!valid){
                    HtmlInputText htmlInputText = (HtmlInputText) uiComponent;
                    FacesMessage facesMessage = new FacesMessage(htmlInputText.getLabel()+
                     ": Email Format is not valid");
                    throw new ValidatorException(facesMessage);
            }
    }
}
```

The following code snippet shows the code to use the custom validator, MyValidator by registering it in the `faces-config.xml` file using the `<validator>` element. by providing an identifier for it

```
<validator>
    <validator-id>myValidator</validator-id>
    <validator-class>com.kogent.validator.MyValidator </validator-class>
</validator>
```

The value provided in the preceding code snippet with `<validator-id>` is used to associate the validator, MyValidator with the input component, which needs to be validated. The use of the <h:inputText> tag is shown in the following code snippet:

```
<h:inputText id="empid" value="#{employee.id}">
    <f:validator validatorId="myValidator"/>
</h:inputText>
```

You have learned about the JSF input validation support provided in terms of validator methods, standard and custom validators.

JSF Type Conversion

The user input is normally a text string, which submitted to the server for further processing. However, when request parameters are mapped to different backing bean properties internally, the string values need to be converted to different Java types, such as Integer, boolean, Short, and Double. On the other hand, when the response is created for the user, these Java types are again changed to strings and in this case JSF converters are used. The JSF converters create the string presentation of an object and object presentation of a string. If the converter is unable to convert any value, error messages are generated and displayed back to the user by using the <h:messages> elements.

JSF provides its own set of standard converters, which can be registered with input as well as output UI components. You can register a converter with a component in the following three ways:

- Setting converter identifier with the converter attribute of the component's tag, as shown in the following code snippet:

```
<h:inputText id="price" value="#{book.price}" converter="javax.faces.Double"/>
```

- Using the <f:converter> element with converter's identifier inside the component tag, as shown in the following code snippet:

```
<h:inputText id="price" value="#{book.price}">
   <f:converter converterId="javax.faces.Double"/>
</h:inputText>
Or
<h:inputText id="price" value="#{book.price}">
   <f:converter converterId="myConverter"/>
</h:inputText>
```

- Using converter's custom tag inside the component tag, as shown in the following code snippet:

```
<h:inputText value="#{book.price}" >
   <f:convertNumber type="currency" currencySymbol="$"/>
</h:inputText>
```

You have learned about standard JSF converters. You can also create your own converter and use it after registering the converter extension in the faces-config.xml file.

Standard JSF Converters

All the JSF standard converters, which convert a string to a simple Java data type, implement the `javax.faces.convert.Converter` interface. Following are the standard JSF converter classes that form the javax.faces.convert package:

- BigDecimalConverter
- BigIntegerConverter
- booleanConverter
- ByteConverter
- CharacterConverter
- DateTimeConverter
- DoubleConverter
- FloatConverter
- IntegerConverter
- LongConverter
- NumberConverter
- ShortConverter

There are two standard JSF converters, `DateTimeConverter` and `NumberConverter`, and these converters contain custom tags. These two standard converters allow us to configure the format of the component data by setting different tag attributes. These standard tag converter tags are:

- <f:convertDateTime/>

- <f:convertNumber/>

These two tags have been discussed with all their attributes and examples in the *JSF Core Tags* section earlier in this chapter. Let's learn about custom converters next.

Creating Custom Converters

Similar to validators, you can also create custom converters by implementing the `javax.faces.convert.Converter` interface, and defining two methods, `getAsObject()` and `getAsString()`. The following code snippet the structure of a simple custom converter:

```
package com.kogent.converter;

import javax.faces.component.UIComponent;
import javax.faces.context.FacesContext;
import javax.faces.convert.Converter;
public class MyConverter implements Converter{
  public Object getAsObject(FacesContext fc, UIComponent comp, String value) {
        //Some Logic
        return null;
  }

  public String getAsString(FacesContext fc, UIComponent comp, Object value) {
        //Some Logic
        return null;
  }

}
```

You need to register the converter that are created in preceding code snippet in the `faces-config.xml` file using the `<converter>` element to use the converter with your component, as shown in the following code snippet:

```
<converter>
  <converter-id>myConverter</converter-id>
  <converter-class>com.kogent.converter.MyConverter</converter-class>
</converter>
```

The value specified in the following code snippet with `<converter-id>` is `myConverter`, which is an identifier for converter created in the preceding code snippet and is used to register this converter with a component, as shown in the following code snippet:

```
<h:inputText id="empid" value="#{employee.empId}" >
  <f:converter converterId="myConverter"/>
</h:inputText>
```

The JSF framework provides support for type conversion using standard and custom converters.

Handling Page Navigation in JSF

One of the important features provided by JSF framework is its support for navigation from one view to another view. JSF allows you to define all possible navigation rules in a centralized location, JSF configuration file. It reduces the need to embed the navigation logic in the components of a JSF page. If the navigation logic is placed at one location, it becomes easy for the developers to maintain the Web application.

The navigation handler plays a vital role in the JSF navigation system. The navigation handler is the code that decides the view to be loaded next and displayed to the user. The default navigation handler operates in response to the action events. Different action resources, such as `HtmlCommandButton` and `HtmlCommandLink`, cause the action events. An action resource may be associated either with a hardcoded outcome string or with an action method, which can return a logical outcome after the execution of an application logic, as shown in the following code snippet:

```
//An HtmlCommandButton associated with hardcode outcome string "home"
<h:commandButton id="home" action="home" value="Home"/>
```

```
//An HtmlCommandButton associated with an action method, which returns a logical
outcome.
<h:commandButton id="add" action="#{student.addNew}" value="Add New"/>
```

The navigation handler defines all possible navigation paths. It is the responsibility of navigation handler to take the outcome string and process it on a set of navigation rules. A navigation rule can be defined as the specification that tells which page can be navigated to from a given page or a set of pages according to different outcomes. The outcome can be any string, such as success, failure, error, and login. The following code snippet shows a simple navigation rule defined in the faces-config.xml file:

```
<navigation-rule>
  <from-view-id>/student.jsp</from-view-id>
  <navigation-case>
        <from-outcome>success</from-outcome>
        <to-view-id>/display.jsp</to-view-id>
  </navigation-case>
</navigation-rule>
```

In preceding code snippet the navigation rule defines that if the action event is generated from `student.jsp` page and the outcome string is success, then the next page that needs to be loaded is `display.jsp`. The `<from-view-id>` and `<to-view-id>` tags take the view id as the filename. The following code snippet shows the code to define different navigation cases from one view:

```
<navigation-rule>
  <from-view-id>/login.jsp</from-view-id>
  <navigation-case>
        <from-outcome>success</from-outcome>
        <to-view-id>/welcome.jsp</to-view-id>
  </navigation-case>
  <navigation-case>
        <from-outcome>failure</from-outcome>
        <to-view-id>/login_failure.jsp</to-view-id>
  </navigation-case>
</navigation-rule>
```

In preceding code snippet, the two different navigation cases are declared. In the first navigation case, the request is passed from the login.jsp page to `welcome.jsp` page. However, according to the other navigation case, the request is passed to the `login_failure.jsp` page. The navigation to either welcome.jsp or login_failure.jsp page depends on the outcome string, which can be `success` or `failure`.

You can define different navigation cases not only for a single page but for all pages. You can define navigation rules globally for a Web application, which works for all the JSP and JSF pages. The outcome string of the action method specifies the view page that will be generated. For example, in the following code snippet, if the outcome string is home then the home.jsp page is generated instead of re-generation of the request page. The following code snippet shows the global navigation rule:

```
<navigation-rule>
  <from-view-id>*</from-view-id>
  <navigation-case>
        <from-outcome>home</from-outcome>
        <to-view-id>/home.jsp</to-view-id>
  </navigation-case>
</navigation-rule>
```

You can even define a particular action method from where you want to receive the outcome. In case when you have two action methods that return same outcome string and have been associated with action resources on the same view you can define a particular action method from where you want to receive the outcome. You can use the `<from-action>` element to specify the action method while declaring navigation cases, as shown in the following code snippet:

```
<navigation-case>

  <from-action>#{user.login}</from-action>
  <from-outcome>success</from-outcome>
```

```
    <to-view-id>/welcome.jsp</to-view-id>

</navigation-case>
```

You have learned about the declarative support in JSF for navigation rules. These rules are defined at a single location; therefore, the development process becomes simpler as well as flexible while implementation and maintenance of the JSF application.

Describing Internationalization Support in JSF

A Web application is accessible from all over the world, so it needs to support localization of messages to display messages according to the language and format preferred by the users.

The UI framework, such as JSF, which supports the creation of rich UI components, supports Internationalization (also known as I18N) and provides different ways to localize the messages of an application without making any change in the code. The most important concept is not to hard code all messages for the user. Instead, the message strings should be fetched from some resource bundle according to the current user Locale. In this section, you learn about all the JSF support provided for Internationalization of an application.

Configuring Supported Locales

The JSF based Web application supports different Locales and you need to configure the Web application for all the supported Locales. You can configure supported Locales for a Web application in the JSF configuration file. The supported Locales can be specified using the `<supported-locale>` and `<locale-config>` elements under the `<application>` element, as shown in the following code snippet:

```
<application>
   <locale-config>
         <default-locale>en</default-locale>
         <supported-locale>en</supported-locale>
         <supported-locale>fr</supported-locale>
   </locale-config>
   <message-bundle>com.kogent.ApplicationMessages</message-bundle>
</application>
```

The Locales supported in the preceding code are `en` (English) and `fr` (French) and the default Locale is en. You can also specify the country for different versions of a language, as shown in the following code snippet:

```
<application>
   <locale-config>
         <default-locale>en</default-locale>
         <supported-locale>en_US</supported-locale>
         <supported-locale>fr_FR</supported-locale>
   </locale-config>
   <message-bundle>com.kogent.ApplicationMessages</message-bundle>
</application>
```

A Web application supports Locales other than the Locale of a Web application's JVM if you configure the supported Locales. You can also declare the base name of the default resource bundle using the <message-bundle> element.

Creating Resource Bundles

Resource bundles are required to make an application to support different Locales. A resource bundle stores Locale-specific text strings, which can be used in a Web application. A resource bundle is a simple properties file, which contains key/value pairs. The properties files have a number of strings placed corresponding to unique keys. You need to create a separate properties file that have the same base name, and the Locale prefixed with the base name for each supported Locale. For example, to provide all text strings to be used for `fr` Locale, you need to create an `ApplicationMessages_fr.properties` file. The structure of `ApplicationMessages_en.properties`, which is the default resource bundle is shown in the following code snippet:

```
welcome=Welcome
```

```
roll=Enter Roll No.
name=Enter Name
showdetail=Show Detail
```

A properties file, which contains all text strings translated to support French language is shown in the following code snippet:

```
welcome=Bienvenue
roll=Entrez Roll No.
name=Entrez Nom
showdetail=Voir Détail
```

In the preceding code snippet, Locales are specified for some keys and the corresponding values are translated into French language. Similarly, you can create resource bundles for other supported Locales also.

Accessing Localized Messages from Resource Bundle

You can load the resource bundle having localized static data for the Locale of current view and use it as a map in the current request. Accessing localized message strings include two basic steps, which are as follows:

- Loading resource bundle in the request scope
- Referencing localized messages

A resource bundle supporting current view Locale can be loaded into the request scope using the `<f:loadBundle>` tag in the JSF page. The key/value pairs stored in the loaded resource bundle are exposed as a map object, which can be accessed using JSF EL. You need to specify the base name of the resource bundle for loading the Locales and the reference name for the map object by setting the basename and var attributes of the `<f:loadBundle>` tag, as shown in the following code snippet:

```
<f:loadBundle basename="com.kogent.ApplicationMessages" var="msg"/>
```

You can use a value-binding expression from an attribute of the component tag that displays the localized data to reference or access a localized message from resource bundle, as shown in the following code snippet:

```
<%@ page language="java" pageEncoding="ISO-8859-1"%>
<%@ taglib uri="http://java.sun.com/jsf/html" prefix="h"%>
<%@ taglib uri="http://java.sun.com/jsf/core" prefix="f"%>
<html>
   <head>
         <title>Welcome</title>
         <link rel="stylesheet" href="mystyle.css" type="text/css" />
   </head>       <body>
         <f:view>
         <f:loadBundle basename="com.kogent.ApplicationMessages" var="msg"/>
         <h:messages/>
         <h:outputText value="#{msg.welcome}"/>
         <h:form id="studentForm">
         <h:panelGrid id="panel" columns="2" border="1">
         <h:outputText value="#{msg.roll}" />
         <h:inputText id="rollno" value="#{student.rollno}"/>
         <h:outputText value="#{msg.name}" />
         <h:inputText id="name" value="#{student.name}" />
         <h:commandButton id="button2" action="#{student.showDetail}"
         value="#{msg.showdetail}"/>
         </h:panelGrid> </h:form> </f:view>
   </body>
</html>
```

In the preceding code snippet the Web page is internationalized; therefore supports customized message strings for the current Locale, while loading the resource bundle. You can change the Locale of a view while using the `<f:view>` tag by setting its Locale property. The Locale of a view can also be changed programmatically in the code, as shown in the following code snippet:

```
public String changeToFrench()
{
   FacesContext context = FacesContext.getCurrentInstance();
```

```
        context.getViewRoot().setLocale(Locale.FRENCH);
        return null;
    }
```

Using the preceding code snippet, you can handle internationalization for all the components created in a Web application by changing the code programmatically.

You can also internationalize all validation and conversion error messages generated by different validators and converters by providing additional key/value pairs in resource bundle. Table 11.50 lists some of the keys for error messages with default text:

Table 11.50: Displaying Keys and their Default Text for Standard JSF Error Messages

Key	Defaut Error Message
javax.faces.validator.NOT_IN_RANGE	Indicates a Validation Error if the given attribute is not in the specified range of {0} and {1}.
javax.faces.validator.NOT_IN_RANGE_detail	Defines that value should be in between {0} and {1}.
javax.faces.validator.DoubleRangeValidator.LIMIT	Indicates Validation Error: value of specified attribute cannot be converted into proper type.
javax.faces.validator.DoubleRangeValidator.MAXIMUM	Indicates Validation Error: value is greater than allowed maximum of {0}.
javax.faces.validator.DoubleRangeValidator.MINIMUM	Indicates Validation Error: value is greater than allowed minimum of {0}.
javax.faces.validator.DoubleRangeValidator.TYPE	Indicates Validation Error: value is not of the correct type.
javax.faces.validator.LengthValidator.LIMIT	Indicates Validation Error: value of specified attribute cannot be converted into proper type.
javax.faces.validator.LengthValidator.MAXIMUM	Indicates Validation Error: the value has exceeded than allowed maximum of {0}.
javax.faces.validator.LengthValidator.MINIMUM	Indicates Validation Error: the allowed minimum is {0} but the value is more than that.
javax.faces.component.UIInput.CONVERSION	Indicates Conversion Error: value cannot be converted during model data update.
javax.faces.component.UIInput.REQUIRED	Indicates Validation Error: value is required.
javax.faces.component.UISelectOne.INVALID	Indicates Validation Error: value is not valid.
javax.faces.component.UISelectMany.INVALID	Indicates Validation Error: invalid value.
javax.faces.validator.RequiredValidator.FAILED	Indicates Validation Error: value is required.
javax.faces.validator.LongRangeValidator.LIMIT	Indicates Validation Error: value of a specified attribute cannot be converted into proper type.
javax.faces.validator.LongRangeValidator.MAXIMUM	Indicates Validation Error: value is greater than allowed maximum {0} of Long type validator.
javax.faces.validator.LongRangeValidator.MINIMUM	Indicates Validation Error: value is greater than allowed minimum {0} of Long type validator.
javax.faces.validator.LongRangeValidator.TYPE	Indicates Validation Error: Incorrect type.

You can override some of the keys in your resource bundle for different Locales. Using a key you can easily localize the error message produced by standard validators and converters in an application.

Configuring JSF Applications

Configuring a Web application involves addition of different mappings in configuration files. In a JSF application, the basic configuration starts with updating deployment descriptors to support JSF framework. In addition, the JSF application has its own configuration file, which helps in implementing various features of the JSF framework in a JSF application. You need to set the deployment descriptor (web.xml) and JSF configuration file (faces-config.xml) while configuring a JSF application.

Setting web.xml

The JSF framework needs to implement its own standard request processing life cycle for all requests. The request processing is handled by the `javax.faces.webapp.FacesServlet` class, which is a simple servlet and works as an engine for JSF based applications. You need to map JSF requests to `FacesServlet` class so that the requests can be processed through the standard phases of JSF framework . Similar any other Servlet, you need to provide servlet mapping for `FacesServlet` with a specific URL pattern. The following code snippet defines the FacesServlet servlet class and its mapping, which is provided in the web.xml file:

```
<?xml version="1.0" encoding="UTF-8"?>
<web-app xmlns="http://java.sun.com/xml/ns/javaee"
xmlns:xsi="http://www.w3.org/2001/XMLSchema-instance" version="3.1"
  xsi:schemaLocation="http://xmlns.jcp.org/xml/ns/javaee
  http:// xmlns.jcp.org/xml/ns/javaee/web-app_3_1.xsd">
  <servlet>
        <servlet-name>Faces Servlet</servlet-name>
        <servlet-class>javax.faces.webapp.FacesServlet</servlet-class>
        <load-on-startup>0</load-on-startup>
  </servlet>

  <servlet-mapping>
        <servlet-name>Faces Servlet</servlet-name>
        <url-pattern>*.faces</url-pattern>
  </servlet-mapping>

  <welcome-file-list>
        <welcome-file>index.jsp</welcome-file>
  </welcome-file-list>
</web-app>
```

In preceding code snippet, all the requests ending with `.faces` are mapped to the `javax.faces.webapp.FacesServlet class`. You can provide any name for a servlet but the use of `javax.faces.webapp.FacesServlet` class is mandatory. It is also known as suffix mapping and the default suffix for resources to load is `.jsp`; therefore, any request ending with `home.faces`, the Servlet searches for `home.jsp` page to handle the request.

You can also set some JSF Web application parameters, which can be used by the `FacesServlet` servlet class. The JSF Web application parameters are set as context parameters using the `<context-param>` element, as shown in the following code snippet:

```
<context-param>
   <param-name>javax.faces.STATE_SAVING_METHOD </param-name>
   <param-value>server</param-value>
</context-param>

<context-param>
   <param-name>javax.faces.CONFIG_FILES</param-name>
   <param-value>/WEB-INF/faces-config.xml</param-value>
</context-param>
```

The context parameters, which can be set in the web.xml file to customize the JSF Web application behavior are listed in Table 11.51:

Table 11.51: Showing the JSF Web Application Configuration Parameters

Context Parameter	Description	Default
javax.faces.CONFIG_FILES	Accepts a comma-delimited list of context-relative JSF configuration file, which the framework loads before it loads the WEB-INF/faces-config.xml file.	None
javax.faces.DEFAULT_SUFFIX	Loads resources when extension mapping is used.	.jsp
javax.faces.LIFE-CYCLE_ID	Serves as an identifier for the life cycle of the JSF instance to be used while processing JSF requests within an application.	The default Life-cycle instance
javax.faces.STATE_SAVING_METHOD	Indicates the location where the component states need to be saved (server side of client side).	Server

After configuring the Web application deployment descriptor, let's learn about the configuration details provided in JSF configuration file.

Setting the faces-config.xml File

Similar to other Web application frameworks, the JSF configuration file provides essential mapping for the Web application. The configuration details, such as navigation rules, managed beans, and Internationalization settings are provided in the faces-config.xml file. In addition, you can configure customized validators, converters, and components in this file. You have learned to define navigation rules and managed beans in the faces-config.xml file earlier in this chapter.

Let's discuss about the common elements, such as <application>, <managed-bean>, <referenced-bean>, and <navigation-rule> used in the faces-config.xml file.

The `<application>` element is used to declare supported Locales to specify the location of resource bundle, and define the default render kit and other pluggable components. The `<managed-bean>` element implements the managed bean creation facility and helps to create and manage different beans in given scopes. The `<navigation-rule>` element is used to define the navigation rules that should be followed in a Web application. The following code snippet shows an example of using these elements in the `faces-config.xml` file:

```
<?xml version='1.0' encoding='UTF-8'?>
<faces-config xmlns="http://java.sun.com/xml/ns/javaee"
  xmlns:xsi="http://www.w3.org/2001/XMLSchema-instance"
  xsi:schemaLocation="http://java.sun.com/xml/ns/javaee
  http://java.sun.com/xml/ns/javaee/web-facesconfig_2_2.xsd"
  version="2.2">
  <application>
        <locale-config>
              <supported-locale>en</supported-locale>
              <supported-locale>fr</supported-locale>
        </locale-config>
        <message-bundle>com.kogent.ApplicationMessages</message-bundle>
  </application>
  <navigation-rule>
        <from-view-id>/login.jsp</from-view-id>
        <navigation-case>
              <from-outcome>success</from-outcome>
              <to-view-id>/welcome.jsp</to-view-id>
        </navigation-case>
        <navigation-case>
```

```
                <from-outcome>failure</from-outcome>
                <to-view-id>/login.jsp</to-view-id>
            </navigation-case>
    </navigation-rule>
    <managed-bean>
            <managed-bean-name>beanName</managed-bean-name>
            <managed-bean-class>com.kogent.BeanClassName</managed-bean-class>
            <managed-bean-scope>request</managed-bean-scope>
    </managed-bean>
</faces-config>
```

Whenever a framework is extended by creating custom UI components, converters, validators, or renderers, the extension should be registered in the JSF configuration file. The elements used in the faces-config.xml file are `<component>`, `<render-kit>`, `<validator>`, and `<converter>`. The basic structure for registering extensions in the faces-config.xml file is shown in the following code snippet:

```
<validator>
   <validator-id>myValidator</validator-id>
   <validator-class>com.kogent.validator.MyValidator</validator-class>
</validator>
<converter>
   <converter-id>myConverter</converter-id>
   <converter-class>com.kogent.converter.MyConverter</converter-class>
</converter>
<component>
   <component-type>SomeType</component-type>
   <component-class>com.kogent.component.MyUIComponent</component-class>
</component>
```

The JSF framework can support multiple configuration files that are defined by setting `javax.faces.CONFIG_FILES` context parameter in the deployment descriptor, web.xml. However, the `faces-config.xml` file does not need to be configured in the `web.xml` file, as this file is by default found in the WEB-INF/faces-config.xml file and is loaded automatically. The `faces-config.xml` file is the location where most of the application configuration details are placed. You need additional configuration files only when you are working on a large application, which is divided into different modules.

You have learned to create components and customize them, manage beans, define navigation rules and handle action events, and apply validations in the Web application with all implementation and configuration details. Now, let's learn to develop a JSF based Web application.

Developing a JSF Application

Let's develop the KogentPro Web application with a number of JSF pages using various JSF UI components, backing beans implementing application logic and a model class handling database interaction for an application. The application created in this section implements all concepts, uses various HTML and Core tags, and other JSF features, such as managed bean, centralized navigation rules, input validation and type conversion support. In addition, the application supports Internationalization through which the localized messages are displayed to a user.

Setting Development Environment

The basic functionality provided by the Web application created in this subsection is maintaining the database of employees, such as adding new employees, editing or deleting details of an existing employee, in an organization. A JSF application is created with the support of following components:

- Set of JSP pages using JSF components.
- A backing bean, `Employee`
- A Model class, `EmployeeDB`
- A custom validator, `EmailValidator`

You cannot declare a faces page as the welcome file; therefore, you have to provide a page to simply create the first JSF request to your home page, which is a JSF page and needs FacesServlet to handle it. Let's create the index.jsp page and provided the `<jsp:forward>` element to access the `home.jsp page` (yet to be created). Listing 11.1 shows the code to create the `index.jsp` page (save this file in the \KogentPro\folder):

Listing 11.1: Showing the Code for the index.jsp Page

```
<%@ page language="java" pageEncoding="ISO-8859-1"%>
<html>
   <body>
         <jsp:forward page="home.jsp"/>
   </body>
</html>
```

Rest of the JSP pages, `such as addNew.jsp and viewAll.jsp` created in the JSF application use JSF components; therefore, those pages are referred as JSF pages instead of JSP pages.let's discuss these JSP pages one by one.

Creating JSF Pages

A JSF application uses different JSF pages, which further use different JSF UI components to create interactive interfaces with the user with proper formats, localized messages, and required fields. Let's create the following JSP pages in the JSF application:

- home.jsp
- addnew.jsp
- viewall.jsp
- detail.jsp
- edit.jsp

Creating home.jsp page

The `home.jsp` page is the first page that is displayed to the users. This page contains header and footer content and an image. The most important components used in the home.jsp page are three `HtmlCommandLink` components, which provide navigational links to other pages. The code of home.jsp page has been provided in Listing 11.2 (save this file in the `\KogentPro\` folder):

Listing 11.2: Showing the Code for the home.jsp Page

```
<%@ page language="java" pageEncoding="ISO-8859-1"%>
<%@ taglib uri="http://java.sun.com/jsf/html" prefix="h"%>
<%@ taglib uri="http://java.sun.com/jsf/core" prefix="f"%>
<html>
   <head>
         <title>Welcome - Kogent Solutions Inc</title>
                  </head>
   <body>
   <f:view>
         <f:loadBundle basename="com.kogent.ApplicationMessages" var="msg"/>
         <table width="700" align="center" height="500" cellpadding="0" cellspacing="0">
         <tr><td height="70" bgcolor="#5577C6" align="center">
         <h2 style="color: white;"><h:outputText value="#{msg.header}"/></h2>
         </td></tr>
         <tr><td>
         <table>
         <tr>
         <td width="300" valign="middle" align="center">
         <h:form>
         <h:commandLink action="addnew" value="#{msg.addnew}"/><br><br>
         <h:commandLink action="edit" value="#{msg.edit}"/><br><br>
         <h:commandLink action="#{employee.getEmployees}"
         value="#{msg.viewall}"/><br><br>
         </h:form>
         </td>
```

```
                <td width="300" align="center">
                <h:graphicImage value="images/people.jpg" width="300" /></td>
                </tr>
                </table>
                </td></tr>
                <tr><td height="40" bgcolor="#C6D1EC" align="center">
                <h:outputText value="#{msg.footer}"/>
                </td></tr>
                </table>
        </f:view>
        </body>
    </html>
```

In Listing 11.2, the home.jsp page uses localized messages, which are accessed by all `HtmlCommandLink` components created on the home.jsp page. The `<f:loadBundle>` tag is used to load resource bundle and value expressions are set for the value attribute by using the `msg` variable.

First two `HtmlCommandLink` components have associated string outcome and help navigation handler to select the next view. These components are set in the `addnew.jsp` and `edit.jsp pages` through navigation rules in faces-config.xml file, which is discussed later in this chapter. The third `HtmlCommandLink` is associated with an action method `getEmployees()` of the backing bean, `employee`. This backing bean has been discussed later in this chapter. The output of home.jsp page is shown in Figure 11.6:

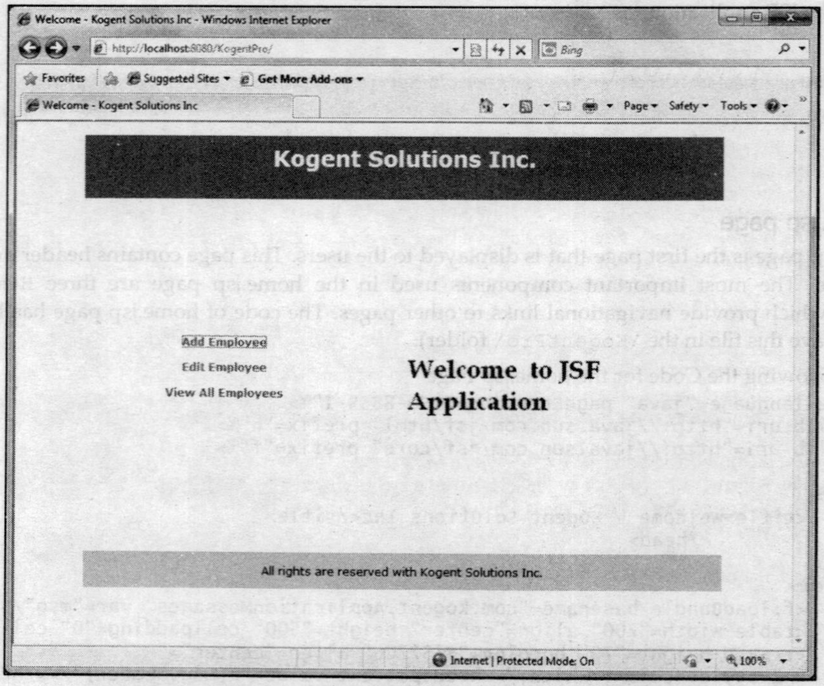

Figure 11.6: Displaying the Output of home.jsp Page

Figure 11.6 shows the the home page of the `KogentPro` Web application and provides links to the `addnew.jsp` and `edit.jsp` pages. Next, let's create the `addnew.jsp` and `edit.jsp` pages.

Creating addnew.jsp page

The addnew.jsp page provides a form with various input fields for giving informations of new employees who need to be added. To get the information about new employees a form and other input components, such as text box, rich text box are created using JSF components. The UI components, such as `HtmlForm`, `HtmlCommandButton`, `HtmlInputText`, `HtmlInputTextarea`, `HtmlSelectOneListbox`, `HtmlSelectOneMenu`, and `HtmlSelectOneRadio are also used in this page`. Let's create a form by using the `HtmlPanelGrid` components, which are used to create a two-column table. Listing 11.3 shows the code for the addnew.jsp file (save this file in the `\KogentPro\web` folder):

Listing 11.3: Displaying the Code for the `addnew.jsp File`

```
<%@ page language="java" pageEncoding="ISO-8859-1"%>
<%@ taglib uri="http://java.sun.com/jsf/html" prefix="h"%>
<%@ taglib uri="http://java.sun.com/jsf/core" prefix="f"%>
<html>
  <head>
        <title>Adding New Employee...</title>

  </head>
  <body>
  <f:view>
        <f:loadBundle basename="com.kogent.ApplicationMessages" var="msg" />
        <table width="700" align="center" height="500" cellpadding="0" cellspacing="0">
        <tr><td height="70" bgcolor="#5577C6" align="center">
        <h2 style="color: white;"><h:outputText value="#{msg.header}" /></h2>
        </td></tr>
        <tr><td align="center" valign="top"><br>
        <h:form>
        <h:panelGrid columns="3" cellspacing="0" cellpadding="5"
        styleClass="menu" border="1">
                <h:commandLink action="home" value="#{msg.home}" />
                <h:commandLink action="edit" value="#{msg.edit}"/>
                <h:commandLink action="#{employee.getEmployees}" value="#{msg.viewall}"/>
                </h:panelGrid>
        </h:form>
        <h5>Enter New Employee Details</h5>
        <h:messages styleClass="error"/>
        <h:form id="addForm">
        <h:panelGrid columns="2" bgcolor="#F1F1F8" width="400" cellpadding="2">
        <h:outputLabel for="empid" value="#{msg.empid}"/>
        <h:inputText id="empid" value="#{employee.id}" required="true">
                <f:validateLongRange minimum="100"/>
        </h:inputText>

        <h:outputLabel for="name" value="#{msg.empname}"/>
        <h:inputText id="name" value="#{employee.name}" required="true"/>
        <h:outputLabel for="address" value="#{msg.address}"/>
        <h:inputTextarea id="address" cols="18" rows="2" value="#{employee.address}"/>

        <h:outputLabel for="city" value="#{msg.city}"/>
        <h:inputText id="city" value="#{employee.city}"/>
        <h:outputLabel for="email" value="#{msg.email}"/>
        <h:inputText id="email" value="#{employee.email}" size="30">
                <f:validator validatorId="emailValidator"/>
        </h:inputText>

        <h:outputLabel for="sex" value="#{msg.sex}"/>
        <h:selectOneRadio id="sex" value="#{employee.sex}">
                <f:selectItem itemValue="Male" itemLabel="Male" />
                <f:selectItem itemValue="Female" itemLabel="Female"/>
        </h:selectOneRadio>

        <h:outputLabel for="department" value="#{msg.department}"/>
        <h:selectOneMenu id="department" value="#{employee.department}" required="true">
        <f:selectItem itemValue="Content Solutions" itemLabel="Centent Solutions"/>
                <f:selectItem itemValue="Testing" itemLabel="Testing"/>
                <f:selectItem itemValue="HR" itemLabel="HR"/>
        </h:selectOneMenu>

        <h:outputLabel for="skills" value="#{msg.skills}"/>
        <h:selectOneListbox id="skills" value="#{employee.skills}">
                <f:selectItem itemValue="Java" itemLabel="Java"/>
```

```
                <f:selectItem itemValue="Struts" itemLabel="Struts"/>
                <f:selectItem itemValue="Spring" itemLabel="Spring"/>
            </h:selectOneListbox>
            <h:outputLabel for="joindate" value="#{msg.joindate}"/>
            <h:panelGroup>
            <h:inputText id="joindate" value="#{employee.joinDate}" required="true">
                        <f:convertDateTime type="date" pattern="dd-MM-yyyy"/>
                </h:inputText>
                <h:outputText value=" [dd-MM-yyyy]"/>
            </h:panelGroup>
            <h:commandButton action="#{employee.addNew}" value="#{msg.addnew}"/>
            <h:commandButton type="reset" value="#{msg.reset}" />
            </h:panelGrid>
            </h:form><br>
            </td></tr>
            <tr><td height="40" bgcolor="#C6D1EC" align="center">
                <h:outputText value="#{msg.footer}" />
            </td></tr>
            </table>
        </f:view>
        </body>
    </html>
```

In Listing 11.3, a `LongRangeValidator` is used with input field, empid and a custom validator, `EmailValidator` to validate the input field, `email`. The output of the `addnew.jsp` file is shown in Figure 11.7:

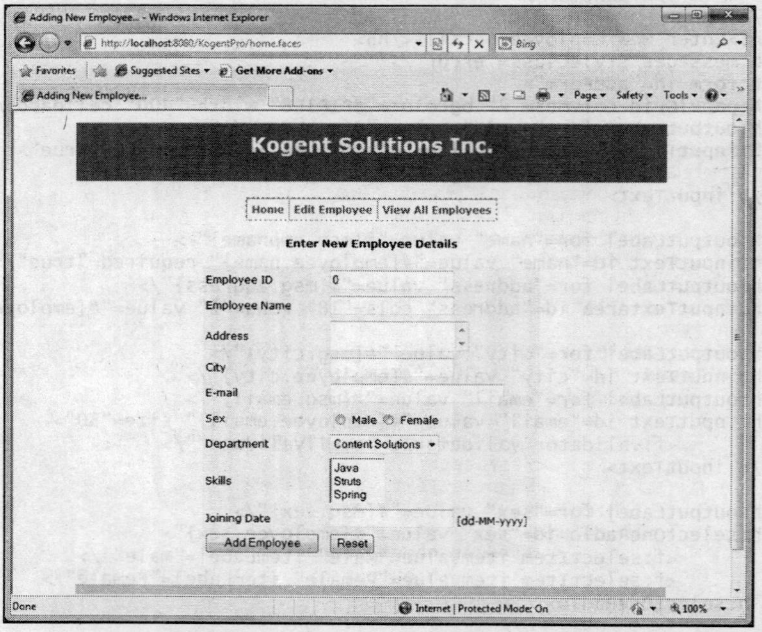

Figure 11.7: Displaying the Output of addnew JSF Page

All the input fields created in the KogentPro application have been associated with different properties of employee backing bean. Listing 11.3. An HTMLCommandButton component is created that binds the request with the action method, addNew() and this method is created in the same backing bean. The `addNew()` method processes the logic of adding a new employee record in the database. The `DateTimeConverter` with `HtmlInputText` component is used for joining date to ensure that the date is entered in the correct format. The `HtmlMessages` component is used to display all components and application level messages.

NOTE

During the execution of the KogentPro application, all JSP pages (.jsp files) get converted into the .faces pages, as configured in the web.xml file of the application.

Creating the viewall.jsp Page

The viewall.jsp page shows the list of all existing employees. This page uses an `HtmlDataTable` component, which iterates over an `ArrayList` in the application scope. The `<h:dataTable>` and `<h:column>` elements are also used in this page. In addition, two `HtmlCommandLink` components (details and delete hyperlinks) are used in each row for getting the details of an employee and deleting an employee from database using the `HtmlDataTable` component. Listing 11.4 shows the the code of the viewall.jsp page (save this file in the \KogentPro\web folder):

Listing 11.4: Showing the Code for the viewall.jsp Page

```
<%@ page language="java" pageEncoding="ISO-8859-1"%>
<%@ taglib uri="http://java.sun.com/jsf/html" prefix="h"%>
<%@ taglib uri="http://java.sun.com/jsf/core" prefix="f"%>
<html>
  <head>
        <title>Listing all Employees</title>
              </head>
  <body>
  <f:view>
        <f:loadBundle basename="com.kogent.ApplicationMessages" var="msg" />
        <table width="700" align="center" height="500" cellpadding="0" cellspacing="0">
        <tr><td height="70" bgcolor="#5577C6" align="center">
        <h2 style="color: white;"><h:outputText value="#{msg.header}"/></h2>
        </td>
        </tr>
        <tr>
        <td align="center" valign="top"><br>
        <h:form>
        <h:panelGrid columns="3" cellspacing="0" cellpadding="5"
        styleClass="menu" border="1">
              <h:commandLink action="home" value="#{msg.home}" />
              <h:commandLink action="addnew" value="#{msg.addnew}" />
              <h:commandLink action="edit" value="#{msg.edit}" />
              </h:panelGrid>
        </h:form>
        <h5 align="left">Listing all employees</h5>
        <h:form>
        <h:dataTable value="#{applicationScope.employees}" var="emp" cellspacing="1"
        cellpadding="4" width="600" headerClass="header" rowClasses="odd-row, even-row">
              <h:column>
                    <f:facet name="header">
                          <h:outputText value="ID" />
                    </f:facet>
                    <h:outputText value="#{emp.id}" />
              </h:column>
              <h:column>
                    <f:facet name="header">
                          <h:outputText value="Employee Name" />
                    </f:facet>
                    <h:outputText value="#{emp.name}" />
              </h:column>
              <h:column>
                    <f:facet name="header">
                          <h:outputText value="Department" />
                    </f:facet>
                    <h:outputText value="#{emp.department}" />
              </h:column>
              <h:column>
                    <f:facet name="header">
                          <h:outputText value="Date of Joining" />
```

```
                        </f:facet>
                        <h:outputText value="#{emp.joinDate}">
                              <f:convertDateTime pattern="dd MMM, yyyy" />
                        </h:outputText>
                  </h:column>
                  <h:column>
                        <f:facet name="header">
                              <h:outputText value="- -" />
                        </f:facet>
                        <h:commandLink value="#{msg.details}"
                        action="#{employee.getDetail}">
                        <f:setPropertyActionListener
                        target="#{employee.id}" value="#{emp.id}" />
                        </h:commandLink>
                  </h:column>
                  <h:column>
                        <f:facet name="header">
                              <h:outputText value="- -" />
                        </f:facet>
                        <h:commandLink action="#{employee.deleteEmployee}"
                        value="#{msg.delete}" onclick="return confirm('Do you want to
                        delete.')">
                        <f:setPropertyActionListener target="#{employee.id}"
                        value="#{emp.id}" />
                        </h:commandLink>
                  </h:column>
                  </h:dataTable>
            </h:form>
            </td></tr>
            <tr><td height="40" bgcolor="#C6D1EC" align="center">
                  <h:outputText value="#{msg.footer}" />
            </td></tr>
            </table>
      </f:view>
      </body>
   </html>
```

In Listing 11.4, two `HtmlCommandLink` components are created for each row and associated with two different action methods, `getDetail()` and `deleteEmployee()`. We have used the `<f:setPropertyActionListener>` element with the `HtmlCommandLink` components to set the employee id before the action method is executed. The output of the `viewall.jsp` page displays the existing three employees in the database, as shown in Figure 11.8:

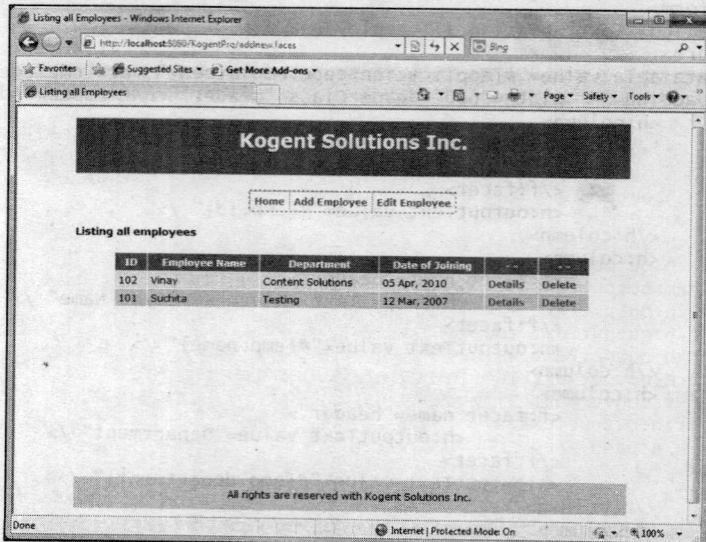

Figure 11.8: Showing the Output of the viewall JSF Page

In Figure 11.8, header and alternative rows are provided in different styles by setting the `headerClass` and `rowClasses` attributes of the `HtmlDataTable` component.

Creating the detail.jsp page

The `detail.jsp` page shows the detail of a particular employee. This page can be accessed from the `viewall.jsp` page, which has the `details` hyperlink (`HtmlCommandLink` component) to view the details corresponding to each employee. The `detail.jsp` page uses the `HtmlOutputText` element associated with individual properties of the `employee` backing bean. Listing 11.5 shows the code for the detail.jsp page (save this file in the \KogentPro\ folder):

Listing 11.5: Showing the Code for the detail.jsp Page

```
<%@ page language="java" pageEncoding="ISO-8859-1"%>
<%@ taglib uri="http://java.sun.com/jsf/html" prefix="h"%>
<%@ taglib uri="http://java.sun.com/jsf/core" prefix="f"%>
<html>
  <head>
        <title>Employee Detail...</title>
              </head>
  <body>
  <f:view>
        <f:loadBundle basename="com.kogent.ApplicationMessages" var="msg"/>
        <table width="700" align="center" height="500" cellpadding="0" cellspacing="0">
        <tr><td height="70" bgcolor="#5577C6" align="center">
        <h2 style="color: white;"><h:outputText value="#{msg.header}"/></h2>
        </td></tr>
        <tr><td align="center" valign="top"><br>
        <h:form>
        <h:panelGrid columns="3" cellspacing="0" cellpadding="5" styleClass="menu"
        border="1">
              <h:commandLink action="home" value="#{msg.home}"/>
              <h:commandLink action="addnew" value="#{msg.addnew}"/>
              <h:commandLink action="#{employee.getEmployees}" value="#{msg.viewall}"/>
                    </h:panelGrid>
        </h:form>

        <br><h5>Employee Details</h5>
        <h:form id="empForm">
        <h:panelGrid columns="2" cellpadding="4" cellspacing="4" border="1" rules="rows">
              <h:outputText value="#{msg.empid}"/>
              <h:outputText id="empid" value="#{employee.id}"/>
              <h:outputText value="#{msg.empname}"/>
              <h:outputText id="name" value="#{employee.name}" />
              <h:outputText value="#{msg.address}"/>
              <h:outputText id="address" value="#{employee.address}"/>
              <h:outputText value="#{msg.city}"/>
              <h:outputText id="city" value="#{employee.city}"/>
              <h:outputText value="#{msg.email}"/>
              <h:outputText id="email" value="#{employee.email}" />
              <h:outputText value="#{msg.sex}"/>
              <h:outputText id="sex" value="#{employee.sex}"/>
              <h:outputText value="#{msg.department}"/>
              <h:outputText id="department" value="#{employee.department}"/>
              <h:outputText value="#{msg.skills}"/>
              <h:outputText id="skills" value="#{employee.skills}"/>
              <h:outputText value="#{msg.joindate}"/>
              <h:outputText id="joindate" value="#{employee.joinDate}">
              <f:convertDateTime type="date" pattern="dd-MM-yyyy"/>
              </h:outputText>
              </h:panelGrid>
        </h:form>
        </td></tr>
        <tr><td height="40" bgcolor="#C6D1EC" align="center">
              <h:outputText value="#{msg.footer}"/>
        </td></tr>
```

```
            </table>
        </f:view>
        </body>
    </html>
```

The output of the detail.jsp page is shown in Figure 11.9:

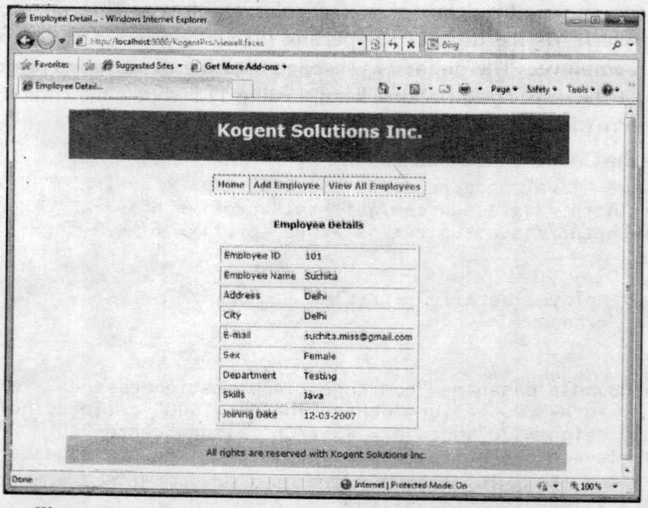

Figure 11.9: Displaying the Output of the detail JSF Page

In Figure 11.9 the detail.jsp page displays the properties of employee backing bean, which is further updated for the selected employee by the `getDetail()` method of the `employee` backing bean.

Creating the edit.jsp Page

The `edit.jsp` page creates two different HtmlForm components, `getEmp` and `editForm`. The `editForm` `HtmlForm` component does not render initially as its render attribute is set to `false`. The `getEmp` HtmlForm component is submitted and handled by the `getEmployee()` action method. The `getEmployee()` method processes the business logic and updates the details of the employee with respect to the entered `employee id`. Listing 11.6 shows the code of the `edit.jsp` page (save this file in the \KogentPro\ folder):

Listing 11.6: Showing the Code for the edit.jsp Page

```
<%@ page language="java" pageEncoding="ISO-8859-1"%>
<%@ taglib uri="http://java.sun.com/jsf/html" prefix="h"%>
<%@ taglib uri="http://java.sun.com/jsf/core" prefix="f"%>
<html>
  <head>
        <title>Editing Employee...</title>
              </head>
  <body>
  <f:view>
        <f:loadBundle basename="com.kogent.ApplicationMessages" var="msg" />
<table width="700" align="center" height="500" cellpadding="0" cellspacing="0">
        <tr><td height="70" bgcolor="#5577C6" align="center">
<h2 style="color: white;"><h:outputText value="#{msg.header}" /></h2>
        </td></tr>
        <tr><td align="center" valign="top"><br>
        <h:form>
<h:panelGrid columns="3" cellspacing="0" cellpadding="5" styleClass="menu" border="1">
              <h:commandLink action="home" value="#{msg.home}" />
              <h:commandLink action="addnew" value="#{msg.addnew}"/>
        <h:commandLink action="#{employee.getEmployees}" value="#{msg.viewall}"/>
              </h:panelGrid>
        </h:form>
        <h:messages styleClass="error"/>
```

```
            <h:form id="getEmp">
                    <h:outputLabel value="#{msg.enterid}" for="intputId"/> 
                    <h:inputText id="empid" value="#{employee.id}"/>
            <h:commandButton value="Enter" actionListener="#{employee.getEmployee}"/>
            </h:form>

            <h:form id="editForm" rendered="false" binding="#{employee.editForm}" >
            <h:inputHidden value="#{employee.id}"/>
            <h:panelGrid columns="2" bgcolor="#F1F1F8" width="400" cellpadding="2">
            <h:outputLabel for="empid" value="#{msg.empid}"/>
            <h:inputText id="empid" value="#{employee.id}" readonly="true"/>

            <h:outputLabel for="name" value="#{msg.empname}"/>
            <h:inputText id="name" value="#{employee.name}" required="true"/>

            <h:outputLabel for="address" value="#{msg.address}"/>
            <h:inputTextarea id="address" cols="18" rows="2" value="#{employee.address}"/>

            <h:outputLabel for="city" value="#{msg.city}"/>
            <h:inputText id="city" value="#{employee.city}"/>

            <h:outputLabel for="email" value="#{msg.email}"/>
            <h:inputText id="email" value="#{employee.email}" size="30">
                    <f:validator validatorId="emailValidator"/>
            </h:inputText>

            <h:outputLabel for="sex" value="#{msg.sex}"/>
            <h:selectOneRadio id="sex" value="#{employee.sex}">
                    <f:selectItem itemValue="Male" itemLabel="Male" />
                    <f:selectItem itemValue="Female" itemLabel="Female"/>
            </h:selectOneRadio>

            <h:outputLabel for="department" value="#{msg.department}"/>
            <h:selectOneMenu id="department" value="#{employee.department}" required="true">
            <f:selectItem itemValue="Content Solutions" itemLabel="Centent Solutions"/>
                    <f:selectItem itemValue="Testing" itemLabel="Testing"/>
                    <f:selectItem itemValue="HR" itemLabel="HR"/>
            </h:selectOneMenu>

            <h:outputLabel for="skills" value="#{msg.skills}"/>
            <h:selectOneListbox id="skills" value="#{employee.skills}">
                    <f:selectItem itemValue="Java" itemLabel="Java"/>
                    <f:selectItem itemValue="Struts" itemLabel="Struts"/>
                    <f:selectItem itemValue="Spring" itemLabel="Spring"/>
            </h:selectOneListbox>

            <h:outputLabel for="joindate" value="#{msg.joindate}"/>
            <h:panelGroup>
            <h:inputText id="joindate" value="#{employee.joinDate}" required="true">
                    <f:convertDateTime type="date" pattern="dd-MM-yyyy"/>
                    </h:inputText>
                    <h:outputText value=" [dd-MM-yyyy]"/>
            </h:panelGroup>
            <h:commandButton action="#{employee.update}" value="#{msg.update}"/>
            </h:panelGrid>
            </h:form><br>
            </td></tr>
            <tr><td height="40" bgcolor="#C6D1EC" align="center">
                    <h:outputText value="#{msg.footer}" />
            </td></tr>
            </table>
        </f:view>
    </body>
</html>
```

In Listing 11.6, the `HtmlForm` component, `editForm` is similar to the `addnew.jsp` page except the fact that the `HtmlInputText` component for employee id is set as readonly and an `HtmlInputHidden` component has been placed. The `HtmlInputHidden` component prohibits the user from changing the employee id, as there is no need to change employee id while modifying the details of an existing employee. The `update()` method of the backing bean is responsible for updating the employee record with the modified detail and this method is bound as action method.

You have learned to create various JSF pages that use a backing bean, Employee. The UI components in these JSF pages are used to either read or set the values of properties of the Employee backing bean. Different action methods of the Employee bean are used to perform these actions. Now, let's learn to create a backing bean for request processing.

Creating the Employee Backing Bean

A single backing bean, employee is created in the `KogentPro` application. This backing bean has a set of properties and their corresponding get and set methods. Different action methods, such as `addNew()`, `update()`, `deleteEmployee()`, `getDetail()`, and `getEmployees()` are defined in the bean. In addition, we have an action listener method, `getEmployee()`. All these action methods have been bound with different command components on various pages to process some logic. Listing 11.7 shows the code for the backing bean class, com.kogent.Employee (save this file in the `\KogentPro\src\com\kogent\` folder):

Listing 11.7: Displaying the Code of Employee.java File

```
package com.kogent;

import java.util.ArrayList;
import java.util.Date;
import java.util.Map;

import javax.faces.application.FacesMessage;
import javax.faces.component.html.HtmlForm;
import javax.faces.context.ExternalContext;
import javax.faces.context.FacesContext;
import javax.faces.event.ActionEvent;

public class Employee {
   int id;
   String name;
   String address;
   String city;
   String email;
   String sex;
   String department;
   String skills;
   Date joinDate;

   ArrayList<Employee> employees;

   HtmlForm editForm;

   public String getAddress() {
         return address;
   }
   public void setAddress(String address) {
         this.address = address;
   }
   public String getCity() {
         return city;
   }
```

```
public void setCity(String city) {
      this.city = city;
}
public String getDepartment() {
      return department;
}
public void setDepartment(String department) {
      this.department = department;
}
public String getEmail() {
      return email;
}
public void setEmail(String email) {
      this.email = email;
}


public int getId() {
      return id;
}
public void setId(int id) {
      this.id = id;
}
public Date getJoinDate() {
      return joinDate;
}
public void setJoinDate(Date joinDate) {
      this.joinDate = joinDate;
}
public String getName() {
      return name;
}
public void setName(String name) {
      this.name = name;
}
public String getSex() {
      return sex;
}
public void setSex(String sex) {
      this.sex = sex;
}
public String getSkills() {
      return skills;
}
public void setSkills(String skills) {
      this.skills = skills;
}

public HtmlForm getEditForm() {
      return editForm;
}
public void setEditForm(HtmlForm editForm) {
      this.editForm = editForm;
}
public String addNew(){
      FacesContext fc=FacesContext.getCurrentInstance();
      EmployeeDB empdb=new EmployeeDB();

      if(!empdb.checkEmployee(id)){
```

```
                empdb.addEmployee(this);
        }
        else{
        fc.addMessage(null, new FacesMessage(FacesMessage.SEVERITY_ERROR, "Employee with
        this ID exists.", ""));
                return "failure";
        }
        Map<String, Object>
    application=FacesContext.getCurrentInstance().getExternalContext().getApplicationMap();
        application.put("employees", empdb.getEmployees());

        return "success";
    }
    public  String getEmployees(){
        EmployeeDB empdb=new EmployeeDB();
        FacesContext fc=FacesContext.getCurrentInstance();
        ExternalContext exc=fc.getExternalContext();
        Map<String, Object> application=exc.getApplicationMap();
        application.put("employees", empdb.getEmployees());
        return "viewall";
    }

    public void getEmployee(ActionEvent event){

        FacesContext fc=FacesContext.getCurrentInstance();
        ExternalContext exc=fc.getExternalContext();
        Map<String, Object> request=exc.getRequestMap();

        EmployeeDB empdb=new EmployeeDB();
        Employee employee=empdb.getEmployee(id);
        if(employee==null){
        fc.addMessage(null, new FacesMessage(FacesMessage.SEVERITY_ERROR, "Employee with
        this ID does not exist.", ""));
                editForm.setRendered(false);
        }
        else{
                request.put("employee", employee);
                editForm.setRendered(true);
        }
    }

    public String update(){
        FacesContext fc=FacesContext.getCurrentInstance();
        EmployeeDB empdb=new EmployeeDB();
        int i=empdb.updateEmployee(this);
        if(i==1){
        Map<String, Object> application=fc.getExternalContext().getApplicationMap();
                application.put("employees", empdb.getEmployees());
                return "success";
        }
        else{
        fc.addMessage(null, new FacesMessage(FacesMessage.SEVERITY_ERROR, "Employee could
        not be Updated.", ""));
                return "failure";
        }
    }

    public String getDetail(){
        EmployeeDB empdb=new EmployeeDB();
        Employee employee=empdb.getEmployee(this.id);

Map<String, Object>
    request=FacesContext.getCurrentInstance().getExternalContext().getRequestMap();
        request.put("employee", employee);
        return "detail";
    }
```

```
    public String deleteEmployee(){

            EmployeeDB empdb=new EmployeeDB();
            int i=empdb.deleteEmployee(this.id);
            System.out.print(i+"row deleted");
  Map<String, Object>
    application=FacesContext.getCurrentInstance().getExternalContext().getApplicationMap();
            application.put("employees", empdb.getEmployees());
            return "viewall";
    }

}
```

In Listing 11.7, the `com.kogent.EmployeeDB` class is used in the `Employee` class. The `EmployeeDB` class is a model class that interacts with database and the backing bean invokes methods on its object to perform various operations, such as adding a record, deleting and modifying a record, and fetching employee records from the `EMPLOYEE` table Let's discuss various action methods of the employee backing bean.

String getEmployees()

The getEmployees() method simply returns an `ArrayList` of Employee objects using the `getEmployees()` method on the `EmployeeDB` object and places this `ArrayList` object in the application scope by the name, employees. This action method returns viewall as the outcome string. You can see the `faces-config.xml` file to configure the mapping for this outcome.

String addNew()

The addNew() method checks whether the employee with the given id already exists or not and adds the new record by calling the `addEmployee()` method on the `EmployeeDB` object. Further, it updates an application scope attribute named employee with a new set of employees. In case, the employee with the given id exists, the FacesMessage object is created and added into the `FacesContext` instance.

String update()

The update() method invokes the `updateEmployee()` method on the `EmployeeDB` object and returns success or failure accordingly. If the record is updated successfully, the application scoped `ArrayList` object, employee is also updated again.

String deleteEmployee()

The `deleteEmployee()` method is invoked to delete the employee with the given employee id. The `deleteEmployee()` method of the Employee class uses the `deleteEmployee()` method of the `EmployeeDB` class. This method also returns `viewall` as outcome string.

String getDetail()

The getDetail() method fetches an Employee object representing a given employee and uses the `getEmployee()` method of the `EmployeeDB` class. After fetching the `Employee` object, this object is placed in the request scope so that it is accessible from the next view to be loaded. Returns `detail` as outcome string.

void getEmployee(ActionEvent)

The getEmployee(ActionEvent) is the only action listener method among other action methods and does not affect navigation. It performs logic and receives an `Employee` object by calling the `getEmployee(int)` method on the `EmployeeDB` object. If the fetched `Employee` object is not null, it simply places the object in the request scope and sets the render property of the `empForm` object to true. After setting the render property to true, the empForm is visible to the user; thereby, allows the user to edit the employee details through the `edit.jsp` page.

Managing Employee Bean

The `com.kogent.Employee` class is a backing bean and needs to be managed in the `faces-config.xml` file. You need to provide a three-line configuration detail to define the identifier for this backing bean, set the class name and the scope of the bean. The configuration details of managed beans is shown in the following code snippet:

```
<managed-bean>
   <managed-bean-name>employee</managed-bean-name>
   <managed-bean-class>com.kogent.Employee</managed-bean-class>
   <managed-bean-scope>request</managed-bean-scope>
</managed-bean>
```

In the preceding code snippet; the employee managed bean is configured by defining its class and scope. Let's now create the `EmployeeDB` class.

Creating the EmployeeDB Class

As we have seen, backing bean has performed varied database operations without executing any JDBC code. The database interaction code has been bundled into a model class that has been used in all action methods of the `Employee` class. Table 11.52 shows the structure of employee table used in the `KogentPro` application:

Table 11.52: Showing the Structure of Employee Table

Name	Type
ID	NUMBER(38)
NAME	VARCHAR2(35)
ADDRESS	VARCHAR2(50)
CITY	VARCHAR2(15)
EMAIL	VARCHAR2(30)
SEX	VARCHAR2(6)
DEPARTMENT	VARCHAR2(25)
SKILLS	VARCHAR2(40)
JOINDATE	DATE

The model class, `com.kogent.EmployeeDB` has various methods created for different database operations. Listing 11.8 shows the code of the EmployeeDB class file (save this file in the `\KogentPro\src\com\kogent\` folder):

Listing 11.8: Showing the Code of EmployeeDB.java File

```
package com.kogent;

import java.sql.Connection;
import java.sql.DriverManager;
import java.sql.PreparedStatement;
import java.sql.ResultSet;
import java.sql.SQLException;
import java.sql.Statement;
import java.util.ArrayList;

public class EmployeeDB {

   Connection con;
   ResultSet rs;
   Statement stmt;

   public EmployeeDB() {
         try {
               Class.forName("oracle.jdbc.driver.OracleDriver");
```

```
con = DriverManager.getConnection
      ("jdbc:oracle:thin:@192.168.1.123:1521:XE","scott","tiger");
      } catch (Exception e) {
              e.printStackTrace();
      }
}

public boolean  checkEmployee(int empid){
      boolean  found=false;
      try {
              stmt=con.createStatement();
              rs=stmt.executeQuery("select * from employee where id="+empid);
              if(rs.next())
                      found=true;
      } catch (SQLException e) {
              e.printStackTrace();
      }
      return found;
}
public ArrayList<Employee> getEmployees(){
      ArrayList<Employee> employees=new ArrayList<Employee>();
      Employee emp=null;

      try {
              stmt=con.createStatement();
              rs=stmt.executeQuery("select * from employee ");
              while(rs.next()){
                      emp=new Employee();
                      emp.setId(rs.getInt(1));
                      emp.setName(rs.getString(2));
                      emp.setAddress(rs.getString(3));
                      emp.setCity(rs.getString(4));
                      emp.setEmail(rs.getString(5));
                      emp.setSex(rs.getString(6));
                      emp.setDepartment(rs.getString(7));
                      emp.setSkills(rs.getString(8));
                      emp.setJoinDate(rs.getDate(9));
                      employees.add(emp);
              }
              rs.close();
      } catch (Exception e) {
              e.printStackTrace();
      }
      return employees;
}

public Employee getEmployee(int empid){
      Employee emp=null;

      try {
              stmt=con.createStatement();
              rs=stmt.executeQuery("select * from employee where id="+empid);
              if(rs.next()){
                      emp=new Employee();
                      emp.setId(rs.getInt(1));
                      emp.setName(rs.getString(2));
                      emp.setAddress(rs.getString(3));
                      emp.setCity(rs.getString(4));
                      emp.setEmail(rs.getString(5));
                      emp.setSex(rs.getString(6));
                      emp.setDepartment(rs.getString(7));
                      emp.setSkills(rs.getString(8));
                      emp.setJoinDate(rs.getDate(9));
              }
      } catch (Exception e) {
              e.printStackTrace();
```

```
        }
        return emp;
    }

    public void addEmployee(Employee emp){
        try {
        PreparedStatement pstmt=con.prepareStatement("insert into employee
        values(?,?,?,?,?,?,?,?,?)");
                pstmt.setInt(1,emp.getId());
                pstmt.setString(2, emp.getName());
                pstmt.setString(3, emp.getAddress());
                pstmt.setString(4, emp.getCity());
                pstmt.setString(5, emp.getEmail());
                pstmt.setString(6, emp.getSex());
                pstmt.setString(7, emp.getDepartment());
                pstmt.setString(8, emp.getSkills());
                java.sql.Date date=new java.sql.Date(emp.getJoinDate().getTime());
                pstmt.setDate(9, date);
                pstmt.executeUpdate();
                pstmt.close();

        } catch (SQLException e) {
                e.printStackTrace();
        }

    }
    public int updateEmployee(Employee employee){
        int i=0;
        try {
                stmt=con.createStatement();
                String query="update employee set name='"+employee.getName()+"', ";
                query+="address='"+employee.getAddress()+"', ";
                query+="city='"+employee.getCity()+"', ";
                query+="email='"+employee.getEmail()+"', ";
                query+="sex='"+employee.getSex()+"', ";
                query+="department='"+employee.getDepartment()+"', ";
                query+="skills='"+employee.getSkills()+"', ";
                query+="joindate=to_date('"+new
                java.sql.Date(employee.getJoinDate().getTime())+"', 'yyyy-MM-dd') ";
                query+="where id="+employee.getId();
                System.out.println(query);
                i=stmt.executeUpdate(query);
        } catch (Exception e) {
                e.printStackTrace();
        }
        return i;
    }
    public int deleteEmployee(int id){
        int i=0;
        try {
                stmt=con.createStatement();
                System.out.println("delete from employee where id="+id);
                i=stmt.executeUpdate("delete from employee where id="+id);
        } catch (Exception e) {
                e.printStackTrace();
        }
        return i;
    }
}
```

In Listing 11.8, the `EmployeeDB` class is all about handling JDBC statements. We have created various methods to perform different database operations. The methods of the EmployeeDB class are as follows:

- boolean checkEmployee(int empid)
- ArrayList<Employee> getEmployees()
- Employee getEmployee(int empid)

- void addEmployee(Employee emp)
- int updateEmployee(Employee employee)
- int deleteEmployee(int id)

The names of these methods are self-explanatory for the functions they perform. Their return types and the argument types further describe their usage in the backing bean.

Creating the **EmailValidator** Class

We have used a custom validator to validate the email id of an employee. The custom validator is used with the `HtmlInputText` component in the `addnew.jsp` and `edit.jsp` pages, as shown in the following code snippet:

```
<h:inputText id="email" value="#{employee.email}" size="30">
   <f:validator validatorId="emailValidator"/>
</h:inputText>
```

In the preceding code snippet, we have created a custom validator by implementing the `javax.faces.validator.Validator` interface and defining its `validate()` method. The logic implemented to validate a string for a valid email id is shown in Listing 11.9 (save this file in the `\KogentPro\src\com\kogent\validator\` folder):

Listing 11.9: Showing the Code of the EmailValidator.java File

```
package com.kogent.validator;

import java.util.regex.Pattern;
import java.util.regex.Matcher;

import javax.faces.application.FacesMessage;
import javax.faces.component.UIComponent;
import javax.faces.component.html.HtmlInputText;
import javax.faces.context.FacesContext;
import javax.faces.validator.Validator;
import javax.faces.validator.ValidatorException;

public class EmailValidator implements Validator {

public void validate(FacesContext facesContext, UIComponent uiComponent, Object value)
   throws ValidatorException {

         String patternStr = ".+@.+\\.[a-z]+"; // For Email
         Pattern pattern = Pattern.compile(patternStr);

         // Passed Value must be type cast into CharSequence
         Matcher matcher = pattern.matcher((CharSequence)value);
         boolean matchFound = matcher.matches();
         if (!matchFound){
                HtmlInputText htmlInputText = (HtmlInputText) uiComponent;
                FacesMessage facesMessage = new FacesMessage(htmlInputText.getLabel()+ ":
                Email Format is not valid");
                throw new ValidatorException(facesMessage);
         }
   }
}
```

After compiling the validator class and placing it in the application's classpath, the custom validator should be registered in the `faces-config.xml` file. The registration of custom validator is required to define its identifier, which is used by the input components. The `com.kogent.validator.EmailValidator` class has been registered in the `faces-config.xml` file, as shown in the following code snippet:

```
<validator>
   <validator-id>emailValidator</validator-id>
   <validator-class>com.kogent.validator.EmailValidator</validator-class>
</validator>
```

Now, let's learn about configuring a JSF application.

Configuring a JSF Application

Configuring a JSF application involves setting the `web.xml` and `faces-config.xml` files. The setting provided in deployment descriptor includes configuring `FacesServlet`, whereas configuring the `faces-config.xml` file includes navigation rules to be followed by the navigation handler, managing backing beans, and registering custom validator used in a Web application.

Enabling JSF Servlet in the web.xml File

A JSF-based application needs all JSF requests to be handled by the `FacesServlet` class. Listing 11.10 shows the code to define `FacesServlet` and provide a servlet mapping for `FacesServlet` in the deployment descriptor (save this file in the \KogentPro\WEB-INF\folder):

Listing 11.10: Showing the Code of the web.xml File

```
<?xml version="1.0" encoding="UTF-8"?>
<web-app xmlns=http:// xmlns.jcp.org/xml/ns/javaee
  xmlns:xsi="http://www.w3.org/2001/XMLSchema-instance" version="23.0"
  xsi:schemaLocation="http:// xmlns.jcp.org/xml/ns/javaee
  http:// xmlns.jcp.org/xml/ns/javaee/web-app_3_1.xsd">

  <servlet>
        <servlet-name>Faces Servlet</servlet-name>
        <servlet-class>javax.faces.webapp.FacesServlet</servlet-class>
        <load-on-startup>0</load-on-startup>
  </servlet>

  <servlet-mapping>
        <servlet-name>Faces Servlet</servlet-name>
        <url-pattern>*.faces</url-pattern>
  </servlet-mapping>

  <welcome-file-list>
        <welcome-file>index.jsp</welcome-file>
  </welcome-file-list>
</web-app>
```

In Listing 11.10, we have used a `*.faces` as the url pattern, which tells that all requests ending with `.faces` will be mapped to `FacesServlet` and handled by the JSF engine. If you need to access the `edit.jsp` page, which is a JSF page, you can access it by requesting the `edit.faces` page.The `index.jsp` page is a welcome file that is forwarded to the `home.jsp` page that requests a JSF Servlet for `home.faces` page..

Navigation Rules Defined in the faces-config.xml File

All the navigation rules for the application are defined in the `faces-config.xml` file. Different action methods are used to return string as an outcome and navigation handler to search for navigation cases defined for matching outcome string to load the next view for the user. All the navigation rules defined in the `faces-config.xml` file are shown in Listing 11.11 (save this file in the \KogentPro\WEB-INF\ folder):

Listing 11.11: Showing the Navigation Rules Provided in faces-config.xml File

```
<?xml version='1.0' encoding='UTF-8'?>
<faces-config xmlns="http:// xmlns.jcp.org/xml/ns/javaee"
  xmlns:xsi="http://www.w3.org/2001/XMLSchema-instance"
xsi:schemaLocation="http:// xmlns.jcp.org/xml/ns/javaee
  http:// xmlns.jcp.org/xml/ns/javaee/web-facesconfig_2_2.xsd"
  version="2.2">

  <navigation-rule>
        <from-view-id>*</from-view-id>
        <navigation-case>
              <from-outcome>home</from-outcome>
              <to-view-id>/home.jsp</to-view-id>
        </navigation-case>
  </navigation-rule>
```

```
<navigation-rule>
      <from-view-id>*</from-view-id>
      <navigation-case>
            <from-outcome>addnew</from-outcome>
            <to-view-id>/addnew.jsp</to-view-id>
      </navigation-case>
</navigation-rule>
<navigation-rule>
      <from-view-id>*</from-view-id>
      <navigation-case>
            <from-outcome>viewall</from-outcome>
            <to-view-id>/viewall.jsp</to-view-id>
      </navigation-case>
</navigation-rule>
<navigation-rule>
      <from-view-id>*</from-view-id>
      <navigation-case>
            <from-outcome>edit</from-outcome>
            <to-view-id>/edit.jsp</to-view-id>
      </navigation-case>
</navigation-rule>

<navigation-rule>
      <from-view-id>/addnew.jsp</from-view-id>
      <navigation-case>
            <from-outcome>success</from-outcome>
            <to-view-id>/viewall.jsp</to-view-id>
      </navigation-case>
      <navigation-case>
            <from-outcome>failure</from-outcome>
            <to-view-id>/addnew.jsp</to-view-id>
      </navigation-case>
</navigation-rule>

<navigation-rule>
      <from-view-id>/edit.jsp</from-view-id>
      <navigation-case>
            <from-outcome>success</from-outcome>
            <to-view-id>/viewall.jsp</to-view-id>
      </navigation-case>
      <navigation-case>
            <from-outcome>failure</from-outcome>
            <to-view-id>/edit.jsp</to-view-id>
      </navigation-case>
</navigation-rule>

<navigation-rule>
      <from-view-id>/viewall.jsp</from-view-id>
      <navigation-case>
            <from-outcome>detail</from-outcome>
            <to-view-id>/detail.jsp</to-view-id>
      </navigation-case>
</navigation-rule>

</faces-config>
```

In Listing 11.11, we have defined different global navigation rules for outcome strings, `home`, `addnew`, `viewall`, and `edit`. The navigation handler loads, `home.jsp`, `addnew.jsp`, `viewall.jsp`, and `edit.jsp` respectively with outcome strings. All navigation rules and cases are shown in Figure 11.10:

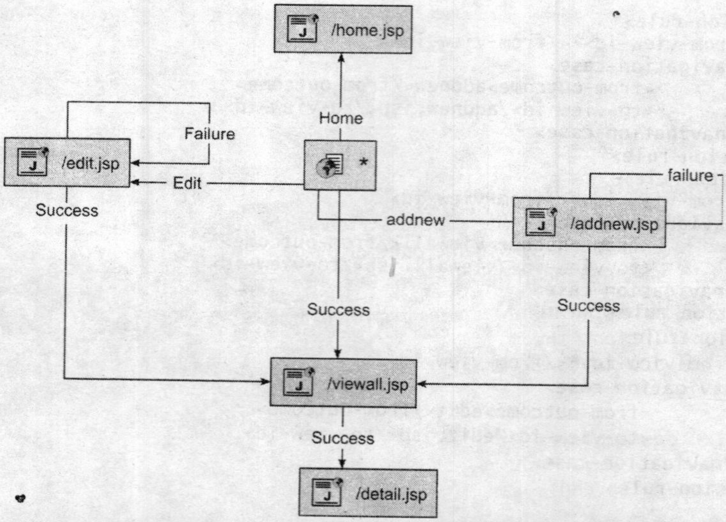

Figure 11.10: Showing the Various Navigational Paths from View to View

Let's learn about internationalization.

Supporting Internationalization

All the Locales supported by an application need to be configured in the `faces-config.xml` file. In addition, the location of resource bundle containing custom and localized messages is also placed under the `<application>` element, as shown in the following code snippet:

```
<application>

   <locale-config>
         <supported-locale>en</supported-locale>
         <supported-locale>fr</supported-locale>
   </locale-config>

   <message-bundle>com.kogent.ApplicationMessages</message-bundle>
</application>
```

In the preceding code snippet, we have created a resource bundle by the base name, `ApplicaitonMessages`. There are two different properties files containing custom messages to support two different Locales, English (`en`) and French (`fr`). The key and corresponding messages created to support default Locale is `ApplicationMessages_en.properties` file, as shown in Listing 11.12 (save this file in the `\KogentPro\WEB-INF\classes\com\kogent\` folder):

Listing 11.12: Showing the ApplicationMessages_en.properties File

```
header=Kogent Solutions Inc.
footer=All rights are reserved with Kogent Solutions Inc.
home=Home
addnew=Add Employee
edit=Edit Employee
viewall=View All Employees
delete=Delete
update=Update
reset=Reset

details=Details
enterid=Enter Employee ID
empid=Employee ID
```

```
empname=Employee Name
address=Address

city=City
email=E-mail
sex=Sex
department=Department
skills=Skills
joindate=Joining Date
```

In Listing 11.12, the other properties file supports French Locale and has the same set of keys but with all messages translated to French. The key/value pairs of the `ApplicationMessages_fr.properties` file are shown in Listing 11.13 (save this file in the `\KogentPro\WEB-INF\classes\com\kogent\` folder):

Listing 11.13: Showing the ApplicationMessages_fr.properties File

```
header=Kogent Solutions Inc.
footer=Tous les droits sont réservés par Kogent Solutions Inc
home=Accueil

addnew=Ajouter des employés
edit=Edit Employee
viewall=Voir tous les employés

delete=Supprimer
update=Update
reset=Reset
details=Détails

enterid=Entrez ID employé
empid=ID employé
empname=Employee Nom
address=Adresse

city=Ville
email=E-mail
sex=Sexe

department=Département
skills=Compétences

joindate=Participer Date
```

In the preceding code snippet, both the properties files, ApplicationMessages_en.properties and ApplicationMessages_fr.properties are placed in the com\kogent folder in the classes folder of the KogentPro application (Figure 11.6).

Exploring the Directory Structure of the Application

Let's create the KogentPro folder to place all the components of the KogenPro application. Figure 11.11 shows the directory structure of the KogentPro JSF application:

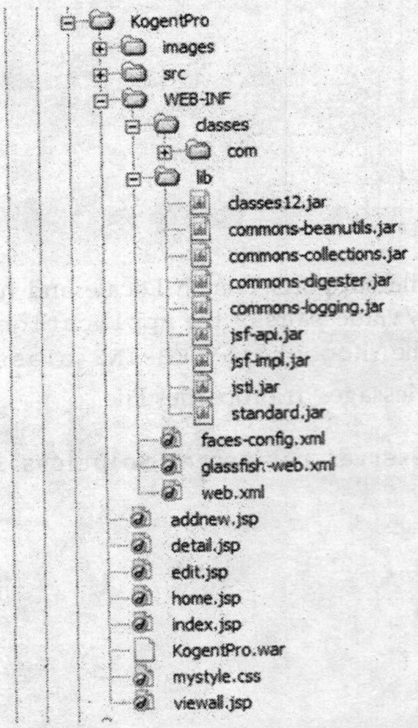

Figure 11.11: Displaying the Directory Structure of KogentPro Application

Let's now run the application.

Running the KogentPro Application

After successfully deploying the KogentPro application, you can launch the KogentPro application and access the home page, as shown in Figure 11.12:

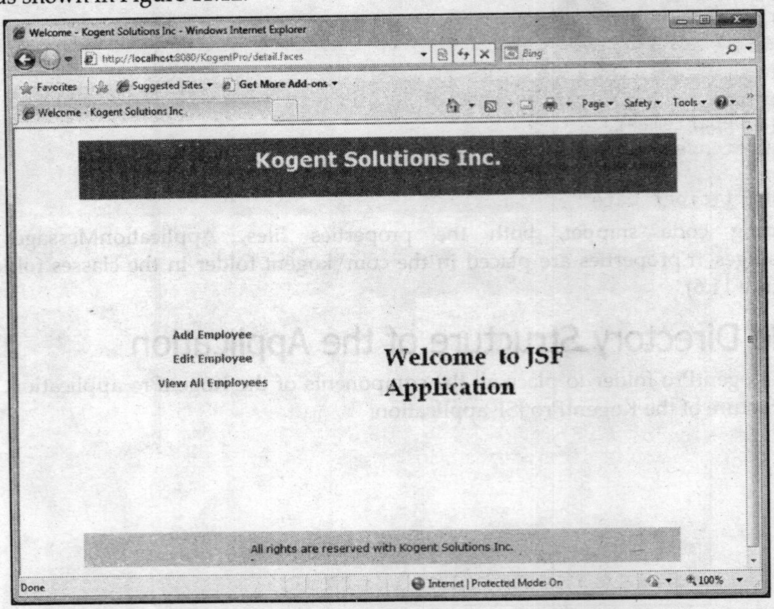

Figure 11.12: Displaying the Home Page of the KogentPro Application

You can also use the three `HtmlCommandLink` components created in the `home.jsp page` to navigate to other views.

Displaying All Employees

You can also click link `View All Employees` (Figure 11.12) to invoke the associated action method, `employee.getEmployees()`. This method returns `viewall` as the outcome string. Consequently, the navigation handler loads the `viewall.jsp page`, which displays all existing employees, as shown in Figure 11.13:

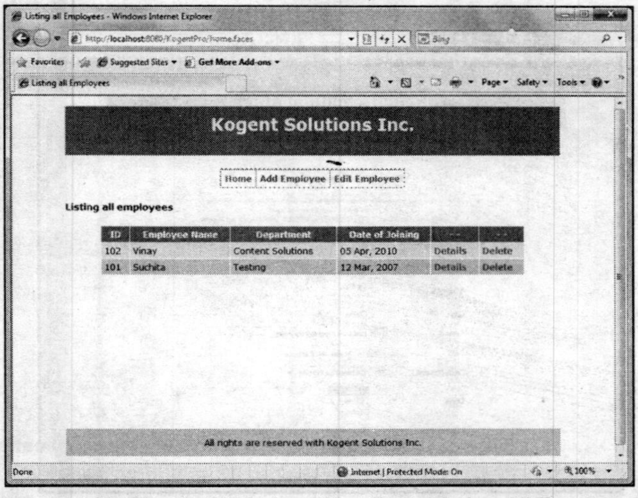

Figure 11.13: Showing the viewall.jsp Page Listing All Employees

In Figure 11.13, the `viewall.jsp` page uses an `HtmlDataTable` component, which iterates on an `ArrayList` of `Employee` objects and processes these objects to renderer rows of the table.

Getting Employee Detail

The `HtmlCommandLink` component (Figure 11.13) with the name, `Details` can be clicked to invoke the associated action method, `employee.getDetail()`. This method sets the given `employee id` in the request scope and returns `Details` as the outcome string. The output `of` the `details.jsp page is` Listing 11.11 shown in Figure 11.14:

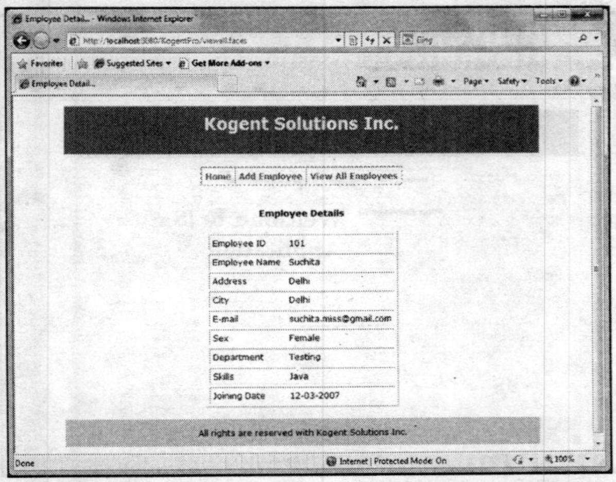

Figure 11.14: Displaying the details JSFPage Showing Employee Details

When you click the Details link of employee with id 101 (Figure 11.13), the details are displayed (Figure 11.14).

Adding New Employee

The `HtmlCommandLink` components is added on almost all pages created in the `KogentPro` application with the text, `Add Employee`, which can be clicked to navigate to the `addnew.jsp` page. This page provides a form with various input field (Figure 11.15). The `HtmlMessages` component used in the `addnew.jsp` page displays all validation and conversion error messages, as shown in Figure 11.15:

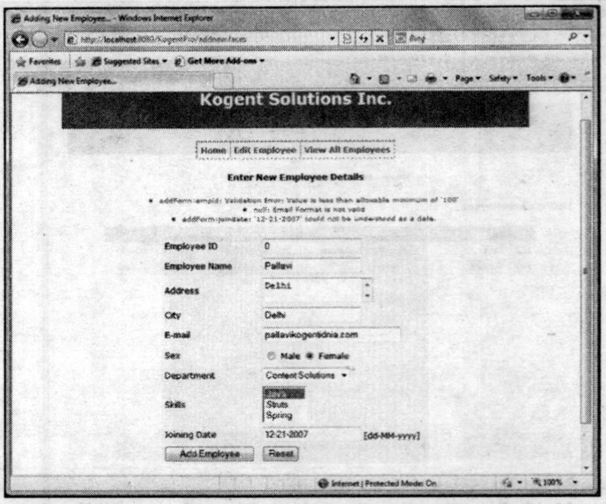

Figure 11.15: Displaying the addnew.jsp Page Showing Validation and Conversion Error Messages

You can submit the addNew form with valid employee id, valid email id, and date of joining for successful addition of new employee in the database. The successful addition of an employee displays the `viewall.jsp` page containing the details of the newly added employee.

Editing Employee Detail

You can access the `edit.jsp` page by clicking the `HtmlCommandLink` component showing the text, `Edit Employee`. The `viewall.jsp` page initially displays a form with single input field for entering employee id to be edited, as shown in Figure 11.16:

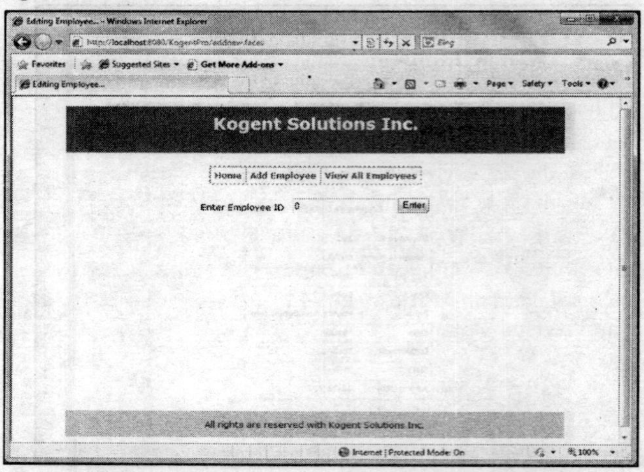

Figure 11.16: Displaying the addnew JSF Page Showing One Input Field

In Figure 11.16, we have used another `HtmlForm` component in the `edit.jsp` page, which has not been rendered, as its `render` attribute is set to `false`. The action listener method, `employee.getEmployee()` sets the `render` property of this `HtmlForm` component to `true` after setting the requested employee in the request scope. The editForm appears, as shown in Figure 11.17:

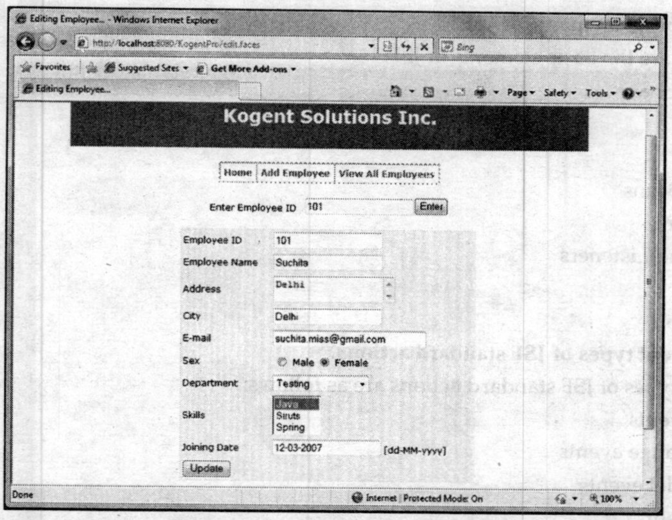

Figure 11.17: Displaying the edit.jsp Page Showing editForm Populated with the Employee Detail

You can modify the detail of an employee and submit the form by clicking the `Update` button, which executes the `employee.update()` method.

Deleting Employee

You can use the `HtmlCommandLink` components created in the `viewall.jsp` page corresponding to each row for individual employee to delete a particular employee. The associated backing bean method executed to delete an employee is `employee.deleteEmployee()`.

You have learned about various JSF pages using different UI components, implementing backing bean and action methods with all declaration of navigation rules, and managing bean in the `faces-config.xml` file.

Summary

In this chapter, we have discussed about the UI framework, JSF. The chapter describes all elements of the JSF framework, such as UI components, backing beans, validators, converters, and event handlers. Various phases of JSF request processing life cycle are also described in detail to clearly display the actual flow in the framework.

All JSF HTML and core tags have been explained with examples and their attributes. The backing bean concept and managed bean facility are the key features of JSF. Further, the chapter discusses JSF's support for input validation, type conversion, and Internationalization.

The chapter includes a full discussion on the development of various components, their implementation and configuration through a running Web application, named KogentPro.

The next chapter discusses JavaMail API in detail and demonstrates its implementation with the help of an application of sending and receiving mail.

Quick Revise

Q1. What is JSF?

Ans. JSF can be defined as a framework, which makes Web application development easy by providing rich, powerful, and ready to use UI components.

Q2. JSF architecture is designed based on .... pattern.

Ans. MVC

Q3. What are the basic elements of JSF?

Ans. The following are the basic elements of JSF:

- UI Component
- Renderer
- Validator
- Backing Beans
- Converter
- Events and Listeners
- Message
- Navigation

Q4. List the different types of JSF standard actions.

Ans. The different types of JSF standard actions are as follows:

- Action events
- Value-change events
- Data model events
- Phase events

Q5. Write the element of the faces configuration file that describes the navigation rules of a JSF view.

Ans. The code that describes navigation rules is as follows:

```
<navigation-rule>
<from-view-id>/login.jsp</from-view-id>
<navigation-case>
<from-outcome>success</from-outcome>
<to-view-id>/welcome.jsp</to-view-id>
</navigation-case>
<navigation-case>
<from-outcome>failure</from-outcome>
<to-view-id>/login.jsp</to-view-id>
</navigation-case>
```

Q6. List the six phases of the JSF request processing life cycle.

Ans. The six phases of the JSF request-processing life cycle are as follow:

- Restore View
- Apply Request View
- Process Validation
- Update Model Values
- Invoke Application
- Render Response

Q7. Which JSF UI component's values are validated in the Apply Request Values phase of the JSF request processing?

Ans. All the JSF UI components configured with immediate property set to true are validated in Apply Request Values phase of JSF request processing.

Q8. The commandButton element is described under the .... JSF tag library.

Ans. HTML

Q9. Write the URI used to refer the JSF HTML tag library.

Ans. http://java.sun.com/jsf/html

12

Understanding JavaMail 1.5

JavaMail is a platform and protocol-independent technology, which is developed by Sun Microsystems to create E-mail applications with the help of the Java programming language. JavaMail provides JavaMail Application Programming Interface (API), which is used to create Java-based E-mail client applications. These E-mail client applications use various protocols, such as Simple Mail Transfer Protocol (SMTP) and Internet Message Access Protocol (IMAP) to transfer E-mails. The SMTP protocol is a mail transfer protocol used to send and receive an E-mail; whereas, IMAP is an Internet protocol that enables an E-mail client to retrieve the E-mails from a mail server. Apart from supporting various protocols, Java-based E-mail client applications provide various features, such as customized personal E-mail applications and the ability to add E-mail functionality to an enterprise application. The latest version of the JavaMail technology is 1.5 that is used in the Java EE 7 platform.

JavaMail consists of various components, such as abstract layer, Internet implementation layer, and JavaBeans Activation Framework (JAF). The abstract layer component consists of classes, interfaces, and abstract methods that perform E-mail handling functions, which are expected to be provided by all E-mail systems. The Internet implementation layer component provides implementation to the abstract layer component with the help of standards defined by RFC822, which is a standard for Internet text message format. Multipurpose Internet Mail Extensions (MIME) is a standard that enables you to include non-ASCII characters in E-mails, such as non-text attachments. ASCII stands for American Standard Code for Information Interchange. JAF encapsulates message data and manages commands needed to make data interaction possible.

In this chapter, you learn about JavaMail, its architecture, and the JavaMail API. You will explore new features introduced in JavaMail 1.5. The chapter also discusses classes, such as Folder, Message, Multipart, Address, and interfaces, such as Part and QuotaAware of the JavaMail API. In the end, you learn how to create E-mail client applications by using the JavaMail API.

Let's start with an overview of JavaMail.

Introducing JavaMail

JavaMail is a technology that provides a protocol-independent framework to create Java-based E-mail client applications. It supports various E-mail protocols, such as HyperText Transfer Protocol (HTTP) and Post Office Protocol (POP). Classes and interfaces of the JavaMail API are utilized to create E-mail client applications. The JavaMail API is broadly divided into the following two parts:

- The first part of the JavaMail API is concerned with how to send and receive messages in a provider/protocol independent manner.
- The second part of the JavaMail API provides the classes and interfaces to use the communication protocols, such as SMTP, POP, IMAP, and News Network Transport Protocol (NNTP), used for transferring E-mails.

To understand the JavaMail API in detail, you first need to understand few important terms related to E-mail, which are as follows:

- **E-mail client**—Refers to an application that is used to compose, read, and send E-mails.
- **Mail server**—Refers to an application that receives E-mails from E-mail client applications or other mail servers. It stores the messages until they are read or deleted by the E-mail client. A computer that is used especially to run applications which receive E-mails from E-mail client applications and various other mail servers is called a mail server. Some examples of mail servers are Eudora's mail server, Microsoft Exchange server, Microsoft Windows POP3 service, and WinGate.
- **Messaging system**—Provides an E-mail delivery system to send and receive E-mails from the mail server. This messaging system is made up of the following functional components:
  - **Mail User Agent (MUA or UA)**—Represents a client E-mail application, such as Outlook and Eudora, which sends or receives a message to or from a mail server. When a user sends a message, MUA sends the message to the Message Transfer Agent (MTA), discussed in next bullet. This MTA passes the message to another MTA. This process continues till the message reaches the mail server.
  - **Message Transfer Agent**—Serves as an agent who is responsible for sending and delivering E-mails between machines, as well as queuing of messages. MTA stores incoming E-mails and delivers them to the right recipient. The most commonly-used MTAs on the Internet `are Sendmail` and `PostFix`. A large organization may have several MTA servers for sending and delivering E-mails over the Internet.

The components (MUA and MTA) of the messaging system are packaged together to successfully send and receive E-mails from the mail server.

- **Message Delivery Agent (MDA)**—Stores a message into an E-mail client's mailbox. As the message reaches to its destination, i.e. correct mail server, an intermediate MTA gives the message to the final MTA. The message is then passed on to an MDA that adds it to the client's mailbox.
- **Message store (MS)**—Serves as a user mailbox that holds E-mails until they are read and deleted by the user.
- **SMTP**—Refers to a protocol that is used to send and receive an E-mail over the Internet.

Apart from the plain text content, an E-mail can also contain Uniform Resource Locator (URL) pages and files sent as attachments. To read such type of content, JavaMail API uses the JAF framework. This framework allows you to identify the type of data contained in an E-mail, access the data, and instantiate the relevant bean to perform the desired operation on the data.

Let's now discuss the protocols used with the JavaMail API.

Exploring the E-Mail Protocols

E-mail protocols can be defined as a set of some rules, formats, and functions used to exchange messages between the components of a messaging system. The JavaMail API provides five protocols, which are as follows:

- SMTP
- POP3
- IMAP
- NNTP
- MIME

Let's discuss these protocols in detail.

SMTP

SMTP is a standard protocol used to transfer E-mails over the Internet. It uses Transmission Control Protocol (TCP)/Internet Protocol (IP) port 25 or 2525 to send the messages to the recipients. SMTP acts just as a delivery agent to transfer messages and is open to abuse by spammers, who usually send numerous unsolicited mails over the Internet. Due to this reason, many system administrators have blocked or restricted the capability of their SMTP protocol of receiving E-mails from the E-mail clients.

In the context of JavaMail API, a JavaMail E-mail client application communicates with a mail server or SMTP server to send or receive E-mails. This SMTP server sends the message onto the recipient SMTP server with the help of POP or IMAP protocol.

POP3

The POP3 protocol allows E-mail client to collect, download, store, and remove the E-mails from the mail server. This protocol describes how E-mail clients interact with E-mail POP3 servers. The POP3 server is a mail server type used to store incoming E-mails, which are collected, downloaded, stored, and removed by the E-mail clients from the POP3 server. The E-mail client application usually connects to a POP3 server to download messages. Some of the popular POP3 servers are Mozilla Thunderbird, Opera, Eudora, KMail, and Novell Evolution.

IMAP

IMAP is a protocol that is used by many E-mail clients to access the E-mails from the mail server. The latest version of IMAP is 4.7. In POP3, the user is responsible for storing E-mails; whereas, in case of IMAP, the server is responsible for storing an E-mail. The main advantage of IMAP over POP3 is that it stores all the incoming E-mails on the mail server, so the E-mail client, having Internet connection, can connect to the mail server and access all his or her E-mails.

The client that uses the POP3 protocol to retrieve an E-mail from the mail server needs to download the E-mail from the mail server to read it. However, if an E-mail is sent through the IMAP protocol, it is stored on the server and the client can directly access it from the server instead of downloading it on his machine.

NNTP

NNTP is an Internet protocol that is used to view and post Usenet articles, which are articles posted to the worldwide discussion group Usenet, as well as share news among news servers. In other words, NNTP is a protocol used to transfer news and articles between a news server and a newsreader.

`Newsreader` is a client program that is used to read messages from discussion groups over the Internet. A newsreader can be a stand-alone application or part of an E-mail program or a Web browser. News server is a server that hosts newsgroups on the Internet.

Examples of some `newsgroup` servers are as follows:

- Giganews (http://www.giganews.com)
- Rhino News (http://www.rhinonewsgroups.com)
- Power Usenet (http://www.powerusenet.com)

MIME

The text content should always be converted into an ASCII format before it is transmitted over the network. Therefore, a standard format is required to encode the binary files (non-ASCII) into the ASCII text format and to decode them again from ASCII to the non-ASCII format. MIME is used in Internet communications to enable the users to attach formatted document in non-ASCII format, such as graphics, audio, video, spreadsheets, and Adobe Acrobat files, in the E-mails. For example, a user writes the message in non-ASCII format, which is then encoded by MIME into ASCII format for the successful transmission over the Internet. When an E-mail client receives the message in ASCII format, the message is again decoded into its original non-ASCII format so that the receiver could read the message. In messages with a Hypertext Markup Language (HTML) attachment, the MIME type header is set to text/html. In addition to the E-mail applications, Web browsers also support other MIME types, such as application/zip and image/gif.

After having a brief understanding about the mail protocols, let's discuss the role of these protocols in establishing communication between an E-mail client and E-mail server.

Establishing Communication between an E-mail Client and E-mail Server

Now, let's see how an E-mail client and an E-mail server interact with each other to send and receive mails. While sending an E-mail, the E-mail server first finds the sender's E-mail address by using Domain Name System (DNS), which is a hierarchical naming system used to identify computers, resources, and services over the Internet, and the SMTP protocol. Then, the E-mail server sends the mail to the E-mail client.

Figure 12.1 shows the process of interaction between the E-mail client and the E-mail server:

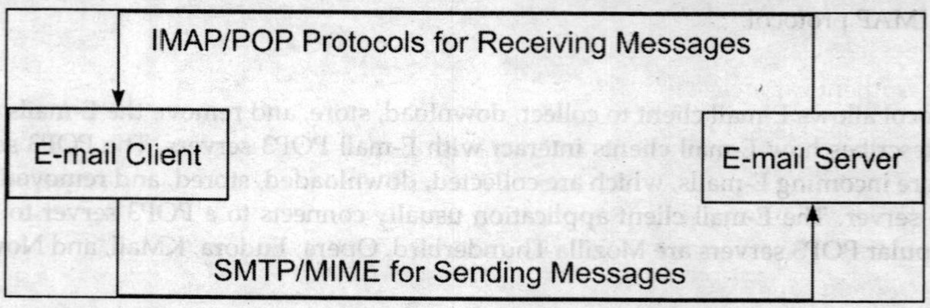

Figure 12.1: Showing the Process of Sending and Receiving Messages

Figure 12.1 shows how the SMTP and IMAP/POP protocols are used to maintain interaction between E-mail client and E-mail server. Let's now discuss the JavaMail architecture.

Exploring the JavaMail Architecture

The JavaMail architecture can be divided into three main layers, the application layer, the JavaMail API, and the implementation layer. This layered architecture permits clients to use the JavaMail API with different protocols, such as POP3, IMAP4, and SMTP, to create an E-mail client application.

Figure 12.2 shows the JavaMail architecture:

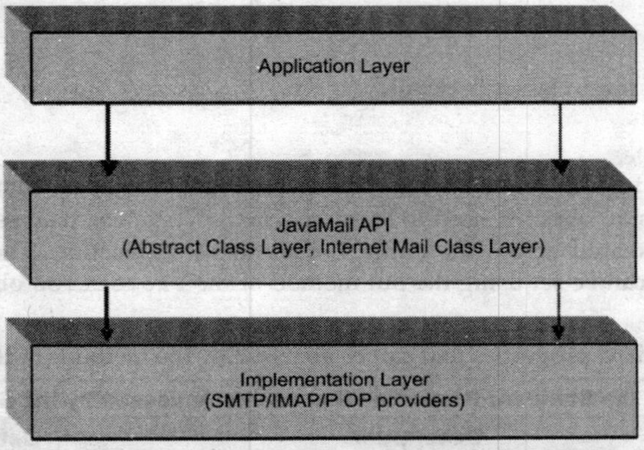

Figure 12.2: Showing the JavaMail Architecture

The application layer is the topmost layer. It uses the JavaMail API to communicate with the E-mail client application. The second layer is the JavaMail API, which is a set of classes and interfaces used to support E-mail client functionality. This layer helps to create E-mail client applications. The implementation layer is the bottom layer of the JavaMail architecture, which uses various protocols, such as POP3, IMAP, and SMTP, to transfer messages between the E-mail client and the mail server.

You can use the classes and interfaces of the JavaMail API to create a JavaMail application. Therefore, you should have a fair knowledge about the JavaMail API, which is discussed in the following section.

Exploring the JavaMail API

As discussed, the JavaMail API provides a set of classes and interfaces to create Java-based E-mail applications. JavaMail API supplies a set of classes and interfaces that enables you to create platform-independent and protocol-independent messaging applications. Some of the important classes and interfaces provided by JavaMail API are as follows:

- The Session class
- The Authenticator class
- The Message class
- The MimeMessage class
- The Part interface
- The MultiPart class
- The ContentType class
- The MimeBodyPart class
- The PreencodedMimeBodyPart class
- The MimeUtility class
- The InternetHeader class
- The ParameterList class
- The QuotaAwareStore interface
- The Resource class
- The Quota class

- The SharedFileInputStream class
- The SharedByteArrayInputStream class
- The ByteArrayDataSource class
- The Address class
- The Store class
- The Folder class
- The Transport class

Let's now discuss each of these classes in detail.

The Session Class

The `javax.mail.Session` class defines the mail session that is used to communicate with remote systems through its object. A session object is used to store information, such as mail server, username, password, and other data that can be shared across the entire E-mail client application. The JavaMail API supports some standard properties that can be set using the put method of the `Properties` object, which is used to create the `session` object.

Table 12.1 describes standard properties that can be accessed by the methods of the `Session` class:

Table 12.1: Explaining the Standard Properties that can be Accessed by the Session Class

Property	Description	Default Value
`mail.transport.protocol`	Represents the default transport protocol. An object that implements this transport protocol is returned when the getTransport() method of the Session class is called.	SMTP
`mail.store.protocol`	Represents the default store protocol. An object that implements this store protocol is returned when the getStore() method of the Session class is called.	POP3
`mail.host`	Represents the default host name of a mail server. Both the transport and host protocols use the host name specified in the E-mail client application, if their own host name is not specified.	Local Machine
`mail.user`	Represents the default user name to connect to a mail server. Both the transport and store protocols use the user name, which is specified in an E-Mail client application.	`user.name`
`mail.from`	Specifies an address of the current user.	`username@host`
`mail.protocol.host`	Specifies the IP address of the default mail server.	`mail.host`
`mail.protocol.user`	Overrides the mail.user standard property with respect to the specified protocol.	`mail.user`
`mail.debug`	Helps to print debug messages of the E-mail client application, when set to true. When the mail.debug property is set to false, the debug messages are not printed.	False

After learning about the standard properties that can be accessed by the Session class, let's learn to create a session object. The constructors of the Session class are private; however, you can get the instance of a session object with the help of the `getInstance()` static method of the Session class. A single default session, which can be shared among multiple applications running in the same Java Virtual Machine (JVM), is returned when the `getDefaultInstance()` static method of the Session class is invoked. The following code snippet shows the use of the `getDefaultInstance()` method:

```
Properties props = new Properties();
// filling props with information
props.put("mail.transport.protocol","smtp");
props.put("mail.smtp.host","yourmail.yourserver.com");
props.put("mail.smtp.port","25");
Session session = Session.getDefaultInstance(props);
```

You can create a private session by calling the `getInstance(Properties prop)` method in the same manner as given in the preceding code snippet.

Table 12.2 describes methods of the `Session` class:

Table 12.2: Describing the Methods of the Session Class

Method	Description
`void addProvider (Provider provider)`	Allows you to add a provider passed through the method to a session object.
`boolean getDebug()`	Returns the debug setting for a session object.
`static Session getDefaultInstance (java.util.Properties props)`	Returns the default session object. In case a default session object does not exist, a new session object is created and considered as default. The `props` parameter passed to the `getDefaultInstance()` method stores properties, such as host name, user name, and protocol used.
`static Session getDefaultInstance (java.util.Properties props, Authenticator authenticator)`	Returns the default session object. In case a default session object does not exist, a new session object is created and considered as default. The authenticator parameter passed to this method specifies that if the authenticator object, which is used to check the access permission, is not available in the session object, a new authenticator object is created and added to the session object. Otherwise, an existing authenticator object available in the session object is used. The props parameter used in this method stores properties, such as host name, user name, and protocol used.
`Folder getFolder(URLName url) throws MessagingException`	Returns a closed folder object, a state in which certain operations are allowed on the folder object, for the url parameter passed to it. If the requested folder cannot be obtained, null is returned. The url parameter represents the desired folder object. This method throws the `MessagingException` exception when a folder object cannot be located or created.
`static Session getInstance (java.util.Properties props)`	Returns a new instance of the Session class. The props parameter stores properties, such as host name, user name, and protocol used.
`static Session getInstance (java.util.Properties props, Authenticator authenticator)`	Returns a new instance of the Session class. The props parameter of the getInstance() method stores properties, such as host name, user name, and protocol used. The authenticator parameter of the getInstance() method defines an authenticator object.
`PasswordAuthentication getPasswordAuthentication (URLName url)`	Returns the PasswordAuthentication object for store or transport URLName. This method is used usually with the store or transport protocol.
`java.util.Properties getProperties()`	Retrieves the properties object related with the current session.
`String getProperty (String name)`	Returns a value of the property whose name is passed to it. Returns null if the property does not exist.

Table 12.2: Describing the Methods of the Session Class

Method	Description
`Transport getTransport (Address address) throws NoSuchProviderException`	Returns a transport object that can send a message to the address passed to this method.
`Transport getTransport (String protocol) throws NoSuchProviderException`	Returns a transport object that implements the specified protocol. In case the transport object is not found, null is returned. This method throws the `NoSuchProviderException` exception when a `protocol` is not found.
`void setProvider (Provider provider)`	Allows you to add the specified provider to the current session.
`void setProtocolForAddress (String addresstype, String protocol)`	Sets the protocol address in the currently used transport protocol.

The Authenticator Class

The `javax.mail.Authenticator` class is used to obtain authentication for a network connection. Authentication is the process used to verify the validity of a user with the help of the login credentials provided by the user. You need to create an authenticator object and call its `getPasswordAuthentication()` method to authenticate the user or find if the user is valid or not. After creating the authenticator object, you must register it with the session object. The session object must have necessary authentication details to send and receive an E-mail.

The following code snippet shows how to register an authenticator object with the session object:

```
static Session getInstance(Properties prop,Authenticator auth);
static Session getDefaultInstance(Properties prop,Authenticator auth);
```

In the preceding code snippet, the props parameter passed to the `getInstance()` method of the Session class is the properties object that contains relevant properties. The auth parameter passed to the `getInstance()` method is an authenticator object used by an application to authenticate a user. In the `getDefaultInstance()` method of the Session object, the prop and auth parameters are the same as in the `getInstance()` method.

The Message Class

The `javax.mail.Message` class is an abstract class used to create a new mail message. All the message structures are based on this class. A mail message consists of the following two main components:

- **Header**—Contains information about message properties, such as subject field, recipient, and sender of the message
- **Content**—Represents the content of the message

The `Message` class implements the `javax.mail.Part` interface. To attach a file with a message, the `javax.mail.internet` package provides the `MimeMessage` class, which extends the `Message` class.

The MimeMessage Class

The `javax.mail.internet.MimeMessage` class is used to create a MIME message, which accepts MIME types and headers. To create a new MIME message, you need to create an empty MimeMessage object and then provide suitable attributes and content to it. The `MimeMessage` class provides two constructors, which are used to create a MIME message, as shown in the following code snippet:

```
Constructor 1    public MimeMessage(Session session)
Constructor 2    public MimeMessage(MimeMessage msg)
```

In the preceding code snippet, constructor 1 creates an empty `MimeMessage` object that is created by passing a session object as a parameter to this constructor. Constructor 2 creates a new `MimeMessage` instance by passing the `MimeMessage` object as a parameter to this constructor.

Table 12.3 lists the methods of the `MimeMessage` class:

Table 12.3: Describing the Methods of the MimeMessage Class

Method	Description
`void addFrom(Address[] addresses)`	Allows you to add multiple addresses that are stored in the addresses parameter to the From property of the MimeMessage class.
`void setRecipients(Message.RecipientType type, Address[] addresses)`	Allows you to set the recipient type specified by the type parameter to the multiple addresses that are stored in the addresses parameter.
`void setSubject(String subject)`	Sets the `Subject` header field. The value of the subject parameter of the `setSubject()` method is assigned to the `Subject` header field.
`void setText(String text)`	Sets a string, which is passed as the text parameter, to the content of a message, whose MIME type is text/plain.
`void setText(String text, String charset)`	Sets a string, which is passed as the text parameter, to the content of a message having MIME type text/plain and the charset as passed to the method.
`void setText(String text, String charset, String subtype)`	Sets a string, which is passed as the text parameter, to the content of a message having the text MIME type and the MIME subtype similar to the subtype parameter passed to this method. Parameter charset represents the encoding scheme that specifies mapping of characters in text parameter string with 8 bits bytes.
`void setFileName (String filename)`	Sets the filename related to a message. In case, the value of the `mail.mime.encodefilename` System property is true, the `MimeMessage` and `MimeBodyPart` `setFileName()` methods invoke the `MimeUtility.encodeText()` method to encode the filename. When the `mail.mime.encodefilename` System property is false, they invoke the `MimeUtility.decodeText()` method to decode the filename. You should note that by default the value of both the properties are set to false.
`void updateMessageID() throws MessagingException:`	Allows you to update the Message-ID header. This method is called by the `updateHeaders()` method of the `MimeMessage` class, which makes it possible to override the algorithm written for selecting a Message-ID.
`MimeMessage createMimeMessage(Session session) throws MessagingException`	Allows you to create and get a `MimeMessage` object.

The most common properties used with the `MimeMessage` class are as follows:

- The From property
- The To, CC, BCC properties
- The Reply-To property
- The Subject property
- The other property

Let's now discuss each of these properties, one by one.

Using the From Property

The `From` property depicts the source of an E-mail message. The `Message` class has a set of methods, such as `getFrom()` and `setFrom()`, to set and get data from this property. The `getFrom()` method is used to get the

E-mail addresses from the `From` property. The following code snippet shows the syntax to read the value of the `From` property:

```
void Address[] getFrom();
```

In the preceding code snippet, an array of E-mail addresses is retrieved from the `javax.mail.Address` object.

The `setFrom()` method is used to set an E-mail address in the `From` property, as shown in the following code snippet:

```
void setFrom(javax.mail.Address senderAddress)
```

Using To, CC, BCC Properties

The `To` property is used to specify recipients of the E-mail message. The carbon copy (`CC`) property is used to specify other recipients, which receive the copy of the original message. The Blind Carbon Copy (`BCC`) property is marked only to those recipients whose name you do not want to reveal to the other recipients of the E-mail.

Using the Reply-To Property

The `Reply-To` property is used to reply an E-mail. The following code snippet shows the implementation of the Reply-to property by using the `setReplyTo()` method:

```
void setReplyTo(Address myaddress);
```

If you do not make a call to the `setReplyTo()` method, then a null argument is set in this method, which means the Reply-To property is not included in the message header of the resulting mail message. The following code snippet shows how to retrieve the `Reply-To header` field:

```
Address[ ] getReplyTo().
```

If header is not present, the `getReplyTo()` method returns the `From` field value.

Using the Subject property

The `Subject` property represents the subject of an E-mail. You can set the value of the `Subject` property by using the `setSubject()` method. The following code snippet shows how to set the Subject property:

```
message.setSubject("MySubject");
```

In the preceding code snippet, the subject of an E-mail is set by using the `setSubject()` method.

Using the Other property

The other property is used to set or get a new header of an E-mail. The following code snippet shows how to set a new header:

```
void setHeader(String username,String passvalue);
```

The following code snippet shows how to get a new header:

```
String getHeader (String username,String delimiter);
```

The Part Interface

The `javax.mail.Part` interface is used to create the message body. The `Part` interface consists of attributes, such as content type and content. The getter and setter methods for the attributes of the `Part` interface gets and sets the values of these attributes. The content attribute of the `Part` instance uses a MIME type, such as text/plain and text/html, to represent the type of data of the message.

Table 12.4 describes the methods of the *`Part`* interface:

Table 12.4: Describing the Methods of the Part Interface

Method	Description
`String getContentType()`	Returns content type of the content of a `Part` instance. Content type of an E-mail is the type of data it contains.
`Object getContent()`	Gets the content of the current `Part` instance as a Java object
`InputStream getInputStream()`	Returns an input stream of text content of an E-mail
`void writeTo(Outputstream os)`	Writes the data passed to it to the output stream of an E-mail
`boolean isMimeType`	Allows you to determine whether the MIME content type of the

Table 12.4: Describing the Methods of the Part Interface

Method	Description
`(String mimeType)`	current `Part` instance is same as the argument `mimeType` passed to it
`String getDescription()`	Allows you to get descriptive information, such as MIME type and file attachment, about the Part instance.
`void setDescription (String desc)`	Allows you to set descriptive notes about the `MimePart` instance
`void setDisposition (String disp)`	Allows you to set the file attachment in a body part of an E-mail
`String getFileName()`	Gets the name of the attachment file of the current Part instance
`void setFileName(String fname)`	Sets the name of the attachment file of the current Part instance
`int getSize()`	Retrieves the length of the content of the current `BodyPart` object in bytes

The JavaMail API provides the `MultiPart` class that implements the `Part` interface. A mail message is constructed using the `Part` interface as well as the `MultiPart` and `BodyPart` classes.

Figure 12.3 shows the use of the `Part` interface, the `MultiPart` class, and the `BodyPart` class in a complex mail message:

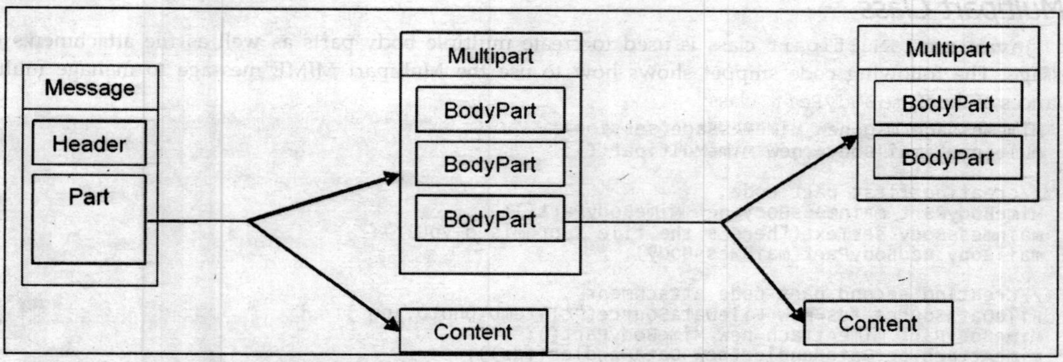

Figure 12.3: Showing the Structure of a Complex Mail Message

Figure 12.3 shows the concept of a complex E-mail implemented by the `Part` interface. In the first block, a message is built by the `Header` and `Part` components. The `Header` component contains information about message properties, such as subject field and recipient. The body of the message is represented by a customized `BodyPart` class that implements the `Part` interface. The `Part` component represents the message body that contains file attachments, which are represented by the `MultiPart` class and `Content`, as shown in the second block. In the second block, the `Multipart` class contains many BodyParts. Each of these BodyParts can further contain a file attachment that is represented using the `MultiPart` class and `Content`. As body of the E-mail message can only contain HTML content; therefore, JavaMail uses JAF to process E-mail content, when it contains non-HTML attachments, such as portable document format (PDF) file or graphics files.

JAF provides services to determine the type of data (PDF or graphic file), determine the operations available on the data, and instantiate the appropriate bean, which is a Java class that performs data access and storage functions to transfer the data to a recipient.

For example, if a browser obtains a PDF file, JAF would enable the browser to use MIME type to determine the type of the received data. This MIME type helps the browser to determine whether it can display the file itself or whether it has to invoke another helper application, such as acrobat reader for reading a PDF file.

JAF provides the `DataHandler` class that acts as the main interface of non-HTML data and handles necessary operations on that data. When the `Part` interface handles the content of an E-mail, all operations are performed through the `DataHandler` class.

Most common MIME types provided by the `DataHandler` class are as follows:

- **text/plain**—Helps in processing only ASCII text messages
- **text/html**—Helps in processing HTML text messages
- **multipart/mixed**—Helps in processing non-HTML data

Now, let's use the `getContentType()` method to return the MIME type of the `DataHandler` object, as shown in the following code snippet:

```
MimeMessage msg=new MimeMessage(session);
String messageBody="Hello from my first E-mail with JavaMail";
DataHandler dh=new DataHandler(messageBody,"text/plain");
msg.setDataHandler(dh);
DataHandler dh=msg.getDataHandler();
if(dh.getContentType().equals("text/plain")) {
  String messageBody=(String)dh.getContent();
}
```

In the preceding code snippet, an object of the DataHandler class (dh) is created by supplying a string value (body of the message) and MIME type to the constructor of the *`DataHandler`* class. The dh object is then passed to the `setDataHandler()` method to create a message by using the `msg` object of the `MimeMessage` class. Similarly, the content stored in the object of the *`DataHandler`* class is retrieved by invoking the *`getContent()`* method on the *`DataHandler`* object.

The Multipart Class

The `javax.mail.Multipart` class is used to create multiple body parts as well as file attachments of a message. The following code snippet shows how to use the Multipart MIME message to manage multiple instances of the `MimeBodyPart` class:

```
MimeMessage msg=new MimeMessage(session);
Multipart mailBody= new MimeMultipart();

//creating first part code
MimeBodyPart mainmessBody=new MimeBodyPart();
mainmessBody.setText("here's the file I promised you.");
mailBody.addBodyPart(mainmessBody);

//creating second part code,attachment
FileDataSource fds=new FileDataSource("c:\temp\photo.jpg");
MimeBodyPart mimeAttach=new MimeBodyPart();
mimeAttach.setDataHandler(new DataHandler(fds));
mimeAttach.setFileName(fds.getName());
mailBody.addBodyPart(mimeAttach);

msg.setContent(mailBody);
```

In the preceding code snippet, we have created a new instance of the `MimeMultipart` class that acts as a container for multiple instances of the Part interface. The path of the file to be attached to a message is stored in the `FileDataSource` object. In our case, the path of the photo.jpg file is stored in the `fds` object of the `FileDataSource` class.

Table 12.5 describes methods of the `Multipart` class:

Table 12.5: Describing the Methods of the Multipart Class

Method	Description
`BodyPart getBodyPart (int index)`	Returns a specified `BodyPart` from the `Multipart` object. It returns zero (0), if there is no `BodyPart` in a message.
`boolean removeBodyPart (BodyPart bp)`	Removes the `BodyPart` object from the `Multipart` object, whose reference is same as the `bp` parameter. If the `BodyPart` object has been removed successfully, the `removeBodyPart()` method returns true; otherwise, it returns false.
`boolean removeBodyPart (int index)`	Removes the `BodyPart` object from the list of `BodyPart` objects in the Multipart object, at the specified position. If the `BodyPart` object has been removed successfully, this method returns true; otherwise, it returns

Table 12.5: Describing the Methods of the Multipart Class

Method	Description
	false.
`int getCount()`	Gets the number of `BodyPart` objects in the list of `BodyPart` objects.
`Part getParent()`	Returns the reference of the Part instance that contains the Multipart object. It returns null, if no Part is available.
`String getContentType()`	Returns the MIME type for the Multipart object.
`public void addBodyPart (BodyPart bp)`	Adds a `BodyPart` object to the end of the list of currently used `BodyPart` objects.
`public void addBodyPart (BodyPart bp, int index)`	Adds the `BodyPart` object at the specified index in the list of `BodyPart` objects of the Multipart object.
`public void setParent (Part parent)`	Sets the parent of the `MultiPart` class as an individual part of a message.

The ContentType Class

The `ContentType` class defines the nature of data contained in a message. The content type is divided into the following two parts:

- **Primary type** – Signifies the general type of data
- **Sub type** – Signifies a particular format for the primary type

The `javax.mail.internet.ContentType` class represents the value of content type. This class provides various methods to perform various operations on a `ContentType` string, such as getting the individual parts of the `ContentType` value and creating the MIME style `ContentType` string.

Table 12.6 describes the methods of the `ContentType` class:

Table 12.6: Describing the Methods of the ContentType Class

Method	Description
`getBaseType()`	Gets the MIME Content Type string, which is a concatenated string of primary type, /, and sub type. For example, the `getBaseType()` method returns the string text/html for the content type of text/html. The returned string comprises primary type, which is text, forward slash, and the sub type, which is html.
`getPrimaryType()`	Gets the primary type part of the content type.
`getSubType()`	Gets the sub type part of the content type.
`setPrimaryType(String pType)`	Allows you to set the primary type of content type. The `pType` parameter sets the primary type of the message.
`setSubType(String sType)`	Allows you to set the passed `sType` argument to the sub type of the message.

The MimeBodyPart Class

The `javax.mail.internet.MimeBodyPart` class specifies MIME body part. The `MimeBodyPart` class extends the `BodyPart` abstract class and implements the `MimePart` interface.

Table 12.7 describes the methods of the `MimeBodyPart` class:

Table 12.7: Describing the Methods of the MimeBodyPart Class

Method	Description
`Void attachFile(java.io.File file) throws java.io.IOException, MessagingException`	Attaches the file to be passed as the file parameter with an E-mail

Table 12.7: Describing the Methods of the MimeBodyPart Class	
Method	**Description**
`void saveFile(java.io.File file) throw java.io.IOException, MessagingException`	Saves the content of the current `MimeBodyPart` object in the file passed as a parameter

The PreencodedMimeBodyPart Class

The `javax.mail.internet.PreencodedMimeBodyPart class` helps to create a message and attaches the encoded data to the message by using the encoding scheme as base64 encoding. Encoding scheme is a scheme used to convert the data into a format that can be transmitted over the network. You can encode the data by using an E-mail client application, a file, or database. The encoded data is sent to the recipient when the object of the `PreencodedMimeBodyPart class` is created.

Table 12.8 describes the methods of the `PreencodedMimeBodyPart` class:

Table 12.8: Describing the Methods of the PreencodedMimeBodyPart Class	
Method	**Description**
`String getEncoding()`	Returns the content transfer encoding. This encoding information is specified when a `PreencodedMimeBodyPart` object is created.
`void updateHeaders()`	Updates the headers of messages.
`void writeTo (java.io.OutputStream os)`	Writes to a body of a message by using the `OutputStream` object.

The MimeUtility Class

The `javax.mail.internet.MimeUtility` class provides various MIME utilities, such as encoding and decoding the message header. This class provides various methods to encode and decode MIME headers to transfer non-HTML files between E-mail client applications. Mail headers should possess US-ASCII characters for successful transmission over the network. The headers containing non US-ASCII characters are encoded to ensure that they contain US-ASCII characters for transmission of text messages over the network. You can use the BASE64 or QP algorithm, which are encoding schemes, to encode non US-ASCII characters.

Table 12.9 describes the methods of the `MimeUtility` class:

Table 12.9: Describing the Methods of the MimeUtility Class	
Method	**Description**
`java.io.InputStream decode (java.io.InputStream is, String encoding)`	Decodes the given input stream for successful transmission.
`String decodeText (String etext)`	Decodes unstructured headers, that is, it decodes *text token according to RFC 822 into the form which is supported by E-mail standards with the help of algorithm defined by RFC 2047. RFC 822 is a standard format for the Internet text message.
`String decodeWord (String eword)`	Uses the rules specified in RFC 2047 for parsing an encoded data. The `decodeWord()` method parses the string passed as a parameter to it. RFC 2047 is a standard set of rules for encoded data to be transmitted over the Internet.
`java.io.OutputStream encode (java.io.OutputStream os, String encoding)`	Allows you to wrap an encoder around the output stream passed as an argument to this method.
`static String encodeText(String text)`	Encodes an RFC 822 text token into the mail-safe form according to RFC 2047.
`String encodeWord`	Encodes an RFC 822 word token into the mail-safe form according to

Table 12.9: Describing the Methods of the MimeUtility Class

Method	Description
(String word)	RFC 2047.
String fold(int used, String s)	Breaks a string at linear whitespace so that each line can contain only upto 76 characters. If there are more than 76 non-whitespace characters, the string is folded at the first whitespace.
String unfold (String s)	Allows you to unfold a folded header.

The InternetHeader Class

The `javax.mail.internet.InternetHeaders.InternetHeader` class extends the Header class and represents an Internet header. An instance of the `InternetHeader` class having a null value is used as a placeholder for headers to maintain the order of headers. A placeholder is an `InternetHeader` object with the : character. The : character indicates a position in the list of headers where new `headerS` can be added. The `getValue()` method of the InternetHeader class is used to access the value of a header.

The ParameterList Class

The `javax.mail.internet.ParameterList` class accepts non US-ASCII characters. RFC 2231 provides support to encode non US-ASCII character to MIME headers. JavaMail makes use of two standard properties of the System class, namely `mail.mime.encodeparameters` and `mail.mime.decodeparameters`, whose values are set using the System class `setProperty() method`, to control parameter encoding and decoding. When the `mail.mime.encodeparameters` property is set to true, the non US-ASCII character is encoded. Similarly, when the `mail.mime.decodeparameters` property is set to true, the non US-ASCII character is decoded.

By default, the `encodeparameters` and `decodeparameters` properties are set to false. The `mail.mime.encodeparameters` and `mail.mime.decodeparameters` system properties determines whether or not the encoded parameters are supported in an E-mail. If the value of the `mail.mime.decodeparameters.strict` system property is set to true, the E-mail client application raises the `ParseException` exception that is thrown for errors that are encountered during the decoding of the encoded parameters.

Table 12.10 describes the methods of the `ParameterList` class:

Table 12.10: Describing the Methods of the ParameterList Class

Method	Description
String get (String name)	Returns the value of the parameter passed as an argument. Note that parameter names are case insensitive.
public void set (String name, String value)	Sets the value of the name parameter. If the name parameter already exists, then the value of the name parameter is replaced by the value parameter.
public void set (String name, String value, String charset)	Allows you to set the value of a parameter. If the `mail.mime.encodeparameters` system property is set to true, the parameter value is converted into non US-ASCII character and encoded with the specified charset, as mentioned by RFC 2231, which is a document that specifies the methods, behaviors, innovations that applies to the working of the Internet.
public void remove (String name)	Removes the parameter name that is passed as an argument to it from the current ParameterList object.
public java.util.Enumeration getNames()	Gets an enumeration object having all the parameter names in the current list of parameters.
public String toString()	Changes the ParameterList object in the form of MIME string.

The QuotaAwareStore Interface

The `javax.mail.QuotaAwareStore` interface is used by the `store` objects to support quotas. Quota allows you to limit the mail storage database for a particular user. The `getQuota()` and `setQuota()` methods of the `QuotaAwareStore` interface provides support to quota, which is defined by the `IMAP QUOTA` extension. The `IMAP QUOTA` extension restricts the usage of resources (quota) that are to be used by IMAP.

Table 12.11 lists the methods of the `QuotaAwareStore` interface:

Table 12.11: Describing the Methods of the QuotaAwareStore Interface

Method	Description
Quota[] getQuota(String root) throws `MessagingException`	Allows you to get the quotas for the quota root passed to it as a string argument. Quotas are controlled with the help of a quota root.
void setQuota(Quota quota) `throws MessagingException`	Allows you to set the quotas for the quota root passed to it as an argument.

The Resource Class

The `javax.mail.Quota.Resource` class represents an individual resource in a quota root. The following code snippet describes the constructors of the Resource class:

```
public Quota.Resource(String name, long usage, long limit)
```

In the preceding code snippet, the constructor of the `Quota.Resource` class creates an object of the `Resource` class with the name, usage, and limit argument passed to it.

The Quota Class

The `javax.mail.Quota` class specifies quotas for a specific quota root. Each quota root is modeled by the `Resource` class, which has resources. Each resource has a name (for example, `KOGENT`), and a usage limit provided by the name and limit attributes.

Table 12.12 describes the method of the `Quota` class:

Table 12.12: Describing the Method of the Quota Class

Method	Description
public void setResourceLimit (String name, long limit)	Allows you to set a resource limit value for the Quota object, with which the setResourceLimit() method has been called

The SharedFileInputStream Class

The `javax.mail.util.SharedFileInputStream` class is a subclass of the `BufferedInputStream` class that buffers data from a file. The `SharedFileInputStream` class permits you to access the file it buffers and also ensures that the file is closed when it is in use.

Table 12.13 describes the methods of the `SharedFileInputStream` class:

Table 12.13: Describing the Methods of the SharedFileInputStream Class

Method	Description
public int available() throws IOException	Retrieves the number of bytes that can be read from a file using the InputStream object. It overrides the `available()` method derived from its superclass, `BufferedInputStream.`
public void reset() throws IOException	Represents the inherited reset() method of its superclass `InputStream` and reposition the pointer to position in an `SharedFileInputStream` object that was last marked by `mark()` method of the `SharedFileInputStream` object.
public void close() `throws IOException`	Closes an input stream and releases system resources that are used by the input stream. This method overrides the close() method of its

Table 12.13: Describing the Methods of the SharedFileInputStream Class	
Method	**Description**
	superclass, `BufferedInputStream`.
public long getPosition()	Gets the current position of the data stored in a buffer of `SharedFileInputStream`, with which the method was called.
public InputStream newStream (long start, long end)	Allows you to create a new input stream object that represents a data substring from the input stream object, starting at start (inclusive) up to end (exclusive). Value of start must be positive. If end value is -1, the new input stream object also ends at the same place as the input stream object. The newly created input stream object from this method also implements the `SharedInputStream` interface.
protected void finalize() `throws Throwable`	Forces the `input stream` object to close. This method overrides the `finalize ()` method of its superclass, Object.

The SharedByteArrayInputStream Class

The `javax.mail.util.SharedByteArrayInputStream` class extends the `ByteArrayInputStream` class and implements the `SharedInputStream` interface. It provides methods that permit multiple readers to read the data from a common byte array.

Table 12.14 describes the methods of the SharedByteArrayInputStream class:

Table 12.14: Describing the Methods of the SharedByteArrayInputStream Class	
Method	**Description**
`long getPosition()`	Retrieves the current input data position from the current input stream object
InputStream newStream (long start, long end)	Retrieves a new input stream object denoting a subset of the data from the input stream object with which the newStream() method has been called, which starts from the start argument position and ends at the end argument position

The ByteArrayDataSource Class

The `javax.mail.util.ByteArrayDataSource` class is used to initialize a byte array using an `InputStream` or a string value. It implements the `javax.activation.DataSource` interface.

Table 12.15 describes the methods of the `ByteArrayDataSource` class:

Table 12.15: Describing the Methods of the ByteArrayDataSource Class	
Method	**Description**
`public java.io.InputStream getInputStream() throws java.io.IOException`	Allows you to retrieve an input stream object of a socket, which is a communication channel between the client and the server. A new input stream object is always returned when this method is called.
`public java.io.OutputStream getOutputStream() throws java.io.IOException`	Gets an output stream object of a socket.
`public String getContentType()`	Allows you to get the MIME content type of data in the form of string.
`public String getName()`	Gets the name of an entity, such as class, interface, and array. By default, an empty string:(" ") is returned.
`public void setName(String name)`	Sets the name of the entity, such as class, interface, and array to the string parameter passed to it.

The Address Class

JavaMail API provides the `javax.mail.Address` abstract class that represents E-mail addresses of the sender or the receiver of the E-mail. The Address class contains the following subclasses:

- `javax.mail.internet.InternetAddress`
- `javax.mail.internet.NewsAddress`

Let's discuss these classes in detail.

The InternetAddress Class

The `javax.mail.internet.InternetAddress` class provides methods to concatenate and parse E-mail addresses in a field. If you want multiple E-mail addresses in the field, then addresses must be separated with commas. The E-mail addresses are passed as an argument to the `setAddress()` method of the `InternetAddress` class.

The following code snippet shows how to set an E-mail address in an E-mail:

```
Internetaddress MyInternetAddress=new InternetAddress();
MyInternetAddress.setAddress("yourEmaiID");
MyInternetAddress.setPersonal("Kogent");
System.out.println("MyAddress="+MyAddress.toString());
```

You can parse an E-mail address by using the `parse()` method, as shown in the following code snippet:

```
InternetAddress[] parse(String)
```

The following code snippet parses more than one E-mail addresses into an array of `InternetAddress` objects:

```
InternetAddress toField[]=InternetAddress.parse
("Test@Mymail.com,Test1@Mymail.com");

for(int i=0;i<toField.length;i++){
   System.out.println("toField["+i+"].Address="+tofield[i].getAddress());
   System.out.println("toField["+i+"].Address="+tofield[i].getPersonal());
```

The NewsAddress Class

The `javax.mail.internet.NewsAddress` class is used to develop a newsgroup message with a newsgroup name and an optional host name. Newsgroups are organized into different hierarchies, such as `alt` (alternative), `biz` (business), `comp` (computing), `misc` (miscellaneous), and `rec` (recreational).

The Store Class

The `javax.mail.Store` class is used to store and receive messages. In addition, it performs other actions on messages, such as storing similar messages in specific folder objects, which are then stored on a mail server. Table 12.16 describes the methods of the `Store` class:

Table 12.16: Describing the Methods of the Store Class

Method	Description
`Folder getFolder(String name)`	Gets a folder object corresponding to the name argument passed to it.
`Folder getFolder(URLName myurl)`	Gets a closed folder object corresponding to the myurl argument passed to it.
`Folder[ ] getPersonalNamespaces()`	Gets a set of folder objects denoting the personal namespaces of the current user. A personal namespace contains personal details, such as username and password, of the authenticated user. Typically, only the authenticated users have access to mail folders in their personal namespace. The INBOX folder object is always contained within the personal namespace, reserved for the user. A particular user can have only personal namespace in a typical case.
`Folder[ ] getSharedNamespaces()`	Allows you to get a folder object array, which represents the namespaces shared among multiple users.
`Folder[] getUserNamespaces(String user)`	Allows you to get a folder object array. This array specifies the user namespace, which is passed as a parameter to the

Table 12.16: Describing the Methods of the Store Class	
Method	**Description**
	getUserNamespaces() method.
`public abstract Folder getDefaultFolder()`	Allows you to get a folder object, which specifies the default namespace root.

You need to connect to mail storage to retrieve the session object, which in turn is used to retrieve the store object. The session object is needed to get the instance of POP server's connection and then retrieve the store object by using the `getStore()` method. The following code snippet shows how to retrieve a store object by connecting to a POP server:

```
//Set up default parameters

Properties myprops=new Properties();
myprops.put("mail.transport.protocol","pop");

//Create the seesion and create a new mail message

Session mymailSession=Session.getInstance(myprops);

//Get the store and connect to the server

Store mymailStore=mymailSession.getStore();
mymailStore.connect("yourpop.server.com",10,"yourname","yourpassword");

//Proceed to manipulate Folder objects
```

In the preceding code snippet, the store object is retrieved by using the `getStore()` method of the `Session` class. After retrieving the store object, you need to retrieve the folder object to store a message. You can use the `getFolder()` method of the `Session` class to retrieve the folder object. The `exists()` method of the folder object verifies whether or not the folder exists in the store object.

The following code snippet shows how to retrieve the inbox folder object by using the object of the `Store` class (mymailStore):

```
//Get the Strore and connect to the server
URLName myurlname=new URLName("pop3://<user>;auth=<auth>@<host>:<port>");
Store mymailStore=mymailSession.getStore(myurlname);
mymailStore.connect();

//proceed to manipulate Folder objects
Folder myinbox=mymailStore.getDefaultFolder();
//or
Folder myinbox=mymailStore.getFolder("INBOX");
```

In the preceding code snippet, the `INBOX` keyword is a special name for a folder object in which the users receive their messages.

The Folder Class

The `javax.mail.Folder` class represents a folder containing messages as well as other subfolders in a structure similar to tree hierarchical structure. A folder object is initially in the closed state. You can perform certain operations on the folder object in its closed state, such as renaming the folder object and monitoring it for new messages. To open the folder object, you need to call the `open()` method. You can perform actions, such as retrieving messages and changing notifications on the folder object in the open state.

You can create the folder objects by calling the `getFolder()` method of the `Store` class and the `Folder` class. Alternatively, you can call the `list()`, `list(String)`, `listSubscribed()`, and `listSubscribed(String)` methods of the `Folder` class to create folder objects.

When a message is deleted from a folder object, the total number of messages is not calculated until expunging occurs on the folder object. The concept of expunging a folder object implies that all the messages which have been marked for deletion are deleted and finally removed from the folder object. When you invoke the `getMessage(msgno)` method, the folder object returns the same message multiple times with the same `message` object, until an expunge is done or the messages marked as deleted are deleted from the folder object.

Table 12.17 describes the fields of the Folder class:

Table 12.17: Describing the Fields of the Folder Class

Field	Description
`HOLDS_FOLDERS`	Contains other folder objects
`HOLDS_MESSAGES`	Contains messages
`READ_ONLY`	Specifies that the folder object is read-only, implying it can cannot be modified
`READ_WRITE`	Specifies that the folder object permits read-write operations
`Store`	Contains the parent object

Table 12.18 describes the methods of the Folder class:

Table 12.18: Describing the Methods of the Folder Class

Method	Description
`boolean hasNewMessages()`	Returns true if any folder object message is flagged with the `Flag.RECENT` flag.
`int getMessageCount()`	Allows you to get the total number of messages of the folder object. The getMessageCount() method can be called on a closed folder object. However, note that for some folder objects implementation, getting the total message count can be an operation that may involve opening of the folder object. In such cases, a provider can select not to support invocation of the getMessageCount() method on the closed folder object.
`int getNewMessageCount()`	Allows you to get number of new messages in a folder object by calling the getMessage(int) method of the folder object to retrieve all its messages, and checking whether or not its RECENT flag is set. If the RECENT flag of a message is set to true then this implies that the message is new and the message is added to the count of new messages, which is to be returned by the getNewMessageCount() method.
`int getUnreadMessageCount()`	Allows you to get number of unread messages from a folder object by calling the getMessage(int) method of the folder object to retrieve all its messages and checking whether or not its SEEN flag is set. If the SEEN flag of a message is set to false then this implies that the message has not been read and the message is added to the count of unread messages, which is to be returned by the getUnreadMessageCount() method.
`Message getMessage(int)`	Allows you to get the message object corresponding to the message number passed as an argument to it. Unlike the folder objects, repeated calls to the getMessage() method with the same message number returns the same message object, as long as no messages in the folder object have been expunged.
`Message[] getMessages()`	Allows you to get all the message objects stored in a folder object. Returns an empty array if the folder object is empty.
`Message[] getMessages(int, int)`	Allows you to get all the message objects corresponding to the message numbers passed as arguments.
`Message[] getMessages(int[])`	Allows you to get the message objects for message numbers given in an array passed to this method.

You can perform the following operations with the Folder class:

- Listing folders
- Opening and closing folders
- Listing messages
- Copying and moving messages
- Searching messages

Let's discuss these in detail.

Listing Folders

If a folder object contains subfolders, you can use the `list()` function of the `Folder` class to list these subfolders. The `list()` function lists only the top-level folder objects within the folder object hierarchy. The following code snippet shows how to list folder objects:

```
//Set up the default parameters
Properties myprops=new Properties();
//create the Session anad create a new mail message
Session mymailSession=Sesion.getInstance(myprops);

//Get the store and connect to the server
URLName myurl=new URLName("imap://alan:ceri@mail.microsoft.com");
Store mymailStore=mailSession.getStore(myurl);

mymailStore.connect();
//proceed to list all the Folder objects
Folder thisFolder=mymailStore.getDefaultInstance();

Folder listOfFolders[]=null;
if((thisFolder.getType() & Folder.HOLDS_FOLDERS)) {
   listOfFolders=thisFolder.list();
}
```

In the preceding code snippet, the `getType()` method of the `Folder` class returns the status field for a Folder object. The `list()` method returns a list of folder objects that match the search string passed as a parameter to it. For example, the following code snippet returns all the folder objects that begin with the string, Client:

```
Folder mylistOfFolders[]=thisFolder.list("Client%");
```

The following code snippet returns all the folder objects, including any subfolder objects, which begin with the letter A:

```
Folder mylistOfFolders[] = thisFolder.list("A*");
```

The following code snippet lists all the folder objects in the folder object hierarchy:

```
//Set up the default parameters
Properties myprops=new Properties();

//create the Session anad create a new mail message
Session mymailSession=Sesion.getInstance(myprops);

//Get the store and connect to the server
URLName myurlname=new URLName("imap://alan:ceri@mail.microsoft.com");
Store mymailStore=mymailSession.getStore(urlname);

mymailStore.connect();
//proceed to list all the Folder objects
Folder thisfolder=mymailStore.getDefaultInstance();

if(thisFolder!=null)
{
   if((thisFolder.getType() & Folder.HOLDS_FOLDERS)!=0)
   {
         Folder[] listOfFolders=thisFolder.list("*");
         for(int i=0;i<listOfFolders.length;i++)
         {
                System.out.println("FolderName="+listOfFolders[i].getName());
         }
   }
}
```

In the preceding code snippet, we have used the list() method to list the folder objects.

Two other methods of the folder objects are used to return a list of folders in the folder. The `listSubscribed()` method of the folder object returns the list of subscribed folders inside a folder and `listSubscribed(String search)` method returns the list of folders in the folder namespace that matches the pattern of the string parameter passed to it.

Opening and Closing Folders

You can use the public void open (int mode) method to open a folder object. This method is called on the folder objects that are not empty and are not opened. To check whether the folder object is open or not, you can call the boolean isOpen() method. The following code snippet shows how to invoke the getType() method on the folder object:

```
if(thisFolder.getType() == Folder.READ_WRITE)
  System.out.println("This folder was opened with READ_WRITE Access both");
else
  System.out.println("This folder was opened with READ_ONLY Access only");
```

This method helps to determine the permission, read or write, with which the folder should be opened.

To close the folder object, you can use the public void close(boolean) method. This method can be called only when the folder object is opened. The Boolean parameter indicates whether the expunge operation should be performed on the folder object or not. If TRUE Boolean value is returned, the expunge() method is invoked.

Listing Messages

As discussed earlier, the Folder object is used to store messages. These messages are returned in a list of array. Each message object returns a reference to the actual message and the returned message reference is stored in a list of messages.

The following code snippet shows all the messages within a POP folder and displays the subject field of each retrieved message:

```
inbox.open(Folder.READ_ONLY);

Message[] allTheMessages=inbox.getMessages();
for(int i=0;i<allTheMessages.length;i++)
System.out.println("ID:"+i+"Subject:"+allTheMessages[i].getSubject());

inbox.close();
mailStore.close();
```

The messages retrieved from a folder are references to the actual messages. Such message objects can be retrieved by calling the get() method. Clients use the FetchProfile class to list the message attributes to be fetched from the server. The following code snippet shows how to fetch message attributes:

```
void fetch(Message[] msgs,FetchProfile fp)
```

The following code snippet shows how to list messages using the FetchProfile class:

```
Message[] mymsgs=thisFolder.getMessages();
FetchProfile myfp=new FetchProfile();
myfp.add("To");
myfp.add("From");
myfp.add("Subject");
thisFolder.fetch(mymsgs,myfp);
for(int i=0;i<thisFolder.getMessageCount();i++)
{
  display(mymsgs[i].getTo());
  display(mymsgs[i].getFrom());
  display(mymsgs[i].getSubject());
}
```

The server-based message access protocols, such as IMAP and SMTP, are used to retrieve attributes of a group of messages sent in a single request. You can fetch group message attributes by using the javax.mail.FetchProfile.Item inner class, which is the base class of all group items that can be fetched from the FetchProfile class.

Copying and Moving Messages

The Folder class provides the copyMessages() method that is used to copy and move messages among different folder objects. The copyMessages() method appends messages to the destination folder object by invoking appendMessages(msgs) on the destination folder object. To append messages to the destination folder object, ensure that the destination folder object is not open.

Searching Messages

JavaMail provides the javax.mail.search package to define classes that can be used to search messages. A search expression searches the message based upon a specific criterion from a SearchTerm object. Search expressions are represented by the SearchTerm class available in the javax.mail.search package. SearchTerm objects are `Serializable`, which allows these objects to be stored between sessions. The folder object contains the following two methods to search messages on the basis of the specified search expression of the `SearchTerm object`:

- Message[] search(SearchTerm myterm)
- Message[] search(SearchTerm myterm, Message[] mymessageList)

The following code snippet shows the use of the `search()` method:

```
SearchTerm myst=new SearchTerm(new FromStringterm("alan@n-ary.com"),
new FromStringTerm("cormac@n-ary.com"));
Message[] mymessageList=thisFolder.search(myst);
```

The subclasses of the `SearchTerm` class implement the following logical methods on the base class:

- `AndTerm`—Allows you to build `AND` expressions. The syntaxes of the overloaded `AndTerm()` method are as follows:
  - `AndTerm(SearchTerm[])`
  - `AndTerm(SearchTerm, SearchTerm)`
- `OrTerm`—Allows you to build `OR` expressions. The syntaxes of the overloaded `OrTerm()` method are as follows:
  - `OrTerm(SearchTerm[])`
  - `OrTerm(SearchTerm, SearchTerm)`
- `NotTerm`—Allows you to build NOT expressions. The syntax of `NotTerm()` is as follows:
  - `NotTerm(SearchTerm)`
- `ComparisonTerm`—Serves as a subclass of the `SearchTerm` class, which is an abstract class. The subclasses of the `ComparisonTerm` class implements particular functionalities. The `ComparisonTerm` class has the following constants for numerical comparison types:
  - `ComparisonTerm.EQ`—Corresponds to equal to
  - `ComparisonTerm.GE`—Corresponds to greater than or equal to comparison
  - `ComparisonTerm.GT`—Corresponds to greater than comparison
  - `ComparisonTerm.LE`—Corresponds to less than or equal to comparison
  - `ComparisonTerm.LT`—Corresponds to less than comparison
  - `ComparisonTerm.NE`—Corresponds to not equal to comparison

Table 12.19 describes the classes of the `javax.mail.search` package and their constructor syntaxes to build different expressions:

Table 12.19: Describing the Classes of the javax.mail.search Package

Class	Description	Constructor Syntax
`AddressStringTerm`	Performs string comparisons for message addresses and extends the StringTerm class in a package.	`AddressStringTerm(String pattern)`
`AddressTerm`	Extends the `javax.mail.search.SearchTerm` class and is used to compare the search expression with message address. The `StringTerm` class and the `AddressTerm` class are different in functionality. The `StringTerm` class performs comparisons on address strings and the `AddressTerm` class performs comparisons on `Address` objects.	`AddressTerm(address Add)`
`BodyTerm`	Implements the `MessageBody` interface and extends the `StringTerm` class. This class performs searches on a message body.	`BodyTerm(String Pattern)`
`DateTerm`	Compares the search expression with dates and	`DateTerm(int comparison,`

Table 12.19: Describing the Classes of the javax.mail.search Package

Class	Description	Constructor Syntax
	extends the `ComparisonTerm` class.	`Date date)`
`FlagTerm`	Compares the search expression with message Flag. The `FlagTerm` class extends `javax.mail.search.SearchTerm`.	`FlagTerm(Flags flags, boolean set)`
`FromStringTerm`	Extends the `javax.mail.search.AddressStringTerm` class and compares the search expression with string address.	`FromStringTerm(String pattern )`
`FromTerm`	Allows you to compare the From address header. The `FromTerm` class extends the `javax.mail.search.AddressTerm` class. The `FromStringTerm` class has a major difference from the `FromTerm` class. This class checks address strings than address objects, as in the case of the `FromTerm` class. The result address string comparison does not depend on whether the string expression contains lowercase letter or uppercase letter.	`FromTerm(Address add)`
`HeaderTerm`	Compares the search expression with message headers. The result of the comparison does not depend on whether the search expression contains lowercase letter or uppercase letter. The `HeaderTerm` class extends the `javax.mail.search.StringTerm` class.	`HeaderTerm(String headerName, String pattern).`
`IntegerComparison Term`	Compares the search expression with integer message number. The `IntegerComparisonTerm` class extends the `ComparisonTerm` class.	`IntegerComparisonTerm(int mycomparison, int mynumber)`
`MessageIDTerm`	Compares the search expression with the MessageId, which is a unique identifier for a message. A message can be searched in a folder object whose ID is same as the messageId argument passed to this method. The MessageIDTerm class extends the javax.mail.search.StringTerm class.	`MessageIDTerm(String messageID).`
`MessageNumberTerm`	Compares the search expression with message number. The `MessageNumberTerm` class extends the `javax.mail.search.IntegerComparisonTerm` class.	`MessageNumberTerm(int number).`
`ReceivedDateTerm`	Compares the search expression with the date on which the message was received. The `ReceivedDateTerm` class extends the `javax.mail.search.DateTerm` class.	`ReceivedDateTerm(int comparison, Date date).`
`RecipientStringTerm`	Compares the search expression with recipient address headers. The `RecipientStringTerm` class extends the javax.mail.search.AddressStringTerm class.	`RecipientStringTerm (Message.RecipientType type, String pattern).`
`RecipientTerm`	Compares recipient address headers with the address object passed to the constructor of the `RecipientTerm` class during the creation of the `RecipientTerm` object and extends the `javax.mail.search.AddressTerm` class. There is a difference between the `RecipientStringTerm` and `RecipientTerm`	`RecipientTerm(Message.RecipientType type, Address address)`

Table 12.19: Describing the Classes of the javax.mail.search Package

Class	Description	Constructor Syntax
	classes. The `RecipientStringTerm` class performs comparisons on address string objects and the `RecipientTerm` class performs comparison on address objects. However, string comparisons are case insensitive	
`SentDateTerm`	Compares the date on which message was sent to the recipient with the date passed to the constructor of the class during the creation of the `SentDateTerm` object. This class extends the `javax.mail.search.DateTerm` class.	`SentDateTerm(int comparison, Date date).`
`SizeTerm`	Compares the search expression of the SearchTerm object with the size of the message. The `SizeTerm` class extends the `javax.mail.search.IntegerComparisonTerm` class.	`SizeTerm (int comparison, int size).`
`StringTerm`	Compares a string with the pattern argument passed to its constructor.	`StringTerm(String pattern, Boolean ignoreCase)` `StringTerm(String pattern)`
`SubjectTerm`	Compares the search expression with message subject header. The result of the comparison does not depend on whether the search expression contains lowercase letter or uppercase letter.	`SubjectTerm(String pattern)`

The Transport Class

The `javax.mail.Transport` class is used to deliver messages to the recipients. This class extends the `Service` class. The `Transport` class provides the following three methods to send messages to the recipient:

- void `send(Message)` – Allows you to send a message
- void `send(Message, Address[])` – Allows you to send a message to the specified addresses
- void `sendMessage(Message, Address[])` – Allows you to send a message to the specified list of addresses

The `Transport` class throws the `SendFailedException` exception, if a recipient address is found incorrect during the message submission.

The following code snippet shows the use of the `Transport` class and the `send()` method:

```
try
{
   Transport myTransport=session.getTransport("smtp");
   myTransport.connect();
   myTransport.send(msg,msg.getAllreciepents());//msg is a MimeMessage object
   myTransport.close();
   }
   catch(SendFailedException sfe)
   {
         Address[] list=sfe.getInvalidAddresses();
         for(int i=0;i<list.length;i++)
               System.out.println("Invalid Address:"+list[i]);
         list=sfe.getUnsentAddresses();
         for(int i=0;i<list.length;i++)
               System.out.println("Unsent Address:"+list[i]);
         list=sfe.getValidAddresses();
         for(int i=0;i<list.length;i++)
               System.out.println("Valid Address:"+list[i]);
   }
```

The following three methods are used to handle errors related to an E-mail address:

- `Address[] getInvalidAddresses()` – Returns an array of Address objects that are not correct.
- `Address[] getUnsentAddresses()`–Returns an array of Address objects that are not accepted for delivery. It may be due to the reason that a server may not send a message to an outside domain user.
- `Address[] getValidAddresses()`–Returns an array of Address objects that are accepted for delivery.

After having a brief knowledge about the classes and interfaces of JavaMail API, let's explore some of the new features that have been introduced in JavaMail 1.5.

Exploring New Features in JavaMail 1.5

Various updates have been introduced in JavaMail 1.5 API including the following new features:

- Support for QRESYNC and CONDSTORE
- Support for WITHIN and ID
- Support for write timeouts

Let's briefly discuss each of these features in this section.

Support for QRESYNC and CONDSTORE

When multiple IMAP client access shared mailbox, they need to quickly synchronize and co-ordinate the state changes in the messages within the mailbox. The Conditional Store (CONDSTORE) facility in JavaMail 1.5 enables these clients to quickly synchronize the state changes of the messages in the shared mailbox. This also implies that at a time only one client can make changes to the messages and the updates will be communicated to all other clients. The CONDSTORE facility associates a modification sequence with every IMAP message which is updated with every modification to the metadata. This enables a disconnected client to quickly resynchronize IMAP flag changes for pre-read messages. This is usually done with the help of CHANGEDSINCE FETCH modifier once the mailbox is opened. In order to identify expunged messages, the client needs to issue UID FETCH or UID SEARCH command.

The Quick Resync (QRESYNC) IMAP extension enables reconnecting clients to perform full resynchronization including the identification of expunged messages, in a single round trip. QRESYNC extension also provides a new response status VANISHED to represent a list of expunged messages. It is greatly beneficial for mobile clients who experience frequent disconnection issues.

Support for WITHIN and ID

The JavaMail 1.5 API introduces WITHIN extension to IMAP SEARCH which returns messages having internal dates within or outside a specified time range. This is accomplished with the help of two new search keys namely, OLDER and YOUNGER which take a specified time interval in seconds as argument. The server calculates the required time range by subtracting client specified time interval from its current date and time and returns the messages older or younger than the calculated time range on the basis of the respective search key used. This extension is beneficial to the networks having limited bandwidth as it minimizes network traffic generated by repeated requests or redundant responses.

The JavaMail 1.5 API also provides the ID command to gather information about the programs used by remote clients along with their contact details. This enables the interested sites to assemble usage statistics data and bug reports about the programs used by remote clients.

Support for Write Timeouts

Prior to JavaMail 1.5, the API provided support for read timeouts however when a timeout occurred on a write, it resulted in hanging the connection for a while before the connection is killed. The support for write timeouts has been incorporated in JavaMail 1.5 API with the help of ScheduledExecutor which requires a separate thread for each connection.

After having a brief review of the new features introduced in JavaMail 1.5, let's now learn how to create an application for sending and receiving mails.

Working with JavaMail

As discussed earlier, JavaMail API provides several classes, such as Address, Authenticator, BodyPart, Flags, and interfaces, such as Part, to develop E-mail client applications.

In this section, let's create a customized E-mail client application, Kogent E-mail client, to understand how JavaMail helps in sending and reading an E-mail from the inbox of the desired E-mail address. Firstly, let's create an E-mail client that sends E-mails through SMTP. To create the E-mail client, create the `SimpleMailSender` class, which sends a message to the desired E-mail address. Next, you learn how to read an E-mail using JavaMail. To read an E-mail, create the `SimpleMailReader` class that reads the mails from the inbox of the desired E-mail address.

Sending Mails

JavaMail allows you to send an E-mail with or without attachments to one or many recipients. To send the E-mail, first you need to specify the domain name of the SMTP server by setting the value of `mail.smtp.host` property to the domain name of the SMTP server using the `put()` method of the property object, which is `smtpout.secureserver.net` in this application. The TCP/IP protocol is used to connect to the SMTP server to send E-mails on a single or multiple computers. You can develop your customize mailing system for sending an E-mail.

Listing 12.1 shows the `SimpleMailSender.java` file, which is created to send an E-mail through SMTP server (save this file in the `\Chapter12` folder):

Listing 12.1: Showing the SimpleMailSender.java File

```
import java.security.Security;
import java.util.Properties;
import javax.mail.Message;
import javax.mail.MessagingException;
import javax.mail.PasswordAuthentication;
import javax.mail.Session;
import javax.mail.Transport;
import javax.mail.internet.InternetAddress;
import javax.mail.internet.MimeMessage;

public class  SimpleMailSender
{
   private static final String SmtpServer = "smtpout.secureserver.net";
   private static final String MsgContent = "Test Message Contents";
   private static final String Subject = "A test Mail";
   private static final String mailFrom= "suchita.jain@kogentindia.com";
   private static final String[] sendTo = {"anuj.dixit@kogentindia.com"};
   public static void main(String args[]) throws Exception
   {

         Security.addProvider(new com.sun.net.ssl.internal.ssl.Provider());
         new SimpleMailSender().sendSSLMessage(sendTo, Subject, MsgContent , mailFrom);
         System.out.println("Sucessfully Sent");
   }
   public void sendSSLMessage(String recipients[], String subject, String message,
   String from) throws MessagingException
   {
         boolean debug = true;
         Properties props = new Properties();
         props.put("mail.smtp.host",  SmtpServer);
         props.put("mail.smtp.auth", "true");
         props.put("mail.debug", "true");
         props.put("mail.smtp.port","3535");
         Session session = Session.getDefaultInstance(props, new
         javax.mail.Authenticator()
         {
                 protected PasswordAuthentication getPasswordAuthentication()
                 {
                 return new PasswordAuthentication("suchita.jain@kogentindia.com",
                 "suchita");
                 }
         });
```

```
            session.setDebug(debug);
            Message msg = new MimeMessage(session);
            InternetAddress addressFrom = new InternetAddress(from);
            msg.setFrom(addressFrom);
            InternetAddress[] addressTo = new InternetAddress[recipients.length];
            for (int i = 0; i < recipients.length; i++)
            {
                    addressTo[i] = new InternetAddress(recipients[i]);
            }
            msg.setRecipients(Message.RecipientType.TO, addressTo);
            // Setting the Subject and Content Type
            msg.setSubject(subject);
            msg.setContent(message, "text/plain");
            Transport.send(msg);
      }
}
```

In Listing 12.1, the `send()` method in the `SimpleMailSender` class is used to send messages. Note that a mail session is created by using the `java.mail.Session class` to send the mail. In the `SimpleMailSender.java` class, the `Session.getDefaultInstance()` method is called to get a shared session, which other applications may reuse. You can also set up an entirely new session by using the `Session.getInstance()` method. To launch a session, you are required to set certain properties, such as the `mail.smtp.host` property.

You can run the `SimpleMailSender` class on your computer by changing the SMTP server name (provided in Listing 12.1) with your SMTP server name.

On the basis of the authentication details of your SMTP server, you also need to modify the value of variables, such as `PasswordAuthentication`, `mailFrom`, and `sendTo` (provided in Listing 12.1). You should ensure that the javax.mail.jar file is mapped to the `classpath` environment variable, before compiling the `SimpleMailSender.java` file. Execute the following commands from Command Prompt to compile and run the `SimpleMailSender` class:

```
javac SimpleMailSender.java
java SimpleMailSender
```

Figure 12.4 shows the output of Listing 12.1:

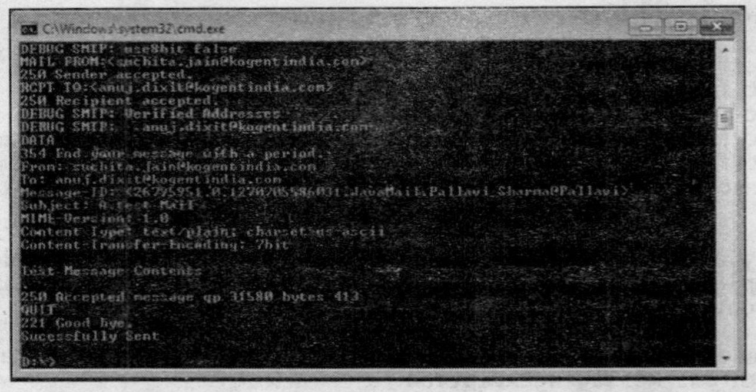

Figure 12.4: Showing the Output of the SimpleMailSender.java File

After creating a session, you need to create a message. The `javax.mail.Transport` class is used to send the message.

Reading Mails

JavaMail provides various features that allow you to read an E-mail using POP3. You can connect to the message store using the `connect()` method of the Store class, download messages, and optionally delete them from the server. Let's create the `SimpleMailReader.java` file that is used to read E-mails from the SMTP server, as shown in Listing 12.2 (save this file in the `\Chapter12` folder):

Listing 12.2: Showing the SimpleMailReader.java File

```
import java.util.Properties;
```

```
import javax.mail.Authenticator;
import javax.mail.Folder;
import javax.mail.Message;
import javax.mail.PasswordAuthentication;
import javax.mail.Session;
import javax.mail.Store;
public class SimpleMailReader
{
  public static void main(String[] args) throws Exception
  {
  Properties mailproperties = new Properties();
  String hostmailserver = "pop.secureserver.net";
  mailproperties.setProperty("mail.pop3.port", "110");
  mailproperties.put("mail.pop3.host", hostmailserver);
  mailproperties.put("mail.store.protocol", "pop3");
  Session session = Session.getDefaultInstance(mailproperties);
  Store store = session.getStore();
  store.connect( hostmailserver,110, "akanksha.saksena@kogentindia.com","akanksha");
  Folder inbox = store.getDefaultFolder().getFolder("INBOX");
  if (inbox == null)
  {
        System.out.println("No INBOX");
        System.exit(1);
  }
  inbox.open(Folder.READ_ONLY);
  Message[] messages = inbox.getMessages();
  for (int i = 0; i < messages.length; i++)
  {
        System.out.println("Message " + (i + 1));
        messages[i].writeTo(System.out);
  }
  inbox.close(false);
  store.close();
  }
}
```

In Listing 12.2, we have used the POP3 server of secureserver.net to access E-mails. To compile the `SimpleMailReader` class, execute the following command from the Command Prompt:

```
javac SimpleMailReader.java
```

To run the SimpleMailReader class, execute the following command from Command Prompt:

```
java SimpleMailReader
```

After executing the preceding command, the E-mails of your inbox are displayed on Command Prompt.

Figure 12.5 shows the output of Listing 12.2:

Figure 12.5: Displaying the Output of the SimpleMailReader.java File

This ends up the discussion on JavaMail. Let's now recall what you have learned in the chapter.

Summary

In this chapter, you have learned about the JavaMail and its API. The JavaMail API provides various classes and interfaces used to develop an E-mail client application in Java. You have also learned about various types of mail protocols, such as SMTP, IMAP, and POP3, which are used by JavaMail to send and receive E-mails. In addition, you have learned how to implement the JavaMail API by creating various E-mail applications.

In the next chapter, you learn about EJB 3.2.

Quick Revise

Q1. **The BodyPart class belongs to the .... package.**

A. **javax.mail.search** B. **javax.mail.event**
C. **javax.mail.internet** D. **javax.mail**

Ans. D

Q2. **The......................... is an abstract class that represents a mail message.**

A. **javax.mail.Folder** B. **javax.mail.Message**
C. **javax.mail.Address** D. **javax.mail.Authenticator**

Ans. B

Q3. **The .... method returns the total number of messages stored in a `folder` object.**

A. **getMessage()** B. **getMessageCount()**
C. **getUnreadMessageCount()** D. **getNewMessageCount()**

Ans. B

Q4. **The `send()` method of the `Transport` class takes an argument of the type.........................**

A. **Message** B. **Folder**
C. **BodyPart** D. **Multipart**

Ans. A

Q5. **The .... class is extended by the `javax.mail.Store` class.**

A. **javax.mail.Session** B. **javax.mail.Transport**
C. **javax.mail.Folder** D. **javax.mail.Service**

Ans. D

Q6. **What is the significance of JavaMail API?**

Ans. The JavaMail API provides a framework to build complete mailing and messaging applications. This framework is both platform and protocol-independent. All the API classes and interfaces have been organized in the `javax.mail` package and its sub packages. The JavaMail API helps the programmers to develop E-mail client applications in an efficient and manageable manner.

Q7. **What is a mail server?**

Ans. An application receiving and storing mails and messages from E-mail clients is known as a mail server.

Q8. **Define SMTP.**

Ans. SMTP is a standard E-mail protocol. It is an application layer protocol supporting messaging functions. It is used for sending mails.

Q9. **Differentiate between SMTP and POP3.**

Ans. Both SMTP and POP3 are Internet protocols. SMTP is used to deliver mails while POP3 is used to retrieve E-mails from the mail server by using an E-mail client. In other words, POP3 is used to download a message from a mailbox and SMTP routes the message from one server to another or from a client to a server.

Q10. **What is the importance of `javax.mail.Authenticator` class?**

Ans. When we send or receive a message, we need to authenticate the connection. The `Authenticator` class provides the methods used to check the authenticity of the connection.

Q11. **Which methods of the `Transport` class help in delivering messages?**

Ans. The following methods of the Transport class help in delivering messages:

- void send(Message)
- void send(Message, Address[])
- void sendMessage(Message, Address[])

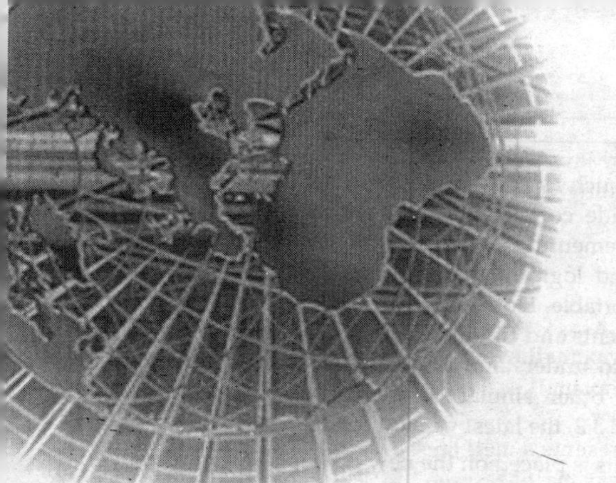

13

Working with EJB 3.2

An enterprise level application should contain various features, such as distributive, transactional, secure, and portable. Java EE introduced a new technology called server-side component architecture, more commonly known as Enterprise JavaBeans (EJB), which helps in implementing these features in Java enterprise applications. Earlier, a developer had to provide extra code and logic in the application to ensure that an enterprise application is distributive, transactional, secure, and portable. However, with the advent of EJB, these features were managed directly by the EJB container. EJB components and containers used in application servers also reduce the efforts of the developers, as they do not need to understand low level transaction and state management details, connection pooling, multithreading, and other similar complex processes related to application development. The Java EE 7 specification supports EJB 3.2, the latest version of EJB.

In this chapter, while discussing the EJB technology, the main focus is placed on the new concepts introduced by EJB 3, and how it has made developing a Web application easier. Firstly, you learn about the fundamental concepts of EJB 3, followed by the discussion on various types of EJBs, such as session beans and Message-Driven Bean (MDB). Next, the chapter helps you to understand how to manage transactions in Java EE applications. In addition, the classes and interfaces used to implement EJB 3 timer services are described. Moreover, the chapter explores how to work with EJB 3 interceptors and implement life cycle callback methods in the MDB and session beans.

Let's start by learning about the fundamentals of EJB 3.

Understanding EJB 3 Fundamentals

EJB is a standard architecture used for enterprise level applications that are object-oriented, transaction-oriented, and distributed. In the EJB architecture, the enterprise beans are managed by the EJB container. To create an enterprise bean application, you first need to create an interface containing various user-defined enterprise bean methods that encapsulate the business logic of an enterprise application. Next, the enterprise bean class implements the interface and provides the body for the enterprise bean methods. Finally, the EJB clients are created to invoke these methods remotely. The configuration details of the enterprise beans are provided in Deployment Descriptor.

In addition to business logic, you can also provide service information in an enterprise bean by using annotations or Deployment Descriptor. The enterprise beans can use the container for all the services defined in Deployment Descriptor. You need to create a client view to access an enterprise bean and display the output of the bean. The client view refers to creating another enterprise component or Java program, such as an applet or a servlet, to access an enterprise bean and its business methods. The client view of the enterprise bean is independent of the type of container and server in which the enterprise bean is deployed.

NOTE

Please note that throughout the chapter, the container refers to the EJB container.

An enterprise bean can be used to:

- Provide all stateless services, where the client state is not required to be maintained. In addition, you can also use an enterprise bean as a Web service endpoint that provides a stateless service.
- Provide stateless service asynchronously with the arrival of some message.
- Provide stateful services, where the conversational state of a client is maintained.
- Represent a persistent object as an entity, which is managed automatically by the container for its persistence and relation with other entities.

Let's now discuss the need, architecture, and features of EJB 3.

Why EJB 3?

The earlier version of EJB, EJB 2.1, was powerful enough to support all the needs of a distributed enterprise application. However, the development of the distributed application using EJB 2.1 was very complex because a developer has to create a number of interfaces and classes for implementing a single enterprise bean application. In addition, all the interfaces and classes created in an enterprise application need to implement interfaces and extend classes from the `javax.ejb` package. Moreover, the client had to use Java Naming and Directory Interface (JNDI) look up to access enterprise bean and invoke its business methods.

EJB 3 introduced with the Java EE 5 specification has made the EJB technology simpler and easier to be implemented in the applications. EJB 3 needs fewer interfaces and classes as it supports metadata annotation to support Dependency Injection (DI). In EJB 3, the use of annotations has removed the need of Deployment Descriptor, which was used to configure an enterprise bean. In other words, in EJB 3, you can directly configure an enterprise bean using annotations instead of providing the configuration details in Deployment Descriptor. Moreover, the introduction of EJB 3 has simplified the use of entity persistence and Object Relational Mapping (ORM). As the EJB container provides various services, such as transaction and security, the developer does not need to provide code for these services in an application. This gives the developer enough time to concentrate on the implementation of the business logic. EJB 3 enhances business logic implementation; thereby, speeding up the process of enterprise bean development.

EJB 3 provides the following functionalities to simplify the development of enterprise applications:

- Leverages Java language metadata, which helps simplify all bean types and resource accesses. It reduces the need of Deployment Descriptors; however, it preserves the ability to use an Extensible Markup Language (XML) file as an alternative mechanism to override annotations.
- Defines an enterprise bean in the form of Plain Old Java Objects (POJO) instead of implementing EJB component interfaces.
- Provides all business interfaces as Plain Old Java Interfaces (POJI).
- Eliminates the use of the Home interfaces.
- Allows you to define all callback methods by using annotations.
- Simplifies the persistence model.
- Provides support for reusability of existing components in a new application. The EJB 3 specification helps in migrating from the EJB 2.1 applications to new EJB 3 applications.

EJB 3—Architecture and Concepts

The EJB 3 architecture comprises the EJB server, EJB container, and EJB client. In an enterprise application server, the third party vendors provide the container to process an enterprise bean or EJB file. Let's discuss how an enterprise bean or EJB file is processed.

The first step in the EJB processing model is to process an EJB file to generate deployment artifacts (required interfaces and Deployment Descriptors) according to the EJB 2.1 deployment model. Then, the EJB component is deployed on the EJB server. The deployment artifacts generated in the EJB processing model can be non-standard; however, they are similar to Deployment Descriptors defined in EJB 2.1.

Figure 13.1 shows the EJB 3 architecture:

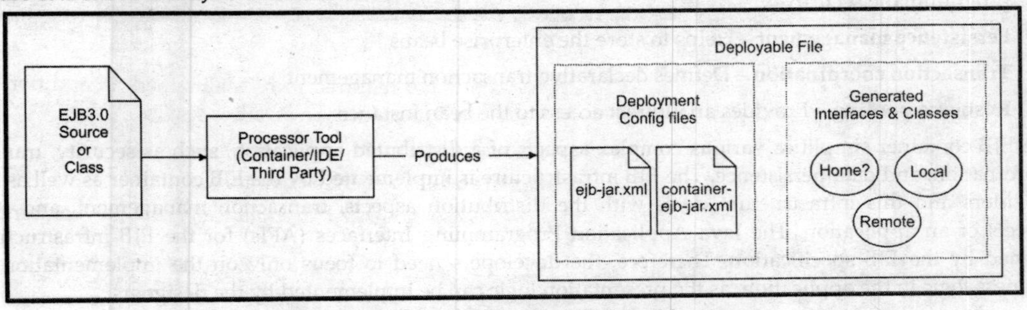

Figure 13.1: Displaying the EJB 3 Architecture

Another EJB 3 processing model is a JavaServer Pages (JSP) drag-and-drop deployment model. This model allows you to add an EJB file into a pre-designated, implementation-defined directory, which can be picked up by the container for processing, deploying, and making it available for use.

Now, let's discuss the EJB architecture in detail by understanding the EJB server, the EJB container, and the EJB client.

The EJB Server

The EJB server provides a runtime environment to execute server applications that use enterprise beans. The EJB server is used to create an infrastructure to deploy server applications also called components. It provides a JNDI-accessible naming service, manages and co-ordinates the allocation of resources to client applications, provides access to system resources, and provides a transaction service.

In the EJB architecture, servers are basically the resource managers. Every server manages the allocation of resources to the containers it controls. It is the resource manager that determines which and how many containers may run within the server.

The EJB server performs the following functions:

- Manages all incoming client requests at the client-level. This also includes providing connections to clients, dispatching client requests to containers, and routing responses back to the clients.
- Manages the processing of the resources that are available to the container at the container-level. This type of management includes allocating available working processes and threads to the running containers.
- Verifies that the container has access to shared services, such as a centralized security manager, a pool of Java Database Connectivity (JDBC) drivers, a transaction service implementation, a global cache manager, and an asynchronous messaging service. This function is done at the server-level.

You can run an EJB application on more than one server. Therefore, the servers must cooperate as a group to allocate resources efficiently across all the containers in a cluster. This cooperation among the servers first provides the status of services to a load balancing process and then assigns the client requests to the least-loaded server to provide the requested services.

The EJB Container

The EJB container provides an environment in which one or more enterprise beans can run. This environment is basically a combination of the available interfaces and classes that the container uses to support enterprise beans throughout their life cycle. The EJB container intercepts all method calls and provides the following services to EJB components:

- **Life cycle management**—Creates and removes enterprise bean instances and handles instance pooling with the activation and passivation of the bean instances
- **Naming services**—Provides JNDI registration of EJB when an enterprise bean is loaded on the Java EE server
- **Security checks**—Performs authentication and access control as well as implements declarative and programmatic security
- **Persistence management**—Helps to store the enterprise beans
- **Transaction coordination**—Defines declarative transaction management
- **Resource pooling**—Provides an indirect access to the bean instance

The EJB container simplifies various complex aspects of a distributed application, such as security, transaction coordination, and data persistence. The EJB infrastructure is implemented by the EJB container as well as service providers and this infrastructure deals with the distribution aspects, transaction management, and security aspects of an application. The Java Application Programming Interfaces (APIs) for the EJB infrastructure are defined by the EJB specification. Therefore, the developers need to focus only on the implementation of the business logic in the application, as the presentation logic can be implemented by the designers.

Figure 13.2 shows the services provided by the EJB container :

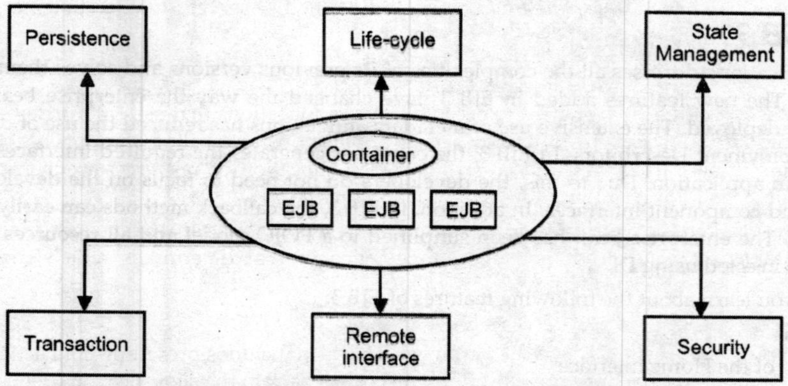

Figure 13.2: Displaying the Services Provided by the EJB Container

The EJB container performs the following tasks for each enterprise bean:

- Registers the object of an enterprise bean on the Java EE server
- Provides a Remote interface for the object
- Creates and destroys object instances
- Checks security for the object
- Manages the active state for the object (activation/passivation)
- Coordinates distributed transactions
- Persists Container-Managed Persistence (CMP) entity beans and saves stateful session beans attributes when passivated

Whenever a client wants to call business methods of an enterprise bean, it needs to connect to the container first. Then, the container verifies that whether or not the call follows the semantics specified in Deployment Descriptor and then dispatches the request to the enterprise bean. This mechanism enables the container to control all the aspects of the execution of an enterprise bean, including the following aspects:

- **Life cycle**—Refers to the invocation of the life cycle methods of an enterprise bean according to the EJB 3 specification. While managing the life cycle of an enterprise bean, the container itself enforces security, transaction, and persistence requirements.
- **Security**—Refers to the permissions set for users to access an enterprise bean. When a client attempts to call a method of EJB, the container looks for the user's permission in an Access Control List (ACL) to verify whether the client has the right to invoke that method. Deployment Descriptor contains the access control declarations about the EJB's methods.
- **Transaction**—Refers to the declarations about the transaction restrictions on the EJB's methods included in the Deployment Descriptor object. When a client attempts to call the method of an EJB, the container verifies whether or not the call obeys the transaction restrictions on that method.
- **Persistence**—Refers to the persistence storage of data of an EJB. There are two different types of persistence-one that is managed by beans and the other that is managed by the container. In the bean managed persistence, the beans are responsible for implementing data access as the code for data access functions need to be provided in the bean class; whereas, in CMP, the implementation of data access functions are done by the container.

The EJB Client

The client code is the code written to execute business logic embedded in an enterprise bean and its methods. An EJB client can be a simple Java program or a Web client. The end-users run these clients to get results from the enterprise bean method invocation. The EJB client can use resource injection or JNDI service to access an enterprise bean. The EJB client can be a simple Java class, applet, servlet, or JSP. An enterprise bean is looked up using resource injection or the lookup() method, irrespective of the different EJB clients.

Features of EJB 3

The EJB 3 specification addresses all the complexities of its previous versions and solves them by implementing new strategies. The new features added in EJB 3 have changed the way the enterprise beans are developed, configured, and deployed. The extensive use of metadata annotations has reduced the use of different interfaces, classes, and Deployment Descriptors. In EJB 3, the container generates the required interfaces and Deployment Descriptor for an application. Due to this, the developers do not need to focus on the development of local or remote home and component interfaces. In addition, in EJB 3, the callback methods can easily be marked in the enterprise bean. The enterprise bean has been simplified to a POJO model and all resources to be used by the components are injected using DI.

In this section, you learn about the following features of EJB 3:

- Annotations
- Elimination of the Home interface
- Elimination of the component interface
- Callback methods
- Simple POJO model
- Java Persistence API
- Dependency injection
- Timer service
- Interceptors

Annotations

The annotation feature is introduced in the Java Platform, Standard Edition 5 (Java SE 5). These annotations are inspected at compile time or runtime by different tools to generate additional constructs, such as Deployment Descriptors, and to customize the component's runtime behavior. You can annotate class fields, methods, and classes. The set of annotations provided by EJB 3 simplifies the development of enterprise beans. You can mark interfaces, classes, fields, and methods created for an EJB implementation with different annotations, such as @Remote, @Stateful, and @Stateless. You should provide annotations only when the default values cannot be used. For example, for an enterprise bean CustomerBean, you do not need to extend `javax.ejb.EnterpriseBean` type of class; instead, you can use @Stateless annotation to declare it as a stateless session bean, as shown in the following code snippet:

```
package com.kogent.ejb;
import javax.ejb.Stateless;
@Stateless
public class CustomerBean
{
   public String sayHello()
   {
        return "Hello from CustomerBean.";
   }
}
```

Elimination of the Home Interface

In EJB 2.1, you need to create a home interface (local or remote) by extending either the `javax.ejb.EJBHome` interface or the `javax.ejb.EJBLocalHome` interface and declaring life cycle methods, such as create() and remove(). In EJB 3, you do not need to create locale or remote home interfaces for an enterprise bean. The EJB 2.1 APIs are still supported in EJB 3 specification and the home interfaces can be used to declare the enterprise bean methods.

Elimination of the Component Interface

The earlier versions of EJB require the local or remote component interfaces to be created for the given enterprise bean. The local component interfaces require extending the `javax.ejb.EJBObject` class; whereas, the remote component interfaces require extending the `javax.ejb.EJBLocalObject` class. The component interfaces were used to declare the business methods that a client could invoke. In EJB 3, you do not need to create component interfaces as they have been replaced by business interfaces that declare all business methods to be provided to the client. The business interface can be local or remote; however, both local and remote home interfaces are simple POJI.

Callback Methods

In EJB 3, you do not need to define all the life cycle callback methods, such as `ejbPassivate()` and `ejbActivate()`, in the enterprise bean class. In the earlier versions, you have to define these callback methods to provide various implementations in an enterprise bean class; however, in EJB 3, they have become optional. In EJB 3, you can mark an arbitrary method as the callback method, which can listen EJB life cycle events. You can use different metadata annotations, such as `@PreDestroy`, `@PostConstruct`, `@PrePassivate`, `@PostActivate`, and `@Remove` to mark a method as callback method, as shown in the following code snippet:

```
@Stateful
public class SomeSessionBean
{
   @PreDestroy
   public void someMethod()
   {
         /*Some Logic to be executed before the destroy() method*/
   }
}
```

Simple POJO Model

In EJB 3, an enterprise bean is a simple Java class that does not implement any interface or extend any class. A simple POJO object can be made a powerful component that can handle concurrency, transactions, and security issues. All these functionalities are provided by the container to the simple POJO objects.

The POJO model also helps in creating enterprise bean classes that do not depend on other APIs. The POJO objects help in implementing the unit testing by using frameworks, such as JUnit, without deploying them on a server. The implementation of the POJO model has simplified the development of enterprise beans to a great extent. To create an EJB application, you just need to create simple business interfaces that are POJIs and implement business methods in an enterprise bean class, which is a POJO. All these resources, such as business interfaces and enterprise bean class are made accessible in the component by resource injection using annotations. In addition, all callback methods can be marked with annotations in the enterprise bean class.

Java Persistence API

EJB 3 includes a new Java Persistence API (JPA) to simplify the task of storing the data of an enterprise bean permanently in a database. ORM and all persistence logic are now handled by the container and you just need to provide proper annotations, such as `@Id`, @Table, `@OneToOne`, and `@OneToMany`, in the enterprise bean class. These annotations are used to map entities and their relationships to application's database.

An enterprise application helps to persistently store data of an organization. Initially, JavaBeans was used to handle the organization's data and the developers need to provide code to directly establish connection of the application with the database. In case of large amount of data, the direct communication with database led to the problem of heavy load on the server. As the solution to this problem, JPA was introduced in the Java EE 5 platform to store the data persistently with the help of an enterprise bean. The first release of JPA lacked many features, such as annotations and brought many problems to the developers. For example, the developer needs to provide the code to manage the relationships of the entities or store the foreign key fields of a database in the bean class. The EJB2.1 specification introduced the container-managed entity beans in which the EJB container was responsible to manage the entity relationships. In addition, in the container-managed entity beans, the EJB server was responsible for generating subclasses to manage the persistent data. The EJB2.1 specification also introduced the Enterprise Java Bean Query Language (EJBQL) – a query language designed to create queries for CMP entity beans. This language is similar to SQL and is used to search the persistent attributes of the enterprise beans.

The EJB 2.1 specification, despite of the improved features than its earlier versions, was still overloaded with the major problems and complexities. The problems and complexities were reduced with the introduction of EJB 3, which provides JPA as a simplified programming model for entity persistence. Now, ORM or persistence approach uses the POJO model instead of the abstract persistence schema model to simplify the complexities of EJB 2.1. ORM maps entities and their relationships to application's database. An EJB 3 entity depicts persistent information stored in a database by using CMP; however, EJB 2.1 entity bean only represents persistent information stored in the database. The optimistic locking technique that was supported only by the TopLink persistence framework is also encapsulated in the EJB 3 specification. This technique allows you to use objects in a disconnected model implying that you can change data and the relationships of objects offline and merge data operations into one transaction. The following are the features and functionalities provided by JPA:

- Requires less number of classes and interfaces
- Introduces a new EntityManager API, similar to Hibernate, which is used to perform various operations, such as creating, removing, and searching entity beans
- Eliminates the use of the lengthy Deployment Descriptors by facilitating the use of annotations
- Provides better ORM
- Eliminates the need for lookup code
- Provides better support for inheritance and polymorphism
- Adds support for named (static) and dynamic queries
- Allows you to perform many database related operations, instead of performing only one operation generating primary key
- Provides a Java Persistence query language—an enhanced EJB QL
- Makes testing the entities without the EJB container easier. Earlier, the developers need to be aware of deployment platform to test EJBs.

The preceding changes in the new JPA are explained in detail in *Chapter 14, Implementing Entities and Java Persistence API 2.1*.

Dependency Injection

The client who wants to use the constructed bean in an application needs to know how to locate and invoke that enterprise bean (constructed bean). The client for an EJB 2.1 session bean gets the reference of the session bean with JNDI. To use an enterprise bean, Calculator, you need to add the following code snippet in the EJB 2.1 client to locate and invoke an enterprise bean method:

```
Context ic = new InitialContext();

Object obj = ic.lookup ("CalculatorJNDI");

CalculatorHome home =

(CalculatorHome)PortableRemoteObject.narrow(obj, CalculatorHome.class);

Calculator calc = home.create();
```

In the preceding code snippet, the JNDI name of the Calculator bean is CalculatorJNDI. The local/remote instance is obtained with the create() method. However, in EJB 3.0, the JNDI lookup and create() method invocation are not required. In EJB 3.0, a reference to a resource is obtained with DI using annotations. EJB, by implementing DI, conveys to the container that a particular resource is dependent on some other resource. A DI comprises the type of resource, the resource properties, and a name to access the resource. The use of annotations in EJB 3 has simplified the task of both the developers and the EJB client. Some examples of DIs are shown in the following code snippet

```
@EJB (name="sessionBeanName", beanInterface=SessionBeanInterface.class)
@Resource (name="Database", type="javax.sql.DataSource.class")
```

The @EJB annotation used in the preceding code snippet injects stubs of a session bean having the sessionBeanName name in a Java class. The @Resource annotation is used to inject a service object having the `Database` JNDI name. This name may be present in either global or local JNDI tree.

DIs may be associated to a bean class or the member variables and methods of a bean class. The information to be specified in DI depends upon the context and the amount of data to be fetched from that context.

Timer Service

In enterprise applications, sometimes you need to implement time-dependent services. For example, you may need to invoke a particular business method provided by an enterprise bean after a given span of time or repeatedly after certain fixed time intervals. Prior to EJB 2.1, developers had to write code manually for building and deploying time-based workflows. However, with EJB 3, the task of creating such applications has been considerably simplified. Equipped with annotations and DIs, developers can use EJB 3 to build and deploy scheduled applications easily.

Interceptors

The interceptors are used to intercept the invocation of business methods of an enterprise bean to provide some additional functionality. The methods of interceptor can be defined in a separate Interceptor class and invoked before the business method. These Interceptor classes are then used with the session beans and MDBs. For example, you can invoke more than one interceptor on an enterprise bean if you need to validate all passed values to the business methods before executing the actual logic.

Let's use the @Interceptors annotation to import a chain of interceptors associated with the bean. You can define interceptor methods by using the @AroundInvoke annotation. The following code snippet shows how to add interceptor methods to a bean:

```
@Stateful
@Interceptors({MethodProfiler.class})
public class SomeServiceBean
{
   ...
   ...
}
```

In addition, various new features have been introduced in EJB 3.2, the latest version of EJB bundled in Java EE 7. These features are as follows:

- Incorporates new features in EJB.Lite with asynchronous session beans, and non-persistent EJB Timer service.
- Prunes technologies including Entity Bean Component Contract for CMP and BMP of EJB 2.1 and earlier, Client View of EJB 2.1 and earlier, EJB QL – Query language for CMP query methods, and JAX-RPC-based Web Service Endpoints and Client View.
- Incorporates following updates and improvements:
  - The stateful session bean lifecycle callback methods viz @PostConstruct, @PreDestroy, @PostActivate, and @PrePassivate can be optionally made transactional which are non-transactional by default
  - The stateful session beans can be opt-out of passivation
  - Simplified rules for defining local and remote views of the beans.
  - A new convenient API namely TimerService.getAllTimers() that returns a list of all timers in the same bean
  - Removal of the restriction of obtaining current class loader to allow using java.io package
  - New activation-config properties defined for JMS 2.0
  - Thread-safe ThreadContext in Singleton
  - Embedded containers inherently implement Autocloseable

After having the basic knowledge of EJB, let's explore different types of EJBs.

Classifying EJBs

There are different scenarios in the enterprise application development where you need to implement different types of enterprise beans. Different enterprise beans provide different functionalities. An entity bean represents an object in a persistent state; whereas; an MDB can be used only when a Java Message Service client is needed, and the user session bean is used to maintain the conversational state of the user. The enterprise beans can be classified into the following three types based on the type of functionality provided by them:

- Session beans
- Message-driven bean
- Entity beans

Now, let's discuss session beans and MDB in detail. The next chapter provides a detailed knowledge of entity beans.

Introducing Session Beans

A session bean is a type of enterprise bean that exists only for the client and server sessions. A session bean is generally created when a client requests a database with the help of a query to retrieve the required data. The bean exists till the client and server session persists. Almost all the services start with session beans, such as LoginVerificationBean and ShoppingCartBean. The session beans hold business processes, such as delivering an order and doing financial calculations for an application. These beans are reusable components, which provide methods that can be accessed by the client. All the services provided by the session bean are in the form of different methods.

As a session bean is never shared among multiple clients, the methods of a particular bean can only be executed by a single client. The length of a session determines the duration for which a session bean remains in use. This implies that a session bean is a short-lived object.

The actions performed using the methods of a session bean may lead to the change of data of an enterprise bean. This results in change in the state of the enterprise bean that may be persistent or transient. A persistent change is available for the multiple sessions of a client; however, a transient change is available for a single session. There are two types of session beans:

- The stateful session bean
- The stateless session bean

The difference between stateful and stateless session beans is that a stateless session bean can be used for another client also, while a stateful session bean cannot be used for another client. These two types will be discussed in detail later in this chapter.

Prior to the discussion on the stateless and stateful session beans, some of the session bean concepts, such as conversational state as well as state management of a session bean are described in the following sections. It would make the concept of working of the whole session bean architecture clear.

Conversational State

An action performed by a method provided by the session bean may change the state of the session bean instance. The state of a session bean instance is known as its conversational state. In other words, a conversational state can also be defined as the state of all the attributes of session bean instances, state of connections (database, open source), and the reference to some other objects.

If the state of a session bean is stored for one client, then a different bean instance is needed for other clients. This may increase the number of session bean instances on the server. This can be avoided by the EJB container by writing the state of the stateful session bean to a secondary storage device. This process of removing the session bean from the active storage is known as passivation—the reverse process of activation. The EJB container uses serialization at the time of passivation and deserialization at the time of activation. In this way, the state can be preserved and the bean instance can be used to hold the new conversation with the new client.

State Management of a Bean

The word state refers to the state of all the attributes of a session bean class. The state of a bean is managed by the EJB container. The way the state of a session bean is maintained depends upon the type of the session bean.

If the session bean is of type stateless, then it holds the state for a single method invocation. The next invocation of any method on the same instance of the bean does not need to know the past invocation results. In other words, there is no conversational state to be managed. All the clients inside the bean pool are equivalent and any client can be serviced by any other client.

In case of a stateful session bean type, the new state of the bean is decided by the action of the next method invoked and the result of the action performed by the last method call. The state of the bean is maintained across multiple method calls or transactions for a particular client, that is, particular session. A single bean instance has a particular state for a particular client and thereby cannot be reassigned to another client. When the number of active beans allowed by the container exceeds, the container passivates the beans and reactivates them when they are required. In other words, the container passivates those active beans which are not required and activates them whenever they are required.

According to the type of the session bean, the state can be maintained either for a single method call (stateless) or the sequence of method invocations (stateful). All the states of a session bean are managed by the container.

The Stateless Session Beans

Some business processes do not need the state of a bean to be saved through multiple method invocations. The session bean representing such business processes will be a stateless session bean. A stateless session bean does not require its conversational state to be stored. The term stateless explains the fact that this type of session bean does not hold the state of a bean between different method calls.

In other words, a stateless session bean does not have any conversational state as the bean does not hold client details after a method call. The algorithm implemented by an EJB container decides whether the bean is to be destroyed or to be retained for reuse by some other client. The information held by a stateless session is not specific to any client.

After having a brief discussion about a stateless session bean, let's now explore its life cycle.

The life cycle of a stateless session bean can be described with various methods that are invoked throughout its life. A stateless session bean can be in one of the following two states:

- Does Not Exist state
- Ready state

You can change the state of a stateless session bean by invoking different methods, such as `ejbCreate()` and `ejbRemove()`.

Figure 13.3 represents the life cycle of a stateless session bean:

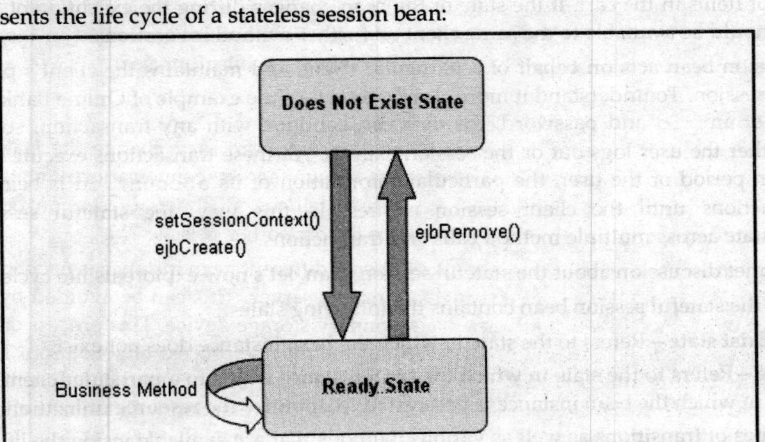

Figure 13.3: Displaying the Life cycle of a Stateless Session Bean

Figure 13.3 shows the two major transitions in the state of a stateless session bean. These transitions are from the Does Not Exist state to the Ready state and from the Ready state to the Does Not Exist state. Let's explain these transitions in brief.

Moving from the Does Not Exist State to the Ready State

There are some callback methods that are used to change the state of a stateless session bean from the Does Not Exist state to the Ready state. These methods are as follows:

- `setSessionContext()` – Contains the reference of the session context. After creating a stateless session bean instance, the EJB container places it into the Ready state. This instance then invokes the `setSessionContext()` method. The main purpose of calling this method is to associate a bean with a session context because the session context behaves as the gateway to interact with the container.
- `ejbCreate()` – Refers to the method that is invoked only once during the lifetime of the session bean. After the `setSessionContext()` callback method is called, the EJB container calls the `ejbCreate()` callback method to initialize the beans. It is important to remember that the `ejbCreate()` method is always called after the `setSessionContext()` method, as the enterprise bean can be created only after the session context has been created.

When the bean instance is in the Ready state, it can service a client's request and invoke the business method. The EJB container uses the available bean instance to execute the business method. After the execution of the business method is finished, the session bean instance moves from the Ready state to the Does Not Exist state.

Moving from the Ready State to the Does Not Exist State

Suppose the EJB container has a large number of session bean instances and one of these instances needs to access some resources or services of the container. In such a situation, the container needs to reduce the number of session bean instances that are in the ready pool. To reduce the number of session bean instances, the EJB container calls the `ejbRemove()` callback method on the session bean instances that are not in use. Using this method, the EJB container invalidates the reference to the bean instance that is in the ready pool. It does not indicate that the bean has been destroyed; it only sets the status of the bean instance as an inactive one.

The Stateful Session Beans

When a business process needs to maintain the client's state, the stateful session bean should be used. The stateful session beans are basically used for the process in which the state of the bean should be retained to be used by the same client during further method invocations. One of the good examples of a stateful session bean is ShoppingCart. Each method call in a ShoppingCart needs to know the current state of the shopping cart, that is, the number of items in the cart. If the state of the bean changes during the execution of the method, then the changed state should be available to the same client on further method invocations.

The stateful session bean acts on behalf of a particular client, and maintains the client's particular information throughout the session. To understand it more clearly, let's take the example of Online Banking. After a user logs on with the `account_id` and password, the user can continue with any transaction, such as withdrawal or deposit until either the user logs out or the session expires. All these transactions execute successfully, because during the login period of the user, the particular information of its `account_id` is being maintained across multiple transactions until the client session expires. In this way, the stateful session bean creates a conversational state across multiple method calls and transactions.

After having a brief discussion about the stateful session bean, let's now explore its life cycle.

The life cycle of the stateful session bean contains the following states:

- **Does Not Exist state** – Refers to the state in which the bean instance does not exist
- **Ready state** – Refers to the state in which the bean instance is tied to a particular client Passive state: Refers to the state in which the bean instance is passivated to optimize the resource utilization

The different types of transitions as well as various methods that are available inside the life cycle of the stateful session bean are shown in Figure 13.4:

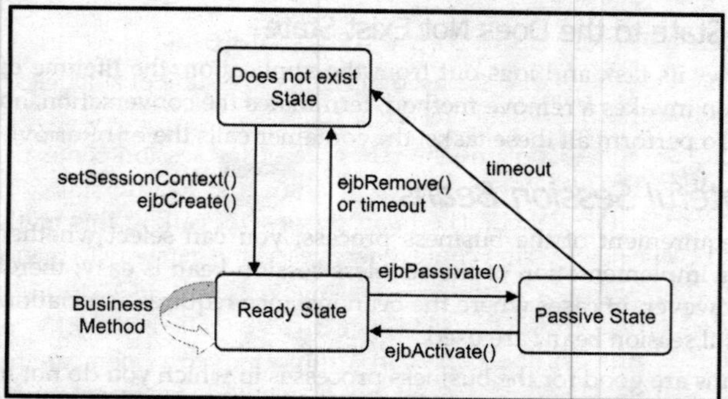

Figure 13.4: Displaying the Life Cycle of a Stateful Session Bean

Let's now discuss different transitions and methods of the life cycle of the stateful session bean.

Moving from the Does Not Exist State to the Ready State

The Ready state of the stateful session bean is similar to the Ready state of the stateless session bean. When there is interaction between the Does Not Exist and Ready states and the state of transition is from the Does Not Exist state to the Ready state, the following methods are used:

- `setSessionContext()`
- `ejbCreate()`

The functionality of both the `setSessionContext()` and `ejbCreate()` methods is similar as described in the stateless session bean section in the chapter.

In the Ready state, the session bean instance is associated with a particular client for the duration of the conversation. During this duration, the instance executes the methods that are invoked by the client.

Moving from the Ready State to the Passive State

Suppose a client does not invoke a bean for a long time and lets it remain in memory. As it is not a good practice to keep a bean in memory; therefore, to save memory, the client employs the process of passivation. In the process of passivation, the bean instances that are no longer used are saved into a disk or in some permanent storage device. The container performs this task by serializing the entire bean instance and then moving it into a permanent storage, such as a database or a file.

The EJB container can passivate a session bean by moving it from the Ready state to the Passive state. During passivation, data will be serialized and written back to the disk. To perform a task, the container calls the `ejbPassivate()` callback method. In the Passive state, the bean instances can be categorized as:

- **Not Recently Used (NRU)** – Lists the items that are not used recently
- **Least Recently Used (LRU)** – Lists the item that is used least recently

In the Passive state, if the stateful session bean is set to use the NRU algorithm, the session bean can perform the time-out operation. It means the lifetime of a session bean has expired and it moves to the Does Not Exist state, leading to the invocation of the `ejbRemove()` method by the container. However, if a stateful session bean is set to use the LRU algorithm, the instance of the stateful session bean cannot be expired while it is in the Passive state.

Moving from the Passive State to the Ready State

When a bean instance is needed again by a client, then the instance should move from the Passive state to the Ready state. The process of moving from the Passive state to the Ready state is known as activation. In this process, the container activates the bean instance by retrieving it from the permanent storage, then deserializes the bean instance, and finally sends it back to the memory for future use.

After passivation, if the client wants to continue the conversation by invoking a business method, then it needs to reactivate the session bean instance. The data stored in the disk is used to restore the bean instance state by calling the `ejbActivate()` callback method.

Moving from the Ready State to the Does Not Exist State

When the client completes its task and logs out from the application, the lifetime of the session expires. In this case, the client application invokes a remove method, terminates the conversation, and informs the EJB container to remove the instance. To perform all these tasks, the container calls the `ejbRemove()` method.

Stateless versus Stateful Session Beans

Depending upon the requirement of the business process, you can select whether to use the stateless or the stateful session bean. As implementation of the stateless session bean is easy; therefore, it is preferred over the stateful session bean. However, in cases where the bean instance requires association with the same client for the whole session, the stateful session beans are used.

The stateless session beans are good for the business processes in which you do not need to maintain the state for a single client among the number of methods invoked. The EJB container can use any free stateless session bean from the pool to serve the client request as the stateless session bean is not associated to a particular client. This makes stateless session beans more scalable.

A stateful session bean helps in preserving the bean state that is used for further business method invocations. Therefore, it is recommended to use the stateful session bean for the implementation of such business processes. The stateful session bean is also used whenever a bean requires storing information about a single particular client. The stateful session bean can be used for a single client only.

Implementing Session Beans

The implementation of the stateless and stateful session beans involves development of different components. Therefore, before developing an application using a stateless session bean, you should get familiar with the following components:

- Business interface
- Bean class

Let's discuss these components, one by one.

Exploring Business Interface

An interface through which a client is able to access a bean is known as a business interface. Generally, this interface contains bean methods that are required for developing applications related to beans. The bean methods declared in business interface are known as business methods. This interface is necessary for the stateless session bean. The business interface can be of two types—local interface and remote interface. You can define the type of a business interface by using annotations, such as `@Remote` and `@Local`. If you do not provide any annotation, then this interface becomes local business interface.

Exploring Bean Class

The stateless session bean is represented by a class known as the bean class, which implements business interfaces to provide implementation to a business method. The bean class can implement multiple business interfaces. A stateless session bean should be defined as stateless in Deployment Descriptor or it must be annotated with the `@Stateless` annotation. Due to the use of the `@Stateless` annotation, you need not to implement the `javax.ejb.SessionBean` interface in a bean class, as it was required in earlier versions of EJB.

NOTE

`javax.ejb.SessionBean` ***contains methods, such as*** *`setSessionContext()`*, *`ejbremove()`*, *`ejbActivate()`*, ***and*** *`ejbPassivate()`*. ***The stateless annotation is denoted as*** *`@Stateless`* ***and it indicates that the bean is a stateless session bean.***

After understanding about the bean interface and bean class, let's develop an application using a stateless session bean.

Working with a Stateless Session Bean

Now, let's develop a simple application, Hello, to demonstrate how to work with a stateless session bean. Perform the following steps to develop the Hello application:

- Create a business interface
- Create a bean class
- Create a client
- Create the directory structure of the Hello application
- Package the application
- Deploy the application
- Run the application

Let's perform these steps, one by one.

Creating a Business Interface

A business interface is designed to perform the following tasks:

- Defines the client view of the bean
- Declares all the business methods

The business interface created in this application is `HelloRemote` and the only business method declared is `hello()`.

Listing 13.1 provides the code for the HelloRemote.java file (save this file in the `\Hello\Hello-ejb\src\com\kogent\ejb\` folder):

Listing 13.1: Showing the Code of the `HelloRemote.java` File

```
package com.kogent.ejb;
public interface HelloRemote
{
   public String hello(String h);
}
```

The `HelloRemote.java` file is stored under the `com.kogent.ejb` package. Save HelloRemote.java under the src directory of the Hello-ejb directory.

NOTE

It is a good practice to write the programs inside the package while developing any application. It avoids the name conflicts among files.

Creating a Bean Class

After creating the business interface, the `HelloBean` class is required to implement the `HelloRemote` interface. The `HelloBean` class is a plain Java class, which implements business methods defined in business interface. This bean class is also known as the implementation class of the stateless session bean class as it provides implementation to all business methods. In our case, the bean class is `HelloBean`, which implements the `HelloRemote` business interface.

Listing 13.2 shows the code to create `HelloBean` class (save this file in the `\Hello\Hello-ejb\src\com\kogent\ejb\` folder):

Listing 13.2: Showing the Code of the `HelloBean.java File`

```
package com.kogent.ejb;
import javax.ejb.*;
@Stateless
public class HelloBean implements HelloRemote
{
  public String hello(String h)
  {
       return  "Hello " + h + "!";
  }
}
```

Listing 13.2 shows that the HelloBean class is created in the com.kogent.ejb package and the @Stateless annotation is used to define the HelloBean class as a stateless session bean. Instead of using the @Stateless annotation, you can configure the bean in Deployment Descriptor (web.xml). In EJB 3, annotations are introduced to reduce the efforts required to create and configure different components of EJB.

Creating a Client

To access an enterprise bean, a client code uses JNDI, which is a directory service that provides a mechanism to find and lookup data and objects by using a naming service. When the client code is executed completely, connection of the naming directory with a bean's container is established. The code used to obtain the JNDI context depends upon the application server being used.

Listing 13.3 shows the code of the JSP client, hello.jsp, of the Hello application (save the hello.jsp file in the \Hello\Hello-war\ folder):

Listing 13.3: Showing the Code of the hello.jsp File

```
<%@ page import="com.kogent.ejb.*, javax.naming.*, java.text.*"%>
<%!
private HelloRemote hel = null;
public void jspInit ()
{
   try
   {
         InitialContext ctx = new InitialContext();
         hel = (HelloRemote) ctx.lookup("java:comp/env/ejb/HelloBean");
   }
   catch (Exception e)
   {
         e.printStackTrace ();
   }
}
%>
<%
String result = null;
String name = null;
try
{
   name=request.getParameter("name");
   if(name!=null)
         result = hel.hello(name);
}
catch (Exception e)
{
   result = "Not valid";
}
%>
<html>
<head>
   <title>Example of Stateless session bean</title>
   <link rel="stylesheet" href="mystyle.css" type="text/css"/>
</head>
<body>
   <h1>Using Stateless session bean</h1>
   <br><br>
   <form action="hello.jsp" method="POST">
         Enter Your Name : <input type="text" name="name">
         <br><br><input type="submit" value="Submit"><br><br>
   </form>
   <%
   if(result!=null)
   out.println("<b>"+result+"</b>");
   %>
</body>
</html>
```

Save the code shown in Listing 13.3 as `hello.jsp` in the Hello-war directory under the root directory, named Hello. After the connection is established and the context is obtained from the `InitialContext()` method, the context can be used to look up the EJB's business interface by using the `lookup()` method. The `hello` JSP page looks up for the business interface, `HelloRemote`, by using the `lookup()` method. The `hello.jsp` file shows a text field and a submit button. Now, when you enter a name in the text field and click the submit button, the `String hello(String)` business method returns a string value.

NOTE

JNDI offers:

- *A mechanism to bind an object to a name*
- *A directory lookup interface*
- *An event interface that define when to modify the directory entries*

Creating the Directory Structure and Configuring the Hello Application

To create the directory structure of the Hello application, you first need to create a folder named Hello, depicting the name of the application that you are creating. The Hello folder contains three subfolders, `Hello-war`, `Hello-ejb`, and `META-INF`. The `Hello-ejb` folder and the Hello-war folder are also known as the bean module and Web module, respectively. The `Hello-ejb` folder contains all the Java files, such as interfaces and bean files that are inside your application. The `Hello-war` folder stores all the JSP files, Hypertext Markup Language (HTML) files, and WEB-INF folder. The META-INF folder contains the `MANIFEST.MF` file, by default.

The directory structure of the Hello application is shown in Figure 13.5:

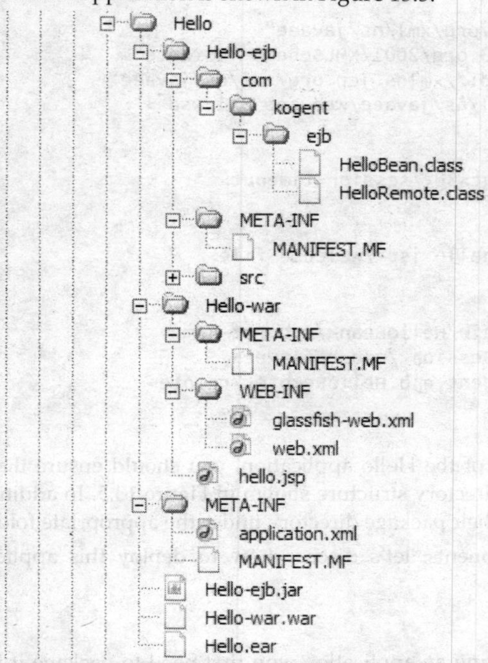

Figure 13.5: Showing the Directory Structure of the Hello Application

In Figure 13.5, the .class files of the bean and remote interface of the Hello application are placed within the Hello-ejb folder, as it is the EJB module of the application where the bean would be looked up.

The only additional file you have to create is `application.xml`. This file is necessary for the EJB 3 applications to provide the application details, such as the name of the EJB and Web modules. Listing 13.4 provides the code for the application.xml file (save this file in the \Hello\META-INF\ folder):

Listing 13.4: Showing the Code for the `application.xml` File

```
<?xml version="1.0" encoding="UTF-8"?>
<application version="7" xmlns="http://xmlns.jcp.org/xml/ns/javaee"
xmlns:xsi="http://www.w3.org/2001/XMLSchema-instance"
xsi:schemaLocation="http://xmlns.jcp.org/ xml/ns/javaee
http://xmlns.jcp.org/xml/ns/javaee/application_7.xsd">
   <display-name>Hello</display-name>
   <module>
          <ejb>Hello-ejb.jar</ejb>
   </module>
   <module>
          <web>
          <web-uri> Hello-war.war</web-uri>
          <context-root>/Hello-war</context-root>
          </web>
   </module>
</application>
```

The `application.xml` file configures two modules used in the `Hello` application. These modules are Hello-war and Hello-ejb.

The code for `web.xml` file of `WEB-INF` is given in Listing 13.5 (save this file in the \Hello\Hello-war\WEB-INF folder):

Listing 13.5: Showing the `web.xml File`

```
<?xml version="1.0" encoding="UTF-8"?>
<web-app version="3.1"
xmlns="http://xmlns.jcp.org/xml/ns/javaee"
xmlns:xsi="http://www.w3.org/2001/XMLSchema-instance"
xsi:schemaLocation="http://xmlns.jcp.org/xml/ns/javaee
http://xmlns.jcp.org/xml/ns/javaee/web-app_3_1.xsd">

   <session-config>
          <session-timeout>30</session-timeout>
   </session-config>
   <welcome-file-list>
          <welcome-file>hello.jsp</welcome-file>
   </welcome-file-list>
   <ejb-ref>
          <ejb-ref-name>ejb/HelloBean</ejb-ref-name>
          <ejb-ref-type>Session</ejb-ref-type>
          <remote>com.kogent.ejb.HelloRemote</remote>
   </ejb-ref>
</web-app>
```

After creating the required files of the Hello application, you should ensure that all the files are stored at the right location according to the directory structure shown in Figure 13.5. In addition, compile all the Java source files and place them along with their package directory under the appropriate folder.

After developing all the components, let's discuss how to deploy this application on the Glassfish server version 4.

Packaging the Application

As you know that before deploying an application, you first need to package it in an archive file. Therefore, in this section, you learn how to package the Hello application into the Hello.ear file. To create the Enterprise ARchive (EAR) file, you the first need to package the `Hello-ejb` module into **Hello-ejb.jar** and the `Hello-war` module into the **Hello-war.war** archive file. You can package the EJB module through Command Prompt by using the following command from the Hello-ejb folder:

```
jar -cvf Hello-ejb.jar *.*
```

Similarly, the Web module can be packaged by executing the following command from the Hello-war folder:

```
jar -cvf Hello-war.war *.*
```

You need to package the Hello-ejb.jar, Hello-war.war, and META-INF files in the EAR file of the Hello application. Now, let's create an EAR file through Command Prompt by executing the following command from the location of the Hello folder:

```
jar -cvf Hello.ear *.*
```

In the Hello application, the EAR file named Hello.ear needs to be deployed on the Glassfish server version 4 to run the Hello application.

Deploying the Application

After packaging the Hello application, let's deploy it on the Glassfish server version 4. Prior to the deployment of the Hello application, ensure that the server is running. Perform the following steps to deploy the Hello application:

1. Browse the `http://localhost:4848/` URL to open the Admin console. The index page appears in which you need to enter the username and password to login to the Admin console.
2. Expand the Applications node from the left panel.

   Figure 13.6 shows the Deployment panel for enterprise applications:

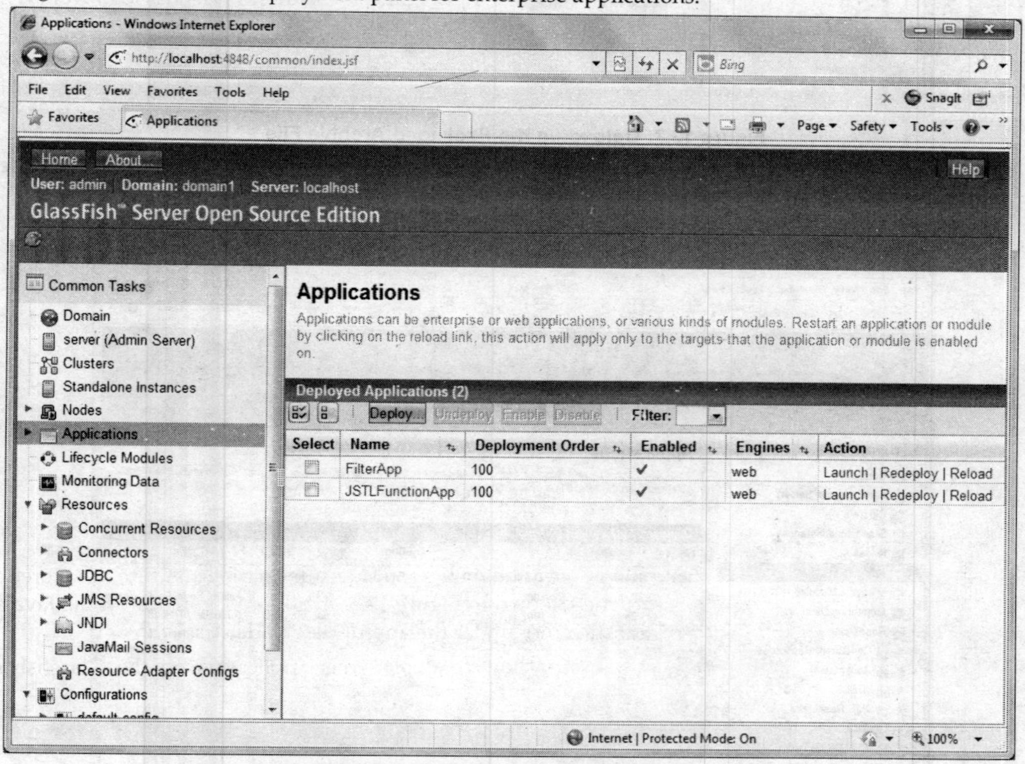

Figure 13.6: Deploying the Enterprise Applications

3. Click the Deploy button to deploy the enterprise application. The Deploy Applications or Modules pane appears (Figure 13.7).
4. Click the Browse button to browse the `Hello.ear` file saved on your computer. After browsing the file, the information required for the `Hello` application gets automatically filled in the relevant fields, as shown in Figure 13.7:

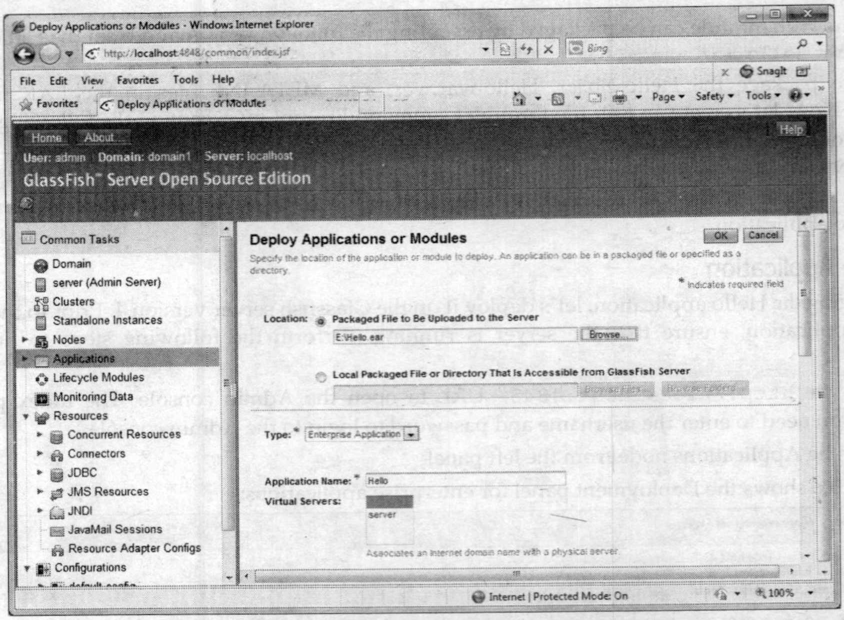

Figure 13.7: Uploading the Packaged Archive File

5. Click the `OK` button to deploy the `Hello` application. Figure 13.8 displays the list of the deployed applications, including the `Hello` application:

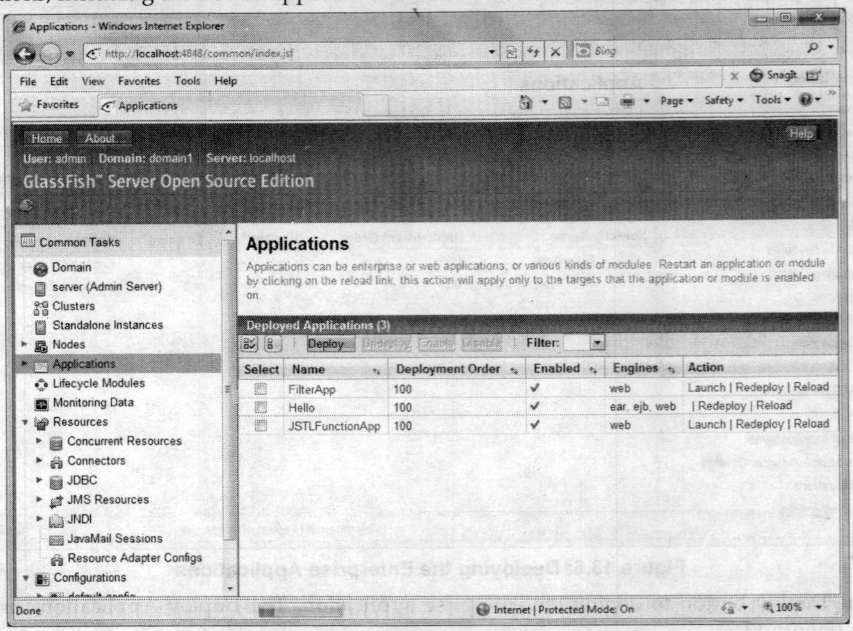

Figure 13.8: Displaying the Deployed Applications

In the `Hello` application, the Enabled column shows the true value, implying that you can execute the application (Figure 13.8). However, if this column shows false, then select the checkbox beside the Hello application, which activates the Enable button. Finally, click the Enable button to enable the application for execution.

Now, let's run the application to see its output.

Running the Application

After deploying the application, you can run it by browsing the `http://localhost:8080/Hello-war/hello.jsp` URL. The hello.jsp page appears, as shown in Figure 13.9:

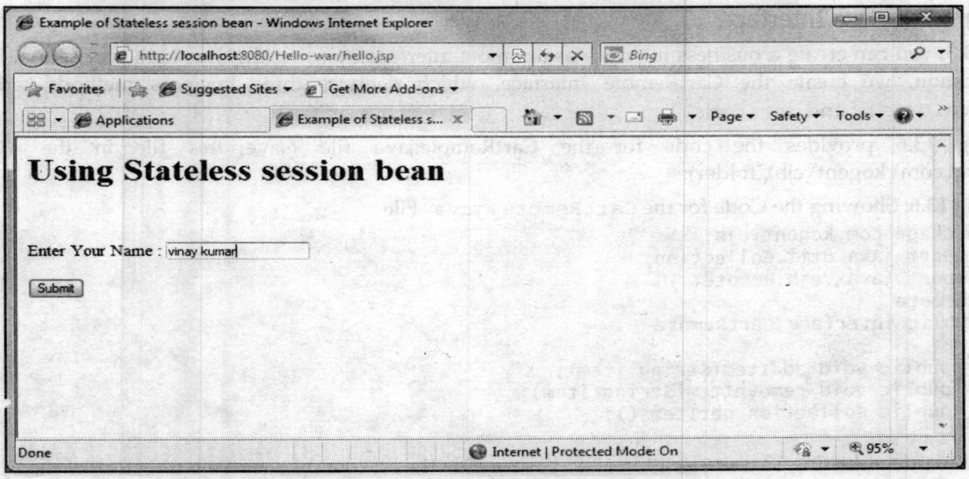

Figure 13.9: Displaying the hello.jsp Page

Enter your name in the textbox shown on the hello.jsp page and click the Submit button (Figure 13.9).

The name entered by you in the text box is displayed, as shown in Figure 13.10:

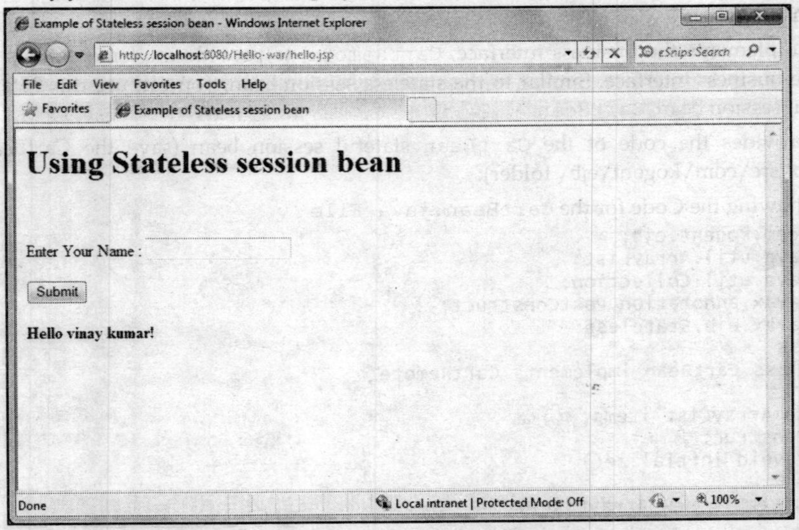

Figure 13.10: Displaying the Output of Hello Application

After developing the Hello application to understand the working of a stateless session bean, let's learn how to work with a stateful session bean.

Working with a Stateful Session Bean

Let's create an application named Cart, which uses a stateful session bean to enable users to insert items into the cart. Perform the following steps to create the Cart application:

- Create a business interface

- Create a bean class
- Create a JSP client
- Package, deploy, and run the application

Let's discuss these steps one by one.

Creating a Business Interface

In EJB 3, you can create a business interface as a remote interface by using the `@Remote` annotation. In the Cart application, we create the CartRemote interface, which declares three business methods—`addItem()`, `removeItem()`, and `getItems()`.

Listing 13.6 provides the code for the CartRemote.java file (save this file in the \Cart\Cart-ejb\src\com\kogent\ejb\ folder):

Listing 13.6: Showing the Code for the `CartRemote.java` File

```
package com.kogent.ejb;
import java.util.Collection;
import javax.ejb.Remote;
@Remote
public interface CartRemote
{
   public void addItem(String item);
   public void removeItem(String item);
   public Collection getItems();
}
```

Save the code of Listing 13.6 as `CartRemote.java` inside the src\com\kogent\ejb directory of the EJB module. Compile the `CartRemote.java` file, the com.kogent.ejb package structure is created containing the `CartRemote` class. The directory structure of the Cart application is similar to the Hello application created in the *Developing a Stateless Session Bean* section.

Creating a Bean Class

A bean class implements the business interface, `CartRemote`, to provide implementations to all the business methods of the business interface. Similar to the stateless session bean, you can use the @Stateful annotation to create a stateful session bean, `CartBean`.

Listing 13.7 provides the code of the `CartBean` stateful session bean (save the CartBean.java file in the \Cart\Cart-ejb\src\com\kogent\ejb\ folder):

Listing 13.7: Showing the Code for the `CartBean.java File`

```
package com.kogent.ejb;
import java.util.ArrayList;
import java.util.Collection;
import javax.annotation.PostConstruct;
import javax.ejb.Stateless;
@Stateless
public class CartBean implements CartRemote
{
   private ArrayList items;
   @PostConstruct
   public void initialize()
   {
         items = new ArrayList();
   }
   @SuppressWarnings("unchecked")
   public void addItem(String item)
   {
         items.add(item);
   }
   public void removeItem(String item)
   {
         items.remove(item);
   }
```

```
    public Collection getItems()
    {
        return items;
    }
}
```

In Listing 13.7, the `initialize()` method that has been annotated with the `@PostConstruct` annotation is invoked just after the bean instance is created to initialize the `items` ArrayList.

Creating a Client

To access a stateful session bean and invoke the `addItem()` or `getItems()` method over it, you need to create a JSP client. Let's create the index.jsp page as a client that invokes the business methods of the CartBean class. Listing 13.8 provides the code for the `index.jsp file` (save this file in the \Cart\Cart-war\ folder):

Listing 13.8: Showing the Code for the `index.jsp File`

```
<%@ page import="com.kogent.ejb.*, javax.ejb.*,javax.naming.*
,java.util.logging.*,java.util.*" %>
<%!
private CartRemote cart ;
public void jspInit() {
   try {
         Context c = new InitialContext();
         cart=(CartRemote) c.lookup("java:comp/env/ejb/CartBean");
   }
   catch(NamingException ne) {
         Logger.getLogger(getClass().getName()).log(Level.SEVERE,"exception
         caught" ,ne);
         throw new RuntimeException(ne);
   }
}
public void jspDestroy() {
   cart = null;
}
%>
<html>
<head>
   <title>A Stateful session bean Implementation.</title>
   <link rel="stylesheet" href="mystyle.css" type="text/css"/>
</head>
<body bgcolor="white">
   <h1>Shopping Cart</h1>
   <hr>
   <h3>Adding Items to Shopping Cart</h3>
   <form method="get">
         Enter Item Name : <input type="text" name="item" size="25">
         <br>
         <input type="submit" value="Add Item">
   </form>
<%
   String item = request.getParameter("item");
   if(item!=null)
   cart.addItem(item);
   Collection items = cart.getItems();
%>
<p>
<%= items %>
</body>
</html>
```

This JSP file works as a client code for the Cart application. Save the `index.jsp` file inside the Web module of the Cart folder. After creating the client, you need to configure various details, such as context root, ejb-ref of the application in the application.xml and web.xml files, respectively.

The `application.xml` file for the `Cart` application is similar to the file given in Listing 13.4 (save this file in the `\Cart\META-INF\`folder). The only difference is that the context-root name is Cart-war, as shown in the following code snippet:

```
<display-name>Cart</display-name>
  <module>
        <ejb>Cart-ejb.jar</ejb>
  </module>
  <module>
        <web>
        <web-uri>Cart-war.war</web-uri>
        <context-root>/Cart-war</context-root>
        </web>
  </module>
```

Listing 13.9 provides the code for the web.xml file of the Cart application (save this file in the \Cart\Cart-war\WEB-INF\ folder):

Listing 13.9: Showing the Code for the `web.xml` File

```
<?xml version="1.0" encoding="UTF-8"?>

<web-app version="3.1" xmlns="http://xmlns.jcp.org/xml/ns/javaee"
xmlns:xsi="http://www.w3.org/2001/XMLSchema-instance"

xsi:schemaLocation="http://xmlns.jcp.org/xml/ns/javaee
http://xmlns.jcp.org/xml/ns/javaee/web-app_3_1.xsd">

  <session-config>
        <session-timeout>
              30
        </session-timeout>
  </session-config>
  <welcome-file-list>
  <welcome-file>
        index.jsp
  </welcome-file>
  </welcome-file-list>
  <ejb-ref>

        <ejb-ref-name>ejb/CartBean</ejb-ref-name>
        <ejb-ref-type>Session</ejb-ref-type>
        <remote>com.kogent.ejb.CartRemote</remote>

  </ejb-ref>

</web-app>
```

Let's now learn to package, deploy, and run the Cart application.

Packaging, Deploying, and Running the Application

To package, deploy, and run the Cart application, you first need to ensure that the Web (Cart-war) and EJB (Cart-ejb) modules of the `Cart` application are arranged according to the directory structure of the `Hello` application (Figure 13.5).

To create the `Cart.ear` file, you first need to create the `Cart-war.war` and `Cart-ejb.jar` files. Let's create an EAR file named `Cart.ear` by using the `jar -cvf Cart.ear *.*` command, as described in the Hello application. Execute this command through Command Prompt from the location at which the `Cart` folder is stored. Now, deploy your corresponding EAR file that is `Cart.ear`. The Glassfish server version 4 is used for deploying this application. After successfully deploying the `Cart.ear` file, open the browser with the corresponding address bar and browse the `http://localhost:8080/Cart-war` URL.

Figure 13.11 shows the output of the Cart application:

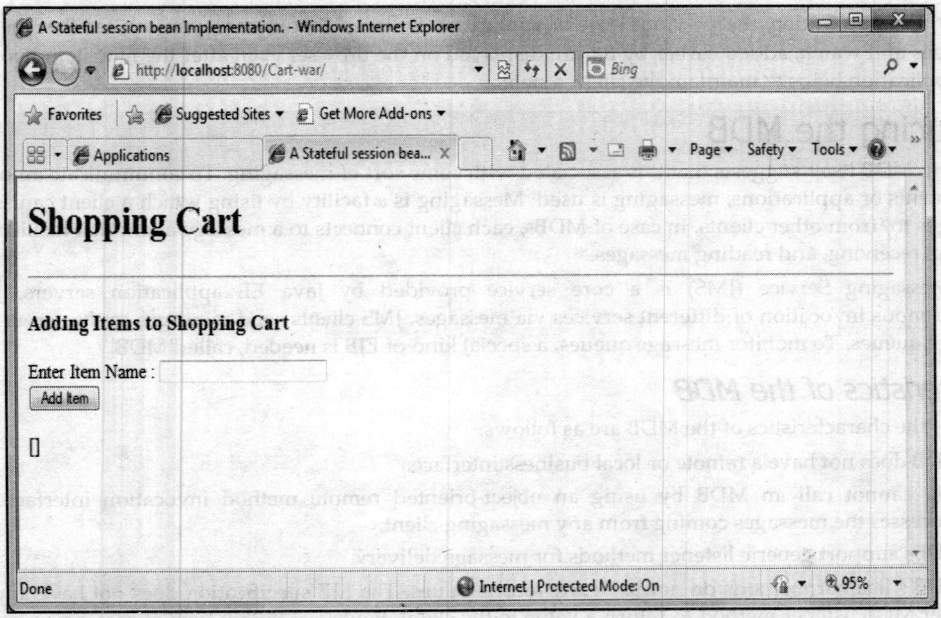

Figure 13.11: Displaying the index JSP Page of the Cart Application

Figure 13.11 displays the client, index.jsp. You can enter an item of your choice in the `Enter Item Name` text box to add it to your shopping cart. Enter the item name in the text field and click the **Add Item** button.

Figure 13.12 shows the list of items added in the shopping cart:

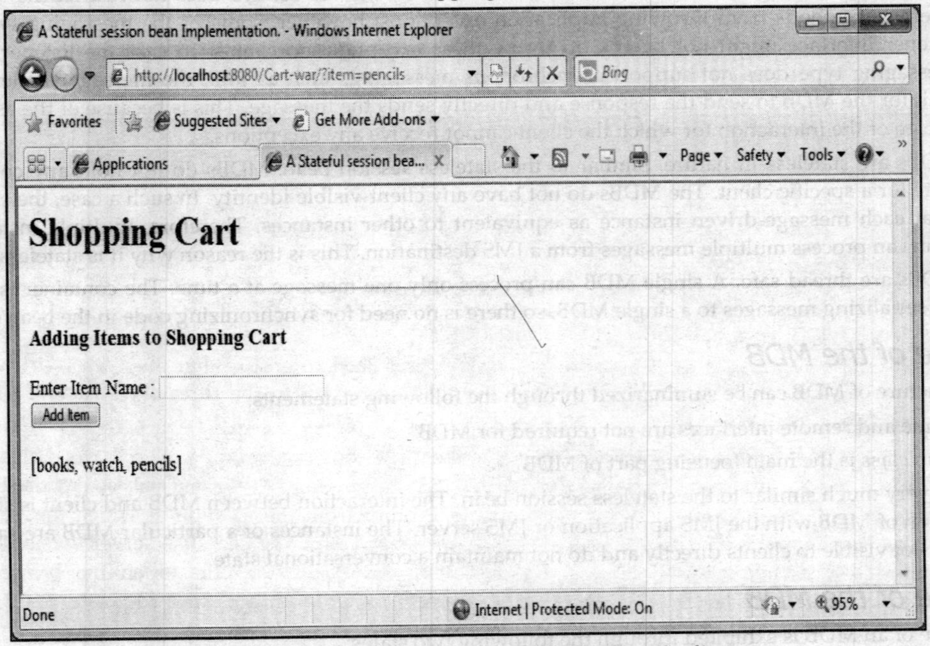

Figure 13.12: Displaying the Cart after Adding the Items

In the `Cart` application, the previous state of application is stored. In our case, you can see that the items, such as pencils and watch, added earlier by us, are displayed on the browser even after the new item books is added. This application helps to maintain the client's state.

Introducing the MDB

The term MDB itself suggests that it is associated with some sort of messaging. To communicate among software components or applications, messaging is used. Messaging is a facility by using which a client can send/receive messages to/from other clients. In case of MDBs, each client connects to a message agent that facilitates creating, sending, receiving, and reading messages.

Java Messaging Service (JMS) is a core service provided by Java EE application servers. JMS allows asynchronous invocation of different services via messages. JMS clients send messages to the server maintained message queues. To monitor message queues, a special kind of EJB is needed, called MDB.

Characteristics of the MDB

Some of the characteristics of the MDB are as follows:

- MDB does not have a remote or local business interface.
- You cannot call an MDB by using an object-oriented remote method invocation interface. The MDB processes the messages coming from any messaging client.
- MDBs support generic listener methods for message delivery.
- MDB's listener methods do not have any return values. The EJB specification does not have any restriction over MDB listener method to return a value to the client; however, certain type of messaging is not suitable for this purpose. For example, let's consider a listener interface of a messaging type, which supports asynchronous messaging, such as JMS. In this case, the message producers do not wait for the MDB to respond as the interaction between the message producers and consumers is asynchronous.
- The exceptions might not be sent back to the clients by the MDBs. EJB does not restrict the MDB listener interface methods from throwing application exceptions; however, some of the messaging types in MDB listener interface might not be able to throw these exceptions to clients. In case the listener interface of messaging type does not support asynchronous messaging, such as JMS, the message sender would not wait for the MDB to send the response and directly sends the message. This is because of the asynchronous nature of the interaction for which the client cannot receive any exceptions.
- MDBs are stateless in nature. Similar to the stateless session bean, MDBs do not hold any conversational state for a specific client. The MDBs do not have any client-visible identity. In such a case, the container can treat each message-driven instance as equivalent to other instances. Therefore, multiple instances of the bean can process multiple messages from a JMS destination. This is the reason why it is stateless in nature.
- MDBs are thread safe. A single MDB can process only one message at a time. The container is responsible for serializing messages to a single MDB, so there is no need for synchronizing code in the bean class.

Structure of the MDB

The structure of MDB can be summarized through the following statements:

- Home and remote interfaces are not required for MDB
- Bean class is the main focusing part of MDB

MDB is very much similar to the stateless session bean. The interaction between MDB and client is similar to the interaction of MDB with the JMS application or JMS server. The instances of a particular MDB are same because they are not visible to clients directly and do not maintain a conversational state.

Life Cycle of the MDB

Life cycle of an MDB is exhibited through the following two states:

- Does Not Exist state
- Method-Ready Pool state

The state of MDB depends upon the container as the container decides when to insert a new instance to its pool. The container creates a new instance by calling the `setMessageDrivenContext()` and `ejbCreate()` methods.

The `setMessageDrivenContext()` method provides access to the runtime message-driven context that the container provides for a message-driven enterprise bean instance. It is called by the container after creating the bean instance and it passes a reference of the `MessageDrivenContext` object to the bean. This means that the container passes the `MessageDrivenContext` reference to an instance after the instance has been created. An MDB can also acquire a reference to the `MessageDrivenContext` object by using DI by simply using the @Resource annotation. The message-driven context remains associated with the corresponding instance as long as the instance is alive, that is throughout its lifetime. After creating the instance and getting the `MessageDrivenContext` reference, the MDB is ready to receive messages. If any annotation, such as `@PostConstruct`, has been used to define a life cycle callback method, then the relevant method is invoked. According to the configuration specified in Deployment Descriptor, the application server generates an initial pool of beans at the startup time. The size of this pool can be expanded as the size of messages increases. When the bean instance is processing a JMS message, the `onMessage()` method is invoked on the bean instance to perform a task. The container can destroy an instance by removing it from the pool while shutting down the system. This can also be done to decrease the size of the pool in the container to conserve memory. To decrease the size of the pool, it needs to call the `ejbRemove()` method, before the instance is ready for the garbage collection.

To take an instance out of the bean pool, the container calls the `@PreDestroy()` method. The diagrammatical representation of the life cycle of the MDB is shown in Figure 13.13:

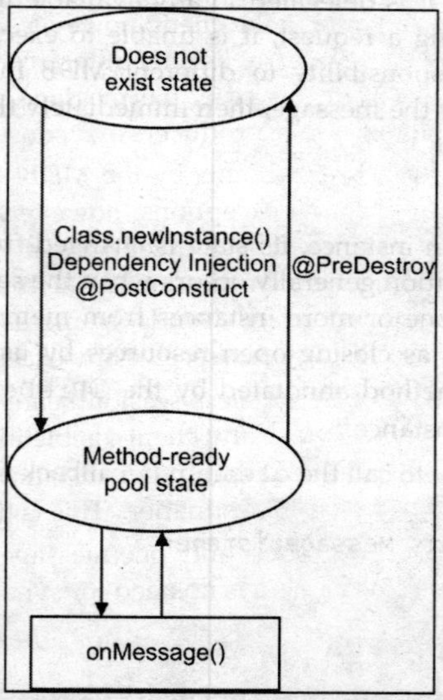

Figure 13.13: Displaying the Life cycle of an MDB

You can observe that the life cycle of the stateless session bean described in the previous section is quite similar to that of the MDB. Let's discuss the two states of the MDB:

- **Does Not Exist state**—Refers to the stage in which an MDB instance is not considered as an instance in the system memory. It means that it has not been instantiated yet.
- **Method-Ready Pool state**—Refers to the stage in which an MDB instance is needed by the container to handle incoming messages. As soon as the EJB server starts, it may create a number of instances and move the instances into the method-ready pool. When the MDB instances are not enough to handle the incoming messages, then more instances of MDB are created and inserted into the pool.

Let's now discuss the transition from one state to another.

Transitioning to the Method-Ready Pool

When an instance moves from the Does Not Exist state to the method-ready pool state, the following three tasks are performed by the container:

- Instantiates a bean instance, when the newInstance() method is invoked on an MDB class
- Injects the required resource with the help of annotation or XML Deployment Descriptor
- Invokes the method annotated by `the @PostConstruct` annotation

The `@javax.ejb.PostConstruct` annotation may or may not be used with any of the methods of the bean class. However, in case it is present, this annotated method will be called by the container only after the bean is instantiated. The return type of the `@PostConstruct` annotated method should always be void and the method should not have any parameter.

The following code snippet shows how to use the `@PostConstruct` annotation:

```
@MessageDriven
public class MyBean implements MessageListener
{
   @PostConstruct
   public void myInit( )
   { }
}
```

Exploring the Life Time of an MDB in the Method-Ready Pool

As soon as an instance reaches to the method-ready pool state, it is ready to handle incoming messages. While a message is being forwarded to MDB, it is delegated to any available instance in the method-ready pool state. When an instance in MDB is executing a request, it is unable to execute or process other messages. In such scenarios, the MDB delegates the responsibility to different MDB instances to handle messages. When an instance has finished the processing of the message, then immediately this instance becomes available to handle another new message in the MDB.

Destroying the MDB Instance

When the server does not need a bean instance, its state is changed from the Method-Ready Pool state to the Does Not Exist state. This type of situation generally occurs when the server decides to decrease the total size of the method-ready pool by releasing one or more instances from memory. At this time, the bean instance can perform any cleanup operation, such as closing open resources by using the `@PreDestroy` annotation. It is important to note that the callback method annotated by the `@PreDestroy` annotation can only be invoked once during the life cycle of an MDB instance.

The following code snippet shows how to call the `cleanup()` callback method annotated with @PreDestroy:

```
@MessageDriven
public class MyBean implements MessageListener
{
   @PreDestroy
   public void cleanup( )
   {
        ...
   }
```

Implementing the MDB

Prior writing an MDB, a developer should take the following tasks into consideration:

- Implementing the `javax.ejb.MessageDrivenBean` and `javax.jms.MessageListener` interfaces in the MDB class.
- Implementing the business logic in the `onMessage()` method.

Now, let's discuss them one by one.

Implementing the MessageDrivenBean and MessageListener Interfaces

JMS MDBs are the classes that implement `javax.jms.MessageListener` and `javax.ejb.MessageDrivenBean` interfaces to define a Java class as an MDB. The `javax.ejb.MessageDrivenBean` interface is optional and must provide a constructor with no argument. In case of the earlier versions of the EJB, it was compulsory to use the MessageDrivenBean interface; however, this is not required in the new version of the EJB, EJB 3.

Implementing Business Logic inside the onMessage() Method

The `onMessage()` method is the only method in the JMS message listener interface `javax.jms.MessageListener`. This accepts JMS messages that can represent a byte message, object message, text message, and map message. The main goal of the `onMessage()` method is to type-cast the incoming message of any type to a text message and to display the text. It acts like a business interface as all the business logic is exhibited inside the `onMessage()` method of the MDB.

Let's now create a sample MDB application and then package, deploy, and run the application.

Creating a Sample MDB Application

Let's create an application, MDB, which displays a message while the investment is calculated by using the investment calculator. While the server is calculating your investment, it will give a message, Please wait while I am checking whether the message has arrived, to let you know that you have to wait for the required result. To create the MDB application, you need to perform the following steps:

- Create the CalculationRecord class
- Create the RecordManager class
- Create the CalculatorBean class
- Create the calculator.jsp file
- Create the check.jsp file

Let's perform these steps, one by one.

Creating the CalculationRecord Class

Let's first create the CalculationRecord class, which has the CalculationRecord (Timestamp, Timestamp, double) constructor, setting three different fields—sent, processed, and result. Listing 13.10 shows the code of the CalculationRecord class (save this file in the \MDB\MDB-ejb\src\jms\ folder):

Listing 13.10: Showing the CalculationRecord.java File

```
package jms;
import java.sql.Timestamp;
public class CalculationRecord
{
   public CalculationRecord(Timestamp sent,
   Timestamp processed, double result)
   {
         this.sent = sent;
         this.processed = processed;
         this.result = result;
   }
   public Timestamp sent;
   public Timestamp processed;
   public double result;
}
```

In Listing 13.10, the constructor of the CalculationRecord class is defined.

Creating the RecordManager Class

The RecordManager class provides different methods, such as `addRecord()`, and `getRecord()` to manipulate records. Listing 13.11 shows the code for the RecordManager class (save the RecordManager.java file in the \MDB\MDB-ejb\src\jms\ folder):

Listing 13.11: Showing the Code for the RecordManager.java File

```
package jms;
import java.sql.Timestamp;
import java.util.ArrayList;
public class RecordManager
{
  public RecordManager()
  {
  }
  public static void addRecord(Timestamp sent, double result)
  {
  if(crs.size() > maxSize)
        crs.remove(0);
        Timestamp processed = new Timestamp(System.currentTimeMillis());
        crs.add(new CalculationRecord(sent, processed, result));
  }
  public static CalculationRecord getRecord(long sent)
  {
        for(int i = 0; i < crs.size(); i++)
        {
              CalculationRecord cr = crs.get(i);
              if(cr.sent.equals(new Timestamp(sent)))
              return cr;
        }
        return null;
  }
  private static ArrayList<CalculationRecord> crs =
  new ArrayList<CalculationRecord>();
  private static int maxSize = 100;
}
```

In Listing 13.11, the addRecord() method is defined to add the time records in the crs ArrayList of the CalculationRecord type. In addition, the getRecord() method is defined to retrieve all the records from the ArrayList.

Creating the CalculatorBean Class

The CalculatorBean class is the MDB class. This class has been annotated with the @MessageDriven annotation to ensure that the container considers it as an MDB. Listing 13.12 provides the code of the CalculatorBean class (save the CalculatorBean.java file in the \MDB\MDB-ejb\src\jms\ folder):

Listing 13.12: Showing the Code for the CalculatorBean.java File

```
package jms;
import java.sql.Timestamp;
import java.util.StringTokenizer;
import javax.ejb.ActivationConfigProperty;
import javax.ejb.MessageDriven;
import javax.jms.Message;
import javax.jms.MessageListener;
import javax.jms.TextMessage;
@MessageDriven(
  mappedName = "jms/Queue", activationConfig = {
  @ActivationConfigProperty(propertyName = "acknowledgeMode",
  propertyValue = "Auto-acknowledge"),
  @ActivationConfigProperty(propertyName = "destinationType",
  propertyValue = "javax.jms.Queue") })
public class CalculatorBean implements MessageListener {
  public void onMessage (Message msg)
  {
        try
        {
              TextMessage tmsg = (TextMessage) msg;
              Timestamp sent =
              new Timestamp(tmsg.getLongProperty("sent"));
              StringTokenizer st = new StringTokenizer(tmsg.getText(),",");
```

```
                int start = Integer.parseInt(st.nextToken());
                int end = Integer.parseInt(st.nextToken());
                double growthrate = Double.parseDouble(st.nextToken());
                double saving = Double.parseDouble(st.nextToken());
                // Pause to simulate a long running task
                Thread.sleep(1000);
                double result = calculate (start, end, growthrate, saving);
                RecordManager.addRecord (sent, result);
                System.out.println ("The onMessage() is called");
            }
            catch (Exception e)
            {
                e.printStackTrace ();
            }
        }
        private double calculate (int start, int end, double growthrate, double
        saving)
        {
        double tmp = Math.pow(1. + growthrate / 12., 12. * (end - start) +    1);
        return saving * 12. * (tmp - 1) / growthrate;
        }
    }
```

In Listing 13.12, we have created a bean class which implements the `javax.jms.MessageListener` interface and is annotated using the `@MessageDriven` annotation that specify EJB 3 characteristics.

Compile the `CalculationRecord.java`, `RecordManager.java` and `CalculatorBean.java` files and the class files are generated in a package named jms, which is present in the MDB-ejb module. The directory structure of the files of this MDB application is similar to that of the session bean.

Creating the calculator.jsp File

Let's create the calculator.jsp file that looks up the required connection with the jms/Queue Queue by using the lookup methods. Listing 13.13 shows the code for the calculator.jsp file (save this file in the \MDB\MDB-war\ folder):

Listing 13.13: Showing the Code for the calculator.jsp File

```
<%@ page import="jms.*,
   javax.naming.*,javax.jms.Queue,javax.jms.*,java.text.*,java.sql.Timestamp"%>

<%
  if ("send".equals(request.getParameter ("action"))) {

    QueueConnection cnn = null;
    QueueSender sender = null;
    QueueSession sess = null;
    Queue queue = null;

    try {
      InitialContext ctx = new InitialContext();
      queue = (Queue) ctx.lookup("jms/Queue");
      QueueConnectionFactory factory =
          (QueueConnectionFactory) ctx.lookup("jms/ConnectionFactory");
      cnn = factory.createQueueConnection();
      sess = cnn.createQueueSession(false,
                QueueSession.AUTO_ACKNOWLEDGE);

    } catch (Exception e) {
      e.printStackTrace ();
    }

    TextMessage msg = sess.createTextMessage(
        request.getParameter ("start") + "," +
        request.getParameter ("end") + "," +
        request.getParameter ("growthrate") + "," +
        request.getParameter ("saving")
```

```
    );
    // The sent timestamp acts as the message's ID
    long sent = System.currentTimeMillis();
    msg.setLongProperty("sent", sent);

    sender = sess.createSender(queue);
    sender.send(msg);
    // sess.commit ();
    sess.close ();
%>

<html>
<head><meta http-equiv="REFRESH" content="3;URL=check.jsp?sent=<%=sent%>">
<link rel="stylesheet" href="mystyle.css" type="text/css"/>
</head>
  <body>
    Please wait while I am checking whether the message has arrived.<br/>
    <a href="calculator.jsp">Go back to Calculator</a>
  </body>
</html>

<%
    return;

  } else {

    int start = 25;
    int end = 65;
    double growthrate = 0.08;
    double saving = 300.0;
%>

<html>
<body>
<p>Investment calculator<br/>
<form action="calculator.jsp" method="POST">
  <input type="hidden" name="action" value="send">
  Start age = <input type="text" name="start" value="<%=start%>"><br/>
  End age   = <input type="text" name="end" value="<%=end%>"><br/>
  Annual Growth Rate = <input type="text" name="growthrate" value="<%=growthrate%>"><br/>
  Monthly Saving = <input type="text" name="saving" value="<%=saving%>"><br/>
  <input type="submit" value="Calculate">
  <INPUT type="button" value="Close Window" onClick="window.close()">
</form>
</p>
</body>
</html>

<%
    return;
  }
%>
```

After creating the calculator.jsp file, let's create the check.jsp file.

Creating the check.jsp File

The code for the `check.jsp` file is given in Listing 13.14 (save this file in the \MDB\MDB-war\ folder):

Listing 13.14: Showing the Code for the check.jsp File

```
<%@ page import="jms.*, java.text.NumberFormat"%>
<%
long sent = Long.parseLong(request.getParameter ("sent"));
CalculationRecord rc = RecordManager.getRecord(sent);
if (rc == null)
{
  %>
```

```
        <html>
                <head><meta http-equiv="REFRESH" content="3;
                        URL=check.jsp?sent=<%=sent%>"></head>
                <body>
                        Please wait while I am checking whether the message has
                        arrived.<br/>
                        <a href="calculator.jsp">Go back to Calculator</a>
                </body>
        </html>
        <% return;
    }
    else
    {
        NumberFormat nf = NumberFormat.getInstance();
        nf.setMaximumFractionDigits(2); %>
        <html>
        <body>
                The message was sent at<br/>
                <b><%=rc.sent%></b>.<br/><br/>
                The message was processed at<br/>
                <b><%=rc.processed%></b>.<br/><br/>
                The calculation result (total investment) is
                <b><%=nf.format(rc.result)%></b>.<br/>
                <a href="calculator.jsp">Go back to Calculator</a>
        </body>
        </html>
    <% return; } %>
```

After creating the required files, you need to configure the calculator.jsp file as the welcome page to be displayed at the starting of the MDB application. You can configure this file in the web.xml file.

The code for the `web.xml` file is given in Listing 13.15 (save this file in the \MDB\MDB-war\WEB-INF\ folder):

Listing 13.15: Showing the web.xml File

```
<?xml version="1.0" encoding="UTF-8"?>
<web-app version="3.1" xmlns="http://xmlns.jcp.org/xml/ns/javaee"
  xmlns:xsi=http://www.w3.org/2001/XMLSchema-instance
  xsi:schemaLocation="http://xmlns.jcp.org/xml/ns/javaee
  http://xmlns.jcp.org/xml/ns/javaee/web-app_3_1.xsd">
  <session-config>
        <session-timeout>
        30
        </session-timeout>
  </session-config>
  <welcome-file-list>
        <welcome-file>calculator.jsp</welcome-file>
  </welcome-file-list>
  </web-app>
```

You should save the `calculator.jsp and check.jsp` files in the Web module (MDB-war) of the MDB application. The Web module created for the MDB application is similar to the Hello application.

Now, you might be thinking why MDB is implemented when the same result could be achieved by using a session bean. This is because MDB allows you to implement the concept of messaging, which is essential for performing different business tasks, such as messaging and calculating. These business tasks are complex and require more time to complete, because they require implementation of entity bean. Now, if you are using the session bean to perform a task, this task would have to wait until the session bean is completed and returns the control to the application. However, in case of MDB, a waiting message is displayed to users while the request sent by the user is processed.

Packaging, Deploying, and Running the Application

To deploy the MDB application on the application server, the Glassfish server version 4, you need to perform the following tasks:

- Create an EAR file

- Configure JMS resources
- Configure JMS connection factories
- Configure destination resources
- Run the application

Now, let's perform these steps, one by one.

Creating the EAR file

After completing the coding part, you should package the MDB application by creating an EAR file that would be deployed on the Glassfish server version 4. You can create the EAR file through Command Prompt by using the `jar -cvf MDB.ear *.*` command after changing your current directory to MDB. The execution of this command adds the beans module, Web module, and META-INF in the MDB.ear file.

Configuring JMS Resources

After packaging the MDB application, start the Glassfish server version 4 and then open the `http://localhost:4848/` URL. The Admin console appears. Now, expand the `Resources` node in the Admin console and select the JMS Resources option. The right panel of Admin console displays two options: Connection Factories and Destination Resources, as shown in Figure 13.14:

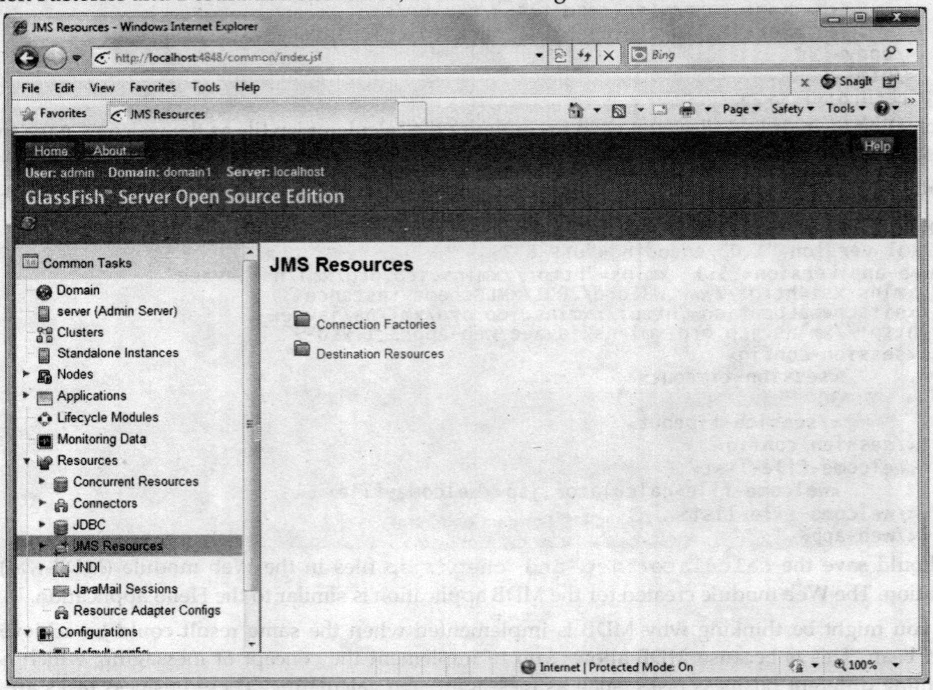

Figure 13.14: Displaying the JMS Resources

Now, select the Connection Factories option to create a JMS connection factory. The following section describes how to create the JMS connection factory for the MDB application created earlier.

Configuring JMS Connection Factories

When you select the Connection Factories option in the JMS Resource pane (Figure 13.14), it displays the existing JMS Connection Factories, as shown in Figure 13.15:

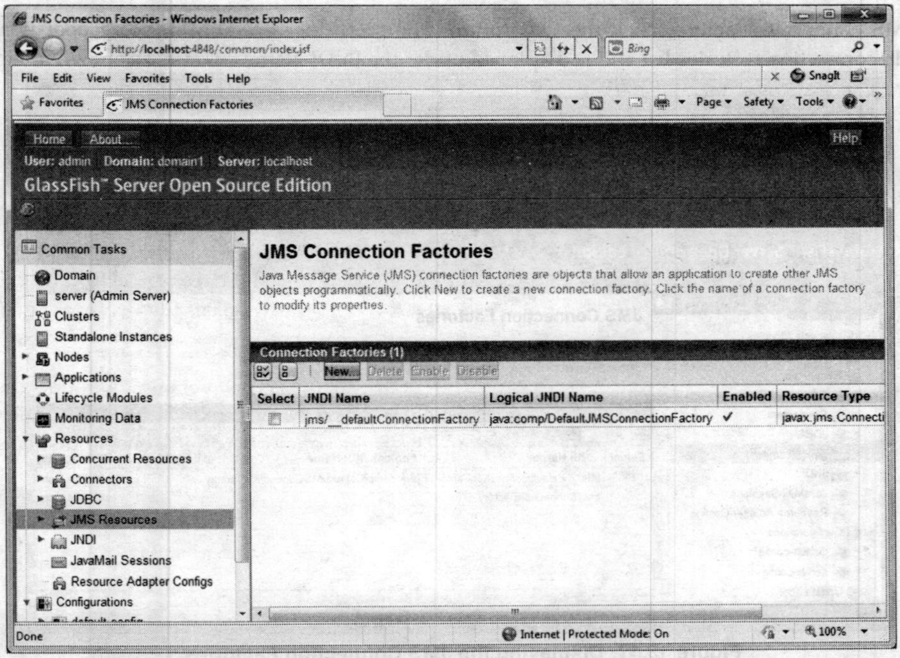

Figure 13.15: Displaying the Existing JMS Connection Factories

To create a new JMS connection factory, click the `New` button and configure the new JMS connection factory, as shown in Figure 13.16:

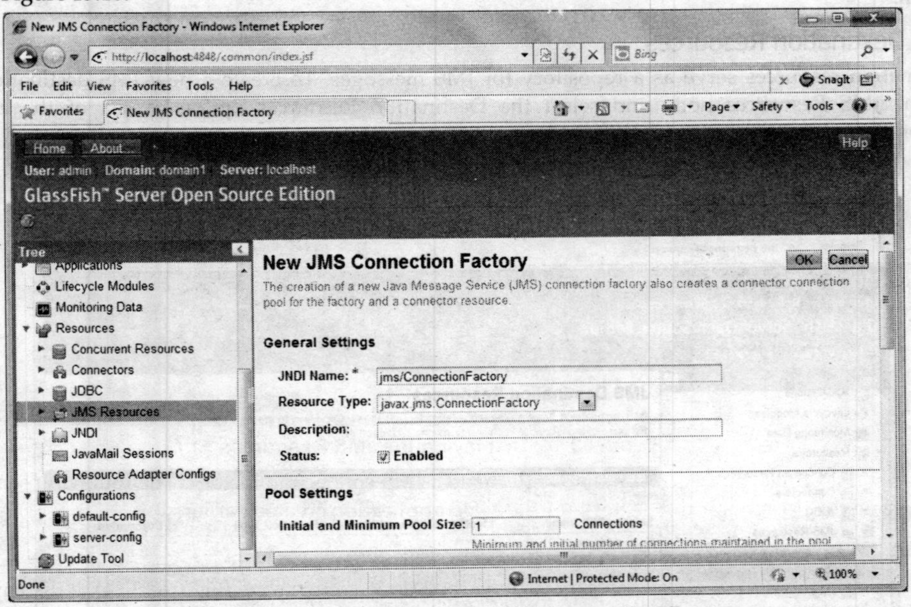

Figure 13.16: Configuring a New JMS Connection Factory

In Figure 13.16, you can see that pool name (JNDI name) for the new JMS connection factory is `jms/ConnectionFactory` and the Resource Type is `javax.jms.ConnectionFactory`. After configuring the new JMS connection factory, click the OK button. The `jms/ConnectionFactory` pool is added to the existing JMS connection factories list and is displayed under the JNDI Name column, as shown in Figure 13.17:

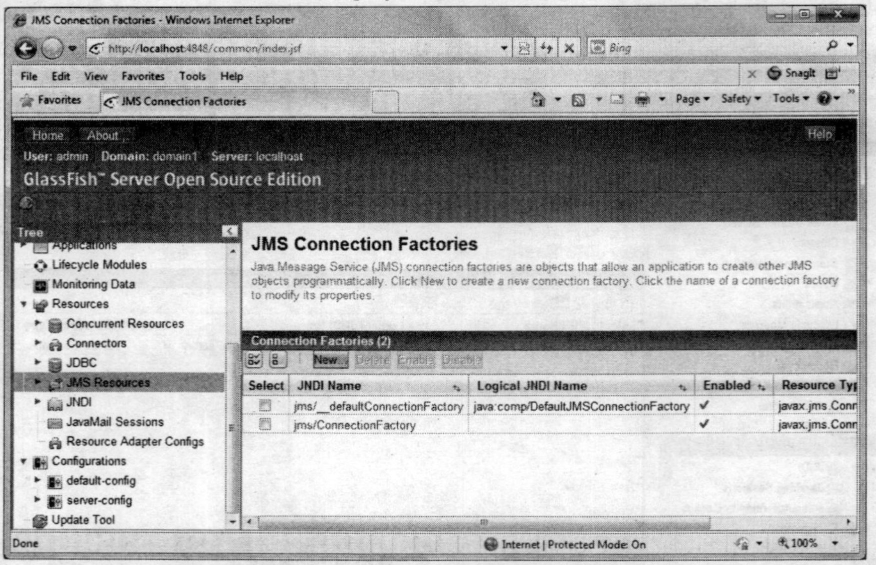

Figure 13.17: Displaying the JMS Connection Factories

After creating a new JMS connection factory for the MDB application, you need to configure new destination resources. The following section describes how to configure new JMS destination resources for the MDB application.

Configuring Destination Resources

JMS destination resources serve as a repository for JMS messages. To create a new JMS destination resource, expand the JMS Resources node and select the Destination Resources option. A list of the existing JMS Destination Resources appears, as shown in Figure 13.18:

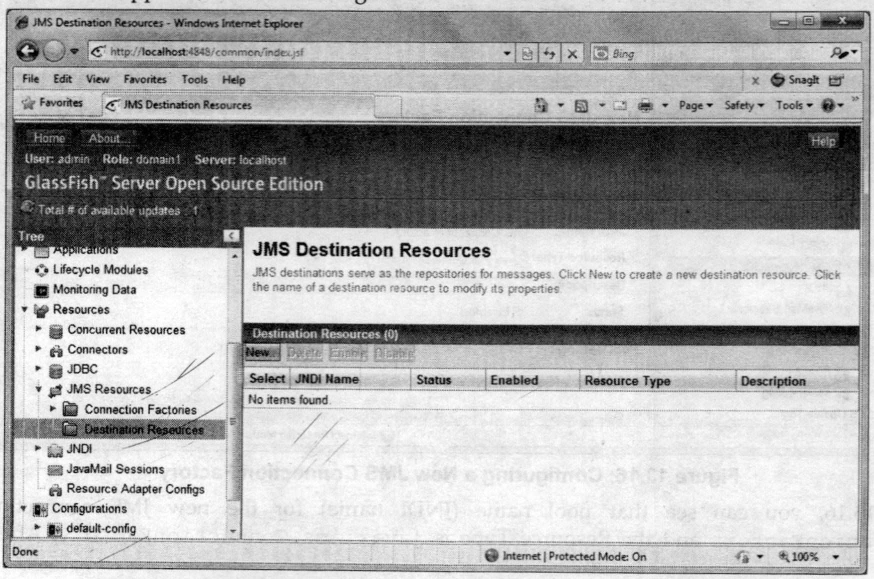

Figure 13.18: Displaying the Existing Destination Resources

Now, click the `New` button to open the `New JMS Destination Resource` pane. In the `New JMS Destination Resource` pane, you need to provide all configuration settings, as shown in Figure 13.19:

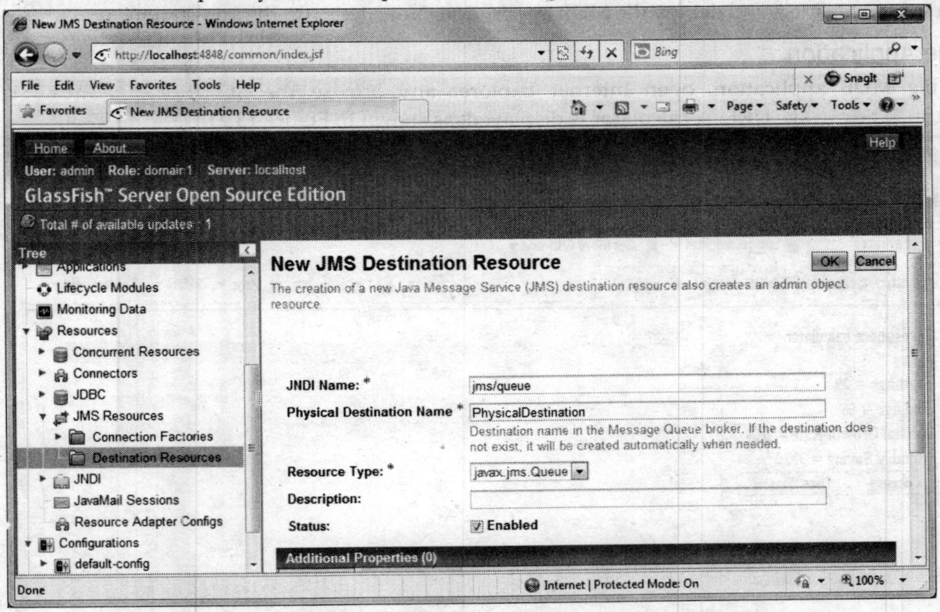

Figure 13.19: Displaying a New JMS Destination Resource

In Figure 13.19, you can see that the JNDI name for the new JMS destination resource for the MDB application is `jms/queue`. In our case, we enter `PhysicalDestination` in the `Physical Destination Name` textbox and `javax.jms.Queue` in the `Resource Type` textbox. Now, click the `OK` button to add the new JMS destination resource, `jms/queue`, in the existing JMS destination resource list, as shown in Figure 13.20:

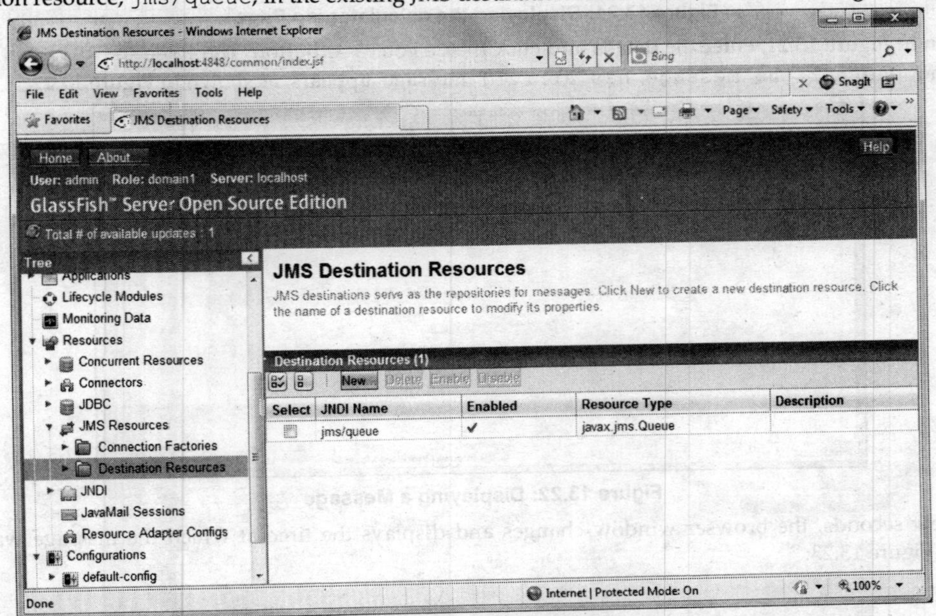

Figure 13.20: Displaying the jms/Queue Destination Resource

After configuring the JMS connection factory and JMS destination resource for the given application, deploy this application in the same way as done for the `Hello` and `Cart` applications. Upload the `MDB.ear` file on the Glassfish server version 4 and deploy the MDB application. Now, let's run the application.

Running the Application

To run the MDB application, open Internet Explorer and browse the `http://localhost:8080/MDB-war/calculator.jsp` URL. A calculator is displayed, as shown in Figure 13.21:

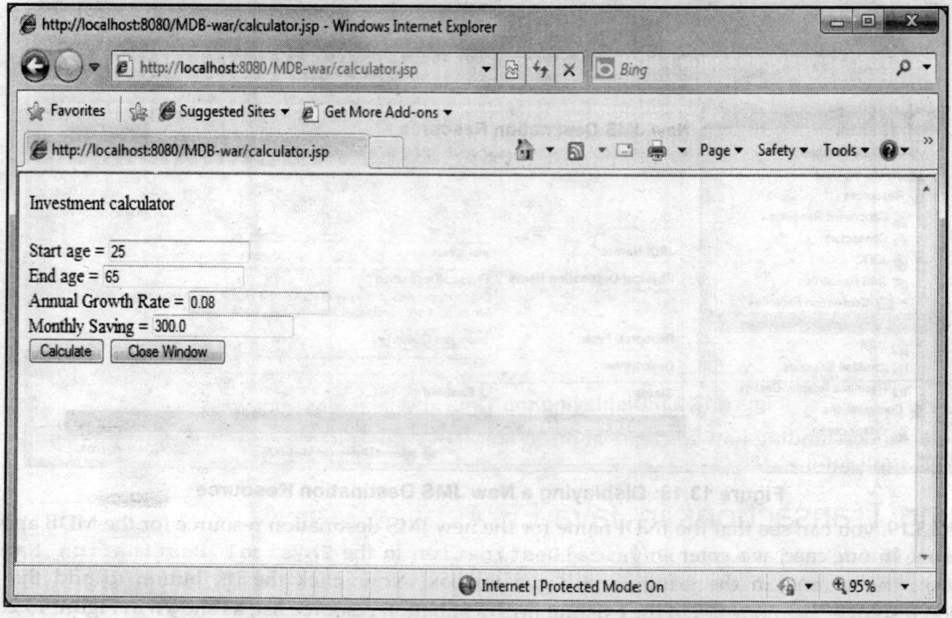

Figure 13.21: Displaying the calculator.jsp Page

As shown in Figure 13.21, enter the details and click the `Calculate` button. The `Please wait while I am checking whether the message has arrived` message appears, as shown in Figure 13.22:

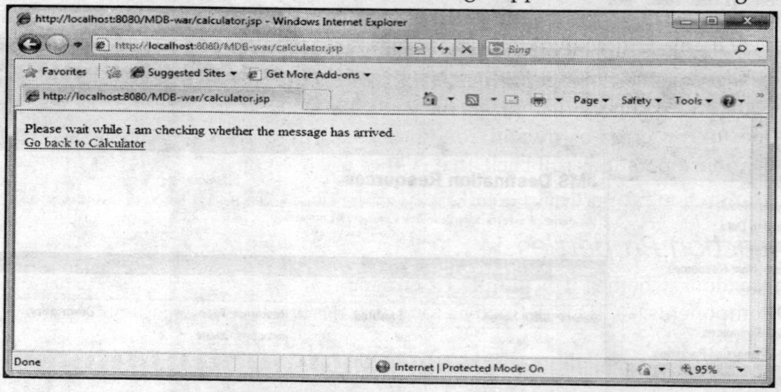

Figure 13.22: Displaying a Message

After a few seconds, the browser window changes and displays the time at which the message was sent, as shown in Figure 13.23:

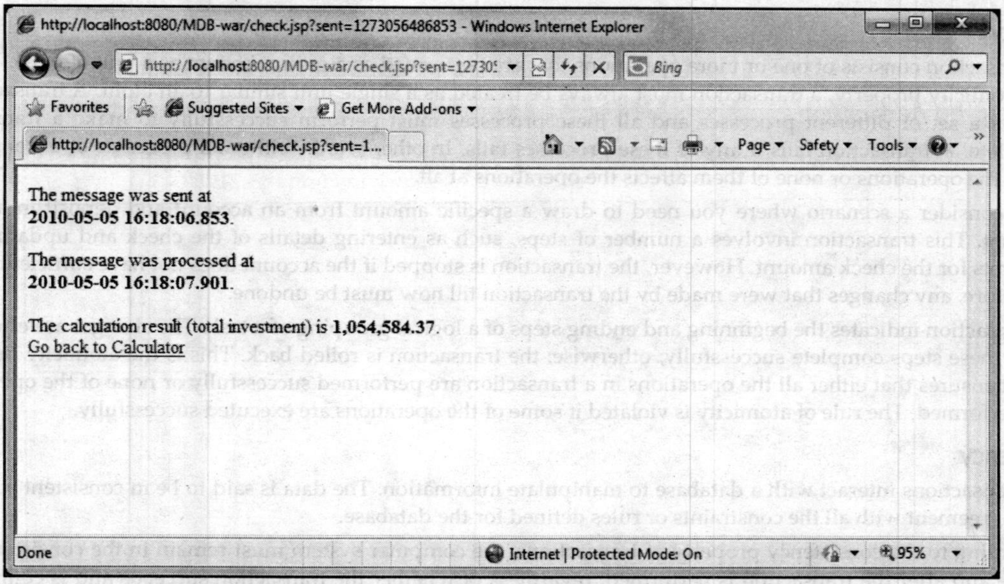

Figure 13.23: Displaying the Time at Which Message was Sent

Now, after understanding how to create and run an MDB application, let's discuss how to manage transactions in Java EE applications.

Managing Transactions in Java EE Applications

A transaction is defined as a group of operations that should be performed as a single unit. These operations can be synchronous or asynchronous, and can involve persisting data objects, sending mails, validating credit cards, and so on. A common example of a transaction involving operations is an online transfer of funds. In this transaction, one operation debits amount from one account and updates the record in a database. The other operation credits the same amount to another account, which updates another row in the same or a different database. This whole process involves two different operations – updating an account by debiting the amount and updating another account by crediting the same amount. This process of money transfer cannot be considered complete if any of these two operations fails.

The operations in a transaction are performed in a sequential or concurrent manner. The transaction is not considered complete and committed until all the operations are not performed successfully. If any of these operations fail due to any error or invalid condition, then the transaction is considered incomplete and all changes done by various operations roll back, that is, they are undone.

Let's discuss the transaction properties in detail.

Exploring Transaction Properties

Any type of transactions whether it is simple or complex, small or large contain some features in common, known as ACID components. ACID is defined as four characteristics for a reliable transaction:

- Atomicity
- Consistency
- Isolation
- Durability

A transaction must comply with these four properties to be considered a transaction.

Let's take a look at each of these four ACID properties.

Atomicity

A transaction consists of one or more operations that are performed as a group, known as a unit of work. As per the atomicity property, a transaction must always be treated as a single unit similar to an atom. A transaction is always a set of different processes and all these processes must perform successfully to make a transaction complete. A transaction fails if any of these processes fails. In other words, either all processes of a transaction affect the operations or none of them affects the operations at all.

Let's consider a scenario where you need to draw a specific amount from an account and deposit in another account. This transaction involves a number of steps, such as entering details of the check and updating two accounts for the check amount. However, the transaction is stopped if the account does not have sufficient funds. Therefore, any changes that were made by the transaction till now must be undone.

A transaction indicates the beginning and ending steps of a logical grouping of a task. The changes are effected if all of these steps complete successfully; otherwise; the transaction is rolled back. This is the atomicity property and it ensures that either all the operations in a transaction are performed successfully or none of the operations are performed. The rule of atomicity is violated if some of the operations are executed successfully.

Consistency

All transactions interact with a database to manipulate information. The data is said to be in consistent state if it is in agreement with all the constraints or rules defined for the database.

According to the consistency property of transactions, the computer system must remain in the consistent state before and after the transaction is performed, regardless of whether the transaction succeeds and is committed, or fails and is rolled back.

The consistency is assured both by transaction manager and developer. Transaction manager ensures that ACID properties of a transaction are intact and the developer ensures its consistency by specifying different constraints.

To maintain consistency of the database when a transaction is committed, the consistency of transaction is validated by Database Management System (DBMS) against all the constraints defined before the changes made by transactions are reflected in the database. If the results do not satisfy the requirements, the transaction is rolled back.

Isolation

The isolation property of a transaction ensures that the data being interacted by the transaction is not accessible by another transaction. In other words, no other transaction is allowed to access the data used by the running transaction until its execution completes.

The isolation property is important to support concurrent access to data. The probability of getting errors and corruption of data is high in a concurrent system, if the operations are not controlled properly.

The transaction manager takes the responsibility of ensuring isolation and managing concurrent execution of transactions.

Transaction isolation specifies that the intermediate state of a transaction is not exposed at all. Outside programs viewing the data objects involved in a transaction must not see the modified data objects until the transaction has been committed.

Durability

After a transaction is committed, the changes that are affected by the transaction should become visible to other applications. The durability property of transactions defines that all the changes made by the transaction must be recorded in some permanent storage. These changes can be recorded in some log files known as transaction log. A transaction log is a list that shows all the changes made by a transaction to the database. This helps in recovering the data to a previous valid state in case of the loss of data due to some error or system failure.

Exploring Transaction Model

A transaction model is a generalized framework that describes a class of transactions. Based on the transaction usage and structure, following are the transactional models:

- Flat transactions
- Nested transactions
- Chained transactions
- Saga transactions

Let's discuss each of them in detail.

Flat Transactions

A flat transaction is the simplest type of transaction. It is a single task comprising a number of steps. If any of the steps of this transaction fails, the transaction is rolled back. Flat transactions are standard for database operations and EJBs.

Nested Transactions

Nested transactions, as the name suggests, are the transactions that are further nested inside another transaction. In the nested transactions model, a transaction A can have another transaction B, as transaction A comprises multiple processes. In other words, a nested transaction has several sub-transactions. A sub-transaction can be either a flat transaction or another nested transaction.

Figure 13.24 shows an example of a nested transaction:

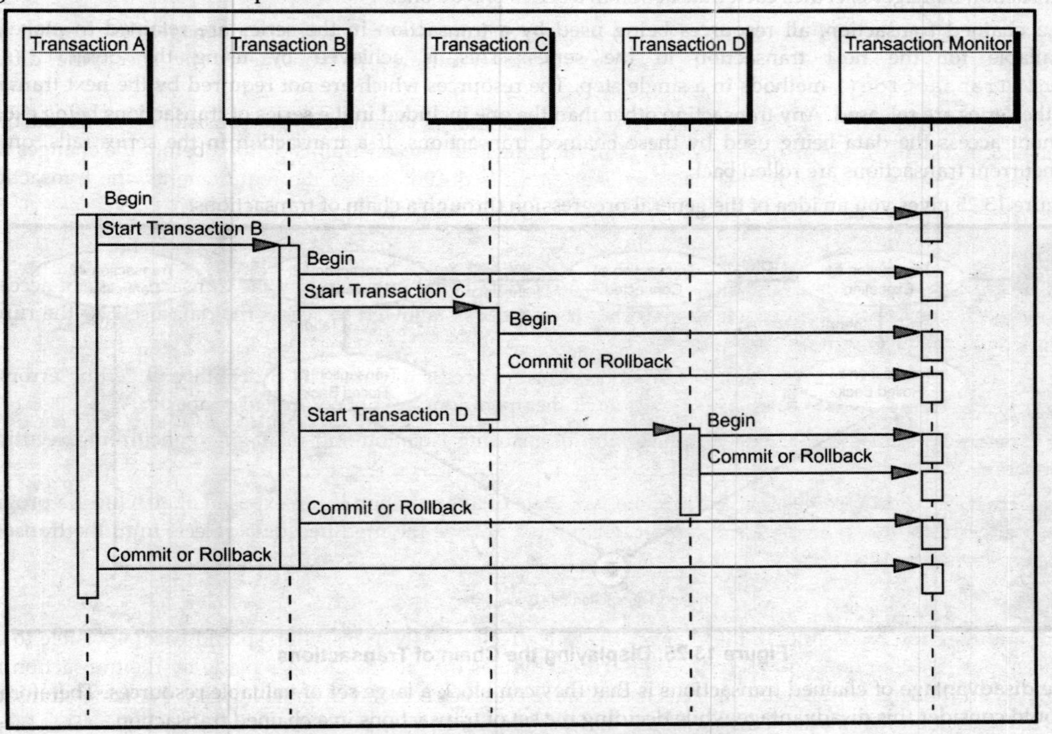

Figure 13.24: Displaying the Nested Transactions

In Figure 13.24, the Transaction A begins and starts the Transaction B. The Transaction B, in turn, first invokes the Transaction C and then invokes the Transaction D.

Another example of nested transactions is an airline reservation system. Let's say that you want to book a flight from New Delhi to Mumbai. Your first transaction (T) entails your attempt to book a direct flight. If there is no direct flight, your transaction fails. This is a flat transaction. Then you start a new transaction (U) and try to find a flight that is available between New Delhi and Pune. You want to hold this reservation, so you keep the transaction open. You then begin a new transaction (V), with your current one that will attempt to book a flight from Pune to Mumbai. There are no direct flights between the two cities, so your transaction fails and rolls back. However, since the transaction is localized at Pune, you will not lose the New Delhi booking. Next, another transaction (W) is started to book a flight between Pune and Hyderabad. You are successful in finding a reservation, so you hold transaction W. Finally, you initiate a new transaction (X) hoping that you will find a flight from Hyderabad to Mumbai. If you are successful, then you commit transaction X. Transaction W checks the status of transaction X and seeing that it was successful, W commits. This continues with W's parent transaction, that is U, and then T. With all of the transactions committed (T, U, W, and X), you have booked your flight. If you decide to scrap the whole affair thinking it a complex affair, X would roll back. W would see that X has failed and, as part of a business rule, would roll back. Finally, the entire tree of transactions (T, U, W, and X) would be aborted canceling the entire transaction.

NOTE

Nested transactions do not roll back the transaction in which they are contained.

Chained Transactions

A series of transactions is referred as serial transactions or chained transactions. These transactions are contiguous and related to each other. The execution of the next transaction in a series of transactions is based on the result of the previous transaction. The set of transactions is submitted to the transaction manager and the transaction manager executes each transaction in a series one by one.

In a chained transaction, all resources being used by a transaction in the series are retained to make them available for the next transaction in the series. This is achieved by using the `commit()` and `beginTransaction()` methods in a single step. The resources which are not required by the next transaction in the series are released. Any transaction other than the one included in the series of transactions being executed cannot access the data being used by these chained transactions. If a transaction in the series fails, only the concurrent transactions are rolled back.

Figure 13.25 gives you an idea of the general progression through a chain of transactions:

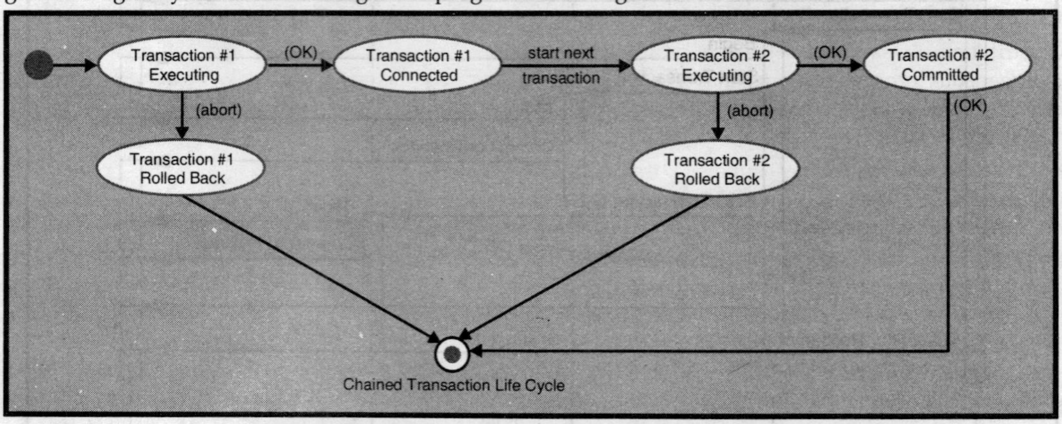

Figure 13.25: Displaying the Chain of Transactions

The disadvantage of chained transactions is that they can block a large set of valuable resources. Therefore, you should consider this disadvantage while deciding the set of transactions in a chained transaction.

Saga Transactions

Saga transactions, similar to the chained transactions, are long-lived transactions. These transactions also consist of multiple transactions. However, each saga transaction has a corresponding compensating transaction. When any of the transactions fail, the compensating transactions for all the successfully executed transactions are invoked automatically by the transaction manager. Therefore, before the execution of the saga transaction, the relationship between the successfully executed transactions and their compensate transactions should be identified by the transaction manager.

Figure 13.26 illustrates a saga transaction that consists of three transactions:

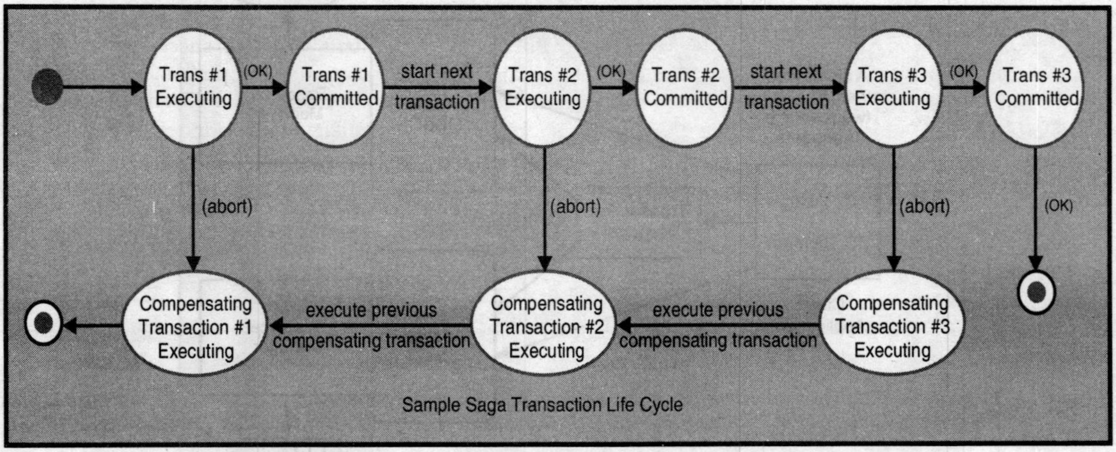

Figure 13.26: Displaying Various Transactions in a Saga Transaction

Explaining Distributed Transactions

A transaction may span more than one resource. This means that the context of some transactions can be propagated or shared by more than one component. Such types of transactions are known as distributed transactions. In other words, a distributed transaction is said to have taken place when the operations in a transaction are performed across database or other resources that reside on separate computers or processes. The distributed transactions support scenarios, such as when a component is required to communicate with multiple resources within the same atomic operation or when multiple components need to operate within the same atomic operation.

A distributed transaction often spans multiple resource managers. Each resource manager may be hosted on a heterogeneous processing node, may manage its own threads of control, and may have a different resource adapter. A distributed transaction model is more complex than the local one because it has more participants involved in it. The participants of a distributed transaction are as follows:

- **Transaction Originator**—Initiates a transaction. The transaction originator can be a Java application in the client tier, a servlet in the Web tier, or a session bean in the EJB tier. In the Web tier or EJB tier, the transaction originator can also be Java Messaging Service (JMS) producer/consumer.
- **Transaction Manager**—Manages transactions on behalf of the originator. It is responsible for enforcing the ACID properties as it coordinates access among all participating resource managers. Whenever resource manager fails to commit the transaction, the transaction manager decides to commit or rollback the pending transactions. In the J2EE architecture, Java Transaction API (JTA) is responsible for implementing the transaction manager.
- **Recoverable Resource**—Provides persistent storage for transaction data to ensure durability of the transaction. In most cases, it is a database or a flat file resource.
- **Resource Manager**—Manages a DBMS, a JMS provider, or a Java Connector Architecture (JCA) resource. It is one of the previously mentioned transaction-aware types.

Figure 13.27 summarizes the protocols and interactions among all participants of a distributed transaction:

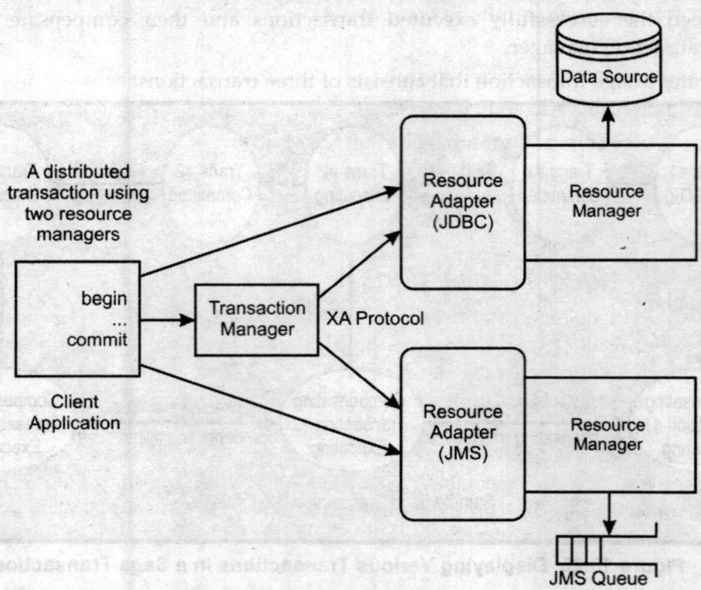

Figure 13.27: Displaying Protocols and Interactions in a Distributed Transaction

To perform a distributed transaction, the transaction manager coordinates the transaction execution across multiple resource managers. As all the participant resource managers are not aware of each other, an algorithm has been established as a standard protocol to control the interactions of all participants. This standard protocol is known as the Two-Phase Commit protocol.

The Two-Phase Commit (2PC) protocol enforces the ACID properties and is implemented into two phases:

- **Phase 1**—Refers to the preparation phase. The transaction manager or coordinator asks each resource manager to be prepared to commit a transaction (also called vote to commit). This process is mainly concerned with providing locks to shared resources without persisting data on permanent storage.
- **Phase 2**—Refers to a phase in which the transaction manager requests all the resource managers to commit their changes as a result of successful transaction execution. Otherwise, the transaction is rolled back, indicating the transaction failure to the application. The transaction succeeds, if and only if all the resource managers commit successfully.

Implementing Transaction Management in EJB 3

EJB 3 handles transaction management through JTA. In EJB 3, you can implement transactions in the following two ways:

- Using Container-Managed Transactions (CMT), which can be implemented by using annotations or Deployment Descriptor.
- Using Bean-Managed Transactions (BMT), which is used to manage transactions programmatically. In this case, all the transactions are not managed by the container; instead, the developer needs to provide code to manage transaction explicitly.

Let's now learn how transactions are supported by the EJB platform. To provide transactional capabilities needed by an EJB application, the EJB container is required to support the high-level interface defined by the JTA for transaction demarcation. The key specifications on transaction processing help you to understand JTA and its role in EJB.

The JTA defines a set of Java interfaces. It specifies how a transaction manager communicates with an application, a resource manager, and the application server in the J2EE architecture. JTA consists of the following primary interfaces:

- The javax.transaction.UserInterface interface
- The javax.transaction.xa.XAResource interface
- The javax.transaction.TransactionManager interface

In context of using JTA in EJB, you need to have the knowledge of the `javax.transaction.UserTransaction` interface. This is because the container takes care of most transaction management details behind the scenes.

Explaining Bean-Managed Transactions

In some cases, the CMTs do not provide the solutions which some enterprise beans require. Let's take an example of a client who wants to call several methods on a session bean even if none of the method commits its work. The EJB handles isolation of transactions in such a way that it terminates this problem. To do this, first turn off the entire container managed services by simply specifying the value of the TransactionManagementType field as BEAN by using the `@TransactionManagement(TransactionManagementType.BEAN)` annotation or by assigning equivalent metadata to the session bean in the ejb-jar.xml file. With BMT isolation, the EJB container provides the transaction support to the bean. The primary difference between CMT and BMT is that the enterprise beans in BMT calls begin, commit, and rollback transactions explicitly. Any given enterprise bean must select either CMT or BMT for the bean methods. Both bean types BMT and CMT can interact with each other within the same transaction context.

BMT is implemented in those enterprise beans that manage their own transactions. BMT can be used only for a session bean and not for an entity bean. The methods of a BMT do not contain transaction attributes. Let's see how a session bean manages transaction explicitly. To isolate transactions, an enterprise bean implements the `javax.transaction.UserTransaction` interface. This interface provides *`begin()`*, *`commit()`*, and *`rollback()`* transaction isolation methods to the bean, so that the EJB manages the transaction isolation explicitly.

A session bean initiates a transaction in one method by using BMT at the isolation level. The bean is then propagated to subsequent method calls until the transaction is finally committed in a separate method. This can be done by specifying the value for the `TransactionManagerType` field as `BEAN`, as shown in the following code snippet:

```
import javax.ejb.* ;
import javax.annotation.* ;
import javax.transaction.UserTransaction;
@Stateless
@TransactionManagement(TransactionManagerType.BEAN)
public class DepartmentManagerBean implements DepartmentManager
{
...}
```

Enterprise beans need to obtain the UserTransaction object to manage their own transactions. The object can be obtained either by using the @Resource annotation or by accepting a reference of the object provided by EJBContext to an enterprise bean, as shown in the following code snippet:

```
import javax.ejb.* ;
import javax.annotation.* ;
import javax.transaction.UserTransaction;
@Stateless
@TransactionManagement(TransactionManagerType.BEAN)
public class DepartmentManagerBean implements
DepartmentManager {
  @Resource SessionContext ejbContext;
  public void someMethod( )
  {
        try
        {
```

```
                    UserTransaction ut = ejbContext.getUserTransaction( );
                    ut.begin( );
                    // Do some work.
                    ut.commit( );
                }
                catch(IllegalStateException ise)
                {
                    ...
                }
                catch(SystemException se)
                {
                    ...
                }
                catch(TransactionRolledbackException tre)
                {
                    ...
                }
                catch(Exception e)
                {
                    throw new EJBException(e);
                }
        . . . .
        . . . .
```

Alternatively, the UserTransaction object can be directly injected into the bean, as shown in the following snippet (see user of `@Resource`):

```
import javax.ejb.* ;
import javax.annotation.* ;
import javax.transaction.UserTransaction;
@Stateless
@TransactionManagement(TransactionManagerType.BEAN)
public class DepartmentManagerBean implements DepartmentManager
{
  @Resource UserTransaction ut;
  ...
}
```

An enterprise bean can also access the `UserTransaction` object from JNDI ENC. The enterprise bean performs the lookup by using the `java:comp/env/UserTransaction` context, as shown in the following code snippet:

```
InitialContext jndiCntx = new InitialContext( );
UserTransaction tran = (UserTransaction)
  jndiCntx.lookup("java:comp/env/UserTransaction");
```

In Java EE, a client application can get the UserTransaction object by using JNDI. The following code snippet shows how a client obtains the `UserTransaction` object if the EJB container is a part of a Java EE system:

```
Context jndiCntx = new InitialContext( );
UserTransaction ut = (UserTransaction)
  jndiCntx.lookup("java:comp/UserTransaction");
ut.begin( );
...
ut.commit( );
```

Explaining Container-Managed Transactions

In case of CMT, the EJB container is responsible for managing the transaction demarcation for every method of the bean. Transaction behavior is described in the bean's Deployment Descriptor or in the annotated class. Transaction attributes are used to define handling of transactions by the EJB container on the invocation of bean's methods. These methods can be associated with any number of transactions at a time. A transaction begins with the execution of the method and commits just before the completion of the execution of the method. Not all the methods of the bean are associated with transactions; however, only those methods are supported that are specified by transaction attributes in the bean's Deployment Descriptor. The following section introduces the transaction attributes that are vital in configuring the bean's methods participating in a CMT.

Enterprise JavaBeans support six types of transactional attributes:

- REQUIRED
- REQUIRES_NEW
- MANDATORY
- SUPPORTS
- NOT_SUPPORTED
- NEVER

Let's discuss these in detail.

REQUIRED

The REQUIRED attribute defines that the specified method always executes within a transaction. In case, the method is invoked within the context of some existing transaction, the same transaction is used to perform a task; otherwise, a new transaction is created by the container.

The new transaction starts with the method invocation and commits just after the execution ends. If the transaction does not commit, then the changes made by the transaction are not reflected and the RollBackException exception is thrown.

The REQUIRED attribute is used when a method is involved to make some serious data change that needs to be protected by a transaction.

REQUIRES_NEW

The `REQUIRES_NEW` transaction attribute assures that a method is always executed within a new transaction. A new transaction is created before the method is invoked. It means that the method is going to be executed into its own transaction and is helpful in implementing local rollback and local commit. The local rollback and local commit mean that a transaction does not affect outcome of other transactions outside the method.

If the method is invoked in context of some existing transaction, this transaction is suspended and the new transaction is started. The suspended transaction is reinstated after the completion of new transaction.

MANDATORY

The MANDATORY attribute assures that a method is going to be executed in the context of some pre-existing transaction only. Therefore, it becomes mandatory that a client should have a transaction running and a method would be invoked in the context of the running transaction. In case there is no transaction context, the container throws the `TransactionRequiredException` or `TransactionRequiredLocalException` exception.

You should use the MANDATORY attribute when the method needs to verify that a component was invoked within the context of a transaction managed by a client.

SUPPORTS

The SUPPORTS attribute assures that a method can be invoked with an existing transaction context; however, if there is no transaction context, the method can be invoked without a transaction.

In case, when a transaction does not need to incur processing overhead or suspend and resume an existing transaction, then you can use the `SUPPORTS` attribute. You must also ensure that your method does not cause any exception which signals a failure within the context of a transaction.

NOT_SUPPORTED

The `NOT_SUPPORTED` transaction attribute informs the container that a method should not be invoked within a transaction. If the method is invoked by using some existing transaction context, the transaction is suspended before the method is invoked. Any exception caused by the method does not affect this suspended transaction.

NEVER

The NEVER transaction attribute specifies that a method should never be invoked in context of another transaction. You should use this attribute when you need to check that the method is not invoked within a transaction managed by a client and the container is not going to attempt to provide a transaction for it.

This attribute is used when the given method is not capable enough to participate in a transaction. If the method is invoked and a transaction context exists, the container throws the `RemoteException` or `EJBException` exception for remote and local clients, respectively.

Explaining EJB 3 Timer Services

The EJB applications are meant for large-scale enterprises that operate on the principle of job scheduling or task scheduling. In simple words, job scheduling refers to the scheduling or managing tasks and activities of an organization within time constraints. These scheduled tasks may be either date-based or time-based, or recurring—that is, performed on a routine basis. In other words, large organizations would perform these tasks at a particular point of time or within a period of time. This would become much clearer with the help of the following scenarios:

- In a customer care center, all complaints are addressed and processed according to the assigned batches. A batch can be the number of complaints received in one hour, a day, or at any fixed period. The complaints are grouped in batches so that necessary action can be promptly taken to resolve these complaints. All the complaints made in one single day are settled together instead of dealing with them separately. This work is usually scheduled in the evening to reduce the load of processing on the system.
- In large-scale enterprises, managers need to run specific reports on a daily basis. A scheduling system can help by running these reports automatically according to the scheduled time and deliver them as e-mail to the managers.
- In a system dealing with mortgages, several different tasks need to be completed before a mortgage can be closed. The operations may concern appraisals, closing appointments, and so on. The processing of this job is time-bound and is, therefore, carried on schedule.
- A company with multiple job shifts needs to run the attendance report after the completion of the job shift. This is done on a regular basis to maintain a daily record of the employees' attendance.

The tasks specified in the preceding scenarios require task scheduling. To implement task scheduling in `Java EE` applications, `EJB 3` has introduced the Timer service facility. Timer services are used for the purpose of building J2EE applications based on time-based services. The time-based services are basically used in scheduling applications. In technical terms, scheduling applications are called workflows, and they define the sequence or batch of tasks to be performed at a particular point of time.

Prior to EJB 2.1, building and deploying time-based workflows need to be performed manually. However, with `EJB 3`, the task of creating such applications has been considerably simplified. Equipped with annotations and DIs, developers can use `EJB 3` to build and deploy scheduled applications easily. The EJB container provides Timed Event API for the Timer service facility. The Timed Event API schedules the timer for a specific date, period, or interval. As soon as the Timed Event API schedules the timer, the timer becomes associated with the enterprise bean responsible for setting it. The Timed Event API calls the `ejbTimeout()` method of the enterprise bean as soon as the `Timer` object expires. Let's now learn about the different types of timers and understand their functions.

Different Types of Timers

EJB supports the following two forms of timer objects:

- The Single Action Timer
- The Interval Timer

The Single Action Timer

The single action timer expires only once, which means that there is no subsequent instantiation and expiration of this timer. It is also known as a single interval timer. EJB provides two ways for constructing a single action timer—one is to create a timer which expires at a specific point of time, such as a specified date, and the other is to create a timer which expires after a certain period of time, such as 6 hours or 3 days. The enterprise bean receives the notification, when the specified time expires. In other words, once the specified time expires, the container calls the `ejbTimeout()` method or the method associated with the `@Timeout` annotation to destroy the timer.

The Interval Timer

The interval timer recurs at multiple intervals of time and expires multiple times at regular intervals. As with the single action timer, there are two ways of constructing an interval timer. The first way is to create a timer having an initial expiration at a particular point of time, and the subsequent expirations happening at specified intervals. The other way is to create the timer having the initial expiration after a certain period of time and subsequent expirations happening after specified intervals.

Strengths and Limitations of EJB Timer Services

The Timer service facility provided by Java EE has eased the work scheduling in Java EE applications. The strengths of Timer service are as follows:

- The timers are persistence objects. It implies that even if the server shuts down, the timers will still be available and become active again as soon as the server restarts. This is possible because the Timer service persists the `Timer` object. The `Timer` object is stored in the database, and becomes active again once the server starts normal functioning.
- The EJB Timer service facility is used to build robust scheduling applications.

However, there are certain flaws as pointed out by Java developers, leaving a lot of scope of improvement as far as the EJB Timer service is concerned. Some limitations of the Timer service facility are as follows:

- Very little information can be retrieved about the `Timer` object itself. It is very difficult to know whether the timer is a single action timer or an interval timer.
- There is no mechanism in an interval timer to predict that timer has executed its first expiration or not.

Timer Service API

The Timer Service API provides an interface to implement the Timer service facility in Java EE applications. The Timer Service API schedules the timers for the specified date or for recurring intervals. To use the Timer service facility, an enterprise bean must implement the `javax.ejb.TimedObject` interface. This interface defines the callback method, `ejbTimeout()`.

Since `EJB 3` focuses on the use of annotations, the `@javax.ejb.Timeout` annotation can be applied to a method. However, the argument passed to this method must be void and should have the `javax.ejb.Timer` object as one of its parameters. The four interfaces provided by the Timer Service API are as follows:

- The `TimerService` interface
- The `Timer` interface
- The `TimedObject` interface
- The `TimerHandle` interface

Let's discuss these interfaces in detail.

The TimerService Interface

The `TimerService` interface is used to create timers. It also helps in retrieving existing timers from the EJB container. Now that you are familiar with the use of the `TimerService` interface, let's study the following in detail:

- Creating Timers
- Listing Existing Timers

Creating Timers

The TimerService interface creates a timer with the help of the createTimer method. Timers can be either single action or interval, depending on their expiry notifications.

The TimerService interface provides the following two methods for creating single action timers:

```
Timer createTimer (long duration, Serializable info)
Timer createTimer (Date expiration, Serializable info)
```

While working with the different types of timers, it was observed that the single action timer lapses after the specified duration of time or after the specified point of time. The first method creates a single action timer that expires after the specified duration of time, while the second method creates a single action timer that expires at a specified date. In both the methods, the first parameter specifies the expiry notification and the second parameter specifies the application information to be passed to the `Timer` object.

NOTE

If there is no application-specific information to be passed, then the second parameter can be ignored by passing a null value. In addition, the duration time must be in milliseconds.

The TimerService interface provides the following two methods to create an interval timer:

```
Timer createTimer (Date initialExpiration, long intervalDuartion, Serializable info)
Timer createTimer (long initialDuration, long intervalDuartion, Serializable info)
```

While creating interval timers, the createTimer method takes three arguments. The first argument, `initialExpiration`, is of the Date type and accepts the date when the expiration of a task would begin. The second argument, `intervalDuration`, specifies the subsequent expiration in milliseconds. Moreover, just as in single action timers, interval timers also provide application-specific information to the Timer object at the time of their creation.

Listing Existing Timers

You can use the getTimers() method to retrieve a list of existing timers that have been already created by the other enterprise beans. The getTimers() method returns the java.util.Collections class, which is essentially an unordered collection of existing javax.ejb.Timer objects. Each Timer object represents a separate timed event for the enterprise bean. This method is also helpful in managing Timer objects. With the help of the getTimers() method, the enterprise bean can cancel any timer which is no longer in use or it can reschedule the timer according to the requirement.

The following code snippet defines the getTimers() methods of the TimerService interface:

```
package javax.ejb;
import java.util.Date;
import java.io.Serializable;
public interface TimerService
{
// retrieves all the active timers associated with this bean
public java.util.Collection getTimers( ) throws
IllegalStateException,EJBException;
}
```

Now, let's discuss the next interface of the Timer Service API called the `Timer` interface.

The Timer Interface

The `Timer` interface holds information of the created `Timer` object throughout the EJB life cycle. This interface is available in the javax.ejb package. After the `Timer` objects are returned by the `TimerService.createTimer()` and `TimerService.getTimers()` methods, the information in these objects is updated. The following code snippet shows the implementation of the `Timer` interface:

```
package javax.ejb;
public interface Timer
{
   public void cancel( )
   throws IllegalStateException,NoSuchObjectLocalException,EJBException;

   public java.io.Serializable getInfo( )
   throws IllegalStateException,NoSuchObjectLocalException,EJBException;

   public java.util.Date getNextTimeout( )
   throws IllegalStateException,NoSuchObjectLocalException,EJBException;

   public long getTimeRemaining( )
   throws IllegalStateException,NoSuchObjectLocalException,EJBException;

   public TimerHandle getHandle( )
   throws IllegalStateException,NoSuchObjectLocalException,EJBException;
}
```

The `Timer` interface provides the following methods:

- `public void cancel()` – Cancels the `Timer` object. When the Timer object is cancelled, all notifications associated with the expiration of the timer are also cancelled. Then, the enterprise bean does not receive timed events. Cancelling a timer is useful when you want to remove the timer or reschedule it. You have to cancel an old timer and create a new one whenever you want to reschedule a timed event.
- `public java.io.Serializable getInfo()` – Returns the application-specific information passed to the `getInfo()` method at the time of creating `Timer` objects. This method must implement the Serializable interface to write the state of the `Timer` object.
- `public java.util.Date getNextTimeout( )` – Returns the time when the next expiration of the `Timer` object is due, as a Date object.
- `public long getTimeRemaining( )` – Returns the time, in milliseconds, left for the next expiration of the `Timer` object. Similar to the `getNextTimeout()` method, this method also returns the time when the next expiration will occur; however, the former returns the date as an object while the latter returns the milliseconds as an object.
- `public TimerHandle getHandle( )` – Provides the reference of the `TimerHandle` interface which can be used later for reconstructing or rescheduling the `Timer` object.

The TimedObject Interface

The TimedObject interface provides callback methods to deliver timer expiration notifications. After the timer expires, the `ejbTimeout()` method is invoked by the EJB container. If the timer is a single action timer, then the `ejbTimeout()` method will be invoked only once; however, if it is an interval timer, then the `ejbTimeout()` method is invoked multiple times. The TimedObject interface is implemented by the enterprise bean to receive time-based notification. When the `Timer` object expires, the EJB container calls the `void ejbTimeout(java.ejb.Timer timer)` method.

The following are the two ways to implement the callback method:

- Implementing the enterprise bean with the `TimedObject` interface. After implementing the enterprise bean, you should implement the `void ejbTimeout(java.ejb.Timer timer)` method, as shown in the following code snippet:

```
@Stateless

@Remote

class FirstBeanImpl implements FirstBean,TimedObject

{
  public void ejbTimeout(Timer timer)
  {
       // code to implement ejbTimeout method
  }
}
```

- Annotating a method with the `@Timeout` annotation. In this way, instead of implementing the Bean class with the `TimedObject` interface, the method defined within the Bean class is annotated. The return type of the method must be void and should accept only one argument of `Timer` type, as shown in the following code snippet:

```
@Stateless
@Remote
class FirstBeanImpl implements FirstBean
{
  @Timeout
  public void TimeOutMethod(Timer timer)
  {
       // code to implement ejbTimeout method
  }
}
```

Let's now learn about the `TimerHandle` interface.

The TimerHandle Interface

The `TimerHandle` interface is used by the container so that the `Timer` object can be rescheduled or reconstructed by the enterprise bean. This interface provides the `Timer.getHandle()` method that returns the `TimerHandle` object. This `TimerHandle` object can then be saved either in a file or at some other resource to regain access to the timer.

The following code snippet shows the implementation of the TimerHandle interface:

```
package javax.ejb;
public interface TimerHandle extends java.io.Serializable {
   Public Timer getTimer() throws NoSuchObjectLocalException, EJBException;
}
```

The TimerHandle objects cannot be used outside the container because these objects are generated by the container and therefore are considered as local objects. The local enterprise beans are located within the same container; thereby, making it possible for the `TimerHandle` objects to pass to the local enterprise bean by using local interfaces. The `TimerHandle` interface is valid until the timer exits. In other words, if the timer expires, then the `TimerHandle` interface becomes invalid. In this case, if you call the `getTimer()` method, then the `javax.ejb.NoSuchObjectException` exception is thrown. Even if the Cancel method is invoked for a timer's explicit expiration before the timer's expiration date, then also the `TimerHandle` becomes invalid.

Now, let's create an application implementing the EJB 3 Timer service.

Implementing EJB 3 Timer Service

The enterprise bean creates an instance of the `Timer` object by using the Timer service facility The Timer service lasts permanently by storing the `Timer` object in the database. Even if the server shuts down, the timer still remains available and becomes active as soon as the server resumes normal functioning.

Figure 13.28 shows the relationship between the enterprise bean and the `Timer` interface:

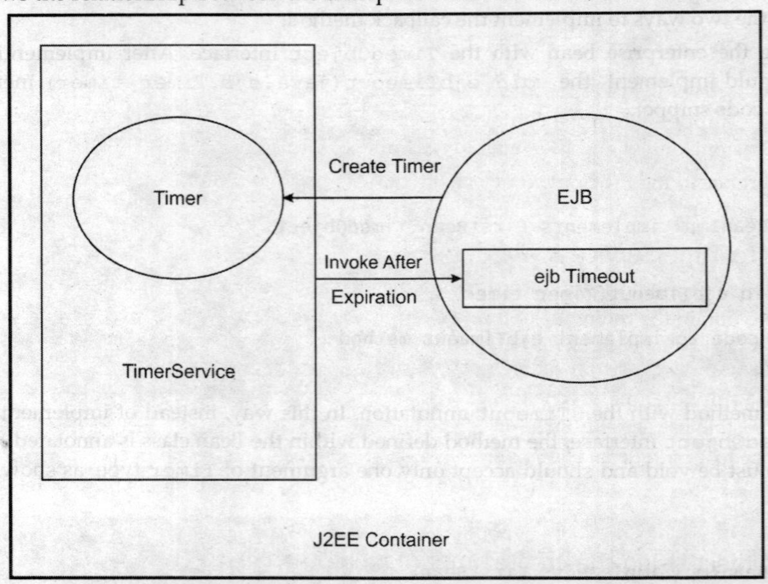

Figure 13.28 Displaying the Relationship between Enterprise Bean and Timer

As shown in Figure 13.28, the enterprise bean creates the `Timer` object with the help of the `TimerService` interface. The `TimerService` interface provides the `createTimer()` method to create the `Timer` object as per the requirement. As soon as the expiry date of the `Timer` object arrives, the `TimerService` interface invokes the `ejbTimeout()` callback method to destroy the `Timer` object (Figure 13.28).

The APIs of the Timer service which help to create and handle Timer objects have been already discussed. Let's now learn how the enterprise bean invokes the various methods of the Timer Service API for creating or cancelling `Timer` objects. To implement the Timer service facility, you need to provide the code to:

- Create the `Timer` object
- Cancel the `Timer` object
- Expire the `Timer` object

Now, let's discuss each of these in detail.

Creating Timer Objects

You can use the createTimer() method of the TimerService interface to create the Timer object. However, you learn how the enterprise bean uses the `createTimer()` method to create the `Timer` object. Stateless beans and MDBs create `Timer` objects. The enterprise bean creates a Timer object by performing the following three tasks:

- Obtaining the reference of the EJBContext object
- Obtaining the reference of the `TimerService` interface using the context object
- Creating the `Timer` object using the `createTimer` method of the `TimerService` object

Let's now look at each task individually.

Obtaining Reference of EJBContext

`EJB 3`, equipped with new features of annotation and DI, has simplified the task of getting the reference to the `EJBContext` object. This class has two subclasses, `SessionContext` and `MessageDrivenContext`. These subclasses have various methods to manipulate runtime environment of session and MDBs, respectively. You have to create only the references of these classes to obtain the `EJBContext` instance.

The following code snippet shows how to obtain the reference for the stateless session bean and the MDB, respectively:

```
@Resource
Private SessionContext sctx;
@Resource
Private MessageDrivenContext msgdrvnctx;
```

In the preceding code snippet, when the container creates session and MDB instances, it implicitly passes both context references, SessionContext and MessageDrivenContext, to the created beans instances, respectively.

After getting the reference to the EJBContext object, let's learn how to obtain the reference to the `TimerService` object.

Obtaining Reference to TimerService

The `getTimerService()` method provides the reference to the `TimerService` interface. The following code snippet shows how to obtain the reference to the `TimerService` object:

```
TimerService timersrvc = sctx.getTimerService();
TimerService timersrvc =msgdrvnctx.getTimerService();
```

In the preceding code snippet, timersrvc is the `TimerService` reference obtained with the help of the reference of `EJBContext`. The stateless session `EJBContext` reference, sctx, invokes the `getTimerService()` method to obtain the reference to `TimerService`.

After getting the `TimerService` reference, the `Timer` object is created by invoking the `createTimer()` method.

Creating the Timer Object Using the createTimer () Method

As discussed earlier, timers are of two types, single action timer and interval timer. You can create a `Timer` object according to your requirement.

Let's first discuss how to create a single action timer. The following code snippet shows how to create a `Timer` object that will expire after 50 seconds from the current time:

```
Calendar today =Calendar.getInstance();
Timer timer =timersrvc.createTimer( today.getTimeInMillis() + (50 * 1000), null);
```

In the preceding code snippet, a `Timer` object (single action) is created by calling the `createTimer()` method through the `TimerService` reference.

The following code snippet shows how to create a single action timer which will expire on a specified date (18th November 2008):

```
Calendar date = new GregorianCalendar(2008, Calendar.NOVEMBER, 18);
Timer timer = timersrvc.createTimer(date, null);
```

Apart from the single action timer, you can also create an interval timer, as shown in the following code snippet:

```
long fiveweeks = 5* 7 * 24 * 60 * 60 * 1000;
Timer timer=timersrvc.createTimer(fiveweeks, (4 * 7 * 24 * 60 * 60 * 1000), null);
```

In the preceding code snippet, the `Timer` object expires after 5 weeks and the subsequent expirations will occur after every 4 weeks.

The following code snippet shows how to create an interval timer, which will elapse on 18th November 2008 for the first time and then the subsequent expirations will take place after every two weeks:

```
Calendar date = new GregorianCalendar (2008, Calendar.NOVEMBER, 18);
long twoweeks = (2 * 7 * 24 * 60 * 60 * 1000);
Timer timer = timersrvc.createTimer( date, twoweeks, null);
```

This is how the enterprise bean creates and uses the `Timer` object. The `Timer` object can also be explicitly cancelled by invoking the `Timer.cancel()` method. Let's now learn how to cancel a Timer object.

Canceling a Timer Object

The container cancels a `Timer` object that is no longer used by the `cancel()` method. After the `cancel()` method of the `Timer` object is invoked explicitly, the enterprise bean will not receive the callback methods, such as `ejbTimeout()`, from the container. In other words, after the cancellation of the `Timer` object, the enterprise bean will not receive any notification from the container. The following code snippet shows how to call the `cancel()` method:

```
Timer timer =timersrvc.createTimer(............);
.......
timer.cancel();
```

In the preceding code snippet, the cancel() method is invoked on the timer object to cancel the timer.

Expiring the Timer Object

Expiration only happens in case of single action timers, and interval timers never expire. Instead, interval timers have to be stopped by invoking the `cancel()` method explicitly. A single action timer expires when its specified date or period of time has elapsed. After the timer expires, the container gives the notification to the enterprise bean by calling the annotated method or the `ejbTimeout()` method.

When you create a single `Timer` object, you have to specify the date after which the container expires the `Timer` object. Similarly, if you specify the period of time (in milliseconds) for a single action timer, the timer will expire after the specified time period.

Exploring EJB 3 Interceptors

Interceptors are useful in situations where you want to add some common features, such as logging, to all EJBs in your application. Now, it is very complex and time consuming task to add code for logging to all EJBs in each EJB class. It requires you to modify many EJB classes. EJB 3 interceptors can solve this problem easily. For example, in this case, you can simply create an EJB interceptor which performs logging and then you can make this interceptor as a default interceptor for your application. The default interceptor will be executed when any bean method is executed. If your requirement further changes, then you need to only change the logging interceptor.

Interceptors are objects that are automatically invoked when an EJB method is invoked. Generally, interceptors are used in session and MDBs. They can be defined within a bean class or in an external class and you can use any number of constructors within these classes. Interceptor encapsulates common code that you can reuse; however, it is not required to include it within the business logic in an application. In case of logging, it is not desirable to include the logging code into the EJB classes. Therefore, the use of interceptors in EJB 3 specification makes applications simpler and easier to use. Interceptors are one of the parts of the changes made in EJB 3 to modularize the application and to extend the EJB container.

Specifying Interceptors

Interceptors are the methods that are used to implement business logic in a business method or in a life cycle callback method. The two types of interceptors available in the EJB 3 specification are as follows:

- Interceptors that intercept the business methods
- Interceptors that intercept the life cycle callback methods

The interceptors can be specified for both the session and MDBs. Interceptors can be specified within a bean class as well as in an external class. You can also use annotations to simplify the use of interceptors in your application. Annotations are used to specify whether an external class or a bean class can be used as an interceptor. The @Interceptor and @Interceptors annotations are used to determine whether an external class is used as an interceptor in an application. The @AroundInvoke annotation is used to identify a method as an interceptor. The method can be either in a bean class or in an external class. The interceptor methods can access the methods that are used to trigger them in an application. The interceptor methods can also be used to stop the processing of business methods. Initially, they check for some security information on the methods; if it is not found, it would halt the processing of the business methods.

The lifetime of an interceptor instance is the same as that of the life cycle of the bean instance with which the interceptors are associated. These interceptors are invoked for JNDI, JDBC, JMS, and other data sources. All interceptors are configured within a single package named javax.interceptor. The following procedure must be followed to specify interceptors for an application:

- Decide whether the interceptor methods are specified within a bean class or within an external class.
- Implement the interceptors within an external class by considering the following instructions:
  - Using the @javax.interceptor.Interceptors annotation in the bean class to associate the interceptor class to the bean class
  - Annotating the business method in the interceptor class with the @javax.interceptor.AroundInvoke annotation.
  - Specifying any number of interceptors within a bean class. Interceptors are executed according to the order specified in the annotation.
  - Specifying an interceptor either at class or method level. If you specify interceptor at the class level, then the interceptor methods can be applied to all appropriate bean class methods. On the other hand, if you specify interceptor at the method level, then the interceptor methods can only be applied to the annotated methods.
- If you decide to implement interceptors within a bean class, then you must consider the following instructions:
  - The methods and classes are annotated with the @javax.interceptor.ExcludeClassInterceptors annotation in the bean class.
  - The classes and methods of a default interceptor are annotated by using the @javax.interceptor.ExcludeDefaultInterceptor annotation. In other words, you can set one or more interceptors as default that you want to define for every EJB.
  - Default interceptors are configured within the ejb-jar.XML Deployment Descriptor and can be applied to all EJBs in the JAR file.

Exploring the Life Cycle of Interceptors

The life cycle of an interceptor is the same as that of the EJBs it intercepts. Interceptor classes are created, activated, and passivated according to the bean instances. The interceptor class also has the limitations of the bean classes with which they are associated. You cannot inject an extended persistent context into an interceptor class if that interceptor class does not intercept a stateful session bean.

The interceptor life cycle events are generated by the EJB container. The life cycle events have internal states that are held by the EJB container. The internal states are useful whenever you want the interceptor class to obtain an open connection to a remote system and to close the connection at the destroy time. Therefore, an internal state is maintained from the time of the creation of a bean instance to the destruction of the instance in which the interceptor class is intercepted. You can hold the internal state of the bean instance within the interceptor class and do the clean up when the interceptor and the bean instances are destroyed.

Working with the Interceptor Class

`Interceptor` classes are the plain Java classes that include the `interceptor annotations` to specify which methods intercept business methods and the life cycle callback methods. All the classes of `interceptors` must be annotated with the `@javax.interceptor.AroundInvoke annotation`. The methods of an `interceptor` must be either within an external class or within a `bean` class. The `annotation` used by the methods has the signature, as shown in the following code snippet:

```
// Signature for @javax.interceptor.InvocationContext //
@AroundInvoke
Object <any-method-name>(javax.interceptor.InvocationContext
invocation)
throws Exception;
```

The `@AroundInvoke annotation` is the primary `annotation` used by all `interceptor` classes and methods. As the name implies, the `@AroundInvoke annotation` wraps the program calls to the business methods that are available in the `interceptor`. The calls to the business methods are made by the `bean` instances in the same transaction. The `javax.interceptor.InvocationContext interface` represents the business method invoked by the client. You can access information of a target `bean` by using the InvocationContext parameter. A reference to the `java.lang.reflect.Method` class is made to determine the actual invoked method. The `javax.interceptor.InvocationContext interface` is used to start the invocation. You should provide the implementation of the business and life cycle callback methods in an `interceptor` class.

The `javax.interceptor.InvocationContext interface` is also used to invoke several methods from a `bean` class. All the methods, as shown in the following code snippet, belong to the `javax.interceptor.` InvocationContext interface:

```
package javax.interceptor;
public interface InvocationContext
{
   public Object getTarget( );
   public Method getMethod( );
   public Object[] getParameters( );
   public void setParameters(Object[] newArgs);
   public java.util.Map<String, Object> getContextData( );
   public Object proceed( ) throws Exception;
}
```

In the preceding code snippet, the `getTarget()` method returns a reference to the current or the target `bean` instance. The `getMethod ()` method is used to invoke the name of the method being called. The `getParameter()` method is used to display the name of the parameters associated with the `bean` instance and the `setParameter()` method is used to set values for the parameters in a `bean` class.

Let's explore more about interceptors by understanding how to:

- Apply interceptors through XML
- Disable interceptors
- Use the business methods
- Use the life cycle callback methods
- Specify default interceptor methods

Let's discuss these one by one.

Applying **Interceptors** through XML

The `@Interceptor` annotation is used to apply the `interceptor` easily to your `bean` class. However, each time when the modifications are done in a bean class, you need to modify and recompile the classes. As `interceptors` are a part of the business logic, they may create complexities in modifying the class again and again as the business logic is changed from time to time. Therefore, the use of XML is a good practice for annotating code in a `bean` class. In EJB 3, source code annotations are used in place of XML Deployment Descriptors and due to this reason, EJB 3 supports partial XML deployment. Applying `interceptors` through XML is better and easier because it is easy to change XML file as the business method changes.

The following code snippet shows the use of `interceptors` in an XML file:

```
<ejb-jar xmlns="http://xmlns.jcp.org/xml/ns/javaee"
   xmlns:xsi="http://www.w3.org/2001/XMLSchema-instance"
   xsi:schemaLocation="http://xmlns.jcp.org/xml/ns/javaee
   http://xmlns.jcp.org/xml/ns/javaee/ejb-jar_3_2.xsd" version="3.2">
   <assembly-descriptor>
   <interceptor-binding>
   <ejb-name> </ejb-name>
   <interceptor-class> </interceptor-class>
   <method-name> </method-name>
   <method-params>
   <method-param> </method-param>
   <method-param> </method-param>
   </method-params>
   </interceptor-binding>
   </assembly-descriptor>
</ejb-jar>
```

If you want to apply the `interceptor` to all the business methods of a particular `EJB`, then you need to modify the XML file (preceding code snippet), as shown in the following code snippet:

```
<ejb-jar
   xmlns="http://xmlns.jcp.org/xml/ns/javaee"
   xmlns:xsi="http://www.w3.org/2001/XMLSchema-instance"
   xsi:schemaLocation="http://xmlns.jcp.org/xml/ns/javaee
   http://xmlns.jcp.org/xml/ns/javaee/ejb-jar_3_2.xsd"
   version="3.2">
   <assembly-descriptor>
   <interceptor-binding>
   <ejb-name> </ejb-name>
   <interceptor-class> </interceptor-class>
   </interceptor-binding>
   </assembly-descriptor>
</ejb-jar>
```

In the preceding code snippet, you can see that `<method-name>` and `<method-param>` have been omitted to make the `XML` file available to all the business methods in a `bean` class.

Disabling **Interceptors**

Whenever you use default or class-level `interceptors`, you may need to disable them for a particular `EJB` or a particular method in an `EJB`. You can disable the `interceptors` either by using the XML file or by using the `annotations`. The following code snippet shows how to disable `interceptors` using an XML file:

```
<ejb-jar
   xmlns="http://xmlns.jcp.org/xml/ns/javaee"
   xmlns:xsi="http://www.w3.org/2001/XMLSchema-instance"
   xsi:schemaLocation="http://xmlns.jcp.org/xml/ns/javaee
   http://xmlns.jcp.org/xml/ns/javaee/ejb-jar_3_2.xsd"
   version="3.2">
   <assembly-descriptor>
   <interceptor-binding>
```

```
        <ejb-name>*</ejb-name>
        <interceptor-class>
        </interceptor-class>
        </interceptor-binding>
        </assembly-descriptor>
    </ejb-jar>
```

In the preceding code snippet, the XML file is deployed and configured in the JAR file. The preceding code snippet disables the default interceptor and the interceptor is made applicable to method level only.

To exclude the default interceptor from a bean class, the @javax.interceptor.ExcludeDefaultInterceptor annotation is used. The following code snippet shows how to disable a default interceptor in a bean class:

```
@Stateful
@ExcludeDefaultInterceptors
@Interceptors
(com.titan.SomeOtherInterceptor.class)
public class ExampleInterceptor implements MyInterceptor
{
   ...
}
```

Using the Business Method Interceptors

Business method interceptors can be specified by using the @AroundInvoke annotation. The @AroundInvoke annotation can be represented only once throughout the program structure. It can be associated with the bean class or with the interceptor class. You can execute multiple interceptor classes for a business method by specifying multiple interceptor classes within a bean file. The interceptor methods are executed according to the order they are specified within the interceptor classes. The @AroundInvoke annotation cannot be used with a business method. The following code snippet shows the signature of the @AroundInvoke annotation for a business method:

```
Object<METHOD>(InvocationContext) throws Exception
```

The invocationContext.proceed() method should be called by the method that is annotated with the @AroundInvoke annotation. No other business method or any subsequent @AroundInvoke methods are invoked. The business method invocation occurs within the same transaction in which the @AroundInvoke method is invoked. The business method interceptor may throw the runtime or the application exception. These exceptions are allowed in the throws clause of the business method.

Using the Life Cycle Callback Methods

The life cycle callback methods are obtained from the life cycle events generated by the EJB life cycle. The life cycle events are generated by the EJB container. The creation, passivation, and destruction of the bean instance in an EJB container are the life cycle events of an EJB. Some annotations are used to specify that the method is a life cycle callback interceptor method. These annotations are given as follows:

- @javax.ejb.PrePassivate—Refers to the annotation used for the method to be notified by the EJB container, when it is about to passivate a stateful session bean.
- @javax.ejb.PostActivate—Refers to the annotation used for the method that is to be notified by the EJB container after re-activation of the stateful session bean.
- @javax.annotation.PostConstruct—Refers to the annotation used for the method that is notified by the EJB container before the business method is invoked and after the DI is applied to a resource. The annotation is in the javax.annotation package instead of the javax.ejb package.
- @javax.annotation.PreDestroy—Refers to the annotation used for the method that is notified by the EJB container before destruction of the bean instance. This annotation is applied to the method used to release the resources held by the bean class. The annotation is in the javax.annotation package instead of the javax.ejb package.

You can annotate the life cycle callback methods either in a bean class or in an external class. These methods can be annotated by more than one annotation. To specify multiple interceptor classes to execute in a given life cycle callback event, you need to associate multiple interceptor classes within the same bean file. The interceptor methods are executed in the order they are listed in the @Interceptor annotation. The signatures of the annotated methods depend on the associated method, as described in the following cases:

- If the life cycle method is defined within a bean class, then the method signature is as shown in the following code snippet:

```
void <METHOD>()
```

- If the life cycle method is defined in the interceptor class, then the method signature is as shown in the following code snippet:

```
void <METHOD>(InvocationContext)
```

The following code snippet shows the use of the @AroundInvoke annotation along with the InvocationContext interface by using both, the business methods and the life cycle callback methods:

```
package examples;
import javax.interceptor.AroundInvoke;
import javax.interceptor.InvocationContext;
import javax.ejb.PostActivate;
import javax.ejb.PrePassivate;
public class ExampleInterceptor
{
   public ExampleInterceptor() {}
   @AroundInvoke
   public Object example(InvocationContext ctx) throws Exception
   {
         System.out.println("Invoking method: "+ ctx.getMethod());
         return ctx.proceed();
   }
   @PostActivate
   public void postActivate(InvocationContext ctx)
   {
         System.out.println("Invoking method: "+ ctx.getMethod());
   }
   @PrePassivate
   public void prePassivate(InvocationContext ctx)
   {
         System.out.println("Invoking method: "+ ctx.getMethod());
   }
}
```

The preceding code snippet initially imports all the metadata annotations used in the ExampleInterceptor class. The interceptor class named ExampleInterceptor is the plain Java class and is followed by a no argument constructor, ExampleInterceptor(). The method-level @AroundInvoke annotation specifies the interceptor method. In the interceptor class, this annotation can be used only once. The @PreActivate annotation defines the methods that are called by the EJB container after reactivating the bean instance; whereas, after passivation, the EJB container should invoke the methods defined by the @PrePassivate annotation. The life cycle callback interceptor methods can only be applied to the stateful session beans.

Specifying Default Interceptor Methods

The business and life cycle callback methods are specified at the method level by using default interceptors. The default interceptor methods can be applied to all the components of a particular EJB JAR file. Therefore, these methods can be configured in the ejb-jar.xml Deployment Descriptor file and not with the metadata annotation. The default interceptors are invoked by the EJB container before all other defined interceptors. To prevent invocation of the default interceptor in a particular EJB, you need to specify the class level by using the @javax.interceptor.ExcludeDefaultInterceptor annotation in the bean class file. The default interceptor can be also specified by using the <interceptor-binding> as parent and <assembly-descriptor> as child element in the ejb-jar.xml file. Then, by setting the <ejb-name> child element to *, which indicates that the corresponding interceptor class is applicable to all EJBs; and the <interceptor-class> child element is applicable to the name of the interceptor class.

The following code snippet shows how to map the default interceptor to the org.mycompany.DefaultIC class:

```
<?xml version="1.0" encoding="UTF-8"?>
<ejb-jar version="3.2"
xmlns="http://xmlns.jcp.org/xml/ns/javaee"
xmlns:xsi="http://www.w3.org/2001/XMLSchema-instance"
xsi:schemaLocation="http://xmlns.jcp.org/xml/ns/javaee
http://xmlns.jcp.org/xml/ns/javaee/ejb-jar_3_2.xsd">
...
<assembly-descriptor>
...
<Interceptor-binding>
<ejb-name>*</ejb-name>
<interceptor-class>org.mycompany.DefaultIC</interceptor-class>
</interceptors>
</assembly-descriptor>
</ejb-jar>
```

Figure 13.29 shows the order in which business method interceptors are invoked:

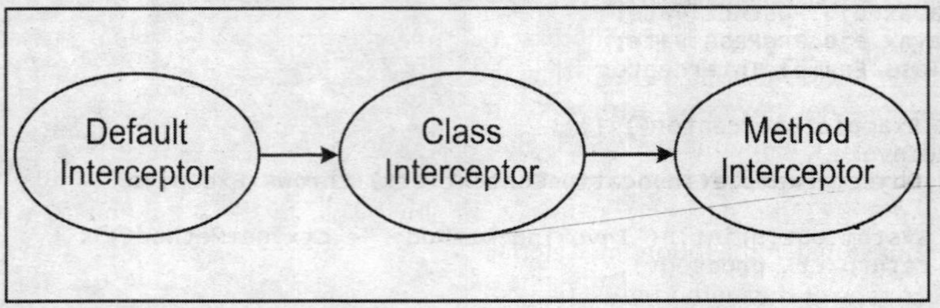

Figure 13.29: Displaying the Order for Invoking Business Method Interceptors

The interceptors are invoked in the order they are represented in the bean file. Default interceptors are invoked first, then the class-level interceptors, and in the end, the method-level interceptors are invoked. The default interceptor, shown in Figure 13.29, is applicable to all the methods of all EJBs in the ejb-jar package; the class-level interceptors are applicable to all the methods specified within that particular class; and the method-level interceptors are applicable to only one method in a particular class.

Exploring the Life Cycle Callback Methods in an Interceptor Class

The annotations named @PreDestroy, @PostConstruct, @PostActivate, and @PrePassivate are used to receive life cycle callback methods. These annotations work in the same way as the life cycle methods of interceptors. The life cycle callbacks defined in an interceptor is known as life cycle callback interceptors or life cycle callback listeners. The life cycle callback methods can be applied to both session and MDBs. Generally, four annotations are used along with the beans. These annotations are as follows:

- @PreDestroy
- @PostConstruct
- @PostActivate
- @PrePassivate

Let's discuss these annotations, one by one.

The @PreDestroy Annotation

The @PreDestroy annotation is specified by the javax.annotation.PreDestroy class. This annotation specifies the life cycle callback method which notifies the bean class that the bean instance is going to be destroyed by the EJB container. Annotation is specifically applied to the methods that release resources held by the bean class. Only a single method can be annotated by using the @PreDestroy annotation. This annotation can be applied to both session and MDBs. The method on which the @PreDestroy annotation is to be applied must match the following criteria:

- The return type of the method must be void
- The method must not throw a checked exception

- The method must be public, protected, or private
- The method must not be static and final
- The method may or may not contain any attribute

The @PostConstruct Annotation

The @PostConstruct annotation is specified by the javax.annotation.PostConstruct class. It specifies the life cycle callback method that the EJB container should execute before invoking the business method and after the DI is implemented to perform any initialization. This annotation can be applied to any bean class that includes the DI. The @PostConstruct annotation can be applied to only one method in a bean class. It can be applied to both session and MDBs. The method on which the @PostConstruct annotation is to be applied should match the criteria as defined for the @PreDestroy annotation.

The @PostActivate Annotation

The @PostActive annotation is specified by the javax.ejb.PostActivate class. This annotation is used to notify the life cycle callback method that the EJB container has been activated in the bean instance. This annotation does not have any attribute and can only be applied to stateful beans because the state of a stateful bean instance is maintained even when the bean is in the Passivate state. Only a single method of the bean class can be annotated by using the @PostActivate annotation. If more than one method is annotated by using this annotation, the EJB will not deploy. The method annotated with the @PostActivate annotation must match the following criteria:

- The return type of the method must be void
- The method must not throw a checked exception
- The method must be public, private, or protected
- The method must not be static and final

The @PrePassivate Annotation

The @PrePassivate annotation is specified by the javax.ejb.PrePassivate class. The @PrePassivate annotation does not contain any attribute. This annotation is used to notify the life cycle callback method that the EJB container is about to passivate the bean instance. It is also applicable to the stateful beans because the EJB container automatically maintains its state of the bean instance. It is not necessary to specify this annotation for the stateful bean instance; however, it can be specified only along with the @PostActivate annotation. If more than one method is annotated by using this annotation, then the EJB will not deploy. The method on which the @PrePassivate annotation is to be applied should match the criteria as defined for the @PostActivate annotation.

The life cycle callback methods are mainly applied to the session and MDBs. The @PreDestroy, @PostConstruct, @PostActivate, and @PrePassivate annotations are used for the stateful session bean. The @PreDestroy and @PostConstruct annotations are used for MDBs, and the @PrePassivate and @PostActivate annotations cannot be applied to MDBs as the activate and passivate states are not available for the life cycle of the MDB. The following section shows the use of life cycle callback methods in MDBs.

Exploring the Life Cycle Callback Interceptor Methods in an MDB

You can use the life cycle callback methods in the interceptor class by using annotations life cycle. To configure life cycle callback methods in an MDB, you need to perform the following tasks:

- Create an interceptor class that can be any POJO class. The methods of the interceptor class are invoked according to the response to business method invocation and the life cycle events on the bean. The following code snippet shows how to specify the AroundInvoke interceptor and the life cycle callback interceptors in a bean class for an MDB:

```
public class ExampleInterceptor
{
   ...
```

```
    @AroundInvoke
    protected Object exampleInterceptor(InvocationContext invctx)
    throws Exception
    {
        Principal p = invctx.getEJBContext().getCallerPrincipal();
        if (!userIsValid(p))
        {
            throw new SecurityException( "Caller: '" + p.getName() +
"' does not have permissions for method " + invctx.getMethod()
            );
        }
        return invctx.proceed();
    }
    @PreDestroy
    public void examplePreDestroyMethod (InvocationContext ctx)
    {
        ...
        invctx.proceed();
        ...
    }
}
```

In the preceding code snippet, the Principal object is used to authenticate the user. If the authentication fails, it throws a SecurityException exception.

- Associate the interceptor class with an MDB by using the `@Interceptor` annotation. The association of the ExampleInterceptor interceptor class with an MDB is shown in the following code snippet:

```
@MessageDriven
@Interceptors(ExampleInterceptor.class)
public class MessageLogger implements MessageListener
{
    @Resource javax.ejb.MessageDrivenContext mc;
    public void onMessage(Message message) {
        ....
    }
    @PostConstruct
    public void initialize()
    {
        items = new ArrayList();
    }
    ...
}
```

In the preceding code snippet, when the `onMessage()` method is called, the methods annotated with the `@AroundInvoke` annotation and the methods of the `ExampleInterceptor` interceptor class are automatically invoked. The life cycle callback interceptor methods are invoked according to the occurrence of appropriate life cycle events.

While creating your interceptor class for an MDB, you must consider the following points:

- The interceptor class that is created must have a public constructor with no argument.
- The life cycle callback `interceptor` method must be implemented in the `bean` class. The callback methods defined in the `bean` class have the following signature:

```
Object <METHOD> (InvocationContext)
```

- A life cycle event is to be associated with the callback `interceptor` method. The life cycle callback event can be associated with one callback `interceptor`; however, a life cycle callback `interceptor` method can be used to associate multiple callback events.

The interceptor class methods can be specified as the life cycle callback methods by using the @PostConstruct and @PreDestroy annotations. The following code snippet shows the use of these annotations in a bean class:

```
public class ExampleInterceptor
{
    ...
    public void InterceptorMethod (InvocationContext invctx) {
        ...
        invctx.proceed ();
        ...
    }
    @PostConstruct
    public void PostContructMethod (InvocationContext invctx)
    {
        ...
        invctx.proceed();
        ...
    }
    @PreDestroy
    public void PreDestroyMethod (InvocationContext invctx)
    {
        ...
        invctx.proceed();
        ...
    }
}
```

The preceding code snippet shows the use of the @PostConstruct and @PreDestroy annotations in a bean class. The postConstructMethod() and preDestroyMethod ()methods are called whenever an appropriate event occurs.

Exploring the Life Cycle Callback Interceptor Methods in a Session Bean

An interceptor method can be associated with an interceptor class as a life cycle callback interceptor method. To configure the life cycle callback interceptor methods in an interceptor class, you must perform the following steps:

- Create an interceptor class that can be any POJO class. The methods of the interceptor class are invoked according to the response to business method invocation and the life cycle events on the bean class. The @AroundInvoke annotation and the exampleInterceptor() method is invoked each time a business method is called. The following code snippet shows how to specify an AroundInvoke interceptor and the life cycle callback interceptors in a bean class for a session bean:

```
public class ExampleInterceptor
{
   ...
   @AroundInvoke
protected Object exampleInterceptor(InvocationContext invctx)
throws Exception {
        Principal p = invctx.getEJBContext().getCallerPrincipal;
        if (!userIsValid(p))
        {
                throw new SecurityException( "Caller: '" + p.getName() +
"' does not have permissions for method " + invctx.getMethod()
                );
        }
        return invctx.proceed();
   }
   @PreDestroy
   public void myPreDestroyMethod (InvocationContext invctx)
```

```
    {
        ...
        invctx.proceed();
        ...
    }
}
```

- Associate an `interceptor` class with a session `bean` by using the `@Interceptors` annotation. The association of an `interceptor` with a Stateful session bean is shown in the following code snippet:

```
@Stateful
@Interceptors(ExampleInterceptor.class)
public class CartBean implements Cart

{
  private ArrayList items;
  @PostConstruct
  public void initialize() {
        items = new ArrayList();
  }
  ...
}
```

While creating an `interceptor` class for a session bean, you must consider the following points:

The interceptor class must have a public constructor without any argument.

- Implement the life cycle callback method in the `bean` class. The callback method defined in the `bean` class has the following signature:

```
Object <METHOD> (InvocationContext)
```

The life cycle callback event should be associated with the callback interceptor method. The life cycle event can only be associated with one callback `interceptor` method; however, a life cycle callback `interceptor` method may be used to associate with multiple callback events.

You can specify the life cycle `interceptor` method in a bean class as an `EJB` 3 session `bean` life cycle method by using any of the following `annotations`:

- @PostConstruct
- @PreDestroy
- @PrePassivate
- @PostActivate

The following code snippet shows the use of annotations for a stateful session `bean`:

```
public class ExampleStatefulSessionBeanInterceptor {
  ...
  protected void exampleInterceptorMethod (InvocationContext invctx)    {
        ...
        invctx.proceed();
        ...
  }
  @PostConstruct
  @PostActivate
protected void examplePostConstructInterceptorMethod
  (InvocationContext invctx) {
        ...
        invctx.proceed();
        ...
  }

  @PrePassivate
```

```
    protected void examplePrePassivateInterceptorMethod
      (InvocationContext invctx) {
            ...
            invctx.proceed();
            ...
    }
```

The preceding code snippet shows an `interceptor` class for a stateful session `bean`. It provides the implementation of the `examplePrePassivateInterceptorMethod` method as the life cycle callback `interceptor` method by using the `@PrePassivate` annotation. It also implements `examplePostConstructInterceptorMethod` as the life cycle callback method by using the `@PostActivate` and `@PostConstruct` annotations.

Summary

The chapter introduced EJB that can be used in distributed, highly secure, and scalable enterprise applications. All characteristics and new features introduced by EJB 3 have been discussed in the chapter. The chapter further explained different types of EJBs, the functionality provided by these EJBs, and their corresponding life cycles. You also learned to implement the different types of enterprise beans with the help of enterprise applications. Next, the chapter discussed the new concepts introduced in EJB 3, such as Interceptors and Timer service.

The next chapter discusses the entity beans and the role of JPA in creating entity beans.

Quick Revise

Q1. What is the use of EJB component?

Ans. The EJB component helps in easy and fast development of distributed, transactional, secure, and portable Java EE applications.

Q2. What is JPA?

Ans. JPA is a framework introduced with the release of EJB 3.0 and simplifies the programming model for entity persistence. It implies that the JPA provides an interface to store the data for persistent use with the help of enterprise beans of an enterprise application.

Q3. What is a session bean? How many types of session beans are there?

Ans. A session bean is a reusable component that consists of business logic of an application. Session beans are of two types:

- The stateless session bean
- The stateful session bean

Q4. How is stateful session bean different from stateless session bean?

Ans. A stateful session bean maintains a client session during the lifetime of an application; whereas, a stateless session bean does not save the client's state.

Q5. Describe the activation and passivation states of a stateful session bean.

Ans. When a bean instance is not used by a client, the EJB container removes the instance from memory and stores it in the secondary storage so that the memory can be reused. This process is known as passivation of stateful session bean. Now, when the client invoked the bean instance again, the EJB container uses the passivated bean instance from secondary storage. Further, the EJB container stores the stateful bean instance in memory to serve the client request. This process is called the activation of a bean instance.

Q6. Define an MDB.

Ans. An MDB is an enterprise bean that allows Java EE applications to process messages asynchronously. It acts as a JMS message listener that receives messages sent by any Java EE component or an application client.

Q7. List different types of transactional models.

Ans. The different types of transactional models are as follows:

- Flat transactions

- ❑ Nested transactions
- ❑ Chained transactions
- ❑ Saga transactions

Q8. Which two forms of Timer objects are supported by EJB 3?

Ans. EJB 3 supports the following two forms of Timer objects:

- ❑ Single Action Timer
- ❑ Interval Timer

Q9. What are interceptors in EJB 3?

Ans. Interceptors are methods that are automatically invoked when an EJB method is invoked. Interceptors provide a logging feature to all EJBs in an application.

Q10. Discuss the role of an EJB container.

Ans. The EJB container provides an environment in which one or more enterprise beans can run. This environment is a combination of available interfaces and classes that the container uses to support enterprise beans throughout their life cycle.

14

Implementing Entities and Java Persistence API 2.1

Java Persistence API (JPA) is the combination of several classes and interfaces used to store the data of the applications persistently in a relational database. JPA also allows you to retrieve the data from a database. The data to be stored or retrieved is managed with the help of the entity classes of an application. An entity class is a simple Java class used to set and retrieve the properties of a bean. To store the data of an entity in a database, you need to create the Java object of the entity class and map the object to the table. This process of mapping the Java objects to the database tables is known as Object Relational Mapping (ORM). To map the Java objects, various details, such as name of the table, row, and column need to be specified in an enterprise application in the form of configuration metadata. This data allows an application to determine the particular rows and columns where the data held by the objects needs to be stored. Configuration metadata refers to the mapping details related to ORM provided in the Deployment Descriptor of an application.

For example, in an online library application, the details of books, such as ISBN number, book name, author name, and name of the publisher are maintained in a database. To store all these details, you need to create an entity class, say Book in our case. The fields of the Book entity class are mapped with the rows and columns of the table in which the data of the books need to be stored. To create the Book entity class and map its details with the table, you need to use the classes and interfaces provided by JPA. The details of mapping the Java object of the Book entity class to the table is provided in the form of configuration metadata in the application.

Initially, Java Database Connectivity (JDBC) was used to store the data of an application in a database. In this process, developers used to write a large amount of code and SQL queries to manage various database operations, such as inserting, updating, and deleting records. The introduction of ORM eliminated these problems by providing a persistent provider that is used to generate the optimized code required for performing database operations. In Enterprise JavaBeans (EJB) 3, JPA was introduced as the ORM mechanism in which the entity beans are mapped to rows and columns of a table to store the data persistently in a database. EJB 3 has facilitated the mapping of an entity by using annotations, such as @Table, @Column, @Enumerated, @Lob, @Temporal, and @Embeddable. Further, many new features have been introduced in JPA 2.1 API as included in Java EE 7.

The chapter begins with the discussion of Java persistence and EntityManager. The chapter then discusses briefly about the new features introduced in JPA 2.1. Next, you learn about entity beans and how they are different from session beans. You also learn how entity fields are mapped to the database columns using JPA. In addition, the chapter explores about various relationships that can exist between two entities, such as one-to-one, one-to-many, and many-to-many. The chapter further discusses about Java Persistence Query Language (JPQL). Finally, the Customer application is developed to demonstrate the use of JPQL to query the data from a database.

Understanding Java Persistence and EntityManager API

JPA provides Plain Old Java Objects (POJO) standard and ORM for maintaining persistent data among the applications. The term persistent refers to the data of an application that needs to be stored permanently in a database. In JPA, the persistent data refers to the entities that serve as a logical collection of the data that needs to be stored or retrieved. For example, in an online book purchasing application, the details of the book to be purchased and the person buying the book need to be maintained in the database. Therefore, in this example, book and person are treated as entities. The personal details of person, such as name, credit card details, and address are logically grouped together to represent the Person entity. Similarly, International Standard Book Number (ISBN), book name, and author name may be grouped together for representing the Book entity. In an enterprise application, you can define an entity by creating a POJO by using annotations.

An entity includes the persistence, transaction ability, and identity as its unique properties. The persistence property refers to storing and retrieving data held by entities in the relational databases. The identity property specifies the unique identification of one entity from other entities. For example, the entity named Person will be uniquely identified by the PersonID. It can also be said that the PersonID will be the primary key of the Person table in a database. Therefore, each person would be assigned a unique ID, whose value cannot be null and would not be similar to the value assigned to other person. In this example, the PersonID serves as the identity for the Person entity or the primary key for the Person table in a database.

After having an overview about the entities in JPA, let's now discuss the EntityManager API that is used to implement the persistence property in the EJB 3 applications. API stands for Application Programming Interface. The `EntityManager API` is an interface used to access entities in an application's persistent context. As discussed earlier, all the entities available in the persistent context must be unique and can be identified by the primary key associated with a table. The `EntityManager` API manages the life cycle of the entities and serves as a connecting bridge between the object-oriented data and relational database, as shown in Figure 14.1. The `EntityManager` translates an entity into a new database record. When the client requests to update the entity, the EntityManager looks at the relational database corresponding to the entity and updates it. Similarly, when the request is to delete an entity, the `EntityManager` deletes the entity from the persistent context. When the request is to save an entity in the persistent context, the `EntityManager` creates an entity object, maps the object to the relational database, and returns the entity object to the application.

Figure 14.1 shows the communication between the object and the relational database with the help of the EntityManager:

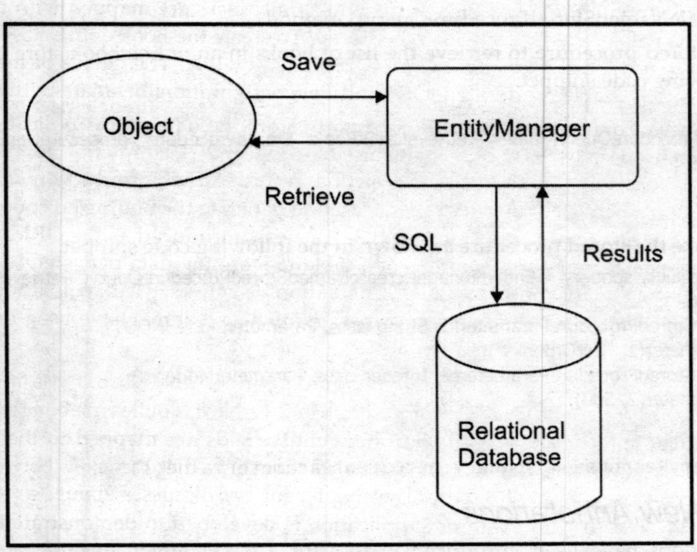

Figure 14.1: Showing the Access Pattern in the EntityManager API

The `EntityManager` provides the following two types of interfaces:

- **Container-managed EntityManager**—Specifies the EntityManager for an application, which is provided by the Java EE runtime container. The `EntityManager` is defined by using the `@PersistenceContext` annotation and the `lookup()` method is used to obtain the `EntityManager` from the persistence context.
- **Application-managed EntityManager**—Creates the `EntityManager` by using the code provided in the application.

Let's now explore some of the new features introduced in JPA 2.1 API as included in Java EE 7.

Exploring New Features in JPA 2.1

The JPA 2.1 API has been released as a part of Java EE 7. Various new features have been introduced in the API which vary from minor updates to major enhancements. Some of these features are:

- Support for Stored Procedures
- Introduction of new Annotations
- Automatic schema generation
- JPQL updates

- Criteria API refactoring
- CDI support for Entity Listeners
- Synchronization of persistence context
- New reserved keywords

Let's briefly discuss each of these features in this section.

Support for Stored Procedures

The new JPA 2.1 API comes with an added support for stored procedures so that predefined database functions as well as user defined functions can be invoked using Java Persistence query language (JPQL). Different variants of EntityManager.createXXXStoredProcedureQuery() have been added in the API that return the respective StoredProcedureQuery to execute a particular stored procedure. On the other hand, stored procedures can be defined using @NamedStoredProcedureQuery annotation and executed using the EntityManager.createNamedStoredProcedureQuery() method.

For example, the stored procedure to retrieve the list of books in an online book store system can be created as shown in the following code snippet:

```
@Entity
@NamedStoredProcedureQuery(name="RetrieveListOfBooks_StoredProcedure", procedureName="RetrieveListOfBooks")
public class Book {
 ...
}
```

JPA client can invoke the stored procedure as shown in the following code snippet:

```
StoredProcedureQuery spquery = EntityManager.createNamedStoredProcedureQuery("RetrieveListOfBooks
_StoredProcedure");
spquery.registerStoredProcedureParameter(1, String.class, ParameterMode.INOUT);
spquery.setParameter(1, "ListOfBooks");
spquery.registerStoredProcedureParameter(2, Integer.class, ParameterMode.IN);
spquery.setParameter(2, 500);
    ... ..
spquery.execute();
String spqueryResponse = spquery.getOutputParameterValue(1);
```

Introduction of New Annotations

Some new annotations have been introduced in the JPA 2.1 API which include @Index and @ForeignKey. @Index annotation can be used to specify additional indexes and their orders as shown in the following code snippet:

```
@Table(indexes={@Index(columnList="Book_Name")
@Index(columnList="Book_ID")})
@Entity
public class Book {
@Id
private Integer bookId;
private String bookName;
....
}
```

The @ForeignKey annotation can be used to specify any foreign key constraint. However, please note that when used, this annotation overrides the default foreign key treatment as provided by the persistence provider. The annotation can be used as shown in the following code snippet:

```
@Entity
public class Book {
@Id
private Integer bookId;
private String bookName;
@JoinColumn(foreignKey=@ForeignKey(foreignKeyDefinition="FOREIGN KEY (CATEGORY_ID) REFERENCES
```

```
    CATEGORY"))
    private Category category;
    . . .
    }
```

Automatic Schema Generation

JPA 2.1 supports automatic scheme generation by using annotations as well as some standard properties which include javax.persistence.schema-generation-action that controls the actions to be taken by the persistence provider for schema creation and javax.persistence.schema-generation-target that specifies whether scheme to be created in database, whether DDL scripts to be created, or both. The javax.persistence.ddl-create-script-target and javax.persistence.ddl-drop-script-target properties can be used to specify the target location of the DDL scripts as java.io.Writer or a URL string. The API also supports javax.persistence.ddl-create-script-source and javax.persistence.ddl-drop-script-source properties which can be used to define the source location of the DDL scripts as java.io.Reader or a URL string.

JPQL Updates

The Java Persistence query language has been updated with new reserved words which include FUNCTION, ON, AND TREAT. The FUNCTION operator has been added in JPQL to enable invocation of predefined and user defined database functions. For example, the following code snippet shows the use of FUNCTION operator in a query string:

```
    SELECT b
FROM Book b
WHERE FUNCTION('publishedInLastTenYears', b.yearOfPublishing)
```

The ON clause helps in specifying the relationship between the tables. Following code snippet shows the query using ON clause:

```
    SELECT v.name, COUNT(b)
FROM Vendor v LEFT JOIN v.book b
ON b.status = 'inStock'
GROUP BY v.name
```

The result of this query will include all the vendors including the ones that have no books in stock.

The support for TREAT keyword has been included in JPA 2.1 to allow downcasting within path expression in the FROM and WHERE clauses as shown in the following code snippet:

```
    SELECT u FROM User u
WHERE TREAT(u AS LibraryManager).leaves > 5
OR TREAT(u AS Visitors).visitingHours > 2
```

Criteria API Refactoring

The Criteria API has been refactored with addition of CriteriaUpdate and CriteriaDelete interfaces to provide support for bulk update and bulk delete queries. Following code snippet shows the use of CriteriaUpdate interface to update the status of those books as OutOfStock for which NumberOfBooksRemaining is less than 1:

```
    CriteriaUpdate<Book> q = cb.createCriteriaUpdate(Book.class);
    Root<Book> b = q.from(Book.class);
    q.set(b.get(Book.status), "OutOfStock")
 .where(cb.lt(b.get(Book.numberOfBooksRemaining), 1));
```

which has the equivalent JPQL as:

```
    UPDATE Book b
    SET b.status = "OutOfStock"
    WHERE b.numberOfBooksRemaining < 1
```

The query can be executed as:

```
    @PersistenceContext
    EntityManager em;
    Query query = em.createQuery(q);
    query.executeUpdate();
```

CDI Support for Entity Listeners

Entity Listeners enable handling of cross-cutting life cycle events for non-persistent listener classes. JPA 2.1 adds support for dependency injection in entity listeners through CDI. Entities can use the usual lifecycle callback methods of @PrePersist, @PostPersist, @PreUpdate, and @PreRemove while entity listeners can be annotated with @PostContruct and @PreDestroy for their lifecycle.

Synchronization of Persistence Context

By default, the persistence context in JPA is synchronized with the resource manager. This implies that resource manager also receives any updates made to the persistence context. JPA 2.1 has introduced the concept of unsynchronized persistence context which allows binding of the persistence context to current transaction only. Thus, the changes are not automatically flushed to the database and the context is only propagated to the jta transaction.

Let's now discuss about entities that are used to store persistent data.

Introducing Entities

Entities are POJOs that are used to store data in a database. Entities hold the data of an application in the form of fields and the methods associated with the details of an entity. All the information regarding an entity is always available in ORM. Entities support relational and object-oriented capabilities, such as entities, inheritance, and polymorphism. A database-driven application is created to collect data from the entities, which are stored in a database. To create a database-driven application, the developer needs to manage entities within the application, as the data is maintained by these entities.

Entity beans are designed to bridge the gap between the object and the relational representation of the application data. Figure 14.2 shows how a client can manipulate the data with the help of entity beans. The client can be the Java application or the Web browser, which does not communicate directly with the relational database. As shown in Figure 14.2, the Web browser accesses the JavaServer Pages (JSP) page available in the Web container. Then, the JSP page calls the appropriate entity bean and Java objects of the entity bean class that holds the data provided by the client in the JSP page. These Java objects, with the help of the EJB container, store the data in the mapped tables of a relational database.

Figure 14.2 shows how entity beans communicate with each other, according to the client's request:

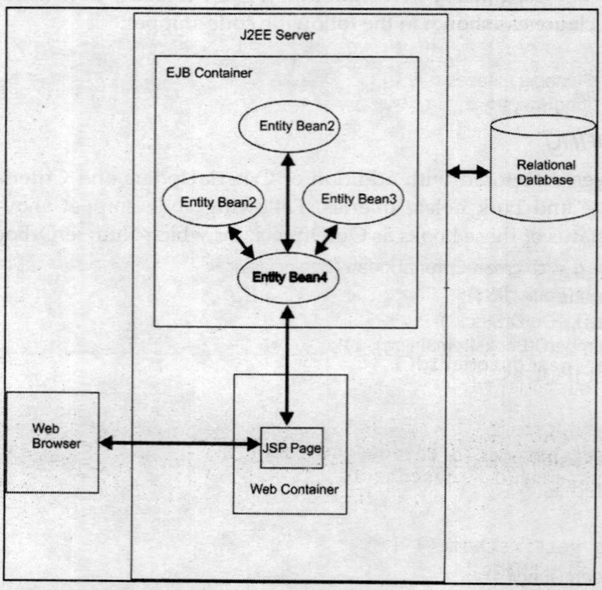

Figure 14.2: Showing the Entities Communication Based on Client's Request

In EJB 3, entity beans are POJOs that are defined by using annotations. These beans are also used to specify how Java objects are stored in the database for persistence usage. The EJB 3 container automatically maps these Java objects to the relational database tables; therefore, the developers need not worry about the details of the data in the relational database.

EJB 3 has made programming simpler for developers as the container handles the data held by entity beans. In EJB 2.x, there were two types of entity beans—container-managed and bean-managed. In the bean-managed entity beans, the code needs to be written by the developer to make the database calls to access the data from a database. In case of the container-managed entity beans, the required database calls are automatically invoked by the EJB container.

In EJB 3.0, the JPA has updated and renewed the concept of the entity beans. To understand how entity beans are created in EJB 3.0, let's first learn to introduce a plain Java class and then convert it into an entity with the help of annotations. The advanced features, such as inheritance, polymorphism, and complex relations, which were not available in EJB 2.x, are supported in JPA.

The code for the plain Java class, Customer.java that contains the getter and setter properties to retrieve and set the data, respectively is shown in Listing 14.1:

Listing 14.1: Showing the Code of the Customer.java Files

```
package com.example.entity;

import java.util.List;
import javax.persistence.*;

public class Customer implements java.io.Serializable {

  private Integer customerId;
  private String firstName;
  private String lastName;
  private String company;
  private String address1;
  private String address2;
  private String city;
  private String state;
  private String zip;
  private String emailAddress;
  private String phoneNumber;

  public Customer() {
       firstName = "";
       lastName = "";
       company = "";
       address1 = "";
       address2 = "";
       city = "";
       state = "";
       zip = "";
       emailAddress = "";
       phoneNumber = "";
  }

  public Integer getCustomerId() {
       return customerId;
  }

  public void setCustomerId(Integer customerId) {
       this.customerId = customerId;
  }

  public String getFirstName() {
       return firstName;
  }
```

```
public void setFirstName(String firstName) {
        this.firstName = firstName;
}

public String getLastName() {
        return lastName;
}
public void setLastName(String lastName) {
        this.lastName = lastName;
}

public String getCompany() {
        return company;
}

public void setCompany(String company) {
        this.company = company;
}

public String getAddress1() {
        return address1;
}

public void setAddress1(String address1) {
        this.address1 = address1;
}

public String getAddress2() {
        return address2;
}

public void setAddress2(String address2) {
        this.address2 = address2;
}

public String getCity() {
        return city;
}

public void setCity(String city) {
        this.city = city;
}

public String getState() {
        return state;
}

public void setState(String state) {
        this.state = state;
}

public String getZip() {
        return zip;
}

public void setZip(String zip) {
        this.zip = zip;
}

public String getEmailAddress() {
        return emailAddress;
}

public void setEmailAddress(String emailAddress) {
        this.emailAddress = emailAddress;
```

```
    }

    public String getPhoneNumber() {
          return phoneNumber;
    }

    public void setPhoneNumber(String phoneNumber) {
          this.phoneNumber = phoneNumber;
    }

}
```

Listing 14.1 defines the Customer class as the Plain Old Java class having 11 variables, namely customerID, firstName, lastName, company, address1, address2, city, state, zip, emailAddress, and phoneNumber. The getter and setter properties are set for all these variables. The getter property returns the value of the variable and the setter property sets the data for the variable. To make the Plain Old Java Class an entity, annotations, such as `@Entity`, `@Table`, `@Column`, and `@ID` are used. Apart from these annotations, `JPQL` is also used to query the database. Moreover, the instance of the `EntityManager` is created to manage the entity.

NOTE

The detailed study of JPQL and EntityManager is provided later in this chapter.

Listing 14.2 provides the code of the Customer entity class containing the required annotations (save the Customer.java file in the `\Customer\Customer-ejb\src\com\kogent\entity` folder):

Listing 14.2: Showing the Code of the `Customer.java` File

```
package com.kogent.entity;

import java.util.List;
import javax.persistence.*;
@Entity
public class Customer implements java.io.Serializable {

   private Integer customerId;
   private String firstName;
   private String lastName;
   private String company;
   private String address1;
   private String address2;
   private String city;
   private String state;
   private String zip;
   private String emailAddress;
   private String phoneNumber;

   public Customer() {
         firstName = "";
         lastName = "";
         company = "";
         address1 = "";
         address2 = "";
         city = "";
         state = "";
         zip = "";
         emailAddress = "";
         phoneNumber = "";
   }

   @Id
   @Column(name="custId", insertable=false, updatable=false)
   public Integer getCustomerId() {
         return customerId;
   }
   public void setCustomerId(Integer customerId) {
```

```
        this.customerId = customerId;
    }
    public String getFirstName() {
        return firstName;
    }

    public void setFirstName(String firstName) {
        this.firstName = firstName;
    }
    public String getLastName() {
        return lastName;
    }
    public void setLastName(String lastName) {
        this.lastName = lastName;
    }
    public String getCompany() {
        return company
    }
    public void setCompany(String company) {
        this.company = company;
    }
    @Column(name="address_1")
    public String getAddress1() {
        return address1;
    }
    public void setAddress1(String address1) {
        this.address1 = address1;
    }
    @Column(name="address_2")
    public String getAddress2() {
        return address2;
    }
    public void setAddress2(String address2) {
        this.address2 = address2;
    }
    public String getCity() {
        return city;
    }
    public void setCity(String city) {
        this.city = city;
    }

    public String getState() {
        return state;
    }
    public void setState(String state) {
        this.state = state;
    }
    public String getZip() {
        return zip;
    }
    public void setZip(String zip) {
        this.zip = zip;
    }
    public String getEmailAddress() {
        return emailAddress;
    }
    public void setEmailAddress(String emailAddress) {
        this.emailAddress = emailAddress;
    }
    public String getPhoneNumber() {
        return phoneNumber;
    }
    public void setPhoneNumber(String phoneNumber) {
        this.phoneNumber = phoneNumber;
```

```
    }

    public static List<Customer> findAllCustomers(EntityManager em) {
          Query query = em.createQuery(
                "SELECT OBJECT(cust) FROM Customer cust");
          List<Customer> customers = query.getResultList();
    return customers;
    }

    public static Customer findCustomerById(EntityManager em, int custId) {

    Query query = em.createQuery(
          "SELECT OBJECT(cust) FROM Customer cust "
                + "WHERE cust.customerId = :custId");
          System.out.println("customerid in customer"+custId);
          query.setParameter("custId",custId);
          Customer customer = (Customer)query.getSingleResult();
          return customer;
    }
}
```

In Listing 14.2, the Customer entity class is defined in the `com.kogent.entity` package.

Let's now discuss about various annotations, such as `@ENTITY`, `@ID`, and `@Column` that can be used in an entity class.

Specifying the @ENTITY Annotation

The use of the `@Entity` annotation before the declaration of a class specifies that the Java class is an entity bean. The `Customer` entity (shown in Listing 14.2) has various fields, such as `customerID`, `firstName`, `lastName`, and `company` to represent the details of each customer. The following code snippet shows the use of the `@Entity` annotation before the declaration of the `Customer` entity bean class:

```
@Entity
public class Customer implements java.io.Serializable {

   private Integer customerId;
   private String firstName;
   private String lastName;
   private String company;
   private String address1;
   private String address2;
   private String city;
   private String state;
   private String zip;
   private String emailAddress;
   private String phoneNumber;
...
...
}
```

Specifying the @Table Annotation

The `@Table` annotation is used to provide the name of the table containing the columns to which an entity is to be mapped. By default, all the persistent data for the entity is mapped to the table with the help of the `name` parameter of the `@Table` annotation. The use of the `@Table` annotation is optional. If it is omitted, then the entity is mapped to the default schema with the same name as the entity class. If you do not provide the name of the table as the value of the `name` parameter, the name of the entity would be taken as the table name. The persistent provider provides a feature of automatic schema generation and creates database objects for entities when the objects do not exist in the database. The following code snippet shows the use of the `@Table` annotation to map an entity:

```
@Entity
@Table(name="Customer", schema=" ")
public class Customer
```

The preceding code snippet shows the use of the @Table annotation. The name parameter specifies the name of the table (in our case, Customer) and the schema parameter denotes the schema associated with the database. If you do not provide a value for the schema parameter, the automatic schema generation process is used to create objects for the entities in the database. The @Table annotation also contains some other parameters, such as catalog and uniqueConstraints, as shown in the following code snippet:

```
@Target(TYPE)
@Retention(RUNTIME)
public @interface Table {
   String name() default "";
   String catalog() default "";
   String schema() default "";
   UniqueConstraint[] uniqueConstraints() default {};
}
```

Now, let's discuss how the @Columns annotation is used in an entity class.

Specifying the @Column Annotation

The @Column annotation is used to map a persisted field to a table column and provides various parameters, such as name, unique, nullable, insertable, updatable, and columnDefinition. The following code snippet shows the type of value accepted by the parameters of the @Column annotation:

```
@Target({METHOD, FIELD})
@Retention(RUNTIME)
public @Column {
   String name() default "";
   boolean unique() default false;
   boolean nullable() default true;
   boolean insertable() default true;
   boolean updatable() default true;
   String columnDefinition() default "";
   String table() default "";
   int length() default 255;
   int precision() default 0;
   int scale() default 0;
}
```

In the preceding code snippet:

- **The** name **parameter**—Defines the column name, which is optional. If the column name is not specified in the name parameter, then by default, the name parameter is set to the property name.
- **The** nullable **parameter**—Defines whether the column supports null values.
- **The** unique **parameter**—Defines whether or not the column supports any unique constraints.
- **The** insertable **and** updatable **parameters**—Control the behavior of the persistent provider. If the insertable parameter is set to false, then the specified field or property is not included in the insert statement. If the updatable parameter is set to false, then the field or property of an entity cannot be updated in the database. These properties are useful for the read-only data, such as the generation of the primary key.
- **The** length **parameter**—Specifies the size of the database column.
- **The** precision **parameter**—Specifies the precision of the decimal field.
- **The** scale **parameter**—Specifies the scale of the decimal column.

The following code snippet shows the use of the @Column annotation in an entity class:

```
@Column(name="custId", insertable=false, updatable=false)
public Integer getCustomerId()
{
  return custId;
}
```

In the preceding code snippet, the column named custId does not allow the inserting and updating of the data in the database, as the value of the insertable and updatable parameters are set to false. This also indicates that the custId column is the primary key in the Customer table.

Specifying the @Enumerated Annotation

The use of the @Enumerated annotation indicates that the field's persistent property should be stored in the form of an Enumeration. The @Enumerated annotation can also be used in conjunction with the @Basic annotation. The possible values of EnumType can be ORDINAL or STRING.

The following code snippet shows the use of the @Enumerated annotation with the ORDINAL EnumType:

```
@Enumerated(EnumType.ORDINAL)
...
protected firstName fName;
```

The preceding code snippet shows that if the value of the field is set to firstName.fName, then the ORDINAL value of fName is stored in the database. You can also specify the enumeration value as strings, as shown in the following code snippet:

```
@Enumerated(EnumType.STRING)
...
protected firstName fName;
```

If the value of the field provided in the preceding code snippet is set to firstName.ADMIN, then the string value, ADMIN is saved in the database. By default, the ORDINAL EnumType is used for the @Enumerated annotation.

Specifying the @Lob Annotation

One of the important features of relational database is its ability to store large objects. These objects are categorized in either Binary Large Object (BLOB) or Character Large Object (CLOB). The categorization depends on the type of available data. These two types correspond to JDBC java.sql.Blob and java.sql.Clob objects. If the data is of the char [] or string type, then the persistent provider maps the data to a CLOB column; otherwise, the data is mapped to the BLOB column. This annotation can be used within the @Basic annotation, which is an auxiliary annotation. If the application is accessing the @Lob object for the first time, the @Basic annotation causes the @Lob object to be loaded from the database.

Specifying the @Temporal Annotation

The @Temporal annotation is used to specify the persistent property or field as a temporal type. You should note that the relational databases support temporal data types. The DATE, TIME, and TIMESTAMP types can be used to map a temporal type. The java.util.Date and java.util.Calender packages are used to access the temporal data types. The following code snippet shows the mapping of temporal types to the database:

```
@Temporal(TemporalType.DATE)
protected Date creationDate;
```

The preceding code snippet defines the creationDate variable as the DATE type, which is specified as the temporal type for the @Temporal annotation. If no value is specified for the TemporalType parameter of the @Temporal annotation, the TIMESTAMP is selected as the default value.

Now after understanding how to create an entity using various annotations, let's discuss how entity beans are different from the session beans.

Exploring Entity and Session Beans

Enterprise Java beans are classified into different categories, such as session beans and entity beans. Session beans are further divided into two types – the stateless session bean and the stateful session bean. As their names suggest, stateful session beans maintain their state across multiple client requests along with the bean instance; whereas, stateless session beans do not maintain their state across multiple client requests. Session beans are used to model business processes, whereas entity beans are used to model business data. The session beans are used to perform various actions, such as accessing the database through its instance or calling the legacy system. However, the Entity beans are the Java objects used to access the database. Session beans along with entity beans are used to accomplish business transactions.

The session bean exists till the client or user runs the application; whereas, the entity bean exists even after the client closes the application, as the data of the entity beans is stored in the database. In other words, the session bean exists till the client or the user exists. On the other hand, entity beans persist till the data is in the database. Entity beans have a persistent state; whereas, session beans have conversational state. In each entity bean, there is a unique object identifier known as a primary key that helps a client to locate a particular entity bean. However, in session beans the fields identifying the client's identity allows a client to create its conversational state with the bean. One instance of session bean is for a single client; whereas, in case of entity beans, a single instance is shared by multiple clients.

Now, let's discuss the conditions where entity beans can be used.

Describing When To Use Entity Beans

Entity beans are used under the following conditions:

- When the bean's state needs to be kept persistent. Even when a user exits an application, the entity bean's state is stored persistently in a database.
- When a bean represents a business entity. Consider an example where a customer makes some purchases online using his credit card. In this case, credit card is an entity containing unique details, such as credit card number, name, and the billing address of the customer. While shopping online, a customer needs to log in with an id and a password. After the customer had logged in, a session is being maintained till the customer logs out or the session expires. During the session, the customer adds the required items in the shopping cart. Next, the customer pays the total amount of the items added in the shopping cart with the help of the credit card. After making the payment, the customer logs out and the session of online shopping expires. The details related to this transaction persist in the database. In other words, the details, such as credit card number used to make payment, number of items purchased, and the billing address of the customer is stored in the database.

In this example, the session of the online shopping by a customer is maintained with the help of the session bean and the shopping details have been saved persistently by using the entity bean. To implement this example in an application, you can create two beans, CreditCardEJB and CreditCardVerifierEJB. The CreditCardEJB bean is used to represent the details of a credit card; therefore, this bean would be an entity bean. The CreditCardVerifierEJB bean is used to validate the credit card number; therefore, this bean would be a session bean.

Describing an Entity Class

An entity class is a simple Java class that contains a metadata annotation or an Extensible Markup Language (XML) Deployment Descriptor. Entity classes have the following features in the persistent API:

- Refers to the Java classes that do not extend any framework classes or interfaces. In addition, the entity classes do not implement the java.io.Serializable interface. If they implement the Serializable interface, then the entity object can be used as a simple data object and can be transferred as an argument in the remote invocation. However, the entity itself does not provide direct remote invocation.
- Maps to a data definition in a relational database. During runtime, the entity instance of the class is mapped to a particular field in a relational database. The Java Persistent API maps entity classes to relational database tables and allows the user to control the mapping by annotations or XML Deployment Descriptors.
- Allows you to declare a primary key in the relational database. This key is useful to differentiate between entities in the relational database. In case of complex relationships, the primary key represents the entire object. JPA provides flexibility to identifiers by including a primary key class with an existing entity. This class must be public, serializable, and should contain a public constructor.
- Allows you to access the persistent state of the entity class by directly accessing its related fields. These fields can be accessed by using the get and set methods similar to JavaBean. The persistent provider determines which methods are to be applied for accessing the fields related with the entity and also determines the use of annotations.
- Provides some business methods. The entity class must provide some callback methods and listeners to apply the business methods. The persistent provider calls these methods to explicitly manage the entities.

After understanding the entity class, let's now discuss the life cycle of an entity.

Describing the Life Cycle of Entity

The life cycle of an entity is managed by the `EntityManager` API, which provides various methods, such as new(), remove(), find(), merge(), and persist() (Figure 14.3). The entity life cycle is based on two main aspects, its relationship to a specific persistence context and the synchronization of its state with the database. The entity life cycle consists of the following four different stages:

- **New**—Refers to the state in which a new instance of an entity is created, which is not associated with any persistent identity or persistent context. Any changes made to the entity at this stage are not synchronized in the database.
- **Managed**—Refers to the state in which an entity is associated with the persistent context. The entity has a persistent identity in the database and is in the managed state after the invocation of the `persist()` method. Changes made to the entity are synchronized in the database after the transactions are committed or the `remove` () method is called.
- **Detached**—Refers to detaching the association of the entity with persistent context. In this stage, the entity also has its persistent identity.
- **Removed**—Removes the entity data from the database. In this stage, the entity also has an association with the persistent context.

Figure 14.3 demonstrates the entity life cycle with the specified methods:

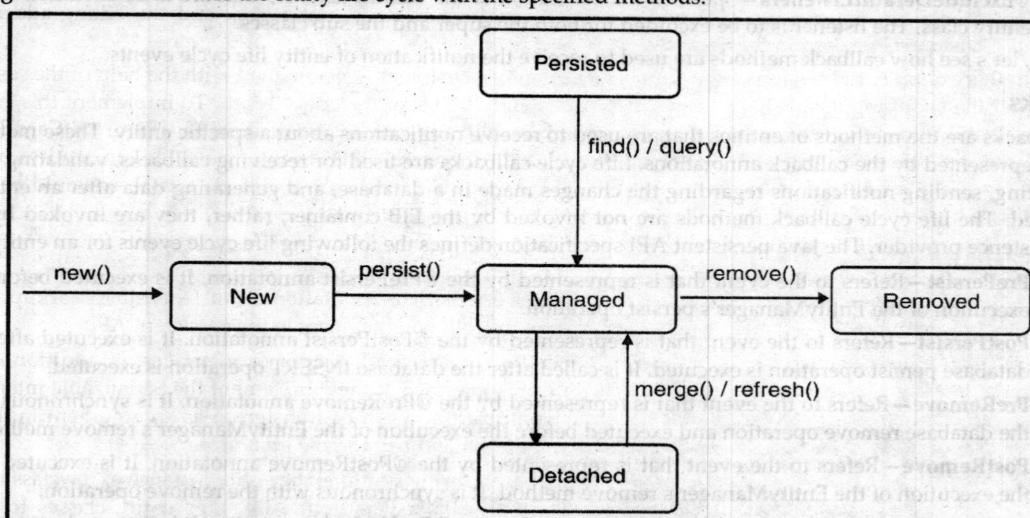

Figure 14.3: Showing the Entity Life Cycle

To destroy the entity data from the database, you need to invoke the `remove()` method. You should note that the invocation of the `remove()` method does not remove the entity from the database; instead, it schedules the entity that is to be removed. The remove operation does not work with new and removed entities. It only works with the managed entities. The `remove()` method cannot be called on the detached entities. Calling the method on a detached entity throws the `IllegalArgumentException` exception. Deletion of a particular entity takes place when transaction is committed or when the `remove()` method is called on the entity. The `merge()` method is used to bring the detached entity back to the persistent context. Entities are detached completely when their persistent context ends. The `merge()` method returns a managed entity.

Entity Listeners and Callbacks

An application reacts with respect to certain events that occur during the persistence mechanism. This process allows implementation of some definite type of generic functionalities and a reference to some built-in functionalities. The EJB 3 specification provides the following two mechanisms for this purpose:

- **Using the** `EntityListener` **class**—Refers to the mechanism in which you need to define an `EntityListener` class that is used to handle the life cycle events of an entity.
- **Using the callback method**—Refers to the mechanism in which the business method of an entity can be defined as the callback method with the help of the `@Callback` annotation. This callback method receives the notifications about the life cycle events of a particular entity.

Let's now discuss each of these mechanisms in detail.

Entity Listeners

The `EntityListener` class is a stateless bean class containing a non-argument constructor. A class can be made as the EntityListener class by using the `@EntityListener` annotation. The entity listeners are applied to entity classes. You can define several entity listeners for a single entity within different levels of hierarchy. However, for the same event within an entity, you cannot define two listeners. The occurrence of an event leads to the execution of the entity listeners according to inheritance hierarchy. Entity listeners for an entity can be defined by using the following annotations:

- **@EntityListeners**—Specifies the callback listener classes that should be used for an entity.
- **@ExcludeSuperclassListeners**—Specifies the invocation of the superclass listeners that are to be excluded for the entity and the subclass.
- **@ExcludeDefaultListeners**—Specifies the invocation of the default listeners that are to be excluded for the entity class. The listener is to be excluded for both the super and the sub classes.

Now, let's see how callback methods are used to receive the notification of entity life cycle events.

Callbacks

Callbacks are the methods of entities that are used to receive notifications about a specific entity. These methods are represented by the callback annotations. Life cycle callbacks are used for receiving callbacks, validating data, auditing, sending notifications regarding the changes made in a database, and generating data after an entity is loaded. The life cycle callback methods are not invoked by the EJB container; rather, they are invoked by the persistence provider. The Java persistent API specification defines the following life cycle events for an entity:

- **PrePersist**—Refers to the event that is represented by the @PrePersist annotation. It is executed before the execution of the EntityManager's persist operation.
- **PostPersist**—Refers to the event that is represented by the @PostPersist annotation. It is executed after the database persist operation is executed. It is called after the database INSERT operation is executed.
- **PreRemove**—Refers to the event that is represented by the @PreRemove annotation. It is synchronous with the database remove operation and executed before the execution of the EntityManager's remove method.
- **PostRemove**—Refers to the event that is represented by the @PostRemove annotation. It is executed after the execution of the EntityManager's remove method. It is synchronous with the remove operation.
- **PreUpdate**—Refers to the event that is represented by the @PreUpdate annotation. It is executed prior to the database UPDATE operation.
- **PostUpdate**—Refers to the event that is represented by the @PostUpdate annotation. It is executed after the database UPDATE operation.
- **PostLoad**—Refers to the event that is represented by the @PostLoad annotation. It is executed after an entity is loaded into the persistent context or the entity is being refreshed.

Packaging a Persistence Unit

The entities of a Java EE application are packaged in a persistence unit. In other words, the entities are not limited to the EJB modules; instead, they are packaged in a Web module, Enterprise ARchive (EAR) module, or the standard jar file. These entities are packaged in a Deployment Descriptor called `persistence.xml`.

The sample code for the `persistence.xml` is given in Listing 14.3:

Listing 14.3: Showing the Code of the persistence.xml File

```
<?xml version="1.0" encoding="UTF-8"?>
<persistence xmlns="http://xmlns.jcp.org/xml/ns/persistence"
```

```
       xmlns:xsi="http://www.w3.org/2001/XMLSchema-instance"
       xsi:schemaLocation="http://xmlns.jcp.org/xml/ns/ persistence
       http://www.oracle.com/webfolder/technetwork/jsc/xml/ns/persistence/persistence_2_1.xsd"
       version="2.1">

       <persistence-unit name="manager1" transaction-type="JTA">
           <provider> </provider>
           <jta-data-source> </jta-data-source>
           <mapping-file> </mapping-file>
           <jar-file> </jar-file>
           <class> </class>
       </persistence-unit>
    </persistence>
```

Let's now discuss the elements and attributes specified in the persistence.xml file under Listing 14.3.

The name Attribute

The `name` attribute of the `persistent-unit` element, listed in Listing 14.3, specifies the name of the entity manager.

The transaction-type Attribute

The value for the `transaction-type` attribute can be `Java Transaction API (JTA)` or `RESOURCE_LOCAL`. If the `jta-data-source` element is used, then the transaction type is `JTA`. However, if the `non-jta-data-source` element is used, then the `RESOURCE_LOCAL` value is used.

The provider Element

The `provider` element is used to specify the class name of the EJB persistence provider. If you are not working with the multiple EJB 3 implementations, then the provider may not be specified.

The jta-data-source and non jta-data-source Elements

The `jta-data-source` element is used to specify the Java Naming and Directory Interface (JNDI) name of the JDBC data source. The name of the specified data source is automatically enlisted in JTA transactions and is used in global transaction. In the `non-jta-data-source` element, the JNDI name of JDBC data source is specified that is not enlisted in JTA transactions.

The mapping-file Element

The `class` element specifies an EJB3 compliant XML mapping file to be mapped, say Customer class. The name of the EJB3 Deployment Descriptor is provided in the mapping-file element, defined in the persistent.xml file in Listing 14.3. The other elements of the persistence.xml file are:

- **Jar file** – Defines the `jar-file` element that specifies the name of the jar file required in an application
- **Class** – Defines the `class` element that specifies the class name that has to be mapped to the entity

Now, let's continue with the sample example in which a simple `Customer` entity class is created in Listing 14.2. Create a persistence.`xml` file for the Customer entity class, as shown in Listing 14.4 (save this file in the `\Customer\Customer-ejb\META-INF` folder):

Listing 14.4: Showing the Code of the persistence.xml File for the Customer Entity

```
    <?xml version="1.0" encoding="UTF-8"?>
    <persistence version="2.1" xmlns="http://xmlns.jcp.org/xml/ns/persistence"
               xmlns:xsi="http://www.w3.org/2001/XMLSchema-instance"
               xsi:schemaLocation="http://xmlns.jcp.org/xml/ns/persistence
     http://www.oracle.com/webfolder/technetwork/jsc/xml/ns/persistence/persistence_2_1.xsd">
      <persistence-unit name="Customer-ejbPU" transaction-type="JTA">
            <provider>oracle.toplink.essentials.PersistenceProvider</provider>
            <jta-data-source>customer</jta-data-source>
            <class>com.kogent.entity.Customer</class>
            <exclude-unlisted-classes>true</exclude-unlisted-classes>
            <properties>
            <property name="toplink.ddl-generation" value="create-tables"/>
```

```
        </properties>
    </persistence-unit>
</persistence>
```

In Listing 14.4, the persistence-unit name is `Customer-ejbPU` and the transaction-type is `JTA`. The `Customer-ejbPU` persistence unit packages all the entities. You have already created a single entity named Customer in Listing 14.2 and the JNDI name for the `Customer-ejbPU` persistence unit is customer, as specified in Listing 14.3. The `persistence.xml` file helps in locating the required entity as it packages the `Customer` entity in the persistence unit named `Customer-ejbPU`. You can save the `persistence.xml` file in the META-INF folder of the application (Figure 14.19).

After the entity bean is created and packaged in a persistence unit, you need to obtain an EntityManager to create an interaction between the client session and the entity instances.

Obtaining an EntityManager

The EntityManager provides the services offered by the EJB 3 persistence framework for the client. The client sessions must have an EntityManager instance for interacting with the entities. The EntityManager helps in querying, updating, removing, and refreshing the entity instances.

The collection of the instances within the transaction context called persistence context is also maintained by the EntityManager. The entity instance can be used either inside or outside of the EJB container. A client can obtain an EntityManager instance with the help of any of the following approaches:

- Using the container injection
- Using the `EntityManagerFactory` interface
- Looking up the `EntityManager` through JNDI

Let's explore each of these approaches in detail.

Using the Container Injection

The session bean uses the container injection to obtain an `EntityManager` instance that is bound to a persistence unit named as `persistence`. The following code snippet shows how to obtain the EntityManager instance, `em` using the container injection:

```
@Stateless
public class Customer {
    @PersistenceContext("Customer-ejbPU")
    private EntityManager em;
    public void createCustomer() {
        final Customer cust = new Customer();
        cust.setName("abc");
        em.persist(cust); }
}
```

In the preceding code snippet, the `em` instance is bound to the persistence unit named, `Customer-ejbPU`. This `EntityManager` is used to persist a new `Customer` instance.

Using the EntityManagerFactory Interface

Sometimes, an application needs to have more control over the life cycle of the EntityManager. In such situations, the client has a better option for obtaining the instance of an EntityManager by using the `EntityManagerFactory` interface. In the following code snippet, the `EntityManager` instance is obtained by using `EntityManagerFactory` factory:

```
public static void main(String[] args) {
    final EntityManagerFactory emf =
    Persistence.createEntityManagerFactory("Customer-ejbPU");
    final EntityManager em = emf.createEntityManager();
    final Customer cust = new Customer();
    cust.setName("abc");
    em.persist(cust);
}
```

In the preceding code snippet, the emf instance of the `EntityManagerFactory` interface is bound to the `Customer-ejbPU` persistence-unit, which includes the customer entity. Next, the `em` instance of the `EntityManager` class is created from the `emf` instance, which is used to manage the data of a new Customer instance, `cust`.

Looking up the `EntityManager` Using JNDI

The `lookup()` method of JNDI is used either by `EntityManagerFactory` or `EntityManager` for finding the reference of the entity. The following code snippet shows how the `EntityManager` instance is obtained by using the JNDI:

```
EntityManager em = (EntityManager)ctx.lookup("Customer-ejbPU");
```

In the preceding code snippet, you can see that the `em` is the instance of the `EntityManager` that is used to look for `Customer-ejbPU` persistence unit.

Interacting with an EntityManager

The process of persisting an entity is similar to the act of injecting an entity in the database. If the persisted entity is not created in the database, then it is automatically created. After the creation of the entity, the properties of the entity are set by using the `setXXX` methods. Next, the relationship of the entity is created with other Java objects by using `EntityManager`.

The `EntityManager` interface is used to interact with the persistence context. The EntityManager API provides the methods to insert and remove entities from the database. To interact with the `Customer-ejbPU` persistence unit using EntityManager, you first need to obtain the instance of the EntityManager interface, as discussed in the previous section, *Obtaining an EntityManager*. Then, the SessionFacade beans are created to interact with the Customer entity using the EntityManager API.

Listing 14.5 provides the code for the CustomerFacade session bean (save this file in the `\Customer\Customer-ejb\src\com\kogent\session` folder):

Listing 14.5: Showing the Code of the CustomerFacade.java File

```
package com.kogent.session;
import com.kogent.entity.Customer;
import java.util.List;
import javax.ejb.Stateless;
import javax.persistence.EntityManager;
import javax.persistence.PersistenceContext;

@Stateless
public class CustomerFacade implements CustomerFacadeLocal {
   @PersistenceContext
   private EntityManager em;

   public void create(Customer customer) {
         em.persist(customer);
   }

   public void edit(Customer customer) {
         em.merge(customer);
   }

   public void remove(Customer customer) {
         em.remove(em.merge(customer));
   }

   public Customer find(Object id) {
         return em.find(com.kogent.entity.Customer.class, id);
   }

   public List<Customer> findAll() {
 return em.createQuery("select object(o) from Customer as o").getResultList();
   }
}
```

In Listing 14.5, the persist(), merge(), remove(), and find() methods of the EntityManager interface are used. The find() method of EntityManager interface helps in finding the Customer entity. The find() method accepts the name of an entity class as a parameter and the instance of entity's primary key. The find() method returns null if the entity is not found in the database. In Listing 14.5, the Customer entity's class is located. The create(), edit(), remove(), find(), and findAll() methods are declared in the CustomerFacadeLocal interface.

Listing 14.6 provides the code for the CustomerFacadeLocal interface (save this file in the \Customer\Customer-ejb\src\com\kogent\session folder):

Listing 14.6: Showing the Code of the CustomerFacadeLocal.java File

```
package com.kogent.session;

import com.kogent.entity.Customer;
import java.util.List;
import javax.ejb.Local;

@Local
public interface CustomerFacadeLocal {

    void create(Customer customer);

    void edit(Customer customer);

    void remove(Customer customer);

    Customer find(Object id);
    List<Customer> findAll();

}
```

In Listing 14.6, the create(), edit(), remove(), find(), and findAll() methods have been declared. The CustomerFacade session bean and the CustomerFacadeLocal interface are defined under the com.kogent.session package. Listing 14.5 interacts with the Customer entity by using the em instance of the EntityManager interface. The em instance invokes the persist() method, as shown in Listing 14.6, to create a new Customer instance. The remove() method is invoked to remove the Customer instance.

After packaging the entity into a persistence unit (persistence.xml) and understanding various ways to obtain the packaged persistence unit, let's now discuss the various types of entity relationships.

Understanding Entity Relationship Types

Entities can have a single reference or collections of references to other entities. A relationship is always implemented with the help of a relationship field on either one or both entities involved in a relationship. An entity relationship can be unidirectional or bidirectional. In contrast to EJB 2.1, the EJB container of EJB 3.0 maintains bidirectional relationships. In a unidirectional relationship between entity A and entity B, updating an instance of entity A leads to updation of some related instance of entity B. However, the same is not entertained by the container in reverse direction, i.e. updating an instance of entity B does not affect any instance of entity A. While using container-managed relationships, you do not need to declare the actual database foreign key constraints for a field of a table. The entities can have any of the following types of relationships:

- One-to-one
- One-to-many
- Many-to-one
- Many-to-many

The use of annotations has further improved the way in which entity relationships are defined in EJB 3.0. The new functionalities introduced in EJB 3.0, such as using annotations, using JPA, and entities being POJOs have greatly simplified EJB programming. In addition to the annotations used in EJB 3 for different Object Relational (O/R) mapping, there are several annotations available for defining different types of relationships.

Table 14.1 lists the annotations used to define different types of entity relationships:

Table 14.1: Showing the Types of Entities and their Corresponding Annotations

Type of Relationship	Annotation
One-to-one	@OneToOne
One-to-many	@OneToMany
Many-to-one	@ManyToOne
Many-to-many	@ManyToMany

Let's now discuss each entity relationship in detail with their real world examples and their implementation in EJB 3.

The One-to-One Relationship

One-to-one relation specifies that an instance of an entity is associated to only a single instance of another entity. For example, there are two entities, Division and Manager. As you know that one division is managed by one manager only; therefore, the Division entity is said to have a one-to-one relationship with the Manager entity. This relationship is unidirectional. However, if it is given that a manager can manage a single division only, this relationship changes to one-to-one bidirectional entity relationship.

Figure 14.4 shows the one-to-one unidirectional and bidirectional relationships between the Division and Manager entities:

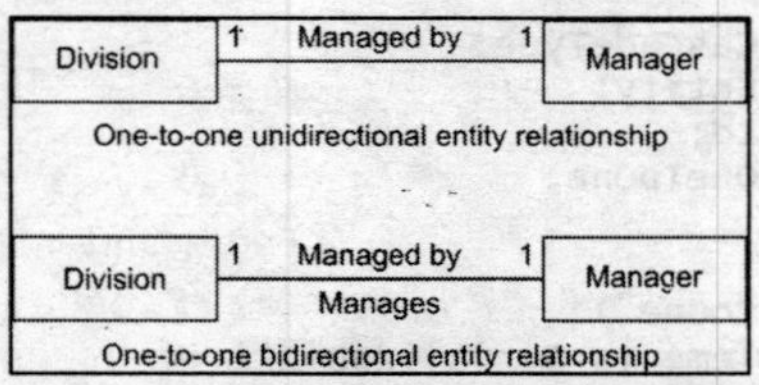

Figure 14.4: Showing One-To-One Unidirectional and Bidirectional Relationship

After understanding the concept of the one-to-one relationship, let's learn how to implement this relationship in an entity class. Consider another example that defines two entities Employee and Department. The Employee entity instance represents a table containing the record of employees working for different departments. The Department entity represents the department details for which different employees are working. There is a one-to-one relationship between the two entities, Employee and Department.

Figure 14.5 shows the two tables, EMPLOYEE and DEPARTMENT, which represents Employee and Department entities:

Employee

ID	Name
A1	Vinay
A2	Ashutosh
A3	Manoj

Department

ID	Department	Manager
A1	Accounts	R. Batra
A2	HRD	P. Sinha
A3	Admin	N. Sarkar

Figure 14.5: Showing the EMPLOYEE and DEPARTMENT Table Representing Entities

Figure 14.5 shows that an employee works only in a single department. For example, an employee with ID A1 has only a single department record in the DEPARTMENT table. Therefore, the Employee entity has a one-to-one unidirectional relationship with the Department entity, as shown in Figure 14.6:

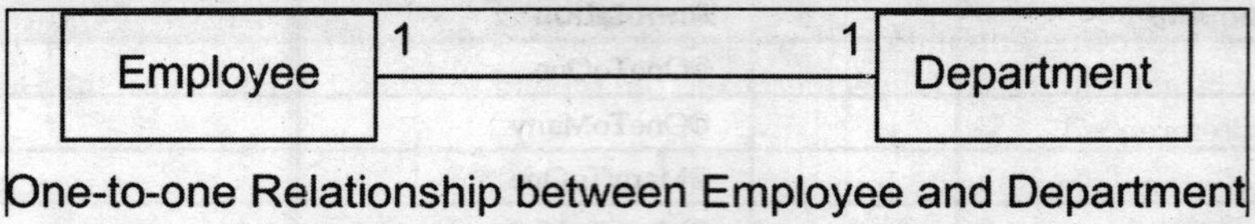

Figure 14.6: Showing a Unidirectional Relationship between Employee and Department Entities

Let's now implement the relationship between Employee and Department entities by creating the entity bean classes for the two entities (Employee and Department), a session bean class, and a class implementing the client code. The client code accesses the session bean and this session bean interacts with the entity beans on behalf of the client. Let's begin with the first entity bean, which is Employee.

The Employee and Department entities have a one-to-one relationship, as shown in Figure 14.6. This can be implemented by providing a single value entity reference at one or both ends of the relationship. Listing 14.7 shows the code of the Employee entity bean class:

Listing 14.7: Showing the Code of Employee.java File Representing One to One Relationship

```
package com.kogent.one_to_one;

import java.io.Serializable;

import javax.persistence.CascadeType;
import javax.persistence.Entity;
import javax.persistence.Id;
import javax.persistence.OneToOne;


@Entity(name="EmployeeOnetoOne")
public class Employee implements Serializable {
   private String id;
   private String employeeName;
   private Department department;

   public Employee() {
        id = "SPM" + java.lang.Math.random();
   }

   @Id
   public String getId() {
        return id;
   }

   public void setId(String id) {
        this.id = id;
   }

   public String getEmployeeName() {
        return employeeName;
   }

   public void setOrderName(String employeeName) {
        this.employeeName = employeeName;
   }

   @OneToOne(cascade={CascadeType.PERSIST})
   public Department getShipment() {
        return department;
   }

   public void setDepartment(Department department) {
```

```
            this.department = department;
        }
    }
```

In Listing 14.7, the @OneToOne annotation is used to define a single-valued association. You do not need to define the associated target entity as it is specified from the type of the object (in this case, the Department entity is used) that is being referenced.

You can use a set of optional elements with the `@OneToOne` annotation, such as cascade and fetch.

Table 14.2 lists the available elements for the `@OneToOne` annotation:

Table 14.2: Describing the Optional Elements of the @OneToOne Annotation

Element	Description
CascadeType[] cascade	Helps to define operations that must be cascaded to the associated target entity
FetchType fetch	Helps to define whether the association should be slowly loaded or must be quickly fetched
String mappedBy	Helps to define the fields from where the relationship exists
boolean optional	Sets whether or not the association is optional
Class targetEntity	Defines the target entity class

Prior to implementing the Department entity bean class, let's have a brief discussion over elements used with the `@OneToOne` annotation. The elements used with the @OneToOne annotation are as follows:

- **Cascade**—Defines operations that must be cascaded to the target entity in the association. By default, no operation is cascaded.

Table 14.3 provides various possible constant values that can be used for the CascadeType[] cascade element:

Table 14.3: Describing the CascadeType Constants

Constants	Description
CascadeType.ALL	Cascades all operations
CascadeType.MERGE	Cascades the merge operation
CascadeType.PERSIST	Cascades the persist operation
CascadeType.REFRESH	Cascades the refresh operation
CascadeType.REMOVE	Cascades the remove operation

- **Fetch**—Sets with FetchType constants, which decide whether the association is lazily loaded or eagerly fetched. The possible two values are FetchType.EAGER and FetchType.LAZY. By default, for performance reasons, all the fields' values are fetched lazily.
- **mappedBy**—Defines the field which owns the relationship. This element is specified on the inverse (non-owning) side of the association.
- **Optional**—Sets to either true or false. False defines a not null relationship; whereas, true defines a null relationship.
- **targetEntity**—Sets the target entity in the relationship.

The other entity in the relationship, which represents the DEPARTMENT table, is the Department entity. Let's now define the Department class that does not contain any annotation to define the relationship between the Employee and Department entity.

Listing 14.8 shows the code of the Department entity class:

Listing 14.8: Showing the Code of the Department.java File

```
package com.kogent.one_to_one;
import java.io.Serializable;
import javax.persistence.Entity;
import javax.persistence.Id;
```

```
@Entity(name="DepartmentOnetoOne")
public class Department implements Serializable {
  private String id;
  private String departmentName;
  private String manager;

  public Department() {
        id = "SPM" + java.lang.Math.random();
  }
  @Id
  public String getId() {
        return id;
  }

  public void setId(String id) {
        this.id = id;
  }

  public String getDepartmentName() {
        return departmentName;
  }
  public void setDepartmentName (String departmentName) {
        this. departmentName = departmentName;
  }

  public String getManager() {
        return manager;
  }

  public void setManager(String manager) {
        this.manager = manager;
  }
}
```

Let's create a session bean class to work as an interface between the client code and entity classes. Therefore, creation of a remote interface is required to implement the session bean class. Listing 14.9 provides the code for the `EmployeeDepartment` remote interface:

Listing 14.9: Showing the Code of the EmployeeDepartment.java File

```
package com.kogent.one_to_one.interfaces;

import java.util.List;
import javax.ejb.Remote;


@Remote
public interface EmployeeDepartment {
  public void setQueries();

  public List getEmployees();
}
```

The two methods defined in the `EmployeeDepartment` interface are `setQueries()` and `getEmployees()`. The session bean class, `EmployeeDepartmentBean`, implements the `EmployeeDepartment` interface. An instance of the `EntityManager` interface is acquired through container injection, which is achieved by using the `@PersistenceContext` annotation. The code for the `EmployeeDepartmentBean` class is shown in Listing 14.10:

Listing 14.10: Showing the Code of the EmployeeDepartmentBean.java File

```
package com.kogent.one_to_one;

import java.util.List;

import javax.ejb.Stateless;
import javax.persistence.EntityManager;
```

```
import javax.persistence.PersistenceContext;
import javax.persistence.Query;

import com.kogent.one_to_one.interfaces.EmployeeDepartment;
@Stateless
public class EmployeeDepartmentBean implements EmployeeDepartment {
  @PersistenceContext
  EntityManager em;

  public void setQueries() {
         Departent d = new Department();
         d.setDepartmentName("Accounts");
         d.setManager("Ashutosh Verma");

         Employee e = new Employee();
         e.setEmployeeName("Vinay");
         e.setDepartment(d);

         em.persist(e);
  }

  public List getEmployees() {
         Query q = em.createQuery("SELECT e FROM EmployeeOto e");
         return q.getResultList();
  }
}
```

In Listing 14.10, the `setQueries()` method creates instances of the Department and Employee entities and sets the department field of the Employee entity with the Department object. Finally, the `persist()` method is called and the Employee entity instance is added to a persistence context as a managed instance. In other words, the record of an employee is inserted in the EMPLOYEE table and the associated DEPARTMENT table.

Let's now create the client class, `EmployeeDepartmentClient` to access this session bean, as shown in Listing 14.11:

Listing 14.11: Showing the Code of the EmployeeDepartmentClient.java File

```
package com.kogent.one_to_one.client;
//import goes here
public class EmployeeDepartmentClient {
  public static void main(String[] args) {
         try {
                InitialContext ic = new InitialContext();
                EmployeeDepartment ed =
               (EmployeeDepartment)ic.lookup(EmployeeDepartment.class.getEmployeeName());

                ed.setQueries();

                System.out.println("Unidirectional One-To-One client\n");

                for (Object o : ed.getEmployees()) {
                       Employee emp = (Employee)o;
                       System.out.println("Employee "+emp.getId()+":
                       "+emp.getEmployeeName());
                       System.out.println("\tDepartment:
                       "+emp.getDepartment().getDepartmentName()+"
                       "+emp.getDepartment().getManager());
                }
         }
         catch (NamingException e) {
                e.printStackTrace();
         }
  }
}
```

Now, you can compile all the Java source files provided in Listing 14.7 to 14.11 and create an EAR file to deploy the application on the application server. You can also run the `EmployeeDepartmentClient` class to see the output.

Let's now discuss the one-to-many relationship.

The One-to-Many Relationship

A one-to-many entity relationship shows the association of an instance of an entity with multiple instances of another entity, for example, many orders can be placed for a single customer. Therefore, if there are two entities named, Customer and Order, there is a one-to-many relationship between them.

Figure 14.7 displays the one-to-many relationship between the Customer and Order entities:

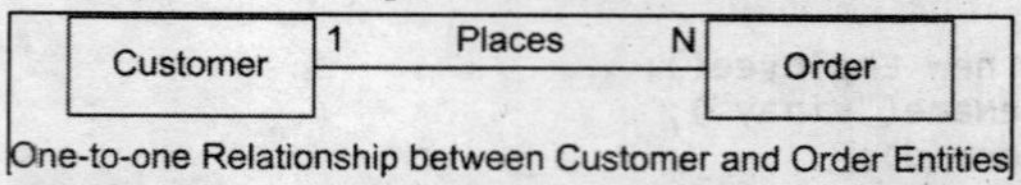

Figure 14.7: Showing the Unidirectional Relationship between CUSTOMER and ORDER Entities

After understanding the concept of the one-to-many relationship, let's learn how to implement this relationship in an entity class. Consider another example that defines two entities, Company and Employee. A company has many employees working for it. The data of these entities is represented by the two tables, COMPANY and EMPLOYEE.

Figure 14.8 shows the two tables, named COMPANY and EMPLOYEE:

Company

Company_ID	Company_Name
C101	Kogent
C102	SBP
C103	Wiley

Employee

Company_ID	Employee_Name
C101	Santosh
C101	Prakash
C101	Ishita
C102	Suman
C103	Jyotsna

Figure 14.8: Showing the COMPANY and EMPLOYEE Table

In Figure 14.8, records of the COMPANY table and the EMPLOYEE table. You should note that the Company_ID field of the EMPLOYEE table contains the records of the COMPANY_ID field of the COMPANY table. You can see the one-to-many relationship between the two entities in Figure 14.9:

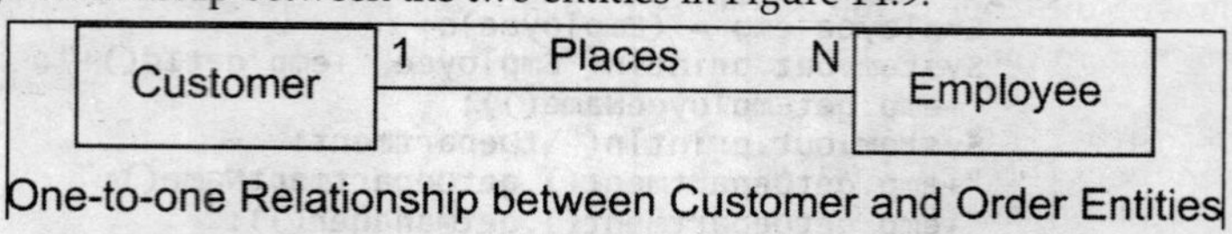

Figure 14.9: Showing the Relationships between Company and Employee Entities

Similar to the one-to-one relationship, let's create the two entity bean classes (Company and Employee), a remote interface, a session bean, and a client class to demonstrate the one-to-many relationship. The `@OneToMany` relationship annotation is used to define the one-to-many relationship. Listing 14.12 provides the code of the Company entity bean class:

Listing 14.12: Showing the Code of the Company.java File

```
package com.kogent.one_to_many;
import java.io.Serializable;
```

```
import java.util.Collection;
import javax.persistence.CascadeType;
import javax.persistence.Entity;
import javax.persistence.FetchType;
import javax.persistence.Id;
import javax.persistence.OneToMany;
@Entity(name="CompanyOMUni")
public class Company implements Serializable {
  private int id;
  private String name;
  private Collection<Employee> employees;

  public Company() {
        id = (int)System.nanoTime();
  }

  @Id
  public int getId() {
        return id;
  }

  public void setId(int id) {
        this.id = id;
  }

  public String getName() {
        return name;
  }

  public void setName(String name) {
        this.name = name;
  }

  @OneToMany(cascade={CascadeType.ALL},fetch=FetchType.EAGER)
  public Collection<Employee> getEmployees() {
        return employees;
  }

  public void setEmployees(Collection<Employee> employees) {
        this.employees = employees;
  }
}
```

The use of generic collection type in Listing 14.12 (Collection<Employee>) enables persistence framework to determine the entity type at the other end of the relationship. Different elements of the `@OneToMany` annotation are the same as those used with the `@OneToOne` annotation except for the optional element, which is not used. The `mappedBy` element is needed only in case when the relationship is unidirectional.

Let's now create the Employee entity bean class, as shown in Listing 14.13:

Listing 14.13: Showing the Code of the Employee.java File Representing One to Many Relationship

```
package com.kogent.one_to_many;

import java.io.Serializable;
import javax.persistence.Entity;
import javax.persistence.Id;

@Entity(name="EmployeeOMUni")
public class Employee implements Serializable {
  private int id;
  private String name;
  private char sex;

  public Employee() {
        id = (int)System.nanoTime();
  }
```

```
    @Id
    public int getId() {
          return id;
    }

    public void setId(int id) {
          this.id = id;
    }

    public String getName() {
          return name;
    }

    public void setName(String name) {
          this.name = name;
    }

    public char getSex() {
          return sex;
    }
    public void setSex(char sex) {
          this.sex = sex;
    }
}
```

In Listing 14.13, a session bean class is used to interact with different entities on behalf of the client code. Let's now create the CompanyEmployeeOM remote interface, as shown in Listing 14.14:

Listing 14.14: Showing the Code of the CompanyEmployeeOM.java File

```
package com.kogent.one_to_many.interfaces;
import java.util.List;
import javax.ejb.Remote;
@Remote
public interface CompanyEmployeeOM {
  public void doSomeStuff();

  public List getCompanies();

  public List getCompanies2(String query);

  public void deleteCompanies();
}
```

In Listing 14.15, the `CompanyEmployeeOM` remote interface defines four different methods--`doSomeStuff()`, `getCompanies()`, `getCompanies2()`, and `deleteCompanies()`. Now, you need to create the session bean class, `CompanyEmployeeOMUniBean`, which implements the `CompanyEmployeeOM` interface. You can see the code of the `CompanyEmployeeOMUniBean` class in Listing 14.15:

Listing 14.15: Showing the Code of the CompanyEmployeeOMUniBean.java File

```
package com.kogent.one_to_many;

import java.util.ArrayList;
import java.util.Collection;
import java.util.List;
import javax.ejb.Stateless;
import javax.persistence.EntityManager;
import javax.persistence.PersistenceContext;
import javax.persistence.Query;

import com.kogent.one_to_many.interfaces.CompanyEmployeeOM;

@Stateless
public class CompanyEmployeeOMUniBean implements CompanyEmployeeOM {
  @PersistenceContext
  EntityManager em;
```

```
public void doSomeStuff() {
        Company c = new Company();
        c.setName("M*Power Internet Services, Inc.");

        Collection<Employee> employees = new ArrayList<Employee>();
        Employee e = new Employee();
        e.setName("Vinay Kumar");
        e.setSex('M');
        employees.add(e);

        e = new Employee();
        e.setName("Prakash Kumar");
        e.setSex('M');
        employees.add(e);

        c.setEmployees(employees);
        em.persist(c);

        c = new Company();
        c.setName("Kogent Solutions Inc.");

        employees = new ArrayList<Employee>();
        e = new Employee();
        e.setName("Shilpa Sharma");
        e.setSex('F');
        employees.add(e);

        e = new Employee();
        e.setName("Vikas");
        e.setSex('M');
        employees.add(e);

        c.setEmployees(employees);
        em.persist(c);

        c = new Company();
        c.setName("ABC Pvt. Ltd.");
        em.persist(c);
}

public List getCompanies() {
        Query q = em.createQuery("SELECT c FROM CompanyOMUni c");
        return q.getResultList();
}
public List getCompanies2(String query) {
        Query q = em.createQuery(query);
        return q.getResultList();
}
```

```
    public void deleteCompanies() {
            Query q = em createQuery("DELETE FROM CompanyOMUni");
            q.executeUpdate();
    }
}
```

The different methods of the `CompanyEmployeeOMUniBean` class either create instances of the entity or invoke the `persist()` method. In addition, the session bean class executes various queries, such as select and delete, to provide the desired results.

Finally, let's create the client class, `CompanyEmployeeClient,` as shown in Listing 14.16:

Listing 14.16: Showing the Code of the CompanyEmployeeClient.java File

```
package com.kogent.one_to_many.client;

//import goes here

public class CompanyEmployeeClient {
    public static void main(String[] args) {
            try {
                    InitialContext ic = new InitialContext();
                    CompanyEmployeeOM ceom =
                    (CompanyEmployeeOM)ic.lookup
                    (CompanyEmployeeOM.class.getName());

                    ceom.deleteCompanies();

                    ceom.doSomeStuff();

                    System.out.println("All Companies:");
                    for (Object o : ceom.getCompanies()) {
                            Company c = (Company)o;
                            System.out.println("Here are the employees for
                            company: "+c.getName());
                            for (Employee e : c.getEmployees()) {
                                    System.out.println("\tName: "+e.getName()+",
                                    Sex: "+e.getSex());
                            }
                            System.out.println();
                    }
            }
            catch (NamingException e) {
                    e.printStackTrace();
            }
    }
}
```

Now, compile all the Java source code files created in Listing 14.12 to 14.16 and bundle them into an EAR file to be deployed on the Glassfish Server 4.0 . You can view the output by executing the `CompanyEmployeeClient` class.

The Many-to-One Relationship

A many-to-one entity relationship shows the association of multiple instances of an entity with a single instance of another entity. For example, there are two entities, `ORDER` and `ORDER_ITEM`. There is always a collection of order items related with a single order placed by any customer. In other words, for a single `Order` entity instance, there are multiple `Order_Item` instances. You can also say that multiple `Order_Item` instances can be associated with a single `Order` instance.

Figure 14.10 shows the many-to-one entity relationship:

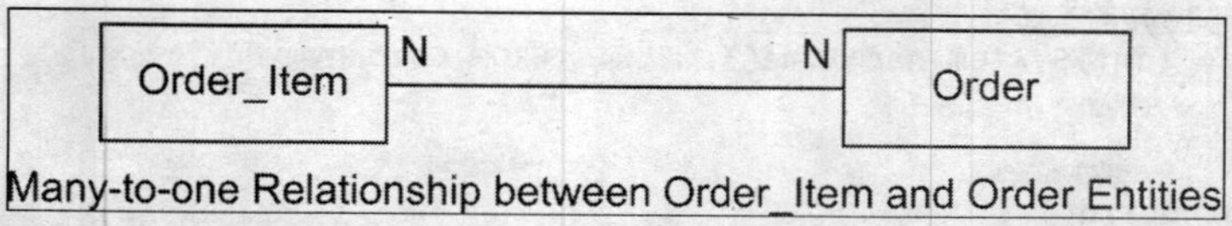

Figure 14.10: Showing Many-To-One Relationship between ORDER_ITEM and ORDER Entities

The two tables representing the `Order_Item` and `Order` entities have been shown in Figure 14.11:

Order_Item

ID	Item_Name	Quantity
1001	Monitor	1
1001	Keyboard	2
1001	Processor	1
1002	Monitor	3
1002	Pen Drive	2

Order

ID	Customer_Name	Payment_Mode
1001	John	Cash
1002	Danish	Credit Card

Figure 14.11: Showing the ORDER_ITEM and ORDER Tables

In Figure 14.11, you can see that there are multiple entries in the `ORDER_ITEM` table, which are associated with a single record in the `ORDER` table.

After understanding the concept of the many-to-one relationship, let's learn how to implement this relationship in an entity class. Consider another example that defines two entities `Employee` and `BusinessAddress`. There can be multiple employees working at a single working place, which is known as their business address. Therefore, you can say that the `Employee` entity has a many-to-one relationship with the `BusinessAddress` entity, as shown in Figure 14.12:

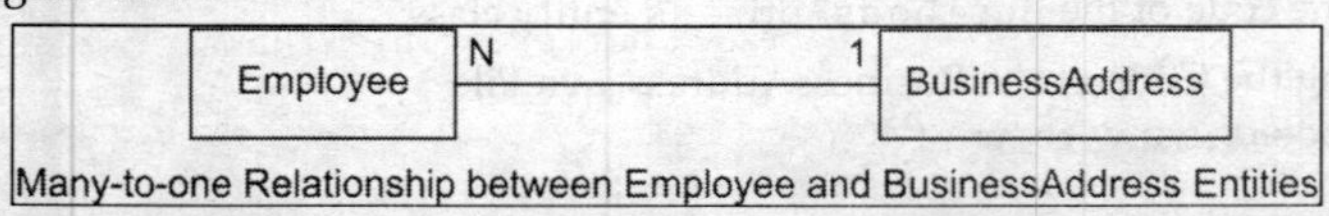

Figure 14.12: Showing Many-To-One Relationships between Employee and BusinessAddress Entities

Let's now implement the relationship between `Employee` and `BusinessAddress` entities by creating the entity bean classes for the two entities (`Employee` and `BusinessAddress`), a session bean class, and a class implementing the client code. The `@ManyToOne` annotation is used to define the many-to-one relationship between `Employee` and `BusinessAddress` entities.

The code of the `Employee` entity is shown in Listing 14.17:

Listing 14.17: Showing the Code of the Employee.java File Representing Many to One Relationship

```
package com.kogent.many_to_one;

import java.io.Serializable;
import javax.persistence.CascadeType;
import javax.persistence.Entity;
import javax.persistence.Id;
import javax.persistence.ManyToOne;

@Entity
public class Employee implements Serializable {
   private int id;
   private String name;
   private BusinessAddress address;
```

```
    public Employee() {
          id = (int)System.nanoTime();
    }

    @Id
    public int getId() {
          return id;
    }

    public void setId(int id) {
          this.id = id;
    }

    public String getName() {
          return name;
    }


    public void setName(String name) {
          this.name = name;
    }

    @ManyToOne(cascade={CascadeType.ALL})
    public BusinessAddress getAddress() {
          return address;
    }

    public void setAddress(BusinessAddress address) {
          this.address = address;
    }
}
```

The `@ManyToOne` annotation can be used with different optional elements, such as `cascade`, `fetch`, `optional`, and `targetEntity`.

The other entity in the many-to-one relationship is `BusinessAddress` in which you need to define the primary key by using the `@Id` annotation with the id field.

Listing 14.18 shows the code of the `BusinessAddress` entity class:

Listing 14.18: Showing the Code of the BusinessAddress.java File

```
package com.kogent.many_to_one;

import java.io.Serializable;
import javax.persistence.Entity;
import javax.persistence.Id;

@Entity
public class BusinessAddress implements Serializable {
    private int id;
    private String city;
    private String zipcode;

    public BusinessAddress() {
          id = (int)System.nanoTime();
    }

    @Id
    public int getId() {
          return id;
    }

    public void setId(int id) {
          this.id = id;
    }

    public String getCity() {
```

```
        return city;
    }

    public void setCity(String city) {
        this.city = city;
    }
    public String getZipcode() {
        return zipcode;
    }

    public void setZipcode(String zipcode) {
        this.zipcode = zipcode;
    }
}
```

The session bean created in this example is `EmployeeAddressMOUniBean` class that implements a remote interface, `EmployeeAddressMOUni`. The code of the `EmployeeAddressMOUni` interface is provided in Listing 14.19:

Listing 14.19: Showing the Code of the EmployeeAddressMOUni.java File

```
package com.kogent.many_to_one.interfaces;

import java.util.List;
import javax.ejb.Remote;
@Remote
public interface EmployeeAddressMOUni {
  public void doSomeStuff();

  public List getEmployees();
}
```

The `EmployeeAddressMOUni` interface declares two methods, `doSomeStuff()` and `getEmployees()`. Now, you need to create the `EmployeeAddressMOUniBean` bean class that implements the `EmployeeAddressMOUni` interface and provides the body to the `doSomeStuff()` and `getEmployees()` methods.

The code of the `EmployeeAddressMOUniBean` entity bean class is shown in Listing 14.20:

Listing 14.20: Showing the Code of the EmployeeAddressMOUniBean.java File

```
package com.kogent.many_to_one;

import java.util.List;

import javax.ejb.Stateless;
import javax.persistence.EntityManager;
import javax.persistence.PersistenceContext;
import javax.persistence.Query;

import com.kogent.many_to_one.interfaces.EmployeeAddressMOUni;

@Stateless
public class EmployeeAddressMOUniBean implements EmployeeAddressMOUni {
  @PersistenceContext
  EntityManager em;

  public void doSomeStuff() {
        BusinessAddress a = new BusinessAddress();
        a.setCity("Mumbai");
        a.setZipcode("400001");

        Employee e = new Employee();
        e.setName("Ishita");
        e.setAddress(a);
        em.persist(e);

        e = new Employee();
```

```
            e.setName("Prakash");
            e.setAddress(a);
            em.persist(e);

            e = new Employee();
            e.setName("Santosh");
            e.setAddress(a);
            em.persist(e);
    }

    public List getEmployees() {
            Query q = em.createQuery("SELECT e FROM Employee e");
            return q.getResultList();
    }
}
```

You can see the `doSomeStuff()` method in Listing 14.20 where the `BusinessAddress` entity instance is being associated with multiple instances of the `Employee` entity before calling the `persist()` method. Finally, you need to create the client code in the form of the `EmployeeAddressClient` class, as shown in Listing 14.21:

Listing 14.21: Showing the Code of the EmployeeAddressClient.java File

```
package com.kogent.many_to_one.client;

//import goes here

public class EmployeeAddressClient {
   public static void main(String[] args) {
        try {
                Initialcontext ic = new InitialContext();
EmployeeAddressMOUni ea =
   (EmployeeAddressMOUni)ic.lookup(EmployeeAddressMOUni.class.getName());

                ea.doSomeStuff();

                for (Object o : ea.getEmployees()) {
                        Employee e = (Employee)o;
System.out.println("Name: "+e.getName()+", Business Address: "+
   e.getAddress().getCity()+", "+e.getAddress().getZipcode());
                }
        }
        catch (NamingException e) {
                e.printStackTrace();
        }
   }
}
```

Now, compile all the Java source code files created in Listing 14.17 to 14.21 and bundle them into an EAR file to be deployed on the Glassfish V3 application server. You can view the output by executing the `EmployeeAddressClient` class.

The Many-to-Many Relationship

A many-to-many relationship is defined as the association between two entities where one instance of an entity is associated with multiple instances of another entity and vice-versa. For example, there are two entities Student and Course. An instance of the Student entity can be associated with multiple instances of the Course entity and a single instance of the Course entity can be associated with multiple instance of the Student entity.

Figure 14.13 shows the many-to-many relationship between the Student and Course entities:

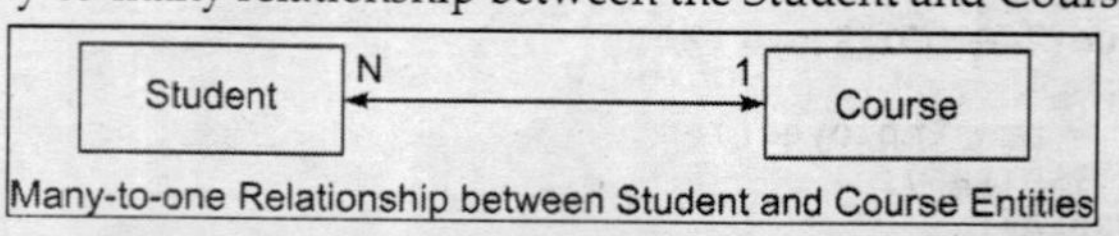

Figure 14.13: Displaying Many-to-Many Relationship between Student and Course Entities

A many-to-many relationship always has two sides called an owning side and a non-owning side. The join operation of a table is defined on the owning side. If the relationship is bidirectional, then either of the side can be designated as the owning side.

To maintain the data of the `Student` and `Course` entities, you need to create various tables in the database, such as `STUDENT`, `COURSE`, and `STU_COURSE`. The `STU_COURSE` table is created by using the join operation between the `STUDENT` and `COURSE` tables and the `STU_COURSE` table specifies many-to-many relationship.

Figure 14.14 shows the `STUDENT`, `COURSE`, and `STU_COURSE` tables:

Student

ST_ID	Name
101	Sujeet Verma
102	Amit Kumar
103	Puneet Saxena

Course

CI_ID	CO_Name
C01	Java EE6
C02	VB.Net
C03	PHP

STU_Course

ST_ID	CO_Name
101	C01
102	C02
102	C02
101	C01
102	C02
103	C03

Figure 14.14: Showing the STUDENT, COURSE, and STU_COURSE Tables

You can see in Figure 14.14 that a student, say 101, may be enrolled in multiple courses (C01, C03). Similarly, a course can be studied by several students, such as C01 and C03 are studied by students with ID 101 and 103.

After understanding the concept of the many-to-many relationship, let's learn how to implement this relationship in an entity class. Consider another example that defines two entities, Author and Book.

An author can work on various books and a book can be written by various authors. Therefore, the many-to-many relationship exists between the Author and Book entities, as shown in Figure 14.15:

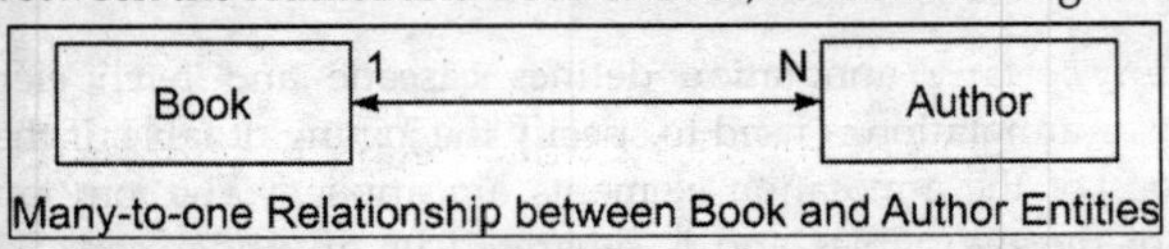

Figure 14.15: Showing the Many to Many Relationship between Book and Author

Let's now implement the relationship between Author and Book entities by creating the entity bean classes for the two entities (Book and Author), a session bean class, and a class implementing the client code. The `@ManyToMany` annotation is used to define many-to-many associations as well as multiplicity of the associations. Whenever you search for the associated entity instance, you always get a collection of objects. You do not need to specify the target entity class if the collection is defined using generics. The code of the Book entity class is shown in Listing 14.22:

Listing 14.22: Showing the Code of the Book.java File

```
package com.kogent.many_to_many;

import java.io.Serializable;
import java.util.ArrayList;
import java.util.Collection;

import javax.persistence.CascadeType;
```

```
import javax.persistence.Entity;
import javax.persistence.FetchType;
import javax.persistence.Id;

import javax.persistence.JoinTable;
import javax.persistence.ManyToMany;
@Entity(name="BookUni")
public class Book implements Serializable {
   private int id;
   private String bookName;
   private Collection<Author> authors = new ArrayList<Author>();
   public Book() {
         id = (int)System.nanoTime();
   }

   @Id
   public int getId() {
         return id;
   }

   public void setId(int id) {
         this.id = id;
   }

   public String getBookName() {
         return bookName;
   }

   public void setBookName(String bookName) {
         this.bookName = bookName;
   }

   @ManyToMany(cascade={CascadeType.ALL},fetch=FetchType.EAGER)
   @JoinTable(name="BOOKUNI_AUTHORUNI")
   public Collection<Author> getAuthors() {
         return authors;
   }

   public void setAuthors(Collection<Author> authors) {
         this.authors = authors;
   }

}
```

In Listing 14.22, the `@ManyToMany` annotation defines cascade and fetch elements of the `@OneToMany` annotation. The `@JoinTable` annotation is used to specify the joining of table. If the `@JoinTable` annotation is not used, the default values of the annotation elements are applied. The join table name can be created by concatenating the names of the two tables and is separated by an underscore. The optional elements of the `@JoinTable` annotation are listed in Table 14.4:

Table 14.4: Showing the Optional Elements of the @JoinTable

Elements	Description
`String catalog`	Sets the catalog of the table
`JoinColumn[] inverseJoinColumns`	Specifies the foreign key columns of the join table with reference to the primary table of the entity that does not own the association
`JoinColumn[] joinColumns`	Specifies the foreign key columns of the join table with reference to the primary table of the entity owning the association
`String name`	Sets the name of the join table
`String schema`	Sets the schema of the table
`UniqueConstraint[] uniqueConstraints`	Sets the unique constraints that are to be placed on the table

The following code snippet shows the implementation of the @JoinTable annotation:

```
@JoinTable(
   name="Book_Author",

   joinColumns=
   @JoinColumn(name="B_ID", referencedColumnName="ID"),
   inverseJoinColumns=
   @JoinColumn(name="A_ID", referencedColumnName="ID")
)
```

The entity on the non-owning side of the relationship is Author. The code of the Author entity class is shown in Listing 14.23:

Listing 14.23: Showing the Code of the Author.java File

```
package com.kogent.many_to_many;
import com.kogent.many_to_many.Book;
import java.io.Serializable;
import java.util.ArrayList;
import java.util.Collection;

import javax.persistence.Entity;
import javax.persistence.Id;
@Entity(name="AuthorUni")
public class Author implements Serializable {
   private int id;
   private String authorName;
   private Collection<Book> bookss = new ArrayList<Book>();

   public Author() {
         id = (int)System.nanoTime();
   }

   @Id
   public int getId() {
         return id;
   }

   public void setId(int id) {
         this.id = id;
   }

   public String getAuthorName() {
         return authorName;
   }

   public void setAuthorName(String authorName) {
         this.authorName = authorName;
   }

   public Collection<Book> getBooks() {
         return books;
   }

   public void setBooks(Collection<Book> books) {
         this.books = books;
   }
}
```

As shown in Listing 14.23, the Author entity has the `getBooks()` method, which returns a collection of the associated `Book` instances. Similarly, the `Book` entity has the `getAuthors()` method, which returns a collection of the `Author` objects that are associated with an instance of the `Book` entity.

To interact with the Book and Author entities, you need to create a session bean class. In our case, create the session bean class named as `BookAuthorUniBean`, which implements the remote interface `BookAuthor`.

Listing 14.24 shows the code for the `BookAuthor` interface:

Listing 14.24: Showing the Code of the BookAuthor.java File

```
package com.kogent.many_to_many.interfaces;
import java.util.List;
import javax.ejb.Remote;
import com.kogent.many_to_many.Book;
@Remote
public interface BookAuthor {
   public void doSomeStuff();

   public List<Book> getAllBooks();
}
```

The two methods declared in the `BookAuthor` interface are `doSomeStuff()` and `getAllBooks()`. These two business methods are defined by the `BookAuthorUniBean` class, which implements the `BookAuthor` interface.

The code for the `BookAuthorUniBean entity bean` class is shown in Listing 14.25:

Listing 14.25: Showing the Code of the BookAuthorUniBean.java File

```
import com.kogent.many_to_many.*;
import java.util.List;
import javax.ejb.Stateless;
import javax.persistence EntityManager;
import javax.persistence PersistenceContext;
import javax.persistence Query;
import com.kogent.many_to_many.interfaces.BookAuthor;
@Stateless
public class BookAuthorUniBean implements BookAuthor {
   @PersistenceContext
   EntityManager em;
   public void doSomeStuff() {
         Author a1 = new Author();
         a1.setAuthorName("Vinay");

         Author a2 = new Author();
         a2.setAuthorName("Ashutosh");

         Book b1 = new Book();
         b1.setBookName("Java EE6");

         b1.getAuthors().add(a1);

         b1.getBooks().add(b1);

         Book b2 = new Book();
         b2.setBookName("Asp 4.0");

         b2.getAuthors().add(a1);
         b2.getAuthors().add(a2);

         a1.getBooks().add(b2);
         a2.getBooks().add(b2);
         em.persist(a1);
         em.persist(a2);
   }
   public List<Book> getAllBooks() {
         Query q = em.createQuery("SELECT b FROM BookUni b");
         return q.getResultList();
   }
}
```

In Listing 14.25, the `doSomeStuff()` method creates two instances each of the `Book` entity and the `Author` entity, respectively. Now, you need to create a client class to access the session bean.

The client code in the `BookAuthorClient` entity bean class is shown in Listing 14.26:

Listing 14.26: Showing the Code of the BookAuthorClient.java File

```
package com.kogent.many_to_many.client;
```

```
import javax.naming.InitialContext;
import javax.naming.NamingException;
import com.kogent.many_to_many.Book;
import com.kogent.many_to_many.Author;
import com.kogent.many_to_many.interfaces.BookAuthor;
public class BookAuthorClient {
  public static void main(String[] args) {
        try {
                InitialContext ic = new InitialContext();
                BookAuthor ba =
                (BookAuthor)ic.lookup(BookAuthor.class.getName());
                ba.doSomeStuff();
                for (Book b : ba.getAllBooks()) {
                       System.out.println("Book: "+b.getBookName());
                       for (Author a : b.getAuthors()) {
                              System.out.println("\tAuthor:
                              "+a.getAuthorName());
                       }
                }
        }
        catch (NamingException e) {
                e.printStackTrace();
        }
  }
}
```

Now, compile the Java source files created in Listing 14.22 to 14.26 and package them in the EAR file that needs to be deployed on the Glassfish Server 4.0. You can view the desired output by executing the `BookAuthorClient` class.

This discussion concludes different types of entity relationships and their implementations in EJB 3.1. Let's now learn how to map collection-based relationships.

Mapping Collection-Based Relationships

The Java persistence specification also allows us to represent a relationship with the `java.util.List` or `java.util.Map` interface. Therefore, the collection-based relationship can now be expressed by the `java.util.List` interface. The List collection type returns the collection of related entity instances based on a specific set of criteria. This List collection requires the additional metadata provided by the `@javax.persistence.OrderBy` annotation. In other words, you can use the `@OrderBy` annotation to specify the sequence of elements of the collection valued association. This ordering is done when the collection object is retrieved from the persistent storage using some method. You can define the ordering element and the required order, that is `ASC` for ascending and `DESC` for descending order, with the `@OrderBy` annotation. If no order is specified, `ASC` is assumed by default and if no ordering element is defined, the collection is ordered on the basis of the primary key defined for the entity.

Let's take the example of the Booking/Customer relationship, which is a many-to-many bidirectional relationship. The `customer's` attribute of the `Booking` entity represents a list of customers that is stored alphabetically by the `Customer` entity's last name. The implementation of the `getCustomers()` method is provided in the following code snippet:

```
. . . . .

@Entity
public class Booking implements Serializable {

  // define some variables relating to booking
  private List<Customer> customers =
  new ArrayList<Customer>( );
  . . . . . .

  @ManyToMany
```

```
    @OrderBy ("lastName ASC")
    @JoinTable(name="BOOKING_CUSTOMER"),
    joinColumns={@JoinColumn(name="BOOKING_ID")},
    inverseJoinColumns={@JoinColumn(name="CUSTOMER_ID")})
    public List<Customer> getCustomers( ) {
        return customers;
    }

    public void setCustomers(Set customers) {
        this.customers = customers;
    }
}
```

After understanding how to map a List type, let's explore the entity inheritance.

Understanding Entity Inheritance

Inheritance is a basic feature of Object Oriented Programming that allows a subclass to derive the state and behavior of a superclass. A superclass refers to the main class from which the subclass is derived and a subclass refers to the derived class. When a subclass is inherited from a superclass, the subclass derives or inherits all the methods and variables of the superclass. This inheritance feature was absent in the earlier version of EJB. In other words, you could not derive/inherit an entity from another entity in the EJB 1.x or EJB 2.x persistence model.

Now, the Java persistence specification supports entity inheritance for enhanced O/R mapping. Entity inheritance is used as a bridge between object-oriented technology (Java) and relational database technology (RDBMS). The strategies for supporting the object-oriented concept of inheritance in relational database are as follows:

- Single table per class hierarchy
- Separate table per subclass
- Single table per concrete entity class

These strategies are described later in this chapter. Figure 14.16 shows the model that is used for each of these strategies. In this model, the base class is Employee. Two classes are inherited by this class--PartTime and FullTime. Moreover, the Admin and NonAdmin classes are inherited from the FullTime class.

Figure 14.16 shows the class hierarchy:

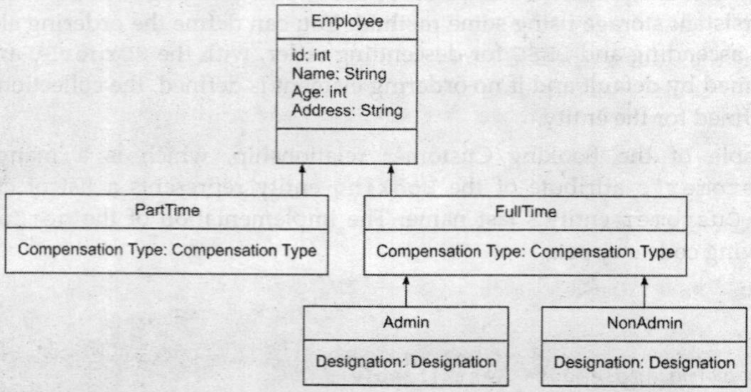

Figure 14.16: Showing the Hierarchical Structure of the Employee Class

Now, create the entity class hierarchy which has been shown in Figure 14.16. Listing 14.27 shows the code implementation of the `Employee` class:

Listing 14.27: Showing the Code of the Employee.java File

```
public class Employee {
public enum Compensation {WAGES, SALARY};
```

```
    protected int id;
    protected int age;
    protected String name;
       protected String address;
    public String getName() {
         return name;
    }

    public void setAddress(String address) {
         this.address = address;
    }
    public String getAddress() {
         return address;
    }

    public void setName(String name) {
         this.name = name;
    }

    public int getId() {
         return id;
    }

    public void setId(int id) {
         this.id = id;
    }
    public int getAge() {
         return age;
    }
    public void setAge(int age) {
         this.age = age;
    }

    public String toString(){
         return "ID="+ id +",Age ="+
               age;
    }
  }
```

In Listing 14.27, the Employee entity is the root class or the superclass used to derive the other entity classes. The code for creating the `PartTime` class is shown in Listing 14.28:

Listing 14.28: Showing the Code of the PartTime.java File

```
  public class PartTime extends Employee {
  public final Compensation compensation = Compensation.WAGES;
    public PartTime() {
         id = 0101170101;
         age = 25;
    }

    public String toString(){
         return "PartTime :"+super.toString();
    }
  }
```

The `PartTime` entity, created in Listing 14.28, is derived from the `Employee` entity. As shown in Figure 14.16, the `FullTime` entity is also derived from the `Employee` entity. Listing 14.29 provides the code for the `FullTime` class:

Listing 14.29: Showing the Code of the FullTime.java File

```
  public class FullTime extends Employee {
  public final Compensation compensation = Compensation.SALARY;
    public FullTime() {
         id = 0101190101;
```

```
            age = 25;
        }

        public String toString(){
            return "FullTime :"+super.toString();
        }
    }
```

In Listing 14.29, the `FullTime` entity is derived from the `Employee` entity class. Listing 14.30 creates the `Admin` entity derived from the `FullTime` entity:

Listing 14.30: Showing the Code of the Admin.java File

```
public class Admin extends FullTime {
public enum Designation {MANAGER, CEO, ACCOUNTANT};
private Designation designation;
public Admin() {
   id = 010280101;
   age = 25;
}
Public Designation getDesignation() {
     Return designation;
}
Public void setDesignation(Designation designation) {
     This.designation = designation;
}
public String toString(){
   return "Admin :"+super.toString();
}
}
```

The code for the `NonAdmin` entity bean class that is derived from the `FullTime` entity bean class, is shown in Listing 14.31:

Listing 14.31: Showing the Code of the NonAdmin.java File

```
public class NonAdmin extends FullTime {
public enum Role {QA, TECHNICAL WRITER, CLEANER};
private Role role;
public NonAdmin() {
   id = 010180101;
   age = 25;
}
Public Role getRole() {
     return role;
}
Public void setRole(Role role) {
     This.role = role;
}
public String toString() {
   return "NonAdmin :"+super.toString();
}
```

Listings 14.27 to 14.31 show the implementation of the entity inheritance. The `Employee` class is the root entity or the superclass from which the `FullTime` and the `PartTime` entities are derived. The `FullTime` and the `PartTime` entities use the `extends` keyword to show that these entities are extended from the root entity, `Employee`. The other two entities, named `Admin.java` and `NonAdmin.java`, are extended from the entity `FullTime`.

Let's now look at the three strategies: single table per class hierarchy, separate table per subclass, and single table per concrete entity class that support the object-oriented concept of inheritance in relational database.

Single Table Per Class Hierarchy

In single table per class hierarchy, the superclass and the subclasses are mapped to a single table. In other words, the mapping of each class is done to a single table. Listing 14.32 shows the implementation of the single table per class strategy:

Listing 14.32: Showing the Code of Employee with the @Entity Annotations

```
//imports go here
@Entity ( name = "EmployeeSingle")
@Inheritance ( strategy = InheritanceType.SINGLE_TABLE )
@DiscriminatorColumn ( name ="DISC", discriminatorType =
DiscriminatorType.STRING)
@DiscriminatorValue ( "EMPLOYEE")

public class  Employee implements  Serializable{
public enum Compensation {WAGES, SALARY};
@Id
protected int id;
protected int age;
protected String name;
protected String address;
public Employee(){
     id = java.lang.Math.random();
}
public String getName() {
  return name;
}
        public void setAddress(String address) {
  this.address = address;
}
public String getAddress() {
  return address;
}
public void setName(String name) {
  this.name = name;
}
public int getId() {
  return id;
}
public void setId(int id) {
  this.id = id;
}
public int getAge() {
  return age;
}
public void setAge(int age) {
  this.age = age;
}
}
```

In Listing 14.32, various new annotations, such as `@Inheritance`, `@DiscriminatorColumn`, and `@DiscriminatorValue`, are used. These annotations are inspected by the Java EE container at the deployment time. These annotations are also known as hint annotations as they give hint to the application server that a hierarchy is being set using the single table strategy. Let's see the use of these annotations in the `FullTime`, `PartTime`, `Admin`, and `NonAdmin` entity classes. The code for the `PartTime` class with entity annotations is provided in the following code snippet:

```
//imports go here

@Entity
@DiscriminatorValue ("PARTTIME")
public class PartTime extends Employee implements Serializable{
public final Compensation compensation = Compensation.WAGES;
public PartTime() {
  super();
     name = "Arjun";
     address = "NewDelhi";
}
}
```

The following code snippet shows the code for the `FullTime` class with entity annotations:

```
// imports go here
```

```
@Entity
@DiscriminatorValue ("FULLTIME")
Public class FullTime extends Employee implements Serializable {
public final Compensation salary = Compensation.SALARY;
public FullTime() {
  super();
     name = "Sujeet";
     address = "NewDelhi";
}
}
```

The following code snippet shows the code for the `Admin` class with entity annotations:

```
// imports go here

@Entity
@DiscriminatorValue (" ADMIN")
public class Admin extends FullTime implements Serializable {
public enum Designation {MANAGER, CEO, ACCOUNTANT};
private Designation designation;
public Admin() {
     super();
  name = "Vinay";
}
Public Designation getDesignation() {
     Return designation;
}
Public void setDesignation(Designation designation) {
     this.designation = designation;
}
}
```

The following code snippet shows code for the `NonAdmin` class with entity annotations:

```
// imports go here

@Entity
@DiscriminatorValue (" NONADMIN")
public class NonAdmin extends FullTime implements Serializable {
public enum Role {QA, TECHNICAL WRITER, CLEANER};
private Role role;
public NonAdmin() {
  super();
  name = "Ashutosh";
}
Public Role getRole() {
     return role;
}
Public void setRole(Role role) {
     This.role = role;
}
}
```

When you deploy the code provided in preceding code snippets on a server, a table is created according to the rules specified by the annotations. The following code snippet shows the structure of the EMPLOYEE table:

```
CREATE TABLE EMPLOYEE {
  ID INTEGER NOT NULL,
  NAME VARCHAR(31),
  AGE INTEGER,
  COMPENSATION INTEGER,
  ADDRESS VARCHAR(255),
  ROLE VARCHAR(20),
  DESIGNATION VARCHAR(20),
     DISC VARCHAR(32)
  };
```

The preceding code snippet shows an extra column called DISC, which is a discriminator column defined by using the `@DiscriminatorColumn` annotation in the Employee class. This field in the database has different values, depending on the type of object being persisted to the database.

The following code snippet shows how to persist the previously defined entities, such as `FullTime`, `PartTime`, `Admin`, and `NonAdmin` in the database:

```
. . . . . . . . . . . . . .
@PersistenceContext
EntityManager emgr;
. . . . . . .
Admin fa = new Admin();
fa.setName ( " Vinay");
fa.setDesignation (Designation.MANAGER);
emgr.persist (fa);

NonAdmin fn = new NonAdmin();
fn.setName ("Ashutosh");
fn.setRole (Role.QA);
emgr.persist(fn);

PartTime pt = new PartTime();
emgr.persist(pt);
. . . . . . . . . .
```

When the `persist()` method is invoked, as shown in preceding code snippet, the data inserted into the database. Table 14.5 describes the structure of the inserted data:

Table 14.5: Showing the Persisted Data

ID	DISC	NAME	DESIGNATION	ROLE
010170101	PARTTIME	Ajay	NULL	NULL
010180101	ADMIN	Ashutosh	QA	NULL
010190101	NONADMIN	Vinay	NULL	TECHNICAL WRITER

Let's now discuss how separate tables are created for each subclass in the hierarchy.

Separate Table Per Subclass

In the separate table per subclass strategy, separate tables are created for each subclass in the hierarchy. The layout of the table shows only those properties that are defined in the subclass and are separate from parent classes in the hierarchy. The code for the `Employee` class in this strategy is shown in the following code snippet:

```
@Entity (name = "EmployeeJoined")
@Table (name = " EMPLOYEEJOINED")
@Inheritance (strategy = InheritanceType.JOINED)
public class Employee
{
    . . . . . . . . .
}
```

In the preceding code snippet, the `InheritanceType.JOINED` strategy is specified by using the `@Inheritance` annotation. This specifies that the separate table per subclass strategy is implemented in the Employee class. In this strategy, a join between tables must be performed to resolve all the properties of subclasses. The `@Table` annotation is used to specify a different table name from the class name. The structure of the `EMPLOYEEJOINED` table is shown in Table 14.6:

Table 14.6: Showing the Data from EMPLOYEEJOINED Table

ID	DTYPE	NAME	DESIGNATION	ROLE
010170101	PARTTIME	Ajay	NULL	NULL
010180101	ADMIN	Ashutosh	QA	NULL
010190101	NONADMIN	Vinay	NULL	TECHNICAL WRITER

Table 14.7 shows the structure of the PARTTIME table:

Table 14.7: Showing the Data from the PARTTIME Table	
ID	**WAGES**
010170101	600

Table 14.8 shows the structure of the FULLTIME table:

Table 14.8: Showing the Data from the FULLTIME Table	
ID	**SALARY**
010160101	0
010160103	0

Table 14.9 shows the structure of the ADMIN table:

Table 14.9: Showing the Data from the ADMIN Table	
ID	**DESIGNATION**
010180101	MANAGER

Table 14.10 shows the structure of the NONADMIN table:

Table 14.10: Showing the Data from the NONADMIN Table	
ID	**DESIGNATION**
010190101	TECHNICAL WRITER

Let's now discuss single table per concrete entity class strategy.

Single Table Per Concrete Entity Class

In the single table per concrete entity class strategy, each concrete class has its own table. Each table has all the properties found in the inheritance chain up to the parent class.

Table 14.11 shows the database layout for the Admin class:

Table 14.11: Showing the Database Table Layout Mapped for Admin.java File					
ID	NAME	AGE	ADDRESS	DESIGNATION	ROLE

Table 14.12 shows the database layout for the NonAdmin class:

Table 14.12: Showing the Database Table Layout Mapped for NonAdmin.java File					
ID	NAME	AGE	ADDRESS	DESIGNATION	ROLE

Table 14.13 shows the database layout for the PartTime class

Table 14.13: Showing the Database Table Layout Mapped for PartTime.java File				
ID	NAME	AGE	ADDRESS	WAGES

Now, let's proceed to discuss a Java Persistence query language (JPQL) used to operate Java classes and objects (entities).

Understanding JPQL

JPQL is the extended version of the EJB Query Language (EJB QL). Although referred as a query language, JPQL is different from `SQL`. `JPQL` operates on classes and objects (entities) available in the Java workspace, while SQL operates on table properties, such as rows and columns in the database space. Using SQL, the columns of a table are selected; however, by using JPQL, the entity fields are selected. JPQL statements can be executed only after they are converted into simple SQL statements, as the SQL statements operate on the table properties and JPQL works on Java classes and objects. The JPQL query parser helps to convert JPQL statements into simple SQL statements. The JPQL query parser is used as an intermediate between the JPQL query and the SQL query, as shown in Figure 14.17. JPQL is a collection of JPQL statements, functions, and operators, which are discussed later in this chapter.

Figure 14.17 demonstrates the conversion of a JPQL query into a simple executable SQL query:

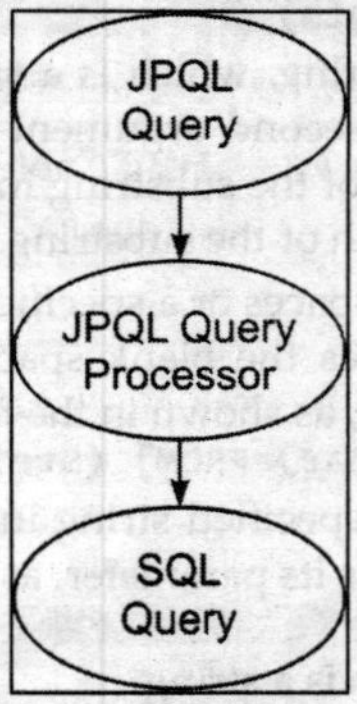

Figure 14.17: Showing the Conversion of JPQL to SQL

Figure 14.17 shows the conversion of a JPQL query into an SQL query with the help of the JPQL Query Processor. The JPQL Query Processor serves as a parser to convert JPQL statements into the SQL statements. To learn how to create a JPQL query, it is essential to know about various statements, functions, and clauses of JPQL.

The following code snippet shows a simple JPQL query, which returns all the employee names from the Employee entity:

```
SELECT e.empname from Employee e
```

In the preceding code snippet, `SELECT` is a JPQL statement used to retrieve the employee names. Apart from SELECT, you can also use various other JPQL statements, such as `UPDATE` and `DELETE`, which are discussed later in the chapter. In the preceding JPQL query, the following elements are used:

- `e.empname`—Refers to an expression resulting in the string type, which means that it represents the result in a sequence of characters.
- from—Refers to the FROM clause of SQL
- Employee—Refers to the Employee entity
- e—Represents an identifier variable for the Employee entity

Let's now discuss each JPQL function in detail.

JPQL Functions

JPQL provides some built-in functions that are to be used by JPQL statements to perform arithmetic and string operations. These functions can be used with the `WHERE` or the `HAVING` clauses of the JPQL statements. The functions available in JPQL are as follows:

- The String functions
- The Arithmetic functions
- The Temporal functions

The String Functions

String functions, used in the `SELECT` clause in JPQL, filter the results returned by a query. They also perform string manipulation on the data. The following is the description of the string functions available in JPQL:

- **The CONCAT function**— Concatenates (or add) two strings or literals (or constants) together. It is used along with the WHERE clause and takes the string parameters, as shown in the following syntax:

```
CONCAT (String, String)
```

The return type of this function is a string.

- **The SUBSTRING function** — Returns a substring of a specified length from the parent string. It accepts a string value, position from where the characters need to be read, and the length of the string as parameters, as shown in the following syntax:

```
SUBSTRING (String, position, length)
```

  The SUBSTRING function returns a string, which is a substring from the first argument and contains the characters from position specified in second argument and contains length-1 characters. The `position` argument defines the starting position of the substring in the parent string (provided as first argument) and the `length` argument defines the length of the substring.

- **The TRIM function** — Trims the whitespaces or a specified character from a string. However, if no character is specified, then this function removes the blank spaces from the string. The TRIM function accepts a character to be trimmed as a parameter, as shown in the following syntax:

```
TRIM ([[LEADING|TRAILING|BOTH] char) FROM] (String)
```

- **The LOWER function** — Converts the specified string into its lower case and returns the converted string. The LOWER function accepts a string as its parameter, as shown in the following syntax:

```
LOWER (String)
```

  The return type of the LOWER function is a string.

- **The UPPER function** — Converts the specified string into upper case and returns the converted string. The UPPER function accepts a string as its parameter, as shown in the following syntax:

```
UPPER (String)
```

  The return type of the `UPPER` function is a string.

- **The LENGTH function** — Returns the length of the specified string. The LENGTH function accepts a string as its parameter, as shown in the following syntax:

```
LENGTH (String)
```

  The return type of this function is an integer.

- **The LOCATE function** — Searches the position of one string within another. The search starts at position 1, if `initialPosition` is not specified. The LOCATE function accepts the `initialPosition`, `searchString`, and `stringToBeSearched` as parameters, as shown in the following syntax:

```
LOCATE (searchString, stringToBeSearched [initialPosition])
```

  The return type of the LOCATE function is an integer.

Now after understanding String functions, let's discuss the arithmetic functions.

The Arithmetic Functions

Arithmetic functions are used to manipulate data for generating analysis reports. These functions can be used with the `WHERE` clause or the `HAVING` clause. The following is the description of the arithmetic functions available in JPQL:

- **The ABS function** — Returns the absolute value of the expression passed to the function. The syntax of the ABS function is as follows:

```
ABS (number)
```

  The return type of this function can be an integer, double, or float.

- **The SQRT function** — Returns the square root of the expression passed to the function. The square root is in the form of a double value. The syntax of the SQRT function is as follows:

```
SQRT (double)
```

  The return type of the SQRT function is double.

- **The MOD function** — Returns the modulus of the operation for the specified number in the function. The syntax of the MOD function is as follows:

```
MOD (int, int)
```

  The preceding function returns the output in the integer format and returns the remainder as a result when the first argument is divided by the second.

- **The SIZE function** — Returns the number of items in a collection. The syntax of the SIZE function is as follows:

```
SIZE (Collection)
```

  The SIZE function returns the number of elements in a given collection in the integer format.

The Temporal Functions

JPQL provides certain time-related functions, known as temporal functions, which are used to obtain the current time, date, or timestamp. These functions are translated into database-specific SQL functions and the requested values can be retrieved from the database as desired. This translation is required as the values of current time, date, or timestamp obtained from JPQL Temporal functions vary from the SQL values retrieved from the database. The following are the temporal functions provided by JPQL:

- **CURRENT_TIME ()** – Returns the current time
- **CURRENT_DATE ()** – Returns the current date
- **CURRENT_TIMESTAMP ()** – Returns the current timestamp

After discussing the various built-in JPQL functions implemented by the JPQL statements, let's now discuss the `SELECT`, `UPDATE`, and `DELETE` statements.

JPQL Statements

JPQL includes SQL statements to represent the query language. Three types of statements are available in JPQL – `SELECT`, `UPDATE`, and `DELETE`. These statements are called queries in JPQL. Let's now look at these statements in detail.

The SELECT Statement

The `SELECT` statement is used to access entity-related data from the Java workspace. An entity is defined as the collection of data that can be stored or retrieved. Entity can also be referred as a class or an object. The `SELECT` statement can use some clauses, such as from, where, and group by, as shown in the following syntax:

```
Select_statement ::= select_clause from_clause [where_clause] [groupby_clause]
[having_clause] [orderby_clause]
```

The clauses used in the preceding syntax are described as follows:

- **Select** – Determines the type of object or value that is to be retrieved or selected
- **From** – Specifies the entity set from where the selection is to be made
- **Where** – Helps to retrieve conditional data
- **Group By** – Aggregates the data retrieved by using the SELECT statement
- **Having** – Filters the aggregated data retrieved by the SELECT statement
- **Order By** – Helps to order the data that are returned by the query

The `SELECT` and `FROM` clauses are mandatory for representation of the `SELECT` statement, while all the other clauses, such as `WHERE` or `ORDER BY`, are optional.

The following code snippet shows the use of the SELECT statement with the WHERE and ORDER BY clauses:

```
SELECT b
FROM Book e
WHERE b.bookName LIKE :bookName
ORDER BY b.id
```

In the preceding code snippet, the `SELECT` statement arranges the returned value according to the id of the `BOOK` table.

The UPDATE Statement

The UPDATE statement is used to update the records of a table. The use of the `UPDATE` statement available in `JPQL` is very similar to the `UPDATE` statement in `SQL`. You should note that at a time, only one entity can be updated in `JPQL`. The `WHERE` clause is used to restrict the number of entities affected by the `UPDATE` statements. The syntax of the `UPDATE` statement is as follows:

```
UPDATE entityName indentifierVariable
SET single_value_path_expression1 = value1, ...
single_value_path_expressionN = valueN
WHERE where_clause
```

The following code snippet shows the `UPDATE` query that sets the status of the employees to inactive if their last working day is less than the date specified in the `inactiveThresholdDate` field:

```
UPDATE EMPLOYEE e
SET e.status = 'inactive'
WHERE e.lastworked < :inactiveThresholdDate
```

In the preceding code snippet, the UPDATE statement is used along with the WHERE clause in which EMPLOYEE is the entity name and e is the identifier variable for the entity.

The DELETE Statement

The use of the `DELETE` statement in JPQL is similar to the `DELETE` statement of SQL. The `DELETE` statement is used to delete an entity. You should note that at a time, only one entity can be deleted by using the `DELETE` statement. The `WHERE` clause can be used to restrict the number of entities that are affected by the `DELETE` statement. The syntax for the `DELETE` statement is as follows:

```
DELETE entityName indentifierVariable
WHERE where_clause
```

The following example shows how to delete all the employees whose status is set to inactive, i.e. they are no longer in the company:

```
DELETE FROM EMPLOYEE e
WHERE e.status = 'inactive'
AND e.company IS EMPTY
```

In the preceding code snippet, the `EMPLOYEE` is the entity and e is used as the identifier variable

Now, you must be aware that JPQL statements are a combination or collection of JPQL clauses, such as `SELECT`, `WHERE`, `FROM`, and `ORDER BY`. Now, let's study these clauses in detail.

The SELECT Clause

In JPQL, the `SELECT` clause is used to retrieve the result of a query. The `SELECT` clause can have more than one identifier, single valued path expressions, or aggregate functions. The following code snippet shows the syntax of using a `SELECT` clause:

```
SELECT [DISTINCT] exp1, exp2, exp3.....expN
```

The `SELECT` clause can have multiple expressions to be retrieved from the database. Therefore, the `SELECT` clause may contain duplicate values. To avoid retrieving duplicate values, the `DISTINCT` keyword is used.

Let's now learn how to use the SELECT clause to retrieve the records of all employees from a table in a database. While using the SELECT clause, an identification variable is followed by a navigational operator (.) and a state field or association field (column name) is called a path expression. Remember that while using the SELECT clause, a single valued path expression must be used, and not a collection value path expression. However, multiple path expressions can be used in a clause, which are separated by commas. The following example shows the use of path expressions in a clause:

```
SELECT e.empName1, e.empName2 FROM Employee e
```

In the preceding example, `e` is the identification variable, followed by the navigational operator (.), forming e.empName1 and e.empName2 as the path expressions.

The `SELECT` clause can also use the aggregate functions, which are used to group the results retrieved by the `SELECT` clause. These functions are described as follows:

- **The AVG function**—Calculates the average value of the fields to which it is applied. The following code snippet shows the use of the AVG function along with the SELECT clause:

```
select AVG(e.empsal) from Employee e
```

The preceding code snippet calculates the average of the salary field of the entity Employee.

- **The COUNT function**—Determines the number of results returned by the `SELECT` clause. The following code snippet shows the use of the COUNT function along with the SELECT clause:

```
select COUNT(e) from Employee e
```

The preceding code snippet counts the number of entities found.

- **The MAX function**—Determines the maximum value of the fields among the results. The following code snippet shows the use of the MAX function along with the SELECT clause:

```
Select MAX(e.empsal) from Employee e
```

The preceding code snippet provides the maximum value of the employee's salary and empsal is passed as an argument to the MAX function.

- **The MIN function**—Determines the minimum value of the fields among the results. The following code snippet shows the use of the MIN function along with the SELECT clause:

```
Select MIN(e.empsal) from Employee e
```

The preceding code snippet provides the minimum value of the employee's salary and empsal is passed as an argument to the MIN function.

- **The SUM function**—Returns the sum of the values of the fields to which it is applied. The following code snippet shows the use of the SUM function along with the SELECT clause:

```
Select SUM(e.empsal) from Employee e
```

The preceding code snippet calculates the sum of the employee's salary and empsal is passed as an argument to the SUM function.

The FROM Clause

The `FROM` clause defines the domain for identifying the variables or expressions used in the `SELECT` clause. The domain of the expressions can be constrained by using conditional expressions. Multiple identification variables, separated by commas, can be used in the `FROM` clause. The following is the syntax of the `FROM` clause within the `SELECT` statement:

```
SELECT e FROM domainName e
```

In the preceding syntax, domainName can be any domain from where the specific data needs to be retrieved and e is used as the identification variable. The identification variables are used in JPQL according to the `FROM` clause and must match the entity specified for the particular query. You can specify multiple identification variables in the `FROM` clause. The following code snippet shows the use of the FROM clause:

```
From Employee e
```

In the preceding code snippet, Employee is the `domainName` to be queried and `e` is the identifier of the type `Employee`.

JPQL imposes the following restrictions while creating the identifiers:

- Must ensure that the name of the identifier does not belong to any of the reserved words available in JPQL
- Must ensure that the name of the identifier does not belong to the stated categories as statements and clauses (SELECT, FROM, UPDATE, DELETE, and WHERE), joins (inner, outer, left, and fetch), conditions, and operators (AND, OR, NOT, true, false, LIKE, IN, and AS), and functions (AVG, MAX, MIN, COUNT, MOD, UPPER, and TRIM)

You can use multiple identification variables in the `FROM` clause. These variables are case sensitive and cannot be used with any other clauses.

The WHERE Clause

The output of the `SELECT` clause occasionally has no limit. Therefore, the `WHERE` clause is used to filter or limit the result of the `SELECT` clause. This clause is also used to restrict or limit the `UPDATE` and `DELETE` clauses as well. The following code snippet shows the use of the `WHERE` clause in the `SELECT` statement:

```
select e FROM Employee e
```

The preceding code snippet results in retrieving all the instances for the Employee entity and does not specify any conditions. Now, look at the following code snippet that specifies a condition by using the WHERE clause:

```
SELECT e FROM Employee e WHERE e.empID > 100
```

In the preceding code snippet, a condition is specified along with the `WHERE` clause. Therefore, only the instances where the `empID` is greater than 100 are displayed in the result. The `WHERE` clause supports most of the Java literals, such as Boolean, float, string, int, and enum. However, it does not support numeric type literals (octal and hexadecimal) and array type (byte [] and char []) values.

The ORDER BY Clause

The `ORDER BY` clause is used to order the values of the data and objects retrieved by the `SELECT` clause. The following is the syntax of the `ORDER BY` clause:

```
ORDER BY path_exp1 [ASC | DESC]. . . . path_expN [ASC | DESC]
```

In the preceding syntax, ASC and DESC are used to order the objects in either ascending or descending order, respectively. The use of ASC and DESC are optional. Even if no such declaration is provided, then the ASC value is taken by default. If you are using single valued path expressions instead of an identification variable, then the SELECT clause must contain the path expressions that is used in the ORDER BY clause. You can include more than one ORDER BY clause in a single statement. These ORDER BY clauses act according to precedence, with the left most ORDER BY clause having the highest precedence among the clauses in the statement. If a JPQL query contains both the WHERE and the ORDER BY clauses, the result is first filtered by the WHERE clause and then ordered by the ORDER BY clause.

Conditional Expressions

Conditional expressions are used in the Where and Having clauses of the JPQL query consisting of any one of the Select, Update, or Delete JPQL statements. These expressions include other conditional expressions, comparison operators, and path expressions that evaluate Boolean values and Boolean literals. A conditional expression can be any arithmetic expression, which returns the Boolean value. JPQL provides various operators used by the conditional expressions, as described in Table 14.14:

Table 14.14: Describing the Operators used in Conditional Expressions

Operator Type	Use	Example
Navigational Operator	Helps to form the path expression used in the query.	.
Unary Operators	Helps to denote the sign of an expression.	+, -
Arithmetic Operators	Helps to perform the arithmetic operations required for conditional expressions.	*, /, +, -
Relational Operators	Returns boolean values. The relational operators are used for checking the conditions.	=,>,<,>=,<=, [NOT] BETWEEN, [NOT] LIKE, [NOT] IN, IS [NOT] NULL, IS [NOT] EMPTY, [NOT] MEMBER [OF]
Logical Operators	Helps to control the program flow by joining two or more conditions.	NOT,AND,OR

The navigational operator (.) is used in the path expressions for navigation purpose. The unary and arithmetic operators are used to perform the arithmetic operations. The relational operators, such as BETWEEN, EMPTY, and IS NULL are used for checking the conditions, such as <, >, =, or >=. The logical operators are used for controlling the flow of a program.

Exploring the Path Expressions

The navigational operator (.) is used in the path expression. Consider the following code snippet to understand the use of the navigational operator:

```
Select e.empname from Employees e
```

In the preceding code snippet e.empname is the path expression, e is the identification variable for the Employee entity, and empname is the state-field. The navigation operator (.) is used after the identification variable and before the state-field.

NOTE

The state-field includes the fields or properties of an entity, which are independent and not interrelated. The association-field, on the other hand, includes those fields of an entity having a relationship.

Let's now discuss relational operators next.

Using the BETWEEN Operator

The BETWEEN operator is used in an arithmetic expression to compare a range of values. A certain range is specified in the expression and the BETWEEN operator compares the values within this range. The following code snippet represents the use of the BETWEEN operator in a query:

```
path_expression [NOT] BETWEEN lowerRange and upperRange
```

In the preceding code snippet, lowerRange refers to the minimum value from where the comparison needs to begin, while upperRange refers to the maximum value to which the comparison can be done.

Let's suppose you need to display the id of the employees between the specified ranges. To do this, upperRange and lowerRange must be specified in the query. The following code snippet shows the use of the BETWEEN operator by specifying the highest and lowest ranges:

```
Select e.empId from Employee e WHERE e.empID BETWEEN :200 AND :300
//this will display the employee ID in between the specified range.
```

In the preceding code snippet, 200 is the lowerRange and 300 is the upperRange for the BETWEEN operator.

Using the IN Operator

The IN operator is used to create conditional expressions within a list of values, which are separated by commas. The following is the syntax of the IN operator in JPQL:

```
Path_expression [NOT] IN (List_of_values)
```

In the preceding syntax, the use of the NOT keyword is optional. The following code snippet shows the implementation of the IN operator:

```
SELECT e FROM Employee e WHERE e.empId IN (1, 2)
```

The preceding code snippet is used to select all the fields of the Employee entity where empId is 1 or 2. If Not is used in this case, the output of the query changes and the query selects all the fields of the Employee entity where empId is neither 1 nor 2. The following code snippet shows the implementation of Not in the IN operator:

```
SELECT e FROM Employee e WHERE e.empId Not IN (1, 2)
```

Using the LIKE Operator

The LIKE operator is used to determine whether a single-value path expression matches with a specified string pattern. The syntax of the LIKE operator is:

```
String_value_path_expression [NOT] LIKE pattern_value
```

The pattern_value specified in the syntax is an input character, which may contain an underscore (_) or a percentage (%). The underscore (_) in a pattern_value is used to represent a single character. The following code snippet shows the implementation of the LIKE operator:

```
WHERE e.empName LIKE '_am'
```

The preceding code snippet evaluates the names of the employees whose names end with the pattern am.

The percentage (%) symbol is used to represent any number of characters. It can be represented as follows:

```
WHERE e.empName LIKE 'ana%'
```

The preceding code snippet evaluates the names of those employees whose names start with ana and end with any number of characters following this pattern.

Using the NULL Operator

The NULL operator is used to test whether a single valued expression contains a null value or not. The IS NULL returns true if a single valued path expression contains a null value. The following code snippet shows the use of the NULL operator:

```
Select e from Employee e WHERE e.empName IS NOT NULL
```

The preceding code snippet results in selecting all the fields of the Employee entity, where empname is not null. If you use the IS NULL value instead of NOT NULL, the query provides all the fields of the Employee entity where empname is NULL. The following code snippet shows the use of IS NULL:

```
Select e from Employee e WHERE e.empName IS NULL
```

Using the EMPTY Comparison Expression

To understand the EMPTY expression, let's consider an example of the Item and Category entities having a many-to-many relationship between them. The following code snippet is used to query all objects in the Category entity that have associated items:

```
SELECT distinct c FROM Category c
WHERE c.items is NOT EMPTY
```

In the preceding code snippet, c.items represents many-to-many association. Such association fields are called collection types and the path expressions that contain collection types are known as collection-value path expressions.

You should note that the NULL comparison operator is not applicable to the path expressions of collection type. Instead, the IS [NOT] EMPTY operator checks whether or not the collection valued path expression is empty.

Using the JPQL Collection Member Expression

The collection member expression tests whether or not a value is a member of the collection specified by the collection_valued expression. If the collection valued path expression defines an empty collection, then the value of the MEMBER OF expression returns false. In this case, the value of the NOT MEMBER OF expression returns true. If the value of the collection_valued path expression is unknown, then the collection member expression is also unknown. The syntax of a MEMBER OF expression in a query is given as follows:

```
Entity_expression [NOT] MEMBER [OF] collection_value_path_expression
```

Using the EXISTS Expression

The EXISTS expression is used to test whether or not a query contains any result set. It returns true if the result set contains one or more values; otherwise, it returns false. The EXISTS expression is mostly used in a subquery. The syntax of the EXISTS expression is given as follows:

```
Exists_expression [NOT] EXISTS subquery
```

Now, consider the following code snippet:

```
Select Distinct emp from Employee emp where EXISTS (Select sal from Employee
emp where sal=5000)
```

In the preceding code snippet, the result of the given query consists of all the employees having the salary equal to 5000.

Using the ALL, ANY, and SOME JPQL Expressions

The ALL conditional expression returns a true value, if the comparison operation is true for all the values in the result of the subquery, or if the result of the subquery is empty. If a single instance of the query returns false, then the ALL conditional expression returns false. The ANY conditional operator is true if the comparison operation is true for some values in the result of the subquery. The ANY conditional operator returns false, if the result of the subquery is empty or if the comparison operation is false for every value of the result of the subquery. The SOME operator is synonymous with the ANY operator. The comparison operators used with the ALL and ANY conditional expressions are =, <, >, <=, >=, and <>.

After learning about the operators used in JPQL statements, let's discuss another important concept, known as Query API.

Query API

The Query API feature of EJB allows you to create custom queries to access a single or a collection of entities from the database. All the query definitions, parameter binding, execution, and pagination are performed by the Query interface. JPA Query API uses JPQL or SQL to create queries. SQL deals with queries used to access database records; whereas, JPQL deals with entities or Java objects and classes. The Query API consists of the EntityManager methods, the Query interface methods, and JPQL. The EntityManager methods are used to create queries and the Query interface methods are used to execute them.

Figure 14.18 shows the structure of the Query API:

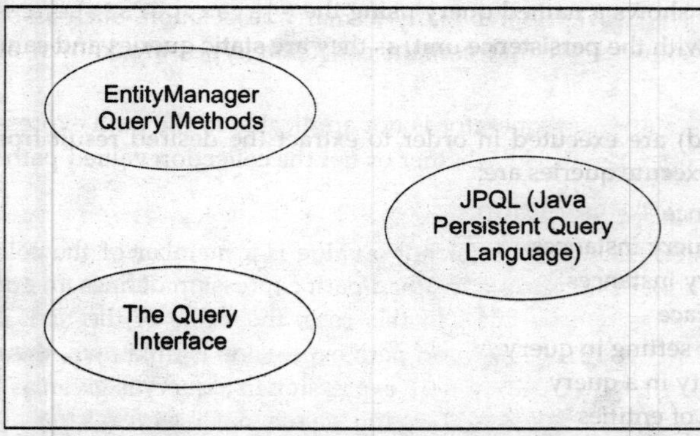

Figure 14.18: Showing Structure of the Query API

The Query API available in JPQL supports two types of queries, called named queries and dynamic queries. The main difference between the named query and the dynamic query is that the dynamic query uses the `createQuery()` method while the named query uses the `createNamedQuery()` method while creating queries.

Defining Dynamic Queries

Dynamic queries are used to create dynamic query statements based on the user input or the conditions of the application logic. The following code snippet shows the use of the dynamic query by retrieving all the results:

```
@PersistenceContext em;
...
public List findAllEmployees() {
   Query query = em.createQuery("SELECT e FROM Employee e"); ...
   return query.getResultList(); ...........
}
```

The preceding code snippet returns all the results retrieved by the `select` clause by using the dynamic query. The preceding code snippet creates an instance of the `EntityManager` with the help of the `@PersistentContext` annotation. The EntityManager then creates an instance of the Query object to get the result using the `EntityManager.createQuery()` method. The `createQuery()` method takes the query string as an object. The final step of the query is to return the result by using the `getResultList()` method. The JPQL and SQL can also be used for defining a dynamic query.

Defining Named Queries

Named queries, also known as static queries, are defined by the entities using metadata annotations or the `XML` file defining the O/R mapping. These queries can be accessed by their name when the EntityManager creates their instance. Named queries are created and saved in the entity specified by the `EntityManager` and can be accessed by the `EntityManager.createNamedQuery()` method. The following are the benefits of the named queries:

- Enhances the performance of execution of code
- Improves the maintenance and reusability of code

Named queries are created and stored by using metadata annotation. The following code snippet shows the use of a named query:

```
@Entity
@NamedQuery(
name = "findAllEmployees",
query = "SELECT e FROM Employee e WHERE e.employeeName
LIKE :employeeName ")
public class Employee implements Serializable {
..
}
```

The preceding code snippet shows a named query using the `@javax.persistence.NamedQuery` annotation. Named queries are scoped with the persistence unit, as they are static queries and cannot be changed.

Executing Queries

Queries (dynamic or named) are executed in order to extract the desired result from a database. The various steps or stages required to execute queries are:

- Creating a Query instance
- Creating the Named Query instances
- Creating dynamic query instances
- Describing query interface
- Establishing parameter setting in query
- Retrieving a single entity in a query
- Retrieving a Collection of entities
- Paginating a result list
- Controlling the flush mode
- Specifying Query hints

Creating a Query Instance

As already discussed, you can create two types of queries in JPQL, called named and dynamic. To execute these queries, you need to create query instances. The `EntityManager` interface provides the following methods to create query instances and SQL queries:

- **createQuery(String sqlString)** – Helps to create dynamic queries using a JPQL statement.
- **createNamedQuery(String name)** – Creates a query instance by using a named query. This method can be used for both JPQL and SQL queries.
- **createNativeQuery(String sqlString)** – Helps to create a dynamic query by using a native SQL statement with the UPDATE or DELETE clauses.
- **createNativeQuery(String sqlString, Class result-class)** – Helps to create a dynamic query by using a native SQL statement that receives a single entity type.
- **createNativeQuery(String sqlString, String result-setMapping)** – Helps to create a dynamic query by using a native SQL statement that retrieves a result set with multiple entity types.

Creating the Named Query Instances

Named queries have global scope because they are static queries and cannot be changed. A named query instance can be created from any instance that has access to the persistence unit. The `EntityManager` interface is needed to create an instance of a named query instance. Named queries are created and saved in the entity specified by the `EntityManager`. You can access a named query by the `EntityManager.createNamedQuery()` method. The following code snippet shows the creation of named query instances by using the stored named query:

```
Query query = em.createNamedQuery("findAllEmployees");
```

The preceding code snippet shows the creation of the named query instance by using the instance of the EntityManager. In this case, findAllEmployees is a named query stored in the entity and name of the query is passed as a parameter to the method. The `EntityManager` instance, em, is used to access the named query and returns the reference to the query object.

Creating Dynamic Query Instances

To create dynamic queries, an `EntityManager` is used. The `EntityManager` includes session beans, message driven beans, Web applications, and some outside containers. Dynamic queries are not supported by previous versions of EJB. The `EntityManager.CreateQuery()` method is used to create dynamic queries in JPQL. This method takes a valid JPQL statement as a parameter and returns the result according to the query. The following code snippet shows how to create a dynamic query by using the `EntityManager.CreateQuery()` method:

```
Query query = em.createQuery ("select e FROM Employee e");
```

In the preceding code snippet, query is the object that stores the result returned from the `em.createQuery()` method. The em is an instance of the `EntityManager` interface. This instance is used to access the method in the `EntityManager` interface. The method evaluates the JPQL query and the result of the selected query is stored in the query object.

Describing the Query Interface

The Query interface contains some methods to execute the query. It also contains methods to set parameters in a query, such as specifying the pagination properties for the query and controlling the flush mode. The flush mode determines whether all the changes in the transaction have been written out. The Query interface works for both JPQL and SQL queries. The `javax.persistence.Query` interface is used to set the parameters for the methods, and control the flush mode. The following are the methods of the Query interface that are used to retrieve the results:

- **getResultList()** – Retrieves a result set for a query
- **getStringResult()** – Returns a single result or object for a query
- **executeUpdate()** – Executes the JPQL UPDATE or DELETE statement
- **setMaxResults()** – Sets the maximum number of results that is to be retrieved
- **setFirstResult()** – Specifies the initial position for the first element or result that is to be retrieved
- **setHint()** – Sets the vendor specific hint for the query
- **setParameter(String name, object value)** – Sets the value for the named parameter
- **setParameter(String name, Date value, TemporalType temporalType)** – Sets the value for the named parameter when the parameter is of the Date type
- **setParameter(String name, Calendar value, TemporalType temporalType)** – Sets the value for Calendar type named parameter
- **setParameter(int position, object value)** – Sets the value for a positional parameter
- **setParameter(int position Calendar value, TemporalType temporalType)** – Sets the value for Calendar type positional parameter
- **setFlushMode(FlushModeType flushMode)** – Helps to set the flush mode

Let's now consider the following code snippet to demonstrate the use of dynamic queries along with the methods of the `EntityManager` interface:

```
query = em.createNamedQuery("findEmployeeByName");
query.setParameter("employeeName", employeeName);
query.setMaxResults(10);
query.setFirstResult(3);
List categories = query.getResultList();
```

In the preceding code snippet, the em instance of the `EntityManager` is used to create the queries. The `query.setParameter()` method is used to set the parameters for the method that is to be executed. The `setMaxResult()` method is used to set the maximum result for the query and the `setFirstResult()` is used to set the initial position of the first element or result to be retrieved.

Establishing Parameter Setting in Query

The number of entities retrieved by a query can be limited by using the `WHERE` clause. You can specify the parameters in a string in two ways: by names or by numbers. If the parameter specified in the method takes an integer value, the parameter is called a positional parameter or a numbered parameter. Positional parameters are common in query languages. EJB 2 does not support positional parameters. You have to specify the parameters before executing a query in JPQL.

When you specify a name for a parameter, that parameter becomes a named parameter. You should note that a named parameter starts with a colon (:), followed by the name of the parameter. These parameters increase the readability of the code. The major difference between a positional and named parameter is their structure. A positional parameter starts with a Question mark (?) and is followed by the position of parameter. A named parameter, on the other hand, starts with a colon (:), followed by the name of the parameter.

Retrieving a Single Entity in a Query

A single query instance can be retrieved by using the methods available in the `Query` interface. The following code snippet shows the implementation of the `query.getSingleResult()` method:

```
query.setParameter(1, "Jhon Smith");
Employee emp = (Employee)query.getSingleResult();
```

The `getSingleResult()` method returns a single query instance, if there is a unique result available for the entity. In case of a repeated entity, the method throws the `NonUniqueResultException` exception. If the query does not retrieve any result, the `getSingleResult()` method throws the `NoResultException` exception. To avoid these exceptions, you can write the query within the try catch statements, as shown in the following code snippet:

```
try {
    ...
    query.setParameter (1, "Jhon Smith");
    Employee emp= (Employee) query.getSingleResult ();
    ...
    }
    catch (NonUniqueResultException ex) {
           handleException (ex);
    }
    catch (NoResultException ex) {
           handleException(ex);
}
```

Retrieving a single result from a query needs an active transaction. In other words, the query should not contain any `UPDATE` or `DELETE` statement.

Retrieving a Collection of Entities

You can retrieve a collection or set of entities in a result set or in a result list. The `getResultList()` method is used to retrieve all the results of a query. If the `getResultList()` method does not return any value for a query, then it returns an empty list and no exceptions are thrown. Retrieving all results from a query does not need any active transactions, as the `getResultList()` method does not throw any exception.

Paginating a Result List

Pagination is the property to deal with a large number of results retrieved by the query. This allows you to iterate through the results of a query, when you need to display only a part of a large number of results on a page or in a report and other results on the next page or report. The following code snippet shows the use of the iterator in a result list:

```
Iterator l =names.iterator();
while (l.hasNext()) {
    Item name = (Item)l.next();
    System.out.println("Id:" + name.getNameId() +
    " Initial Name:"+name.getInitialName());
}
```

In the preceding code snippet, an iterator is specified to navigate the result list obtained by the query. JPA provides the ability to paginate through the result list of a query. The following code snippet is used to set the pagination property in a result list:

```
query.setMaxResults (10);
query.setFirstResult (10);
List names = query.getResultList ();
```

The preceding code snippet uses two methods: the `setMaxResult()` method and the `setFirstResult()` method. The `setMaxResult()` method is used to set the maximum number of entities to be displayed to the user and the `setFirstResult()` method is used to indicate the location from where the pagination takes place. The values passed to these functions are the indicators to the result lists of the query. In this case, 10 entities are to be displayed to the user in a single page and the iteration starts from the 10th entry in the result list.

Controlling the Flush Mode

The flush mode determines the working of the EntityManager. The result of a query depends on the setting of the flush mode, whose function is to check whether or not all changes in a transaction are written on the database. The `Query.setFlushMode()` method is used to set the flush mode for a query. The default flush mode is AUTO. In the default mode, the persistent provider is responsible for the updates made to the entities in the persistent context. If the flush mode is set to `FlushModeType.COMMIT`, then the updates made to the entities are not defined by the persistent provider.

Specifying Query Hints

The persistent provider provides some extensions during the execution of the queries. These are the performance optimizations and are called query hints. In other words, a query hint is a tip that is provided by the persistent provider while executing or retrieving an entity. The hints specified by the persistent provider are implementation-specific. You can specify the hint for a query by using the `Query.setHint()` method. The following are some specified links available to provide hints for queries:

- **toplink.jdbc.fetch-size**—Provides information about the number of rows fetched by the JDBC driver
- **toplink.cache-usage**—Specifies the usage of cache
- **toplink.refresh**—Specifies whether or not the cache is refreshed from the database
- **toplink.jdbc.timeout**—Specifies the timeout for a query

After understanding how entities are created using JPA, let's create an enterprise application using the Customer entity (Listing 14.2) and CustomerFacade (Listing 14.5) session bean classes created earlier in the chapter.

Developing Sample Application

Let's consider a scenario of the ABC company where the employees need to view all the customers of their company. The employees also want to look up the details of each customer on the basis of the customer id. To do this, you need to create Customer enterprise application having the Customer entity. As seen in Listing 14.2, `Customer.java` can be considered as the Customer entity under this scenario. In the Customer application, some JSP pages are designed to view the customer details. In addition, some Java classes, such as FormConstants and UrlUtils, are also designed in the following sections.

Let's first understand the directory structure for Customer application, which helps in understanding the locations for JSP pages and servlets.

Exploring the Directory Structure

In the Customer application, two modules are created namely, Customer-war and Customer-ejb. The Customer-war module is a Web module containing the JSP pages and servlets. The Customer-ejb module comprises the entity class (Customer) and the session façade bean (CustomerFacade).

Figure 14.19 displays the complete directory structure for Customer enterprise application:

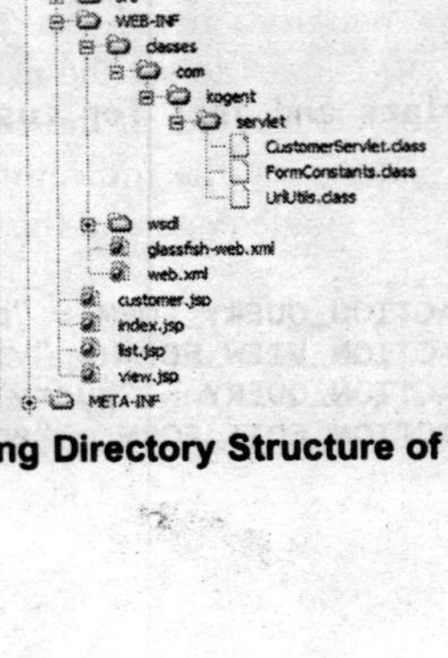

Figure 14.19: Displaying Directory Structure of Customer Application

Figure 14.19 shows the directory structure of the Customer application, in which various Java classes, such as CustomerServlet (a servlet class), FormConstants, and UrlUtils, which are located under the classes subfolder (along with the package directory) of the WEB-INF folder of the Customer-war directory. The Customer, CustomerFacade, and CustomerFacadeLocal Java classes are located under the classes subfolder of the Customer-ejb directory. The web.xml is a configuration file and a persistence-unit for the application is packaged in the persistence.xml file. The JSP pages for the application are index.jsp, list.jsp, view.jsp, and customer.jsp. In the Customer application, oracle is used as the data source. The database name is XE and the table name is Customer.

The table structure of the Customer table is provided in Table 14.15:

Table 14.15: Showing Structure of the Customer Table

Field Name	Data Type
custId	NUMBER(10)
firstName	VARCHAR2(20)
lastName	VARCHAR2(20)
Company	VARCHAR2(20)
address_1	VARCHAR2(30)
address_2	VARCHAR2(30)
City	VARCHAR2(10)
State	VARCHAR2(10)
Zip	VARCHAR2(8)
emailAddress	VARCHAR2(20)
PhoneNumber	VARCHAR2(12)

NOTE

The table name must be customer, as it maps the customer entity; whereas, the database name can be any name of your choice

Now, let's create the servlet classes and JSP pages for the Customer-war module.

Creating the Web Module

The Web module for the Customer enterprise application is Customer-war. The Customer-war module comprises FormConstants and UrlUtils Java classes. It also contains a servlet class named as CustomerServlet. Apart from servlets, the Web module also contains various JSP pages, such as list.jsp, view.jsp, and customer.jsp. The FormConstants Java source file is used to declare the constants that are used throughout the Customer application. This source file also declares and initializes the form fields, request attributes, form actions, and the controller servlet for the Customer-war module.

Listing 14.33 provides the code for the FormConstants class (save the FormConstants.java file in the `\Customer\Customer-war\src\com\kogent\servlet` folder):

Listing 14.33: Showing the Code of the FormConstants.java File

```
package com.kogent.servlet;

/**
 * Some constants used in servlets and jsps for Customer application
 */
public class FormConstants {

  // Form Actions
  public static final String ACTION_QUERY_FORM = "queryForm";
  public static final String ACTION_VIEW_FORM = "viewForm";
  public static final String ACTION_QUERY = "query";
  public static final String ACTION_EDIT_FORM = "edit";
```

```
    // Form Fields
    public static final String FIELD_ACTION = "action";
    public static final String FIELD_COMPANY = "company";
    public static final String FIELD_FNAME = "fname";
    public static final String FIELD_LNAME= "lname";
    public static final String FIELD_CUSTOMER_ID = "customer_id";
    public static final String FIELD_EMAIL = "email";
    public static final String FIELD_PHONE = "phone";
    public static final String FIELD_ADDRESS1 = "address1";
    public static final String FIELD_ADDRESS2 = "address2";
    public static final String FIELD_CITY = "city";
    public static final String FIELD_STATE = "state";
    public static final String FIELD_ZIP = "zip";

     // Request attributes
     public static final String ATTRIBUTE_CUSTOMER = "customer";
     public static final String ATTRIBUTE_CUSTOMER_LIST = "customer_list";

     // Controller Servlet
     public static final String CONTROLLER = "CustomerServlet";
}
```

The FormConstants class is defined under the com.kogent.servlet package and is saved at the location shown in the directory structure (Figure 14.19). The other Java class, UrlUtils, is used to manipulate the Uniform Resource Locators (URLs) depending upon the request made to the server.

Listing 14.34 provides the code for the UrlUtils Java class (save the UrlUtils.java file in the `\Customer\Customer-war\src\com\kogent\servlet` folder):

Listing 14.34: Showing the Code of the UrlUtils.java File

```
package com.kogent.servlet;

import static com.kogent.servlet.FormConstants.*;
/**
* Utility class to generate URLs for Customer application
*/
public class UrlUtils {

   private static String makeActionUrl(String action) {
         return CONTROLLER + "?" + FIELD_ACTION + "=" + action;
   }

   public static String makeCustomerViewUrl(String customerId) {
         return makeActionUrl(ACTION_VIEW_FORM) + "&" + FIELD_CUSTOMER_ID
         + "=" + customerId;
   }
}
```

In Listing 14.34, the UrlUtils class is created to generate URLs for Customer application. Now, let's create the CustomerServlet is class, which the Controller servlet class, which is used to handle the type of request sent by the various JSP pages.

Listing 14.35 provides the code for the CustomerServlet servlet class (save the CustomerServlet.java file in the `\Customer\Customer-war\src\com\kogent\servlet` folder):

Listing 14.35: Showing the Code of the CustomerServlet.java File

```
package com.kogent.servlet;

import com.kogent.entity.Customer;
import com.kogent.session.CustomerFacadeLocal;
import java.io.*;
import java.net.*;
import java.util.*;
import javax.ejb.EJB;
import javax.persistence.*;
import javax.servlet.*;
import javax.servlet.http.*;
```

```
public class CustomerServlet extends HttpServlet {
   @EJB
   private CustomerFacadeLocal customerFacade;

protected void processRequest(HttpServletRequest request, HttpServletResponse response)
   throws ServletException, IOException
   {

String action = request.getParameter(com.kogent.servlet.FormConstants.FIELD_ACTION);
if (com.kogent.servlet.FormConstants.
ACTION_QUERY_FORM.equals(action)) {
                displayQueryForm(request, response);
} else if (com.kogent.servlet.FormConstants.ACTION_VIEW_FORM.equals(action)) {
                displayViewForm(request, response);
} else if (com.kogent.servlet.FormConstants.ACTION_QUERY.equals(action)) {
                doQueryAll(request, response);
        }
        else {
                displayQueryForm(request, response);
        }
   }
   private void displayQueryForm(HttpServletRequest request,
   HttpServletResponse response) throws ServletException, IOException
   {

getServletConfig().getServletContext().
getRequestDispatcher("/index.jsp").forward(request, response);
   }
   @Override
protected void doGet(HttpServletRequest request, HttpServletResponse response)
   throws ServletException, IOException {
        processRequest(request, response);
   }

   @Override
protected void doPost(HttpServletRequest request, HttpServletResponse response)
   throws ServletException, IOException {
        processRequest(request, response);
   }

   @Override
   public String getServletInfo() {
        return "Short description";
   }

private void displayViewForm(HttpServletRequest request, HttpServletResponse response)
   throws IOException, ServletException
   {
int custId = Integer.parseInt(request.getParameter(com.kogent.
servlet.FormConstants.FIELD_CUSTOMER_ID));
        Customer customer = customerFacade.find(custId);
request.setAttribute(com.kogent.servlet.FormConstants.
ATTRIBUTE_CUSTOMER, customer);
getServletConfig().getServletContext().getRequestDispatcher
 ("/view.jsp").forward(request, response);

   }

private void doQueryAll(HttpServletRequest request, HttpServletResponse response) throws
IOException, ServletException
   {
        List<Customer> cust = customerFacade.findAll();
request.setAttribute(com.kogent.servlet.FormConstants.
ATTRIBUTE_CUSTOMER_LIST, cust);
getServletConfig().getServletContext().getRequestDispatcher
("/list.jsp").forward(request, response);
   }
}
```

When the CustomerServlet class is called, the request is being forwarded to the index page, by default. Depending upon the action, the respective method is called in the Customer application. For example, if the action form is ACTION_QUERY_FORM, the displayQueryForm() method is called and the request is forwarded to the index page. If the action is ACTION_VIEW_FORM, the displayViewForm() method is called, which uses CustomerFacade, an instance of the CustomerFacadeLocal interface to find the customer details on the basis of custId. The custId, an integer variable, contains the customer id that is retrieved from the FIELD_CUSTOMER_ID field defined in the FormConstants class. Next, the request is forwarded to the list page. If the form action is ACTION_QUERY_FORM, the doQueryAll method is invoked, which further calls the findAll() method of the session façade bean and stores the data in the List form. This data is set to the ATTRIBUTE_CUSTOMER_LIST attribute defined in the FormConstants class.

After creating and understanding the servlet required for the Customer-war module, let's now create the JSP pages. In this module, four JSP pages are designed namely: index, list, view, and customer.

Listing 14.36 provides the code for the index.jsp file (save this file in the \Customer\Customer-war folder):

Listing 14.36: Showing the Code of the index.jsp File

```
<%@page import="com.kogent.servlet.*"%>
<%@page contentType="text/html"%>
<%@page pageEncoding="UTF-8"%>
<!DOCTYPE html>
<html>
   <head>
         <meta http-equiv="Content-Type" content="text/html; charset=UTF-8">
         <title>Customer Database</title>
   </head>
   <body>
         <center><h1>Sample Customer Database</h1></center>

<p>This application highlights Java Persistence API and its usage from a Java Servlet to
  build a sample customer database. </p>

         <p>You can start the application and go to the list of customers by
         clicking the "Go" button below. </p>
         <hr/>
<form action="<jsp:expression>FormConstants.CONTROLLER
</jsp:expression>" method="post">
<input name="<jsp:expression>FormConstants.FIELD_ACTION
</jsp:expression>" type="HIDDEN"
         value="<jsp:expression>FormConstants.ACTION_QUERY</jsp:expression>">
         </input>
         <input name="Submit" type="submit" value="Go"/>
         </form>
         <hr/>
   </body>

</html>
```

In Listing 14.36, the index JSP page is designed to forward the request to the CustomerServlet class. The list JSP page is used to display the list of the customers along with their company names.

Listing 14.37 provides the code for the list.jsp file (save this file on CD in the \Customer\Customer-war folder):

Listing 14.37: Showing the Code of the list.jsp File

```
<%@page import="java.util.List"%>
<%@page import="com.kogent.entity.Customer"%>
<%@page import="com.kogent.servlet.*"%>
```

```
<%@page contentType="text/html"%>
<%@page pageEncoding="UTF-8"%>

<!DOCTYPE html>
<html>
  <head>
        <meta http-equiv="Content-Type" content="text/html; charset=UTF-8">
        <title>Customer List</title>
  </head>
  <body>
        <center><h1>Sample Customer List</h1></center>
   <p>Here is the list of customers. You can view more details on a customer by clicking
  the customer name.
        <hr/>
        <table>
                <tr bgcolor="#99CCCC">
                        <td><strong>Company Name</strong></td>
                        <td><strong>Customer Name</strong></td>
                </tr>
                <%
                List<Customer> customers =
  (List<Customer>)request.getAttribute(FormConstants.
   ATTRIBUTE_CUSTOMER_LIST);
                if (customers == null || customers.size() == 0) {
                %>
                <tr>
                        <td colspan="2"><i>No customers</i></td>
                </tr>
                <%
                        } else {
                        for (Customer cust: customers) {
                        String actionUrl = UrlUtils.makeCustomerViewUrl(
                        cust.getCustomerId().toString());
                %>
                <tr>
                <td><jsp:expression>cust.getCompany()</jsp:expression></td>
                <td><a href="<jsp:expression>actionUrl</jsp:expression>">
<jsp:expression>cust.getFirstName() +  " " +  cust.getLastName()</jsp:expression>
                </a>
                </td>
                </tr>
                <%
                }
                }
                %>
        </table>
        <hr/>
  </body>
</html>
```

In Listing 14.37, the list JSP page is designed. The required packages are imported and the `<jsp:expression>` tag is used to display customer name and company name in a table format. The `getCompany()` and `getFirstName()` methods are used to retrieve customer's name and the company's name.

Figure 14.20 displays the list JSP page:

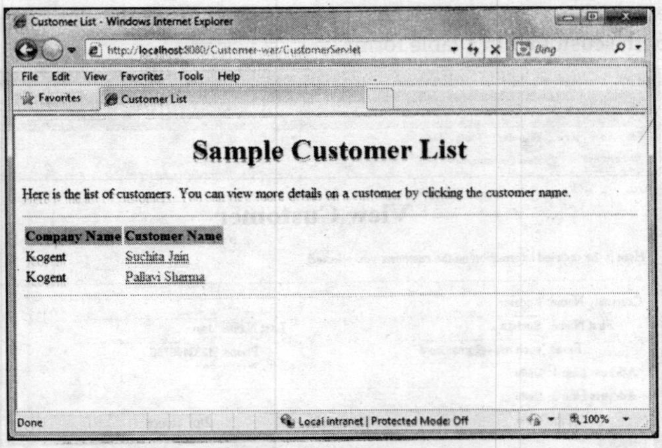

Figure 14.20: Showing the List of Customers

When the user clicks the name of a customer, the view page displays the details of the customer, such as address, city, and state of the customer.

Listing 14.38 provides the code for the view.jsp file (save this file in the `\Customer\Customer-war` folder):

Listing 14.38: Showing the Code of the view.jsp File

```
<%@page import="com.kogent.entity.Customer"%>
<%@page import="com.kogent.servlet.*"%>
<%@page contentType="text/html"%>
<%@page pageEncoding="UTF-8"%>
<!DOCTYPE HTML PUBLIC "-//W3C//DTD HTML 4.01 Transitional//EN"
"http://www.w3.org/TR/html4/loose.dtd">
<html>
  <head>
        <meta http-equiv="Content-Type" content="text/html; charset=UTF-8">
        <title>View Customer</title>
  </head>
  <body>
        <center><h1>View Customer</h1></center>
<p>Here is the detailed information on the customer you selected.</p>
        <hr/>
        <%
  Customer customer = (Customer)request.getAttribute(FormConstants.ATTRIBUTE_CUSTOMER);
        %>
        <form method="post" action=
        "<jsp:expression>FormConstants.CONTROLLER</jsp:expression>">
        <%@include file="customer.jsp"%>
<input type="hidden" name="<jsp:expression>FormConstants.FIELD_ACTION</jsp:expression>"
value="<jsp:expression>FormConstants.
ACTION_QUERY</jsp:expression>"/>
        <input type="submit" name="Submit" value="Back"/>
        </form>
        <hr/>
<p><a href="<jsp:expression>FormConstants.CONTROLLER
</jsp:expression>">Return to the application top page</a></p>
        <hr/>
  </body>
</html>
```

When a customer name is clicked in the `list` JSP page, then the request is forwarded to the CustomerServlet class. The `CustomerServlet` class then forwards the request to the `view` JSP page. In Listing 14.38, the com.kogent.entity.Customer and com.kogent.servlet packages are imported. The `view` JSP page includes the customer JSP page, which retrieves the details of a customer from the Customer entity class. Figure 14.21 displays the details of the customer in a table form:

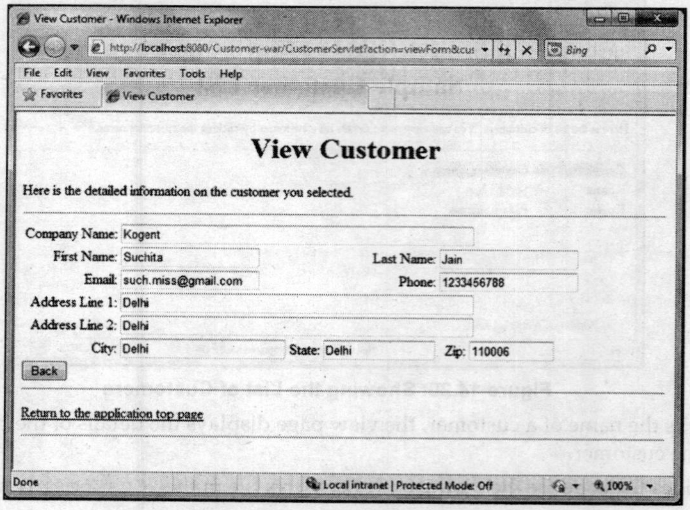

Figure 14.21: Showing the Customer Details

In Figure 14.21, the customer details, such as email address, customer address, city, and state are displayed. Listing 14.39 provides the code for the customer.jsp file (save this file in the \Customer\Customer-war folder):

Listing 14.39: Showing the Code of the customer.jsp File

```
<table>
  <tr>
        <td colspan="1" align="right">Company Name: </td>
        <td colspan="5">
<input type="text" name="<jsp:expression>FormConstants.FIELD_COMPANY</jsp:expression>"
        value="<jsp:expression>customer.getCompany()</jsp:expression>"
        size="60"/>
  </td>
  </tr>
  <tr>
        <td align="right">First Name: </td>
        <td colspan="2">
<input type="text" name="<jsp:expression>FormConstants.FIELD_FNAME</jsp:expression>"
        value="<jsp:expression>customer.getFirstName()</jsp:expression>"
        size="20"/>
        </td>
        <td align="right">Last Name: </td>
        <td colspan="2">
<input type="text" name="<jsp:expression>FormConstants.FIELD_LNAME</jsp:expression>"
        value="<jsp:expression>customer.getLastName()</jsp:expression>"
        size="20"/>
        </td>
  </tr>
  <tr>
        <td align="right">Email: </td>
        <td colspan="2">
<input type="text" name="<jsp:expression>FormConstants.FIELD_EMAIL</jsp:expression>"
        value="<jsp:expression>customer.getEmailAddress()</jsp:expression>"
        size="20"/>
        </td>
        <td align="right">Phone: </td>
        <td colspan="2">
<input type="text" name="<jsp:expression>FormConstants.FIELD_PHONE</jsp:expression>"
```

```
            value="<jsp:expression>customer.getPhoneNumber()</jsp:expression>"
            size="20"/>
            </td>
    </tr>
    <tr>
            <td colspan="1" align="right">Address Line 1: </td>
            <td colspan="5">
    <input type="text" name="<jsp:expression>FormConstants.FIELD_ADDRESS1</jsp:expression>"
            value="<jsp:expression>customer.getAddress1()</jsp:expression>"
            size="60"/>
            </td>
    </tr>
    <tr>
            <td colspan="1" align="right">Address Line 2: </td>
            <td colspan="5">
    <input type="text" name="<jsp:expression>FormConstants.FIELD_ADDRESS2</jsp:expression>"
            value="<jsp:expression>customer.getAddress2()</jsp:expression>"
            size="60"/>
            </td>
    </tr>
    <tr>
            <td align="right">City: </td>
            <td>
    <input type="text" name="<jsp:expression>FormConstants.FIELD_CITY</jsp:expression>"
            value="<jsp:expression>customer.getCity()</jsp:expression>"
            size="25"/>
            </td>
            <td align="right">State: </td>
            <td>
    <input type="text" name="<jsp:expression>FormConstants.FIELD_STATE</jsp:expression>"
            value="<jsp:expression>customer.getState()</jsp:expression>"
            size="15"/>
            </td>
            <td align="right">Zip:</td>
            <td>
    <input type="text" name="<jsp:expression>FormConstants.FIELD_ZIP</jsp:expression>"
            value="<jsp:expression>customer.getZip()</jsp:expression>"
            size="10"/>
            </td>
    </tr>
    </table>
```

In Listing 14.39, various fields and methods are used to display the details of the customer, such as customer address, city, state, zip, phone number, and email address. The servlet-mapping is done in the web.xml file and the code is provided as Listing 14.40 (save this file in the `/Customer/Customer-war/WEB-INF` folder):

Listing 14.40: Showing the Configuration File of the Customer Application

```
<?xml version="1.0" encoding="UTF-8"?>
<web-app version="3.1" xmlns="http://xmlns.jcp.org/xml/ns/javaee"
xmlns:xsi="http://www.w3.org/2001/XMLSchema-instance"
 xsi:schemaLocation="http://xmlns.jcp.org/xml/ns/javaee
  http://xmlns.jcp.org/xml/ns/javaee/web-app_3_1.xsd">
   <servlet>
         <servlet-name>CustomerServlet</servlet-name>
         <servlet-class>com.kogent.servlet.CustomerServlet</servlet-class>

   </servlet>

   <servlet-mapping>
         <servlet-name>CustomerServlet</servlet-name>
         <url-pattern>/CustomerServlet</url-pattern>
   </servlet-mapping>
   <session-config>
         <session-timeout>
               30
         </session-timeout>
```

```
    </session-config>

    <welcome-file-list>
        <welcome-file>index.jsp</welcome-file>
    </welcome-file-list>

</web-app>
```

In the web.xml file, the CustomerServlet servlet is mapped and the index page is defined as the welcome page. The customer details are displayed if the JDBC resource is configured on the server.

Let's now configure the connection pool and the JDBC resource customer to run the application.

Configuring Connection Pool and JDBC Resource

You need to configure the JDBC resource, customer, for the `Customer` application. To store, organize, and retrieve data, most applications use relational database. A relational database can be accessed by the Java EE applications with the help of the JDBC API.

Let's create a new connection for the Customer application to access a database. To create a new connection pool, start the Glassfish Server 4.0 and open the Admin console by browsing http://localhost:4848 URL. Next, expand the Resources node from the left pane of the Admin console. Then select the JDBC node, which displays a hierarchy of nodes. Finally, select the Connection Pools node.

Figure 14.22 displays the list of existing connection pools:

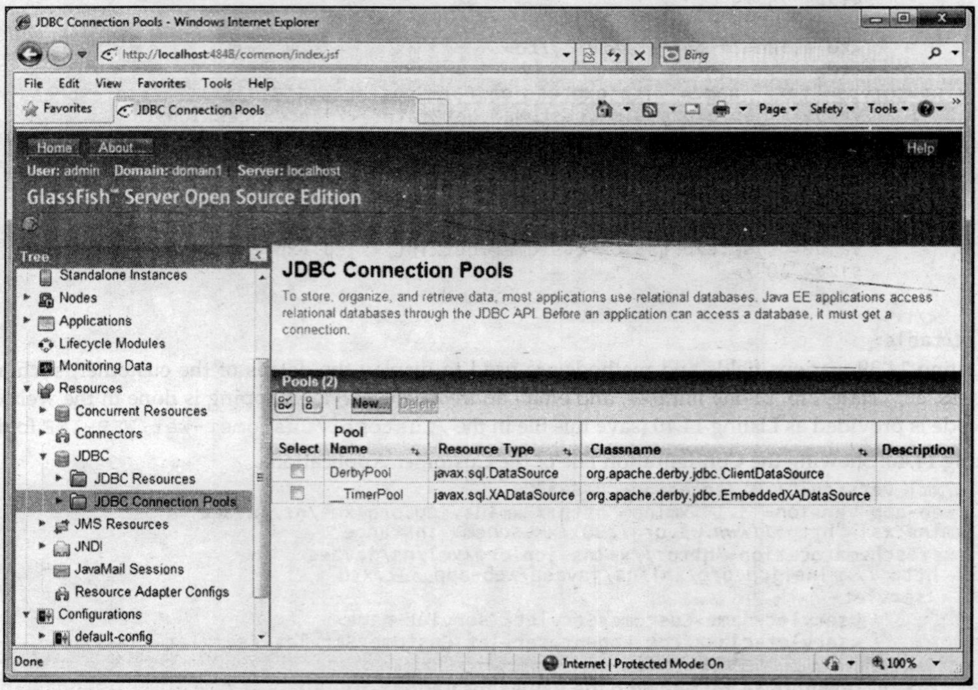

Figure 14.22: Showing the JDBC Connection Pools

To create a new connection pool, click the `New` button. As a result, the right pane displays general settings for configuring a new connection, as shown in Figure 14.23:

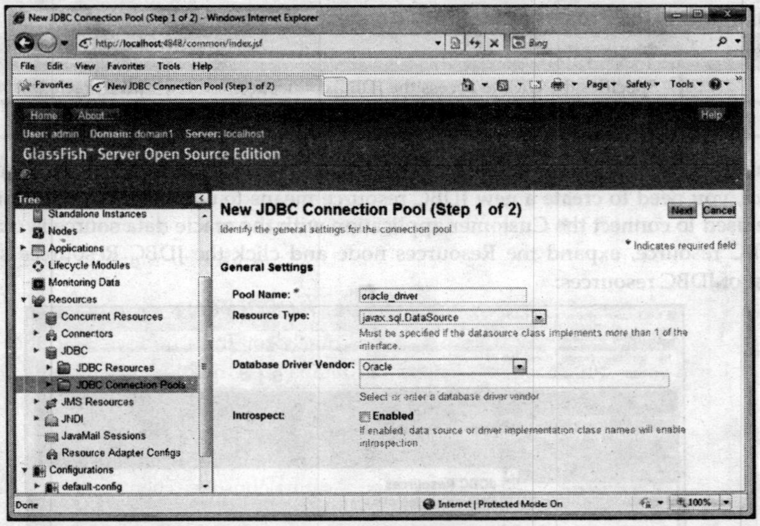

Figure 14.23: Showing the General Settings for New JDBC Connection Pool

In Figure 14.23, specify the name for the new connection pool; in our case, the name specified is `oracle_driver`. Then, select the `javax.sql.DataSource` option in the Resource Type field for the connection pool and Oracle as the Database Vendor, as shown in Figure 14.23. Now, click the `Next` button to provide further settings for this connection pool, as shown in Figure 14.24:

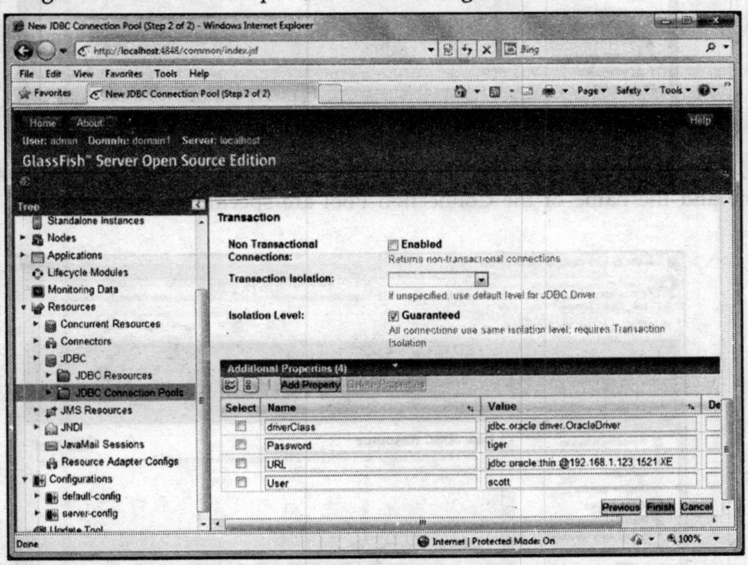

Figure 14.24: Showing the Values for Various Properties of New JDBC Connection Pool

Table 14.16 describes the properties to configure a new connection pool:

Table 14.16: Showing the Properties for JDBC Connection Pool

Property Name	Description	Value
`User`	Specifies the user name used to connect the database server	scott
`driverClass`	Specifies the driver class for the JDBC connection	jdbc.oracle.driver.OracleDriver

Table 14.16: Showing the Properties for JDBC Connection Pool

Property Name	Description	Value
`URL`	Specifies the URL to access the JDBC connection	jdbc:oracle:thin:@192.168.1.123:1521:XE
`Password`	Specifies the password for the database connection	tiger

Now, click the `Finish` button (Figure 14.24) to create a new connection pool. After establishing a new connection pool, you need to create a new JDBC resource means to connect an application with a database. The JDBC resource used to connect the Customer application with the oracle data source is `customer`. To create the `customer` JDBC resource, expand the Resources node and click the JDBC Resources sub node. Figure 14.25 displays the list of JDBC resources:

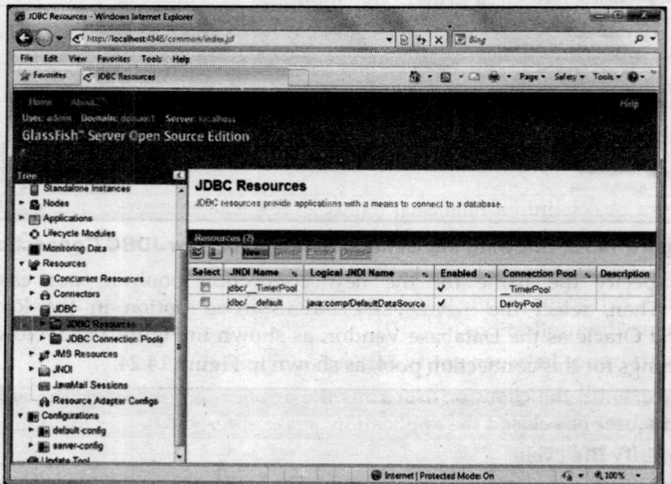

Figure 14.25: Showing the List of Existing JDBC Resources

In Figure 14.25, the existing JDBC resources are provided. Click the New button to create a new JDBC resource. The JNDI Name and the name of the Connection Pool are specified for a new JDBC resource, as shown in Figure 14.26:

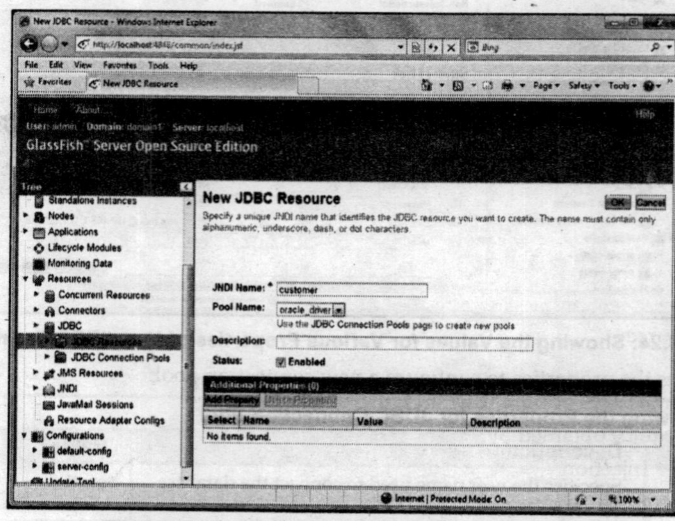

Figure 14.26: Configuring New JDBC Resource

In Figure 14.26, the JNDI name specified is `customer` and the pool name is the `oracle_driver`. Now, click the OK button to add the `customer` JDBC resource in list. After configuring the connection pool and JDBC resource for the `Customer` application, deploy and run the application by opening the http://localhost:8080/Customer/Customer-war URL.

Summary

This chapter introduced you to the concepts of ORM, JPA, and EntityManager. The chapter has also explained how to package and obtain a persistence unit in an application. You have also learned how to interact with a persistence unit using EntityManager. Next, has the chapter explored various types of entity relationships, such as one-to-one, one-to-many, and many-to-many. The concept of JPQL has also been explored by describing about JPQL statements, functions, and clauses. Further, the mapping of collection-based relationships has been discussed in the chapter. Towards the end, you learned to create the `Customer` enterprise application by configuring new connection pools and JDBC resources.

The next chapter discusses about the implementation of Java persistence using Hibernate 3.5.

Quick Revise

Q1. What is ORM?

Ans. The mapping of Java objects into a relational database is termed as ORM. The Java objects are saved in the tables available in the databases.

Q2. What is JPA?

Ans. JPA stands for Java Persistence API, which provides POJO standard and ORM for the maintaining persistent data among the applications.

Q3. What is the main difference between entity and session beans?

Ans. The session bean exists till the client or user runs the application; whereas, the entity bean exists even after the client or the user has closed the application, as the data is stored in the database.

Q4. List the stages of entity life cycle.

Ans. The following are the different stages of an entity life cycle:

- New
- Managed
- Detached
- Removed

Q5. What are entity listeners?

Ans. An entity listener is a stateless bean class that has non-argument constructor and the @EntityListeners annotation is used to specify it. The entity listeners are applied to entity classes.

Q6. Specify the elements and attributes of the persistence.xml file.

Ans. The following are the elements and attributes of the persistence.xml file:

- name
- transaction-type
- provider
- jta-data-source
- non jta-data-source
- mapping-file

Q7. What are the different ways of obtaining an EntityManager?

Ans. An EntityManager can be obtained by:

- Using Container Injection
- Using EntityManagerFactory
- Using JNDI

Q8. What are the different types of entity relationship?

Ans. The entities can have any of the following types of relationships:

- One-to-one
- One-to-many
- Many-to-one
- Many-to-many

Q9. What are the different strategies for supporting the object-oriented concept of inheritance in relational database?

Ans. The different strategies for supporting the object-oriented concept of inheritance in relational database are as follows:

- Single table per class hierarchy
- Separate table per subclass
- Single table per concrete entity class

Q10. What is JPQL?

Ans. The full form of JPQL is `Java Persistence Query Language,` which is the extended version of the EJB-QL. JPQL operates on classes and objects (entities) available in the Java workspace.

15

Implementing Java Persistence Using Hibernate 4.3

If you need an information on:	*See page:*

Hibernate is an Object Relational Mapping (ORM) framework that is used to map an object-oriented domain model to a relational database. Initially, the developers used Structured Query Language (SQL) to query and retrieve data from a database. In such a scenario, the developers need to provide additional Java code in the application to handle the resultsets containing the data retrieved from the database.

With the introduction of the Hibernate framework, the JavaBean classes can now directly be mapped to the database tables, eliminating the need to provide the additional Java code in the applications to handle query results. The Hibernate framework automatically generates the SQL calls and ensures that a Web application is portable with all SQL supported databases. This framework also provides the persistence feature for Plain Old Java Objects (POJOs). You can use the Hibernate framework not only in a Java Platform, Standard Edition (Java SE) application but also in the Java EE applications using servlets or Enterprise JavaBeans (EJB) session beans.

The chapter discusses features and architecture of Hibernate. You also learn Hibernate Query Language (HQL), which is a very powerful and simple query language to retrieve data from databases. Next, you learn to create a simple Hibernate Web application by using create, read, update, and delete (CRUD) operations by using HQL instead of the Java DataBase Connectivity (JDBC) resultset.

Introducing Hibernate

The Hibernate framework is a lightweight ORM, which is a technique for mapping an object model to a relational model. This framework handles mapping from Java classes to database tables and provides Application Programming Interface (API) for querying and retrieving data from a database.

Earlier, JDBC and SQL were used to retrieve data from a database; however, writing queries using SQL to insert, retrieve, update, or delete data from a database was a time consuming process. This was simplified with the introduction of Hibernate that provides HQL. As compared to SQL, in HQL, you do not need to write code to perform common data persistence related programming tasks.

Hibernate uses a transparent programming model for mapping Java objects to the relational databases. To provide mapping for Java objects, you need to write a simple POJO class and create an Extensible Markup Language (XML) mapping file. This XML file describes the relationship of the database with the class attributes and calls the Hibernate APIs to load/store the persistent objects. Hibernate establishes the relationship between object-oriented systems and relational databases. It allows transparent persistence that enables the applications to use any Relational Database Management System (RDBMS) software.

Hibernate works efficiently with applications that use swings, servlets, and EJB session beans. The developer does not need to implement interfaces or extend classes for persistence, as Hibernate provides extensive support of Java collections API (Map, Set, List, SortedMap, SortedSet, and Collection).

After being familiar with the Hibernate framework, let's now try to understand the need Hibernate framework to develop Web application in the next section.

Why Hibernate?

The Hibernate framework provides an extensive approach to manage the object relational mapping and persistence management. The following are the reasons due to which Hibernate in a Web application can be used to query or retrieve data from a database:

- Supports object-oriented programming models, such as inheritance, polymorphism, composition, abstraction, and the Java collections framework.
- Provides developers with persistence feature and a code generation library (CGLIB) that helps in extending Java classes and implementing Java interfaces at runtime environment. The changes that are made to objects associated with a transaction are automatically addressed in the database. This saves the time spent in extra coding for bytecode processing.
- Provides object-oriented query language called HQL, which is similar to SQL. It helps in writing multi-criteria search and dynamic queries.
- Provides Object/Relational mapping for bridging the gap between object-oriented systems and relational databases.

- Enables the developer to build a Hibernate Web application very efficiently in MyEclipse by using Hibernate eclipse plug-ins that provide mapping editor, interactive query prototyping, and schema reverse engineering tool.
- Reduces the development time, as it supports object-oriented programming, such as inheritance, polymorphism, composition, and Java Collection framework.
- Provides ID generator classes to generate surrogate keys also called unique keys/identifiers. Some of the classes are:
  - Native
  - Identity
  - Sequence
  - Increment
  - Hilo and seqhilo (HI/LO) algorithm
  - Universally Unique Identifier (UUID) algorithm
- Provides a Multi Level Cache Architecture that ensures thread safety and continuous data access.
- Provides features, such as lazy initialization and eager or batch fetching to improve the performance of an application.
- Provides integration with Java EE.
- Operates transactions in a managed or non-managed environment. It can run outside an application server container, within standalone applications. This facilitates the following tasks:
  - SessionFactory can be easily bound to Java Naming and Directory Interface (JNDI)
  - Stateful session bean or a HttpSession servlet with loadbalancing to handle a session
  - JDBC connections may be provided by application data source
  - Hibernate Transaction system integrates with Java EE applications through Java Transaction API (JTA)
  - Automatic binding of the Hibernate session to the global JTA transaction scope

Let's now see how the information flows in the Hibernate framework by understanding its architecture.

What is New in Hibernate 4.3?

Hibernate 4.3 framework provides support for JPA 2.1, which is a part of JavaEE 7 specification. JPA provides an object/relational mapping facility that allow using the data from relational database in Java-based applications. JPA is Java based solutions for mapping the persistence with the relational databases.

The main features of JPA 2.1 are as follows:

- **Converters**— Allows you to perform custom code conversions between database and object types
- **Criteria Update or Delete**—Allows you to update or delete data through the Criteria API
- **Stored procedure**—Allows you to define queries for database using stored procedures
- **Schema Generation**—Allows you to generate schemas
- **Entity Graphs**—Allows you to perform partial or specified fetching or merging of objects

Exploring the Architecture of Hibernate

The Hibernate architecture consists of two technologies— Hibernate and Java EE. Hibernate makes use of the existing Java APIs, including JDBC, JTA, JNDI. JDBC loads database driver and establishes a connection for accessing relational database. It uses all types of database drivers that are supported by Hibernate. JNDI and JTA allow Hibernate to be integrated with application servers.

Figure 15.1 shows the architecture of Hibernate:

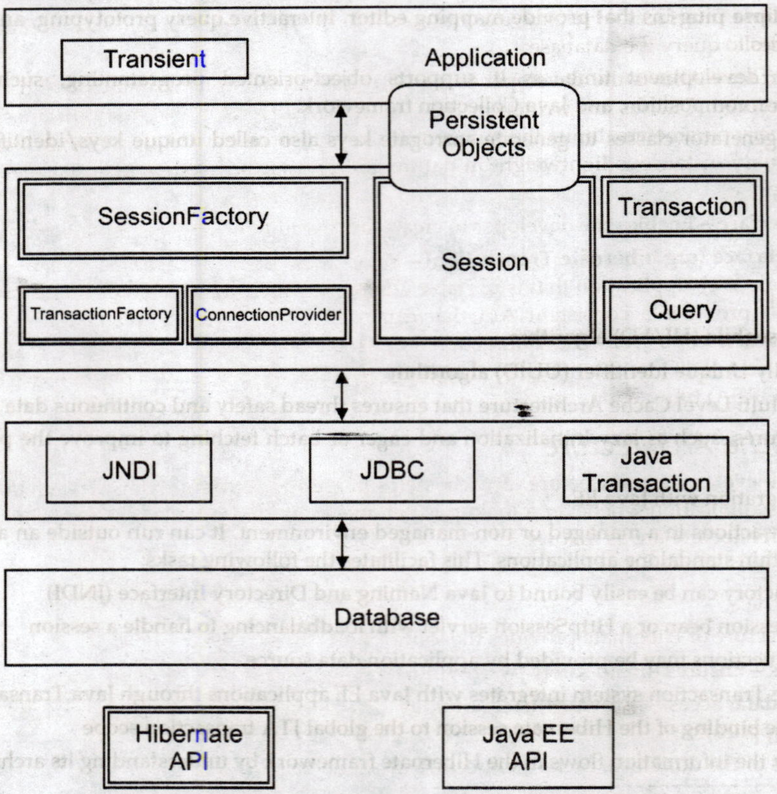

Figure 15.1: Displaying the Hibernate Architecture

Now, let's explore the important interfaces of the Hibernate architecture in detail.

Noteworthy Interfaces of Hibernate

Hibernate provides various interfaces, such as org.hibernate.SessionFactory and org.hibernate.cfg.Configuration, to develop applications. Some of the important interfaces which are necessary to understand the architecture of Hibernate are:

- **Session interface (org.hibernate.Session)** – Maintains a session between a connection and transaction. All applications need to maintain a session for a particular process. Sessions are lightweight and thread safe and can be created or destroyed several times in an application. A session caches all the loaded objects in a session and can keep track of any changes made to these objects. In this way, it maintains the persistence of these objects and is called the Persistence manager.

  The org.hibernate.Session interface represents a Hibernate session and abstracts the notion of a persistence service. The Hibernate session performs mainly CRUD operations for objects of the mapped entity classes.
- **SessionFactory interface (org.hibernate.SessionFactory)** – Creates a session factory interface during application initialization. The SQL statements and other mapping metadata that Hibernate uses at runtime are cached by the SessionFactory interface. It holds the cached data that has been read in the current operation and may be further reused in other operations.
- **Configuration interface (org.hibernate.cfg.Configuration)** – Allows you to configure the `Configuration` object. A configuration instance is used to specify the location of the configuration files, such as Hibernate-specific properties. Further, the configuration instance is used to create the SessionFactory object.

- **Query and Criteria interfaces**—Helps to execute a query. The developer needs to obtain an instance of one of these interfaces to query the database:
  - **Query interface**—Allows the developer to perform queries against the database and control how the query is executed. Queries are written in HQL or in the native SQL. A Query instance binds concrete values to query parameters, limits the number of results returned by the query, and finally executes the query. A Query instance is lightweight in nature and can not be used outside the session that creates this instance.
  - **Criteria interface**—Enables the developer to create and execute the object-oriented criteria queries.
- **Transaction interface (org.hibernate.Transaction)**—Refers to an optional interface. This interface is used to create a Hibernate Web application that is portable among different kinds of Web containers and execution environments. It provides a consistent API that can control the transaction boundaries. A Transaction abstracts application code from the transaction implementation code that is used in application. The transaction can be a JDBC transaction, a JTA user transaction, or even a Common Object Request Broker Architecture (CORBA) transaction.

The Hibernate Cache Architecture

Hibernate has a dual-level cache architecture. A cache helps to keep the current database state (local copy of the data) available to the application whenever a lookup is performed or lazy initialization is needed. The elements of Hibernate cache architecture are as follows:

- First-level cache
- Second-level cache

The dual-level architecture of Hibernate provides the following features:

- **Thread safeness**—Ensures thread safety by providing a unique set of persistent instances for each session
- **Non-blocking data access**—Provides a continuous data access by avoiding threads in the wait state throughout an application

The various elements of the dual-level cache architecture can be seen in Figure 15.2:

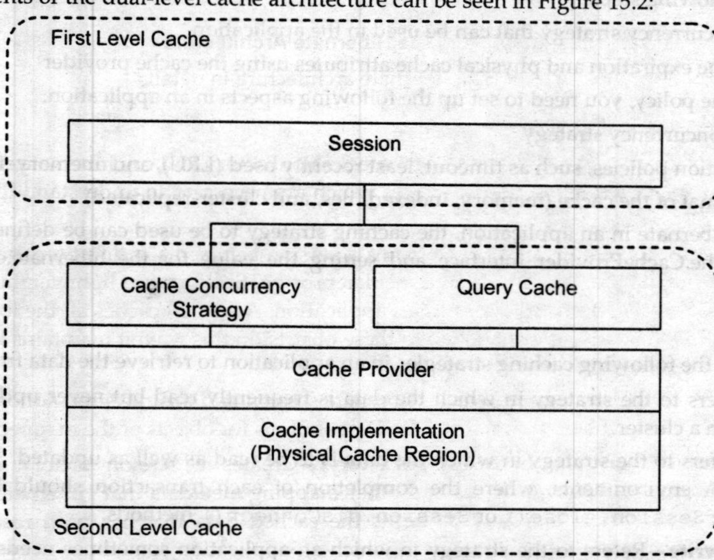

Figure 15.2: Displaying the Hibernate Dual-level Cache Architecture

Let's now discuss about both first-level and second-level cache.

First-Level Cache

The first-level cache is always associated with the session object. It is active for a single user that handles a database transaction or an application transaction. The first-level cache is mandatory and cannot be turned off. It also maintains the object identity inside a transaction and helps in avoiding database traffic. The benefits of first-level cache are as follows:

- Can be used with repeated requests for the same instance in a particular session.
- Can be used in O/R mapping, which facilitates mapping a database row to a single object. This results in updating the changes made to the object in the database.

When the operations, such as save() or update() are used on an object or if an object is retrieved using the load(), find(), list(), iterate(), or filter() method, then that object is added to the session cache.

To synchronize the object with the database, the flush() method can be used. In order to manage memory and avoid synchronization, the evict() method can be used. The evict() method removes the object (invokes the evict() method) and its data from the first-level cache. The Session.clear() method completely removes all the objects from the session cache.

Second-Level Cache

The second-level cache in Hibernate has process scope cache or cluster scope cache. The process scope cache stores either the persistent context or persistent state of the processes in a disassembled format. The cluster scope cache shares multiple processes on the same machine or between multiple machines in a cluster. In the second-level cache, network communication is very important and requires some kind of remote process communication to maintain consistency of the processes among multiple machines. The second-level cache stores the persistent instances in the disassembled form, which is similar to the deserialization of an object (save the state of an object) in Java programming. The cache policies include caching strategies and physical cache providers, which are used on the basis of various factors, such as the ratio of reads to writes, the size of the database tables, and the number of tables shared with external applications. The second-level cache can be used for both immutable and mutable data. The Hibernate second-level cache can be implemented in an application by performing the following steps:

- Selecting the concurrency strategy that can be used in the application
- Configuring cache expiration and physical cache attributes using the cache provider

According to the cache policy, you need to set up the following aspects in an application:

- The Hibernate concurrency strategy
- The cache expiration policies, such as timeout, least recently used (LRU), and memory-sensitive
- The physical format of the cache (memory, indexed files, and cluster-replicated)

While configuring Hibernate in an application, the caching strategy to be used can be defined by implementing the org.hibernate.cache.CacheProvider interface and setting the value for the hibernate.cache.provider_class property.

Caching Strategies

You can use either of the following caching strategies in an application to retrieve the data from a database:

- **Read-only**—Refers to the strategy in which the data is frequently read but never updated. This is simple and safe to use in a cluster.
- **Read/write**—Refers to the strategy in which the data is to be read as well as updated. This type of cache is used in non-JTA environments, where the completion of each transaction should be done before the invocation of the `Session.close()` or `Session.disConnect()` methods.
- **Nonstrict read/write**—Refers to the strategy in which an application sometimes needs to update the data along with reading a large amount of data. This strategy can also be used to restrict two or more transactions from modifying the same data simultaneously.
- **Transactional**—Refers to a fully transactional cache that can only be used in a JTA environment.

Query Cache

Hibernate also implements a cache for query resultsets that integrate closely with the second-level cache. This is an optional feature and is useful for applications involving few insert, delete, or update operations. The query cache caches just the identifier values and not the returned query results. To enable the query cache, the hibernate.cache.use_query_cache property is set to true.

Hibernate uses the timestamp cache to decide whether or not the resultset should be cached. The most recent resultset obtained by executing the insert, update, or delete queries is cached. If the timestamp of a resultset query is more than the timestamp of the cached query results, then the cached results are discarded and a new query is issued.

Cache Provider

Hibernate provides various cache providers from which you can select the appropriate cache provider for your application. It also supports some of the following open source cache providers:

- **ECHCache**—Supports the read-only, nonstrict read/write, and read/write caching strategies. This cache provider is used for the simple process scope cache in a single Java Virtual Machine (JVM). This type of cache provider can be in memory or on disk.
- **OpenSymphony cache (OSCache)**—Enables caching to memory as well as disk in a single JVM with a query cache. The caching strategy, such as read-only, nonstrict read/write, and read/write, are supported by the OSCache cache provider.
- **JBoss Cache**—Refers to a fully transactional replicated clustered cache that is based on JGroup, which is a communication protocol that is purely written in Java and used to create groups of processes whose members can send messages to each other. It supports read-only and transactional caching strategies.

Downloading Hibernate

Hibernate is a free open source software, which can be downloaded from http://www.hibernate.org/. Visit http://www.hibernate.org/ and then click the 'ORM' menu option go to the download page. Click the 'Download(4.3.1.Final)' button from the download page to download the current latest release of the Hibernate 4.3 ORM (hibernate-release-4.3.1.Final.zip, (Hibernate 4.3)).

Let's now understand one of the most powerful features of Hibernate— HQL.

Exploring HQL

HQL is an easy-to-learn and powerful query language designed as an object-oriented extension to SQL that bridges the gap between the object-oriented systems and relational databases. The HQL syntax is very similar to the SQL syntax. It has a rich and powerful object-oriented query language available with the Hibernate ORM, which is a technique of mapping the objects to the databases. The data from object-oriented systems are mapped to relational databases with a SQL-based schema.

HQL queries are case insensitive; however, the names of Java classes and properties are case-sensitive. HQL is used to execute queries against database. If HQL is used in an application to define a query for a database, the Hibernate framework automatically generates the SQL query and executes it. Unlike SQL, HQL uses classes and properties in lieu of tables and columns. HQL supports polymorphism as well as associations, which in turn allows developers to write queries using less code as compared to SQL. In addition, HQL supports many other SQL statements and aggregate functions, such as sum() and max() and clauses, such as group by and order by.

HQL can also be used to retrieve objects from database through O/R mapping by performing the following tasks:

- Apply restrictions to properties of objects
- Arrange the results returned by a query by using the order by clause
- Paginate the results
- Aggregate the records by using group by and having clauses
- Use Joins
- Create user-defined functions
- Execute subqueries

Need of HQL

As already discussed, it is more beneficial to use HQL instead of native SQL to retrieve data from databases. The following are some of the reasons why HQL is preferred over SQL:

- Provides full support for relational operations. It is possible to represent SQL queries in the form of objects in HQL, which uses classes and properties instead of tables and columns.
- Returns results as objects. In other words, the query results are in the form of objects rather than the plain text. These objects can be used to manipulate or retrieve data in an application. This eliminates the need of explicitly creating objects and populating the data from the resultset retrieved from the execution of a query.
- Supports polymorphic queries. Polymorphic queries return the query results along with all the child objects (objects of subclasses), if any.
- Easy to learn and use. The syntax of HQL is quite similar to that of SQL. This makes Hibernate queries easy to learn and implement in the applications.
- Support for advanced features. HQL provides many advanced features as compared to SQL, such as pagination, fetch join with dynamic profiling (initialization the associations or collection of values with their parent objects can be done using a single select statement), inner/outer/full joins, and Cartesian product. It also supports projection, aggregation (max, avg), grouping, ordering, sub queries, and SQL function calls.
- Provides database independency. HQL helps in writing database independent queries that are converted into the native SQL syntax of the database at runtime. This approach helps to use the additional features that the native SQL query provides.

Now, let's learn about the HQL syntax and its usage.

HQL Syntax

HQL is considered to be the most powerful query language designed as a minimal object-oriented extension to SQL. HQL queries are easy to understand and use persistent class and property names, instead of table and column names. HQL consists of the following elements:

- Clauses
  - from
  - select
  - where
  - order by
  - group by
- Aggregate functions
- Subqueries

Clauses in HQL

Clauses are HQL keywords that make up queries. HQL allows you to express a SQL query in object-oriented terms, i.e. by using classes and their properties.

The from Clause

The from clause is the simplest form of HQL query used with the select statement that specifies the object whose instances are to be returned as the query result. The syntax of the from clause is:

```
from object [as object_alias]
```

In the preceding syntax, the object_alias refers to an object.

Consider the following code snippet which depicts the use of the from clause:

```
from org.kogent.baseclass.User
or
from User
```

In the preceding code snippet, the from clause is used to retrieve all the instances of the org.kogent.baseclass.User class.

If there is a need to refer to the `User` class in other parts of the query, an alias name can be assigned to the class by using the following code snippet:

```
from User as user
```

The preceding code snippet assigns the alias name user to the User instances. The alias name user can be used as reference in other queries for the User class. The as keyword is optional, so the preceding code snippet can be written as follows:

```
from User user
```

In case of cross join, you can use the following code snippet to assign an alias name for multiple tables:

```
from User, Group
or
from User as user, Group as group
```

In the preceding code snippet, the user alias name is assigned for the `User` class and the group alias name is assigned for the `Group` class.

The select Clause

The select clause refers to the objects and properties returned as query resultset. The returned properties may be of any value type, including the properties of the component type. The syntax of the select clause is shown in the following code snippet:

```
select [object.property]
```

The following code snippet shows the use of the select clause along with the from clause:

```
select user.name from User user
or
select cust.contact.firstName from Customer as cust
```

In the preceding code snippet, the execution of the first query returns the names of all the users from the details stored in the User table. The next query returns the firstname from the details of the customers stored in the Customer table.

The where Clause

The where clause is used to specify a condition based on which the resultset is obtained from a database. The syntax of the where clause is:

```
where condition
```

In the preceding syntax, condition refers to a combination of logical and relational operators, such as >, <, AND, and NOT used to specify the type of value you want to retrieve from the database. The where clause can be used with the select and/or select, and/or, and from clause.

The following code snippet returns the details of the user whose name is mary:

```
from User as user where user.name='mary'
```

Compound path expressions can also be used with the where clause to get classified results. Consider the following example in which the cust.contact.name expression is used to retrieve the details of a customer whose first name is not null in the database:

```
from org.applabs.base.Customer cust where cust.contact.name is not null
```

The preceding example results in an SQL query with a table (inner) join condition. In the where clause, the = operator can be used to compare properties and instances, as shown in the following code snippet:

```
from Document doc, User user where doc.user.name = user.name
```

In the preceding code snippet, the value of an expression (doc.user.name) is assigned with the help of the user.name expression. Instead of using an expression for assigning a value, you can directly provide a unique value, as shown in the following code snippet:

```
from Document as doc where doc.id = 131512
or
from Document as doc where doc.author.id = 69
```

In the preceding code snippet, a unique value is assigned for the id on the basis of which the data is retrieved.

The order by Clause

The order by clause is used to order (ascending/descending) the properties of objects that are returned as query resultset. It is used with the select and from clauses. The syntax of the order by clause is shown in the following code snippet:

```
Order by object1.property1 [asc|desc] [object1.property2]
```

By default, the order is ascending.

The following code snippet shows the use of the order by clause:

```
from User user order by user.name asc, user.creationDate desc, user.email
```

The group by Clause

The group by clause is used to group the object properties (returned as query resultset) on a specific criteria. This clause is used with the select, and/or, and from clause. The syntax of the group by clause is:

```
group by object1.property0, object1.property1
```

The following code snippet shows the use of the group by clause:

```
select dept.emp_no from department as dept group by dept.mgr
```

The preceding code snippet returns a list of all the emp_no instances from the department group corresponding to the values of the mgr instances.

The `having` clause is used with either the select and from clause or the select or from clause, as shown in the following code snippet:

```
select sum(document) from Document document group by document.category
having document.category in (Category.HIBERNATE, Category.STRUTS)
```

Associations and Joins

Join is used to assign aliases to associated entities or elements of a collection of values. The join types supported by HQL are as follows:

- Inner join
- Left outer join
- Right outer join
- Full join

Aggregate Functions

HQL queries use aggregate functions to perform mathematical operations in a query to retrieve the desired output from the database. You can use these functions along with the `distinct` or `all` option. The supported aggregate functions are as follows:

- avg(...)
- sum(...)
- min(...)
- max(...)
- count()

There are four variant or subfunctions of count() function that are given as follows:

- count(*)
- count(...)
- count(distinct ...)
- count(all...)

Expressions

Expressions are used with the where clause to extract some rows from the database table. The where clause uses the following expressions:

- Mathematical operators — +, -, *, /
- Binary comparison operators — =, >=, <=, <>, !=

- ❑ Logical operators—and, or, not
- ❑ String concatenation— | |
- ❑ SQL scalar functions— upper() and lower()
- ❑ Parentheses indicate grouping —( )
- ❑ In, between, is null
- ❑ JDBC IN parameters?
- ❑ Named parameters—:name, :end_date, : x1
- ❑ SQL literals— 'abc', 60, '1990-01-01 10:00:01.0'
- ❑ Java public static final constants, such as Color.LOBBY

Subqueries

A query within a query is known as a subquery and is surrounded by parentheses. Hibernate supports creation of a subquery (a query within another query), which is an important and powerful feature of SQL. An example of a subquery is subselect in which a select clause is embedded in another clause, such as select, from, and where clause.

You should note that a subquery is executed before the execution of the main query. You can use the following quantifiers in HQL:

- ❑ any
- ❑ all
- ❑ some (a synonym for any)
- ❑ in (similar to the = operator)

For example, the following query returns items where all bids are less than 100:

```
from Item item where 100 > all ( select b.amount from item.bids b )
```

To retrieve the items with bids greater than 100, you can use the following query:

```
from Item item where 100 < any ( select b.amount from item.bids b )
```

Now, let's understand the concept of O/R mapping that provides mapping between the object and database table.

Understanding Hibernate O/R Mapping

ORM is a technique to map object-oriented data with the relational data. In other words, it is used to convert the datatype supported in object-oriented programming language to a datatype supported by a database. This facilitates the transfer of object-oriented data to the database without the occurrence of an exception due to incompatibility of datatypes.

ORM is also known as O/RM, ORM, and O/R mapping. ORM involves mapping of the object-oriented data to relational data. Mappings should be in a format that can define the mapping of the classes with tables, properties with columns, foreign keys with associations, and SQL types with Java types. The document should be in such a mapping format that it can be easily read and edited. ORM is used to reduce programming code and map the object-oriented programming objects with relational databases that can be oracle, DB2, MySql, Sybase, and any other relational database software. The programming code can be reduced through caching, and by using an embedded SQL or call-level interface, such as JDBC. XML documents are used to define O/R mapping. They can be easily manipulated by version-control systems and text editors, and may be customized at deployment time or runtime. XML mapping documents allows you to:

- ❑ Bridge the gap between object-oriented systems and relational databases
- ❑ Define the object-relational mapping
- ❑ Help to generate and export database table
- ❑ Use XDoclet support that allows mappings to be generated from javadoc-style source comments

In complex applications, a class can be inherited by other classes, which may lead to the problem of class mismatching. To overcome such problems, the following approaches can be used:

- ❑ **table-per-class-hierarchy**—Removes polymorphism and inheritance relationships completely from the relational model
- ❑ **table-per-subclass (normalized mapping)**—Denormalizes the relational model and enables polymorphism
- ❑ table-per-concrete-class: Represents inheritance relationships as foreign key relationships

Multiple-objects can be mapped to a single row. Polymorphic associations for the three mapping strategies are as follows:

- ❑ **Many-to-one**—Serves as an association in which an object reference is mapped to a foreign key association
- ❑ **One-to-many**—Serves as an association in which a collection of objects is mapped to a foreign key association
- ❑ **Many-to-many**—Serves as an association in which a collection of objects is transparently mapped to a match table
- ❑ **One-to-one**—Serves as an association in which an object reference is mapped to a primary key or unique foreign key association
- ❑ **Ternary**—Serves as an association in which a Map contained and keyed by objects is mapped to a ternary association (with or without match table)

Indexes collections, such as Maps, Lists, and Arrays can be maintained and persisted as key-value pairs. Mappings are done using persistent class declarations and not by table declarations. The example of Hibernate XML mapping file is shown in the following code snippet:

```
<?xml version="1.0"?>
<!DOCTYPE hibernate-mapping
PUBLIC "-//Hibernate/Hibernate Mapping DTD//EN"
"http://hibernate.sourceforge.net/hibernate-mapping-3.0.dtd">------DTD
                                                          declaration
<hibernate-mapping>----Mapping declaration
<class
name="com.kogent.hibernate.Employee" table="EMPLOYEE">---Class Mapped to table
<id name="id" column="EMP_ID " type="long">----Identifier Mapped
<generator class="native"/>
</id>
<property name="name" column="NAME" type="String"/>----Property Mapped
</class>
</hibernate-mapping>
```

The preceding code snippet shows a Hibernate mapping file in which the Employee class is mapped to the EMPLOYEE table. The important elements of the hibernate.cfg.xml Hibernate mapping file are as follows:

- ❑ **DOCTYPE**—Refers to the Hibernate mapping Document Type Declaration (DTD) that should be declared in every mapping file for syntactic validation of the XML.
- ❑ **<hibernate-mapping> element**—Refers as the first or root element of Hibernate. Inside the <hibernate-mapping> tag, any number of class elements may be present. The attributes of the <hibernate-mapping> tag are as follows:
  - **schema (optional)**—Specifies the name of a database schema.
  - **catalog (optional)**—Specifies the name of a database catalog.
  - **default-cascade (optional-defaults to none)**—Specifies a cascade style.
  - **default-access (optional-defaults to property)**—Defines a strategy by using which Hibernate can access all the properties. In addition, this strategy can be a custom implementation of the PropertyAccessor interface.
  - **default-lazy (optional-defaults to true)**—Specifies the default value for lazy attributes of class and collection mappings.
  - **auto-import (optional-defaults to true)**—Specifies whether unqualified class names (of classes in this mapping) can be used in the query language.
  - **package (optional)**—Specifies a default package prefix so that the unqualified class names can be located in the mapping document.

The following code snippet shows the syntax of the <hibernate-mapping> element:

```
<hibernate-mapping
  schema="schemaName"
  catalog="catalogName"
  default-cascade="cascade_style"
  default-access="field|property|ClassName"
  default-lazy="true|false"
  auto-import="true|false"
  package="package.name"
 />
```

- **<class> element**—Maps a class object with its corresponding entity in the database. It also specifies the table name in the database that has to be accessed along with the column of that table. Within one <hibernate-mapping> element, several <class> mappings are possible. All attributes of the class element and their description are described as follows:
  - **name (optional)**—Specifies the fully qualified Java class name of the persistent class (or interface). In the absence of this attribute, it is assumed that the mapping is for a non-POJO entity.
  - **table (optional)**—Specifies the name of its database table.
  - **discriminator-value (optional)**—Specifies a value. This value defines polymorphic behavior to distinguish individual subclasses. Its values are null and not null.
  - **mutable (optional, defaults to true)**—Specifies whether instances of the class are mutable or immutable.
  - **schema (optional)**—Overrides the schema name that is defined by the root element (<hibernate-mapping>).
  - **catalog (optional)**—Overrides the catalog name that is defined by the root element (<hibernate-mapping>).
  - **proxy (optional)**—Specifies the name of the interface to use for lazy initializing proxies. The name of the class itself may be specified.
  - **dynamic-update (optional, defaults to false)**—Specifies that generation of UPDATE SQL should be done at the runtime and contains only those columns whose values have been changed.
  - **dynamic-insert (optional, defaults to false)**—Specifies that generation of INSERT SQL should be done at the runtime and contains only those columns whose values are not null.
  - **select-before-update (optional, defaults to false)**—Specifies that SQL UPDATE operation can not be performed by Hibernate, until the object is not modified. In some cases (when a transient object become associated with a new session by using update() method), Hibernate should perform an extra SQL SELECT that determines whether an UPDATE operation is required or not.
  - **polymorphism (optional, defaults to implicit)**—Specifies values to determine whether implicit or explicit query polymorphism is used.
  - **where (optional)**—Specifies an arbitrary SQL WHERE condition to be used when retrieving objects of this class.
  - **persister (optional)**—Specifies a custom ClassPersister interface. Refers to a custom interface of ClassPersister interface.
  - **batch-size (optional, defaults to 1)**—Specifies a batch size for fetching instances of the class implements ClassPersister interface.
  - **optimistic-lock (optional, defaults to version)**—Specifies the optimistic locking strategy.
  - **lazy (optional)**: Disables the lazy fetching by setting lazy="false".
  - **entity-name (optional)**—Allows multiple mapping of a class (a class to multiple tables). It also allows entity mappings between Bean classes and databases.
  - **check (optional)**—Specifies the SQL expression. This attribute is also used to generate a multi row check constraint whenever the schema generation is automatic.

- **rowid (optional)**—Specifies the physical location of a stored tuple. If this option is set to true, Hibernate can use ROWIDs on databases (Oracle) for fast updates.
- **subselect (optional)**—Maps an immutable and read-only entity to a database subselect. This is useful when there is a need to have a view instead of a base table.
- **abstract (optional)**—Marks abstract superclasses in <union-subclass> hierarchies.

The following code snippet shows the syntax of the <class> element:

```
<class
  name="ClassName"
  table="tableName"
  discriminator-value="discriminator_value"
  mutable="true|false"
  schema="owner"
  catalog="catalog"
  proxy="ProxyInterface"
  dynamic-update="true|false"
  dynamic-insert="true|false"
  select-before-update="true|false"
  polymorphism="implicit|explicit"
  where="arbitrary sql where condition"
  persister="PersisterClass"
  batch-size="N"
  optimistic-lock="none|version|dirty|all"
  lazy="true|false"
  entity-name="EntityName"
  check="arbitrary sql check condition"
  rowid="rowid"
  subselect="SQL expression"
  abstract="true|false"
  node="element-name"
/>
```

- **<id> element**—Serves as a unique identifier used to map primary key column of database table. The attributes of the id element are as follows:
  - **name**—Specifies the property name that is used by the persistent class.
  - **column**—Specifies the column, which is used to store the primary key value.
  - **type**—Specifies the Java data type used.
  - **unsaved-value**—Specifies the value that is used to determine if a class has been made persistent. The null value for the id attribute indicates that the object has not been persisted.
  - **access (optional-defaults to property)**—Specifies the strategy Hibernate used for accessing the property value.

The following code snippet shows the syntax of the <id> element:

```
<id
  name="propertyName"
  type="typename"
  column="column_name"
  unsaved-value="null|any|none|undefined|id_value"
  access="field|property|ClassName">
  node="element-name|@attribute-name|element/@attribute|."
  <generator class="generatorClass"/>
</id>
```

- **<generator> element**—Helps in generation of the primary key for the new record. The following are some of the commonly used generators:
  - **increment**—Helps to generate primary keys of the long, short, and int type. It should not be used in the clustered deployment environment. This generator takes the maximium primary key column value from the table and increments this value by one each time when a row is inserted. It returns an identifier of type long, short, or int. This generator is useful in case when the Hibernate Web application has exclusive access to the database and it can not be used in other scenarios.

- **sequence**—Generates the primary key. It can be used with DB2, PostgreSQL, Oracle, and SAP DB databases.
- **assigned**—Requires invocation when application code generates the primary key.
- **identity**—Returns an identifier of type long, short, or int. In addition, this is used for identity columns in DB2, MySQL, MS SQL Server, Sybase, and HypersonicSQL.
- **hilo (A high/low algorithm)**—Refers to an algorithm that helps to generate identifiers of int, long, or short type that are given in a table and its column. By default these identifiers are hibernate_unique_key and nrxt_hi values and acts as a source of hi value. The identifiers that are generated by hilo are unique for a particular database only.
- **uuid**—Allows you to use 128-bit UUID to return identifier of the CHAR type. 128-bit UUID algorithm is used to generate String type identifiers and these identifiers are unique with in a network. The IP address is used in combination with a unique timestamp. The UUID attribute is encoded in a hexadecimal digit of length 32 bit.
- **native**—Selects any one of the identity generators, such as sequence or hilo, depending on the database.
- **guid**—Returns a String MS SQL Server and MySQL.

The following code snippet shows the syntax of the <generator> element:

```
<id name="id" type="long" column="cat_id">
   <generator class="org.hibernate.id.TableHiLoGenerator">
         <param name="table">uid_table</param>

         <param name="column">next_hi_value_column</param>
   </generator>
</id>
```

The developer may create a user-defined identifier generator by implementing Hibernate's IdentifierGenerator interface.

- **<property> element**—Defines standard Java attributes and their mapping into database schema. This element supports the column child element that specifies additional properties, such as the index name given on a column or a specific column type. The property name of the String type is mapped to a database column name. The attributes of the <property> element are described as follows:
  - **name**—Specifies the name of the property, started with a lowercase letter.
  - **column (optional-defaults to the property name)**—Specifies the name of the mapped database table column.
  - **type (optional)**—Specifies the Hibernate type.
  - **update, insert (optional - defaults to true)**—Refers to optional attributes, whose values are by default true. These attributes specified that all the mapped columns should be included in the UPDATE and/or INSERT statements of a SQL query.
  - **formula (optional)**—Defines a value for stored attribute, and this expression is specified as an arbitrary SQL expression.
  - **not-null (optional)**—Enables a column to have a null or not null constraint.
  - **unique (optional)**—Enables a column to have a unique constraint.
  - **lazy (optional-defaults to false)**—Specifies that lazy fetching of this property should be done when the instance variable is first accessed.
  - **access (optional-defaults to property)**—Specifies how the container accesses the property at runtime. For example, when access is set to property, the container calls the property of getter or setter method and when access is set to field, the container bypasses the getter or setter method and calls the corresponding field directly.

The following code snippet shows the <property> attribute:

```
<property
   name="propertyName"
   column="column_name"
```

```
    type="typename"
    update="true|false"
    insert="true|false"
    formula="arbitrary SQL expression"
    access="field|property|ClassName"
    lazy="true|false"
    unique="true|false"
    not-null="true|false"
    optimistic-lock="true|false"
    generated="never|insert|always"
    node="element-name|@attribute-name|element/@attribute|."
    index="index_name"
    unique_key="unique_key_id"
    length="L"
    precision="P"
    scale="S"
/>
```

- **<many-to-one> element**—Specifies a many-to-one association to a persistent class that is declared using a many-to-one element. The relational model is a many-to-one relationship, i.e. a foreign key is referenced as the primary key column in the target table. The attributes of the <many-to-one> element are described as follows:
  - **name**—Specifies the name of the property.
  - **column (optional)**—Specifies the name of the foreign key columns, which may also be specified by nested <column> element(s).
  - **class (optional-defaults to the property type determined by reflection)**—Specifies associated class name.
  - **cascade (optional)**—Specifies the operations to be cascaded from parent object to the associated object.
  - **update, insert**—Refers to the optional attributes, by default whose values are true. This attribute specified that all the mapped columns should be included in SQL UPDATE and/or INSERT statements. If both the attributes update and insert are set to be "false", then a pure "derived" association is allowed.
  - **property-ref (optional)**—Specifies the name of a property of the associated class that is joined to this foreign key. By default, the primary key of the associated class is used.
  - **access (optional-defaults to property)**—Specifies the strategy to be used for accessing the property value.
  - **unique (optional)**—Allows the DDL of a unique constraint to be generated for the foreign-key column.
  - **not-null (optional)**—Enables a foreign key column to have a null or not null value.
  - **optimistic-lock (optional-defaults to true)**—Specifies if the updates to this property require acquisition of the optimistic lock.
  - **lazy (optional-defaults to false)**—Specifies that the lazy fetching of this property should be done when the instance variable is first accessed.

The following code snippet shows the <many-to-one> attribute:

```
<many-to-one
   name="propertyName"
   column="column_name"
   class="ClassName"
   cascade="cascade_style"
   fetch="join|select"
   update="true|false"
   insert="true|false"
   property-ref="propertyNameFromAssociatedClass"
   access="field|property|ClassName"
   unique="true|false"
   not-null="true|false"
   optimistic-lock="true false"
   lazy="proxy|no-proxy|false"
   not-found="ignore|exception"
```

```
entity-name="EntityName"
formula="arbitrary SQL expression"
node="element-name|@attribute-name|element/@attribute|."
embed-xml="true|false"
index="index_name"
unique_key="unique_key_id"
foreign-key="foreign_key_name"
/>
```

- **<one-to-one> element**—Specifies a one-to-one association to a persistent class and that is declared by using one-to-one element. The attributes of the <one-to-one> element are described as follows:
  - **name**—Specifies the name of the property.
  - **class (optional-defaults to the property type determined by reflection)**—Specifies the name of an associated class with this attribute.
  - **cascade (optional)**—Specifies the operations to be cascaded from the parent object to the associated object.
  - **constrained (optional)**—Specifies a foreign key constraint on the primary key of mapped table. This mapped table references the table of the associated class. This option specifies the order in which the save() and delete() methods are cascaded.
  - **fetch (optional-defaults to select)**—Specifies whether to choose outer-join fetching or sequential select fetching.
  - **property-ref (optional)**—Specifies the name of a property of an associated class. This property is to be joined with primary key of this class. If the property is not specified then the primary key of the class should be used.
  - **access (optional-defaults to property)**—Specifies a strategy. This strategy is then used by Hibernate for accessing the property value.
  - **formula (optional)**—Specifies a value for a computed property in an arbitrary SQL expression. The following code snippet shows <one-to-one> attribute:

```
<one-to-one
  name="propertyName"
  class="ClassName"
  cascade="cascade_style"
  constrained="true|false"
  fetch="join|select"
  property-ref="propertyNameFromAssociatedClass"
  access="field|property|ClassName"
  formula="any SQL expression"
  lazy="proxy|no-proxy|false"
  entity-name="EntityName"
  node="element-name|@attribute-name|element/@attribute|."
  embed-xml="true|false"
  foreign-key="foreign_key_name"
/>
```

Hibernate can persist instances of java.util.Map, java.util.Set, java.util.SortedMap, java.util.SortedSet, java.util.List, and any array of persistent entities or values. Properties of the java.util.Collection or java.util.List type may also be persisted with the bag semantic.

The elements, such as <set>, <list>, <map>, <bag>, <array>, and <primitive-array> are used to declare Collections. The <map> element contains the following attributes:

- **name**—Specifies the collection property name.
- **table (optional-defaults to property name)**—Specifies the name of the collection table (not used for one-to-many associations).
- **schema (optional)**—Specifies the name of a table schema to override the schema declared in the root element.
- **lazy (optional-defaults to false)**—Enables lazy initialization (not used for arrays).

- **inverse (optional-defaults to false)**—Marks this collection as the inverse end of a bidirectional association.
- **cascade (optional-defaults to none)**—Specifies operations to cascade to the child entities.
- **sort (optional)**—Specifies a Collection, defined with either natural order or with a given comparator class.
- **order-by (optional, JDK1.4 only)**—Specifies a single column or multiple columns of a table that defines the iteration order of the Map, Set, or Bag with either an optional asc or desc.
- **where (optional)**—Refers to an arbitrary SQL condition that is to be used when query is executed for retrieving or removing the collection (it is useful in case when the collection should contain only a subset of the available data).
- **fetch (optional, defaults to select)**—Provides the capability to choose among outer-join fetching, fetching by sequential select, and fetching by sequential subselect.
- **batch-size (optional, defaults to 1)**—Specifies the batch size for the fetching instances of a Collection.
- **access (optional-defaults to property)**—Specifies the strategy that Hibernate should use for accessing the property value.
- **optimistic-lock (optional-default to true)**—Specifies the changes that are made to the state of the collection results.
- **mutable (optional - defaults to true)**—Specifies that whether the elements of the Collection can be altered or not. The following code snippet shows the <map> element:

```
<map
name="propertyName"
table="table_name"
schema="schema_name"
lazy="true|extra|false"
inverse="true|false"
cascade="all|none|save-update|delete|all-delete-orphan|delete-orphan"
sort="unsorted|natural|comparatorClass"
order-by="column_name asc|desc"
where="arbitrary sql where condition"
fetch="join|select|subselect"
batch-size="N"
access="field|property|ClassName"
optimistic-lock="true|false"
mutable="true|false"
node="element-name|."
>
```

After being familiar with HQL and O/R mapping, let's understand how a JavaBean is configured in Hibernate Web application.

Working with Hibernate

Let's consider a Hibernate example in which a JavaBean sets and retrieves the employee details from a database. For this example, let's create EmployeeData table to store employee details and configure the connection details, such as dialect, connection Uniform Resource Locator (URL), username, and password in hibernate.cfg.xml file. Then a JavaBean is created to set or retrieve the employee details from the database table. The EmployeeData.hbm.xml file is created to configure the `EmployeeData` table to the JavaBean. The following steps help in understanding configuration in Hibernate application:

- Setting up the Development Environment
- Creating database table
- Writing Hibernate configuration file, JavaBean, and Hibernate mapping file

Now, let's study each of them in detail.

Setting up the Development Environment

First, let's create necessary directories and move the required files to the appropriate directory by performing the following steps:

- Create a directory named Chapter 15 to represent the chapter number.

- Create the MyHibernateApp directory under the Chapter15 directory.
- Now, add the Hibernate code to the application development environment. Extract hibernate-release-4.3.1.Final.zip in a directory on your system.
- Copy all the JAR files, such as hibernate-core-4.3.1.Final.jar from the lib directory of the Hibernate 4.3 dowloaded directory into the lib of your application. In our case, we have copied the JAR files into the lib directory of the MyHibernateApp directory.

After setting the development environment of the MyHibernateApp application, let's create a database table to be used in O/R mapping.

Creating Database Table

To work with the Hibernate application discussed in this chapter, create a table named EmployeeData. The following code snippet shows the query to create the EmployeeData table:

```
CREATE TABLE EmployeeData (Employee_id NUMBER(5),
   Employee_name VARCHAR2(25), Employee_title VARCHAR2(20));
```

This table is required to be mapped with the Hibernate mapping file.

Writing Hibernate Configuration File, JavaBean, and Hibernate Mapping File

In this section, the code samples of the files required to configure and develop a Hibernate Web application are provided. These configuration files are hibernate.cfg.xml, Hibernate mapping (in our case it is EmployeeData.hbm.xml), and JavaBean (POJO) class that is required to map database table. You can configure the variables of JavaBean to map the column of database table.

Creating the hibernate.cfg.xml File

Let's create the hibernate.cfg.xml file to configure Hibernate by declaring the environmental details. In the hibernate.cfg.xml file, you need to provide various details, such as table name that maps to a class, and JavaBean properties mapping to column names of the specified table. The hibernate.cfg.xml file should be placed in \WEB-INF\classes folder of your application. The Hibernate configuration file (hibernate.cfg.xml) is shown in the following code snippet:

```
<!DOCTYPE hibernate-configuration PUBLIC
  "-//Hibernate/Hibernate Configuration DTD 3.0//EN"
  "http://hibernate.sourceforge.net/hibernate-configuration-3.0.dtd">
<hibernate-configuration>
  <session-factory>
  <!-- properties -->
  <property name="connection.username">scott</property>
  <property
  name="connection.url"> jdbc:oracle:thin:@192.168.1.123:1521:XE</property>
  <property name="dialect"> org.hibernate.dialect.OracleDialect</property>
  <property name="connection.password">tiger</property>
  <property name="connection.driver_class"> oracle.jdbc.driver.OracleDriver </property>
<!-- mapping files -->


<mapping resource="com/kogent/hibernate/EmployeeData.hbm.xml"/>
</session-factory>
</hibernate-configuration>
```

Creating a JavaBean

A JavaBean stores the data retrieved from the database table. The AbstractEmployeedata class is a sample JavaBean class for the MyHibernateApp application. The AbstractEmployeedata class has three variables—EmployeeId, EmployeeName, and EmployeeTitle. The EmployeeId variable allows the application to access database identity that serves as the primary key of the EmployeeData table. This JavaBean also has getter methods, such as getEmployeeId() and getEmployeeName(), which are used to get data from the EmployeeData table and also has some setter methods, such as setEmployeeId() and setEmployeeName(), which are used to set data in the EmployeeData table. The AbstractEmployeedata JavaBean is shown in the following code snippet:

```
package com.kogent.hibernate;
import java.io.Serializable;
public abstract class AbstractEmployeedata
implements Serializable
{
/** The cached hash code value for this instance. Settting to 0 triggers re-
  calculation. */
  private int hashValue = 0;

  /** The composite primary key value. */
  private java.lang.Integer EmployeeId;

  /** The value of the simple EmployeeName property. */
  private java.lang.String EmployeeName;

  /** The value of the simple EmployeeTitle property. */
  private java.lang.String EmployeeTitle;

  /**
  * Simple constructor of AbstractEmployeedata instances.
  */
  public AbstractEmployeedata()
  {
  }

  /**
  * Constructor of AbstractEmployeedata instances given a simple primary key.
  * @param EmployeeId
  */
  public AbstractEmployeedata(java.lang.Integer EmployeeId)
  {
        this.setEmployeeId(EmployeeId);
  }

  /**
  * Return the simple primary key value that identifies this object.
  * @return java.lang.Integer
  */


  public java.lang.Integer getEmployeeId()
  {
        return EmployeeId;
  }

  /**
  * Set the simple primary key value that identifies this object.
  * @param EmployeeId
  */
  public void setEmployeeId(java.lang.Integer EmployeeId)
  {
  this.hashValue = 0;
  this.EmployeeId = EmployeeId;
  }

  /**
  * Return the value of the Employee_name column.
  * @return java.lang.String
  */
  public java.lang.String getEmployeeName()
  {
        return this.EmployeeName;
  }

  /**
  * Set the value of the Employee_name column.
```

```
     * @param EmployeeName
     */
    public void setEmployeeName(java.lang.String EmployeeName)
    {
           this.EmployeeName = EmployeeName;
    }

    /**
     * Return the value of the Employee_title column.
     * @return java.lang.String
     */
    public java.lang.String getEmployeeTitle()
    {
           return this.EmployeeTitle;
    }

    /**
     * Set the value of the Employee_title column.
     * @param EmployeeTitle
     */
    public void setEmployeeTitle(java.lang.String EmployeeTitle)
    {
           this.EmployeeTitle = EmployeeTitle;
    }

    /**
     * Implementation of the equals comparison on the basis of equality of the
    primary key values.
     * @param rhs

     * @return boolean
     */
    public boolean equals(Object rhs)
    {
           if (rhs == null)
                   return false;
           if (! (rhs instanceof Employeedata))
                   return false;
           Employeedata that = (Employeedata) rhs;
           if (this.getEmployeeId() != null && that.getEmployeeId() != null)
           {
                   if (! this.getEmployeeId().equals(that.getEmployeeId())) {
                           return false;
                   }
           }
           return true;
    }

    public int hashCode() {
           if (this.hashValue == 0) {
                   int result = 17;
                   int EmployeeIdvalue = this.getEmployeeId() == null ? 0 :
                    this.getEmployeeId().hashCode();
                   result = result * 37 + EmployeeIdvalue;
                   this.hashValue = result;
           }
           return this.hashValue;
    }
}
```

Now, you need to map this JavaBean with the database table.

Creating the EmployeeData.hbm.xml File

Hibernate maps the columns of the EmployeeData table to the properties of the JavaBean, so that you can use HQL query language. The following code sinippet shows Hibernate mapping in the Hibernate mapping file (EmployeeData.hbm.xml):

```
<?xml version="1.0"?>
<!DOCTYPE hibernate-mapping PUBLIC
  "-//Hibernate/Hibernate Mapping DTD//EN"
  "http://hibernate.sourceforge.net/hibernate-mapping-3.0.dtd" >
<hibernate-mapping package="com.kogent.hibernate">
  <class name="AbstractEmployeedata" table="Employeedata">
  <id name="EmployeeId" column="Employee_id" type="java.lang.Integer">
  <generator class="native"/>
  </id>
  <property name="EmployeeName" column="Employee_name"
  type="java.lang.String" not-null="true" />
  <property name="EmployeeTitle" column="Employee_title"
  type="java.lang.String" not-null="true" />
  </class>
</hibernate-mapping>
```

Let's now learn to implement the O/R mapping using Hibernate by developing the HibernateApplication application.

Implementing O/R Mapping with Hibernate

Hibernate Web application, named HibernateApplication, acts as an employee directory service that allows a user to create, read, update, and delete employee details stored in the company database. In this section, you learn to define all the components of the HibernateApplication application including the Hibernate configuration (hibernate.cfg.xml, provided as Listing 15.2) , Hibernate mapping file (in this Web application it is Employee.hbm.xml, provided as Listing 15.3), and JavaBean (Employee.java, provided in Listing 15.1). You also learn to develop some Controller components with the help of Java Servlet and the View components by using the JSP technology. The Oracle database is used as backend that stores employee record by implementing Hibernate O/R mapping and HQL.

Developing a JavaBean

The first step in creating Hibernate application (HibernateApplication) is to build the JavaBean that is used to store the data persistently in a database. This Java class contains the getter and setter methods that maps to the EMPLOYEE table. The Employee JavaBean is shown in Listing 15.1 (save the Employee.java file in the `\HibernateApplication\src\com\kogent\hibernate` folder):

Listing 15.1: Displaying the Employee JavaBean File

```
package com.kogent.hibernate;
public class Employee

{
  int employeeId;
  String name;
  int age;
  double salary;
  public int getEmployeeId()

  {
        return employeeId;
  }
  public String getName()
  {
        return name;
  }
  public int getAge()
```

```
    {
        return age;
    }
    public double getSalary()
    {
        return salary;
    }
    public void setEmployeeId(int employeeId)
    {
        this.employeeId = employeeId;
    }
    public void setName(String name)
    {
        this.name = name;
    }
    public void setAge(int age)
    {
        this.age = age;
    }
    public void setSalary(Double salary)
    {
        this.salary = salary;
    }
}
```

The code shown in Listing 15.1 (Employee JavaBean) sets the values of the fields of a table that can be created by executing the following query on the Oracle datasource:

```
Create table EMPLOYEE (EMPLOYEE_ID number(5), NAME varchar2(20),
  AGE number(3), SALARY number(7,2),
  constraint Pk_Employee_EmployeeID Primary key(EMPLOYEE_ID));
```

Developing Hibernate Configuration File

As discussed ealier, you can provide the Hibernate configuration details in the hibernate.cfg.xml file. This file contains connection details, such as driver class, username, and password of database software (Oracle), and Hibernate mapping file that you are using in the HibernateApplication application. The Hibernate configuration file is shown in Listing 15.2 (save the hibernate.cfg.xml file in the `\HibernateApplication\WEB-INF\classes` folder):

Listing 15.2: Showing the Code for the hibernate.cfg.xml File

```
<?xml version='1.0' encoding='UTF-8'?>
<!DOCTYPE hibernate-configuration PUBLIC
  "-//Hibernate/Hibernate Configuration DTD 3.0//EN"
  "http://hibernate.sourceforge.net/hibernate-configuration-3.0.dtd">
<hibernate-configuration>
  <session-factory>
        <property name="connection.username">scott</property>
        <property name="connection.password">tiger</property>
        <property name="connection.url">
             jdbc:oracle:thin:@192.168.1.123:1521:XE
        </property>
        <property name="dialect">
              org.hibernate.dialect.Oracle10gDialect

        </property>
        <property name="connection.driver_class">
              oracle.jdbc.driver.OracleDriver
        </property>
        <mapping resource="com/kogent/hibernate/Employee.hbm.xml" />
  </session-factory>
</hibernate-configuration>
```

Developing Hibernate Mapping File

As discussed earlier, the Hibernate mapping file maps the columns of the EMPLOYEE table to the properties of the Employee JavaBean. The mapping of the EMPLOYEE table to the Employee JavaBean is known as O/R mapping.

The Hibernate mapping file (Employee.hbm.xml) is shown in Listing 15.3 (save the Employee.hbm.xml file in the `\HibernateApplication\WEB-INF\classes\com\kogent\hibernate` folder):

Listing 15.3: Showing the Code for the Employee.hbm.xml File

```
<?xml version="1.0" encoding="utf-8"?>
<!DOCTYPE hibernate-mapping PUBLIC "-//Hibernate/Hibernate Mapping DTD 3.0//EN"
"http://hibernate.sourceforge.net/hibernate-mapping-3.0.dtd">
<hibernate-mapping>
  <class name="com.kogent.hibernate.Employee" table="EMPLOYEE" schema="SCOTT">
  <id name="employeeId" type="java.lang.Integer">
  <column name="EMPLOYEE_ID" precision="5" scale="0" />
  <generator class="assigned" />
  </id>
  <property name="name" type="java.lang.String">
        <column name="NAME" length="20" />
  </property>
  <property name="age" type="java.lang.Integer">
        <column name="AGE" precision="3" scale="0" />
  </property>
  <property name="salary" type="java.lang.Double">
        <column name="SALARY" precision="7" scale="0" />
  </property>
  </class>
</hibernate-mapping>
```

Creating the EmployeeData.java File

The EmployeeData.java file is used to develop business objects that store the data of an employee. This Java file contains methods, such as getEmployees(), addEmployee(), editEmployee(), and deleteEmployee() that provide the CRUD operation to access data from the EMPLOYEE table through the Hibernate SessionFactory interface. This interface is used to get the connection detail information, such as connection URL, username, and password from the hibernate.cfg.xml configuration file and build the factory for session instances. This session provides transaction to query the database table. The code for the EmployeeData.java file is shown in Listing 15.4 (save the EmployeeData.java file in the `\HibernateApplication\src\com\kogent\hibernate` folder):

Listing 15.4: Showing the Code for the EmployeeData Class

```
package com.kogent.hibernate;
import java.util.ArrayList;
import java.util.Iterator;
import org.hibernate.Session;
import org.hibernate.SessionFactory;
import org.hibernate.Transaction;
import org.hibernate.Query;
import org.hibernate.cfg.Configuration;
import com.kogent.hibernate.Employee;
public class EmployeeData
{
  public static Employee getEmployee(String employeeId) throws Exception
  {
        Session session = null;
        Employee employee=null;
        try
        {
              // This step will read hibernate.cfg.xml
              //and prepare hibernate for use
              SessionFactory sessionFactory = new
```

```
                Configuration().configure().buildSessionFactory();
                session =sessionFactory.openSession();
                //Create new instance of Employee and set
                //values in it by reading them from form object
                Transaction tx = session.beginTransaction();
                System.out.println("Getting Record");
                employee = new Employee();
                tx.commit();
                System.out.println("Done");
        Query query = session.createQuery("select employee1.employeeId, employee1.name,
        employee1.age, employee1.salary from Employee employee1 where employeeId =
        '"+employeeId +"'");
                for(Iterator it=query.iterate();;)
                {
                        Object[] row = (Object[]) it.next();
                        employee.setEmployeeId((int) new Integer(row[0].toString()));
                        employee.setName((String) row[1]);
                        employee.setAge((int) new Integer(row[2].toString()));
                        employee.setSalary((Double) row[3]);
                }
        }
        catch(Exception e)
        {
                System.out.println(e.getMessage());
        }
        finally
        {
                session.flush();
                session.close();
        }
        return employee;
   }
   // method to read employee of CRUD operation
   public static ArrayList getEmployees()
   {
        Session session = null;
        Employee employee=null;
        ArrayList<Employee> employees = new ArrayList<Employee>();
        try
        {
                // This step will read hibernate.cfg.xml
                //and prepare hibernate for use
                SessionFactory sessionFactory = new
                Configuration().configure().buildSessionFactory();
                session =sessionFactory.openSession();
Query query = session.createQuery("select employee1.employeeId, employee1.name,
employee1.age, employee1.salary from Employee employee1");
                for(Iterator it=query.iterate();it.hasNext();)
                {
                        employee = new Employee();
                        Object[] row = (Object[]) it.next();

                        employee.setEmployeeId((int) new Integer(row[0].toString()));
                        employee.setName((String) row[1]);
                        employee.setAge((int) new Integer(row[2].toString()));
                        employee.setSalary((Double) row[3]);
                        employees.add(employee);
                }
        }
        catch(Exception e)
        {
                System.out.println(e.getMessage());
        }
        finally
        {
                session.flush();
```

```
                session.close();
        }
        return employees;
}
// method to create employee of CRUD operation
public void addEmployee(Employee emp) throws Exception
{
        Employee employee = null;
        Session session = null;
        try
        {
                // This step will read hibernate.cfg.xml
                //and prepare hibernate for use
                SessionFactory sessionFactory = new
                Configuration().configure().buildSessionFactory();
                session =sessionFactory.openSession();
                Transaction tx = session.beginTransaction();
                System.out.println("Selecting Record");
                employee = new Employee();
                employee.setEmployeeId(emp.getEmployeeId());
                employee.setName(emp.getName());
                employee.setAge(emp.getAge());
                employee.setSalary(emp.getSalary());
                session.save(employee);
                tx.commit();
                System.out.println("Done");
        System.out.println("Employee fffId Name Age Salary");
        }
        catch(Exception e)
        {
        System.out.println("Exception caught in EmployeeData.addEmployee" + e);
        }
}
// method to delete employee of CRUD operation
public static void deleteEmployee(String employeeId) throws Exception
{
        Session session = null;
        try
        {
                // This step will read hibernate.cfg.xml
                //and prepare hibernate for use
                SessionFactory sessionFactory = new
                Configuration().configure().buildSessionFactory();
                session =sessionFactory.openSession();
 String hqlDelete ="delete Employee employee where employeeId='" + employeeId + "'";
                Transaction tx = session.beginTransaction();
                System.out.println("Deleting Record");
                Query query = session.createQuery(hqlDelete);
                int row = query.executeUpdate();
                System.out.println("Number of rolw deleted " + row);
                tx.commit();
                System.out.println("Done");
        }
        catch(Exception e)
        {
 System.out.println("Exception caught in EmployeeData.deleteEmployee" + e);
        }
}
// method to edit employee of CRUD operation
public void editEmployee(Employee emp) throws Exception
{
        Session session = null;
        try
        {
                // This step will read hibernate.cfg.xml
```

```
                //and prepare hibernate for use
                SessionFactory sessionFactory = new
                Configuration().configure().buildSessionFactory();
                session =sessionFactory.openSession();
                Transaction tx = session.beginTransaction();
                System.out.println("Updating Record...");
                String hqlUpdate = "update Employee employee set name = :newName, age =
                :newAge, salary = :newSalary where employeeId = :NewEmployeeId";
                Query query = session.createQuery(hqlUpdate);
                query.setInteger("NewEmployeeId", emp.getEmployeeId());
                query.setString("newName", emp.getName());
                query.setInteger("newAge", emp.getAge());
                query.setDouble("newSalary", emp.getSalary());
                int rowCount = query.executeUpdate();
                System.out.println("Rows affected: " + rowCount);
                tx.commit();
                System.out.println("Done");
            }
            catch(Exception e)
            {
            System.out.println("Exception caught in EmployeeData.EditEmployee " + e);
            }
        }
    }
```

Developing Controller Component

In a Web application, the business logic is handled by controller components. In our case, the business logic of the HibernateApplication application is to perform the CRUD operations. Let's now develop servlets as controller components that are used to retrieve data from the database by using the EmployeeData.java file. The following files are required to perform the CRUD operations in the HibernateApplication application:

- AddEmployeeServlet.java
- DeleteEmployeeServlet.java
- EditEmployeeServlet.java
- EmployeeListServlet.java

Creating the AddEmployeeServlet.java File

The AddEmployeeServlet servlet is used to add a row (or record) in the EMPLOYEE table by using the addEmployee() method of the EmployeeData.java file and forward it to the EmployeeList JSP page to display a list of the employees working in a company. The code for the AddEmployeeServlet servlet is shown in Listing 15.5 (save the AddEmployeeServlet.java file in the `\HibernateApplication\src\com\kogent\hibernate` folder):

Listing 15.5: Showing the Code for the AddEmployeeServlet.java File

```
package com.kogent.hibernate;
import com.kogent.hibernate.Employee;
import com.kogent.hibernate.EmployeeData;
import java.io.IOException;
import java.util.ArrayList;
import javax.servlet.ServletException;
import javax.servlet.http.HttpServlet;
import javax.servlet.http.HttpServletRequest;
import javax.servlet.http.HttpServletResponse;
import javax.servlet.http.HttpSession;
import javax.servlet.RequestDispatcher;
public class AddEmployeeServlet extends HttpServlet {

   public void doGet(HttpServletRequest request, HttpServletResponse response)
   throws ServletException, IOException
   {
          String employeeId = request.getParameter("employeeId");
          String name = request.getParameter("name");
          String age = request.getParameter("age");
          String salary = request.getParameter("salary");
```

```
            Employee emp = new Employee();
            EmployeeData emplData = new EmployeeData();
            try
            {
                    emp.setEmployeeId(Integer.parseInt(employeeId));
                    emp.setName(name);
                    emp.setAge(Integer.parseInt(age));
                    emp.setSalary(Double.parseDouble(salary));
                    emplData.addEmployee(emp);
                    ArrayList employees = EmployeeData.getEmployees();
                    HttpSession session = request.getSession(true);
                    session.setAttribute("employees", employees);
            }

            catch(Exception e)
            {
            System.out.println("Exception caught in AddEmployeeServlet" + e);
            }
            RequestDispatcher rd=request.getRequestDispatcher("/EmployeeList.jsp");
            rd.forward(request,response);
    }
}
```

Creating the DeleteEmployeeServlet.java File

This DeleteEmployeeServlet servlet is used to delete a row from the EMPLOYEE table and forward the EmployeeList JSP page to display the remaining row of the EMPLOYEE table. The deletion is done by the delete HQL query mentioned in the deleteEmployee() method in the EmployeeData.java file (Listing 15.4). The code for the DeleteEmployeeServlet servlet is shown in Listing 15.6 (save DeleteEmployeeServlet.java file in the `\HibernateApplication\src\com\kogent\hibernate` folder):

Listing 15.6: Showing the Code for the DeleteEmployeeServlet.java File

```
package com.kogent.hibernate;
import java.io.IOException;
import java.io.PrintWriter;
import java.util.ArrayList;
import javax.servlet.RequestDispatcher;
import javax.servlet.ServletException;
import javax.servlet.http.HttpServlet;
import javax.servlet.http.HttpServletRequest;
import javax.servlet.http.HttpServletResponse;
import javax.servlet.http.HttpSession;
public class DeleteEmployeeServlet extends HttpServlet
{
  public void doGet(HttpServletRequest request, HttpServletResponse
   response) throws ServletException, IOException
   {
        String employeeId = request.getParameter("employeeId");
        System.out.println("employee Idddddd  "+employeeId);
        try {
                EmployeeData.deleteEmployee(employeeId);
                ArrayList employees = EmployeeData.getEmployees();
                HttpSession session = request.getSession(true);
                session.setAttribute("employees", employees);
        }

        catch(Exception e)
        {
        System.out.println("Exception caught in AddEmployeeServlet" + e);
        }
        RequestDispatcher
        rd=request.getRequestDispatcher("/EmployeeList.jsp");
        rd.forward(request,response);
   }
}
```

Creating the EditEmployeeServlet.java File

The `EditEmployeeServlet` servlet is used to edit a row of the EMPLOYEE table and display the edited row by using the EmployeeList JSP page. The `EditEmployeeServlet` servlet calls the editEmployee() method of the EmployeeData.java file and updates the desired row by using the HQL update query. The code for the EditEmployeeServlet servlet is shown in Listing 15.7 (save the EditEmployeeServlet.java file in the `\HibernateApplication\src\com\kogent\hibernate` folder):

Listing 15.7: Showing the EditEmployeeServlet.java File

```
package com.kogent.hibernate;
import java.io.IOException;
import java.io.PrintWriter;
import java.util.ArrayList;
import javax.servlet.RequestDispatcher;
import javax.servlet.ServletException;
import javax.servlet.http.HttpServlet;
import javax.servlet.http.HttpServletRequest;
import javax.servlet.http.HttpServletResponse;
import javax.servlet.http.HttpSession;

public class EditEmployeeServlet extends HttpServlet
{
  public void doGet(HttpServletRequest request, HttpServletResponse response)
  throws ServletException, IOException
  {
        String employeeId = request.getParameter("employeeId");
        String name = request.getParameter("name");
        String age = request.getParameter("age");
        String salary = request.getParameter("salary");
        System.out.println("dsfdsf empid  "+employeeId);
        Employee emp = new Employee();
        EmployeeData emplData = new EmployeeData();
        try
        {
                emp.setEmployeeId(Integer.parseInt(employeeId));
                emp.setName(name);
                emp.setAge(Integer.parseInt(age));
                emp.setSalary(Double.parseDouble(salary));

                emplData.editEmployee(emp);
                ArrayList employees = EmployeeData.getEmployees();
                HttpSession session = request.getSession(true);
                session.setAttribute("employees", employees);
        }
        catch(Exception e)
        {
        System.out.println("Exception caught in EditEmployeeServlet " + e);
        }
        RequestDispatcher rd=request.getRequestDispatcher("/EmployeeList.jsp");
        rd.forward(request,response);
  }
}
```

Creating the EmployeeListServlet.java File

The EmployeeListServlet servlet is used for getting all the rows of the EMPLOYEE table by using getEmployees() method of the EmployeeData.java file and forwarding to the EmployeeList JSP page to display a list of the employees working in a company. The code for the EmployeeListServlet servlet is shown in Listing 15.8 (save the EmployeeListServlet.java file in the `\HibernateApplication\src\com\kogent\hibernate` folder):

Listing 15.8: Showing the Code for the EmployeeListServlet.java File

```
package com.kogent.hibernate;

import java.io.IOException;
import java.util.ArrayList;
import javax.servlet.RequestDispatcher;
import javax.servlet.ServletException;
import javax.servlet.http.HttpServlet;
import javax.servlet.http.HttpServletRequest;
import javax.servlet.http.HttpServletResponse;
import javax.servlet.http.HttpSession;
```

```
public class EmployeeListServlet extends HttpServlet

{
   public void doGet(HttpServletRequest request, HttpServletResponse response)
   throws ServletException, IOException

   {
         ArrayList employees = EmployeeData.getEmployees();
         HttpSession session = request.getSession(true);
         session.setAttribute("employees", employees);
         ArrayList employees1=((ArrayList) session.getAttribute("employees"));
         if(employees1!= null && employees1.size()>0)
         {
                for(int i=0;i<employees1.size();i++)
                {
                       Employee emp= (Employee) employees1.get(i);
                       System.out.println(emp.getEmployeeId());
                       System.out.println(emp.getName());
                       System.out.println(emp.getAge());
                       System.out.println(emp.getSalary());

                 }
         }
         RequestDispatcher rd=request.getRequestDispatcher("/EmployeeList.jsp");
         rd.forward(request,response);
   }

}
```

After developing all the servlets for performing CRUD operation of EMPLOYEE table, let's now develop some JSP pages that display the CRUD operation of the EMPLOYEE table.

Developing View Components

The view components are JSP pages that are used to display the resultant view page of the CRUD operations of the EMPLOYEE table in a company. The following JSP files are developed as view components of the HibernateApplication application:

- AddEmployee.jsp
- EditEmployee.jsp
- EmployeeList.jsp

Now let's develop these JSP files one by one.

Creating the AddEmployee.jsp File

The AddEmployee.jsp file displays the Add Employee Page screen that is used to add a row (or record) of an employee. This page contains four text fields, such as Employee Id, Employee Name, Employee Age, and Employee Salary along with a submit button. The code for the AddEmployee page is shown in Listing 15.9 (save the AddEmployee.jsp file in the `\HibernateApplication` folder):

Listing 15.9: Showing the Code for the AddEmployee.jsp File

```
<%@ page language="java" %>
<html>
<head>
   <title>Add Employee Page</title>
   </head>
<body>
   <form action="/HibernateApplication/AddEmployeeServlet">
   <table width="500" border="0">
   <tr>
         <td>Employee Id</td>
         <td><input type="text" name="employeeId"></td>
   </tr>
   <tr>
```

```
            <td>Employee Name</td>
            <td><input type="text" name="name"></td>
    </tr>
    <tr>
            <td>Employee Age</td>
            <td><input type="text" name="age"></td>
    </tr>
    <tr>
            <td>Employee Salary</td>
            <td><input type="text" name="salary"></td>
    </tr>
    <tr>
            <td> <input type="submit" name ="submit" value="submit"> </td>
    </tr>
    </table>
</form>
</body>
</html>
```

Creating the EditEmployee.jsp File

The EditEmployee JSP page displays the Edit Employee Page screen that is used to edit the details of an employee. The code for the EditEmployee JSP page is shown in Listing 15.10 (save the EditEmployee.jsp file in the `\HibernateApplication` folder):

Listing 15.10: Showing the Code for the EditEmployee.jsp File

```
<%@ page language="java" %>
<%@ page import="com.kogent.hibernate.EmployeeData,
com.kogent.hibernate.Employee" %>
<html>
<head>
  <title>Edit Employee Page</title>
  </head>
<body>
  <%
  String employeeId = request.getParameter("employeeId");
  Employee emp = null;
  emp= EmployeeData.getEmployee(employeeId);
  %>
  <form action="/HibernateApplication/EditEmployeeServlet">
  <table width="500" border="0">
  <tr>
        <td>Employee Id</td>
        <td> <%=emp.getEmployeeId() %> <input type = "hidden" name ="employeeId"
        value=<%=emp.getEmployeeId() %>></td>
  </tr>
  <tr>
        <td>Employee Name</td>
        <td><input type="text" name="name" value=<%=emp.getName()%>></td>
  </tr>
  <tr>
        <td>Employee Age</td>
        <td><input type="text" name="age" value=<%=emp.getAge() %>></td>
  </tr>
  <tr>
        <td>Employee Salary</td>
 <td><input type="text" name="salary" value=<%=emp.getSalary() %>></td>
  </tr>
  <tr>
        <td> <input type="submit" name ="submit" value="submit"> </td>
  </tr>
  </table>
</form>
</body>
</html>
```

Creating the EmployeeList.jsp File

The EmployeeList JSP page displays the Employee List Page screen that is used to display a list of the employees working in a company. This JSP page contains three hyperlinks that are used to add, delete, and update the details of an employee. The code for the EmployeeList JSP page is shown in Listing 15.11 (save the EmployeeList.jsp file in the `\HibernateApplication` folder):

Listing 15.11: Showing the Code for the EmployeeList.jsp File

```
<%@ page import="java.util.ArrayList, com.kogent.hibernate.Employee" %>
<%@ taglib uri="http://java.sun.com/jstl/core" prefix="c" %>
<html>
<head>
  <title>Employee List Page</title>

</head>
<body>
  <table width="700"
  border="0" cellspacing="0" cellpadding="0">
  <tr align="left">
        <th>Employee Id</th>
        <th>Name</th>
        <th>Age</th>
        <th>Salary</th>
  </tr>
  <!-- iterate over the results of the query -->
<% ArrayList employees=((ArrayList) session.getAttribute("employees"));
if(employees!= null && employees.size()>0)
{
  for(int i=0;i<employees.size();i++)
  {
        Employee emp= (Employee) employees.get(i);
        %>
        <tr>
              <td> <%=emp.getEmployeeId() %> </td>
              <td> <%=emp.getName() %> </td>
              <td> <%=emp.getAge() %> </td>
              <td> <%=emp.getSalary() %> </td>
        <td><A href
        ="/HibernateApplication/DeleteEmployeeServlet?employeeId=<%=emp.getEmployeeId()
        %>"> Delete</A>
        <td><A href
        ="/HibernateApplication/EditEmployee.jsp?employeeId=<%=emp.getEmployeeId() %>">
        Edit</A>
        </tr>
        <%
  }
} %>
</table>
<A href ="/HibernateApplication/AddEmployee.jsp">Add New Employee </A>
</body>
</html>
```

Creating the web.xml File

The web.xml file contains the configuration details of the HibernateApplication application and the mapping of various servlets that are used in the application. The code for the web.xml file is shown in Listing 15.12 (save the web.xml file in the `\HibernateApplication\WEB-INF` folder):

Listing 15.12: Showing the Web Configuration File web.xml of the HibernateApplication

```
<?xml version="1.0" encoding="UTF-8"?>

<web-app version="3.1"
  xmlns="http:// xmlns.jcp.org/xml/ns/javaee"
  xmlns:xsi="http://www.w3.org/2001/XMLSchema-instance"
  xsi:schemaLocation="http:// xmlns.jcp.org/xml/ns/javaee
```

```
   http:// xmlns.jcp.org/xml/ns/javaee/web-app_3_1.xsd">

<servlet>
   <servlet-name>EmployeeList</servlet-name>
   <servlet-class>com.kogent.hibernate.EmployeeList</servlet-class>

</servlet>

<servlet>
   <servlet-name>EmployeeListServlet</servlet-name>
   <servlet-class>com.kogent.hibernate.EmployeeListServlet</servlet-class>

</servlet>

<servlet>
   <servlet-name>AddEmployeeServlet</servlet-name>
   <servlet-class>com.kogent.hibernate.AddEmployeeServlet</servlet-class>

</servlet>

<servlet>
   <servlet-name>DeleteEmployeeServlet</servlet-name>
   <servlet-class>com.kogent.hibernate.DeleteEmployeeServlet</servlet-class>

</servlet>

<servlet>
   <servlet-name>EditEmployeeServlet</servlet-name>
   <servlet-class>com.kogent.hibernate.EditEmployeeServlet</servlet-class>
</servlet>

<servlet-mapping>
   <servlet-name>EmployeeList</servlet-name>
   <url-pattern>/EmployeeList</url-pattern>

</servlet-mapping>

<servlet-mapping>
   <servlet-name>EmployeeListServlet</servlet-name>
   <url-pattern>/EmployeeListServlet</url-pattern>
</servlet-mapping>

<servlet-mapping>
   <servlet-name>AddEmployeeServlet</servlet-name>
   <url-pattern>/AddEmployeeServlet</url-pattern>

</servlet-mapping>

<servlet-mapping>
   <servlet-name>DeleteEmployeeServlet</servlet-name>
   <url-pattern>/DeleteEmployeeServlet</url-pattern>
</servlet-mapping>

<servlet-mapping>
   <servlet-name>EditEmployeeServlet</servlet-name>
   <url-pattern>/EditEmployeeServlet</url-pattern>

</servlet-mapping>

</web-app>
```

After developing the files related to view, logic, Hibernate configuration, and Web configuration for the HibernateApplication, let's now describe the directory structure of the application to understand where these files are located.

Exploring Directory Structure

The HibernateApplication is the root directory in which all the JSPs, servlets, and configuration files are stored. To execute the HibernateApplication application properly, you must store the following JAR files in the \WEB-INF\lib directory:

- antlr 2.7.7.jar
- hibernate-commons-annotations-4.0.4.Final.jar
- hibernate-core-4.3.1.Final.jar
- hibernate-jpa-2.1-api-1.0.0 Final.jar
- classes12.jar
- jandex-1.1.0.Final.jar
- javassist-3.18.1-GA.jar
- jboss-logging-3.1.3.GA.jar
- dom4j-1.6.1.jar
- ojdbc14.jar
- poi-2.5.1.jar
- jboss-logging-annotations-1.2.0.Beta1.jar
- jboss-transaction-api_1.2_spec-1.0.0.Final.jar

The directory structure of the HibernateApplication application is shown in Figure 15.3:

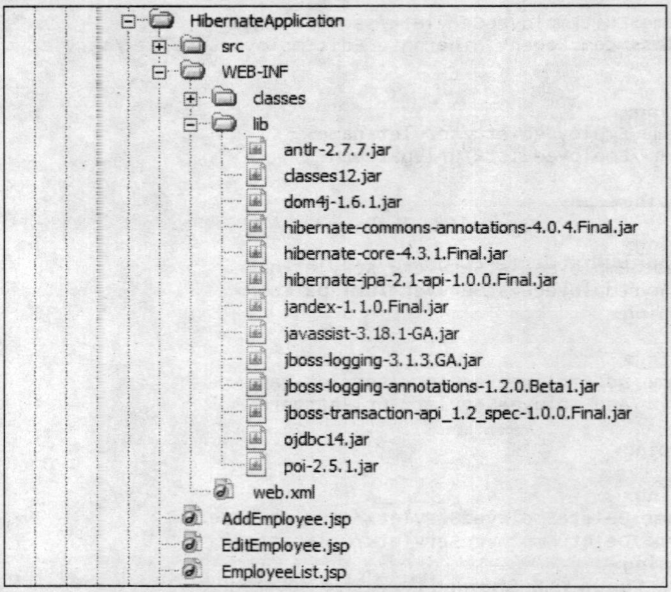

Figure 15.3 Showing the Directory Structure of HibernateApplication

Now, let's learn to run the HibernateApplication application on Glassfish Server 4.0 server

Running the Application

After developing the servlets, JSP pages, and configuration files, you should store them at the appropriate location in the HibernateApplication directory structure, as described in Figure 15.3. Create a Web ARchive (WAR) file and name it as HibernateApplication.war. Deploy the HibernateApplication.war file on the Glassfish Server 4.0. After successful deployment of this Hibernate Web application, perform the following steps to run the application:

1. Open the Internet Explorer Web browser and type the following URL:

```
http://localhost:8080/HibernateApplication/EmployeeListServlet
```

The details of employees appear, as shown in Figure 15.4:

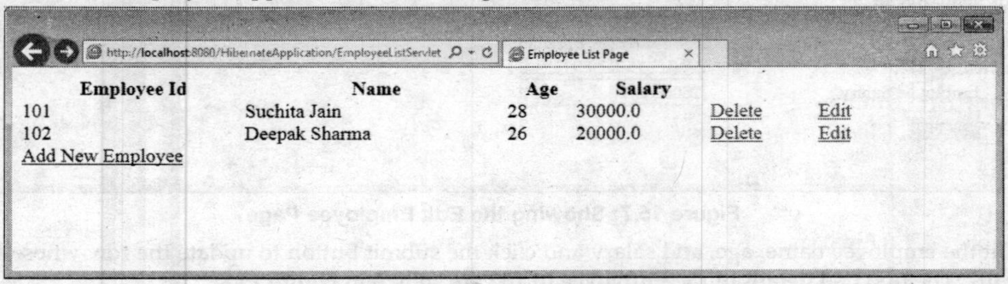

Figure 15.4: Showing the Employee List Page

Figure 15.4 shows the Add New Employee hyperlink used to add a new employee record in the database.

2. Click the Add New Employee hyperlink (Figure 15.4). The Add Employee Page appears, as shown in Figure 15.5.
3. Enter Employee Id, Employee Name, Employee Age, and Employee Salary in the corresponding text fields, as shown in Figure 15.5:

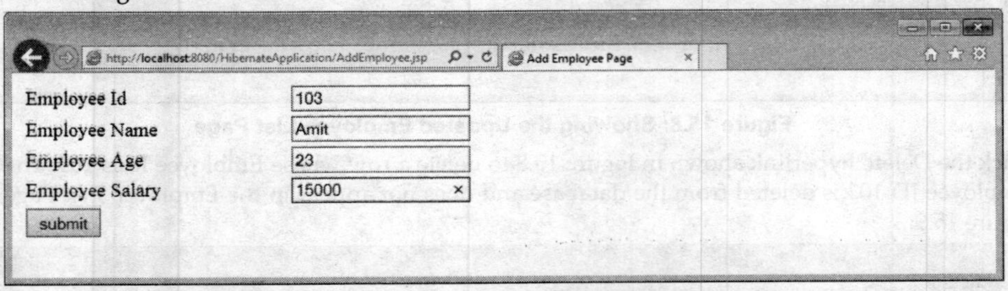

Figure 15.5: Showing the Add Employee Page

4. Click the **submit** button displayed on the Add Employee page to add a row in the EMPLOYEE table. The updated Employee List Page is as shown in Figure 15.6:

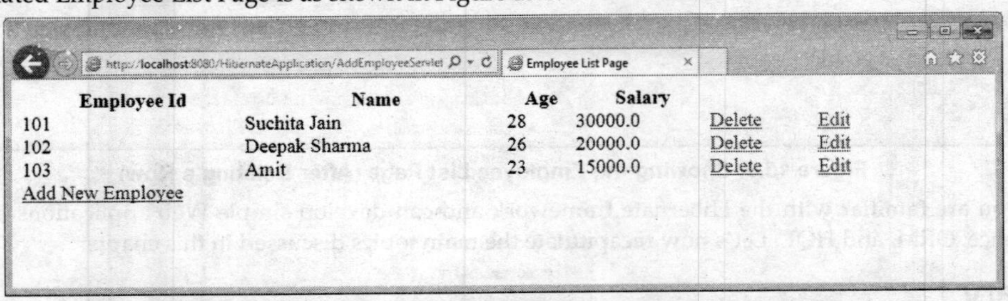

Figure 15.6: Showing the Added Record in the Employee List Page

5. Click the Edit hyperlink to edit the corresponding row. When you click the Edit hyperlink of employee whose Employee Id is 102, you can see the Edit Employee Page, as shown in Figure 15.7:

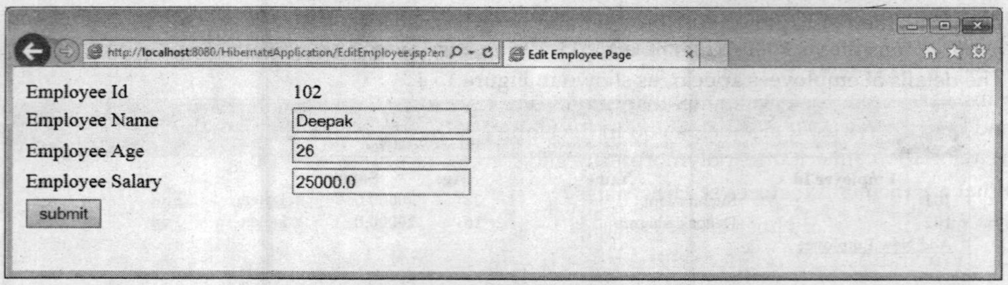

Figure 15.7: Showing the Edit Employee Page

6. Edit the employee name, age, and salary and click the submit button to update the row whose Employee Id is 102. The updated details of the Employee Id 102 are shown in Figure 15.8:

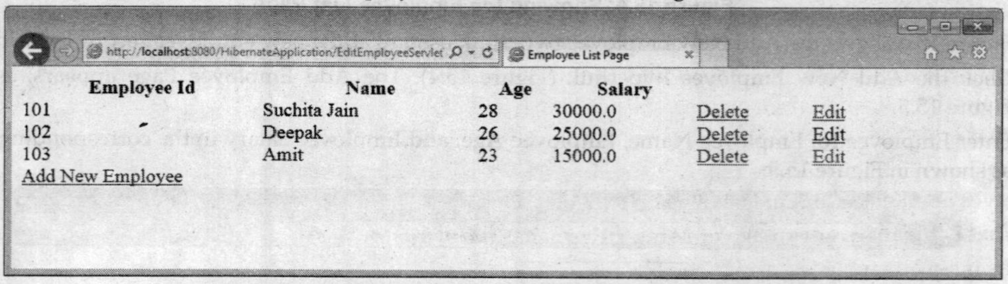

Figure 15.8: Showing the Updated Employee List Page

7. Click the Delete hyperlink shown in Figure 15.8 to delete a row whose Employee Id is 103. The record of the Employee ID 103 is deleted from the database and does not appear in the Employee List Page, as shown in Figure 15.9:

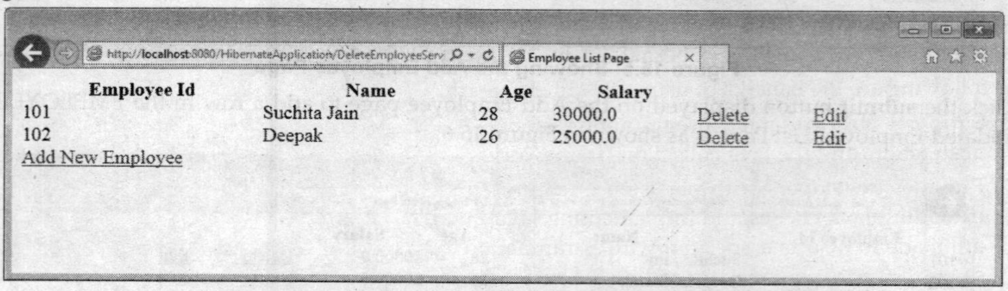

Figure 15.9: Showing the Employee List Page (After Deleting a Row)

Now, you are familiar with the Hibernate framework and can develop simple Web applications by using Java Persistence, ORM, and HQL. Let's now recapitulate the main topics discussed in this chapter.

Summary

The chapter has discussed the architecture and features of the Hibernate framework. You have also learned to retrieve data from the database table by using the O/R mapping and HQL. The chapter has also explored various clauses, such as select, from, where, and group by that can be used in HQL to query the database. You have also learned how to configure Hibernate for developing Hibernate Web applications. Towards the end, you have learned how to implement Hibernate in an application by developing a simple Hibernate Web application performing the CRUD operations.

In the next chapter, you learn the JBoss Seam framework.

Quick Revise

Q1. What is Hibernate?

Ans. Hibernate is a persistence model that provides powerful, high performance object/relational persistence, and query services. It also helps you in developing persistent classes with object-oriented features, such as association, inheritance, polymorphism, and composition.

Q2. What are the main features of Hibernate?

Ans. The main features of Hibernate are:

- Provides HQL to query database to retrieve the desired results
- Provides a way to store the Java object directly in the database table
- Provides O/R mapping in such a manner that reduces the difference between object-oriented and relational database systems

Q3. What is O/R mapping?

Ans. O/R mapping is the technique of mapping the data representation from an object-oriented system to a relational database system. The ORM feature allows you to perform various operations, such as insert, delete, update, and select, on the data stored in a database.

Q4. What is HQL?

Ans. HQL stands for Hibernate Query Language. This language is based on the relational object models and serves as an object-oriented extension to SQL.

Q5. What is the main advantage of using Hibernate than using the SQL?

Ans. The main advantage of using the Hibenate is that it allows you to map Java objects to tables in a database for persistent storage of data.

Q6. What is the difference between sorted and ordered collection in Hibernate?

Ans. A sorted collection in Hibernate is a collection that are sorted in memory using Java Comparator interface, whereas the ordered collections are the collections that are ordered in the database using the order by clause.

Q7. List the benefits of using the Hibernate framework.

Ans. The following are the benefits of using the Hibernate framework:

- Supports object-oriented programming models, such as inheritance, polymorphism, composition, abstraction, and the Java collections framework.
- Provides developers with persistence feature and a code generation library (CGLIB) that helps in extending Java classes and implementing Java interfaces at runtime environment. The changes that are made to objects associated with a transaction are automatically addressed in the database. This saves the time spent in extra coding for bytecode processing.
- Provides object-oriented query language called HQL, which is similar to SQL. It helps in writing multi-criteria search and dynamic queries.
- Provides Object/Relational mapping for bridging the gap between object-oriented systems and relational databases.
- Enables the developer to build a Hibernate Web application very efficiently in MyEclipse by using Hibernate eclipse plug-ins that provide mapping editor, interactive query prototyping, and schema reverse engineering tool.
- Reduces the development time, as it supports object-oriented programming, such as inheritance, polymorphism, composition, and Java Collection framework.

Q8. What are the benefits of HQL?

Ans. The following are the benefits of HQL:

- Provides full support for relational operations
- Returns results as objects
- Supports polymorphic queries

- Easy to learn
- Supports advanced features
- Provides database independence

Q9. Define Session interface.

Ans. All applications need to handle the session details of a user to carry out further transactions. Sessions are created and destroyed several times in an application. Sessions are lightweight and inexpensive. Hibernate maintains a session between a connection and a transaction. It caches all the loaded objects in a session and can keep track of any changes made to these objects.

Q10. What is Transaction interface?

Ans. The Transaction interface is an optional API that resides in the `net.sf.hibernate` package. The use of this API makes Hibernate applications portable on different platforms as well as on different containers.

16

Implementing JBoss Seam

In Java EE, Enterprise JavaBeans 3 (EJB 3) is used to implement the business logic in an enterprise application. JavaServer Faces (JSF) helps in creating the user interfaces (UI) of these enterprise applications. However, developers need to provide a lot of code in an application to create UI components by using JSF. JBoss Seam (Seam) a light weight framework that helps to integrate the EJB and JSF technologies and facilitates efficient development of UI components. Consequently, while using Seam, the developers can focus more on the business logic of the enterprise applications. Seam is developed and designed by JBoss, a division of RedHat.

The Seam framework is based on a three-tier architecture that supports the Model, View, Controller (MVC) architecture. The three-tier architecture of the Seam framework consists of the presentation tier, business logic tier, and persistent tier. The presentation tier and the business logic tier integrate with JSF and EJB, respectively. The persistent tier represents the backend database support for the database access.

In this chapter, you learn about the Seam framework and its features. In addition, you learn about the Seam context, Seam components, and built-in Seam components, such as context injection, internationalization, and Mail and Java Message Service (JMS). You also learn about the configuration of the Seam components and how Business Process Management (BPM) and page flow are implemented in the Seam application. Finally, you learn how to configure the Seam framework to develop a Seam application.

Listing the Features of the Seam Framework

The Seam framework provides a simplified programming model, which is a combination of various frameworks, such as EJB and JSF. The features of the Seam framework are as follows:

- **Support for using JSF with EJB 3**—Provides support for integrating JSF and EJB 3. Integration of JSF and EJB in the Seam framework speeds up the process of creating enterprise applications, as the developers only need to focus on the business logic that is to be implemented in the application.
- **Support for AJAX**—Provides support for AJAX-based applications. Seam uses the JBoss, RichFaces, and ICEFaces frameworks, also known as JSF with AJAX frameworks, to create AJAX-based applications. Using these frameworks, developers do not need to write JavaScript code to implement the AJAX functionality. Seam makes the use of the JavaScript remoting layer to asynchronously call a component from the client side.
- **Support for jBPM**—Provides support for Java Business Process Management (jBPM), which is a workflow management system provided by JBoss. It reduces the time spent in implementing the complex workflows, collaboration, and task management features of enterprise applications.
- **Support for declarative application state management**—Provides support for declarative application state management, which overcomes the problems, such as navigation with back button, refresh button, and duplicate form submission, during the application sessions. Seam provides the conversational and business process contexts, which automate the manual technique of state management.
- **Support for Bijection**—Provides support for Bijection technique, which helps in aliasing the variables used in a context and assigning the aliased variable to attributes of the components. This automatically assembles the component tree. The Bijection technique also defines the scope of stateful components with sufficient flexibility, which was not possible with the Inversion of Control (IoC) or Dependency Injection (DI) features of JSF and EJB 3.
- **Support for annotations**—Provides support for the annotations feature of EJB 3. Earlier, while creating Seam applications, you need to provide Extensible Markup Language (XML) based configuration details in Deployment Descriptors. Seam extends the annotations feature of EJB 3 and uses the same with declarative state management and context demarcation annotations, which help in reducing the time required for writing JSF-based managed bean declarations. In addition, the use of annotations provides a flexible approach of configuring the components of an application without using Deployment Descriptors; thereby, saving the time that was spent earlier in creating Deployment Descriptors.
- **Support for workspace management**—Provides support for workspace management, which allows a user to switch between multiple workspaces in a single tab window. This helps in implementing transaction management at isolation level and multi-window browsing.

- **Other supports**—Provides support for other Java Persistence API (JPA) and Hibernate 3.6 integration, which deals with persistence objects.

After having a brief overview of the features of the Seam framework, let's now learn to use the Seam framework in an application.

Working with the Seam Framework

The Seam framework is based on three fundamental concepts: contexts, components, and annotations. Contexts and components of the Seam framework are implemented in an application as stateful EJB objects. Generally, the enterprise beans, along with instances of the Seam components, are associated with the Seam context. This provides a naming convention context to develop stateful Web applications. The @In annotation injects Seam components in a Seam application and the @Out annotation outjects the components from a Seam application.

Let's now explore these three fundamental concepts of the Seam framework in detail.

Understanding Contexts

A context is a set of namespaces and data items that are associated with the Seam components. Seam contexts are used to maintain the state of sessions in a Web application. These contexts are generated and destroyed by the Seam framework. The basic Seam contexts are as follows:

- **Stateless context**—Deals with stateless session beans. In this context, the state of a bean is active during the invocation of the bean. When a client invokes a stateless context bean, the bean instance variables remain in a session only till the time the bean is being invoked.
- **Event or request context**—Provides functionalities to manage short time events, such as remotely calling a resource and request invocations. The event or request context is the simple and most used context throughout the Seam context. This context is activated at the time of its generation and gets destroyed at the end of the event life-cycle.
- **Page context**—Allows you to maintain the state of a particular task, such as retrieving information using the dynamic list, on the Web page. You can initialize the state of a page context in the event listener, which is defined in the web.xml Deployment Descriptor, and then access it from linked events. This context is specifically used in case of dynamic Web pages.
- **Conversation context**—Holds the state of a client that supports multiple conversations in multiple windows. The conversation context is one of the most important contexts in the Seam framework. A conversation may consist of several user interactions, requests, responses, and database transactions in a Web application. One of the most important tasks of conversation context is to ensure that the states of the different conversations do not collide and cause errors. For example, using the Airlines website involves multiple conversations, such as selecting the flight, hotel, and car. If a user performs these tasks simultaneously, the respective conversations might collide. To overcome this problem, the conversation context holds the state for the current task, while the other tasks are running in the background.

NOTE

Conversation may also be nested, which means that one large conversation can contain multiple smaller conversations.

- **Session context**—Holds the state of the HyperText Transfer Protocol (HTTP) session throughout the scope of a Seam application. The session context is used as a Web request, which is used to share the global application information across multiple conversations. In the session context, the stateful session bean is used to maintain the state of several conversations throughout the Seam application.
- **Business process context**—Holds the state of the business processes involved in a Seam application. The state is managed, created, and destroyed by the Seam's jBPM. The business process holds multiple interactions with multiple users, so the state involved in a business process is shared among multiple users. The state of the current task defined by the business process instance and the life cycle of the business process is managed by the jBPM Process Definition Language (jPDL), so there are no special annotations for business process demarcation.

- **Application context**—Holds static information, such as configuration of data and data models of an application. The application context is similar to the servlet context.

The variables defined in a Seam context are known as context variables. In Seam, a developer can bind any value to a context variable, similar to defining the session and request attributes in servlets. Within a Seam framework, the Seam component variables are accessed by using the context variable names and the context class. This context class provides the component instance that can be retrieved from the Context interface, as shown in the following code snippet:

```
User user = (User) Contexts.getSessionContext().get("user"); //Method for accessing the
   value of the context variable.

Contexts.getSessionContext().set("user", user); // Method for setting the value of context
   variable.
```

The context variable name can be changed or set according to the user's choice, as shown in the preceding code snippet. The components from the application context can be accessed by injecting a component using the `@In` annotation, and can be outjected to the context by using the `@Out` annotation. In the preceding code snippet, `user` is the context variable used in the context interface. The value for the `user` context variable can be retrieved by using the `Contexts.getSessionContext().get("user")` method; whereas, the value for the variable can be set by using the `Contexts.getSessionContext().set("user")` method.

However, when you need to obtain the components, injection is used to get components from a context, and outjection is used to outject the component instances into a context.

NOTE

Seam components instances are obtained from a defined scope. All stateful scopes are searched in the priority order, which is as follows:

1. *Event context*
2. *Page context*
3. *Conversation context*
4. *Session context*
5. *Business process context*
6. *Application context*

You can perform priority search by calling the `Contexts.lookupInStatefulContexts()` method.

Working with Seam Components

The Seam components are similar to Plain Old Java Object (POJO) components that integrate JavaBeans or EJBs and JSF to implement the business and presentation logic. The Seam framework supports the following types of beans:

- JavaBeans
- EJB session beans
- EJB stateless session beans
- EJB stateful session beans
- EJB entity beans
- EJB message driven beans

NOTE

You can learn more about EJB 3.2 in Chapter 13, Working with EJB 3.2 and Chapter 14, Implementing Entities and JPA 2.1.

The Seam components must be intercepted before they are used in the Seam framework. For example, to access the session beans, you must register an EJB interceptor in a class through the `@Interceptors` annotation. The interceptors for the session bean component can be defined, as shown in the following code snippet:

```
@Stateless
```

```
@Interceptors (SeamInterceptor.class)
public class LoginAction implements Login {
  // codes for login module
}
```

You can also define the interceptors in the ejb-jar.xml file. The representation of the interceptors within the ejb-jar.xml file is shown in the following code snippet:

```
<interceptors>
<interceptor>
  <interceptor-class> org.jboss.seam.ejb.SeamInterceptor </interceptor-class>
</interceptor>
</interceptors>
<assembly-descriptor>
  <interceptor-binding>
        <ejb-name>*</ejb-name>
        <interceptor-class> org.jboss.seam.ejb.SeamInterceptor </interceptor-class>
  </interceptor-binding>
</assembly-descriptor>
```

In the Seam framework, all Seam components must be assigned a name. The @Name annotation is used to assign a name to a component. The following code snippet shows how to assign a name to a component:

```
@Name("loginAction")
@Stateless
public class LoginAction implements Login {
...
}
```

In the preceding code snippet, we have created the `loginAction` Seam component for the `LoginAction` class that implements the `Login` interface.

Apart from creating a Seam component, you can also use the built-in Seam components in a Seam application. Let's discuss about the built-in Seam components and how to configure a Seam component in the following subsections.

Exploring Built-in Seam Components

The Seam framework provides some built-in components, such as context injection and internationalization, which help to access entity beans and stateful session beans in a Seam application. These built-in components are used to customize the basic functionalities of Seam applications and can be defined at runtime. You can define built-in components in the components.xml file by overriding the default properties, such as `localeSelector.localeString`, `localeSelector.language`, and `localeSelector.cookieEnabled`.

To use the built-in components, you first need to replace the existing Seam components with the built-in components. The built-in components can be replaced by specifying the name of the corresponding Seam component, such as stateless, stateful, and entity, in a class by using the `@Name` annotation. A built-in Seam component must be qualified with a name. However, you cannot replace some existing Seam components as they are aliased to unqualified names, by default. This implies that you cannot assign a name to these Seam components. In such cases, you can use the `auto-create` property to create an instance of Seam built-in component corresponding to a Seam component that cannot be replaced. You can set the `auto-create` property as true in the components.xml file.

The built-in components are defined in the Seam API of the `org.jboss.seam.core` package. Some important built-in Seam components provided by the Seam framework are listed as follows:

- Context injection component
- Internationalization component
- Mail and Java Messaging Service (JMS) related components
- Infrastructural component
- Special components

These Seam built-in components can be used in Seam applications to extend the security, internationalization, and message services functionalities.

The Context Injection Component

The context injection Seam built-in component is used to inject various contextual objects, such as `sessionContext` and `applicationContext`, in a class. The following syntax is used to inject and instantiate a Seam session context object in a Seam application:

```
@In private Context <Name of the context>;
```

The preceding syntax allows you to specify the `org.jboss.seam.core.contexts` class to access a Seam context object. For example, the `org.jboss.seam.core.contexts.sessionContext[loginUser]` object is used to access a user object in a session context.

The Internationalization Components

The internationalization built-in component provides an easy way to build internationalized Seam applications with support for multiple languages.

The following components are used to implement internationalization in Seam applications:

- `org.jboss.seam.international.locale`—Serves as a built-in Seam component used to handle Locales, such as geographical, political, or cultural regions. You can use the `org.jboss.seam.international.localeSelector` object to implement Locale-specific functionalities at either configuration level or runtime. The select() method is used to set a specific Locale. You can use the following properties with the `localeSelector object:`
  - `localeSelector.localeString`—Provides string representation of a Locale
  - `localeSelector.language`—Represents the language of the specified Locale
  - `localeSelector.country`—Denotes a particular country for the specified Locale
  - `localeSelector.cookieEnabled`—Helps to select a Locale that should be persisted through a cookie
- `org.jboss.seam.international.timezone`—Serves as a built-in Seam component used to set time zone for the current session. You can use the `org.jboss.seam.international.timezoneSelector` component to set the time zone at either configuration level or runtime. The following method and properties are used with the `timezoneSelector` component:
  - `select()`—Helps to select a specified Locale
  - `timezoneSelector.timeZoneId`—Specifies the time zone, represented as a String value
  - `timezoneSelector.cookieEnabled`: Helps to select the time zone that should persist throughout a cookie
- `org.jboss.seam.core.resourceBundle`—Serves as a built-in Seam component that is used to search the resource bundles associated with the current session. The Seam resource bundle performs a detailed search to locate the required information for internationalization in a list of Java resource bundles.

The Mail and JMS Related Components

The Seam framework provides mail related built-in component, `MailSession`, which is used to send and receive email messages. The `org.jboss.seam.mail.MailSession` component is a manager component with session scope that can be looked up either by Java Naming and Directory Interface (JNDI) or can be created by configuring a host. A manager component is used to manage the life cycle of a component. Any component used with the `@Unwrap` method can be a manager component.

The properties of the `org.jboss.seam.mail.mailSession` component are as follows:

- **org.jboss.seam.mail.mailSession.host**—Specifies the hostname of the Simple Mail Transfer Protocol (SMTP) server.
- **org.jboss.seam.mail.mailSession.port**—Denotes the port number of the SMTP server.
- **org.jboss.seam.mail.mailSession.username**—Denotes the username used to connect to the SMTP server.
- **org.jboss.seam.mail.mailSession.password**—Specifies the password used to connect to the SMTP server.
- **org.jboss.seam.mail.mailSession.debug**—Helps in debugging JavaMail.

- **org.jboss.seam.mail.mailSession.ssl**—Helps to enable Secure Sockets Layer (SSL) connection to SMTP. The default port number for this property is 465.
- **org.jboss.seam.mail.mailSession.sessionJndiName**—Helps to specify the name of the current session, represented by the javax.mail.Session object, which is bound to JNDI. If this property is passed to the MailSession component, all the properties are ignored.

The JMS built-in components are used with the `TopicPublishers` and `QueueSenders` managed properties. The `org.jboss.seam.jms.queueSession` property is a manager component of the `JMS QueueSession` component and `org.jboss.seam.jms.topicSession` is a manager component of the `JMS TopicSession` component.

The Infrastructural Component

The infrastructural built-in component provides an environment to integrate Seam annotation, EJB, JSF, and Hibernate to develop JBoss Seam applications. However, this component is not installed by default; you need to set the `install` property to `true` in the components.xml file to install this component.

The properties of the infrastructural component are as follows:

- **org.jboss.seam.core.init.jndiPattern**—Helps to look up session beans by using the JNDI pattern.
- **org.jboss.seam.core.init.debug**: Helps to enable the Seam debug mode.
- **org.jboss.seam.core.init.clientSideConversations**—Helps to save the conversation context variables. When this property is set to true, the conversation context variables are saved at the client side instead of an HttpSession.
- **org.jboss.seam.core.init.userTransactionName**—Helps to look up Java Transaction API (JTA) UserTransaction objects with the help of JNDI name.
- **org.jboss.seam.core.manager.conversationTimeout**—Specifies the conversation context timeout, in milliseconds.
- **org.jboss.seam.core.manager.concurrentRequestTimeout**—Specifies the maximum wait time of a thread. This property also attempts to lock a long-running conversation context after the specified maximum wait time.
- **org.jboss.seam.core.manager.conversationIsLongRunningParameter**—Specifies whether or not a conversation is long-running.

The Special Components

Some special Seam components are manager components that manage the entity manager with extended persistence context. For example, the following code snippet installs and configures the two Seam components in the components.xml file, which serve as the entity managers:

```
<component name="loginDatabase"
   class="org.jboss.Seam.persistence.ManagedPersistenceContext">
<property name="persistenceUnitJndiName">java:/comp/emf/loginPersistence</property>
</component>

   <component name="employeeDatabase"
   class="org.jboss.Seam.persistence.ManagedPersistenceContext">
<property name="persistenceUnitJndiName">java:/comp/emf/employeePersistence</property>
</component>
```

In the preceding code snippet, `loginDatabase` and `employeeDatabase` are special Seam components.

Now, let's discuss how to configure Seam components.

Configuring Seam Components

The Seam components are configured by using XML files, such as web.xml and components.xml, available in the Seam framework. You also need to set the configuration details in the property file. Configuring Seam components helps a developer to isolate deployment-specific information from Java code, and provides reusability. The web.xml and component.xml files are also used to configure the built-in Seam components.

You can configure the Seam components by using:

- Property settings
- The components.xml file
- Sliced configuration files
- XML namespaces

Let's discuss these in detail.

Using Property Settings

The properties of the Seam components can be configured by using the servlet context parameters or the Seam properties file, named `seam.properties`. The `seam.properties` file is available in the root of the `classpath`. To understand how to configure Seam components, let's look at an example. Suppose we have a property, `com.jboss.myapp.setting` and a setter method, `setLocale()` in the Seam framework. The property name for the `setLocale()` method can be specified as `com.jboss.myapp.setting.locale` in the `seam.properties` file or in the servlet context parameter. The Seam framework sets the value of the locale attribute while instantiating the Seam component.

To configure Seam in an application, you need to provide the property settings in the web.xml or seam.properties file. For example, to store the state of conversation timeout, you must provide a value for the `org.jboss.seam.core.manager.conversationTimeout` property in the `web.xml` or `seam.properties` file.

Using the components.xml File

Using the components.xml file to configure Seam components is a more powerful approach than setting a property in the web.xml or seam.properties file. The components.xml file has the following advantages over the seam.properties file:

- Configures the installed component automatically. This includes both the built-in Seam components as well as other Seam components, such as stateless session bean and entity bean, which have been annotated with the `@Name` annotation.
- Helps to configure Seam components that have the `@Name` annotation but have not been installed automatically. This is because the `@Install` annotation indicates whether or not the component is already installed.

The components.xml file can be stored either in the WEB-INF directory of a WAR, in the META-INF directory of a jar, or within any directory of a jar that contains the classes with the `@Name` annotation. In general, Seam components are installed when the deployment scanner finds a class annotated with the `@Name` annotation stored in an archive with the `seam.properties` file or the `META-INF/components.xml` file.

The annotations used in the classes may be overridden. The `components.xml` files handle these special cases of overriding annotations within the `seam.properties` file.

The following code snippet shows the code to be provided in the `components.xml` file to install jBPM in an application:

```
<components xmlns=http://jboss.com/products/Seam/components"
   xmlns:xsi=http://www.w3.org/2001/XMLschema-instance
   xmlns:bpm=http://jboss.com/products/Seam/bpm >
   <bpm:jBPM/>
</components>
```

jBPM can also be installed by making some changes in the `components.xml` file, as shown in the following code snippet:

```
<components>
   <component class="org.jboss.Seam.bpm.jbpm">
</components>
```

The Seam managed persistence context can be installed by using EJB as well. In this case, you need a database and the persistence context unit used for that database. You can include the scope of the persistence context in an application while configuring the persistence context, as shown in the following code snippet:

```
<components xmlns=http://jboss.com/products/Seam/components
  Xmlns:persistence=http://jboss.com/products/Seam/persistence >
  <persistence:managed-persistence-context name="StudentEntityManagerFactory"
        scope="session"
        auto-create="true"
  persistent -unit-jndi-name="java:/studentEntityManagerFactory"/>
  <persistent:managed-persistence-context name="employeeDatabase"
        scope="session"
        auto-create="true"
  persistence-unit-jndi-name="java:/employeeEntityManagerFactory"/>
</components>
```

While configuring infrastructure components, you need to explicitly specify the `create` property as true in the `components.xml` file. To avoid this, you can create an instance of the component by using the `auto-create` method. Generally, `auto-create` is used along with the `@In` annotation in the `components.xml` file.

Alternatively, you can also install the Seam persistence context by making changes in the `components.xml` file, as shown in the following code snippet:

```
<components>
<component name="studentDatabase">
  Class="org.jboss.Seam.persistenceManagedPersistenceContext"
  Scope="session"
  auto-create="true">
<property name="PersistentUnitJndiName">java:/customerEntityManageFactory
</property>
</component>
<component name="employeeDatabase"
  Class="org.jboss.Seam.persistence.ManagedPersistenceContext"
  Scope="session"
  auto-create="true">
<property name="PersistentUnitJndiName">java:/employeeEntityManagerFactory
</property>
</component>
</components>
```

Using the Sliced Configuration Files

Configuring multiple components using XML in the components.xml file is a cumbersome task. To avoid this, you can divide the information specified in the components.xml file into small files. Let's consider that we have a class named `com.JavaEE.Java` in an application. Seam specifies the configuration information for this class into a resource file named com/JavaEE/Java.component.xml. The root of the resource file can be either the <component> element or the <components> element. The following code snippet shows the definition of components in the `Java.component.xml` file:

```
<components>
  <component class="com.JavaEE.Java" name="Java">
        <property name="name">#{user.name}</property>
  </component>
  <factory name="message" value="#{Java.message}"/>
</components>
```

In the preceding code snippet, the Java component is configured by providing the `com.JavaEE.Java` class name. However, in the following code snippet, the class name has not been specified to configure the Java component in the `Java.component.xml` file:

```
<component name="Java">
  <property name="name">#{user.name}</property>
</component>
```

In the preceding code snippet, the class name is implied by the file in which the component definition appears.

Using XML Namespaces

You can also declare the Seam components with or without the XML namespaces. The following code snippet shows the declaration of a component without using namespaces:

```
<?xml version="1.0" encoding="UTF-8"?>
<components xmlns=http://jboss.com/products/Seam/components
xsi:schemaLocation=http://jboss.com/products/Seam/components
http://jboss.com/products/Seam/components-2.0.xsd">
  <component class="org.jboss.Seam.core.init">
        <property name="debug">true</property>
        <property name="jndiPattern">@jndiPattern@</property>
</component>
</components>
```

The following code snippet shows how to configure components by using namespaces:

```
<?xml version="1.0" encoding="UTF-8"?>
<components xmlns="http://jboss.com/products/Seam/components"
  xmlns:core="http://jboss.com/products/Seam/core"
  xmlns:xsi="http://www.w3.org/2001/XMLSchema-instance"
xsi:schemaLocation="http://jboss.com/products/Seam/core
http://jboss.com/products/Seam/core-2.0.xsd
http://jboss.com/products/Seam/components http://jboss.com/products/Seam/components-
2.0.xsd">
  <core:init debug="true" jndi-pattern="@jndiPattern@"/>
</components>
```

XML namespaces provide detailed information about each component and attribute in the file you want to configure. The use of the namespaced elements makes the components.xml file much simpler. The Seam framework supports the mixing of both the models (with or without the usage of the namespaces). It also allows the use of the <component> generic component declaration or quick declarations of the namespaces for the components. You can also associate a Java package with an XML namespace by using the `@Namespace` annotation.

Table 16.1 shows some namespaces provided by the Seam framework:

Table 16.1: Namespaces of the Seam framework

Namespaces	Namespace representation
components	Helps to handle Seam components. Its namespace representation is `http://jboss.com/products/seam/components.`
core	Helps to handle core classes of the Seam framework, such as `BusinessProcess`, `Ejb`, and `Pageflow`. Its namespace representation is `http://jboss.com/ products/seam/core.`
drools	Helps to handle Seam drools classes, such as `DrollsActionHandler`, `DrollsDecisionHandler`, and `RuleBase`. You can define its namespace as `http://jboss.com/products/seam/drools.`
security	Helps to handle security features of Seam applications. It can be defined as `@Namespace(value="http:// jboss.com/products/seam/security", prefix="org.jboss.seam.security")` in your Seam application.
mail	Helps to handle email functionalities, such as receiving and sending emails by using Seam framework. Its namespace representation is `http://jboss.com/ products/seam/mail.`
web	Helps to handle Web classes, such as `CharacterEncodingFilter`, `ContextFilter`, and `MultipartRequest`, to handle client requests and responses. It can be defined as `@Namespace(value="http://jboss.com/products/seam/web", prefix="org.jboss.seam.web")` in Seam applications.
pdf	Helps to handle the Portable Document Format (PDF) files. Its namespace representation is `http://jboss.com/prod'ucts/seam /pdf.`
Spring	Helps to add Spring framework functionality in an application. Its namespace representation is `http://jboss.com/ products/seam/spring.`

Let's now move ahead and explore the annotations of the Seam framework.

Using Annotations

The Seam framework supports annotations, allowing you to directly configure a Seam component instead of creating an instance of the component. This simplifies the code used for a Seam component in a class. Seam introduces the bijection mechanism for injecting and outjecting Seam components. As already discussed, Seam is an integration of the JSF and EJB frameworks; therefore, it supports the annotations defined in the EJB 3.0 specification. The annotations for Seam component life cycle methods are also discussed in this subsection as these annotations allow a Seam component to interact with its life cycle events. The `@Logger` annotation has also simplified the code for providing a simple log message. The Seam framework provides the annotation support for:

- Bijection mechanism
- Life cycle callback methods
- Conditional installation
- Logging

Now let's discuss these in detail.

Understanding the Bijection Mechanism

DI allows you to separate the construction and implementation of an object. It allows a component to obtain a reference of another component by injecting a setter method or an instance variable in a class. The injection mechanism occurs only when the component is created and the reference of the component is changed during the lifetime of the component instance.

All the instances of a stateless component are interchangeable in a Seam application. Therefore, DI is not very useful in this scenario. As a result, the bijection mechanism has been introduced in the Seam framework. The usage of DI in the Seam framework is often referred as bijection, because the injection is performed in a two-way format, injection and outjection. For example, a component named A creates another component named B, which can outject to another component, C, for use at a later point of time. This process in the Seam framework is known as bijection.

The bijection mechanism is used to assemble the Seam components from different contexts, such as event, page session, and business process. The values of context variables are injected to the Seam components and can again be outjected from the Seam components. Consequently, bijection occurs each time a Seam component is invoked. In other words, the bijection mechanism is contextual, bidirectional, and dynamic in the Seam framework.

The Seam components can be injected and outjected by using the `@In` and the `@Out` annotations. The `@In` annotation specifies the Seam component that needs to be injected. The following code snippet shows the use of the `@In` annotation with a Seam component:

```
@Name ("HelloUser")
@Stateless
public class HelloUser implements User
{
  @In Username name;
  …
}
```

The `@In` annotation can also be used with setter methods, such as the `setUserName()` method of a Seam component. The following code snippet shows the use of `@In` annotation with a setter method:

```
@Name ("HelloUser")
@Stateless
public class HelloUser implements User
{
  Username name;
  @In
  public void setUsername (Username name)
  {
        this.name=name;
  }
  …
}
```

Similarly, you can use the @Out annotation for outjection in a Seam component. The @Out annotation can also be used with the getter method. The following code snippet shows the use of the @Out annotation:

```
@Name ("HelloUser")
@Stateless
public class HelloUser implements User
{
   @In Username name;
   …
}

// Using @Out annotation in the getter method

@Name ("HelloUser")
@Stateless
public class HelloUser implements User
{
   Username name;
   @In
   public void setUsername (Username name)
   {
         this.name=name;
   }
   @Out
   public Username getUserName() {
         return name;
   }
   …
}
```

Understanding Life Cycle Callback Methods

The life cycle of the Seam components is managed with the help of various annotated methods, such as @Create, @PreDestroy, @PostConstruct, and @Destroy. These methods are known as life cycle callback methods. When the first object of a class is created, the life cycle callback methods get attached to the object and are available throughout the session of the object. A Seam component, such as session bean or entity bean, supports all common EJB life cycle callback methods, such as @PostConstruct and @PreDestroy. In addition, the Seam life cycle callback methods are also supported by JavaBeans.

The Seam framework also supports two additional life cycle callback methods, @Create and @Destroy, which are equivalent to @PostConstruct and @PreDestroy. The @Create callback method is defined whenever the Seam framework instantiates a Seam component and the @Destroy callback method is called whenever the Seam framework destroys a Seam component. In the Seam framework, the @Startup callback method is used to instantiate a Seam component when the life cycle of a Seam application starts.

Understanding Conditional Installation

When you install Seam, some of its components are installed by default. However, you can install other components by using the @Install annotation in the Seam framework. In other words, the @Install annotation allows you to control the conditional installation of Seam components required to deploy Web applications. When you use the @Install annotation, you need to specify the precedence value of the corresponding Seam component. The precedence of a component is a numeric number, which specifies the component that needs to be installed if multiple classes with the same component name exist in the classpath of the Seam application.

The components in the Seam framework are selected according to the pre-defined precedence values, as shown in Table 16.2:

Table 16.2: Pre-defined Precedence Value of Seam Components

Precedence Value	Description
BUILT_IN	Specifies the lowest precedence value among all the precedence values available in the Seam framework.
FRAMEWORK	Specifies the component defined by a third party framework that overrides the built-in components. This precedence value can be overridden by the application components.
APPLICATION	Specifies the default component in the Seam framework. This precedence value is applicable for most application frameworks, such as JSF.
DEPLOYMENT	Specifies the precedence value for application components used for deployment purpose.
MOCK	Specifies the precedence value used for testing Seam components.

In case you unknowingly begin to install an already installed component, the `@Install` annotation automatically prevents the installation.

Implementing Logging

Earlier, you had to write multiple lines of code for implementing even simple functionalities in an application. For example, more lines of code need to be provided for implementing logging than for implementing the business logic. The following code snippet shows the code that need to be written to implement logging in an application without using Seam:

```
private static final Log log = LogFactory.getLog(CreateOrderAction.class);
public Order createOrder(User user, Product product, int quantity) {
  if (log.isDebugEnabled()) {
         log.debug("Creating new order for user: " + user.username() +
         " product: " + product.name()
         + " quantity: " + quantity);
  }
  return new Order(user, product, quantity);
}
```

In the preceding code snippet, the `log.isdebugEnabled()` method is verified, because string concatenation is preformed inside the `debug()` method. To overcome this problem, Seam provides a logging API that simplifies the code for implementing logging. The following code snippet shows the use of the logging API:

```
@Logger private Log log;
public Order createOrder(User user, Product product, int quantity) {
log.debug("Creating new order for user: #0 product: #1 quantity: #2", user.username(),
product.name(), return new Order(user, product, quantity);
}
```

In the preceding code snippet, the `log` variable is not static, but it should be declared static for entity bean components. Moreover, in the preceding code snippet, we do not need to provide the `log.isDebugEnabled()` method as we do not need to explicitly specify the log category when the Seam component is injected.

NOTE

If log4.jar is set in the classpath environment variable, Seam uses it for logging; else it uses JDK logging.

Now, let's discuss business process management (BPM) and page flow of Seam framework, which allow you to create business processes.

Implementing BPM and Page Flow in Seam

A business process is a well defined group of tasks that need to be performed by the users or applications. jBPM is integrated with the Seam application to create and implement business processes. jBPM is a business process management engine for the Java environments. BPM is the process to manage the set of tasks in a business process. jBPM also supports the Java Standard Edition (SE) and the Enterprise Edition (EE) environments to create and implement business processes.

jBPM provides well-defined rules specifying who can perform a task, and when it should be performed. It represents the tasks of a business process as nodes of a Seam application. The nodes represent the wait states, decisions, tasks, and Web pages. jBPM is introduced in the Seam framework for the following two reasons:

- Defining page flow by using jPDL, which allows you to define a single user interaction and a single jPDL process for single conversation. Therefore, a Seam conversation is referred to be a short running interaction for a single user.
- Providing facilities to manage multiple user tasks and conversations.

NOTE

jPDL is an extendable language that is used to design long range Seam applications and define the page flow of the Seam applications.

The Seam framework stores the associated business process tasks in the BUSINESS_PROCESS context. The states of the tasks are persisted by the jBPM variables. The business process definition of the Seam framework looks similar to the page flow definition, except the <page> nodes. In case of business process definition, we use the <task-node> as the node of a task, as shown in the following code snippet:

```
<process-definition name="todo">

   <start-state name="start">
         <transition to="todo"/>
   </start-state>

   <task-node name="todo">
         <task name="todo" description="#{todoList.description}">
                <assignment view-id="#{view.id}"/>
         </task>
         <transition to="done"/>
   </task-node>

   <end-state name="done"/>

</process-definition>
```

You can use the jPDL business process definition along with the jPDL pageflow definition in the same component. The similarity between these two definitions is that a single <task> element in a business process corresponds to the page flow in the <pageflow-definition> tag.

Depending on the work flow and task management of the Seam application, the page flow can be categorized into the following three different groups:

- Stateless navigation model
- Stateful navigation model
- jPDL Pageflows

Let's discuss these in detail.

Stateless Navigation Model

The stateless navigation model defines a mapping of a set of logical outcome of events with the resources of a Seam application. The logical outcomes of the events are represented in a view page. The navigation rules for a Web page depend on the source of the event, i.e. from where the event has been generated. The stateless navigation model can be represented by using the JSF navigation rules or Seam navigation rules. For example, suppose we have a page named Guess.jsp in a Seam application. In case of a successful event, the view page is forwarded to the success.jsp page. In case of a failure event, the failure.jsp file is displayed. The JSF navigation rules for this example are shown in the following code snippet:

```
<navigation-rule>
   < from-view-id>/Guess.jsp</from-view-id >
   <navigation-case>
         <from-outcome>guess</from-outcome>
         <to-view-id>/Guess.jsp</to-view-id>
         <redirect/>
   </navigation-case>
   <navigation-case>
         <from-outcome>success</from-outcome>
         <to-view-id>/success.jsp</to-view-id>
         <redirect/>
   </navigation-case>
   <navigation-case>
         <from-outcome>failure</from-outcome>
         <to-view-id>/ failure.jsp</to-view-id>
         <redirect/>
   </navigation-case>
</navigation-rule>
```

The stateless navigation model can be represented by using the Seam navigational rules as well, as shown in the following code snippet:

```
<page view-id="/Guess.jsp">
   <navigation>
         <rule if-outcome="guess">
               <redirect view-id="/Guess.jsp"/>
         </rule>
         <rule if-outcome="success">
               <redirect view-id="/success.jsp"/>
         </rule>
         <rule if-outcome="failure">
               <redirect view-id="/failure.jsp"/>
         </rule>
   </navigation>
</page>
```

Stateful Navigation Model

The stateful navigation model works on the principle of jPDL. This model defines the flow of the pages of a Seam application by using a set of defined elements, such as <start-page> and <transition>.

To implement stateful navigation, the action listener methods for a particular event are used to define the flow of multiple pages in a Seam application, as shown in the following code snippet:

```
<pageflow-definition name="numberGuess">
   <start-page name="viewGuess" view-id="/Guess.jsp">
   <redirect/>
         <transition name="guess" to="evaluateGuess">
               <action expression="#{Guess.guess}" />
         </transition>
   </start-page>
   <decision name="evaluateGuess" expression="#{Guess.correctGuess}">
         <transition name="true" to="success"/>
         <transition name="false" to="evaluateRemainingGuesses"/>
   </decision>
   <decision name="evaluateRemainingGuesses" expression="#{Guess.lastGuess}">
         <transition name="true" to="failure"/>
```

```
            <transition name="false" to="viewGuess"/>
      </decision>
      <page name="success" view-id="/success.jsp">
            <redirect/>
            <end-conversation />
      </page>
      <page name="failure" view-id="/failure.jsp">
            <redirect/>
            <end-conversation />
      </page>
  </pageflow-definition>
```

Using jPDL Pageflows

The installation of the jBPM components specifies the position of the jPDL pageflows in an application. The Seam configuration for the pageflows can be stored within the components.xml file of a Seam application. The specification of the pageflows within the components.xml file is shown in the following code snippet:

```
  <core:jbpm>
      <core:pageflow-definitions>
            <value>pageflow.jpdl.xml</value>
      </core:pageflow-definitions>
  </core:jbpm>
```

In the preceding code snippet, the <core> element installs the jBPM component; whereas, the <value> element, which contains the pageflow.jpdl.xml file, specifies the jPDL based pageflow definition.

After installing the required components, you need to start the jPDL pageflows. The jPDL pageflows are initiated by providing the name of the process definitions along with the @Begin, @BeginTask, or @StartTask annotations. The following code snippet shows how to start a jPDL pageflow by using the @Begin annotation:

```
  @Begin(pageflow="guess")

  public void begin() { ... }
```

The pageflows can be started by using the pages.xml file as well, as shown in the following code snippet:

```
  <page>
      <begin-conversation pageflow="guess"/>
  </page>
```

If the pageflow is started by using the @Create annotation or during the RENDER-RESPONSE phase, you need to use the <start-page> element in the pages.xml file as the starting node of the pageflow. If the pageflow is started by the invocation of the action listener, the <start-state> element is specified as the starting node of the particular pageflow. The following code snippet demonstrates the use of the starting nodes within a pageflow:

```
  <pageflow-definition name="viewEditRecord">
      <start-state name="start">
            <transition name="RecordFound" to="displayRecord"/>
            <transition name="RecordNotFound" to="notFound"/>
      </start-state>

      <page name="displayRecord" view-id="/Record.jsp">
            <transition name="edit" to="editRecord"/>
            <transition name="done" to="main"/>
      </page>
      ...

      <page name="notFound" view-id="/404.jsp">
            <end-conversation/>
      </page>

  </pageflow-definition>
```

Each page node defined in the pages.xml file is used to define a state of the pageflow. The state is meant to accept input from the user. The view-id element is used in this file to represent the JSF view-id. The transition name specifies the JSF outcome, which is triggered by the action event listener.

The pageflow can be controlled by using the <decision> elements. The name of the control structure is given in the <decision> element, and the value for the <decision> element is given in the <expression> element. The decision is made by evaluating JSF Expression Language (EL) expressions within the Seam contexts.

After the successful completion of the pageflow, the associated conversation needs to be terminated by the Seam framework. The conversation can be terminated by using the `<end-conversation>` element or by specifying the `@End` annotation in the pages.xml file, as shown in the following code snippet:

```
<page name="success" view-id="/success.jsp">
   <redirect/>
   <end-conversation/>
</page>
```

You can also end a conversation by specifying the jBPM transition name in the `pages.xml` file, as shown in the following code snippet:

```
<page name="success" view-id="/success.jsp">
   <redirect/>
   <end-task transition="success"/>
</page>
```

Let's now learn how to configure the Seam framework to develop Seam applications.

Configuring JBoss Seam

Prior to the configuration of JBoss Seam, you need to download the compressed version of JBoss Seam framework and decompress its Seam API. It can be downloaded as a gun-zipped Tape ARchive (TAR) file or as a ZIP file from the http://www.seamframework.org/Seam3/Downloads Uniform Resource Locator (URL).

NOTE

The JBoss Seam (jboss-seam-3.1.0) is used in this chapter to develop Seam applications.

A large number of configurations are possible with the Seam framework, which contains many external library files associated with it. You only need the jboss-seam-ui.jar and jboss-seam.jar files to compile the source code of a Seam application.

A Seam application generally uses JSF to create a view. You need to define the JSF support to create the view within the <servlet element> element, as shown in the following code snippet:

```
<servlet>
   <servlet-name>Faces Servlet</servlet-name>
   <servlet-class>javax.faces.webapp.FacesServlet</servlet-class>
   <load-on-startup>1</load-on-startup>
</servlet>


<servlet-mapping>
   <servlet-name>Faces Servlet</servlet-name>
   <url-pattern>*.Seam</url-pattern>
</servlet-mapping>
```

In addition, you also need to specify the following code snippet in the web.xml file to support event handling:

```
<listener>
   <listener-class>org.jboss.seam.servlet.SeamListener</listener-class>
</listener>
```

In the preceding code snippet, the listener is responsible for destroying the session and application contexts, and loading the Seam application.

NOTE

If you face a problem with conversation propagation during form submission, then the following mapping in web.xml, switches you to the client side state:

```
<context-param>
    <param-name>javax.faces.STATE_SAVING_METHOD</param-name>
    <param-value>client</param-value>
</context-param>
```

Configuring JSF in Seam

The Seam framework allows you to configure JSF to develop view components of an application. To use JSF with Seam, you need to configure the following resources:

- Facelets
- Seam Resource Servlet
- Seam Servlet Filters

Let's discuss these configurations in detail.

Configuring Facelets

Facelets are viewhandlers that are used with JSF pages having no JSP code. The facelets do not need any Tag Library Descriptor (TLD) file or tag classes to define a UI component and is faster than using JSF. When you want to use facelets instead of JSF, the following code snippet needs to be added in the faces-config.xml file:

```
<application>
    <view-handler>com.sun.facelets.FaceletViewHandler</view-handler>
</application>
```

You need to provide the <context-param> element to call the .xhtml page in the web.xml file at the time of running the default.xhtml page, as shown in the following code snippet:

```
<context-param>
    <param-name>javax.faces.DEFAULT_SUFFIX</param-name>
    <param-value>.xhtml</param-value>
</context-param>
```

Configuring Seam Resource Servlet

The Seam Resource Servlet represents the servlet provided with Seam to access various runtime resources, such as a view required by Seam components. This servlet provides resources, such as a view that is required for security and JSF UI controls. You need to add the following code snippet in the web.xml file to configure the Seam Resource Servlet:

```
<servlet>
    <servlet-name>Seam Resource Servlet</servlet-name>
    <servlet-class>org.jboss.seam.servlet.SeamResourceServlet</servlet-class>
</servlet>

<servlet-mapping>
    <servlet-name>Seam Resource Servlet</servlet-name>
    <url-pattern>/seam/resource/*</url-pattern>
</servlet-mapping>
```

Configuring Seam Servlet Filters

Seam provides a facility to add and configure servlet filters in Seam components. The SeamFilter class is used to support servlet filter to perform the filter operation. The following code snippet shows how to use Seam servlet filters to filter and compress data:

```
<filter>
    <filter-name>Seam Filter</filter-name>
    <filter-class>org.jboss.seam.servlet.SeamFilter</filter-class>
</filter>
```

```
<filter-mapping>
   <filter-name>Seam Filter</filter-name>
   <url-pattern>/*</url-pattern>
</filter-mapping>
```

Let's now learn how to configure Seam with EJB 3.

Configuring EJB components in Seam

To integrate EJB with the Seam framework, you need the ejb-jar.xml file. The SeamInterceptor is configured in the ejb-jar.xml file and is used to perform all session beans of the Seam application. The following code snippet shows how to integrate the Seam framework with EJB:

```
<interceptors>
   <interceptor>
   <interceptor-class>org.jboss.seam.ejb.SeamInterceptor</interceptor-class>
   </interceptor>
   </interceptors>

   <assembly-descriptor>
   <interceptor-binding>
   <ejb-name>*</ejb-name>
   <interceptor-class>org.jboss.seam.ejb.SeamInterceptor</interceptor-class>
   </interceptor-binding>
</assembly-descriptor>
```

The Seam components also need to provide the JNDI within the EJB specification so that they can be looked up with their JNDI names. The `@JndiName` annotation is used to work with session beans. This is due to the fact that no standard mapping is specified in the EJB specification. Therefore, you must include the JNDI specification in the components.xml file. The following code snippet shows the use of JNDI with the EJB specification:

```
<core:init jndi-name="myEarName/#{ejbName}/local" /> // inside the context of an EAR

<core:init jndi-name="#{ejbName}/local" />    // outside the context of an EAR
```

The seam.properties file must be placed within the META-INF/seam.properties or META-INF/components.xml file. If you include the Seam components within the WAR files, you must add the seam.properties file in the WEB-INF/classes directory.

Let's now move ahead and learn to create a Seam application.

Creating a Jboss Seam Application

You can also integrate some other technologies, such as Hibernate, Spring, and AJAX, with Seam to provide persistence, Object Relational Mapping (ORM), POJO, and other services to a Seam application. We explore the integration of these technologies, as well as EJB and JSF, with Seam by developing a Seam application, UserLogin. To develop the UserLogin Seam application, you need to perform the following tasks:

- ❑ Create an EJB component
- ❑ Create Views
- ❑ Create Resources
- ❑ Package and deploy the Seam application
- ❑ Run the application

Let's discuss these tasks, one by one.

Creating an EJB Component

The EJB component contains the business logic, datasource, and persistence services of the UserLogin application. All EJB components must be stored under the `src` directory of the `UserLogin` Seam application.

The following files are required to create the EJB component of the UserLogin Seam application:

- User.java
- AuthenticatorAction.java
- RegisterAction.java

Let's discuss these files one by one.

The User.java File

The User.java file is an entity bean that contains the data model of the UserLogin Seam application. It also contains username, password, and the name property used to handle user requests. The @Entity annotation is used to create an entity bean. Listing 16.1 shows the code for the User.java file (save the User.java file in the \UserLogin\src\com\kogent\seam folder):

Listing 16.1: Displaying the Code for the User.java File

```
package com.kogent.seam;

import static org.jboss.seam.ScopeType.SESSION;

import java.io.Serializable;

import javax.persistence.Entity;
import javax.persistence.Id;
import javax.persistence.Table;

import org.hibernate.validator.Length;
import org.hibernate.validator.NotNull;
import org.hibernate.validator.Pattern;
import org.jboss.seam.annotations.Name;
import org.jboss.seam.annotations.Scope;

@Entity
@Name("user")
@Scope(SESSION)
@Table(name="Customer")
public class User implements Serializable
{
  private String username;
  private String password;
  private String name;

  public User(String name, String password, String username)
  {
        this.name = name;
        this.password = password;
        this.username = username;
  }

  public User() {}

  @NotNull
  @Length(max=100)
  public String getName()
  {
        return name;
  }
  public void setName(String name)
  {
        this.name = name;
```

```
    }

    @NotNull
    @Length(min=5, max=15)
    public String getPassword()
    {
          return password;
    }
    public void setPassword(String password)
    {
          this.password = password;
    }

    @Id
    @Length(min=5, max=15)
    @Pattern(regex="^\\w*$", message="not a valid username")
    public String getUsername()
    {
          return username;
    }
    public void setUsername(String username)
    {
          this.username = username;
    }
    @Override
    public String toString()
    {
          return "User(" + username + ")";
    }
}
```

The AuthenticatorAction.java File

The AuthenticatorAction.java file is used to verify whether or not the user is an authenticated user. The `@Name("authenticator")` annotation is used to identify the method, authenticate(), which must be used to authenticate a user. The `authenticate()` method returns a boolean value, which indicates whether or not the authentication is successful. The username and password can be obtained from the `identity.username` and `identity.password` fields.

Listing 16.2 shows the code for the AuthenticatorAction.java file (save the AuthenticatorAction.java file in the \UserLogin\src\com\kogent\seam folder):

Listing 16.2: Displaying the Code for the AuthenticatorAction.java File

```
package com.kogent.seam;

import static org.jboss.seam.ScopeType.SESSION;

import java.util.List;

import javax.persistence.EntityManager;

import org.jboss.seam.annotations.In;
import org.jboss.seam.annotations.Name;
import org.jboss.seam.annotations.Out;

@Name("authenticator")
public class AuthenticatorAction
{
  @In EntityManager em;
```

```
    @Out(required=false  scope = SESSION)
    private User user;

    public boolean authenticate()
    {
  List results = em.createQuery("select u from User u where u.username=#{identity.username}
  and u.password=#{identity.password}").getResultList();

         if ( results.size()==0 )
         {
              return false;
         }
         else
         {
              user = (User) results.get(0);
              return true;
         }
    }
}
```

The RegisterAction.java File

The RegisterAction.java file is used to verify the username and password of a user. If the username and password match the session's username and password, the main.xhtml page is displayed. The @In annotation is used to inject the context variable or attribute of the bean of the `UserLogin` Seam application. The EntityManager API uses the register() action listener method and interacts with a database to return a valid JSF outcome.

Listing 16.3 shows the code for the RegisterAction.java file (save the RegisterAction.java file in the \UserLogin\src\com\kogent\seam folder):

Listing 16.3: Displaying the Code for the RegisterAction.java File

```
package com.kogent.seam;

import static org.jboss.seam.ScopeType.EVENT;
import java.util.List;
import javax.persistence.EntityManager;
import org.jboss.seam.annotations.In;
import org.jboss.seam.annotations.Name;
import org.jboss.seam.annotations.Scope;
import org.jboss.seam.faces.FacesMessages;

@Scope(EVENT)
@Name("register")
public class RegisterAction
{

   @In
   private User user;

   @In
   private EntityManager em;

   @In
   private FacesMessages facesMessages;

   private String verify;

   private boolean registered;

   public void register()
   {
        if ( user.getPassword().equals(verify) )
```

```
            {
    List existing = em.createQuery("select u.username from User u where
    u.username=#{user.username}").getResultList();
                    if (existing.size()==0)
                    {
                            em.persist(user);
    facesMessages.add("Successfully registered as #{user.username}");
                            registered = true;
                    }
                    else
                    {
    facesMessages.addToControl("username", "Username #{user.username} already exists");
                    }
            }
            else
            {
                    facesMessages.add("verify", "Re-enter your password");
                    verify=null;
            }
        }
        public void invalid()
        {
            facesMessages.add("Please try again");
        }

        public boolean isRegistered()
        {
            return registered;
        }

        public String getVerify()
        {
            return verify;
        }

        public void setVerify(String verify)
        {
            this.verify = verify;
        }
    }
```

After developing the EJB components, you need to create the view components to interact with EJB components.

Creating Views

In this application, let's use the JSF framework to develop the view pages. All views must be under the view directory of the UserLogin Seam application. The following views are required for developing the `UserLogin` Seam application:

- index.xhtml
- home.xhtml
- main.xhtml
- register.xhtml
- conversations.xhtml
- template.xhtml

Let's create these views one by one.

The index.xhtml View

The index.xhtml view is used to forward a request to the home.xhtml view. The forwarding of request is done through the `<url-pattern>` mapping specified in the web.xml file.

Listing 16.4 shows the code for the index.xhtml view (save the index.xhtml file in the \UserLogin\view folder):

Listing 16.4: Displaying the Code for the index.xhtml File

```
<html>
  <head>
        <meta http-equiv="Refresh" content="0; URL=home.seam">
  </head>
</html>
```

The home.xhtml View

The home.xhtml view displays the home page of the `UserLogin` Seam application. This view contains two textboxes, username and password, and one submit button. Listing 16.5 shows the code for the home.xhtml view (save the home.xhtml file in the \UserLogin\view folder):

Listing 16.5: Displaying the Code for the home.xhtml File

```
    <!DOCTYPE html PUBLIC "-//W3C//DTD XHTML 1.0 Transitional//EN"
"http://www.w3.org/TR/xhtml1/DTD/xhtml1-transitional.dtd">
    <html xmlns="http://www.w3.org/1999/xhtml"
      xmlns:h="http://xmlns.jcp.org/jsf/html"
      xmlns:f="http://xmlns.jcp.org/jsf/core"
      xmlns:s="http://jboss.com/products/seam/taglib">
      <head>
            <title>home</title>
      </head>
      <h1>User Login </h1>
      <body id="pgHome">
            <f:view>
                    <div id="document">
                    <div id="container">
                    <div id="sidebar">
                    <h:form id="login">
                    <fieldset>
                    <div>
                    <h:outputLabel for="username">Login Name:       </h:outputLabel>
                    <h:inputText id="username"
                    value="#{identity.username}" style="width: 175px;"/>
                    <div class="errors"><h:message for="username"/></div>
                    </div>
                    <div>
                    <h:outputLabel for="password">Password :</h:outputLabel>
                    <h:inputSecret id="password"
                    value="#{identity.password}" style="width: 175px;"/>
                    </div>
                    <div class="errors"><h:messages globalOnly="true"/></div>
                    <div class="buttonBox"><h:commandButton id="login"
                    action="#{identity.login}" value="User Login"/></div>
                    <div class="notes"><s:link id="register"
                    view="/register.xhtml" value="Register New User"/></div>
                    </fieldset>
                    </h:form>
                    </div>
                    </div>
                    </div>
          </f:view>
    </body>
  </html>
```

The main.xhtml View

The main.xhtml view is used to display the successful login information when a user has successfully logged on to the application. The main.xhtml view uses the template.xhtml file to add images and template text. Listing 16.6 shows the main.xhtml view (save the main.xhtml file in the \UserLogin\view folder):

Listing 16.6: Displaying the Code for the main.xhtml File

```
    <!DOCTYPE composition PUBLIC "-//W3C//DTD XHTML 1.0 Transitional//EN"
"http://www.w3.org/TR/xhtml1/DTD/xhtml1-transitional.dtd">
    <ui:composition xmlns="http://www.w3.org/1999/xhtml"
      xmlns:ui="http://xmlns.jcp.org/jsf/facelets"
      xmlns:h="http://xmlns.jcp.org/jsf/html"
      xmlns:f="http://xmlns.jcp.org/jsf/core"
      xmlns:s="http://jboss.com/products/seam/taglib"
      xmlns:a="https://ajax4jsf.dev.java.net/ajax"
      template="template.xhtml">

      <!-- content -->
            <ui:define name="content">

            <div class="section">
                   <h:form id="main">

                                 <span class="errors">
                                        <h:messages globalOnly="true"/>
                                 </span>
      </h:form>
            </div>

      </ui:define>
    </ui:composition>
```

The register.xhtml View

The register.xhtml view is used to register a new user. This view contains various textboxes, such as username, name, password, and verify. If any text box is left blank, the view displays a validation error. Listing 16.7 shows the code for the register.xhtml view (save the register.xhtml file in the \UserLogin\view folder):

Listing 16.7: Displaying the Code for the register.xhtml File

```
    <!DOCTYPE html PUBLIC "-//W3C//DTD XHTML 1.0 Transitional//EN"
      "http://www.w3.org/TR/xhtml1/DTD/xhtml1-transitional.dtd">
    <html xmlns="http://www.w3.org/1999/xhtml"
      xmlns:h="http://xmlns.jcp.org/jsf/html"
      xmlns:f="http://xmlns.jcp.org/jsf/core"
      xmlns:s="http://jboss.com/products/seam/taglib"
      xmlns:a="https://ajax4jsf.dev.java.net/ajax">
      <head>
            <title>Registration Page</title>
      </head>
      <body id="pgHome">
            <div id="document">

                   <div id="container">

                   <div id="content">
                   <div class="section">
                   <h1>
                          Register
                   </h1>
                   </div>
                   <div class="section">

                   <h:form id="register">
                   <fieldset>

                   <s:validateAll>

                   <f:facet name="aroundInvalidField">
                   <s:span styleClass="errors" />
                   </f:facet>
```

```
<f:facet name="afterInvalidField">
<s:div styleClass="errors">
<s:message />
</s:div>
</f:facet>

<div class="entry">
<div class="label">
<h:outputLabel for="username">Username:</h:outputLabel>
</div>
<div class="input">
<s:decorate id="usernameDecorate">
<h:inputText id="username" value="#{user.username}"
required="true">
<a:support event="onblur" reRender="usernameDecorate" />
</h:inputText>
</s:decorate>
</div>
</div>

<div class="entry">
<div class="label">
<h:outputLabel for="name">Real Name:</h:outputLabel>
</div>
<div class="input">
<s:decorate id="nameDecorate">
<h:inputText id="name" value="#{user.name}" required="true">
<a:support event="onblur" reRender="nameDecorate" />
</h:inputText>
</s:decorate>
</div>
</div>

<div class="entry">
<div class="label">
<h:outputLabel for="password">Password:</h:outputLabel>
</div>
<div class="input">
<s:decorate>
<h:inputSecret id="password" value="#{user.password}"
required="true" />
</s:decorate>
</div>
</div>

<div class="entry">
<div class="label">
<h:outputLabel for="verify">Verify Password:</h:outputLabel>
</div>
<div class="input">
<s:decorate>
<h:inputSecret id="verify" value="#{register.verify}"
required="true" />
</s:decorate>
</div>
</div>

</s:validateAll>
```

```
                <div class="entry errors">
                <h:messages globalOnly="true" />
                </div>

                <div class="entry">
                <div class="label">
                 
                </div>
                <div class="input">
                <h:commandButton id="register" value="Register"
                action="#{register.register}" />
                 
                <s:button id="cancel" value="Cancel" view="/home.xhtml" />
                </div>
                </div>

                </fieldset>
                </h:form>

                </div>
                </div>
                </div>

        </div>
    </body>
</html>
```

The conversations.xhtml View

The conversations.xhtml view is used to maintain a list of concurrent conversations in the current user session. The concurrent conversations for the current user session is maintained in a component named `#{conversationList}`. You can iterate a list of current information of a user, such as description of the conversations, their starting time, and the time the conversation was last used.

Listing 16.8 shows the code for the conversations.xhtml view (save the conversations.xhtml file in the \UserLogin\view folder):

Listing 16.8: Displaying the Code for the conversations.xhtml File

```
<div xmlns="http://www.w3.org/1999/xhtml"
  xmlns:h="http://xmlns.jcp.org/jsf/html"
  xmlns:s="http://jboss.com/products/seam/taglib">

  <div class="section">
<h1><h:outputText rendered="#{not empty conversationList}" value="Workspaces"/></h1>
  </div>

  <div class="section">
      <h:form>
            <h:dataTable value="#{conversationList}" var="entry">
                  <h:column>
<h:commandLink action="#{entry.select}" value="#{entry.description}"/>
                         
<h:outputText value="[current]" rendered="#{entry.current}"/>
                  </h:column>
                  <h:column>
                        <h:outputText value="#{entry.startDatetime}">
<s:convertDateTime type="time" pattern="hh:mm"/>
                        </h:outputText>
                        -
                        <h:outputText value="#{entry.lastDatetime}">
<s:convertDateTime type="time" pattern="hh:mm"/>
                        </h:outputText>
```

```
                    </h:column>
                </h:dataTable>
            </h:form>
        </div>

    </div>
```

The template.xhtml View

The template.xhtml view is used as a template page to create other pages, such as main.xhtml. The purpose of this page is to add extra information, such as an image and a cascade style sheet, on a specified page. Listing 16.9 shows the code for the template.xhtml view (save the template.xhtml file in the \UserLogin\view folder):

Listing 16.9: Displaying the Code for the template.xhtml File

```
    <!DOCTYPE html PUBLIC "-//W3C//DTD XHTML 1.0 Transitional//EN"
"http://www.w3.org/TR/xhtml1/DTD/xhtml1-transitional.dtd">
    <html xmlns="http://www.w3.org/1999/xhtml"
      xmlns:ui="http://xmlns.jcp.org/jsf/facelets"
      xmlns:h="http://xmlns.jcp.org/jsf/html">
      <head>
            <title>Successful login page</title>
      </head>
      <body>

            <div id="document">
            <div id="header">
            <div id="status">
            You have successfully login as #{user.name}
            | <s:link id="logout" action="#{identity.logout}" value="Logout"/>
            </div>
            </div>
            <div id="container">
                    <div id="sidebar">
                    <ui:insert name="sidebar"/>
            </div>
            <div id="content">
                    <ui:insert name="content"/>
                    <ui:include src="conversations.xhtml" />
            </div>
            </div>

            </div>
      </body>
    </html>
```

Creating Resources

In an application, various resources, such as name of the database and entity manager need to be configured. These resources are configured in various resources files, such as components.xml, pages.xml, and persistence.xml. These files are stored in the resources directory of an application. In the UserLogin Seam application, the JSF and EJB 3 technologies are used with the Seam framework; therefore, you need to configure these technologies while deploying the UserLogin Seam application. For example, you need the pages.xml file to configure the JSF framework, and the persistence.xml file to configure Java persistency. All these files must exist in the resources directory of the UserLogin Seam application. To deploy the `UserLogin` Seam application, you need to create the following configuration files:

- components.xml
- web.xml
- pages.xml
- persistence.xml
- jboss-web.xml

Let's create these configuration files one by one.

The components.xml File

The components.xml file is stored in the resources directory of the WAR file. It is used to declare and configure the application component and various Seam runtime services, such as jBPM, pageflow, and security. Listing 16.10 shows the code for the components.xml file (save the components.xml file in the \UserLogin\resources folder):

Listing 16.10: Displaying the Code for the components.xml File

```
<?xml version="1.0" encoding="UTF-8"?>
<components xmlns="http://jboss.com/products/seam/components"
  xmlns:core="http://jboss.com/products/seam/core"
  xmlns:persistence="http://jboss.com/products/seam/persistence"
  xmlns:transaction="http://jboss.com/products/seam/transaction"
  xmlns:security="http://jboss.com/products/seam/security"
  xmlns:xsi="http://www.w3.org/2001/XMLSchema-instance"
  xsi:schemaLocation=
"http://jboss.com/products/seam/core http://jboss.com/products/seam/core-2.0.xsd
http://jboss.com/products/seam/persistence http://jboss.com/products/seam/persistence-
2.0.xsd
http://jboss.com/products/seam/security http://jboss.com/products/seam/security-2.0.xsd
http://jboss.com/products/seam/components http://jboss.com/products/seam/components-
2.0.xsd">
  <core:manager conversation-timeout="120000"
  concurrent-request-timeout="500"
  conversation-id-parameter="cid"/>

  <!-- <transaction:entity-transaction entity-manager="#{em}"/>  -->

  <persistence:entity-manager-factory name="bookingDatabase"/>

  <persistence:managed-persistence-context name="em"
  auto-create="true"
  entity-manager-factory="#{bookingDatabase}"/>

  <security:identity authenticate-method="#{authenticator.authenticate}"/>

</components>
```

The web.xml File

The web.xml file is used to configure the UserLogin Seam application as well as the Seam and JSF frameworks. It is also used to configure a servlet and Seam listener. Listing 16.11 shows the code for the web.xml file (save the web.xml file in the \UserLogin\resources folder):

Listing 16.11: Displaying the Code for the web.xml File

```
<?xml version="1.0" encoding="UTF-8"?>
<web-app>

  <context-param>
        <param-name>org.ajax4jsf.VIEW_HANDLERS</param-name>
        <param-value>com.sun.facelets.FaceletViewHandler</param-value>
  </context-param>

  <!-- Seam -->

<listener>
        <listener-class>org.jboss.seam.servlet.SeamListener</listener-class>
  </listener>

  <filter>
        <filter-name>Seam Filter</filter-name>
        <filter-class>org.jboss.seam.servlet.SeamFilter</filter-class>
  </filter>

  <filter-mapping>
```

```
        <filter-name>Seam Filter</filter-name>
        <url-pattern>/*</url-pattern>
    </filter-mapping>

    <servlet>
        <servlet-name>Seam Resource Servlet</servlet-name>
        <servlet-class>org.jboss.seam.servlet.ResourceServlet
        </servlet-class>
    </servlet>

    <servlet-mapping>
        <servlet-name>Seam Resource Servlet</servlet-name>
        <url-pattern>/seam/resources/*</url-pattern>
    </servlet-mapping>

    <!-- Faces Servlet -->

    <servlet>
        <servlet-name>Faces Servlet</servlet-name>
        <servlet-class>javax.faces.webapp.FacesServlet</servlet-class>
        <load-on-startup>1</load-on-startup>
    </servlet>

    <servlet-mapping>
        <servlet-name>Faces Servlet</servlet-name>
        <url-pattern>*.seam</url-pattern>
    </servlet-mapping>

    <!-- JSF parameters -->

    <context-param>
        <param-name>javax.faces.DEFAULT_SUFFIX</param-name>
        <param-value>.xhtml</param-value>
    </context-param>

    <context-param>
        <param-name>facelets.DEVELOPMENT</param-name>
        <param-value>true</param-value>
    </context-param>
</web-app>
```

The pages.xml File

The pages.xml configuration file is used to configure various properties of the views of the UserLogin Seam application. This file is stored in the WEB-INF directory. It defines action, navigation, and error handling events of the UserLogin application. The `action` attribute is used to invoke the action class before a page is invoked. Listing 16.12 shows the code for the pages.xml file (save the pages.xml file in the \UserLogin\WEB-INF folder):

Listing 16.12: Displaying the Code for the pages.xml File

```
<?xml version="1.0" encoding="UTF-8"?>
<pages xmlns="http://jboss.com/products/seam/pages"
  xmlns:xsi="http://www.w3.org/2001/XMLSchema-instance"
xsi:schemaLocation="http://jboss.com/products/seam/pages
http://jboss.com/products/seam/pages-2.0.xsd"

  no-conversation-view-id="/main.xhtml"
  login-view-id="/home.xhtml">

  <page view-id="/register.xhtml">

        <action if="#{validation.failed}"
        execute="#{register.invalid}"/>
```

```
        <navigation>
                <rule if="#{register.registered}">
                        <redirect view-id="/home.xhtml"/>
                </rule>
        </navigation>

    </page>

    <page view-id="/home.xhtml">

        <navigation>
                <rule if="#{identity.loggedIn}">
                        <redirect view-id="/main.xhtml"/>
                </rule>
        </navigation>

    </page>

    <page view-id="/main.xhtml"
        login-required="true">

        <navigation from-action="#{hotelBooking.selectHotel(hot)}">
                <redirect view-id="/hotel.xhtml"/>
        </navigation>

    </page>

    <page view-id="*">

        <navigation from-action="#{identity.logout}">
                <redirect view-id="/home.xhtml"/>
        </navigation>

        <navigation from-action="#{hotelBooking.cancel}">
                <redirect view-id="/main.xhtml"/>
        </navigation>

    </page>

    <exception class="org.jboss.seam.security.NotLoggedInException">
        <redirect view-id="/home.xhtml">
  <message severity="warn">You must be logged in to use this feature</message>
        </redirect>
    </exception>

  </pages>
```

The persistence.xml File

The persistence.xml file is used to connect to the datasource provided by EJB persistence. This file contains some vendor-specific information, such as persistence-unit and datasource information. Listing 16.13 shows the code for the persistence.xml file (save the persistence.xml file in the \UserLogin\resources folder):

Listing 16.13: Displaying the Code for the persistence.xml File

```
  <?xml version="1.0" encoding="UTF-8"?>
  <persistence xmlns="http://xmlns.jcp.org/xml/ns/persistence"
    xmlns:xsi="http://www.w3.org/2001/XMLSchema-instance"
 xsi:schemaLocation="http://xmlns.jcp.org/xml/ns/persistence

    http://xmlns.jcp.org/xml/ns/persistence/persistence_2_1.xsd"
    version="2.1">
    <persistence-unit name="bookingDatabase" transaction-type="JTA">
    <provider>org.hibernate.ejb.HibernatePersistence</provider>
    <jta-data-source>jdbc/__default</jta-data-source>
    <properties>
        <property name="hibernate.dialect"
```

```
        value="GlassfishDerbyDialect"/>
        <property name="hibernate.hbm2ddl.auto" value="create-drop"/>
        <property name="hibernate.show_sql" value="true"/>
<property name="hibernate.cache.provider_class"
value="org.hibernate.cache.HashtableCacheProvider"/>
<property name="hibernate.transaction.manager_lookup_class"
  value="org.hibernate.transaction.SunONETransactionManagerLookup"/>
        </properties>
   </persistence-unit>
</persistence>
```

The jboss-web.xml File

The jboss-web.xml file is a Deployment Descriptor that specifies how to deploy a WAR application on the JBoss application server. Listing 16.14 shows the jboss-web.xml file (save the jboss-web.xml file in the \UserLogin\resources folder):

Listing 16.14: Displaying the Code for the jboss-web.xml File

```
<jboss-web>

   <class-loading java2ClassLoadingCompliance="false">
        <loader-repository>
                seam.jboss.org:loader=jboss-seam-jpa

<loader-repository-config>java2ParentDelegation=false</loader-repository-config>
        </loader-repository>

   </class-loading>
</jboss-web>
```

You need the `seam.properties` file, which is a blank file, to deploy the `UserLogin` Seam application. You also need to arrange the files created for the `UserLogin` Seam application in the directory structure, as shown in Figure 16.1:

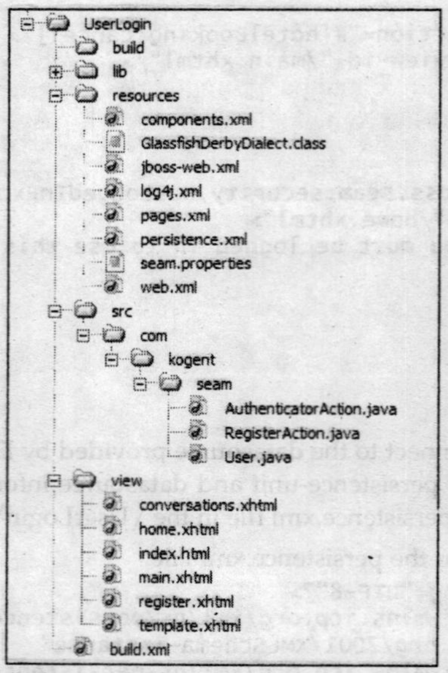

Figure 16.1: Showing the Directory Structure of the UserLogin Seam Application

You need to add various JAR files in the lib folder to compile the UserLogin Seam application. These JAR files are required to provide the functionalities of different frameworks used in the application, such as AJAX and Hibernate. These JAR files are as follows:

- ajax4jsf-1.1.1.jar
- commons-logging.jar

- hibernate-3.6.6.jar
- hibernate-jpa-2.1-api-1.0.0.Final.jar
- hibernate-validator.jar
- jboss-el.jar
- jboss-logging-3.1.3.GA.jar
- jboss-seam-2.1.0.GA.jar
- jboss-seam-debug.jar
- jboss-seam-ui.jar
- jsf-api.jar
- jsf-facelets.jar
- thirdparty-all.jar

Packaging and Deploying the Seam Application

You need the Ant tool to package the `UserLogin` Seam application. Ant is a Java tool used to compile and package Web applications. Ant uses an XML file, build.xml, to compile and package Web applications. You can download the apache-ant-1.9.3-bin.zip file from the Apache website (`http://ant.apache.org/bindownload.cgi`). After downloading the apache-ant-1.9.3-bin.zip file, install the Ant tool in your system and set the path for the `ANT_HOME` environment variable in the class path.

You can deploy a Seam application by using the following servers:

- Glassfish
- JBoss

Let's explore these next.

Using Glassfish

Packaging and deploying the Seam application on the Glassfish Server 4.0 can be done by using the Ant tool. Run the `ant glassfish` command at command prompt to obtain the WAR file of the UserLogin Seam application, For example, type the following command at command prompt from the application directory:

```
ant glassfish
```

Figure 16.2 shows the output of the preceding command:

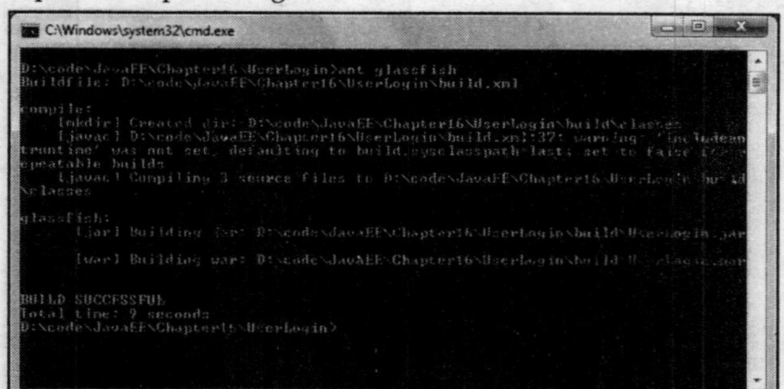

Figure 16.2: Packaging the UserLogin Application on Glassfish

The `ant glassfish` command generates the `UserLogin.war` file, which is stored in the `build` directory of the `UserLogin` Seam application. Now, open the Admin Console of the Glassfish Server 4.0 (`http://localhost:4848/`) and deploy the `UserLogin` Seam application.

Using JBoss

The JBoss application server is a free Java EE certified application server. It can be downloaded from the SourcdForge.net website by clicking the hyperlink of the required version, for example `http://www.jboss.org/jbossas/downloads/` URL for jboss-as-7.1.1.Final.zip. After downloading the

JBoss application server (jboss-as-7.1.1.Final.zip), extract the zip file and install it on the working drive (C:\ drive).

NOTE

The JBoss Seam 3.0 framework supports only JBoss application server 5 or higher version.

After installing the JBoss application server on your system, you need to package and deploy the UserLogin Seam application on it. Prior to the process of packaging and deploying the UserLogin application, you need to ensure that the following code snippet is added to the build.xml file:

```
<!-- JPA and Seam POJO on JBoss AS 7.1.0-->
  <target name="jboss" depends="compile">

    <mkdir dir="${build.jars}"/>

    <jar destfile="${build.jars}/${projname}.jar">
      <fileset dir="${build.classes}">
        <include name="**/*.class"/>
      </fileset>
      <fileset dir="${resources}">
        <include name="seam.properties" />
        <include name="import.sql" />
      </fileset>
      <metainf dir="${resources}">
        <include name="persistence.xml" />
      </metainf>
    </jar>

    <war destfile="${build.jars}/${projname}.war"
         webxml="${resources}/web.xml">

      <webinf dir="${resources}">
        <include name="faces-config.xml" />
        <include name="pages.xml" />

        <include name="jboss-web.xml" />
        <include name="components.xml" />
      </webinf>
      <lib dir="${seamlib}">
        <include name="jboss-seam.jar" />

        <include name="jboss-seam-ui.jar" />
        <include name="jboss-seam-debug.jar" />
      </lib>
      <lib dir="${lib}">

        <include name="jboss-el.jar" />
        <include name="jsf-facelets.jar" />
        <include name="ajax4jsf-*.jar" />

        <!-- needed by ajax4jsf -->
        <include name="commons-digester*.jar" />
        <include name="commons-beanutils*.jar" />

        <include name="oscache*.jar" />
      </lib>
      <lib dir="${build.jars}">

        <include name="${projname}.jar" />
```

```
        </lib>
        <fileset dir="${view}"/>

      </war>
    </target>
```

Run the ant jboss command at command prompt; you will get a WAR file of the `UserLogin` Seam application. For example, type the following command at command prompt:

```
ant jboss
```

After the preceding command is executed, the generated WAR file (UserLogin.war) is saved in the build directory of the UserLogin application.

Next, you need to start the JBoss application server. To start the server, change the working directory to the bin subdirectory, where the JBoss application server is installed, at command prompt. Type the `standalone` command at command prompt to start the JBoss application server. The JBoss application server is started, as shown in Figure 16.3:

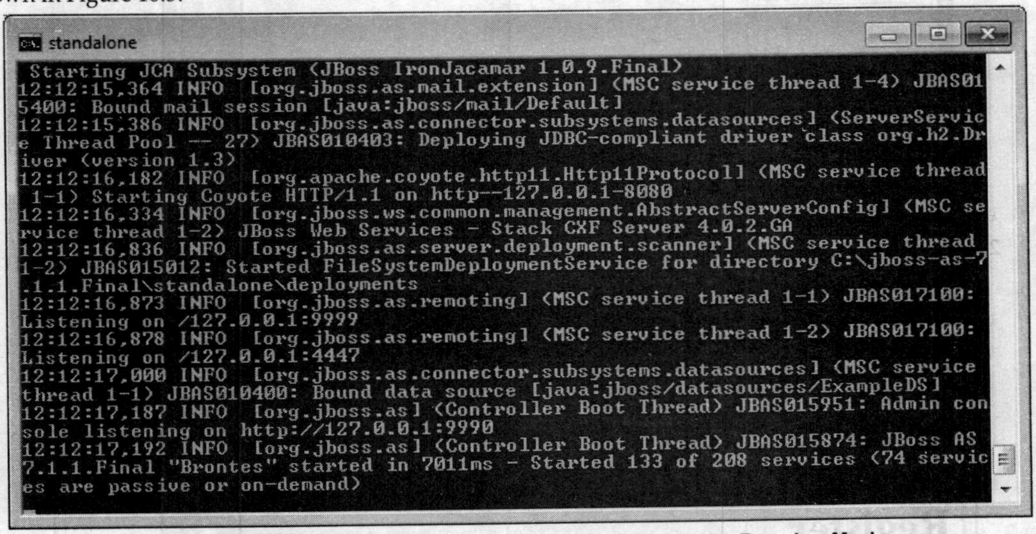

Figure 16.3: Showing the JBoss Application Server in the Running Mode

Now, deploy the `UserLogin` Seam application by copying it from the `\UserLogin\build` directory and pasting it in the `C:\jboss-as-7.1.1.Final\standalone\deployments` directory.

After successfully deploying the `UserLogin` Seam application, you need to run the application.

Running the Application

Perform the following steps to run the UserLogin application deployed on the Glassfish Server 4.0:

- Open the Web browser and type the following URL:

```
http://localhost:8080/UserLogin/
```

The home page of the application appears, as shown in Figure 16.4:

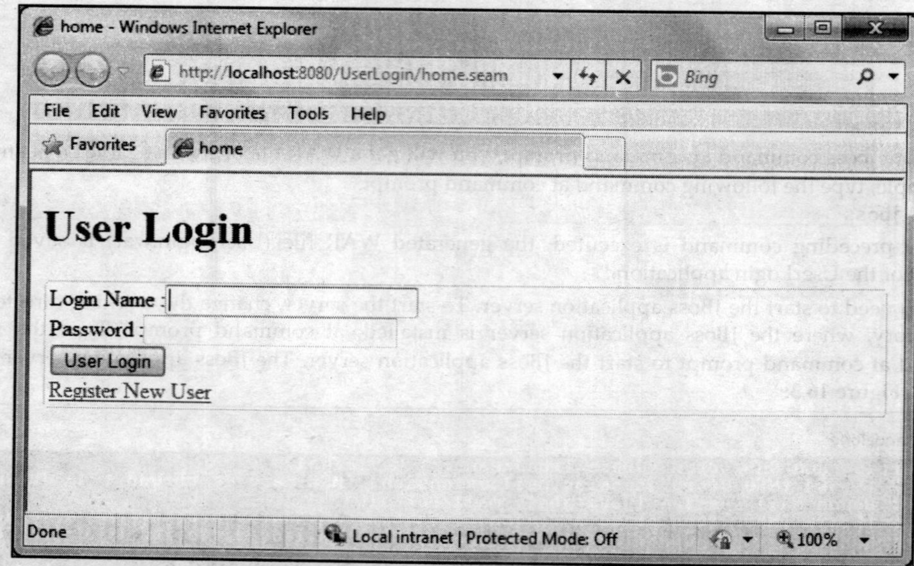

Figure 16.4: Displaying the Home Page Running on Glassfish Server 4.0

1. Click the `Register New User` hyperlink to open the `Register` page.
2. Enter the values in the Username, Real Name, Password, and Verify Password text boxes and click the `Register` button to register a new user, as shown in Figure 16.5:

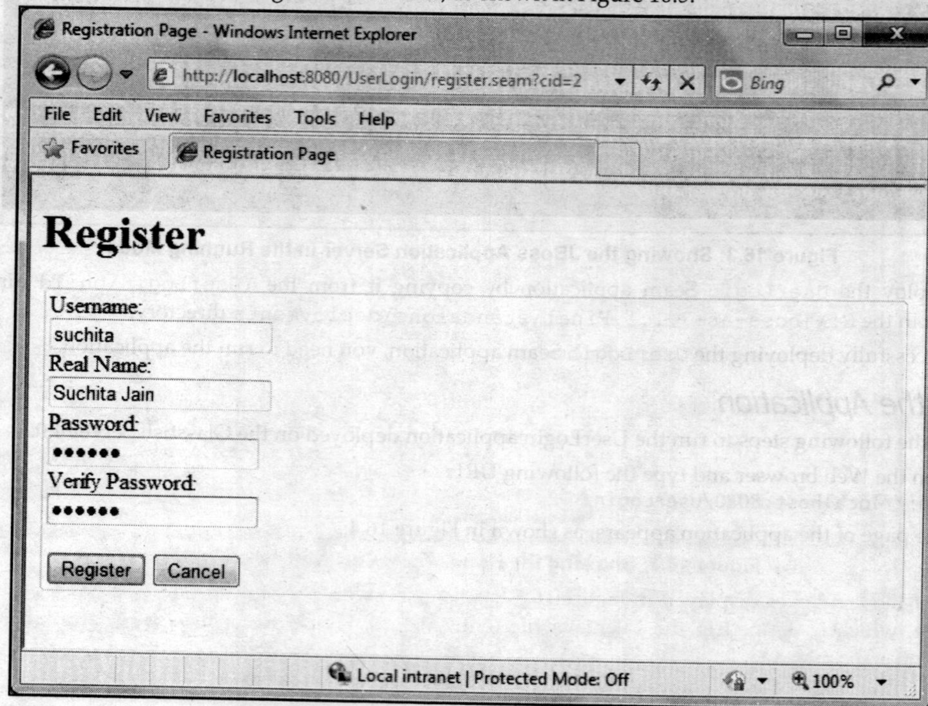

Figure 16.5: Displaying the Registration Page

Figure 16.6 shows the successful registration message:

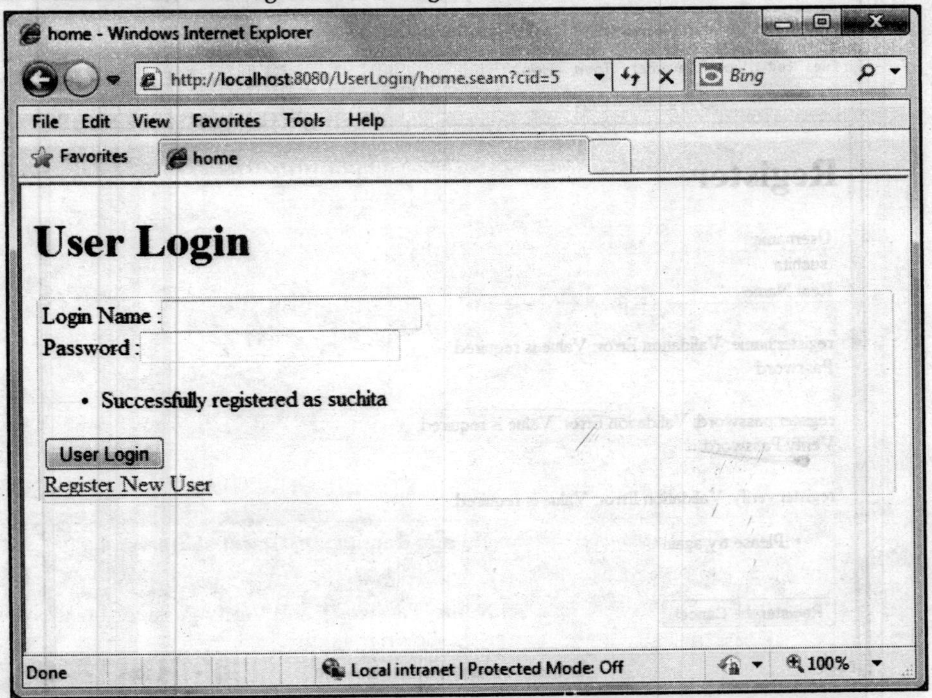

Figure 16.6: Showing the Home Page with a Message on Successful Registration

4. Enter the Login Name as `suchita`, password as `kogent`, and click the `User Login` button. The successful login page with the welcome message appears, as shown in Figure 16.7:

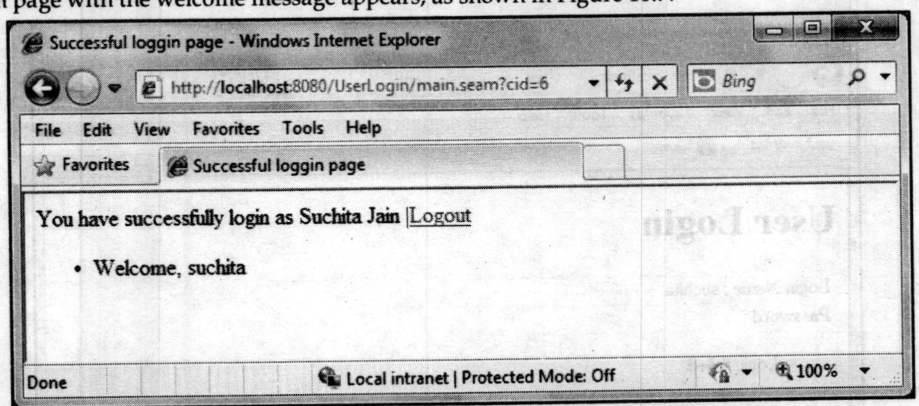

Figure 16.7: Showing the Home Page with Welcome Message

If any of the text boxes displayed in Figure 16.5 has been left blank, the application generates a validation error message, which is defined in the User.java file (entity bean). Figure 16.8 shows a registration page with the validation error message:

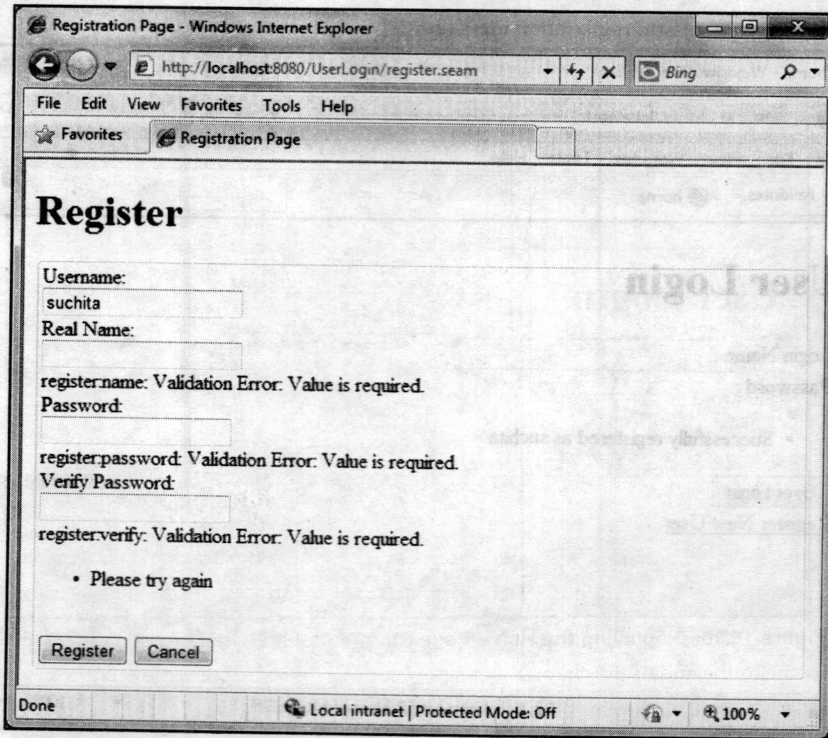

Figure 16.8: Displaying the Registration Page with Validation Error Messages

If you enter an invalid username or password, the application displays the `Login failed` message, as shown in Figure 16.9:

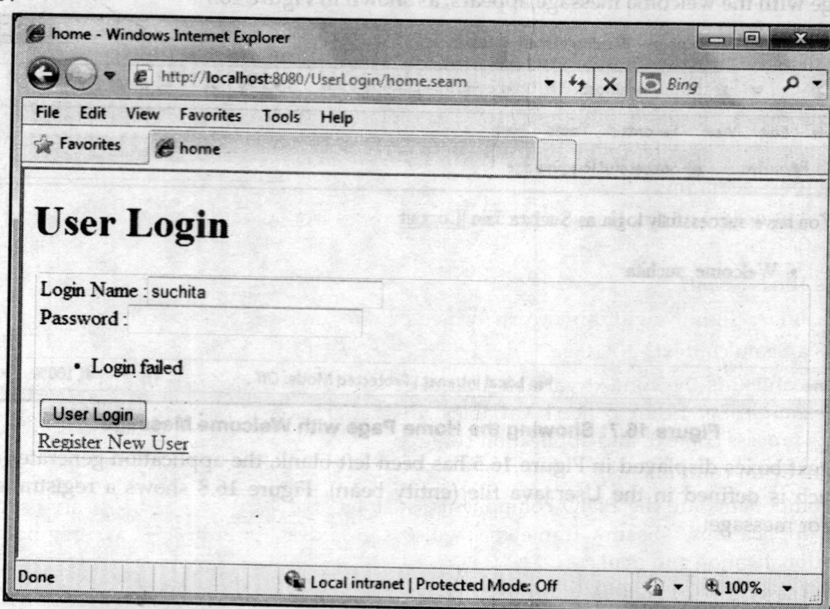

Figure 16.9: Displaying the Home Page with the Login Failed Message

If you have used JBoss to deploy the application, use the following URL to run the application:

```
http://localhost:8080/UserLogin
```

The home page of the UserLogin application appears, as shown in Figure 16.10:

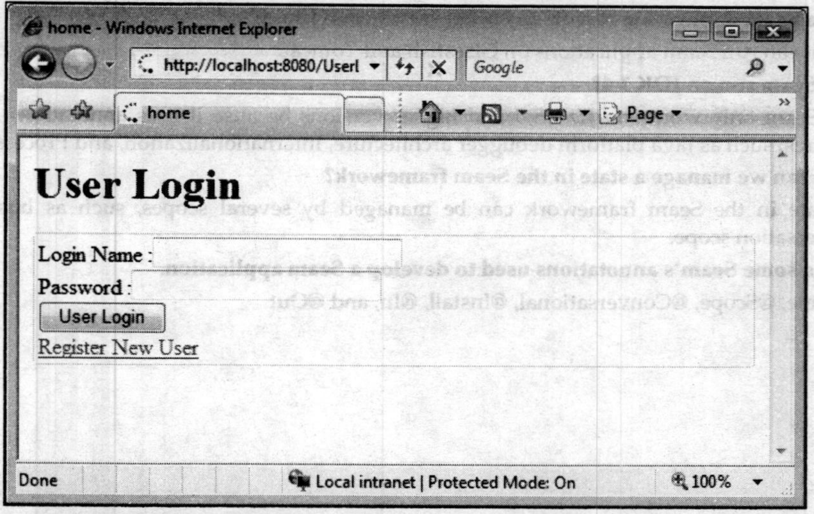

Figure 16.10: Displaying the Home Page Running on the JBoss Application Server

With this, we come to the end of the chapter. Let's now summarize the main points of the chapter.

Summary

In this chapter, you have learned about the JBoss Seam framework and its features. You have also learned about Seam context, Seam components, and built-in Seam components. In addition, you have learned how to configure Seam components that are used for developing Seam applications. Finally, you have learned to develop a Seam application, `UserLogin`.

In the next chapter, you learn about the Java EE connector architecture.

Quick Revise

Q1. The .... package provides Seam's annotation.

A. org.jboss.seam.jms **B. org.jboss.seam.core**

C. org.jboss.seam.annotations **D. org.jboss.seam.servlet**

Ans. C

Q2. What is JBoss Seam?

Ans. JBoss Seam is a light weight framework formed by integration of EJB 3 and JSF.

Q3. What is a Seam context?

Ans. A Seam context is the context variable that is generated as well as destroyed by the Seam framework. Some examples of Seam context variables are page context, conversation context, session context, business process context, and application context.

Q4. What are Seam components?

Ans. Seam components are the POJO components, such as JavaBeans and EJB that are used for developing Seam applications. Seam framework also provides built-in Seam components, such as internationalization and mail.

Q5. What is jBPM?

Ans. jBPM stands for Java Business Process Management. It is used to develop Business Process Management (BPM) of an organization.

Q6. **What is BPM?**

Ans. BPM is a well-defined group of tasks which is to be performed by the users or by the well defined software systems.

Q7. **Can a Seam application run on any other server than JBoss?**

Ans. Yes, it can run Seam applications on Glassfish and Tomcat.

Q8. **Can Seam run on JDK 1.4?**

Ans. No, Seam only works on JDK 5.0 and higher versions because it uses annotations and other JDK 5.0 features, such as Java platform debugger architecture, internationalization, and ProcessBuilder.

Q9. **How can we manage a state in the Seam framework?**

Ans. A state in the Seam framework can be managed by several scopes, such as business process and conversation scope.

Q10. **Name some Seam's annotations used to develop a Seam application.**

Ans. @Name, @Scope, @Conversational, @Install, @In, and @Out.

17

Java EE Connector Architecture 1.7

Enterprise applications run on Java EE, which supports the application server. An enterprise application is a distributed application that can handle large amounts of data required in the day to day working of an organization. To manage such voluminous data efficiently, enterprise applications need Enterprise Information Systems (EIS). EIS is a computing system that facilitates an organization to integrate and coordinate their business transactions in an efficient manner.

Java EE Connector Architecture (JCA) is a Java-based technology that is used to connect a Java EE-compliant application server with EIS. JCA enables enterprise applications to deal with large volumes of data. Both the application server and EIS together constitute a part of Enterprise Application Integration (EAI) solutions. In the Java EE platform, separate containers for client applications and application components, such as servlets, JavaServer Pages (JSP), and Enterprise JavaBeans (EJB) provide deployment as well as runtime support for the components used in an enterprise application.

In Java, containers are able to run on existing systems, such as Web servers, Transaction Processing (TP) monitors, application servers, and database systems. This enables an organization to take advantage of the features of both the existing system as well as Java EE. Using the capabilities of Java EE, developers can write new applications as well as encapsulate parts of existing applications in EJBs, JSPs, or servlets. JCA also formalizes the interactions, relationships, and packaging of the integration layer that connects the application server with EIS; thereby, enabling the EIS system to handle large amounts of data. With the help of application servers, it is possible for enterprise applications to connect with heterogeneous EIS systems, and this connectivity is bi-directional. Note that bi-directional connectivity is provided by JCA with the help of standard contracts. Various tools and frameworks are provided by EAI vendors to simplify the integration of EIS with an enterprise application.

JCA is an EAI initiative that provides a standards-based mechanism to access legacy systems from Java or Java EE applications, which significantly reduces the difficulties faced in legacy system integration. JCA is able to solve problems relating to the integration of EIS with enterprise applications by using the Common Client Interface (CCI) Application Programming Interface (API). Earlier, developers used the Java Database Connectivity (JDBC) API to manage data. The JDBC API allows Java programs to access data in a standardized and easy way. However, the JDBC technology does not provide the advantage of platform independency, which is provided by JCA.

JCA is used for legacy data and application integration just as JDBC is used for database interaction. Compared to JDBC, JCA provides an easy-to-use, standardized, legacy system-independent way to interact with different backend systems. The use of JCA provides the benefits of Java technology, such as code reusability, platform independency, and code manageability.

This chapter begins by describing important concepts of JCA. You are then acquainted with new features of JCA 1.7, the Lifecycle Management contract that controls the life cycle of a resource adapter that is used to connect EIS with an enterprise application. Moreover, the chapter explores the Workflow management process of a resource adapter and lists the differences between the JDBC and JCA technologies, both of which are used to access a data store. Apart from this, you learn about the Inbound Communication model, EJB invocation, and the CCI API. The chapter also explores JCA exceptions. Toward the end, you learn how to package and deploy a resource adapter.

Let's begin by describing the important concepts of JCA.

Describing the Key Concepts of the JCA

With the help of JCA, enterprise application components can communicate with EIS efficiently. JCA is a Java-based technology that connects an application server to various types of EIS. Examples of EIS are Enterprise Resource Planning (ERP), mainframe transaction processing, and non-relational databases. Knowledge of these and several other concepts is necessary to understand JCA. We discuss the concepts under the following broad-level headings:

- EIS
- Resource manager
- Resource adapter

- Managed environment
- Non-managed environment
- Connection of an application client with a resource manager
- System contracts
- CCI

Let's now start by discussing EIS.

Enterprise Information Systems

EIS is the backend computing system with which components of an enterprise application must integrate to retrieve the required data. EIS provides system-level services to the clients of an enterprise application. The main components of EIS are as follows:

- **The ERP system—**Handles the internal and external resources of an organization, including tangible assets, financial resources, materials, and human resources
- **The mainframe transaction processing system—**Contains information needed to process data transactions in a database system
- **The legacy database system—**Controls the storage, retrieval, security, and integrity of data in a database

To connect an enterprise application with EIS, a suitable EIS connector (a JCA-compliant resource adapter) needs to be installed on an application server. After connecting the enterprise application with EIS, you can develop the components of the enterprise application to communicate with EIS by using the CCI API.

Figure 17.1 shows the use of EIS along with a resource adapter and an application server:

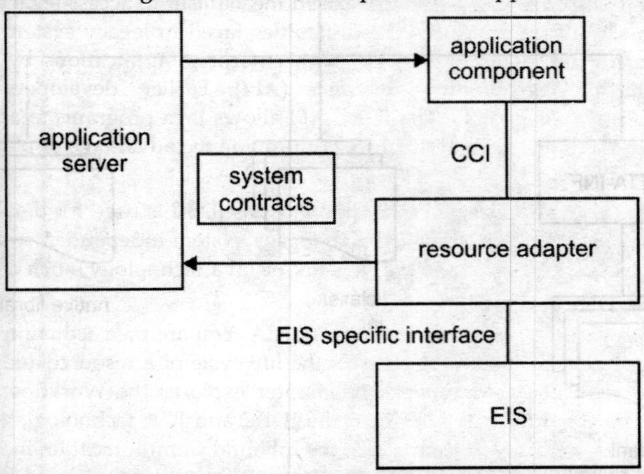

Figure 17.1: Displaying the Java EE Application Server with JCA Components and EIS

As shown in Figure 17.1, an application server communicates with the application components with the help of the CCI API. In addition, the system-level contracts define the rules on the basis of which a resource adapter can communicate with the application server. You must note that the resource adapter plays an important role in maintaining the communication between the application component and EIS.

JCA services are provided by an application server vendor and EIS is provided by an EIS vendor. By supporting JCA, all Java EE-compliant application servers can handle multiple and heterogeneous EIS resources. In this way, JCA helps to boost the productivity of a Java EE application developer while reducing development costs and protecting the existing investment in EIS systems by providing a scalable integration solution through Java EE. An EIS resource provides EIS-specific services to its clients.

Some examples of EIS resources are as follows:

- A record or set of records in a database system
- A business object in an ERP system

- A transaction processing application containing a transaction program

Next, let's discuss the resource manager.

Resource Manager

The role of a resource manager is to manage a group of sharable EIS resources. The resource manager can participate in data transactions, which are coordinated and controlled by a transaction manager. In JCA, a resource manager may have two types of clients, a client tier application or a middle-tier application server. The resource manager and the clients in JCA are located on different machines. A resource manager may be a mainframe transaction processing system, a database system, or an ERP system.

Now, let's discuss the resource adapter.

Resource Adapter

JCA, for a particular EIS type, is implemented by a Java EE component called resource adapter. A resource adapter improves the interaction between an enterprise application and EIS. The resource adapter is usually stored in a Resource Adapter ARchive (RAR) module (also known as .rar file) and is deployed on any Java EE application server. The `.rar` file can also be stored in an Enterprise ARchive (EAR) file.

Figure 17.2 shows the structure of a resource adapter:

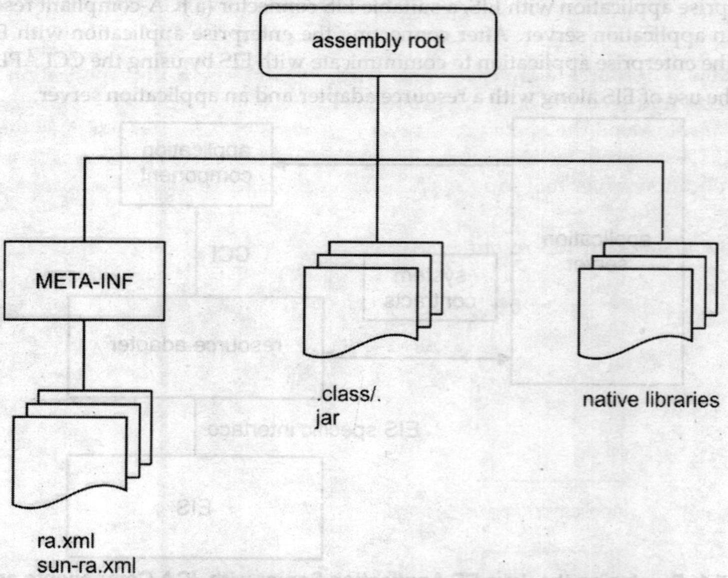

Figure 17.2: Showing the Structure of a Resource Adapter

As you can see in Figure 17.2, a resource adapter comprises the class file of the ResourceAdapter JavaBean, Deployment Descriptor of a resource adapter, and native libraries. All these are packaged under the assembly root of the resource adapter and are required to execute the resource adapter.

A resource adapter is similar to a JDBC driver used in relational database programming. The resource adapter and EIS both provide classes and interfaces that help an enterprise application to access resources not contained within an application server.

After learning about the resource adapter, let's discuss the concepts of managed and non-managed environments.

Managed Environment

In a managed environment, a resource adapter is deployed inside an application server. The methods of the resource adapter are called from inside an EJB container. An enterprise application may consist of application components, such as EJBs, JSPs, and servlets, which are deployed on their corresponding containers. These application components possess the capability to access the EIS system. In the context of JCA, these enterprise applications are known as managed applications.

Non-Managed Environment

In a non-managed environment, a resource adapter is separated from an application server and is used outside the application server as a library. In a non-managed environment, with the help of JCA, clients such as applets or Java client applications can access an EIS system. In other words, in an application, a client can directly use a resource adapter library. This allows the resource adapter to offer low-level transactions and security to its clients. In the context of JCA, such applications are called non-managed applications.

Now, let's discuss the connection between an application client and a resource manager.

Connection of an Application Client with a Resource Manager

An application client and a resource manager are linked through a connection, so that the client application can access the services provided by the resource manager. These connections are classified into two categories, namely transactional connections and non-transactional connections. At a single point of time, only one type of connection is possible. A connection between a resource manager and an application client can be bi-directional; however, connection type is mainly based on the capabilities of a resource manager.

System Contracts

System contracts enable a resource adapter to link with the services of an application server to manage connections, transactions, and security. If an application server vendor wants the application server to support JCA, then the vendor must extend the application server only once so that connectivity between the application server and multiple EIS is assured. Similarly, an EIS vendor should provide a resource adapter that is able to integrate with any application server that supports JCA. You should note that only JCA can provide system-level pluggability.

Figure 17.3 shows how a standard EIS resource adapter can connect to multiple application servers and vice versa:

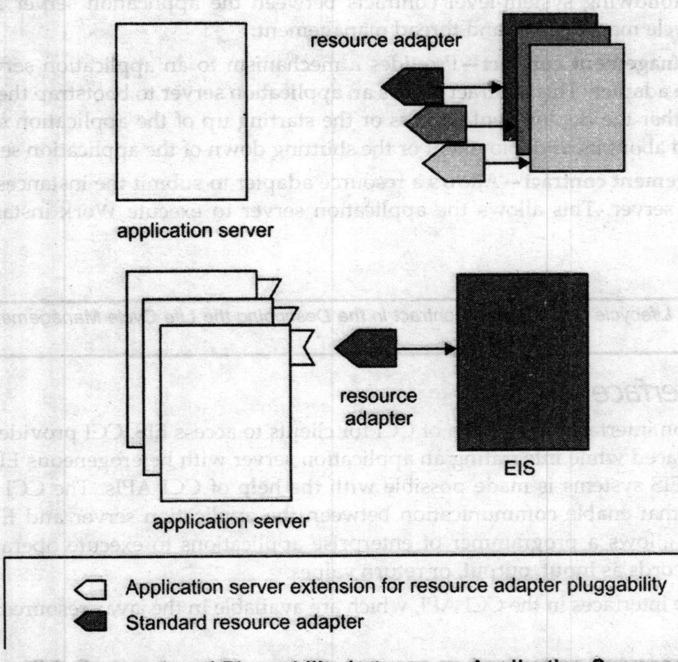

Figure 17.3: System-Level Pluggability between an Application Server and EIS

Figure 17.3 shows how an application server integrates with EIS. Prior to the introduction of JCA, application server and EIS were integrated manually by connecting them in a vendor-specific and non-standard way. As the number of EIS systems increased, it became difficult to manually manage integration between the application server and EIS. This problem was resolved with the introduction of JCA.

To understand how JCA helps in the problem of integration, let's consider an example in which there are p application servers and q EIS. JCA reduces the scope of the integration problem by changing it from a p x q problem to a p + q problem.

JCA defines the following standard system-level contracts between an application server and EIS, enabling outbound connectivity to the EIS system:

- **The Connection Management contract**—Allows an application server to offer its own services to create and manage connection pools with an underlying EIS resource. The creation and management of connection pools with EIS resources provide a scalable connection-management facility to support multiple clients.
- **The Transaction Management contract**—Extends the transactional capability of an application server to the underlying EIS resource management. This contract makes it possible for an application server to monitor a transaction by using a transaction manager across multiple resource managers.
- **The Security Management contract**—Allows an application server to access the information stored in EIS in a secured manner. This prevents security threats, such as loss of valuable information related to resources that are managed by EIS.

Apart from the preceding system-level contracts, JCA also defines the following system-level contracts between an application server and EIS, enabling inbound connectivity to an EIS system:

- **The Message Inflow contract**—Allows a resource adapter to deliver messages to their endpoints asynchronously. In addition, this contract allows various message providers, such as Java Message Service (JMS) to be plugged in an application server with the help of a resource adapter.
- **The Transaction Inflow contract**—Allows propagation of an imported transaction to an application server. In addition, this contract helps a resource adapter to manage the inflow of a transaction and prevent the atomicity, consistency, isolation, and durability (ACID) properties of the imported transactions.

JCA also defines the following system-level contracts between the application server and EIS to enable the resource adapter life cycle management and thread management:

- **The Lifecycle Management contract**—Provides a mechanism to an application server to manage the life cycle of a resource adapter. This contract allows an application server to bootstrap the instance of a resource adapter during either the deployment process or the starting up of the application server. In addition, the instance is notified about its undeployment or the shutting down of the application server.
- **The Work Management contract**—Allows a resource adapter to submit the instances of the Work interface to an application server. This allows the application server to execute Work instances by dispatching a' thread.

NOTE

You learn more about the Lifecycle Management contract in the Describing the Life Cycle Management of a Resource Adapter section.

Common Client Interface

JCA provides a common interface in the form of CCI for clients to access EIS. CCI provides standard client APIs to solve the problems faced while integrating an application server with heterogeneous EIS systems. Integration across heterogeneous EIS systems is made possible with the help of CCI APIs. The CCI API provides a set of classes and interfaces that enable communication between the application server and EIS through a resource adapter. The CCI API allows a programmer of enterprise applications to execute operations with EIS and to manage data object/records as input, output, or return values.

Table 17.1 describes the interfaces in the CCI API, which are available in the javax.resource.cci package:

Table 17.1: Describing the Interfaces of the javax.resource.cci Package

Interface	Description
`ConnectionFactory`	Provides an interface used by a resource adapter to establish a connection to an EIS instance. In other words, a client looks up the instance of the `ConnectionFactory` interface from Java Naming and Directory Interface (JNDI) to establish an EIS connection.
`Connection`	Represents a connection to a particular EIS.
`ConnectionSpec`	Passes the connection-specific properties to the `ConnectionFactory` interface when a connection request is made.
`Interaction`	Allows application components to execute EIS methods, such as procedures stored in a database.
`InteractionSpec`	Contains the properties for application components, which interact with EIS.
`Record`	Contains record instances. Classes of record instances include `MappedRecord`, `IndexedRecord`, and `ResultSet`.
`RecordFactory`	Creates the `MappedRecord` and `IndexedRecord` instances.
`Indexedrecord`	Represents an ordered collection of a record instance of the `java.util.List` type.

A client application component uses the CCI API to interact with EIS. Connection with the resource manager is established by using the `ConnectionFactory` instance. The instance of the `Connection` interface corresponds to an EIS connection and is used to perform EIS transactions. Application components interact with EIS to perform multiple tasks, such as accessing data from a specific table and using an iteration object. The `InteractionSpec` object provides the specifications for the interaction objects described in JCA. Data from EIS can be read and written to a table by using an instance of the class that implements the Record interface of the CCI API. The Record instance is classified into three main categories, namely the `MappedRecord` instance, the `IndexedRecord` instance, and the `ResultSet` instance.

After understanding the main concepts of JCA, let's discuss the new features of JCA 1.7.

What Is New in JCA 1.7

The latest release of JCA architecture is 1.7, which is also required by Java EE 7 platform in order to create resource adapters that support access to EIS systems. After that these EIS systems are plugged in to any Java EE product.

The JCA 1.7 release provides deployment annotations for connection factories and administration objects. Figure 17.4 shows how to use deployment annotations:

```
@ConnectionDefinition(
  connection="MyConnection.class",
  connectionImpl="MyConnectionImpl.class",
  connectionFactory="MyConnectionFactory.class",
  connectionFactoryImpl="MyConnectionFactoryImpl.class"
)

@AdministeredObjectDefinition(
  className="MyQueueImpl.class",
  name="java:comp/MyQueue",
  resourceAdapter="myAdapter",
)
```

Figure 17.4: Annotations for Connection Factories and Administration Objects

After understanding the new features of JCA 1.7, let's discuss the life cycle management of a resource adapter.

Describing the Life Cycle Management of a Resource Adapter

The Lifecycle Management contract plays an important role in managing the life cycle of a resource adapter. It provides an environment to connect and integrate an application server with EIS and vice versa. Therefore, you can say that the resource adapter is the main means of communication among application servers, enterprise application components, and EIS. JCA provides well-defined contracts by which a resource adapter can communicate with the other components of an enterprise application.

The life cycle of a resource adapter starts when an application server bootstraps a resource adapter instance, after the deployment of the resource adapter or the starting of an application server. Next, some useful instances, such as WorkManager, XATerminator, and Timer are provided to the instance of the resource adapter. Finally, when the application server shuts down or the resource adapter is undeployed, a notification is sent from the application server to the resource adapter.

JCA introduces life cycle management interfaces that consist of methods. The implementation of these methods manages the life cycle of a resource adapter. A resource adapter must implement the `ResourceAdapter` interface to enable the Lifecycle Management contract to control the life cycle of the resource adapter.

Figure 17.5 shows the interfaces of the Lifecycle Management contract in JCA:

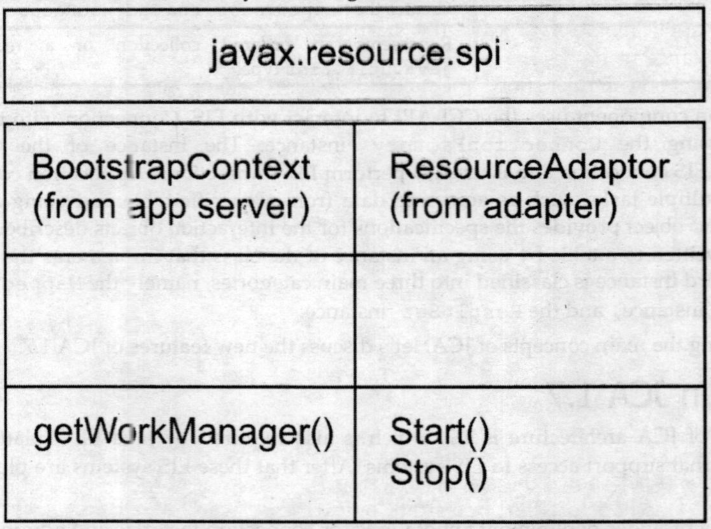

Figure 17.5: Showing the Interfaces in the Lifecycle Management Contract

Figure 17.5 shows the various interfaces needed to manage the life cycle of a resource adapter, which are available in the javax.resource.spi package. The start() and stop() methods of the ResourceAdapter interface allow an application server to start and stop, respectively, the execution of a resource adapter. You can control the process in which a resource adapter submits the instances of the Work interface to an application server for execution. This process is called Workflow management. The workflow of a resource adapter is managed by the instance of the `WorkManager` interface, which is returned by the getWorkManager() method of the BootstrapContext interface.

Figure 17.6 shows the object diagram of the Lifecycle Management contract:

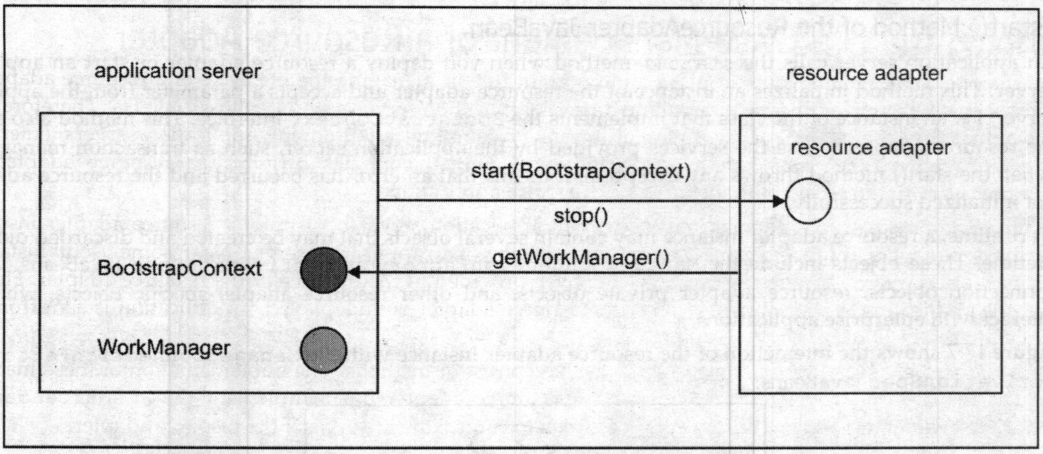

Figure 17.6: Showing the Lifecycle Management Contract by using an Object Diagram

In Figure 17.6, an application server calls the start() method to start the ResourceAdapter instance. The ResourceAdapter instance then uses the getWorkManager() method to access the application server's bootstrap context. The following code snippet shows the methods declared in the ResourceAdapter and BootstrapContext interfaces of JCA:

```
package javax.resource.spi;

import javax.resource.spi.work.WorkManager;

public interface ResourceAdapter {
   void start(BootstrapContext)
   throws ResourceAdapterInternalException;  // startup notification
   void stop(); // shutdown notification
   ... // other operations
}

public interface BootstrapContext{
   WorkManager getWorkManager();
   ... // other operations
}
```

The preceding code snippet shows the start() and stop() methods of the ResourceAdapter interface and the `getWorkManager()` method of the BootstrapContext interface. A resource adapter implements the `ResourceAdapter` interface and provides implementation for the start() method, which accepts the `BootstrapContext` instance as an argument. In addition, the class implementing the `BootstrapContext` interface should provide implementation for the `getWorkManager()` method.

Let's now discuss how an application server bootstraps a ResourceAdapter instance.

Bootstrapping a Resource Adapter Instance

The `ResourceAdapter` interface enables an application server to manage the deployment and undeployment of a resource adapter. A `JavaBean` implements the `ResourceAdapter` interface, which is configured in Deployment Descriptor of the resource adapter. The application server uses Deployment Descriptor to find the `JavaBean` class and calls its two important methods, `start` () and `stop()` to start and stop, respectively, the execution of a resource adapter.

To deploy a resource adapter, an instance of the resource adapter is bootstrapped in its address space. The application server must use the configured `ResourceAdapter` JavaBean and call the `start()` method to bootstrap a resource adapter instance.

Let's discuss the start() and stop() methods of the ResourceAdapter JavaBean.

The start() Method of the ResourceAdapter JavaBean

An application server calls the `start()` method when you deploy a resource adapter or start an application server. This method initializes an instance of the resource adapter and accepts a parameter from the application server, i.e. an instance of the class that implements the `BootstrapContext` interface. This method also enables the resource adapter to use the services provided by the application server, such as transaction management. When the start() method throws any exception, it means that an error has occurred and the resource adapter is not initialized successfully.

At runtime, a resource adapter instance may contain several objects that may be created and discarded during its lifetime. These objects include the `ManagedConnectionFactory` and `ActivationSpec` JavaBeans, various connection objects, resource adapter private objects, and other resource adapter-specific objects, which can interact with enterprise applications.

Figure 17.7 shows the interaction of the resource adapter instance with the `ManagedConnectionFactory` and `ActivationSpec` JavaBeans:

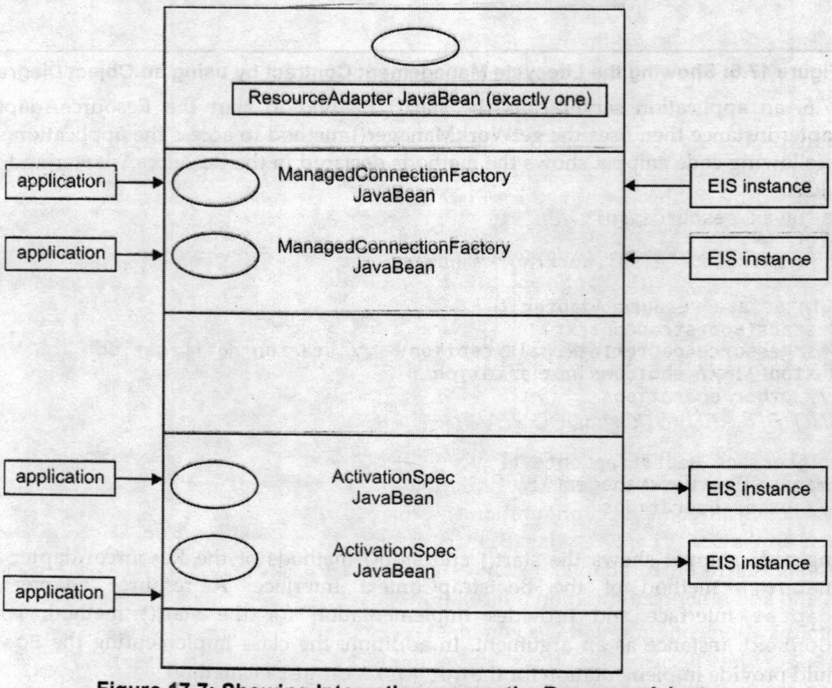

Figure 17.7: Showing Interaction among the Resource Adapter, ManagedConnectionFactory, and ActivationSpec Instances

In Figure 17.7, you can see that an application communicates with the ManagedConnectionFactory instance, which further communicates with the EIS instance to retrieve the required data. When the data is retrieved, the EIS instance communicates with the ActivationSpec instance, which in turn communicates with the application.

The stop() Method of the ResourceAdapter JavaBean

The stop() method of a JavaBean, which implements the ResourceAdapter interface, is invoked to stop the resource adapter functionality. This method is invoked during the shutdown process of the application server or when the resource adapter is undeployed.

Let's now learn about the ManagedConnectionFactory JavaBean that holds the configuration information related to outbound connectivity from an enterprise application component to an EIS instance.

Understanding a ManagedConnectionFactory JavaBean and Outbound Communication

Information about the outbound connectivity between an enterprise application and EIS is represented by the `ManagedConnectionFactory` JavaBean instance through a particular ResourceAdapter instance. The ManagedConnectionFactory JavaBean instance holds the configuration information related to outbound connectivity to an EIS instance. An enterprise application initiates outbound communication with EIS through a resource adapter. The configuration of outbound communication is a combination of the configurations of the `ResourceAdapter` and `ManagedConnectionFactory` JavaBeans. The following code snippet shows a JavaBean that implements the ManagedConnectionFactory and ResourceAdapterAssociation interfaces:

```
import javax.resource.spi.ResourceAdapterAssociation;
import javax.resource.spi.ManagedConnectionFactory;
import java.io.Serializable;
public class ManagedConnectionFactoryImpl implements ManagedConnectionFactory,
ResourceAdapterAssociation, Serializable
{
   ResourceAdapter getResourceAdapter();
   void setResourceAdapter(ResourceAdapter) throws ResourceException;
   ... // other methods
}
```

The association of the `ManagedConnectionFactory` JavaBean with a `ResourceAdapter` JavaBean is specified by the methods of the `ResourceAdapterAssociation` interface. The association between these two JavaBeans is created by calling the `setResourceAdapter()` method on the `ManagedConnectionFactory` JavaBean. You should note that the setResourceAdapter() method should be called only once. If the association is successfully created, the setResourceAdapter() method executes without raising an exception. The association established between the `ManagedConnectionFactory` and `ResourceAdapter` JavaBeans does not change during the lifetime of the `ManagedConnectionFactory` JavaBean.

Let's now learn about the ActivationSpec JavaBean, which contains the configuration information related to the inbound connectivity from an EIS instance to an enterprise application component.

Understanding an ActivationSpec JavaBean and Inbound Communication

Inbound connectivity is represented by a JavaBean that implements the `ActivationSpec` interface, which originates from an EIS instance to an enterprise application through a specific resource adapter instance. The ActivationSpec JavaBean contains configuration information pertaining to inbound connectivity from an EIS instance. When an `ActivationSpec` JavaBean is created, it may inherit the `ResourceAdapter` JavaBean (which represents the resource adapter instance) configuration information, override specific global default values, if any, and add other configuration information specific to the inbound connectivity.

Inbound communication configuration is a combination of the configuration of the `ResourceAdapter` and `ActivationSpec` JavaBeans. This type of communication is initiated by an EIS instance and the communication occurs in the context of a resource adapter thread. You should note that application threads are not involved in such type of communication.

The following code snippet shows the code of the `MyActivationSpecImpl` class, which implements the `ActivationSpec and Serializable` interface:

```
import javax.resource.spi.ActivationSpec;
import java.io.Serializable;
// ActivationSpec interface extends ResourceAdapterAssociation interface.
public class MyActivationSpecImpl implements ActivationSpec, Serializable
{
   ResourceAdapter getResourceAdapter();
   void setResourceAdapter(ResourceAdapter) throws ResourceException;
   ... // other methods
}
```

The `setResourceAdapter()` method of the `ActivationSpec` JavaBean establishes an association between the ActivationSpec and ResourceAdapter JavaBeans. This method must be called by the application server before the invocation of the other methods of the `ActivationSpec` JavaBean. A successful association is established only when the setResourceAdapter() method of the ActivationSpec JavaBean is executed successfully without throwing an exception. The setResourceAdapter() method of the ActivationSpec JavaBean is invoked only once. The association between the ResourceAdapter and ActivationSpec instances must not change during the lifetime of the ActivationSpec JavaBean. The reason for this is that the ActivationSpec instance contains the configuration information pertaining to inbound connectivity.

Now, let's learn how to manage the life cycle of a resource adapter.

Managing the Life Cycle of a Resource Adapter

An application server manages the life cycle of a resource adapter. The following are some of the tasks performed by the application server to manage the life cycle of the resource adapter:

- Uses a new ResourceAdapter JavaBean to manage the life cycle of each resource adapter instance and discards the ResourceAdapter JavaBean after its stop () method has been called. In other words, the application server must not reuse the same ResourceAdapter JavaBean object to manage multiple instances of a resource adapter, as the ResourceAdapter JavaBean object may contain resource adapter instance-specific state information.
- Calls the start() method on the ResourceAdapter JavaBean to make a resource adapter instance functional, before accessing other methods on the ResourceAdapter JavaBean instance or before using other objects that belong to the same resource adapter instance.
- Invokes the start() and stop() methods of the ResourceAdapter JavaBean in an unspecified context. To invoke these methods, it is mandatory for the application server to possess the same security permission level as that of the resource adapter instance.

Irrespective of the cause for the shutdown of a resource adapter, an application server uses two phases to shut down the resource adapter. These phases are described in the following sections.

Phase One

An application server must ensure that all dependant applications using a specific resource adapter instance are stopped before calling the stop () method by using the instance of the ResourceAdapter JavaBean. This includes deactivating all the message endpoints that are receiving messages through a specific resource adapter. However, the dependant applications cannot be stopped until they are undeployed. Therefore, the application server may have to delay destruction of the resource adapter instance till all dependant applications are undeployed. The successful completion of phase one guarantees that the threads of an application will not use the resource adapter instance, even though the instance-specific objects of the resource adapter may still be in the memory heap. This ensures that all application activities, including transactional activities, are completed.

Phase Two

In phase two of the shutdown process of an application server, the stop() method is called by an application server thread on the ResourceAdapter JavaBean. The invocation of the stop() method notifies the instance of the ResourceAdapter JavaBean to stop its functioning and to unload the instance safely. The ResourceAdapter JavaBean is responsible for performing a proper shutdown of the resource adapter instance when the stop() method is called. Proper shutdown of a resource adapter may include closing network endpoints, relinquishing threads, and releasing all active Work instances. When all the Work instances are released during the shutdown, the resource adapter is allowed to complete the internal in-flight transactions, if the transactions are already in the process of doing a commit and flushing any cached data to EIS. If the stop() method throws any unchecked exception, the shutdown process of an application server and the undeployment process of a resource adapter instance are not rolled back. The application server may log or store the information about exceptions that may have occurred when various activities are performed on the server.

Figure 17.8 describes the life cycle of a resource adapter in JCA:

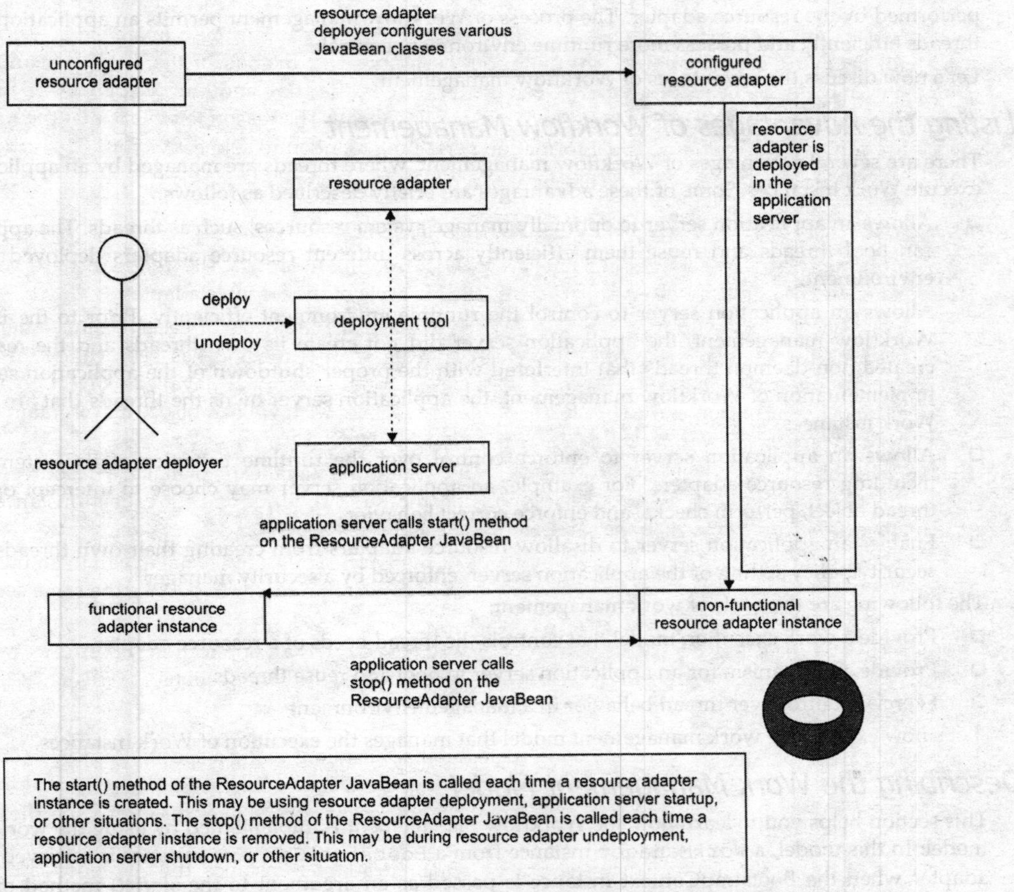

Figure 17.8: Showing the Resource Adapter Life Cycle (State Diagram)

Figure 17.8 shows the state diagram depicting the life cycle of a resource adapter in JCA. The resource adapter deployer maps various JavaBean classes to configure a resource adapter. The configured resource adapter is then deployed on the application server to create the instance of the resource adapter.

NOTE

The instance of the resource adapter is non-functional until the start() method is invoked.

Next, the `start()` method is invoked to make the instance functional or active. Later, when all the necessary tasks are performed by using the instance of the resource adapter, the `stop()` method is invoked on the ResourceAdapter JavaBean. The `stop()` method is generally invoked during the undeployment of the resource adapter instance or shutdown of the application server.

After understanding the life cycle of a resource adapter, let's explore Workflow management.

Exploring Workflow Management

Workflow management refers to the process of monitoring the Work instances submitted by a resource adapter to an application server for their execution. The instances of the `Work` interface can be managed by specifying the Work Management contract between the application server and the resource adapter. Threads are dispatched by the application server to run the submitted Work instances, which in turn prevent a request dispatcher to create or manage threads directly. The submitted Work instances contain the implementation of the tasks to be performed by the resource adapter. The process of Workflow management permits an application server to pool threads efficiently and possess more runtime environment control.

Let's now discuss the advantages of Workflow management.

Listing the Advantages of Workflow Management

There are several advantages of Workflow management, where threads are managed by an application server to execute Work instances. Some of these advantages are briefly described as follows:

- Allows an application server to optimally manage system resources, such as threads. The application server can pool threads and reuse them efficiently across different resource adapters deployed in its runtime environment.
- Allows an application server to control the runtime environment efficiently. Prior to the introduction of Workflow management, the application server did not create its own threads and the resource adapter created non-daemon threads that interfered with the proper shutdown of the application server. With the implementation of Workflow management, the application server owns the threads that are needed to run Work instances.
- Allows an application server to enforce control over the runtime behavior of its system components, including resource adapters. For example, an application server may choose to intercept operations on a thread object, perform checks, and enforce correct behavior.
- Enables an application server to disallow resource adapters from creating their own threads based on the security policy setting of the application server, enforced by a security manager.

The following are the goals of work management:

- Provide a work execution model that controls the thread needs of a resource adapter
- Provide a mechanism for an application server to pool and reuse threads
- Exercise control over thread behavior in a managed environment

Let's now explore the work management model that manages the execution of Work instances.

Describing the Work Management Model

This section helps you to learn how the Workflow management is implemented by using the work management model. In this model, a `WorkManager` instance from a `BootstrapContext` instance is retrieved by a resource adapter when the BootstrapContext instance is passed as an argument to the start () method of the resource adapter, during the deployment of the resource adapter. The resource adapter may create `Work` instances to do its work and submit them to the `WorkManager` instance along with an optional execution context for the execution of the Work instances. A thread pool, where threads wait for the submission of Work instances, is maintained by an application server. When a Work instance is submitted, a free thread from the thread pool retrieves the Work instance, establishes a suitable executable context, and invokes the run() method. After the `run()` method is executed successfully, the application server can reuse the thread for execution of other Work instances.

To reclaim an active thread, an application server invokes the `release()` method on a particular `Work` instance in a separate thread. This method instructs a resource adapter to release the active thread executing the `Work` instance and performs internal cleanup. A mandatory condition for work management is that same priority level threads must be used by the application server to execute the run() method of the Work instances, which are submitted by a particular resource adapter.

Figure 17.9 shows the interfaces and classes used to manage the Work instances submitted by a resource adapter:

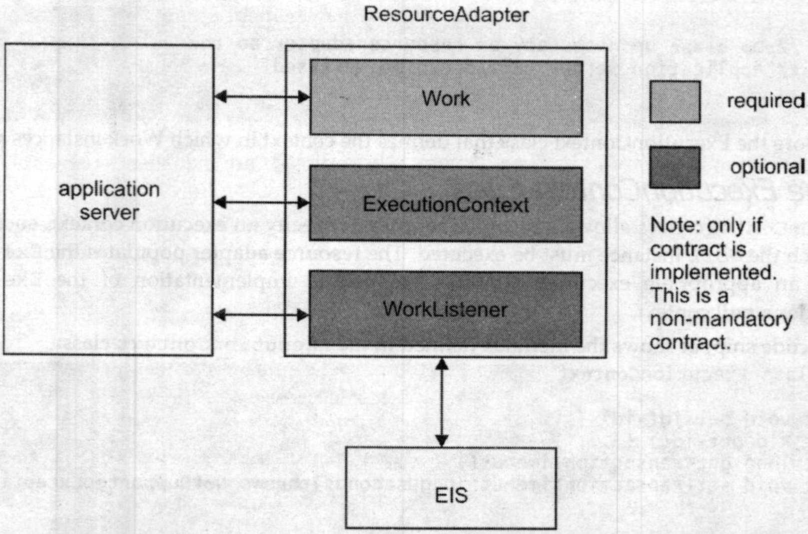

Figure 17.9: Displaying the Interfaces and Classes for Workflow Management

In Figure 17.9, the Work, ExecutionContext, and WorkListener interfaces are used by the application server to interact with EIS. In other words, Workflow management includes some predefined methods and interfaces that are used by the application server to manage Work instances. The BootstrapContext instance available in the Work Management contract is used to deploy the resource adapter in the application server.

Now, let's explore the interfaces used in Workflow management.

Describing the Work Interface

A resource adapter creates Work instances with the help of the `Work` interface. These Work instances are provided to an application server for their execution. Initially, the resource adapter creates the `Work` instances and then submits them to the `WorkManager` instance of the application server. The `WorkManager` instance is obtained from the `BootstrapContext` instance that is passed in the `start()` method at the time of the initialization of the resource adapter. The following code snippet shows the implementation of the methods of the Work interface:

```
public interface Work extends Runnable{
   void release();
      }
```

In the preceding code snippet, the `Work` interface extends the `Runnable` interface; therefore, apart from the `release()` method, the methods of the `Runnable` interface are also extended by the `Work` interface. The following is a brief description of the methods of the `Work` interface:

- The `run()` **method**—Initiates the execution of a `Work` instance. The `WorkManager` instance dispatches a thread that calls the `run()` method of the `Work` instance. The execution of the Work instance is completed when the `run()` method returns, with or without an exception. The `Work` instance treats the calling thread as a Java thread.
- The `release()` **method**—Allows a resource adapter to free a thread. This method is invoked by an application server. You cannot declare the `run ()` and `release()` methods as synchronized methods; however, these methods can have synchronized blocks.

The following code snippet shows the implementation of the MyEISWork class implementing the Work interface:

```
import javax.resource.spi.work;
public class MyEISWork implements Work
{
   void run () { }
   void release()
```

```
    {
        // Do clean up necessary on resource adapter so the
        // Application Server thread can be released.
    }
}
```

Next, let's explore the ExecutionContext class that defines the context in which Work instances are executed.

Describing the ExecutionContext Class

The `ExecutionContext` class allows a resource adapter to specify an execution context, such as a transaction context in which the `Work` instance must be executed. The resource adapter populates the `ExecutionContext` instance with an appropriate execution context. The default implementation of the `ExecutionContext` instance provides a null context.

The following code snippet shows the methods defined in the `ExecutionContext` class:

```
public class ExecutionContext
{
   public void setXid(xid) { ... }
   public Xid getXid() { ... }
   public long getTransactionTimeout() { ... }
   public void setTransactionTimeout(long seconds)throws NotSupportedException
   {}
}
```

After exploring the `ExecutionContext` class, let's explore the `WorkListener` interface, which listens to various events, such as accepting, rejecting, and starting the Work instances as well as completing the execution of Work instances.

Describing the WorkListener Interface

The `WorkListener` interface is optionally implemented by a resource adapter. When a resource adapter submits a `Work` instance, an instance of the class that implements the `WorkListener` interface is also passed. After the instance is passed, the resource adapter must provide updates corresponding to the Work instance of the class implementing the `WorkListener` interface, through application server threads. The `WorkListener` interface listens to the notifications for accepting, rejecting, and starting the Work instance as well as completing the execution of the Work instance. The class implementing the `WorkListener` interface provides thread safety and allows variation in the sequence of notifications based on your requirements.

The following code snippet shows the code of the WorkListener interface:

```
public interface WorkListener extends EventListener
{
   void workAccepted(WorkEvent);
   void workRejected(WorkEvent);
   void workStarted(WorkEvent);
   void workCompleted(WorkEvent);
}
```

The following code snippet shows the code of the class implementing the `WorkListener` interface:

```
import javax.resource.spi.work;
public class MyWorkListener implements WorkListener
{
   void workAccepted(WorkEvent e){…}
   void workRejected(WorkEvent e) {…}
   void workStarted(WorkEvent e) {…}
   void workCompleted(WorkEvent e) {…}
}
```

Next, let's explore the `WorkEvent` class, which encapsulates various events that occur during the execution of a Work instance.

Describing the WorkEvent Class

The `WorkEvent` class encapsulates the events that take place when a `Work` instance is executed. An instance of the `WorkEvent` class performs the following functions:

- Provides the type of the event that occurs during the execution of a Work instance
- Provides source objects, i.e., the Work instance on which an event initially occurs
- Accesses the Work instance associated with the event
- Provides an interval in milliseconds with which the execution of a Work instance is delayed
- Provides probable exceptions that are thrown during work processing, such as `WorkRejectedException` and `WorkCompletedException`

The following code snippet shows the implementation of the methods of the `WorkEvent` class:

```
public class WorkEvent extends EventObject
{
   public static final int WORK_ACCEPTED = 1;
   public static final int WORK_REJECTED = 2;
   public static final int WORK_STARTED = 3;
   public static final int WORK_COMPLETED = 4;
   public WorkEvent(Object source, int type, Work work,
   WorkException exc) {...}
   public WorkEvent(Object source, int type, Work work,
   WorkException exc, long startDuration) {...}
   public int getType() { ... }
   public Work getWork() { ... }
   public long getStartDuration() { ... }
   public WorkException getException() { ... }
}
```

Now, let's explore the WorkAdapter class, which is used to override the methods of the WorkListener interface.

Describing the WorkAdapter Class

A developer can create a class that extends the `WorkAdapter` class, which implements the `WorkListener` interface. This allows the developer to override the required methods of the `WorkListener` interface in the class extending the `WorkAdapter` class. The following code snippet shows the implementation of the methods of the `WorkListener` interface in the `WorkAdapter` class:

```
public class WorkAdapter implements WorkListener
{
   public void workAccepted(WorkEvent e) {}
   public void workRejected(WorkEvent e) {}
   public void workStarted(WorkEvent e) {}
   public void workCompleted(WorkEvent e) {}
}
```

In the preceding code snippet, the `WorkAdapter` class implements the `WorkListener` interface; thereby, providing body to all the methods of the interface.

You know that in Java, JDBC is used to establish connections to a data source. A similar functionality is also provided by JCA. In the following section, we differentiate the implementation and working of both these technologies in establishing connections.

Exploring the Differences between JDBC and JCA

JCA and JDBC have an identical mechanism for establishing a connection to a data source and managing transactions. JDBC provides drivers and a client API to connect and integrate with relational database applications; whereas, JCA provides resource adapters and the CCI API to enable seamless integration with EIS resources. Resource adapters for EIS systems correspond to JDBC drivers for relational databases.

Table 17.2 differentiates JDBC and JCA:

Table 17.2: Differences between JDBC and JCA

Points of Difference	JDBC	JCA
API	Defines a standard Java API to access relational databases	Uses CCI to provide an EIS-independent API
Connection	Uses JDBC drivers specific to a	Uses an EIS resource adapter to

Table 17.2: Differences between JDBC and JCA

Points of Difference	JDBC	JCA
	relational database management system (RDBMS).	interact with EIS
Definition	Provides a generic interface to interact with relational databases	Provides a standard architecture for Java EE and Java applications to integrate and interact with EIS resources
Java Transaction API (JTA) support	Provides an interface to support JTA and Java Transaction Service (JTS)	Supports JTA by providing a contract between the Java EE transaction manager and the EIS resource manager
Server implementation	Allows Java EE servers to implement the JDBC connection pool mechanism to create a connection to a database	Allows Java EE servers to implement JCA service contracts to establish a connection factory and manage connections with EIS
Service Provider Interface (SPI) support	Provides support (since JDBC 3.0) for the JCA SPI, which is a contract between an application server and a resource adapter.	Defines SPI to integrate application server services, such as transactions, connections, and security
Support for non-managed applications	Supports non-managed applications that use JDBC	Supports non-managed applications that use CCI
Transaction support	Supports eXtended Architecture (XA) and non-XA transactions with underlying XA data sources	Supports XA and non-XA transactions with underlying EIS resources

After differentiating the JDBC and JCA technologies, let's explore the inbound communication model, which allows an enterprise application component to get information or messages from EIS, with the help of a resource adapter.

Exploring the Inbound Communication Model

You can learn about the inbound communication model only after understanding the communication types supported by a resource adapter. These two types of communication can be explained as follows:

- **Synchronous communication**—Refers to a direct communication process in which all parties engaged in the process are available at a single point of time. Examples of synchronous communication are telephonic communications and board meetings.
- **Asynchronous or event notification-based communication**—Refers to a process in which all parties may not be available at a single point of time. Examples of asynchronous communication are sending messages through mobile phones and blogging.

In JCA, inbound communication is maintained between EIS and an enterprise application component through a resource adapter. Both these types of communication processes are supported by the resource adapter. In case of synchronous communication, the message sent by EIS to the enterprise application component waits for the response from the application. However, in case of asynchronous communication, the message sent by EIS to the enterprise application component does not wait for the response from the application. In other words, it is not essential for the response to be sent to EIS in the same exchange when the message is sent to the application.

In the inbound communication model, all communication to an enterprise application is started by EIS. In this communication model, an enterprise application may be a combination of EJBs (session, entity, and singleton), which is contained in an EJB container. To enable inbound communication, you need a mechanism to invoke the EJBs from a resource adapter as well as propagate transaction information from EIS to the enterprise application residing in the EJB container.

In the following section, we discuss a situation that explains the flow of a message from EIS to an enterprise application component in the inbound communication model.

Discussing a Scenario using Inbound Communication

In the inbound communication model, EIS sends a message to a resource adapter that forwards the message to the enterprise application component by using the contracts defined for inbound communication.

Figure 17.10 shows a diagrammatic representation of the inbound communication model used to send a message:

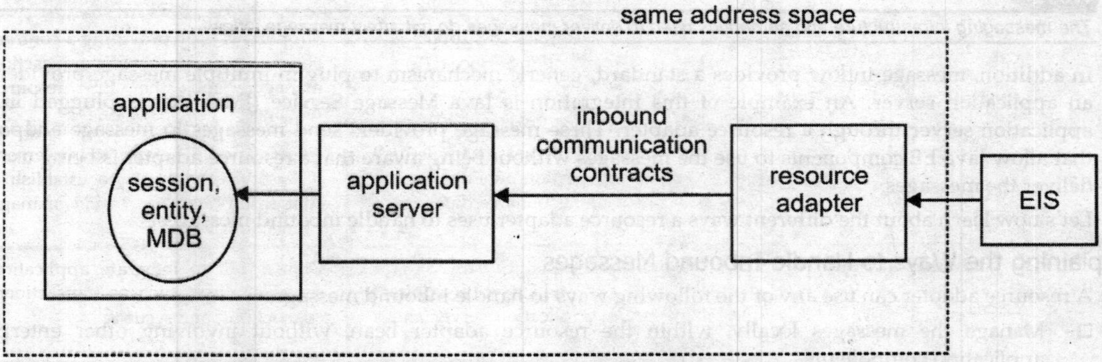

Figure 17.10: Showing the Structure of the Inbound Communication Model

In Figure 17.10, you can see that communication with an enterprise application starts from EIS.

The steps involved in the inbound communication are as follows:

1. EIS sends a message to a resource adapter.
2. The resource adapter receives the message and identifies its type.
3. The `Work` object is created by the resource adapter and submitted to the `WorkManager` object that executes the submitted `Work` object in a separate thread. After submitting the `Work` object, the resource adapter continues waiting for other incoming messages.
4. The resource adapter, based on the message type, looks up the name of the message endpoint in the message endpoint factory. A message endpoint is a proxy of an Message Driven Bean (MDB) instance available in the MDB pool.
5. The resource adapter creates a message endpoint by using the message endpoint factory.
6. The resource adapter calls the onMessage() method on the message endpoint and passes the content of the message received from EIS to the message endpoint.
7. On the invocation of the onMessage() method, an MDB (message endpoint) manages a message in the following ways:
   - Handles the message directly and returns a response to EIS through a resource adapter
   - Sends the message to some other application component
   - Stores the message in a queue, from where it is picked up by a client
   - Communicates directly with the client application

Let's now explore how message inflow works in inbound communication.

Exploring Message Inflow from EIS to Resource Adapter

The inflow of a message through a resource adapter is based on the concept of inbound communication, which provides a standard, generic contract between a resource adapter and an application server. This standard contract is known as the Message Inflow contract, which allows the resource adapter to transfer messages asynchronously or synchronously to message endpoints contained in the application server. In the message inflow process, a message is sent by EIS to a resource adapter, which further transfers the message to a message listener.

A resource adapter uses a communication protocol to establish a connection to EIS and a proprietary communication channel to communicate with EIS. The use of a communication protocol and a channel is an internal process and is not visible to the application server on which the resource adapter is deployed. In addition, the resource adapter also uses a dispatching mechanism to transfer a particular type of message to an application component in the application server.

NOTE

The messaging infrastructure and semantics used to deliver messages do not affect message inflow.

In addition, message inflow provides a standard, generic mechanism to plug in multiple message providers in an application server. An example of this integration is Java Message Service (JMS) that is plugged in the application server through a resource adapter. These message providers send messages to message endpoints that allow Java EE components to use the messages without being aware that a resource adapter is being used to deliver the messages.

Let's now learn about the different ways a resource adapter uses to handle inbound messages.

Explaining the Ways to Handle Inbound Messages

A resource adapter can use any of the following ways to handle inbound messages:

- Manage the messages locally, within the resource adapter bean, without involving other enterprise application components.
- Propagate the messages to another enterprise application component. For example, a resource adapter can look up an EJB component and call its method.
- Send the messages to a message endpoint, which is usually an MDB.

Now, let's discuss the proprietary communication protocol and channel, which are used by a resource adapter in the message inflow process.

Understanding the Proprietary Communication Protocol and Channel

A deployer provides configuration details, such as the communication channel or protocol to be used by a resource adapter to establish a connection between EIS and an enterprise application component. Apart from configuring the resource adapter, the deployer also deploys the resource adapter on an application server. One way to configure the resource adapter is to provide the configuration details in the properties represented by the `ResourceAdapter` bean or the `ActivationSpec` object. Another way of configuring the resource adapter is to provide the same communication channel for both inbound and outbound connectivity.

After learning about the protocol and channel used for message inflow, let's understand the message inflow model that will help to further clarify the concept of message inflow.

Understanding the Message Inflow Model

The message inflow model explains how a message is delivered from a resource adapter to a message listener or an MDB. In other words, this model explains the process of message inflow between an application server and a resource adapter in asynchronous or synchronous manner.

Figure 17.11 shows the message inflow model:

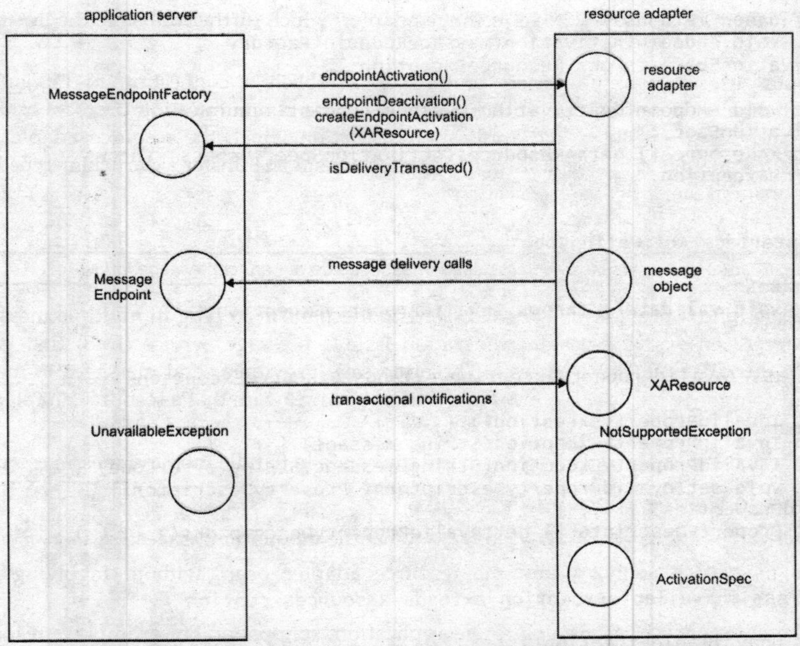

Figure 17.11: Showing the Message Inflow Model (Object Diagram)

As shown in Figure 17.11, the endpointActivation() or endpointDeactivation() method is invoked to activate or deactivate a message endpoint, respectively. During the activation or deactivation of the message endpoint, the MessageEndpointFactory instance is provided to the resource adapter and the ActivationSpec instance is configured. The MessageEndpointFactory instance is used by the resource adapter to obtain the message endpoint to deliver messages synchronously or asynchronously. You should note that the createEndpoint() method may throw the UnavailableException exception due to any of the following reasons:

- Activation of an endpoint is not completed by the application server
- Concurrent message deliveries may be limited by the application server
- Shut down of the application server is in progress
- Internal error condition may have occurred on the application server

As shown in Figure 17.11, the `isDeliveryTransacted()` method can also be invoked by using the MessageEndpointFactory instance to verify whether or not the message deliveries can be transacted.

The methods and instances discussed in the message inflow model are provided by the javax.resource.spi and javax.resource.spi.endpoint packages. Let's now explore the classes and interfaces of these packages.

Describing the javax.resource.spi Package

The `javax.resource.spi` package contains the classes and interfaces, such as ActivationSpec, ResourceAdapter, InvalidPropertyException, and UnavailableException that are used in the message inflow model. You have learned about the use of the endpointActivation() and endpointDeactivation() methods in the preceding section. These methods are also provided by the ResourceAdapter interface defined in the `javax.resource.spi` package.

The following code snippet shows the noteworthy classes and interfaces of the `javax.resource.spi` package:

```
package javax.resource.spi;
import java.beans.PropertyDescriptor;
import javax.resource.NotSupportedException;
import javax.resource.spi.endpoint.MessageEndpointFactory;
public interface ResourceAdapter
{
```

```
   ... // other methods
   public void endpointActivation(MessageEndpointFactory
   , ActivationSpec) throws ResourceException;

   public void endpointDeactivation(MessageEndpointFactory
   , ActivationSpec);
   public XAResource[] getXAResources(ActivationSpec[] specs) throws
   ResourceException;
}

public interface ActivationSpec
{
   // JavaBean
   public void validate() throws InvalidPropertyException;
}

public class InvalidPropertyException extends ResourceException
{
   public InvalidPropertyException() { ... }
   public InvalidPropertyException(String message) { ... }
   public InvalidPropertyException(String message,String errorCode) { ... }
   public void setInvalidPropertyDescriptors( PropertyDescriptor[]
   invalidProperties) { ... }
   public PropertyDescriptor[] getInvalidPropertyDescriptors() {... }
}

public class UnavailableException extends ResourceException
{
   public UnavailableException() { ... }
   public UnavailableException(String message) { ... }
   public UnavailableException(Throwable cause) { ... }
   public UnavailableException(String message, Throwable cause) {... }
}
```

Next, let's explore the javax.resource.spi.endpoint package, which provides classes and interfaces to create a message endpoint that acts as a proxy for an MDB.

Describing the javax.resource.spi.endpoint Package

A resource adapter needs to create a message endpoint before delivering a message to that endpoint. To do this, the resource adapter invokes the createEndpoint() method of the `MessageEndpointFactory` interface, present in the `javax.resource.spi.endpoint` package and then calls the `onMessage()` method of an MDB through the message endpoint to process the message. The javax.resource.spi.endpoint package is implemented by an application server.

The following code snippet shows the noteworthy interfaces defined in the javax.resource.spi.endpoint package:

```
package javax.resource.spi.endpoint;
import java.lang.Exception;
import java.lang.Throwable;
import java.lang.NoSuchMethodException;
import javax.transaction.xa.XAResource;
import javax.resource.ResourceException;
import javax.resource.spi.UnavailableException;
public interface MessageEndpointFactory
{
   MessageEndpoint createEndpoint(XAResource) throws UnavailableException;
   boolean isDeliveryTransacted(java.lang.reflect.Method) throws
   NoSuchMethodException;
}
public interface MessageEndpoint
{
   void beforeDelivery(java.lang.reflect.Method) throws NoSuchMethodException,
   ResourceException;
   void afterDelivery() throws ResourceException;
   void release();
}
```

After the message is sent by an application server to a resource adapter, the adapter delivers the message to a message endpoint. Let's now learn the message inflow process from the resource adapter to the message endpoint.

Exploring the Message Inflow to Message Endpoints

Various entities, such as the resource adapter, application server, and deployer play an important role to deliver messages to a message endpoint. A message provider or third party provides a resource adapter that is capable of sending or delivering messages. In addition, the application server provides a runtime environment for the deployment and execution of an application.

Let's first recall what you mean by the message endpoint. The message endpoint is a proxy to an MDB that is deployed on an application server, which asynchronously or synchronously uses the messages provided by message providers. You should note that the developer creating an MDB must provide various activation configuration details related to the style of the message and to the message provider. These configuration details are provided in Deployment Descriptor of the MDB and are used to activate the MDB (message endpoint).

A message delivery to an MDB should contain the following elements:

- Specific type of inbound message
- The ActivationSpec object implemented by a resource adapter
- Configuration details, such as those related to mapping of message types to message listener interfaces
- An MDB implementing a message listener interface
- The MDB that is bound to a resource adapter

Let's now learn how you can bind an MDB to a resource adapter.

Binding an MDB and a Resource Adapter

You can deploy a resource adapter either independently, i.e. as a standalone RAR file or as a part of an EAR file. Similarly, you can deploy an MDB independently (as a standalone JAR file). It can also be a part of an EAR file. In each case, an MDB must be bound to a resource adapter.

You should perform the following steps to bind an MDB and a resource adapter:

1. Configure the `jndi-name` element in the `sun-ra.xml` Deployment Descriptor for a resource adapter.
2. Configure the `adapter-jndi-name` element in the `sun-ejb-jar.xml` Deployment Descriptor with a value similar to the value set in the corresponding `jndi-name` element.
3. Deploy an MDB only after the resource adapter is deployed on an application server. The bean that represents the `ResourceAdapter` instance is bound to the adapter with a Java Naming and Directory Interface (JNDI) name that is indicated at the time of the deployment of the resource adapter.
4. Allow an MDB container to use an application server-specific API, which looks up the resource adapter with the help of its JNDI name, after the deployment of the MDB. Now, the application server-specific API calls the `endpointActivation(MessageEndpointFactory,ActivationSpec)` method on the resource adapter instance.
5. Provide permission to the resource adapter to use a configured `ActivationSpec` instance (containing configuration information) provided by the MDB container. The resource adapter also possesses a factory of message endpoints by which you can create instances of the message endpoint.

The configured information is saved by the resource adapter and used later to deliver a message to the appropriate message endpoint. The resource adapter contains information about the `MessageListener` interface that is implemented by an MDB. This information is used to determine the kind of messages required to be delivered to the MDB.

Let's learn how a resource adapter dispatches a message to an MDB.

Dispatching a Message

On receiving a message from EIS, a resource adapter determines where the message is to be dispatched. The sequence of events to dispatch a message is as follows:

1. A message comes from EIS to a resource adapter.
2. The resource adapter identifies the type of the message by looking up the message in an internal table located in an application server. The type of the messages is determined with the help of a particular pair of the `MessageEndpointFactory` and `ActivationSpec` instances.
3. The resource adapter, based on the type of the message, decides whether or not the message should be sent to an MDB.
4. The `MessageEndpointFactory` interface decides the message endpoint type. Then, the resource adapter creates an MDB instance by invoking the `createEndpoint()` method on the `MessageEndpointFactory` instance.
5. The resource adapter invokes the `onMessage()` method on the MDB instance and passes the required information, such as the body of an incoming message, to the MDB.
6. If a message listener does not return a value, it is assumed that the message dispatching process has been successfully completed.
7. If the message listener returns a value, this value is handled by the resource adapter.

This ends our discussion on the process of message inflow and how a message is transferred from EIS to a message endpoint. You have also learned about the classes and interfaces that provide the methods used to implement the message inflow model. Apart from this, you also need to understand the activation specifications for a resource adapter. In other words, the resource adapter has an instance of the ActivationSpec class that provides support for each type of message.

Exploring Activation Specifications (JavaBean)

A resource adapter gives a class name for each `ActivationSpec` JavaBean. The resource adapter also provides a class name for each supported message listener type. A JavaBean providing the activation specifications implements the ActivationSpec interface defined in the `javax.resource.spi` package. The configuration information required to activate an endpoint is used during deployment and is provided in Deployment Descriptor (ra.xml). During configuration, an `ActivationSpec` JavaBean instance may check the validity of the configuration settings provided by the deployer for a message endpoint serving as a proxy for an MDB. To check the overall activation configuration information given by the deployer, the `validate()` method of the `ActivationSpec` JavaBean is used while deploying an application on the endpoint.

Let's learn about administered objects that are needed to perform various tasks. For example, the Connection administered object helps to connect an application server to EIS.

Exploring Administered Objects

A resource adapter gives a Java class name and an interface type to an optional set of JavaBean classes that defines administered objects. These classes may represent various administered objects, which are specific to the style of a message or to a message provider. Enterprise applications may use special administered objects to synchronously send and receive messages through connection objects by using APIs, which are specific to the messaging style. Moreover, the administered objects are not used to set up asynchronous message deliveries to message endpoints. However, the `ActivationSpec` JavaBean is used to hold all the necessary activation information needed for an asynchronous message delivery setup. You can configure administered objects in the admin-objects elements of the `ra.xml` and `sun-ra.xml` Deployment Descriptor files.

You can define administered objects in three configuration scope levels similar to outbound connections and other GlassFish resource adapter configuration elements. The three configuration scopes are as follows:

- **Global**—Represents the scope that is acceptable for all administered objects in a resource adapter, which are defined in the ra.xml Deployment Descriptor by using the `default-properties` element.
- **Group**—Represents the scope that is acceptable for all administered objects in a resource adapter, which are defined in the ra.xml Deployment Descriptor using the `admin-object-group` element. The administered objects defined in the group level possess properties that override any property defined at the global level.

- **Instance**—Represents specific administered objects for a resource adapter. Instance-level properties can be defined at the instance level by using the `admin-object-properties` element in the ra.xml Deployment Descriptor. Instance-level properties override group and global level properties.

Now, let's learn how a resource adapter invokes a session or an entity bean.

Understanding EJB Invocation

This section discusses the process of invoking session and entity beans from a resource adapter. Session or entity beans are invoked by a resource adapter to perform the following two main tasks:

- Dispatch the calls from EIS to a bean in order to execute the business logic of an enterprise application
- Use the EJB Container-Managed Persistence (CMP) mechanism for persistence

Note that to dispatch calls to a session or entity bean, the resource adapter needs to know the target bean type and the name as well as parameters of the method to be invoked. When the resource adapter receives a request from EIS through a remote protocol, the adapter selects an appropriate bean and a target method name. In addition, the resource adapter deserializes the request parameters received from EIS and calls the target bean method.

To invoke a session or an entity bean, the resource adapter can use the bean client view model through an MDB. The EJB specification defines the EJB client view and describes how the client view is used to access session or entity beans. The EJB client view is available to an MDB.

Bean dispatch logic is implemented in an MDB. The MDB selects an appropriate session or entity bean and a target method, deserializes the request parameters, and invokes the selected bean based on the request information received from the EIS system. The resource adapter uses the Message Inflow contract to invoke an MDB and then uses the invoked MDB through the EJB client view model to dispatch or send calls to the appropriate session and entity beans.

You can say that an MDB can be used as a replaceable unit of the resource adapter, which plays the role of a bean dispatcher. The Message Inflow contract allows the creation of multiple endpoint instances (MDBs) at runtime. This facilitates the concurrent dispatching of messages to an MDB.

Figure 17.12 shows the EJB invocation model with a resource adapter:

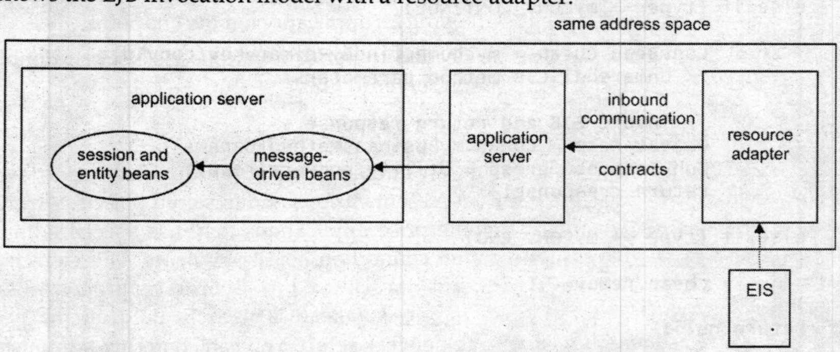

Figure 17.12: Showing the EJB Invocation Model

In Figure 17.12, an MDB is used along with the resource adapter. The resource adapter invokes the MDB to transfer a message to the application server.

Let's now discuss how an MDB is invoked by using the resource adapter in an enterprise application.

A resource adapter supports inbound communication from an EIS system to the application components residing in an application server container. The resource adapter uses the Message Inflow contract to call MDBs that serve as a dispatcher for session and entity bean invocations. The resource adapter and MDBs may be provided by separate or the same resource adapter vendor. An example of a resource adapter providing both the resource adapter and the MDBs is Wombat Inc.

The EIS system uses multiple concurrent conversations in its interactions with a resource adapter. Each conversation may involve multiple serial requests. The resource adapter has a set of `Work` objects (threads), each of which is used to carry on a specific conversation. The resource adapter manages the multiple concurrent conversations and calls an MDB instance whenever a request message arrives as part of a conversation.

The following code snippet shows the implementation of MDB with a resource adapter:

```
import javax.ejb.MessageDrivenBean;
import javax.naming.InitialContext;
public class WombatMDB
implements MessageDrivenBean, WombatMessageListener
{
    public static int myCONV_START = 0;
    public static int myCONV_CONTINUE = 1;
    public static int myCONV_END = 2;
    private Context myjndiContext = null;
    private ConvBeanHome mychome = null;
    public void ejbCreate()
    {
            myjndiContext = new InitialContext();
            mychome = (ConvBeanHome)
            jndi.lookup("java:comp/env/ConvBeanHome");
    }

    ConvResponse onMessage(ConvRequest requestMsg) {
            // get conversation id and request type from the request
            // message
            int convId = ...;
            int type = ...;

            if (type == myCONV_START)
            {
                    // create Entity EJB for holding the specific
                    // conversation state
                    ConvBean cbean = mychome.create(convId);
            }
            else if (type == myCONV_CONTINUE)
            {
                    ConvBean cbean = mychome.findByPrimaryKey(convId);
                    // Unmarshal EJB method parameters
                    ...;
                    // invoke EJB and return response
                    Object resp = cbean.myBusinessMethod(params);
                    ConvResponse cresp = Utility.convert(resp);
                    return cresponse;
            }
            else if (type == myCONV_END)
            {
                    cbean.remove();
            }
            return null;
    }
    public void ejbRemove()
    {
            myjndiContext = null;
            mychome = null;
    }
}
```

The resource adapter uses an MDB as a generic dispatcher for session and entity bean invocations and relies on the application server to efficiently pool MDB instances. When a thread from a resource adapter accesses an MDB method, the JNDI context of the MDB is available to the thread. The resource adapter may take advantage of this and use the MDB as a dispatcher. The bean method may be used in a while loop by a resource adapter. The thread in the bean's while loop is used to process specific data structures, such as Queue and List of the resource adapter. The instances of these data structures are passed to the bean method as parameters. In such a case, the bean becomes a special Java object that has access to the JNDI context, which the resource adapter may use. This usage pattern illustrates a tight coupling between the resource adapter and the MDB.

After understanding the concept of EJB invocation, let's discuss the CCI API.

Understanding the CCI API

The classes and interfaces included in the CCI API provide the methods that allow enterprise application components to access data across heterogeneous EIS systems, such as database systems, legacy applications coded in other programming languages, and ERP. By using the CCI API, EAI frameworks and application components can communicate across heterogeneous EIS systems. Some advantages of the CCI API are as follows:

- Enhances application development tools and EAI frameworks.
- Provides a remote function-call interface that can be used to execute EIS application functions and retrieve their results. The CCI API provides the basic classes and interfaces to connect to EIS.
- Serves as a simple functionality that component developers may use to develop complex enterprise applications. It also provides an extensible application programming model.
- Provides classes and interfaces that can be used in the Java EE and J2SE platforms.
- Provides EIS independence that can be derived by EIS-specific metadata present in the repository.

Let's now briefly discuss the interfaces and classes of CCI.

The CCI API contains the following interfaces:

- `Connection-related` **interfaces**—Represent a connection factory and an application-level connection. The following code snippet lists the connection-related interfaces along with their packages:

```
javax.resource.cci.ConnectionFactory
javax.resource.cci.Connection
javax.resource.cci.ConnectionSpec
javax.resource.cci.LocalTransaction
```

- `Interaction-related` **interfaces**—Allow an enterprise application component to maintain an interaction that is determined by the `InteractionSpec` interface by using an EIS instance. The following code snippet lists the interaction interfaces available in the CCI API:

```
javax.resource.cci.Interaction
javax.resource.cci.InteractionSpec
```

- `Data representation-related` **interfaces**—Represent the data structures that are used in an interaction with an EIS instance. The following code snippet lists the data representation-related interfaces along with their packages:

```
javax.resource.cci.Record
javax.resource.cci.MappedRecord
javax.resource.cci.IndexedRecord
javax.resource.cci.RecordFactory
javax.resource.cci.Streamable
javax.resource.cci.ResultSet
```

- `Metadata-related` **interfaces**—Specifies metadata information for a resource adapter implementation and an EIS connection. The following code snippet lists the metadata-related interfaces along with their packages:

```
javax.resource.cci.ConnectionMetaData
javax.resource.cci.ResourceAdapterMetaData
javax.resource.cci.ResultSetInfo
```

- **Additional classes**—Provide the `ResourceException` and `ResourceWarning` exception classes used to handle an exception raised with respect to a resource adapter. The following code snippet lists the additional classes that are available in the CCI API:

```
javax.resource.ResourceException
javax.resource.cci.ResourceWarning
```

Now, let's discuss the noteworthy interfaces of the CCI API that are needed to connect an application server with heterogeneous EIS systems.

The ConnectionFactory Interface

The javax.resource.cci.ConnectionFactory interface allows you to establish a connection with an EIS instance through a resource adapter. An EIS resource adapter usually provides this interface. The following code snippet shows the methods of the ConnectionFactory interface:

```
public interface javax.resource.cci.ConnectionFactory implements
java.io.Serializable, javax.resource.Referenceable
{
   public RecordFactory getRecordFactory() throws ResourceException;
   public Connection getConnection() throws ResourceException;
   public Connection getConnection(
   javax.resource.cci.ConnectionSpec properties)
   throws ResourceException;
   public ResourceAdapterMetaData getMetaData() throws ResourceException;
}
```

The methods used in the preceding code snippet can be briefly described as follows:

- getConnection()– Retrieves a connection to an EIS instance. In the case of container-managed sign-on, no security information is passed by an enterprise application component. If you need to pass any resource adapter-specific security information and connection parameters, the enterprise application component may decide to use a getConnection variant with the javax.resource.cci.ConnectionSpec type of parameter.
- getRecordfactory()– Creates the RecordFactory instance.
- getMetaData() – Retrieves metadata information about the ResourceAdapter instance.

The ConnectionSpec Interface

Application components use the javax.resource.cci.ConnectionSpec interface to provide a connection request and specific properties to the getConnection() method of the ConnectionFactory interface. Parameters, such as user name and password, are passed to the getConnection() method of the ConnectionFactory interface, while establishing a connection to the EIS system. The following code snippet shows the declaration of the ConnectionSpec interface:

```
public interface javax.resource.cci.ConnectionSpec {}
```

Let's now describe the standard properties for the ConnectionSpec interface.

Table 17.3 shows the properties of the ConnectionSpec interface:

Table 17.3: Properties of the ConnectionSpec Interface

Property	Description
UserName	Specifies the name of a user connecting to an EIS instance
Password	Specifies the password for a user connecting to an EIS instance

The Connection Interface

The javax.resource.cci.Connection interface represents a connection to an EIS resource and is used to perform various operations with an underlying EIS. The following code snippet lists the methods of the Connection interface:

```
public interface javax.resource.cci.Connection
{
   public Interaction createInteraction() throws ResourceException;
   public ConnectionMetaData getMetaData() throws ResourceException;
   public ResultSetInfo getResultSetInfo() throws ResourceException;
   public LocalTransaction getLocalTransaction() throws ResourceException;
   public void close() throws ResourceException;
}
```

The methods used in the preceding code snippet can be briefly described as follows:

- createInteraction()—Creates an instance of the Interaction interface with reference to the Connection instance. This method is invoked on the instance of the Construction interface and allows an enterprise application component to access EIS functions and data.
- getMetaData()—Provides information about the EIS instance associated with a Connection instance. In other words, you can use the ConnectionMetaData interface to find EIS instance-specific information.
- getResultSetInfo()—Returns information about the ResultSet supported by the connected EIS system to a message listener.
- **close()**—Closes an established connection and destroys the instance of the Connection interface.

The Interaction Interface

The javax.resource.cci.Interaction interface interacts with a connected EIS system to perform various operations, such as retrieving data from an EIS system. The following code snippet defines the methods of the Interaction interface:

```
public interface javax.resource.cci.Interaction
{
   public Connection getConnection();
   public void close() throws ResourceException;
   public boolean execute(InteractionSpec ispec,Record input,Record output)
   throws ResourceException;
   public Record execute(InteractionSpec ispec, Record input) throws
   ResourceException;
   ...
}
```

An Interaction instance is used to perform the following tasks with an EIS instance:

- Update the output record and returns a Boolean value. The first execute() method defined in the preceding code snippet accepts three parameters: an input record, output record, and an InteractionSpec instance. The EIS functions specified by the InteractionSpec interface are also executed by the first execute() method.
- Produce and return an output record. The second execute() method defined in the preceding code snippet accepts two parameters, an input record and an InteractionSpec instance. The EIS function specified by the InteractionSpec interface is also executed by the second execute() method.

The InteractionSpec Interface

The InteractionSpec interface defines interactions by providing EIS-specific object properties, such as data types and schema, which are associated with an EIS system. The following code snippet shows the methods defined in the InteractionSpec interface:

```
public interface javax.resource.cci.InteractionSpec implements java.io.Serializable
{
   // Standard Interaction Verbs
   public static final int MYSYNC_SEND = 0;
   public static final int MYSYNC_SEND_RECEIVE = 1;
   public static final int MYSYNC_RECEIVE = 2;
}
```

The LocalTransaction Interface

The javax.resource.cci.LocalTransaction interface represents a local transaction (similar to the UserTransaction interface). Local transaction is controlled internally in a resource manager. The following code snippet shows the methods defined in the LocalTransaction interface:

```
public interface javax.resource.cci.LocalTransaction
{
   public void begin() throws ResourceException;
   public void commit() throws ResourceException;
   public void rollback() throws ResourceException;
}
```

If CCI implementation supports the `LocalTransaction` interface, the `Connection.getLocalTransaction` method returns a `LocalTransaction` instance. To perform a local transaction on an underlying EIS instance, the instance of the `LocalTransaction` interface is usually used by the enterprise application component. A resource adapter is allowed to implement the `javax.resource.spi.LocalTransaction` interface while it does not implement the application-level `javax.resource.cci.LocalTransaction` interface.

Now, let's explore JCA exceptions.

Exploring JCA Exceptions

JCA provides exceptions to handle unexpected circumstances in implementing application components. JCA provides the following two types of exceptions:

- The application exception
- The system exception

Let's describe both these exceptions in the following sections.

The Application Exception

An application exception is thrown whenever application components access an EIS resource. An application exception reports an error in the execution of a function on a target EIS. An application component is capable of handling these exceptions directly.

The System Exception

System exceptions are unexpected error conditions that may be thrown by an invocation of a method of system contracts, such as transaction management-related errors. These exceptions are handled by an application server or a resource adapter, depending on cause of the exception. You should note that the system exceptions are not reported in their original form directly to an application component.

Next, let's discuss the various system exceptions in JCA.

ResourceException

The `javax.resource.ResourceException` class is at the root of the System exception hierarchy, specified by JCA. The `ResourceException` class extends the `java.lang.Exception` class and is a checked exception. In CCI, the `ResourceException` class is the root of the hierarchy of the application exceptions. The `ResourceException` class provides the following information:

- Shows the error code for a particular resource adapter. This error code specifies the error condition.
- Represents an error by a String, which is resource adapter-specific. This String represents an exception message and can be retrieved by the `getMessage()` method of the ResourceException object.

A `ResourceException` exception can point to another exception and occurs as a result of some low level problem, such as hardware failure.

SecurityException

The javax.resource.spi.SecurityException class is a subclass of the ResourceExeption class. An error condition represented by this subclass corresponds to the Security contract, consisting of an application server and a resource adapter as its members. The SecurityException exception may occur due to the following reasons:

- Unsuccessful authentication of a resource or unsuccessful creation of a connection to EIS
- Incorrect security information, which is stored in a Subject instance that is passed to the Security contract
- Unsuccessful authentication of an EIS principal resource
- Unsuccessful establishment of a secure association between an enterprise application component and an EIS instance
- Unsupported security mechanism used by an EIS system or a resource adapter

LocalTransactionException

The `javax.resource.spi.LocalTransactionException` class is a subclass of the `ResourceException` class. The error conditions represented by this class correspond to the contract that is defined for local transaction management. The `LocalTransactionException` exception occurs due to the following reasons:

- Rollback of a transaction without the invocation of the commit() method in the `LocalTransaction` interface
- Incorrect transaction context during the execution of a transaction operation
- Initiation of a transaction with a thread on a `ManagedConnection` instance, which is related to the active local transaction

ResourceAdapterInternalException

The `javax.resource.spi.ResourceAdapterInternalException` class is a subclass of `ResourceException`, which represents all system-level error conditions that are associated with a resource adapter. The ResourceAdapterInternalException exception occurs due to the following reasons:

- Unsuccessful creation of EIS connection, probably because of an error in the communication protocol or resource adapter implementation
- Incorrect configuration of the ManagedConnectionFactory instance, which is used to create a new connection
- Incorrect implementation of a resource adapter

ApplicationServerInternalException

The `javax.resource.spi.ApplicationServerInternalException` class is a subclass of `ResourceException`. The exceptions depicted by the `ApplicationServerInternalException` class point particularly to application server errors. These errors generally occur due to errors made in the configuration of an application server.

ResourceAllocationException

The `javax.resource.spi.ResourceAllocationException` class is a subclass of `ResourceException`. Exceptions defined in this subclass are thrown when an application server or resource adapter fails to allocate system resources, such as threads and connections. Application server-specific `ResourceAllocationException` exceptions occur when the number of connections created is more than can be managed by a connection pool.

NOTE

The javax.resource.spi.CommException exception is a subclass of the ResourceException exception and occurs due to unsuccessful or interrupted communication between an enterprise application component and an EIS instance. Common CommException exceptions are raised due to communication protocol errors and invalid connections that occur because of server failure.

After learning about JCA exceptions, let's discuss how to package and deploy a resource adapter.

Packaging and Deploying a Resource Adapter

JCA specifies the interfaces that are generally used to package and deploy a resource adapter on an application server. Using these interfaces, you can plug in various resource adapters to an application server. Integration between a resource adapter and a Java EE application server is modular and portable. This modular integration is called a resource adapter module (the `.rar` file), which is similar to a Java EE application module (the `.ear` file) and includes Web and EJB components.

Now let's learn about the directory structure of a resource adapter.

Understanding Directory Structure of a Resource Adapter

A resource adapter provider creates and provides adapter interfaces and implementation classes, which are put in a `.rar` file or deployment directory. A resource adapter can be deployed either with the help of the `.rar` file or deployment directory. The `.rar` file or deployment directory contains the compiled classes that are required for the deployment of a resource adapter. These compiled classes are stored within subdirectories and the structure of these subdirectories is exactly the same as their Java package structures.

Resource adapters follow a common directory format. When the required classes and files are packaged in a `.rar` file, the same format is followed in the .rar file. Now, let's know the directory structure of the resource adapter.

Figure 17.13 displays the directory structure of a resource adapter:

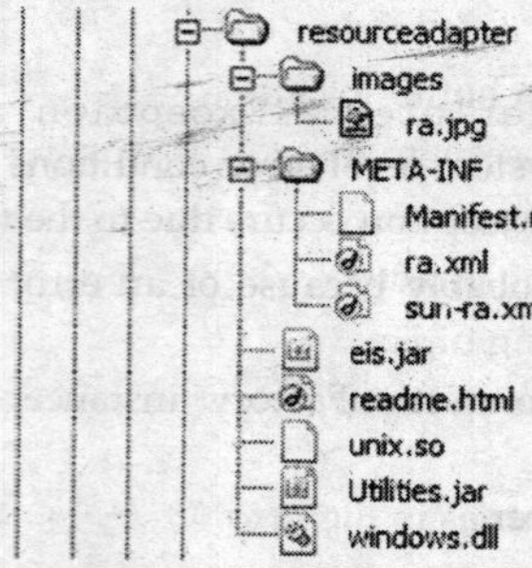

Figure 17.13: Showing the Directory Structure of a Resource Adapter

As you can see in Figure 17.13, the directory structure of a resource adapter consists of the following files:

- **ra.xml** – Contains standard deployment information
- **sun-ra.xml** – Contains additional deployment description
- **eis.jar** – Contains the Java classes and interfaces required by a resource adapter
- **readme.html** – Represents the documentation and related files that are required by a resource adapter
- **unix.so** – Represents the native library that is required by a resource adapter to interact with EIS on UNiplexed Information Computing System (UNICS), later known as the UNIX operating system
- **utilities.jar** – Contains the Java classes and interfaces required by a resource adapter
- **windows.dll** – Represents the native library that is required by a resource adapter to interact with EIS on Windows operating system

Let's now discuss the points to consider while packaging a resource adapter.

Packaging Considerations

As discussed earlier, you can deploy a resource adapter by using either a `.rar` file or deployment directory. Both the `.rar` file and the deployment directory include the compiled resource adapter interfaces and implementation classes developed by the resource adapter provider. Therefore, packaging a resource adapter is an important step in the successful deployment of the resource adapter. A `.rar` file may contain the following files:

- Deployment Descriptors (`ra.xml` and `sun-ra.xml`), which are contained in a subdirectory called `META-INF`.
- The `MANIFEST.MF` file that contains metadata information about an archive. A `JAR` tool implicitly creates a `MANIFEST.MF` file, which is an optional file.
- A resource adapter that contains multiple JAR files, such as `eis.jar` and `utilities.jar`. These JAR files provide the Java classes and interfaces used by a resource adapter.
- The documentation and related files, such as `readme.html` and `/images/ra.jpg`, which are used by the resource adapter.

- An `.ear` file containing resources required to deploy a resource adapter. In other words, if a resource adapter is packaged within a Java EE application, then you first need to create an .ear file that contains the resources required in the application. In addition, instead of deploying a `.rar` file, you can deploy the `.ear` file of the application server, which contains the resource adapter. The `MANIFEST.MF` file is automatically created while packaging the resource adapter on the application server. This file contains the `CLASSPATH` entry supported by the server.

Let's now learn to package a resource adapter.

Packaging a Resource Adapter

After arranging one or more resource adapters in a directory, you can package them in `.rar` files to successfully deploy the resource adapters. The following list indicates the typical sequence followed in packaging a resource adapter:

1. Develop a staging directory, which serves as a buffer to store updates
2. Copy the compiled resource adapter Java classes into the staging directory
3. Create JAR files by using JAR tools, which contain resource adapter Java classes
4. Add the JAR files at the top level of the staging directory
5. Create a META-INF subdirectory in the staging directory
6. Create Deployment Descriptor for the resource adapter, which is ra.xml file, and place it in the META-INF subdirectory
7. Add all the resource adapter configuration entries in the ra.xml file
8. Create another Deployment Descriptor of the resource adapter in the META-INF subdirectory, which is a `sun-ra.xml` file.
9. Add various details used at the time of deployment of the resource adapter, such as configuration details related to connection pooling and mapping a security role in the `sun-ra.xml` file.
10. Use the following command to create a `.rar` file:

```
jar cvf jar-file.rar -C staging-dir
```

By executing the preceding command, a `.rar` file is created that can be deployed on the Glassfish Server 4.0. The -C staging-dir option used in the preceding command informs the JAR tool to change the staging directory to the directory specified in the command. In our case, the staging-dir directory is used as the staging directory. By doing this, you can store directory paths in the `.rar` file, which are relative to the directory where you have staged the resource adapters.

Now, let's learn how to deploy a resource adapter.

Deploying a Resource Adapter

The process of deploying a resource adapter is the same as deploying Web and enterprise applications. A resource adapter can be deployed in an exploded directory format or as an archive (the `.rar` file).

Let's learn about Deployment Descriptor of a resource adapter, which contains information related to the deployment of a resource adapter.

Explaining the Deployment Descriptor for a Resource Adapter

A resource adapter requires two Deployment Descriptors to define its operational parameters. The JCA specification, Version 1.0 final release contains the definition of the `ra.xml` Deployment Descriptor, which is provided by Sun Microsystems. The `sun-ra.xml` Deployment Descriptor is specific to the Glassfish server 4.0 and specifies the operational parameters unique to the server. The Java EE Deployment API specification describes the general deployment procedure in detail.

Deployment Descriptor is defined by a resource adapter provider, which contains certain configuration details for the adapter. In other words, Deployment Descriptor for a resource adapter defines the following general information:

- Name of the resource adapter

- ❑ Description of the resource adapter
- ❑ Uniform Resource Identifier (URI) of a user interface for the resource adapter
- ❑ Name of the vendor providing the resource adapter
- ❑ Description of the licensing requirement for using the resource adapter
- ❑ Type of EIS system supported by the resource adapter, for example, the name of a specific database, ERP system, or mainframe transaction processing system without any versioning information
- ❑ String representing the version of the JCA specification supported by the resource adapter

Apart from providing Deployment Descriptor, you also need to provide the configuration properties file for the resource adapter. This file allows a resource adapter provider to give the `ResourceAdapter` instance configuration properties, which can be used by the resource adapter deployer to configure a `ResourceAdapter` JavaBean instance.

Let's now learn about the deployer of a resource adapter, which configures the resource adapter during the deployment of the adapter.

Explaining the Role of Parties Involved in Deployment of a Resource Adapter

Various parties, such as deployer, application server vendor, and application component provider play an important role in the deployment of a resource adapter. The following is the description of the tasks performed by these parties:

- ❑ **Deployer**—Configures a resource adapter in the target Java EE environment in which the adapter is to be deployed. The deployer provides the attributes in Deployment Descriptor needed for the configuration of the resource adapter. The deployer performs the following tasks in Deployment Descriptor:
  - Configures a property set for each ManagedConnectionFactory instance, which creates connections to multiple underlying EIS instances
  - Configures an application server for transaction management based on the level of transaction support specified by a resource adapter
  - Configures security in the operational environment, based on the security requirements specified by a resource adapter in its Deployment Descriptor.
- ❑ **Application server vendor**—Provides the JCA implementation in the Java EE application server provided by the vendor. Support for JCA in the application server helps to package, deploy, and run JCA component-based applications. The role of the application server vendor is also to provide a container and insulate the Java EE application components from the underlying system-level services.
- ❑ **Application component provider**—Develops enterprise application components that interact with EIS so that the EIS can use the functionalities of an enterprise application. The provider develops the components by using CCI, but does not provide implementations for the transaction, security, concurrency, and distribution services. Instead, these services are used by the application component from an application server.

With this, we come to the end of the chapter. Let's now recap the main points discussed in the chapter.

Summary

The chapter has described JCA and its key components. It has explained the life cycle management as well as the Workflow management of a resource adapter. In addition, the chapter has differentiated the JDBC and JCA technologies. Apart from this, you have learned about the Inbound Communication model, EJB invocation, the CCI API, and JCA exceptions. Towards the end, you have learned to package and deploy resource adapters. The next chapter deals with Java EE design patterns.

Quick Revise

Q1. The package containing the `ActivationSpec` interface is ………………………………….

A. javax.resource.spi | **B. javax.resource.cci**

C. javax.resource | **D. javax.resource.spi.endpoint**

Ans. The correct option is A.

Q2. WorkListener interface belongs to the ………………………………. package.

A. javax.resource.spi.endpoint | **B. javax.resource.cci**

C. javax.resource.spi.security | **D. javax.resource.spi.work**

Ans. The correct option is D.

Q3. What is common between interaction and connection?

A. Both are from the same package, `javax.resource.cci`.

B. Both are classes.

C. Both are methods.

D. Both are packages.

Ans. The correct option is A.

Q4. The `getConnection()` method declared in the `ConnectionFactory` interface throws an exception of type …………………………………………………

A. UnavailableException | **B. ResourceException**

C. NotSupportedException | **D. None**

Ans. The correct option is B.

Q5. What is the need of JCA?

Ans. JCA is a Java technology that is used to connect an application server and EIS. Prior to the introduction of JCA, EAI was the only solution to connect an application server with EIS; however, the connection through EAI was not portable among various application servers. JCA served as a solution to allow an application server to connect with heterogeneous EIS systems. .

Q6. Define EIS.

Ans. EIS is an information system used by an entity such as an organization to manage large amounts of data to perform its day to day activities. EIS software consists of ERP, mainframe transaction processing, and non-relational databases.

Q7. Differentiate between JDBC and JCA.

Ans. JDBC provides an interface that enables applications to interact with only relational databases while JCA provides the architecture to integrate enterprise applications and EIS. JDBC uses a specific driver to establish a connection to a database, but JCA uses an EIS-resource adapter to interact with an EIS system.

Q8. What is a resource adapter?

Ans. A resource adapter is a system-level software driver, which allows an application client or server to connect to EIS. It provides a contract for the services offered by the application server, such as underlying mechanisms, transactions, security, and connection pooling.

Q9. Define work exceptions.

Ans. When an exception related to the Work Management contract is reported, an application server throws work exceptions. The following are some examples of work exceptions:

- WorkException
- WorkRejectedException
- WorkCompletedException

Q10. What is CCI?

Ans. CCI is a standard API that helps enterprise application components to access EIS. It provides common classes and interfaces to interact with various EIS. This interaction can be derived by application components and EAI frameworks.

Q11. How is a resource adapter packaged?

Ans. A resource adapter is packaged into a `.rar` file by using the `JAR` tool. The `.rar` file must have a configuration file, i.e. `ra.xml`, which stores deployment related information for the resource adapter.

Q12. Define the WorkEvent class.

Ans. The `WorkEvent` class is an abstract class that provides information about an event type, a source object, a listener associated with the `Work` instance, and any exception thrown during the processing of submitted Work instances.

Q13. What are System contracts?

Ans. JCA defines a number of system-level contracts to be implemented by a resource adapter and application server. These system-level contracts are classified into three categories: the Connection Management contract, the Transaction Management contract, and the Security contract. These contracts specify the simple interfaces between the application server and EIS.

18

Java EE Design Patterns

If you need an information on:	*See page:*

With the advent of Web technologies, almost all the industries use the Internet in many ways. Web applications are developed to reach customers, expand business domains, and provide better services to the clients. Java EE provides a platform for the development of distributed enterprise or Web applications. As the size of the enterprise increases, there arises a need for more effective Web solutions; thereby, resulting in an increase in the size and complexity of Web applications. Therefore, the Web applications need to be scalable, easily expandable, and reusable to ensure effective management of increasing complexity and size. Development of such Web applications requires some standard architecture. A lot of work has been done in this domain of developing Web applications. All the Web applications follow the 3-tier architecture, which provides a clear separation between business logic and presentation logic of the Web application. This ensures a standard format to be followed in the development and maintenance of the basic infrastructure of Java EE enterprise applications. Along with a standard architecture, various standard design patterns are also applied to enterprise applications to ensure consistency and delivery of high quality business solutions.

In this chapter, you learn about the Java EE application architecture. Next, you learn about the design patterns. Further, you learn about the role of design patterns in Web applications. Finally, the chapter discusses the different types of design patterns.

Let's start the chapter by learning about the Java EE application architecture.

Describing the Java EE Application Architecture

A proper technical architecture is necessarily required to ensure development and management of an enterprise application, which is scalable, robust, flexible, and reusable. Java EE allows various architectures to be used for managing enterprise applications. However, the 3-tier architecture is the most commonly used architecture. Java EE employs a component-based approach for developing, managing, and deploying enterprise applications. The 3-tier architecture consists of three tiers or layers, namely presentation tier or client tier, business tier or application tier, and data tier or enterprise information service tier. The client tier or presentation tier manages the user interface of the application. This tier is responsible for handling user inputs and interactions as well as presentation of data to the user. The business tier or application tier implements the business logic for the application. This tier is responsible for processing the input data and generating response accordingly. The data tier or enterprise information service tier handles the data for the application. This tier manages a database and stores persistent data for the application. Figure 18.1 shows a representation of the 3-tier architecture:

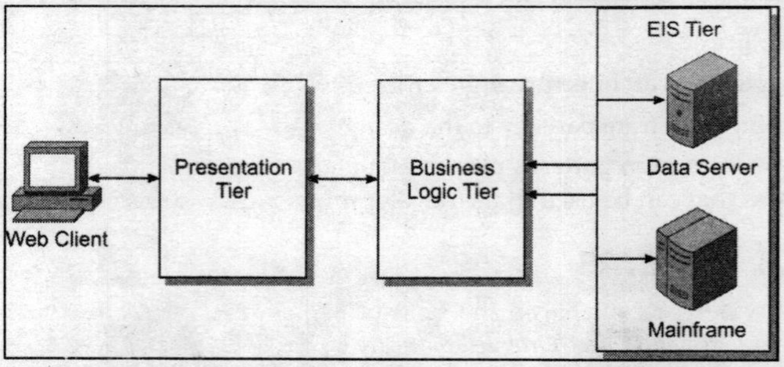

Figure 18.1: Displaying the 3-tier Architecture

Figure 18.1 shows a representation of the 3-tier architecture, where a client interacts with the presentation tier, which provides the user interface; the requests made by the client are processed at the business tier, which provides the business logic; and the client data is stored at the enterprise information service tier. For example, if a client wants to store some data on the data server, then instead of forwarding the request directly to the data server, the request is first forwarded to the presentation tier; the business tier then processes the request and validates the user before forwarding the data to the data server. In this way, the 3-tier architecture is used to design the enterprise applications.

However, designing Web applications is not an easy task. A lot of considerations need to be examined before reaching to a conclusion about how to develop a Web application or an enterprise application. To facilitate the development process for developing Web applications, a lot of design patterns have been proposed. Before discussing about the various available design patterns that are applied in Web application development and designing, let's first examine what is meant by a design pattern in context to a Web or an enterprise application.

Introducing a Design Pattern

Design patterns refer to language-independent solutions provided for solving commonly recurring design problems. A design pattern first describes the problem and then the solution that can be applied to the problem. The design patterns are implemented in the form of objects and classes that provide solutions to the problem. The concept of design patterns was first applied to object oriented programming. Later, this concept was also applied to the development of enterprise applications.

There are various problems concerning the designing issues of Web applications that may arise while developing the application. Some of the problems occur more often and creating a solution from scratch all over again every time the problem occurs, results in wastage of time and effort involved in the process of development of the Web or enterprise application. Therefore, design patterns have been developed which provide well examined and proven solution to recurring problems while designing applications. The design patterns can be divided into various categories on the basis of their application domains.

After understanding about a design pattern, let's learn in what ways it can be helpful in designing enterprise applications.

Discussing the Role of Design Patterns

Design patterns are used while designing the enterprise applications to provide standardized, proven, and tested solutions to recurring problems that arise during the development of enterprise applications. Design patterns offer various benefits to enterprise application development. The application of design patterns greatly speeds up the development process. Moreover, reusing design patterns help in recognizing and avoiding subtle issues that can later become a bottleneck to the development process. Design patterns provide code reusability and improve readability of code for developers who are familiar with the design patterns. They also help in improving communication between the developers by providing a vocabulary which uses well-known and well-understood names and terms for software interaction. The important benefits of design patterns can be summed up as follows:

- Provides tested solutions to frequently and repeatedly occurring problems
- Provides code reusability
- Helps in defining application architecture more efficiently and clearly
- Provides more reliability and transparency to the design of the application

After discussing the roles that design patterns play in an enterprise application, let's move forward and explore the types of design patterns that can be used in the development of such applications.

Exploring Types of Patterns

Design patterns became widely acceptable in the field of computer science after the publication of the book *Design Patterns: Elements of Reusable Object-Oriented Software* by Erich Gamma, Richard Helm, Ralph Johnson, and John Vlissides in 1994. Java EE design patterns help in recognizing potential problems that have been observed while using various Java EE technologies and finding appropriate implementable solutions to those problems according to the application architecture. The various available patterns can be categorized on the basis of the architectural tier in which they are applied. Figure 18.2 shows some patterns as provided by Sun Java Center:

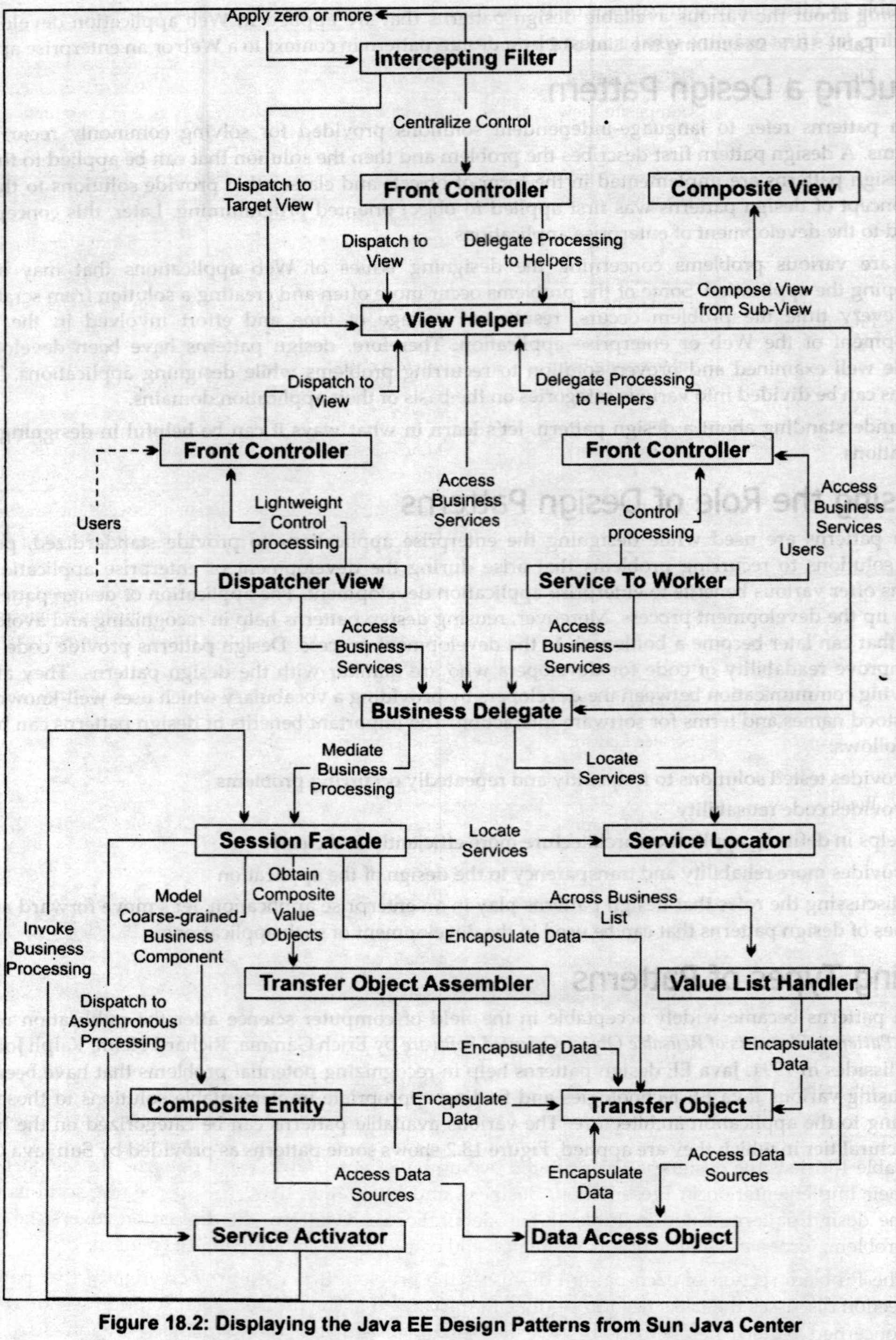

Figure 18.2: Displaying the Java EE Design Patterns from Sun Java Center

Table 18.1 lists the design patterns on the basis of the architectural tiers to which they belong:

Table 18.1: Describing the List of Design Patterns

Tier	Pattern Name	Description
Presentation Tier	Composite View	Manages the layout of a Web page and presentation of data on it. It represents a composite view, in which data is presented in the form of sections which are built by using reusable sub-views.
	Dispatcher View	Provides services for data processing, such as authentication; and request handling by offering limited amount of business processing. It solves a combination of problems handled by the Front Controller and View Helper patterns.
	Front Controller	Implements a central controller in an enterprise application to process the requests.
	Intercepting Filter	Intercepts the request reception and response transmission. It also helps in pre-processing or redirection of a request; and post-processing or content replacement of a response.
	Service to Worker	Maintains a separation between the models, views, and controllers. The workers and views are managed by a dispatcher object.
	View Helper	Helps in maintaining a separation between the presentation logic and business logic. The business logic is implemented for a view using the view helper class.
Business Tier	Business Delegate	Manages the complexity involved in lookup and exception handling for distributed components by introducing an intermediate business delegate class which reduces coupling between presentation tier and business tier.
	Composite Entity	Manages a network of interrelated persistent objects.
	Service Locator	Allows the users to uniformly access business components and services. To accomplish this, the Service Locator pattern uses Java Naming and Directory Interface (JNDI).
	Session Façade	Provides a simple interface to a client by hiding all the complexities involved in the interaction between various business components by encapsulating the complex implementation details in a session bean that acts as a facade.
	Transfer Object	Provides a way to transfer bulk data from a remote server by using a serialized Java object.
	Value List Handler	Provides a handler object that enables the users to iterate over a read only list.
Integration Tier	Data Access Object	Allows the code for accessing and manipulating data to be encapsulated in a separate layer.
	Service Activator	Allows asynchronous invocation of the business services.

Table 18.1 lists the design patterns offered by Sun Java Center. The design patterns are categorized according to their implementation in Presentation, Business, and Integration tiers. The succeeding sections discuss some of the design patterns listed in Table 18.1 in detail. For each pattern, the discussion covers the definition of the problem, forces, possible solution, strategies, and consequences of applying the pattern.

The Problem section of each pattern discusses the problem that led to the creation of that pattern. The Forces section discusses the tasks need to be done in the context of the problem. The Solution section discusses how the concerned pattern has helped to solve the discussed problem. The Strategies section discusses the various strategies that can be used to implement the pattern and the result of the pattern is discussed in the Consequences section.

Let's start exploring some of the design patterns listed in Table 18.1, starting with the Front Controller pattern, in the next section.

The Front Controller Pattern

The Front Controller pattern provides a centralized control to the application request processing. It introduces a central controller component that acts as a common entry point for all application requests. The controller component provides the logic for handling user requests, invoking security services, managing content retrieval, delegating business processing, and selecting appropriate views. The controller component may delegate some processing to a helper component or dispatcher component. The helper component takes the responsibility of helping a view or controller in completing its processing. For example, the helper component may help in gathering the data required by the view. The data can be provided as raw data, or the helper component may format that data as required by the view. The dispatcher component helps the controller in managing and selecting the next view to be presented to a user.

Problem

The Presentation tier requires a centralized control to handle multiple user requests for effectively managing the activities of content retrieval, view management, and security service invocation. However, users can access the views directly without following a centralized mechanism. This approach requires the code for processing logic and system services to be duplicated for each view. When the responsibility of view navigation and management is left to the views themselves, then this may lead to commingled view content and navigation. For example, in an online shopping Web site, multiple user requests need to be handled at the same time and the sequence of steps involved in shopping process also needs to be controlled. There may be multiple users logged in the Web site at a time. This scenario requires that consistency and security should be maintained across multiple requests. A lot of code duplication can occur if the code that controls the input is scattered across multiple objects.

Forces

The problem described in the preceding section results in the following forces:

- Replication of code in multiple views
- Similar business requests responded by multiple views
- Complex logic for view management
- Completion of common system services on a per request basis

Solution

The solution is obtained by introducing a `Front Controller` component that acts as a common entry point for handling multiple client requests. The `Front Controller` component provides a centralized control mechanism for request handling that reduces code duplication and encourages code reusability. The Front Controller pattern helps to achieve the following tasks:

- Calling up the security services, such as authentication and access control
- Managing request handling
- Managing view selection and navigation
- Managing client's state
- Handling errors

Figure 18.3 shows the representation of the Front Controller pattern:

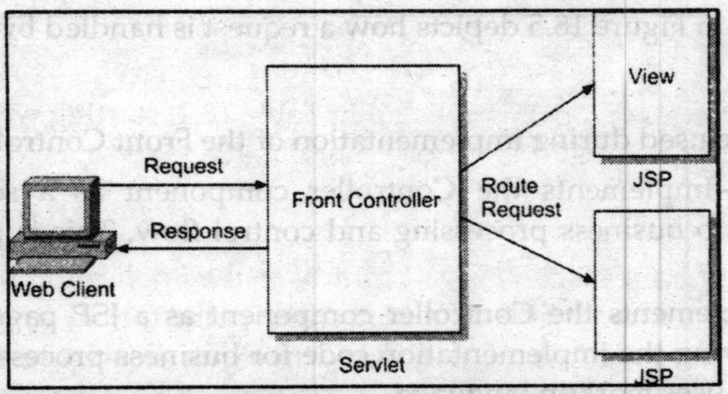

Figure 18.3: Displaying the Role of Front Controller

As shown in Figure 18.3, the central Front Controller component implemented as a servlet receives a request from a client and redirects it to respective views. It also forwards back the response to the client. Multiple controllers can also be used in an application, where each controller is mapped to a distinct set of services. Figure 18.4 shows the class diagram of `Front Controller`:

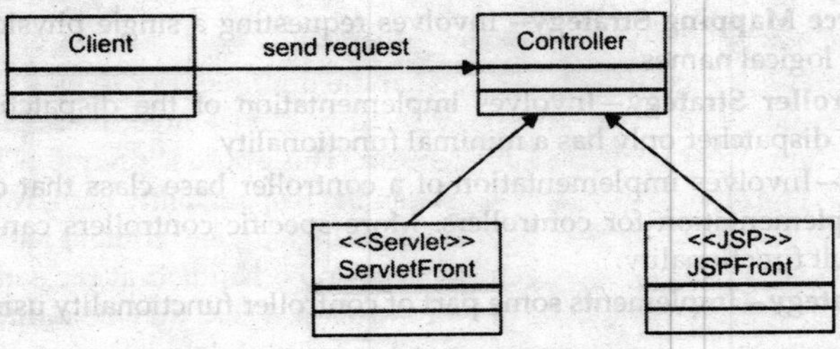

Figure 18.4: Displaying the Front Controller Class Diagram

The `Front Controller` component may use a separate dispatcher component for implementing the required workflow. It can also use helper components, which are implemented as JavaBean components and custom tags. Figure 18.5 shows a sequence diagram representing the interaction between the components involved in the Front Controller pattern:

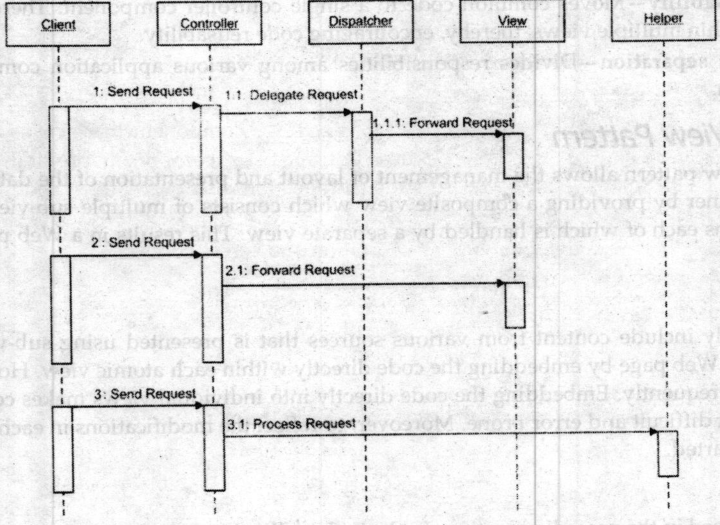

Figure 18.5: Displaying the Sequence Diagram for the Front Controller Pattern

The sequence diagram shown in Figure 18.5 depicts how a request is handled by the Controller component.

Strategies

The following strategies can be used during implementation of the Front Controller pattern:

- **Servlet Front Strategy**—Implements the Controller component as a servlet, which manages request handling aspects related to business processing and control flow. This is preferred over JavaServer Pages (JSP) Front strategy.
- **JSP Front Strategy**—Implements the Controller component as a JSP page. However, this strategy is not preferred because modifying the implementation code for business processing logic involves modifications to be made in a page that uses markup language.
- **Command and Controller Strategy**—Specifies that a generic interface should be provided to the helper components to reduce coupling between them.
- **Physical Resource Mapping Strategy**—Involves requesting resources by their specific physical resource name instead of logical names.
- **Logical Resource Mapping Strategy**—Involves requesting resources by their logical names.
- **Multiplexed Resource Mapping Strategy**-- Involves requesting a single physical resource by not just one but a complete set of logical names.
- **Dispatcher in Controller Strategy**—Involves implementation of the dispatcher functionality within the controller, where the dispatcher only has a minimal functionality.
- **Base Front Strategy**—Involves implementation of a controller base class that contains common code and provides default implementation for controllers. More specific controllers can extend the controller base class to acquire default functionality.
- **Filter Controller Strategy**—Implements some part of controller functionality using a filter.

Consequences

Following consequences are observed when the `Front Controller` pattern is used:

- **Centralizes control**—Implements a central controller component for handling requests and implementing business logic. Therefore, requests can be easily tracked and logged.
- **Improves manageability**—Provides a single entry point for all requests, which requires fewer resources; thereby, improving manageability.
- **Improves reusability**—Moves common code to a single controller component. Therefore, the code is not duplicated within multiple views; thereby, encouraging code reusability.
- **Improves role separation**—Divides responsibilities among various application components for effective role separation.

The Composite View Pattern

The Composite View pattern allows the management of layout and presentation of the data on a Web page in a more effective manner by providing a composite view which consists of multiple sub-views. The Web page is divided into sections each of which is handled by a separate view. This results in a Web page that consists of a set of views.

Problem

Web pages normally include content from various sources that is presented using sub-views. The content is incorporated in the Web page by embedding the code directly within each atomic view. However, the content of the views changes frequently. Embedding the code directly into individual views makes code modification and layout management difficult and error prone. Moreover, to reflect the modifications in each sub-view; the server may need to be restarted.

Forces

The problem discussed in the preceding section results in the following forces:

- The atomic content of the view more often changes

- ❑ Multiple composite views utilize similar sub-views which are presented either by using surrounding template text, or may be displayed at different location within the Web page
- ❑ It is difficult and error-prone to maintain and manage changes in the layout and code
- ❑ The frequent embedding of code, which controls the frequently changing portions, directly into views greatly affects the availability and maintenance of the system

Solution

The solution to the problem mentioned with respect to Composite View pattern is to implement a composite view which is made up of multiple atomic sub-views. This involves dynamic inclusion of each component of the Web page template into the page. This allows you to manage the layout independent of the content of the page. The composite view pattern provides the following benefits:

- ❑ Encourages code reusability and modular design
- ❑ Allows you to create pages using components that can be incorporated dynamically by combining them in a variety of ways
- ❑ Allows layout of the page to be modified independent of the page content
- ❑ Helps in creating a prototype for examining the layout of a site

The responsibilities of various components which participate in the Composite View pattern are listed as follows:

- ❑ **Composite view**—Provides a view which is an aggregate of multiple independent atomic sub-views.
- ❑ **View Manager**—Manages page structure and layout by managing and controlling the inclusion of code fragments in the composite view. It can be implemented as a JavaBean helper or custom tag helper.
- ❑ **Included view**—Refers to a sub-view which is an atomic portion of a larger view. The sub-view can either be composite or can itself include multiple views.

Figure 18.6 shows the class diagram representing the `Composite View` pattern:

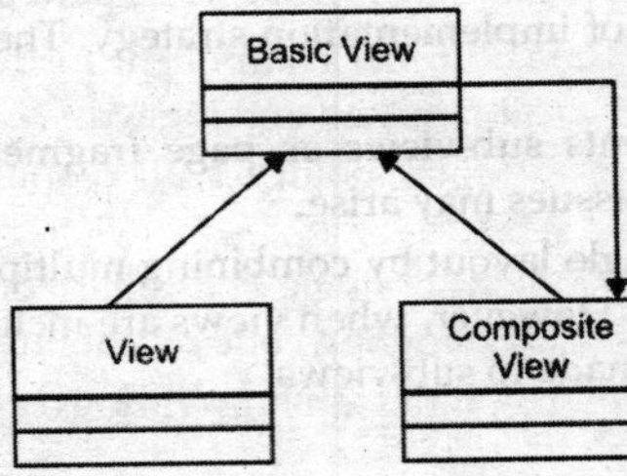

Figure 18.6: Displaying the Class Diagram Representing the Composite View Pattern

Figure 18.7 shows the sequence diagram for the Composite View pattern:

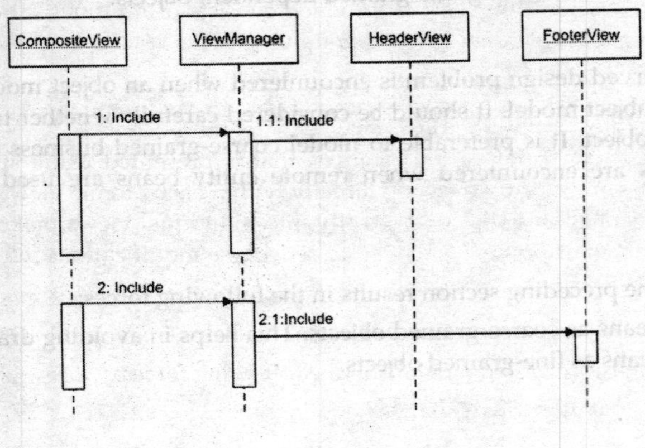

Figure 18.7: Displaying the Sequence Diagram for the Composite View Pattern

Figure 18.7 describes the sequence of interaction between the components of the Composite View pattern. The CompositeView component partitions the user interface into multiple views, and then, the ViewManager component controls the layout and structure of the Web page.

Strategies

The strategies to implement the Composite View pattern are as follows:

- **JavaBeans View Management Strategy**—Implements a JavaBean component for handling view management.
- **Standard Tag View Management Strategy**—Uses standard JSP page tags for managing views.
- **Custom Tag View Management Strategy**—Uses custom tags for implementing view management.
- **Transformer View Management Strategy**—Uses an Extensible Stylesheet Language (XSL) Transformer for handling view management.
- **Early-Binding Resource Strategy**—Refers to translation time content inclusion. As the name suggests, content is included in the page at translation time. This strategy is appropriate to be used for maintaining and updating static templates.
- **Late-Binding Resource Strategy**—Refers to runtime-content inclusion. As the name suggests, content is included in the page at runtime. This strategy is appropriate to be used for maintenance of composite pages.

Consequences

The following consequences are observed when Composite View pattern is used:

- **Enhances modular design**—Encourages modular design. The code of atomic portions of a template can be used in multiple views and at different locations of a page; thereby, improving maintainability.
- **Enhances flexibility**—Includes views conditionally at runtime on the basis of user role or security policy.
- **Enhances Maintainability**—Allows you to make changes to the content of portions of a template, without affecting its layout as the template code is not directly hard coded into a view. The changes made can be reflected immediately, on the basis of implementation strategy. The page layout can also be changed easily since modifications are centralized.
- **Reduces Manageability**—Implements sub-views as page fragments. When these atomic fragments are aggregated together, manageability issues may arise.
- **Performance Impact**—Creates a single layout by combining multiple sub-views. When views are included at runtime, some delay is observed. However, when views are included at translation time, some problems are encountered while changes are made to sub-views.

The Composite Entity Pattern

The Composite Entity pattern helps in effectively modeling a set of dependent interrelated objects when they are mapped to an Enterprise JavaBean object model. The interface of composite entity is itself coarse-grained, which internally manages communication among fine-grained dependent objects.

Problem

One of the repeatedly observed design problem is encountered when an object model is directly mapped to an Enterprise JavaBean (EJB) object model. It should be considered carefully whether to implement an object as an entity EJB or a plain Java object. It is preferable to model coarse-grained business entities using remote entity beans. However, problems are encountered when remote entity beans are used for modeling fine-grained entities.

Forces

The problem discussed in the preceding section results in the following forces:

- Implementing entity beans as coarse-grained objects. This helps in avoiding drawbacks observed in case of implementing entity beans as fine-grained objects.

- Mapping relational database schema to entity beans. This involves large number of fine-grained entity beans to be created. It is more preferable to have coarse-grained entity beans. At the same time, it is also recommended that the overall number of entity beans should be kept less.
- Mapping object model to EJB model. This results in creation of fine-grained entity beans which map to database schema. This mapping leads to problems concerning performance security issues, manageability, and transaction processing. Moreover, it is difficult and expensive to manage inter-entity bean relationship.
- Mapping of entity beans to database schema. This results in a tight coupling between entity beans and database schema where changes made to one are reflected in the other.

Solution

The solution to the problem stated with respect to the Composite Entity pattern is to implement the set of dependent persistent objects by using a composite entity instead of implementing the dependent objects as individual fine-grained entity bean. A persistent object stores its state in a data store and is shared by multiple clients. These persistent objects can either be coarse-grained objects or dependent objects. Dependent objects are usually managed by the coarse-grained parent objects and are not directly accessible by the client. A composite entity bean represents a coarse-grained object and all its dependent objects as well. It aggregates interrelated dependent persistent objects into single entity bean; thereby, reducing the overall number of entity beans in the application.

Figure 18.8 shows the class diagram representing Composite Entity pattern:

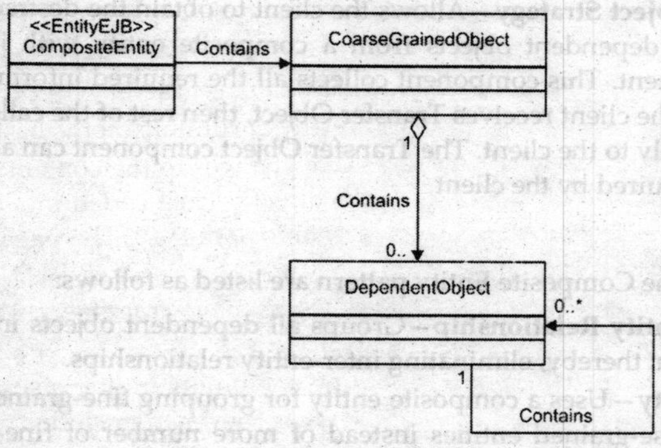

Figure 18.8: Showing the Class Diagram Representing the Composite Entity Pattern

The class diagram in Figure 18.8 shows that the CompositeEntity component contains the CoarseGrainedObject component, which in turn contains the DependentObject component. Figure 18.9 shows the sequence diagram for the Composite Entity pattern displaying the interaction among its various components:

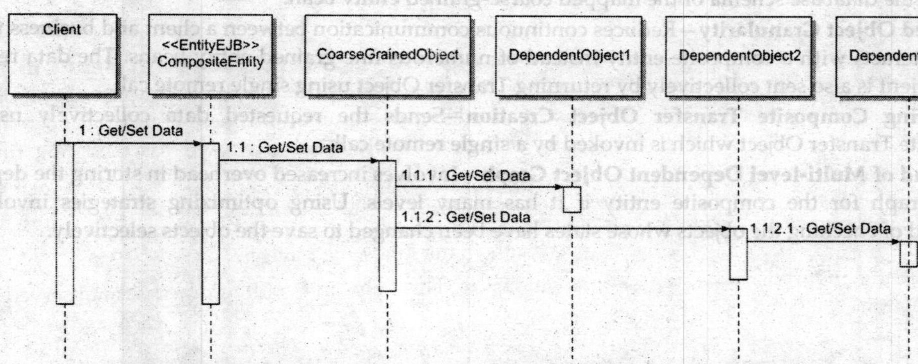

Figure 18.9: Showing the Sequence Diagram for Composite Entity Pattern

Strategies

The strategies used for implementing the Composite Entity pattern are as follows:

- **Composite Entity Contains Coarse-Grained Object Strategy**—Specifies that the coarse-grained entity object is contained by the composite entity. The coarse-grained entity object maintains connection with the dependent objects as well.
- **Composite Entity Implements Coarse-Grained Object Strategy**—Implies that composite entity is itself a coarse-grained entity object which implements the coarse-grained entity and thereby contains its attributes and methods. The dependent objects are represented as attributes of the composite entity which maintains and manages the relationship between the coarse-grained object and its dependent objects.
- **Lazy Loading Strategy**—Implies that all the dependent objects related to the composite entity are not loaded in an application while the composite entity bean is initialized by the EJB container. Only the most important required dependent objects are loaded during initialization. The remaining dependent objects are loaded on an on-demand basis when they are required or accessed by the client.
- **Store Optimization (Dirty Marker) Strategy**—Involves the creation, implementation, and usage of the `DirtyMarker` interface that contains methods, which can be used by the dependent objects to let the caller be aware of the changes in their state. This enables the caller of the objects to selectively save only the dependent objects that have changed since the last call to the `ejbStore()` operation while persisting the composite entity. Otherwise, the complete dependent object graph needs to be persisted to the database whenever the `ejbStore()` method is called by the EJB container.
- **Composite Transfer Object Strategy**—Allows the client to obtain the desired information about the coarse-grained object and its dependent objects from a composite entity with just one remote call using the Transfer Object component. This component collects all the required information into a single object using one remote call. When the client receives Transfer Object, then rest of the calls made by the client to Transfer Object are invoked locally to the client. The Transfer Object component can also gather data from a subset of dependent objects if required by the client.

Consequences

The consequences of using the Composite Entity pattern are listed as follows:

- **Elimination of Inter-Entity Relationship**—Groups all dependent objects into a single entity bean using a composite entity pattern; thereby, eliminating inter-entity relationships.
- **Improved Manageability**—Uses a composite entity for grouping fine-grained entities; thereby, resulting in fewer numbers of coarse-grained entities instead of more number of fine-grained entities. This, in turn, improves manageability.
- **Improved Network Performance**—Reduces inter-entity bean communication between fine-grained entity bean objects; thereby, resulting in an improved network performance.
- **Reduction in Database Schema Dependency**—Hides the database schema, which is mapped internally to the coarse-grained entity bean, from the client. Therefore, the client is not affected whenever changes are made to the database schema of the mapped coarse-grained entity bean.
- **Increased Object Granularity**—Reduces continuous communication between a client and business tier. The client interacts with a composite entity instead of numerous fine-grained entity beans. The data requested by the client is also sent collectively by returning Transfer Object using single remote call.
- **Facilitating Composite Transfer Object Creation**—Sends the requested data collectively using the composite Transfer Object which is invoked by a single remote call.
- **Overhead of Multi-level Dependent Object Graph**—Involves increased overhead in storing the dependent object graph for the composite entity if it has many levels. Using optimizing strategies involves the overhead of checking the objects whose states have been changed to save the objects selectively.

The Intercepting Filter Pattern

The Intercepting Filter pattern introduces a filter that intercepts and intermediates the request to be received and the responses to be transmitted. The filter allows pre-processing and post-processing of the request and response, respectively. Therefore, the filter can either modify or redirect the request; and post-process or replace the content in the response.

Problem

All the requests received by the presentation tier cannot be directly forwarded to a request handler. Sometimes, the request needs to be modified or pre-processed before it is handed over to the request handler. Similarly, the responses generated in response to a request cannot always be forwarded back to the client directly. Sometimes, the content of the response need to be post-processed or replaced before it is sent to the client. The Intercepting Filter pattern solves this problem by introducing an intercepting filter between incoming requests and outgoing responses; thereby, allowing requests to be pre-processed and responses to be post-processed.

Forces

Following forces are involved in the problem stated in the preceding section:

- Implementation of common processing logic, such as, logging client information, and authentication by a centralized filter. This allows the processing to be carried out on a per request basis.
- Centralization of common logic.
- Addition and removal of services without affecting existing components.

Solution

The problem stated in the preceding section can be solved by introducing intercepting filters that implement common code to process common services for pre-processing incoming requests and post-processing outgoing responses. In this approach, whenever a change is required to be introduced in the processing logic for common services, the core request processing code need not be modified. The intercepting filters implementing the code for common services are independent of the main application and can be added or removed without affecting the application. The intercepting filters can also be chained together in sequence, one after the other.

Figure 18.10 shows the class diagram depicting the Intercepting Filter pattern:

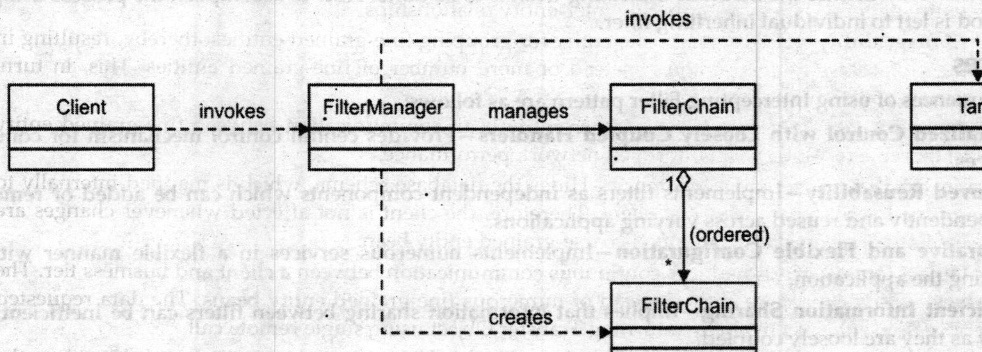

Figure 18.10: Showing the Class Diagram for the Intercepting Filter Pattern

Figure 18.11 shows the sequence diagram representing the interactions between various components of the Intercepting Filter pattern:

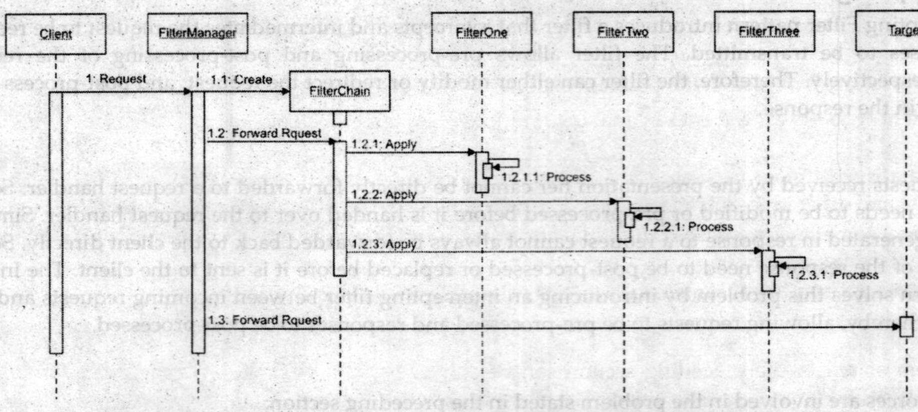

Figure 18.11: Showing the Sequence Diagram for the Intercepting Filter Pattern

Strategies

The Intercepting Filter pattern can be implemented by using the following strategies:

- **Custom Filter Strategy**—Implements the filter by using a user-defined custom strategy. However, it is less effective and less preferable because it does not request and response object in a standard manner.
- **Standard Filter Strategy**—Declares filters using the Deployment Descriptor. Creation of filter chains as well as addition and removal of filters to those chains follow a standard mechanism. Filters are added and removed declaratively by modifying the Deployment Descriptor.
- **Base Filter Strategy**—Implements a base filter that acts as a common superclass for all filters. Common features are implemented in the base filter and shared among all the other filters.
- **Template Filter Strategy**—Implements a base filter that is inherited by all other filters and provides template methods whose specific implementations are provided by the respective inheriting filters. The base filter only defines the methods indicating what is to be done. How to accomplish the process using the method is left to individual inheriting filter.

Consequences

The consequences of using Intercepting Filter pattern are as follows:

- **Centralized Control with Loosely Coupled Handlers**—Provides central control mechanism for common services.
- **Improved Reusability**—Implements filters as independent components which can be added or removed independently and reused across varying applications.
- **Declarative and Flexible Configuration**—Implements numerous services in a flexible manner without affecting the application.
- **Inefficient Information Sharing**—Implies that information sharing between filters can be inefficient and costly as they are loosely coupled.

The Transfer Object Pattern

The Transfer Object pattern, also termed as Value Object pattern, implements a Transfer Object component, which is a serializable class that aggregates related attributes together to form a composite value that can be returned as a return type by the methods. The instance of Transfer Object can be obtained by calling the coarse-grained business methods. The fine-grained values can be accessed locally within Transfer Object.

Problem

Sometimes the client requires to access bulk data from an enterprise bean. The requested data may include a set of attributes that are to be accessed together. In such a case, the business object's get method needs to be invoked multiple times for each attribute to fetch the values for all the attributes. This results in increased network traffic, high latency, and unnecessary consumption of server resources.

Forces

Following forces are involved in the problem stated in the preceding section:

- The client requests for the data by making multiple remote method calls through the remote interface to the bean.
- The data is read more frequently than being modified. The data is required by the client for presentation, display, and other read-only operations. The data is modified and updated less frequently.
- The client sometimes request for multiple attributes, which are accessed by making multiple remote method calls to the enterprise bean.
- The increased number of remote calls affects network traffic and performance.

Solution

The problem stated in the preceding section can be solved by using Transfer Object that aggregates related attributes together into a composite object. The client can access Transfer Objects by a single remote method call. Individual attributes can then be accessed locally from Transfer Object. This significantly helps in reducing network traffic as well as latency, and also provides better resource utilization.

Figure 18.12 shows the class diagram representing the Transfer Object pattern:

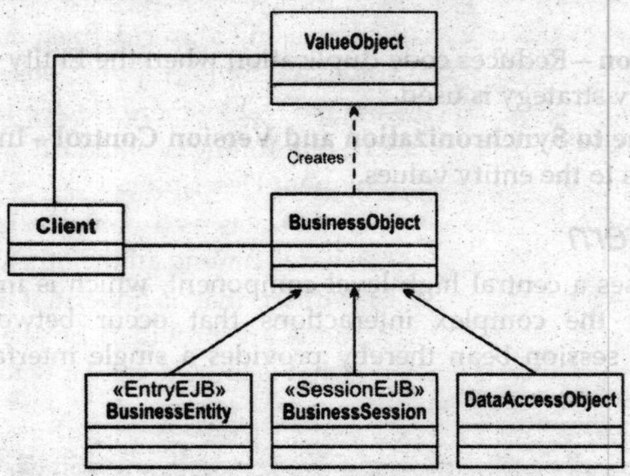

Figure 18.12: Showing the Class Diagram Representing the Transfer Object Pattern

As shown in Figure 18.12, Transfer Object is created on an on-demand basis by the enterprise bean. Figure 18.13 shows the sequence diagram depicting the interaction between various components of the Transfer Object pattern:

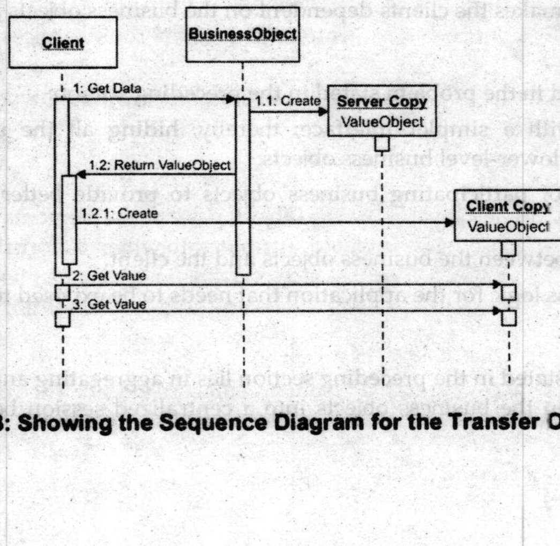

Figure 18.13: Showing the Sequence Diagram for the Transfer Object Pattern

Strategies

Following strategies can be applied to implement the Transfer Object pattern:

- **Updatable Transfer Object Strategy**—Implements Transfer Object that can make data accessible from the business object to the client, as well as from the client back to the business object.
- **Multiple Transfer Object Strategy**—Creates multiple Transfer Objects to manage a single business object.
- **Entity Inherits Transfer Object Strategy**—Specifies that the entity bean inherits the Transfer Object class. Therefore, the attributes specified in the Transfer Object class do not get duplicated in the entity bean.
- **Transfer Object Factory Strategy**—Allows on-demand creation of Transfer Objects by using the concept of reflection. Therefore, multiple Transfer Objects can be created dynamically.

Consequences

The consequences of using Transfer Object pattern are as follows:

- **Entity Bean and Remote Interface Simplification**—Uses entity bean's getData() method to fetch Transfer Object that contains the attribute values. Therefore, multiple get methods need not be implemented in the bean's remote interface.
- **More data Transfer in Fewer Remote Calls**—Involves only a single remote call to be made to Transfer Object. Individual attributes can then be accessed locally from Transfer Object.
- **Reduced Network Traffic**—Results in reduction of network traffic, as only one remote call to Transfer Object needs to be made.
- **Reduced Code Duplication**—Reduces code duplication when the Entity Inherit Transfer Object strategy or the Transfer Object Factory strategy is used.
- **Increased Complexity due to Synchronization and Version Control**—Increases complexity when multiple clients request for updates to the entity values.

The Session Facade Pattern

The Session Facade pattern uses a central high level component, which is implemented as a session bean and contains the functionality of the complex interactions that occur between various lower-level business components. The higher-level session bean thereby provides a single interface to the client for accessing the functionality of an application.

Problem

Applications sometimes involve complex business processes that comprise many business objects. In such cases, the participating business objects or business classes can be tightly coupled, resulting in higher dependence between the business objects, lower design clarity, and less flexibility towards modifications. Moreover, multiple method invocations need to be made in case of numerous business classes, which affects the network performance. In addition, the direct interaction between the client and the business objects results in tight coupling between them and makes the clients dependent on the business objects implementation.

Forces

Following forces are involved in the problem stated in the preceding section:

- Providing the client with a simpler interface; thereby, hiding all the underlying complexities in the interaction between the lower-level business objects.
- Reducing the number of participating business objects to provide better manageability, flexibility, and enhanced code clarity.
- Reducing the coupling between the business objects and the client.
- Centralizing the business logic for the application that needs to be exposed to the client.

Solution

The solution to the problem stated in the preceding section lies in aggregating and encapsulating the code for the complex interactions between the business objects into a centralized session bean. The session bean acts as a facade for the lower-level business processes. The session facade provides a simpler centralized higher-level interface for the application's functionality and manages the interaction between the lower-lever business processes. Figure 18.14 shows the class diagram representing the Session Facade pattern:

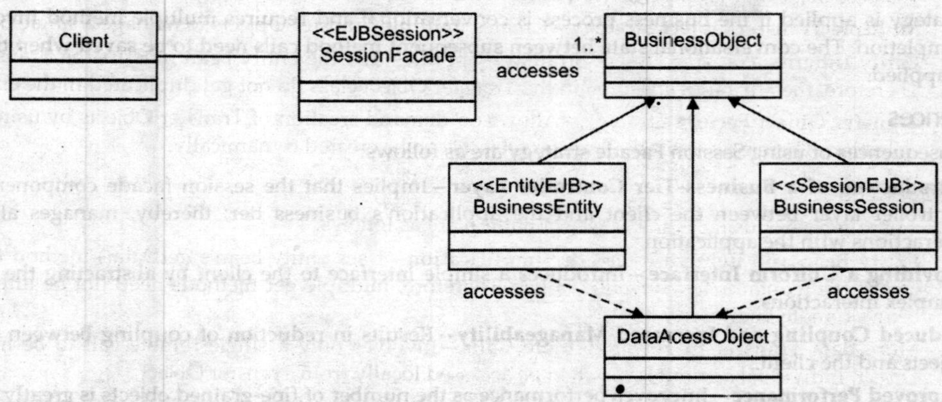

Figure 18.14: Showing the Class Diagram Representing the Session Facade Pattern

As shown in Figure 18.14, the business objects are not accessed directly by the client; however, every request to the business object is made through the session bean. Figure 18.15 shows the sequence diagram depicting the interaction between various components of the Session Facade pattern:

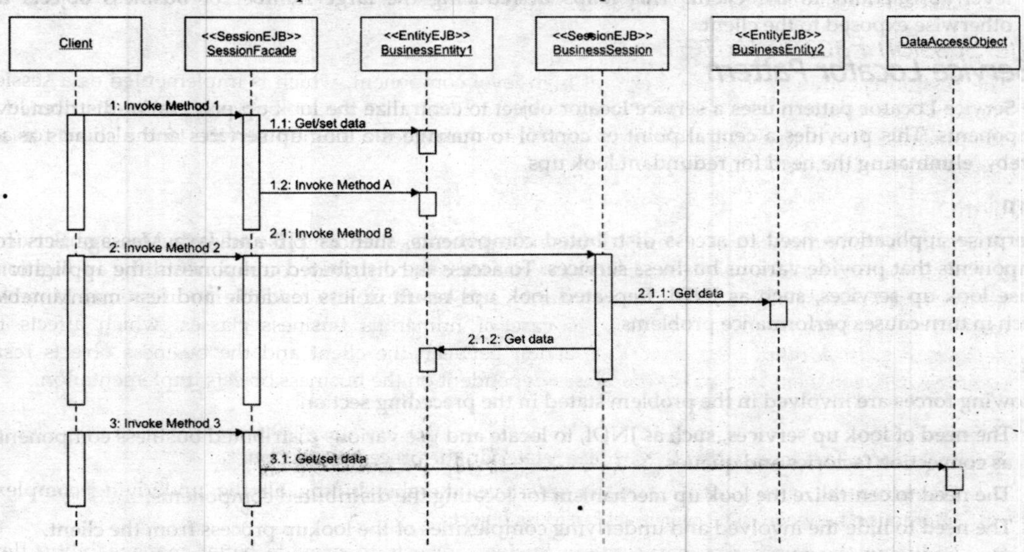

Figure 18.15: Showing the Sequence Diagram for the Session Facade Pattern

Strategies

Following strategies can be used to implement the Session Facade pattern:

- **Stateless Session Facade Strategy** – Implements a business process as a stateless session facade object by using a stateless session bean if the process is non-conversational. Being non-conversational means that the process implemented using stateless session faced strategy gets completed in a single call. The conversational state between subsequent method calls need not be saved.

- **Stateful Session Facade Strategy**—Implements the session facade as a stateful session bean object. This strategy is applied if the business process is conversational and requires multiple method invocations for completion. The conversational state between subsequent method calls need to be saved when this strategy is applied.

Consequences

The consequences of using Session Facade strategy are as follows:

- **Introduction of a Business-Tier Controller Layer**—Implies that the session facade component acts as a controller layer between the client and the application's business tier; thereby, manages all the client interactions with the application.
- **Providing a Uniform Interface**—Introduces a simple interface to the client by abstracting the underlying complex interactions.
- **Reduced Coupling and Increased Manageability**—Results in reduction of coupling between the various objects and the client.
- **Improved Performance**—Improves performance as the number of fine-grained objects is greatly reduced.
- **Providing Coarse-Grained Access**—Provides a coarse-grained abstraction of the application's functionality.
- **Centralized Security Management**—Implements security policy only at the level of the session facade.
- **Centralized Transaction Control**—Applies transaction control at the level of the session façade.
- **Exposing fewer remote interfaces to the client**—Offers a coarse-grained interface that provides higher-level abstractions to the client. This helps in reducing the large number of business objects that are otherwise exposed to the client.

The Service Locator Pattern

The Service Locator pattern uses a service locator object to centralize the look up process for distributed service components. This provides a central point of control to manage the look up services and also acts as a cache; thereby, eliminating the need for redundant look ups.

Problem

Enterprise applications need to access distributed components, such as EJB and Java Message Service (JMS) components that provide various business services. To access the distributed components, the application needs to use look up services, such as JNDI. Repeated look ups result in less readable and less maintainable code, which in turn causes performance problems.

Forces

Following forces are involved in the problem stated in the preceding section:

- The need of look up services, such as JNDI, to locate and use various distributed business components, such as connection factories and queues.
- The need to centralize the look up mechanism for locating the distributed components.
- The need to hide the involved and underlying complexities of the lookup process from the client.
- The need of repeated look up operations. These are resource-intensive and affect performance.
- The requirement of re-establishing the connection to an enterprise bean instance that has been accessed previously.

Solution

The solution to the problem stated in the previous section can be obtained by providing a service locator object that offers a centralized mechanism for the look up process to locate various requested distributed components required by the client. The service locator object abstracts the underlying complexities involved in the look up process. It also provides caching facilities; thereby, providing better management for repeated look up operations. Figure 18.16 shows the class diagram representing the Service Locator pattern:

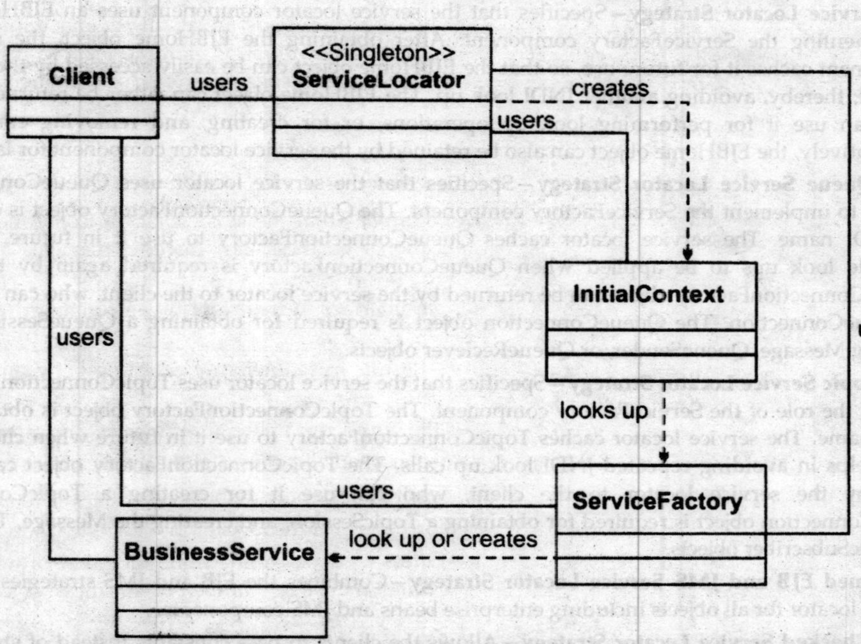

Figure 18.16: Showing the Class Diagram Representing the Service Locator Pattern

Figure 18.17 shows the sequence diagram depicting the interaction between various components of the Service Locator pattern:

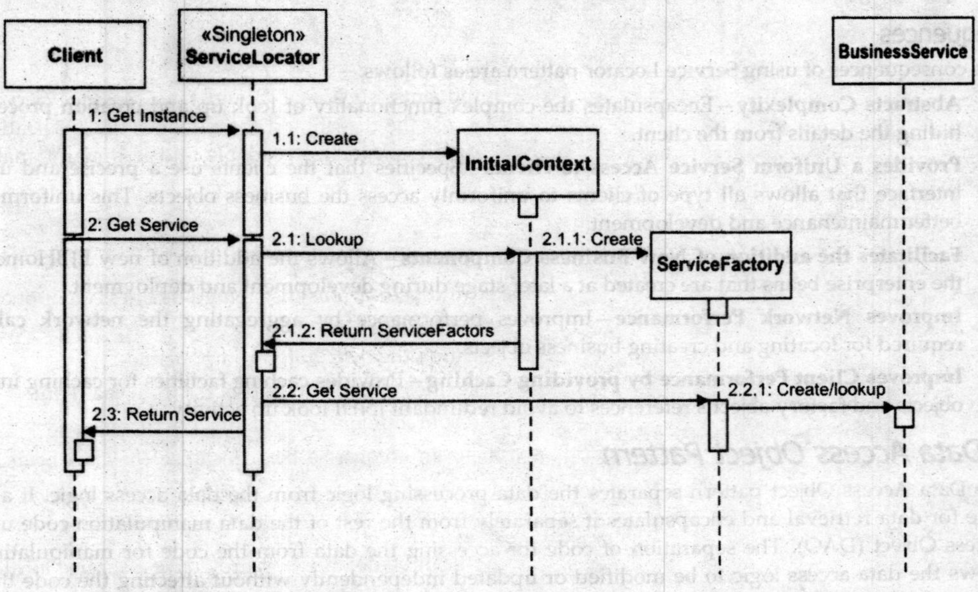

Figure 18.17: Showing the Sequence Diagram of the Service Locator Pattern

Strategies

The Service Locator pattern can be implemented using the following strategies:

- **EJB Service Locator Strategy**—Specifies that the service locator component uses an EJBHome object for implementing the ServiceFactory component. After obtaining the EJBHome object, the service locator component caches it for future use, so that the EJBHome object can be easily accessed by the client on next request; thereby, avoiding another JNDI look up. The EJBHome object can either be returned to the client who can use it for performing look up operations, or for creating, and removing enterprise beans. Alternatively, the EJBHome object can also be retained by the service locator component for later use.
- **JMS Queue Service Locator Strategy**—Specifies that the service locator uses QueueConnectionFactory objects to implement the ServiceFactory component. The QueueConnectionFactory object is obtained using its JNDI name. The service locator caches QueueConnectionFactory to use it in future, which avoids multiple look ups to be applied when QueueConnectionFactory is required again by the client. The QueueConnectionFactory object can be returned by the service locator to the client, who can use it to create a QueueConnection. The QueueConnection object is required for obtaining a QueueSession object, and creating Message, QueueSender, or QueueReciever objects.
- **JMS Topic Service Locator Strategy**—Specifies that the service locator uses TopicConnectionFactory objects to play the role of the ServiceFactory component. The TopicConnectionFactory object is obtained using its JNDI name. The service locator caches TopicConnectionFactory to use it in future when client requires it. This helps in avoiding repeated JNDI look up calls. The TopicConnectionFactory object can be returned back by the service locator to the client, who can use it for creating a TopicConnection. The TopicConnection object is required for obtaining a TopicSession, and creating the Message, TopicPublisher, or TopicSubscriber objects.
- **Combined EJB and JMS Service Locator Strategy**—Combines the EJB and JMS strategies for providing service locator for all objects including enterprise beans and JMS components.
- **Type Checked Service Locator Strategy**—Allows the clients to pass constants instead of string names for JNDI service name and EJBHome class object to the getHome() method as arguments.
- **Service Locator Properties Strategy**—Allows property files or deployment descriptors to be used for specifying JNDI names and EJBHome class name.

Consequences

The consequences of using Service Locator pattern are as follows:

- **Abstracts Complexity**—Encapsulates the complex functionality of look up and creation process; thereby, hiding the details from the client.
- **Provides a Uniform Service Access to clients**—Specifies that the clients use a precise and user-friendly interface that allows all type of clients to uniformly access the business objects. This uniformity helps in better maintenance and development.
- **Facilitates the addition of New Business Components**—Allows the addition of new EJBHome objects for the enterprise beans that are created at a later stage during development and deployment.
- **Improves Network Performance**—Improves performance by aggregating the network calls that are required for locating and creating business objects.
- **Improves Client Performance by providing Caching**—Provides caching facilities for caching initial context objects and factory object's references to avoid redundant JNDI look up activity.

The Data Access Object Pattern

The Data Access Object pattern separates the data processing logic from the data access logic. It abstracts the code for data retrieval and encapsulates it separately from the rest of the data manipulation code using a Data Access Object (DAO). The separation of code for accessing the data from the code for manipulating the data allows the data access logic to be modified or updated independently without affecting the code that uses the data.

Problem

In many cases, applications that provide code, which depends on a specific feature of data resources, combine the data processing logic with data access logic. Sometimes, applications need to access data from different resources. The data access code, in such cases, also varies according to the source of data. For example, the code for accessing data from a relational database will be different than the code that accesses data from a flat file. However, when the data processing code is combined with data access code, the code that accesses the data cannot be flexibly replaced or modified as and when the source of data changes.

Forces

Following forces are involved in the problem stated in the preceding section:

- Implementing the code for accessing the data into a persistent storage.
- Providing a uniform data access Application Programming Interface (API) and persistent storage APIs to various data sources.
- Separating persistent storage implementation from the rest of the code.
- Managing the data access logic by encapsulating it into a separate code block; thereby, facilitating maintainability and portability.
- Allowing the code to be flexibly modified and being adaptable when there is a change in the data source, storage type, or product vendor type.

Solution

The solution to the problem stated in the previous section lies in using a DAO that abstracts and encapsulates the logic for accessing the data from various data sources. DAO manages the establishment of a connection with the respective data source. It also fetches and stores the data that can be further used by some other processing block for manipulation and further processing. DAO hides the entire implementation details from the clients. The clients always see a uniform interface that does not change with the change in the data source. Therefore, the Data Access Object pattern allows DAO to flexibly adapt to the changes in the data sources without affecting the clients or the rest of the code. Figure 18.18 shows the class diagram for the Data Access Object pattern:

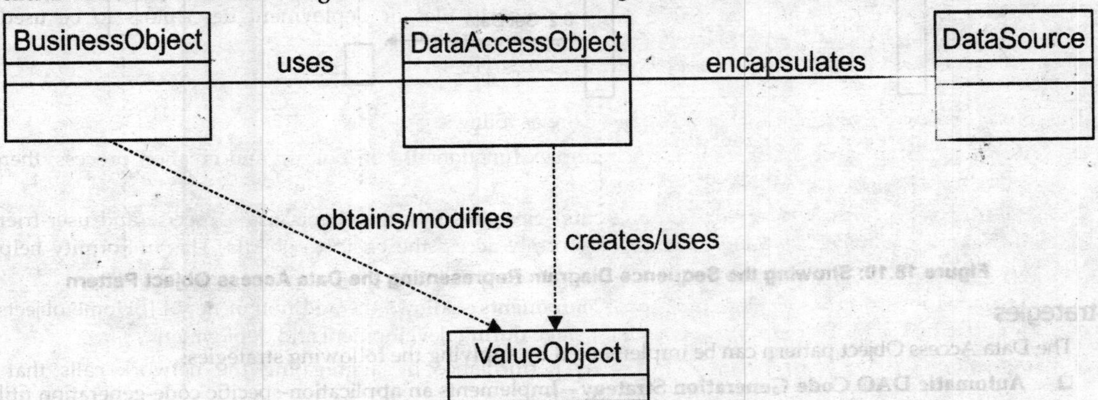

Figure 18.18: Showing the Class Diagram Representing the Data Access Object Pattern

Figure 18.19 shows the sequence diagram for the Data Access Object pattern depicting the relationship between its various participants:

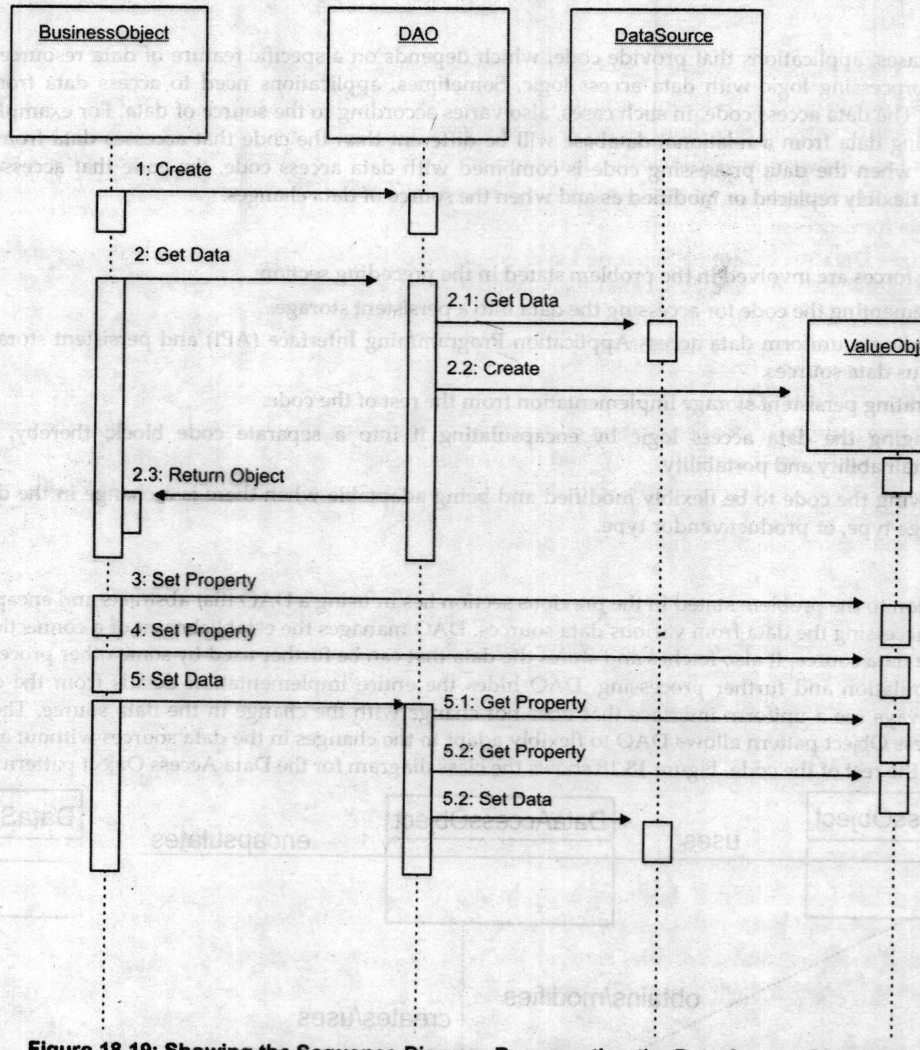

Figure 18.19: Showing the Sequence Diagram Representing the Data Access Object Pattern

Strategies

The Data Access Object pattern can be implemented by applying the following strategies:

- **Automatic DAO Code Generation Strategy**—Implements an application-specific code-generation utility to generate the code for all DAOs that the application requires. To implement this strategy, a relationship between the BusinessObject component, the DAO component, and the underlying implementation needs to be established.
- **Factory for Data Access Objects Strategy**— Uses Abstract Factory and Factory Method patterns to create DAO. This strategy is implemented using the Factory Method pattern to create the DAOs required by the application when the storage does not change between multiple implementations. When the storage is expected to change between various implementations, this strategy is implemented using the Abstract Factory pattern, which in turn uses the Factory Method pattern.

Consequences

The following consequences are observed when the Data Access Object pattern is used:

- **Enables Transparency**—Hides implementation details in DAO; thereby, providing a transparent access to the data source without revealing its specific implementation details.
- **Enables Easier Migration**—Allows the clients to switch between various database implementations.
- **Reduces Code Complexity in Business Objects**—Simplifies the code in business objects that use DAOs to fetch data for processing.
- **Centralizes Data Access into a Separate Layer**—Separates the data access code from the rest of the code of the application; thereby, allowing better management and maintenance of the application.
- **Adds Extra Layer**—Creates an additional layer between the data source and the data client that requires additional effort for implementation.

The View Helper Pattern

The View Helper pattern enforces separation of presentation and business logic. In this pattern, the presentation and formatting logic is handled by the view and the processing and data retrieval logic is handled by the View Helper class. JSP pages are used to create the views for handling the presentation part of the application, while JavaBeans helper classes are created to manage the business logic for the application. The separation of presentation and business logic promotes code reusability and makes the application more manageable.

Problem

The presentation logic of an application changes very often. However, it becomes very difficult to modify or change the presentation logic when it is tightly mingled with the code handling the business logic for the application. This is because when the code for business logic and presentation logic is tightly intermingeled, then any changes to be applied on the code handling the presentation logic also require that considerable relevant changes be made in the associated code handling the business logic. Therefore, the application becomes less manageable and flexible to change. This also results in a poor separation of roles between the Web developers who write the code for presentation logic and the software developers who write the code for business logic.

Forces

The following forces are involved in the problem stated in the preceding section:

- Avoiding the embedding of business logic in the view handling the presentation logic because that promotes copy-and-paste type of reuse which results in maintenance problems and bugs.
- Promoting a clear separation of roles between the Web developers and the software developers.
- Using one view to handle the responses to a specific business request.

Solution

The solution to the problem stated in the previous section is to provide a clear separation between the presentation logic and the business logic. The presentation logic is provided by the views which are JSP pages in most of the cases. The views handle formatting and presentation of content, and delegate the responsibility of processing to the helper classes. The helper classes, normally implemented as JavaBeans or custom tags, handle the business logic for the application. These classes also store any intermediate data for the views. This separation of presentation logic from business logic makes the code more manageable and flexible to change as any change in the presentation logic can be made without affecting the business logic for the application. The View Helper pattern also provides a clear separation of roles between the Web developers and the software developers. Figure 18.20 shows the class diagram representing the View Helper pattern:

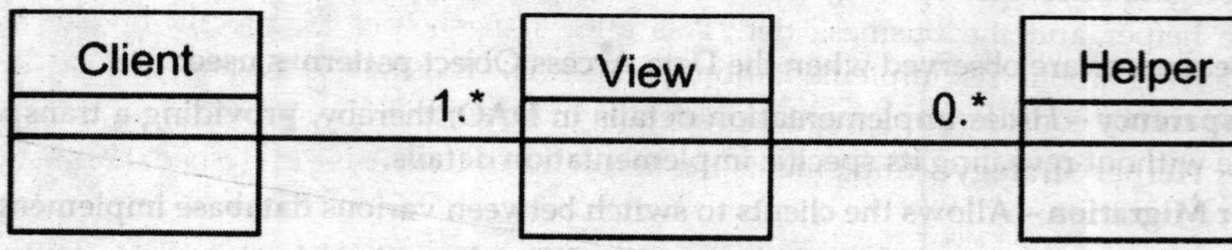

Figure 18.20: Showing the Class Diagram Representing the View Helper Pattern

Figure 18.21 shows the sequence diagram for the View Helper pattern depicting the interaction between its various participants:

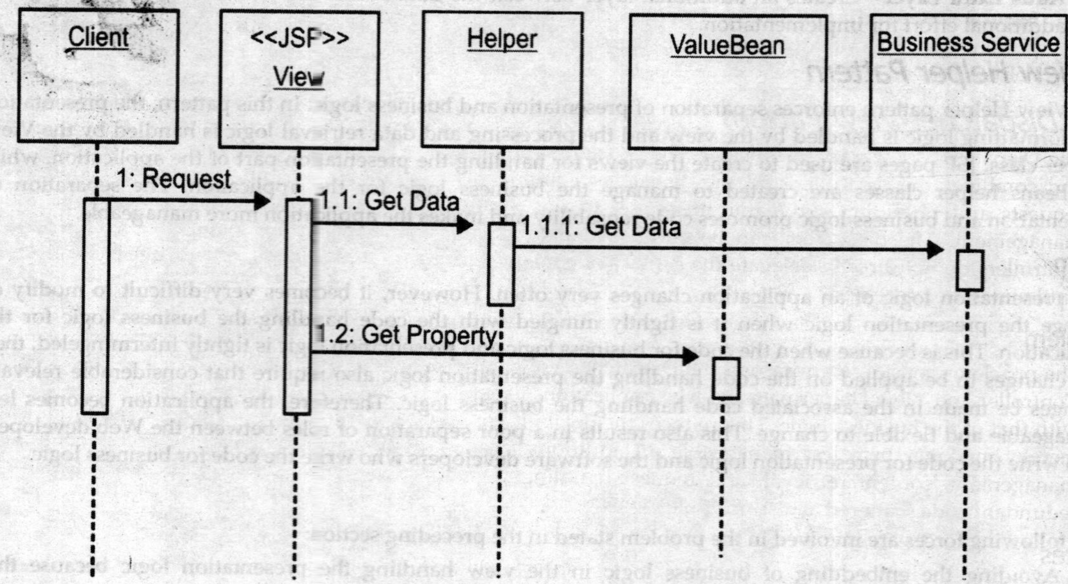

Figure 18.21: Showing the Sequence Diagram for the View Helper Pattern

Strategies

Following strategies can be applied for implementing the View Helper pattern:

- **JSP View Strategy** – Specifies that a view is implemented as JSP page. This strategy is preferred over the Servlet View strategy. JSP pages are used more commonly and provide a more elegant solution for creating the views as it is easier to code JSP pages as compared to creating servlets.
- **Servlet View Strategy** – Uses a servlet for implementing a view. However, it is more difficult to code servlets because servlets have mark up tags embedded directly within Java code. This makes it very difficult to modify and update the code.
- **JavaBean Helper Strategy** – Uses a JavaBean to implement a helper. The JavaBean helper encapsulates the code for implementing the business logic. Using JavaBeans to implement helper classes makes the code more manageable. Moreover, it is easier to create JavaBeans.
- **Custom Tag Helper Strategy** – Uses a custom tag component to implement the helper that encapsulates the business logic. However, developing custom tags is a complicated task as compared to creating JavaBeans. To use the Custom Tag Helper strategy, the environment is required to be configured with various tags, tag library descriptors, and configuration files.

- **Business Delegate as Helper Strategy**—Specifies that a Business Delegate component should be introduced between the helper and the business tier. This allows the helper to directly invoke a business service without worrying about its implementation details. The business delegate can be implemented as a JavaBean and can be considered as a specialized type of helper.
- **Transformer Helper Strategy**—Implements the helper as an Extensible Stylesheet Language Transformer.

Consequences

The consequences of using the View Helper pattern are as follows:

- **Improves reusability, manageability and application partitioning**—Makes the application more manageable by clearly separating business logic from presentation logic. This also improves code reusability and maintainability.
- **Improves Separation of Roles**—Provides clear role separation between the Web developers who code the presentation logic for the views and the software developers who code the business logic for the view helper classes.

The Dispatcher View Pattern

The Dispatcher View pattern considers the problems solved by the Front Controller and View Helper patterns, and combines the controller and the dispatcher components with the views and helpers for handling client requests and providing a dynamic response. In this strategy, the dispatcher handles view navigation and management. The dispatcher can be encapsulated by a controller, a view, or some other component. The controllers do not directly delegate the activity of content retrieval to the handlers. The activities are postponed until views are processed.

Problem

The problems considered in case of the Dispatcher View pattern comprise the problems considered in the Front Controller and View Helper patterns. The applications usually have the code for presentation logic intermingled with that of the business logic. This reduces the flexibility of applications to adapt to changes and modifications; thereby, making them less manageable. In addition, a central component for handling access control, view management, content retrieval, and request handling is not available. Moreover, applications usually have redundant code scattered across multiple views.

Forces

Following forces are involved in the problem stated in the preceding section:

- Complete authentication and authorization checks performed per request
- Minimized scriptlet code within views
- Encapsulation of business logic in separate components other than views
- Simplified control flow based on values supplied with request
- Limited and simpler view management logic

Solution

The solution to the problem stated in the previous section lies in combining the controller and the dispatcher with the views and helpers for handling the client requests and preparing a dynamic presentation as the response. In this strategy, the controllers do not delegate the content retrieval activities directly to the helpers. The dispatcher plays a minimized role and forwards the request to the views on the basis of input received from the controller; thereby, handling view navigation and management. On processing, the views handle the request and generate a response by accessing the helper classes. Figure 18.22 shows the class diagram for the Dispatcher View pattern:

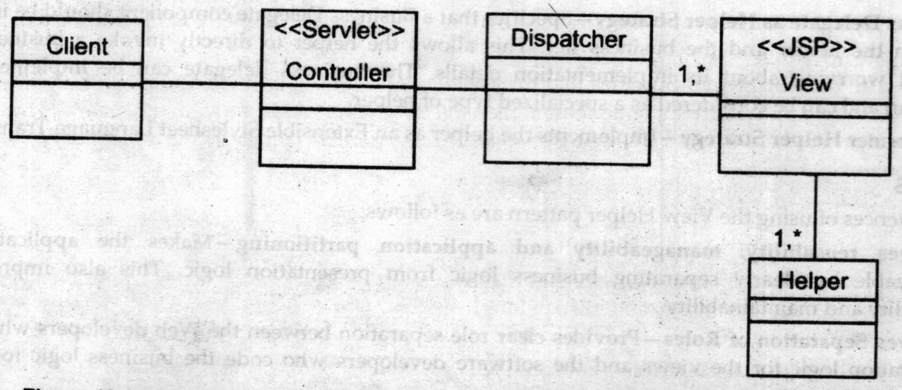

Figure 18.22: Showing the Class Diagram Representing the Dispatcher View Pattern

Figure 18.23 shows the sequence diagram for the Dispatcher View pattern depicting the interactions between its various participants:

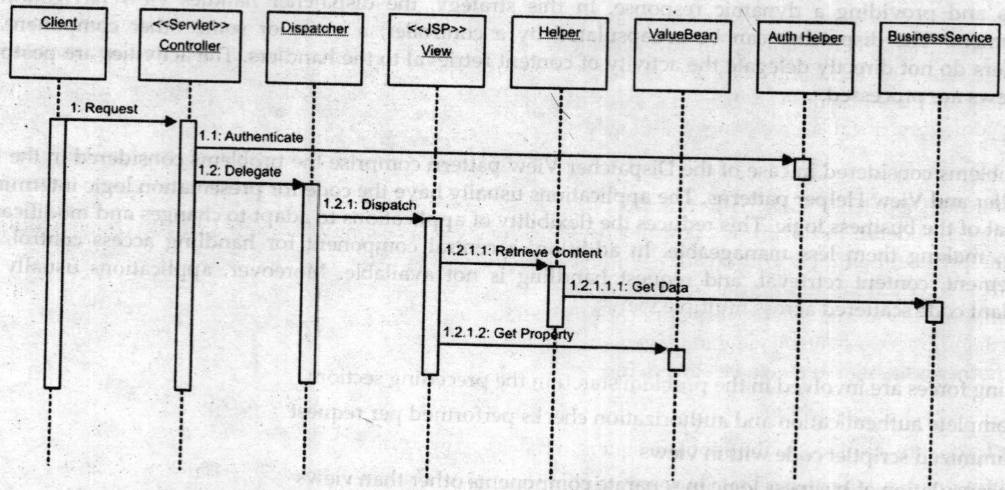

Figure 18.23: Showing the Sequence Diagram for the Dispatcher View Pattern

Strategies

The Dispatcher View pattern can be applied by using various strategies which have already been discussed in the previous sections. They are listed as follows:

- Servlet Front Strategy
- JSP Front Strategy
- JSP View Strategy
- Servlet View Strategy
- JavaBean Helper Strategy
- Custom Tag Helper Strategy
- Dispatcher in Controller Strategy
- Transformer Helper Strategy

Besides the preceding strategies, another strategy that can be used for implementing the Dispatcher View pattern is described as follows:

- **Dispatcher in View Strategy**—Specifies that in case when the controller has a limited role and therefore, is removed from the application implementation; then the dispatcher can be moved into a view. This design is found useful when there is one view that is mapped to a particular request while a secondary view can be used infrequently.

Consequences

The consequences of using Dispatcher View pattern are as follows:

- **Centralizes control thereby improving reusability and maintainability**—Provides a centralized control for the process of request handling and dispatching; thereby, enhancing code reusability and making the application more manageable.
- **Improves application partitioning**—Provides clear separation between the presentation logic coded in views and the business logic coded in helpers.
- **Improves the separation of roles**—Provides clear role separation between Web developers who code the views and the software developers who code the helper classes.

The Service To Worker Pattern

The Service to Worker pattern shows various similarities with the Dispatcher View pattern. This pattern also deals with the problems considered in the Dispatcher View pattern; however, the solution is obtained and implemented slightly differently. In the Service to Worker pattern also, the focus is to deal with the intermingling of presentation and business logic as well as the need to implement a central component for managing content retrieval, access control, and views.

Problem

As stated for the Dispatcher View pattern in the previous sections, the Service to Worker pattern also focuses on the problems considered in the Front Controller and View Helper patterns. There is usually no clear separation between the presentation logic and business logic in the applications. The code providing presentation logic is mixed with the code representing the business logic. This makes the applications less flexible to adapt to new changes and modifications. Moreover, applications usually do not have a centralized component that can effectively handle access control, view management, content retrieval, and request handling. Code duplication in views is another issue that needs to be considered.

Forces

Following forces are involved in the problem stated in the preceding section:

- Executing particular business logic for servicing a request to fetch content that can be used for generating a dynamic response
- Managing view selection that may depend on the responses generated from invoking various business services
- Minimizing scriptlet code within views
- Encapsulating business logic in separate components other than views
- Generating content dynamically
- Using multiple views for responding to similar requests

Solution

As in case of the Dispatcher View pattern, the solution in this case is also obtained by combining the controller and the dispatcher with the views and helpers for handling the client requests and preparing a dynamic presentation as the response. However, in the Service to Worker pattern, unlike the Dispatcher View pattern, the controller delegates the content retrieval activities directly to the helpers. The dispatcher, in this case, submits the request to the appropriate view; thereby, handling view navigation and management. The views then handle the request and generate a dynamic response accordingly with the help of the helper classes. In the Service to

Worker pattern, the dispatcher plays a comparatively larger role as compared to the Dispatcher View pattern, and can be implemented as a separate component or within a controller. Figure 18.24 shows the class diagram for the Service to Worker pattern:

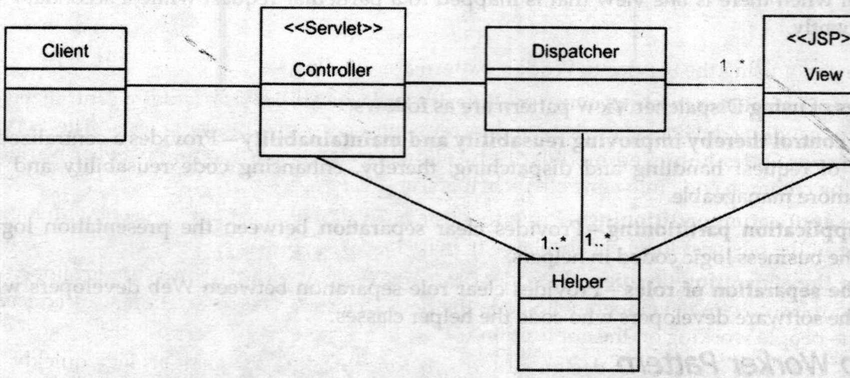

Figure 18.24: Showing the Class Diagram Representing the Service to Worker Pattern

Figure 18.25 shows the sequence diagram depicting the relationship between various participants of the Service to Worker pattern:

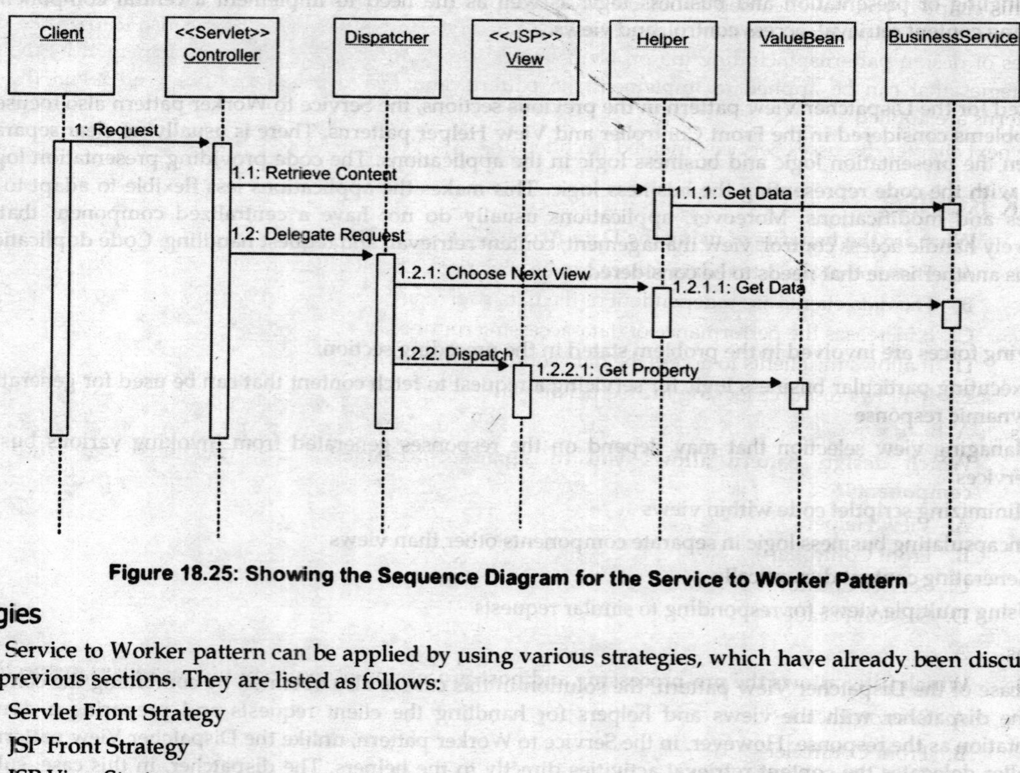

Figure 18.25: Showing the Sequence Diagram for the Service to Worker Pattern

Strategies

The Service to Worker pattern can be applied by using various strategies, which have already been discussed in the previous sections. They are listed as follows:

- Servlet Front Strategy
- JSP Front Strategy
- JSP View Strategy
- Servlet View Strategy

- JavaBean Helper Strategy
- Custom Tag Helper Strategy
- Dispatcher in Controller Strategy
- Transformer Helper Strategy

Consequences

The consequences of using the Service to Worker pattern are as follows:

- **Centralizes control thereby improving modularity and reusability**—Provides a centralized control for the process of handling business services and processing across multiple requests. The Service to Worker pattern also provides improved modularity by allowing clearer partitioning between various components and moving common code into controllers, helpers, and views.
- **Improves application partitioning**—Provides clear separation between the presentation logic encapsulated in views and the business logic encapsulated in helpers.
- **Improves the separation of roles**—Provides clear role separation between Web developers who code the views and the software developers who code the helper classes. This separation also reduces dependencies among the people working on the application.

This completes the discussion about design patterns. Before finishing the chapter, let's quickly summarize the topics covered throughout the chapter, in the next section.

Summary

In this chapter, you have learned about the Java EE application architecture. Next, the chapter introduced the concept of design patterns. Further, it discussed the role of design patterns. You have also learned the different types of design patterns, including the problems faced, forces involved, solution implemented by the pattern, strategies that can be applied to implement the pattern, and the consequences observed when the various patterns are applied.

The next chapter discusses Service Oriented Architecture (SOA) using Java Web Services in detail.

Quick Revise

Q1. What are the benefits of using the Data Access Object pattern?

A. The type of the actual data source can be specified at deployment time.

B. The data clients are independent of the data source vendor API.

C. It increases the performance of data-accessing routines.

D. It allows the clients to access the data source through EJBs.

E. It allows resource locking in an efficient way.

Ans. A, B

Q2. Which design pattern allows you to separate presentation and business logic into distinct components?

A. View Helper

B. Front Controller

C. Service Locator

D. Session Facade

Ans. A

Q3. Which filter allows the pre-processing and post-processing of requests and responses, respectively?

A. Session Facade

B. Front Controller

C. Intercepting Filter

D. Composite Entity

Ans. C

Q4. Which of the following is true in case of the Transfer Object design pattern?

A. The Transfer Object pattern is also termed as Value Object pattern

B. The Transfer Object pattern provides a centralized control to the application request processing

C. A Transfer Object aggregates related attributes together to form a composite value that can be returned as a return type by the methods

D. The Transfer Object pattern defines a separation between data access and data processing logic.

Ans. A, C

Q5. What is a design pattern?

Ans. Design patterns refer to language-independent solutions provided for solving commonly recurring design problems. A design pattern first describes the problem and then the solution that can be applied to the problem. The design patterns are implemented in the form of objects and classes that provide solutions to the problem.

Q6. What are the benefits of using design patterns?

Ans. **The important benefits of design patterns are as follows:**

- Provides tested solutions to frequently and repeatedly occurring problems
- Provides code reusability
- Helps in defining application architecture more efficiently and clearly
- Provides more reliability and transparency to the design of the application

Q7. What are the benefits of using the Front Controller pattern?

Ans. **The Front Controller pattern provides following benefits:**

- **Centralizes control**—Implements a central controller component for handling requests and implementing business logic. Therefore, requests can be easily tracked and logged.
- **Improves manageability**—Provides a single entry point for all requests, which requires fewer resources; thereby, improving manageability.
- **Improves reusability**—Moves common code to a single controller component. Therefore, code is not duplicated within multiple views; thereby, encouraging code reusability.
- **Improves role separation**—Divides responsibilities among various application components for effective role separation.

Q8. What is Session Facade?

Ans. Session Facade is a design pattern that is used for developing enterprise applications. The Session Facade pattern uses a central high level component, which is implemented as a session bean and contains the functionality of the complex interactions that occur between various lower-level business components. The higher-level session bean thereby provides a single interface to the client for accessing the functionality of an application.

Q9. What is a Data Access Object (DAO)?

Ans. Data Access Object provides application components with a user-friendly and common interface to access the data from various multiple data sources. It reduces the dependency of various components on the details of the database implementations. The DAO communicates with the actual underlying database and handles the different types of data access mechanisms.

Q10. What is the use of Service Locator pattern?

Ans. The Service Locator pattern is useful for locating various business components and services. This pattern uses a service locator object to centralize the look up process for distributed service components. This provides a central point of control to manage the look up services and also acts as a cache; thereby, eliminating the need for redundant look ups.

19

Implementing SOA using Java Web Services

Service Oriented Architecture (SOA) defines how different components of a software application interact to execute the business logic of an enterprise application. In other words, SOA is a software design pattern that defines how loosely-coupled software application components interact to implement the business logic of the entire application. In SOA, the independent software application components involved in implementing the business logic are termed as software services, or simply services. These services may be defined as independent and self-sustained units of a software application that implement specific functionalities to execute the business logic. These functionalities are generally a part of the overall business logic of the software application. For example, consider a software application of a bank. The bank can provide specific functionalities, such as submitting an online registration form for opening a new bank account, and oreviewing the online bank account statement. These functionalities can be implemented using independent services. That is, we can have independent services to submit an online form and view the online bank statement. Though these services work independently, they are part of the banking software application. As a design pattern, SOA defines how these individual and independent services fit into the banking software application.

SOA primarily focuses on binding large and independent services, which normally interact through interfaces. It provides a feature of orchestration, which ensures scalability of SOA-based applications. You learn in detail about the concept of orchestration later in the chapter.

SOA is mostly implemented for a specific category of software services, known as Web services, which are interoperable software applications that work on the client/server model. As the name suggests, Web services can be accessed over a network, such as the Internet, through standard communication protocols, such as Hyper Text Transfer Protocol (HTTP). A Web service performs the standard task of an application based on the client/server model, i.e., receiving requests from a client, processing the requests, and providing the requested resources or appropriate responses. A simple E-Commerce Web site, such as eBay provides Web services for online shopping. The Java EE 7 specification defines various standards to develop and deploy Web services. This specification also specifies the guidelines to develop and deploy Web services based on SOA. In this chapter, we explore how to use these Web service specifications to implement SOA in Java EE 7 Web services. The chapter is divided into three sections: A, B, and C. Section A introduces the basic concepts of SOA and Java Web Services (JWS). Section B creates the theoretical base to understand the Java EE 7 Web service specifications that are used to implement SOA. Section C focuses on the implementation of these Web service specifications.

Section A: Exploring SOA and Java Web Services

This section provides an overview of SOA and JWS. It also extends the discussion about implementing SOA in JWS. Implementing SOA through Web services makes data portable by ensuring consensus on the use of XML-based standards and protocols for data transmission, such as Simple Object Access Protocol (SOAP), Web Services Description Language (WSDL), and Universal Description, Discovery, and Integration (UDDI). You explore these concepts in detail next.

Note that this and the next section help you to explore the concepts of SOA in relation to its implementation with JWS.

Overview of SOA

SOA integrates the business logic of applications, which are modularized into loosely-coupled Web services. These Web services are consumed by client applications to implement specific business logic. A basic model of a software application based on SOA is shown in Figure 19.1:

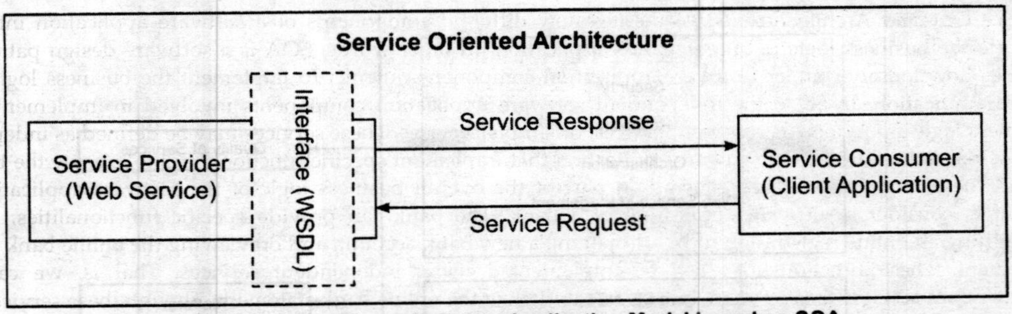

Figure 19.1: Showing a Software Application Model based on SOA

Figure 19.1 shows that the software application implementing SOA works on the client/server model. This type of application generally contains a Web service, which is hosted on the server side and acts as the service provider. Service requests are sent to the service provider, which processes and returns a response message or requested resources back to the client application, also known as the service consumer. For example, consider a simple Web service used to convert currencies. The Web service contains the logic to accept the input (in the form of a currency) and convert it into the required format (in terms of the other currency). This Web service, hosted on the server side, is provided by a third party that is considered as the service provider. A Web browser is used to access the currency converter Web service and this Web browser acts as the service consumer. When the Web browser accesses the currency converter Web service to process a conversion request, the process is termed as consuming the Web service.

SOA-based applications are platform independent, i.e., service providers can implement Web services in different platforms and languages, such as .NET or J2EE, and a service consumer or client application can use the service on a different platform or language. Enterprise applications can also add in new services or upgrade the existing services for implementing new business requirements.

The key characteristics of SOA are as follows:

- Ensures that the interfaces are implemented in a standard way, as well-formed XML documents Interfaces of SOA-based applications are described using a platform-independent Extensible Markup Language (XML) document, known as a WSDL document. .
- Uses XML schemas to define a message to communicate between service consumers and providers in heterogeneous environments.
- Allows you to register SOA-based enterprise applications in a service registry so that client applications can look up and invoke them. The service registry is defined by using UDDI.

Let's now explore the SOA environment in detail in the next section.

Describing the SOA Environment

In the previous section, we saw a basic model of an SOA-based application, which had one service provider and one service consumer. However, in real-life situations, SOA-based applications might span across numerous service providers and consumers. At times, big enterprise applications might also be based on SOA. These enterprise applications must conform to the SOA environment to run and manage SOA-based applications. The SOA environment specifies the required standards and runtime containers needed to implement SOA. Figure 19.2 displays the different layers of the SOA environment:

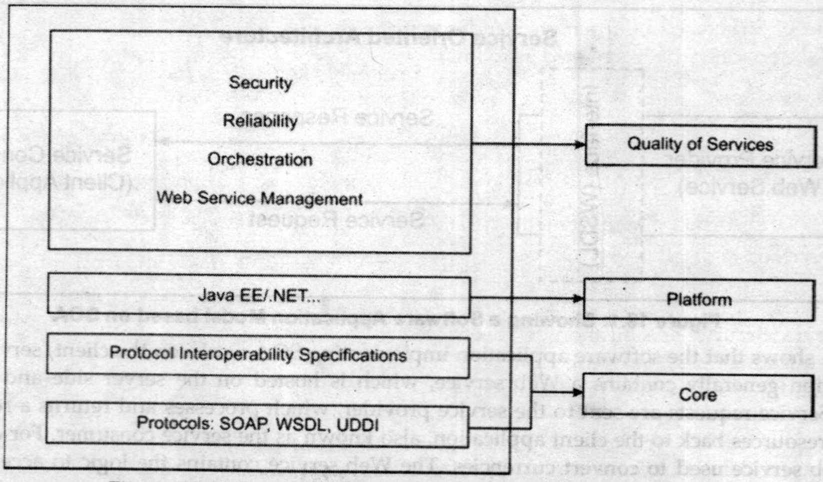

Figure 19.2: Displaying the Layers of the SOA Environment

Let's now explore these layers in detail.

The Core Layer

The Core layer of the SOA environment includes the following components:

- Protocols
- Protocol Interoperability Specification

Protocols

The protocols component includes the following protocols:

- **SOAP**—Acts as transport layer protocol to transmit messages between service clients and service providers.
- **WSDL**—Provides a format to describe the Web service interfaces. A WSDL file contains data type and message definitions, and defines how the Web services need to be bound to specific network addresses. To interact with a SOA-based Web service, service consumers need to obtain the WSDL of a Web service and then call the service by using SOAP.
- **UDDI**—Represents the protocol used by service providers to register services. Service consumers also use UDDI to search Web services in the UDDI registry.

Protocol Interoperability Specification

Web Services Interoperability (WS-I) Basic Profile is a specification that defines the standards for SOAP, WSDL, and UDDI protocols to ensure interoperability of Web services. WS-I Basic Profile is one of the core components required to test whether a Web service can be accessed across multiple platforms. The version of WS-I Basic Profile, i.e., 1.0, was released in 2004. Upgrade to version 2.0 of the specification is under progress.

The Platform Layer

The Platform layer contains different development platforms, such as Java EE and .NET, used for developing SOA-based applications. The Java EE platform provides features, such as scalability, reliability, and high performance, to the SOA environment. The Java EE specification includes Web services specifications, such as Java API for XML Binding (JAXB) to map XML documents to Java classes, in Web services. You learn about the different Java EE specifications used to develop Java EE Web services in detail, later in the chapter.

The Quality of Services Layer

The Quality of Services layer of the SOA environment caters to the requirements of enterprise applications, such as security, reliability, and transaction management. Organizations such as W3C and Organization for the

Advancement of Structured Information Standards (OASIS) have developed many specifications related to the quality of Web services, which are listed as follows:

- Security
- Reliability
- Policy
- Orchestration
- Web Service Distributed Management (WSDM)

These are described in detail next.

Security

The Web Service Security specification defines processes and methods to secure messages in various ways, such as by authenticating messages based on certain user credentials, or by using Security Assertion Markup Language (SAML) to secure Web service messages.

Reliability

Reliability means delivering a message to the recipient with an acknowledgement back to the sender and avoiding delivery of duplicate messages. The `WS-Reliability` and `WS-Reliable Messaging` standards handle reliability of Web service messages.

Policy

The WS-Policy standard defines a set of rules that an application uses to process a WS-Policy message. These set of rules are called policy standards or policy rules that must be followed to exchange Web service messages between service providers and service consumers. For example, a policy rule can implement encryption of a request to a Web service or declare the maximum acceptable size of a message by a Web service.

Orchestration

Web Service Orchestration (WSO), or simply orchestration, defines the interaction, automated arrangement, and management of different components of an SOA-based application. To be more specific, WSO defines the deployment structure of Web service components of an SOA-based application to automatically process the required business logic. Consequently, WSO also ensures that an SOA-based application is scalable, i.e., new components can be added or existing components can be modified with minimum effort as and when a business need arises. In other words, WSO can be understood as an extension of business process management that defines the interaction of individual components of a software application to process business logic. WSO is implemented by using orchestration scripts. These scripts map either to business processes or the workflow of an SOA-based enterprise application. WSO can be implemented by using different programming languages such as Business Process Execution Language for Web Services (BPEL4WS) and Web Service Choreography Interface (WSCI).

Web Service Distributed Management

The status of Web services need to be managed and monitored when the number of Web services increases in an SOA-based enterprise application. For example, you can manage and monitor the status of a Web service by verifying various parameters. Some of the parameters that can be used for managing and monitoring Web services are listed as follows:

- Examining the state of the Web service; whether or not the Web service is processing client requests
- Verifying the number of requests processed by the Web service
- Verifying the number of requests that could not be processed by the Web service due to some errors
- Verifying the number of requests that have been responded by the Web service
- Verifying the number of requests that have timed out

The status of Web services need to be monitored according to the WSDM standard, so that the WSDM-complaint management infrastructure of Web services can manage services running in a heterogeneous environment. The Web Service Coordination (WS-Coordination) and WS-Transaction specifications manage the interaction between service providers and consumers, and handle transactions involving numerous Web services. The third-party Web service monitoring tools, such as Actional SOAPstation developed by Progress Actional, can also be integrated to manage and monitor the status of Web services in an SOA-based application.

After exploring the SOA environment, let's now proceed to the discussion about JWS.

Overview of JWS

The Web service technology is the best way to implement SOA. JWS, or simply Web services, are composed of modularized services (which encapsulate the business logic) that can be registered, searched, and called over the Internet, and provide standard interfaces for service consumers. The modular services are loosely coupled, which allows them to be accessed by anyone at any location using any platform.

NOTE

The generic term Web services is used instead of JWS throughout the chapter.

Let's take an example of a hypothetical SOA application to explain the theoretical integration between SOA and Web services. The application manages the orders placed by customers. It accepts customer orders in the form of SOAP requests and sends acknowledgements for confirmed orders in the form of SOAP responses. Let's label this application as SOA Composite App, as it is built using a set of two Web services, Purchase Order and Inventory Management. Figure 19.3 illustrates the process flow of the SOA Composite App application:

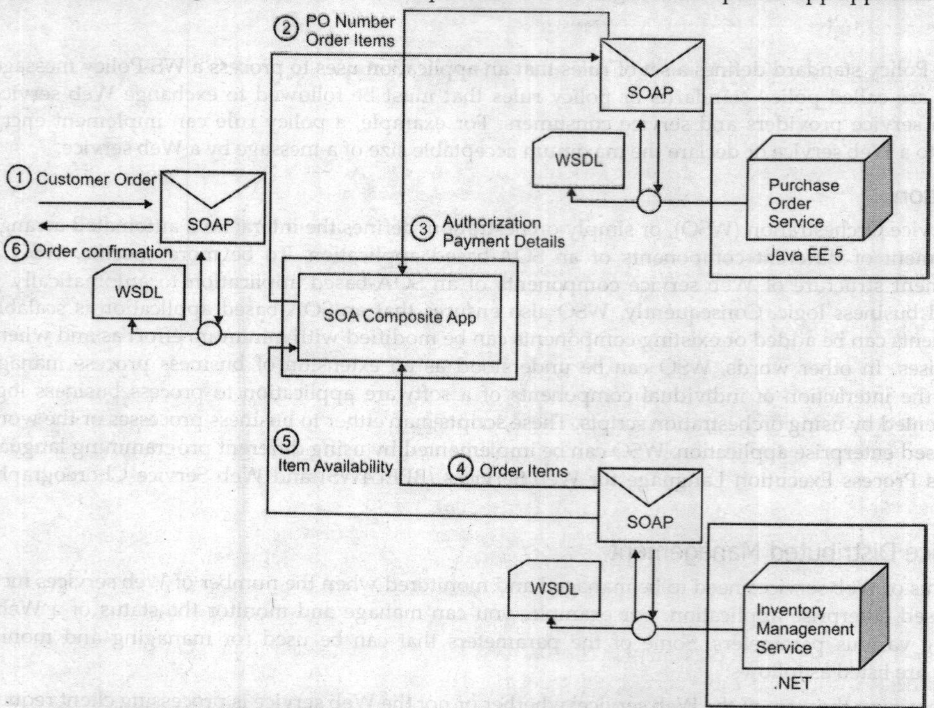

Figure 19.3: Displaying the Process Flow of the SOA Composite App Application

The process flow of the SOA Composite App application can be summarized through the following steps:

- A customer or service consumer sends an order, which contains the purchase order (PO) number and a list of products with their respective quantities. PO is sent in the form of a SOAP message.
- The PO number and list of products are entered in the `Purchase Order Service` Web service in the form of a PO. This Web service checks whether or not the PO contains all the required details. If the PO contains the required details, then the Web service prepares payment details of the order.

- The user credentials of the service consumer sending the PO are verified. If the verification succeeds, the authorization and payment details are sent to the `SOA Composite App` application.
- The list of product items is then sent to the `Inventory Management Service` Web service, which further verifies whether or not these items are available in the stock. The `Inventory Management Service` Web service then identifies the anticipated delivery dates for the product items ordered.
- The information regarding the availability of product items and their delivery dates are returned to the `SOA Composite App` application.
- Finally, an order confirmation message is sent to the customer. This message contains payment details and anticipated delivery dates of the ordered items.

As you can see in Figure 19.3, the `SOA Composite App` application uses two underlying Web services, `Purchase Order Service` and `Inventory Management Service`, to execute the business logic of the `SOA Composite App` application. It first processes the customer order with the `Purchase Order Service` Web service and then with the `Inventory Management Service` Web service. It then combines the output from both the Web services and finally creates an order confirmation message for the customer.

Role of WSDL, SOAP, and Java/XML Mapping in SOA

This section helps you to understand the role of Web service standards such as WSDL and SOAP, which are used to implement SOA by using JWS. Java/XML mapping is required to implement SOA in JWS as Java instances need to be converted to XML representations, and vice-versa. SOA-based applications are written by using XML messages and WSDL operations. As the WSDL document is a well-formed XML document, every SOA component in the SOA-based application is in the XML format. On the other hand, in the Java environment, applications are written by using classes and methods. Therefore, Java/XML mapping is required to use SOA components in the Java environment.

It is assumed that you have a basic knowledge of WSDL, SOAP, and XML; therefore, the chapter does not provide detailed information on these concepts.

NOTE

If you need to refresh your knowledge about WSDL, SOAP, and XML, you can refer to the W3C Web site, http://www.w3c.org.

Role of WSDL in SOA

WSDL is an XML-based language used by SOA components to interact with each other. A WSDL document defines the guidelines for communication between the components of an SOA-based application. Custom communication guidelines can also be provided for the interaction of SOA components. However, different enterprise applications might implement specific guidelines as per their requirements, which would reduce the scalability and reusability of SOA-based applications. In addition, these enterprise application-specific guidelines do not follow generalized standards that results in reduced interoperability of SOA-based applications. Therefore, the WSDL standard has been introduced to act as a generalized standard for communication between SOA components. This ensures enhanced scalability and interoperability of SOA-based applications. The WSDL standard specifies that XML messages be transferred over HTTP by using SOAP.

Let's take an example of a WSDL document. It describes a Web service that retrieves orders placed during a particular time period. This document accepts a date range as an input and generates an output containing the orders placed during the time period between the dates specified in the date range. Listing 19.1 shows the content of the WSDL document:

Listing 19.1: Showing the Code for a Sample WSDL Document

```
<?xml version="1.0" encoding="UTF-8"?>
<wsdl:definitions targetNamespace="http://www.example.com/oeps/retrieveorders"
  xmlns:soap="http://schemas.xmlsoap.org/wsdl/soap/"
  xmlns:wsdl="http://schemas.xmlsoap.org/wsdl/"
  xmlns:xs="http://www.w3.org/2001/XMLSchema"
  xmlns:oeps="http://www.example.com/oeps"
  xmlns:getord="http://www.example.com/oeps/retrieveorders"
```

```
    xmlns:faults="http://www.example.com/faults">
    <wsdl:types>
    <xs:schema targetNamespace="http://www.example.com/oeps">
    <xs:include schemaLocation="http://soabook.com/example/oms/orders.xsd"/>
    </xs:schema>
    <xs:schema targetNamespace="http://www.example.com/faults">
    <xs:include schemaLocation="http://soabook.com/example/faults/faults.xsd"
    />
    </xs:schema>
    <xs:schema elementFormDefault="qualified"
          targetNamespace="http://www.example.com/getord">
          <xs:element name="retrieveOrdersPeriod">
                <xs:complexType>
                      <xs:sequence>
                            <xs:element name="beginDate" type="xs:date"/>
                            <xs:element name="endDate" type="xs:date"/>
                      </xs:sequence>
                </xs:complexType>
          </xs:element>
          <xs:element name="retrieveOrdersPeriodResponse">
                <xs:complexType>
                      <xs:sequence>
                      <xs:element name="orders" type="oeps:OrderType"/>
                      </xs:sequence>
                </xs:complexType>
          </xs:element>
    </xs:schema>
    </wsdl:types>
  </wsdl:definitions>
```

In Listing 19.1, the wsdl:types element contains two xs:schema definitions, which include two XML schemas located at different locations. The targetNamespace attribute of the first xs:schema element specifies that the orders.xsd schema belongs to the schema library of the Order Entry and Processing System Web services (oeps). Similarly, the second attribute, schemaLocation, specifies the location of the orders.xsd schema.

The second xs:schema element in Listing 19.1 specifies the relationship between the WSDL interface and the faults.xsd schema in the Web services infrastructure. The xs:include element is used to reference these schemas in the WSDL document. The wsdl:types element also contains two wrapper elements: retrieveOrdersPeriod and retrieveOrdersPeriodResponse.

A service consumer calls a WSDL document to invoke the required Web service. The call to the WSDL document is made through the SOAP protocol. Therefore, you must provide the SOAP binding declaration of a WSDL while implementing a Web service. You can provide the SOAP binding declaration by using the wsdl:binding element, as shown in Listing 19.2:

Listing 19.2: Showing the Code for SOAP Binding of a WSDL Document

```
<wsdl:binding name="RetrieveOrdersSOAPBinding"
  type="retrieveorder:RetrieveOrdersPort">
  <soap:binding style="document"
  transport="http://schemas.xmlsoap.org/soap/http"/>
  <wsdl:operation name="retrieveOrders">
        <wsdl:input>
              <soap:body use="literal"/>
        </wsdl:input>
        <wsdl:output>
              <soap:body use="literal"/>
        </wsdl:output>
        <wsdl:fault name="retrieveOrdersInFault">
              <soap:fault name="retrieveOrdersInFault"/>
        </wsdl:fault>
  </wsdl:operation>
</wsdl:binding>
```

In Listing 19.2, the `name` attribute of the `wsdl:operation` element accepts the name of the WSDL document for which the SOAP binding declaration is provided.

Role of SOAP in SOA

SOAP is a protocol that allows SOA-based applications to exchange messages. In an SOA-based application, a service consumer sends a request to the service provider in the SOAP format. The service provider might be implemented on a platform different from the service consumer, such as Java EE 6. Therefore, the SOAP request received by a service provider is converted into the native format of the service provider. The response provided by the service provider is again converted in a SOAP message when it is received by the service consumer.

SOAP is based on XML and HTTP, and can be used across multiple platforms. It uses the Internet application layer protocol as the transport protocol to access Web services. In addition, SOAP defines the XML structure of the messages being exchanged among the SOA components. SOAP adds headers and envelopes to the message body of SOAP messages. A SOAP header provides information about the quality of service of the messaging infrastructure, such as security and reliability. The SOAP specification also provides a standard way of defining SOAP fault messages. The SOAP standard uses a processing model with multiple nodes, which can transmit and receive messages. Messages can be simply relayed from one SOAP node to the other.

The SOAP standard provides some header attributes, such as `env:mustUnderstand`, which specifies whether or not a SOAP node must process a SOAP header. If this attribute is set to true, the last SOAP node must either process the header block or return a SOAP fault message to the sender.

The example of a SOAP request message for the retrieveOrdersPeriod Web service is shown in Listing 19.3:

Listing 19.3: Showing the Code for theRetrieveOrdersPeriodSOAPRequest.xml File

```
<?xml version="1.0" encoding="UTF-8"?>
<env1:Envelope xmlns:env1="http://schemas.xmlsoap.org/soap/envelope">
  <env1:Body>
<retrieveorder:retrieveOrdersPeriod
  xmlns:retrieveorder="http://www.example.com/oms/getorders">
        <retrieveorder:beginDate>2008-03-10</retrieveorder:beginDate>
        <retrieveorder:endDate>2008-03-13</retrieveorder:endDate>
        </retrieveorder:retrieveOrdersPeriod>
  </env1:Body>
</env1:Envelope>
```

Listing 19.3 represents a SOAP request message that has no headers. The message body of the SOAP envelope contains only one element, `retrieveorder:retrieveOrdersPeriod`.

When a Web service receives a SOAP response message to this SOAP request, the response message must have the date value of the PURCHASE_DATE attribute set between the date ranges specified in the SOAP request message, as shown in Listing 19.4:

Listing 19.4: Showing the Code for a Sample SOAP Response

```
<?xml version="1.0" encoding="UTF-8"?>
<env1:Envelope xmlns:env1="http://schemas.xmlsoap.org/soap/envelope">
  <env1:Body>
        <retrieveorder:retrieveOrdersPeriodResponse
                xmlns:retrieveorder="http://www.example.com/oeps/getorders">
                <Orders xmlns="http://www.example.com/oeps"
                xmlns:xsi="http://www.w3.org/2001/XMLSchema-instance"
                xsi:schemaLocation="http://www.example.com/oeps
                http://soabook.com/example/oeps/orders.xsd">
                <Order>
                        <OrderId>ABC1234567</OrderId>
                        <OrderHeader>
                        <SALES_ORG>Coca-Cola India</SALES_ORG>
                        <PURCHASE_DATE>2008-02-01</PURCHASE_DATE>
                        <CUST_ID>ABC0072123</CUST_ID>
                        <PAYMENT_METHOD>PO</PAYMENT_METHOD>
                        <PURCHASE_ORD_NO>PO-72123-0007</PURCHASE_ORD_NO>
                        <DELIVERY_DATE>2008-03-20</DELIVERY_DATE>
                        </OrderHeader>
                        <Products>
```

```
                    <product>
                    <PROD_ID>012345</PROD_ID>
                    <AMOUNT>50</AMOUNT>
                    <UNIT_OF_MEASURE>liter</UNIT_OF_MEASURE>
                    <PRICE_PER_UNIT>15</PRICE_PER_UNIT>
                    <DESCRIPTION>2 liter Fanta soft drink </DESCRIPTION>
                    </product>
                    <product>
                    <PROD_ID>543210</PROD_ID>
                    <AMOUNT>20</AMOUNT>
                    <UNIT_OF_MEASURE>liter</UNIT_OF_MEASURE>
                    <PRICE_PER_UNIT>21</PRICE_PER_UNIT>
                    <DESCRIPTION></DESCRIPTION>
                    </product>
                    </Products>
                    <OrderDescription>This order is rush.</OrderDescription>
                    </Order>
                </Orders>
        </retrieveorder:retrieveOrdersPeriodResponse>
    </env1:Body>
</env1:Envelope>
```

In Listing 19.4, the message body of the SOAP envelope contains only one element, `retrieveorder:retrieveOrdersPeriodResponse`, according to the `RetrieveOrders.wsdl` document. The content of this element is of the `oeps:Orders`Type, which is defined in the `orders.xsd` imported schema. Therefore, the structure of the SOAP message depends on both the WSDL document and the schema library of the associated Web services.

If a SOAP request is not valid, a SOAP fault message is returned to the sender, as shown in Listing 19.5:

Listing 19.5: Showing the Code for a Sample SOAP Fault Message

```
<?xml version="1.0" encoding="UTF-8"?>
<env1:Envelope xmlns:env1="http://schemas.xmlsoap.org/soap/envelope/">
  <env1:Body>
        <env1:Fault xmlns:faults="http://www.example.com/faults">
              <faultcode>env1:Client</faultcode>
              <faultstring>Invalid input message.</faultstring>
              <detail>
                    <faults:inputMessageValidationFailure
                    msg="The startDate is larger than the endDate."/>
              </detail>
        </env1:Fault>
  </env1:Body>
</env1:Envelope>
```

Listing 19.5 represents a simple SOAP fault message. The `env1:Client` value specifies that there is an error in the request message, which the Web service is unable to process. It uses the `detail` element to give specific details about the error.

Role of Java/XML Mapping in SOA

Java/XML mapping transforms a SOAP request message to a Java-compatible format to execute the SOA component in the Java environment. Let's take the example of a Web service implemented in Java EE. This Web service acts as a service provider, and can interpret messages in the Java format only. A service consumer, such as a Web browser, can interpret messages in the XML format (by using the SOAP protocol). Figure 19.4 shows the processing of a message by a service provider and a service consumer:

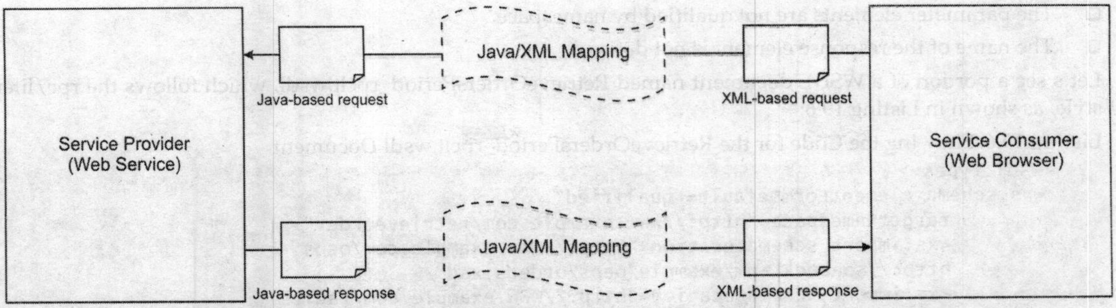

Figure 19.4: Showing the Transformation of Messages through Java/XML Mapping

Figure 19.4 shows the role of Java/XML mapping in message transformations. As you can see from Figure 19.4, an XML-based request from a service consumer is transformed into a Java-based request when it is sent to the service provider. This ensures that the service provider is able to interpret the request. Similarly, the service provider sends a Java-based response, which is transformed into an XML-based response, so that the service consumer can understand and interpret the response.

You need to determine the WSDL port for the message before associating a SOAP request message with a WSDL operation. According to the WSDL specification, the request dispatching process searches for the location of the HTTP port in the `soap:address` element of the `wsdl:port` element. From the `wsdl:port` element, you can also retrieve the `RetrieveOrdersPeriodSOAPBinding` binding, which implements the `RetrieveOrdersPeriodPort` element. It is not necessary to use the `soap:address` element inside the `wsdl:port` element as you can set the value for the `soap:address` element from the underlying HTTP request.

After determining the `wsdl:port` element, the request dispatching process determines the `wsdl:operation` element. Identifying the WSDL operation depends on the WSDL styles used in the `wsdl:binding` element. The `style` and `use` attributes of the `wsdl:operation` element define SOAP binding. These attributes describe how a Web service maps SOAP messages to WSDL operations. The `style` attribute can take two values, `rpc` or `document`, depending on the structure of the SOAP Body element, `env:Body`. The `use` attribute can also take two values, `literal` or `encoded`, depending on the serialization of the SOAP message. If the `use` attribute takes a `literal` value, the data of the SOAP message must conform to XML schema constraints defined in the WSDL's types section. If the `use` attribute takes an `encoded` value, the serialization of data is based on SOAP encoding in the SOAP 1.1 specification.

The possible values for the entire WSDL style of the WSDL document are as follows:

- rpc/literal
- Document/literal (by default unwrapped)
- Document/literal wrapped

Let's explore each WSDL style in detail and see the differences in the output of the SOAP messages when we use these styles.

The rpc/literal Style

The WSDL document based on the rpc/literal style has the following characteristics:

- The request message can have many parts and these parts must be defined by using the type attribute
- If the type attribute of any part of the request message uses complex type, it must be defined in the wsdl:types element

The SOAP message generated according to the rpc/literal style has the following characteristics:

- The root element under the env:Body element must be a wrapper element and must have the same name as that of the wsdl:operation element
- The parameter elements under the root element must have the same names as those specified in the name attribute of the wsdl:part elements

- The parameter elements are not qualified by namespace
- The name of the response element is not defined

Let's see a portion of a WSDL document named RetrieveOrdersPeriod_rpclt.wsdl, which follows the rpc/literal style, as shown in Listing 19.6:

Listing 19.6: Showing the Code for the RetrieveOrdersPeriod_rpclt.wsdl Document

```
<wsdl:types>
 <xs:schema elementFormDefault="qualified"
        targetNamespace="http://www.example.com/retrieveorder">
        <xs:import schemaLocation="http://www.example.com/oeps
        http://soabook.com/example/oeps/orders.xsd"/>
        <xs:import schemaLocation="http://www.example.com/faults
        http://soabook.com/example/faults/faults.xsd"/>
 </xs:schema>
</wsdl:types>
<wsdl:message name="rec">
 <wsdl:part name="beginDate" type="xs:date"/>
 <wsdl:part name="endDate" type="xs:date"/>
</wsdl:message>
<wsdl:message name="res">
 <wsdl:part name="orders" element="oeps:OrdersType"/>
</wsdl:message>
```

The code of a SOAP request message which is written according to the rpc/literal style is shown in Listing 19.7:

Listing 19.7: Showing a Soap Request Message Based on the rpc/literal Style

```
<?xml version="1.0" encoding="UTF-8"?>
<env:Envelope xmlns:env="http://www.w3.org/2003/05/soap-envelope">
 <env:Body>
        <retrieveOrdersPeriod>
                <beginDate>2005-11-19</beginDate>
                <endDate>2005-11-22</endDate>
        </retrieveOrdersPeriod>
 </env:Body>
</env:Envelope>
```

Notice that the request message in Listing 19.7 does not contain namespaces.

The SOAP message based on the rpc/literal style is easy to understand but the contents of this SOAP message do not follow any XML schema.

The document/literal Style

The document/literal style is unwrapped; therefore, if you need to send multiple parameters in a SOAP message, the message body of the SOAP request message would contain the corresponding number of child nodes. A WSDL document based on the document/literal style has following characteristics:

- The input message can have multiple parts, and these parts must be defined using the element attribute.
- Full schema of SOAP messages needs to be written within the wsdl:types element. The element attribute of each part refers to element definition in the xs:schema element.

The SOAP message generated according to the document/literal style has the following characteristics:

- The SOAP-ENV:Body element does not need to specify the name of the wsdl:operation element.
- The parameter elements under the root element must have the same names as those specified in the name attribute of the wsdl:part elements.
- The parameter elements must be qualified by appropriate namespaces.
- Both request and response messages are unwrapped.

A portion of a WSDL document, named RetrieveOrdersPeriod_doclit.wsdl, which follows the document/literal style is shown in Listing 19.8:

Listing 19.8: Showing the Code for the RetrieveOrdersPeriod_doclit.wsdl Document

```
<wsdl:types>
 <xs:schema elementFormDefault="qualified"
         targetNamespace="http://www.example.com/retrieveorder">
         <xs:import schemaLocation="http://www.example.com/oeps
         http://soabook.com/example/oeps/orders.xsd"/>
         <xs:import schemaLocation="http://www.example.com/faults
         http://soabook.com/example/faults/faults.xsd"/>
         <xs:element name="beginDate" type="xs:date"/>
         <xs:element name="endDate" type="xs:date"/>
         <xs:element name="orders" type="oeps:OrdersType"/>
 </xs:schema>
</wsdl:types>
<wsdl:message name="req">
 <wsdl:part name="param1" element="retrieveorder:beginDate"/>
 <wsdl:part name="param2" element="retrieveorder:endDate"/>
</wsdl:message>
<wsdl:message name="res">
 <wsdl:part name="param1" element="retrieveorder:orders"/>
</wsdl:message>
```

The code for a SOAP request message which is written according to the document/literal style, is shown in Listing 19.9:

Listing 19.9: Showing the Code for a SOAP Request Message Based on the document/literal Style

```
<?xml version="1.0" encoding="UTF-8"?>
<env:Envelope xmlns:env="http://www.w3.org/2003/05/soap-envelope">
 <env:Body xmlns:getord="http://www.example.com/oeps/retrieveorders">
         <retrieveorder:beginDate>2005-11-19</retrieveorder:beginDate>
         <retrieveorder:endDate>2005-11-22</retrieveorder:endDate>
 </env:Body>
</env:Envelope>
```

The document/literal wrapped Style

The document/literal wrapped style is derived from the document/literal style by using wrapper elements around the parameter elements.

The WSDL document based on the document/literal wrapped style has the following characteristics:

- The input message must have only one part, and this part must be defined by using the element attribute.
- The single message part is a wrapper element and the full schema of the message must be written in the wsdl:types element.
- All parameters must be the immediate child nodes of the wrapper element.
- The response message contains the response in a wrapper element, and the local name of this wrapper element must be in the `wsdl:operationRS` form, where RS represents the response string.

The SOAP message generated according to the document/literal wrapped style has the following characteristics:

- The root element under the env:Body element must be a wrapper element and must have the same name as that of the wsdl:operation element.
- The root element must be qualified by the appropriate namespace.
- All parameter elements must be the immediate child nodes of the wrapper element. The local names of the parameter elements can be different from the names specified in the name attributes of the wsdl:part definition.
- The parameter elements must be qualified by the appropriate namespaces.

Listing 19.10 shows a portion of a WSDL document, named RetrieveOrdersPeriod.wsdl, which follows the document/literal wrapped style:

Listing 19.10: Showing the Code for the RetrieveOrdersPeriod.wsdl Document

```
<wsdl:types>
 <xs:schema targetNamespace="http://www.example.com/oeps">
 <xs:include schemaLocation="http://soabook.com/example/oeps/orders.xsd"/>
 </xs:schema>
 <xs:schema targetNamespace="http://www.example.com/faults">
 <xs:include schemaLocation="http://soabook.com/example/faults/faults.xsd"
 />
 </xs:schema>
 <xs:schema elementFormDefault="qualified"
         targetNamespace="http://www.example.com/retrieveorder">
         <xs:element name="retrieveOrdersPeriod">
         <xs:complexType>
                 <xs:sequence>
                         <xs:element name="beginDate" type="xs:date"/>
                         <xs:element name="endDate" type="xs:date"/>
                 </xs:sequence>
         </xs:complexType>
 </xs:element>

 <xs:element name="retrieveOrdersPeriodResponse">
         <xs:complexType>
                 <xs:sequence>
                         <xs:element name="orders" type="oeps:OrdersType"/>
                 </xs:sequence>
         </xs:complexType>
 </xs:element>
 </xs:schema>
</wsdl:types>
<wsdl:message name="req">
 <wsdl:part name="parameters" element="retrieveorder:retrieveOrdersPeriod/>
</wsdl:message>
<wsdl:message name="res">
<wsdl:part name="parameters" element="retrieveorder:retrieveOrdersPeriodResponse"/>
</wsdl:message>
```

Listing 19.11 shows the code for a SOAP request message which is written according to the document/literal wrapped style:

Listing 19.11: Showing the Code for a SOAP Request Message Based on the document/literal wrapped Style

```
<?xml version="1.0" encoding="UTF-8"?>
<env1:Envelope xmlns:env1="http://schemas.xmlsoap.org/soap/envelope">
 <env1:Body>
<retrieveorder:retrieveOrdersPeriod
 xmlns:retrieveorder="http://www.example.com/oeps/retrieveorders">
         <retrieveorder:beginDate>2008-03-10</retrieveorder:beginDate>
         <retrieveorder:endDate>2008-03-13</retrieveorder:endDate>
         </retrieveorder:retrieveOrdersPeriod>
 </env1:Body>
</env1:Envelope>
```

Let's now move ahead and explore the Web service specifications to implement SOA and the advanced features of Web services in the next sections.

Section B: Understanding Web Service Specifications to Implement SOA

Java EE has evolved as a premiere solution for server-side scripting of Web services. To ensure scalability and interoperability of Web applications, World Wide Web Consortium (W3C) has introduced various standards for Web services. These standards have also been integrated in the Java EE 7 specification, which includes various Web service specifications, such as WSEE 1.3, JAX-WS 2.2, JAXB 2.2, JAX-RS 2.0, and WebSocket 1.0. The main purpose of Java Web service specifications is to make the development and deployment of Web services easy.

NOTE

W3C is a standards organization that defines the specifications for creating, configuring, deploying, and managing Web services.

Table 19.1 lists the Web service specifications included in the Java EE 7 specification:

Table 19.1: Web Service Specifications of Java EE 7

Specification	Version	Java Specification Request (JSR) ID No.
Java Application Programming Interface (Java API) for XML based Web Services	JAX-WS 2.2	JSR 224
Java Architecture for XML Binding	JAXB 2.2	JSR 222
Implementing Web Services	WSEE 1.3	JSR 109
Web Service Metadata for the Java platform	WS-Metadata 2.0	JSR 181
Simple Object Access Protocol (SOAP) with Attachments API	SAAJ 1.3	JSR 67
Java API for XML Registries	JAXR 1.0	JSR 93
Streaming API for XML	StAX 1.0	JSR 173
Java API for WebSocket	WebSocket 1.0	JSR 356
Java API for RESTful Web Services (JAX-RS)	JAX-RS 2.0	JSR 339
Java API for JSON Processing	JSON-P	JSR 353

The succeeding sections provide a detailed description of the Web service specifications.

Exploring the JAX-WS 2.2 Specification

The JAX-WS 2.2 specification provides a Java API that you can use to create Web services. The primary objective of JAX-WS 2.2 is to simplify the development and deployment of clients and endpoints of Web services. An endpoint refers to an interface of a service provider or consumer, exposed as the destination of a SOAP message. The JAX-WS Web services specification can be divided into three categories: invocation, serialization, and deployment. These categories define specific standards and sub-specifications to invoke, serialize, and deploy Web services. Table 19.2 lists the sub-specifications of the JAX-WS Web service specification:

Table 19.2: Sub-Specifications of the JAX-WS Web Service Specification

Invocation Sub-Specification	Serialization Sub-Specification	Deployment Sub-Specification
Web service invocation with Java interface proxies	WSDL styles	Java/WSDL mapping
Web service invocation with XML		Static WSDL

Table 19.2: Sub-Specifications of the JAX-WS Web Service Specification

Invocation Sub-Specification	Serialization Sub-Specification	Deployment Sub-Specification
Message context		XML service providers
Handler framework		XML catalogs
SOAP binding		Run-time endpoint publishing
HTTP binding		
Converting exceptions to SOAP faults		
Asynchronous invocation of Web service		
One-way operation		
Client-side thread management		
Pseudo reference passing		

Let's discuss each of these briefly.

The Invocation Sub-Specification Category

The Invocation sub-specification category defines the standards to invoke Web services. In addition, this sub-specification category defines the standards related to transmission and processing of messages between Web services. Some provisions offered by this sub-specification category are:

- Web service invocation with Java interface proxies
- Web service invocation with XML
- Message context
- Handler framework
- SOAP binding
- HTTP binding
- Conversion of exceptions to SOAP faults
- Asynchronous invocation
- One-way operations
- Client-side thread management
- Pseudo reference passing

Let's explore these in detail.

Web Service Invocation with Java Interface Proxies

JWSs are invoked by static or dynamic service instances by using the service endpoint interface (SEI) as a proxy. You can use the `Service.getPort()` method to create an instance of the Web SEI. This instance corresponds to the `wsdl:port` element of a WSDL document of the Web service. The SEI must follow the JAX-WS Java/WSDL and JAXB XML/Java mapping.

Web Service Invocation with XML

You can also invoke Web services by sending and receiving XML messages. In order to do so, you need to invoke the `createDispatch()` method, which returns a `javax.xml.ws.Dispatch` instance on an instance of the Web service. You only need to build SOAP messages and send them to the Web service instance.

Message Context

A message context specifies the namespaces and metadata about the elements of an XML message. The instance of the `javax.xml.ws.handler.MessageContext` class represents the message context. JAX-WS allows handlers, endpoints, and clients to access and modify the message context of XML request/response messages. Let's consider an example of message sequencing to understand the use of the message context:

- When multiple SOAP messages are sent to a destination, the request handler extracts the sequence of messages from the SOAP header elements
- The endpoint then processes the messages concurrently and sends the responses after processing all the previous messages in the sequence
- The sequence of responses can be changed according to the sequence information specified in the message context

Endpoint implementations access the message context with the help of Dependency Injection. (To learn more about dependency injection, refer to *Chapter 13, Working with EJB 3.1, Chapter20, Working with Struts2.1,* and *Chapter 21, Working with Spring3.0.)* The clients can access the message context by invoking the `getRequestContext()` and `getResponseContext()` methods of the `javax.xml.ws.BindingProvider` interface.

Handler Framework

The JAX-WS 2.2 specification defines request and response handlers to post-process requests and pre-process responses. You can use these handlers at both the client and the server side. For example, you can use a handler to post-process a client message to be sent to a Web service, and append some headers to the message. You can use another handler on the server side to pre-process the response messages and verify the appended headers to the response messages. You can configure a chain of handlers at runtime by using either deployment metadata with the `@HandlerChain` annotations or the `HandlerResolver` interface.

Two types of handlers are supported by JAX-WS namely, protocol and logical. Protocol handlers can access the entire structure of a SOAP message. However, logical handlers, can only access the information about the payload of a message by using either the `javax.xml.transform.Source` interface or the instance of the JAXB annotated class.

SOAP Binding

SOAP binding refers to the process of setting the message addressing properties in the SOAP header of a SOAP message to simplify the transmission of the SOAP message from one endpoint to other. W3C standards define detailed specifications for SOAP binding in terms of notational conventions and XML namespaces. The following properties of the SOAP header must be in conformation with the specifications provided by W3C:

- **Destination**—Specifies the destination property of a SOAP header. Destination represents the destination endpoint of the corresponding SOAP message.
- **SourceEndpoint**—Defines the source endpoint property of the SOAP header. The source endpoint specifies the endpoint from which the corresponding SOAP message was sent.
- **ReplyEndpoint**—Represents the reply endpoint property of the SOAP header. The reply endpoint represents the endpoint to which the SOAP response for the corresponding SOAP message must be sent.
- **FaultEndpoint**—Specifies the fault endpoint property of the SOAP header. If a SOAP message contains a fault and cannot be delivered to the destination, it is sent to the fault endpoint.
- **Action**—Represents the action property of the SOAP header.
- **MessageID**—Specifies the message ID property of the SOAP header.
- **Relationship**—Defines the relationship property of the SOAP header.
- **ReferenceParameters**—Specifies the reference parameters property of the SOAP header.

The JAX-WS 2.2 specification conforms to the specifications of W3C for SOAP binding.

HTTP Binding

The JAX-WS 2.2 specification provides support for XML/HTTP binding to deploy and consume RESTful Web services, which send and receive XML messages over the HTTP protocol, instead of using the SOAP protocol.

Conversion of Exceptions to SOAP Faults

The JAX-WS 2.2 specification provides mapping among the `java.lang.Exception` instances to SOAP fault messages. Consider the example of Java/XML mapping described earlier. As stated previously, the SOAP requests originating from a service consumer need to be mapped to Java, so that the service provider can interpret the SOAP requests. This mapping is required in case of Java exceptions as well. JWSs are implemented in Java, and can raise exceptions due to various reasons. If the service consumer receives a Java exception, it would not be able to interpret the same. To ensure that exceptions are appropriately interpreted and handled by the service consumers, Java exceptions must be converted to the corresponding SOAP faults.

In earlier specification of JAX-WS, you had to map service exceptions to SOAP faults by writing the code for the same. In the JAX-WS 2.2 specification; however, the `WebFault` annotation maps service exceptions to SOAP fault messages and you do not need to write discrete code for the same.

At times, exceptions in Web services might not be Java-specific and might arise due to reasons, such as faulty construction of SOAP messages. Therefore, we need to convert these exceptions into SOAP fault messages. You can also convert application-specific exceptions to SOAP fault messages. However, you must ensure that Java runtime exceptions are not converted into SOAP fault messages.

Asynchronous Invocation

The JAX-WS 2.2 specification supports asynchronous invocation. In asynchronous invocation, the Web service being called does not wait for the request or response to be delivered before performing other operations. That is, in asynchronous invocation, the Web service can simultaneously perform other operations, which are not dependent on the request or response being called, while the request or response is being delivered to the specified destination. Consequently, the request or response performance of the application using the Web service is enhanced. JAX-WS facilitates asynchronous request-response communication by using two techniques: polling and callback. In polling, a client checks frequently to verify whether a response has arrived. In callback, a handler processes the response asynchronously when the response is available.

One-Way Operations

The JAX-WS 2.2 specification allows you to map Java methods to WSDL one-way operations. The WSDL of a Web service provides four types of operations that an endpoint can support, which are listed as follows:

- **One-Way**—Specifies that an endpoint needs to only receive a message
- **Request-Response**—Specifies that an endpoint must receive a message and send a response to the message
- **Solicit-Response**—Specifies that an endpoint must send a message and receive a response for the message
- **Notification**—Specifies that an endpoint only needs to send a message

These operations allow developers to use reliable messaging protocols, such as Web services reliable messaging, to implement the business logic using Web services.

Client-Side Thread Management

The JAX-WS 2.2 specification provides the option to set the `java.util.concurrent.Executor` instance inside the `javax.xml.ws.Service` instance to manage multiple threads that invoke a Web service. This type of thread management is usually done during asynchronous Web service invocation.

Pseudo Reference Passing

When you pass an instance of a Java class to a Java method call and assign this call to an object, the object gets the reference of the passed instance, and not a copy of the instance. When we make a call to a Web service by passing an instance, the copy of this instance is serialized, wrapped in a SOAP message, and sent over the network.

You cannot pass a reference of an instance of a Java class residing on your local address space by using SOAP. The JAX-WS specification supports a pseudo reference passing mechanism to pass references of these instances. The `Holder<name>` class holds the reference of the Java class name. Now, when you invoke a Web service, JAX-WS sends a duplicate copy of the instance of the `Holder<name>`class to the Web service and returns the changed instance of the `Holder<name>` class. The `Holder<name>` instance also stores the changed instance of the `Holder<name>` class received from a Web service.

The Serialization Sub-Specification Category

The serialization sub-specification category defines the standards for serializing the Web services. These standards are defined in the WSDL of a Web service. JAXB serializes request and response parameters; however,

JAXB needs some instructions to package the serialized parameters into a SOAP message. The WSDL styles are used to specify these instructions. For example, serialized parameters are packaged either as separate child nodes of the SOAP body element or as a single element child node that contains all parameters.

The JAX-WS 2.2 specification supports commonly used WSDL styles, such as rpc/literal and document/literal wrapped. You can specify the rpc style by using the `javax.jws.SOAPBinding` annotation with properties, such as style of RPC, LITERAL, and parameterStyle. You can specify the document wrapped style by using the `javax.jws.SOAPBinding` annotation with properties, such as style of DOCUMENT, LITERAL, and parameterStyle. The JAX-WS 2.2 specification uses request and response beans to wrap request parameters and the response value.

The Deployment Sub-Specification Category

The deployment sub-specification category specifies the standards to deploy Web applications. These sub-specifications include the following components:

- Java/WSDL mapping
- Static WSDL
- XML service providers
- XML catalogs
- Runtime endpoint publishing

Let's explore these in detail next.

Java/WSDL Mapping

Java/WSDL mapping defines the binding between WSDL operations and Java methods. Initially, the SOAP message requests for a WSDL operation. Then, Java/WSDL mapping is used to invoke the associated Java method and map the SOAP message to the parameters of this method. Java/WSDL mapping is also used to map the return value of the method to the SOAP response.

With the help of this mapping, a developer can first create a Java class, use the JAX-WS processor (java2wsdl or wsgen utility), and create a WSDL document of a Web service end point.

You can customize standard Java/WSDL mapping with embedded binding declarations. These binding declarations are provided by using the `jaxws:bindings` extension elements.

Following are some restrictions while performing Java/WSDL mapping:

- One-to-one mapping exists between the `wsdl:portType` element and the Java interface (in our case SEI), irrespective of the number of operations in this element
- Mappings for parameters of the SEI and its return type should necessarily be compatible with JAXB

Static WSDL

A `javax.xml.ws.Service` instance represents a JAX-WS Web service client. This instance corresponds to the `wsdl:service` element of the WSDL document of a Web service. You can create service instances statically or dynamically. To generate a service instance dynamically, use the `Service.create` factory method. You can generate your own service instance from the WSDL document by using the JAX-WS processing tool. For example, the wsimport processing tool of JAX-WS is provided by the Glassfish server.

XML Service Providers

You can deploy a Web service to send and receive XML messages without JAXB binding annotations. The JAX-WS API provides the `javax.xml.ws.Provider` interface to create Web services that do not require JAXB binding annotations. JAX-WS Java/WSDL and JAXB Java/XML mappings are not used during the invocation of this type of Web services.

XML Catalogs

The JAX-WS specification supports the feature of XML catalogs. This feature allows a WSDL document to import external schemas. In this way, the same schema information need not be duplicated in different WSDL documents. XML catalogs contain the mapping information where external references to imported schemas are mapped to local instances of these schemas.

Runtime Endpoint Publishing

JAX-WS supports the publishing of Web service endpoints at runtime. The instance of the `javax.xml.ws.EndPoint` class is used to assign an instance of the Web service implementation class to a URL. Dynamic publishing of endpoints is supported only by Java SE 6, while Java EE 6 does not support dynamic publishing of endpoints.

JAX-WS runtime creates the required server infrastructure to invoke a Web service. Initially, the HTTP context is created and finally SOAP requests are listened on a specified URL. During this process, WSDL document for endpoint is created dynamically. The generated WSDL document depends on source code annotations in the class implementing the Web service or metadata files deployed during invocation of the `Endpoint.setMetadata` method. The location for accessing the generated WSDL document is specified in the publish mechanism.

Exploring the JAXB 2.2 Specification

The JAXB 2.2 specification provides the standards to bind Java classes to XML schema components. It is necessary to know the difference between certain terms, which are listed as follows, before exploring JAXB 2.2:

- **Java/XML binding**—Specifies that each Java class is mapped to a unique XML schema component depending on its annotations. The Java/XML binding is defined by using JAXB 2.2 annotations in Java classes.
- **Java/XML type mapping**—Specifies the relationship between a Java element and an XML schema component. The serializer and deserializer define this type of mapping. The serializer changes the instances of the Java class into XML instances, which correspond to a specific XML schema. The deserializer does the opposite. A type mapping framework is usually used to create layered architecture applications.
- **Java/XML map**—Consists of a collection of type mappings. The Java/XML map contains the mapping information where a Java element is mapped to XML instances of different schema types.

While implementing SOA with Web services, you need to define the mapping between existing XML schemas and Java classes. Java/XML maps are also used when there may be numerous Java classes that need to map to a single XML schema. However, the schema compiler or the schema generator cannot be used to provide such type of mapping as they are used for one-to-one mapping. In such cases, you need to specify the mappings in Java classes by using JAXB 2.2 annotations. The JAXB 2.2 specification is restricted in the sense that you cannot use JAXB 2.2 annotations for mapping a Java class to XML instances of all the XML schema types.

Figure 19.5 shows the architecture of JAXB implementation:

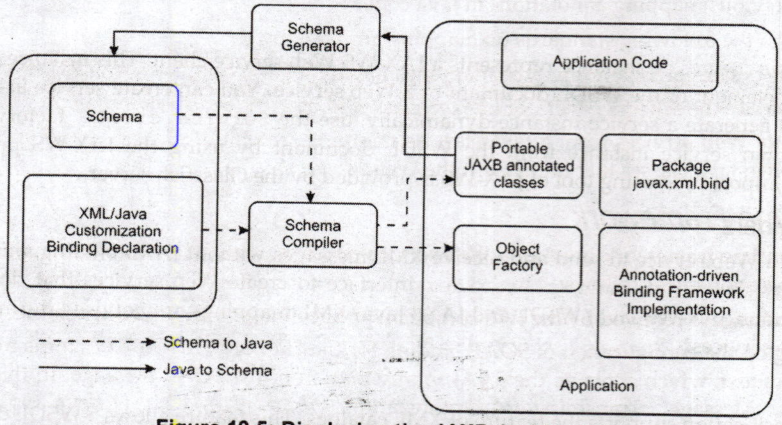

Figure 19.5: Displaying the JAXB Architecture

Figure 19.5 shows the following three main components of the JAXB architecture:

- **The schema compiler**—Binds a source schema to a collection of schema-based program elements by using the JAXB binding language.
- **The schema generator**—Performs the reverse operation to that of the schema compiler. It maps a collection of schema-based program elements to a source schema by using Java annotations.
- **The binding runtime framework**—Performs unmarshal and marshal operations. During unmarshalling, this framework accesses and validates XML content using schema-based program elements and converts the XML content into Java objects. During marshalling, this framework creates an XML document from the Java objects.

The sub-specifications of the JAXB specification are as follows:

- Mapping annotations
- Binding runtime framework
- Validation
- Marshal event callbacks
- Partial binding
- Binary data encoding
- JAXB binding language
- Probability

Let's briefly discuss each of these next.

Mapping Annotations

The JAXB 2.2 mapping annotations are used to customize standard Java/XML binding. The schema generator accepts Java classes and mapping annotations to define customized mapping. In case there is no mapping annotation present in the Java class, the schema generator applies the default Java/XML binding.

The following code snippet uses a mapping annotation to map a Java bean property to an XML schema element:

```
public class PO
{
    ....
    @XmlElement(name="POnum") } )
    String getPONumber();
    void setPONumber();
};
```

When you need to bind an XML element to a Java bean property in the reverse direction, the schema compiler generates the previous mapping annotations in Java code.

JAXB 2.2provides the following standards on mapping annotations:

- You need to create corresponding type mappings in parallel to creation of Java classes
- You need to run the schema generator on Java classes to determine type mappings

It's easy to create Web services from a Java class as mapping annotations allow you to specify type mappings and serialization in Java classes that implement the Web services.

Binding Runtime Framework

The binding runtime framework invokes a Web service deployed in a JWS-complaint application. The steps to perform this operation are as follows:

- A SOAP message is received by the JWS compliant application at a deployed endpoint.
- Depending on the configuration of SOAP binding for the endpoint, the JAX-WS implementation creates the message context, which contains the SAAJ representation of the SOAP message. In this case, JAXB can be used for Message Transmission Optimization Mechanism/XML-binary Optimized Packaging (MTOM)/XOP processing, which creates the SAAJ representation of the SOAP message.
- The JAX-WS implementation calls the request handlers. The application uses the SAAJ interface to retrieve the request parameters of the SOAP message.

- After the request handlers complete the processing, the JAXB runtime binding framework unmarshals the contents of the SOAP message into a request bean. The JAX-WS implementation defines the request bean depending on the parameter and return type packaging of deployment. The JAXB implementation binds the request bean to the SOAP message request. The terms marshal and unmarshal also mean serialize and deserialize, respectively.
- The request bean consists of Java objects that are passed as parameters to the Java method that invokes the Web service.
- The JAX-WS implementation uses the Java object that has been returned by the Java method to construct the instance of the response bean.
- Next, the JAXB runtime marshals the response bean.
- The JAX-WS modifies the message context to provide the SAAJ representation of the response, which is rendered as the SAAJ interface.
- The JAX-WS implementation calls the response handlers.
- The JAX-WS implementation delegates control to JAXB runtime to process the MTOM of the response message. You learn more about MTOM later in the chapter.
- The JAX-WS implementation transmits the response message to the transport protocol.

Figure 19.6 summarizes this process of invoking a Web service deployed as a JWS-complaint application:

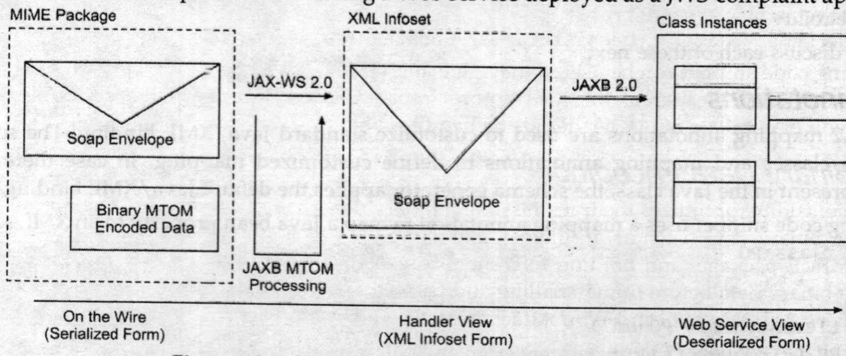

Figure 19.6: Displaying Java Web Service Invocation

In Figure 19.6, a SOAP request comes from the network wire in the form of a MIME package. The JAX-WS implementation converts the serialized SOAP request message into an XML infoset representation. The JAXB implementation unmarshals the infoset representation into JAXB annotated Java elements. The Java method that implements the Web service accepts these elements to invoke the Web service.

Implementing Validation

To successfully implement Web services, you need to handle invalid XML instances. An XML instance is invalid if it is not valid according to the WSDL/XML schema that defines the Web service. JAXB, by default, supports unmarshalling of invalid XML instances. This is done through the flexible unmarshalling mode that ignores some invalid conditions, such as out-of-order elements found in XML instances.

To unmarshal only valid XML instances, turn on the JAXB validation by invoking the `Unmarshaller.setSchema()` method with the `javax.xml.Validation.Schema` instance as a parameter. After the JAXB validation is turned on, by default, unchecked exception is thrown on the first error in an XML instance. You can define your own event handler by setting a `javax.xml.bind.ValidationEventHandler` instance with the `Unmarshaller.setEventHandler()` method to handle errors. Use the `javax.xml.bind.util.ValidationEventCollector` instance inside an event handler to collect all the errors that have occurred during unmarshalling.

Exploring Marshal Event Callbacks

Marshalling is the process of changing instances of JAXB annotated classes to XML infoset representations. This conversion is based on the changed JAXB standard Java/XML binding. Unmarshalling is a process of changing XML infoset representations to content objects that are represented in the form of XML tree structures. The content objects are either JAXB schema-derived program elements or existing program elements mapped to the XML schema generated by the schema generator.

Callbacks allow application-specific processing during serialization. You can invoke callbacks before or after the serialization.

Exploring Partial Binding

The `javax.xml.bind.Binder` class binds a part of an XML document. For example, you can use this class for creating the JAXB binding of a SOAP header without processing the message body of the SOAP message. The following code snippet shows an example of partial binding of an XML document:

```
JAXBContext jaxbContext= JAXBContext.newInstance(…);
org.w3c.dom.Element persistElt = ... // get from SOAP header
Binder<org.w3c.dom.Node> myBinderDemo = jaxbContext.createBinder();
PersistedValueClass persistVC = (PersistedValueClass)
myBinderDemo.unmarshal(persistElt);
persistVC.setPersisted(true);
myBinderDemo.updateXML(persistVC); // updates the XML infoset
```

The preceding code snippet can be used to navigate and update the Document Object Model (DOM) interface to manipulate the SOAP header of the XML infoset representation. You do not need to work with the DOM interface if you manipulate SOAP header inside handlers.

Exploring Binary Data Encoding

Binary data encoding optimizes the transmission of binary data in SOAP messages. The optimization is achieved by encoding binary data (such as an image), extracting it from the SOAP envelope, attaching its compressed form to a MIME package, and holding references to encoded parts in the SOAP envelope. In addition, JAXB unpackages binary data before unmarshalling and packages it after marshalling. JAXB supports two binary data encoding types: MTOM/XOP and WS-I Attachments Profile Version (WSIAP).

MTOM is a W3C standard to accept content from an XML infoset, compress it, package it as a MIME attachment, and finally replace it with a reference in the infoset. The encoding used during packaging is XML-binary Optimized Packaging (XOP).

Exploring JAXB Binding Language

The binding language is used to make Java types compatible with XML types, so that Java types can be accepted as parameters and return types by Web SEIs. The JAXB binding language annotates XML instances to customize Java representation of XML schema. In other words, the JAXB binding language fine tunes the structure of Java elements generated by the schema compiler. The annotations in the binding language are generated by the schema compiler by using the source schema and binding declarations. Therefore, binding declarations indirectly control the serialization of Web services.

Mapping annotations are provided in a Java class; however, binding language customizations (or binding language declarations) can be given in the following three ways:

- With a global scope
- With a component scope
- As an XML schema or a separate configuration file

Let's explore these three ways to map the annotations next.

Binding Declaration with a Global Scope

The following code snippet shows a binding declaration with a global scope:

```
<jaxb:globalBindings>
```

```
        <jaxb:javaType name="long" xmlType="xs:date"
              parseMethod="pkg.DatatypeConverter.parseDate"
              printMethod="pkg.DatatypeConverter.printDate"/>
        </jaxb:javaType>
    </jaxb:globalBindings>
```

The binding declaration in the preceding code snippet maps the XML instances of the `xs:date`type to a Java long type. By default, XML instances of the `xs:date`type are mapped to `javax.xml.datatype.XMLGregorianCalendar class`. The `parseMethod` and `printMethod` attributes denote the location of the methods used to unmarshal and marshal the type mapping to the JAXB implementation.

Binding Declaration with a Component Scope

The binding declaration may have a component scope if the `<jaxb:name>`binding tag is nested inside the `<xs:appinfo>` element. The following code snippet shows a binding declaration with a component scope:

```
<xs:complexType name="ComplexPO">
    <xs:sequence>
          <xs:element name="PO" type="javector:PurchaseOrder"
          maxOccurs="unbounded"/>
                 <xs:annotation><xs:appinfo>
                        <jaxb:dom/>
                 </xs:appinfo></xs:annotation>
          </xs:element>
    </xs:sequence>
</xs:complexType>
```

In the preceding code snippet, the PO element is mapped to the `org.w3c.dom.Element` instance of a DOM representation. When you are mapping an XML element to a DOM representation, you can specify the `javector:PurchaseOrder` custom serializer to serialize the DOM representation.

Binding Declaration as an External Configuration File

The external binding file uses XPath expressions to refer to specific schemas associated with the XML elements. The following code snippet shows an external binding file:

```
<jaxb:bindings xmlns:jaxb="http://java.sun.com/xml/ns/jaxb"
   xmlns:xs="http://www.w3.org/2001/XMLSchema" version="1.0">
   <jaxb:bindings schemaLocation=".../mySchema.xsd">
          <jaxb:bindings node="//xs:complexType[@name='ComplexPO']">
                 <jaxb:bindings node=".//xs:element[@name='PO']">
                        <jaxb:dom/>
                 </jaxb:bindings>
          </jaxb:bindings>
   </jaxb:bindings>
</jaxb:bindings>
```

The use of external binding file ensures that you do not require XML-based execution process to implement the WSDL of a Web service. However, including JAXB implementation-specific XML in the WSDL document makes the document insecure.

Explaining Portability

JAXB mapping annotations help in achieving JAXB portability, which simply means that a runtime marshaller of any JAXB implementation can serialize a JAXB annotated class to an instance of the XML schema defining a Web service, or deserialize a schema instance to the instance of the JAXB annotated class.

In other words, JAXB portability allows you to deploy a Web service, implemented through a Java class with JAXB annotations, on any JAXB platform, such as JBoss or GlassFish. You do not need to recompile the schema or change the Web service to use vendor-specific implementation classes.

Exploring the WSEE 1.3 Specification

The WSEE 1.3 specification deals with the service architecture, packaging, and deployment of Web services. The objective of this specification is to make Web services portable on different Java EE application server implementations. The WSEE specification solves the problems related to the deployment of Web services as observed in case of J2EE 1.4. These problems can be solved through the use of annotations and easy packaging architecture. The WSEE specification provides the following sub-specifications:

- Port component
- Servlet endpoints
- Enterprise Java Beans (EJB)endpoints
- Simple packaging
- Handler programming model

Let's look at each feature in detail.

Port Component

The WSEE specification defines a port component as a component that is packaged and deployed on the Web container to implement a Web service. In J2EE 1.4, the WSEE 1.0 specification includes some other artifacts that are required to be deployed along with the port component, such as Service Endpoint Interface (SEI), the Web services Deployment Descriptor (`webservices.xml`), and the JAX-RPC mapping Deployment Descriptor. In Java EE 5, the WSEE 1.2 specification makes certain artifacts, such as the WSDL document, SEI, and webservices.xml, optional. That is, if you define the `webservices.xml` Deployment Descriptor, it overrides the deployment information specified in annotations.

Servlet Endpoints

The WSEE 1.3 specification uses Plain Old Java Objects (POJO) to implement a Web service if it is defined according to the requirements mentioned in the WS-Metadata for a Service Implementation Bean (SIB). This POJO is also known as a Servlet endpoint.

EJB Endpoints

The WSEE 1.3 specification allows a stateless session bean to implement a Web service deployed in an EJB container. This stateless session bean is also known as an EJB endpoint. You also need to create a service implementation bean from the EJB endpoint to execute the Web service functionality.

Simple Packaging

The WSEE 1.3 specification eliminates the need for Deployment Descriptors in simple cases. Even those used in complex situations are simpler when compared to the ones in J2EE 1.4.

Handler Programming Model

WS-Metadata defines many handler annotations. The WSEE 1.3 specification defines the programming and runtime behavior of these handler annotations. For example, the @HandlerChain annotation binds a chain of handlers with a port component. The WSEE 1.3 specification describes how to define a structure for the chain of handlers in the Web services Deployment Descriptor, `webservices.xml`.

Exploring the WS-Metadata 2.2 Specification

The JAX-WS and JAXB specifications cover most of the sub-specifications for the invocation and serialization of JWSs. The WS-Metadata specification provides standards for deploying the JWSs. As per the WS-Metadata 2.2 specification, you can now use annotations to deploy Java classes as Web services. The WS-Metadata 2.2 API provides annotations that are used to develop and deploy Web services on the Java SE 6 and Java EE 6 platforms. You can use the `Start From WSDL` Java development mode to develop and deploy JWSs by using the annotations feature.

For example, let's assume that you need to deploy the createPurchaseOrder() method of the PurchaseOrder Java class as a Web service operation, ns:createPO. This Web service operation includes the ns:PurchaseOrder element based on the given XML schema. You also want to publish the Web service as a WSDL interface for allowing users to access it.

If you want to include WS-Metadata annotations in the PurchaseOrder class, you should have access to its code and access rights to recompile and redeploy the application with the annotations. After you have redeployed the application with metadata annotations, you need to map the PurchaseOrder program elements to the ns:PurchaseOrder element with JAXB annotations. Assume that you create a customized mapping class with JAXB mapping annotations to perform this mapping. To verify that the customized mapping is valid, you need to run the WSDL/XML schema generator and check the final WSDL document to verify whether it conforms with the given schema.

The `Start From WSDL` development mode can be used to generate the WSDL using wrapper classes. To generate the wrapper classes, you need to run the WSDL/XML schema compiler on the given WSDL standard, retrieve the required Java classes, and convert them into wrapper classes. This entire process invokes the PurchaseOrder class.

The sub-specifications of the WS-Metadata specification are:

- WSDL mapping annotations
- SOAP binding annotations
- Handler annotations
- Service implementation bean
- Start From WSDL and Java
- Automatic deployment

Let's look at these in detail.

WSDL Mapping Annotations

WSDL mapping annotations are also known as Web services annotations. These annotations are packaged in the `javax.jws` package. WSDL mapping annotations modify the default WSDL/Java mapping. For example, they are used to assign the WSDL operation name to a specific Java method. Annotation type declarations are contained in the `javax.jws` package, which need to be imported.

The `javax.jws package` defines the enumerations and annotations. The data types of the `javax.jws` package are described in Table 19.3:

Table 19.3: Data Types of the javax.jws Package

Name	Type	Description
WebParam.Mode	Enum	Specifies the flow control of the parameters
HandlerChain	Annotation	Links a Web service with an external handler chain
Oneway	Annotation	Indicates that the given @WebMethod annotation does not have any output messages but only input message
WebMethod	Annotation	Customizes a method that is exhibited as a Web service operation
WebParam	Annotation	Specifies the mapping between an individual parameter and a Web service message part along with an XML element
WebResult	Annotation	Customizes the mapping of parameter's return value to a WSDL part and an XML element
WebService	Annotation	Indicates that a Web service is implemented by a Java class or an interface used for implementing Web service is defined by the Java interface

SOAP Binding Annotations

WS-Metadata 2.2 SOAP binding annotations are present in the `javax.jws.soap` package. These annotations modify the SOAP binding style when performing SOAP mapping. You learned earlier that JAX-WS uses the document/literal wrapped value for the binding style by default.

Handler Annotations

Some WS-Metadata 2.2 annotations are used to deploy handlers. The `javax.jws.HandlerChain` annotation associates a Web service with a chain of handlers defined in an external file, which you can reference by using the `@HandlerChain.file` annotation. Note that JAX-WS-compliant endpoints cannot use the `javax.jws.soap.SOAPMessageHandlers` annotation to deploy SOAP handlers as this annotation has been deprecated.

Service Implementation Bean

WS-Metadata specifies some conditions for a Java class to be deployed as a Web service. The Java classes that satisfy these conditions are known as Service Implementation Beans (SIBs). WS-Metadata annotations prevent you from container-specific deployment of Web services.J2EE 1.4 complies with the JAX-RPC specification, a previous version of JAX-WS 2.2, which requires SEIs to inherit the `java.rmi.Remote` class for implementing Java classes as Web services. However, as per the WS-Metadata 2.2 specification, both POJOs and EJBs acting as SIBs may be deployed as Web services.

Start From WSDL and Java

The `Start From WSDL and Java` development mode uses some WS-Metadata annotations to map the elements of a Java class or interface to the elements of a WSDL document. For example, the `@WebMethod.operationName` annotation associates a Java method to the `wsdl:operation` element. The demerits of using the `Start From WSDL and the Java` development mode have already been discussed earlier in the chapter. To avoid those demerits, you can use a well-implemented tool, such as Castor, which identifies nonconformance errors when a Web service implementation deviates from a standard WSDL contract.

Automatic Deployment

The WS-Metadata specification allows a Web service to be deployed by using the drag and drop option. Runtime deployment of Web services only depends on annotations used in Java class and there is no need for a vendor-specific deployment tool. GlassFish V3, a Java EE 6 implementation provides the drag and drop deployment model for deploying Web services.

Describing the SAAJ 1.3 Specification

The SAAJ specification lays down the standards for transmitting and processing SOAP messages in compliance with the JAX-WS handlers and JAXR implementations. You can write SOAP messaging applications directly by using this specification. The SAAJ API defined by the SAAJ specification, works on SOAP 1.1, 1.2, and SOAP with attachments specifications. The SAAJ 1.3 API provides the `javax.xml.soap` package that provides classes to create and send request-response messages.

Working with SAAJ and DOM APIs

The interfaces and classes of the SAAJ API extend the corresponding interfaces and classes present in the `org.w3c.dom` package. The `Node` interface of the SAAJ API inherits the `org.w3c.dom.Node` interface of the DOM API. Similarly, the `SOAPElement` interface of the SAAJ API inherits both the `Node` and `org.w3c.dom.Element` interfaces of the DOM API. In addition, the `org.w3c.dom.Document` interface is also implemented by the `SOAPPart` class.

As SAAJ nodes implement the DOM `Node` and `Element` interfaces, you can manipulate contents of a message by using any of the following:

- Only the DOM API

- Only the SAAJ API
- The SAAJ API first, and then using the DOM API
- The DOM API first, and then using the SAAJ API

The first three ways are easy to implement, as after creating a message, you can use either the DOM or the SAAJ API to manipulate the message content. However, when you use the DOM API first, retrieving the references to objects using the DOM API within the source tree of the message is not possible.

Let's look at a few examples to use the SAAJ API. To be precise, we perform the following actions:

- Creating a simple SOAP message
- Accessing the different message parts of the SOAP message
- Adding content to the SOAP Body object
- Sending a message
- Retrieving the content of a message
- Adding content to the header element
- Creating and adding attachments
- Retrieving Attachments

Let's explore these in detail.

Creating a Simple SOAP Message

You can create an instance of a message by invoking the `newInstance()` static method of the `MessageFactory` class. As `MessageFactory` is an abstract class, the SAAJ API uses the default implementation class of the `MessageFactory` class. The following code snippet shows how to create an instance of a message:

```
MessageFactory mfactory = MessageFactory.newInstance();
SOAPMessage msg = mfactory.createMessage();
```

The previous code snippet creates an instance of the `MessageFactory` class for SOAP 1.1 messages. The SOAP message contains the `SOAPPart` object, which further contains the `SOAPEnvelope` object in turn containing empty `SOAPHeader` and `SOAPBody` objects.

In order to create an instance of the `MessageFactory` class for SOAP 1.2 messages, pass the SOAP_1_2_PROTOCOL constant as an argument to the `newInstance()` method, as shown in the following code snippet:

```
MessageFactory mfactory =
MessageFactory.newInstance(SOAPConstants.SOAP_1_2_PROTOCOL);
```

In order to create an instance of the `MessageFactory` class that enables you to create either SOAP 1.1 or SOAP 1.2 messages, call the `newInstance()` method, as shown in the following code snippet:

```
MessageFactory mfactory =
MessageFactory.newInstance(SOAPConstants.DYNAMIC_SOAP_PROTOCOL);
```

Accessing the Different Message Parts of a SOAP Message

The SAAJ API provides different methods to access the parts of a SOAP message. Table 19.4 lists the methods to access the different message parts of a SOAP message:

Table 19.4: Methods to Access Message Parts

Message Part	Syntax	
SOAPPart	`SOAPPart soapPrt = msg.getSOAPPart();`	
SOAPEnvelope	`SOAPEnvelope spEnv= soapPrt.getEnvelope();`	
SOAPHeader and SOAPBody	`SOAPHeader soapheadr = spEnv.getHeader();` `SOAPBody soapbdy = spEnv.getBody();`	`SOAPHeader soapheadr = msg.getSOAPHeader();` `SOAPBody soapbdy = msg.getSOAPBody();`

Adding Content to the SOAPBody Object

To add content to the `SOAPBody` object, you need to first create one or more `SOAPBodyElement` objects, and then add sub elements to these `SOAPBodyElement` objects by invoking the `addChildElement()` method. Finally, add content by invoking the `addTextNode()` method. You should create an associated `javax.xml.namepace.QName` object for each new `SOAPBodyElement` element that uniquely identifies the element. The `QName` object consists of a fully qualified namespace URI, local part, and a namespace prefix.

The following code snippet associates a QName object to a SOAPBodyElement object:

```
SOAPBody soapbdy = msg.getSOAPBody();
QName soapbdyElemName = new QName("http://wombat.ztrade.com",
"GetLastTradePrice", "n");
SOAPBodyElement soapbdyElem = soapbdy.addBodyElement(soapbdyElemName);
```

In the previous code snippet, as the `soapbdyElem` element contains no content, we need to add the stock symbol SUNW as a child element of the `soapbdyElem` element, as shown in the following code snippet:

```
QName qname = new QName("symb");
SOAPElement symb = soapbdyElem.addChildElement(qname);
symb.addTextNode("SUNW");
```

In the preceding code snippet, the symb local name is specified while creating the instance of the QName class, named qname. Further, the qname instance inherits namespace prefix and URI from the parent element.

As you know that SOAP part can contain only XML content, SAAJ API creates appropriate XML elements automatically on invocation of methods, such as `addBodyElement()`, `addChildElement()`, and `addTextNode()`.

> **NOTE**
> *You cannot invoke the addTextNode() method on a SOAPHeader or SOAPBody object, as they contain only elements.*

Let's now explore how a SOAP-based XML document is generated by using the SAAJ API. The following code snippet shows the SAAJ API code for generating the XML document:

```
SOAPMessage msg = mFactory.createMessage();
SOAPHeader soapheadr = msg.getSOAPHeader();
SOAPBody soapbdy = msg.getSOAPBody();
QName soapbdyElemName = new QName("http://wombat.ztrade.com",
"GetLastTradePrice", "n");
SOAPBodyElement soapbdyElem = soapbdy.addBodyElement(soapbdyElemName);
QName qname = new QName("symb");
SOAPElement symb = soapbdyElem.addChildElement(qname);
symb.addTextNode("SUNW");
```

After executing the code provided in the preceding code snippet, the XML document is created as shown in the following code snippet:

```
<SOAP-ENV:env
  xmlns:SOAP-ENV="http://schemas.xmlsoap.org/soap/envelope/">
  <SOAP-ENV:body>
        <n:GetLastTradePricexmlns:n="http://wombat.ztrade.com">
                <symb>SUNW</symb>
        </n:GetLastTradePrice>
  </SOAP-ENV:body>
</SOAP-ENV:env>
```

Sending a Message

All SOAP messages are transmitted over a connection between a sender and destination endpoint. The SAAJ API provides the `SOAPConnection` class to facilitate the sending and receiving of SOAP messages. Two types of messages are sent using the SAAJ API, request and response. You can send request messages by making a call to the `SOAPConnection.call()` method. The following code snippet shows how to send a request message:

```
SOAPConnectionFactory soapConnectFactory =
  SOAPConnectionFactory.newInstance();
SOAPConnection con = soapConnectFactory.createConnection();
```

```
. . .// code to create a request message and give it content
java.net.URL endpointURL =
  new URL("http://wombat.ztrade.com/quotes");
SOAPMessage responsemsg = con.call(msg, endpointURL);
con.close();
```

The `call()` method sends the request message `msg` to the specified endpoint `endpointURL`. The first argument to the `call()` method specifies the request message to be sent, and the second argument to this method specifies the destination of the request message.

Retrieving the Content of a Message

You need to invoke the `getValue()` method on the SOAPBodyElement object to retrieve the content of a SOAP message, as shown in the following code snippet:

```
SOAPBody soapBdy = responsemsg.getSOAPBody();
java.util.Iterator it =soapBdy.getChildElements(soapbdyElemName);
SOAPBodyElement bdyElem =(SOAPBodyElement)it.next();
String lstPrice = bdyElem.getValue();
System.out.print("The last price for SUNW is ");
System.out.println(lstPrice);
```

In the preceding code snippet, after retrieving the instance of the `SOAPBody` object, the `getChildElements()` method is invoked to get an iterator, `it`. The iterator object `it` contains child elements associated with the `soapbdyElemName` object. As we inserted only one `SOAPBodyElement` element earlier, the `next()` method call on the `Iterator` object returns a Java object that is further typecasted to the `SOAPBodyElement` type. The call to the `getValue()` method on the `bdyElem` instance returns the last price of the `SUNW` stock symbol.

Adding Content to the Header Element

You can add content to a header element of a SOAP message by creating the instance of the `SOAPHeader` class. The following code snippet adds the required content to the `Claim` header:

```
SOAPHeader soapheadr = msg.getSOAPHeader();
QName soapheadrElemName = new QName(
  "http://ws-i.org/schemas/conformanceClaim/","Claim", "wsi");
SOAPHeaderElement soapheadrElem =soapheadr.addHeaderElement(soapheadrElemName);
soapheadrElem.addAttribute(new QName("conformsTo"),
  "http://ws-i.org/profiles/basic/1.1/");
```

The `soapheadrElem` object contains an attribute that specifies information about WS-I conformance claim header. The `addHeaderElement()` method first creates a SOAPHeaderElement instance `soapheadrElem` and adds it to the `soapheadr` header. The header elements can contain only text strings. The following code snippet shows how to add a text string to the header element:

```
soapheadrElem.addTextNode("order");
```

Creating and Adding Attachments

To create and add attachments to a SOAP message, you first need to create an attachment by creating an `AttachmentPart` object, which can be created by invoking the `createAttachmentPart()` method on an instance of `SOAPMessage`, as shown in the following code snippet:

```
AttachmentPart attachmntPart = msg.createAttachmentPart();
```

The preceding code snippet creates an attachment having no content. You can add content to the empty attachment by using the `setContent()` method of the `AttachmentPart` object. The `setContent()` method accepts two parameters, a String object that represents the content and another `String` object that represents the MIME content type. The Java object may be String, stream, a `javax.xml.transform.Source` or `javax.activation.DataHandler` object. After adding content to the attachment, you need to add the attachment to a message. The following code snippet shows the code for adding a text-based attachment to a message:

```
String str = "Update address for Kogent Solutions Inc., " +
  "to  4435/7, ANSARI ROAD, DARYA GANJ, NEW DELHI 110002";
attachmntPart.setContent(str, "text/plain");
```

```
attachmntPart.setContentId("update_addr");
msg.addAttachmentPart(attachmntPart);
```

The preceding code snippet uses the `String` object in the first parameter as a Java `Object` and `text/plain` as the second parameter in the `setContent()` method. The preceding code snippet also adds the `ContentId` header with a value `update_addr`. Finally, the attachment is added to the `msg` instance.

Apart from adding plain text, you can also add images to the attachments by calling the `createAttachmentPart()` method with a `DataHandler` object as parameter. Again, after creating the attachment with an image, you need to add it to a message. The following code snippet shows how to add an image as an attachment to a message:

```
java.net.URL imageurl = new URL(".../img.jpg");
DataHandler dataHandlr = new DataHandler(imageurl);
AttachmentPart attachmntPart=msg.createAttachmentPart(dataHandlr);
attachmntPart.setContentId("image");
msg.addAttachmentPart(attachmntPart);
```

Retrieving Attachments

To manipulate the content of an attachment, you need to access the attachment. Two overloaded versions of the `getAttachments()` method are provided by the `SOAPMessage class` to retrieve the `AttachmentPart` objects. The first version of the `getAttachments()` method accepts no argument and returns a `java.util.Iterator` object for all the `AttachmentPart` objects in a message. The second version of the `getAttachments()` method accepts the `MimeHeaders` object as an argument and returns the `AttachmentPart` objects corresponding to headers present in the `MimeHeaders` object. The following code snippet retrieves and prints the content of all the attachments in a SOAP message:

```
java.util.Iterator it = msg.getAttachments();
while (it.hasNext())
{
  AttachmentPart attachmntPart= (AttachmentPart)it.next();
  String attachmntId = attachmntPart.getContentId();
  String attachmntType = attachmntPart.getContentType();

  System.out.print("Attachment " + attachmntId +
  " has content type " + attachmntType);
  if (attachmntType.equals("text/plain"))
  {
       Object attachmntContent = attachmntPart.getContent();
       System.out.println("Attachment has content:\n" + attachmntContent);
  }
}
```

Describing the JAXR Specification

JAXR helps in accessing standard business registries over the Internet. Business registries normally consist of listings of businesses and the products or services the businesses offer. Therefore, business registeries are often described as electronic yellow pages.

In the Web service architecture, a registry plays a key role as it is used to publish, search, and use Web services. Business registries allow businesses to collaborate with each other dynamically in a loosely coupled way.This is one reason why business registries are gaining popularity as important components of Web services. Consequently, the need for JAXR, which enables enterprises to access standard business registries, is also growing. JAXR provides various APIs to access different XML registries. It also helps in describing the content and the metadata in an XML registry. In addition, it helps in writing portable registry client programs.

Let's now explore the JAXR architecture in detail.

JAXR Architecture

The JAXR architecture can be broadly divided into the following parts:

- ❑ **JAXRclient**—A client program accessing registry through JAXR provider
- ❑ **JAXRprovider**—A JAXR implementation providing access to some registry provider

Figure 19.7 shows the JAXR architecture:

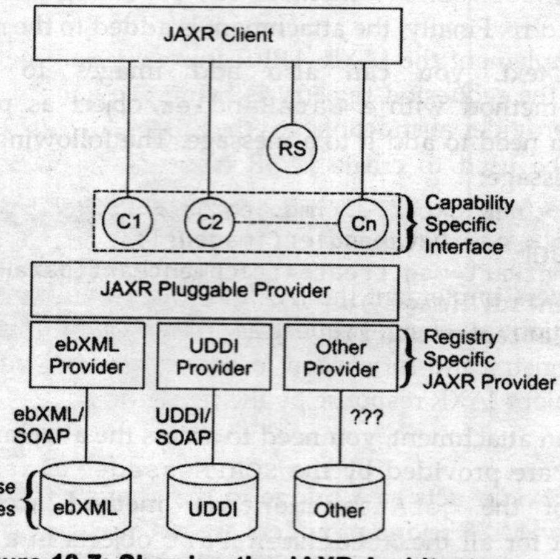

Figure 19.7: Showing the JAXR Architecture

JAXR Client

Any Java application or enterprise component can become a JAXR client by using the JAXR API. A JAXR client can contain the following interfaces:

- ❑ **Connection interface**—Represents a client session along with a registry provider by using the JAXR provider. Creating a connection object by using this interface with the registry provider is necessary to use the services of that registry. The `ConnectionFactory` interface is used to create the connection.
- ❑ **RegistryService interface**—Provides various getter methods used to retrieve `capability-specific` interfaces.
- ❑ **Other capability-specific interfaces**—Helps to perform activities, such as life-cycle management and query management.

JAXR Provider

A JAXR provider represents an implementation of the JAXR API. The JAXR provider helps a JAXR client to access a registry. A JAXR provider needs to implement the following two packages:

- ❑ **javax.xml.registry**—Contains interfaces and classes used to access a specific registry. It has four main interfaces:
- ❑ **Connection**—Represents the connection that exists between a client and a JAXR provider.
- ❑ **RegistryService**—Enables a client to access the registery.
- ❑ **BusinessQueryManager**—Allows clients to find information in a registry according to the `javax.xml.registry.infomodel` interfaces.
- ❑ **BusinessLifeCycleManager** —Allows clients to manipulate the information in a registry.
- ❑ **javax.xml.registry.infomodel**—Provides interfaces that define the types of objects residing in a registry, and how these objects are related to each other. `RegistryObject` is the key interface of this package. The sub-interfaces of the `RegistryObject` interface are `Organization`, `Service`, and `ServiceBinding`.

  JAXR providers can be of differnet types, such as:

  - JAXR Pluggable Provider
  - Registry-Specific JAXR Provider
  - JAXRBridge Provider

- Registry Provider

Let's describe these in detail next.

JAXR Pluggable Provider

JAXR pluggable providers implement the JAXR API features that are not dependent on any particular type of registry. When the access to the requested registry is being provided by multiple JAXR providers, the use of JAXR pluggable provider provide abstraction to the client. It also provides the `ConnectionFactory` implementation, which can be used to create JAXR connections by using different registory-specific JAXR providers.

Registry-Specific JAXR Provider

Registry-specific JAXR providers implement the JAXR API in a manner that is specific to a registry. In case of registry-specific implementation, a client request is transformed into equivalent requests based on the specifications of the target registry and forwarded to the registry provider. Finally, registry-specific responses are also converted into equivalent JAXR response by the registry-specific JAXR provider.

JAXRBridge Provider

If a registry-specific JAXR provider acts as a bridge to the existing registry providers, it is known as a JAXR bridge provider. Consequently, JAXRbridge providers are not specific to a particular registry type; instead, they may be specific to a group of registries (such as OASIS, ebXML, or UDDI).

Registry Provider

Registry providers are implementations of various registry specifications, such as ebXML or UDDI.

Exploring the StAX 1.0 Specification

The StAX 1.0 specification is a joint effort of BEA Electronics and Sun Microsystems. The StAX specification provides various APIs to control the parsing of XML documents. The StAX APIs address the limitations of other parsing APIs, such as Simple API for XML (SAX) and DOM. Following are some uses of the StAX APIs:

- Help in unmarshalling and marshalling and parallel document processing of an XML document
- Parse simple predictable structures, graph representations, and WSDL, while processing a SOAP message
- Navigate a DOM tree in the form of stream of events
- Help parse particular XML vocabularies

Let's discuss the StAX APIs and factory classes in detail next.

StAX APIs

The StAX APIs allow you to perform iterative and event-based processing of XML documents. The XML documents are considered as filtered series of events. The StAX API comprises of two APIs, cursor API and iterator API.

The Cursor API

The StAX `cursor` API provides a cursor to navigate through an XML document. This cursor can point to an element of the XML document and can move in the forward direction only. Key interfaces in the cursor API are `XMLStreamReader` and `XMLStreamWriter`.

The `XMLStreamReader` interface provides methods to retrieve information, such as document encoding, element names, attributes, text nodes, and processing instructions. The following code snippet shows the syntax of some of the methods of the `XMLStreamReader` interface:

```
public interface XMLStreamReader
{
  public int next() throws XMLStreamException;
  public boolean hasNext() throws XMLStreamException;
  public String getText();
  public String getLocalName();
```

```
    public String getNamespaceURI();
    ...
}
```

You can call the `getText()` and `getName()` methods of the `XMLStreamReader` interface to retrieve the data at the current cursor location.

The `XMLStreamWriter` interface provides methods to handle event types, such as `StartElement` and `EndElement`. The following code snippet shows the syntax of some of the methods of the `XMLStreamWriter` interface:

```
public interface XMLStreamWriter
{
    public void writeStartElement(String localName)
            throws XMLStreamException;
    public void writeEndElement()
            throws XMLStreamException;
    public void writeCharacters(String text)
            throws  XMLStreamException;
    ...
}
```

The Iterator API

The StAX `iterator` API represents the data of an XML document in the form of a set of discrete event objects. When an XML parser reads the source XML document, these events are retrieved by the application in the order in which the parser reads them.

`XMLEvent` is the main interface of the iterator API, which contains the `XMLEventReader` and `XMLEventWriter` interfaces to read and write the iterator events, respectively.

The `XMLEventReader` interface has five methods. The following code snippet shows the syntax of some of the methods of the `XMLEventReader` interface:

```
public interface XMLEventReader extends Iterator
{
    public XMLEvent nextEvent() throws XMLStreamException;
    public boolean hasNext();
    public XMLEvent peek() throws XMLStreamException;
    ...
}
```

In the preceding code snippet, the `XMLEventReader` interface extends the `Iterator` interface.

The following code snippet shows the syntax of some of the methods of the `XMLEventWriter` interface:

```
public interface XMLEventWriter
{
    public void flush() throws XMLStreamException;
    public void close() throws XMLStreamException;
    public void add(XMLEvent e) throws XMLStreamException;
    public void add(Attribute attribute)
            throws XMLStreamException;
    ...
}
```

StAX Factory Classes

You can create XML stream readers, writers, and events by using the StAX factory classes, such as `XMLInputFactory`, `XMLOutputFactory`, and `XMLEventFactory`. You can configure these readers, writers, and events by setting properties of factory classes.

Let's explore these factory classes in detail next.

The XMLInputFactory Class

The `XMLInputFactory` class is an abstract class that creates instances of `XMLStreamReader` interface and then configures the implementation instances of XML stream reader processors. An instance of the `XMLInputFactory` class can be created by invoking the `XMLInputFactory.newInstance()` method. The `newInstance()` method finds a particular `XMLInputFactory` implementation class by performing the following operations:

- Using the javax.xml.stream.XMLInputFactory system property
- Using the `lib/xml.stream.properties` file in the Java SE JRE directory
- Finding the class name in the `META-INF/services/javax.xml.stream.XMLInputFactory` files in JAR files of an application
- Using the platform default `XMLInputFactory` instance

The XMLOutputFactory Class

An instance of the `XMLOutputFactory` class can be created by invoking the `XMLOutputFactory.newInstance()` method. The `newInstance()` method of this class references the `javax.xml.stream.XMLOutputFactory` system property. The `XMLOutputFactory` class has only one property, `javax.xml.stream.isRepairingNamespaces`. This property creates default prefixes and links them with namespace URIs.

The XMLEventFactory Class

You can create an instance of the `XMLEventFactory` class by invoking its `newInstance()` method. The `newInstance()` method of this class references the `javax.xml.stream.XMLEventFactory` system property. The `XMLEventFactory` class has no default property.

Exploring the WebSocket 1.0 Specification

The WebSocket 1.0 specification has been introduced to provide a low latency two-way communication solution for communicating peers over single TCP connection. The WebSocket API allows Web application developers to implement client endpoints in the form of annotated Plain Old Java Objects (POJOs). The annoted POJO can respond on invocation of particular events, such as, on request of connection from a client, on reception of a message, and on disconnection from a client. The WebSocket API supports exchange of simple text and binary messages and ensures secure communication by laverging the Web container security model for authentication, authorization, and transport.

The WebSocket API has various interfaces, classes, and annotations. Some of the annotations provided by the API are shown in the Table 19.5 below:

Table 19.5: WebSocket API Annotations

Annotation	Description
ClientEndpoint	A class level annotation to specify a POJO as a Web socket client.
OnClose	Method level annotation to specify the method that should be called on closure of a Web socket session.
OnError	Method level annotation to specify the method that should be called for error handling.
OnMessage	Method level annotation to specify the method that should recieve incoming messages.
OnOpen	Method level annotation to specify the method that should be called when a web socket session is open.

Describing the JAX-RS 2.0 Specification

The JAX-RS 2.0 specification provides APIs to develop Representational State Transfer (REST) based Web services which support asynchronous response processing. With the JAX-RS APIs, a thread that is processing a client request on the server side can keep executing without blocking other clients while waiting for any other process to complete. Similarly, a client that has generated the request can carry out other activities in parallel and keep executing without blocking or waiting for the response for the request. The API also supports the use of various Filters and Entity Interceptors that can be executed before and after processing request and response respectively.

Exploring the JASON-P 1.0 Specification

The JavaScript Object Notation (JSON) is a data exchange format that is used by Web services to transfer and receive textual data. The JASON-P 1.0 specification provides APIs to effectively parse, transform, and query JSON data without requiring the need to bundle third party implementation libraries for the same. JSON data can be produced and consumed using a streaming model or an object model. Following code snippet shows a JSON-formatted object:

```
"address": [
   {
         "type": "home"
         "number":  "234-123-2426"
   },
   {
         "type": "office"
         "number":  "286-331-9802"
   }
]
```

Section C: Using the Web Service Specifications

In Section B, you learned about the various Web service specifications used to implement SOA. In this section, let's look at the practical implementation of these Web service specifications to implement SOA with JWSs. Let's start by developing client-side SOA application components by using the JAX-WS 2.2 specification. Next, you learn to implement Java/XML binding and type mapping by using the JAXB 2.2 specification. You also learn to deploy Web services by using the WSEE 1.3 specification. After that, you create a simple messaging application by using the SAAJ 1.3 specification. You use the JAXR 1.0 specification to develop JAXR clients. Finally, you learn to use the StAX 1.0 specification to read and write to XML streams and XML files.

Using the JAX-WS 2.2 Specification

JAX-WS is primarily used to create client-side SOA components that consume (or invoke and use) Web services. JAX-WS is similar to Remote Message Invocation (RMI) in Java as it allows you to make a local method call to invoke a Web service deployed on a remote host. However, RMI requires that a Web service on remote host should be implemented as a Java application. In JAX-WS, service must provide a WSDL interface having a `wsdl:portType` definition. While creating the client-side SOA components, you need to ensure that proper Java/WSDL mapping has been configured. You can use JAX-WS to map the `wsdl:portType` element of the WSDL interface to the corresponding Java interface. This Java interface is known as Service Endpoint Interface (SEI), as it is the Java representation of a Web service endpoint.

A Web service endpoint can be a referenceable entity, processor or resource by which you can send or receive Web service messages. JAX-WS dynamically generates an instance of SEI, and you can invoke a Web service by making a call to a method of the implementation class of SEI. This implementation class is also known as the JAX-WS dynamic proxy class.

After you have created a SOA component, you can use the annotations provided by the JAX-WS runtime environment to marshal and unmarshal method calls to SEI.

In this section, let's explore the use of JAX-WS proxies to invoke Web services. You also learn to perform Java/WSDL mapping by using JAX-WS annotations. In addition, you learn to marshal and unmarshal method calls to SEI.

Invoking Web Services by using JAX-WS Proxies

The JAX-WS runtime environment provides the implementation class of SEI, which is an instance of `java.lang.relect.Proxy` class, or the proxy class. To invoke a Web service, the proxy class uses an instance of the `java.lang.reflect.InvocationHandler` class to implement standard WSDL to Java and Java to WSDL mapping. The `InvocationHandler` object changes the passed parameters into SOAP messages, which are sent to the Web service endpoint. Similarly, SOAP response messages are converted back into an instance of the return type of SEI.

Figure 19.8 shows the process of invoking a Web service by using a JAX-WS proxy:

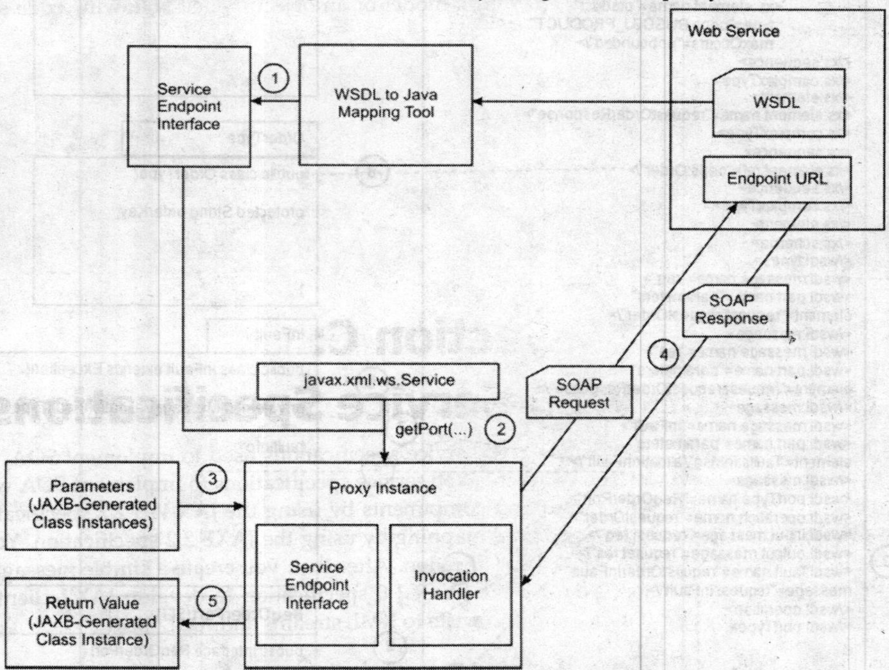

Figure 19.8: Invoking a Web Service Using a Java Proxy

Let's understand each step in Figure 19.8:

- A WSDL to Java mapping tool, such as wsimport tool of the GlassFish server, reads the WSDL and creates an SEI.
- The JAX-WS runtime invokes the appropriate `getPort()` method of the `javax.xml.ws.Service` class to create a proxy instance that implements the SEI.
- The Web service is invoked by a call to a method with different parameters. These parameters are instances of JAXB generated classes of the SEI.
- The dynamic proxy class uses an instance of the `java.lang.reflect.InvocationHandler` class to convert the passed parameters into a SOAP message, which is then sent to the Web service endpoint.
- Finally, the dynamic proxy class converts the SOAP response message into an instance of the return type of SEI.

Implementing JAX-WS WSDL to Java Mapping

To understand the concept of WSDL to Java mapping, let's consider a WSDL, `RequestOrder`. Figure 19.9 illustrates WSDL to Java mapping for the `RequestOrder` WSDL:

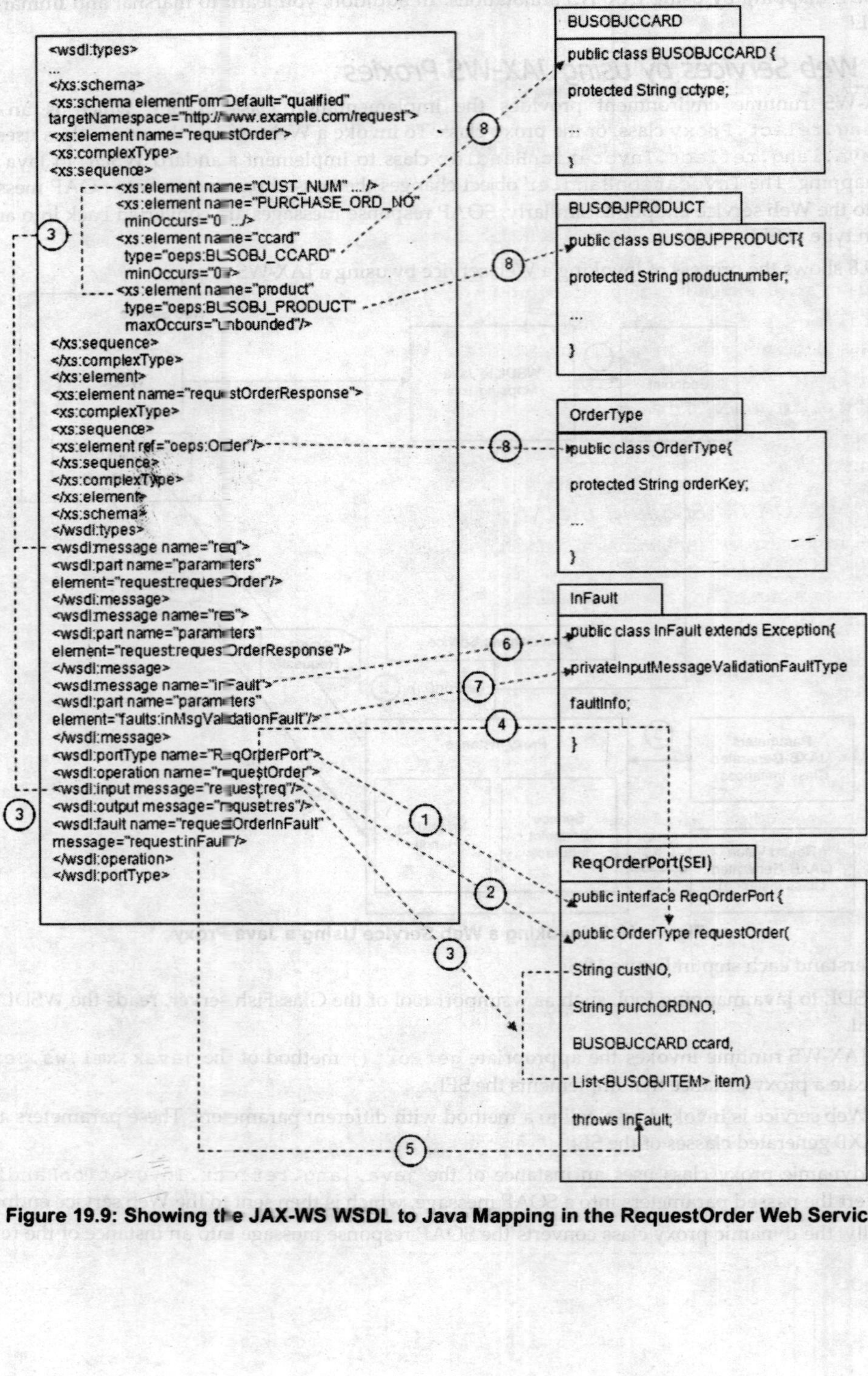

Figure 19.9: Showing the JAX-WS WSDL to Java Mapping in the RequestOrder Web Service

In Figure 19.9, the large box on the left shows the code of the RequestOrder WSDL. Remaining five boxes represent the mapping Java classes generated after the WSDL to Java mapping. The mapping is performed as per the following steps:

1. The `wsdl:portType` element of the WSDL with name `ReqOrderPort` is mapped to the SEI with the same name.
2. The `wsdl:operation` element named as `requestOrder`, inside the `wsdl:portType` element is mapped to a method of the SEI, with the same name, `requestOrder`.
3. The `wsdl:inputmessage` is mapped to the parameters of the `requestOrder()` method, such as `custNO`, `purchORDNO`, and `ccard`. The input message `request:req` has a single wrapper element `request:requestOrder` as declared by the `wsdl:part` element. The wrapper element is in turn defined within the `wsdl:types` section.
4. The `wsdl:outputmessage` element is mapped to the response type `OrderType`, which acts as a return type of the `requestOrder()` method.
5. The`wsdl:fault` element is mapped to thrown exception clause of the `requestOrder()` declaration.
6. The `wsdl:message element`, which refers to the `wsdl:fault element`, is mapped to the `InFault` Java class that extends the `java.lang.Exception` class.
7. The `wsdl:fault` element uses `wsdl:messageinFault` that has a single part. This part refers to a global element that is mapped to the `InputMessageValidationFaultType` fault bean.
8. The types defined in the `wsdl:types` element is mapped to Java classes using JAXB XML Schema to Java mapping.

Marshalling and Unmarshalling Method Calls to SEI

The JAX-WS runtime uses annotations to marshal a method call on SEI into a SOAP request message and unmarshal a SOAP response message into an instance of return type of SEI's method. The annotations used for marshalling and unmarshalling are given as follows:

- WebService
- WebMethod
- WebParam
- WebResult
- RequestWrapper
- ResponseWrapper

Let's discuss these in detail.

The WebService Annotation

The WebService annotation is used to annotate a class or an interface. The use of this annotation with an interface declares that this interface defined a Web service interface. When this annotation is used with a class, it declares that the class is the implementation of a Web service. The list of optional elements for the WebService annotation is provided in Table 19.5:

Table 19.5: Elements of the WebService Annotation

Element	Description
Name	Specifies Web service name
targetNamespace	Specifies the namespace for the wsdl:portType element (and associated XML elements)
serviceName	Specifies the service name of the Web service
portName	Specifies the port name of the Web service
wsdlLocation	Specifies the location of the WSDL describing the Web service
endpointInterface	Specifies the complete name of the SEI

The WebMethod Annotation

The WebMethod annotation is used to annotate a method of a Web service. It customizes a method exposed as a Web service operation. The list of elements for the WebMethod annotation is provided in Table 19.6:

Table 19.6: Elements of the WebMethod Annotation

Element	Description
operationName	Specifies the name of wsdl:operation that matches the method annotated by using the WebMethod annotation
action	Specifies the action for the corresponding operation
exclude	Marks a method not to be exposed as a Web service operation

The WebParam Annotation

The WebParam annotation customizes the mapping for an individual parameter of an SEI method to a single WSDL message part or element. The list of elements for the WebParam annotation is specified in Table 19.7:

Table 19.7: Elements of the WebParam Annotation

Element	Description
name	Specifies the parameter name as listed in the WSDL document. In case of RPC binding, it refers to the name of the wsdl:part element that represents the parameter. In case of document binding, it refers to the name of XML element that represents the parameter.
partName	Specifies the name of the wsdl:part element representing the parameter.
targetNamespace	Specifies the namespace for the parameter.
mode	Specifies the direction of the flow control of the parameter (IN, OUT, or INOUT).
header	Specifies whether the parameter is to be carried as part of the header or not. If true, the parameter is retrieved from a message header rather than the message body.

The WebResult Annotation

The WebResult annotation is used to customize the mapping of the return value of an SEI method to a WSDL part or XML element. Table 19.8 lists the elements of the `WebResult` annotation:

Table 19.8: Elements of the WebResult Annotation

Element	Description
name	Specifies the return value name as listed in the WSDL document. In case of RPC binding, it refers to the name of the wsdl:part element that represents the return value. In case of document binding, it refers to the local name of the XML element that represents the return value.
partName	Specifies that name of the wsdl:part element that represents the return value.
targetNamespace	Specifies the XML namespace for the return value.
header	Specifies whether return value is to be carried as part of the header or not. Its value is set to true, if result is to be pulled from header.

The RequestWrapper Annotation

The RequestWrapper annotation is used to annotate methods in an SEI with the request wrapper bean used at runtime.

Table 19.9 lists the elements of the `RequestWrapper` annotation:

Table 19.9: Elements of the RequestWrapper Annotation

Element	Description
localName	Specifies the local name of XML element that represents the request wrapper
className	Specifies the fully qualified name of the Java class implementing the request wrapper
targetNamespace	Specifies the namespace for the XML request wrapper element

The ResponseWrapper Annotation

The ResponseWrapper annotation is used to annotate methods in an SEI with the response wrapper bean used at runtime.

Table 19.10 lists the elements of the ResponseWrapper annotation:

Table 19.10: Elements of the ResponseWrapper Annotation

Element	Description
localName	Specifies the local name of XML element that represents the response wrapper
className	Specifies the fully qualified name of the Java class implementing the response wrapper
targetNamespace	Specifies the namespace for the XML response wrapper element

Invoking a Web Service using a Proxy

You can use the methods of the dynamic proxy class to invoke a Web service by retrieving a proxy instance of the Web service. You can obtain a proxy instance by any of the following three ways:

- Using the @WebServiceRef annotation
- Using a generated service class
- Using a dynamically configured service

The following code snippet shows how to use the `@WebServiceRef` annotation to invoke a Web service:

```
@WebServiceRef(RequestOrderService.class)
public static RequestOrderPort reqport;
```

You can also use the generated service class to invoke a Web service. In the following code snippet, we use the `RequestOrderService` generated service class to invoke the `RequestOrder` Web service:

```
RequestOrderService reqorderservice = new RequestOrderService();
RequestOrderPort reqport = reqorderservice.getRequestOrderPort();
```

The third method to invoke a Web service is by using a dynamically configured service class. You can use the `javax.xml.ws.Service` class to dynamically create an instance of an SEI proxy at runtime, as shown in the following code snippet:

```
URL wsdlURL = new URL("http://"+hostName+":"+portVal+"/chap19-endpoint-endpoint-
   1.0/requestOrder?wsdl");
QName servQName =
new QName("http://www.example.com/req", "RequestOrderService");
QName portQName =
new QName("http://www.example.com/req", "RequestOrderPort");
Service serv = Service.create(wsdlURL, servQName);
RequestOrderPort port =
(RequestOrderPort) serv.getPort(portQName, RequestOrderPort.class);
```

Using the JAXB 2.2 Specification

The Java/XML binding is defined by using JAXB 2.2 annotations in Java classes. Each Java class maps to unique XML schema components depending on the annotations. You can use the JAXB 2.2 specification to bind XML instances with Java classes by:

- Creating Java classes and using the JAXB 2.2 schema generator to generate XML schema from these Java classes
- Using the XML schema to generate Java classes by using the JAXB 2.2 schema compiler

Binding between XML Schema and Java Classes

The JAXB Java/XML binding defines a standard map from Java classes to an XML schema. The JAX-WS API uses this map to produce WSDL from a Java class deployed as a Web service. The JAXB implementation uses a schema complier to generate Java class elements from XML schema components. Each XML schema component consists of complex type elements. These elements are known as Java value classes. Each value class has get/set methods to access the content of the corresponding XML schema component. This implies one-to-one mapping between the elements and attributes of a complex type and the properties of a Java value class.

The JAXB binding language can change external characteristics, such as the names of the properties of Java value classes. For example, you can map the XML element, which occurs many times in an XML document, to a collection, as shown in the following code snippet:

```
<xs:element name="abc" type="Bar" maxOccurs="unbounded"/>
```

Let's consider another example of mapping a complex XML schema component to a single Java property, as shown in the following code snippet:

```
<xs:element name="phone">
  <xs:complexType>
       <xs:attribute name="acode" type="xs:string"/>
       <xs:attribute name="phno" type="xs:string"/>
  </xs:complexType>
</xs:element>
```

To define the binding between the `<xs:element name= "phone">` complex element and the related Java property, you need to write the custom mapping class, which extends the `javax.xml.bind.annotation.adapters.XmlAdapter` class. The built-in XML schema types, such as `xs:string`, are mapped to basic Java primitive types, such as `java.lang.String`.

The schema compiler is used in conjunction with JAXB value classes to produce factory classes and create valid XML instances from a schema. If you use the Java implementation of the DOM API to create valid schema instances, an additional JAXP validator is required to fix the validation errors. If you use the JAXB API, schema compiler tools, such as `XmlBeans`, are required to validate XML instances.

The JAXB implementation uses a schema generator to generate schemas from existing classes by using a standard map. The schema generator searches for Java bean properties in a Java class, and maps them to attributes and elements of XML instances. If the Java class is not a Java bean, the schema generator is unable to generate appropriate XML schemas from the Java class.

Let's now learn how to customize the Java/XML binding.

Customizing JAXB Binding

You can customize JAXB binding in the following two ways:

- Schema to Java
- Java to Schema

Let us discuss each in detail.

Schema to Java

XML-specific constraints cannot customize JAXB classes to create Java-specific program elements, such as a package. For this, you can use custom JAXB binding declarations in an XML schema to customize machine-generated JAXB classes. You can customize XML schemas by:

- Using annotations inside a source XML schema
- Passing an external binding file containing all the binding customizations to a compiler

Java to Schema

In this binding, you need to customize Java program elements by using JAXB annotations so that they can be mapped to specific XML schema. The `javax.xml.bind.annotations` package includes various JAXB annotations to perform Java to schema mapping. Let's discuss each annotation one by one.

@XmlSchema Annotation

The @XmlSchema annotation is used for mapping a package to an XML target namespace. The following code snippet shows the default setting of the `@XmlSchema` annotation:

```
@XmlSchema (
  xmlns = {},
  namespace = "",elementFormDefault= XmlNsForm.UNSET;
  attributeFormDefault = XmlNsForm.UNSET,
)
```

@XmlAccessorType Annotation

The @XmlAccessorType annotation handles default serialization of fields and properties in a Java class. The following code snippet shows the default setting of the `@XmlAccessorType` annotation:

```
@XmlAccessorType (
  value = AccessType.PUBLIC_MEMBER)
```

@XmlAccessorOrder Annotation

The @XmlAccessorOrder annotation handles the default ordering of properties and fields of a Java class that are mapped to XML elements. The following code snippet shows the default setting for the `@XmlAccessorOrder` annotation:

```
@XmlAccessorOrder (
  value = AccessorOrder.UNDEFINED
)
```

@XmlSchemaType Annotation

The @XmlSchemaType annotation maps a Java type to an XML schema built-in type. The following code snippet shows the default setting of the `@XmlSchemaType` annotation:

```
@XmlSchemaType (
  namespace = "http://www.w3.org/2001/XMLSchema",
  type = DEFAULT.class
)
```

@XmlSchemaTypes Annotation

The @XmlSchemaTypes annotation contains multiple `@XmlSchemaType` annotations to be applied on a Java program element. It is used to define the value for the XMLSchemaType element for different types in a package and it has no default settings.

@XmlType Annotation

The @XmlType annotation maps a Java class or Enum type to an XML schema type. You can use the `@XmlType` annotation with an Enum type and a top level class. The following code snippet shows the default setting of the @XmlType annotation:

```
@XmlType (
  name = "##default",
  propOrder = {""},
  namespace = "##default",
  factoryClass = DEFAULT.class,
  factoryMethod = ""
)
```

@XmlRootElement Annotation

The @XmlRootElement annotation is used to map a top level Java class or an Enum type to an XML element. The following code snippet shows the default setting of the `@XmlRootElement` annotation:

```
@XmlRootElement (
  name = "##default",
  namespace = "##default"
)
```

@XmlEnum Annotation

The @XmlEnum annotation maps a Java Enum type to an XML simple type. The following code snippet shows the default setting of the `@XmlEnum` annotation:

```
@XmlEnum ( value = String.class )
```

@XmlEnumValue Annotation

The @XmlEnumValue annotation maps an Enum constant in the Enum type to its XML representation. You can use the `@XmlEnumValue` annotation with an Enum constant. It has no default settings.

@XmlElement Annotation

The @XmlElement annotation maps a JavaBean property to a local element of complex type of an XML schema. The name of the local element is same as that of the JavaBean property. You can use the `@XmlElement` annotation with a JavaBean property, non-static field, and a `@XmlElements` annotation. The following code snippet shows the default setting of the @XmlElement annotation:

```
@XmlElement (
   name = "##default",
   nillable = false,
   namespace = "##default",
   type = DEFAULT.class,
   defaultValue = "\u0000"
)
```

@XmlElements Annotation

The @XmlElements annotation contains numerous `@XmlElement` annotations to be applied on Java program elements. You can use the `@XmlElements` annotation with a JavaBean property and a non-static field. This annotation has no default settings and is usually meant for a JavaBean collection property, such as a list.

@XmlElementRef Annotation

The @XmlElementRef annotation maps a JavaBean property to a local element of complex type of an XML schema at runtime. The name of the local element is the same as that of the JavaBean property. You can also use the `@XmlElementRef` annotation with a non-static field, and a `@XmlElementRefs` annotation. The following code snippet shows the default setting of the @XmlElementRef annotation:

```
@XmlElementRef (
   name = "##default",
   namespace = "##default",
   type = DEFAULT.class
)
```

@XmlElementRefs Annotation

The @XmlElementRefs annotation contains numerous `@XmlElementRef` annotations to be applied on Java program elements. It has no default settings.

@XmlElementWrapper Annotation

The @XmlElementWrapper annotation generates a wrapper XML element around collections. You can use the `@XmlElementWrapper` annotation with a JavaBean collection property and a non-static field. The following code snippet shows the default setting of the @XmlElementWrapper annotation:

```
@XmlElementWrapper (
   name = "##default",
   namespace = "##default",
   nillable = false
)
```

@XmlAnyElement Annotation

The @XmlAnyElement annotation maps a JavaBean property to both an XML infoset representation and a JAXB element, or to one of them. The following code snippet shows the default setting of the `@XmlAnyElement` annotation:

```
@XmlAnyElement (
   lax = false,
   value = W3CDomHandler.class
)
```

@XmlAttribute Annotation

The @XmlAttribute annotation maps a JavaBean property to an XML attribute. You can use the `@XmlAttribute` annotation with a JavaBean property and a field. The following code snippet shows the default setting of the annotation:

```
@XmlAttribute (
  name =##default,
  required = false,
  namespace = "##default"
)
```

@XmlAnyAttribute Annotation

The @XmlAnyAttribute annotation maps a `java.util.Map` JavaBean property or field to a map of wildcard attributes. It has no default settings.

@XmlTransient Annotation

The @XmlTransient annotation avoids a JavaBean property being mapped to an XML representation. This annotation is usually used to resolve name collisions that may occur between a JavaBean property name and a field name. It has no default settings.

@XmlValue Annotation

The @XmlValue annotation maps a Java class to an XML schema complex type with a `simpleContent` or an XML schema simple type. You can use the `@XmlValue` annotation with a JavaBean property and a non-static field. It has no default settings.

@XmlID Annotation

The @XmlID annotation maps a JavaBean property to an XML ID. This annotation is used to maintain the referential integrity of an object during serialization and deserialization. It has no default settings.

@XmlIDREF Annotation

The @XmlIDREF annotation maps a JavaBean property to an XML IDREF. This annotation is also used to maintain the referential integrity of an object during serialization and deserialization. It has no default settings.

@XmlList Annotation

The @XmlList annotation maps a JavaBean property or field to a list simple type. This annotation allows the representation of multiple values as whitespace-separated tokens in a single XML element. It has no default settings.

@XmlMixed Annotation

The @XmlMixed annotation marks a multi-valued JavaBean property so that it can support mixed content. You can use the `@XmlMixed` annotation with the `@XmlElementRef`, `@XmlElementRefs`, and `@XmlAnyElement` annotations. It has no default settings.

@XmlMimeType Annotation

The @XmlMimeType annotation associates a MIME type with a JavaBean property to handle the XML corresponding representation. It has no default settings.

@XmlAttachmentRef Annotation

The @XmlAttachmentRef annotation enforces an XML representation of a JavaBean property or field of the `DataHandler` type to be a URI reference to the MIME content, which is stored separately in the form of an attachment. It has no default settings.

@XmlJavaTypeAdapter Annotation

The @XmlJavaTypeAdapter annotation uses an adapter that implements the `@XMLAdapter` annotation to perform custom marshalling. You can use the `@XmlJavaTypeAdapter` annotation with a JavaBean property, field, parameter, package, and the `@XmlJavaTypeAdapters` annotation. It has no default settings.

@XmlJavaTypeAdapters Annotation

The @XmlJavaTypeAdapters annotation contains numerous @XmlJavaTypeAdapter annotations to be applied on a Java program element. It has no default settings.

Exploring an Example of JAXB 2.2 Java/XML Binding

Let's take an example to demonstrate standard binding of a company record.

Listing 19.12 shows the schema as coded in the `company.xsd` file (save the `company.xsd` file in the `/customjaxb` folder):

Listing 19.12: Showing the Code for the company.xsd File

```
<schema targetNamespace="http://www.example.com/kogent"
  elementFormDefault="qualified" xmlns="http://www.w3.org/2001/XMLSchema"
  xmlns:kogent="http://www.example.com/kogent">
<element name="Company">
<complexType>
<sequence>
<element name="CompanyAddress">
<complexType>
<sequence>
<element name="name" type="string"/>
<element name="street" type="string"/>
<element name="city" type="string"/>
<element name="state" type="string"/>
<element name="zipcode" type="string"/>
<element name="phnum" type="string"/>
</sequence>
 </complexType>
</element>
<element name="departments">
<complexType>
<sequence>
<element name="department" type="kogent:DeptType" maxOccurs="unbounded"/>
</sequence>
</complexType>
</element>
</sequence>
</complexType>
</element>
<complexType name="DeptType">
<sequence>
<element name="deptmanager" type="string"/>
<element name="cost" type="double"/>
</sequence>
<attribute name="deptname" use="required" type="string"/>
</complexType>
</schema>
```

Listing 19.12 shows a schema that has one global element with the name `Company`. The type of this element has not been specified. This element contains a sequence of two elements, `CompanyAddress` and `departments`. The `CompanyAddress` element represents the company address of the anonymous address type. The `departments` element represents the list of departments of the company. The sub-elements of the departments element include the `DeptType` type, which is defined later in Listing 19.12. The `DeptType` type contains two elements, `deptmanager` and `cost`, and an attribute, `deptname`. The `cost` element is of `xs:double`type. The `deptname` attribute is of `xs:string` type.

The Java mapping of the `company.xsd` document is shown in Figure 19.10:

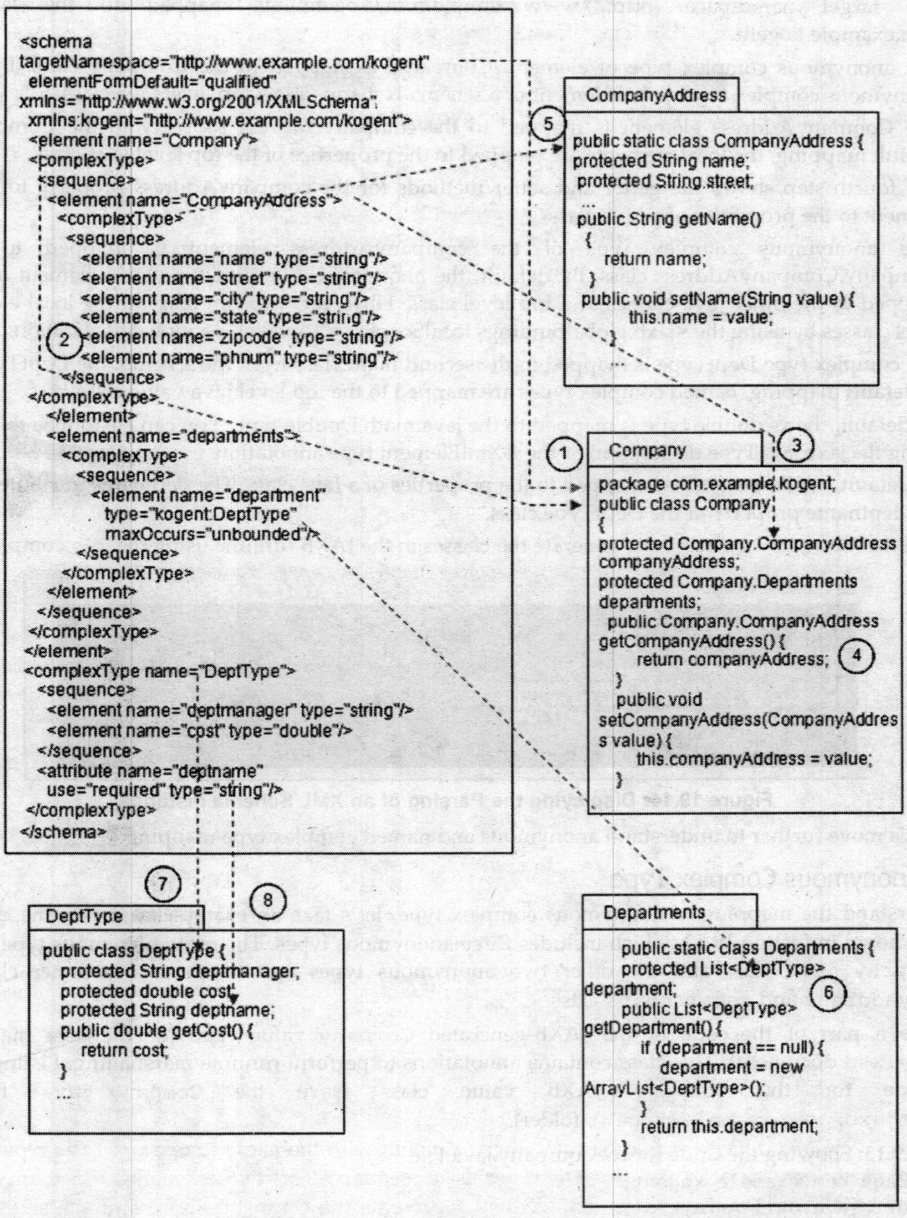

Figure 19.10: Showing the Standard JAXB Binding of the Company Schema

As shown in Figure 19.10, the JAXB standard binding generates two main Java classes from the `company.xsd` schema: `Company` and `DeptType`. The `Company` class has two nested classes, `Company.CompanyAddress` and `Company.Departments`.

The following is the sequence of steps required for binding in JAXB:

1. The target namespace, http://www.example.com/kogent, is mapped to the Java package, com.example.kogent.
2. The anonymous complex type of element, Company, is mapped to the Company class. By default, the anonymous complex type global element of a schema is mapped to a top level Java class.
3. The CompanyAddress element is mapped to the companyAddress property in the Company class. In default mapping, the local elements are mapped to the properties of the top level Java class.
4. The fourth step shows the getter and setter methods for the companyAddress property to map an XML element to the properties of a Java class.
5. The anonymous complex type of the companyAddress element is mapped to the nested Company.CompanyAddress class. By default, the anonymous complex type local element of a schema is mapped to the inner Java classes of a top level class. However, you can map all the local elements to top level classes by using the <jaxb:globalBindings localScoping="toplevel"/> global declaration.
6. The complex type DeptType is mapped to the second main class from the schema, the DeptType Java class. In default mapping, named complex types are mapped to the top level Java value class.
7. By default, the xs:double type is mapped to the java.math.Double type. You can customize this mapping by using the jaxb:javaType declaration or the @XmlElement.type annotation.
8. By default, attributes are also mapped to the properties of a Java class. The deptname attribute is mapped to the deptname property of the DeptType class.

Figure 19.11 shows how to manually generate the classes in the JAXB runtime using the `xjc` compiler:

Figure 19.11: Displaying the Parsing of an XML Schema Instance

Now, let's move further to understand anonymous and named complex type mapping.

Mapping Anonymous Complex Type

To understand the mapping of anonymous complex type, let's take an example based on the `company.xsd` schema shown in Listing 19.12, which includes three anonymous types. The root anonymous type is mapped to the `Company.java` class and the other two anonymous types are mapped to its inner classes named, `CompanyAddress` and `departments` class.

Let's see a part of the code of the JAXB-generated `Company` value class (or the Java mapping of the `company.xsd` document). This class contains annotations to perform runtime marshalling. Listing 19.13 shows the code for the `Company` JAXB value class (save the `Company.java` file in the `/customjaxb/com/example/kogent` folder):

Listing 19.13: Showing the Code for theCompany.java File

```
package com.example.kogent;
import java.util.ArrayList;
import java.util.List;
import javax.xml.bind.annotation.XmlAccessType;
import javax.xml.bind.annotation.XmlAccessorType;
import javax.xml.bind.annotation.XmlElement;
import javax.xml.bind.annotation.XmlRootElement;
import javax.xml.bind.annotation.XmlType;
@XmlAccessorType(XmlAccessType.FIELD)
@XmlType(name = "", propOrder = {
```

```
    "companyAddress",
    "departments"
})
@XmlRootElement(name = "Company")
public class Company {
 @XmlElement(name = "CompanyAddress", required = true)
 protected Company.CompanyAddress companyAddress;
 @XmlElement(required = true)
 protected Company.Departments departments;
 public Company.CompanyAddress getCompanyAddress() {
        return companyAddress;
 }
 public void setCompanyAddress(Company.CompanyAddress value) {
        this.companyAddress = value;
 }
 public Company.Departments getDepartments() {
        return departments;
 }
 public void setDepartments(Company.Departments value) {
        this.departments = value;
 }
 @XmlAccessorType(XmlAccessType.FIELD)
 @XmlType(name = "", propOrder = {
        "name",
        "street",
        "city",
        "state",
        "zipcode",
        "phnum"
 })
 public static class CompanyAddress {
        @XmlElement(required = true)
        protected String name;
        @XmlElement(required = true)
        protected String street;
        @XmlElement(required = true)
        protected String city;
        @XmlElement(required = true)
        protected String state;
        @XmlElement(required = true)
        protected String zipcode;
        @XmlElement(required = true)
        protected String phnum;
        public String getName() {
               return name;
        }
        public void setName(String value) {
               this.name = value;
        }
        public String getStreet() {
               return street;
        }
        public void setStreet(String value) {
               this.street = value;
        }
        public String getCity() {
               return city;
        }
        public void setCity(String value) {
```

```
                this.city = value;
            }
            public String getState() {
                return state;
            }
            public void setState(String value) {
                this.state = value;
            }
            public String getZipcode() {
                return zipcode;
            }
            public void setZipcode(String value) {
                this.zipcode = value;
            }
            public String getPhnum() {
                return phnum;
            }
            public void setPhnum(String value) {
                this.phnum = value;
            }
        }
        @XmlAccessorType(XmlAccessType.FIELD)
        @XmlType(name = "", propOrder = {
            "department"
        })
        public static class Departments {
            @XmlElement(required = true)
            protected List<DeptType> department;
            public List<DeptType> getDepartment() {
                if (department == null) {
                    department = new ArrayList<DeptType>();
                }
                return this.department;
            }
        }
    }
```

Listing 19.13 does not specify any value for the `name` attribute. Therefore, all complex types defined by using `@XmlType` annotations are anonymous types.

As you can see that, the `propOrder` attribute of the `@XmlType` annotation specifies the order of fields of complex types. This order must match with the order specified in the `<sequence>` definition of complex types in the `company.xsd` schema. The `@XmlType` annotation is necessary, as the Java class does not sequence the properties by itself. Listing 19.13 uses `@XmlRootElement` annotation that specifies the `Company` value for its `name` attribute and this value is the same as the name of the global element of the `company.xsd` schema. Listing 19.13 uses the `@XmlAccessorType` annotation to map fields and properties of Java class with the corresponding elements in a schema. Listing 19.13 uses `@XmlElement` annotations to map a specific property to a schema element definition. For example, properties such as `companyAddress` and `departments` are mapped to the `CompanyAddress` and `departments` elements of the `company.xsd` schema.

Listing 19.13 contains two inner classes, `CompanyAddress` and `Departments`, as there are only two anonymous complex types in the `company.xsd` schema. By default, schema element definitions with anonymous complex types are mapped to inner classes. The `CompanyAddress` class is simple to understand.

By default, the element which occurs several times is mapped to java.util.List<T> schema element, where T is the Java class of the element's type.

Mapping Named Complex Type

The `company.xsd` schema also contains a named complex type, `DeptType`. As we know that, the named complex types are not mapped to inner classes. Therefore, the `DeptType` named complex type is mapped to the external `kogent.DeptType` (Listing 19.14) Java class. Listing 19.14 shows the source code of the `DeptType.java` file (save the `DeptType.java` file in the `/customjaxb /com/example/kogent` folder):

Listing 19.14: Showing the Code for the DeptType.java File

```
package com.example.kogent;
import javax.xml.bind.annotation.XmlAccessType;
import javax.xml.bind.annotation.XmlAccessorType;
import javax.xml.bind.annotation.XmlAttribute;
import javax.xml.bind.annotation.XmlElement;
import javax.xml.bind.annotation.XmlType;
@XmlAccessorType(XmlAccessType.FIELD)
@XmlType(name = "DeptType", propOrder = {
   "deptmanager",
   "cost"
})
public class DeptType {
   @XmlElement(required = true)
   protected String deptmanager;
   protected double cost;
   @XmlAttribute(required = true)
   protected String deptname;
   public String getDeptmanager() {
          return deptmanager;
   }
   public void setDeptmanager(String value) {
          this.deptmanager = value;
   }
   public double getCost() {
          return cost;
   }
   public void setCost(double value) {
          this.cost = value;
   }
   public String getDeptname() {
          return deptname;
   }
   public void setDeptname(String value) {
          this.deptname = value;
   }
}
```

In Listing 19.14, the `cost` element of the `DeptType` complex type is mapped to the `cost` property with the `Double` type of the `DeptType` Java class. The `deptname` attribute of the schema is mapped to the `deptname` property of the `DeptType` Java class by using the `@XmlAttribute` annotation.

Implementing Type Mappings with JAXB 2.2

The section focuses on using custom Java classes with JAXB standard mapping to implement your own type mapping. The standard Java/XML type mapping of JAXB maps Java classes to XML schema elements using the following notation:

```
<{http://www.example.com/kogent}company,com.example.kogent.Company>
```

The preceding notation is of the <XMLType, JavaType> form; where XML type is the fully qualified name of the XML schema element and JavaType is the fully qualified name of the Java class.

You can map XML schema elements to custom Java classes. Let's try to implement the mapping between the `<kogent:Company>` and `<CustomCompany>` classes. In this mapping, the `CustomCompany` class is not a JAXB generated class; rather, we create this class. This mapping happens in two steps. In the first step, JAXB creates the JAXB-generated com.example.kogent.Company class and then maps this class to the CustomCompany Java class.

Listing 19.15 shows the code of the CustomCompany.java file (save the CustomCompany.java file in the /customjaxb folder):

Listing 19.15: Showing the Code for the CustomCompany.java File

```
package classes;
import java.util.ArrayList;
import java.util.List;
public class CustomCompany {
  private CustomAddress companyAddress;
  private List<CustomDept> deptList;
  public CustomCompany(String name, String street, String city, String state,
  String zip, String phone) {
        this(new CustomAddress(name, street, city, state, zip, phone));
  }
  public CustomCompany(CustomAddress addr) {
        this.companyAddress = addr;
        deptList = new ArrayList<CustomDept>();
  }
  public CustomAddress getCompanyAddress() {
        return companyAddress;
  }
  public List<CustomDept> getDeptList() {
        return deptList;
  }
}
```

Listing 19.15 uses the companyAddress property of the CustomAddress Java type instead of the JAXB-generated com.example.kogent.CompanyAddress type. It uses the deptList property of the List<CustomDept> type rather than the JAXB-generated com.example.kogent.departments type. The deptList property stores the information about the departments of the company.

Mapping an instance of the classes.CustomCompany class to an instance of the kogent:Company element requires that the companyAddress property is mapped to the classes.CustomAddress type and the List<classes.CustomDept> type is mapped to the kogent:departments element. Listing 19.16 shows the source code of the CustomAddress.java file (save the CustomAddress.java file in the /customjaxb folder):

Listing 19.16: Showing the Code for the CustomAddress.java File

```
package classes;
public class CustomAddress {
  protected String name;
  protected String street;
  protected String city;
  protected String state;
  protected String zipcode;
  protected String phnum;
  public CustomAddress(String name, String street, String city, String state,
  String zipcode, String phnum) {
        this.name = name;
        this.street = street;
        this.city = city;
        this.state = state;
        this.zipcode = zipcode;
        this.phnum = phnum;
  }
}
```

In Listing 19.16, CustomAddress class is not a Java bean and acts only as a container for its sub properties, such as name, street, and city.

Let's take a look at the CustomDept.java class. Listing 19.17 shows the source code of the CustomDept.java file (save the CustomDept.java file in the /customjaxb folder in the CD):

Listing 19.17: Showing the Code for the CustomDept.java File

```
package classes;
public class CustomDept {
    private String deptmanager;
    private float cost;
    private String deptname;
    public CustomDept(String deptmanager, float cost, String deptname)
    throws Exception {
          if (deptname == null) {
                 throw new Exception("department must has some name");
          }
          this.deptname = deptname;
          this.cost = cost;
          this.deptmanager = deptmanager;
    }
    public float getCost() {
          return cost;
    }
    public void setCost(float cost) {
          this.cost = cost;
    }
    public String getDeptname() {
          return deptname;
    }
    public void setDeptname(String deptname) {
          this.deptname = deptname;
    }
    public String getDeptmanager() {
          return deptmanager;
    }
    public void setDeptmanager(String deptmanager) {
          this.deptmanager = deptmanager;
    }
}
```

In Listing 19.17, the `CustomProduct.cost` property is of float type while the `ProdType.cost` property is of double type.

Let's see the Java class that maps the JAXB-generated `com.example.kogent.Company` class to the `CustomCompany` Java class. Listing 19.18 shows the source code of the `CustomCompanySerializer.java` file (save the `CustomCompanySerializer.java` file in the `/customjaxb` folder):

Listing 19.18: Showing the Code for the CustomCompanySerializer.java File

```
package classes;
import java.io.ByteArrayOutputStream;
import java.io.StringReader;
import java.math.BigInteger;
import java.io.File;
import java.util.List;
import javax.xml.XMLConstants;
import javax.xml.bind.JAXBContext;
import javax.xml.bind.Marshaller;
import javax.xml.transform.OutputKeys;
import javax.xml.transform.Source;
import javax.xml.transform.Transformer;
import javax.xml.transform.TransformerFactory;
import javax.xml.transform.stream.StreamResult;
import javax.xml.transform.stream.StreamSource;
import javax.xml.validation.Schema;
import javax.xml.validation.SchemaFactory;
import com.example.kogent.DeptType;
import com.example.kogent.Company;
public class CustomCompanySerializer{
```

```
    public static void main(String[] args) throws Exception {
            CustomCompanySerializer serializer =
            new CustomCompanySerializer();
            CustomCompany customCompany = new CustomCompany(
            "ABC",
            "Street No . 1",
            "Shakarpur", "ND", "110092",
            "9971782025");
            customCompany.getDeptList().add(new  CustomDept( "Mr  .Singh",  (float)  2.99,
            "Content Solutions"));
            customCompany.getDeptList().add(new CustomDept("Mrs. Gupta", (float) 3.99, "HR
            Solutions"));
            customCompany.getDeptList().add(new  CustomDept("Mr.  Kumar",  (float)  5.34,
            "Production"));
            Transformer xform = TransformerFactory.newInstance().newTransformer();
            xform.setOutputProperty(OutputKeys.INDENT, "yes");
            xform.transform(
            serializer.getXML(customCompany),
            new StreamResult(System.out));
    }
    public Source getXML(CustomCompany company) {
    // create the JAXB SimpleOrder
    Company jaxbCompany = new Company();
    // map the addresses
    CustomAddress customAddress = company.getCompanyAddress();
    Company.CompanyAddress companyAddress = new Company.CompanyAddress();
    companyAddress.setName(customAddress.name);
    companyAddress.setCity(customAddress.city);
    companyAddress.setPhnum(customAddress.phnum);
    companyAddress.setState(customAddress.state);
    companyAddress.setStreet(customAddress.street);
    companyAddress.setZipcode(customAddress.zipcode);
    jaxbCompany.setCompanyAddress(companyAddress);
    // map the items
   jaxbCompany.setDepartments(new Company.Departments()); // needed to avoid NPE
    List<DeptType> jaxbDeptList = jaxbCompany.getDepartments().getDepartment();
    for (CustomDept customDept : company.getDeptList()) {
    DeptType jaxbDept = new DeptType();
    //     jaxbItem.setPrice((double) myItem.getPrice());
    jaxbDept.setCost(Double.parseDouble(Float.toString(customDept.getCost())));
    jaxbDept.setDeptname(customDept.getDeptname());
    jaxbDept.setDeptmanager(customDept.getDeptmanager());
    jaxbDeptList.add(jaxbDept);
    }
    try {
    JAXBContext jaxbContext = JAXBContext.newInstance("com.example.kogent");
    Marshaller jaxbMarshaller = jaxbContext.createMarshaller();
    SchemaFactory sf =
    SchemaFactory.newInstance(XMLConstants.W3C_XML_SCHEMA_NS_URI);
    Schema schema = sf.newSchema(
    new File("company.xsd"));
    jaxbMarshaller.setSchema(schema);
    ByteArrayOutputStream baos = new ByteArrayOutputStream();
    jaxbMarshaller.marshal(jaxbCompany, baos);
    return new StreamSource(new StringReader(baos.toString()));
    } catch (Exception e) {
           throw new RuntimeException(e);
    }
    }
  }
```

Listing 19.18 imports an instance of the JAXB-generated `com.example.kogent.Company` class, populates it with the data of the `CustomCompany` Java class, and marshals the JAXB instance to get an XML representation. Listing 19.18 first populates an instance of the `CustomCompany` Java class with the respective values. It invokes the `marshal()` method of the `Transformer` object with two arguments. The first argument makes a call to the `getXML()` method by passing the `CustomCompany` object. The second argument is of the `StreamResult` type.

The `getXML()` method creates an instance of the JAXB generated `Company` Java class. This method populates the `Company.CompanyAddress (companyAddress)` instance from the instance of `CustomAddress` obtained using the `company.getCompanyAddress()` method.

Then, the code provided in Listing 19.18 initializes a list of `departments` of the company to the empty list. This initialization is necessary as JAXB does not map the `kogent:departments` element to the `List<T>` type. The `for loop` populates the members of `List<DeptType>` from the members of the `company.getDeptList()` method that is of the `List<CustomAddress>` type. The setter methods of the JAXB generated `DeptType` class are invoked to set its members.

Listing 19.18 also creates an instance of the `JAXBContext class` by passing the `com.example.kogent` package to the location where JAXB generated classes are found. It then creates an instance of the `Marshaller` class and activates validation on this instance by calling its `setSchema()` method. Finally, `jaxbCompany` is marshaled into `the ByteArrayOutputStream type` and returned as a StreamSource.

Figure 19.12 shows the output of the `customjaxb` application:

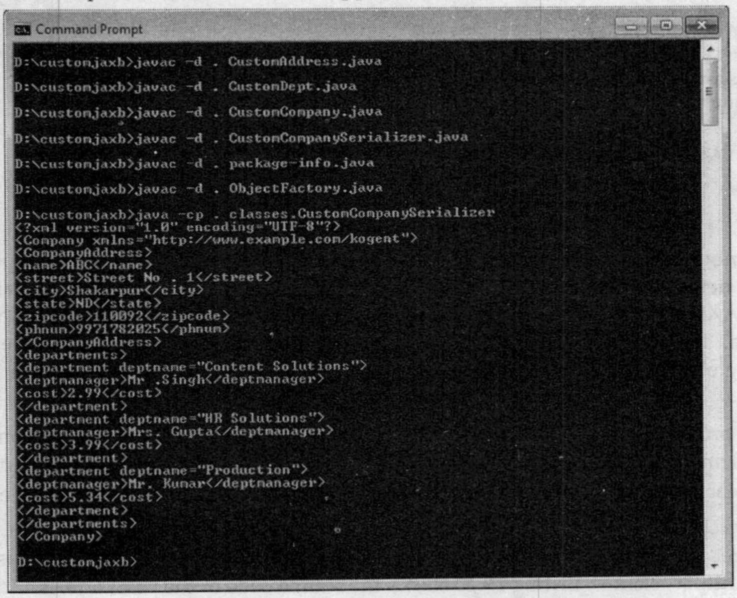

Figure 19.12: Showing the Output of the customjaxb Application

Implementing Type Mappings with JAXB 2.2 Annotations

The section focuses on the use of annotations in existing POJOs to eliminate the need of mapping code. The annotated POJOs are directly mapped to target schema.

Listing 19.19 shows the annotated version of the `CustomCompany.java` file (save the `CustomCompany.java` file in the `/customjaxb_with_annotations` folder):

Listing 19.19: Showing the Code for the CustomCompany.java File

```
package classes;
import javax.xml.bind.annotation.XmlRootElement;
import javax.xml.bind.annotation.XmlElementWrapper;
import javax.xml.bind.annotation.XmlElement;
import java.util.ArrayList;
import java.util.List;
@XmlRootElement(name="Company")
```

```
public class CustomCompany {
   private CustomAddress companyAddress;
   private List<CustomDept> deptList;
   public CustomCompany() {}
   public CustomCompany(String name, String street, String city, String state,
   String zip, String phone) {
         this(new CustomAddress(name, street, city, state, zip, phone));
   }
   public CustomCompany(CustomAddress addr) {
         this.companyAddress = addr;
         deptList = new ArrayList<CustomDept>();
   }
   public CustomAddress getCompanyAddress() {
         return companyAddress;
   }
   public void setCompanyAddress(CustomAddress addr) {
         this.companyAddress = addr;
   }
   @XmlElementWrapper(name="departments")
   @XmlElement(name="department")
   public List<CustomDept> getDeptList() {
         return deptList;
   }
   public void setDeptList(List<CustomDept> deptList) {
         this.deptList = deptList;
   }
}
```

Listing 19.19 does not use annotations on all its components as some components are mapped by the JAXB Java to XML binding default standard. Listing 19.19 uses some additional annotations as compared to the `Company.java` JAXB generated class. It uses the `@XmlRootElement` annotation to map this class to the global element of schema. The `@XmlRootElement` annotation has an optional `namespace` element to specify the namespace of the global element of schema. It uses `@XmlElement` annotation to map an XML element to the `deptList` type.

Note that another property `companyAddress` does not use the `@XmlElement` annotation, as this property is mapped to XML element named `companyAddress` by default. Listing 19.19 uses the `@XmlElementWrapper` annotation so that each element in `deptList` list must wrapped under the `departments` element.

As earlier said, `@XmlRootElement` annotation does not specify namespace of target XML schema. By default, JAXB obtains target namespace from package name. For example, if package name is classes, the target namespace will be http://classes. Listing 19.20 shows the source code of the `package-info.java` file (save the `package-info.java` file in the `/customjaxb_with_annotations` folder):

Listing 19.20: Showing the Code for the package-info.java File

```
@XmlSchema(
   namespace = "http://www.example.com/kogent",
   elementFormDefault=XmlNsForm.QUALIFIED)
   package classes;
import javax.xml.bind.annotation.XmlNsForm;
import javax.xml.bind.annotation.XmlSchema;
```

Listing 19.20 uses the `@XmlSchema` annotation to map a package to an XML schema. The `namespace` element maps package `classes` to the `http://www.example.com/kogent` namespace.

Listing 19.21 shows the annotated version of the `CustomAddress` Java class (save the `CustomAddress.java` file in the `/customjaxb_with_annotations` folder):

Listing 19.21: Showing the Code for the CustomAddress.java File

```
package classes;
import javax.xml.bind.annotation.XmlAccessType;
import javax.xml.bind.annotation.XmlAccessorType;
```

```
import javax.xml.bind.annotation.XmlElement;
import javax.xml.bind.annotation.XmlType;
@XmlAccessorType(XmlAccessType.FIELD)
@XmlType(name = "",
propOrder = {"name", "street", "city", "state", "zipcode", "phnum"})
public class CustomAddress {
  @XmlElement(namespace = "http://www.example.com/kogent")
  protected String name;
  @XmlElement(namespace = "http://www.example.com/kogent")
  protected String street;
  @XmlElement(namespace = "http://www.example.com/kogent")
  protected String city;
  @XmlElement(namespace = "http://www.example.com/kogent")
  protected String state;
  @XmlElement(namespace = "http://www.example.com/kogent")
  protected String zipcode;
  @XmlElement(namespace = "http://www.example.com/kogent")
  protected String phnum;
  // need a no-arg constructor
  public CustomAddress() {};
  //! </example>
  public CustomAddress(String name, String street, String city, String state,
  String zipcode, String phnum) {
        this.name = name;
        this.street = street;
        this.city = city;
        this.state = state;
        this.zipcode = zipcode;
        this.phnum = phnum;
  }
}
```

Listing 19.21 uses the `@XmlAccessorType` annotation, as this class does not have setter or getter methods for its properties. Listing 19.21 requires the use of `@XmlType` annotation as the `CustomAddress` class is mapped to an anonymous complex type. The value of the `name` element indicates that this class is mapped to an anonymous complex type. The `propOrder` element specifies the order of properties in the target XML schema `<sequence>` element. Listing 19.21 also uses the `@XmlElement` annotation for each property to specify namespace of each target XML element. The `@XmlElement` annotation is required as the `CustomAddress` class is mapped to anonymous complex type and there is no namespace to be inherited from parent class.

Listing 19.22 shows the annotated version of the `CustomDept` class (save the `CustomDept.java` file in the `/customjaxb_with_annotations` folder):

Listing 19.22: Showing the Code for the CustomDept.java File

```
package classes;
import javax.xml.bind.annotation.XmlAttribute;
import javax.xml.bind.annotation.XmlType;
@XmlType(name = "DeptType", propOrder = {"deptmanager", "cost"})
public class CustomDept {
  private String deptname;
  private float cost;
  private String deptmanager;
  public CustomDept() {};
  public CustomDept(String deptmanager, float cost, String deptname)
  throws Exception {
        if (deptname == null) {
              throw new Exception("department must has some name");
        }
        this.deptname = deptname;
        this.cost = cost;
        this.deptmanager = deptmanager;
  }
  public float getCost() {
        return cost;
```

```
    }
    public void setCost(float cost) {
          this.cost = cost;
    }
    @XmlAttribute
    public String getDeptname() {
          return deptname;
    }
    public void setDeptname(String deptname) {
          this.deptname = deptname;
    }
    public String getDeptmanager() {
          return deptmanager;
    }
    public void setDeptmanager(String deptmanager) {
          this.deptmanager = deptmanager;
    }
}
```

Listing 19.22 uses the `@XmlType` annotation to map the `kogent:DeptType` complex type to the `CustomDept` Java class. As it does not use any `@XmlAccessorType` annotation, mapping of properties to schema elements is performed by default. However, the `deptname` property needs to be mapped to the attribute of an XML element. Therefore, it associates the `@XmlAttribute` annotation with the `deptname` property.

Listing 19.23 marshals and unmarshals the instance of the `CustomCompanySerializer.java` class (save the `CustomCompanySerializer.java` file in the `/customjaxb_with_annotations` folder):

Listing 19.23: Showing the Code for the CustomCompanySerializer.java File

```
package classes;
import java.io.ByteArrayOutputStream;
import java.io.StringReader;
import java.io.File;
import javax.xml.XMLConstants;
import javax.xml.bind.JAXBContext;
import javax.xml.bind.Marshaller;
import javax.xml.bind.Unmarshaller;
import javax.xml.validation.Schema;
import javax.xml.validation.SchemaFactory;
import classes.CustomCompany;
public class CustomCompanySerializer {
   public static void main(String[] args) throws Exception {
   CustomCompanySerializer serializer =
   new CustomCompanySerializer();
   CustomCompany customCompany = new CustomCompany(
   "ABC",
   "Street No . 1",
   "Shakarpur", "ND", "110092",
   "9971782025");
   customCompany.getDeptList().add(new CustomDept( "Mr .Singh", (float) 2.99, "Content
   Solutions"));
   customCompany.getDeptList().add(new CustomDept("Mrs. Gupta", (float) 3.99,
   "HR Solutions"));
   customCompany.getDeptList().add(new CustomDept("Mr. Kumar", (float) 5.34,
   "Production"));
   try {
   JAXBContext jaxbContext = JAXBContext.newInstance(CustomCompany.class);
   Marshaller jaxbMarshaller = jaxbContext.createMarshaller();
   jaxbMarshaller.setProperty(Marshaller.JAXB_FORMATTED_OUTPUT,
   Boolean.TRUE);
   ByteArrayOutputStream ba = new ByteArrayOutputStream();
   jaxbMarshaller.marshal(customCompany, ba);
   System.out.println(ba.toString());
   Unmarshaller u = jaxbContext.createUnmarshaller();
   CustomCompany cc =
   (CustomCompany) u.unmarshal(new StringReader(ba.toString()));
```

```
            System.out.println("phone = " + cc.getCompanyAddress().phnum);
        } catch (Exception e) {
            e.printStackTrace();
        }
    }
}
```

Listing 19.23 creates an instance of the `CustomCompany` Java class and initializes it. It then creates a `JAXBcontext` instance by passing `CustomCompany.class` parameter value to the `newInstance()` method. Listing 19.23 both marshals the `CustomCompany` instance into XML representation and output XML representation on to the `System.out` stream. It also unmarshals XML representation into the `CustomCompany` Java class, and then prints the phone number of the company specified in the Java instance.

Figure 19.13 shows the output of the `customjaxb_with_annotations` application:

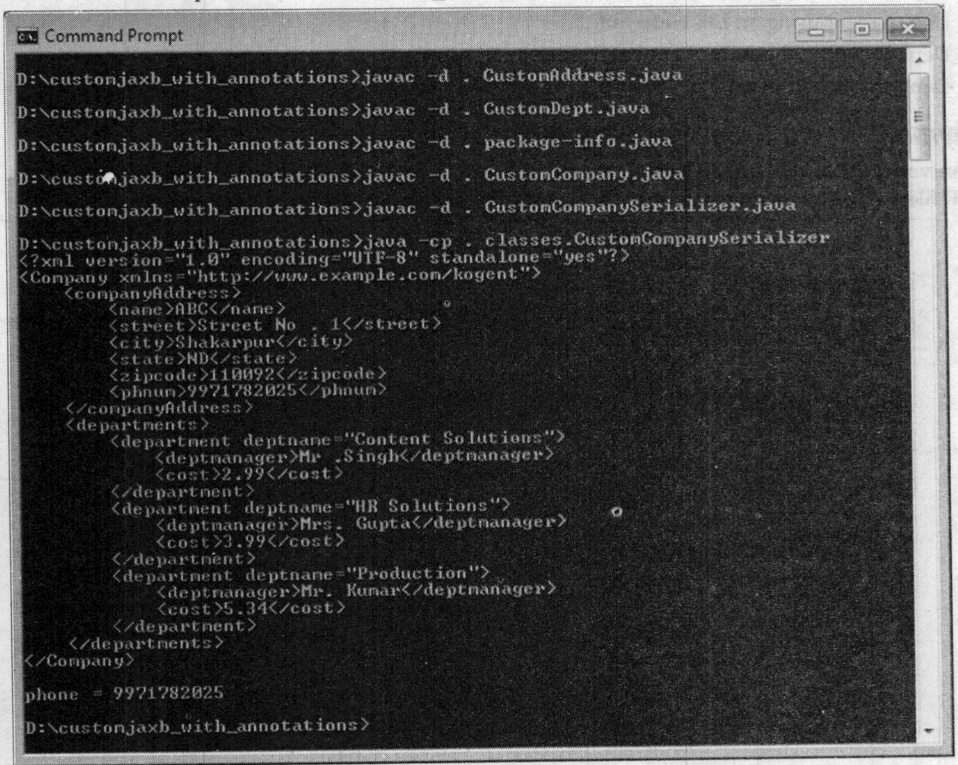

Figure 19.13: Showing the Output of the customjaxb_with_annotations Application

Using the WSEE and WS-Metadata Specifications

The WSEE and WS-Metadata specifications provide information about packaging and deployment of Web services. WS-Metadata provides a set of standard annotations to configure the JWS container and deploy a Java class as a Web service. The container generates artifacts, such as WSDL representation of a Web service, from these annotations. In earlier version of Java, such as J2EE, developers needed to provide a configuration file, such as the `webservices.xml Deployment Descriptor`, to configure a Java class as a Web service. As WS-Metadata provides annotations to deploy Java class declaratively as a Web service, use of `Deployment Descriptor` becomes optional in Java EE5 and Java EE 6.

The WSEE specification makes Web service applications portable across various Java EE application server implementations. It defines how the Java class and generated artifacts are packaged for deployment of a Web service application. It also defines the type of the Java class to be deployed as a Web service. The Java class can be either a servlet or an EJB endpoint. This specification also provides information about packaging these endpoints and Deployment Descriptors, if required.

In brief, WS-Metadata makes development and deployment of Web services easier by providing annotations. WSEE specification describes the correct use and packaging of WS-Metadata annotated classes and other generated artifacts.

The different deployment methods provided by these specifications are given as follows:

- Deployment using a servlet endpoint
- Deployment using an EJB endpoint
- Deployment without Deployment Descriptors
- Deployment with Deployment Descriptors

Deployment using a Servlet Endpoint

When you implement SIBs as servlet endpoints, you need to package them and other generated artifacts in a WAR file. Figure 19.14 shows the structure of this WAR file:

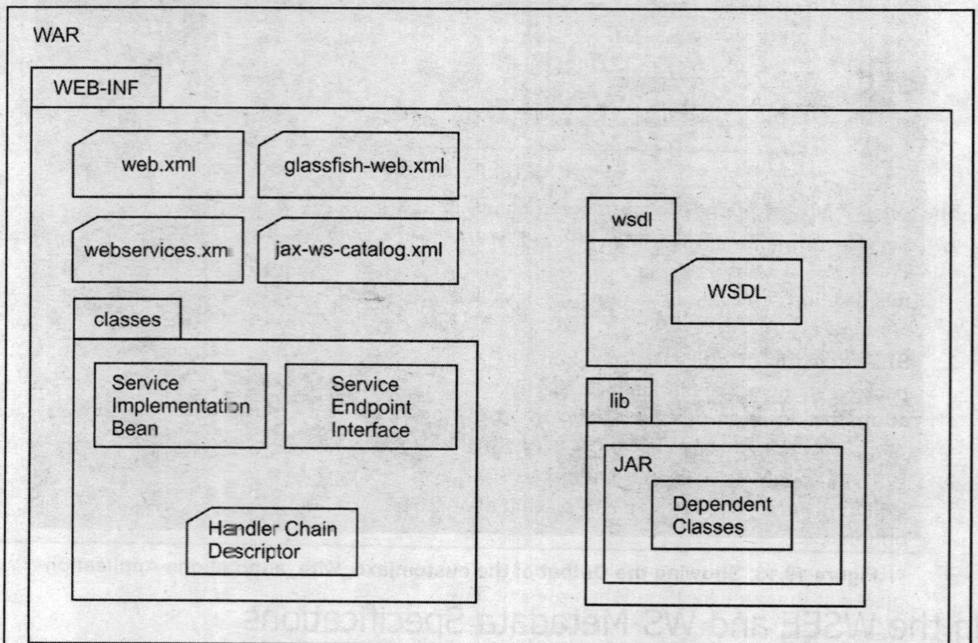

Figure 19.14: Packaging a Servlet Endpoint

Deployment using an EJB Endpoint

When you implement an SIB as an EJB endpoint (stateless session bean), you need to package it and other generated artifacts in an EJB-JAR file. Figure 19.15 shows the structure of this EJB-JAR file:

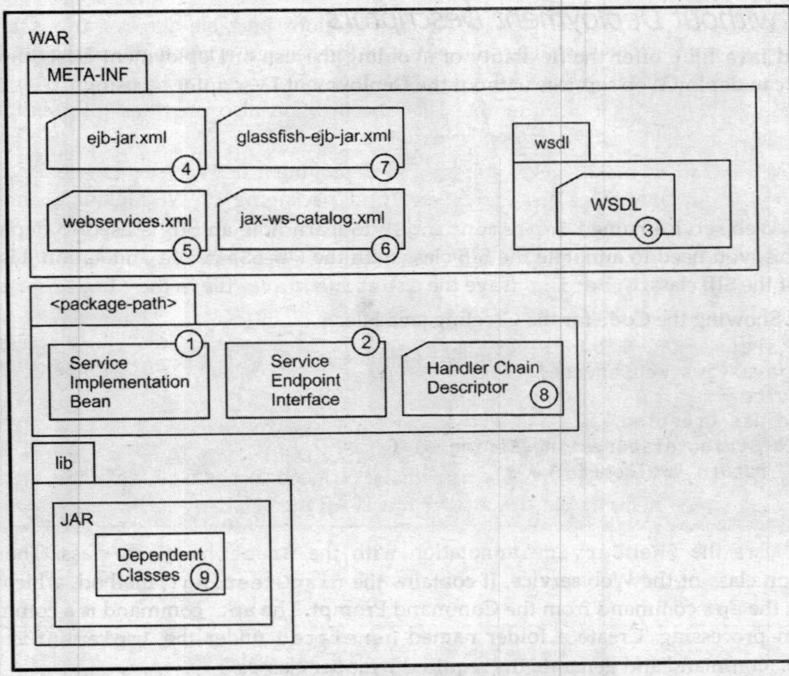

Figure 19.15: Packaging an EJB Endpoint

The following list explains each numbered component in Figure 19.15:

1. **Service implementation bean**—Remains inside the `<package-path>/` directory by convention, where `<package-path>` is a package name of the SIB bean class. You are not restricted to place the bean class in this location rather you can store the bean class in another jar file. The SIB class must use the `@Stateless` annotation and the `@WebService` or `@WebServiceProvider` annotation.
2. **SEI**—Remains inside the `<package-path>/` directory by convention, where `<package-path>` is a package name of the SEI bean class. This location is not restricted for the SEI interface rather you can place it at another location in your application directory. When SEI is present inside a port component, then the `@WebService.endpointInterface` attribute of SIB must have value equal to the name of the SEI.
3. **WSDL**—Remains inside the `META-INF/wsdl` directory by convention. This location is not restricted for the WSDL document rather you can place it at another location in your application directory. This document is optional.
4. **ejb-jar.xml**—Remains always under the `META-INF` directory. The `ejb-jar.xml` file must always be placed at the same location when present. However, this file is optional.
5. **webservices.xml**—Remains always under the `META-INF` directory. The `webservices.xml` file must always be placed at the same location when present. However, this document is optional.
6. **jax-ws-catalog.xml**—Remains always under the `META-INF` directory. The `jax-ws-catalog.xml` descriptor file is optional and is used when you use `OASIS XML` catalogs.
7. **sun-ejb-jar.xml**—Remains under the `META-INF` directory. The `sun-ejb-jar.xml` file is optional. It is Glassfish's EJB Deployment Descriptor.
8. **Handler chain descriptor**—Remains under the `<package-path>/` directory. This location is not restricted for the `Handler Chain Descriptor` document rather you can place it at external location. This file has no standard name and is optional.
9. **Dependent classes**—Represents the classes on which SIB or SEI depends upon. These are bundled in a JAR file at the root of the EAR file.

Deployment without Deployment Descriptors

Java EE 5 and Java EE 6 offer the flexibility of avoiding the use of Deployment Descriptors to configure Web services. You can deploy Web services without the Deployment Descriptor by using:

- An SIB
- A SEI

Using an SIB

Let's create a Web service named `ImplementingSB` to learn how an SIB is used to deploy a Web service. In order to do this, you need to annotate the SIB class with the `@WebService` annotation. Listing 19.24 shows the source code of the SIB class, `Greeting` (save the `Greeting.java` file in the `/ImplementingSB/src` folder):

Listing 19.24: Showing the Code for the Greeting.java File

```
package src;
import javax.jws.WebService;
@WebService
public class Greeting {
   public String dispGreeting(String s) {
         return "Welcome: " + s;
   }
}
```

Listing 19.24 uses the `@WebService` annotation with the `Greeting.java` class. Therefore, it acts as an implementation class of the Web service. It contains the `dispGreeting()` method, which displays a welcome message. Run the `apt` command from the Command Prompt. The `apt` command is a command line utility used for annotation processing. Create a folder named `generated` under the `ImplementingSB` folder. Run the following `apt` command and generate the required wrapper classes:

```
D:\ImplementingSB>apt -d generated src/Greeting.java
```

The `apt` command generates JAX-WS source files in the `src` folder under the `jaxws` directory and JAX-WS class files in the `generated/src/jaxws` directory. This tool also compiles the `Greeting.java` SIB class and places it under `generated/src` folder, as shown in Figure 19.16:

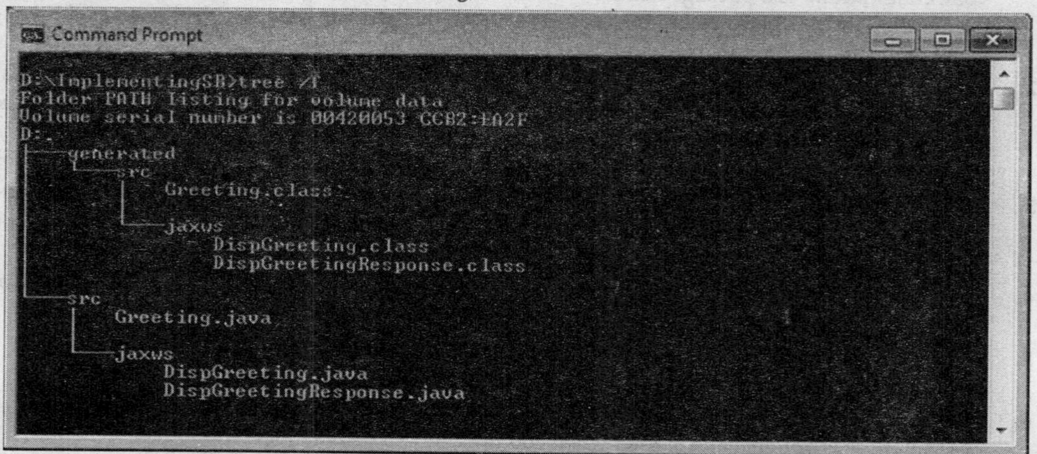

Figure 19.16: Showing the Generated JAX-WS Source and Class Files

You now need to package the `ImplementingSB` application. Create another folder c:\\`ImplementingSB`. Directory structure of c:\\`ImplementingSB` folder is as shown in Figure 19.17:

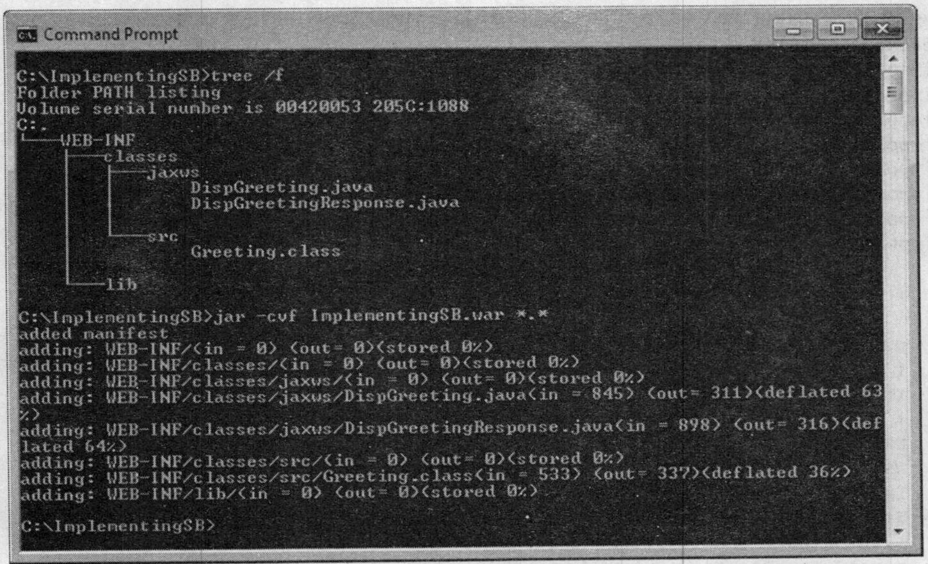

Figure 19.17: Showing the Directory Structure of ImplementingSB Web Service Application

Figure 19.17 also shows the command to package the ImplementingSB application, which generates the ImplementingSB.war file. Next, copy the `ImplementingSB.war` file in the `autodeploy` directory of the domain of the Glassfish V3 application server. GlassFish server automatically generates internal descriptors and WSDL. WSDL document is published on the URL `http://localhost:8080/ImplementingSB/GreetingService?wsdl`. Run `wsimport` command on the deployed WSDL URL to generate some classes. Execute the following command to run `wsimport`:

```
    D:\ImplementingSB>wsimport -p client -keep
http://localhost:8080/ImplementingSB/GreetingService?wsdl
```

Verify all the generated classes and Java source files in the `d:\ImplementingSB\client` folder, as shown in Figure19.18:

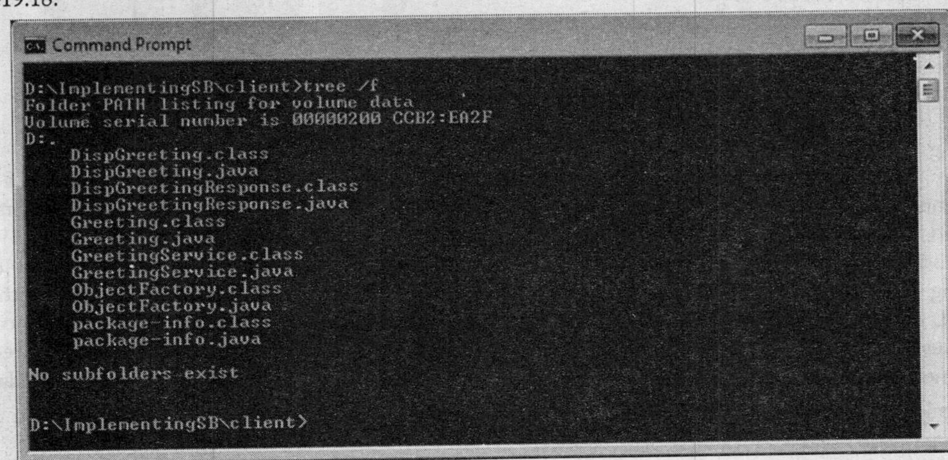

Figure 19.18: Showing all the Java and Class Files Generated by the wsimport Tool

Let's create a Web service client, `ClientApp.java`, to invoke the Web service endpoint and its `dispGreeting()` method. Listing 19.25 shows the source code of the `ClientApp.java` file (save the `ClientApp.java` file in the `/ImplementingSB` folder):

Listing 19.25: Showing the Code for the ClientApp.java File

```
package client;
import java.io.ByteArrayOutputStream;
import java.io.InputStream;
import java.lang.Exception;
import java.net.URL;
import javax.xml.namespace.QName;
import javax.xml.ws.Service;
import javax.xml.transform.*;
import javax.xml.transform.stream.*;

public class ClientApp
{
  public static void main(String args[])
  {
  try
  {
  URL wsdlURL = null;
  wsdlURL= new URL("http://localhost:8080/ImplementingSB/GreetingService?wsdl");
  InputStream is = (InputStream) wsdlURL.getContent();
  Transformer t = TransformerFactory.newInstance().newTransformer();
  t.setOutputProperty(OutputKeys.INDENT,"yes");
  t.setOutputProperty(OutputKeys.METHOD,"xml");
  t.setOutputProperty(OutputKeys.MEDIA_TYPE,"text/xml");
  t.setOutputProperty(OutputKeys.OMIT_XML_DECLARATION,"yes");
  t.transform(new StreamSource(is), new StreamResult(System.out));
  System.out.println();
  QName srvcQName = new QName("http://src/", "GreetingService");
  QName portQName =    new QName("http://src/", "GreetingPort");
  Service srvc = Service.create(wsdlURL, srvcQName);
  Greeting port = (Greeting) srvc.getPort(portQName, Greeting.class);
  String result = port.dispGreeting("Java Programmer");
  System.out.println(result);
  }
  catch (Exception e)
  {
       System.out.println(e);
  }
  }
}
```

Listing 19.25 creates a URL instance with the generated URL of the `http://localhost:8080/ImplementingSB/GreetingService?wsdl` WSDL. Listing 19.25 retrieves the contents of the WSDL document and places it into the InputStream, `is`. The listing then sets some properties related to how the WSDL document should be displayed at the command prompt. Listing 19.25 uses the `transform()` method of the `Transformer` object to transform the source stream into the output stream. Listing 19.25 then uses the `Service.create()` method to configure a `Service` instance with the URL of WSDL document and the `srvcQName` instance of the QName class. After creating the service instance, it invokes the `Service.getPort()` method, which accepts the Qname of `wsdl:portType` and Greeting.class as parameters. The `getPort()` method returns the implementation instance of the `GreetingPort` class.

Compile the `ClientApp.java` file using the `javac` command and place the generated `ClientApp.class` file in the `D:\ImplementingSB\client` folder.

Figure 19.19 shows the output of the compilation and execution of the `ClientApp.java` file:

Figure 19.19: Showing the Output of the ImplementingSB Web Service Application

Figure 19.19 displays the generated WSDL document, `GreetingService.wsdl`, and the output string `Welcome: Java Programmer`, of the `dispGreeting()` method.

Using a SEI

You can also use an SEI to deploy a Web service. Let's create a Web service named `sibwithsei` to learn how a SEI can be used to deploy a Web service. Let's first create an SIB class. Listing 19.26 shows the source code of the SIB class named `Greeting` (save the `Greeting.java` file in the `/sibwithsei/src` folder):

Listing 19.26: Showing the Code for the Greeting.java File

```
package src;
import javax.jws.WebService;
@WebService(endpointInterface="src.GreetingInf")
public class Greeting {
  public String dispGreeting(String s) {
        return "Welcome: " + s;
  }
  public String dispGoodbye(String s) {
        return "Goodbye: " + s;
  }
}
```

Listing 19.26 uses the `@webService` annotation with the `Greeting` class. This SIB class references an endpoint interface using the `src.GreetingInf` location. Listing 19.27 shows the code for the `GreetingInf.java` file (save the `GreetingInf.java` file in the `/sibwithsei/src` folder):

Listing 19.27: Showing the Code for the GreetingInf.java File

```
package src;
import javax.jws.WebService;
@WebService
public interface GreetingInf {
  public String dispGreeting(String s);
}
```

Compile the `GreetingInf.java` class using the following command:

```
D:\sibwithsei>javac -d . src/GreetingInf.java
```

Compile the `Greeting.java` class using the following command:

```
D:\sibwithsei>javac -d . src/Greeting.java
```

Run the `apt` command and generate the required wrapper classes. Make sure that the `d:\sibwithsei\generated` folder is created before the execution of the following command:

```
D:\sibwithsei>apt -d generated src/Greeting.java
```

To deploy the `sibwithsei` application, create another folder `c:\sibwithsei`. The directory structure of the `c:\sibwithsei` folder is shown in Figure 19.20:

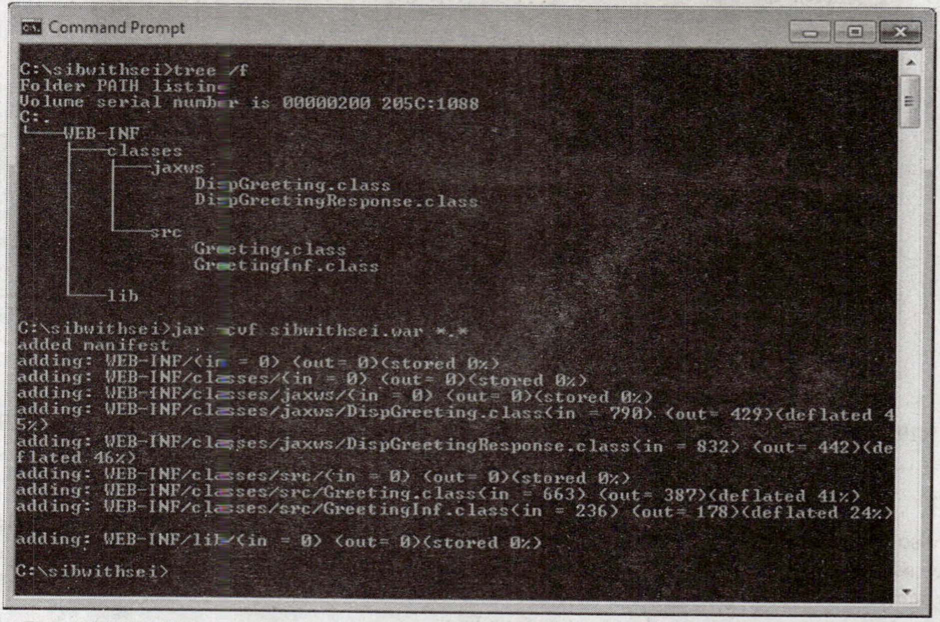

Figure 19.20: Showing the Directory Structure of the sibwithsei Web Service Application

Create the required WAR file using the command shown in Figure 19.20. Copy the `sibwithsei.war` file in the `autodeploy` directory of the domain of the Glassfish V3 application directory. GlassFish server automatically generates WSDL and internal descriptors. WSDL document is published on the URL `http://localhost:8080/sibwithsei/GreetingService?wsdl`.

Run the `wsimport` command on the deployed WSDL URL by executing the following command:

```
D:\sibwithsei>wsimport -p client -keep http://localhost:8080/sibwithsei/Greeting
Service?wsdl
```

Verify all the generated classes and Java source files in the `d:\sibwithsei\client` folder.

Next, let's create a Web service client to invoke the Web service endpoint and its `dispGreeting()` method. Listing 19.28 shows the source code of the Web service client file named as `ClientApp.java` (save the `ClientApp.java` file in the `/sibwithsei` folder):

Listing 19.28: Showing the Code for the ClientApp.java File

```
package client;
import java.io.ByteArrayOutputStream;
import java.io.InputStream;
import java.lang.Exception;
import java.net.URL;
import javax.xml.namespace.QName;
import javax.xml.ws.Service;
import javax.xml.transform.*;
import javax.xml.transform.stream.*;
public class ClientApp
{
  public static void main(String args[])
  {
  try
  {
  URL wsdlURL = null;
  wsdlURL= new URL("http://localhost:8080/sibwithsei/GreetingService?wsdl");
  InputStream is = (InputStream) wsdlURL.getContent();
  Transformer t = TransformerFactory.newInstance().newTransformer();
  t.setOutputProperty(OutputKeys.INDENT,"yes");
  t.setOutputProperty(OutputKeys.METHOD,"xml");
  t.setOutputProperty(OutputKeys.MEDIA_TYPE,"text/xml");
  t.setOutputProperty(OutputKeys.OMIT_XML_DECLARATION,"yes");
  t.transform(new StreamSource(is), new StreamResult(System.out));
  System.out.println();
  QName srvcQName = new QName("http://src/", "GreetingService");
  QName portQName =    new QName("http://src/", "GreetingPort");
  Service srvc = Service.create(wsdlURL, srvcQName);
  GreetingInf port = (GreetingInf) srvc.getPort(portQName, GreetingInf.class);
  String result = port.dispGreeting("Java Programmer");
  System.out.println(result);
  }
  catch (Exception e)
  {
         System.out.println(e);
  }
  }
}
```

Listing 19.28 is same as Listing 19.25; however, it creates a URL instance with the URL of the generated WSDL document, `http://localhost:8080/sibwithsei/GreetingService?wsdl`. Listing 19.28 uses the `Service.create()` method to configure the `Service` instance with the URL of WSDL document and the QName of the `wsdl:service` element. After creating the service instance, it invokes the `Service.getPort()`

method, which accepts the Qname of `wsdl:portType` and `GreetingInf.class` as parameters. The `getPort()` method returns the implementation instance of the `GreetingPort` class.

Compile the `ClientApp.java` file by using the `javac` command, and place the generated `ClientApp.class` file in the `D:\sibwithsei\client` folder.

Figure 19.21 shows the output of the compilation and execution of the `ClientApp.java` file:

```
C:\Windows\system32\cmd.exe
D:\sibwithsei>javac -d . ClientApp.java

D:\sibwithsei>java -cp . client.ClientApp
<!-- Published by JAX-WS RI at http://jax-ws.dev.java.net. RI's version is JAX-W
S RI 2.2.1-hudson-28-. -->
<!-- Generated by JAX-WS RI at http://jax-ws.dev.java.net. RI's version is JAX-W
S RI 2.2.1-hudson-28-. -->
<definitions xmlns:wsu="http://docs.oasis-open.org/wss/2004/01/oasis-200401-wss-
wssecurity-utility-1.0.xsd" xmlns:wsp="http://www.w3.org/ns/ws-policy" xmlns:wsp
1_2="http://schemas.xmlsoap.org/ws/2004/09/policy" xmlns:wsam="http://www.w3.org
/2007/05/addressing/metadata" xmlns:soap="http://schemas.xmlsoap.org/wsdl/soap/"
 xmlns:tns="http://src/" xmlns:xsd="http://www.w3.org/2001/XMLSchema" xmlns="htt
p://schemas.xmlsoap.org/wsdl/" targetNamespace="http://src/" name="GreetingServi
ce">
<types>
<xsd:schema>
<xsd:import namespace="http://src/" schemaLocation="http://localhost:8080/sibwit
hsei/GreetingService?xsd=1"/>
</xsd:schema>
</types>
<message name="dispGreeting">
<part name="parameters" element="tns:dispGreeting"/>
</message>
<message name="dispGreetingResponse">
<part name="parameters" element="tns:dispGreetingResponse"/>
</message>
<portType name="GreetingInf">
<operation name="dispGreeting">
<input wsam:Action="http://src/GreetingInf/dispGreetingRequest" message="tns:dis
pGreeting"/>
<output wsam:Action="http://src/GreetingInf/dispGreetingResponse" message="tns:d
ispGreetingResponse"/>
</operation>
</portType>
<binding name="GreetingPortBinding" type="tns:GreetingInf">
<soap:binding transport="http://schemas.xmlsoap.org/soap/http" style="document"/
>
<operation name="dispGreeting">
<soap:operation soapAction=""/>
<input>
<soap:body use="literal"/>
</input>
<output>
<soap:body use="literal"/>
</output>
</operation>
</binding>
<service name="GreetingService">
<port name="GreetingPort" binding="tns:GreetingPortBinding">
<soap:address location="http://localhost:8080/sibwithsei/GreetingService"/>
</port>
</service>
</definitions>

Welcome: Java Programmer

D:\sibwithsei>
```

Figure 19.21: Showing the Output of the sibwithsei Web Service Application

Figure 19.21 displays the generated WSDL document, GreetingService.wsdl, and the output string Welcome: Java Programmer of the dispGreeting() method.

Deployment with Deployment Descriptor

The JAX-WS specification makes the use of the `webservices.xml` Deployment Descriptor optional, as annotations specify the information required to deploy a Web service. However, you need to use the `webservices.xml` Deployment Descriptor when you are either overriding or not using annotations in the source code of a Web application.

Let's look at an example to use a Deployment Descriptor to deploy a Web service. Let's create the `WelcomeHandler` class to extract the environment information from the `web.xml` file. The `WelcomeHandler` class accesses env-entrys of the `port` component using either the JNDI lookup or the `@Resource` annotation. Listing 19.29 shows the source code of the `WelcomeHandler.java` file (save the `WelcomeHandler.java` file in the `/descwebservice/src` folder):

Listing 19.29: Showing the Code for the WelcomeHandler.java File

```
package src;
import java.util.Set;
import javax.annotation.Resource;
import javax.xml.namespace.QName;
import javax.xml.ws.WebServiceException;
import javax.xml.ws.handler.MessageContext;
import javax.xml.ws.handler.soap.SOAPHandler;
import javax.xml.ws.handler.soap.SOAPMessageContext;
public class WelcomeHandler implements SOAPHandler<SOAPMessageContext> {
  public static final String APPEND_STRING = "src.WelcomeHandler.appendStrg";
  @Resource(name="appendedString")
  String injectedString = "undefined";
  public boolean handleMessage(SOAPMessageContext context) {
  if ( ((Boolean)context.get(MessageContext.MESSAGE_OUTBOUND_PROPERTY)).
  booleanValue() ) return true;
  try {
        context.put(APPEND_STRING, injectedString);
        context.setScope(APPEND_STRING, MessageContext.Scope.APPLICATION);
        System.out.println("WelcomeHandler has appendedString = " + injectedString);
        return true;
  } catch (Exception e) {
        e.printStackTrace();
        throw new WebServiceException(e);
  }
  }
  public Set<QName> getHeaders() {
        return null;
  }
  public boolean handleFault(SOAPMessageContext context) {
        return true;
  }
  public void close(MessageContext context) {}
}
```

Create the `SecondHandler.java` file to allow the `webservices.xml` Deployment Descriptor to configure the associated SIB class, as shown in Listing 19.30 (save the `SecondHandler.java` file in the `/descwebservice/src` folder):

Listing 19.30: Showing the Code for the SecondHandler.java File

```
package src;
import java.util.Set;
import javax.annotation.Resource;
import javax.xml.namespace.QName;
import javax.xml.ws.WebServiceException;
import javax.xml.ws.handler.MessageContext;
import javax.xml.ws.handler.soap.SOAPHandler;
import javax.xml.ws.handler.soap.SOAPMessageContext;
public class SecondHandler implements SOAPHandler<SOAPMessageContext> {
  public static final String APPEND_STRING = "src.WelcomeHandler.appendStrg";
  @Resource(name="appendedString")
  String injectedString = "undefined";
  public boolean handleMessage(SOAPMessageContext context) {
  if ( ((Boolean)context.get(MessageContext.MESSAGE_OUTBOUND_PROPERTY)).
  booleanValue() ) return true;
  try {
        context.put(APPEND_STRING, "NEW !!! "+injectedString);
        context.setScope(APPEND_STRING, MessageContext.Scope.APPLICATION);
        System.out.println("The second handler has appended this: " + injectedString);
```

```
            return true;
        } catch (Exception e) {
            e.printStackTrace();
            throw new WebServiceException(e);
        }
        }
        public Set<QName> getHeaders() {
            return null;
        }
        public boolean handleFault(SOAPMessageContext context) {
            return true;
        }
        public void close(MessageContext context) {}
    }
```

Create the `Handler` chain configuration file, required to configure handlers, as shown in Listing 19.31 (save the `handler.xml` file in the `/descwebservice` folder):

Listing 19.31: Showing the Code for the handler.xml File

```
<?xml version="1.0" encoding="UTF-8"?>
<handler-chains xmlns:jws="http://java.sun.com/xml/ns/javaee">
  <handler-chain>
      <handler>
          <handler-class>src.WelcomeHandler</handler-class>
      </handler>
  </handler-chain>
</handler-chains>
```

Create the SIB class `Greeting.java` that implements the Web service, as shown in Listing 19.32 (save the `Greeting.java` file in the `/descwebservice/src` folder):

Listing 19.32: Showing the Code for the Greeting.java File

```
package src;
import javax.annotation.Resource;
import javax.jws.HandlerChain;
import javax.jws.WebService;
import javax.xml.ws.WebServiceContext;
@HandlerChain(file="handler.xml")
@WebService
public class Greeting {
  @Resource
  WebServiceContext websrvccntxt;
  public String dispGreeting(String s) {
  String appStr =
  (String) websrvccntxt.getMessageContext().get(WelcomeHandler.APPEND_STRING);
  return "Welcome: " + s + "[appended by handler: " + appStr + "]";
  }
}
```

To deploy the Servlet based Web service, create the `web.xml` Deployment Descriptor, as shown in Listing 19.33 (save the `web.xml` file in the `/descwebservice/WEB-INF` folder):

Listing 19.33: Showing the Code for the web.xml File

```
<?xml version="1.0" encoding="UTF-8"?>
<web-app xmlns="http://java.sun.com/xml/ns/javaee"
  xmlns:j2ee="http://java.sun.com/xml/ns/javaee"
  xmlns:xsi="http://www.w3.org/2001/XMLSchema-instance" version="2.5"
  xsi:schemaLocation="http://java.sun.com/xml/ns/javaee
  http://java.sun.com/xml/ns/javaee/web-app_2_5.xsd">
  <servlet>
        <servlet-name>Greeting</servlet-name>
        <servlet-class>src.Greeting</servlet-class>
        <load-on-startup>0</load-on-startup>
```

```
        </servlet>
        <servlet-mapping>
              <servlet-name>Greeting</servlet-name>
              <url-pattern>/my-pattern</url-pattern>
        </servlet-mapping>
        <env-entry>
              <env-entry-name>appendedString</env-entry-name>
              <env-entry-type>java.lang.String</env-entry-type>
              <env-entry-value>ABCDEFGHI...</env-entry-value>
        </env-entry>
    </web-app>
```

The Web service requires GlassFish-specific `sun-web.xml` descriptor to specify the context root of the application. Listing 19.34 shows the code for the `sun-web.xml` descriptor file (save the `sun-web.xml` file in the `/descwebservice/WEB-INF` folder):

Listing 19.34: Showing the Code for the sun-web.xml File

```
    <sun-web-app>
    <context-root>descwebservice</context-root>
    </sun-web-app>
```

Listing 19.35 shows the generated `webservices.xml` descriptor (save the `webservices.xml` file in the `/descwebservice/WEB-INF` folder):

Listing 19.35: Showing the Code for the webservices.xml File

```
    <?xml version="1.0" encoding="UTF-8"?>
    <webservices xmlns="http://java.sun.com/xml/ns/javaee"
      xmlns:xsi="http://www.w3.org/2001/XMLSchema-instance" version="1.2"
      xsi:schemaLocation="http://java.sun.com/xml/ns/javaee
      http://www.ibm.com/webservices/xsd/javaee_web_services_1_2.xsd">
      <webservice-description>
      <webservice-description-name>GreetingService</webservice-description-name>
      <port-component>
      <port-component-name>Greeting</port-component-name>
      <wsdl-service xmlns:ns1="http://src/">ns1:GreetingService</wsdl-service>
      <wsdl-port xmlns:ns1="http://src/">ns1:GreetingPort</wsdl-port>
      <service-impl-bean>
            <servlet-link>Greeting</servlet-link>
      </service-impl-bean>
      <handler-chains>
            <handler-chain>
                  <handler>
                        <handler-name>handler</handler-name>
                        <handler-class>src.SecondHandler</handler-class>
                  </handler>
            </handler-chain>
      </handler-chains>
      </port-component>
      </webservice-description>
    </webservices>
```

Compile the `WelcomeHandler` and `SecondHandler` Java classes from the Command Prompt using the following commands:

```
    D:\descwebservice>javac -d . src/WelcomeHandler.java
    D:\descwebservice>javac -d . src/SecondHandler.java
```

Compile the `Greeting.java` class using the following command:

```
D:\descwebservice>javac -d . src/Greeting.java
```

Run the `apt` command and generate the required wrapper classes. Make sure that the `d:\descwebservice\generated` folder is created before the execution of the following command:

```
D:\descwebservice>apt -d generated src/Greeting.java
```

To deploy the Web service, create another folder `c:\descwebservice`. The directory structure of the `c:\descwebservice`folder is shown in Figure 19.22:

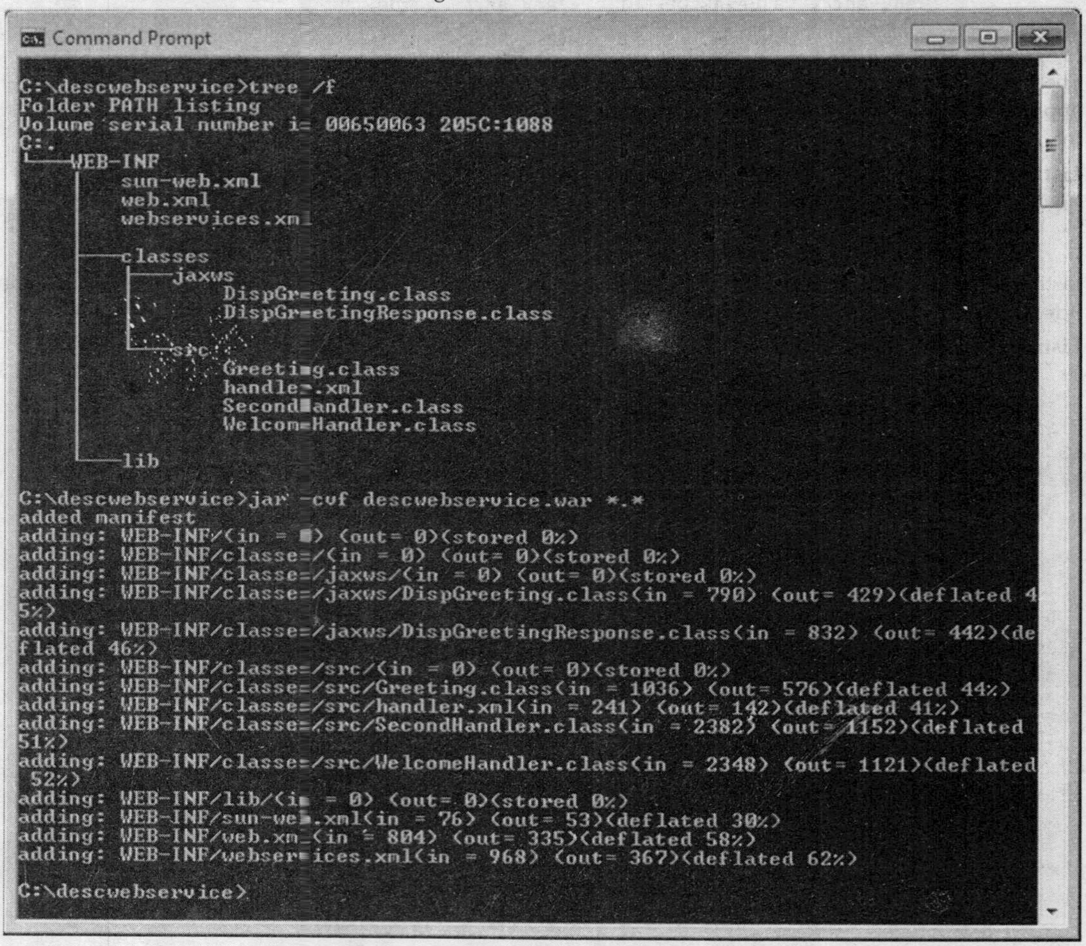

Figure 19.22: Showing the Directory Structure and Packaging of the descwebservice Application

Create the required WAR file by using the command shown in Figure 19.22. Copy the `descwebservice.war` file in the `autodeploy` directory of the domain of the Glassfish V3 application server. GlassFish server automatically generates WSDL and internal descriptors. WSDL document is published on the URL `http://localhost:8080/descwebservice/my-pattern?wsdl`.

Run `wsimport` command on the deployed WSDL URL, as shown in the following command:

```
D:\descwebservice>wsimport -p client -keep http://localhost:8080/descwebservice/
my-pattern?wsdl
```

Verify all the generated classes and the Java source files in the `d:\descwebservice\client` folder.

Let's create a Web service client to invoke the Web service endpoint and its `dispGreeting()` method. Listing 19.36 shows the source code of the Web service client:

Listing 19.36: Showing the Code for the ClientApp.java File

```
package client;

import java.io.ByteArrayOutputStream;
import java.io.InputStream;
import java.lang.Exception;
import java.net.URL;
import javax.xml.namespace.QName;
import javax.xml.ws.Service;
import javax.xml.transform.*;
import javax.xml.transform.stream.*;

public class ClientApp {
   public static void main(String args[]){
   try{
   URL wsdlURL = null;
   wsdlURL= new URL("http://localhost:8080/descwebservice/my-pattern?wsdl");
   InputStream is = (InputStream) wsdlURL.getContent();
   Transformer t = TransformerFactory.newInstance().newTransformer();
   t.setOutputProperty(OutputKeys.INDENT,"yes");
   t.setOutputProperty(OutputKeys.METHOD,"xml");
   t.setOutputProperty(OutputKeys.MEDIA_TYPE,"text/xml");
   t.setOutputProperty(OutputKeys.OMIT_XML_DECLARATION,"yes");
   t.transform(new StreamSource(is), new StreamResult(System.out));
   System.out.println();
   QName srvcQName = new QName("http://src/", "GreetingService");
   QName portQName =    new QName("http://src/", "GreetingPort");
   Service srvc = Service.create(wsdlURL, srvcQName);
   Greeting port = (Greeting) srvc.getPort(portQName, Greeting.class);
   String result = port.dispGreeting("Java Programmer");
   System.out.println(result);
   }
   catch (Exception e){
          System.out.println(e);
   }
   }
 }
```

Listing 19.36 is same as Listing 19.25 but it creates a URL instance with the generated URL of the WSDL, `http://localhost:8080/descwebservice/my-pattern?wsdl`.

Compile the `ClientApp.java` file by using the `javac` command and place the generated `ClientApp.class` file in the `D:\descwebservice\client` folder.

Figure 19.23 shows the output of the compilation and execution of the `ClientApp.java` file:

Figure 19.23: Showing the Output of the descwebservice Application

Implementing the SAAJ Specification

In this section, we create a simple SAAJ-based application. This application sends a simple SOAP Message using the `SendingServlet` servlet class to the specified destination, which is another servlet class, `ReceivingServlet`. The `ReceivingServlet` servlet class gives a reply in the form of another SOAP message.

Listing 19.37 shows the code for the `SendingServlet` servlet class (save the `SendingServlet.java` file in the `/saaj` folder):

Listing 19.37: Showing the Code for the SendingServlet.java File

```
import java.io.*;
import java.net.URL;
import java.util.Properties;
import javax.activation.DataHandler;
import javax.servlet.*;
import javax.servlet.http.*;
import javax.xml.soap.*;
```

```
public class SendingServlet extends HttpServlet {
 String dest = null;
 private SOAPConnection con;
 public void init(ServletConfig servletConfig) throws ServletException {
          super.init( servletConfig );
          try {
          SOAPConnectionFactory scf = SOAPConnectionFactory.newInstance();
          con = scf.createConnection();
          } catch(Exception e) {
                  System.out.println(  "Unable to open a SOAPConnection"+ e);
          }
 }
 public void doGet(HttpServletRequest req, HttpServletResponse resp)
 throws ServletException {
          String SerResp ="<html><H4>";
          try {
                  MessageFactory msgfact = MessageFactory.newInstance();
                  SOAPMessage msg = msgfact.createMessage();
                  SOAPPart sp = msg.getSOAPPart();
                  SOAPEnvelope env = sp.getEnvelope();
                  SOAPHeader head = env.getHeader();
                  SOAPBody body = env.getBody();
                  SOAPBodyElement sbe
                  = body.addBodyElement(env.createName("GetLastTradePrice",
                  "ztrade",
                  "http://wombat.ztrade.com"));
                  sbe.addChildElement(env.createName("symbol",
                  "ztrade",
                  "http://wombat.ztrade.com")).addTextNode("SUNW");
                  StringBuffer sbUrl=new StringBuffer();
                  sbUrl.append(req.getScheme()).append("://").
                  append(req.getServerName());
                  sbUrl.append(     ":"      ).append(     req.getServerPort()     ).append(
                  req.getContextPath() );
                  String reqBase=sbUrl.toString();
                  URL url = new URL(reqBase + "/index.html");
                  AttachmentPart ap = msg.createAttachmentPart(new DataHandler(url));
                  ap.setContentType("text/html");
                  msg.addAttachmentPart(ap);
                  if(dest==null) {
                          dest=reqBase + "/ReceivingServlet";
                  }
                  URL urlEP = new URL(dest);
                  SerResp += "Please see sentmsg.txt file which contains recently sent
                  message and ";
                  File f1 = new File("D:\\saaj\\sentmsg.txt");
                  FileOutputStream sentFile = new FileOutputStream(f1);
                  msg.writeTo(sentFile);
                  sentFile.close();
                  SOAPMessage reply = con.call(msg, urlEP);

                  if (reply != null) {
                  File f2 = new File("D:\\saaj\\replymsg.txt");
                  FileOutputStream replyFile = new FileOutputStream(f2);
                  reply.writeTo(replyFile);
                  replyFile.close();
                  SerResp += " see received reply in replymsg.txt file.</H4></html>";
                  } else {
                          System.out.println("No reply");
```

```
                    SerResp += " no reply was received. </H4></html>";
                }
            } catch(Throwable t) {
            System.out.println("Error in constructing or sending message "+t);
                    SerResp += " There was an error " +
                    "in constructing or sending message. </H4></html>";
            }
            try {
                    OutputStream os = resp.getOutputStream();
                    os.write(SerResp.getBytes());
                    os.flush();
                    os.close();
            } catch (IOException e) {
            System.out.println("Error in outputting servlet response "+e);
            }
    }
  }
```

In Listing 19.37, the `doGet()` method creates an instance of `SOAPMessage` from message factory. Empty `SOAPPart`, `SOAPEnvelope`, and `SOAPBody` parts are received in sequence. The SOAP body element, `GetLastTradePrize`, is added to the SOAP body. The request URL to send this message is prepared. An attachment part is created from a URL and added to the SOAP message. The URL for recipient of this message is created. The entire SOAP message is written to the `sentmsg.txt` file. The SOAP message is sent to the recipient by using the `call()` method of the `con` object.

Listing 19.38 shows the code for the `ReceivingServlet.java` file (save the `ReceivingServlet.java` file in the `/saaj` folder):

Listing 19.38: Showing the Code for the ReceivingServlet.java File

```
import javax.xml.soap.SOAPEnvelope;
import javax.xml.soap.SOAPMessage;
import com.sun.xml.messaging.soap.server.SAAJServlet;
public class ReceivingServlet extends SAAJServlet
{
        public SOAPMessage onMessage(SOAPMessage message) {
        System.out.println("The onMessage() method called in the
                        receiving servlet");
        try {
                System.out.println("The message is as follows: ");
                message.writeTo(System.out);
                SOAPMessage messg = msgFactory.createMessage();
                SOAPEnvelope envlp = messg.getSOAPPart().getEnvelope();
                envlp.getBody()
                .addChildElement(envlp.createName("MsgResponse"))
                .addTextNode("This is a response");
                return messg;
        } catch(Exception excp) {
        System.out.println("Error in processing or replying to a message"+
                        excp);
        return null;
        }
  }
}
```

The onMessage() method of Listing 19.38 is executed when it receives a SOAP message.

The `index.html` file acts as a home page of this application. It contains a hyperlink, `here`, and a simple text description about the application. Listing 19.39 shows the code for the `index.html` file (save the `index.html` file in the `/saaj` folder):

Listing 19.39: Showing the Code for the index.html File

```
<html>
   <body>
         This is a simple example of a SAAJ message exchange.
         <p> Click <a href="SendingServlet">here</a> to send the message
   </body>
</html>
```

Clicking the `here` hyperlink sends a request to the `SendingServlet` servlet, class which sends a message to the `ReceivingServlet` servlet class.

Each servlet-based Web service needs the `web.xml` Deployment Descriptor for deployment. Listing 19.40 shows the `web.xml Deployment` Descriptor of this application (save the `web.xml` file in the `/saaj` folder):

Listing 19.40: Showing the Code for the web.xml File

```
<?xml version="1.0" encoding="UTF-8"?>
<web-app version="3.0" xmlns="http://java.sun.com/xml/ns/javaee"
  xmlns:xsi="http://www.w3.org/2001/XMLSchema-instance"
  xsi:schemaLocation="http://java.sun.com/xml/ns/javaee
  http://java.sun.com/xml/ns/javaee/web-app_3_0.xsd">
  <servlet>
        <servlet-name>SendingServlet</servlet-name>
        <servlet-class>SendingServlet</servlet-class>
        <load-on-startup>1</load-on-startup>
  </servlet>
  <servlet>
        <servlet-name>ReceivingServlet</servlet-name>
        <servlet-class>ReceivingServlet</servlet-class>
        <load-on-startup>2</load-on-startup>
  </servlet>
  <servlet-mapping>
        <servlet-name>SendingServlet</servlet-name>
        <url-pattern>/SendingServlet</url-pattern>
  </servlet-mapping>
  <servlet-mapping>
        <servlet-name>ReceivingServlet</servlet-name>
        <url-pattern>/ReceivingServlet</url-pattern>
  </servlet-mapping>
  <welcome-file-list>
        <welcome-file>index.html</welcome-file>
  </welcome-file-list>
</web-app>
```

Compile the `SendingServlet` and `ReceivingServlet` classes using the `javac` command. Create the `D:\saaj` folder whose directory structure is shown in Figure 19.24:

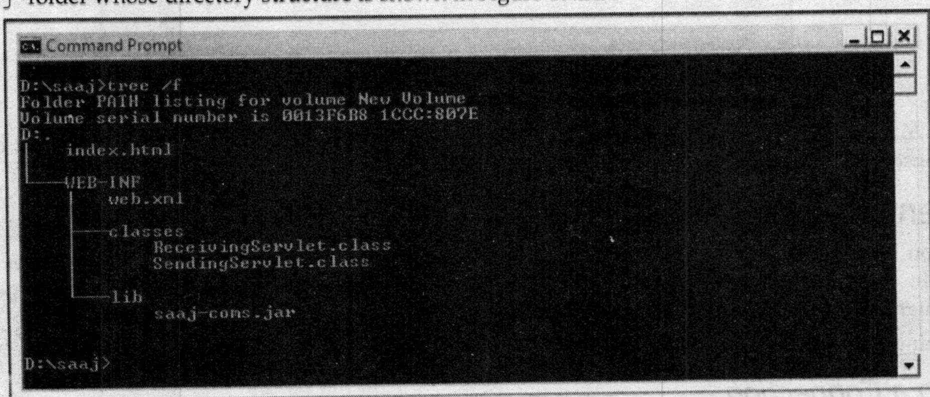

Figure 19.24: Showing the Directory Structure of the sibwithsei Web Service

Package the `D:\saaj` folder in a .WAR file, `saaj.war`. Copy this WAR file in the `C:\Program Files\glassfish\domains\domain1\autodeploy` folder. Start the GlassFish application server. Type `http://localhost:8080/saaj/` on the address bar of the browser and press the Enter key on the keyboard. You can see the `index.html` page, as shown in Figure19.25:

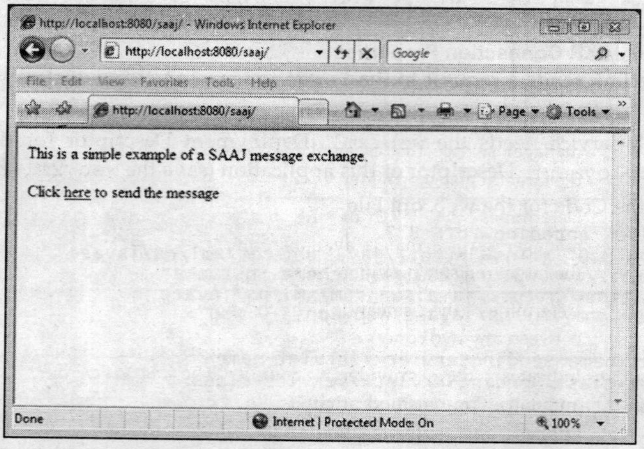

Figure 19.25: Showing the Home Page of the saaj Web Application

When you click the `here` hyperlink, you can see the response generated by the SendingServlet servlet class, as shown in Figure 19.26:

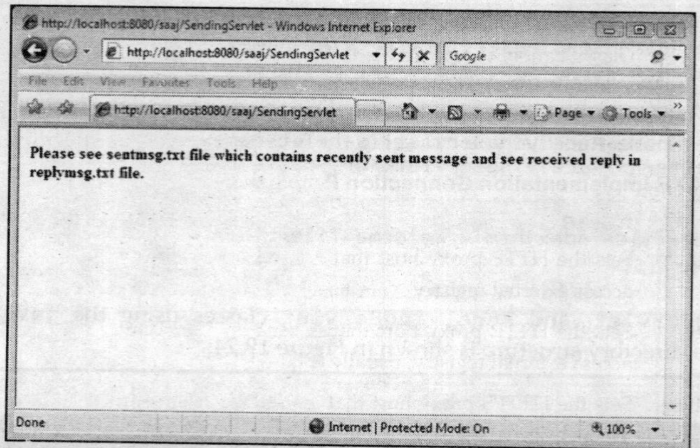

Figure 19.26: Response of the SendingServlet Servlet Class

Figure 19.26 indicates that SOAP message has been successfully sent. It also specifies the locations of the request and response SOAP messages.

Implementing the JAXR Specification

The section helps you in developing a JAXR client that can perform queries and modifications in the UDDI registry. In this application, the Glassfish V3 application server has been used, which provides a JAXR implementation. This server provides JAXR implementation in the form of a resource adapter.

To query and modify the entries in the UDDI registry, you first need to set up a connection.

Setting up a Connection

To set up a connection, you now need to create an instance of the connection factory. Some JAXR implementations provide one or more preconfigured connection factories. JAXR clients implemented as the Java

EE component can access these factories using a resource injection. You need to specify the JNDI name of the connector resource (i.e., /JAXR) to access the preconfigured connection factory.

A JAXR client needs to specify the URLs of registries to be accessed. This is done by setting the properties of the `Properties` instance. JAXR specification defines some standard connection properties on a JAXR connection, as listed in Table 19.11:

Table 19.11: Standard JAXR Connection Properties

Property	Description	Data Type	Default value
javax.xml.registry.queryManagerURL	Determines the URL of the query manager service that is available within the target registry provider	String	None
javax.xml.registry.lifeCycleManagerURL	Determines the URL of the lifecycle manager service that is available within the target registry provider	String	Same as the value specified for queryManagerURL
javax.xml.registry.semanticEquivalences	Determines the semantic equivalence between any two concepts	String	None
javax.xml.registry.security.authenticationMethod	Indicates the provider about the authentication method that is to be applied for authentication with the registry provider	String	None
javax.xml.registry.uddi.maxRows	Indicates the maximum number of rows which a find operation can return.	Integer	None
javax.xml.registry.postalAddressScheme	Represents the ID of a ClassificationScheme that is to be used as a default postal address scheme	String	None

Let us look at connection properties that you can set in the Sun Java server, as specified in Table 19.12:

Table 19.12: Sun's JAXR Implementation Connection Properties

Property	Name	Data Type	Default Value
com.sun.xml.registry.http.proxyHost	Sets the HTTP proxy host that is used to access external registry	String	None
com.sun.xml.registry.http.proxyPort	Sets the HTTP proxy port that is used to access external registry, usually 8080	String	None
com.sun.xml.registry.https.proxyHost	Sets the HTTPS proxy host that is used to access external registry	String	Same as the value of HTTP proxy host
com.sun.xml.registry.https.proxyPort	Sets the HTTPS proxy port that is used to access external registry	String	Same as the value of HTTP proxy port
com.sun.xml.registry.http.proxyUserName	Sets the proxy host's user name for HTTP proxy authentication	String	None
com.sun.xml.registry.http.proxyPassword	Sets the proxy host's password for HTTP proxy authentication	String	None
com.sun.xml.registry.useCache	Instructs the JAXR implementation to first search the registry objects in cache and then in the registry in case they are not found in the cache	Boolean (passed as String)	True
com.sun.xml.registry.userTaxonomyFilenames	Adds user-defined taxonomy structures to the JAXR provider	String	None

The following code snippet shows how to access a connection factory:

```
import javax.annotation.Resource;.*;
import javax.xml.registry.ConnectionFactory;
...
@Resource(mappedName="eis/JAXR")
  public ConnectionFactory connfact;
```

In a standalone JAXR client, use the following code snippet to access a connection factory:

```
import javax.xml.registry.ConnectionFactory;
 ...
ConnectionFactory connFact =ConnectionFactory.newInstance();
```

In order to set up a connection, a client needs to first create a set of properties to specify the details about the URLs of the registries to be accessed. The following code snippet shows how to set up the properties, by providing the URL referring to the query service for a hypothetical registry:

```
Properties propty = new Properties();
Propty.setProperty("javax.xml.registery.queryManagerURL",
              "http://localhost:8080/RegisteryServer/");
...
```

If you are accessing an external registry, you also need to specify the proxy host and port for a network on which you are running your JAXR client program. The following code snippet shows how to set the connection properties on a JAXR connection for accessing external registries:

```
propty.setProperty("com.sun.xml.registry.http.proxyHost",
              "yourhost.yourdomain");
propty.setProperty("com.sun.xml.registry.http.proxyPort",
              "8080");
propty.setProperty("com.sun.xml.registry.https.proxyHost",
              "yourhost.yourdomain");
propty.setProperty("com.sun.xml.registry.https.proxyPort",
              "8080");
connFact.setProperties(propty);
Connection con = connFact.createConnection();
```

The last two lines in the preceding code snippet set the properties for the connection factory and create the connection.

Querying a Registry

After getting the connection instance, let us obtain a `RegistryService` object and its interfaces to perform queries on the registry, as shown in the following code snippet:

```
RegistryService <Registry service object name>= <connection
              object>.getRegistryService();
BusinessQueryManager <object name>= <registry Service Object
              name>.getBusinessQueryManager();
BusinessLifeCycleManager <object name>=<registry Service Object
              name>.getBusinessLifeCycleManager();
```

You need to get only the `BusinessQueryManager` instance for performing simple queries on the registry. In case of complex queries, the `BusinessLifeCycleManager` instance is also required.

The `BusinessQueryManager` interface provides several find methods to search data on the basis of JAXR information model. Important methods used for search purpose are listed as follows:

- **findOrganizations**—Returns a `BulkResponse` object that represents a collection of organizations according to a specified criteria, such as a specified name pattern or a specific classification scheme.
- **findServices**—Returns a `BulkResponse` object that represents a collection of services which a particular organization offers.
- **findServiceBindings**—Returns a `BulkResponse` object that represents a set of service bindings supported by a particular service.

The `JAXRQuery` tool queries a registry on the basis of the name of organizations. There are three classification systems used for classifying registries:

- **NAICS**—Stands for North American Industry Classification System. You can visit the `http://www.census.gov/epcd/www/naics.html` link to get more information on this system.
- **UNSPSC**—Stands for Universal Standard Products and Services Classification. You can visit the `http://www.unspsc.org/`link to get more information on this system.
- **ISO**—Stands for International Organization for Standardization. This organization specifies a 3166 country codes classification system for accessing registries. You can visit the `http://www.iso.org/iso/country_codes` link to get more information on this system.

Finding Organizations by Name

Let us find organizations by name, by using the `findOrganizations()` method. The following code snippet shows the syntax of this method:

```
public BulkResponse findOrganizations(Collection findQualifiers,
                                      Collection namePatterns,
                                      Collection classifications,
                                      Collection specs,
                                      Collection extIds,
                                      Collection extLinks)
                      throws JAXRException
```

The `findOrganizations()`method returns a collection of organization objects after performing logical AND operation on the criteria specified by the parameters. Some parameters can take null values. Some of the parameters required by the `findOrganizations()`method are described as follows:

- **findQualifiers**—Represents a parameter that is a collection of the find qualifiers defined in the `FindQualifier` interface, which has several constants that affect the search of the `findOrganizations()`method. Some of the constants defined in this interface are EXACT_NAME_MATCH, SORT_BY_DATE_ASC and SORT_BY_NAME_ASC.
- **namePatterns**—Specifies a parameter that is a collection of either the String or the LocalizedString object. Each String or LocalizedString value contains a wildcard name matching the pattern used in the SQL-92 LIKE operator.

Finding Organizations by Classification

Let us now find the organizations by classification. To perform this task, you first need to create the `Classification` objects of different classification schemes. Then, you need to instantiate the `Collection` instance containing these `Classification` objects. The following code snippet shows the syntax to search all the organizations corresponding to the classification scheme designed by NAICS:

```
String uuid_naics =
"uuid:C0B9FE13-179F-413D-8A5B-5004DB8E5BB2";
ClassificationScheme <object name>=
   (ClassificationScheme) <business query manager object
   name>.getRegistryObject(uuid_naics,
   LifeCycleManager.CLASSIFICATION_SCHEME);
InternationalString <object name> = <business life cycle manager object
   name>.createInternationalString(
   <Enter Search String here in quotes>));
String <Variable name>= "Enter corresponding value of search string";
Classification <object name> =
   <business life cycle manager object name>.createClassification(<enter
   classification scheme object name>, <Enter international string object
   name, <Enter Search value>);
Collection<Classification><Collection of Classification object name>=
   new ArrayList<Classification>();
<Collection of Classification object names>.add(<Classification object name>);
BulkResponse <Object name>= <business query manager object
   name>.findOrganizations(null, null,
   <Collection of Classification object name>, null, null, null);
Collection <object name>= <BulkResponse Object name>.getCollection();
```

Let's now use classifications to search organizations whose services are based on some technical specifications. These technical specifications are in the form of WSDL documents. To perform this task, you need to use the `Concept` class that holds information for a single specification. After finding the specification concepts, we need to search for the organizations that use these concepts, as shown in following code snippet:

```
String <variable name> = "uddi-org:types";
ClassificationScheme <Object Name>=
   <business query manager object name>.findClassificationSchemeByName(null,
   <Enter variable name>);
Classification <object name>=
   <business life cycle manager object name>.createClassification(uddiOrgTypes,
   "wsdlSpec","wsdlSpec");
Collection<Classification><collection of classification object name> =
   new ArrayList<Classification>();
<collection of classification object name>.add(<Enter
   classification object name>);
// Find concepts
BulkResponse <Object name>=<business query manager object
   name>.findConcepts(null, null,
   <collection of classification object names>, null, null);
```

Manipulating Registry Objects

You must ensure that you have the required authorization before manipulating the registry objects. To perform submit, update, and delete operations, use the `BusinessLifeCycleManager` interface.

If you have the authorization, you need to send authorization credentials, such as user name and password, to the registry before manipulating the registry objects. The following code snippet shows how to send the authorization credentials:

```
String <user name variable> = <Enter value in Quotes>;
String <password variable> = <Enter value in Quotes>;
// Get authorization from the registry
PasswordAuthentication <object name> =
   new PasswordAuthentication(<enter password authentication name>,
   <password variable>.toCharArray());
HashSet<PasswordAuthentication><HashSet of PasswordAuthentication object name>=
   new HashSet<PasswordAuthentication>();
<HashSet of PasswordAuthentication object name>.add(<Enter PasswordAuthentication object
   name>);
con.setCredentials(<Enter HashSet  of PasswordAuthentication object name>);
```

In the preceding code snippet, con object is the Connection object. Let's now learn how to manipulate registry objects. You specifically learn about the following tasks for manipulating the registry objects:

- Add an organization to the registry
- Add classifications
- Add services and service bindings
- Publish the organization
- Delete entries from the registry

Adding an Organization to the Registry

The following code snippet creates an organization, adds it to the registry, and sets other details, such as its name, description, and primary contact:

```
// Create organization name and description
InternationalString <object name> =
   <business life cycle manager object name>.createInternationalString(<Enter
   name of service>);
Organization <object name> = <business life cycle manager object
   name>.createOrganization(<InternationalString object name>);
<InternationalString object name> = <business life cycle manager object
   name>.createInternationalString("Indo-Asian News Service (IANS) - formerly
   India Abroad News Service - was employedin 1986 to act as an
   information bridge between India and North America and chronicle their
   growing ethnic, business and cultural links.");
<Organization object name>.setDescription(<Enter InternationalString object
```

```
    name>);
User <User object name> = <business life cycle manager object
    name>.createUser();
PersonName <PersonName object name> = <business life cycle manager object
    name>.createPersonName(<Enter real name of person>);
<User object name>.setPersonName(<Enter PersonName object name>);
TelephoneNumber <Enter TelephoneNumber object name> = <business life cycle manager
    object name>.createTelephoneNumber();
<TelephoneNumber object name>.setNumber(<Enter phone number of the person>);
Collection<TelephoneNumber><Collection of TelephoneNumber object name> =
    new ArrayList<TelephoneNumber>();
<Collection of TelephoneNumber object names>.add(<Enter TelephoneNumber object
    name>);
<User object name>.setTelephoneNumbers(<Collection of TelephoneNumber object
    names>);
    EmailAddress <EmailAddress object name> =
    blcm.createEmailAddress(<enter actual email address of the person>);
Collection<EmailAddress><Collection of EmailAddress object name> =
    new ArrayList<EmailAddress>();
<Collection of EmailAddress object names>.add(<Enter EmailAddress object name>);
<User object name>.setEmailAddresses(<Collection of EmailAddress object names>);
<Organization object name>.setPrimaryContact(<Enter User object name>);
```

The preceding code snippet creates and adds an organization name and description in the registry. It uses the `InternationalizationString` object for setting the name and description of the organization.

Adding Classifications

Usually all organizations come under some classifications. Each classification is based on a classification scheme, which is defined by the JAXR specification. Let us associate a classification scheme to our organization, as shown in following code snippet:

```
// Set classification scheme to NAICS
ClassificationScheme <ClassificationScheme object> =
    <BusinessQueryManager object name>.findClassificationSchemeByName(null,
    "ntis-gov:naics:1997");
// Create and add classification
InternationalScring <InternationalString object name> =
    <business life cycle manager object name>.createInternationalString(
    <enter search string in quotes>));
String <variable name>= <Enter value related to search string>;
Classification <classification object name> =
<business life cycle manager object name>.createClassification(<ClassificationScheme
    object name>,<Enter InternationalString object name>, <enter corresponding value of
    search string>);
Collection<Classification><collection of ClassificationScheme object name>
        =new ArrayList<Classification>();
<collection of ClassificationScheme object names>.add(<enter Classification object
    name>);
<Organization object name>.addClassifications(<collection of
        ClassificationScheme object name>);
```

The preceding code snippet uses the `findClassificationSchemeByName()` method to create the `ClassficationScheme` instance corresponding to the `NAICS` system.

Adding Services and Service Bindings to an Organization

We now need to add services and associated service bindings in the registry. Similar to an `Organization` object, a `Service` object has members, such as `Name`, `Description`, and `Key` objects. A `ServiceBinding` object also has `description`, access URI of service, and `link` that relates service binding with a technical specification.

Following code snippet shows how to add services and service bindings to an organization:

```
// Create services and service
Collection<Service><name of the collection of Service object name> = new
    ArrayList<Service>();
InternationalString <InternationalString object name> =
    <business life cycle manager object name>.createInternationalString(<Enter
```

```
        Your Service Name>);
    Service <Service object name> = <business life cycle manager object
        name>.createService(<InternationalString object name>);
    <InternationalString object name> = <business life cycle manager object
        name>.createInternationalString(<enter Your Service Description>);
    <Service object name>.setDescription(<enter InternationalString object name>);
    // Create service bindings
    Collection<ServiceBinding><name of a Collection of ServiceBinding object name> =
        new ArrayList<ServiceBinding>();
    ServiceBinding <ServiceBinding object name> = <business life cycle manager object
        name>.createServiceBinding();
    <InternationalString object name> = <business life cycle manager object
        name>.createInternationalString(<enter Your Service Binding Description in quotes>);
    <ServiceBinding object name>.setDescription(<Enter InternationalString object
        name>);
    <ServiceBinding object name>.setValidateURI(false);
    <ServiceBinding object name>.setAccessURI("http://ians.com:8080/ns/");
    <name of a Collection of ServiceBinding object name>.add(<Enter ServiceBinding
        object name>);
    <ServiceBinding object name>.addServiceBindings(<enter name of a Collection of
        ServiceBinding objects>);
    <name of the collection of Service objects>.add(<enter ServiceObject name>);
    <Organization object name>.addServices(<enter name of the collection of Service
        objects>);
```

The preceding code snippet creates a collection of `Service` objects. It also creates a `ServiceBinding` instance and adds it to the collection of the `ServiceBinding` objects.

Publishing an Organization

Our organization object is now ready to be published to a registry. The JAXR client uses the `saveOrganizations()` method to submit or update data of organizations to a registry. Publishing an organization implies that the data of the organization has been made public. After successful execution of the `saveOrganizations()` method, the registry assigns a unique key to the organization. Following code snippet shows how an organization can be published with a registry:

```
    Collection<Organization><name of a collection of Organization object name > =
        new ArrayList<Organization>();
    <name of a collection of Organization object name>.add(<enter Organization
            object name>);
    BulkResponse<BulkResponse object name> = <business life cycle manager object
        name>.saveOrganizations(<name of a collection of Organization object names
        >);
    Collection <name of a collection of Exception objects> = <enter BulkResponse
        object name>.getException();
    if (<name of a collection of Exception object names> == null) {
        System.out.println("Organization saved to registry");
        Collection <collection of Key instances> = <enter BulkResponse object
            name>.getCollection();
        Iterator <Iterator Object name> = <collection of Key instances>.iterator();
        if (<Iterator Object name>.hasNext()) {
            Key <Key object name> = (Key)<Iterator Object name>.next();
            String <variable name> = <enter Key object name>.getId();
            System.out.println("Organization key is " + <variable name>);
        }
    }
```

The preceding code snippet publishes an organization to the registry by invoking the `saveOrganizations()` method.

Deleting Data from the Registry

You can also delete data published to a registry when the data becomes obsolete. You can delete organizations, services, service bindings, and concepts. To do this, the BusinessLifeCycleManager interface provides certain methods, such as `deleteOrganizations()`, `deleteServices()`, `deleteServiceBindings()`, and `deleteConcepts()`.

The following code snippet shows how an organization can be deleted from the registry:

```
String <variable name> = <Key object name>.getId();
System.out.println("Deleting organization with id " + <String variable name>);
Collection<Key><name of a collection of Key instances>= new ArrayList<Key>();
<name of a collection of Key instances>.add(<enter Key object name>);
BulkResponse<BulkResponse object name> = <business query life cycle manager
  object>.deleteOrganizations(<name of a collection of Key instances>);
Collection <name of a collection of Exception objects > = res.getException();
if (<collection of Exception object names> == null) {
  System.out.println("Organization deleted");
Collection <name of a collection of Key objects> = (<collection of Exception
  objects>.getCollection();
  Iterator <Iterator object> = <collection of Key objects>.iterator();
  Key <Key object name> = null;
  if (<Iterator object>.hasNext()) {
       <Key object name> = (Key) <Iterator object>.next();
       <variable name> = <Key object name>.getId();
       System.out.println("Organization key was " + <variable name>);
  }
}
```

The preceding code snippet uses the `deleteOrganizations()` method that takes a collection of keys to delete an organization from the registry.

Implementing the StAX Specification

You can use the StAX specification to read and write data in XML streams and documents. Let's learn about these in detail next.

Reading XML Streams

You can use the `XMLStreamReader` and `XMLEventReader` interfaces to read XML streams.

Using the XMLStreamReader Interface

You can use the `XMLStreamReader` interface of StAX `cursor` API to read XML documents or streams in a forward direction only, one element at a time. You can perform the following operations using the `XMLStreamReader` interface:

- Retrieve the value of an attribute
- Read XML data
- Determine whether or not an element contains data
- Access a collection of attributes using indexes
- Access a collection of namespaces using indexes
- Access name and contents of the current event

The following code snippet shows some of the methods used to retrieve information about the namespaces and attributes of an XML stream:

```
int getAttributeCount();
String getAttributeNamespace(int index);
String getAttributeName(int index);
String getAttributePrefix(int index);
String getAttributeType(int index);
String getAttributeValue(int index);
String getAttributeValue(String namespaceUri,
              String localName);
boolean isAttributeSpecified(int index);
```

You can access the namespaces of XML streams by using the methods shown in the following code snippet:

```
int getNamespaceCount();
String getNamespacePrefix(int index);
String getNamespaceURI(int index);
```

You can access individual elements of an XML stream by instantiating an input factory, creating a reader, and iterating over elements using the methods of the `XMLStreamReader` interface, as shown in the following code snippet:

```
XMLInputFactory xifact = XMLInputFactory.newInstance();
XMLStreamReader xsread = xifact.createXMLStreamReader( ... );
while(xsread.hasNext()) {
  xsread.next();
}
```

Using the XMLEventReader Interface

The `XMLEventReader` interface of the StAX event iterator API maps events in an XML stream to the allocated event objects. It provides four methods, next(), nextEvent(), hasNext(), and peek(), to iterate XML streams. The following code snippet shows the syntax of these methods of the `XMLEventReader` interface:

```
package javax.xml.stream;
import java.util.Iterator;
public interface XMLEventReader extends Iterator {
  public Object next();
  public XMLEvent nextEvent() throws XMLStreamException;
  public boolean hasNext();
  public XMLEvent peek() throws XMLStreamException;
  ...
}
```

In the preceding code snippet, the `next()` method of the `XMLEventReader` interface returns the next event in the stream. The next typed `XMLEvent` is returned by the `nextEvent()` method. The `hasNext()` method checks whether or not any event is left for processing in the stream. The `peek()` method returns the current event.

The following code snippet shows how to read and print all the events of a stream:

```
while(streamObj.hasNext()) {
  XMLEvent evt = streamObj.nextEvent();
  system.out.print(evt);
}
```

Writing XML Streams

It has already been discussed that the StAX API can both read and write XML streams or XML documents. The interfaces of the `cursor` and `event` iterator APIs for reading XML streams are similar, but the interfaces for writing XML streams are significantly different. The interfaces for writing to the XML stream are given as follows:

- XMLStreamWriter
- XMLEventWriter

Let's explore these interfaces for writing XML stream next.

Using the XMLStreamWriter Interface

The `XMLStreamWriter` interface of the StAX cursor API is used either to create a new XML stream or to write to an existing XML stream. The implementation class of the `XMLStreamWriter` interface performs operations defined in the `XMLOutputFactory` class.

Let's consider an example that creates an instance of the XMLOutputFactory class and XMLStreamWriter interface, and finally writes the XML output, as shown in the following code snippet:

```
XMLOutputFactory xofact= XMLOutputFactory.newInstance();
XMLStreamWriter xswrite= xofact.createXMLStreamWriter( ... );
xswrite.writeStartDocument();
xswrite.setPrefix("y","http://y");
xswrite.setDefaultNamespace("http://y");
xswrite.writeStartElement("http://y","w");
xswrite.writeAttribute("x","abc");
xswrite.writeNamespace("y","http://y");
xswrite.writeDefaultNamespace("http://y");
xswrite.setPrefix("z","http://y");
xswrite.writeEmptyElement("http://y","z");
```

```
    xswrite.writeAttribute("http://y","fname","lname");
    xswrite.writeNamespace("z","http://y");
    xswrite.writeCharacters("Character Content");
    xswrite.writeEndElement();
    xswrite.flush();
```

In the preceding code snippet, the `writeCharacters()` method escapes special characters, such as &, <, and ". The `setPrefix()` method binds the prefixes passed as an argument to it. The `setDefaultNamespace()` method sets the default namespace. The `writeStartElement()` method adds the `StartElement` event to the XML stream.

Using the XMLEventWriter Interface

The `XMLEventWriter` interface of the StAX event iterator API is also used either to create a new XML stream or to write to an existing XML stream. The following code snippet shows the methods of the `XMLEventWriter` interface:

```
public interface XMLEventWriter {
   public void flush() throws XMLStreamException;
   public void close() throws XMLStreamException;
   public void add(XMLEvent e) throws XMLStreamException;
   // ... other methods not shown.
}
```

In the preceding code snippet, the `add()` method is used to add stream events represented by the `XMLEvent` parameter. Note that you cannot modify the event after adding it to an event writer instance.

Reading an XML File using the Cursor API

Let's create an application that parses an XML file, `ProductDetails.xml`, using the cursor API.

Listing 19.41 shows the source code of the `ProductDetails.xml` file (save the `ProductDetails.xml` file in the `/cursor` folder):

Listing 19.41: Showing the Code for the ProductDetails.xml File

```
<?xml version="1.0" encoding="UTF-8"?>
<ProductDetails xmlns="http://www.kogentindia.com">
   <Product>
         <Name>LG DVD Player</Name>
         <Category>Entertainment</Category>
         <LaunchDate>June, 2008</LaunchDate>
         <DESC>You can play DVD, CD in latest formats </DESC>
         <Price>2050</Price>
   </Product>
   <Product>
         <Name>Dish TV </Name>
         <Category>Education</Category>
         <LaunchDate>May,2008</LaunchDate>
         <DESC>You can see programs on various air channels</DESC>
         <Price>2250</Price>
   </Product>
</ProductDetails>
```

The `ProductDetails.xml` file contains two `Product` elements, where each element contains information about the `Name`, `Category`, `LaunchDate`, `DESC`, and `Price of a product`.

Listing 19.42 parses the `ProductDetails.xml` file using the cursor API (save the `ParseUsingCursor.java` file in the `/cursor` folder):

Listing 19.42: Showing the Code for the ParseUsingCursor.java File

```
import java.io.FileInputStream;
import javax.xml.namespace.QName;
import javax.xml.stream.XMLInputFactory;
import javax.xml.stream.XMLStreamException;
import javax.xml.stream.XMLStreamReader;
import javax.xml.stream.events.XMLEvent;
public class ParseUsingCursor {
   public static void main(String[] args) throws Exception {
          int cnt = 0;
          String XMLFName = "ProductDetails.xml";
```

```
        cnt = Integer.parseInt(args[0]);
        XMLInputFactory xmlinfact = null;
        try {
                xmlinfact = XMLInputFactory.newInstance();
                xmlinfact.setProperty(
                XMLInputFactory.IS_REPLACING_ENTITY_REFERENCES,
                Boolean.TRUE);
                xmlinfact.setProperty(
                XMLInputFactory.IS_SUPPORTING_EXTERNAL_ENTITIES,
                Boolean.FALSE);
                xmlinfact.setProperty(XMLInputFactory.IS_COALESCING,
                Boolean.FALSE);
        } catch (Exception ex) {
                ex.printStackTrace();
        }
        System.out.println("");
        System.out.println("FACTORY: " + xmlinfact);
        System.out.println("");
        try {
                for (int i = 0; i < cnt; i++) {
                XMLStreamReader xsr = xmlinfact.createXMLStreamReader(
                        XMLFName,new FileInputStream(XMLFName));
                int evntcat = xsr.getEventType();
                //printEventType(eventType);
                dispStartDocument(xsr);
                //check if there are more events in the input stream
                while (xsr.hasNext()) {
                        evntcat = xsr.next();
                        //printEventType(eventType);
                        //these functions prints the information about the
                        // particular event by calling relevant function
                        dispStartElement(xsr);
                        dispEndElement(xsr);
                        dispText(xsr);
                        dispPIData(xsr);
                        dispComment(xsr);
                }
        }
        } catch (XMLStreamException e) {
                System.out.println(e.getMessage());
                if (e.getNestedException() != null) {
                        e.getNestedException()
                        .printStackTrace();
                }
        } catch (Exception e) {
                e.printStackTrace();
        }
}
public static final String getEventTypeString(int evntcat) {
        switch (evntcat) {
        case XMLEvent.START_ELEMENT:
        return "START_ELEMENT";
        case XMLEvent.END_ELEMENT:
        return "END_ELEMENT";
        case XMLEvent.PROCESSING_INSTRUCTION:
        return "PROCESSING_INSTRUCTION";
        case XMLEvent.CHARACTERS:
        return "CHARACTERS";
        case XMLEvent.COMMENT:
        return "COMMENT";
        case XMLEvent.START_DOCUMENT:
        return "START_DOCUMENT";
        case XMLEvent.END_DOCUMENT:
        return "END_DOCUMENT";
        case XMLEvent.ENTITY_REFERENCE:
        return "ENTITY_REFERENCE";
        case XMLEvent.ATTRIBUTE:
        return "ATTRIBUTE";
        case XMLEvent.DTD:
        return "DTD";
```

```
        case XMLEvent.CDATA:
        return "CDATA";
        case XMLEvent.SPACE:
        return "SPACE";
}
return "UNKNOWN_EVENT_TYPE , " + evntcat;
}
private static void dispEventType(int evntcat) {
        System.out.println(
        "EVENT TYPE(" + evntcat + ") = "
        + getEventTypeString(evntcat));
}
private static void dispStartDocument(XMLStreamReader xsr) {
        if (xsr.START_DOCUMENT == xsr.getEventType()) {
                System.out.println(
                "<?xml version=\"" + xsr.getVersion() + "\""
                + " encoding=\"" + xsr.getCharacterEncodingScheme() + "\""
                + "?>");
        }
}
private static void dispComment(XMLStreamReader xsr) {
        if (xsr.getEventType() == xsr.COMMENT) {
                System.out.print("<!--" + xsr.getText() + "-->");
        }
}
private static void dispText(XMLStreamReader xsr) {
        if (xsr.hasText()) {
                System.out.print(xsr.getText());
        }
}
private static void dispPIData(XMLStreamReader xsr) {
        if (xsr.getEventType() == XMLEvent.PROCESSING_INSTRUCTION) {
                System.out.print(
                "<?" + xsr.getPITarget() + " " + xsr.getPIData() + "?>");
        }
}
private static void dispStartElement(XMLStreamReader xsr) {
        if (xsr.isStartElement()) {
                System.out.print("<" + xsr.getName().toString());
                dispAttributes(xsr);
                System.out.print(">");
        }
}
private static void dispEndElement(XMLStreamReader xsr) {
        if (xsr.isEndElement()) {
                System.out.print("</" + xsr.getName().toString() + ">");
        }
}
private static void dispAttributes(XMLStreamReader xsr) {
        int cnt = xsr.getAttributeCount();
        if (cnt > 0) {
                for (int i = 0; i < cnt; i++) {
                        System.out.print(" ");
                        System.out.print(xsr.getAttributeName(i).toString());
                        System.out.print("=");
                        System.out.print("\"");
                        System.out.print(xsr.getAttributeValue(i));
                        System.out.print("\"");
                }
        }
        cnt = xsr.getNamespaceCount();
        if (cnt > 0) {
                for (int i = 0; i < cnt; i++) {
                        System.out.print(" ");
                        System.out.print("xmlns");
                        if (xsr.getNamespacePrefix(i) != null) {
                        System.out.print(":" + xsr.getNamespacePrefix(i));
                        }
                        System.out.print("=");
                        System.out.print("\"");
```

```
                            System.out.print(xsr.getNamespaceURI(i));
                            System.out.print("\"");
                    }
            }
    }
}
```

Create a folder named cursor in the D: drive and place the `ParseUsingCursor.java` and `ProductDetails.xml` files inside this folder. Compile and run the`ParseUsingCursor.java` class as shown in Figure 19.27:

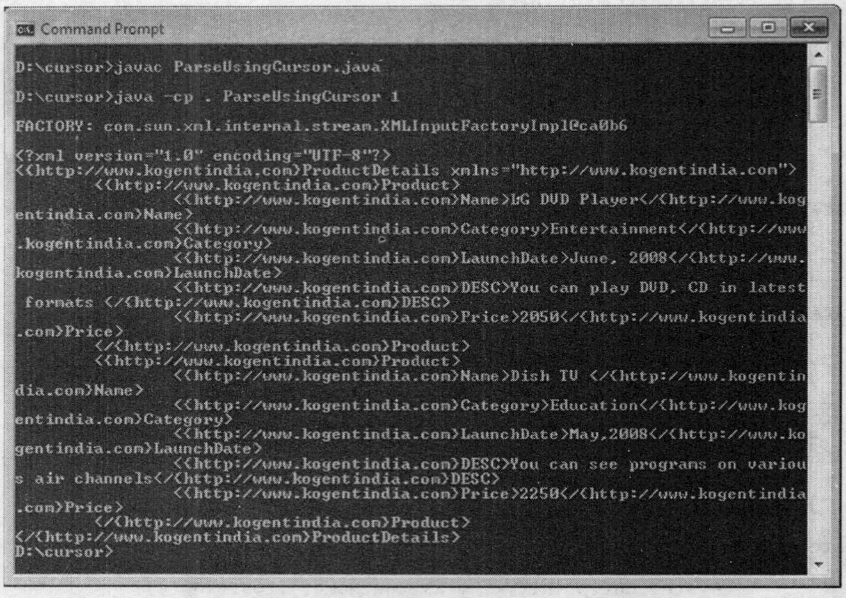

Figure 19.27: Showing the Compilation and Execution of the ParseUsingCursor.java File

Reading an XML File using the Event Iterator API

In this section, you learn to create a Java class, `ParseUsingEvent.java`, which parses the `ProductDetails.xml` file described in the previous section. This class creates an instance of the `XMLInputFactory` class. Listing 19.43 shows the source code of the`ParseUsingEvent.java` file (save the `ParseUsingEvent.java` file in the `/EventIterator` folder):

Listing 19.43: Showing the Code for the ParseUsingEvent.java File

```
import java.io.FileInputStream;
import javax.xml.stream.*;
import javax.xml.stream.events.*;
import javax.xml.namespace.QName;
public class ParseUsingEvent {
  public static void main(String[] args) throws Exception {
        String XMLFName = "ProductDetails.xml";
        XMLInputFactory factory = XMLInputFactory.newInstance();
        System.out.println("FACTORY: " + factory);
        XMLEventReader xer = factory.createXMLEventReader(
        XMLFName,new FileInputStream(XMLFName));
        while (xer.hasNext()) {
                XMLEvent xet = xer.nextEvent();
                System.out.println(xet.toString());
        }
  }
  public static final String getEventTypeString(int eventcat) {
        switch (eventcat) {
                case XMLEvent.START_ELEMENT:
```

```
                return "START_ELEMENT";
                case XMLEvent.END_ELEMENT:
                return "END_ELEMENT";
                case XMLEvent.PROCESSING_INSTRUCTION:
                return "PROCESSING_INSTRUCTION";
                case XMLEvent.CHARACTERS:
                return "CHARACTERS";
                case XMLEvent.COMMENT:
                return "COMMENT";
                case XMLEvent.START_DOCUMENT:
                return "START_DOCUMENT";
                case XMLEvent.END_DOCUMENT:
                return "END_DOCUMENT";
                case XMLEvent.ENTITY_REFERENCE:
                return "ENTITY_REFERENCE";
                case XMLEvent.ATTRIBUTE:
                return "ATTRIBUTE";
                case XMLEvent.DTD:
                return "DTD";
                case XMLEvent.CDATA:
                return "CDATA";
                case XMLEvent.SPACE:
                return "SPACE";
        }
        return "UNKNOWN_EVENT_TYPE " + "," + eventcat;
    }
}
```

Create a folder named `EventIterator` in the D: drive and place the `ParseUsingEvent.java` and `ProductDetails.xml` files (described in the previous section) inside this folder. Compile and run the `ParseUsingEvent.java` class, as shown in Figure 19.28:

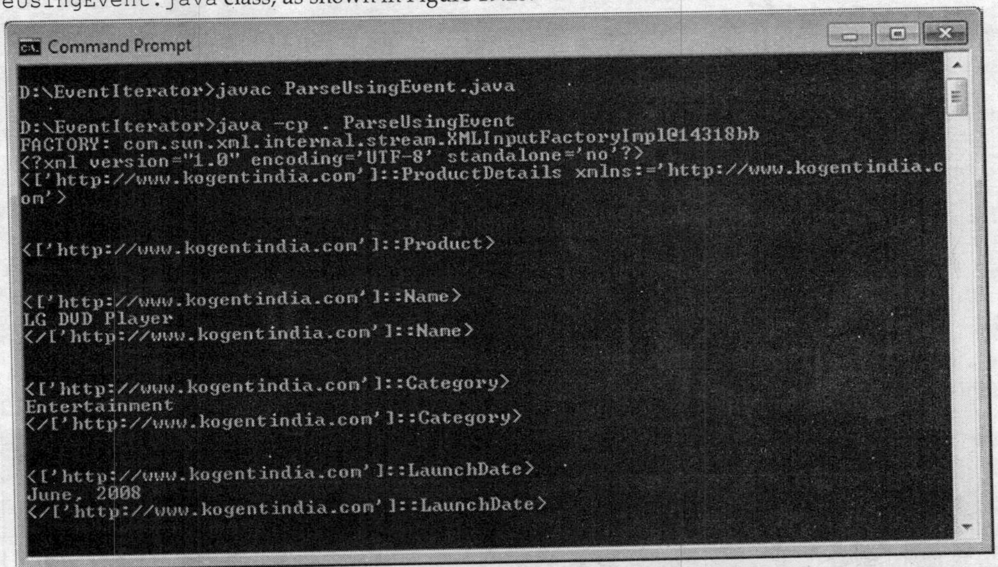

Figure 19.28: Showing the Output of the ParseUsingEvent Class

Writing an XML File using the Cursor API

In this section, you learn to create an XML file using the cursor API. This application that you are going to create in this section, has one Java class, `GenerateXMLUsingCusror`, which writes XML data to the output.xml file. Listing 19.44 shows the source code of the `GenerateXMLUsingCursor.java` file (save the `GenerateXMLUsingCursor.java` file in the `/CursorWriter` folder):

Listing 19.44: Showing the Code for the GenerateXMLUsingCursor.java File

```
import java.io.File;
import java.io.FileOutputStream;
import javax.xml.stream.XMLOutputFactory;
import javax.xml.stream.XMLStreamWriter;
public class GenerateXMLUsingCursor {
   public static void main(String[] args) throws Exception
   {
          try
          {
          XMLOutputFactory xmlof = XMLOutputFactory.newInstance();
          XMLStreamWriter xmlsw = null;
          File file= new File("output.xml");
          xmlsw = xmlof.createXMLStreamWriter(new FileOutputStream(file));
          xmlsw.writeComment(
          "The namespace of price element is http://ecommerce.org/schema");
          xmlsw.writeStartDocument( );
          xmlsw.setPrefix("ecom", "http://ecommerce.org/schema");
          xmlsw.writeStartElement("http://ecommerce.org/schema", "x");
          xmlsw.writeNamespace("x", "http://ecommerce.org/schema");
          xmlsw.writeStartElement("http://ecommerce.org/schema", "price");
          xmlsw.writeAttribute("units", "Euro");
          xmlsw.writeCharacters("35.47");
          xmlsw.writeEndElement();
          xmlsw.writeEndElement();
          xmlsw.writeEndDocument();
          xmlsw.flush();
          xmlsw.close();
          } catch (Exception e) {
                 System.err.println(
                 "Exception occurred while running writer samples");
          }
   }
}
```

Create a folder named `CursorWriter` in the D: drive and place the `GenerateXMLUsingCursor.java` file inside this folder. Compile and run the `GenerateXMLUsingCusror.java` file, as shown in Figure 19.29:

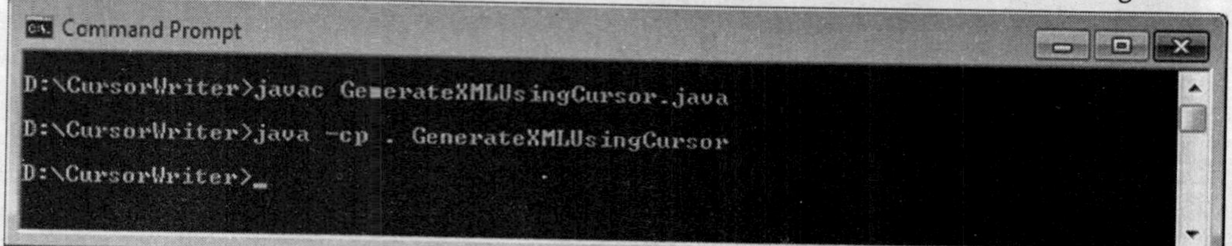

Figure 19.29: Showing the Output of the GenerateXMLUsingCursor Class

Running the `GenerateXMLUsingCursor` Java class creates the `output.xml` file shown in Listing 19.45:

Listing 19.45: Showing the output.xml File

```
<!--The namespace of price element is http://ecommerce.org/schema-->
<?xml version="1.0" ?>
<ecom:x xmlns:x="http://ecommerce.org/schema">
<x:price units="Euro">35.47</x:price>
</ecom:x>
```

Summary

In this chapter, you have learned about SOA and Java Web services. Section A has helped you to explore the basic concepts of SOA and JWSs. You have also learned about the role of WSDL, SOAP, and Java/XML mapping in SOA. In Section B, we have explored the different Web service specifications required to implement SOA. For example, the JAX-WS 2.2 specification provides a Java API that you can use to create Java Web services. The JAXB 2.2 specification provides the standards to bind Java classes to XML schema components. The WSEE 1.3 specification deals with the service architecture, packaging, and deployment of Web services. The WS-Metadata 2.2 specification provides the standards for deploying the JWSs. The SAAJ specification lays down the standards for transmitting and processing SOAP messages in compliance with the JAX-WS handlers and JAXR implementations. The JAXR specification helps access standard business registries over the Internet. Finally, we have learned that the StAX specification provides various APIs to control the parsing of XML documents. We also explored how to implement these Web service specifications in detail in Section C of the chapter.

Quick Revise

Q1. What is a Web service?

Ans. Web services present model by which tasks of e-business processes are distributed widely through Internet. This model is not restricted to specific business model. Web services are not graphical user interfaces but they can be used into software meant for user interaction. They describe their inputs and outputs in a manner that second party can predict its functionality, how to call it, and expected results. The Web services are reusable software components and let developers to reuse basic elements of code made by others. A simple example of Web service is auction engine, such as eBay. This website provides successful auction service. Nowadays, businesses that sell products wish to add auction process to own business model. For this auction process, these businesses or companies require to build the auction software from start or alternatively they can send the customers of products to an auction website, such as eBay. Using Web services, eBay leverage its auction process to other websites and applications for some fee. Businesses only need to subscribe to eBay's Web service and provide some lines of code to their applications to use Web service. Other uses of Web services are payroll management, credit scoring, shipping, business intelligence, and mapping services.

Q2. What is SOAP?

Ans. SOAP, i.e., Simple Object Access Protocol, is a protocol which allows applications to exchange information. It is not a language or platform specific protocol, and; thereby, allows communication between applications running on different platforms. SOAP is a text-based protocol and uses XML-based rule to allow applications interchange information over HTTP.

Q3. What is WSDL?

Ans. Web Services Description Language (WSDL) is an Interface Definition Language (IDL) on the basis of which SOA components can easily communicate with each other. It is a standard language to write guidelines for communicating with a component. Without this language, service providers must provide different documentations for communication with a component for different clients.

Q4. What is a relationship between SOA and Web Services?

Ans. Web Service technology is a best method to implement service-oriented architecture. Web services have self describing interfaces for clients and distributed into modularized services (which encapsulate business logic) that can be registered, searched, and called over the Internet. The modular services are loosely coupled which allows them to access by anyone at any location using any platform.

Q5. What is Java/XML binding?

Ans. The Java/XML binding are defined by using JAXB 2.2 annotations in Java classes. Each Java class maps to a unique XML schema component depending upon its annotations. You can implement type mappings in the Java/XML binding process in the following two ways:

- Begin with an existing Java application and takes help of schema generator to produce machine-generated XML schema. In this way, JAXB user develops Java application and use JAXB annotations or binding language inside the application to map it to a particular schema.
- Begin with an existing XML schema and takes help of a schema compiler to produce a machine-generated Java application. In this way, XML developer writes XML schema, creates a Java application from schema using the schema compiler, and customize it using annotations or binding language.

Q6. What is Java/XML type mapping?

Ans. Java/XML type mappings are implemented between existing Java application and existing XML schema definitions. This mapping is done by using user defined mappings between XML and Java. In this process, there is no generation of machine generated artifacts at runtime.

Q7. What is Java/WSDL mapping?

Ans. Java/WSDL mapping defines the binding between WSDL operations and Java methods. Initially, the SOAP message requests for a WSDL operation. Then, Java/WSDL mapping is used to invoke the associated Java method and map the SOAP message to the parameters of this method. Java/WSDL mapping is also used to map the return value of the method to the SOAP response.

Q8. What is runtime endpoint publishing?

Ans. JAX-WS supports publishing of Web service endpoints at runtime. The instance of the javax.xml.ws.EndPoint class used to assign the instance of the Web service implementation class to a URL. Dynamic publishing of end point is only supported by Java SE 6 while the Java EE 6 container does not support publishing of endpoint dynamically. The Java EE experts are trying to include this feature in future versions of Java EE.

Q9. Define Java API for XML- based Web Services (JAX-WS) Specification.

Ans. JAX-WS is a Java Web services specification that is used for deploying and invoking Web services. JAX-WS server side facilities helps us deploying a Web service partially and JAX-WS on client side helps us in building an SOA based client to consume or invoke a Web service.

Q10. Define Web Services Metadata (WS-Metadata) Specification.

Ans. The WS-Metadata specification provides annotations which are used to develop and deploy Web services on Java SE 6 and Java EE 6 platforms. This API makes development, deployment, and invocation of Web service easy.

Q11. Define Java for XML Binding (JAXB).

Ans. The JAXB 2.2 specification helps to bind XML instances with Java classes. This can be done in the following ways:

- Developers first create Java classes and then the JAXB 2.2 schema generator is used for generating the XML schema from these Java classes
- Developers first have XML schema which is used for generating Java classes using the JAXB 2.2 schema compiler

Q12. Define Streaming API for XML (StAX).

Ans. The StAX 1.0 specification is a joint effort of BEA and Sun Microsystems. The StAX API allows programmers to perform iterative and event based processing of XML documents, which are considered as filtered series of events.

Q13. Define Java API for XML Registries (JAXR).

Ans. The Java API for XML Registries (JAXR) API allows the different kinds of XML registries to be accessed in a uniform and standardized manner. XML registries provide an enabling infrastructure that aids in building, deployment, and discovery of Web services.

Q14. Define SOAP with Attachments API for Java (SAAJ).

Ans. You can build Web service applications directly using XML messages instead of using JAX-WS API. These applications work with SOAP messages using SOAP with Attachments API for Java (SAAJ). SAAJ specification helps in creating a SOAP message on sender side and in transmitting on receiver side.

Q15. What is schema generator?

Ans. Schema generator performs the reverse operation to that of the schema compiler. It maps a collection of schema-based program elements to a source schema by using Java annotations.

Q16. What is schema compiler?

Ans. Schema compiler binds a source schema to a collection of schema-based program elements by using the JAXB 2.2 binding language.

Q17. What is port component?

Ans. The WSEE specification defines port component as a component which is packaged and deployed on container to implement a Web service. In JAVA EE 1.4, WSEE 1.0 specification includes artifacts for deployment in a port component, such as SEI, Web services Deployment Descriptor (webservices.xml), and JAX-RPC mapping Deployment Descriptor. In Java EE 6, WSEE 1.3 specifications makes optional to include artifacts, such as WSDL document, SEI, and webservices.xml. If developer defines the webservices.xml Deployment Descriptor, then descriptor overrides the deployment information specified in annotations.

Q18. Define servlet and EJB endpoints.

Ans. Servlet endpoint: Refers to the Service implementation bean which when implemented as a servlet class is known as servlet endpoint.

EJB Endpoint: Implies that the WSEE 1.3 specification allows a stateless session bean to implement a Web service deployed in an EJB container. This stateless session bean is also known as EJB endpoint.

Q19. Define Service Implementation Bean (SIB).

Ans. WS-Metadata 2.2 specifies some conditions on Java class to deploy it as a Web service. The Java classes that satisfy these conditions are known as Service Implementation Beans.

Q20. Define SEI.

Ans. The SEI is key artifact in a port component that is deployed on application server.

Q21. What is a registry?

Ans. A registry can be defined as a shared resource among number of different business to make Business to Business (B2B) interaction possible in a flexible way and in the form of web-based service. In the Web service architecture, the registry plays a key role as it is used to publish, find, and utilize Web services.

Q22. What find methods BusinessQueryManager interface provides to search data from a JAXR registry?

Ans. The BusinessQueryManager interface provides several find methods to search data on the basis of JAXR information model. Important methods used for search purpose are given as follows:

- **findOrganizations** – Returns a BulkResponse object that is a collection of organizations having a specified name pattern a specific category
- **findServices** – Returns a BulkResponse object that is a collection of services which a particular organization offers
- **findServiceBindings** – Returns a BulkResponse object that is a set of service bindings supported by a particular service

Q23. What are the various ways of deploying Java EE 6Web services?

Ans. The different deployment methods provided by WSEE specification are given as follows:

- Deployment using a servlet endpoint
- Deployment using an EJB endpoint
- Deployment without Deployment Descriptors
- Deployment with Deployment Descriptor

20

Working with Struts 2

Struts 2 is an open source framework for creating Java Web applications; or in other words, it is released to the public domain free of charge. The Struts 2 Framework is designed for creating Web applications based on MVC architecture. As Struts 2 is based on the MVC architecture; it separates the business logic code, page design code, and navigational code into three different components called model, view, and controller. The introduction of these three components helps developers to easily maintain large Web applications. The Struts 2 Framework includes a library of markup tags, which are used to create dynamic data. These markup tags interact with the validation mechanism of Struts 2 to ensure that the output is correct. The tag library can be used with JavaServer Pages (JSP), Velocity, FreeMarker, JavaServer Pages Standard Tag Library (JSTL), and Asynchronous JavaScript and XML (AJAX) technology. The Struts Framework was introduced to support the development of a Web application with its set of Application Programming Interfaces (APIs). These APIs provide a specific architecture and a mechanism to reuse the model, view, and controller parts of a Web application.

This chapter describes the key features of Struts 2, such as interceptors, results, XWork Validation framework support, integration with Object Graph Navigation Language (OGNL), and implementation of Inversion of Control (IoC), which make this framework stand apart from other frameworks.

Introducing Struts 2

Struts1 was the first version of the Struts Framework. With the changing technology, the need for new enhancements and changes was felt in the original design of Struts 1. These changes include development of new and lightweight MVC-based frameworks, such as Spring, Stripes, Tapestry, and so on, to enable rapid development of Web applications. Therefore, it became necessary to modify the Struts Framework. Two new frameworks, Shale and Struts Ti were introduced in response to the growing need for rapid development of Web applications. Then in March 2002, the WebWork Framework was released. WebWork includes new ideas, concepts and functionality with the original Struts code. In December 2005, WebWorks and the Struts Ti merged to develop Struts 2.

Struts 2 has features similar to Struts 1, but the Struts 2 Framework has some architectural differences as compared to Struts 1. In general, the Struts 2 Framework implements the MVC 2 architecture by centralizing the control using a front controller strategy similar to Struts 1. However, the basic code of components and their configuration is quite different in Struts 2.

Explaining MVC 2 Design Pattern for Struts 2

The Struts 2 Framework follows the MVC framework, where model, view, and controller components are represented by Action, Result, and FilterDispatcher classes, respectively. Figure 20.1 shows the implementation of the MVC pattern by Struts 2 components:

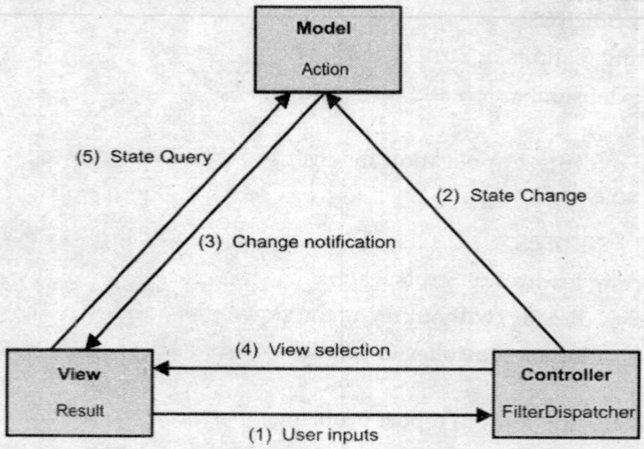

Figure 20.1: Implementing the MVC Pattern in Struts 2

According to Figure 20.1, the following are the steps for the work flow in Struts 2:

1. The user sends a request through a user interface provided by the view, which further passes this request to the controller, represented by `FilterDispatcher` class in Struts 2.

2. The controller servlet filter receives the input request coming from the user through the interface provided by the view, instantiates an object of the suitable action class, and executes different methods over this object.
3. If the state of model is changed, all the associated views are notified about the changes.
4. Next, the controller selects the new view to be displayed according to the result code returned by the action class.
5. The view presents the user interface. The view queries about the state of the model to show the current data, which is retrieved from the action class.

The Need for Struts 2

Struts 2 is created with the intention to streamline the entire development cycle of Web applications, which includes building, deploying, and maintaining these Web applications. Each Web application development framework has its own architecture; and the way the components are designed and configured using these frameworks is also different. What makes Struts 2 a better option amongst the other frameworks can be explained with the help of the features provided by Struts 2. These features are categorized into build supporting features, deployment supporting features, and maintenance supporting features.

Build Supporting Features

The build supporting features of Struts 2 are:

- The stylesheet-driven form tags: Decrease coding effort and reduce the requirement for input validation.
- Smart checkboxes: Provide the capability to select or clear checkboxes in a form with a single click.
- Support for AJAX tags: Help design interactive Web applications.
- Integration with Spring application framework: Provides support to integrate applications created by using Struts 2 with the Spring application framework. Integration with Spring application framework provides more control on struts actions and allows applying Aspect Oriented Programming (AOP) technique rather than object-oriented code.
- Support for action chaining and file downloading: Specifies that results obtained after processing of a request can be processed further for action chaining and file downloading.
- Use of JavaBeans for form inputs: Helps in placing binary and String properties directly on Action class with the help of JavaBeans.
- Support for controller and model: Provides the controller and model to handle the role of interfaces in Struts 2, as interfaces are not used in the Struts 2 Framework.

Deployment Supporting Features

The deployment supporting features of Struts 2 are:

- Allows framework extension, automatic configuration, and use of plugins to enhance the capabilities of the framework
- Helps in debugging a Struts 2 application by ensuring that errors are reported precisely by indicating the location and line of an error

Maintenance Supporting Features

The maintenance supporting features of Struts 2 are:

- Help test Struts actions directly, without using the conventional HTTP objects to debug the application
- Allows easy customization of controller to handle the requests per action, since a new class is invoked for every new request
- Provides built-in debugging tools to report problems; therefore, less time is wasted in manual testing
- Supports JSP, FreeMarker, and Velocity tags that encapsulate the business logic

Processing Request in Struts 2

Similar to Struts 1, Struts 2 implements the front controller approach with the MVC 2 pattern, which means that there is a single controller component here. All requests are mapped to this front controller called org.apache.struts2.dispatcher.FilterDispatcher class. The main work of this controller is to map user requests to the appropriate action classes. Unlike Struts 1, where actions are used to hold the business logic and the model part is represented by JavaBeans, in Struts 2, both the business logic and the model are implemented as action components. In addition to JSP pages, view can be implemented by using other presentation layer technologies, such as the Velocity template, in Struts 2.

The request flow in Struts 2 Web application framework is shown in Figure 20.2:

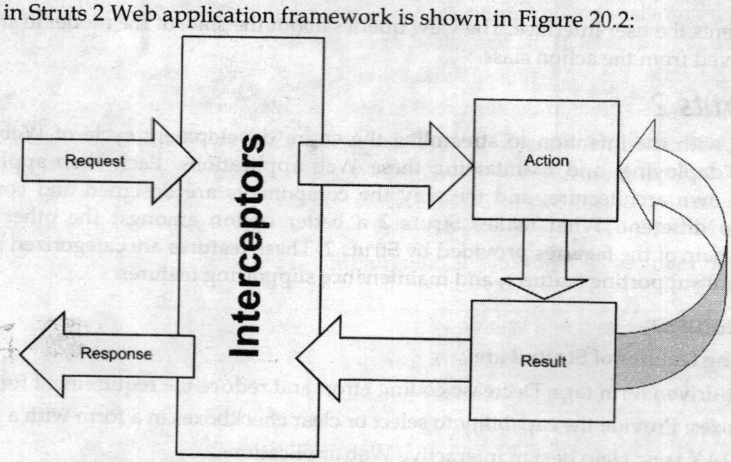

Figure 20.2: Processing Request in Struts 2

As evident from Figure 20.2, Struts 2 processes a request in the following steps:

1. **Request received**—Refers to the step in which the framework matches the request received from the user with the configuration file, struts-config.xml, to invoke the required interceptors, action class, and result class.
2. **Pre-processing by Interceptors**—Refers to the step in which the request passes through a series of interceptors. These interceptors perform certain tasks, such as initialization required to process a request.
3. **Invoke the Action class method**—Refers to the step in which a new instance of an action class is created and the method providing the logic for handling the request is invoked. Note that in Struts 2, a method to be invoked by an action class is specified in the configuration file.
4. **Invoke Result class**—Refers to the step in which the `Result` class determines the mapped class (in struts.xml) on the basis of the obtained result. Then, a new instance of this return class is created and invoked.
5. **Processing by Interceptors**—Refers to the step in which the response is passed through the interceptors in reverse order to perform any clean up or additional processing.
6. **Responding user**—Refers to the step to display the processed response back to the user by the servlet engine.

Exploring Relation between WebWork 2 and Struts 2

Struts 2 Framework is dependent on the WebWork 2 framework, and includes features of both the WebWork 2 and Struts 1 frameworks. Struts 2 inherits certain features from the WebWork 2 framework, such as interceptors, results, and so on. Several files and packages have been included from WebWork 2 in the Struts 2 Framework.

In addition, some features of WebWork 2 have been removed from Struts 2; while some new features have been added in the Struts 2 Framework.

Some features of WebWork 2 included in Struts 2 (with some modifications) are as follows:

- ❑ ConfigurationManager is not a static factory in Struts 2; instead, an instance is created through Dispatcher.
- ❑ The tooltip library used by the xhtml theme has been replaced by Dojo's tooltip component.
- ❑ Tiles integration is available as a plug-in in Struts 2.

- Use of wildcards in action mappings is allowed.
- The MessageStoreInterceptor class has been introduced in Struts 2 so that field errors or action errors can be stored and retrieved through a session. Action's messages are also stored and retrieved through the session.

The features that have been removed from WebWork 2 to develop Struts 2 are:

- **AroundInterceptor**—Refers to the class that has been removed from WebWork 2. If you are extending the AroundInterceptor class in your application, you need to import the AroundIntercepter class into the source code and modify it to serve as the base class, or rewrite the interceptor.
- **oldSyntax**—Refers to the oldSyntax attribute that has been removed from WebWork 2.
- **Rich text editor tag**—Refers to the tag that has been removed and replaced by the Dojo's rich text editor.
- **Default method**—Refers to the doDefault() method, which is not supported in Struts 2.
- **Inversion of Control Framework**—Refers to the framework that has been deprecated in WebWork 2.2 and removed in Struts 2. The Struts 2 Framework provides a Spring plugin to implement IoC. This is implemented by using the ObjectFactory factory.

In addition, certain features of WebWork 2, inherited by Struts 2, have been renamed in Struts 2, as listed in Table 20.1:

Table 20.1: Comparing Struts 2 and WebWork 2

Basis Of Comparison	WebWork 2	Struts 2
Action Support Class	com.opensymphony.xwork.*	com.opensymphony.xwork2.*
Interface	com.opensymphony.webwork.*	org.apache.struts2.*
Configuration File	xwork.xml	struts.xml
Properties File	webwork.properties	struts.properties
RequestDispatcher class	DispatcherUtil	Dispatcher
Configuration Settings class	com.opensymphony.webwork. config.Configuration	org.apache.struts2.config.Settings

Let's now discuss the implementation of MVC 2 architecture by Struts 2 Framework.

Describing Struts 2 Architecture

Struts 2 contains various framework components, such as built-in classes, servlets, and Struts tags. All the framework components work together in a standard manner. The architecture of Struts 2-based application defines the relationship and interaction between these framework components.

Components of a Struts 2-Based Application

The architecture of a Struts 2-based application has been shown in Figure 20.3:

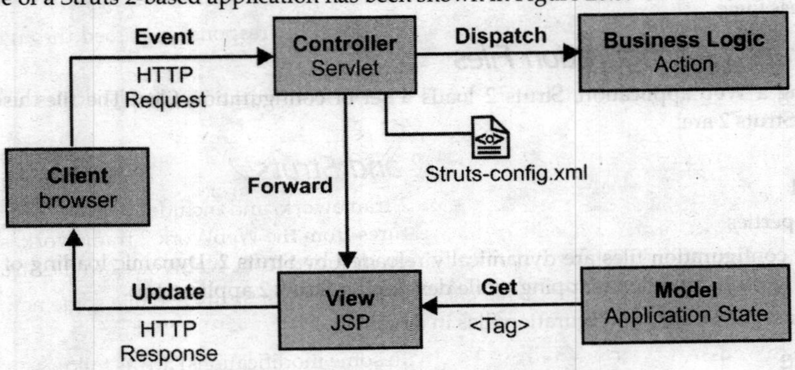

Figure 20.3: Displaying the Struts 2 Architecture

If we compare Figure 20.3 with Figure 20.1, we notice that a new group of components, called Business Logic, has been created. This can be seen as the separation of business logic from the model layer of the traditional

MVC architecture. The business logic component allows the model layer to store only the state of a Web application. The components created in the new group are known as action classes.

Let's discuss different Struts 2 components one by one next.

Controller

The controller receives the requests from users and decides where to send the request. The main aim of the controller is to map the request Uniform Resource Identifier (URI) to an action class using the mappings provided in the struts-config.xml file. There is a single controller Servlet and all requests go through this Servlet, which is provided by the framework itself.

The controller component available in Struts 2 Framework is the `ActionServlet` class that represents the controller in the MVC design pattern. In addition, `ActionServlet` class implements both the front controller and the singleton pattern. The front controller pattern allows a centralized access point for presentation-tier request handling, and the singleton pattern provides a single instance of an object.

You should note that the `ActionServlet` instance selects the appropriate action class that needs to perform the requested business logic and then invokes the `action` class. The action classes do not produce the next page of the user directly; rather it is the duty of the `RequestDispatcher` class to forward the control to an appropriate JSP page. Generally, the Servlet engine uses the `RequestDispatcher.forward()` method of the Servlet API to perform this task.

The struts-config.xml File

The `struts-config.xml` file contains the transformation and configuration information for the Struts application. It provides information regarding various Struts resources, such as action, classes, and interceptors. The relation between user requests, the action class to be invoked, the ActionForm class to be used, and the next possible views are defined in the struts-config.xml file using appropriate mappings.

Action Classes

Action classes implement the business logic; or, in other words, they behave as wrappers around the business logic and interact with the model of the application. They are basically responsible for executing the business service according to user requests.

Model

In the MVC architecture, model represents the data objects that are defined with the help of JavaBeans. In Struts 2, the model is represented by org.apache.struts.action.ActionForm class, which provides the methods to get and set data fields with methods to validate the data.

View

The view represents a JSP or HTML page, which encapsulates the presentation semantics. A view does not include business logic.

Exploring Struts 2 Configuration Files

For configuring a Web application, Struts 2 loads a set of configuration files. The files used to configure an application in Struts 2 are:

- web.xml
- struts.xml
- struts.properties

The preceding configuration files are dynamically reloaded by Struts 2. Dynamic loading of configuration files helps in reconfiguring the action mapping while developing Struts 2 application.

Let's now discuss the Struts 2 configuration files in detail.

The web.xml File

As Struts 2 applications include Servlet programs, it is necessary to keep the mapping functions inside the web.xml file. The web.xml file must reside in the WEB-INF folder of the Web application. The web.xml file is a deployment descriptor file, which represents the core of the Web application. The web.xml file defines the front controller, i.e. the `FilterDispatcher` class, which is a Servlet filter class used to initialize the Struts 2 Framework and manage all the incoming requests.

The FilterDispatcher class can contain initialization parameters to process any additional configuration files that are loaded by the Struts 2 Framework. These key initialization parameters are processed with the help of the <filter> element of the web.xml file. The following are key initialization parameters of the `FilterDispatcher` class:

- **config** – Loads a comma-delimited list of XML configuration files
- **actionPackages** – Provides a comma-delimited list of Java packages to locate the required action classes
- **configProviders** – Loads a comma-delimited list of Java classes used for configuring the action classes

The following code snippet shows how to process the key initialization parameters of the FilterDispatcher class with the help of the<filter> and <filter-mapping> elements of the web.xml file:

```
<?xml version="1.0" encoding="UTF-8"?>
<web-app version="3.1"
  xmlns="http://xmlns.jcp.org/xml/ns/javaee"
  xmlns:xsi="http://www.w3.org/2001/XMLSchema-instance"
  xsi:schemaLocation="http://xmlns.jcp.org/xml/ns/javaee
  http://xmlns.jcp.org/xml/ns/javaee/web-app_3_1.xsd">

<filter>
  <filter-name>struts</filter-name>
  <filter-class>
  org.apache.struts2.dispatcher.FilterDispatcher
  </filter-class>
</filter>
  <filter-mapping>
  <filter-name>struts</filter-name>
  <url-pattern>/*</url-pattern>
  </filter-mapping>

  <!-- ... -->
</web-app>
```

In the preceding code snippet, the <url-pattern>, which is set to /*, ensures that all requests are handled by the FilterDispatcher class. The `FilterDispatcher` class further handles the client requests and uses other configuration details given in different configuration files.

The struts.xml File

The struts.xml file is a default file for the Struts 2 Framework, also known as the core configuration file for this framework. The struts.xml file must be stored in the WEB-INF/classes folder of the Web application. This file contains various configuration details for framework specific components, such as actions, results, and interceptors.

If required, you can also insert other configuration files into the struts.xml file. The following code snippet shows how to load different configuration files in the struts.xml file:

```
<struts>
  <include file="struts-default.xml"/>
  <include file="config-browser.xml"/>
  <package name="default" extends="struts-default">
       ..........
  </package>
  <include file="other.xml"/>
</struts>
```

In the preceding code snippet, the first include statement instructs the Struts Framework to load the struts-default.xml file, which is found in the struts2-core-2.3.16.jar file. The struts-default.xml file defines the default bundled results, interceptors, and interceptor stacks. The files included in the struts.xml file are loaded in the order of their mappings.

The following code snippet shows an implementation of some of the important elements of the struts.xml file:

```
<?xml version="1.0" encoding="UTF-8" ?>
```

```
<!DOCTYPE struts PUBLIC
"-//Apache Software Foundation//DTD Struts Configuration 2.3//EN"
"http://struts.apache.org/dtds/struts-2.3.dtd">
<struts>
  <include file="struts-default.xml"/>
  <package name="default" extends="struts-default">
        <result-types>
              <result-type name="result1" class="SomeResultClass1"/>
              <result-type name="result2" class="SomeResultClass2"/>
        </result-types>
        <interceptors>
        <interceptor name="interceptor1" class="SomeInterceptorClass1"/>
        <interceptor name="interceptor2" class="SomeInterceptorClass2"/>
        <interceptor-stack name="SomeStack1">
              <interceptor-ref name="somename1" />
              <interceptor-ref name="somename2" />
        </interceptor-stack>
        </interceptors>
        <default-interceptor-ref name="defaultStack1"/>
        <global-results>
              <result name="resultname" type="resulttype1">/XXX</result>
        </global-results>
        <action name="action" class="SomeActionClass">
              <result name="success">some_page.jsp</result>
        </action>
  </package>
</struts>
```

In the preceding code snippet, the components of Struts 2 are configured in the struts.xml file. The various components or elements are configured under the opening and closing tags of the <struts> element. The default configuration file, struts-default.xml, has also been included in the struts.xml file. Only the elements usually configured in the struts.xml file are currently shown in the file. These elements include <result-types>, <interceptors>, <interceptorstack>, <global-results>, and <action>.

The struts.properties File

A Struts 2 application uses a number of properties, which can be changed according to the requirement of a user. These properties are specified in the struts.properties file, which is located in the WEB-INF/classes folder of the Web application. This property file is similar to other resource bundle files with the .properties extension. The property file contains key-value pairs, representing various properties and their values.

The struts.properties file can be used to override the default values of the keys set in the struts-default.properties file. For example, setting the struts.devMode property to true helps in debugging Struts-based applications. Table 20.2 describes different properties, which are defined in the struts-default.properties file and can be overridden in the struts.properties file:

Table 20.2: Properties of the struts-default.properties File

Properties	Description
struts.configuration = org.apache.struts2.config. DefaultConfiguration	Defines the configuration class required to configure Struts, and retrieves the configuration parameter.
struts.locale=en_US struts.i18n.encoding=UTF-8	Sets the default locale and encoding scheme in the Struts application.
struts.objectFactory=spring	Specifies that the default object factory can be overridden.
struts.objectFactory.spring. autoWire = name	Defines the autowiring logic when using the SpringObjectFactory class. The autowire property can be set to four options, such as name, type, auto, and constructor. The default value is name.
struts.objectFactory.spring.useClassCache = true	Specifies the Struts-Spring integration. If the class instance is cached, it should be set to true. By default, the value of this property is true.

Table 20.2: Properties of the struts-default.properties File

Properties	Description
`struts.objectTypeDeterminer = tiger`	Specifies that the default object type, determiner, can be overridden.
`struts.objectTypeDeterminer = notiger`	Specifies that the notiger value is used to disable tiger support.
`struts.enable.SlashesInActionNames = false`	Allows slashes in your action names. You need to set a boolean value for the `SlashesInActionNames` property. If false, action names cannot have slashes and will be accessible through any directory prefix. The value true is useful when you use wildcards and store the value in the URLs.
`struts.tag.altSyntax= true`	Uses alternative syntax containing %{} in most places used to evaluate the expression for String attributes of tags.
`struts.devMode = false`	Sets development mode by setting a boolean value for this property. When the true value is set, Struts 2 provides additional logging and debug information, which can speed up the process of Web application development.
`struts.configuration.xml.reload=false`	Reloads the struts.xml configuration file, when the file is changed.
`struts.url.http.port = 80` `struts.url.https.port =443`	Allows you to build URLs.
`struts.url.includeParams=get`	Sets the three possible options for this property: none, get or, all.
`struts.custom.i18n.resources=testmessages, testmessages2`	Loads the custom default resource bundles.
`struts.xslt.nocache=false`	Allows you to use stylesheet caching, by configuring the XSLTResult class and setting the value of this property to true.
`struts.mapper.alwaysSelectFullNamespace=false`	Defines whether or not to always select the namespace before the last slash provided in the namespace.

Let's now discuss Struts 2 applications that do not need XML files for configuration related matters.

Explaining Zero Configuration Applications

Zero configuration Struts 2 applications are Web applications that do not use additional files, such as XML and properties files, to configure different components of the Web application. Instead, annotations are used to provide details about the action class to be executed, the result to be used, validations, and type conversions.

Struts 2 support annotations, which provide information regarding configuring zero configuration Struts 2 applications. Let's discuss annotations in the next section.

Exploring Struts 2 Annotations

Annotations provide information to configure Zero configuration Struts 2 applications. In case of Java, annotation can be defined as a code segment that describes the Java classes, methods, and fields. Annotations are implemented as an interface and can be packaged, compiled, and imported similar to any other classes. Most of the time, the user wants to give more information to a particular piece of code. This is where annotation plays an important role. One of the benefits of the new annotation specification is that annotation enables you to create quite complex structures of Java classes or interfaces, while maintaining type safety.

Annotations in Struts 2 are generally divided into four different types:

- **Action annotations**—Represents the annotations used while creating an action class. There are different annotations available to configure namespace and results for a given action. Action classes need not be configured in the struts.xml file for their associated mapping. This results in Zero configuration for actions. There are different annotations, which help in defining namespace for the action, extending a class from the parent package, and associating the results with the actions. Generally, these annotations are collectively known as action annotations. There are various types of action annotations, such as Namespace annotation, ParentPackage annotation, Result annotation, and Results annotation.

- **Interceptor annotations**—Represents the annotations used to configure different methods of the action class. This ensures that an action class method is invoked before or after the execute() method; consequently intercepting the execution path. There are three types of interceptor annotations: @After annotation, @Before annotation, and @BeforeResult annotation.
- **Validation annotations**—Represents the validation annotations that help in implementing validation rules on various validation fields, without mapping them in the XML files. Different validation annotations are provided for corresponding validation rules. We can use different validation annotation in methods to validate the data being set. Similar to other annotations, these annotations have their own set of attributes. The most frequently used validation annotations are @ConversionErrorFieldValidator, @DateRangeFieldValidator, @DoubleRangeFieldValidator, @EmailValidator, @IntRangeFieldValidator, @RequiredFieldValidator, @RequiredStringValidator, and @StringLengthFieldValidator, @UrlValidator, @CustomValidator.
- **Type conversion annotations**—Represents the type conversion annotation that provides the mechanisms to avoid the use of any ClassName-conversion.properties file. There are six kinds of type conversion annotations: @Conversion annotation, @CreateIfNull annotation, @Element annotation, @Key annotation, @KeyProperty annotation, and @TypeConversion annotation.

We learned about the rich set of annotations available in Struts 2, which can be used with the code to reduce the declaration in configuration files. Let's now discuss mechanism to implement actions in Struts 2.

Understanding Actions in Struts 2

Struts 2 is a front controller based framework, i.e., there is a single controller that handles all the requests and executes an appropriate action in response to those requests. Specific classes, known as *action classes,* are executed to process the response to requests. We can have a number of action classes that embed different business logics for a particular user action. The flow of execution of an action class involves a sequential invocation of different methods. This sequence of method invocation is handled by different interceptors, which simply pre-process the request before executing the main logic embedded in the action class.

Struts 2 has introduced a simpler implementation for the action class, which can be created by implementing some interfaces, extending some classes, or even using Plain Old Java Objects (POJOs). In other words, creating and configuring action classes have become more flexible and simpler in Struts 2.

Let's now discuss the mechanism of creating, configuring, and using action classes in Struts 2.

Action ***Classes***

The action classes are configured to be executed when a particular request for these actions is submitted. An action class contains the execute() method as the default entry point where the execution of the action class starts. The next process to be performed depends on the result returned by the action class, which may include rendering the next JSP page or invoking another action. The following code snippet provides the execute() method of action classes in Struts 2:

```
//execute() method of Struts 2 action classes
public String execute() throws Exception {
  //some logic implementation
}
```

In the preceding code snippet, the execute() method returns a String value from a set of standard values that are defined to be returned by the execute() method. These standard values are success, input, error, none, and login, which are returned by the execute() method of Struts 2 action classes. When the String value returned by the execute() method of an action class is matched with a result configured for that action class in struts.xml file, the JSP page set for that result is executed.

In Struts 1, an action class can be created by extending the org.apache.struts.action.Action class only, while in Struts 2 there are different ways to create an action class. Struts 2 provides flexibility in creating a new action class by implementing the com.opensymphony.xwork2.Action interface or by extending the com.opensymphony.xwork2.ActionSupport class. In addition, Struts 2 supports pure Java classes to be treated as actions classes, known as POJO actions, which enable us to create action classes without implementing any interface and extending any class. The only convention to be followed is the availability of the execute() method in the action classes.

We can create different action classes for different use cases. For every request, an action mapping is searched and the associated action class methods are invoked. Struts 2 actions are not singletons; in other words, for each request, a different instance of the action class is created. Therefore, Struts 2 action need not be thread safe, as in case of Struts 1 actions. So, how can we access different objects to work with, such as request, response, and session? The solution to this problem is Dependency Injection (DI) pattern.

The Dependency Injection pattern used in Struts 2 is interface injection. This means that we can implement various interfaces that provide different methods to the action class. These implemented methods should be invoked in the predefined order, which is assured by the use of appropriate interceptors configured for the action.

Let's now discuss the various interfaces and classes used to create, configure, and execute the action class. Some of these interfaces and classes are:

- The Action interface
- The ActionSupport class
- The ActionMapping class
- The DefaultAction class
- The ActionContext class

The Action Interface

Though we can create action classes without implementing any interface and extending any class, the Struts 2 Framework provides an interface that can be used to create action classes to simplify the code in the action classes. The com.opensymphony.xwork2.Action interface provides the `execute()` method to execute the action class. In addition, the Action interface provides common results (SUCCESS and ERROR) as string constants, which are described in Table 20.3:

Table 20.3: String Constants of the Action Interface

Field Name	Description
`static String ERROR`	Specifies that the execution of action has failed
`static String INPUT`	Specifies that the action class requires more input to be executed
`static String LOGIN`	Specifies that the execution of the action class needs a logged in user
`static String NONE`	Specifies that the execution of the action class has been successful, but no view is provided
`static String SUCCESS`	Specifies that the execution of action was successful

The `Action` interface provides the execute() method, which all action classes implementing this interface must override. The following code snippet shows how to create a sample action class by using the `Action` interface:

```
import com.opensymphony.xwork2.Action;
public class SomeAction implements Action{
  public String execute() throws Exception {
       return SUCCESS;
  }
}
```

In the preceding code snippet, an action class called `SomeAction` implements the `Action` interface. The `Action` interface provides the `execute()` method to the `SomeAction` class. The `execute()` method returns `SUCCESS` as a result type for this action class.

The ActionSupport Class

The `ActionSupport` class provides basic implementation for common actions, such as validation. The ActionSupport class implements various interfaces, such as `Action`, `LocaleProvider`, `TextProvider`, `Validateable`, `ValidationAware`, and `Serializable`. We can create the action classes by extending the `ActionSupport` class and overriding the required methods.

We will now briefly discuss some of these interfaces.

The Validateable Interface

The `com.opensymphony.xwork2.Validateable` interface provides a `validate()` method to validate an action class. You must override the `validate()` method in the action class to implement your logic to validate the data.

The LocaleProvider Interface

The `com.opensymphony.xwork2.LocaleProvider` interface provides a getLocale() method to specify the locale to be used for getting localized messages. This locale is used in an action class to override the default locale, whenever needed. A locale refers to an object representing a particular geographical, political, or cultural region.

The ValidationAwareInterface

The `com.opensymphony.xwork2.ValidationAware` interface provides methods to save and retrieve class-level actions and field-level error messages. Collections classes are used to store/retrieve action level error messages, and maps classes are used to store/retrieve field-level error messages. Table 20.4 describes the methods of the `ValidationAware` interface:

Table 20.4: Methods of the ValidationAware Interface

Methods	Description
`void addActionError(String anErrorMessage)`	Adds an action-level error message to the current action
`void addActionMessage(String aMessage)`	Adds an action-level message to the current action
`void addFieldError(String fieldName, String errorMessage)`	Adds an error message for the specified field
`Collection getActionErrors()`	Retrieves the collection of action-level error messages for this action
`Collection getActionMessages()`	Retrieves the collection of action-level messages for this action
`boolean hasErrors()`	Verifies whether there are any errors (action level or field level) set or not
`boolean hasFieldErrors()`	Verifies whether there are any field errors associated with this action
`void setActionErrors (Collection errorMessages)`	Sets the collection of action-level String error messages
`void setActionMessages (Collection messages)`	Sets the collection of action-level String messages instead of errors
`void setFieldErrors(Map errorMap)`	Sets the field error map of fieldname (String) to collection of String error messages

The TextProvider Interface

The `com.opensymphony.xwork2.TextProvider` interface provides methods for getting localized message texts. The `TextProvider` interface is used to access the text messages in the resource bundle. Table 20.5 describes various methods of the `TextProvider` interface:

Table 20.5: Methods of the TextProvider Interface

Methods	Description
`String getText(String key)`	Retrieves a message on the basis of a message key. However, if the message is not found, the null value is returned.

Table 20.5: Methods of the TextProvider Interface

Methods	Description
`String getText(String key, List args)`	Retrieves a message on the basis of the message key using the specified `args` provided in the form of a list, as defined in `MessageFormat`. However, if no message is found, the null value is returned.
`String getText(String key, String defaultValue)`	Retrieves a message on the basis of the message key. However, if the message is not found, the supplied default value is returned.
`String getText(String key, String[] args)`	Retrieves a message on the basis of a key and using the args supplied in the form of String type array, as defined in MessageFormat. However, if no message is found, the null value is returned.
`String getText(String key, String defaultValue, List args)`	Retrieves a message on the basis of a key and using the supplied args, as defined in MessageFormat. However, if the message is not found, a supplied default value is returned.
`String getText(String key, String defaultValue, List args, ValueStack stack)`	Retrieves a message on the basis of a key using the supplied args provided in the form of a list, as defined in MessageFormat and the specified value stack. However, if the message is not found, the supplied default value is returned.
`String getText(String key, String defaultValue, String obj)`	Retrieves a message on the basis of a key using the supplied obj, as defined in MessageFormat. However, if the message is not found, the supplied default value is returned.
`String getText(String key, String defaultValue, String[] args)`	Retrieves a message on the basis of a key using the supplied args in the form of the String type array, as defined in MessageFormat. However, if the message is not found, a supplied default value is returned.
`String getText(String key, String defaultValue, String[] args, ValueStack stack)`	Retrieves a message on the basis of a key using the supplied args provided in the form of String type array, as defined in MessageFormat, and value stack. However, if the message is not found, a supplied default value is returned.
`ResourceBundle getTexts()`	Retrieves the resource bundle related to the implementing class (usually an action).
`ResourceBundle getTexts(String bundleName)`	Retrieves the named bundle, such as com/kogent/demo

The `com.opensymphony.xwork2.ActionSupport` class provides default definitions of the methods of all the interfaces implemented by it. Therefore, we can create the action classes by extending the `ActionSupport` class and use these methods in our action classes. The following code snippet shows an action class, `LoginAction`, which extends the `ActionSupport` class:

```
import com.opensymphony.xwork2.ActionSupport;
public class LoginAction extends ActionSupport {
   private String username;
   private String password;
   public String getUsername() {
        return username;
   }
   public void setUsername(String username) {
        this.username = username;
   }
   public String getPassword() {
        return password;
   }
   public void setPassword(String password) {
        this.password = password;
   }
   public String execute() throws Exception {
        if(username.equals(password))
```

```
            return SUCCESS;
            else{
                    this.addActionError(getText("app.invalid"));
                    return ERROR;
            }
        }
        public void validate() {
            if ( (username == null ) || (username.length() == 0) ) {
            this.addFieldError("username", getText("app.username.blank"));
            }
            if ( (password == null ) || (password.length() == 0) ) {
            this.addFieldError("password", getText("app.password.blank"));
            }
        }
    }
```

In the preceding code snippet, the action class called `LoginAction` is created by implementing the `ActionSupport` class.

The ActionMapping Class

The `ActionMapping` class is used to provide configuration associated with an action name and action class. It specifies a mapping between HTTP requests and action invocation requests, and vice-versa. For a given HttpServletRequest, the `org.apache.struts2.dispatcher.mapper.ActionMapper` interface may return null if no action invocation request matches; otherwise it may return an instance of the `org.apache.struts2.dispatcher.mapper` type. The `ActionMapping` class describes an action invocation for the Web application.

Let's now discuss the methods of the ActionMapping class, as described in Table 20.6:

Table 20.6: Methods of the ActionMapping Class

Method	Description
`String getMethod()`	Returns the method name
`String getName()`	Returns the name of the action
`String getNamespace()`	Returns the namespace for the action
`Map getParams()`	Returns the Map containing name/value pairs for action parameters
`Result getResult()`	Returns the result
`void setMethod(String method)`	Sets the method name
`void setName(String name)`	Sets the action name
`void setNamespace(String namespace)`	Sets the namespace name
`void setParams(Map params)`	Sets a Map of parameters
`void setResult(Result result)`	Sets the result

The action mappings are the basic units of work in the Struts 2 Framework, which map an identifier to a handler class. When a request matches with the name of the action, the specified mapping is used by the Struts Framework to determine how to process the request. Action mapping provides a set of result types, a set of exception handlers, and an Interceptor stack. In a Web application, every resource should be referred to a Uniform Resource Identifier (URI), which includes HTML pages, custom actions, and JSP pages. The Struts Framework provides this facility by using action mapping, which is defined in the struts.xml configuration file. A sample action mapping is shown in the following code snippet:

```
<?xml version="1.0" encoding="UTF-8" ?>
<!DOCTYPE struts PUBLIC
"-//Apache Software Foundation//DTD Struts Configuration 2.3//EN"
"http://struts.apache.org/dtds/struts-2.3.dtd ">
<struts>
   <include file="struts-default.xml"/>
   <package name="default" extends="struts-default">
```

```
            <action name="login" class="com.kogent.action.LoginAction">
                    <interceptor-ref name="exception"/>
                    <interceptor-ref name="params"/>
                    <interceptor-ref name="workflow"/>
                    <result name="success">/login_success.jsp</result>
                    <result name="error">/login.jsp</result>
                    <result name="input">/login.jsp</result>
            </action>
    </package>
</struts>
```

The Default Action

The default action class is used when an action is requested but is not configured in the struts.xml. In such a case, a default action class can be invoked, which performs an action to prevent error pages from being displayed if a request does not map with the appropriate action. In other words, if no action matches in the struts configuration file, the default action class is used to display JSP result of an application.

The following code snippet shows a default action configured in a struts configuration file:

```
<package name="my-default" extends="struts-default">
   <default-action-ref name="remove">
   <action name="remove" >
           <result>/index.jsp</result>
   </action>
</package>
```

In the preceding code snippet, a default action called remove is configured to generate a view in case Struts 2 is unable to locate the requested action class. In the preceding code snippet, the remove action returns a JSP page called index.jsp as a default view to the user. Let's now discuss the methods of an action class.

The main method in any action class is its String execute() method, which is executed by default to accomplish some defined business logics. Struts 2 action classes provide flexibility of defining methods and invoking them directly by using action configuration. Therefore, for different requests, we can execute different methods of the same action class, provided these methods have a signature similar to the execute() method. This eliminates the need for creating different action classes for different actions.

Let's suppose we have two different action classes for adding and editing an employee. We can group similar type of actions into a single action class. The execute() methods of both these classes operate on a similar set of data and require similar set of validation rules to be followed. We can create a single action class (UpdateEmployeeAction), and two execute() methods of the two action classes can be converted into two different methods of this new class. These methods can be String addEmployee() and String editEmployee(). The following code snippet shows an action class using the `methodName()` method:

```
package com.kogent.action;
import com.opensymphony.xwork2.ActionSupport;
public class UpdateEmployeeAction extends ActionSupport {
   public String execute() throws Exception {
           //some logic
           return SUCCESS;
   }
   public String addEmployee() throws Exception {
           //Logic fo add new employee
           return SUCCESS;
   }
   public String editEmployee() throws Exception {
           //Logic to edit employee
           return SUCCESS;
   }
}
```

In the preceding code snippet, the addEmployee() and editEmployee() methods provide logic for adding and editing employees' details in a single class called `UpdateEmployeeAction`. Keeping these methods in a single class eliminates the need to create two separate classes for adding and editing employee details.

Let's now explore how to configure these action methods in the struts.xml file, as shown in the following code snippet:

```
<?xml version="1.0" encoding="UTF-8" ?>
<!DOCTYPE struts PUBLIC
"-//Apache Software Foundation//DTD Struts Configuration 2.3//EN"
"http://struts.apache.org/dtds/struts-2.3.dtd ">
<struts>
   <include file="struts-default.xml"/>
   <package name="default" extends="struts-default">
          <action name="add"
                 class="com.kogent.action.UpdateEmployeeAction"
                 method="addEmployee">
                 <result name="success">/add_success.jsp</result>
                 <result name="error">/add.jsp</result>
                 <result name="input">/add.jsp</result>
          </action>
          <action name="edit"
                 class="com.kogent.action.UpdateEmployeeAction"
                 method="editEmployee">
                 <result name="success">/edit_success.jsp</result>
                 <result name="error">/edit.jsp</result>
                 <result name="input">/edit.jsp</result>
          </action>
   </package>
</struts
```

The preceding code snippet adds and edits employee details by mapping the addEmployee() and editEmployee() methods in the struts.xml file.

The **ActionContext** Class

The ActionContext class provides objects required to execute an action class. The ActionContext class provides objects such as request, response, session, parameters locale, and so on. We can obtain the reference of this class by using its own static getContext() method, as shown in the following syntax:

```
ActionContext context = ActionContext.getContext();
```

As the execute() method of Struts 2 action classes does not take any argument, we need a mechanism to access objects, such as request, response, and session. The `ActionContext` class helps obtain these objects in the action class. The following code snippet shows the use of the `ActionContext` class:

```
import javax.servlet.http.HttpServletRequest;
import javax.servlet.http.HttpSession;
import com.opensymphony.xwork2.ActionSupport;
import com.opensymphony.xwork2.ActionContext;
import org.apache.struts2.ServletActionContext;
public class SomeAction extends ActionSupport {
   public String execute() throws Exception {
          ActionContext acx=ActionContext.getContext();
          HttpServletRequest request=
          (HttpServletRequest)acx.get(ServletActionContext.HTTP_REQUEST);
          request.setAttribute("name", "John");
          HttpSession session=
          (HttpSession)acx.get(ServletActionContext.SESSION);
          session.setAttribute("user", "kogent");
          return SUCCESS;
   }
}
```

After obtaining the reference of the `ActionContext` class using `getContext()` method, the `getContext()` method returns the value stored in the current `ActionContext` class by looking up the value for the key passed as an argument to it.

Table 20.7 describes the fields of the `ActionContext` class:

Table 20.7: Fields of the ActionContext Class

Field Name	Description
`static String ACTION_INVOCATION`	Represents a constant for the invocation context of an action
`static String ACTION_NAME`	Represents a constant for the name of the action being executed

Table 20.7: Fields of the ActionContext Class

Field Name	Description
static String APPLICATION	Represents a constant for an action application context
static String CONVERSION_ERRORS	Represents a constant for the map of type conversion errors
static String LOCALE	Represents a constant for an action locale
static String PARAMETERS	Represents a constant for an action parameters
static String SESSION	Represents a constant for an action session
static String TYPE_CONVERTER	Represents a constant for an action type converter
static String VALUE_STACK	Represents a constant for the OGNL value stack

Let's now discuss the methods of the ActionContext class, as specified in Table 20.8:

Table 20.8: Methods of the ActionContext Class

Method	Description
Object get(Object key)	Performs a lookup by using the specified key and returns a value that is stored in the current ActionContext class
ActionInvocation getActionInvocation()	Retrieves the action invocation (the execution state)
Map getApplication()	Returns a map of the ServletContext class
static ActionContext getContext()	Returns the ActionContext class associated with the current thread
Map getContextMap()	Returns the context map object
Map getConversionErrors()	Returns the map of conversion errors occurred during execution of an action
Locale getLocale()	Returns the locale of the current action
String getName()	Gets the name of the current action
Map getParameters()	Returns a map of the HttpServletRequest parameters
Map getSession()	Returns a map of HttpSession values
ValueStack getValueStack()	Returns the OGNL value stack
void put(Object key, Object value)	Stores a specified value against a specified key in the current ActionContext
void setActionInvocation(ActionInvocation actionInvocation)	Sets the action invocation (the execution state)
void setApplication(Map application)	Sets the application context of the action
static void setContext(ActionContext context)	Sets the action context for the current thread
void setContextMap(Map contextMap)	Sets the action's context map
void setConversionErrors(Map conversionErrors)	Sets conversion errors occurred during the execution of the action
void setLocale(Locale locale)	Sets the Locale for the current action
void setName(String name)	Sets the name of the current Action in the ActionContext class
void setParameters(Map parameters)	Sets the action parameters
void setSession(Map session)	Sets a map of action session values
void setValueStack(ValueStack stack)	Sets the OGNL Value Stack

Another class that stores Web-specific context information for actions is `ServletActionContext` class, which is a subclass of `ActionContext`. In addition to extending fields and methods from ActionContext, the ServletActionContext class also implements the `org.apache.struts2.StrutsStatics` interface. Table 20.9 describes the fields of the `ServletActionContext` class:

Table 20.9: Fields of the ServletActionContext Class

Field Name	Description
`static String ACTION_MAPPING`	Refers to the static final String type field having value struts.actionMapping
`static String STRUTS_VALUESTACK_KEY`	Represents the key for the associated value stack and its value is struts.valueStack

Let's now discuss the methods of the `ServletActionContext` class in Table 20.10:

Table 20.10: Methods of the ServletActionContext Class

Method	Description
`static ActionContext getActionContext (HttpServletRequest req)`	Returns the current action context
`static ActionMapping getActionMapping()`	Returns the action mapping for the current context
`static PageContext getPageContext()`	Returns the HTTP page context
`static HttpServletRequest getRequest()`	Returns the HTTP Servlet request object
`static HttpServletResponse getResponse()`	Returns the HTTP servlet response object
`static ServletContext getServletContext()`	Returns the Servlet context
`static ValueStack getValueStack (HttpServletRequest req)`	Returns the current value stack for this request
`static void setRequest (HttpServletRequest request)`	Sets the HTTP Servlet request object
`static void setResponse (HttpServletResponse response)`	Sets the HTTP Servlet response object
`static void setServletContext (ServletContext servletContext)`	Sets the current Servlet context object

Let's now discuss about POJO to create action classes.

POJO as Action

POJOs are Java objects that neither implement an interface nor extend a Java class. A POJO object is a pure Java object and does not depend on other APIs. The creation of POJO objects is simple; and therefore, better to design, debug, and test. Struts 2 provides the facility to use POJO as an action class. The methods of POJO action must agree with the contracts defined for them in the Struts 2 specification; for example the signature of the execute() method (). The following code snippet shows a POJO as an action class:

```
public class SomeAction{
public String execute() throws Exception {
return "success";
```

The importance of POJO as action is that we do not need to use extra objects in the Struts Framework. It is faster, simpler, and easier to develop. POJO organizes and manages the business logic, database communication, transactions, and database concurrency.

Implementing Actions in Struts 2

Let's create an application to learn how to implement actions in Struts 2. The application created in this subsection adds some users in the application context and the list of available users is maintained throughout the running application. We can also edit and delete user information. To do this, we create JSP files and action classes, along with modifications in the configuration files, followed by the deployment and testing of our Struts 2 based Web application. Perform the following steps to create the Struts2App Web application:

- Setting Struts 2 environment
- Creating Home page
- Creating action class and JSP file
- Creating UserAction as ActionForm
- Creating Action class and JSP file for editing
- Exploring the directory structure of the application
- Packaging, Deploying, and Running the application

Now, let's study each of them in detail.

Setting Struts 2 Environment

Before getting started with developing Struts applications, you need to first prepare the development environment. This includes getting Struts 2 APIs in the form of JARs. The JAR files provide support to Web container for managing the Web application with the components of Struts Framework.

To develop a Struts 2 based Web application, you need to install Struts 2 APIs. You can download the latest version of Struts 2 APIs from the Apache Web site (`https://struts.apache.org/release/2.3.x/`). The latest available release of Struts 2 is Struts 2.3.16. Download the binary distribution of Struts 2.3.16 on your computer system.

After you have downloaded the Struts 2.3.16 distribution, you can develop Web application using Struts 2 APIs, which are available in the form of JARs. Extract the Struts 2 archive (struts-2.3.16-all.zip) and save it on your local disk, say `D:\Struts2`. A directory named struts-2.3.16 will be created in `D:\Struts2`.

Other important subdirectories that can be found in the struts-2.3.16 directory are as follows:

- **D:\Struts2\struts-2.3.16\apps**—Contains .war files for sample Struts 2 applications.
- **D:\Struts2\struts-2.3.16\lib**—Contains all Struts 2 JAR files that are required for Struts 2 based Web applications. These JAR files contain Strut 2 API in the form of interfaces, classes, and some default configuration files.

Creating Home Page

Let's create a home page in the `Struts2App` application, index.jsp. This page simply contains some hyperlinks to run different JSP pages and actions.

Let's create a client view, `index.jsp` page, which acts as the home page of our application. Listing 20.1 shows the index.jsp page (save the index.jsp file in the \Struts2App folder):

Listing 20.1: Displaying the Code of the `index.jsp File`

```
<%@page contentType="text/html;charset=UTF-8" language="java"%>
<%@taglib uri="/struts-tags" prefix="s"%>
<html>
   <head>
          <title>Struts 2 Actions<title>
          </head>
   <body>
          <center>
                   <h2>
                            Struts 2 Actions
                   </h2>
                   <br>
                   <br>
                   Welcome
                   <s:property value="#session.user" default="Guest" />!
                   <s:if test="#session.user!=null">
                            <s:url id="logout" action="logout" />
                            | <s:a href="%{logout}">Logout</s:a> |
                   </s:if>
```

```
                <br>
                <table cellspacing="5" width="180">
                        <tr bgcolor="#f0edd9" height="25" align="center">
                        <td>
                        <s:url id="hello" action="hello" />
                        <s:a href="%{hello}">Hello Action</s:a>
                        </td>
                        </tr>
                        <tr bgcolor="#f0edd9" height="25" align="center">
                        <td>
                        <s:a href="add_user.jsp">Add User</s:a>
                        </td>
                        </tr>
                        <tr bgcolor="#f0edd9" height="25" align="center">
                        <td>
                        <s:a href="user.jsp">View Users</s:a>
                        </td>
                        </tr>
                        <tr bgcolor="#f0edd9" height="25" align="center">

                        </tr>
                </table>
            </center>
        </body>
    </html>
```

In Listing 20.1, the hyperlinks, such as Add User, View User, and Logout, map to different JSP pages that are yet to be created. To make these hyperlinks work, we need to create different JSP pages, action classes, and other helping Java classes in the following sections.

Creating Action class and JSP file

Let's design some action classes for the `Struts2App` application. The first action class to be created is HelloAction. This action class is created by implementing the `com.opensymphony.xwork2.Action` interface. The action class can use String constants from the `Action` interface, such as SUCCESS and ERROR. Perform the following steps to create and configure the `HelloAction` class and also create the `hello.jsp` file:

- Creating the `HelloAction` class
- Configuring the `HelloAction` class
- Creating the `hello.jsp` file

Creating the HelloAction class

Let's create the HelloAction class that sets a String message field with the `Hello From Struts!` value. Listing 20.2 shows the `HelloAction` class (save the HelloAction.java file in the `\Struts2App\src\com\kogent\action` folder):

Listing 20.2: Displaying the Code of the HelloAction.java File

```
package com.kogent.action;

import com.opensymphony.xwork2.Action;

public class HelloAction implements Action {

   String message;

   public String getMessage() {
         return message;
   }

   public void setMessage(String message) {
         this.message = message;
   }

   public String execute() throws Exception {
```

```
            setMessage("Hello From Struts!");
            return SUCCESS;
        }
    }
```

Compile the HelloAction.java file and place HelloAction.class file in the WEB-INF/classes/com/kogent/action folder, as shown in the directory structure (Figure 20.4). All the properties defined in an action are pushed into its value stack. The value of these properties can be accessed in the next JSP page to be based on the result of String returned from this action class. The action class must have getter methods for all properties to access their values.

Configuring the HelloAction Class

All action classes need to be configured in Struts configuration file struts.xml, which provides action mapping for the corresponding action class. Listing 20.3 shows the struts.xml file; in which HelloAction class is configured (save thestruts.xml file in the \StrutsApp\WEB-INF\classes folder):

Listing 20.3: Displaying the Code of the struts.xml File

```
<?xml version="1.0" encoding="UTF-8" ?>
<!DOCTYPE struts PUBLIC
"-//Apache Software Foundation//DTD Struts Configuration 2.3//EN"
"http://struts.apache.org/dtds/struts-2.3.dtd ">
<struts>
   <include file="struts-default.xml"/>
   <package name="my-default" extends="struts-default">
          <action name="hello" class="com.kogent.action.HelloAction" >
                 <result name="success">hello.jsp</result>
          </action>
   </package>
</struts>
```

The action mapping for the `HelloAction` action class is provided in `struts.xml`. We can configure the list of interceptors and results for a particular action. The request path containing hello.action invokes the `HelloAction` action class, and executes the `execute()` method.

Creating the hello.jsp file

The `HelloAction` class returns the String, such as success or failure. If the String returned is success, then the action class consequently invokes the hello page. The `org.apache.struts2.dispatcher.mapper.ActionMapper` interface provides the mapping between HTTP requests and action invocation requests. If the action invocation request matches, this returns an object `org.apache.struts2.dispatcher.mapper.ActionMapping`; otherwise, it returns null. The object of the ActionMapping class holds action mapping information that is used to invoke a Struts action.

Listing 20.4 shows the code of the hello.jsp file (save the hello.jsp file in the `\Struts2App` folder):

Listing 20.4: Displaying the Code of the hello.jsp Page

```
<%@page contentType="text/html;charset=UTF-8" language="java"%>
<%@taglib uri="/struts-tags" prefix="s"%>
<html>
   <head>
          <title>Struts 2 Actions</title>

   </head>
   <body>
          <center>
                 <h2>
                 <s:property value="message" default="Struts Actions" />
                 </h2>
                 Welcome <s:property value="#session.user" default="Guest" />!
                 <br><br>
                 <s:if test="#session.user!=null">
                        <s:url id="logout" action="logout" />
                        | <s:a href="%{logout}">Logout</s:a> |
                 </s:if>
                 <br><br>| <s:a href="index.jsp">Back</s:a> |
```

```
        </center>
    </body>
</html>
```

The hello.jsp simply displays a text message from the value stack available.

The <s:property value="message" default="Struts Action" /> tag invokes the `getMessage()` method and obtains the message set by the `HelloAction` action. If not set, the default message is printed. Another `<s:property/>` tag displays the value of the user attribute from the session. If there is no user attributes in the session scope, the default `Guest` string is displayed.

Creating UserAction as ActionForm

Struts 2 eliminates the requirement of creating a separate ActionForm class, which is invoked when the user enters the input data. We can use the action fields as input properties by providing their setter and getter methods. For example, for a request parameter named `username`, we can declare a field `username` of String type in the action class with two methods—`void setUsername(String)` and `String getUsername()`. The action class field will automatically be populated with the data sent as the request parameter. This becomes possible only when the ParameterInterceptor is configured as one of the interceptors for the action. Let's now design some JSPs and an action class to show how it works. Let's perform the following broad-level steps:

- Creating UserAction class
- Creating add_user.jsp file
- Creating user.jsp file

Now, let's discuss each of them in detail.

Creating UserAction Class

Let's create the UserAction action class, which extends the ActionSupport class. Listing 20.5 shows the code of the UserAction action class (save the UserAction.java file in the `\Struts2App\src\com\kogent\action` folder):

Listing 20.5: Displaying the Code of the UserAction.java File

```
package com.kogent.action;
import java.util.ArrayList;
import java.util.Iterator;
import java.util.Map;
import org.apache.struts2.interceptor.ApplicationAware;
import com.kogent.User;
import com.opensymphony.xwork2.ActionSupport;
public class UserAction extends ActionSupport implements ApplicationAware{
   String username;
   String password;
   String city;
   String email;
   String type;
   Map application;
   public void setApplication(Map application) {
         this.application=application;
   }
   public String getUsername() {
         return username;
   }
   public void setUsername(String username) {
         this.username = username;
   }
   public String getPassword() {
         return password;
   }
   public void setPassword(String password) {
         this.password = password;
   }
   public String getCity() {
         return city;
```

```
    }
    public void setCity(String city) {
          this.city = city;
    }
    public String getEmail() {
          return email;
    }
    public void setEmail(String email) {
          this.email = email;
    }
    public String getType() {
          return type;
    }
    public void setType(String type) {
          this.type = type;
    }
    public String execute() throws Exception {
          ArrayList users=(ArrayList)application.get("users");
          if(users==null){
                users=new ArrayList();
          }
          if(getUser(username)==null){
                users.add(buildUser());
                application.put("users", users);
          }else{
                return ERROR;
          }
          return SUCCESS;
    }
    public User buildUser(){
          User user=new User();
          user.setUsername(username);
          user.setPassword(password);
          user.setCity(city);
          user.setEmail(email);
          user.setType(type);
          return user;
    }
    public User getUser(String username){
          User user=new User();
          boolean found=false;
          ArrayList users=(ArrayList)application.get("users");
          if(users!=null){
                Iterator it=users.iterator();
                while(it.hasNext()){
                      user=(User)it.next();
                      if(username.equals(user.getUsername())){
                            found=true;
                            break;
                      }
                }
                if(found){
                      return user;
                }
          }
          return null;
    }

}
```

The `UserAction` class extends the `ActionSupport` class and implements the `ApplicationAware` interface. The `ActionSupport` class itself implements different interfaces, such as Action, LocaleProvider, TextProvider, Validateable, and ValidationAware, and provides default implementations for the methods from these interfaces, which we can use in our action class.

The extending of the ActionSupport class enables you to use methods such as addFieldError(), addActionError(), and getText(). The implementation of the ApplicationAware interface uses an instance of the Map class, which can be used to store attributes within the application scope. The objects stored in the Map class are available in the whole application.

In the UserAction action class, the execute() method provides the implementation of the business logic to add a new user into an ArrayList, which is maintained in the application scope. The getUser() method searches for the user with the given username and returns an object of the User class. This class is a simple JavaBean that is used to group single user information. The users ArrayList in application scope basically contains the objects of the User class.

Listing 20.6 shows the code of the User class (save the User.java file in the \Struts2App\src\com\kogent folder):

Listing 20.6: Displaying the Code of the User.java File

```
package com.kogent;
public class User {
   String username;
   String password;
   String city;
   String email;
   String type;
   public String getUsername() {
         return username;
   }
   public void setUsername(String username) {
         this.username = username;
   }
   public String getPassword() {
         return password;
   }
   public void setPassword(String password) {
         this.password = password;
   }
   public String getCity() {
         return city;
   }
   public void setCity(String city) {
         this.city = city;
   }
   public String getEmail() {
         return email;
   }
   public void setEmail(String email) {
         this.email = email;
   }
   public String getType() {
         return type;
   }
   public void setType(String type) {
         this.type = type
   }
}
```

Another method of the UserAction action class is buildUser() that returns an object of the User class to be added into the ArrayList after populating it with the values of corresponding input properties. The execute() method makes sure that no two User objects with the same username are added into the application scoped ArrayList.

Now, add the action mapping shown in the following code snippet for the UserAction action class in the struts.xml file:

```
<struts>
  <include file="struts-default.xml"/>
  <package name="my-default" extends="struts-default">
  <action name="hello" . . . .>
```

```
        . . . .
    </action>
          <action name="adduser" class="com.kogent.action.UserAction" >
          <result name="input">add_user.jsp</result>
          <result name="error">add_user.jsp</result>
          <result name="success">user.jsp</result>
    </action>
    </package>
  </struts>
```

Creating the add_user.jsp File

The two JSP files, add_user.jsp and user.jsp, are configured based on the results provided by the action class. The add_user.jsp page provides a form with five input fields with names matching the input properties defined in the UserAction class.

Listing 20.7 shows the code of the add_user.jsp page (save the add_user.jsp file in the `\Struts2App` folder):

Listing 20.7: Displaying the Code of the add_user.jsp File

```
<%@page contentType="text/html;charset=UTF-8" language="java"%>
<%@taglib uri="/struts-tags" prefix="s"%>
<html>
   <head>
          <title>Struts 2 Actions
          </title>

   </head>
   <body>
          <center>
                 Adding User!
                 <br><br>
                 <table bgcolor="#f0edd9">
                 <tr><td>
                 <s:form action="adduser">
                 <s:textfield name="username" label="User Name" />
                 <s:password name="password" label="Password" size="15" />
                 <s:textfield name="city" label="City" />
                 <s:textfield name="email" label="E-Mail" />
                 <s:select label="Type" name="type" headerKey="1" headerValue="Select
                 Type" list="#@java.util.HashMap@{'Admin':'Admin', 'Client':'Client'}"
                 ></s:select>
                 <s:submit value="Add User" />
                 </s:form>
                 </td></tr>
                 </table>
                 <br>| <s:a href="index.jsp">Back</s:a> |
          </center>
   </body>
</html>
```

Listing 20.7 provides the action attribute of <s:form/> having the value adduser. This action attribute will use UserAction class for the processing of data entered into this form. We can click on "Add User" hyperlink, created in index.jsp, to display the add_user.jsp page.

Creating the user.jsp File

After entering the user information in the add_user.jsp page, click the Add User button to add a new user. If the username entered is unique, a new User object is added into an ArrayList, which is added into application scope. After the successful addition of a new user, the user.jsp page is displayed, which lists all the users added.

Listing 20.8 shows the code for user.jsp page (save the user.jsp file in the `\Struts2Action folder`):

Listing 20.8: Displaying the Code of the user.jsp File

```
<%@page contentType="text/html;charset=UTF-8" language="java" %>
<%@taglib uri="/struts-tags" prefix="s" %>
<html>
   <head>
          <title>Struts 2 Actions</title>
```

```
    </head>
    <body>
            <s:set name="users" value="#application.users"/>
            <table cellspacing="5" cellpadding="2" width="600">
                    <tr bgcolor="#f0edd9">
                            <td>User Name</td>
                            <td>Password</td>
                            <td>City</td>
                            <td>Email</td>
                            <td>Type</td>
                            <td colspan="2"> </td>
                    </tr>
                    <s:iterator id="user" value="users">
                    <tr>
                            <td><s:property value="username"/></td>
                            <td><s:property value="password"/></td>
                            <td><s:property value="city"/></td>
                            <td><s:property value="email"/></td>
                            <td><s:property value="type"/></td>
                            <td>
                            <s:url id="url" action="getuser">
                            <s:param name="username"><s:property value="username"/></s:param>
                            </s:url>
                            <s:a href="%{url}">Edit</s:a>
                            </td>
                            <td>
                            <s:url id="url" action="delete">
                            <s:param name="username"><s:property value="username"/></s:param>
                            </s:url>
                            <s:a href="%{url}">Delete</s:a>
                            </td>
                    </tr>
                    </s:iterator>
            </table>
   <br>| <s:a href="index.jsp">Home</s:a> | <s:a href="add_user.jsp">Add More</s:a>
    </body>
   </html>
```

Listing 20.8 uses the <s:iterator/> tag to iterate over the ArrayList and displays the values of all fields set for each user.

The user.jsp file contains two hyperlinks, Edit and Delete, rendered in front of each user record. These hyperlinks are not functional yet; therefore, we need to create action classes and JSP pages to make these two hyperlinks perform the specified functions.

Creating Action Class and JSP file for Editing User Data

Let's now create the `GetUserAction` class, which is invoked when the client clicks the `Edit` hyperlink of the user.jsp page. The `GetUserAction` class executes the `edit_user.jsp` page. Perform the following steps to create and configure the `GetUserAction` class as well as create the `edit_user.jsp` file:

- Creating the GetUserAction class
- Configuring the GetUserAction class
- Creating the edit_user.jsp file
- Configuring Action Class methods

Creating the GetUserAction Class

The `GetUserAction` class implements the `Action`, `ServletRequestAware`, and `ApplicationAware` interfaces. In the GetUserAction class, the `setServletRequest(HttpServletRequest request)` method of the `ServletRequestAware` interface is used to set the `HttpServletRequest` object to be used in the action.

The execute() method of the GetUserAction action class simply obtains a User object having username matching with the username passed as the request parameter to this action. The HttpServletRequest object is used to get this username parameter as well as to save the obtained User object into the request scope.

Listing 20.9 shows the code of the GetUserAction action class (save the GetUserAction.java file in the \Struts2App\src\com\kogent\action folder):

Listing 20.9: Displaying the Code of the GetUserAction.java File

```
package com.kogent.action;

import java.util.ArrayList;
import java.util.Iterator;
import java.util.Map;
import javax.servlet.http.HttpServletRequest;

import com.opensymphony.xwork2.Action;
import org.apache.struts2.interceptor.ApplicationAware;
import org.apache.struts2.interceptor.ServletRequestAware;
import com.kogent.User;
public class GetUserAction implements
   Action, ServletRequestAware, ApplicationAware {
   HttpServletRequest request;
   Map application;
   public void setServletRequest(HttpServletRequest request) {
         this.request = request;
   }
   public void setApplication(Map application) {
         this.application = application;
   }
   public String execute() throws Exception {
         String username=request.getParameter("username");
         ArrayList users=(ArrayList)application.get("users");
         User user;
         if(users!=null){
                  Iterator it=users.iterator();
                  while(it.hasNext()){
                           user=(User)it.next();
                           if(username.equals(user.getUsername())){
                                    request.setAttribute("user", user);
                                    break;
                           }
                  }
         }
         return SUCCESS;
   }
}
```

Configuring the GetUserAction class

Configure the GetUserAction class by adding new action mapping into the struts.xml file. The following code snippet provides the new action mapping for the GetUserAction class:

```
<action name="getuser" class="com.kogent.action.GetUserAction" >
   <result name="success">edit_user.jsp</result>
</action>
```

In the preceding code snippet, if the result obtained from the GetUserAction class is success, the edit_user.jsp page is invoked.

Creating the edit_user.jsp file

The Edit hyperlink invokes the GetUserAction class and passes a request parameter named username having different values for different user records. The execution of the GetUserAction class gives edit_user.jsp. Listing 20.10 shows the code of the edit_user.jsp page (save the edit_user.jsp file in the \Struts2App folder):

Listing 20.10: Displaying the Code of the edit_user.jsp File

```
<%@page contentType="text/html;charset=UTF-8" language="java" %>
<%@taglib uri="/struts-tags" prefix="s" %>
```

```
<html>
  <head>
        <title>Struts 2 Actions</title>
  </head>
  <body>
        <center>
              Editing User!<br><br>
              <table bgcolor="#f0edd9">
              <tr>
                    <td>
                    <s:form action="edit">
                    <s:textfield name="username" label="User Name" readonly="true">
                    <s:param name="value"><s:property
                    value="#request.user.username"/></s:param>
                    </s:textfield>
                    <s:textfield name="password" label="Password" size="15">
                    <s:param name="value"><s:property
                    value="#request.user.password"/></s:param>
                    </s:textfield>
                    <s:textfield name="city" label="City">
                    <s:param name="value"><s:property
                    value="#request.user.city"/></s:param>
                    </s:textfield>
                    <s:textfield name="email" label="E-Mail">
                    <s:param name="value"><s:property
                    value="#request.user.email"/></s:param>
                    </s:textfield>
                    <s:select label="Type" name="type" headerKey="1"
                    headerValue="Select Type" list="#@java.util.HashMap@{'Admin':
                    'Admin', 'Client':'Client'}" ></s:select>
                    <s:param name="value"><s:property
                    value="#request.user.type"/></s:param>
                          <s:submit value="Edit"/>
                          </s:form>
                    </td>
              </tr>
              </table>
              <br>| <s:a href="index.jsp">Home</s:a> |
        </center>
  </body>
</html>
```

The edit_user JSP page creates a form similar to add_user.jsp. However, the fields in the edit_user JSP page are populated with the values of different fields of the `User` object. This `User` object is set into request scope by the `GetUserAction` class, according to the username passed as the request parameter when the `Edit` hyperlink is clicked.

Configuring Action Class Methods

To edit the user record, a client needs to click the `Edit` hyperlink. However, prior to that, the developer needs to decide which action will be performed to handle this edit action form. The edit _user.jsp page is similar to the add_user.jsp page; therefore, we need the same set of input properties to be set as that of the `UserAction` action class. Similarly, the validation logic for these fields will be same as that implemented in the `validate()` method of UserAction. Therefore, when all these things are similar and can be reused, there is no need for creating a new action class here.

Struts 2 allows configuration of any method, having signature String methodName(), which can work similar to the execute() method of action class.

Add a new method into your existing UserAction class. This method contains the logic to edit the users. The logic is to replace the existing User object in the ArrayList with the new `User` object created with new data. The following code snippet shows the code of the edit() method of the UserAction class:

```
public class UserAction extends ActionSupport implements ApplicationAware{
String username;
String password;
String city;
String email;
String type;
```

```
Map application;
public void setApplication(Map application) {
  this.application=application;
}
//Setter and getter methods..
. . .
. . .
public String execute() throws Exception {
  . . . . .
  return SUCCESS;
  }
  //New method added.
  public String edit() throws Exception{
        ArrayList users=(ArrayList)application.get("users");
        User user=null;
        int index=0;
        Iterator it=users.iterator();
        while(it.hasNext()){
              user=(User)it.next();
              if(user.getUsername().equals(username)){
                    break;
              }
              index++;
        }
        User newuser=buildUser();
        users.set(index, newuser);
        application.put("users", users);
        return SUCCESS;
  }


  public User buildUser(){
  }
  public User getUser(String username){
  }
}
```

Recompile the `UserAction` action class and place the `UserAction.class` file in the `WEB-INF\classes\com\kogent\action` folder. The `<s:form/>` tag used in `edit_user.jsp` page is set with the value edit. Add a new action mapping with the name edit, which invokes the `edit()` method of the `UserAction` class to edit the user information. This is done by appending the code for mapping the edit() method in the struts.xml file, as shown in the following code snippet:

```
<action name="edit" class="com.kogent.action.UserAction" method="edit" >
  <result name="input">edit_user.jsp</result>
  <result name="success">user.jsp</result>
</action>
```

Now, the client can click on the Edit hyperlink, which invokes the `edit()` method of the `UserAction` class.

Similarly, to delete the user record, we need to click the Delete hyperlink. The action generated by the Delete hyperlink is handled by the `deleteUser()` method, which needs to be appended to the existing code of the UserAction.java file. The `deleteUser()` method removes the matching user object from the ArrayList object. The following code snippet shows the deleteUser() method of the UserAction class:

```
public class UserAction extends ActionSupport implements ApplicationAware{
String username;
String password;
String city;
String email;
String type;
Map application;
public void setApplication(Map application) {
this.application=application;
}
//Setter and getter methods..
. . .
. . .
```

```
public String execute() throws Exception {
. . . . .
return SUCCESS;
}
//New method added.
public String deleteUser() throws Exception{

        ArrayList users=(ArrayList)application.get("users");
        User user=null
        int index=0;
        Iterator it=users.iterator();
        while(it.hasNext()){
                user=(User)it.next();
                if(user.getUsername().equals(username)){
                        break;
                }

                index++;
        }
        users.remove(index);
        application.put("users", users);
        return SUCCESS;
    }

}
```

Add a new action mapping with the name delete, which invokes the deleteUser() method of the UserAction class to delete the user information. This is done by appending the code for mapping the deleteUser() method in the struts.xml file, as shown in the following code snippet:

```
<action name="delete" class="com.kogent.action.UserAction" method="deleteUser" >
  <interceptor-ref name="basicStack"/>
  <result name="input">edit_user.jsp</result>
  <result name="success">user.jsp</result>
</action>
```

The mapping shown in the preceding code snippet invokes the `deleteUser()` method of the `UserAction` action class, instead of executing its execute() method, as the method configured in the preceding code snippet is `deleteUser`. Then the validate() method is executed, as username is the only request parameter passed to the action.

You now need to configure the Web application according to the components within the directory structure. To do this, you must make modifications in the web.xml file, as shown in Listing 20.11 (save the web.xml file in the `/Struts2App/WEB-INF` folder):

Listing 20.11: Displaying the Code of the web.xml File

```
<?xml version="1.0" encoding="UTF-8"?>
<web-app version="3.1"
  xmlns="http://xmlns.jcp.org/xml/ns/javaee"
  xmlns:xsi="http://www.w3.org/2001/XMLSchema-instance"
  xsi:schemaLocation="http://xmlns.jcp.org/xml/ns/javaee
  http://xmlns.jcp.org/xml/ns/javaee/web-app_3_1.xsd">
  <display-name>Struts 2 Actions</display-name>
  <filter>
       <filter-name>struts2</filter-name>
<filter-class>org.apache.struts2.dispatcher.FilterDispatcher
  </filter-class>
  </filter>
  <filter-mapping>
       <filter-name>struts2</filter-name>
       <url-pattern>/*</url-pattern>
  </filter-mapping>
  <welcome-file-list>
       <welcome-file>index.jsp</welcome-file>
  </welcome-file-list>
</web-app>
```

Let's now explore the directory structure of the application.

Creating Directory Structure

We now need to create a sample Web application called Struts2App, according to the directory structure shown in Figure 20.4:

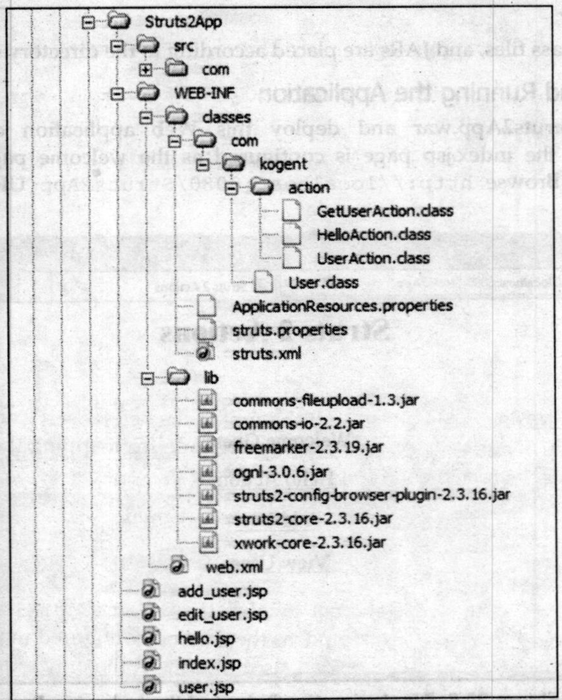

Figure 20.4: Displaying the Directory Structure of Struts2App

Table 20.11 describes the directory structure of the `Struts2App` Web application, and a list of files that should exist in this directory:

Table 20.11: The Directory Structure of Struts2App

Directory	Contains
`/Struts2App`	Serves as the root directory of the Web application. All the JSP and HTML files are stored in this directory. You can also put JSP and HTML pages in separate folders under this directory.
`/Struts2App/WEB-INF`	Contains all resources used in the application. The web.xml file, which contains the configuration/deployment details of the Web application, must exist in this directory.
`/Struts2App/WEB-INF/classes`	Contains Java class file, Struts 2 action class files, and other utility classes. For developing this application, the struts.xml, struts.properties, and ApplicationResources.properties (used in the application) must exist in this directory.
`/Struts2App/WEB-INF/lib`	Contains JAR files to which the components of the Web application are dependent.
`/Struts2App/src`	Contains the source code, which is used to develop the Web application.

Copy the following Struts 2 JARs from struts-2.3.16\lib folder to `\Struts2App\WEB-INF\lib` folder:

- commons-fileupload-1.3.jar
- commons-io-2.2.jar
- freemarker-2.3.19.jar

- ognl-3.0.6.jar
- struts2-config-browser-plugin-2.3.16.jar
- struts2-core-2.3.1.jar
- xwork-core-2.3.16.jar

Make sure that all JSPs, class files, and JARs are placed according to the directory structure shown in Figure 20.4.

Packaging, Deploying, and Running the Application

We will now create Struts2App.war and deploy this Web application on the Glassfish Server 4.0. You should ensure that the index.jsp page is configured as the welcome page in the web.xml file of the Struts2App application. Browse `http://localhost:8080/Struts2App` URL to run the application, as shown in Figure 20.5:

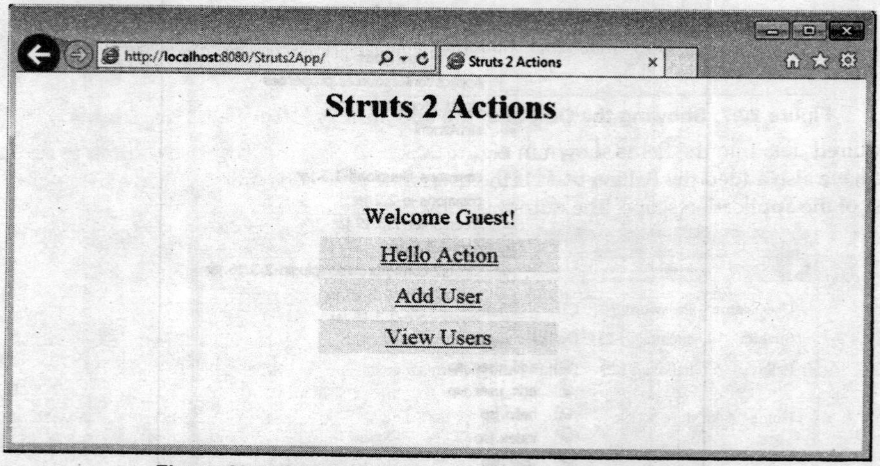

Figure 20.5: Displaying the Output of the index.jsp Page

In Figure 20.5, the hyperlink Hello Action creates a request for `hello.action` and invokes the action named hello configured in the struts.xml. As a result, the hello.jsp page appears, which has been configured to display the result for this action. The output of the hello.jsp page is shown in Figure 20.6:

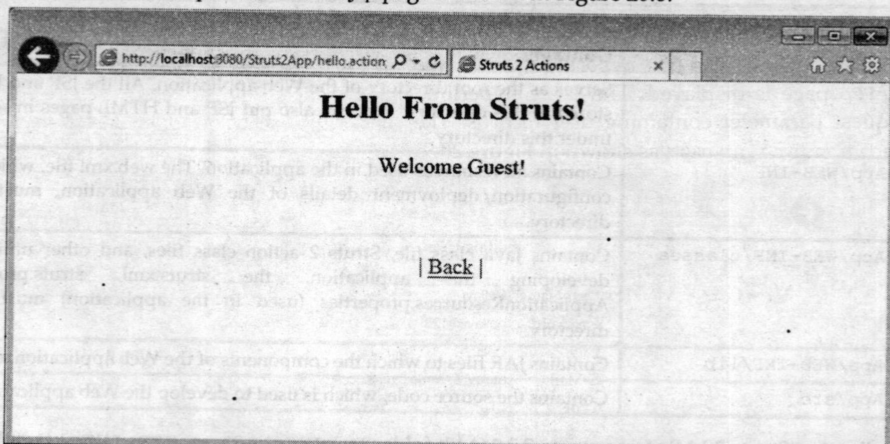

Figure 20.6: Showing the hello.jsp Page with a Message

Now, click the `Back` link to go to the `index.jsp` page. You should note that the hello.jsp page is displayed as hello.action depending upon the mapping of the action done in the web.xml file of the application. Then, click the `Add User` link, as shown in index.jsp (Figure 20.5). As a result, the `add_user.jsp` page appears. The output of `add_user.jsp` page is shown in Figure 20.7:

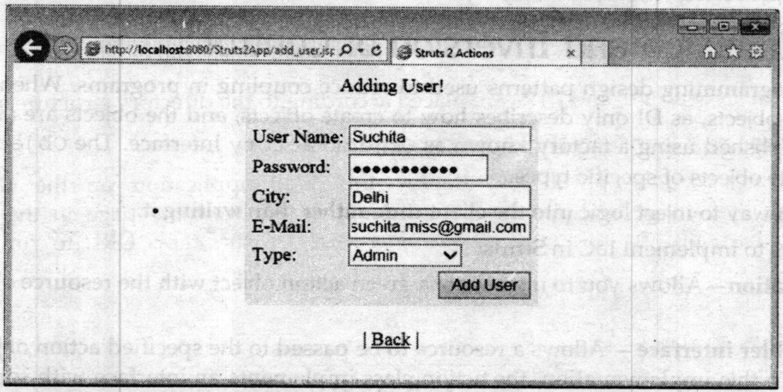

Figure 20.7: Showing the Output of the add_user.jsp Page with User Details

Enter the required data into the fields shown in Figure 20.7 and click the Add User button to add a new user. In our case, we have also added the Pallavi user. If the username entered is unique, a new User object is added into the ArrayList of the application scope. The output is shown in Figure 20.8:

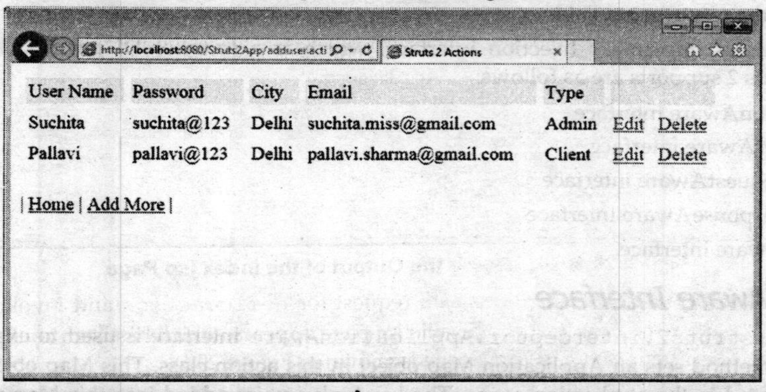

Figure 20.8: Displaying the Output of the user.jsp Page with a List of Users Added

In Figure 20.8, each record has two hyperlinks, `Edit` and `Delete`. When you click the `Edit` hyperlink, the `edit_user.jsp` page is displayed. The `Edit` hyperlink invokes the `GetUserAction` class and passes the username request parameter containing user records. The successful execution of the `GetUserAction` class invokes the `edit_user.jsp` page, as shown in Figure 20.9:

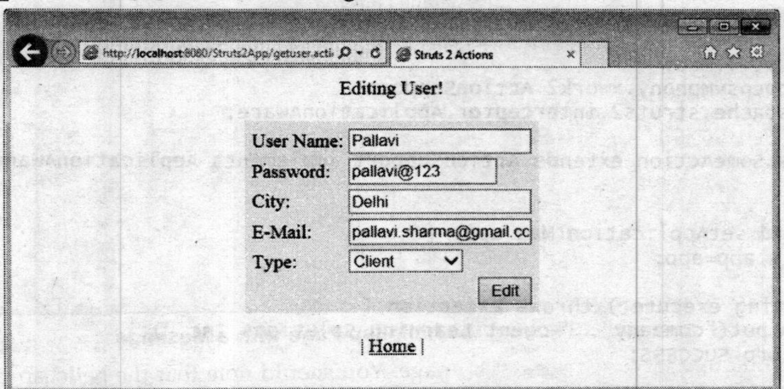

Figure 20.9: Displaying the Output of the edit_user.jsp Page

Similarly, to delete the user information, click the Delete hyperlink shown in Figure 20.8.

Let's now explore the concept of dependency injection and inversion of control in the Struts 2 framework.

Dependency Injection and Inversion of Control

DI and IoC are programming design patterns used to reduce coupling in programs. When you use DI, you do not need to create objects, as DI only describes how to create objects, and the objects are automatically created. This task is accomplished using a factory known as `ObjectFactory` interface. The `ObjectFactory` interface allows you to create objects of specific types.

The IoC provides a way to inject logic into the client code rather than writing it.

There are two ways to implement IoC in Struts:

- **With instantiation**—Allows you to instantiate a given action object with the resource object as a constructor parameter.
- **Using an enabler interface**— Allows a resource to be passed to the specified action object after the object is instantiated. In this implementation, the action class implements an interface with some methods, such as `setResources(ResourceObject r)`.

To use HTTP-specific objects in Struts action classes, Struts 2 uses DI and IoC. While using these techniques, the `Aware` interfaces are injected in an action class. These interfaces are called `Aware` interfaces because the interface names always end with aware. These interfaces have methods to set specific resources into the implementing class and to make the resource available.

Struts 2 action classes implement Injection interface, which is a form of DI pattern. The Common aware interfaces that Struts 2 supports are as follows:

- The ApplicationAware interface
- The ParameterAware interface
- The ServletRequestAware interface
- The ServletResponseAware interface
- The SessionAware interface

The ApplicationAware Interface

The `org.apache.struts2.interceptor.ApplicationAware` interface is used to expose a method to an action class. This method sets an Application Map object in this action class. This Map object contains different objects that are stored in the application scope. The key/value pairs added into this Map can now be accessed similar to other attributes of the application scope. The `ApplicationAware` interface has one method, `setApplication()`, which sets the map of application properties in implementing class.

The code for action that implements the `ApplicationAware` interface is provided in Listing 20.12:

Listing 20.12: Displaying the Code for an Action Implementing the ApplicationAware Interface

```
package com.kogent.action;

import java.util.Map;
import com.opensymphony.xwork2.ActionSupport;
import org.apache.struts2.interceptor.ApplicationAware;

public class SomeAction extends ActionSupport implements ApplicationAware {

   Map app;
   public void setApplication(Map app) {
         this.app=app;
   }
   public String execute() throws Exception {
         app.put("company", "Kogent Learning Solutions Inc.");
         return SUCCESS;
   }
}
```

The Interceptor places the Map application into the SomeAction action class before it is executed.

All key/value pairs stored in Map object can be accessed from any action or JSP page. The Struts 2 tags support the display of different application scope objects using a corresponding key. For example, the single key/value pair stored in Map object, shown in Listing 20.12, can be accessed in a JSP page, as shown in the following code snippet:

```
<s:property value="#application.name"/>
or
<s:property value="#application['name']"/>
```

The ParameterAware Interface

The `org.apache.struts2.interceptor.ParameterAware` interface is used when an action class handles input parameters. All the input parameters, with their name/value pairs, are set in a parameter map. When the actions require the HTTP request parameter map, this interface is implemented within an action. Another common use of this interface is to use parameters to internally instantiate data objects.

The `setParameter(Map map)` method of the ParameterAware interface sets the map of input parameters in an action class. An action that implements the `ParameterAware` interface is shown in Listing 20.13:

Listing 20.13: Displaying the Code for an Action Implementing the ParameterAware Interface

```
package com.kogent.action;

import java.util.Map;

import com.opensymphony.xwork2.ActionSupport;
import org.apache.struts2.interceptor.ParameterAware;

public class SomeAction extends ActionSupport implements ParameterAware {
   Map params;

   public void setParameters(Map params) {
          this.params=params; }
   public String execute() throws Exception {
          return SUCCESS;
   }
}
```

In Listing 20.13, params is a Map containing all input parameters set as the key/value pairs. The action class can use this map to process input parameters or to propagate them to another object. These input parameters can also be displayed on JSP using the following syntax, which displays two input parameters, name and city:

```
<s:property value="#parameters.name"/>
<s:property value="#parameters.city"/>
or
<s:property value="#parameters['name']"/>
<s:property value="#parameters['city']"/>
```

The ServletRequestAware Interface

The HttpServletRequest object is not available in the action class by default. However, this can be injected into the action class by implementing the org.apache.struts2.interceptor.ServletRequestAware interface. The exposed method setServletRequest(HttpServletRequest request) sets the HttpServletRequest object in the action class. This allows an action to use the HttpServletRequest object in a Servlet environment. Listing 20.14 shows an action that implements the ServletRequestAware interface:

Listing 20.14: Displaying the Code for an Action Implementing the ServletRequestAware Interface

```
package com.kogent.action;

import java.util.Map;

import com.opensymphony.xwork2.ActionSupport;
import org.apache.struts2.interceptor.ServletRequestAware;
```

```
import javax.servlet.http.HttpServletRequest;
import javax.servlet.http.HttpSession;

public class SomeAction extends ActionSupport implements ServletRequestAware{
  HttpServletRequest request;
  public void setServletRequest(HttpServletRequest request) {
        this.request=request;   }
  public String execute() throws Exception {
        request.setAttribute("userid", 101);
        HttpSession session=request.getSession();
        return SUCCESS;
  }
}
```

The ServletResponseAware Interface

The org.apache.struts2.interceptor.ServletResponseAware interface is similar to the ServletRequestAware interface. This interface is used to inject the HttpServletResponse object into an action. This interface has the setServletResponse(HttpServletResponse response) method, which sets the HttpServletResponse object. The following code snippet shows the code for an action that implements the ServletResponseAware interface and gets an HttpServletResponse object:

```
package com.kogent.action;
import java.util.Map;
import com.opensymphony.xwork2.ActionSupport;
import org.apache.struts2.interceptor.ServletResponseAware;
import javax.servlet.http.HttpServletResponse;
public class SomeAction extends ActionSupport implements ServletResponseAware {
  HttpServletResponse response;
  public void setServletResponse(HttpServletResponse response) {
        this.response=response;
  }
  public String execute() throws Exception {
        response.setContentType("text/html");
        int buffer=response.getBufferSize();
        . . . .
        . . . .
        return SUCCESS;
  }
}
```

The SessionAware Interface

The `org.apache.struts2.interceptor.SessionAware` interface is used to handle client sessions within an action class. The `SessionAware` interface provides the `setSession()` method to set the map of session attributes while implementing an action class. The action class implementing the `SessionAware` interface can access session attributes in the form of a Session map. We can add, remove, and obtain different session attributes by manipulating this map. Listing 20.15 shows an action class implementing the `SessionAware` interface:

Listing 20.15: Displaying the Code for an Action Implementing the SessionAware Interface

```
package com.kogent.action;
import java.util.Map;
import com.opensymphony.xwork2.ActionSupport;
import org.apache.struts2.interceptor.SessionAware;
public class SomeAction extends ActionSupport implements SessionAware {
  Map session;
  public void setSession(Map session) {
        this.session=session;
  }
  public String execute() throws Exception {
        session.put("user", "John");
        return SUCCESS;
  }
}
```

The single key/value pair stored in session Map session, shown in Listing 20.15, can be accessed in a JSP page, as shown in the following code snippet:

```
<s:property value="#session.user"/>
or
<s:property value="#session['user']"/>
```

Preprocessing with Interceptors

The Interceptor class allows you to define the piece of code that can be executed before or after the execution of an action class. Interceptors also have the ability to prevent an action from being executed. Interceptors provide developers a way to encapsulate common functionality in a reusable form, which can then be applied to one or more action classes. These common functionalities may include validation of input data, pre-processing of file upload, protection from double submit, and sometimes pre invocation of controls with some data before a Web page is displayed. The Interceptor helps in modularizing common code into reusable classes.

The Struts 2 Framework provides a set of Interceptors that can be used to provide the required functionalities to an action class. Interceptor or a stack of Interceptors is configured and executed before the action is executed, to provide all pre-processing of the request. Similarly, these configured interceptors are again executed after the execution of action to provide additional processing, if any. Let's now discuss the basic concept of interceptors, their configuration, and implementation in the Struts 2 Framework.

What are Interceptors?

Interceptor is a class that contains business logic implementation to provide a specific functionality. Interceptors provide additional processing information before the execution of an action class.

Every interceptor is pluggable, and the required interceptor or interceptor stack can be configured on a per-action basis. The separation of core functionality code in the form of interceptors eliminates the chances of implementing an extra code and references in an action class. The purpose of using interceptors is to allow greater control over controller layer and separate some common logic that applies to multiple actions.

An Interceptor class can be created by implementing the `com.opensymphony.xwork2.interceptor.Interceptor` interface or by extending `com.opensymphony.xwork2.interceptor.AbstractInterceptor` class. An intercept(ActionInvocation inv) method is associated with an Interceptor class to perform some processing on the request before and/or after rest of the processing of the request by the `ActionInvocation` interface, which stores the state of an action.

Interceptors as RequestProcessor

In Struts 2, interceptors have been replaced with the `RequestProcessor` interface, which was used in Struts 1 for processing the requests. Similar to `RequestProcessor`, interceptors provide all basic pre-processing required before executing an action class. Similar to the `RequestProcessor` class, we now have Interceptors that contain common logic to be applied to a number of actions. Only a small percentage of Struts 2 applications need to define their custom Interceptors for specific functionality.

How to Configure Interceptors?

Interceptors to be used in an application must be declared in the `struts.xml` file. Interceptor classes can be defined using a name-class pair specified in the Struts configuration file. The other approach is to include another `.xml` file containing the configuration of interceptors into the `struts.xml` file. All the interceptors, which are required to pre-process the request for an action class, should be defined in the action mapping provided for that specified action class in the struts.xml file.

For example, let's assume that we have two custom interceptor classes, `Interceptor1_class_name.class`, and `Interceptor2_class_name.class`. These two Interceptor classes are defined in the `struts.xml` file using the `<interceptor>` element, as shown in the following code snippet:

```
<?xml version="1.0" encoding="UTF-8" ?>
<!DOCTYPE struts PUBLIC
"-//Apache Software Foundation//DTD Struts Configuration 2.3//EN"
"http://struts.apache.org/dtds/struts-2.3.dtd ">
```

```
<struts>
  <include file="struts-default.xml"/>
  <package name="default" extends="struts-default">
  <interceptors>
       <interceptor name="interceptor1" class="Interceptor1_class_name"/>
       <interceptor name="interceptor2" class="Interceptor2_class_name "/>
  </interceptors>
  <action name="login" class="LoginAction">
       <interceptor-ref name="interceptor1"/>
       <interceptor-ref name="interceptor2"/>

       <result name="input">login.jsp</result>
       <result name="success">success.jsp</result>
  </action>
  </package>
</struts>
```

In the preceding code snippet, interceptors, such as Interceptor1_class_name and Interceptor2_class_name, are configured in the struts.xml file with the help of the <interceptor> element. The <interceptor> element uses an attribute called name to provide a simple name for an interceptor class specified in the `class` attribute. In the preceding code snippet, the `name` attribute is set to values, such as interceptor1 and interceptor2, representing interceptor classes, such as Interceptor1_class_name and Interceptor2_class_name, respectively.

Further, a list of interceptor classes used to intercept the action request is declared in action mapping using the `<interceptor-ref name=". . .">` element. The interceptors are executed in the same order in which they are declared in action mapping. The corresponding interceptor classes ar executed to provide all pre-processing before the execution of an action class for which the interceptors are defined.

Stacking of Interceptors

Stacking of interceptors refers to the grouping of a set of interceptors. Stacking of interceptors is important as we may need to apply the same set of interceptors for any number of action classes. Therefore, instead of writing the whole list of interceptors in every action mapping repeatedly, we can just write the name of the interceptor stack. In most of the Struts 2 applications, we do not need to create our custom Interceptors as all the required pre-processing is provided by the default Interceptor stack, which is declared in the `struts-default.xml` file. An Interceptor stack is a set of Interceptors configured in a specific order. Therefore, the default Interceptor stack can be taken as the `RequestProcessor` interface in Struts 2. The action mapping provided in the following code snippet uses a single `<interceptor-ref>` element to declare interceptor stack, instead of using separate `<interceptor-ref>` elements for each interceptor class:

```
<?xml version="1.0" encoding="UTF-8" ?>
<!DOCTYPE struts PUBLIC
"-//Apache Software Foundation//DTD Struts Configuration 2.3//EN"
"http://struts.apache.org/dtds/struts-2.3.dtd ">
<struts>
  <include file="struts-default.xml"/>
  <package name="default" extends="struts-default">
  <interceptors>
       <interceptor name="interceptor1" class="Interceptor1_class_name"/>
       <interceptor name="interceptor2" class="Interceptor2_class_name "/>
              <interceptor-stack name="custom_stack">
              <interceptor-ref name="interceptor1"/>
              <interceptor-ref name="interceptor2"/>
       </interceptor-stack>
  </interceptors>
  <action name="login" class="LoginAction">
       <interceptor-ref name="custom_stack"/>
       <result name="input">login.jsp</result>
       <result name="success">success.jsp</result>
  </action>
  </package>
</struts>
```

In preceding code snippet, we have defined two interceptors, and an interceptor stack (`custom_stack`) containing these two interceptors. Interceptor stack is defined using the `<interceptor-stack>` element.

The name attribute of `<interceptor-ref>` can take the name of an interceptor or an interceptor stack.

Bundled Interceptors

Bundled interceptors are a set of pre-defined interceptors, which are used in a Web application to provide required processing before and after an action class is executed. These pre-defined interceptors are known as bundled interceptors since they are bundled inside the Struts 2 Framework and are defined in the `struts-default.xml` file. Each of these pre-defined interceptors is designed to implement logic for a specific function, which is common to almost all the Web applications. Interceptors can be seen as a reusable component, which is commonly used in different application and different `action` invocations in an application. To use these bundled interceptors in our application, we can extend the `struts-default` package or define these bundled interceptors in our package with name-class pair specified in the `<interceptor>` element. The noteworthy bundled interceptors available in the Struts 2 Framework are described in Table 20.12:

Table 20.12: Noteworthy Bundled Interceptors of the Struts 2 Framework

Name of the Interceptor	Description
alias	Converts the parameters that are named differently but work similar to each other between requests
chain	Provides the properties of the previous action for the current action
checkbox	Allows you to use a hidden field to add a checkbox automatically to detect the unsubmitted checkboxes
conversionError	Allows you to add the errors related to conversion of values from the ActionContext to the field defined for an action
createSession	Allows you to create an HttpSession automatically to facilitate the working of the interceptors that require the HttpSession
Exception	Allows you to map an execption to a specific result
execAndWait	Allows an action to be executed in the background and then forwards the request of a user to the page displaying the progress of the background process
fileUpload	Provides support of uploading a file at the specified target
i18n	Holds the details of the locale selected for the session of a user
model-driven	Pushes the result of the getModel () method to the Value Stack
prepare	Invokes the prepare() method
roles	Verifies the JAAS role of a user, and if the role is correct, the required action is executed
scope	Stores the state of an action in either session or application scope
scoped-model-driven	Retrieves the models from a scope and sets it on the action invoking the setModel() method
servletConfig	Allows you to acess the Maps representing HttpServletRequest and HttpSeervletResponse instances
staticParams	Sets the parameters defined in the struts.xml file to the action

In addition to these bundled interceptors, Struts 2 Framework also allows you to create customized interceptors. Let's now discuss about writing our own interceptors, or customized interceptors.

Writing Interceptors

Struts 2 Framework provides the flexibility to create our own interceptor classes that provide additional logic in a reusable form, which can be applied to one or more action classes.

When customized interceptor classes are created, they are declared in the struts.xml file of the Web application. Further, we can define a default interceptor stack, including the newly designed interceptor, to use it with the action classes.

The main method in every interceptor is its `intercept (ActionInvocation invocation)` method, which takes a reference of the `com.opensymphony.xwork2.ActionInvocation` interface. The `ActionInvocation` interface represents the execution state of the action. The `ActionInvocation interface` holds the instances of all the interceptors and action classes.

The processing of `ActionInvocation` is performed in steps, and every step is invoked by the `ActionInvocation.invoke()` method. First, the `invoke()method` is called on ActionInvocation by the ActionProxy factory and then, `each` Interceptor calls the invoke() method to execute the next Interceptor. Interceptors can also quit the execution of `ActionInvocation` and return a code piece, such as `Action.SUCCESS`, or it may choose to do some processing before or after delegating the rest of the processing by using `ActionInvocation.invoke()`.

The action class is executed only after all the interceptors defined for an action class are executed.

An interceptor class can access various resources by invoking methods on the `ActionInvocation` object, which is passed as an argument to its `intercept()` method. The methods of ActionInvocation are listed in Table 20.13:

Table 20.13: Methods of ActionInvocation Interface

Method	Description
Object getAction()	Returns the action associated with the ActionInvocation interface.
ActionContext getInvocationContext()	Returns the instance of ActionContext class associated with the ActionInvocation interface.
ActionProxy getProxy()	Returns the ActionProxy holding the ActionInvocation interface.
ValueStack getStack()	Returns an object of ValueStack, which represents the value stack of the action.
String invoke()	Invokes the next step in the processing of the ActionInvocation interface. This may be the execution of next Interceptor or the action itself.
Result getResult()	Returns a non-chain result from a chain of ActionChainResults, if the object of the ActionInvocation interface has been executed earlier.
String getResultCode()	Returns the code returned from the current ActionInvocation.

The `ActionContext` returned by `getInvocationContext()` method can further provide details for `HttpServletRequest` and `HttpSession`. The following code snippet shows the sample `intercept()` method of an interceptor:

```
package com.kogent.interceptors;
public class SimpleInterceptor extends AbstractInterceptor
{
        public String intercept (ActionInvocation invocation) throws Exception {
        final ActionContext context = invocation.getInvocationContext();
        HttpServletRequest request = (HttpServletRequest) context.get(HTTP_REQUEST);
        HttpSession session = request.getSession (true);
        Object user = session.getAttribute (USER_HANDLE);
        if (user == null) {
                String loginAttempt = request.getParameter(LOGIN_ATTEMPT);
                if (! StringUtils.isBlank (loginAttempt) ) {
                if (some condition ) {
                        return "success";
                }
                else {
                        Object action = invocation.getAction ();
                        if (action instanceof ValidationAware) {
                        ((ValidationAware) action).addActionError("Username
                        or password incorrect.");
                        }
                }
```

```
            }
            // Either the login attempt failed or the user hasn't tried to login yet,
            // and we need to send the login form.
            return "login";
            } else {
                    return invocation.invoke ();
            }
        }
    }
```

After creating an interceptor, the mapping of this custom interceptor is provided in the struts.xml to configure this custom interceptor so that it can be used in the interceptor stacks defined in the action mappings provided in the struts.xml file. The sample configuration of a custom interceptor is shown in the following code snippet:

```
<struts>
    <package name="my-default" extends="struts-default">
            <interceptors>
<interceptor name="login" class=" com.kogent.interceptors.SimpleInterceptor " />
            </interceptors>
    </package>
</struts>
```

In the preceding code snippet, a custom interceptor, called the `SimpleInterceptor` class, is declared in the struts.xml file to intercept action classes. In the preceding code snippet, the `class` attribute of the `<interceptor>` element is used to specify a path of an interceptor class. The `name` attribute of the `<interceptor>` element specifies a name to the current interceptor class.

Let's now move on to discuss Object Graph Navigation Language (OGNL) support in Struts 2.

OGNL Support in Struts 2

OGNL is an expression language used to manipulate and retrieve different properties of Java objects. OGNL has its own syntax, which is very simple in structure; therefore, it is easy to learn and use and also makes the code more readable. OGNL acts as an expression language for the GUI elements to model objects. You can utilize OGNL for multiple uses. The uses of OGNL are as follows:

- Provides a `TypeConverter` mechanism that is used to convert values of a given data type to another data type. For example, it converts `String` type to numeric type.
- Serves as a data source language used to create a map between table columns and a Swing `TableModel`.
- Works as a binding language between Web components and the underlying model objects.
- Serves as a replacement to other property getting languages used by Jakarta Commons BeanUtils package or JSTL's expression languages, as it is more expressive in terms of getting and setting the objects properties.

OGNL syntax provides a high-level abstraction for navigating object graphs by specifying paths through JavaBeans properties, collection indices, and so on. The following code segment shows how to find the difference between the two Java code segments and the corresponding OGNL expression to access a session scoped object (say, student) and obtain value of a property (say name). In Web frameworks, expression languages have similar goals to eliminate the repetitive code. For example, without an Expression Langugae (EL), getting a Student object from the session and then displaying its name on the Web page requires a few lines of Java code in a JSP, as can be seen in the following code snippet:

```
//Using Java Code - First way
<%
Student student = (Student) session.get("student");
String name = student.getName();
%>
<%= name %>
//Using Java Code - Second way
<%= ((Student) session.get("student")).getName() %>
//OGNL expression - Third Way
#session.student.name
```

In the preceding code snippet, we have used three ways to get the name of a student from a session. First two ways use Java code in JSP page. It is to be noted that the second way has reduced the code to a single line, but the code now looks complex and difficult to read. The third way shows the use of OGNL expression to get the name of a student from a session.

Syntax of OGNL

The most commonly used unit in OGNL expression language is the navigation chain, which is also termed as chain. The chain consists of the following parts:

- Property names, such as `name` and `text`
- Method calls, such as the `hashCode()`
- Array indices, such as `listeners [0]`

All OGNL expressions are evaluated in the context of the current object. Chains work by inheriting the output of the previously executed link and present the same as the current object for the next link. A chain can be extended upto any limit. For example, consider the following chain:

```
name.toCharArray()[0].numericValue.toString()
```

The preceding expression is evaluated in the following manner:

- First, it extracts the `name` property of the initial or root object. This root object is provided to the OGNL through the OGNL context.
- Then, it calls the toCharArray() method of the resulting string.
- After calling the toCharArray()method, the first character at 0 index is extracted from the resulting array.
- It then gets the numericValue property from the first character. The character is represented as a Character object, and numeric value can be retrieved by using the getNumericValue() method of the Character class.
- Finally, the String is returned after calling the toString() method on the resulting Integer object.

Using OGNL in Struts 2

With the help of a standard naming context, the Struts 2 Framework evaluates the OGNL expression. The topmost object dealing with OGNL is a Map, usually called as a context map or context. You should note that the properties of the root object in the OGNL expressions can be referenced without a special marker notion.

In addition, the Struts 2 Framework maps the value stack to the OGNL root object and OGNL context to the `ActionContext class`. Apart from mapping the value stack, the Struts 2 Framework also places other objects in the `ActionContext` class.

The `Action` instance is always pushed onto the value stack as the Action is on the stack, and the stack is the OGNL root. To access other objects in the `ActionContext class`, we must use the # notation so that the object is looked for in the `ActionContext class`. The following code shows how to reference an `Action` property:

```
<s:property value="state"/>
```

The other non-root objects in the `ActionContext` class can be referenced using the # notation as follows:

```
<s:property value="#session.mySesPropKey"/> or
<s:property value="#session["mySesPropKey"]"/> or
<s:property value="#request["mySesPropKey"]/>
```

The following are the examples of using the `select` tag:

- **Syntax for list** (`{e1, e2, e3}`)– Creates a list that contains the String `n1`, `n2`, as well as `n3` and selects `n2` as the default value, as shown in the following code snippet:

```
<s:select label="label1" name="name1"
list="{'n1','n2','n3'}" value="%{'n2'}" />
```

- **Syntax for map** (`#{key1:value1,key2:value2}`)– Creates a map used to configure the String `name` to the String `namevalue` and `desg` to the string `desgvalue`:

```
<s:select label="label2" name="name2" list="#{
'name':'namevalue', 'desg':'desgvalue'}" />
```

The following code snippet shows the implementation of `in` and `not in` to determine if an element exists in a Collection or not:

```
<s:if test="'name' in {'name','desg'}">
```

```
    muhahaha
  </s:if>
  <s:else>
    boo
  </s:else>
  <s:if test="'name' not in {'name','desg'}">
    muhahaha
  </s:if>
  <s:else>
    boo
  </s:else>
```

The following wildcards are used within the collection to select a subset of a collection (called projection):

- ?—Refers to the wildcard depicting that all elements should match the selected logic
- ^—Refers to the wildcard depicting that only the first element should match the selected logic
- $—Refers to the wildcard depicting that only the last element should match the selected logic

For example, the following snippet shows how to obtain a subset of just female relatives from the object person:

```
person.relatives.{? #this.gender == 'female'}
```

You should note that OGNL also provides support for the basic lambda expression syntax to write simple functions. The following code snippet shows that the nth element in Fibonacci series is returned:

```
fib: if n==0 return 0; elseif n==1 return 1; else return fib(n-2)+fib(n-1);
//Output of different method calls with argument 0, 1 and 11
fib(0)= 0

fib(1)= 1
fib(11)= 89
```

The following code shows the usage of lambda expression for the same fib method in Struts 2 Framework:

```
<s:property
value="#fib =:[#this==0 ? 0 : #this==1 ? 1 : #fib(#this-2)+#fib(#this-1)],
#fib(11)" />
```

In the preceding code snippet, the code within the brackets is the lambda expression. The # notation is used to hold the argument to the expression, which initially starts at 11.

Implementing Struts 2 Tags

The 's' prefix has been used in JSP pages to implement Struts 2 tags. The tags in Struts 2 can be divided into two categories:

- Generic tags
- UI tags

Generic Tags

Generic tags are used for controlling the flow of data and data extraction from the value stack or other locations. In other words, the Generic tags are developed to control the flow of execution in the page, and obtain and display data.

Similar to other tags, Generic tags are also contained in a tag library, which is a collection of predefined tags. We have been using Struts 2 tag library in our previous applications, and designed a number of JSP pages using them. Each tag has a specific work and many attributes. You can use these tags in your JSP page by simply importing a tag library in your JSP page, as follows:

```
<%@ taglib prefix="s" uri="/struts-tags" %>
```

The <%@ %> directive identifies the URI defined in the previously listed `<taglib>` element and states that all the tags should be prefixed with string 's'. In Struts 1, there are many tag libraries; but in Struts 2, only one tag library, struts-tags, is specified. The Struts 2 tags are grouped into different categories. The Generic tags are one of the most important tags of the Struts 2 tag library. The Generic tags control the execution flow of the rendered pages. The Generic tags are specified in the `/struts-tags` tag library. There are two types of Generic tags:

- Control tags
- Data tags

Control Tags

Control tags are used to control the behavior of data on a page. Control tags, as the name suggests, are designed to control the path of execution with the help of some decision making constructs, such as `if`, `else`, and `elseif` tags. Another controlling structure is looping constructs, which is supported by the `iterator` tag. You can use the `iterator` tag with the `append` and `merge` tags to loop over data and the `if\else\elseif` tag to make decisions, you can develop more sophisticated and dynamic Web pages. Table 20.14 lists the control tags of the Struts 2 Framework:

Table 20.14: Control Tags of the Struts 2 Framework

Tag	Description
`if`	Allows you to implement the conditional flow of execution
`elseIf`	Allows you to extend the decision making to a number of conditions, and is used along with the if tag
`else`	Allows you to provide alternate execution path if all conditions given in the if tag and the elseif tag(s) fail
`append`	Allows you to append iteratable lists together to form an appended iterator
`generator`	Generates an iterator on the basis of a given value
`iterator`	Allows you to iterate over the given value
`merge`	Allows you to merge iteratable lists together to form a merged iterator
`sort`	Allows you to sort a given List
`subset`	Accepts an iterator and provides output for its subset

Data Tags

Data tags are used for creating and manipulating data. These tags allow you to either get data out of the value stack or place variables and objects in the value stack. Before discussing data tags, let's explain the meaning of the value stack, which is just a stack of objects. Initially, the stack contains input properties of the action executed. This is why when we write value="name", it calls the `getName()` method of the action class. New objects are placed onto the stack when the `<s:iterator>` or `<s:property>` tags are used. The data tags available in Struts 2 are listed in Table 20.15:

Table 20.15: Data Tags Available in Struts 2

Tag	Description
`a`	Helps to create an hyperlink, and is similar to HTML <a href = " " /> tag.
`action`	Helps to call actions directly from a page.
`bean`	Helps to create an instance of a class, which is in agreement with JavaBean specification.
`date`	Helps to format and display date objects in different ways.
`debug`	Helps to create a link, which can be clicked to view all value stack contents with different items available in the stack context. This helps in debugging.
`i18n`	Helps to get a resource bundle and place it on value stack, so that in addition to the bundle associated with action, other resource bundles could be used.
`include`	Includes output of some Servlet or JSP page.
`param`	Helps to define parameters to other tags.
`push`	Pushes the value stack.
`set`	Helps to assign a value to a variable. It is similar to setting a variable with the given value.
`text`	Helps to render an internationalized message from the resource bundle.
`url`	Helps to create a URL.
`property`	Helps to get the property of a value and returns the object from the top of the stack, by default.

Struts 2 comes with another set of tags, which can be used to design a JSP page with quality components for the required user interface, for example a form with some input fields and a submit button.

After discussing Generic tags, let's now start exploring another category of Struts tags, UI Tags.

UI Tags

The UI tags provide a way to create user interface (UI) components on the screen. The UI tags are basically used to design the Web page with high quality UI components that may include a form with other individual components contained in it, such as text box, combo box, submit buttons, radio buttons, and checkboxes. There is a tag associated with each UI component that is used to create and place these components on the page. These UI components can be customized by setting different values for different attributes of the corresponding tags.

The UI tags provide the logic behind the flow of an execution. These tags involve the use of data in an application and focus on how the data is entered by the user and accepted by the application. This data can be retrieved from the actions, stack values, or from the data tags available in the Struts 2 Framework. The UI tags represent the tags and generate the reusable HTML format. The UI tags work on the basis of templates. Templates again group together to form the themes, which are used to perform the actual operation. The UI tags are classified into the following two categories:

- Form tags
- Non-form tags

Form Tags

Form tags allow the display of data in a simple and reusable format. These tags also include the HTML representation, which provides the feature of reusability. These tags are used to create a basic HTML form and other form components. Table 20.16 lists the form tags of the Struts 2 Framework:

Table 20.16: Form Tags of the Struts 2 Framework

form	checkboxlist
file	Token
password	Label
textarea	Hidden
checkbox	doubleselect
select	combobox
radio	Submit
head	DateTimePicker
optiontransferselect	optgroup
reset	textfield
updownselect	

These tags are described in the coming headings, with all their syntaxes and the attributes that control the behaviors of the UI components rendered using these tags.

Non-Form Tags

We have seen a number of form UI tags used to create various components, which are used in a simple form created in a Web page. There is another category of UI tags, known as the Non-form UI tags, which are used to display the output texts, such as action-level messages, action-level errors, and field-level errors. These tags also create some other UI components, such as tabbed panel and table.

Non-form tags are grouped under certain templates. The templates are again combined to form a theme. The themes available for Non-form tags are the same as that of the Form tags. All Non-form tags must extend one of these themes to draw the output of the page. Table 20.17 lists the Non-form tags:

Table 20.17: Non-form Tags of the Struts 2 Framework

actionerror	div	tabbedpanel
actionmessage	fielderror	tree
component	table	treenode

These Non-form tags are used for creating UI components, such as tabs, div, tables, and trees. In addition, these tags include tags to display action errors, action messages, and field errors. The Non-form tags are used to display the output to the user without using the forms. It does not take the input from a form tag to generate the output.

Controlling Results in Struts 2

Action classes are used for the processing of user action, which has been requested with the data sent as input parameters. Interceptors provided for all required pre-processing are executed before the execution of the action class. The processing of request must consequently provide some result, which is to be sent as the response back to the user. After the execution of action class, we always get a string as result code. This result code is mapped to a specific source to be rendered as view to the user, which may be a JSP page, or an HTML page but it is not limited to these two things. There are different classes implementing `com.opensymphony.xwork2.Result` interface, which are responsible for rendering output to the user. Struts 2 provides a set of result classes that needs to process different types of results, such as rendering JSP or HTML page, generating output for the users that are using freemarker or velocity templates or sometimes invoking other actions to get results.

Now, let's explore the result classes along with their need, implementation, and configuration details.

What is Result?

Struts 2, similar to Struts 1, is based on MVC architecture and the results in Struts 2 are purely associated with the view part of the MVC implementation. The term result is used to refer to the output to be displayed to the user as a consequence of the action performed for its request. All user requests are processed by some action class, and each user request needs some response in return. Result in Struts 2 can be defined as something that can be obtained with the help of the result code returned by the action and the result class, which renders the associated source (JSP or HTML) as the next view to the user.

Action classes can return one or many types of result codes (success or error), and the results generated and returned to the user for these different result codes need not be of the same type. The different JSP or HTML pages are returned to generate view in response to results codes returned by the action classes.

The supported result classes are configured in the Struts configuration file so that they can be used by different actions. The association between action and the possible results is also mapped through the result configuration provided with each action mapping in the `struts.xml` file.

Types of Results

The different JSP or HTML pages that are returned to generate view in response to result returned by action classes are not same. For example, the result `success` may render a JSP or HTML page and another result `error` may need to send a HTTP header to the user. Struts 2 comes bundled with several inbuilt result types. The Struts 2 Framework provides several implementation of the `com.opensymphony.xwork2.Result` interface. These implementations can be directly used in your application. Although you can make your own Result class and use it, generally these inbuilt implementations are sufficient for developing the View portion of the Web application. We can define a group of supported `<result-type>` under `<result-types>` elements in `struts.xml`. We can alternately include the `struts-default.xml` file and extend the struts-default package to make all the `<result-type>` definitions available in the `struts.xml file`.

The result types, which are configured in the `struts-default.xml` file, are given in the following code snippet:

```
<package name="struts-default">
   <result-types>
```

```
        <result-type name="chain"
        class="com.opensymphony.xwork2.ActionChainResult"/>
        <result-type name="dispatcher"
        class="org.apache.struts2.dispatcher.ServletDispatcherResult"
        default="true"/>
        <result-type name="freemarker"
        class="org.apache.struts2.views.freemarker.FreemarkerResult"/>
        <result-type name="httpheader"
        class="org.apache.struts2.dispatcher.HttpHeaderResult"/>
        <result-type name="redirect"
        class="org.apache.struts2.dispatcher.ServletRedirectResult"/>
        <result-type name="redirect-action"
        class="org.apache.struts2.dispatcher.ServletActionRedirectResult"/>
        <result-type name="stream"
        class="org.apache.struts2.dispatcher.StreamResult"/>
        <result-type name="velocity"
        class="org.apache.struts2.dispatcher.VelocityResult"/>
        <result-type name="xslt"
        class= "org.apache.struts2.views.xslt.XSLTResult"/>
        <result-type name="plaintext"
        class="org.apache.struts2.dispatcher.PlainTextResult" />
    </result-types>
</package>
```

Struts 2 provides various result types that are configured in the `struts-default.xml` file with their associated result classes. The result types are described in Table 20.18:

Table 20.18: Result Types Available in the Struts 2 Framework

Result name	Description
`Chain`	Helps to implement action chaining
`Dispatcher`	Helps to integrate Web resource, such as JSP
`Redirect`	Helps to redirect the browser to a new URL
`Velocity`	Helps to integrate Velocity
`FreeMarker`	Helps to integrate FreeMarker
`HttpHeader`	Helps to control special HTTP behaviors
`Redirect-Action`	Helps to redirect the request to another action mapping
`Stream`	Helps to stream an InputStream back to the browser, usually for tasks such as file downloading
`XSL`	Helps to integrate the XML/XSLT in the output
`PlainText`	Helps to display the raw content of a particular page, such as HTML and JSP

You can also create additional result types and plug them in your Web application, by implementing the `com.opensymphony.xwork2.Result` interface. You can make result types for different operations, such as generating e-mails, generating images, and so on. Out of these result types, certain result types, such as chain, dispatcher, and redirect, are used frequently as compared to other Result types.

Configuring Results

The method of the action class that processes the user request returns a string as a result code. The String value could be `success`, `error`, `input`, and so on. The string result values returned by an action class are matched with the result elements configured in the struts.xml file for that action class. The action mapping defines the set of possible results, which describes the different possible outcomes. The Action interface has a defined standard set of result tokens. The result tokens describe the names of the predefined result. These result names are mentioned as follows:

- String SUCCESS = "success";
- String NONE = "none";

- String ERROR = "error";
- String INPUT = "input";
- String LOGIN = "login";

The preceding mentioned names of results are predefined, but you can also add your own result name to match the specific cases in your Web application. For example, when the `execute()` method of your Action returns `success` string value, this string value is matched with the result element having `name=success` in `struts.xml`.

We need to configure all supported result types to be used in an application. In addition, the set of possible results to be rendered are also defined in the `struts.xml` file for different action mappings. Consequently, the basic elements used while configuring results, are `<result-types>`, `<result-type>`, and `<result>`.

Configuring Result Types

We have two approaches to configure result types for an action class. The first one is to define all the result types to be used in the application providing a set of `<result-type>` elements for each. This is always required if you want to configure your customized result types. The following code snippet shows the configuration of result types for an action class in the struts.xml file:

```
<struts>
    <package name="mypackage">
            <result-types>
            <result-type name="dispatcher"
            class=" org.apache.struts2.dispatcher.ServletDispatcherResult"
            default="true"/>
            <result-type name="redirect"
            class=" org.apache.struts2.dispatcher.ServletRedirectResult"/>
            </result-types>
            <interceptors>
            //Interceptors declaration.
            </interceptors>
            <action name="login" class="com.kogent.LoginAction">
            <result name="input">login.jsp</result>
            <result name="success" type="redirect">/secure/admin.jsp</result>
            </action>
    </package>
</struts>
```

In the preceding code snippet, results returned by the LoginAction class are configured along with some interceptors. In the preceding code snippet, the login.jsp page is set as a view if the LoginAction class returns `input` as a result type. Similarly, admin.jsp is set as a view in case LoginAction class returns `success`.

The second approach to configure the result types is to include `struts-default.xml` file in your copy of the `struts.xml` file. The `struts-default.xml` file defines a package named `mypackage` with all the available result types configured. The package defined in `struts.xml` can extend the `struts-default` package to make all result types available for all action mappings provided in our package. The following code snippet shows the second approach to configure result types for an action class:

```
<struts>
    <include file="struts-default.xml"/>
    <package name="mypackage" extends="struts-default">
            <action name="login" class="com.kogent.LoginAction">
                    <result name="input">login.jsp</result>
                    <result name="success" type=
                            "redirect">/secure/admin.jsp</result>
            </action>
    </package>
</struts>
```

In the preceding code snippet, a standard way of implementing all results types for action mapping is shown. We can use all kinds of result types directly without providing any `<result-type>` element for them.

After having this general discussion over results in Struts 2, let's learn how to implement validations in Struts 2.

Performing Validation in Struts 2

In this section, we discuss about validation framework of Struts 2 applications, which is based on XWork Validation framework. It is a powerful addition to the Struts 2 Framework. This framework allows you to manage the validations in a separate configuration file, where they can be reviewed and modified without changing Java or JSP code, because localization and validations are tied to the business tier, not to the presentation tier. The XWork Validation framework also provides several basic validators that perform validations. The XWork Validation framework allows developers to add custom validators to support user-defined validation. You can also use the original Struts 2 `validate()` method in tandem with the Struts validators, if required. Struts validator also provides the localization feature that is similar to the validate() method. The validate() method allows you to share the standard message resource file with the main framework, providing an error free solution for the translators you are working with. Struts 2 validators provide validating input for meeting the requirements of complex applications.

Let's now discuss about the XWork Validation framework, which provides validation in the Struts 2 based Web applications.

XWork Validation framework

When a client submits data through a form, it is necessary to check whether the data is valid and in proper format, as required. Validating form data is essential to prevent incorrect data from getting into your applications. Validations can also be performed on the database used in your Web application. Suppose, you perform validation on databases and the welcome page of your application is displayed before the client. This welcome page contains a simple login form, which requires an email address. The proper format of the required email address is defined on the database, which is not known to the client. Now, if the client enters the email address in the wrong format, an error message is displayed. Providing meaningful error messages is one of the keys to providing feedback to the user.

Validations can be performed in your action class, but this approach can make your code very complicated. The code for an action class becomes complicated as while implementing various validation mechanisms, the code for an action class becomes large and difficult to maintain. For example, the code of an action class becomes complicated if we also provide the validation logic for checking empty fields in an action class. Therefore, implementing validation checks declaratively is always preferred over hard coding of logic in an action class. These concerns led to the development of the `XWork Validation` framework, which is part of XWork and describes the validations to be performed on an action with the help of metadata provided in XML files.

Bundled Validators

A class that implements `com.opensymphony.xwork2.validator.Validator` interface can be defined as a validator class or simply a validator. Validators are called by the framework to validate an object by accessing its properties. We have a set of validators, which are already defined by the XWork Validation framework, and the associated classes are bundled in Struts 2 API. Therefore, these validators are also known as bundled validators. These bundled validators are defined in an XML file called `validators.xml`. The `validators.xml` file must be available in your classpath (`/WEB-INF/classes`). However, in case there is no custom validator used in the application, there is no need to put this file in the classpath. All the bundled validators are automatically registered with `ValidatorFactory`, when the `com/opensymphony/xwork2/validator/validators/default.xml` file containing the configuration for all bundled validators is loaded.

All the bundled validators should be configured in the validators.xml file if a custom validator is defined and placed in a classpath. When a `validators.xml` is detected in the classpath, the `com/opensymphony/xwork2/validator/validators/default.xml` file is not automatically loaded; it is only loaded when a custom `validators.xml` cannot be found in the classpath. The following code snippet shows the code of the validators.xml file that contains all the bundled validators:

```
<validators>
<validator name="required"
class="com.opensymphony.xwork2.validator.validators.RequiredFieldValidator"/>
<validator name="requiredstring"
class="com.opensymphony.xwork2.validator.validators.RequiredStringValidator"/>
```

```
<validator name="int"
class="com.opensymphony.xwork2.validator.validators.IntRangeFieldValidator"/>
<validator name="double"
class="com.opensymphony.xwork2.validator.validators.DoubleRangeFieldValidator"/>
<validator name="date"
class="com.opensymphony.xwork2.validator.validators.DateRangeFieldValidator"/>
<validator name="expression"
class="com.opensymphony.xwork2.validator.validators.ExpressionValidator"/>
<validator name="fieldexpression"
class="com.opensymphony.xwork2.validator.validators.FieldExpressionValidator"/>
<validator name="email"
class="com.opensymphony.xwork2.validator.validators.EmailValidator"/>
<validator name="url"
class="com.opensymphony.xwork2.validator.validators.URLValidator"/>
<validator name="visitor"
class="com.opensymphony.xwork2.validator.validators.VisitorFieldValidator"/>
<validator name="conversion"
class="com.opensymphony.xwork2.validator.validators
  .ConversionErrorFieldValidator"/>
<validator name="stringlength"
class="com.opensymphony.xwork2.validator.validators
  .StringLengthFieldValidator"/>
<validator name="regex"
class="com.opensymphony.xwork2.validator.validators.RegexFieldValidator"/>
<validator name="conditionalvisitor"
class="com.opensymphony.xwork2.validator.validators.ConditionalVisitorFieldValidator"/>
</validators>
```

The preceding code snippet shows the bundled validators with their names and descriptions. All validators have their properties, such as `defaultMessage`, `messageKey`, and `shortCircuit`, configured using built-in attributes in the XML file. In addition, all `validators`, except the Expression validator, support a `fieldName` property that is normally set by the Field `validators` inside a <field> element. Table 20.19 describes bundled validators available in the Struts 2 Framework:

Table 20.19: Shows Bundled Validators

Validator	Description
`RequiredFieldValidator`	Checks whether your input field is not null.
`RequiredStringValidator`	Checks whether a String field does not contain null value or has a length greater than 0.
`IntRangeFieldValidator`	Checks whether an Integer value entered in the field is within the specified range.
`DoubleRangeFieldValidator`	Checks whether the double or double value is in the specified range.
`DateRangeFieldValidator`	Checks whether the date is within the specified range.
`ExpressionValidator`	Refers to a non-field validator that evaluates the Boolean value in the OGNL expression.
`FieldExpressionValidator`	Checks whether your input field contains OGNL expression and returns a Boolean value.
`EmailValidator`	Checks whether a given String field is in a valid Email address format.
`URLValidator`	Checks whether your input text field contains valid URL or not.
`VisitorFieldValidator`	Allows the validation to be run against the value of the field to which this validator is applied.

Table 20.19: Shows Bundled Validators	
Validator	**Description**
ConversionErrorFieldValidator	Checks if any conversion error had occurred for this field. The ConversionErrorFieldValidator validator checks whether a type conversion error had occurred while setting the value on this field. It also uses the type-conversion framework to create the correct field error message to be added for this field.
StringLengthFieldValidator	Validates a string for the number of character. This validator checks and makes sure that the length of a String property's value is within a specified range.
RegexFieldValidator	Validates a String field using a regular expression. This validator checks the value of a field against the given regular expression.

Registering Validators

Validators must be registered with the `com.opensymphony.xwork2.validator.ValidatorFactory` `class` by using the `registerValidator()` static method of the `ValidatorFactory` class. The signature for `registerValidator()` method is `public static void registerValidator (String valname, String classname)`. This method allows you to register the specified validator to the existing map of validators. In this method, the parameter `valname` is the name of the validator to be added and `classname` is the fully qualified classname of the validator.

You can register a validator simply by adding the `validators.xml` file in the root of the classpath (`/WEB-INF/classes`), which declares all the validators that you need to use. The following code snippet shows the code for the `validators.xml` file where all the bundled validators are registered:

```
< validators >
<validator name ="required"
class="com.opensymphony.xwork2.validator.validators.RequiredFieldValidator" />
<validator name ="requiredstring"
class="com.opensymphony.xwork2.validator.validators.RequiredStringValidator"/>
<validator name ="int"
class="com.opensymphony.xwork2.validator.validators.IntRangeFieldValidator" />
<validator name ="double"
class="com.opensymphony.xwork2.validator.validators.DoubleRangeFieldValidator"/>
<validator name ="date"
class="com.opensymphony.xwork2.validator.validators.DateRangeFieldValidator" />
<validator name ="expression"
class="com.opensymphony.xwork2.validator.validators.ExpressionValidator" />
<validator name ="fieldexpression"
class="com.opensymphony.xwork2.validator.validators.FieldExpressionValidator" />
<validator name ="email"
class="com.opensymphony.xwork2.validator.validators.EmailValidator" />
<validator name ="url"
class="com.opensymphony.xwork2.validator.validators.URLValidator" />
<validator name ="visitor"
class="com.opensymphony.xwork2.validator.validators.VisitorFieldValidator" />
<validator name ="conversion"
class="com.opensymphony.xwork2.validator.validators.
  ConversionErrorFieldValidator" />
<validator name ="stringlength"
class="com.opensymphony.xwork2.validator.validators
  .StringLengthFieldValidator"/>
<validator name ="regex"
class="com.opensymphony.xwork2.validator.validators.RegexFieldValidator" />
< / validators >
```

In the preceding code snippet, all the pre-defined validators or bundled validators are registered in the validators.xml file.

Defining Validation Rules

Struts 2 Framework provides validation rules for action classes. There are two different ways to define validation rules to validate business logic defined in the action classes.

Validation rules for Struts 2 Framework can be defined in the following ways:

- Per Action class
- Per Action alias

Per Action Class

We can define validation rules for a single action class by creating an XML file, named ActionName-validation.xml. This is known as Action-level validation. To create an Action-level validation, create a file, ActionClass-validation.xml, at the same location where an action class is located. For example, if the name of the action class is MyAction, the name of the validation XML file would be MyAction-validation.xml. The following code snippet shows the Action level validation:

```
< action name="myAlias" class=" action.level.validation.MyAction" >
< / action>
   <action name="myAnotherAlias" class=" action.level.validation.MyAction"
   method = "another" >
< / action>
```

In the preceding code snippet, both the actions, myAlias and myAnotherAlias, are validated according to the same validation configuration file named MyAction-validation.xml file.

Per Action Alias

We can also implement validation rules per action alias by creating a validation configuration file, named as ActionClassName-alias-validation.xml. This is known as Action Alias-level validation. To create an Action Alias-level validation, create a file ActionClassName-alias-validation.xml at the same location where the action class is located. For example, if the name of the action class is MyAction with an alias myAlias, the name of the validation XML file would be MyAction-myAlias-validation.xml. The following code snippet shows the code for the MyAction-myAlias-validation.xml file:

```
< action name="myAlias" class="action.level.validation.MyAction" >
   < / action>
<action name="myAnotherAlias" class="action.level.validation.MyAction"
method = "another">
< / action>
```

In the preceding code snippet, Action Alias-level validation allows the validation to be applied to all action classes with alias named myAlias. This validation mechanism is configured in the MyAction-myAlias-validation.xml. The MyAction-myAlias-validation.xml file will not validate myAnotherAlias action alias as it is not been defined in the validation configuration file representing its alias.

Custom Validators

In addition to using bundled Struts 2 validators, you can build your own custom validators for providing user-defined validation logic in your Web applications. The validation framework allows custom validators to be built and applied in the same declarative fashion as other bundled validators. Implementing a custom validator is as simple as creating a class that extends the com.opensymphony.xwork2.validator.validators.ValidatorSupport (for Global validator) or com.opensymphony.xwork2.validator.validators.FieldValidatorSupport (for FieldValidator). The following code snippet shows the code to build a custom validator named MyStringLengthFieldValidator:

```
package com.kogent.validators;
import com.opensymphony.xwork2.validator.ValidationException;
import com.opensymphony.xwork2.validator.validators.FieldValidatorSupport;
public class MyStringLengthFieldValidator extends FieldValidatorSupport{
   private int maxLength = -1;
   private int minLength = -1;
   private boolean dotrim = true;
```

```
    public void setMinLength ( int minLength )
    {
          this.minLength = minLength;
    }
    public void setMaxLength ( int maxLength )
    {
          this.maxLength = maxLength;
    }
    public void setTrim ( boolean trim )
    {
          dotrim = trim;
    }
    public int getMinLength ( )
    {
          return minLength;
    }
    public int getMaxLength ( )
    {
          return maxLength;
    }
    public boolean getTrim ( )
    {
          return dotrim;
    }
    public void validate ( Object obj ) throws ValidationException
    {
          String fieldName = getFieldName( ) ;
          String val = ( String ) getFieldValue( fieldName , obj )      ;
          if ( dotrim )
          {
                val = val.trim ( );
          }
          if (( minLength > -1 ) && ( val.length ( ) <  minLength ) )
          {
                addFieldError ( fieldName , obj );
          }
          else if (( maxLength > -1 ) && ( val.length ( ) > maxLength ) )
          {
                addFieldError ( fieldName , obj );
          }
    }
  }
```

In the preceding code snippet, a custom validator named `MyStringLengthFieldValidator class` is created by extending the `FieldValidatorSupport` class. The `MyStringLengthFieldValidator` class adds the properties `maxLength`, `minLength`, and `trim`, and uses them to check against the length of the String. The `getFieldName()`, `getFieldValue()`, and `addFieldError()` methods are implemented in the abstract base class. The `MyStringLengthFieldValidator class` needs to be registered with the validation framework by adding the code in the validation.xml file, as shown in the following code snippet:

```
  <validator name="mystringlength"
  class="com.kogent.validators.MyStringLengthFieldValidator"/ >
```

In the preceding code snippet, custom validator named `MyStringLengthFieldValidator` class is registered in the validators.xml file to validate any number of action classes available in a Web application.

When implementing custom validators and registering them using `validators.xml` file, all the required bundled validators should also be configured in the `validators.xml` file.

Short-Circuiting Validators

Short-circuiting validators are those validators that cause the other validators to quit validation, if the first validator itself fails to validate. For example, if an email field is left blank, you do not need to check whether it is a valid email address. In order to implement this function, XWork 1.0.1 added a short-circuit property to the Validation framework. By using this validation, it is possible to short-circuit a stack of validators. The following code snippet shows the configuration for the short-circuit validation:

```
< validators >
< ! - - Field Validator Syntax for EmailValidator  - - >
  < field   name = "EnterEmail" >
        < field-validator type = "requiredstring" short-circuit = "true" >
                < message > You must enter a value for  Email Address
                < /message >
        < /field-validator >
        < field-validator type = "email" short-circuit = "true" >
                < message > Enter a valid Email Address < /message >
        < /field-validator >
  < /field >
< / validators >
```

The preceding code snippet shows that if the `Email` field is null or empty, the EmailValidator is not called because an attribute named short-circuit is set to `true` for the required string validator.

Validation Annotation

Validation annotations help in implementing validation rules on different fields without configuring them in some XML files. Different validation annotations are provided for corresponding validation rules. Let's now discuss each of these validation annotations.

ConversionErrorFieldValidator *Annotation*

The `ConversionErrorFieldValidator` annotation checks whether there are any conversion errors for a field and corrects them. This validator must be applied at the method level. It has five parameters, namely message, key, fieldName, shortCircuit, and type. Among these five parameters, only the message and type are the required parameters; others are the optional. The following code snippet shows the implementation of the `ConversionErrorFieldValidator` annotation:

```
@ConversionErrorFieldValidator(message = "Default message",
key = "i18n.key", shortCircuit = true)
```

The DateRangeFieldValidator Annotation

The DateRangeFieldValidator annotation checks the information regarding the date field; whether the date field has a value within a specified range. The parameters of `DateRangeFieldValidator` annotation are listed in Table 20.20.

Table 20.20: Parameters of DateRangeFieldValidator Annotation

Parameters	Description
message	Specifies an error message for a field
key	Specifies i18n key from language specific properties file
fieldName	Specifies the name of a field to be validated
shortCircuit	Specifies if the current validator class should be used as shortCircuit
type	Specifies Enum value from the ValidatorType element
min	Specifies a minimum date set for the field to be validated
max	Specifies a maximum date set for the field to be validated

Of these parameters, the `message` and `type` parameters are the necessary fields along with the `min` and `max` fields for the checking operations. All the other parameters are optional.

The implementation of the `DateRangeFieldValidator` annotation is shown in the following code snippet:

```
@DateRangeFieldValidator(message = "Default message",
  key = "i18n.key",
  shortCircuit = true,
  min = "2010/01/01", max = "2010/12/31")
```

The DoubleRangeFieldValidator Annotation

The DoubleRangeFieldValidator annotation checks whether or not a double field has a value within the given range. Therefore, for the DoubleRangeFieldValidator annotation also, you have to provide min and max properties; otherwise, no validation is performed. The parameters of DoubleRangeFieldValidator annotation are listed in Table 20.21.

Table 20.21: Parameters of DoubleRangeFieldValidator Annotation

Parameters	Description
message	Specifies an error message for a field
key	Specifies i18n key from language specific properties file
fieldname	Specifies the name of a field to be validated
shortCircuit	Specifies if the current validator class should be used as shortCircuit
type	Specifies Enum value from the ValidatorType element
minInclusive	Specifies a minimum inclusive number for the field to be validated
maxInclusive	Specifies a maximum inclusive number for the field to be validated
minExclusive	Specifies a minimum exclusive number for the field to be validated
maxExclusive	Specifies a maximum exclusive number for the field to be validated

The implementation of the DoubleRangeFieldValidator annotation is shown in the following code:

```
@DoubleRangeFieldValidator(message = "Default message",
    key = "i18n.key",
    shortCircuit = true,
    minInclusive = "1.567", maxInclusive = "99.678")
```

The EmailValidator Annotation

The EmailValidator annotation checks whether the field contains a valid email address. It has the parameters similar to that of the ConversionErrorFieldValidator annotation.

The implementation of the EmailValidator annotation is shown in the following code snippet:

```
@EmailValidator(massage = "Default message",
    key = "i18n.key", shortCircuit = true)
```

The ExpressionValidator Annotation

The ExpressionValidator annotation is used to validate an expression. This annotation must be applied at the method level. The parameters of ExpressionValidator annotation are listed in Table 20.22.

Table 20.22: Parameters of ExpressionValidator Annotation

Parameters	Description
message	Specifies an error message for a field
key	Specifies i18n key from language specific properties file
shortCircuit	Specifies if the current validator class should be used as shortCircuit
expression	Specifies an OGNL expression returning a boolean value

The implementation of the ExpressionValidator annotation is shown in the following code snippet:

```
@ExpressionValidator(message = "Default message",
    key = "i18n.key",
    shortCircuit = true, expression = "Sample OGNL Expression")
```

The FieldExpressionValidator Annotation

The `FieldExpressionValidator` annotation performs validation with the help of an OGNL expression. If the expression returns false at the time it is evaluated against the value stack, the error message gets added to the field. The parameters of `FieldExpressionValidator` annotation are listed in Table 20.23:

Table 20.23: Parameters of FieldExpressionValidator Annotation

Parameters	Description
message	Specifies an error message for a field
key	Specifies i18n key from language specific properties file
fieldName	Specifies the name of a field to be validated
shortCircuit	Specifies if the current validator class should be used as shortCircuit
expression	Specifies an OGNL expression returning a boolean value

Of these parameters, only the message and type are the required fields. The others are optional. The implementation of the `FieldExpressionValidator` annotation is shown in the following code snippet:

```
@FieldExpressionValidator(message = "Default message",
   key = "i18n.key",
   shortCircuit = true,
   expression = "Sample OGNL expression" )
```

The IntRangeFieldValidator Annotation

The `IntRangeFieldValidator` annotation validates whether or not the numeric field has a value within a specified range. The parameters of `IntRangeFieldValidator` annotation are listed in Table 20.24:

Table 20.24: Parameters of IntRangeFieldValidator annotation

Parameters	Description
message	Specifies an error message for a field
key	Specifies i18n key from language specific properties file
fieldName	Specifies the name of a field to be validated
shortCircuit	Specifies if the current validator class should be used as shortCircuit
type	Specifies Enum value from the ValidatorType element
min	Specifies a minimum date set for the field to be validated
max	Specifies a maximum date set for the field to be validated

When you are using this annotation, you have to provide `min` and `max` values in such a way that `0` can also be considered as a possible value.

The implementation of the `IntRangeFieldValidator` annotation is shown in the following code snippet:

```
@IntRangeFieldValidator(message = "Default message",
   key = "i18n.key",
   shortCircuit = true, min = "10", max = "50" )
```

The RegexFieldValidator Annotation

The `RegexFieldValidator` annotation uses a regular expression to validate a String field. It is also applied at the method level. The parameters of the `RegexFieldValidator` annotation are listed in Table 20.25.

Table 20.25: Parameters of the RegexFieldValidator Annotation

Parameters	Description
message	Specifies an error message for a field
key	Specifies i18n key from language specific properties file

Table 20.25: Parameters of the RegexFieldValidator Annotation	
Parameters	**Description**
fieldName	Specifies the name of a field to be validated
shortCircuit	Specifies if the current validator class should be used as shortCircuit
type	Specifies Enum value from the ValidatorType element
expression	Specifies an OGNL expression returning a boolean value

The implementation of the RegexFieldValidator annotation is shown in the following code snippet:

```
@RegexFieldValidator (key = "regex. Field", expression="your regex")
```

The RequiredFieldValidator Annotation

The RequiredFieldValidator annotation checks whether or not a field is required, and is applied at the method level. The parameters of RequiredFieldValidator annotation are listed in Table 20.26:

Table 20.26: Parameters of the RequiredFieldValidator Annotation	
Parameters	**Description**
message	Specifies an error message for a field
key	Specifies i18n key from language specific properties file
fieldName	Specifies the name of a field to be validated
shortCircuit	Specifies if the current validator class should be used as shortCircuit
type	Specifies Enum value from the ValidatorType element

The implementation of @RequiredFieldValidator annotation is shown in the following code snippet:

```
@RequiredFieldValidator (message = "Default message",
   key = "i18n.key", shortCircuit = true)
```

The RequiredStringValidator Annotation

The RequiredStringValidator annotation checks whether a string field is empty or not. In other words, it verifies whether the length of a string field is greater than zero (0). The parameters of the RequiredStringValidator annotation are listed in Table 20.27:

Table 20.27: Parameters of the RequiredStringValidator Annotation	
Parameters	**Description**
message	Specifies an error message for a field
key	Specifies i18n key from language specific properties file
fieldName	Specifies the name of a field to be validated
shortCircuit	Specifies if the current validator class should be used as shortCircuit
type	Specifies Enum value from the ValidatorType element
trim	Specifies a boolean property that determines whether the specified String is trimmed before checking its length

The use of @RequiredStringValidator annotation is shown in the following code snippet:

```
@RequiredStringValidator (message = "Default message",
   key = "i18n.key",
   shortCircuit = true, trim = true)
```

The StringLengthFieldValidator Annotation

The `StringLengthFieldValidator` annotation checks the right length of the string field. To utilize this annotation, you need to set `minLength` and `maxLength`. The parameters of the `StringLengthFieldValidator` annotation are listed in Table 20.28:

Table 20.28: Parameters of StringLengthFieldValidator Annotation

Parameters	Description
message	Specifies an error message for a field
key	Specifies i18n key from language specific properties file
fieldName	Specifies the name of a field to be validated
shortCircuit	Specifies if the current validator class should be used as shortCircuit
type	Specifies Enum value from the ValidatorType element
trim	Specifies a boolean property that determines whether the provided String is trimmed before checking its length
minLength	Specifies the minimum length the String must be
maxLength	Specifies the maximum length the String can be

The implementation of `@StringLengthFieldValidator` annotation is shown in the following code snippet:

```
@StringLengthFieldValidator (message = "Default message",
    key = "i18n.key",
    ShortCircuit = true,
    trim = true,
    minLength = "10", maxLength = "50")
```

The StringRegexValidator Annotation

The `StringRegexValidator` annotation validates the entered string against some configured regular expression. The parameters of the `StringRegexValidator` annotation are listed in Table 20.29:

Table 20.29: Parameters of StringRegexValidator Annotation

Parameters	Description
message	Specifies an error message for a field
key	Specifies i18n key from language specific properties file
fieldName	Specifies the name of a field to be validated
shortCircuit	Specifies if the current validator class should be used as shortCircuit
Type	Specifies Enum value from the ValidatorType element
caseSensitive	Determines whether the matching alpha characters in the expression should be checked keeping case-sensitivity in view or not
regex	Specifies the Regular Expression for which to check a match

The implementation of `@StringRegexValidator` annotation is shown in the following code snippet:

```
@StringRegexValidator(message = "Default message",
    key = "i18n.key",
    shortCircuit = true,
    regex = "a regular expression",
    caseSensitive = true)
```

The **UrlValidator** Annotation

The `UrlValidator` annotation checks for a valid URL. It must be applied at the method level. The parameters of `UrlValidator` annotation are listed in Table 20.30:

Table 20.30: Parameters of the UrlValidator Annotation	
Parameters	**Description**
message	Specifies an error message for a field
key	Specifies i18n key from language specific properties file
fieldName	Specifies the name of a field to be validated
shortCircuit	Specifies if the current validator class should be used as shortCircuit
type	Specifies Enum value from the ValidatorType element

The implementation of the `UrlValidator` annotation is shown in the following code snippet:

```
@UrlValidator (message = "Default message",
   key = "i18n.key", shortCircuit = true)
```

The Validation Annotation

Whenever you want to use annotation-based validation, you have to annotate the class or interface with the Validation annotation. The parameters of Validation annotation are listed in Table 20.31:

Table 20.31: Parameters of the Validation Annotation	
Parameters	**Description**
message	Specifies an error message for a field
key	Specifies i18n key from language specific properties file
fieldName	Specifies name of a field to be validated
shortCircuit	Specifies if the current validator class should be used as shortCircuit
type	Specifies Enum value from the ValidatorType element

The following code snippet shows the implementation of the `Validation` annotation:

```
@Validation()
public interface AnnotationDataAware {
   void setDesignationObj(Designation b);
   Designation getDesignationObj();
   @RequiredFieldValidator(message = "You must enter your designation.")
   @RequiredStringValidator(message = "You must enter your designation.")
   void setData(String data);
   String getData();
}
```

In the preceding code snippet, you have to mark the interface with `@Validation annotation` as well as apply standard or custom annotations at the method level. The following code snippet shows an action class using the `@Validation` annotation:

```
@Validation()
public class MyAnnotationAction extends ActionSupport {
   @RequiredFieldValidator(type = ValidatorType.FIELD, message =
   "You must enter a number.")
   @IntRangeFieldValidator(type = ValidatorType.FIELD, min = "5", max =
   "20", message = "number must be between ${min} and ${max},
   current value is ${number}.")
   public void setNumber(int number) {
         this.number = number;
   }
   public int getNumber() {
         return number;
   }
   public String execute() throws Exception {
         return SUCCESS;
   }
}
```

The **Validations** Annotation

You can use various annotations of the same type by nesting the annotations within the `@Validations` annotation at the method level. The parameters of the Validations annotation are listed in Table 20.32:

Table 20.32: Parameters of Validations Annotation

Parameters	Description
requiredFields	Adds the list of RequiredFieldValidators
customValidator	Adds the list of CustomValidators
conversionErrorFields	Adds the list of ConversionErrorFieldValidators
dateRangeFields	Adds the list of DateRangeFieldValidators
emails	Adds the list of `EmailValidators`
fieldExpressions	Adds the list of FieldExpressionValidators
intRangeFields	Adds the list of IntRangeFieldValidators
requiredStrings	Adds the list of RequiredStringValidators
stringLengthFields	Adds the list of StringLengthFieldValidators
urls	Adds the list of `URLValidators`
visitorFields	Adds the list of VisitorFieldValidators
stringRegex	Adds the list of StringRegexValidators
regexFields	Adds the list of RegexFieldValidators
expressions	Adds the list of ExpressionValidators

The following code snippet shows an action class using the `@Validations` annotation:

```
@Validations(
   requiredFields={
          @RequiredFieldValidator(type = ValidatorType.SIMPLE,
          fieldName = "namefield",
          message = "You must enter your name in this field.")
   },
   requiredStrings ={
          @RequiredStringValidator(type = ValidatorType.SIMPLE,
          fieldName = "stringfield",
          message = "You must enter String value for this field.")
   },
   emails = {
          @EmailValidator(type = ValidatorType.SIMPLE,
          fieldName = "emailaddress",
          message = "You must enter your email address for this field.")
   },
)
public String execute() throws Exception {
   return SUCCESS;
}
```

The VisitorFieldValidator Annotation

The `VisitorFieldValidator` annotation allows you to forward the validator to the properties of your action class to use the validation files of the same action class. This annotation lets you use the Model-Driven development pattern and handles the validation logic in an action class. The parameters of VisitorFieldValidator annotation are listed in Table 20.33:

Table 20.33: Parameters of the VisitorFieldValidator Annotation

Parameters	Description
message	Specifies an error message for a field.
key	Specifies i18n key from language specific properties file.
fieldName	Specifies the name of a field to be validated.
shortCircuit	Specifies if the current validator class should be used as shortCircuit.
type	Specifies Enum value from the ValidatorType element.
appendPrefix	Determines whether the name of this field validator should be appended to the field name of the visited field. The name must be appended as it helps in determining the full field name when an error occurs.
context	Determines the context used to validate the Object property.

The implementation of the VisitorFieldValidator annotation is shown in the following code snippet:

```
@VisitorFieldValidator(message = "Default message",
  key = "i18n.key",
  shortCircuit = true,
  context = "sample action alias", appendPrefix = true)
```

The CustomValidator Annotation

The `CustomValidator` annotation can be used for custom validators. You need to use the `ValidationParameter` annotation to provide additional parameters. The parameters of `CustomValidator` annotation are listed in Table 20.34:

Table 20.34: Parameters of the CustomValidator Annotation

Parameters	Description
message	Specifies an error message for a field
key	Specifies i18n key from language specific properties file
fieldName	Specifies the name of a field to be validated
shortCircuit	Specifies if the current validator class should be used as shortCircuit
type	Specifies Enum value from the ValidatorType element

The implementation of `@CustomValidator` annotation is shown in the following code:

```
@CustomValidator(type = “CustomValidatorName”, fieldname = “customField” )
```

We have learned about various annotations for validation in Struts 2 Application. Let's now discuss about validating a Struts2 application in the following subsection.

Validating Stuts2App Application

In order to induce validation into our application, we have to get back to our previous application called Struts2App. This application was a simple Struts 2 application without any validation mechanism. To validate this application, we first have to edit our action class, UserAction.java, to incorporate validation into this action class. The code for validating application named Struts2App is given in Listing 20.16 (you can find the UserAction.java file in the \Struts2App\src\com\kogent\action folder):

Listing 20.16: Displaying the Code of the UserAction.java File

```
package com.kogent.action;
import java.util.ArrayList;
import java.util.Iterator;
import java.util.Map;
import org.apache.struts2.interceptor.ApplicationAware;
import com.kogent.User;
import com.opensymphony.xwork2.ActionSupport;
```

```
public class UserAction extends ActionSupport implements ApplicationAware{
  String username;
  String password;
  String city;
  String email;
  String type;
  Map application;
  public void setApplication(Map application) {
        this.application=application;
  }
  public String getUsername() {
        return username;
  }
  public void setUsername(String username) {
        this.username = username;
  }
  public String getPassword() {
        return password;
  }
  public void setPassword(String password) {
        this.password = password;
  }
  public String getCity() {
        return city;
  }
  public void setCity(String city) {
        this.city = city;
  }
  public String getEmail() {
        return email;
  }
  public void setEmail(String email) {
        this.email = email;
  }
  public String getType() {
        return type;
  }
  public void setType(String type) {
        this.type = type;
  }
  public String execute() throws Exception {
        ArrayList users=(ArrayList)application.get("users");

        if(users==null){
              users=new ArrayList();
        }
        if(getUser(username)==null){
              users.add(buildUser());
              application.put("users", users);
        }else{
              this.addActionError("User Name is in use.");
              return ERROR;
        }
        return SUCCESS;
  }
  public String edit() throws Exception{
        ArrayList users=(ArrayList)application.get("users");
        User user=null;
        int index=0;
        Iterator it=users.iterator();
        while(it.hasNext()){
              user=(User)it.next();
              if(user.getUsername().equals(username)){
                    break;
              }
```

```
                index++;
            }
            User newuser=buildUser();
            users.set(index, newuser);
            application.put("users", users);
            return SUCCESS;
    }
    public String deleteUser() throws Exception{
            ArrayList users=(ArrayList)application.get("users");
            User user=null;
            int index=0;
            Iterator it=users.iterator();
            while(it.hasNext()){
                    user=(User)it.next();
                    if(user.getUsername().equals(username)){
                            break;
                    }
                    index++;
            }
            users.remove(index);
            application.put("users", users);
            return SUCCESS;
    }
    public User buildUser(){
            User user=new User();
            user.setUsername(username);
            user.setPassword(password);
            user.setCity(city);
            user.setEmail(email);
            user.setType(type);
            return user;
    }
    public User getUser(String username){
            User user=new User();
            boolean found=false;
            ArrayList users=(ArrayList)application.get("users");
            if(users!=null){
                    Iterator it=users.iterator();
                    while(it.hasNext()){
                            user=(User)it.next();
                            if(username.equals(user.getUsername())){
                                    found=true;
                                    break;
                            }
                    }
                    if(found){
                            return user;
                    }
            }
            return null;
    }
    public void validate() {
            if ( (username == null ) || (username.length() == 0) ) {
            this.addFieldError("username", getText("app.username.blank"));
            }
            if ( (password == null ) || (password.length() == 0) ) {
            this.addFieldError("password", getText("app.password.blank"));
            }
            if ( (email == null ) || (email.length() == 0) ) {
                    this.addFieldError("email", getText("app.email.blank"));
            }
    }
}
```

Recompile the UserAction.java and replace the .class file at the location `\Struts2App\WEB-INF\classes\com\kogent\action`. Now, add some property files named struts.properties and ApplicationResources.properties to the application.

The ApplicationResources file is mapped to struts.custom.i18n.resources in the `struts.properties` file, as shown in the following code snippet:

```
struts.custom.i18n.resources=ApplicationResources
```

Save the struts.properties file at the location `\Struts2App\WEB-INF\classes` folder. Similarly, save the ApplicationResources.properties file at the location `\Struts2App\WEB-INF\classes` folder. The code for the ApplicationResource.properties file is shown in the following code snippet:

```
# Resources for parameter 'ApplicationResources'
# Project Struts2Action
app.username.blank=User Name is Required.
app.password.blank=Password is Required.
app.email.blank=Email is Required.
```

After making the above mentioned changes, re-create and deploy Struts2App.war on Glassfish Server 4.0. Browse `http://localhost:8080/Struts2App` URL to run the Web application, as shown in Figure 20.10:

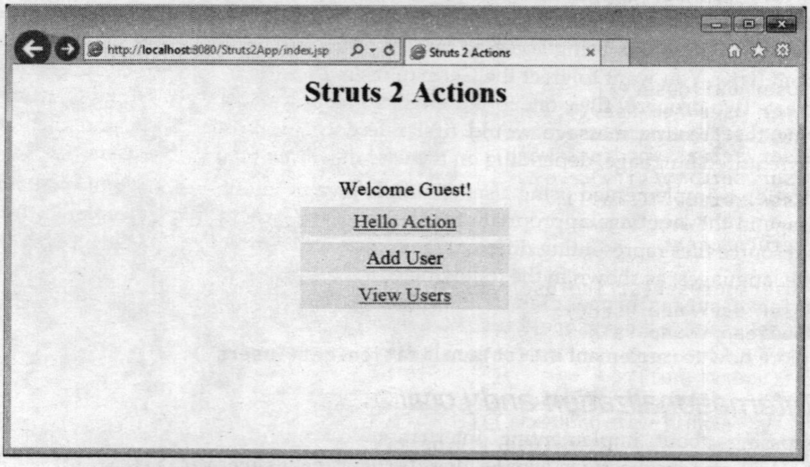

Figure 20.10: Showing the Output of the index.jsp Page

Click the `Add User` hyperlink to add a new user. The output of `add_user.jsp` page is shown in Figure 20.11:

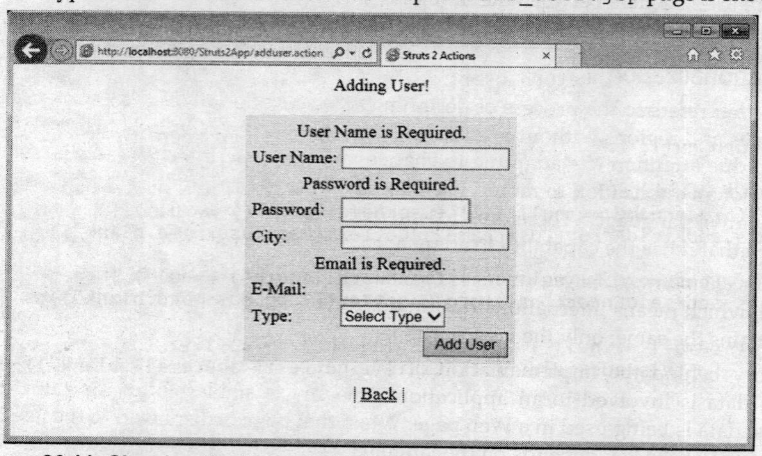

Figure 20.11: Showing the Support for Validation Errors in the add_user.jsp page

Figure 20.11 shows the `add_user.jsp` page, which provides validation by checking whether the fields are empty or not. If the fields are empty, a message is displayed to prompt the user to provide information in them.

Internationalizing Struts 2 Applications

The Struts 2 framework has built-in support for internationalization, which allows Web pages to be displayed according to a client's requirements. In other words, it reduces the effort of the developer to customize the Web pages in different languages. Internationalization provides the translation of messages in a user's native language or locale. It also provides other culture-sensitive data according to the user's locale, such as time, money, and number system representation. Not only this, internationalization also provides the conversion of various non-textual elements, embedded in a Web page, in the form relevant to the user.

While implementing internationalization, you need to create a property file for each language in which you want to display the Web pages. These property files are referenced by the Web pages to ascertain the specific locale or language customization before they are rendered. The property file contains titles, messages, and other text in a specific language. The naming format for the property file is `ResourceBundleName.properties`. For example, the name of a property file with English as default language would be `ApplicationResources.properties`.

Let us suppose your Web site is being accessed by two categories of users from different locales, Germany and United Kingdom (UK). You want to greet the German users in German and the UK users in English. To do this, you need to create two property files, one for an English greeting and the other for a German greeting. The Web page displaying the greeting message would first reference the property file and then render the greeting message in the required language, depending on the user details entered by the users.

Internationalization is implemented using a set of simple Java property files. Each file contains a key/value pair for each message in the language appropriate for the requesting client. For example, in the previous example, two different resource files representing different languages are created to greet the English and German users in their respective languages, as shown in the following code snippet:

```
ApplicationResources.properties // English user
ApplicationResources_de.properties // German user
```

Let's now explore how to implement internationalization in Struts 2.

Describing Internationalization and Localization

Prior to discussing about implementing internationalization in Struts 2, let's explore the concepts of internationalization and localization. Two terms—internationalization and localization are used to describe the internationalization feature of the Struts 2. You should have noticed that internationalization is often abbreviated as `i18n`, as there are 18 letters between the first letter *I*, and the last letter *n*. For the same reason, Localization is sometimes abbreviated as `l10n`. Let's explore these concepts in detail next.

Exploring Internationalization

Internationalization refers to the process of designing an application in such a manner that it can be adapted to various languages and regions without engineering changes. In this definition of internationalization, two terms need to be paid due attention to—adapting to changes and engineering changes. The first term, *adapting*, refers to the capability of an application to mould itself according to the culture of a user by representing all messages in the user's native language. Therefore, to internationalize the application would mean developing the application such that it has the capability to adapt according to the user's regional details.

The second term, *engineering changes,* refers to the changes in the code. The regional details are not hard-coded in the application, which means internationalization does not require engineering changes. The control logic of the application remains the same; only the view is changed.

The main theory behind the implementation of internationalization feature involves using a key whenever region-specific data is involved in an application. This key is similar to an indicator, which indicates that a region-sensitive data is being used in a Web page. When that page is displayed to the user, the key is replaced by its value. The value of the key depends on the language of the user. Therefore, there are different values of a key for different languages. All the possible values for this key are available in a file called `Resource Bundle`, which is stored outside the source code.

When a session begins, the Web browser provides local details of the user to the Web server. According to these local details of the user, a corresponding resource bundle is selected. Wherever there is a key in the page, an appropriate value of the key is retrieved from the selected resource bundle. The retrieval of key-value and its insertion is dynamic. In other words, it takes place at runtime.

It is to be noted that the local details provided by the browser are stored in the server as objects of the `ActionContext class`. This detail is temporarily saved for a single user session only. For different user sessions, these user-details are saved as different `ActionContext`. That is, the objects of the `ActionContext` class are unique for every session.

The `I18n` interceptor is used to remember the locale selected for a user's session. With every HTTP request, a new thread is created, and the interceptor pushes the locale into the `ActionContext` associated to the thread. All the locale-sensitive methods utilize this locale.

The class associated with i18n inceptor is `com.opensymphony.xwork2.interceptor.I18nInterceptor`. This class is directly derived from the `com.opensymphony.xwork2.interceptor.AbstractInterceptor` class, which implements all the methods of the `com.opensymphony.xwork2.interceptor.Interceptor` `interface`, such as `init()`, `destroy()`, and `intercept()`.

Whenever an HTTP request is received, the I18n interceptor looks for the parameters in the request header and sets the locale according to the parameters. This locale remains the same for the entire session of the request. However, it is also possible to change the locale for a session dynamically, which allows the user to select a language of his/her choice at any point in the entire session.

Let's suppose the current locale for a user's session is for the default language. A request, `someAction?request_locale=en_EN`, made by a browser is processed by the interceptor to set the locale for the session to the English language. It is important to configure an interceptor before a request is processed by it.

The following code snippet shows the configuration of the `i18n` interceptor for an action class:

```
<package name="some-default" extends="struts-default">
   <action name="someAction" class="examples.SomeAction">
          <interceptor-ref name="i18n"/>
          <interceptor-ref name="basicStack"/>
          <result name="success">secondPage.jsp</result>
   </action>
</package>
```

In the preceding code snippet, the i18n interceptor is configured in the struts.xml file to intercept the action class called `SomeAction by` using the `<interceptor>` element.

The next example shows the setting of a parameter to be processed by the `i18n` interceptor. Now, we can pass a request parameter named `parameterName` to the `i18n` interceptor to set a new locale according to the value of this parameter, as shown in the following code snippet:

```
<package name="some-default" extends="struts-default">
   <action name="someAction" class="examples.SomeAction">
          <interceptor-ref name="i18n">
                 <param name="parameterName">newlocale</param>
          </interceptor-ref >
          <interceptor-ref name="basicStack"/>

          <result name="success">secondPage.jsp</result>
   </action>
</package>
```

Let's now explore the concept of localization in detail.

Exploring Localization

Localization plays a major role in implementing internationalization. It is a process of adding locale-specific components, such as property files in Web applications to customize them according to specific languages.

Locale is an object representing the regional settings of the user's machine. In the definition, the term to be focused is `locale-specific`, which emphasizes on those elements of the application that are dependent on the local settings of the user's machine.

The main purpose of localization is to translate the region-specific information in the application into the corresponding language and data format. This includes changing the language used, along with the language of the currency, the time and date format, and so on, into the local terms specified by the user's machine.

Global Resource Bundle

A resource bundle is a file that contains the key-value pairs for a particular language. Different resource bundles are required for different languages. A resource bundle file is created in a text editor and saved with the `.properties` extension. Therefore, resource bundles are also known as property files. As resource bundles are global to all classes, these are also known as global resource bundles. The global resource bundles are saved as a property file with a name, as shown in the following code snippet:

```
ResourceBundleName.properties
```

A property file for a language is distinguished from other property files by specifying a two-letter International Ogranization for Standards (ISO) language code in the file name. This code is appended with the file name before the file extension.

Let's consider the property files for different languages, as described in Table 20.35:

Table 20.35: Property Files for Different Languages

Property File Name	Description	File Content
ResourceBundle_fr.properties	Properties file for the French language	app.greeting= Bonjour app.username= usager nom app.submit= s'assujettir
ResourceBundle_es.properties	Properties file for the Spanish language	app. Greeting= Hola app.username= Nombre de Usuario app.submit=somete
ResourceBundle.properties	Properties file for default language, which is English	app.greeting=Welcome app.username=Username app.submit=SUBMIT

These entries tell Struts that when the user has a locale that uses the French language, and the key `app.greeting` is encountered in the code, the value `Bonjour` should be substituted at in place of the app.greeting key. Similarly, when the `app.username` key is encountered, the `usager nom` value must be substituted. Similarly, for the Spanish language Locale, `Hola` and `Nombre de Usuario` must be substituted in place of the `app.greeting` and `app.username` keys, respectively.

It is for the developer to decide how many property files to be included in an application. When the locale specific property file for a user is not available in a Web application, a default property file is used to customize Web pages. In this example, the default property file contains the values of the keys in the English language. Therefore, for the users other than French and Spanish, `Welcome` and `Username` will be substituted for every occurrence of the `app.greeting` and `app.username` keys in the code.

After the property files are created, the next step is to deploy these files in the framework. In Struts 2, the deployment of property files is comparatively easier than Struts 1. In Struts 2, the property files are stored in the `ApplicationName/WEB-INF/classes` folder. Struts 2 applications map the property files with the help of a file, called `struts.properties`. This file contains the location of the property files. The following code snippet shows the entry of a property file in the struts.properties file:

```
struts.custom.i18n.resources=NameOfPropertyFile
```

The preceding code line shows an entry in the `struts.property` file, which describes the global resource for an application.

It is also possible to specify more than one global resource bundles by separating the filenames using commas, as shown in the following code snippet:

```
struts.custom.i18n.resources= File_1, File_2
```

If more than one resource bundles are specified, the action class is associated with all the specified files, and searches for the required key-value in both the resource bundles.

Implementing Plugins in Struts 2

A plugin is a computer program that communicates with a main or host application. For example, a Web browser or an email program serves as a plugin that helps you to communicate with the application to provide a specific function, on request. The term plugin itself suggests that it is something, which can be plugged into the framework to introduce some extension points, such as new functionalities, classes, result types, interceptors, or packages into the existing framework. Struts 2 Framework provides support for integration with other frameworks with the help of some plugins, such as Spring and JSF.

Therefore, these plugins are used to add extra functionality, function on demand, and component to make your Web application more efficient.

Plugins are used in Struts 2 applications with the help of JAR files available in the Struts Framework. Some of these JAR files are struts2-tiles-plugin-2.3.16.jar, struts2-jsf-plugin-2.3.16, and struts2-spring-plugin-2.3.16, which are added into the applications' class path. The JAR file for a plugin may contain a `struts-plugin.xml` file, providing configuration information for the plugin. This `struts-plugin.xml` file follows the same pattern as that of the `struts.xml` file.

Let's now discuss the plugins available in Struts 2 Framework in the following section.

Struts 2 Bundled Plugins

The plugins that come along with the distribution of the Struts 2 Framework are also known as Struts 2 bundled plugins. Table 20.36 describe some of bundled plugins in Struts 2:

Table 20.36: Bundled Plugins in Struts 2

PLUGIN	DESCRIPTION
Codebehind	Reduces the required configuration for the action class and the results by adding the Page Controller conventions.
Config Browser	Enables viewing of the configuration details such as action mapping, exception mapping, result mappings, and so on.
JasperReports	Enables the actions to generate reports through JasperReports.
JFreeChart	Enables the actions to return charts and graphs based on some data.
JSF	Provides support for Java Server Faces (JSF) components, and that too without any additional configuration.
Pell Multipart	Enables the Struts 2 Framework to use the Jason Pell's multipart parser, which is used to process the file uploads.
Plexus	Enables the creation and injection of actions, interceptors, and results by Plexus framework. Plexus is a dependency injection framework, such as Spring.
SiteGraph	Creates a graphical representation showing the flow amongst actions, interceptors, and results in a Struts 2 application.
SiteMesh	Provides support for features, such as headers and menu bars in Web pages.
Spring	Provides the support for creating actions, interceptors, and results by the Spring Framework.
Struts 1	Enables the use of Struts 1 actions and ActionForms in Struts2 applications.
Tiles	Provides a common look to the pages in the Web application by dividing pages into different fragments, known as `tiles`.

Table 20.36 describes various plugins available in Struts 2 Framework. To understand the implementation of a plugin in a Struts 2 application, let's discuss about a commonly used and most popular plugin called Tiles plugin.

Tiles Plugin

The tiles plugin allows the actions to return tile pages containing different JSP pages. This is useful when a developer needs to implement a common look and feel among all the pages of an application. The tile layout is similar to a template layout.

Implementing Tiles Plugin

Let's now create an application named `Struts2Tiles` to understand Struts 2 tiles plugin and to see how an action class can be integrated. Perform the following broad-level steps to create the Web application:

- Creating template
- Creating tiles enabled JSP pages
- Creating Action class
- Configuring struts.xml
- Creating tiles.xml
- Creating body.jsp
- Creating manager_menu.jsp
- Creating clerk_menu.jsp
- Configuring web.xml
- Exploring the directory structure of the application
- Packaging, running, and deploying the application

Creating Template

Template is a JSP page that defines a rectangular region to specify where other pages, such as header, footer, menu, and body should be positioned. A sample of template is shown in Figure 20.12:

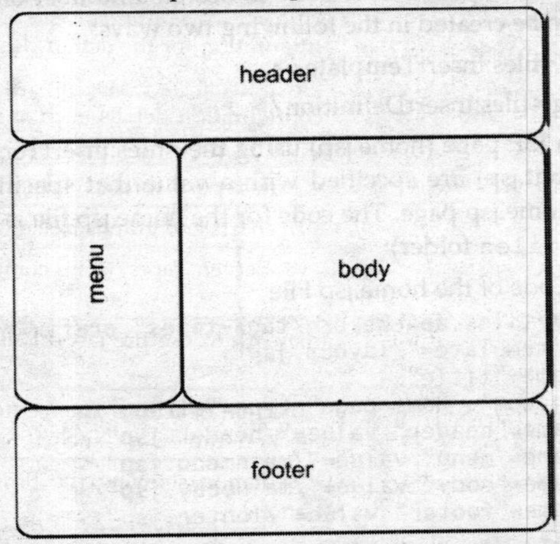

Figure 20.12: Displaying the Layout of a Template

In our application, template is represented by a JSP page, named layout.jsp. The code for layout.jsp is shown in Listing 20.17 (save the layout.jsp file in the `\Struts2Tiles` folder):

Listing 20.17: Displaying the Code of the layout.jsp Page

```
<%@ taglib uri="http://tiles.apache.org/tags-tiles" prefix="tiles" %>
<html>
   <head>
         <title>
                <tiles:getAsString name="title"/>
         </title>
   </head>
```

```
    <body topmargin="0">
        <table width="800" cellspacing="0" align="center" >
            <tr>
                <td colspan="2" height="70">
                    <tiles:insertAttribute name="header"/>
                </td>
            </tr>
            <tr height="300">
                <td width="200" valign="top">
                    <tiles:insertAttribute name="menu"/>
                </td>
                <td width="600">
                    <tiles:insertAttribute name="body"/>
                </td>
            </tr>
            <tr>
                <td colspan="2" height="70">
                    <tiles:insertAttribute name="footer"/>
                </td>
            </tr>
        </table>
    </body>
</html>
```

In Listing 20.17, the <tiles:getAsString/> and <tiles:insertAttribute/> tags are used to specify attributes, such as header, footer, menu, and body in layout.jsp page. These attributes are specified with values representing the name of JSP pages in the home.jsp page.

Creating Tiles Enabled JSPs

A JSP page can be easily changed to a tiled page (fragmented into tiles) using tiles tags. This type of page design using tiles tags helps in reducing duplication of code to design a number of pages having the same structure in an application. A tiles page can be created in the following two ways:

- Inserting template using <tiles:insertTemplate/>
- Inserting definition using <tiles:insertDefinition/>

The template is inserted into a JSP page (home.jsp) using the <tiles:insertTemplate/> tag. The attributes that are declared in the template (layout.jsp) are specified with a value that specifies the path of JSP pages using the <tiles:putAttribute/> tag in the home.jsp page. The code for the home.jsp file is shown in the Listing 20.18 (save the home.jsp file in the `\Struts2Tiles` folder):

Listing 20.18: Displaying the Code of the home.jsp File

```
<%@ taglib uri="http://tiles.apache.org/tags-tiles" prefix="tiles" %>
<tiles:insertTemplate template="/layout.jsp">
<tiles:putAttribute name="title"
value="www.simplylogin.com - Home page" type="string"/>
<tiles:putAttribute name="header" value="/header.jsp" />
<tiles:putAttribute name="menu" value="/mainmenu.jsp"/>
<tiles:putAttribute name="body" value="/mainbody.jsp"/>
<tiles:putAttribute name="footer" value="/footer.jsp"/>
</tiles:insertTemplate>
```

In Listing 20.18, the `<tiles:putAttribute/>` tag is used to fill all the four attributes declared in the layout.jsp page with a value specifying the path of JSP pages. The first attribute is of type String and the content directly gets displayed using <tiles:getAsString/> tag in the layout.jsp template. The basic structure of the home.jsp page is rendered by inserting the template (layout.jsp). Therefore, before you access home.jsp page, make sure that you have created all the four JSP pages, which are specified as values to the attributes, such as header, footer, menu, and body, in the home.jsp page. Therefore, let's create the following JSP pages before accessing the home.jsp file:

- header.jsp
- footer.jsp
- mainmenu.jsp

- mainbody.jsp

In addition, you also need to create login.jsp and loginform.jsp pages.

Creating header.jsp

The header.jsp creates a banner to be displayed in the Web pages. Listing 20.19 shows the code for header.jsp (save the header.jsp file in the \Struts2Tiles folder):

Listing 20.19: Displaying the Code of the header.jsp File

```
<%@ taglib prefix="s" uri="/struts-tags" %>
<table width="100%" height="100%" bgcolor="#5a84da">
   <tr>
         <td align="left" valign="bottom" class="text">
         <s:date name="new java.util.Date()" format="dd MMMM yyyy"/> | </td>
         <td align="right">
         <h1 style="color:#ffffff;font-family:Book
         Antiqua">www.simplylogin.com</h1></td>
   </tr>
</table>
```

Creating footer.jsp

The content provided in the footer.jsp page is displayed at the bottom of the Web page. The code for the footer.jsp page is shown in Listing 20.20 (save the footer.jsp file in the \Struts2Tiles folder):

Listing 20.20: Displaying the Code of the footer.jsp File

```
<hr>
<div align=center style="font-size:10;letter-spacing:2">
All Rights are reserved with <br><b>Kogent Learning Solutions Inc.</b><br>
4435/7, Ansari Road, Daryaganj, New Delhi 110002.
</div>
</hr>
```

Creating mainbody.jsp

The mainbody.jsp is created to display textual content in the body of the Web pages. Listing 20.21 shows the code for the mainbody.jsp file (save the mainbody.jsp file in the \Struts2Tiles folder):

Listing 20.21: Displaying the Code of the mainbody.jsp File

```
<table width="400" align="center" cellpadding="10" bgcolor="#a362b3" >
<tr><td class="text">
<h2 align="center" style="font-family:Book Antiqua">A Tiles 2 Implementaion</h2>
<p align="justify">
This application is the result of Tiles 2 integration with
Struts 2 Framework. A Tiles Plugin is bundled with the Struts 2
distribution to support this integration.
The application uses Tiles 2 (version 2.0.6) and Struts 2 (version 2.3.16).
</p>
</td></tr>
</table>
```

Creating mainmenu.jsp

The mainmenu.jsp creates two hyperlinks named Home and Login. Listing 20.22 shows the mainmenu.jsp page providing these two hyperlinks (save the mainmenu.jsp file in the \Struts2Tiles folder):

Listing 20.22: Displaying the Code of the mainmenu.jsp File

```
<p> </p>
<table width="150" cellpadding="3" cellspacing="0" align="center">
   <tr height="30" valign="middle">
         <td valign="middle" width="10">
                  <img src="images/icon.gif">
         </td>
         <td align="left">
         <a href="home.jsp">Home</a></td>
   </tr>
   <tr height="30" valign="middle">
         <td valign="middle" width="10">
```

```
                <img src="images/icon.gif">
            </td>
            <td align="left">
            <a href="login.jsp">Login</a></td>
        </tr>
    </table>
```

The login hyperlink created in mainmenu.jsp is mapped to a JSP page called login.jsp. Let's now create login.jsp.

Creating login.jsp

The login.jsp is created to include definitions from login.def, which is configured in tiles.xml. The login.def contains view components, such as header.jsp, footer.jsp, mainmenu.jsp, and loginform.jsp.

Listing 20.23 shows code for the login.jsp page (save the login.jsp file in the `\Struts2Tiles` folder):

Listing 20.23: Displaying the Code of the login.jsp Page

```
<%@ taglib uri="http://tiles.apache.org/tags-tiles" prefix="tiles" %>
<tiles:insertDefinition name="login.def"/>
```

In Listing 20.23, the <tiles:insertDefinition/> element sets login.def from tiles.xml into login.jsp. Let's now create the loginform.jsp page.

Creating loginform.jsp

The loginform.jsp page simply gives a form with three input fields, which have been named as loginid, password, and type. The code for the loginform.jsp page is given in Listing 20.24 (save the loginform.jsp file in the `\Struts2Tiles` folder):

Listing 20.24: Displaying the Code of the loginform.jsp Page

```
<%@ taglib prefix="s" uri="/struts-tags" %>
<table bgcolor="#a362b3" width="400" align="center" cellpadding="10">
<tr><td class="text" align="center">
| Login |
<br><s:actionerror/>
<s:form action="login" method="post" cssClass="text">
  <s:textfield name="loginid" key="app.loginid"/>
  <s:password name="password" key="app.password"/>
  <s:selectkey="app.type"name="type"list="#@java.util.HashMap@{'manager':
  'Manager', 'clerk':'Clerk'}"/>
  <s:submit value="Login"/>
</s:form>
</td></tr>
</table>
```

In Listing 20.24, the loginform.jsp uses Struts 2 tags to create a form and input fields.

Let's now create action classes for processing the loginform.jsp page.

Creating Action Class

The login.jsp page shows a login form, which, when submitted, has to be handled by some action class. The action class execution may give some result code, based on which the next view is decided. Listing 20.25 shows the code for the LoginAction class (save the LoginAction.java file in the `\Struts2Tiles\src\com\kogent\action` folder):

Listing 20.25: Displaying the Code of the LoginAction.java File

```
package com.kogent.action;
import com.opensymphony.xwork2.ActionSupport;
public class LoginAction extends ActionSupport {
String loginid;
String password;
String type;
public String getLoginid() {
  return loginid;
}
public void setLoginid(String loginid) {
  this.loginid = loginid;
}
```

```
public String getPassword() {
  return password;
}
public void setPassword(String password) {
  this.password = password;
}
public String getType() {
  return type;
}
public void setType(String type) {
  this.type = type;
}
public String execute() throws Exception {
  if(loginid.equals(password)){
  if("manager".equals(type)){
  return "manager";
}else{
return "clerk";
}
}else{
  this.addActionError(getText("app.invalid"));
  return ERROR;
  }
}
public void validate() {
  if ( (loginid == null ) || (loginid.length() == 0) ) {
  this.addFieldError("loginid", getText("app.loginid.blank"));
}
if ( (password == null ) || (password.length() == 0) ) {
  this.addFieldError("password", getText("app.password.blank"));
  }
}
}
```

In Listing 20.25, the possible result codes returned by the LoginAction class are manager, clerk, error, and input.

Configuring struts.xml

Let's see the action mapping provided in struts.xml file to process the login form submission. Listing 20.26 shows the code for the action mapping for login action (save the struts.xml file in the `\Struts2Tiles\WEB-INF\classes` folder):

Listing 20.26: Displaying the Code of the struts.xml File

```
<?xml version="1.0" encoding="UTF-8" ?>
<!DOCTYPE struts PUBLIC
"-//Apache Software Foundation//DTD Struts Configuration 2.3//EN"
"http://struts.apache.org/dtds/struts-2.3.dtd ">
<struts>
  <package name="default" extends="tiles-default">
  <action name="login" class="com.kogent.action.LoginAction">
  <result name="error">/login.jsp</result>
  <result name="input" type="tiles">login.def</result>
  <result name="manager"
  type="tiles">manager.welcome.def</result>
  <result name="clerk"
  type="tiles">clerk.welcome.def</result>
  </action>
  </package>
</struts>
```

In Listing 20.26, there are four results named error, input, manager, and clerk, configured with an action named login. If a JSP page is being used as the location, the result type should be the default dispatcher. However, the powerful feature added by tiles plugin is the use of tiles as result type, which helps in rendering a page definition from the tiles configuration file. We can use a JSP page and a page definition, instead of generating a view to the user, as shown in the following code snippet:

```
<result name="error">/login.jsp</result>
```

```
<result name="input" type="tiles">login.def</result>
```

In the preceding code snippet, the result named input is configured to read definition from login.def. We can, instead, give a page definition easily in tiles.xml file. The action may return two more result codes other than input and error. These result codes are manager and clerk, which are returned according to the type selected by the user while logging. The user should get two different consoles as their type is different. This can be implemented by giving new definitions using the same template, but different attributes. The two new definitions used are manager.welcome.def and clerk.welcome.def. The following code snippet shows the two results, manager and clerk, being configured in the struts.xml (Listing 20.26):

```
<result name="manager" type="tiles">manager.welcome.def</result>
<result name="clerk" type="tiles">clerk.welcome.def</result>
```

We need to provide these new definitions in the tiles.xml file to generate an appropriate view for two different types of users. Note that we only need to define different attributes to be used in these two definitions.

Creating tiles.xml

All the definitions used in this application are provided in tiles.xml file. Therefore, let's create the tiles.xml file and save it in the WEB-INF folder. Listing 20.27 shows the code for the tiles.xml file (save the tiles.xml file in the `\Struts2Tiles\WEB-INF` folder):

Listing 20.27: Displaying the Code of the tiles.xml File

```
<?xml version="1.0" encoding="ISO-8859-1" ?>
<!DOCTYPE tiles-definitions PUBLIC
  "-//Apache Software Foundation//DTD Tiles Configuration 2.1//EN"
  "http://tiles.apache.org/dtds/tiles-config_2_1.dtd">
<tiles-definitions>
   <definition name="login.def" template="/layout.jsp">
<put-attribute name="title"value=www.simplylogin.com/Login type="string"/>
         <put-attribute name="header" value="/header.jsp"/>
         <put-attribute name="menu" value="/mainmenu.jsp"/>
         <put-attribute name="body"   value="/loginform.jsp"/>
         <put-attribute name="footer" value="/footer.jsp"/>
   </definition>
   <definition name="manager.welcome.def" template="/layout.jsp">
         <put-attribute name="title" value="www.simplylogin.com/Login
         Successfull - Manger" type="string"/>
         <put-attribute name="header" value="/header.jsp"/>
         <put-attribute name="menu" value="/manager_menu.jsp"/>
         <put-attribute name="body"   value="/body.jsp"/>
         <put-attribute name="footer" value="/footer.jsp"/>
   </definition>
   <definition name="clerk.welcome.def" extends="manager.welcome.def">
         <put-attribute name="title" value="www.simplylogin.com/Login
         Successfull - Clerk" type="string"/>
         <put-attribute name="menu" value="/clerk_menu.jsp"/>
   </definition>
   <definition name="manager.def" extends="manager.welcome.def">
         <put-attribute name="title" value="www.simplylogin.com -
         Manager" type="string"/>
         <put-attribute name="body"   value="/actionbody.jsp"/>
   </definition>
   <definition name="clerk def" extends="manager.def">
<put-attribute name="title" value="www.simplylogin.com - Clerk" type="string"/>
         <put-attribute name="menu" value="/clerk_menu.jsp"/>
   </definition>
</tiles-definitions>
```

In Listing 20.27, `login.def` is created in the tiles.xml. This definition uses the template called layout.jsp and fills all its attributes with different view components, such as header.jsp, mainmenu.jsp, loginform.jsp, and footer.jsp. The definition, `manager.welcome.def` is also filled with all the required attributes. The `clerk.welcome.def` definition is created by extending the `manager.welcome.def` definition, and all the attributes from `manager.welcome.def` are filled with values according to the user.

The definition manager.def is created by extending manager.welcome.def definition. Similarly, clerk.def is created by extending the manager.def. These definitions use some previously created and used JSP pages. Now, let's create the following JSP pages:

- body.jsp
- manager_menu.jsp
- clerk_menu.jsp

Creating body.jsp

The body.jsp is created to display links and content according to the `Type` specified by the user, which is either `manager` or `clerk`. Listing 20.28 shows the code for the body.jsp page (save the body.jsp file in the `\Struts2Tiles` folder):

Listing 20.28: Displaying the Code of the body.jsp File

```
<%@ taglib prefix="s" uri="/struts-tags" %>
<table bgcolor="#a362b3" width="400" align="center" cellpadding="10">
   <tr><td class="text" align="center">
         | Successful Login!|
         <br><br><br><br>
         You have logged in as : <b><s:property value="loginid"/></b>
         <br><br><br><br>
         | Use Navigation Links provided in Menu Bar. |
   </td></tr>
</table>
```

The manager_menu.jsp and clerk_menu.jsp pages provide different sets of navigational links and are designed for two different types of user.

Creating manager_menu.jsp

The manager_menu.jsp is displayed only to the users belonging to type `manager`. Listing 20.29 shows the code for the manager_menu.jsp page (save the manager_menu.jsp file in the `\Struts2Tiles` folder):

Listing 20.29: Displaying the Code of the manager_menu.jsp File

```
<p> </p>
<table width="150" cellpadding="3" cellspacing="0" align="center">
   <tr height="30" valign="middle">
         <td valign="middle" width="10">
               <img src="images/icon.gif">
         </td>
         <td align="left"><a href="home.jsp">Home</a></td>
   </tr>
   <tr height="30" valign="middle">
         <td valign="middle" width="10">
               <img src="images/icon.gif">
         </td>
         <td align="left"><a href="manager.action">New</a></td>
   </tr>
   <tr height="30" valign="middle">
         <td valign="middle" width="10">
               <img src="images/icon.gif">
         </td>
   <td align="left"><a href="manager.action">Edit</a></td></tr>
   <tr height="30" valign="middle">
         <td valign="middle" width="10">
               <img src="images/icon.gif">
         </td>
         <td align="left"><a href="manager.action">Delete</a></td>
   </tr>
   <tr height="30" valign="middle">
         <td valign="middle" width="10">
               <img src="images/icon.gif">
         </td>
         <td align="left"><a href="logoff.action">Logoff</a></td>
   </tr>
</table>
```

Creating clerk_menu.jsp

The clerk_menu.jsp is displayed only to the users belonging to type `clerk`. Listing 20.30 shows the code for the clerk_menu.jsp page (save the clerk_menu.jsp file in the `\Struts2Tiles` folder):

Listing 20.30: Displaying the Code of the clerk_menu.jsp File

```
<p> </p>
<table width="150" cellpadding="3" cellspacing="0" align="center">
  <tr height="30" valign="middle">
        <td valign="middle" width="10">
              <img src="images/icon.gif">
        </td>
        <td align="left"><a href="home.jsp">Home</a></td>
  </tr>
  <tr height="30" valign="middle">
        <td valign="middle" width="10">
              <img src="images/icon.gif">
        </td>
        <td align="left"><a href="clerk.action">Deposit</a></td>
  </tr>
  <tr height="30" valign="middle">
        <td valign="middle" width="10">
              <img src="images/icon.gif">
        </td>
        <td align="left"><a href="clerk.action">Withdraw</a></td>
  </tr>
  <tr height="30" valign="middle">
        <td valign="middle" width="10">
              <img src="images/icon.gif">
        </td>
        <td align="left"><a href="clerk.action">Transfer</a></td>
  </tr>
  <tr height="30" valign="middle">
        <td valign="middle" width="10">
              <img src="images/icon.gif">
        </td>
        <td align="left"><a href="logoff.action">Logoff</a></td>
  </tr>
</table>
```

Configuring the web.xml File

In Struts 2 applications, all the requests are mapped to a filter class named `FilterDispatcher`. In addition to this, we also need to register a listener provided by the tiles plugin to integrate tiles with Struts 2. The class `org.apache.struts2.tiles.StrutsTilesListener` provides a better support for Struts 2 features and, therefore, it is preferred over the traditional TilesListener. The configuration for the filters and listeners is provided in the web.xml file, shown in Listing 20.31 (save the web.xml file in the `\Sturts2Tiles\WEB-INF` folder):

Listing 20.31: Displaying the Code for the web.xml File

```
<?xml version="1.0" encoding="UTF-8"?>
<web-app version="3.1"
  xmlns="http://xmlns.jcp.org/xml/ns/javaee"
  xmlns:xsi="http://www.w3.org/2001/XMLSchema-instance"
  xsi:schemaLocation="http://xmlns.jcp.org/xml/ns/javaee
  http://xmlns.jcp.org/xml/ns/javaee/web-app_3_1.xsd">
<display-name>Tiles 2 Plugin Example</display-name>
<filter>
  <filter-name>struts2</filter-name>
  <filter-class>org.apache.struts2.dispatcher.FilterDispatcher</filter-class>
</filter>
<filter-mapping>
  <filter-name>struts2</filter-name>
  <url-pattern>/*</url-pattern>
</filter-mapping>
```

```
<listener>
<listener-class>org.apache.struts2.tiles.StrutsTilesListener</listener-class>
</listener>
<welcome-file-list>
<welcome-file>home.jsp</welcome-file>
</welcome-file-list>
</web-app>
```

In Listing 20.31, we have not provided any context parameter to configure the CONTEXT_FACTORY and tiles configuration file. Therefore, the defaults are implied in Listing 20.31. The default tiles configuration file is tiles.xml, and the context factory used is StrutsTilesContainerFactory.

Save the files according to the directory structure that is discussed in the following section.

Exploring the Directory Structure of the Application

A directory structure of an application depicts the location where all the required files are stored. The directory structure of the application being developed is shown in Figure 20.13:

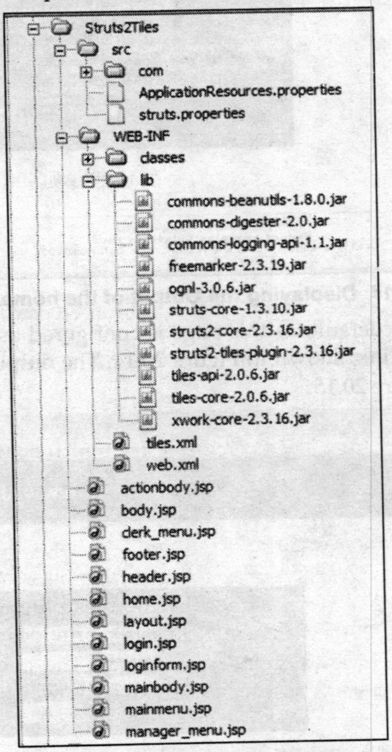

Figure 20.13: Displaying the Directory Structure of Struts2Tiles Web Application

Prior to packaging our application, we must have all the required JAR files in our WEB-INF/lib folder. Therefore, add the following JAR files to your WEB-INF/lib folder:

- tiles-core-2.0.6.jar
- tiles-api-2.0.6.jar
- commons-beanutils-1.8.0.jar
- commons-digester-2.0.jar
- commons-logging-api-1.1.jar
- struts2-tiles-plugin-2.3.61.jar
- struts2-core-2.3.16.jar
- xwork-core-2.3.16.jar

- freemarker-2.3.19.jar
- ognl-3.0.6.jar

Let's now package, deploy, and run the application.

Packaging, Deploying, and Running the Application

We will now create Struts2Tiles.war and deploy it on the Glassfish Server 4.0. Browse the `http://localhost:8080/Struts2Tiles` URL to run the application, as shown in Figure 20.14:

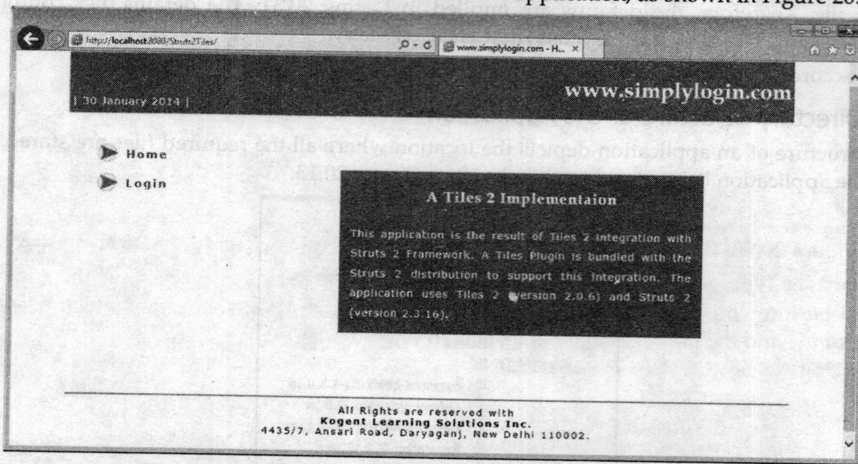

Figure 20.14: Displaying the Output of the home.jsp Page

The home.jsp page is displayed, by default, as this page is configured as the welcome page of the Struts2Tiles application. Click the `Login` hyperlink, shown in Figure 20.14. The output of the login.jsp page, which uses the definition login.def, is shown in Figure 20.15:

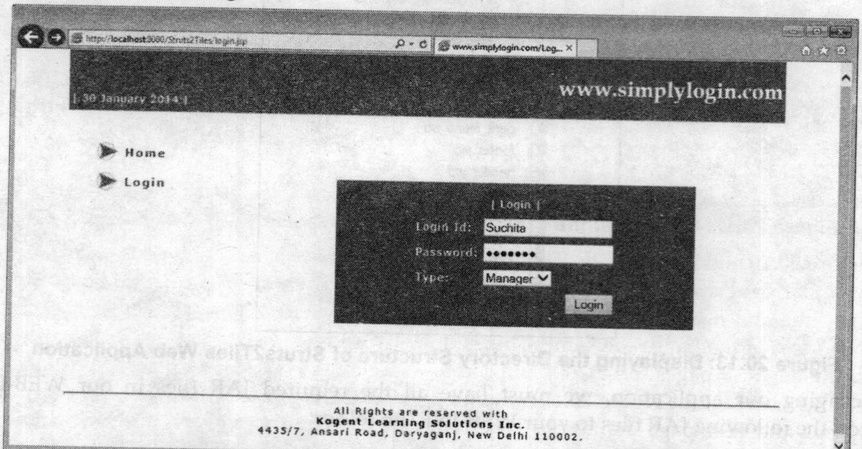

Figure 20.15: Displaying the Output of the login.jsp Page

Enter the login id and password and select `Manager` as type of user. This results in the rendering of the definition manager.welcome.def with its output shown in Figure 20.16. Observe the list of options shown in the menu bar created using manager_menu.jsp page:

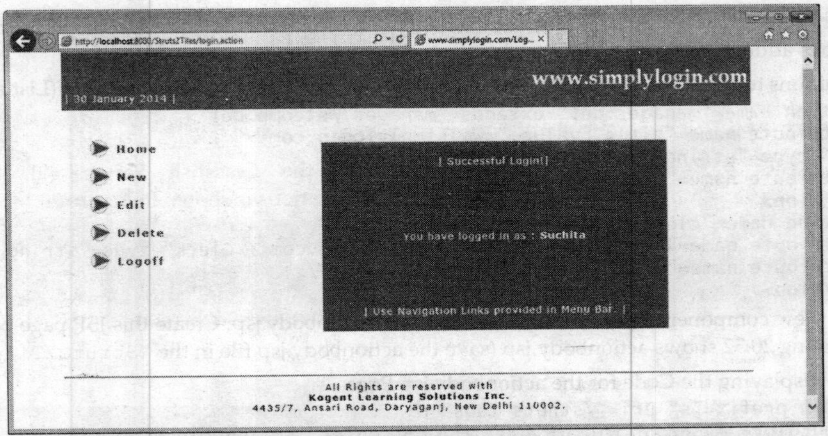

Figure 20.16: Displaying the Output of the manager.welcome.def Definition

Similar to the manager type, you can select `Clerk` as the type of user. After selecting the Clerk type and clicking the Login button, you get a different output using clerk.welcome.def definition, which uses a different value for menu attribute and the list of options, as displayed in Figure 20.17:

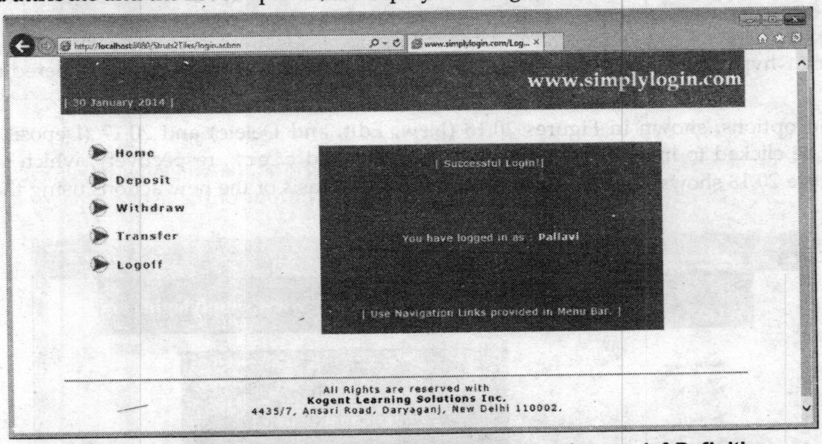

Figure 20.17: Displaying the Output of the clerk.welcome.def Definition

Now, compare Figure 20.16 and Figure 20.17. These figures are designed using the same template layout.jsp and, therefore, have a similar structure. They both use reusable tiles, such as header, footer, and body. However, they are different for the title and menu attributes, which simply make the two pages distinct from each other, even though the look and feel of the pages are same. This is done by adding few definitions in the struts.xml file as compared to creating new JSP pages for `clerk` and `manager` actions. The Home, Deposit, Withdraw, Transfer, and Logoff hyperlinks provided in Figure 20.17 may not be working; so to activate them, we can provide some new action mappings and new page definitions. The following code snippet shows the new action mappings added in the struts.xml file (Listing 20.26):

```
<action name="clerk">
  <result type="tiles">clerk.def</result>
</action>
<action name="manager">
  <result type="tiles">manager.def</result>
</action>
<action name="logoff">
  <result type="tiles">login.def</result>
</action>
```

The new definitions required are clerk.def and manager.def, which can be added to our tiles.xml file similar to other definitions added.

The two definitions to be added to the tiles.xml file are given in the following code snippet (Listing 20.27):

```
<definition name="manager.def" extends="manager.welcome.def">
<put-attribute name="title" value="www.simplylogin.com -
Manager" type="string"/>
<put-attribute name="body" value="/actionbody.jsp"/>
</definition>
<definition name="clerk.def" extends="manager.def">
<put-attribute name="title" value="www.simplylogin.com - Clerk" type="string"/>
<put-attribute name="menu" value="/clerk_menu.jsp"/>
</definition>
```

The only new view component used in these definitions is actionbody.jsp. Create this JSP page before using new definitions. Listing 20.32 shows actionbody.jsp (save the actionbody.jsp file in the `\Struts2Tiles` folder):

Listing 20.32: Displaying the Code for the actionbody.jsp Page

```
<%@ taglib prefix="s" uri="/struts-tags" %>
<table bgcolor="#a362b3" width="400" align="center" cellpadding="10">
  <tr><td class="text" align="center">
        <br><br>
              <h2>| Under Construction |</h2>
        <br><br><br><br>
        This page is underconstruction. <br>Please try after some time.
  </td></tr>
</table>
```

Click the `Logoff` hyperlink, shown in Figures 20.16 and 20.17, to return to the page rendered using definitions login.def.

The new menu options, shown in Figures 20.16 (New, Edit, and Delete) and 20.17 (Deposit, Withdraw, and Transfer), can be clicked to invoke actions named `manager` and `clerk`, respectively, which are configured in struts.xml. Figure 20.18 shows the Web page displayed on the basis of the new actions using the `manager.def` definition:

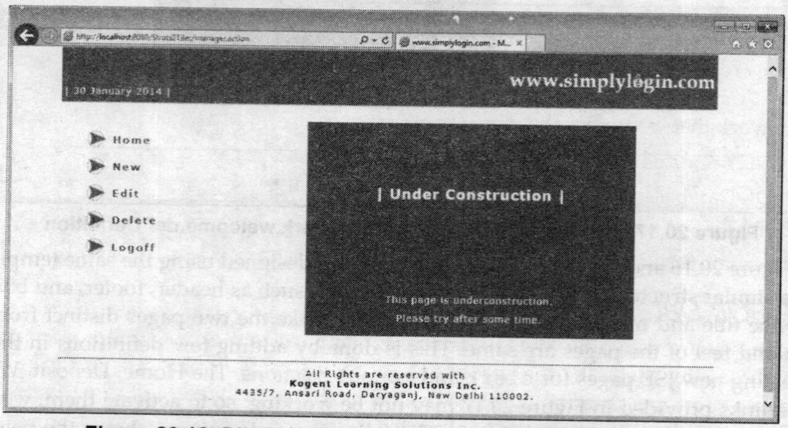

Figure 20.18: Displaying the Output of manager.welcome.def

In this application, we have implemented Struts 2 tiles plugin to integrate our Struts 2 based application with tiles. This integration results in the development of Web pages having a consistent look and feel throughout the application. The Web page development using tiles surely makes life easy for Web page designers, as it reduces the duplicated codes and thereby the efforts to design a new page.

Integrating Struts 2 with Hibernate

Struts 2 Framework does not support the data persistence and Object Relational Mapping features in a Struts 2 application. Integrating Struts 2 with Hibernate incorporates these features in an application. Hibernate is an

Object Oriented Mapping technology that maps object view of data to a relational database. In addition, Hibernate allows you to perform various database operations, such as create, read, update, and delete (CRUD) to store and maintain data persistently in the database.

While integrating Struts 2 with Hibernate in an application, we need to include the relevant JAR files in the lib directory of the application. The relevant JAR files are shown in Figure 20.19:

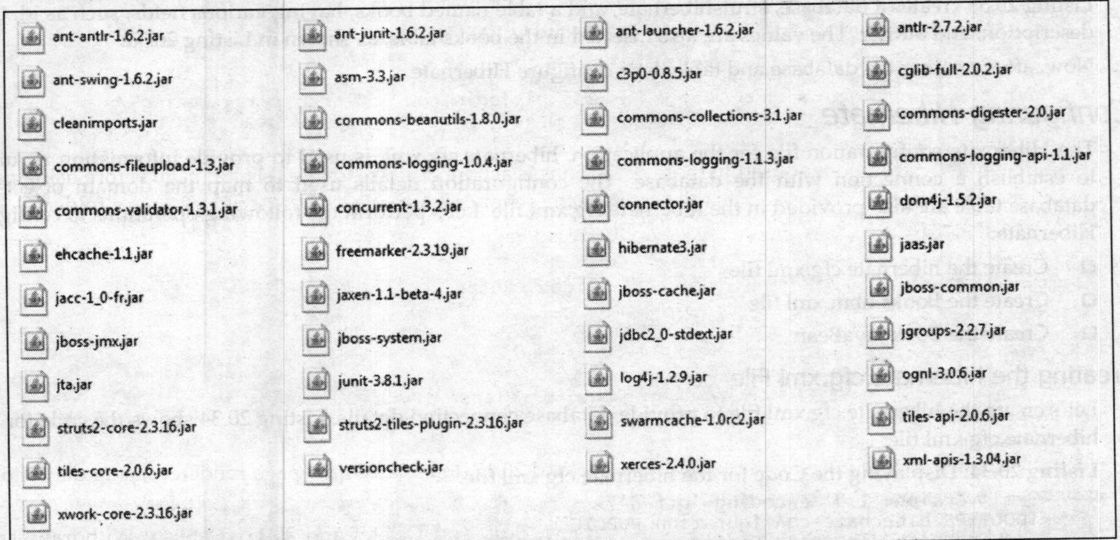

Figure 20.19: JAR files for integrating Struts 2 and Hibernate

NOTE

For more information about Hibernate, refer Chapter 15, Implementing Java Persistence Using Hibernate 4.3.

In this section, we create an application, `StrutsHibernateApp`, demonstrating the integration of Struts 2 and Hibernate 4.3. In `StrutsHibernateApp`, a user enters the text to be searched and clicks the `Search` button. The Struts Framework then processes the request and passes the result to the action class for further processing.

To create `StrutsHibernateApp`, perform the following broad-level steps:

- Set the MySQL Database and table
- Configure Hibernate
- Develop Hibernate Struts Plugin

Setting the MySQL Database and Table

In this application, we are using the MySQL database; you need to enter the valid username and password to access the database. By default, the password of MySQL is `root`. Now, let's create a database, `strutshibernate`, for the `StrutsHibernateApp` application. The `StrutsHibernateApp` application searches for title entered by the user in the books table of the `strutshibernate` database. The books table of the `strutshibernate` database contains relevant book details, such as book id, author, and description of the book. Listing 20.33 provides the SQL script for setting up the database and table:

Listing 20.33: Displaying the Code of the SQL Script for StrutsHibernateApp

```
Create database strutshibernate;
Use strutshibernate;
Create table books(
id int not null auto_increment,
title varchar(50) not null,
description varchar(50) not null,
author varchar(50) not null,
```

```
primary key ( id )
) type = myisam;

insert into books values (1, 'JSP', 'Discussing JSP and Servlets', 'Suchita');
insert into books values (2, 'Struts', 'Integrating Struts with Hibernate', 'Vikash');
insert into books values (3, 'AJAX', 'Understanding AJAX', 'Deepak');
insert into books values (4, 'Servlets', 'Understanding Servlets', 'Shalini');
```

Listing 20.33 creates a database, strutshibernate, and a table named books, having various fields, such as id, title, description, and author. The values are also inserted in the books table, as shown in Listing 20.33.

Now, after creating the database and table, let's configure Hibernate.

Configuring Hibernate

The Hibernate configuration file for the application, hibernate.cfg.xml, is used to provide information required to establish a connection with the database. The configuration details used to map the domain objects to database table are also provided in the hibernate.cfg.xml file. Let's perform the following operations to configure Hibernate:

- Create the hibernate.cfg.xml file
- Create the Books.hbm.xml file
- Create the Book JavaBean

Creating the hibernate.cfg.xml File

Let's create the hibernate.cfg.xml file to provide database connection details. Listing 20.34 shows the code for the hibernate.cfg.xml file:

Listing 20.34: Displaying the Code for the hibernate.cfg.xml file

```
<?xml version='1.0' encoding='utf-8'?>
<!DOCTYPE hibernate-configuration PUBLIC
"-//Hibernate/Hibernate Configuration DTD//EN"
"http://hibernate.sourceforge.net/hibernate-configuration-3.0.dtd">
<hibernate-configuration>
<session-factory>
<property name="hibernate.connection.driver_class">com.mysql.jdbc.Driver
</property>
<property name="hibernate.connection.url">jdbc:mysql://localhost/struts-
 hibernate</property>
<property name="hibernate.connection.username">root</property>
<property name="hibernate.connection.password"></property>
<property name="hibernate.connection.pool_size">10</property>
<property name="show_sql">true</property>
<property name="dialect">org.hibernate.dialect.MySQLDialect</property>
<property name="hibernate.hbm2ddl.auto">update</property>
<!-- Mapping files -->
<mapping resource="/com/kogent/hibernate/Books.hbm.xml"/>
</session-factory>
</hibernate-configuration>
```

In Listing 20.34, the <mapping resource=" "> tag is used to specify the mapping of the Books.hbm.xml file. Save the hibernate.cfg.xml file in the \StrutsHibernateApp\src\ folder.

Now, let's create the Books.hbm.xml file.

Creating the Books.hbm.xml File

The hibernate.cfg.xml file maps the Books.hbm.xml file for configuring the columns of the books table. The Books.hbm.xml file provides the Hibernate mapping for the fields of the books table. Listing 20.35 shows the code for the Hibernate mapping in the Books.hbm.xml file:

Listing 20.35: Displaying the Code of the Books.hbm.xml File

```
<?xml version="1.0" encoding="UTF-8"?>
<!DOCTYPE hibernate-mapping PUBLIC "-//Hibernate/Hibernate Mapping DTD//EN"
  "http://hibernate.sourceforge.net/hibernate-mapping-3.0.dtd">
<hibernate-mapping auto-import="true" default-lazy="false">
<class name="com.kogent.dao.hibernate.Books" table="books">
  <id name="id" type="java.lang.Integer" column="id">
        <generator class="increment" />
```

```
    </id>
    <property name="title" type="java.lang.String" column="title" not-null="true"
      length="50"/>
      <property name="description" type="java.lang.String" column="description"
    not-null="true" length="50"/>
      <property name="author" type="java.lang.String" column="author" not-null="true"
      length="50"/>
    </class>
    </hibernate-mapping>
```

Listing 20.35 specifies the mapping for each column of the books table and configures the Books JavaBean class. Now, let's create the Books JavaBean object.

Creating the Books JavaBean

In this subsection, we create a JavaBean named Books, which is used to store and retrieve the book details from the database. Listing 20.36 shows the code for the Books JavaBean:

Listing 20.36: Displaying the Code for the Books.java File

```
package com.kogent.dao.hibernate;
import java.io.Serializable;
public class Books implements Serializable
{
   private Integer id;
   private String title;
   private String description;
   private String author;
   public Books(Integer id, String title, String description, String author)
   {
          this.id = id;
          this.title = title;
          this.description = description;
          this.author = author;
   }
   public Books()
   {
   }
   public Integer getId()
   {
          return this.id;
   }
   public void setId(Integer id)
   {
          this.id = id;
   }
   public String getTitle()
   {
          return this.title;
   }
   public void setTitle(String title)
   {
          this.title = title;
   }
   public String getDescription()
   {
          return this.description;
   }
   public void setDescription(String description)
   {
          this.description = description;
   }
   public String getAuthor()
   {
          return this.author;
   }

   public void setAuthor(String author)
   {
          this.author = author;
   }
}
```

Listing 20.36 provides setter and getter methods for the id, title, description, and author fields of the books table.

Developing Struts Hibernate Plugin

We now develop the Struts Hibernate Plugin. This plugin creates the Hibernate Session factory and caches the session details in the servlet context. This strategy of creating Hibernate Session factory enhances the performance of the application. Listing 20.37 shows the code required to integrate Struts and Hibernate:

Listing 20.37: Displaying the Code for the Struts Hibernate Plugin

```
package com.kogent.plugin;
//import required packages
public class HibernatePlugIn implements PlugIn
{
   private String configfilepath = "/hibernate.cfg.xml";
   public static final String SESSION_FACTORY_KEY =
          SessionFactory.class.getName();

   private SessionFactory sessionfactory = null;

   public void destroy()
   {
         try {
                sessionfactory.close();
         }catch(HibernateException e)
         {
                System.out.println("Unable to close Hibernate
                 Session Factory: " + e.getMessage());
         }
   }
 public void init(ActionServlet servlet, ModuleConfig config) throws ServletException {
         System.out.println("*************************************");
         System.out.println("**** Initilizing HibernatePlugIn   **********");
         Configuration configuration = null;
         URL configFileURL = null;
         ServletContext context = null;

         try
         {
         configFileURL = HibernatePlugIn.class.getResource(configfilepath);
         context = servlet.getServletContext();
         configuration = (new Configuration()).configure(configFileURL);
         sessionfactory = configuration.buildSessionFactory();
         context.setAttribute(SESSION_FACTORY_KEY, sessionfactory);
         }catch(HibernateException e)
         {
                System.out.println("Error while initializing hibernate: " +
                       e.getMessage());
         }
         System.out.println("*************************************"); }
   public void setConfigFilePath(String configFilePath)  {
   if ((configFilePath == null) || (configFilePath.trim().length() == 0))
   {
         throw new IllegalArgumentException("configFilePath cannot be
         blank or null.");
   }
   System.out.println("Setting 'configFilePath' to '"  +
   configFilePath + "'...");
   configfilepath = configFilePath;
   }
}
```

In Listing 20.37, the configfilepath variable stores the name of the Hibernate configuration file and defines `SESSION_FACTORY_KEY` to store the session factory instance in the servlet context. Therefore, during the startup of the application, the init() method is invoked, which initializes the session factory and caches the session factory instance in the servlet context. The Struts Hibernate plugin created in Listing 20.37 also needs to be configured in the struts-config.xml file, as shown in the following code snippet:

```
<plug-in classname="com.kogent.plugin.HibernatePlugIn"></plugin-in>
```

Summary

This chapter discusses the need for Struts2 framework for creating an enterprise-ready Java Web application. It introduces the concept of action classes with the mechanism to configure these classes using various configuration files and also the concept of interceptors, along with the support of OGNL in Struts2. It further discusses the mechanism to perform validation in Struts 2 and an in-built feature of Struts2, known as internationalization. The implementation of tiles plugin in Struts2 is also discussed in this chapter.

In the next chapter, we learn about another interesting framework of Java, known as Spring 4.0.

Quick Revise

Q1. What is Struts 2?

Ans. Struts 2 is an open source framework used to create Java Web applications based on MVC architecture.

Q2. Explain the work flow of an application in Struts 2.

Ans. The steps for the work flow in Struts 2 are as follows:

- The user sends a request through a user interface provided by the view, which further passes this request to the controller represented by the FilterDispatcher class in Struts 2.
- The controller servlet filter receives the input request coming from the user through the interface provided by the view, instantiates an object of the suitable action class, and executes different methods over this object.
- If the state of model is changed, all the associated views are notified about the changes.
- Then the controller selects the new view to be displayed according to the result code returned by the action class.
- The view presents the user interface. The view queries about the state of the model to show the current data, which is retrieved from the action class.

Q3. List the steps used by Struts 2 to process a client's request.

Ans. Struts 2 processes a request in the following steps:

- Receiving of request
- Pre-processing by Interceptors
- Invoking the Action class method
- Invoking the Result class
- Processing by Interceptors
- Responding to the user

Q4. What is IoC?

Ans. IoC is a programming design pattern used to reduce copuling in programs and is implemented by using the `ObjectFactory` factory.

Q5. List the components of Struts 2 based applications.

Ans. The following are the components of Struts 2 based applications:

- Controller
- struts-config.xml
- struts.xml
- Action classes
- Model
- View

Q6. List the different types of annotations in Struts2.

Ans. Annotations in Struts 2 can be generally divided into four different types:

- Action annotation
- Interceptor annotation
- Validation annotation
- Type Conversion annotation

Q7. What is the use of Action interface in Struts 2?

Ans. Struts 2 Framework provides Action interface that can be used to create action classes to simplify the code in the action classes.

Q8. What is Dependency Injection and Inversion of Control?

Ans. Dependency Injection (DI) and Inversion of Control (IoC) are programming design patterns that help to reduce coupling in a program.

Q9. List the common aware interfaces supported by Struts 2.

Ans. The common aware interfaces that Struts 2 supports are:

- The ApplicationAware Interface
- The ParameterAware Interface
- The ServletRequestAware Interface
- The ServletResponseAware Interface
- The SessionAware Interface

Q10. What is OGNL?

Ans. Object Graph Navigation Language (OGNL) is an expression language used to manipulate and retrieve different properties of Java objects.

21

Working with Spring 4.0

Prior to the advent of Enterprise Java Beans (EJB), Java developers needed to use JavaBeans to create Web applications. Although JavaBeans helped in the development of user interface (UI) components, they were not able to provide services, such as transaction management and security, which were required for developing robust and secure enterprise applications. The advent of EJB was seen as a solution to this problem. EJB extends the Java components, such as Web and enterprise components, and provides services that help in enterprise application development. However, developing an enterprise application with EJB was not easy, as the developer needed to perform various tasks, such as creating Home and Remote interfaces and implementing lifecycle callback methods, which lead to complexity of providing code for EJBs. Due to this complication, developers started looking for an easier way to develop enterprise applications.

The Spring framework has emerged as a solution to all these complications. This framework uses various new techniques, such as Aspect-Oriented Programming (AOP), Plain Old Java Object (POJO), and dependency injection (DI), to develop enterprise applications, thereby removing the complexities involved while developing enterprise applications using EJB. Spring is an open-source, lightweight framework that allows Java EE 7 developers to build simple, reliable, and scalable enterprises applications. This framework mainly focuses on providing various ways to help you manage your business objects. It makes the development of Web applications much easier as compared to classic Java frameworks and Application Programming Interfaces (APIs), such as Java Database Connectivity (JDBC), JavaServer Pages (JSP), and Java Servlet.

This chapter provides an overview of the Spring 4.0 framework. First, you learn about the basic features of Spring framework, newly introduced or updated features of its 4.0 release. Next, you learn about the architecture of Spring framework. In addition, the chapter explores Spring Inversion of Control (IoC), Spring AOP, and transaction management. This chapter also discusses about the Spring Web Model View Controller (MVC) Framework along with its implementation using a simple Spring-based application.

Features of the Spring Framework

The Spring framework can be considered as a collection of subframeworks, also called layers, such as Spring AOP, Spring Object-Relational Mapping (Spring ORM), Spring Web Flow, and Spring Web MVC. You can use any of these modules separately while constructing a Web application. The modules may also be grouped together to provide better functionalities in a Web application.

The features of the Spring framework, such as IoC, AOP, and transaction management, make it unique among the list of frameworks. Some of the most important features of the Spring framework are as follows:

- **IoC container**—Refers to the core container that uses the DI or IoC pattern to implicitly provide an object reference in a class during runtime. This pattern acts as an alternative of service locator pattern. The IoC container contains assembler code that handles the configuration management of application objects.

  The Spring framework provides two packages, namely, `org.springframework.beans` and `org.springframework.context`, which helps in providing the functionality of the IoC container. We will discuss more about the IoC container in the *Exploring Dependency Injection and Inversion of Control* section of this chapter.

- **Data access framework**—Allows the developers to use persistence APIs, such as JDBC and Hibernate, for storing persistence data in database. It helps in solving various problems of the developer, such as how to interact with a database connection, how to make sure that the connection is closed, how to deal with exceptions, and how to implement transaction management. It also enables the developers to easily write code to access the persistence data throughout the application.
- **Spring MVC framework**—Allows you to build Web applications based on MVC architecture. All the requests made by a user first go through the controller and are then dispatched to different views, that is, to different JSP pages or Servlets. The form-handling and form-validating features of the Spring MVC framework can be easily integrated with all popular view technologies such as JSP, JasperReport, FreeMarker, and Velocity.
- **Transaction management**—Helps in handling transaction management of an application without affecting its code. This framework provides Java Transaction API (JTA) for global transactions managed by an application server and local transactions managed by using the JDBC, Hibernate, Java Data Objects (JDO),

or other data access APIs. It enables the developer to model a wide range of transactions on the basis of Spring's declarative and programmatic transaction management. We will discuss declarative and programmatic transactions later in this chapter.

- **Spring Web Service**—Generates Web service endpoints and definitions based on Java classes, but it is difficult to manage them in an application. To solve this problem, Spring Web Service provides layered-based approaches that are separately managed by Extensible Markup Language (XML) parsing (technique of reading and manipulating XML). Spring provides effective mapping for transmitting incoming XML message request to any object, and helps the developer to easily distribute XML message (object) between two machines.
- **JDBC abstraction layer**—Helps the users in handling errors in an easy and efficient manner. The JDBC programming code can be reduced when this abstraction layer is implemented in a Web application. This layer handles exceptions such as DriverNotFound. All `SQLExceptions` are translated into the `DataAccessException class`. Spring's data access exception is not JDBC specific and hence Data Access Objects (DAO) are not bound to JDBC only.
- **Spring TestContext framework**—Provides facilities of unit and integration testing for the Spring applications. Moreover, the Spring `TestContext` framework provides specific integration testing functionalities such as context management and caching, DI of test fixtures, and transactional test management with default rollback semantics.

What's New in Spring 4.0

The Spring framework was first released in 2004. After that there have been significant major revisions, such as Spring 2.0 provided XML namespaces and AspectJ support, Spring 2.5 provided annotation-driven configuration, Spring 3.0 provided Java-based @Configuration model. The latest release of the Spring framework is 4.0. It is released with the support for Java 8 and Java EE 7 technologies. Though you can still use Spring with older versions of Java, but the minimum requirement is restricted to Java SE 6. Spring 4.0 also support Java EE 7 technologies, such as Java Message Service (JMS) 2.0, Java Persistence API (JPA) 2.1, Bean Validation 1.1, Servlet 3.1, and JCache.

Some noteworthy new features of the Spring 4.0 framework are as follows:

- **Support for Java 8 language and API features**—Spring framework 4.0 supports various features of Java 8. For example, you can use lambda expressions and method references in callback interfaces. Spring framework 4.0 also supports JSR-310 date and time, and various existing annotations are remodified as @Repeatable. In addition, Spring 4.0 framework also supports the compilation of code using Java 8's parameter name discovery.
- **Core container improvements**—The Spring 4.0 framework provides various improvements to the core container. For example, generic types are used as qualifiers when injected to the beans. Take for instance, you can inject @Autowired Repository<User> userRepository, while using a Spring Data Repository.

  Now, beans can be ordered when they are autowired into lists and arrays. The @Lazy annotation is used on injection points and on @Bean definitions. The @Description annotation is newly introduced to perform Java-based configuration. The @Conditional annotation is used for conditional filtering beans.
- **General Web improvements**—The Spring 4.0 framework now supports Servlet 3.0+ environments. You can use the new @RestController annotation in case of developing Spring MVC applications, so that there is no need to add @ResponseBody to each of your @RequestMapping methods. Moreover, a class, named AsyncRestTemplate, has been added that allows non-blocking asynchronous support for Representational State Transfer (REST) clients.
- **Support for WebSocket-based communication**—Spring 4.0 framework now supports WebSocket-based communication between client and server in Web applications. It is compatible with JSR-356, and offers a WebSocket API on top of JSR-356 containers. Spring 4.0 framework also provides fallback options for use in browsers and networks that don't support the use of WebSocket, with the help of using the SockJS protocol.
- **Support for Streaming Text Oriented Messaging Protocol (STOMP) messaging protocol**—Spring 4.0 framework supports a new protocol, STOMP, which acts as a sub-protocol of WebSocket, for providing

message facility in Web applications. STOMP acts as a lightweight message broker to Web clients. It can automatically handle subscriptions without any server code and allow controller methods to handle incoming messages and subscriptions.

Spring 4.0 framework also uses an annotation programming model that helps in routing and processing of STOMP messages from WebSocket-connected clients. Therefore, the @Controller annotation is used to contain both @RequestMapping and @MessageMapping methods for handling Hyper Text Transfer Protocol (HTTP) requests and messages from WebSocket-connected clients, as shown in the following code snippet.

```
@Controller
public class GreetingController
{
@RequestMapping(value="/hellotext", method=POST)
public void httpGreet(String str)
{
        // ...
}
@MessageMapping("/hellotext")
public void stompGreet(String str)
{
 // ...
}
  }
```

- **Dependency upgrades**—In Spring 4.0 framework, various deprecated features are removed. The minimum dependency is raised to Java 6+. Table 21.1 lists removed packages from Spring 4.0 framework:

Table 21.1: Removed Packages from Spring 4.0 Framework		
org.springframework.core.enums	org.springframework.orm.ibatis.support	org.springframework.test.context.junit38
org.springframework.ejb.support	org.springframework.remoting.jaxrpc	org.springframework.test.jpa
org.springframework.instrument.classloading.oc4j	org.springframework.scheduling.backportconcurrent	org.springframework.web.servlet.view.tiles
org.springframework.orm.ibatis	org.springframework.scheduling.timer	org.springframework.web.struts

Table 21.2 lists added packages to Spring 4.0 framework:

Table 21.2: Added Packages to Spring 4.0 Framework		
org.springframework.beans.factory.groovy	org.springframework.messaging.simp.config	org.springframework.websocket.config
org.springframework.cache.guava	org.springframework.messaging.simp.stomp	org.springframework.websocket.config.annotation
org.springframework.format.datetime.standard	org.springframework.messaging.simp.user	org.springframework.websocket.handler
org.springframework.messaging	org.springframework.messaging.support	org.springframework.web.socket.messaging
org.springframework.messaging.	org.springframework.messaging.	org.springframework.web.

Table 21.2: Added Packages to Spring 4.0 Framework

converter	tcp	socket.server
org.springframework.messaging.core	org.springframework.messaging.tcp.reactor	org.springframework.web.socket.server.jetty
org.springframework.messaging.handler	org.springframework.util.concurrent	org.springframework.web.socket.server.standard
org.springframework.messaging.handler.annotation	org.springframework.web.socket	org.springframework.web.socket.server.support
org.springframework.messaging.handler.annotation.support	org.springframework.web.socket.adapter	org.springframework.web.socket.sockjs
org.springframework.messaging.handler.invocation	org.springframework.web.socket.adapter.jetty	org.springframework.web.socket.sockjs.frame
org.springframework.messaging.simp	org.springframework.web.socket.adapter.standard	org.springframework.web.socket.sockjs.support
org.springframework.messaging.simp.annotation	org.springframework.web.socket.client	org.springframework.web.socket.sockjs.transport
org.springframework.messaging.simp.annotation.support	org.springframework.web.socket.client.jetty	org.springframework.web.socket.sockjs.transport.handler
org.springframework.messaging.simp.broker	org.springframework.web.socket.client.standard	org.springframework.web socket.sockjs.transport.session

NOTE

Besides the listed packages in Table 21.1 and Table 21.2, Spring 4.0 also modified various existing packages from technical aspects. For which, you can refer the http://docs.spring.io website.

- **Testing improvements**—Spring 4.0 framework also introduces various features used in unit and integration testing. For example, annotations used in testing, such as @ContextConfiguration, @WebAppConfiguration, @ContextHierarchy, and @ActiveProfiles can now be used as meta-annotations to create customized composed annotation. Another change is that an active bean definition can be created programmatically, by implementing a custom ActiveProfilesResolver and registering this profile resolver with the help of @ActiveProfiles.

After having a brief overview about the new features of the Spring 4.0 framework, let's explore the Spring architecture.

Exploring the Spring Framework Architecture

The Spring framework consists of seven modules, which are shown in Figure 21.1. These modules are Spring Core, Spring AOP, Spring Web MVC, Spring DAO, Spring ORM, Spring context, and Spring Web flow. These modules provide different platforms to develop different enterprise applications; for example, you can use Spring Web MVC module for developing MVC-based applications. Figure 21.1 shows the modules of the Spring framework architecture:

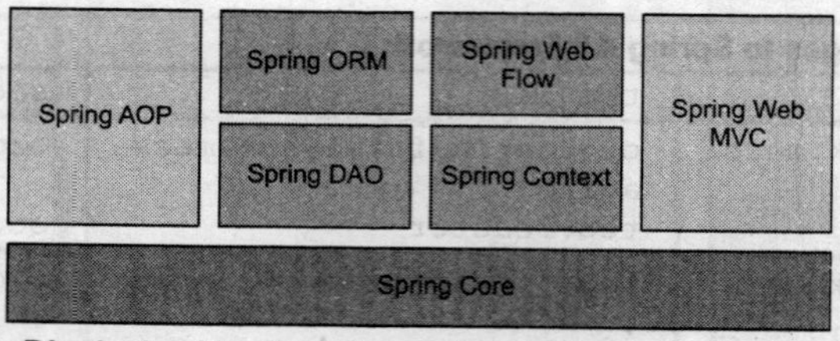

Figure 21.1: Displaying the Modules of the Spring Framework Architecture

Now, let's discuss each module shown in Figure 21.1 in the following subsection.

Explaining the Spring Core Module

The Spring Core module, which is the core component of the Spring framework, provides the IoC container. There are two types of implementations of the Spring container, namely, bean factory and application context. Bean factory is defined using the org.springframework.beans.factory.BeanFactory interface, and acts as a container for beans. The Bean factory container allows you to decouple the configuration and specification of dependencies from program logic.

In the Spring framework, the Bean factory acts as a central IoC container that is responsible for instantiating application objects. It also configures and assembles the dependencies between these objects. There are numerous implementations of the `BeanFactory` interface. The `XmlBeanFactory` class is the most common implementation of the `BeanFactory` interface. This allows you to express the object to compose your application and remove interdependencies between application objects.

Explaining the Spring AOP Module

Similar to Object-Oriented Programming (OOP), which breaks down the applications into hierarchy of objects, AOP breaks down the programs into `aspects` or `concerns`. Spring AOP module allows you to implement concerns or aspects in a Spring application. In Spring AOP, the aspects are the regular Spring beans or regular classes annotated with @Aspect annotation. These aspects help in transaction management, and logging and failure monitoring of an application. For example, transaction management is required in bank operations such as transferring an amount from one account to another. Spring AOP module provides a transaction management abstraction layer that can be applied to transaction APIs.

Explaining the Spring ORM Module

The Spring ORM module is used for accessing data from databases in an application. It provides APIs for manipulating databases with JDO, Hibernate, and iBatis. Spring ORM supports DAO, which provides a convenient way to build the following DAOs-based ORM solutions:

- Simple declarative transaction management
- Transparent exception handling
- Thread-safe, lightweight template classes
- DAO support classes
- Resource management

Explaining the Spring Web MVC Module

The Web MVC module of Spring implements the MVC architecture for creating Web applications. It separates the code of model and view components of a Web application. In Spring MVC, when a request is generated from the browser, it first goes to the DispatcherServlet class (Front Controller), which dispatches the request to a controller (SimpleFormController class or AbstractWizardFormController class) using a set of handler mappings. The controller extracts and processes the information embedded in a request and sends the result to the DispatcherServlet class in the form of model object. Finally, the DispatcherServlet class uses ViewResolver classes to send the results to a view, which displays these results to the users.

Explaining the Spring Web Flow Module

The Spring Web Flow module is an extension of the Spring Web MVC module. Spring Web MVC framework provides form controllers, such as SimpleFormController class and AbstractWizardFormController class, to implement predefined workflow. The Spring Web Flow helps in defining XML file or Java Class that manages the workflow between different pages of a Web application. The Spring Web Flow is distributed separately and can be downloaded through http:\\`www.springframework.org` website.

The following are the advantages of Spring Web Flow:

- The flow between different UIs of the application is clearly provided by defining Web flow in XML file
- Web flow definitions help you to virtually split an application in different modules and reuse these modules in multiple situations

Spring Web Flow lifecycle can be managed automatically

Explaining the Spring DAO Module

The DAO package in the Spring framework provides DAO support by using data access technologies such as JDBC, Hibernate, or JDO. This module introduces a JDBC abstraction layer by eliminating the need of providing tedious JDBC coding. It also provides programmatic as well as declarative transaction management classes. Spring DAO package supports heterogeneous Java Database Connectivity and O/R mapping, which helps Spring work with several data access technologies

For easy and quick access to database resources, the Spring framework provides abstract DAO base classes. Multiple implementations are available for each data access technology supported by the Spring framework. For example, in JDBC, the `JdbcDaoSupport` class and its methods are used to access the `DataSource` instance and a preconfigured `JdbcTemplate` instance. You need to simply extend the `JdbcDaoSupport` class and provide a mapping to the actual `DataSource` instance in an application context configuration to access a DAO-based application.

Explaining the Spring Application Context Module

The Spring Application context module is based on the Core module. Application context `org.springframework.context.ApplicationContext` is an interface of `BeanFactory`. This module derives its feature from the `org.springframework.beans` package and also supports functionalities such as internationalization (I18N), validation, event propagation, and resource loading. The Application context implements MessageSource interface and provides the messaging functionality to an application.

In the next section, we discuss how DI and IoC are used in the Spring framework.

Exploring Dependency Injection and Inversion of Control

IoC is a principle of software construction, where the developers no longer need to create objects from classes. Instead, an application gets the objects from outside sources such as an XML configuration file. The concept of IoC is used to reduce coupling in an application. Coupling is a term that describes the degree to which one module depends on another module for proper functioning of an application. Loose coupling allows easier maintainability and higher reusability of an application. In this way, IoC facilitates better software design. Spring IoC container is the core of the Spring framework. The two interfaces, such as ApplicationContext and BeanFactory, allow you to manage beans in the Spring IoC container.

DI is a programming design pattern, which is used to reduce coupling in an application. DI allows the developers to inject (use) an object directly in a class, which means that they no longer need to depend on a class to create an object. Spring framework supports loose coupling between one module and other module of an application by using DI. The basic principle of DI is that objects define their dependencies (other objects they work with) using constructor argument or argument to a factory method. It means that objects should only have as many dependencies as are required to perform their job. In other words, we can say that the number of dependencies should be minimum in an application.

The key benefit of injecting objects in an application is that you can modify implementation part of dependencies without being concerned about the depending object. For example, if the Car class knows about its dependency on the Petrol class through an interface, any other effect of changes in the implementation of the Petrol class to the Car class is not required. Even if we modify the implementation of the Petrol class, it does not affect the Car class.

Let's now discuss both these concepts in detail.

Explaining DI

As already learned, DI is a concept of injecting an object into a class rather than explicitly creating the object in a class, since the IoC container injects object into the class during runtime. The three important types of DIs are setter injection, constructor injection, and method injection. Setter injection is implemented through JavaBeans setter methods. The Constructor Injection is implemented through Constructor arguments, where the IoC container is responsible for implementing methods at runtime. The method injection is implemented through a number of callback methods and an API for traditional lookup.

The benefits of DI are as follows:

- Ensures that components are simpler to write and maintain, as they do not require runtime collaboration lookup
- Reduces coding effort, as JavaBeans can be injected in a class using DI
- Allows business objects to run in different DI frameworks or outside any framework without any change in the code.

Explaining IoC Container

The actual representation of the Spring IOC container is the `BeanFactory` interface. This interface is an implementation of the factory design pattern, which creates and destroys beans. Various implementations of the BeanFactory interface exist; the `XmlBeanFactory` class being the most commonly used BeanFactory implementation. This `XmlBeanFactory` class loads its beans based on the definitions specified in an XML file, and takes this XML configuration metadata to create a fully configured system or application.

The two models of objects supported by the `BeanFactory` interface are as follows:

- **Singleton**—Serves as the default and most commonly used model in which the only shared instance of the object is retrieved on lookup with a particular name. This object model is ideal for stateless service objects.
- **Prototype**—Refers to the non-singleton model. Every new retrieval of a bean results in the creation of a new object, and in this way, it is used to allow each caller to have its own distinct object references.

Two important methods in the `BeanFactory` interface are getBean(String name) and getBean(String name, Class requiredType) methods. The getBean(String name) method allows you to get a bean on the basis of the value of the name parameter. The getBean(String name, Class requiredType) method allows you to specify the required class of the returned bean and throws an exception if it doesn't exist.

Sub-interfaces of BeanFactory provide extra functionality, such as message lookup, and configuring metadata of a bean. The following are the sub-interfaces of the BeanFactory interface:

- **ListableBeanFactory**—Provides methods to enumerate the beans in a bean factory. For example, the getBeanDefinitionNames() method of the ListableBeanInterface interface returns the names of all the beans defined in the factory, the getBeanNamesForType(Class type) method returns the names of all the bean classes of a certain type, and the getBeanDefinitionCount() method returns the number of bean classes defined in the factory.
- **AutowireCapableBeanFactory**—Helps in configuring an existing external object and facilitates its dependencies. This is done through the autowireBeanProperties() and applyBeanPropertyValues() methods. By using the specified autowire strategy, the autowire() method creates a new bean instance of the given class.
- **ConfigurableBeanFactory**—Provides additional configuration options on a bean factory that can be applied during the bean initialization stage.
- **ApplicationContext**—Provides extra functionality of Bean Factory. This interface provides support for message lookup, internationalization, and an event handling mechanism.

One of the most striking features of Spring is AOP, which will be discussed in the next section.

Exploring AOP with Spring

AOP is a complement of OOP, which is defined as a programming technique. The important unit of modularity in AOP is aspect; whereas in OOP, the units of modularity are classes and objects. Aspects provide the modularization of various concerns, such as transaction management, which crosscut multiple types and objects. In AOP, such concerns are termed as cross-cutting concerns. For example, security is a cross-cutting concern in an application, as EmployeeService, SalaryService, and other services of that application must implement the security functionality.

The Spring IoC containers don't depend on AOP; however, you can use these containers with AOP, depending on the requirements of the application. The following are the uses of AOP in Spring:

- Replaces the EJB declarative services with new declarative enterprise services such as declarative transaction management.
- Allows you to implement custom aspects by using OOP with AOP.
- Allows AOP to be combined with Acegi security framework to provide declarative security service. Acegi security framework is a kind of Spring security framework that provides security solutions for Java EE-based Web applications.

Describing the AOP Concepts

The following list defines and explains the various key terms of the AOP module:

- **Advice**– Defines both what and when of an aspect. We know that each aspect has a purpose in AOP; the purpose of an aspect is known as advice. In real world, an advice defines what the job is and when it can be performed. The advice can be applied either before or after method invocation by using the `@Aspect` annotation.
- **Joinpoint**–Refers to a point where an aspect can be plugged in. It is the single location in the code where an advice should be executed (i.e., method invocation). For specifying a joinpoint, you have to implement the `org.springframework.aop.Pointcut` interface, and the information about the joinpoint can be accessed by the MethodInvocation interface.
- **Pointcut**–Refers to many joinpoints that are grouped together to perform an advice, which makes a pointcut. As we know that in Spring, a joinpoint is always a method invocation; therefore, we can say that a pointcut is a set of methods invocation.
- **Aspect**–Combines both advice and pointcuts. Therefore, an aspect consists of information such as what is the role of the aspect, and where and when to apply the aspect.
- **Introduction**–Adds methods and fields to an existing object. For using this concept, Spring has introduced some interfaces that must be implemented by the advised class.
- **Target object** –Refers to an object that is being adviced by one or more aspects.
- **AOP proxy**–Refers to an object created by the Spring AOP to implement the aspect. In Spring, there are two types of AOP proxies-JDK dynamic proxy and code generator library (CGLIB) proxy.
- **Weaving**–Refers to the process that links aspects with other application types or objects to create an advised object. This process can be performed at compile time, load time, and runtime.

Explaining Types of Advices

The different types of advices are as follows:

- **Around advice**– Specifies whether to proceed to the joinpoint or to make a cross-cutting concern by returning its own return value or throwing an exception. The around advice is used in context of a joinpoint such as a method invocation.
- **Before advice**–Fires an advice before the execution of a joinpoint.
- **After throws advice**–Fires an advice when a method throws an exception. To handle this exception, you have to write the corresponding try and catch block in a class.

- **After returning advice**—Fires an advice when a method invocation or joinpoint is completed. For example, if the return statement of a method is executed, it returns an appropriate value without throwing an exception.
- **After finally advice**—Fires an advice regardless of whether a joinpoint exits with a normal or exceptional return.

Most of the AOP frameworks provide only around advice. However, at other instances, you might need to use other types of advices. For example, if you want to update a cache with a method that returns a result, you need to implement an after returning advice instead of an around advice.

Spring AOP Capabilities and Its Goals

Since Spring AOP is a fully OOP-based concept, the compilation process of a Spring application is the same as that of the simple Java applications. As a result, AOP can be used successfully in Java EE compatible application server and Web container.

The classes that represent pointcuts and different advice types are provided by Spring. The term advisor is used for an object that represents an aspect. This aspect has both an advice and a pointcut, which targets a particular joinpoint.

In Spring, different types of method interceptors are used with advice. The org.springframework.aop package has defined all the advices. The org.aopalliance.aop.Advice tag interface must be implemented by every advice. Some of the common advice interfaces in Spring AOP are MethodInterceptor, ThrowsAdvice, BeforeAdvice, and AfterReturningAdvice.

Generally, the features of Spring AOP are used with a Spring IoC container. AOP's advice is defined by using simple bean definition syntax. Spring IoC is capable of managing both advice and pointcuts. There are some situations where Spring AOP is very difficult to use. For example, when an advice is very fine-grained, it is difficult to implement Spring AOP. In such a situation, AspectJ annotation should be use.

Java EE 5 application server provides secondary services, which are heavy weight. These secondary services are managing transactions, implementing security, and logging errors of an application. Therefore, heavy weight Java EE 5 application server should be run while accessing the business logic of an enterprise application. However, in case of Spring application, only AOP framework of the Spring framework (a lightweight container) should be use.

Managing Transactions

The Spring framework provides declarative and programmatic transaction management services that offer a consistent programming model in every environment. The transaction management services are implemented by using different transaction APIs such as JTA, JDBC, Hibernate, JPA, and JDO. Spring transaction management provides the following benefits:

- Supports declarative transaction management for handling transactions
- Provides simple API for programmatic transaction management as compared to complex transaction APIs such as JTA
- Provides easier integration with various data access abstractions

Need of Transaction Management Support

Transaction management supported by the Spring framework provides an easy solution for handling transactions such as declarative and programmatic transactions. Some application servers support JTA that can be easily used with Spring's declarative transaction management, which is more powerful than EJB Container Management Transaction (CMT). The only scenario in which we need an application server's JTA capability is when we need to handle transactions across multiple resources. This scenario is not common in many high-end applications as they use single, highly scalable database.

There are two types of transactions to be managed by the application server:

- Global transactions: Help work with multiple transactional resources

- Local transactions: Represent resource-specific transactions such as transactions associated with a JDBC connection
- JTA is normally available in an application server environment; therefore, the reusability of application code is limited to global transactions.

Prior to the advent of the Spring framework, the first choice to use global transactions was by using EJB CMT. CMT provides declarative type of transaction management, which is always preferred over the programmatic version. While using EJB CMT, the code for transaction management and Java Naming and Directory Interface (JNDI) lookup are not required. EJB CMT needs JTA and a Deployment Descriptor, that is, `ejb-jar.xml`, for providing metadata information. Therefore, we can say that implementing business logic in EJB is more complex (requiring more configuration) as compared to its implementation in Spring.

Local transactions are easy to handle, but do not support transactions over multiple transactional resources. For example, the code to manage transaction through JDBC will not run in a global JTA environment.

Programmatic transaction management solves the problem of managing transactions over multiple transactional resources. Consequently, application developers can use consistent programming model, irrespective of the environment.

Spring Transaction Abstraction

In the Spring framework, the `org.springframework.transaction.PlatformTransactionManager` interface defines the manner in which the transaction should take place. The following code snippet lists the methods of the `PlatformTransactionManager` interface:

```
public interface PlatformTransactionManager {
   TransactionStatus getTransaction(TransactionDefinition definition)
   throws TransactionException;
   void commit(TransactionStatus status) throws TransactionException;
   void rollback(TransactionStatus status) throws TransactionException;
}
```

The `PlatformTransactionManager` interface is a Serial Peripheral Interface (SPI) that provides a serial exchange of data between two systems. `PlatformTransactionManager` implementations are defined similar to any other object or bean in the IoC container. All the methods of this interface throw an object of the `TransactionException` class, and this exception class extends java.lang.Exception. The developer can choose to catch and handle the `TransactionException` instance where the application code can be recovered, in case of transaction failure. One of the salient features of Spring is that the developer is not necessarily required to handle the exceptions.

The `getTransaction()` method of the `PlatformTransactionManager` interface returns a `TransactionStatus` object and also passes TransactionDefinition parameter. The properties of a transaction that are specified by the TransactionDefinition interface are as follows:

- **Isolation**—Specifies that the degree of all transactions is isolated from each other. For example, the uncommitted updates of one transaction are kept isolated from the other transaction.
- **Propagation**—Specifies that the transaction code is executed within a scope of transaction. The Spring framework allows all types of transaction propagation such as suspending the existing transaction and creating a new transaction if the transaction is not executed due to network failure.
- **Timeout**—Specifies the duration for which the transaction may run before being timed out. A timed out transaction is automatically rolled back by the underlying infrastructure.
- **Read-only status**—Specifies a transaction that does not modify any data.

The transaction code is required to manage the transaction execution and query transaction status. The following code snippet shows the execution of transaction by using the `TransactionStatus` interface:

```
public interface TransactionStatus {
   boolean isNewTransaction();
   void setRollbackOnly();
   boolean isRollbackOnly();
}
```

You can use declarative or programmatic transaction management in Spring. For this, you need to define the correct `PlatformTransactionManager` implementation in your application to handle transaction. This implementation is given by IoC. The following code snippet shows the configuration details of datasource (dataSource), such as username, password, and URL, to handle transactions:

```
<bean id="dataSource" class="org.apache.commons.dbcp.BasicDataSource" destroy-
  method="close">
<property name="driverClassName" value="${jdbc.driverClassName}" />
<property name="url" value="${jdbc.url}" />
<property name="username" value="${jdbc.username}" />
<property name="password" value="${jdbc.password}" />
</bean>
```

The preceding code snippet defines the JDBC DataSource, dataSource.

The following code snippet is the related PlatformTransactionManager bean definition:

```
<bean id="txManager"
  class="org.Springframework.jdbc.datasource.DataSourceTransactionManager">
  <property name="dataSource" ref="dataSource"/>
</bean>
```

The preceding code snippet uses the Spring `DataSourceTransactionManager` class for transaction management and provides a reference of this class to the `DataSource`.

When using JTA in Java EE container, a DataSource instance is required, which is obtained through JNDI. In Spring, a JtaTransactionManager implementation is provided to manage transactions of a bean and to lookup a datasource through JNDI. In other words, the JtaTransactionManager implementation uses only container DataSource. The following code snippet shows the implementation of `JtaTransactionManager`:

```
<?xml version="1.0" encoding="UTF-8"?>
<beans xmlns="http://www.Springframework.org/schema/beans"
xmlns:xsi="http://www.w3.org/2001/XMLSchema-instance"
xmlns:jndi="http://www.Springframework.org/schema/jndi"
xsi:schemaLocation="
http://www.Springframework.org/schema/beans
  http://www.Springframework.org/schema/beans/Spring-beans.xsd
http://www.Springframework.org/schema/jee
  http://www.Springframework.org/schema/jee/Spring-jee.xsd">
<jee:jndi-lookup id="dataSource" jndi-name="jdbc/sample"/>
<bean id="txManager"
  class="org.Springframework.transaction.jta.JtaTransactionManager" />
  <!-- other <bean/> definitions here -->
</beans>
```

The preceding code snippet uses the <jndi-lookup/> tag from the <jee:jndi-lookup id="dataSource" jndi-name="jdbc/sample"/> schema inside the definition of a dataSource bean.

We can also use Hibernate dialect in place of JDBC to configure a datasource in an application, as shown in the following code snippet:

```
<bean id="sessionFactory"
  class="org.Springframework.orm.hibernate.LocalSessionFactoryBean">
<property name="dataSource" ref="dataSource" />
<property name="mappingResources">
  <list>
<value>com/kogent/hibernate/hospital.hbm.xml</value>
  </list>
  </property>
        <property name="hibernateProperties">
        <value>
                hibernate.dialect=${hibernate.dialect}
        </value>
  </property>
</bean>
<bean id="txManager"
  class="org.Springframework.orm.hibernate.HibernateTransactionManager">
  <property name="sessionFactory" ref="sessionFactory" />
</bean>
```

In the preceding code snippet, the Hibernate LocalSessionFactoryBean object can be identified by a unique ID, that is, sessionFactory. The `sessionFactory` bean is used to obtain Hibernate Session instances. The DataSource definition is the same as provided when using the JDBC transaction API. The txManager bean is of HibernateTransactionManager type. The `HibernateTransactionManager` class needs reference to the sessionFactory bean, and the DataSourceTransactionManager instance needs a reference to the DataSource instance.

Similar to JDBC, we can also use JtaTransactionManager implementation in Hibernate and JTA transactions. Replace the definition of the txManager bean, given in the preceding code snippet, with the following:

```
<bean id="txtManager"
    class="org.Springframework.transaction.jta.JtaTransactionManager"/>
```

The way in which transactions are managed can be changed by just changing the configuration; there is no need to change the application code even if you are changing the local transactions to global transactions.

Resource Synchronization with Transactions

Now, you know how different transaction managers are created and linked to related resources that need to be synchronized to transactions. For example, the `DataSourceTransactionManager` class is needed to create a JDBC DataSource. Now you need to consider how to ensure that the resources, such as JDBC DataSource, Hibernate SessionFactory, and JDO, are obtained and handled properly in an application. Various techniques, such as creation, reuse, and cleanup, are performed to handle these resources.

There are three approaches to synchronize the resources with transactions—high-level approach, low-level approach, and using the `TransactionAwareDataSourceProxy` class.

The High-Level Approach

High-level approach is the most preferred approach for handling resources using the Spring framework. The resource handling techniques, such as creation, reuse, and cleanup, are handled internally by this approach. It means that the user does not need to create, reuse, and cleanup the resources as these functions are performed by the Spring framework automatically. You should note that commonly the classes, such as JdbcTemplate, HibernateTemplate, and JdoTemplate, are used in this approach to handle transactions.

The Low-Level Approach

In low-level approach, classes, such as `DataSourceUtils` for JDBC, `SessionFactoryUtils` for Hibernate, and `PersistenceManagerFactoryUtils` for JDO, are used to handle resources. A developer provides the application code to handle transaction directly with the resource type of the native persistence APIs. In this approach, these classes ensure that the Spring managed instances are obtained, transactions are synchronized, and the exceptions that occur in the process are mapped to a consistent API. For example, the `org.springframework.jdbc.datasource.DataSourceUtils` class is used to get an instance of connection, instead of calling the `getConnection()` method on the `DataSource` instance. The following code snippet shows how to use the `DataSourceUtils` class to establish connection with a datasource:

```
Connection conn = DataSourceUtils.getConnection (dataSource);
```

If an existing transaction establishes a connection by using the `getConnection()` method, it returns an instance of this connection. Otherwise, a new connection is created and synchronized to any existing transaction. In the Spring framework, the `SQLException` instance is wrapped in a `CannotGetJdbcConnectionException` instance. Therefore, the `CannotGetJdbcConnectionException` instance raises more exceptional errors that cannot be easily obtained from the `SQLException instance`.

The TransactionAwareDataSourceProxy Class

The `TransactionAwareDataSourceProxy` class can be used as a proxy for a target `DataSource`. This class is used to handle resource synchronization with transactions at the lowest level. The target `DataSource` is wrapped into this proxy class. Therefore, it is similar to transactional JNDI `DataSource` as provided by Java EE technology.

Declarative Transaction Management

The Spring framework helps the developers to make few changes in application code to handle transaction through declarative transaction management. The Spring framework's declarative transaction management is implemented by using Spring AOP because transactional aspect code is executed with the help of AspectJ annotation of AOP. The following are the similarities and differences of EJB CMT and Spring declarative transaction management:

- The Spring framework's declarative transaction management is capable of working in any environment with JDBC, JDO, or Hibernate; while EJB CMT is bound to JTA only
- Spring's declarative transaction management can be applied to any class; while EJB CMT is for special classes such as an enterprise Java bean class
- Spring offers declarative rollback that can be used with both programmatic and declarative rollback; whereas these are not supported by EJB
- You can build customized transactions by using Spring's AOP; but you cannot build customized transactions using EJB

Rollback rules enable us to define which type of exception should cause a transaction rollback automatically. Rollback rules are declarative and provided in the configuration file, not in the Java code. This declarative approach is preferred over rolling back transactions programmatically by calling the `setRollbackOnly()` method. In declarative approach, the business logic is not dependent on the transaction infrastructure and you do not need to import any Spring APIs.

Programmatic Transaction Management

Programmatic transaction management is a type of transaction management defined by the developer in the source code using the Spring transaction API. This type of transaction management can be implemented in the Spring framework in the following two ways:

- Using the TransactionTemplate class
- Using a PlatformTransactionManager interface

Using the TransactionTemplate Class

The method of implementing the TransactionTemplate class in an application is similar to the implementation of the JdbcTemplate class. Programmatic transactions can be performed with a callback approach, and the application code is not required to explicitly acquire and release transactional resources such as JDBC datasource. The application code must be executed in a transactional context to explicitly use the TransactionTemplate class. For this, you need to implement a TransactionCallback interface that contains all the code you need to execute in the transaction context. Next, you have to pass an instance of TransactionCallback interface to the execute() method of the TransactionTemplate object. The following is an example of application code using the `TransactionTemplate` class:

```
public class SampleService implements Service {
  private final TransactionTemplate tTemplate;
  public SimpleService(PlatformTransactionManager tManager)    {
Assert.notNull(tManager, "The 'transactionManager' argument must not be null.");
this.tTemplate = new TransactionTemplate(tManager);
  }
  public Object sampleServiceMethod() {
       return tTemplate.execute(new TransactionCallback() {
             public Object doInTransaction(TransactionStatus status) {
                   updateOperation1();
                   return resultOfUpdateOperation2();
             }
       });
  }
}
```

The following code snippet shows the use of the `TransactionCallbackWithoutResult` class when the return type is `void`:

```
    tt.execute(new TransactionCallbackWithoutResult() {
      protected void doInTransactionWithoutResult(TransactionStatus status) {
            updateOpt1();
            updateOpt2();
      }
    });
```

Transactions can be rolled back by using the `setRollbackOnly()` method. This method is called on the `TransactionStatus` object, as shown in the following code snippet:

```
    tTemplate.execute(new TransactionCallbackWithoutResult() {
      protected void doInTransactionWithoutResult(TransactionStatus status) {
            try {
                    updateOperation1();
                    updateOperation2();
            }
            catch (SomeBusinessExeption e) {
                    status.setRollbackOnly();
            }
      }
    });
```

Using the PlatformTransactionManager Interface

You can use the org.springframework.transaction.PlatformTransactionManager interface to manage your transaction. For using the PlatformTransactionManager interface, you need to pass the object reference of the PlatformTransactionManager interface to the bean. Transactions can be executed with the help of TransactionDefinition and TransactionStatus instances. The code snippet to manage a transaction through the PlatformTransactionManager interface is as follows:

```
    public class SampleService implements Service {
      // single TransactionTemplate shared all methods
      private final TransactionTemplate tTemplate;
      // use constructor-injection to supply the PlatformTransactionManager
      public SampleService(PlatformTransactionManager tManager){
            Assert.notNull(tManager, "The 'transactManager'
            argument must not be null.");
            this.tTemplate = new
            TransactionTemplate(tManager);
      }
      public Object sampleServiceMethod() {
            return tTemplate.execute(new TransactionCallback() {
            // the code in this method executes in a transactional context
            public Object doInTransaction(TransactionStatus status) {
                    updateOperation1();
                    return resultOfUpdateOperation2();
            }
      });
    }
```

Choosing between Programmatic and Declarative Transaction Managements

Choosing which type of transactional management, that is, programmatic or declarative, is dependent on the number of transactional operations required by an enterprise application. If you have small number of transactional operations, you can implement programmatic transactional management. In this scenario, the use of TransactionTemplate class is preferred since you do not need to set up transactional proxies using Spring.

In case of large number of transactional operations, we use declarative transaction management, since it separates business logic from the transaction management.

Application Server-Specific Integration

Spring's transaction management is dependent on the application server. The JtaTransactionManager class needs to perform JNDI lookup for the JTA `UserTransaction` and `TransactionManager` objects, which are auto detected. The JTA `UserTransaction` and `TransactionManager` objects vary in different application servers, such as IBM WebSphere and BEA WebLogic.

NOTE

IBM stands for International Business Machines.

BEA WebLogic

While using WebLogic 7.1 or higher as an application server, the `WebLogicJtaTransactionManager` class, which is a subclass of the JtaTransactionManager class, is used for handling transaction management. The `WebLogicJtaTransactionManager` class handles suspended transactions, which have been marked for rollback, and resumes all types of transactions. In WebLogic 8.1, the transaction manager can be configured, as shown in the following code snippet:

```
<!-- WebLogic 8.1 transaction manager -->
<bean id="tManager"
   class="org.springframework.transaction.jta.WebLogicJtaTransactionManager">
</bean>
```

IBM WebSphere

When using IBM WebSphere as an application server, the WebSphereTransactionManagerFactoryBean class may be used to retrieve the instances of JTA TransactionManager using WebSphere's static access methods. In IBM WebSphere, the transaction manager can be configured as follows:

```
<!-- WebSphere transaction manager -->
<bean id="tmanagerWebSphere"
class="org.springframework.transaction.jta.WebSphereTransactionManagerFactoryBean"/>
   <bean id="tManager"
   class="org.springframework.transaction.jta.JtaTransactionManager">
   <property name="tnManager">
   <ref local="tmanagerWebSphere"/>
   </property>
</bean>
```

The instance of JTA TransactionManager can be obtained by configuring Spring's org.springframework.transaction.jta.JtaTransactionManager class. In the preceding code snippet, the WebSphereTransactionManagerFactoryBean class is used for checking WebSphere version to handle the transactions.

Let's move ahead to learn about Spring tag library, which allows you to generate dynamic Web pages.

Exploring Spring Form Tag Library

Spring provides a set of custom tag libraries that allow you to generate dynamic Web pages and other Web page content. The tab library contains a set of tags for using JSP and Spring Web MVC. A set of attributes is attached with each tag. The Spring form tag library has simplified the task of creating JSPs.

Spring form tag library is bundled in the JAR file named spring.jar. A Tag Library Descriptor (TLD), namely, spring-form.tld, is used to provide tag-related information in an application. You can use taglib declaration for a JSP view implementation by adding the Spring form tag library at the beginning of a JSP page, as shown in the following code snippet:

```
%@taglib prefix="forms" uri=" http://www.springframework.org/tags/forms" %
```

In the preceding directive, the form tag name is denoted by a prefix, which is used to access different tags, such as form and input, from the Spring form tag library.

Classifying the Types of Tags

The tags present in the Spring form tag library are as follows:

- form tag
- input tag
- checkbox tag
- checkboxes tag
- radiobutton tag
- radiobuttons tag
- password tag

- select tag
- option tag
- options tag
- textarea tag
- hidden tag
- errors tag

The form Tag

The `form` tag is used to create an UI form. The client enters some data and submits the form, which is then sent to the server.

In the following code snippet, a domain object is used, that is, Client, which contains a JavaBeans with various properties such as `userName` and `age`. The following code snippet provides an example of the `forms.jsp` page:

```
<form:form>
  <table>
        <tr>
                  <td>Your Name:</td>
                  <td><form:input path="userName" /></td>
        </tr>
        <tr>
                  <td>Age:</td>
                  <td><form:input path="age" /></td>
        </tr>
        <tr>
                  <td colspan="4">
                           <input type="submit" value="Save" />
                  </td>
        </tr>
  </table>
</form:form>
```

The `Client` object, which resides in the `PageContext` object, returns the values of `userName` and `age`. There are many inner tags, such as <input type=text ...>, which can be used with the form tag. The following code snippet provides the code for the generated HyperText Markup Language (HTML) page:

```
<form method="POST">
  <table>
        <tr>
                  <td>Your Name:</td>
                  <td><input name="userName" type="text" value="San"/></td>
                  <td></td>
        </tr>
        <tr>
                  <td>Age:</td>
                  <td><input name="age" type="text" value="24"/></td>

        </tr>
        <tr>
                  <td colspan="4">
                           <input type="submit" value="Save" />
                  </td>
        </tr>
  </table>
</form>
```

In the preceding HTML page, it is assumed that the variable name of the form object is Client. You can bind the form into a Client object, as provided in the following code snippet:

```
<form:form commandName="Client">
  <table>
        <tr>
                  <td>Name:</td>
                  <td><form:input path="userName" /></td>
        </tr>
        <tr>
                  <td>Age:</td>
                  <td><form:input path="age" /></td>
        </tr>
```

```
        <tr>
                <td colspan="4">
                        <input type="submit" value="Save" />
                </td>
        </tr>
    </table>
</form:form>
```

The input Tag

The `input` tag is used to accept input from a user. The `type` attribute of the `input` tag provides the type of the input that a user can enter. The preceding code snippet also shows the usage of the `input` tag.

The checkbox Tag

The `checkbox` tag is used to input multiple selections by a user. Let's assume that a user has to choose a newspaper and a list of hobbies. For this, a class, that is, `Prefer`, is described in the following example:

```
public class Prefer {
   private boolean letter;
   private String[] interest;
   private String favWord;
   public boolean isletter() {
         return letter;
   }
   public void setletter(boolean letter) {
         this.letter = letter;
   }
   public String[] getInterest() {
         return interest;
   }
   public void setInterest(String[] interest) {
         this.interest = interest;
   }
   public String getFavWord() {
         return favWord;
   }
   public void setFavWord(String favWord) {
         this.favWord = favWord;
   }
}
```

The following code snippet provides the code of the `forms.jsp` with the `checkbox` tag:

```
<form:form>
   <table>
         <tr>
         <td>Find the letter :</td>
         <%--First Approach : This Property is of type java.lang.Boolean --%>
         <td><form:checkbox path="prefer.letter"/></td>
         </tr>
         <tr>
         <td> Your Interests:</td>
         <td>
         <%--Second Approach : This Property is of an array or of type
         java.util.Collection --%>
         Trekking: <form:checkbox path="prefer.interest" value="Trekking"/>
         Tennis: <form:checkbox path="prefer.interest" value="Tennis"/>
         Hypnotizing: <form:checkbox path="prefer.interest"
         value=" Hypnotizing"/>
         </td>
         </tr>
         <tr>
         <td>This is the favourite Word:</td>
         <td>
         <%--Third Approach : This Property is of type java.lang.Object --%>
         Cosmopolitan: <form:checkbox path="prefer.favWord" value="Cosmopolitan"/>
         </td>
         </tr>
   </table>
</form:form>
```

The following are three approaches to input multiple selections by using the checkbox tag:

- **First approach**— Allows you to use the java.lang.boolean type as a bound value. The checkbox is marked as checked when the bound value is `TRUE`. The `value` attribute of input corresponds to the resolved value of the `setValue(Object)` method of the `value` property.
- **Second approach**— Allows you to use the java.util.collection type or array as a bound value. The checkbox is marked as checked when the `setvalue(Object)` method of the `value` property exists in the bound collection.
- **Third approach**— Refers to the approach in which the checkbox is defined as checked when the bound value is equal to the value returned by the `setValue(Object)` method, provided the bound value is of any other type. The following code snippet provides the code of an HTML page with some checkboxes:

```
<tr>
   <td>Your Interests:</td>
   <td>
   Trekking: <input name="prefer.interest" type="checkbox"
   value="Trekking"/>
   <input type="hidden" value="1" name="_prefer.interest "/>
   Tennis: <input name="prefer.interest" type="checkbox"   value="Tennis"/>
   <input type="hidden" value="1" name="_prefer.interest"/>
   Hypnotizing: <input name="prefer.interest" type="checkbox"
   value="Hypnotizing"/>
   <input type="hidden" value="1" name="_prefer.interest"/>
   </td>
</tr>
```

If a form is submitted and a checkbox is selected, the unchecked value is not sent to the server. An underscore (_) is used for each checkbox to include hidden parameters.

The checkboxes Tag

The `checkboxes` tag is used for rendering multiple input tags. For example, to list all the possible hobbies in a JSP page, you can either provide a list of the available options during runtime or provide the list as the value for the items attribute of the `checkboxes` tag. For doing this, you have to pass the list of options in the form of an array, a list, or a `Map` interface. The use of this tag is shown in the following code snippet:

```
<form:form>
   <table>
         <tr>
               <td>Interests:</td>
               <td>
                     <form:checkboxes path="prefer.interest"
                     items="${userInterestList}"/>
               </td>
         </tr>
   </table>
</form:form>
```

In the preceding code snippet, `userInterestList` is a type of the `List` interface. The `userInterestList` interface is available as a model attribute and contains strings values of the options of the checkboxes to be selected from.

The radiobutton Tag

The `radiobutton` tag is used to select a single option at a time in a JSP page. It is used when there are many tag instances with different values in the same property. The following code snippet shows how to use the `radiobutton` tag:

```
<tr>
   <td> Your Initials:</td>
      <td>Mr.:  <form:radiobutton path="initials" value="Mr"/> <br/>
      Mrs.: <form:radiobutton path="initials" value="Mrs"/> </td>
</tr>
```

The radiobuttons Tag

The `radiobuttons` tag is used to display a pair of radiobuttons on a JSP page. It is similar to the `checkboxes` tag, which is used to pass all possible options during runtime. You can pass the available options in the item property, in the form of array, or a `List` or `Map` interface. You can also use custom object, as discussed earlier in the `checkboxes` tag. You can use the `radiobuttons` tag as follows:

```
<tr>
   <td>Marital status:</td>
   <td><form:radiobuttons path="maritalStatus"items="${maritalOptions}"/></td>
</tr>
```

The password Tag

The `password` tag is used for displaying the password entered by a user. The password text is generally displayed as asterisks (*). The following code snippet uses the `password` tag:

```
<tr>
   <td>Enter Password:</td>
   <td> <form:password path="password" /> </td>
</tr>
```

The select Tag

The `select` tag is used for binding data to the selected option. The `option` and `options` tags are nested tags in the `select` tag. Suppose a user knows languages of many countries; the `select` tag can be used to select multiple options of languages simultaneously. The following code snippet shows an example of the `select` tag:

```
<tr>
   <td> Language known :  </td>
         <td><form:select  path="language"  items="$(language)"  /> </td>
</tr>
```

For example, if the user knows French language, the HTML code would appear as follows:

```
<tr>
   <td>Language known:</td>
   <td><select name="language" multiple="true">
         <option value="Hindi">Hindi</option>
         <option value="French" selected="true">French</option>
         <option value="English">English</option></select></td>
</tr>
```

The option Tag

The `option` tag is used to provide multiple options for a client. The following code snippet shows how to use the `option` tag:

```
<tr>
   <td>Place:</td>
   <td>
         <form:select path= "place">
         <form:option value="Canada"/>
         <form:option value="Switzerland"/>
         <form:option value="New Delhi"/>
         <form:option value="Singapore"/>
         </form:select>
   </td>
</tr>
```

Suppose a user's native place is Switzerland, then the HTML source would appear as follows:

```
<tr>
   <td>Place:</td>
   <td>
   <select name="place">
         <option value="Switzerland" selected="selected">Switzerland</option>
         <option value="Canada" selected="true">Canada</option>
         <option value="New Delhi">New Delhi</option>
         <option value="Singapore">Singapore</option>
   </select> </td>
</tr>
```

The options Tag

The `options` tag is used to represent a list of option tags for a view page. The following code snippet shows how to use the `options` tag:

```
<tr>
   <td>Native Place :</td>
   <td>
   <form:select path="place">
   <form:option value="-" label="--Please Select--"/>
   <form:options items="${placeList}" itemValue="code" itemLabel="name"/>
   </form:select>
   </td>
</tr>
```

The preceding code snippet provides a list of places in the form of an Array. All options are populated using the options tag.

For example, if a user's native place is Germany, the HTML source code would appear as follows:

```
<tr>
   <td>Native Place:</td>
   <tr>
         <td>Place:</td>
         <td>
                  <select name="place">
                  <option value="-">--Please Select--</option>
                  <option value="France">France</option>
                  <option value="US">United States</option>
                  <option value="Germany" selected="selected">Germany</option>
                  </select>
         </td>
   </tr>
```

The textarea Tag

The `textarea` tag is used to represent an HTML `textarea`. The following code snippet shows how to use the `textarea` tag:

```
<tr>
   <td>Important Tips:</td>
   <td><form:textarea path="tips" rows="5" cols="30" /></td>
   <td><form:errors path="tips" /></td>
</tr>
```

The hidden Tag

The `hidden` tag is used for submitting a hidden value, after the form submission. The HTML input tag with the hidden type is written as follows:

```
<form:hidden path="place" />
```

For submitting `place` value as a hidden field, the HTML code is as follows:

```
<input name="place" type="hidden" value="Switzerland"/>
```

The errors Tag

The `errors` tag is used to represent a field that may lead to an error. The `errors` tag is useful to generate errors created by a `controller` or by any validators associated with the `controller`.

For example, you can use the `errors` tag if you need to raise an error on the basis of the text entered in the name and age fields. The following code snippet shows the use of the `ClientValidator` class to show error messages:

```
public class ClientValidator implements Validator {
   public boolean support(Class candidate) {
          return Client.class.isAssignFrom(candidate);
   }
   public void validate(Object obj, Errors errors) {
   ValidationUtils.rejectIfEmptyorWhitespace(errors, "name", required", " Name field is
   required.");
   ValidationUtils.rejectIfEmptyorWhitespace(errors, "age", "required", "Age field is
   required.");
   }
}
```

The JSP page would appear as follows:

```
<form:form>
  <table>
        <tr>
              <td>Name:</td>
              <td><form:input path="name" /></td>
              <%-- It show the errors for name field --%>
              <td><form:errors path="name" /></td>
        </tr>
        <tr>
              <td>Age:</td>
              <td><form:input path="age" /></td>
              <%-- It show the errors for Age field --%>
              <td><form:errors path="age" /></td>
        </tr>
        <tr>
              <td colspan="4">
                    <input type="submit" value="Save" />
              </td>
        </tr>
  </table>
</form:form>
```

If there are empty values in the name and age fields, the HTML form would appear as follows:

```
<form method="POST">
  <table>
        <tr>
              <td>Name:</td>
              <td><input name="name" type="text" value=""/></td>
              <%-- Errors associated to name field is displayed --%>
              <td><span name="name.errors">Name field is required.</span></td>
        </tr>
        <tr>
              <td>Age:</td>
              <td><input name="age" type="text" value=""/></td>
              <%-- Errors associated to name field is displayed --%>
              <td><span name="age.errors">Age field is required.</span></td>
        </tr>
        <tr>
              <td colspan="4">
                    <input type="submit" value="Save" />
              </td>
        </tr>
  </table>
</form>
```

Some wildcard facilities support the errors tag. For displaying the entire list of errors for a given page, the single wildcard character (such as * and #) or a sequence of wildcard characters is used. For example, the wildcard for the path attribute is as follows:

- **path="*"** – Displays all errors
- **path="age"** – Displays all errors associated with the age field

The following code snippet displays a list of errors at the top of an HTML page with the field-specific errors:

```
<form:form>
  <form:errors path="*" cssClass="errorList" />
  <table>
        <tr>
              <td>Name:</td>
              <td><form:input path="name" /></td>
              <td><form:errors path="name" /></td>
        </tr>
        <tr>
              <td>Age:</td>
              <td><form:input path="age" /></td>
              <td><form:errors path="age" /></td>
        </tr>
        <tr>
              <td colspan="4">
                    <input type="submit" value="Save" />
              </td>
        </tr>
  </table>
```

```
</form:form>
```

In the preceding code snippet the cssClass attribute of the form tag i used to specify the class that would be displayed on the occurrence of an error. The following code snippet provides the source of the HTML page:

```
<form method="POST">
   <span name="*.errors" class="errorList">Field is required.<br/>Field is
   required.</span>
   <table>
        <tr>
                <td>Name:</td>
                <td><input name="name" type="text" value=""/></td>
                <td><span name="name.errors">Name field is required.</span></td>
        </tr>
        <tr>
                <td>Age:</td>
                <td><input name="age" type="text" value=""/></td>
                <td><span name="age.errors">Age field is required.</span></td>
        </tr>
        <tr>
                <td colspan="4">
                        <input type="submit" value="Save" />
                </td>
        </tr>
</form>
```

Now, let's discuss about Spring's MVC framework.

Exploring Spring's Web MVC Framework

The Spring Web MVC framework is built on generic Servlet known as a `DispatcherServlet` class. The `DispatcherServlet` class is also known as `Front Controller`. This `DispatcherServlet` class sends the request to the handlers with configurable handler mappings, theme resolution, and locale and view resolution along with file uploading. The `handleRequest(request, response)` method is given by the default handler called the `Controller` interface. The application controller implementation classes of the `Controller` interface are as follows:

`AbstractController`

`AbstractCommandController`

`SimpleFormController`

These are super classes of the application controllers, and you can choose an appropriate super class while developing MVC Web applications. Any object can be used as a command or form object—it is not required to implement an interface or inherit a base class. The data binding of Spring considers type mismatches as validation errors that can be evaluated by the application; not as system errors.

Key Features of Spring Web MVC

Spring's Web module provides a set of Web support features, which are as follows:

- **Powerful configuration of both framework and application classes**—Provides powerful configuration of both framework and application classes. It also contains the information about validators and business objects.
- **Separation of roles**—Allows each component of the MVC framework to perform a different role during request handling. Request is handled by components such as controller, validator, command object, form object, model object, view resolver, handler mapping, and so on. Request handling is dependent among these roles and provides clear separation of roles.
- **Flexibility in choosing subclasses**—Allows you to use subclasses of any controller in an MVC Spring application.
- **Model transfer flexibility**—Provides the flexibility in model transferring through name/value pair of Map. This model transfer is easily integrated by any view technology.
- **No need of the duplication of code**—Allows you to use the existing business code. Therefore, there is no redundancy of code and the existing objects can be used as a form or command objects.
- **Specific validation and binding**—Displays the errors to the client if any validation error occurs.

- **Specific local and theme resolution**—Provides the facility of tag library of Spring and Java Server Pages with or without support for JavaServer Pages Standard Tag Library (JSTL).
- **Facility of JSP form tag library**—Helps in writing forms in JSP pages, which was introduced in the Spring Web MVC framework.

After discussing the features of Spring Web MVC framework, let's now discuss the components of Spring Web MVC framework.

The DispatcherServlet Class

The `DispatcherServlet` class is an important part of the Spring Web MVC framework, which is used for dispatching the request to application controllers. The `DispatcherServlet` class is configured with the IoC container. It is a Servlet that is inherited from the `HttpServlet` base class. The `DispatcherServlet` class is configured in the web.xml file of a Web application. You have to map the request using Uniform Resource Locator (URL) mapping in the same web.xml file when you want any request to be handled by it. The following code snippet shows how to map DispatcherServlet class in the web.xml file:

```
<web-app>
   ...
   <servlet>
         <servlet-name>examples</servlet-name>
         <servlet-class> org.springframework.web.servlet.DispatcherServlet</servlet-class>
         <load-on-startup>1</load-on-startup>
   </servlet>
   <servlet-mapping>
         <servlet-name>examples</servlet-name>
         <url-pattern>*.form</url-pattern>
   </servlet-mapping>
</web-app>
```

In the preceding code snippet, the `DispatcherServlet` class handles all the requests.

After initialization of DispatcherServlet class, the Spring framework creates the beans, which are defined in the Spring configuration file.

There are many special beans in Spring DispatcherServlet, which are used to process the requests and provide the appropriate views for displaying the resultant Web page. These beans can be configured in the `WebApplicationContext` context. Table 21.3 lists the special beans in the `WebApplicationContext` context:

Table 21.3: Special Beans in the WebApplicationContext Context

Expression	Explanation
`Controller(s)`	Handles the client's request.
`handler mapping(s)`	Manages the execution of controllers, provided they match the specified criteria. For instance, a specified URL matches with the controller.
`handler exception resolver`	Facilitates mapping of exceptions to views or providing code to handle complex exceptions.
`locale resolver`	Resolves the locale that a client is using to offer internationalized views
`Multipart file resolver`	Helps you to process file uploads
`theme resolver`	Resolves themes that an Web application can use
`view resolver`	Resolves view names to views used by the `DispatcherServlet class`

The `DispatcherServlet` class handles the client's request by:

- Using the `WebApplicationContext reference` to search and bind request so that the controller and other elements in an application can use it. It is attached by default under the `DispatcherServlet.WEB_APPLICATION_CONTEXT_ATTRIBUTE` key.
- Using the locale resolver to resolve the locale, such as client date, and language used in an application. It is a component capable of resolving the locale of a client, such as internationalized views. We use it when processing the request such as preparing the data and also rendering the view.

You can customize the Spring DispatcherServlet class by adding context parameters in the web.xml file or Servlet init parameters. Table 21.4 lists the various initialization parameters of the Spring Dispatcher class:

Table 21.4: Various Initialization Parameters

Parameter	Explanation
contextClass	Allows you to instantiate the context for the class that implements the WebApplicationContext interface. The context is used by the Servlet. If we don't provide the contextClass parameter, the XmlWebApplicationContext class is used.
contextConfigLocation	Allows you to locate the context. For this, a String is passed to the context instance. The corresponding String is divided into many Strings by using comma as a delimiter.
namespace	Allows you to provide the description of the namespace.

Let's now discuss about the controller classes that can be extended by controllers of a Spring application.

Controllers

In Spring MVC framework, a controller plays the key role of handling the client request. It is used for defining the attributes of an application. The user input is interpreted by the Controllers, which also transforms the user input into a model and then displays the view page by using this model. The org.Springframework.web.servlet.mvc.Controller interface is very important for the Controller architecture.

The Controller interface is implemented as follows:

```
public interface Controller {
    // Process the request and return a ModelAndView object which the
    DispatcherServlet  will render.
    ModelAndView handleRequest( HttpServletRequest req, HttpServletResponse
    res) throws Exception; }
```

A single method of the Controller interface handles the request and returns an appropriate model and view. ModelAndView and Controller's references are the main components of the Spring MVC implementation. The controllers in the Spring framework are as follows:

AbstractController class

MultiActionController class

Command Controllers (include classes such as AbstractCommandController and SimpleFormController)

The AbstractController Class

The AbstractController class is the basic controller in the Spring MVC framework. All Spring Controllers are inherited from the AbstractController class. This class also offers caching support. Table 21.5 lists the properties of this controller class:

Table 21.5: Properties of the AbstractController Class

Property	Explanation
cacheSeconds	Generates caching directives in the Hypertext Transfer Protocol (HTTP) response provided by the Controller. Its default value is -1.
requiresSession	Indicates whether or not the session is required for Controller.
supportedMethods	Allows you to find the methods that support the Controller. You can set this property to either GET or POST method.
synchronizeOnSession	Allows the Controller to synchronize a user session.
useCacheHeader	Allows the Controllers to provide the HTTP 1.1 compatible Cache-Control header. The default value of this property is true.
useExpiresHeader	Allows the Controllers to provide the HTTP 1.0 compatible "Expires" header. The default value of this property is true.

In the following code snippet, we override the handleRequestInternal(HttpServletRequest, HttpServletResponse) method to handle request. This method returns the ModelAndView object to forward a Web page. The following code snippet shows a `Controller` class that returns an object of the `ModelAndView` class:

```
package sample;
public class SampleController extends AbstractController {
  public ModelAndView handleRequestInternal(
  HttpServletRequest req, HttpServletResponse res)
  throws Exception {
        ModelAndView mv = new ModelAndView("fo");
        mv.addObject("message", "Have a Nice Day!");
        return mv; }
}
```

The preceding declared class allows you to set up a handler mapping for a Controller. A hard-coded view is also returned by this Controller.

The MultiActionController Class

The `MultiActionController` class is a special type of `Controller` used to group related functionality mapped to different request. It is defined in the following package:

```
org.springframework.web.servlet.mvc.multiaction
```

The `MultiActionController` class maps requests to method names and then invokes the right method name. Table 21.6 lists the main properties of the `MultiActionController` class:

Table 21.6: Properties of the MultiActionController Class

Property	Explanation
`delegate`	Defines a delegate object used to invoke the methods that are resolved by the Resolver. For this, you need to define the delegate using configuration parameter as a collaborator.
`methodNameResolver`	Helps to resolve the method specified in a subclass of the MultiActionController class. It has to invoke a method based on the incoming request. You can define a Resolver that uses the configuration parameter.

The Command Controllers

Command controllers, such as `AbstractCommandController` and `SimpleFormController`, are the essential parts of Spring MVC package. The Command controllers provide an easy way to handle requests by binding the request parameter to data objects. The role of the Command Controllers classes is similar to the ActionForm class of Struts.

The following are the types of Command Controller classes:

- **AbstractCommandController**—Helps to create a customize Command Controller. It is used for binding the request parameter to a data object. This class does not provide the form functionality, but provides the validation features.
- **AbstractFormController**—Models and populates the forms by using a command object retrieved in the Controller. This controller supports many features such as validation and normal Workflow.
- **SimpleFormController**—Creates a form with corresponding command objects. It specifies a command object, a viewname for the form, and a viewname for the page, which is displayed to the user after successful submission of the form.
- **AbstractWizardFormController**—Serves as an abstract class that should be extended by the `WizardController` class. The `AbstractWizardFormController` class consists of various methods such as `validatePage()`, `processFinish()`, and `processCancel()` methods. The `validatePage()` method is used for forwarding the next view. The `processFinish()` method is used for exiting from the wizard, and the `processCancel()` method is used to cancel the wizard before it performs the final action.

Handler Mappings

Handler mapping is used for mapping the incoming requests to the appropriate handlers. The SimpleUrlHandlerMapping class and the BeanNameUrlHandlerMapping class are the examples of handler mapping. It is used for delivering a HandlerExecutionChain object. The main task of the HandlerMapping's reference is to provide the HandlerExecutionChain object. The `HandlerExecutionChain` object must contain the handlers that should match with the incoming request and also contain a list of handler interceptors.

When the user sends the request, the DispatcherServlet instance passes the incoming request to the handlers to inspect the request and forward to the HandlerExecutionChain object. After that, the `DispatcherServlet` instance executes the handler and handler interceptors in the chain.

A subclass of HandlerMappings class chooses a handler, based on the URL of the incoming request, as well as a state of the session associated with the incoming request.

Views and View Resolvers

Each Spring MVC framework renders a way for resolving the views. In Spring, you do not need a specific view technology for providing models in a browser. This facility is provided by view resolvers. Spring supports JavaServer Pages, Velocity templates, and XSLT view technologies to display the model's data in a browser.

The Spring framework provides ViewResolver interface to handle views. The ViewResolver interface is used to map between view names and actual views, whereas the View interface is used for preparation of request and handling over the request to one of the view technologies.

The ViewResolver Interface

ViewResolver is an interface used for resolving views by name. It is used for providing a mapping between views and view names. The state of a view cannot be changed while running an application. In Spring, views are addressed by a view name and resolved by a view resolver. Table 21.7 lists the various ViewResolver classes:

Table 21.7: Various ViewResolver Classes

ViewResolver	Description
`AbstractCachingViewResolver`	Caches the views.
`FreeMarkerViewResolver/ VelocityViewResolver`	`Supports FreeMarkerView` and `VelocityView`, such as Velocity templates. It is a subclass of the `UrlBasedViewResolver` class.
`InternalResourceViewResolver`	Supports the `InternalResourceView` class, such as Servlets and JSPs. Apart from `InternalResourceView`, the `InternalResourceViewResolver` class also supports subclasses, such as `JstlView` as well as `TilesView`, and is a subclass of the `UrlBasedViewResolver class.`
`ResourceBundleViewResolver`	Implements the `ViewResolver interface;` the bean definitions in a `ResourceBundle` interface are used by this class.
`UrlBasedViewResolver`	Implements `ViewResolver`, and is used for direct resolution of symbolic view names to URLs, without an explicit mapping definition. There's no need of arbitrary mappings when your symbolic names match the names of your view resources.
`XmlViewResolver`	Implements `ViewResolver`, which accepts an XML file with the same Document Type Definition (DTD) as the bean factories of Spring.

The `UrlBasedViewResolver` class allows you to choose JSP for a view technology. The following code snippet defines the `ViewResolver` bean using the `UrlBasedViewResolver` class for viewing JSP page:

```
<bean id = "viewresolverex"  class =
  "org.springframework.web.servlet.view.UrlBasedViewResolver">
<property name = "prefix"  value ="/WEB-INF/view/"/>
<property name = "suffix"  value=".jsp"/>
</bean>
```

If the `ViewResolver bean` returns a viewname tests, the request will be passed on to the `RequestDispatcher` object. The `RequestDispatcher` object sends the request to /WEB-INF/view/tests.jsp.

The `RequestBundleViewResolver` class is used for mixing of different view technologies. The following code snippet defines the `ViewResolver` bean using the `RequestBundleViewResolver` class:

```
<bean id="viewresolverex"
   class="org.springframework.web.servlet.view.ResourceBundleViewResolver">
   <property name="base"  value="views"/>
   <property name="defaultParent"  value="parentViews"/>
</bean>
```

In the bean definition, the ResourceBundleViewResolver class examines the ResourceBundle, which is recognized by the property name base. It is resolved by using the property value [viewname.class], which acts as a view class, and the property value [viewname].url, which acts as a view URL. A parent view can be recognized by the value of the property parentViews, from which all views in the properties file can be sorted.

Chaining ViewResolvers

When there are more than one view resolvers for handling a view, the Spring framework supports a chain of view resolvers, such as displaying both JSP and Excel views. You can create a chain of the resolvers by adding more resolvers in application context and setting the order property of multiple view resolvers for forwarding Web pages in an application. The order property is used for specifying the order of execution of the resolvers when it is found that there is more than one resolver in the application context.

There are two resolvers—`InternalResourceViewResolver` class and `XmlViewResolver` class—in the chain of view resolvers. The `InternalResourceViewResolver` object is always the last resolver in the chain of view resolvers, whereas the `XmlViewResolver` object is used for displaying Excel view. Excel view is an Excel worksheet that is used for displaying as a Web page without using Microsoft Excel. The chaining view resolver is described in the following examples of bean definition:

```
<bean
  id="jspResolver"
  class="org.springframework.web.servlet.view.InternalResourceViewResolver">
  <property name="viewClass"
  value="org.springframework.web.servlet.view.JstlView"/>
  <property name="prefix' value="/WEB-INF/view/"/>
  <property name="suffix' value=".jsp"/>
</bean>
<bean id="excelResolver"
  class="org.springframework.web.servlet.view.XmlViewResolver">
  <property name="order" value="1"/>
  <property name="location" value="/WEB-INF/view.xml"/>
</bean>
<beans>
<bean name="reports" class="org.springframework.example.ReportExcelView"/>
</beans>
```

When a particular view resolver of Spring does not give a view, then Spring examines the application context to find the other configured view resolver. If Spring finds an additional view resolver, it inspects it; otherwise, it throws an Exception. If a view resolver does not find any view, then it returns null.

Implementing Spring Web MVC Framework

In this section, we develop a simple Spring MVC application (`springapp`) that separates the business logic, presentation logic, and allows a controller servlet to handle the requests of the clients. The controller is responsible for accepting the user's request and interacting with the business objects to fulfill the request. Based on the user's request, the controller decides which view is used to display the result. In the `springapp` application, we need to develop the following modules for creating the springapp Spring MVC application:

- The controller (DemoController.java)
- The View (hello.jsp)
- Spring configuration file
- Web configuration file (web.xml)

Creating the Controller

Create a controller called DemoController.java and place it in the src\com\kogent\spring directory of the application directory. The DemoController.java Controller handles the request and returns a ModelAndView named hello.jsp (/jsp/hello.jsp). Listing 21.1 shows the code of the DemoController.java file (located in the `\springapp\src\com\kogent\spring` folder):

Listing 21.1: Showing the Code of the DemoController.java File

```
package com.kogent.spring
import org.springframework.web.servlet.mvc.AbstractController;
import org.springframework.web.servlet.mvc. Controller;
```

```
import org.springframework.web.servlet.ModelAndView;
import javax.servlet.ServletException;
import javax.servlet.http.HttpServletRequest;
import javax.servlet.http.HttpServletResponse;
import org.apache.commons.logging.Log;
import org.apache.commons.logging.LogFactory;
import java.io.IOException;
import java.util.Date;
public class DemoController implements Controller {
    protected final Log logger = LogFactory.getLog(getClass());
    public ModelAndView handleRequest(HttpServletRequest request, HttpServletResponse
    response)
    throws ServletException, IOException {
            String now = (new Date()).toString();
            logger.info("Returning hello view with " + now);
            return new ModelAndView("hello", "now", now);
    }
```

In Listing 21.1, the ViewResolver is used to return the view, hello.jsp and forward it to the URL that matches the name of the view specified in the firstspring-servlet.xml file. It also sets the current date and time value to the now key identifier, and makes the model available to the hello.jsp view.

Creating the Views

In this subsection, we need to create two JSP pages that are used to display the view page based on the Spring MVC paradigm. The two JSP pages are as follows:

- index.jsp
- hello.jsp

The index.jsp Page

The index.jsp page is used to forward client requests to the hello.htm page, which is mapped with the <servlet-mapping> element in the web.xml file. Listing 21.2 shows the index.jsp file (save the index.jsp file in the `\springapp\jsp` folder):

Listing 21.2: Showing the Code of the index.jsp File

```
<html>
 <head>
        Index.jsp page
 </head>
 <body>
        <jsp:forward page="/hello.html"></jsp:forward>
 </body>
</html>
```

The hello.jsp Page

Now, you need to create the hello JSP page (/jsp/hello.jsp) that is used to forward the user request matched to the HelloController.java file. Add the JSTL capability in your JSP page to display current date and time by using the <c:out/> tag, which is retrieved from the model mentioned in DemoController.java. Listing 21.3 shows the hello.jsp file (save the hello.jsp file in the `\springapp\jsp` folder):

Listing 21.3: Displaying the Code of the hello.jsp File

```
<%@taglib prefix="c" uri="http://java.sun.com/jstl/core_rt"%>
<%@taglib prefix="fmt" uri="http://java.sun.com/jstl/fmt_rt"%>
<html>
<head><title>Hello, Welcome to the Spring Application</title></head>
<body>
<h1>Welcome to the Spring Application</h1>
<p>Greetings, it is now <c:out value="${now}"/></p>
</body>
</html>
```

Creating the Spring Configuration File

Now, you need to create an XML file called firstspring-servlet.xml in the springapp/WEB-INF directory. This file contains a bean definition that is used by the DispatcherServlet object. The name of this file is determined by two identifiers: one is firstspring, specified in the <servlet-name /> element in the web.xml file, and the other is servlet, appended with firstspring. This is the standard naming convention followed by Spring's MVC framework. This file contains bean entry named /hello.html, which specifies the class named `com.kogent.spring.DemoController`. This class acts as a controller that forwards the request to hello.html. Listing 21.4 shows the `firstspring-servlet.xml` file (save the XML file in the `\springapp\WEB-INF` folder):

Listing 21.4: Displaying the Code of the `firstspring-servlet.xml` File

```
<?xml version="1.0" encoding="UTF-8"?>
<beans xmlns="http://www.springframework.org/schema/beans"
 xmlns:xsi="http://www.w3.org/2001/XMLSchema-instance"
 xmlns:context="http://www.springframework.org/schema/context"
 xsi:schemaLocation="http://www.springframework.org/schema/beans
http://www.springframework.org/schema/beans/spring-beans-3.0.xsd">
<!-- the application context definition for the firstspring DispatcherServlet -->
<bean name="/hello.html" class="com.kogent.spring.DemoController"/>
<bean                                                          id="viewResolver"
 class="org.springframework.web.servlet.view.InternalResourceViewResolver">
<property name="prefix" value="/jsp/"/>
<property name="suffix" value=".jsp"/>
</bean>
</beans>
```

Creating the Web Configuration File

The web.xml file contains the configuration of the Spring MVC application, that is, springapp. It contains a DispatcherServlet instance, which acts as a Front Controller. All client requests are routed through this Front Controller. It also contains the <servlet-mapping> element that maps to the URL pattern with .htm extension, which is to be routed by the DispatcherServlet instance. Listing 21.5 shows the code of the web.xml file (save the web.xml file in the `\springapp\WEB-INF` folder):

Listing 21.5: Showing the Code for the web.xml File

```
<?xml version="1.0" encoding="UTF-8"?>
<web-app version="3.1"
   xmlns="http://xmlns.jcp.org/xml/ns/javaee"
   xmlns:xsi="http://www.w3.org/2001/XMLSchema-instance"
   xsi:schemaLocation="http://xmlns.jcp.org/xml/ns/javaee
   http://xmlns.jcp.org/xml/ns/javaee/web-app_3_1.xsd">
 <servlet>
        <servlet-name>firstspring</servlet-name>
        <servlet-class>
               org.springframework.web.servlet.DispatcherServlet
        </servlet-class>
        <load-on-startup>1</load-on-startup>
 </servlet>
 <servlet-mapping>
        <servlet-name>firstspring</servlet-name>
        <url-pattern>*.html</url-pattern>
 </servlet-mapping>
 <welcome-file-list>
        <welcome-file>index.jsp</welcome-file>
 </welcome-file-list>
</web-app>
```

Exploring the Directory Structure

The springapp is the root directory of Spring MVC application created here. All the JSP, Controller, and Spring configuration files are placed in this directory. You need to download and place the following .jar files in the springapp\WEB-INF\lib directory, as springapp application uses the APIs of JSTL, Servlet, and Spring Web MVC module:

- commons-logging.jar
- spring-web-4.0.1.RELEASE.jar
- spring-webmvc-4.0.1.RELEASE.jar
- spring-core-4.0.1.RELEASE.jar
- spring-beans-4.0.1.RELEASE.jar
- spring-context-support-4.0.1.RELEASE.jar
- spring-context-4.0.1.RELEASE.jar
- spring-expression-4.0.1.RELEASE.jar
- spring-aop-4.0.1.RELEASE.jar

These JAR files help in successful compilation and execution of the `springapp` application. The directory structure of the `springapp` application is shown in Figure 21.2:

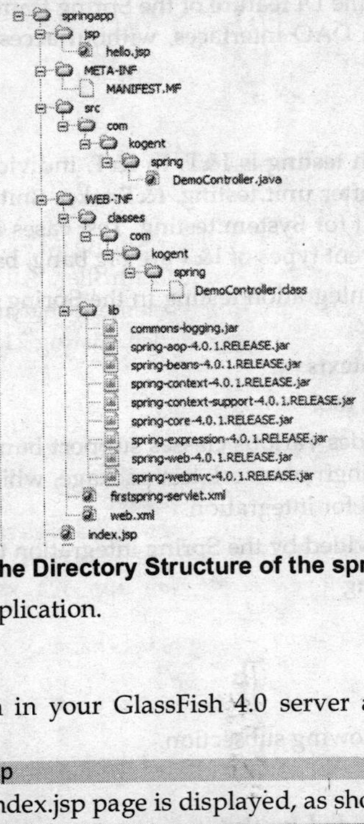

Figure 21.2: Displaying the Directory Structure of the springapp Application

Now, it's time to run the Spring MVC application.

Running the Application

Now, deploy the springapp application in your GlassFish 4.0 server and run the application by typing the following URL on your browser:

```
http://localhost:8080/springapp
```

After accessing the preceding URL, the index.jsp page is displayed, as shown in Figure 21.3:

Figure 21.3: Displaying the Spring MVC Application

Testing Spring Applications

Testing is an integral part of enterprise software development. It is a process of finding bugs in the software under development to give reliable solution to the client. The software testing process is performed by testers to improve the quality of the application by checking the result and performance of the software application for various types of inputs. The process involves steps such as defining and executing test cases, and identifying problems and fixing them. There are many types of testing; however, this section focuses on unit and integration testing with Spring.

The Unit Testing

Unit testing is the basic type of testing in the development process. The smallest part of source code consisting of modules is called a unit. For procedural language, a unit can be a program, function, and so on; however, in object-oriented language, a unit is generally represented by a class. The test performed on these units is called unit test. The purpose of unit testing is to separate each piece of program and ensure that individual pieces of the code are correct.

While performing unit testing in the Spring framework, you do not need to set up the runtime infrastructure. If your application uses the **Plain Old Java Object** (POJO) concept, it can be tested in the Junit tests with objects whose instance is created by using the new operator.

Spring facilitates unit testing due to the DI feature of the Spring framework. For example, you can test the objects of the service layer by mocking the DAO interfaces, without accessing the persistent data while running unit tests.

The Integration Testing

The abbreviated name of integration testing is I&T. In I&T, individual modules are combined and tested as a group. I&T is normally performed after unit testing. I&T takes unit tested modules as input, groups them into larger units, and prepares the output for System testing. Test cases are designed to test that all the modules are functioning appropriately. The different types of I&T are big bang, backbone, top-down, and bottom-up.

The spring-mock.jar file is used for integration testing in the Spring framework. You can perform I&T to ensure the following in a Spring application:

- The correct wiring of Spring contexts
- Data access using JDBC or ORM tool

For integration testing, Spring provides various classes support bundled in the form of the spring-test JAR file. In this JAR file, you find the org.springframework.test package, which contains classes such as TestContext and TestContextManager, which are used for integration.

The following functionalities are provided by the Spring integration testing:

- Context management and caching
- DI of the test fixtures
- Transaction management
- Inherited instance variables

Let's discuss these in detail in the following subsection.

Context Management and Caching

There are two types of support provided by the `org.springframework.test` package: first for consistent loading of Spring contexts, and second for caching the loaded contexts. You should note that the caching of loaded contexts support is used if you are working on a large project. Spring container instantiates objects when you start the container, which consumes time and resource. To solve this problem, the AbstractDependencyInjectionSpringContextTests class provides an abstract protected method to provide the location of contexts:

```
protected abstract String[] getConfigLocations();
```

In the preceding code snippet, the signature of the `getConfigLocations()` method is provided. This method provides an array that contains the resource locations of XML configuration metadata, typically in the `WEB-INF/classes` folder of the application. The location of the XML configuration metadata is the same as the list of configuration locations specified in the web.xml file. The set of configuration is loaded once and reused later for each test case. This reusability of configuration ensures that subsequent tests are executed fast.

Dependency Injection of Test Fixtures

When the application context is loaded by the AbstractDependencyInjectionSpringContextTests class (and its subclasses), it provides an optional way to configure instances of the test classes by using Setter Injection. For this, you have to define the instance variable and the corresponding setters. The AbstractDependencyInjectionSpringContextTests class automatically finds the corresponding object in the set of configuration files passed as a parameter to the getConfigLocations() method.

Let's consider a scenario that you have a class, TestTitleDao, which implements the data access logic. Now, we want to write the integration tests to test the following aspects:

- **The Spring configuration**—Checks whether or not every information about TestTitleDao bean configuration is correct
- **The Hibernate mapping file configuration**—Verifies whether or not objects of the application are mapped correctly and the correct lazy-loading settings are specified in the Hibernate mapping file
- **The logic of the HibernateTitleDao**—Checks whether or not the configured instance performs its expected functionality successfully

An example of a test class is provided in the following code snippet:

```
package com.kogent.hibernate;
public class TestTitleDao extends
   AbstractDependencyInjectionSpringContextTests {
   // this instance will be (automatically) dependency injected
   private TestTitleDao titleDao;
   // a setter method to enable DI of the 'titleDao' instance variable
   public void setTitleDao(TestTitleDao tDao) {
         this.titleDao = tDao;
   }
   public void loadtestTitle() throws Exception {
         //provide code to load the title
   }
   // specifies the Spring configuration to load for this fixture
   protected String[] getConfigLocations() {
         return new String[] { "classpath:com/kogent/conf.xml" };
   }
}
```

In the preceding code snippet, the attendant file referenced by the `getConfigLocations()` method (`'classpath:com/kogent/conf.xml'`) is specified in the following code snippet:

```
<?xml version="1.0" encoding="UTF-8"?>
<!DOCTYPE beans PUBLIC "-//SPRING//DTD BEAN//EN"
"http://www.springframework.org/dtd/http://www.springframework.org/dtd/spring-
   beans.dtd">
<beans>
<!-- this bean will be injected into the TestTitleDao class -->
<bean id="titleDao" class="com/kogent/ hibernate/TestTitleDao">
<property name="sessionFactory" ref="sessionFactory"/>
</bean>
<bean id="sessionFactory"
   class="org.springframework.orm.hibernate3.LocalSessionFactoryBean">
<!-- dependencies elided for clarity -->
</bean>
</beans>
```

You can use the AbstractDependencyInjectionSpringContextTests class to test the autowire relationship between the beans in a Spring application. However, if you have multiple beans of the same type, you cannot apply this autowire approach for these beans. In this case, you can use the `applicationContext` instance variable for explicit lookup and explicitly call the applicationContext.getBean("titleDao") bean.

If you don't need DI in your test case, you can create a customize class that is extended by the AbstractSpringContextTests class of the org.springframework.test package.

Transaction Management

One common issue in testing is that it requires a database to observe and test the state of the persistence store. If the state of a database is changed during testing, you need to ensure that the changes are rolled back so that the database can be used for testing in future.

The Spring integration testing supports frameworks to perform insert or update operations for multiple test cases on the same database. By default, the frameworks create and roll back a transaction for each test. Transactional support is provided to the test class through a PlatformTransactionManager bean defined in the test's application context. The benefit of transaction management in the Spring framework is that you can reuse the application contexts across various testing scenarios such as configuring Spring-managed object graphs, transactional proxies, and DataSources.

For example, if the test methods delete the contents of selected tables while running a transaction, the transaction will roll back to the default state, and the database will return to its prior state.

There are some useful methods to commit transactions, such as the following:

- **setComplete()**—Helps to commit a transaction. This method is inherited from the `AbstractTransactionalSpringContextTests` class.
- **endTransaction()**—Rollbacks a transaction, and commits it only if the `setComplete()` method has been called earlier.

Inherited Instance Variables

You can access the following protected instance variables by extending the AbstractTransactionalDataSourceSpringContextTests class:

- **applicationContext (ConfigurableApplicationContext)**—Helps to perform the bean lookup explicitly and also test the complete state of the context. This method is inherited from the `AbstractDependencyInjectionSpringContextTests` super class.
- **jdbcTemplate**—Inherites from the AbstractTransactionalDataSourceSpringContextTests class. It is used for querying a database to confirm its state.

The following example illustrates the use of the `AbstractTransactionalJUnit4SpringContextTests` class for performing integration testing:

```
@ContextConfiguration
public abstract class AbstractHospitalTests
extends AbstractTransactionalJUnit4SpringContextTests {
   protected Hospital hospital;
   public void setHospital(Hospital hospital) {
          this.hospital = hospital;
   }
   public void testGetVets() {
          //provide code to retrieve data from the datasource

   }
```

The following code snippet illustrates the JDBC implementation of the tests containing the `getConfigLocations()` method:

```
@ContextConfiguration
public class HibernateHospitalTests extends AbstractHospitalTests {
   protected String[] getConfigLocations() {
          return new String[]      {
                 //provide the location of the hibernate.xml file in the form of String};
   }
}
```

In the preceding code snippet, the Hibernate implementation of the `HibernateHospitalTests` class contains the `@ContextConfiguration` annotation, which is used to load the application context of a bean. Testing is performed by inheriting the `AbstractHospitalTests` class.

Integrating Spring with Hibernate

The integration of the Spring framework with Hibernate provides functionalities such as resource management, DAO implementation support, and transaction management. Although Hibernate supports ORM, the problem is that the Hibernate Web application uses the Hibernate APIs, such as `Configuration`, `SessionFactory`, and `Session`, to access a database through Hibernate DAO object. The Hibernate DAO object is scattered across the code throughout the Hibernate Web Application. In case of the Spring framework, the business objects are not scattered as they are configured with the help of IoC Container. Therefore, it is possible to use the Hibernate objects with Spring beans through the IoC Container. It is also possible to use all the functionalities, such as ORM and DAO implementation of Hibernate, with the Spring framework.

The following are some of the benefits of using the Spring framework to create Hibernate ORM DAOs:

- **Easy to test**—Facilitates the Spring's IoC container to use the implementations and configuration of Hibernate SessionFactory instances, JDBC DataSource instances, transaction managers, and ORM object implementations. This makes it easier to test each piece of persistence code by isolating the code in the Spring Web application.
- **Integrated transaction management**—Allows you to wrap the ORM code with either declarative transaction management or AOP style method interceptor. In either case, if any exception occurs during the execution of the transaction, the transaction can be easily rollbacked. JDBC-related code provides full transactional support by using ORM.

Integrating Struts 2 with Spring

Struts 2.x, which was known as WebWork earlier, can be treated as a new Web framework. It has very few similarities with Struts 1.x. Struts 2.x is an integration of WebWork and Struts 1.x.

Struts 2 is a very simple way of implementing MVC pattern in our applications. It has a servlet filter, called FilterDispatcher, as the controller. All the requests pass through this FilterDispatcher. The FilterDispatcher takes the requests and passes it through a series of interceptors before it invokes an Action class. The Action class receives the requests, processes the requests, and returns a result that is sent to the user.

Struts 2 applications consist of application objects that help in controlling the application functionality. These application objects include service objects, along with actions and interceptors components. The Struts 2 framework creates and instantiates these objects. In Struts 2, an action class is created and mapped to appropriate URL using XML or Java annotations. The Struts 2 framework uses the `ObjectFactory` component to automatically create the application objects, except the service objects, which are required for implementing actions in Struts 2 applications. Since the actions need to obtain the reference of service objects for implementing any functionality, this reference to a service object is provided manually using the `new operator`. Due to this, the service objects and actions may get tightly coupled with each other at some point of time. To overcome this, we need a framework that manages the creation of service object and solves the problem of tightly coupled objects. The solution to this problem is the Spring framework, which can be used for managing the creation of objects and reducing the coupling between objects.

Let's understand how to integrate Spring with Struts 2 next.

Configuring Spring in a Struts 2 Application

To integrate Spring and Struts 2 in an application, we need to perform the following broad-level steps:

- Add the Spring plug-in and explicitly define the objects in the source code of the application. Spring plug-in specifies how to integrate Spring and Struts 2 by manipulating the application and service objects.
- Download the Spring.jar file to create a Spring container in the Struts 2 application. Then, configure the Spring listener in the web.xml file.
- Set the mode of autowiring to inject dependencies in the created objects.

Let's explore these steps in detail.

Adding the Spring Plug-In

You need to download and add the Spring plug-in to the Struts 2 application. Struts 2 supports the Spring plug-in, which enhances the Struts 2 ObjectFactory component class for managing the created objects. This plug-in deals with objects that are explicitly specified in the source code of the application. You can download the spring plug-in file, that is, spring-plugin-2.0.9.jar, from the URL `http://cwiki.apache.org/S2PLUGINS/home.html`.

Downloading the Spring.jar File and Configuring the Spring Listener

You also need to download the Spring JAR, that is, spring.jar, from the URL `http://springframework.org` ,for creating a Spring container to implement Spring functionality in the Struts 2 application. Next, the Spring listener is configured in the web.xml file of a Web application for using the Spring application Context listener, as shown in following code snippet:

```
<listener>
<listener-class>org.springframework.web.context.ContextLoaderListener</listener-class>
</listener>
```

To specify the objects explicitly, we need to declare the objects as Spring beans in the applicationcontext.xml file located in the WEB-INF folder. The ContextLoaderListener Spring listener searches for metadata information in the applicationcontext.xml file and then injects the object in a class, based on the metadata information.

Let's move further and set the autowiring mode required to inject dependencies in the objects.

Setting the Autowiring Mode

The Spring framework provides a feature to autowire dependencies of resources. Autowiring refers to the technique where you do not need to explicitly declare the object for injecting the dependencies; Spring automatically looks up for an object based on the object property. There are various modes of implementing autowiring, which can be set in the configuration files. The modes of autowiring are as follows:

- Autowiring by name
- Autowiring by type
- Autowiring by constructor
- Autowiring by auto

Now let's discuss each of them in detail.

Implementing the Name Mode

Autowiring by name is the default mode of autowiring. This mode uses the setter method to match the ID of a bean with the name of the property specified in the bean action.

The following code snippet shows how to implement the autowiring by name mode in the applicationcontext.xml file:

```
<?xml version="1.0" encoding="UTF-8"?>
<beans xmlns="http://www.springframework.org/schema/beans "
   xmlns:xsi=
   xsi:schemaLocation="http://www.springframework.org/schema/beans
   http://www.springframework.org/schema/beans/spring-beans-2.0.xsd">
<bean id="strutsservice" class = "com.kogent.StrutsServiceJPA"/>
......
</beans>
```

The preceding code snippet declares the ID for the bean to be injected in a resource. Spring automatically matches this ID with the setter method name for injecting the dependencies.

The following code snippet shows the setter method for receiving the dependencies:

```
StrutsServiceInterface strutsservice;
public void setStrutsService(StrutsServiceInterface strutsservice)
this.strutsservice=strutsservice;
}
```

Implementing the Type Mode

Spring provides the type mode of autowiring, which helps search registered Spring beans that match the property specified in the defined action. For using this mode, you need to change the autowiring mode in the struts.properties file, as shown in the following code snippet:

```
Struts.objectFactory.spring.autowire=type
```

You can also specify the type mode in the struts.xml file, as shown in the following code snippet:

```
<constant name=" Struts.objectFactory.spring.autowire" value=type />
```

Implementing the Constructor Mode

The autowiring by constructor mode allows you to autowire the parameters specified in the bean constructor. This mode works with constructor objects, which take the dependencies as parameters. If more than one Spring bean has the same matching type, an exception is thrown instead of deciding which bean to be injected. The syntax to implement the autowiring by constructor mode is as follows:

```
Struts.objectFactory.spring.autowire=constructor
```

Implementing the Auto Mode

The autowiring by auto mode allows you to automatically detect the mode for injecting the dependencies. Usually, the autowiring by auto mode injects the dependencies by using the constructor mode and then the type mode. The syntax to implement the autowiring by auto mode is as follows:

```
Struts.objectFactory.spring.autowire=auto
```

Summary

The chapter has described Spring, a lightweight framework for developing Java EE applications. First, the chapter has described about the basic features and newly introduced features in its 4.0 release. Then, the chapter has described about the architecture of Spring framework and about is seven modules, namely Spring Core, Spring AOP, Spring Web MVC, Spring DAO, Spring ORM, Spring context, and Spring Web flow, have also been discussed. In addition, the chapter describes the key terms and advices of Spring AOP. The chapter has also helped you to create an application, that is, springapp, to demonstrate the implementation of Spring. Finally, the chapter has discussed the integration of Spring with Hibernate and Struts 2.

In the next chapter, you learn how to implement security in Java EE 7 applications.

Quick Revise

Q1. .... is not a module in the Spring architecture.

A. Spring AOP **B. Spring ORM**

C. Spring APO **D. Spring DAO**

Ans. C

Q2. The .... package provides the core JDBC framework.

A. org.springframework.beans.factory **B. org.springframework.aop**

C. org.springframework.jdbc.core **D. org.springframework.beans**

Ans. C

Q3. Name the package containing the super classes for integration testing.

A. org.springframework.test **B. org.springframework.jdbc.core**

C. org.springframework.beans.factory **D. org.springframework.aop**

Ans. A

Q4. What is Spring framework?

Ans. Spring framework is a collection of subframeworks, also called layers, such as Spring AOP, Spring ORM, Spring Web Flow, and Spring Web (Model View Controller) MVC. You can use any of these layers separately while creating a Web application. These modules may also be grouped together to provide better functionalities in a Web application.

Q5. Give the full form of AOP.

Ans. Full form of AOP is Aspect-Oriented Programming

Q6. What are the different types of advices in Spring AOP?

Ans. Different types of advices in Spring AOP are as follows:

- Around
- Before
- After throws
- After returning
- After finally

Q7. What is Dependency Injection?

Ans. Dependency Injection can be defined as a form of Inversion of Control (IoC). It is an object-oriented programming technique that is used to invert the control for object creation and linking.

Q8. What is the role of the DispatcherServlet class in the Spring framework?

Ans. The `DispatcherServlet` class plays the role of a central Servlet, which extends the `HttpServlet` class, and is fully configured with the IoC container. All the client requests to the controller are processed by this class.

Q9. What is a BeanFactory?

Ans. A BeanFactory is an implementation of the factory pattern that instantiates, configures, and manages Beans and Java objects.

Q10. Why do we need to implement the JDBC abstraction layer?

Ans. JDBC abstraction layer helps in reducing the amount of code and simplifying the process of error handling.

Q11. Which interface is responsible for handling the exceptions in the Spring framework?

Ans. The `HandlerExceptionResolvers` interface is responsible for exception handling. This interface is defined in the `web.xml` file.

Q12. What is the role of the `JdbcTemplate` class?

Ans. The JdbcTemplate class is the main class in the core package of the Spring framework that helps in avoiding common errors. This class is used to execute SQL queries, stored procedures, and operations on Resultsets in JDBC.

Q13. The _____ annotation is used on injection points and on @Bean definitions.

A. @MessageMapping

B. @Lazy

C. @Description

D. @Conditional

Ans. B

Q14. The _______ annotation is used for conditional filtering beans.

A. @Bean

B. @RestController

C. @ResponseBody

D @Conditional

Ans. D

Q15. STOMP stands for _____________

A. Streaming Text Oriented Messaging Protocol

B. Socket Text Oriented Messaging Protocol

C. Streaming Text Object Messaging Protocol

D. Streaming Text Object Mapping Protocol

Ans. A

22

Securing Java EE 7 Applications

If you need an information on:	See page:

In today's scenario, every organization faces numerous security threats that can expose the confidential information of the organization to unauthorized access. These threats may occur due to system failure, lack of availability of resources, access to data by unauthorized users, and so on. The security threats to an organization can include disclosure of confidential information, modification or destruction of information, misappropriation of protected resources, and compromise on accountability. These security threats may appear depending upon the environment in which an enterprise application is executed. For example, sharing of confidential information stored in files over a network that is not protected may pose a security threat.

Therefore, organizations must take steps to identify these threats; and take the necessary corrective actions to eliminate them. Java EE platform provides various security mechanisms, such as authentication, authorization, encryption, and auditing, which allow you to expose data to authorized users.

In this chapter, you learn about the concept of security in Java EE 7. Next, you learn about different security mechanisms. You also learn how to implement security on an application server. Further, you learn how to secure enterprise beans and application clients. In addition, you learn how to implement security on Web applications. In the end, you learn how to implement security using different approaches.

Let's start by learning the concept of security in Java EE 7.

Introducing Security in Java EE 7

The Java EE 7 applications consist of Web components, such as Java Servlet and JavaServer Pages (JSP). These components are deployed in different Web containers to build an enterprise application. After creating an enterprise application, you need to consider various security issues so that the data in the system can be protected from unauthorized access. In a Java EE 7 application, a security mechanism is configured to allow only authenticated users to access functions and data of the application. Java EE uses the Java EE container to supply low level platform specific functionality to the Web components. The Java EE container provides the following two types of security:

- **Declarative security**—Refers to the type of security provided to the Web components by using the Deployment Descriptor, which is an Extensible Markup Language (XML) file that explains the deployment of Web and enterprise applications. The Deployment Descriptor includes the mapping for application specific components, which provide security roles, users, and policies to protect the Web application and enterprise application components from unauthorized and unauthenticated access. Security roles, users, and policies are discussed later in this chapter.
- **Programmatic security**—Refers to the type of security that is embedded in an application and is used to make security decisions, such as determining whether or not a user is authorized to access a resource. Programmatic security defines the security model of the application.

  Security deals with authentication and protection of Web resources for various clients. Let's discuss about authentication and protection domain next.

Authentication

Authentication is a security mechanism in which callers and service providers validate each other on behalf of specific users or systems in a distributed computing environment. While implementing authentication call, identities are created to validate whether or not the user is authenticated. The type of authentication in which the identity of caller is validated by a service provider and the identity of the service provider is validated by the caller is called mutual authentication. An entity is called unauthenticated if it participates in a call without setting up or proving its identity.

The caller identity refers to a user, who is running a client program and trying to access the server using the client end program.

When a client program, which is executed by the user, requests for an application component, the caller identity propagated to the requested component is of the user. In case request to an application component is made from another application component, which is between the user originating the request and the requested application component, caller identity propagated to the final application component may be of the intermediate application component or of the user.

Authentication is a mechanism that involves two phases. In the first phase, the service independent authentication is performed to establish an authentication context that encapsulates and verifies the user's identity. In the second phase, the authentication context authenticates the user's identity with entities on the server. Therefore, providing control over access to the authentication context, and authenticating the associated identity, becomes the base of authentication. To control access to an authentication context, you can perform the following tasks:

- Perform the initial authentication to allow a user to access the authenticated context
- Provide the authenticity of a component in any other trusted or related component of the same application
- Delegate the authenticated context from the caller to its called component when the component impersonates its caller

Protection Domain

A collection of entities that are expected or known to trust each other is called a protection domain. An entity in a protection domain is not required to prove its authenticity to others in the domain. In such cases, authentication is only needed when interactions span the protection domain boundary, as illustrated in Figure 22.1. When a component interacts with another component within the same protection domain, no constraint is enforced on the caller identity emanated from these components. Based on trust, instead of authentication, the caller, which is a component, can claim its identity in the following ways:

- Propagating an identity
- Selecting an identity on the basis of the authorization constraints implemented by the called components

If you implement the concept of protection domain, you should define the boundaries of the protection domain to restrict the unproven identities. This will also avoid the authentication of entities in the protection domain as only proved identities are allowed within the domain.

In the Java EE architecture, the authentication boundary is established by the container, which lies between external callers and the components hosted by the container. A container does not usually host different protection domain components; but exceptionally, it might host components from different protection domains. Figure 22.1 shows the details of protection domain:

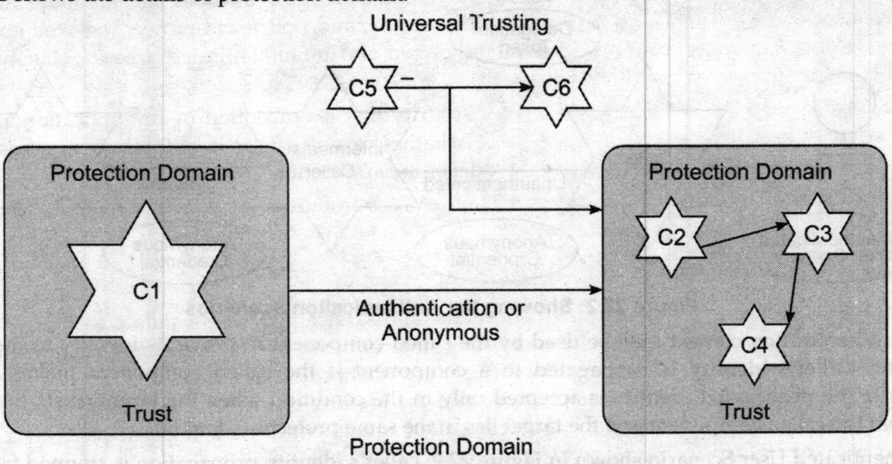

Figure 22.1: Showing Protection Domain

A caller identity is accessible to the components as credentials; for example a X.509 certificate or a Kerberos service ticket, which is mainly used for inbound calls. The bi-directional authentication functionality is provided by the container to impose protection domain boundaries of the deployed applications in the container.

The interacting containers need to decide if there is enough inter-container trust for accepting the container-provided depiction of component identities. In some environments, trust may simply be assumed, while in others, inter-container authentication need to be evaluated and the container identities may be compared with the trusted identities. In case the required information regarding the identity of the user is not provided and sufficient inter-container trust relationship does not exist, the container would reject the call. Figure 22.2 explains the authentication concepts using two scenarios, an authenticated user scenario and an unauthenticated user scenario:

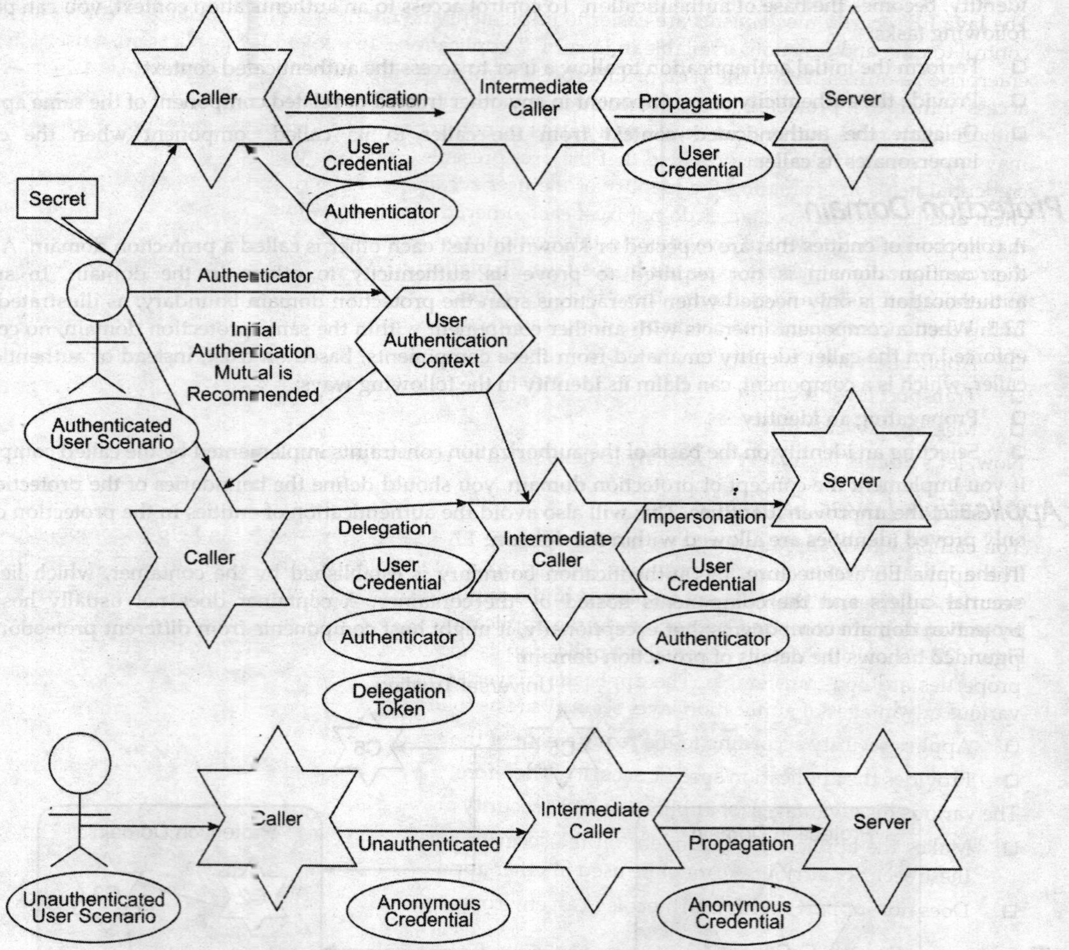

Figure 22.2: Showing the Authentication Scenarios

A user's authentication context may be used by the called component to prove its identity to the intermediate component. Caller's identity is propagated to a component if the called component makes a call to that component. The propagated identity is accepted only in the condition when the target trusts the caller, which implies that the called component and the target lies in the same protection domain.

In Unauthenticated User Scenario shown in Figure 22.2, caller's identity propagation is stopped from delegation and subsequent impersonation as it is found unauthenticated by the service provider. It is the responsibility of service providers to identify whether the propagated identities should be accepted as authentic during propagation. The user provides the accessibility to a called component for its authentication context so that the called component can impersonate the user during calls in delegation. The only requirement of impersonation is that it is expected from the user to trust the impersonator, which acts on behalf of the user. Figure 22.2 also describes how the propagation of an unauthenticated user identity can be done in the form of an anonymous credential. An anonymous credential is a form of unproven identity that may be propagated even if there is no mutual trust between the caller and the service provider.

After having a brief idea about the implementation of security in the Java EE 7 application, let's explore various mechanisms used to implement security.

Exploring Security Mechanisms

The Java EE security mechanisms are easier to implement and configure. These mechanisms provide fine access control to data and functions available in Java EE 7 applications. In a Java EE 7 application, a user interacts with enterprise resources within the Web or Enterprise JavaBeans (EJB) tiers, through a client container. A user may access either the protected or unprotected resources. Protected resources are distinguished by using the authorization rules that restrict access to a subset of non-anonymous identities. Therefore, a protected resource may be accessed by the user provided that the user presents a non-anonymous credential. This non-anonymous credential helps in evaluating the identity of the user according to the resource authorization policy. When the client and the resource container do not trust each other, the credential must be associated with an authenticator that approves the credential's validity. In this section, you learn about various authentication mechanisms and their configurations that are expected by the Java EE platform. The Java EE security mechanisms provide a way to authenticate users and authorize them to access application functions and associated data at different layers. In this section, the security mechanism is discussed in context of the following three layers of security:

- Application layer security
- Transport layer security
- Message layer security

Now, let's discuss each layer of security in detail with its advantages and disadvantages.

Application Layer Security

You can provide an application layer security in Java EE 7 applications with the help of component containers. The application layer security provides security to a specific application type. In case of application layer security, application firewalls are employed in the application layer to enhance protection to a Web application by preventing unauthorized user access to the application stream, and all application resources. The security is provided to an application when the application is executed on different application servers. The security properties are non-transferable. The application layer security has certain advantages and disadvantages. The various advantages of application layer security are as follows:

- Applies security according to the requirement of the application.
- Provides the application specific security. Therefore, it is applied while executing the application.

The various disadvantages of application layer security are as follows:

- Makes the application dependent on the security attributes, which are non-transferable. This implies that these security attributes cannot be used in other application types.
- Does not support multiple protocols in an environment.

Transport Layer Security

The transport layer security is provided by transport mechanism associated with a specific type of application. The transport mechanism includes transferring information over the client-server network. Therefore, the transport layer security relies on secure Hypertext Transfer Protocol (HTTP) transport using Secure Sockets Layer (SSL). The transport layer security is a point-to-point security used for authorization, message integrity, and confidentiality. The server and client can authenticate one another during execution of an application over SSL-protected session. In addition, the server and the client agree on an encryption algorithm and cryptographic keys, which are source of information that determines the result of encryption algorithm, prior to transmission and reception of data by the application protocol. In case of transport layer security, the message must be encrypted before it is sent.

Security mechanism through the transport layer is performed in three stages, which are as follows:

- The client and the server accede to utilize the same algorithm for encryption and decryption.
- A key is exchanged between the client and the server using the public key encryption and certificate-based authentication

- A symmetric cryptography chipper, which is an algorithm for encryption or decryption of data, is used while exchanging the information. It is symmetric, as it uses a key that is common during encryption and decryption of data. In the absence of a key, no result is produced during encryption or decryption of the data.

The transport layer security has various advantages and disadvantages. The advantages of transport layer security are as follows:

- Provides a standard approach for securing the Java EE 7 platform. Therefore, it is simple and easily understandable security, in comparison to the application layer security.
- Pertains to both the message body and the attachments.

The disadvantages of transport layer security are as follows:

- Remains tightly coupled with the transport layer protocol.
- Provides transient protection to messages during their transmission. The protection is automatically removed after the message leaves this layer.
- Provides point to point security; therefore, it is not an end solution for securing the systems.

Message Layer Security

When the message layer security mechanism is followed, the security information is transmitted to the appropriate recipient using a Simple Object Access Protocol (SOAP) message or SOAP message attachment. This SOAP attachment allows the message content to travel along the message or the attachment. In this case, a portion of the message may be signed by a particular sender and encryption may be provided for a specific receiver. The message is passed through intermediate nodes prior to its delivery to the receiver. The encrypted message remains opaque at intermediate nodes and can only be decrypted at the intended receiver. The message layer security is also known as the end-to-end security, as it completely secures the message content from the sender end to the receiver end, which was not possible in the transport layer security. This security mechanism also has certain advantages and disadvantages.

The advantages of the message layer security are as follows:

- Provides security that lasts until a message is received by the intended receiver
- Provides security to different portions of a message
- Provides interaction with intermediaries in case the message passes through multiple hops or devices in its way to the receiver over the network.
- Provides security to the message only, which is independent of the application environment or transport protocol

The disadvantages of message layer security are as follows:

- Is complex as compared to other security mechanisms
- Adds some overhead to processing in terms of operating cost

Now, after discussing each layer of security mechanism, let's discuss how to implement security on an application server.

Implementing Security on an Application Server

The deployment of a Web application on an application server offers highly secure, interoperable, and distributed component computing based on the Java EE security model. The security model is supported by the application server. The application server can be configured to perform the following tasks:

- Adding, deleting, and modifying authorized users. This can be done by adding realms, users, groups, and roles to the Web application.
- Configuring the HTTP and the Internet Inter-ORB Protocol (IIOP) listeners.
- Configuring the Java Management Extensions (JMX) connectors.
- Adding, modifying, and deleting existing or custom realms.

- Defining an interface using Java Authorization Contract for Containers (JACC) for the pluggable authorization providers. Security contracts between the application server and the authorization policy modules are provided with the help of JACC. These contracts specify the instructions for installing, configuring, and using authorization providers while making access decisions.
- Setting and changing an application's policy permissions.

To implement the security on the application server, it must be ensured that only authorized users are given access to the resources. Controlled access to protected resources is made possible with the help of authorization. Authorization is based on two concepts, which include identification and authentication. Identification is a technique using which a system can recognize an entity. Authentication is a process with the help of which it is possible to verify the user's identity, a device, or other entity in a computer system. You must perform the following steps to authenticate a user:

1. Write the code to prompt the users for their username and password
2. Provide information in the Deployment Descriptor to establish security for the application
3. Set authorized users and groups on the application server
4. Map the application's security roles to users, groups, and principals defined on the application server

Prior to creating an application that implements security, you need to understand how to work with realms, users, groups, and roles.

Realm

In terms of Java EE 7 application security, a realm is a database of users and groups that is used to identify valid users of a Web application. The authentication services available in Java EE 7 manage the realms available in an application server. In the application server, the admin-realm, file and the certificate realm are configured. In the file realm, the server stores information of files in a file named `keyfile`. The file realm is used to check the authentication mechanism for entities. It is used for authenticating all clients, except the Web browser client containing the HTTP protocol and certificate.

In case of certificate realm, the server stores user's information in a certificate database. The application server uses the HTTP protocol and the certificates to authenticate clients. The Java EE authentication service verifies the identity of the user by verifying an X.509 certificate. The common field name of the X.509 certificate is utilized as the principal name to verify the identity of the user

The admin-realm file can also be considered as a file realm, which is used to store user information in a local file named `admin-keyfile`. Users in an `admin-realm` are managed in the same way as they are managed in case of the file realm.

User

A user is an individual identity defined by the application server. It can have multiple roles corresponding with that identity. These multiple roles help the user to access all resources protected by the roles. The users can be related to a group. Note that a user in Java EE is same as a user in an operating system, but the security mechanisms involved in both the cases are different.

Group

A group is a collection of authenticated users, which have common traits specified in an application server. A Java EE user, who is also the user of the file realm, can belong to an application server group. An application server group is a category of user's type identified by the common traits, such as job title or customer profile. For example, it may be possible that majority of customers of an e-commerce application are associated with the CUSTOMER group, while the more profitable customers are associated with the PREFERRED group. In such situations, to manage and control the access of large number of users, classifying users into groups is the best strategy.

Categorizing users into groups makes it easier to control the access of application components by the large numbers of users. An application server group possesses a wider scope of accessibility as compared to a role. A group is declared for all the applications that are deployed on the application server, while a role is related to a particular application deployed on the application server.

Role

To grant permission to access a particular collection of resources in an application, an abstract name called role is provided. A role may be considered as a key that is capable of opening a lock. Various users might possess a copy of the key, needed to open a lock; or the role, needed to access the application resources. An application's resources can be accessed by the original or the copy of the role.

After understanding implementation of security on the application server, let's understand security in the context of enterprise beans and application clients.

Securing Enterprise Beans

Enterprise beans are Java EE components that implement the EJB technology to create distributed, scalable, platform independent, and secure enterprise applications. They are executed inside the EJB container to provide security to the beans associated with the application. The EJB container provides application level security to enterprise beans associated with the application. These security services permit a user to rapidly build and deploy enterprise beans, forming the core of transactional Java EE applications. The declarative and programmatic security is used to protect enterprise beans from unauthorized and unauthenticated access. The resources present over the Internet that are protected from unauthorized and unauthenticated access include methods of EJBs, Web components and other enterprise beans. Figure 22.3 displays the basic configuration of a Java EE application:

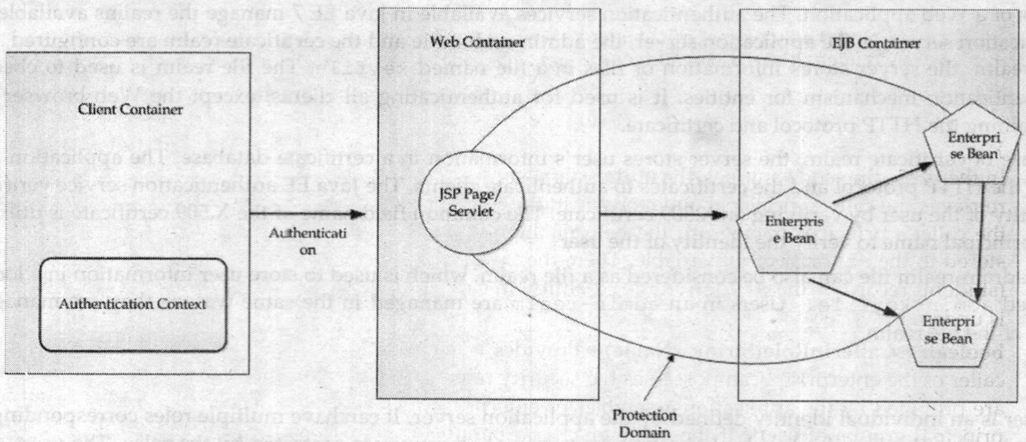

Figure 22.3: Showing the Configuration of a Typical Java EE Application

According to the Java EE 7 platform specification, there is no requirement of interoperable caller authentication at the EJB container. The direct connection of client containers and enterprise beans through Remote Method Invocation (RMI) is also avoided by the use of network firewall technology. The only way in which the EJB container can protect EJBs from unauthorized access is by entrusting the Web container to assure the user identity. This would restrict the accessibility of the enterprise beans through protected Web components only. Figure 22.3 shows how the protection domain boundaries are imposed for Web components, and enterprise beans that are called by the Web components.

Now, after learning about the basic configuration of a Java EE application, let's discuss about the role of programmatic approach and security identity propagation in implementing security in an application.

Using the Programmatic Security Approach

Enterprise beans can be secured programmatically by providing the code to implement security in the business methods of the bean. The programmatic security approach should be used when declarative security alone cannot provide full security to the enterprise bean. The programmatic security approach is particularly used in situations when security context information and caller's identity are to be retrieved by the enterprise bean business methods. The caller's identity is utilized to take security decisions. For example, you may need to grant access to the users of the enterprise application at a specific time of a day.

The following two methods of the `javax.ejb.EJBContext` interface are used to retrieve the security information of the caller of the enterprise bean:

- **Principal getCallerPrincipal()**—Allows you to access the current caller principal's name. The `getCallerPrincipal()` method enables the enterprise bean's method to obtain the caller's principal name that can be used to identify the caller of the enterprise bean. The following code snippet shows the use of the `getCallerPrincipal()` method:

```
public void UseCallerPrincipal(...) {
    ... @Resource SessionContext myctx;
        @PersistenceContext EntityManager myem;

    // acquire the caller principal.
    mycallerPrincipal = myctx.getCallerPrincipal();

    // acquire the caller principal's name.
    studnameKey = mycallerPrincipal.getName();

    // use studnameKey as primary key to find StudentRecord
    StudentRecord myStudentRecord =
        myem.find(StudentRecord.class, studnameKey);

    // update address of Student
    myStudentRecord.setAddress(...);

        ...
    }
}
```

  In the preceding code snippet, the address of a student is updated. The `getCallerPrincipal()` method retrieves the callers' principal and stores it in the `mycallerPrincipal` variable, which is used to retrieve the caller's principal name with the help of the `getName()` method. The principal name of the caller is stored in the `studnameKey` variable. Then, the `EntityManager` instance uses this name to find the caller (student) record or the `StudentRecord` entity. In case student record is found, the address of the student is updated.

- **boolean isCallerInRole(String rName)**—Provides a mechanism to determine whether or not the current caller of the enterprise bean possesses the security role passed as a parameter to this method. Security roles are provided by the application assembler or enterprise bean developer. The security roles are assigned to principal groups of users. If the value of `rName` parameter matches with the security role specified in the Deployment Descriptor, the `isCallerInRole()` method returns true; otherwise, it returns false.

Using Security Identity

Security in enterprise beans can be implemented by propagating the security identity. To execute a specific method of an enterprise bean, security identity of a caller or the specific run-as identity of the enterprise bean is used. Consider a situation in which a Web client invokes an enterprise bean method in an EJB container. Consecutively, this enterprise bean's method invokes another enterprise bean method deployed in another container. In the call from the Web client to an enterprise bean method, the security identity propagated is the identity of the Web client. The security identity propagated to the target enterprise bean, in the call from an intermediate enterprise bean method to the target enterprise bean method, can be either of the following:

- **Web client**—Applies in situations when the trust exists between the target container and the intermediate container.
- **Specific run-as identity**—Applies in situations when the target container only supports specific run-as identity. The run-as identity represents the whole intermediate enterprise bean.

The run-as identity is applicable to the entire enterprise bean, which includes all the enterprise bean business methods, business interfaces, home interface, component interface, time-out callback method, and Web service endpoint interfaces. The run-as identity of a message-driven bean is applied to all its methods and message listener methods.

Securing Application Clients

The authentication mechanism for application clients is same as for the Java EE components or Java EE 7 application components. To access the protected Web resources, a user requires various authentication mechanisms, such as HTTP basic authentication, SSL client authentication, and HTTP login form authentication. These mechanisms are useful while accessing an enterprise Java bean in an application server.

Services offered by the application client containers, specifically used for authenticating the users, are utilized by the application client for authentication.

The users may be authenticated by the application container when an application server starts its operation. When the user accesses any protected resource in the application server, the container authenticates the user. An application client offers a class to hold the authentication data. To gather authenticated data, the application client must implement the `javax.security.auth.callback.CallbackHandler` interface. The class for gathering the data must be specified in the Deployment Descriptor. The application's callback handler must support callback objects defined in the `javax.security.auth.callback` package.

Now, let's discuss how to implement security in Web applications.

Implementing Security in Web Applications

You need to protect Web applications and their resources from malicious users who can harm the applications in numerous ways, such as disclosing confidential information, modifying or destroying original information, and using the resources inappropriately. Although it is not possible to completely secure a Web application, the threats to it can be reduced to an acceptable level by using security mechanisms, such as authentication and authorization. The Java platform provides various security technologies, which include a large set of Application Programming Interfaces (APIs), implementations for commonly used security mechanisms, and protocols. The Java security APIs provide various features including cryptography, public key infrastructure, secure communication, authentication, and access control, to secure the application from unauthorized and unauthenticated access.

This section describes various security mechanisms used in Web applications, such as authentication and authorization, and explains how these mechanisms are used to secure the applications. It also discusses various HTTP authentication mechanisms. In addition, it explains how to implement Web security using declarative security and programmatic security. However, before discussing these security mechanisms, let's first look at the Java Authentication and Authorization Service (JAAS) API, which is used to implement authentication in Web applications.

Using JAAS

JAAS API is used to implement authentication and authorization in Java applications. JAAS was introduced as an optional package in the Java 2 Platform, Standard Edition, version 1.3; and has been integrated into the Java 2 Platform, Standard Edition, version 1.4. The JAAS authentication is based on the Pluggable Authentication Module (PAM) framework or architecture, described later in the chapter. JAAS enables Java applications to be independent of the underlying technologies that are used for authentication purposes. The JAAS API is a collection of classes particularly used to make authentication services available and impose access controls on users. The JAAS API is used for three purposes:

- Finding out who is running the Java code, irrespective of whether the code is a standalone Java application, an applet, a bean, or a servlet
- Authorizing users to ensure that they possess the right permissions required to perform the respective actions
- Allowing implementation of data integrity

Let's now look at authentication, authorization, and data integrity in detail.

Implementing Authentication with JAAS

Authentication is the process of checking the validity of the security details submitted by a user. It is used by Web applications to relate a user identity to an HTTP session accessing a resource of the Web application. This resource may be protected; and authentication is used to validate the user identity and check whether the user is authorized to access the resource. To understand the concept of authentication better, let's consider the example of Internet banking or Web-based emails. In these cases, identity of a user is related to a real person and access depends on some proof of the identity based on authentication parameters.

An application that performs authentication is known as authenticator. An authenticator requires certain security details, which vary for different applications. Therefore, different authenticators (or different authentication technologies) are required to handle different securit quirements. This, in turn, has brought in third party vendors to provide various authenticators. Apart from this, you can also develop your own authenticators using the JAAS API. The JAAS API provides a standard abstraction through which a Java application can communicate with any vendor-provided authenticators.

As already stated, JAAS authentication is based on the PAM framework. Figure 22.4 shows the authentication architecture of the PAM framework:

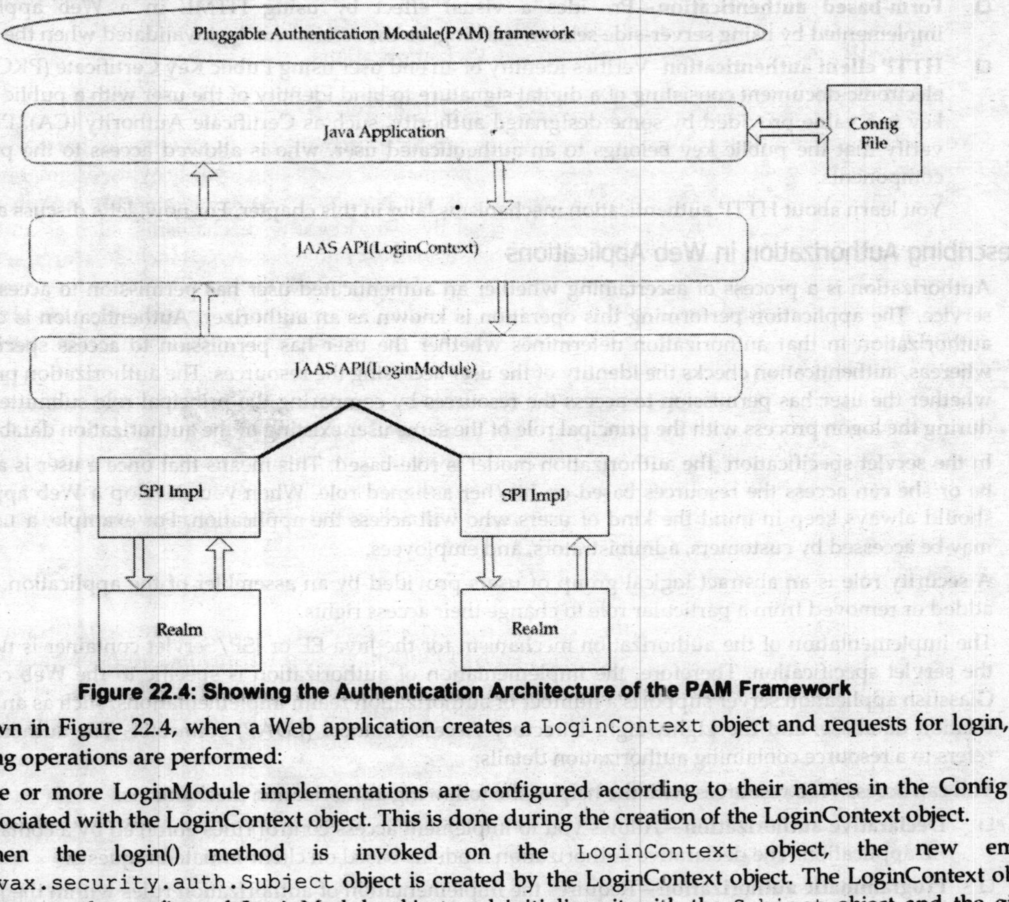

Figure 22.4: Showing the Authentication Architecture of the PAM Framework

As shown in Figure 22.4, when a Web application creates a `LoginContext` object and requests for login, the following operations are performed:

1. One or more LoginModule implementations are configured according to their names in the Config file associated with the LoginContext object. This is done during the creation of the LoginContext object.
2. When the login() method is invoked on the `LoginContext` object, the new empty `javax.security.auth.Subject` object is created by the LoginContext object. The LoginContext object constructs the configured LoginModule object and initializes it with the `Subject` object and the given `CallBackHandler` object, which receives all JAAS events, and then returns the results back to JAAS.

3. The login() method of the LoginContext object calls the methods in the `LoginModule` object to perform login and authentication. The `LoginModule` object utilizes the given `CallBackHandler` class to obtain the security details and check their validity.
4. If authentication is successful, the `LoginModule` object creates a relation between the relevant `principals` (authenticated identities), credentials (authentication data such as cryptographic keys), and the `Subject` object.

The servlet specification provides support for the Web container to perform authentication through the <security-constraint> element in the Deployment Descriptor, web.xml. The servlet specification provides the following types of authentication:

- **HTTP basic authentication**—Refers to the authentication mechanism used to protect Web resources through specified username and password. This is the simplest authentication method supported by a Web application.
- **HTTP digest authentication**—Refers to the authentication mechanism in which the information is transmitted from the Web browser to the server in HTTP basic authentication containing a password. However, HTTP digest authentication is rarely used because only few Web browsers support this type of authentication.
- **Form-based authentication**—Provides a visual effect by using HTML in a Web application. It is implemented by using server-side session tracking, so the session can be invalidated when the user logs out.
- **HTTP client authentication**- Verifies identity of an end user using Public Key Certificate (PKC), which is an electronic document consisting of a digital signature to bind identity of the user with a public key. A public key is a value provided by some designated authority, such as Certificate Authority (CA). PKC is used to verify that the public key belongs to an authenticated user, who is allowed access to the protected Web components.

You learn about HTTP authentication mechanisms later in this chapter. For now, let's discuss authorization.

Describing Authorization in Web Applications

Authorization is a process of ascertaining whether an authenticated user has permission to access a requested service. The application performing this operation is known as an authorizer. Authentication is different from authorization in that authorization determines whether the user has permission to access specific resources; whereas, authentication checks the identity of the user accessing the resources. The authorization process verifies whether the user has permission to access the resources by comparing the principal role submitted by the user during the logon process with the principal role of the same user existing in the authorization database.

In the servlet specification, the authorization model is role-based. This means that once a user is authenticated, he or she can access the resources based on his/her assigned role. When you develop a Web application, you should always keep in mind the kind of users who will access the application. For example, a `Login` module may be accessed by customers, administrators, and employees.

A security role is an abstract logical group of users provided by an assembler of the application. Users can be added or removed from a particular role to change their access rights.

The implementation of the authorization mechanism for the Java EE or JSP/Servlet container is not defined by the servlet specification. Therefore, the implementation of authorization is specific to the Web container. The Glassfish application server supports a number of authorization realm implementations, such as an XML file, the relation database, and the Lightweight Directory Access Protocol (LDAP) connector. The authorization realm refers to a resource containing authorization details.

You can access Web resources with the help of the following authorization mechanisms:

- **Declarative authorization**—Allows you to implement access control rules enforced by a container in a Java EE application. The declarative authorization model is based on client-initiated requests.
- **Programmatic authorization**—Requires the implementation of authorization rules within the Java code of a Web application, but it uses the servlet security framework to authenticate the users.

These authorization models are discussed in detail later in this chapter. After discussing about authentication and authorization, let's now discuss data about integrity with reference to JAAS API.

Implementing Data Integrity with JAAS API

Data integrity is the property that restricts or prevents data from being modified during transmission. The servlet container is responsible for maintaining data integrity. Additionally, you can use the HTTP/SSL connection, which provides the data integrity feature, to provide security in the transport layer.

Now, after understanding the concept of security in the context of authorization, authentication, and data integrity, let's learn about HTTP authentication mechanisms.

Using Authentication Mechanisms

The authentication mechanism for a Web resource is configured in the web.xml file. This configured authentication mechanism is activated only when a user tries to access the protected Web resource. You can use the following authentication mechanisms to protect your resources:

- HTTP basic authentication
- Form-based authentication
- Client-certificate authentication or HTTPS client authentication
- HTTP digest authentication

NOTE

If you do not specify any of these mechanisms in the web.xml file, authentication will not be performed.

Let's now discuss these mechanisms in detail, one by one.

Describing HTTP Basic Authentication

The HTTP basic authentication mechanism is the simplest way of implementing authenticity in Java EE 7 applications. In this authentication mechanism, the resource requested by the user is accessible by providing the valid username and password. Figure 22.5 shows the process of HTTP basic authentication:

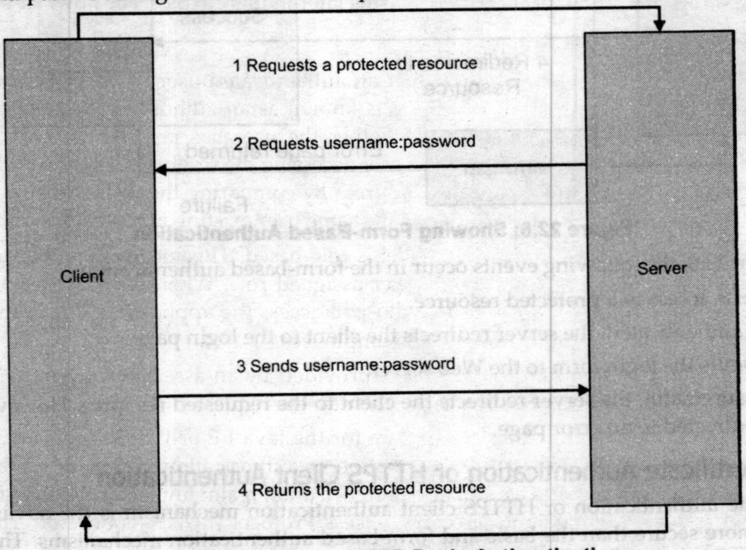

Figure 22.5: Showing HTTP Basic Authentication

As shown in Figure 22.5, the following events occur in HTTP basic authentication:

1. A client requests access to a protected resource
2. The Web server requests the client's name and password of the client, which are entered through a dialog box
3. The Web server validates the user credentials

4. If successful, the server returns the requested resource

There is a drawback of using the HTTP basic authentication. It is not secure because it transfers usernames and passwords over the Internet as Unix-to-Unix encoded (UU-encoded) encrypted text, which can be easily decoded.

Describing Form-Based Authentication

In form-based authentication, the username and password of a client are transferred in form of plain text, and no authentication is enforced on the target server. This authentication mechanism can disclose usernames and passwords, which can be easily decoded unless the connections are established over SSL. SSL is a technology that permits secure data transmission from the Web server to the Web browser. With the help of form-based authentication, you can alter the login and error pages of an application, which are displayed for the user. Figure 22.6 shows the working of form-based authentication:

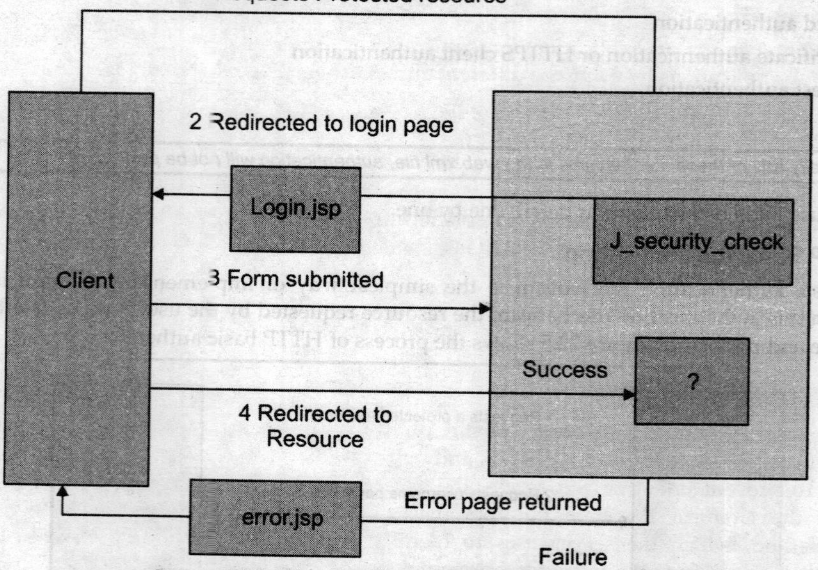

Figure 22.6: Showing Form-Based Authentication

As shown in Figure 22.6, the following events occur in the form-based authentication:

1. A client requests access to a protected resource.
2. If the client is authenticated, the server redirects the client to the login page.
3. The client submits the login form to the Web server.
4. If the login is successful, the server redirects the client to the requested resource. However, if the login fails, the client is redirected to an error page.

Describing Client-Certificate Authentication or HTTPS Client Authentication

The client-certificate authentication or HTTPS client authentication mechanism is the advanced authentication method which is more secure than the basic and form-based authentication mechanisms. This is because it uses HTTP over SSL (HTTPS).

In the client-certificate authentication, the server and, sometimes, the client, authenticate each other by using public key certificates. A public key certificate is a digitally signed document used to validate a username and other user credentials. It is provided by a trusted organization called certificate authority (CA), and gives identification for the bearer. HTTPS offers data encryption, server authentication, and message integrity. HTTPS may also offer client authentication for a Transmission Control Protocol/Internet Protocol (TCP/IP) connection.

If you specify client-certificate authentication, the Web server authenticates the client by using the client's X.509 certificate, which is a public key certificate that conforms to a standard defined by X.509 Public Key Infrastructure (PKI). Before running an application that uses SSL (HTTPS), you must configure SSL (HTTPS) support on the Web server and set up the public key certificate.

Describing HTTP Digest Authentication

Similar to HTTP basic authentication, HTTP digest authentication authenticates users based on their username and password. In the HTTP digest authentication, the password is transmitted as encrypted data and in basic authentication; password is transmitted as simple base64 encoded data. You should note that transferring encrypted data is more protected than transferring base64 encoded data. Therefore, the HTTP digest authentication mechanism is more secure than the HTTP basic authentication mechanism. Digest authentication is currently not widely used since it is a new HTTP 1.1 feature and not supported by all browsers. If a non-compliant browser makes a request on a server that requires digest authentication, the server rejects the request and sends an error message.

After learning about various authentication mechanisms, let's learn about Web security, and see how to implement it in Web applications by using the different authentication mechanisms.

Implementing Security

A Web application consists of various resources, which can be used by multiple users. These resources often move through unprotected and open networks, such as the Internet. Consequently, a Web application needs to implement security. Web containers provide support to implement security for Web applications through the JAAS API. As already learned, Web security can be implemented using the following two ways:

- Declarative security
- Programmatic security

Let's discuss these two mechanisms in detail.

Describing Declarative Security

In declarative security, application's security structure can be demonstrated by a Web application provider. The Web application may include roles, access control, and authentication requirements, in a form that is external to the application. To prevent unauthorized access, the Web application's Deployment Descriptor (web.xml) is used to declare the Uniform Resource Locators (URLs) that need protection. You can also declare an authentication method, which the server uses to identify the users requesting the resources of the Web application. The server prompts the users for username and password when they access restricted resources, validates the user credentials against a pre-defined set of usernames and passwords, and keeps track of previously authenticated users. These processes are performed in a transparent manner in servlets and JSP pages.

Declarative security is server-based in most cases. This means that the server's configuration is used to provide protection to a resource or a set of resources. To secure a Web application's resources against unauthorized access, a Web container provides the authentication and authorization schemes. The authentication and authorization scheme is applied to the static content of a Web application and to the dynamic code (servlets, filters and JSP pages) requested by a client within the application.

Now, let's create an application that implements the declarative security.

Using Declarative Security

In this subsection, we create a simple application, simpledeclarativeex, to demonstrate the implementation of declarative security through the basic authentication mechanism. In this application, the Windows Security dialog box appears when a user submits an HTML form. The validation of the credentials is done by the server and on successful validation; the protected resource requested by the user is displayed. Otherwise, an error message is displayed..

Now, perform the following broad-level steps to create the simpledeclarativeex application:

1. Create a Web client for HTTP basic authentication

2. Configure the application
3. Create the Web resource servlet
4. Create roles and users
5. Explore the directory structure of the application
6. Run the application

Creating a Web Client for HTTP Basic Authentication

In this subsection, we create a Web client, Hello.html, which initiates the request for a protected resource. Listing 22.1 provides the code for the Hello.html file. The Hello.html file creates two HTML `submit` type buttons. When a user submits a form by clicking either of these buttons, the control is forwarded to the URL path testser. The mapping between the URL path tester and TestServlet servlet is provided in Listing 22.2. Listing 22.1 shows the code for the Hello.html file (save the Hello.html file in the `\simpledeclarativeex` folder):

Listing 22.1: Showing the Code for the Hello Page

```
<html>
   <body>
           <form method=post action="testser">
<input type="submit" value="Make a POST Request to access TestServlet"/>
           </form><br><br>
           <form method=get action="testser">
<input type="submit" value="Make a GET Request to access TestServlet"/>
           </form>
   </body>
</html>
```

In Listing 22.1, Hello.html is the Web client for HTTP basic authentication. Let's now learn how to configure the `simpledeclarativeex` application and implement the HTTP basic method of authentication.

Configuring the Application

To configure this application, you need to use the `web.xml` file. This file maps the action URL path `testser` forwarded by Home.html with the `TestServlet` class, and defines the security constraints. Listing 22.2 provides the code for the webxml file (save the web.xml file in the `\simpledeclarativeex\`WEB-INF folder):

Listing 22.2: Showing the Code for the web.xml File

```
<?xml version="1.0" encoding="UTF-8"?>
<web-app version="3.1"
xmlns="http://xmlns.jcp org/xml/ns/javaee" xmlns:xsi="http://www.w3.org/2001/XMLSchema-
   instance" xsi:schemaLocation="http://xmlns.jcp.org/xml/ns/javaee
   http://xmlns.jcp.org/xml/ns/javaee/web-app_3_1.xsd">
   <servlet>
           <servlet-name>ts</servlet-name>
           <servlet-class>com.kogent.servlets.TestServlet</servlet-class>
   </servlet>
   <servlet-mapping>
           <servlet-name>ts</servlet-name>
           <url-pattern>/testser</url-pattern>
   </servlet-mapping>
   <security-constraint>
           <web-resource-collection>
                   <web-resource-name>myres</web-resource-name>
                   <url-pattern>/testser</url-pattern>
                   <!--<http-method>POST</http-method>-->
                   <!--Uncomment the above line to perform security
                           check only for HTTP POST method request-->
           </web-resource-collection>
           <auth-constraint>
                   <role-name>myrole1</role-name>
           </auth-constraint>
   </security-constraint>
   <login-config>
           <auth-method>BASIC</auth-method>
```

```
    </login-config>
    <security-role>
          <role-name>myrole1</role-name>
    </security-role>

    <welcome-file-list>
          <welcome-file>Hello.html</welcome-file>
    </welcome-file-list>

  </web-app>
```

In Listing 22.2, the <security-constraint> and </security-constraint> tags define the Web resource being protected. In Deployment Descriptor provided in Listing 22.2, the `<auth-constraint>` element is used to protect the Web resources, having the `testser` url-pattern defined using the <url-pattern> element. This protection is specified for the users that are assigned the `myrole1` role. The users are assigned myrole1 role using <role-name> sub element of <security-role> element of the Deployment Descriptor. In the <auth-constraint> element, role name is specified using the <role-name> element.

The <security-role> element defines the logical grouping of the users defined by the application developer or assembler. Note that the authentication method specified in Listing 22.2 is BASIC.

The `com.kogent.servlets.TestServlet` class is mapped to the URL path testser. Therefore, the TestServlet class is a protected Web resource for the users assigned the myrole1 role group. The following code snippet shows how to map the group role in the glassfish-web.xml file:

```
<security-role-mapping>
    <role-name>myrole1</role-name>
    <group-name>myrole1</group-name>
</security-role-mapping>
```

In the preceding code snippet, the myrole1 group is mapped to the myrole1 role.

Creating the Web Resource Servlet

As discussed, TestServlet is the Web resource accessed by users defined under the myrole1 role group. The `TestServlet.java` file is created in the com.kogent.servlets package. Listing 22.3 provides the code for the `TestServlet.java` file (save the TestServlet.java file in the `\simpledeclarativeex\src\com\kogent\servlets` folder):

Listing 22.3: Showing the TestServlet.java File

```
package com.kogent.servlets;

import javax.servlet.*;
import javax.servlet.http.*;
import java.security.*;
import java.io.*;

public class TestServlet extends HttpServlet
{
  public void service(HttpServletRequest req, HttpServletResponse res)
  throws ServletException,IOException
  {
              Principal p=req.getUserPrincipal();
        String principal_name="UnAuthenticated";
        if (p!=null)
              principal_name=p.getName();
        PrintWriter out=res.getWriter();
out.println("User <b>"+principal_name+"</b> has requested for TestServlet");
  }// end service
}// end class
```

In Listing 22.3, `TestServlet` is the `HttpServlet` class, which calls the `getUserPrincipal ()` method on the request object. The `getUserPrincipal ()` method returns a `java.security.Principal` object, which holds the current authenticated user's name.

Compile the TestServlet.java file and place the .class file under the simpledeclarativeex\WEB-INF\classes\com\kogent\servlets folder.

After compiling TestServlet.java, start the Glassfish Server 4.0 to create roles and users for the simpledeclarativeex application.

Creating Roles and Users

To create roles and users for the simpledeclarativeex application, perform the following steps:

1. Navigate to the http://localhost:4848 URL. This URL displays the Glassfish server administrator's Console page. Now, use either the administrator's username and password or the default username admin and password adminadmin to log on to the Admin Console.
2. Expand the server-config node under the Configurations node and further expand the Security node and then select the Realms node, as shown in Figure 22.7:

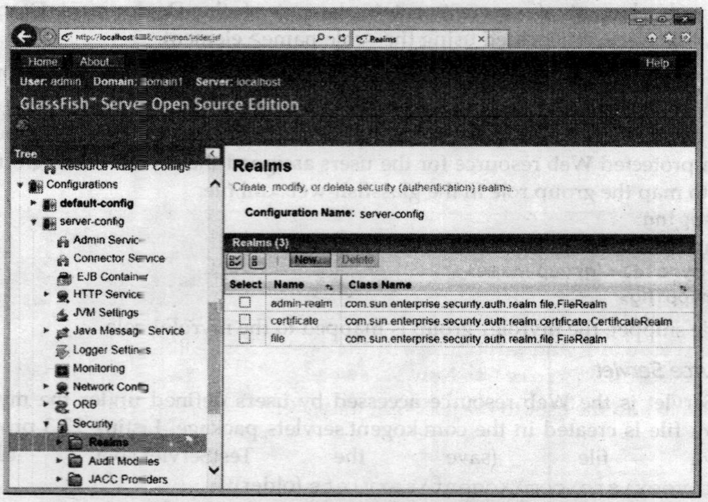

Figure 22.7: Displaying the Realms Panel

3. Select the file realm displayed in the Realms panel. The Edit Realm panel appears, as shown in Figure 22.8:

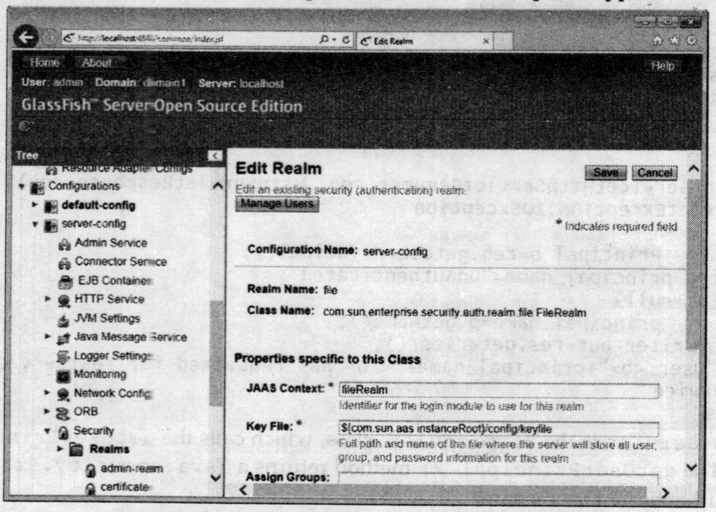

Figure 22.8: Displaying the Edit Realm Panel

4. Click the Manage Users button (Figure 22.8), as a result the File Users panel appears as shown in Figure 22.9:

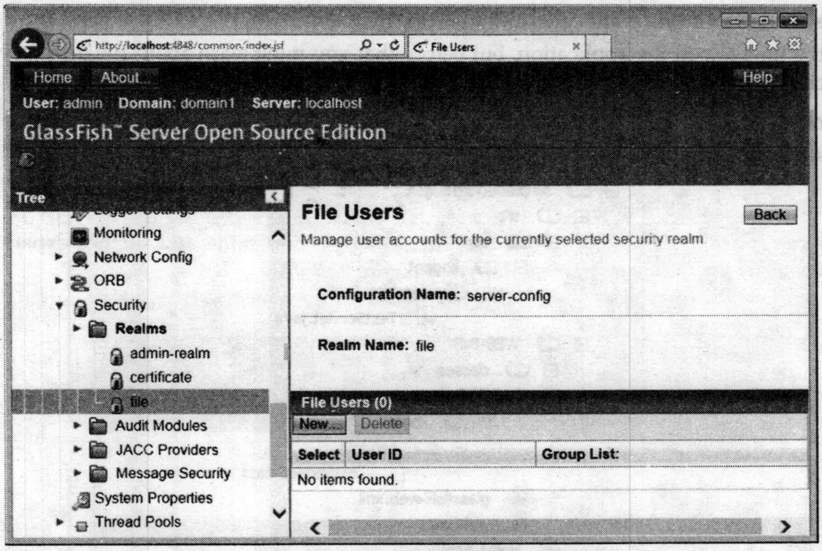

Figure 22.9: Displaying the File Users Panel

5. Click the New button to create a new user, the New File Realm User panel appears (Figure 22.10).
6. Enter the User Id, Password, and Group List in the New File Realm User panel. In our case, we have entered `santosh` as User ID, `myrole1` as New Password, and `myrole1` as Group List.
7. Click the OK button to add the user to the users list in the realm, as shown in Figure 22.10:

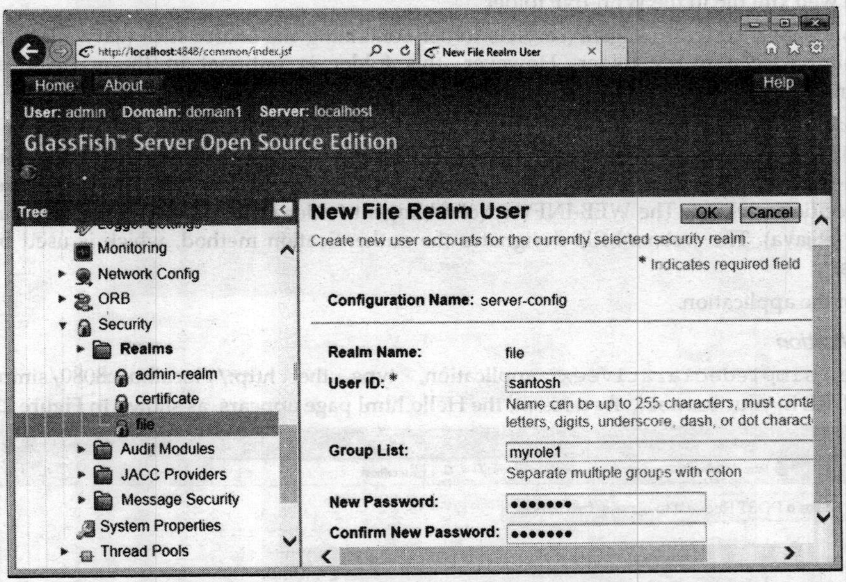

Figure 22.10: Displaying the New File Realm User Panel

There are three types of realms under the realms pane, which are as follows:

- **file**—Allows adding users who have the permission to access applications running in this realm

- **admin-realm**—Allows adding users who have the permission to become system administrators of the application server
- **certificate**—Allows adding certificates to the certificate realm

Now it's the time to run the application, but before that you must learn about the directory structure of the simpledeclarativeex application which is discussed next.

Exploring the Directory Structure of the Application

The directory structure of the simpledeclarativeex application is shown in Figure 22.11:

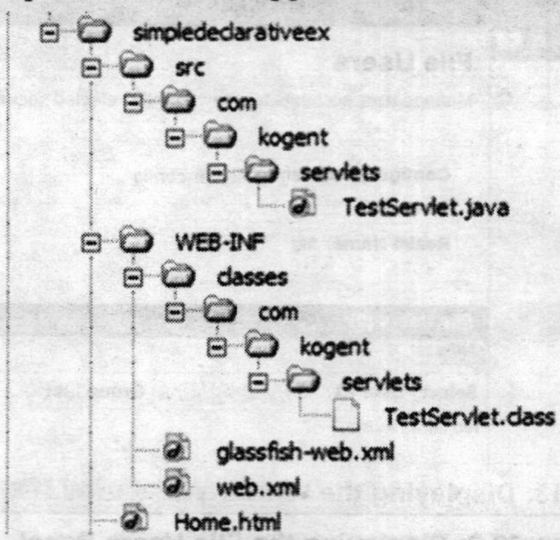

Figure 22.11: Displaying the Directory Structure

To create this structure, you need to create a folder for your application say, simpledeclarativeex (Figure 22.11). Now, save the different types of files at their proper locations in the directory structure in the following manner:

- Save all packages containing class files in the WEB-INF\classes folder
- Save the web.xml file in the WEB-INF folder

You can also create a src\com\kogent\servlets folder containing the source files (.java files) for all class files under the simpledeclarativeex folder. However, this folder is optional in the `simpledeclarativeex` application and you can save the source files of this folder at any other location.

The `simpledeclarativeex` folder is the root folder containing the src folder, the WEB-INF folder, and the Hello.html file (Figure 22.11). The WEB-INF folder has the classes folder, and two XML files, which are web.xml and glassfish-web.xml. As discussed previously, the WEB-INF\classes folder contains the TestServlet class file, with fully specified package. The WEB-INF\src\com\kogent folder is an optional folder containing the source file (TestServlet.java). The web.xml file designates the authentication method, which is used by the server to identify users.

Let's now run the application.

Running the Application

To run the `simpledeclarativeex` application, type the http://localhost:8080/simpledeclarativeex/Hello.html URL in your browser. As a result, the Hello.html page appears, as shown in Figure 22.12:

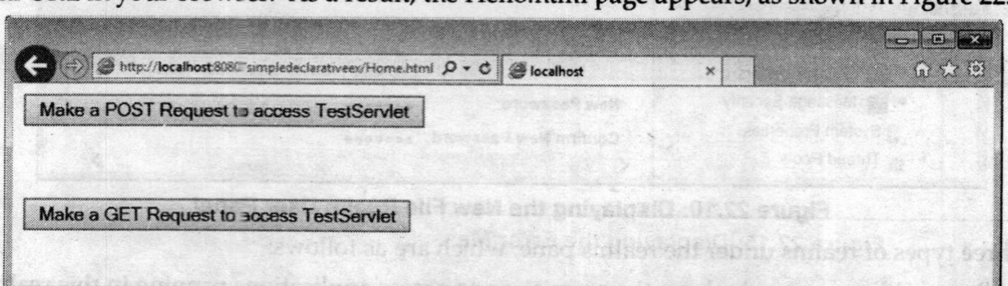

Figure 22.12: Displaying the Hello.html Page

The buttons displayed in Figure 22.12 are used to make requests through the GET and POST methods. Clicking either of these buttons displays the associated dialog box with blank username and password fields, as shown in Figure 22.13:

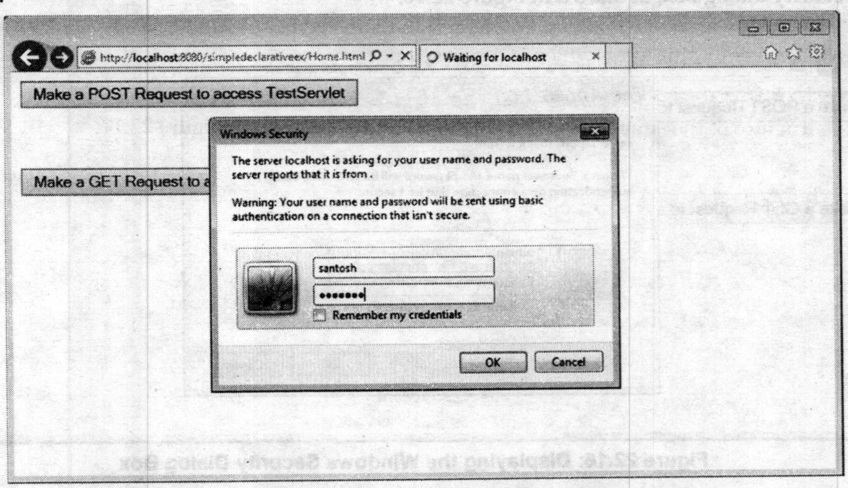

Figure 22.13: Displaying the Windows Security Dialog Box

In this dialog box, enter the username as `santosh` and password as `myrole1`. If the given username and password are valid, the user will be able to access `TestServlet`, as shown in Figure 22.14:

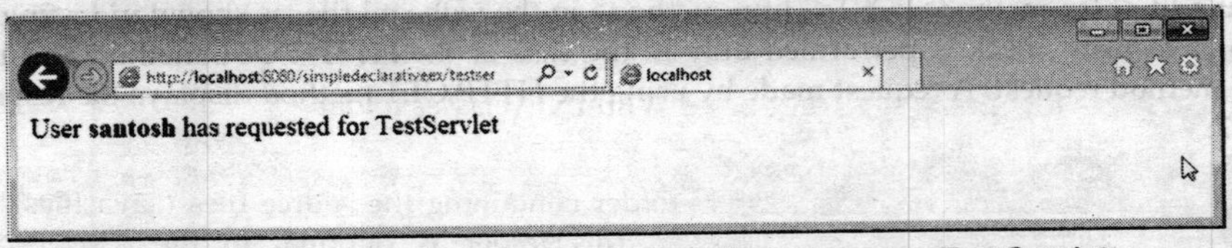

Figure 22.14: Displaying the Response after Accessing TestServlet

Figure 22.14 shows the result of entering a valid username and password. However, if this information is incorrect, the server displays an error page with 401 status code, as shown in Figure 22.15:

Figure 22.15: Displaying the Error Message for Incorrect User Details

Alternatively, if the username and password are correct, but the user is not associated with the myrole1 role (for example, if we type the username as `admin` and leave the password field blank), the server displays the Windows Security dialog box, as shown in Figure 22.16:

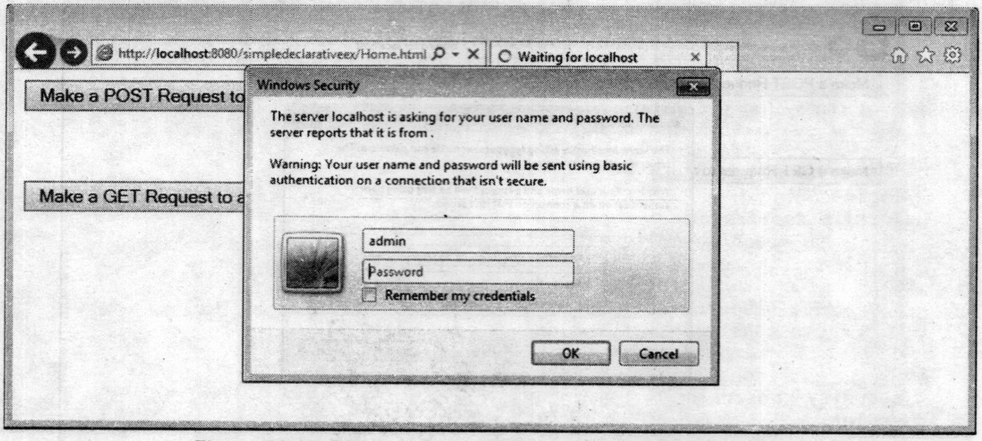

Figure 22.16: Displaying the Windows Security Dialog Box

NOTE

In this case, the user is authenticated but is not authorized to access the request resource.

Now, if you add <http-method>POST</http-method> in the web.xml file, as shown in Listing 22.2, and run the application, a security check is performed only in the case of the HTTP POST method and not in the default HTTP GET method request. A request made by using the HTTP GET method displays the response, as shown in Figure 22.17:

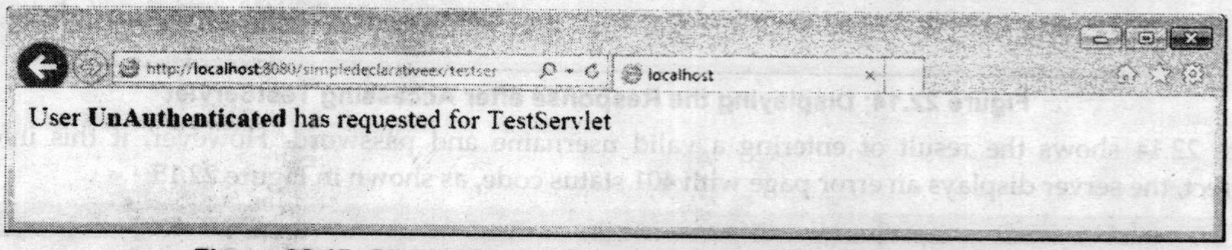

Figure 22.17: Displaying the Response for the HTTP GET Method

In this application, we used the <auth-method>BASIC</auth-method> element to implement basic authentication. However, if you want to display your own login page instead of a dialog box, you can use the <auth-method>FORM</auth-method> element.

Let's now learn how to implement the form-based authentication.

Using the Form-based Authentication for Declarative Security

Next, let's convert the `simpledeclarativeex` application from HTTP basic authentication to form-based authentication. For this, you need to perform the following broad-level steps:

1. Change the web.xml file for form-based authentication
2. Create the Login.jsp and MyError.jsp files
3. Change the directory structure
4. Run the application

Changing the web.xml File

To implement form-based authentication in the simpledeclarativeex application, the <login-config></login-config> element defined in Listing 22.2 must be changed to provide form-based authentication. Listing 22.4 provides the updated code for the web.xml file:

Listing 22.4: Showing the Code for the web.xml File in Form-based Authentication

```
<?xml version="1.0" encoding="UTF-8"?>
<web-app version="3.1"
xmlns="http://xmlns.jcp.org/xml/ns/javaee" xmlns:xsi="http://www.w3.org/2001/XMLSchema-
instance" xsi:schemaLocation="http://xmlns.jcp.org/xml/ns/javaee
  http://xmlns.jcp.org/xml/ns/javaee/web-app_3_1.xsd">
  <login-config>
        <auth-method>FORM</auth-method>
        <form-login-config>
              <form-login-page>/Login.jsp</form-login-page>
              <form-error-page>/MyError.jsp</form-error-page>
        </form-login-config>
  </login-config>
  <security-constraint>
        <web-resource-collection>
              <web-resource-name>myres</web-resource-name>
              <url-pattern>/testser/*</url-pattern>
        </web-resource-collection>
        <auth-constraint>
              <role-name>myrole1</role-name>
        </auth-constraint>
  </security-constraint>
  <servlet>
        <servlet-name>ts</servlet-name>
        <servlet-class>com.kogent.servlets.TestServlet</servlet-class>
  </servlet>
  <servlet-mapping>
        <servlet-name>ts</servlet-name>
        <url-pattern>/testser/*</url-pattern>
  </servlet-mapping>
  <security-role>
        <role-name>myrole1</role-name>
  </security-role>
  <welcome-file-list>
        <welcome-file>Home.html</welcome-file>
  </welcome-file-list>
</web-app>
```

In Listing 22.4, the authentication method has been changed from BASIC to FORM. Login.jsp is declared as the login page by using the <form-login-page> element of the <form-login-config> tag; and the MyError.jsp page is declared as the error page by using the <form-error-page> element of the <form-login-config> tag.

Let's now create the login form and error pages for the application.

Creating the Login.jsp and MyError.jsp Files

While discussing form-based authentication, we have seen that a login page is displayed when a user requests for a protected resource. When the user submits the login page, the server verifies the credentials. If the login is successful, the requested protected resource is displayed; otherwise, an error page appears. Therefore, to implement form-based authentication in the simpledeclarativeex application, you must create the login and error pages. Listing 22.5 provides the code for the Login page (save the Login.jsp file in the \simpledeclarativeex folder):

Listing 22.5: Showing the Code for the Login.jsp File

```
<!DOCTYPE html>
<html>
   <head>
   </head>
   <body>
         <form action="j_security_check" method="POST">
               Username:<input type="text" name="j_username"><br>
               Password:<input type="password" name="j_password">
               <input type="submit" value="Login">
         </form><br>
   </body>
</html>
```

Listing 22.5 shows a login form that consists of two textboxes, to let the user enter the username and password, respectively. As seen in Listing 22.5, the form action is `j_security_check;` and the field names, `j_username` and `j_password`, which take the username and password, respectively.

Next, we create an error page to display an error message for unauthenticated usernames and passwords. Listing 22.6 provides the code for the MyError.jsp file (save the MyError.jsp file in the `\simpledeclarativeex` folder):

Listing 22.6: Displaying the Code for the MyError.jsp File

```
<!DOCTYPE html>
<html>
   <head>
         <title>Login Test: Error logging in</title>
   </head>
   <body>
         <h1>User Name Password entered are not valid</h1>
         <br/>
   </body>
</html>
```

In Listing 22.6, a JSP page is created to display an error message for unauthenticated users.

The directory structure of the `simpledeclarativeex` application is changed to implement form-based authentication.

Changing the Directory Structure

The directory structure for the `simpledeclarativeex` application, shown in Figure 22.11, has to be changed; since we have added two JSP pages to the application. Figure 22.18 shows the modified directory structure:

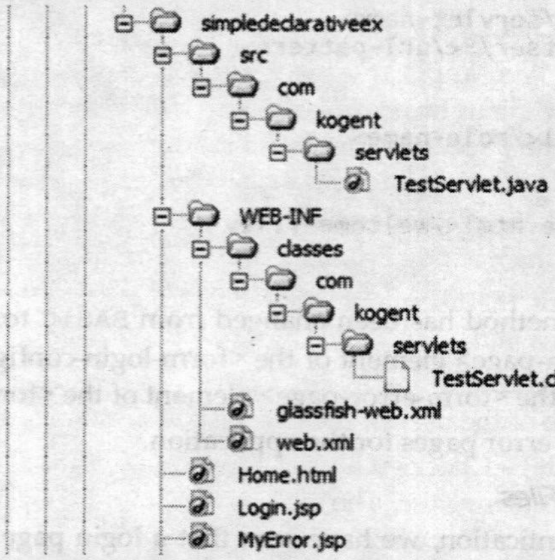

Figure 22.18: Displaying the Changed Directory Structure

In Figure 22.18, the two JSP pages, Login.jsp and MyError.jsp, have been added under the `simpledeclarativeex` folder.

Now, let's run the `simpledeclarativeex` application to see its output.

Running the Application

To run the simpledeclarativeex application, open the Web browser and type the http://localhost:8080/simpledeclarativeex/Hello.html URL.

The Hello.html page is displayed (Figure 22.12). After clicking any of the two buttons of the Hello.html page, the `Login` page is displayed, as shown in Figure 22.19:

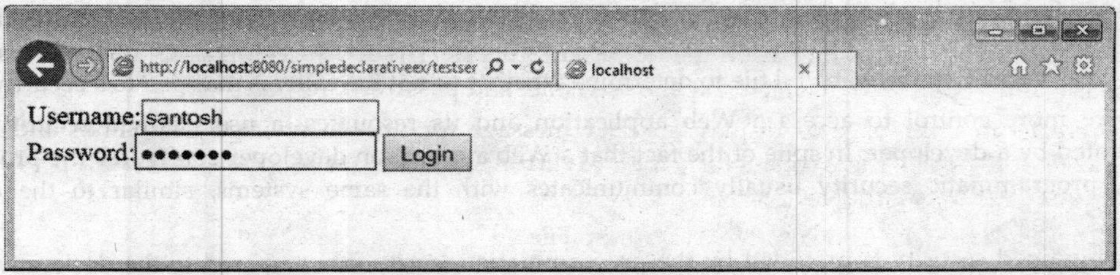

Figure 22.19: Displaying the Login Form for Form-Based Authentication

Figure 22.20 is displayed when a user enters `santosh` in the username and `myrole1` in the password fields, respectively:

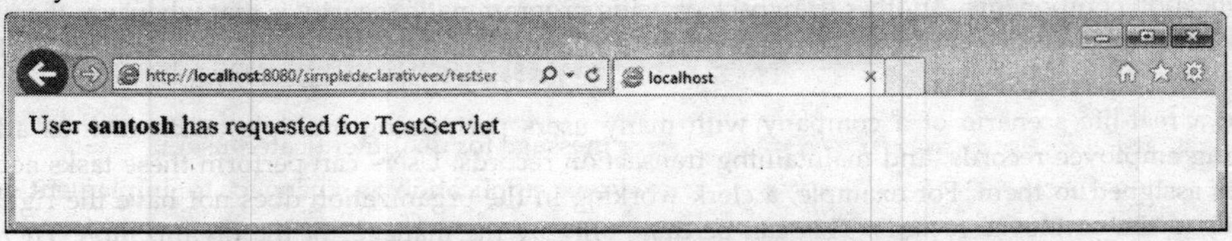

Figure 22.20: Displaying the Form-Based Authentication Response

We have learned that declarative security only verifies the user credentials. To implement security for accessing resources, we should implement programmatic security, which is discussed next.

Implementing Programmatic Security

In case of programmatic security, a Web application is responsible for authorizing a client; that is, the Web application verifies whether or not the client has permissions to access the resource(s). This mechanism is called programmatic security because the security implementation is coded into the Web application programmatically. The servlet specifications include some methods in the `HttpServletRequest` interface to implement programmatic security. These methods allow servlets to take business logic decisions based on the user's information. Some methods of the `HttpServletRequest` interface used in programmatic security are:

- **String getRemoteUser()** – Returns the username provided by a client for authentication. If the user is not authenticated, this method returns *null*.
- **Principal getUserPrincipal()** – Returns a `java.security.Principal` object. The `Principal` object is used to get the `Principal` name of the user. If the user is not authenticated, this method returns *null*.
- **boolean isUserInRole(String role)** – Checks if a user is included in the specified security role. If the user is not authenticated, this method returns *false*. The `isUserInRole()` method takes a string, which has the same value as that of the role-name parameter.

The Deployment Descriptor contains the <security-role-ref> element with the <role-name> sub-element, which must be declared for a particular role. The <role-name> sub-element denotes the role name that is passed as an argument to the isUserInRole () method. The <security-role-ref> element must contain the <role-link> sub-element, signifying the security role name, with which the user is mapped to. The Web container utilizes the mapping provided within the <security-role-ref> tag to determine the return value of the call to the `HttpServletRequest.isUserInRole (String rolename)` method. The following code snippet shows how to define the `myrole1ref` role using the <role-name> element and map the role with the `myrole1` role link using the <role-link> element:

```
<security-role-ref>
<role-name>myrole1ref</role-name>
<role-link> myrole1</role-link>
</security-role-ref>
```

According to this mapping, only a user belonging to the `myrole1` security role can call the specified servlet. To check the role of the user, you can use the `isUserInRole ("myrole1ref")` method, which returns the Boolean value, true.

If the <security-role-ref> elements are not declared, the Web container uses default role references to verify the role-names of the security-role elements for a Web application. The `isUserInRole()` method references the security roles defined in the web.xml file to determine whether or not the caller is mapped to a security role.

To enforce more control to access a Web application and its resources, a user-defined security model is implemented by a developer. In spite of the fact that a Web application developer configures the programmatic security, programmatic security usually communicates with the same systems, similar to the declarative security.

More fine-grained security is provided by the programmatic security, as compared to the declarative security; however, programmatic security can reduce a Web application component's reusability. Integrating various components to form a Web application, in which each application component uses the programmatic security, is difficult in case the programmed security model, which provides programmatic security, is inconsistent between the application components. Another drawback of using programmatic security is that whenever there is change in the security policy, each protected component must be revised and modified with new security authorization information.

Imagine a real-life scenario of a company with many users performing multiple tasks, such as adding and modifying employee records, and maintaining transaction records. Users can perform these tasks according to the roles assigned to them. For example, a clerk working in the organization does not have the right to make additions to the employee records. This can be done only by the manager of the organization. Therefore, the manager, as a user, is assigned the admin role, authorizing him or her to make changes in the employee records.

In this subsection, we create an application named `programmaticex`, to authenticate users based on their username and password. An invalid username or password displays an error message. A successful login allows users to perform the tasks based on the roles assigned to them. For example, users who are assigned the administrator role can modify or add the records of the employees, but if their assigned role is that of a clerk's role, they will be prevented from making such changes.

Perform the following broad-level steps to create the `programmaticex` application:

1. Create the JSP pages for programmatic security
2. Create the Login.java and User.java files
3. Configure the application
4. Explore the directory structure of the application
5. Run the application

Creating JSP Pages

In the `programmaticex` application, various JSP pages are used to validate user details, add employee details, view employee details, and display the welcome page to authenticated users. In the application, we need six JSP pages to perform different tasks, which are as follows:

- **index.jsp**—Displays the login screen for users to enter their username and password.
- **validateuser.jsp**–Redirects users to the validateuser page. The validateuser page uses the Login class to verify the user.
- **retry.jsp**—Displays an error message if an invalid username or password is entered. The error message prompts the user to enter a valid or correct username and password.
- **welcome.jsp**—Displays a welcome message and provides the reference for the addemployee and viewemployee pages if the login is successful.
- **addemployee.jsp**—Redirects a user to the addemployee page. If the entered username has been assigned an administrator role, the form to add employee records is displayed; otherwise, a message of non-authorization is displayed.
- **viewemployee.jsp**—Displays a table with the name of the employees and their designation.

Let's now create these pages.

Creating the index.jsp File

The index.jsp file displays the login screen for entering the username and password. Listing 22.7 provides the code for the index.jsp file (save the index.jsp file in the `\programmaticex` folder):

Listing 22.7: Displaying the Code for the index.jsp File

```
<%@ page language="java" session="true" pageEncoding="ISO-8859-1"%>
<!DOCTYPE html>
<html>
  <head>
        <title>Programmatic Security</title>
  </head>
  <body>
        <form action="validateuser.jsp" method="POST" name="theForm">
        <table align="center">
                  <tr>
                            <td><font size=2> Enter the User Name </font> </td>
                            <td><input type="text" name="userName"> </td>
                  </tr>
                  <tr>
                            <td><font size=2> Enter the Password </font></td>
                            <td><input type="password" name="passWord"></td>
                  </tr>
                  <tr>
                            <td>
                                      <br/>
                                      <input type="submit" value="Submit"/>
                                      <input type="reset" value="Reset"/>
                            </td>
                  </tr>
        </table>
        </form>
  </body>
</html>
```

Creating the validateuser.jsp File

As shown in Listing 22.7, two textboxes, userName and passWord, are created to accept the username and password from the user, respectively. When the user enters these details and submits the form, the validateuser.jsp file is displayed. Listing 22.8 provides the code for the validateuser.jsp file (save the validateuser.jsp file in the `\programmaticex` folder):

Listing 22.8: Displaying the Code for the validateuser.jsp File

```
<%@ page language="java" session="true" pageEncoding="ISO-8859-1"%>
<jsp:useBean id="idHandler" class="com.kogent.login.Login" scope="request">
<jsp:setProperty name="idHandler" property="*"/></jsp:useBean>
<!DOCTYPE html>
<html>
  <head>
        <title>Programmatic Security</title>
  </head>
  <body>
  <%
        String userName = request.getParameter("userName");
        ServletContext context=getServletContext();
        context.setAttribute("name",userName);
        String passWord = request.getParameter("passWord");
        if(idHandler.authenticate(userName, passWord))
        {
                  response.sendRedirect("welcome.jsp");
        }
        else
        {
                  response.sendRedirect("retry.jsp");
        }
  %>
  </body>
</html>
```

The validateuser.jsp file implements authentication by verifying the username and password entered by the user, with the username and password defined in the Login class.

In Listing 22.8, idHandler is created to handle the Login class, defined in the `com.kogent.login` package. The username and password entered by the user in the index.jsp file is retrieved in the validateuser.jsp file, and the `authenticate()` method of the Login class is then invoked. The `authenticate()` method of the Login class is discussed later in the chapter.

Creating the retry.jsp File

The `authenticate()` method in Listing 22.8 returns a `boolean` value; if this value is true, the welcome.jsp file is called; otherwise, the retry.jsp file is invoked. The retry.jsp file displays an error message for invalid username and password, and prompts the user to re-enter the details. Listing 22.9 shows the code for the retry.jsp file (save the retry.jsp file in the `\programmaticex` folder):

Listing 22.9: Displaying the Code for the retry.jsp File

```
<%@ page language="java" session="true" pageEncoding="ISO-8859-1"%>
<!DOCTYPE html>
<html>
<head>
   <body>
         <h1>
                  Invalid User name and Password.
                  Please Try Again!!!!!
         </h1>
         <jsp:include page="index.jsp"/>
   </body>
</html>
```

In Listing 22.9, the retry.jsp file displays an error message and includes the output of the index.jsp file.

Creating the welcome.jsp File

The welcome.jsp file is displayed if the username and password are correct and the login is successful. Listing 22.10 provides the code of the welcome.jsp file (save the welcome.jsp file in the `\programmaticex` folder):

Listing 22.10: Displaying the Code for the welcome.jsp File

```
<%@ page language="java" session="true" pageEncoding="ISO-8859-1" %>
<html>
   <head>
         <title>Programmatic Security</title>
   </head>
   <body>
         <br/>
         <h1>Welcome!!!! </h1>
         <h2>You have successfully Logged In</h2>
         <a href="addemployee.jsp">Add Employee</a><br/>
         <a href="viewemployee.jsp">View Employee</a>
   </body>
</html>
```

Creating the addemployee.jsp File

The welcome.jsp file in Listing 22.10 displays a welcome message and the reference link for the Add Employee and View Employee pages. Clicking the `Add Employee` link displays the `addemployee.jsp` file. This page determines the role assigned to the user based on the username entered by him or her. In other words, the `addemeployee.jsp` file implements the authorization. If the username entered by the authenticated user has been assigned the administrator role, the employee form is displayed. However, if the user has been assigned the role of a clerk, he or she is unauthorized to modify the employee records. Listing 22.11 provides the code for the addemployee.jsp file (save the addemployee.jsp file in the `\programmaticex` folder):

Listing 22.11: Displaying the Code for the addemployee.jsp File

```
<%@ page language="java" session="true" pageEncoding="ISO-8859-1" %>
<jsp:useBean id="idHandler" class="com.kogent.login.Login" scope="request">
<jsp:setProperty name="idHandler" property="*"/></jsp:useBean>
```

```
<!DOCTYPE html>
<html>
  <head>
        <title>Programmatic Security</title>
  </head>
  <body>
        <br/><br/><br/>
        <%
        ServletContext context=getServletContext();
        String userName = context.getAttribute("name").toString();
        if(idHandler.authorize(userName))
        {
        %>
        <br/>
        <h1 align=center>Enter the Employee Details</h1>
        <table border=4 cellpadding=1 align=center>
                  <tr>
                            <td>Enter the Employee Name</td>
                            <td><input type="text" name="empname"/></td>
                  </tr>
                  <tr>
                            <td>Enter the Designation</td>
                            <td><input type="text" name="empdesg"/></td>
                  </tr>
                  <tr>
                            <td>
                                      <input type="submit" value="Add Employee"/>
                            </td>
                  </tr>
        </table>
        <%
        }
        else {
                  out.println("<h2>" + "you are Unauthorized to add records" + "</h2>");
                  out.println("<a href=viewemployee.jsp>" + "View Employee" + "</a>");
        }
        %>
  </body>
</html>
```

In Listing 22.11, the addemployee.jsp file uses a Login class, and invokes the authorize () method of the Login class to check if the authenticated username entered by the user has been assigned the administrator role. If the user has been assigned the administrator role, the `authorize()` method of the Login class returns true; otherwise, it returns false.

If the value is true, the employee form is displayed to enter employee details. However, if the value retuned is false, an unauthorization message is displayed.

Creating the viewemployee.jsp File

If the user clicks the View Employee reference link in the welcome.jsp file, the viewemployee.jsp file is displayed. Listing 22.12 provides the code for the viewemployee.jsp file (save the viewemployee.jsp file in the `\programmaticex` folder):

Listing 22.12: Displaying the Code for the viewemployee.jsp File

```
<%@ page language="java" session="true" pageEncoding="ISO-8859-1" %>
<!DOCTYPE html>
<html>
  <head>
        <title>Programmatic Security</title>
  </head>
  <body>
        <h1 align=center>Employee Records</h1>
        <table border=4 cellpadding=1 align=center>
                  <tr>
                            <td>Ambika Sharma</td>
```

```
                    <td>Project Manager</td>
                </tr>
                <tr>
                    <td>Sam Malik</td>
                    <td>Technical Consultant</td>
                </tr>
                <tr>
                    <td>John Smith</td>

                    <td>Technical Writer</td>
                </tr>
            </table><br> </body>
</html>
```

The viewemployee.jsp file displays the employee names and their designation, as shown in Listing 22.12. This page can be accessed by an authenticated user defined in the Login class. However, only the authenticated user with the administrator role can make additions in employee records.

The `authenticate()` and `authorize()` methods of the Login class checks the authenticity and authorization of the user, respectively.

Creating the Login.java and User.java Files

In this section, we create the `Login.java` and `User.java` files used in the `programmaticex` application. However, before creating these files, let's understand what we are going to implement in the `Login.java` file and why it is required. In declarative security, a Web server manages users and their roles, as was done in the `simpledeclarativeex` application. However, in programmatic security, users and their roles are not managed by the server; instead, these are defined by the developer. Therefore, the Login class defines the users and associates the roles to these users. The Login class also implements the authorization and authentication modes of security based on these roles. Listing 22.13 provides the code for the Login class (save the Login.java file in the `\programmaticex\src\com\kogent\login folder`):

Listing 22.13: Displaying the Code for the Login Class

```
package com.kogent.login;
import java.io.*;
import java.util.HashMap;
import java.util.Map;
public class Login
{
   private Map users;
   private static final String ADMIN_ROLE = "administrator";
   private static final String CLERK_ROLE = "clerk";
   public Login(){
          users = new HashMap();
users.put("manager", new User("manager","manager",new String[] {ADMIN_ROLE, CLERK_ROLE}));
users.put("clerk", new User("clerk", "clerk", new String[] {CLERK_ROLE}));
   }
public boolean authenticate(String username, String password)throws IOException
   {
          User user = (User) users.get(username);
          boolean passwordIsValid = user.passwordMatch(password);
          if(user != null && !passwordIsValid )
          {
                 return false;
          }
          else
          {
                 return true;
          }
   }
   public boolean authorize(String username) throws IOException
   {
          User user = (User) users.get(username);
          boolean role = user.isAdministrator();
          if (!role)
```

```
            {
                    return false;
            }
            else
            {
                    return true;
            }
        }
    }
```

In Listing 22.13, we have created a `users` object of type `HashMap, which contains two user objects, namely manager and clerk`. The manager user has been assigned the administrator role and the clerk user has been assigned the clerk role. This indicates that the manager and clerk are authenticated usernames; however, only the manager user is authorized to add employee records.

The manager and clerk users are defined with the help of the `User` class by passing three parameters (username, password, and role assigned) in the `User` class constructor. In Listing 22.13, the `authenticate()` method checks the password assigned in the User class for the username based on the parameters passed by the validateuser.jsp file. If the password is correct, the true `boolean` value is returned; otherwise, false is returned to the validateuser.jsp page.

Similarly, in Listing 22.13, the `authorize()` method invokes the isAdministrator() method of the User class. The `isAdministrator()` method returns true if the user has the administrator role assigned to him or her; otherwise, it returns false. Based on this `boolean` value, the `authorize()` method also returns the `boolean` value to the addemployee.jsp file. Listing 22.14 provides the code for the User.java file (save the User.java file in the `\programmaticex\src\com\kogent\login folder`):

Listing 22.14: Displaying the Code for the User.java File

```
package com.kogent.login;
import java.io.Serializable;
public class User implements Serializable {
   private String username;
   private String password;
   private String[] roles;
   public User() {
   }
   public User(String name, String pwd, String[] assignedRoles) {
          username  = name;
          password  = pwd;
          roles=assignedRoles;
   }
   public String getUsername() {
          return username;
   }
   boolean passwordMatch(String pwd) {
          return password.equals(pwd);
   }
   public boolean hasRole(String role) {
          if (roles.length > 0) {
                 for (int i=0; i<roles.length; i++) {
                        if (role.equals(roles[i]))
                        return true; }
          }
          return false;
   }
   public boolean isAdministrator() {
          return hasRole("administrator");
   }
}
```

In Listing 22.14, the `User` class is defined in the `com.kogent.login` package. The username, password, and role are assigned through the Login class. In the `User` class, the `getUsername()` method returns the username and the `passwordMatch()` method returns the `boolean` value after verifying whether the password entered by the user is same as provided in the User class. The `isAdministrator()` method verifies whether the user has been assigned the administrator role; if yes, it returns true; otherwise, it returns false.

After compiling the Login.java and User.java files, place the resultant .class files in `programmatice\WEB-INF\classes\com\kogent\login` folder. Let's now configure the `programmaticex` application.

Configuring the Application

The web.xml file is used to configure the programmaticex application. Listing 22.15 provides the code for web.xml file (save the web.xml file in the `\programmaticex\WEB-INF folder):`

Listing 22.15: Displaying the Code for the web.xml File

```
<?xml version="1.0" encoding="UTF-8"?>
<web-app version="3.1"
xmlns="http://xmlns.jcp.org/xml/ns/javaee" xmlns:xsi="http://www.w3.org/2001/XMLSchema-
   instance" xsi:schemaLocation="http://xmlns.jcp.org/xml/ns/javaee
   http://xmlns.jcp.org/xml/ns/javaee/web-app_3_1.xsd">
        <welcome-file-list>
                <welcome-file>index.jsp</welcome-file>
        </welcome-file-list>
</web-app>
```

In Listing 22.15, the <welcome-file> element contains the index.jsp file, which is the home page of the programmaticex application.

Let's now explore the directory structure of the application.

Exploring the Directory Structure

The directory structure of the `programmaticex` application is shown in Figure 22.21:

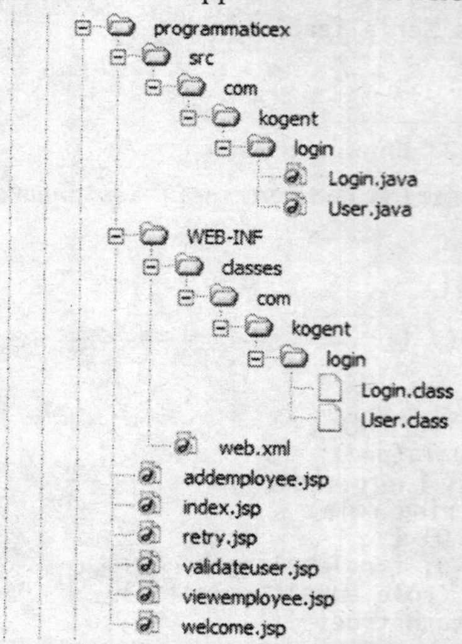

Figure 22.21: Displaying the Directory Structure of programmaticex

To create this structure, create a folder for the application as shown in Figure 22.21, which in our case is named programmaticex. Now, store the different types of files at their proper locations in the directory structure in the following manner:

- Store all packages containing class files in the WEB-INF/classes folder
- Store the Deployment Descriptor (web.xml) in the WEB-INF folder
- Store all JSP pages in the root directory, `programmaticex`

You can also create the `src` folder containing the source files (.java files) for all class files. This folder is optional in the `programmaticex` application; you can save your source files at any other location as well.

Let's now package, deploy, and run the programmaticex application to see its output.

Running the Application

To run the programmaticex application, start the Glassfish Server 4.0 and navigate to the `http://localhost:8080/programmaticex/` URL. Figure 22.22 displays the index page:

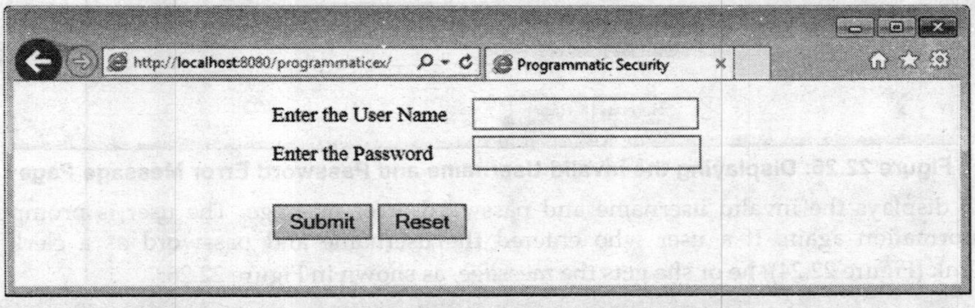

Figure 22.22: Displaying the Login Screen

Now, enter the username and password and click the Submit button, as shown in Figure 22.23:

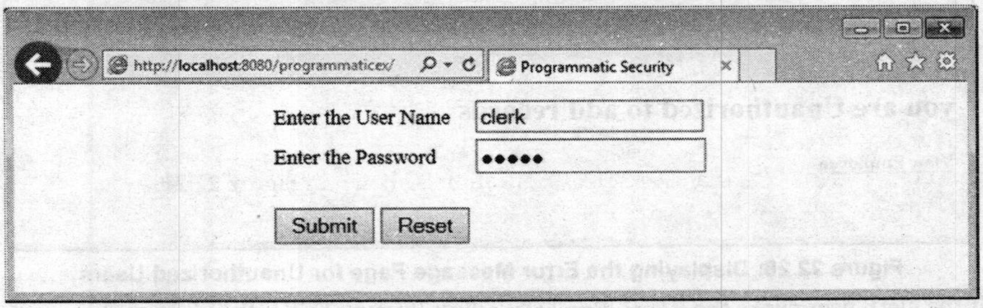

Figure 22.23: Entering a Username and Password

If the username and password are authentic, the welcome page is displayed, as shown in Figure 22.24:

Figure 22.24: Displaying the welcome Page

If the information entered by the user is incorrect, the retry page is displayed, as shown in Figure 22.25:

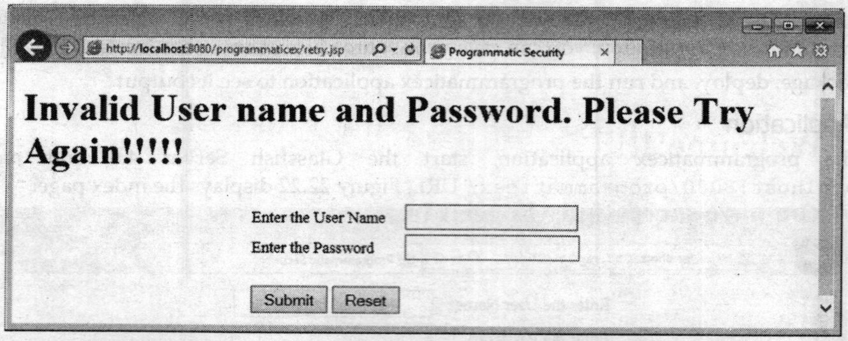

Figure 22.25: Displaying the Invalid Username and Password Error Message Page

Figure 22.25 displays the invalid username and password error message. The user is prompted to enter the required information again. If a user who entered the username and password as a clerk clicks the `Add Employee` link (Figure 22.24), he or she gets the message, as shown in Figure 22.26:

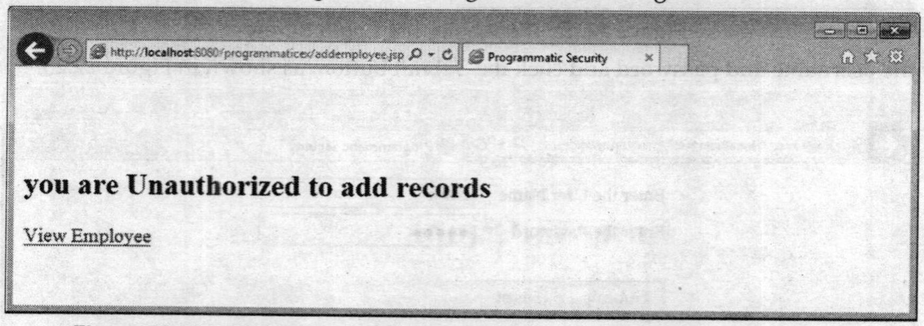

Figure 22.26: Displaying the Error Message Page for Unauthorized Users

However, if the clerk user clicks the `View Employee` link (Figure 22.26), the viewemployee page is displayed, as shown in Figure 22.27:

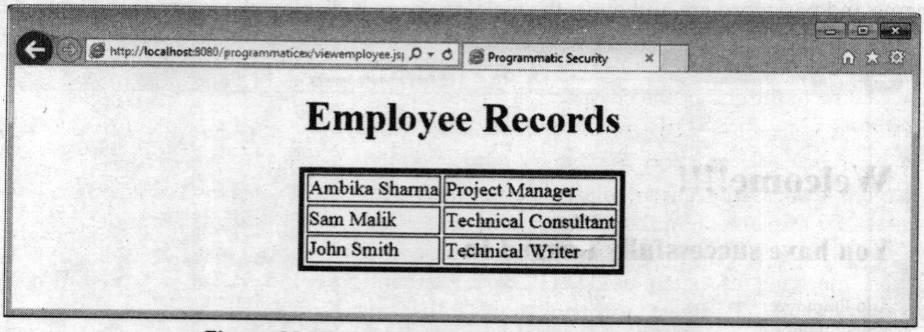

Figure 22.27: Displaying the viewemployee Page

If the user uses `manager` as a username and password to login (Figure 22.22), the user is authorized to add employee records. After logging with the `manager` username and password, the `welcome.jsp` page is displayed as shown in Figure 22.28:

Figure 22.28: Displaying the Welcome Page

In the welcome page, when the user clicks the `Add Employee` link (Figure 22.28) the `addemployee page` is displayed.

Figure 22.29 shows the `addemployee` page:

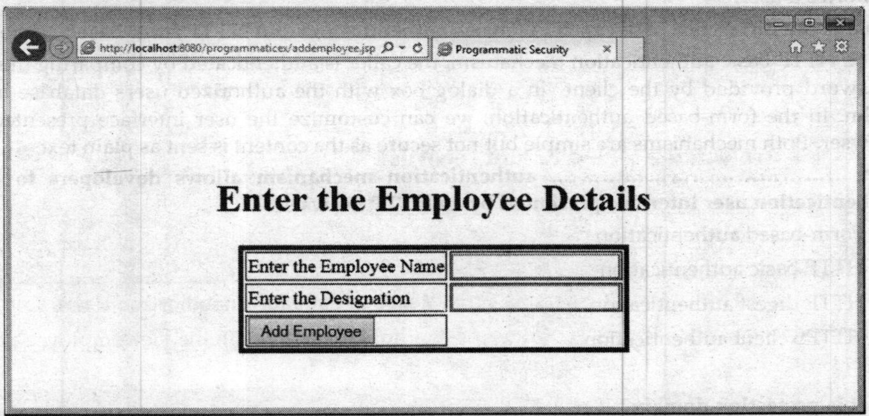

Figure 22.29: Displaying the addemployee Page for Authorized Users

With this, we come to the end of the chapter. Let's now summarize the main points of the chapter.

Summary

This chapter has discussed security related issues with respect to Web applications. It has introduced JAAS, which is used to implement authentication and authorization in Web applications, as well as the PAM framework on which the JAAS authentication is based. The chapter has also described various types of authentication mechanisms, such as HTTP basic authentication, form-based authentication, HTTP client authentication, and HTTP digest authentication. It has also explained the declarative and programmatic authorization mechanisms. Finally, we create two Web applications, `simpledeclarativeex` and `programmaticex`, to demonstrate the implementation of declarative and programmatic security, respectively.

Quick Revise

Q1. What is authentication?

Ans. Authentication is the process of checking the validity of the security details submitted by a user.

Q2. What is authorization?

Ans. Authorization is a process to determine whether the user has the appropriate access control rights to perform the requested action. The authorization mechanism restricts the access to resources according to the identity property.

Q3. What is data integrity?

Ans. Data integrity is the property that restricts or prevents data from being modified during transmission.

Q4. List the two ways to implement Web security.

Ans. The two ways of implementing Web security are as follows:

- Declarative security
- Programmatic security

Q5. List the HTTP authentication mechanisms that can be used to protect Web resources.

Ans. The following four types of authentication mechanisms are used to protect Web resources:

- HTTP basic authentication
- Form-based authentication
- Client-certificate authentication or HTTPS client authentication
- HTTP digest authentication

Q6. What is the use of JAAS?

Ans. Java Authentication and Authorization Service (JAAS), as the name suggests, is used to authenticate and authorize a user.

Q7. What is the difference between HTTP basic authentication and HTTP form-based authentication?

Ans. In the HTTP basic authentication mechanism, the caller is authenticated by comparing the username and password provided by the client in a dialog box with the authorized users database in the specified realm. In the form-based authentication, we can customize the user interface presented by an HTTP browser. Both mechanisms are simple but not secure as the content is sent as plain text.

Q8. The ………………………………… authentication mechanism allows developers to customize the authentication user interface presented by an HTTP browser.

A. Form-based authentication

B. HTTP basic authentication

C. HTTP digest authentication

D. HTTPS client authentication

Ans. A

Q9. What is protection domain?

Ans. A protection domain is a collection of entities that are expected to trust one another. There is no need of authentication of entities in such a domain.

Q10. List the three layers in context of security mechanism.

Ans. Security mechanism is discussed in context of the following three layers of security:

- Application layer security
- Transport layer security
- Message layer security

23

People Management Solutions

Every organization has to perform certain functions, such as recruitment, maintenance of attendance records, and payroll management, to appoint and manage its human resources. In large organizations, managing the records of thousands of employees manually is a cumbersome task. As a result, a system is required that can help the human resource (HR) management to perform all these tasks in an automated and efficient manner.

In this project, you learn to develop a system, People Management Solutions (`PeopleMgmt`) that facilitates an organization to manage the details of each employee, such as salary and leaves status. In addition, this system helps the HR management to maintain the records of the candidates that are being interviewed. This system is basically designed to reduce the workload of the HR and administrative departments, as it allows you to automatically manage the data related to various processes, such as recruitment, leave management, and payroll. The software requirement for this project should be identified before the project development process begins.

The next section discusses about the software requirements of the proposed system.

Software Requirements

The following are the software requirements for developing the PeopleMgmt project:

- JDK 1.6 or JDK 1.7 and Java EE related Technologies
- Glassfish Server 4.0
- Oracle 10g Server as well as Client Editions

The latest versions of Servlet 3.1, and JSP 2.3 technologies are used in this project. In addition, for backend data handling, Oracle 10g is used as the database and Java DataBase Connectivity (JDBC) 4.0 provides Application Programming Interfaces (APIs) for connectivity of the database to the application program. The Glassfish Server 4.0 is used to deploy and execute this project.

The next section discusses the Software Development Life Cycle (SDLC) that identifies the stages of development of the project.

SDLC of the Project

Software Development Life Cycle (SDLC) entails the different stages of the project development. The SDLC of this project is discussed under the following heads:

- Requirement analysis
- Software design
- Database design
- Development
- Testing
- Implementation and maintenance

Let's now discuss the requirement analysis phase of SDLC.

Requirement Analysis

Any new software application is created to fulfill certain requirements that have not been met by the existing system. Therefore, the development process of any system starts with identifying the requirements. This process of analyzing the existing system to define the objectives of the new application is known as requirement analysis. The requirement analysis can be done by collecting feedbacks using questionnaires and surveys. In this case, automating the existing system to reduce manual labour and ensure greater accuracy in maintaining attendance, leave, and salary records of employees are some of the primary objectives for developing the proposed system.

Let's now describe the software design phase of the `PeopleMgmt` project.

Software Design

The `PeopleMgmt` project consists of various modules that are required to fulfill the requirements analyzed in the requirement analysis phase of the SDLC. The project can be divided into the following modules:

- The Login module

- The Profile Management module
- The Recruitment module
- The Attendance Management module
- The Leave Management module
- The Payroll module

Let's begin the next section by discussing the `Login` module of the project.

The Login Module

Every system designed to perform administrative functions requires to be fully secured in a distributed environment. The most commonly-used security mechanism is to provide a login based authentication for users. The Login module of this project implements the login authentication mode in the system. This module ensures that only an authenticated and authorized user can access the links and navigation paths to perform operations, such as adding or editing employees, adding or updating applicants for recruitment, and updating daily attendance of the employees. A user name and password is provided to the users who perform these people management and administration related tasks. When the user enters the specified user name and password in the login page, the system verifies the user name and password. If the user is authenticated and authorized, the home page of the system is displayed.

The Profile Management Module

The Profile Management module manages the profiles of the employees of an organization. This module provides the interface to enter and update the information of the employees. You can insert, edit, update, and delete the profile of a person in this section. The information regarding a person, such as name, date of birth, address, joining date, and contact number are stored in the PEOPLE_EMPLOYEE table in the database.

The Recruitment Module

The Recruitment module keeps track of the recruitment process, which consists of different stages, such as written round, technical round, and HR round. When an applicant applies for an interview, the registration details of the applicant are maintained with the help of this module. After entering the registration details of the applicant, the automated system displays the applicant's name for different levels of tests to be conducted during the interviewing process. The Recruitment module also helps in scheduling tests and uploading the results of each applicant. This module also displays a list of finally selected candidates who have cleared all the tests according to the organization's expectations.

The next section discusses the Attendance Management module.

The Attendance Management Module

The Attendance Management module manages the attendance details of the employees. The interface of this module provides fields to enter the incoming and outgoing time of each employee for each day. The administrator is authorized to view the daily attendance report for the employees.

The next section discusses the Leave Management module.

The Leave Management Module

The Leave Management module manages leave-related functions, such as providing a leave form, submission of leave request to the management, and approval of a leave. In any organization, there is a limited amount of leave allocated to every employee. When an employee applies for leaves, this module provides a leave request form to be filled up by the employee. After filling and submitting the leave form, the information provided in the form is stored in the database. This module also displays whether or not the leave has been approved by the management. All this information is considered while calculating the working days, and consequently, the salary of an employee at the end of each month.

The next section discusses about the Payroll module.

The Payroll Module

To calculate the salary of an employee, different aspects need to be considered, such as number of working days, tax induced, or incentives and other allowances. All this makes the task of calculating salaries of each and every employee manually a cumbersome task. The Payroll module is designed to reduce the workload of calculating salaries from the HR management. This module retrieves the details of the number of leaves taken by an employee from the Leave Management module to evaluate the salary.

The next section discusses about the database design.

Database Design

The PeopleMgmt project adds as well as updates the details of both employees and applicants by interacting with the database. Now, let's develop the database for this project. Table 23.1, 23.2, 23.3, 23.4, 23.5, 23.6, 23.7, and 23.8 provide the structure of different tables of the database, with their column names and data types.

Table 23.1 shows the structure of the PEOPLE_USER_LOGIN table:

Table 23.1: Showing the Structure of the PEOPLE_USER_LOGIN Table

Field name	Data type	Size	Primary key	Null
USER_ID	VARCHAR2	10	Y	N
USER_NAME	VARCHAR2	30		N
OLD_PSWD	VARCHAR2	10		
NEW_PSWD	VARCHAR2	10		
PSWD_EFF_DATE	DATE			
PSWD_EXP_DATE	DATE			

Table 23.2 shows the structure of the PEOPLE_EMPLOYEE table:

Table 23.2: Showing the Structure of the PEOPLE_EMPLOYEE Table

Field name	Data type	Size	Primary key	Null
EMP_ID	VARCHAR2	10	Y	N
EMP_F_NAME	VARCHAR2	20		N
EMP_M_NAME	VARCHAR2	20		
EMP_L_NAME	VARCHAR2	20		
ORG_ID	VARCHAR2	10		N
LEVEL_ID	VARCHAR2	10		N
DEPT_ID	VARCHAR2	10		N
DOB	DATE			
DOJOIN	DATE			
ADDRESS_1	VARCHAR2	50		
ADDRESS_2	VARCHAR2	50		
CITY	VARCHAR2	15		
STATE	VARCHAR2	20		
NATIONALITY	VARCHAR2	15		

Table 23.3 shows the structure of the PEOPLE_APPLICANT table:

Table 23.3: Showing the Structure of the PEOPLE_APPLICANT Table

Field name	Data type	Size	Primary key	Null
APPLICANT_ID	VARCHAR2	10	Y	N
APPLICANT_NAME	VARCHAR2	50		N

Table 23.3: Showing the Structure of the PEOPLE_APPLICANT Table

Field name	Data type	Size	Primary key	Null
ADDRESS_1	VARCHAR2	100		
ADDRESS_2	VARCHAR2	100		
EMAIL	VARCHAR2	50		
PHONE	NUMBER	15		
MOBILE	NUMBER	11		
DOB	DATE			
GENDER	VARCHAR2	10		
NATIONALITY	VARCHAR2	30		
WORK_EXP	NUMBER	10		
SKILL	VARCHAR2	100		
INDUSTRY	VARCHAR2	30		
CATEGORY	VARCHAR2	30		
ROLES	VARCHAR2	30		
CURRENT_EMPLOYER	VARCHAR2	100		
CURRENT_SAL	NUMBER	7,2		
HIGHEST_DEGREE	VARCHAR2	100		
SECOND_HIGHEST_DEGREE	VARCHAR2	100		
DOMAIN	VARCHAR2	50		
CURRENT_LOCATION	VARCHAR2	30		

Table 23.4 shows the structure of the APPLICANT_TEST_DETAIL table:

Table 23.4: Showing the Structure of the APPLICANT_TEST_DETAIL Table

Field name	Data type	Size	Primary key	Null
TEST_ID	VARCHAR2	10	Y	N
TEST_NAME	VARCHAR2	30	Y	N
APPLICANT_ID	VARCHAR2	10	Y	N
APPLICANT_NAME	VARCHAR2	50		
TEST_DATE	DATE			
TEST_TIME	DATE			
PRESENT_STATUS	VARCHAR2	15		
TOTAL_MARKS	NUMBER	3		
MARKS_GAINED	NUMBER	3		
TEST_STATUS	VARCHAR2	10		
PASS_FAIL	VARCHAR2	10		
NEXT_ROUND	VARCHAR2	10		

Table 23.5 shows the structure of the EMPLOYEE_DAILY_ATTENDANCE table:

Table 23.5: Showing the Structure of the EMPLOYEE_DAILY_ATTENDANCE Table				
Field name	**Data type**	**Size**	**Primary key**	**Null**
EMP_ID	VARCHAR2	10	Y	N
EMP_NAME	VARCHAR2	30		
TODAY_DATE	VARCHAR2	10	Y	N
MONTH	VARCHAR2	10		
DAY	VARCHAR2	10		
YEAR	NUMBER	4		
IN_TIME	DATE			
OUT_TIME	DATE			
REMARK	VARCHAR2	50		

Table 23.6 shows the structure of the LEAVE_REQUEST table:

Table 23.6: Showing the Structure of the LEAVE_REQUEST Table				
Field name	**Data type**	**Size**	**Primary key**	**Null**
REQ_ID	VARCHAR2	10	Y	N
EMP_ID	VARCHAR2	10		N
EMP_NAME	VARCHAR2	30		
TODAY_DATE	DATE			
LEVEL_ID	VARCHAR2	10		
DEPT_ID	VARCHAR2	10		
FROM_DATE	DATE			
TO_DATE	DATE			
DAYS	NUMBER	2		
REASON	VARCHAR2	100		
LEAVE_TYPE	VARCHAR2	2		
ACTIVITY_1	VARCHAR2	50		
ACTIVITY_2	VARCHAR2	50		
ACTIVITY_3	VARCHAR2	50		
PERSON_1	VARCHAR2	50		
PERSON_2	VARCHAR2	50		
PERSON_3	VARCHAR2	50		
DETAIL_1	VARCHAR2	100		
DETAIL_2	VARCHAR2	100		
DETAIL_3	VARCHAR2	100		
ADDRESS	VARCHAR2	100		
REMARK	VARCHAR2	100		
LEAVE_STATUS	VARCHAR2	5		

Table 23.7 shows the structure of the EMPLOYEE_AGREEMENT table:

Table 23.7: Showing the Structure of the EMPLOYEE_AGREEMENT Table				
Field name	**Data type**	**Size**	**Primary key**	**Null**
EMP_ID	VARCHAR2	10	Y	N
EMP_NAME	VARCHAR2	30		N

Table 23.7: Showing the Structure of the EMPLOYEE_AGREEMENT Table

Field name	Data type	Size	Primary key	Null
LEVEL_ID	VARCHAR2	10		
ALLOWANCE_TYPE	VARCHAR2	10		N
ALLOWANCE_NAME	VARCHAR2	20	Y	N
AMT	NUMBER	7,2		N
TAXABLE	VARCHAR2	5		
PERCENTAGE	NUMBER	3,2		
AGREEMENT_DATE	DATE			

Table 23.8 shows the structure of the EMP_SAL table:

Table 23.8: Showing the Structure of the EMP_SAL Table

Field name	Data type	Size	Primary key	Null
EMP_ID	VARCHAR2	10	Y	N
YEAR	NUMBER	4	Y	N
MONTH	NUMBER	2	Y	N
ALLOWANCE_TYPE	VARCHAR2	10		N
ALLOWANCE_NAME	VARCHAR2	20	Y	N
AMT	NUMBER	7,2		N
TAXABLE	VARCHAR2	5		
PERCENTAGE	NUMBER	3,2		

Development

The `PeopleMgmt` project is developed using the Model View Controller (MVC) architecture, which allows a developer to concentrate on building business logic in the Controller servlet and other helper classes, while a designer can design the JSP pages. In the MVC architecture, a central Controller servlet handles all the business logic with the help of some helper classes. The Model part of the MVC architecture can be defined by JavaBeans that are used as data transfer objects to hold client data. They may be initialized automatically or manually using the ResultSet object. Finally, the View part of the architecture is implemented through the JSP pages. When the development process of a project is separated, the development becomes complex; however, it increases the reusability of the components.

To implement the MVC architecture, the designing of the PeopleMgmt project is divided into three layers—presentation, business logic, and data, which are developed separately. The presentation layer is designed using JSP to create user interface, the business logic is embedded in the Controller servlet, and the JavaBean classes hold the data to be stored in the database. In the `PeopleMgmt` project, every module has its own Controller servlet to handle client requests. Each Controller servlet has a helper class that defines all the required methods used by the servlet to implement a functionality. The JavaBean classes are populated manually using the methods of the helper classes of the Controller servlet. The packaging, deployment, and execution of the PeopleMgmt project are performed on the Glassfish Server 4.0.

Testing

You need to test the project to ensure proper navigation and validity of data being entered into the User Interface (UI) forms before providing the PeopleMgmt project to clients for their use. As a best practice, a project is considered ready to be implemented and used by the clients in the real environment only after performing a thorough testing process.

Implementation and Maintenance

The last stage in the SDLC is implementation and maintenance, in which you need to deploy the project in the real environment. Implementation includes proper deployment of the project on the application server. The maintenance of a project means updating the project for the required changes in the implemented system. While running the project in the real environment, many loopholes and areas of improvement may be discovered. The user may also suggest some changes or report some problems in the system, based on which the project is updated from time-to-time.

Summary

In this chapter, you learn about the phases of SDLC and their implementations in the `PeopleMgmt` project. The chapter also describes about the requirements of the project and approaches to develop the project. Next, you learned about the designing process, role, and functionality of various modules. In addition, you have also learned how to design database that includes number of tables and the column data types used in the project to store the data.

The next sections discuss about the development of different modules by using Java EE 7 and its related technologies. The PeopleMgmt project is divided into six different modules, which are described in the following sections:

- **Section A** – Developing the Login Module
- **Section B** – Developing the Profile Management Module
- **Section C** – Developing the Recruitment Module
- **Section D** – Developing the Attendance Management Module
- **Section E** – Developing the Leave Management Module
- **Section F** – Developing the Payroll Module

All these modules are created using Java EE 7 technologies and deployed on the Glassfish Server, which is the standard Oracle application server.

Section A

Developing the Login Module

The PeopleMgmt system is used to maintain and update the employee-related data, such as recruitment details, employee salary, and employee attendance. These records are of great importance for any organization and should always be protected from unauthorized access. The Login Module of the PeopleMgmt project is developed to verify the authentication of users. If the user is authentic, various links and interfaces are displayed to the user to add, update, and search important data.

The entire project is being developed on the basis of the MVC architecture. All the modules consist of JSP pages, servlets, and some other Java classes. These Java classes are used to handle the basic business logic for holding the data similar to JavaBeans.

The development of this module includes writing code for the following files:

- UserLoginDBObj.java
- UserLoginDBMethods.java
- people_user_login.java
- people_user_login.jsp
- people_user_login_pswd_change.jsp
- people_default.jsp
- people_footer.jsp
- people_header.jsp
- people_main_menu.jsp

The code for all files has been discussed in detail in the following sections. You can use notepad or any Integrated Development Environment (IDE), such as NetBeans or Eclipse, to develop these code files.

Designing Login User Interface

Any user interface through which a user can interact with the system is called a *JSP* page (View). In the Login module, the people_user_login JSP page serves as a login interface for the users. This page contains three text boxes to enter User Id, User Name, and Password along with the Submit button. After entering the details in these text boxes, the user can submit the people_user_login JSP page by clicking the Submit button.

The code of the people_user_login.jsp file is shown in Listing 23.1 (save the people_user_login.jsp file in the people-mgmt\jsp folder):

Listing 23.1: Showing the Code of the people_user_login.jsp File

```
<html>
<head><title>www.peoplemanagementsolutions.com/User Login</title>
<link rel="stylesheet" href="../css/mystyle.css" type="text/css" />
</head>
<body>
        <form name = "form1" method="post">
        <table width="900" align=center>
                <tr>
                <td colspan="2"><%@ include file="\jsp\people_header.jsp" %></td>
                </tr>
                <tr >
                <td colspan="2">
                <table border ="0"  align="center" >
                <tr><td>User Id</td>
                <td align="center" ><input type =
                "text" name="user_id" id="user_id" value=""
                        /></td></tr>
                <tr><td>User Name</td>
                <td align="center" ><input type ="text" name=
                "user_name" id="user_name" value=""
                        /></td></tr>
                <tr><td>Password</td>
```

```
                <td align="center" ><input type =
                "password" name="user_pswd" id="user_pswd"
                        value="" /></td></tr>
                <tr><td colspan="2" align="center" >
                <input type ="submit" name="submit"
                        id="submit" value="Submit" />
                <input type="hidden" name="action_submit" id="action_submit"
                        value="people_user_login_submit"/>
                </td></tr>
                <tr><td colspan="2" align="center">
                <input type ="submit" name="submit" id=
                "submit" value="ChangePassword" />
                <input type="hidden" name="action_chngpswd" id="action_chngpswd"
                value="people_change_pswd_submit"/>
                </td></tr>
                <%
                String msg  = (String)session.getAttribute("lErrorMsg");
                if ( msg != null && msg.length() > 0 ){
                %>
                <tr>
                <td colspan="2" align="center">
                <%      out.println("<div class=boldred>"+msg+"</div>"); %>
                </td>
                </tr>
                <%      }       %>
                </table>
                </td></tr>
                <tr>
        <td colspan="2"><%@include file="../jsp/people_footer.jsp"%></td>
        </tr>
        </table>
        </form>
    </body>
</html>
```

In Listing 23.1, the `people_user_login.jsp` file includes two JSP files, `people_header.jsp` and `people_footer.jsp` using the `<%@include %>` directive.

Creating the people_user_login Servlet

The `people_user_login.java` file is a servlet that contains the business logic to authenticate a user. After a user is successfully authenticated, this servlet displays a default page from where the user can access details of employees or applicants. The `people_default` JSP page serves as the default page and shows various navigation menus, such as Employee, Recruitment, Time Management, and Payroll. In the `people_user_login.java` file, annotations are used to specify `servlet-mapping` instead of Deployment Descriptor (`web.xml` file).

NOTE

Java Servlet 3.1 provides the support for annotations instead of Deployment Descriptors to provide configuration or mapping details of a resource.

The code of the `people_user_login.java` file is shown in Listing 23.2 (save the `people_user_login.java` file in the `people-mgmt\WEB-INF\src` folder):

Listing 23.2: Showing the Code of the people_user_login.java File

```
import javax.servlet.*;
import javax.servlet.http.*;
import java.io.*;
import javax.servlet.annotation.*;
import com.UserLogin.UserLoginDBMethods;
import com.UserLogin.UserLoginDBObj;
```

```
@WebServlet(name="people_user_login", urlPatterns="/servlet/people_user_login")
public class people_user_login extends HttpServlet
{
 String lDBUser  = "";
 String lDBPswd  = "";
 String lDBUrl   = "";
 /**Initialize global variables*/
      @Override
 public void init(ServletConfig config) throws ServletException
 {
          System.out.println("initializing controller servlet.");
          ServletContext context = config.getServletContext();
          lDBUser = "scott";
          lDBPswd = "tiger";
          lDBUrl  = "jdbc:oracle:thin:@localhost:1521:"+"orcl";
          super.init(config);
 }
 /**Process the HTTP Get request*/
 @Override
 public void doGet(HttpServletRequest request, HttpServletResponse response)
 throws ServletException, IOException
 {
          doPost(request, response);
 }
 /**Process the HTTP Post request*/
 @Override
 public void doPost(HttpServletRequest request, HttpServletResponse response)
 throws ServletException, IOException
 {
          response.setContentType("text/html");
          PrintWriter out = response.getWriter();
          HttpSession session = request.getSession();
          session.setAttribute("lErrorMsg",null);
          String target = "/jsp/people_user_login.jsp";
          String action = request.getParameter("action");
          String action_submit = request.getParameter("action_submit");
          String action_chngpswd = request.getParameter("action_chngpswd");
          System.out.println("action_submit=="+action_submit);
          if ( action_submit != null || action_chngpswd != null )
          {
                   if ( request.getParameter("submit").equals("Submit") )
                   {
                            System.out.println("in the  Submit");
                            if ( action_submit.equals("people_user_login_submit") )
                            {
                            System.out.println("in the people_user_login_submit");
                                     action = "people_user_login_submit";
                            }
                            else
                            if (action_submit.equals("login_pswd_change_submit"))
                            {
                                     action = "login_pswd_change_submit";
                            }
                   }
                   else
                   if (request.getParameter("submit").equals("ChangePassword") )
                   {
                   if (action_chngpswd.equals("people_change_pswd_submit") )
                            action = "people_change_pswd_submit";
```

```
            }
        }
        if (action!=null)
        {
                System.out.println("in the  "+action);
                if (action.equals("people_user_login_submit"))
                {
                        String lUserId = "";
                        String lUserName = "";
                        String lUserPswd = "";
                        lUserId = (String)request.getParameter("user_id");
                        lUserName = (String)request.getParameter("user_name");
                        lUserPswd = (String)request.getParameter("user_pswd");
                        UserLoginDBObj userLoginDBObj = new UserLoginDBObj();
                        UserLoginDBMethods userLoginDBMethods = new
                        UserLoginDBMethods(lDBUser,lDBPswd,lDBUrl);
                        userLoginDBObj=(UserLoginDBObj)
                  userLoginDBMethods.getRecordByPrimaryKey(lUserId,lUserName,lUserPswd);
                        if ( userLoginDBObj != null && (userLoginDBObj.user_id !=null &&
                        (userLoginDBObj.user_id).length() > 0) )
                        {
                                target = "/jsp/people_default.jsp";
                        }
                        else
                        {
                                String lErrorMsg = "User Does Not Exist!!";
                                session.setAttribute("lErrorMsg",lErrorMsg);
                                target = "/jsp/people_user_login.jsp";
                        }
                }
                else
                if (action.equals("people_change_pswd_submit"))
                {
                        target = "/jsp/people_user_login_pswd_change.jsp";
                }
                else
                if (action.equals("login_pswd_change_submit"))
                {
                        UserLoginDBObj popUserLoginDBObj = new UserLoginDBObj();
                        UserLoginDBMethods userLoginDBMethods = new
                        UserLoginDBMethods(lDBUser,lDBPswd,lDBUrl);
                        String lUserId = "";
                        String lUserName = "";
                        String lCurPswd = "";
                        String lNewPswd = "";
                        String lRetypePswd = "";
                        popUserLoginDBObj =(UserLoginDBObj)
                        userLoginDBMethods.populateUser LoginDBObjFromReq(request);
                        lRetypePswd =
                        (String)request.getParameter("retype_pswd");
                        if ((popUserLoginDBObj.new_pswd).equals(lRetypePswd))
                        {
                        UserLoginDBObj userLoginDBObj = new UserLoginDBObj();
                        userLoginDBObj = (UserLoginDBObj)userLoginDBMethods.
                                getRecordByPrimaryKey(popUserLoginDBObj.
                                user_id,popUserLoginDBObj.user_name,
                                popUserLoginDBObj.old_pswd);
                        if ( userLoginDBObj != null && (
                                userLoginDBObj.user_id != null &&
                                (userLoginDBObj.user_id).length() > 0) )
                                {
```

```
                            int rval =
                                    userLoginDBMethods.updateUserLogin
                                    ByPrimaryKey(popUserLoginDBObj);
                                    if ( rval > 0 )
                                    {
                                            target =
                                            "/jsp/people_user_login.jsp";
                                    }
                                    else
                                    {
                                            target =
                                            "/jsp/people_user_login_
                                            pswd_change.jsp";
                                    }
                            }
                            else
                            {
                            String lErrorMsg = "User Does Not Exist!!";
                            session.setAttribute("lErrorMsg",lErrorMsg);
                            target = "/jsp/people_user_login_pswd_change.jsp";
                            }
                    }
                    else
                    {
                            String lErrorMsg = "Retype Correct Password!!";
                            session.setAttribute("lErrorMsg",lErrorMsg);
                            target = "/jsp/people_user_login_pswd_change.jsp";
                    }
            }
        }
        // (action== null )
        /* forwarding the request/response to the targeted view */
        RequestDispatcher requestDispatcher =
                getServletContext().getRequestDispatcher(target);
        requestDispatcher.forward(request, response);
 }
 // doPost closed
 /* write the methods that are used in class  */
}
// class closed
```

Creating the UserLoginDBObj Class

The `UserLoginDBObj` Java class provides various variables, such as `user_id`, `user_name`, `old_pswd`, and `new_pswd` to handle a user's login details. The object of this class represents a record in the PEOPLE_USER_LOGIN table of the Oracle 10g database.

The code of the `UserLoginDBObj.java` file is shown in Listing 23.3 (save the `UserLoginDBObj.java` file in the `people-mgmt\WEB-INF\src\com\UserLogin` folder):

Listing 23.3: Showing the Code of the UserLoginDBObj.java File

```
package com.UserLogin;
public class UserLoginDBObj
{
   public String user_id ;
   public String user_name;
   public String old_pswd ;
   public String new_pswd ;
   public String pswd_eff_date;
   public String pswd_exp_date;
}
```

Creating the UserLoginDBMethods Class

The UserLoginDBMethods class provides various methods to update and retrieve the login information of a user. This class also contains the code to establish a connection with the database to retrieve or update records in the PEOPLE_USER_LOGIN table. In the `UserLoginDBObj` class, the parameterized constructor is defined to assign the values to the `DBUser`, `DBPswd`, and `DBUrl` variables on the basis of the String arguments passed to the constructor. The values of these variables are used to establish the database connection.

The code of the `UserLoginDBMethods.java` file is shown in Listing 23.4 (save the `UserLoginDBMethods.java` file in the `people-mgmt\WEB-INF\src\com\UserLogin` folder):

Listing 23.4: Showing the Code of **the** UserLoginDBMethods.java File

```
package com.UserLogin;
import java.sql.*;
import javax.servlet.http.*;
public class UserLoginDBMethods
{
 public String DBUser;
 public String DBPswd;
 public String DBUrl ;
 public UserLoginDBMethods()
 {
 }
 public UserLoginDBMethods(String inDBUser, String inDBPswd, String inDBUrl )
 {
        DBUser = inDBUser ;
        DBPswd = inDBPswd;
        DBUrl  = inDBUrl;
 }
 public void initializeUserLoginDBObj(UserLoginDBObj inUserLoginDBObj )
 {
        inUserLoginDBObj.user_id =  "";
        inUserLoginDBObj.user_name = "";
        inUserLoginDBObj.old_pswd = "";
        inUserLoginDBObj.new_pswd = "";
        inUserLoginDBObj.pswd_eff_date = "";
        inUserLoginDBObj.pswd_exp_date = "";
 }
 public UserLoginDBObj getRecordByPrimaryKey(String inUserId, String inUserName, String
 inUserPswd)
 {
        UserLoginDBObj  userLoginDBObj = new UserLoginDBObj();
        try
        {
               System.out.println("DBUser=="+DBUser+",DBPswd=="+DBPswd+",
               DBUrl=="+DBUrl);
               DriverManager.registerDriver(new oracle.jdbc.driver.OracleDriver());
               Connection conn= DriverManager.getConnection(DBUrl,DBUser,DBPswd);
               Statement stmt = conn.createStatement();
               String lSqlString =     "select * from PEOPLE_USER_LOGIN ";
               lSqlString = lSqlString + "where user_id='"+inUserId+"' ";
               lSqlString = lSqlString + "and user_name='"+inUserName+"' ";
               lSqlString = lSqlString + "and new_pswd='"+inUserPswd+"' ";
               ResultSet rs  = null;
               rs  = stmt.executeQuery(lSqlString);
               System.out.println("lSqlString====trtrt==within
                      getRecordByPrimaryKey== "+lSqlString);
               if( rs.next())
               {
               userLoginDBObj.user_id =  rs.getString("user_id");
```

```
                    userLoginDBObj.user_name = rs.getString("user_name");
                    userLoginDBObj.old_pswd = rs.getString("old_pswd");
                    userLoginDBObj.new_pswd = rs.getString("new_pswd");
                    userLoginDBObj.pswd_eff_date = rs.getString("pswd_eff_date");
                    userLoginDBObj.pswd_exp_date = rs.getString("pswd_exp_date");
                }
                else {
                          initializeUserLoginDBObj(userLoginDBObj);
                }
                               }
          catch(SQLException  ex)
          {
                ex.printStackTrace();
          }
          return userLoginDBObj;
     }
     public int updateUserLoginByPrimaryKey(UserLoginDBObj inUserLoginDBObj)
     {
          int recupd = 0
          String lQuery = "";
          lQuery = lQuery +"update PEOPLE_USER_LOGIN set
          old_pswd='"+inUserLoginDBObj.old_pswd+"'  ";
          lQuery = lQuery +" , new_pswd='"+inUserLoginDBObj.new_pswd+"' ";
          lQuery = lQuery + "where user_id='"+inUserLoginDBObj.user_id+"' ";
          lQuery = lQuery + "and user_name='"+inUserLoginDBObj.user_name+"' ";
          lQuery = lQuery + "and new_pswd='"+inUserLoginDBObj.old_pswd+"' ";
          System.out.println("lSqlString===:"+lQuery);
          try
          {
               DriverManager.registerDriver(new
               oracle.jdbc.driver.OracleDriver());
               Connection conn= DriverManager.getConnection(DBUrl,DBUser,DBPswd);
               Statement stmt = conn.createStatement();
               recupd  = stmt.executeUpdate(lQuery);
          }
          catch(SQLException  ex) {
               ex.printStackTrace();
          }
          return recupd;
     }
     public UserLoginDBObj populateUserLoginDBObjFromReq(HttpServletRequest inReq)
     {
          UserLoginDBObj  userLoginDBObj = new UserLoginDBObj();
          userLoginDBObj.user_id    =  (String)inReq.getParameter("user_id");
          userLoginDBObj.user_name = (String)inReq.getParameter("user_name");
          userLoginDBObj.old_pswd  = (String)inReq.getParameter("old_pswd");
          userLoginDBObj.new_pswd  = (String)inReq.getParameter("new_pswd");
          userLoginDBObj.pswd_eff_date = (String)inReq.getParameter("pswd_eff_date");
          userLoginDBObj.pswd_exp_date =
          (String)inReq.getParameter("pswd_exp_date");
          return userLoginDBObj;
     }
}
```

In Listing 23.4, the following methods are defined in the UserLoginDBMethods class:

- **The** `initializeUserLoginDBObj (UserLoginDBObj)` **method**—Initializes the passed object with empty String values

- **The** `getRecordByPrimaryKey()` **method**—Returns the `UserLoginDBObj` object with all member variables that are set with the retrieved login information of a user
- **The** `updateUserLoginByPrimaryKey(UserLoginDBObj)` **method**—Updates the login information of the user
- **The** `populateUserLoginDBObjFromReq(HttpServletRequest)` **method**—Accepts the `HttpServletRequest` object as an argument and returns the `UserLoginDBObj` object after populating it with the information stored in the request scope

Creating the people_default.jsp File

The `people_default` JSP page serves as the home page of the PeopleMgmt project. This home page contains the menus used to access other pages and modules of the project.

The code of the `people_default.jsp` file is shown in Listing 23.5 (save the `people_default.jsp` file in the `people-mgmt\jsp` folder):

Listing 23.5: Showing the Code for the people_default.jsp File

```
<%@ page contentType="text/html; charset=iso-8859-1" language="java"  errorPage="" %>
<!DOCTYPE html>
<html xmlns="http://www.w3.org/1999/xhtml">
<head>
<meta http-equiv="Content-Type" content="text/html; charset=iso-8859-1" />
<title>www.peoplemanagementsolutions.com-Welcome</title>
<link rel="stylesheet" href="../css/mystyle.css" type="text/css" />
</head>
<body>
<table width="900" border="0" align="center">
<tr>
<td colspan="2"><%@ include file="../jsp/people_header.jsp" %></td>
</tr>
<tr>
<td width="900">
 <%@ include file="../jsp/people_default_menu.jsp" %>
</td>
</tr>
<tr>
<td width="750" align="center" valign="top">
 <%@include file="../jsp/design.jsp"%>
</td>
</tr>
<%
 String msg  = (String)session.getAttribute("lErrorMsg");
 if ( msg != null && msg.length() > 0 ){
%>
<tr><td align='center'>
<% out.println("<div class=boldred>"+msg+"</div>"); %>
<br/>
</td></tr>
<%}%>
<tr>
<td colspan="2"><%@include file="../jsp/people_footer.jsp"%></td>
</tr>
</table>
</body>
</html>
```

The people_default JSP page is created by using the following four reusable JSP pages:

- `people_header`—Provides a header to a page. The `people_header` JSP page contains a logo of the company and the information that needs to be displayed on all JSP pages.

- people_default_menu—Provides the menus to be added to all user interfaces of the PeopleMgmt project.
- people_footer—Contains the footer information, such as copyright as well as company's basic information that needs to be added in all JSP pages of the project.
- design—Contains the design of the default (home) page.

The code for the preceding JSP pages has been provided in the people-mgmt\jsp folder and can be used within that specified location.

Let's now discuss the code of the people_default_menu.jsp file.

The people_default_menu JSP page shows the menus and submenus that need to be added to all user interfaces of the PeopleMgmt project. These menus and submenus are used to perform various functions, such as creating or updating the profile of an employee, registering a new applicant, and scheduling a written test, updating test results for each applicant, and selecting the applicants for the next round.

The code of the people_default_menu.jsp file is shown in Listing 23.6 (save the people_default_menu.jsp file in the people-mgmt\jsp folder):

Listing 23.6: Showing the Code for the people_default_menu.jsp File

```
<%@ page contentType="text/html; charset=iso-8859-1" language="java"  errorPage=""
%>
<!DOCTYPE html>
<html>
<head>
<link rel="stylesheet" href="../css/CascadeMenu.css" type="text/css"></link>
<script language="JavaScript" type="text/JavaScript"
src="../css/CascadeMenu.js">
</script>
</head>
<body onload="InitMenu()" onclick="HideMenu(menuBar)" id="Bdy">
<div id="menuBar" class="menuBar" >
<div id="Bar5" class="Bar" menu="menu9" title="About Us/Log Out">,
</div>
<div id="Bar1" class="Bar" menu="menu1">Employee</div>
<div id="Bar2" class="Bar"  menu="menu2">Recruitment</div>
<div id="Bar3" class="Bar"  menu="menu3">Time Management</div>
<div id="Bar4" class="Bar"  menu="menu4">PayRoll</div>
</div><div align="right"><a href="/people-mgmt/jsp/people_default.jsp">Home
Page</a></div>
<div id="menu9" class="menu" >
<div id="menuItem9_1" class="menuItem" title="About Us" cmd="/people-
mgmt/jsp/people_aboutus.jsp" class="whitelink">About Us </div>
<div id="menuItem9_2" class="menuItem" title="Log Out" cmd="/people-
mgmt/servlet/people_user_login" class="whitelink">Log Out</div>
</div>
<div id="menu1" class="menu" >
<div id="menuItem1_1" class="menuItem" title="Add Employees" cmd="/people-
mgmt/servlet/people_employee?dbopr=create" class="whitelink">Add New
Employee</div>
<div id="menuItem1_2" class="menuItem" title="Edit Employee"cmd="/people-
mgmt/servlet/people_employee?dbopr=edit" class="whitelink">Edit Employee</div>
<div id="menuItem1_3" class="menuItem" title="Employee Profile" cmd="/people-
mgmt/servlet/people_employee?dbopr=show" class="whitelink">Employee Profile</div>
</div>
<div id="menu2" class="menu">
<div id="menuItem2_1" class="menuItem" title="Register Applicants"
cmd="/people-mgmt/servlet/people_applicant?dbopr=register" class="whitelink">New
Applicant</div>
<div id="menuItem2_2" class="menuItem" title="Update Applicants" cmd="/people-
mgmt/servlet/people_applicant?dbopr=select" class="whitelink">Update
```

```
Applicant</div>
<div id="menuItem2_3" class="menuItem" title="Shortlisted Candidate"
menu="menu5">Written Round</div>
<div id="menuItem2_4" class="menuItem" menu="menu6" title="Technical Round" >
Technical Round</div>
<div id="menuItem2_5" class="menuItem" menu="menu7" title="HR Round" > HR
Round</div>
</div>
<div id="menu3" class="menu">
<div id="menuItem3_1" class="menuItem" title="Enter/Update Attendance"
cmd="/people-mgmt/servlet/time_management?dbopr=daily_attendance_entry"
class="whitelink">
Update Attendance</div>
<div id="menuItem3_2" class="menuItem" title="Attendance Summary" cmd="/people-
mgmt/servlet/time_management?dbopr=daily_attendance_summary" class="whitelink">
Attendance Summary</div>
<div id="menuItem3_3" class="menuItem" menu="menu8">Leave Management</div>
</div>
<div id="menu4" class="menu">
<div id="menuItem4_1" class="menuItem" title="Employee Agreement" cmd="/people-
mgmt/servlet/people_payroll?dbopr=employee_agreement" class="whitelink"><br />
Salary BreakUp</div>
<div id="menuItem4_2" class="menuItem" title="employee Salary" cmd="/people-
mgmt/servlet/people_payroll?dbopr=calc_employee_salary" class="whitelink">
Employee Salary</div>
</div>
<div id="menu5" class="menu">
<div id="menuItem5_1" class="menuItem" title="call for written" cmd="/people-
mgmt/servlet/applicant_test_dtl?dbopr=call_for_written" class="whitelink">Call for
Written</div>
<div id="menuItem5_2" class="menuItem" title="Update Results" cmd="/people-
mgmt/servlet/applicant_test_dtl?dbopr=upd_wrtn_performance"
class="whitelink">Results</div>
</div>
<div id="menu6" class="menu">
<div id="menuItem6_1" class="menuItem"title="Shortlisted For Tech.Round"
cmd="/people-mgmt/servlet/applicant_test_dtl?dbopr=shortlist_after_wrtn"
class="whitelink">
Shortlist For Tech. Round</div>
<div id="menuItem6_2" class="menuItem" title="Update Results" cmd="/people-
mgmt/servlet/applicant_test_dtl?dbopr=upd_tech_performance" class="whitelink">
Update Result</div>
</div>
<div id="menu7" class="menu">
<div id="menuItem7_1" class="menuItem" title="Shortlisted for HR Rounds"
cmd="/people-mgmt/servlet/applicant_test_dtl?dbopr=shortlist_after_tech"
class="whitelink">
Shortlist  for HR Round </div>
<div id="menuItem7_2" class="menuItem" title="Update Results" cmd="/people-
mgmt/servlet/applicant_test_dtl?dbopr=upd_hr_performance" class="whitelink">
Update Result</div>
<div id="menuItem7_3" class="menuItem" title="Shortlisted for Selection"
cmd="/people-mgmt/servlet/applicant_test_dtl?dbopr=shortlist_after_hr"
class="whitelink">
Shortlist For Selection</div>
<div id="menuItem7_4" class="menuItem" title="Selected" cmd="/people-
mgmt/servlet/applicant_test_dtl?dbopr=final_selected" class="whitelink">
Selected Candidate</div>
</div>
```

```
<div id="menu8" class="menu">
<div id="menuItem8_1" class="menuItem" title="Leave Application" cmd="/people-
mgmt/servlet/leave_management?dbopr=leave_request" class="whitelink">Leave Apply
</div>
<div id="menuItem8_2" class="menuItem" title="Approval Status" cmd="/people-
mgmt/servlet/leave_management?dbopr=leave_approve" class="whitelink">Leave
Approval</div>
  <div id="menuItem8_3" class="menuItem" title="Approved/Rejected" cmd="/people-
  mgmt/servlet/leave_management?dbopr=approved_leave" class="whitelink">Approved
       Request</div>
</div></body>
</html>
```

In Listing 23.6, you can see that almost all the submenus, such as `Edit Employee`, `New Applicant`, `Update Applicant`, and `Call for Written`, invoke the appropriate servlet instead of calling JSP pages. According to the MVC architecture, this project also provides various servlets to handle user requests. The servlets process the requests and forward the response to the View page requested by the user.

Let's now explore the directory structure of the project in the next section.

Directory Structure of the Project

Let's now create a directory structure of the PeopleMgmt project to place all the files at a specific location. Perform the following steps to create the directory structure of the project:

1. Create a project folder and give it a name, say `people-mgmt`.
2. Create four more folders, namely `css`, `images`, `jsp`, and `WEB-INF`.
3. Place all the source files (.java) in the `WEB-INF/src` folder.
4. Put all the class files in the `WEB-INF/classes` folder within specific package folders, if any, and put all the jar files in the `WEB-INF/lib` folder.
5. Save all the JSP pages in the `people-mgmt/jsp` folder. The recently compiled files, `UserLoginDBObj.class` and `UserLoginDBMethods.class`, are placed in the src/`com/UserLogin` folder.

NOTE

The mapping of a servlet is not provided in the web.xml file, as it is already defined in the servlet by using annotations.

Figure 23.1 shows the directory structure of the PeopleMgmt project:

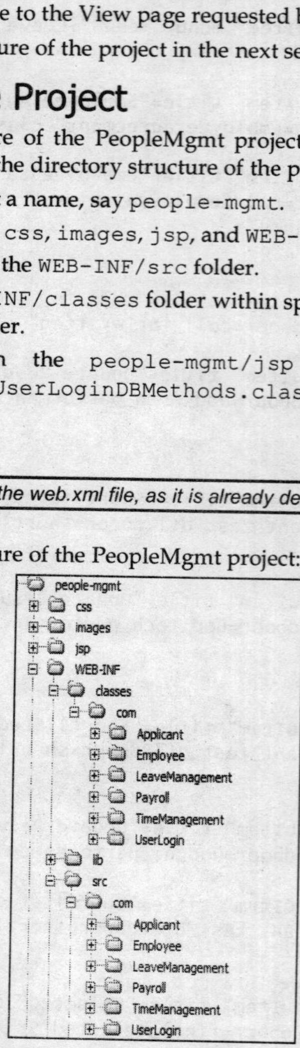

Figure 23.1: Showing the Directory Structure for the Project

The compiled Java source files (class files) are placed in the `classes` directory, along with their package directories. In the Login module, the `people_user_login` servlet is mapped within itself using the `@WebServlet` annotation. Use of this annotation removes the need of mapping a servlet in the `web.xml` file. In this project, the `web.xml` file is used for Web specification.

The code of the `web.xml` file is shown in Listing 23.7 (save the web.xml file in `people-mgmt\WEB-INF` folder):

Listing 23.7: Showing the Code of the web.xml File

```
<?xml version="1.0" encoding="UTF-8"?>
<web-app version="3.1" xmlns="http://xmlns.jcp.org/xml/ns/javaee
  xmlns:xsi="http://www.w3.org/2001/XMLSchema-instance"
  xsi:schemaLocation="http://xmlns.jcp.org/xml/ns/javaee
  http://xmlns.jcp.org/xml/ns/javaee/web-app_3_1.xsd">
<display-name>PEOPLE</display-name>
    <description>
  Kogent Learning Solutions
</description>
</web-app>
```

After configuring the resources of the `PeopleMgmt` project in the `web.xml` file, you can execute the project. You must ensure that you have compiled all the source files of the project and placed them in the classes directory. Next, you also need to package the project in a war file and deploy the war file on the Glassfish Server 4.0.

Login and Navigating to Home Page

To run the PeopleMgmt project, you first need to ensure that the project has been packaged and deployed on the server. Then, start the Glassfish application server and open the `http://localhost:8080/people-mgmt/servlet/people_user_login Uniform Resource Locator (URL)` in the Internet Explorer. Next, you need to access the main login servlet, i.e. `people_user_login` to execute the project. This servlet automatically redirects you to the `people_user_login` JSP page.

Figure 23.2 shows the `people_user_login` JSP page:

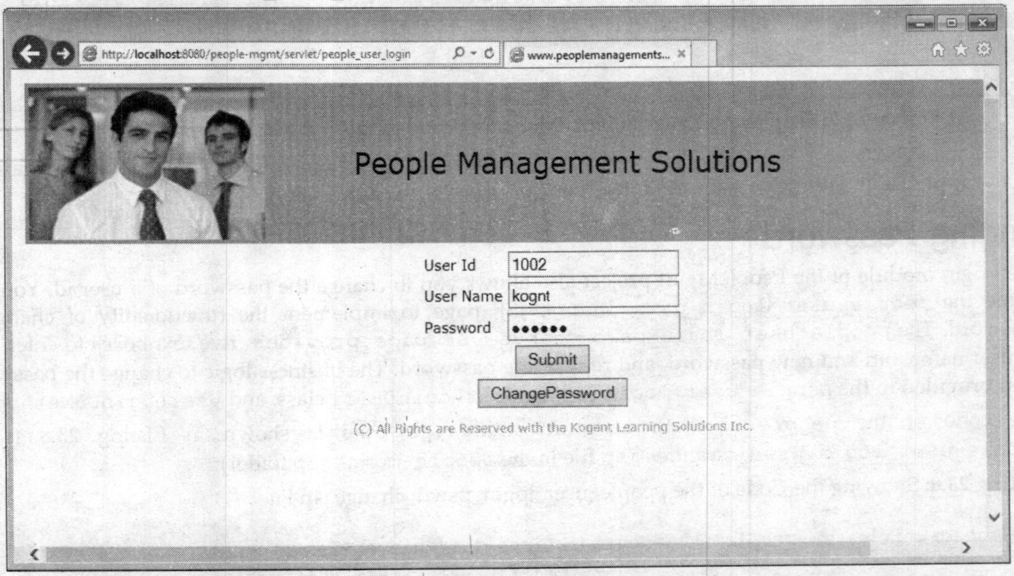

Figure 23.2: Displaying the people_user_login JSP Page with the Login User Interface

In the people_user_login JSP page, you need to enter a valid `user id`, `user name`, and `password` details, which are used for authentication purpose. In our case, we have entered 1002 as the user id and kogent as user name and password, as shown in Figure 23.2.

NOTE

In the http://localhost:8080 URL, 8080 is the port number on which the Glassfish Server is running. This port number can vary depending on the port number on which the server is running on your system. You also need to create the required tables in the Oracle database from which the user id and password are retrieved to authenticate a user. The Structured Query Language (SQL) queries used to create the required tables are provided in the queries.txt file in the people-mgmt folder. You need to execute the following SQL query to insert a record in the PEOPLE_USER_LOGIN table of the Oracle database:

```
insert into PEOPLE_USER_LOGIN values ('1002', 'kogent',
'kogent', 'kogent', '02-Feb-2007', '28-Feb-14');
```

After entering the user id and password, click the Submit button. You should note that the form tag defined in the people_user_login JSP page does not contain the action attribute. Due to this, the form is submitted to the same servlet from where the user has forwarded the request to the `people_user_login` *JSP page. If* `user id`*,* `user name`*, and* `password` *do not match with the details provided in the database, the people_user_login servlet redirects the user to the login page with an error message. However, if the user is authenticated, the request is forwarded to the home page of the project.*

Figure 23.3 shows the home page of the project:

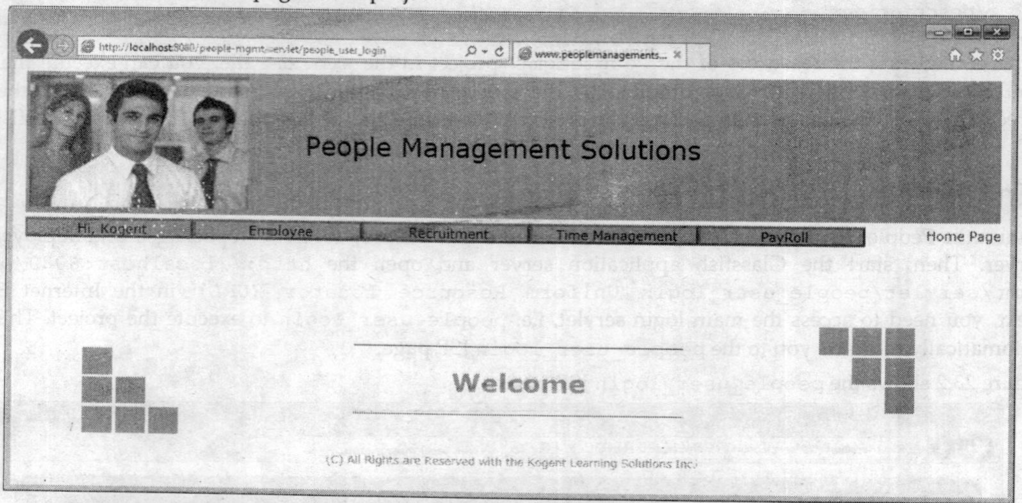

Figure 23.3: Displaying the Welcome Page after Validating All the Requested Login Data

The `people_default_menu JSP page` is inserted in the default page, as it contains all the navigation links for the application. This page is inserted in all the JSP pages of the application.

Changing Password

The Login module of the PeopleMgmt project also allows you to change the password of a user id. You need to create the `people_user_login_pswd_change` JSP page to implement the functionality of changing the password. The `people_user_login_pswd_change JSP page provides` five text boxes to enter the user id, user name, old and new password, and re-type the password. The business logic to change the password has been provided in the `people_user_login` servlet, `UserLoginDBObj` class, and `UserLoginDBMethods` class.

The code of the `people_user_login_pswd_change.jsp` file is shown in Listing 23.8 (save the `people_user_login_pswd_change.jsp` file in the `people-mgmt\jsp` folder):

Listing 23.8: Showing the Code of the people_user_login_pswd_change.jsp File

```
<html>
<head><title>www.peoplemanagementsolutions.com/Change Password</title>
<link rel="stylesheet" href="../css/mystyle.css" type="text/css" />
</head>
<body>
<form name = "form1" method="post">
<table width="100%" >
<tr>
<td colspan="2">
```

```
    <%@ include file="\jsp\people_header.jsp" %>
   </td>
   </tr>
   <tr >
   <td colspan="2">
   <table border ="0"  align="center" >
   <tr><td>User Id</td>
   <td align="center" ><input type ="text" name="user_id" id="user_id" value=""
   /></td></tr>
   <tr><td>User Name</td>
   <td align="center" ><input type ="text" name="user_name" id="user_name" value=""
   /></td></tr>
   <tr><td>Old Password</td>
   <td align="center" ><input type ="password" name="old_pswd" id="old_pswd"
   value=""/></td></tr>
   <tr><td>New Password</td><td align="center" >
   <input type ="password" name="new_pswd" id="new_pswd" value="" /></td></tr>
   <tr><td>Retype Password</td><td align="center" >
   <input type ="password" name="retype_pswd" id="retype_pswd" value="" /></td></tr>
   <tr><td colspan="2" align="right">
   <input type ="submit" name="submit" id="submit" value="Submit" />
   <input type="hidden" name="action_submit" id="action_submit"
   value="login_pswd_change_submit"/>
   </td></tr>
   <%String msg  = (String)session.getAttribute("lErrorMsg");
     if ( msg != null && msg.length() > 0 ){        %>
   <tr><td colspan="2" align="right">
   <%out.println("<div class=boldred align=center>"+msg+"</div>"); %>
   </td></tr>
   <% } %>
   </table></td>
   </tr>
   <tr><td colspan="2"><%@include file="../jsp/people_footer.jsp"%></td></tr>
   </table></form></body></html>
```

In Listing 23.8, the hidden field value is used to specify the path of a servlet to which the request is redirected. Figure 23.4 shows the interface provided to change the password which is the output of the `people_user_login_pswd_change JSP` page:

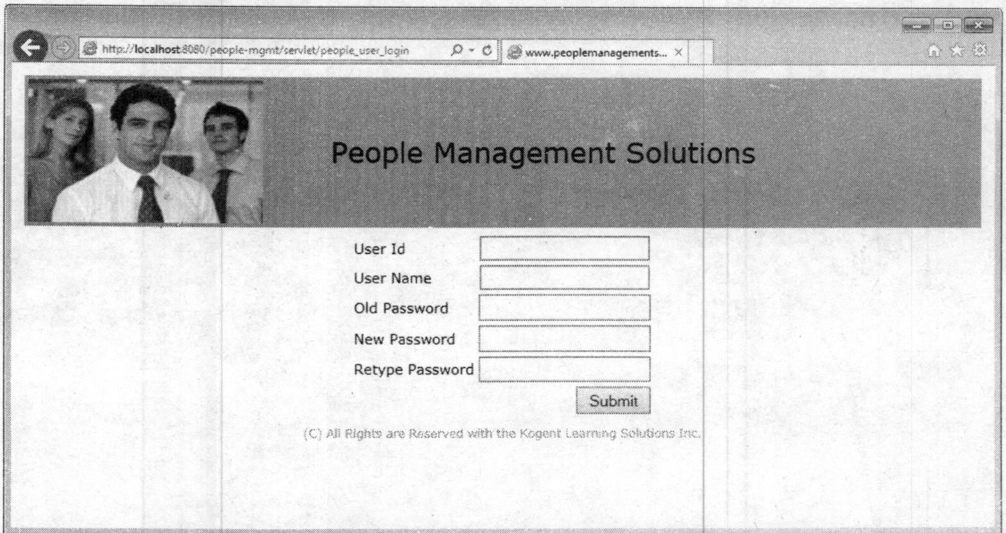

Figure 23.4: Displaying the Page Used to Change the password of a User

Figure 23.4 shows various fields to be filled to change the password.

This section has discussed how the MVC architecture is being used in the development of this project and how to implement the login process in the project. A single servlet, `people_user_login`, and two more Java classes, `UserLoginDBObj` and `UserLoginDBMethods`, help the servlet to perform the functionality of user login. This servlet acts as a central controller as it intercepts all the requests. The `UserLoginDBObj` class is being used as a data transfer object, which represents Model in the MVC architecture. `people_default` is the home page of the application, which is designed for working with different modules.

The next section describes the development of module to handle profile details of all employees of the organization.

Section B

Developing the Profile Management Module

The Profile Management module of the PeopleMgmt project enables an organization to maintain the profiles of all its employees. This module provides user interfaces to create or edit the profile of a person whose records are already maintained in the database. The profile-related information includes personal details, such as department name, designation, and date of joining. In this module, the details of a person are stored in the PEOPLE_EMPLOYEE table of the database. In addition, there is a search form used to search the records of the database on the basis of the employee id and the first name of an employee.

To develop this module, you need to create the following files:

- people_employee.java
- EmployeeDBObj.java
- EmployeeDBMethods.java
- GenerateId.java
- employee_insert.jsp
- employee_search.jsp
- employee_edit.jsp

Let's begin the discussion with the logic implementation using Java Servlet in the next section.

Implementing Logic with Servlet

The logic implementation of the Profile Management module is performed with the help of the people_employee servlet. The request is forwarded to the next JSP page on the basis of the parameters passed from the request page to a servlet. The people_employee servlet uses three more classes (EmployeeDBObj, EmployeeDBMethods, and GenerateId) to complete the task. This servlet decides the next JSP page according to the parameters passed from the page to the servlet. The servlet uses two more classes to complete this task, i.e. EmployeeDBObj and EmployeeDBMethods. The code for the GenerateId.java, people_employee.java, EmployeeDBObj.java, and EmployeeDBMethods.java files has been discussed in the next subsections.

Creating the people_employee Servlet

The people_employee servlet controls the navigation of the user from one JSP page to another while updating the profile of an employee. This servlet uses the forward() method of the RequestDispatcher object after setting values for target and action variables accordingly. The people_employee servlet is a controller servlet for this module.

Listing 23.9 shows the code of the people_employee.java file (save the people_employee.java file in the people-mgmt\WEB-INF\src folder):

Listing 23.9: Showing the Code of the people_employee.java File

```
import javax.servlet.*;
import javax.servlet.http.*;
import java.util.ArrayList;
import java.io.*;
import java.util.*;
import java.sql.*;
import javax.servlet.annotation.*;
import javax.servlet.annotation.WebServlet;
import com.Employee.EmployeeDBMethods;
import com.Employee.EmployeeDBObj;

@WebServlet(name="people_employee", urlPatterns="/servlet/people_employee")
public class people_employee extends HttpServlet
{
    String lDBUser  = "";
    String lDBPswd  = "";
    String lDBUrl   = "";
   /**Initialize global variables*/
   @Override
   public void init(ServletConfig config) throws ServletException{
```

```
    System.out.println("initializing controller servlet.");
    ServletContext context = config.getServletContext();
    lDBUser = "scott";
    lDBPswd = "tiger";
    lDBUrl  = "jdbc:oracle:thin:@192.168.1.123:1521:"+"XE";
       super.init(config);
     }
  /**Process the HTTP Get request*/
    @Override
  public void doGet(HttpServletRequest request, HttpServletResponse response) throws
  ServletException, IOException{
                 doPost(request, response);
  }
  /**Process the HTTP Post request*/
    @Override
  public void doPost(HttpServletRequest request, HttpServletResponse response)
  throws ServletException, IOException{
    response.setContentType("text/html");
    PrintWriter out = response.getWriter();
    HttpSession session = request.getSession();
    session.setAttribute("lErrorMsg",null);
    String target = "";
    String action = request.getParameter("action");
    String lDBOpr = "";
    EmployeeDBMethods employeeDBMethods = new
       EmployeeDBMethods(lDBUser,lDBPswd,lDBUrl);
       lDBOpr = (String)request.getParameter("dbopr");
    if( (lDBOpr != null && lDBOpr.length() > 0) && (lDBOpr.equals("create")) ){
         target = "/jsp/employee_insert.jsp";
    }
    else if( (lDBOpr != null && lDBOpr.length() > 0) && (lDBOpr.equals("edit"))
        ){
         target = "/jsp/employee_search.jsp";
    }
    else if( (lDBOpr != null && lDBOpr.length() > 0) && (lDBOpr.equals("show"))
       ){
         ArrayList employeeList = new ArrayList();
         String criteria = "";
         employeeList =
             (ArrayList)employeeDBMethods.selectEmployeeByCriteria(criteria);
         session.setAttribute("EmployeeList",employeeList);
         target = "/jsp/employee_list.jsp";
         }
    else if( (lDBOpr != null && lDBOpr.length() > 0) &&
       (lDBOpr.equals("detail")) ){
         String lEmpId = "";
         String lEmpFName = "";
         lEmpId = (String)request.getParameter("emp_id");
         lEmpFName = (String)request.getParameter("emp_f_name");
         EmployeeDBObj employeeDBObj = new EmployeeDBObj();
         employeeDBObj =
  (EmployeeDBObj)employeeDBMethods.getRecordByPrimaryKey(lEmpId,lEmpFName);
  System.out.println("iiiii="+employeeDBObj.emp_id+"ffff="+employeeDBObj.emp_f_name);
  session.setAttribute("employeeDBObj",employeeDBObj);
  target = "/jsp/employee_profile.jsp";
  }
  else if ( (lDBOpr != null && lDBOpr.length() > 0) && (lDBOpr.equals("delete")) ){
    String emp_Id = "";
    emp_Id = (String)request.getParameter("emp_id");
    employeeDBMethods.deleteEmployee(emp_Id);
    String criteria = "";
    ArrayList employeeList = new ArrayList();
    employeeList =
       (ArrayList)employeeDBMethods.selectEmployeeByCriteria(criteria);
    session.setAttribute("EmployeeList",employeeList);
```

```
    target = "/jsp/employee_list.jsp";
  }
  String action_submit = request.getParameter("action_submit");
  String action_edit = request.getParameter("action_edit");
  System.out.println("action_submit=="+action_submit);
  if ( action_submit != null || action_edit != null ){
    if ( request.getParameter("submit").equals("Submit") ){
          System.out.println("in the  Submit");
          if ( action_submit.equals("people_employee_insert_submit") ){
          System.out.println("in the people_employee_insert_submit ");
                 action = "people_employee_insert_submit";
          }
          else
          if (action_submit.equals("login_pswd_change_submit")){
                 action = "login_pswd_change_submit";
          }
          else
          if (action_submit.equals("people_employee_search_submit")){
                 action = "people_employee_search_submit";
          }
    }
    else
    if ( request.getParameter("submit").equals("Edit") ){
          if ( action_edit.equals("people_employee_edit_submit") ){
                 action = "people_employee_edit_submit";
                 EmployeeDBObj popEmployeeDBObj = new EmployeeDBObj();
                 popEmployeeDBObj =
      (EmployeeDBObj)employeeDBMethods.populateEmployeeDBObjFromReq(request);
                 int rval =
              employeeDBMethods.updateEmployeeByPrimaryKey(popEmployeeDBObj);
          if ( rval > 0 ){
                 EmployeeDBObj employeeDBObj = new EmployeeDBObj();
               employeeDBObj =
(EmployeeDBObj)employeeDBMethods.getRecordByPrimaryKey(popEmployeeDBObj.emp_id,pop
EmployeeDBObj.emp_f_name);
                 session.setAttribute("employeeDBObj",employeeDBObj);
                 String lErrorMsg = "Employee is Updated!!";
                 session.setAttribute("lErrorMsg",lErrorMsg);
                 target = "/jsp/employee_list.jsp";
          }
    }
  }
  }
    if (action!=null){
          System.out.println("in the  "+action);
          if (action.equals("people_employee_search_submit")){
                 String lEmpId = "";
                 String lEmpFName = "";
                 lEmpId = (String)request.getParameter("emp_id");
                 lEmpFName = (String)request.getParameter("emp_f_name");
                        EmployeeDBObj employeeDBObj = new EmployeeDBObj();
                 employeeDBObj =
     (EmployeeDBObj)employeeDBMethods.getRecordByPrimaryKey(lEmpId,lEmpFName);
System.out.println("iiii="+employeeDBObj.emp_id+"ffff="+employeeDBObj.emp_f_name)
;
if ( (employeeDBObj.emp_id != null && employeeDBObj.emp_f_name != null) ){
          session.setAttribute("employeeDBObj",employeeDBObj);
          target = "/jsp/employee_edit.jsp";
    }
    else{
          String lErrorMsg = "Employee doesn't Exist";
          session.setAttribute("lErrorMsg",lErrorMsg);
          System.out.println("Employee:" + lErrorMsg);
          target = "/jsp/people_default.jsp";
       }
```

```
    }
    else
    if (action.equals("people_change_pswd_submit")){
            target = "/jsp/people_user_login_pswd_change.jsp";
    }
    else
    if (action.equals("people_employee_insert_submit")){
            EmployeeDBObj popEmployeeDBObj = new EmployeeDBObj();
            popEmployeeDBObj =
(EmployeeDBObj)employeeDBMethods.populateEmployeeDBObjFromReq(request);
            EmployeeDBObj employeeDBObj = new EmployeeDBObj();
            employeeDBObj =
(EmployeeDBObj)employeeDBMethods.getRecordByPrimaryKey(popEmployeeDBObj.emp_id,pop
EmployeeDBObj.emp_f_name);
     if ( (popEmployeeDBObj.emp_id).equals(employeeDBObj) &&
            (popEmployeeDBObj.emp_f_name).equals(employeeDBObj.emp_f_name) ){
                    String lErrorMsg = "Employee Already Exist";
                    session.setAttribute("lErrorMsg",lErrorMsg);
                    System.out.println("Employee:" + lErrorMsg);
                    target = "/jsp/people_default.jsp";
     }
     else{
            int rval =  employeeDBMethods.insertEmployee(popEmployeeDBObj);
            EmployeeDBObj sEmployeeDBObj = new EmployeeDBObj();
            sEmployeeDBObj =
(EmployeeDBObj)employeeDBMethods.getRecordByPrimaryKey(popEmployeeDBObj.emp_id,pop
EmployeeDBObj.emp_f_name);
            session.setAttribute("employeeDBObj",sEmployeeDBObj);
            String lErrorMsg = "Employee is Added!!";
            session.setAttribute("lErrorMsg",lErrorMsg);
            target = "/jsp/people_inserted.jsp";
        }
  }
  else
  if (action.equals("people_employee_edit_submit")){
     EmployeeDBObj popEmployeeDBObj = new EmployeeDBObj();
     popEmployeeDBObj =
(EmployeeDBObj)employeeDBMethods.populateEmployeeDBObjFromReq(request);
     int rval = employeeDBMethods.updateEmployeeByPrimaryKey(popEmployeeDBObj);
     if ( rval > 0 ){
            EmployeeDBObj employeeDBObj = new EmployeeDBObj();
            employeeDBObj =
(EmployeeDBObj)employeeDBMethods.getRecordByPrimaryKey(popEmployeeDBObj.emp_id,pop
EmployeeDBObj.emp_f_name);
            session.setAttribute("employeeDBObj",employeeDBObj);
            String lErrorMsg = "Employee is Updated!!";
            session.setAttribute("lErrorMsg",lErrorMsg);
            target = "/jsp/employee_list.jsp";
     }
     else
     if (action.equals("people_employee_detail")){
            ArrayList employeeList = new ArrayList();
            String criteria="";
            employeeList =
(ArrayList)employeeDBMethods.selectEmployeeByCriteria(criteria);
            session.setAttribute("EmployeeList",employeeList);
            target = "/jsp/employee_list.jsp";
     }
     else
     if (action.equals("people_employee_delete")){
            String emp_Id = "";
     }
  }
  } // (action== null )
  /* forwarding the request/response to the targeted view */
```

```
        RequestDispatcher requestDispatcher =
            getServletContext().getRequestDispatcher(target);
        requestDispatcher.forward(request, response);
    } // doPost closed
    }// class closed
```

In Listing 23.9, the `@WebServlet` annotation is used to define the `servlet` mapping, while the `@Override` annotation specifies that the methods, such as `doPost()`, and `doGet()` are overridden. The business logic embedded in this servlet uses various set of variables, such as action and target and the parameters passed with the request to find out the proper execution path. The value of the next page to be executed depends on the value held by the dbopr parameter. The two class files, i.e. `EmployeeDBObj` and `EmployeeDBMethods`, used in the `people_employee` servlet are discussed in the following sections.

Creating the EmployeeDBObj Class

`EmployeeDBObj` is a Java class having member variables matching the columns of the PEOPLE_EMPLOYEE table. It is used as a JavaBean to hold the data related to the profile of an employee. An instance of this class represents a single record in the PEOPLE_EMPLOYEE table.

Listing 23.10 shows the code of the `EmployeeDBObj.java` file (save the `EmployeeDBObj.java` file in the `people-mgmt\WEB-INF\src\com\Employee` folder):

Listing 23.10: Showing the Code of the EmployeeDBObj.java File

```
package com.Employee;
public class EmployeeDBObj
{
   public String emp_id ;
   public String emp_f_name ;
   public String emp_m_name ;
   public String emp_l_name ;
   public String org_id  ;
   public String level_id ;
   public String dept_id ;
   public String dob ;
   public String dojoin  ;
   public String address_1;
   public String address_2 ;
   public String city ;
   public String state;
   public String nationality ;
}
```

Creating the EmployeeDBMethods Class

EmployeeDBMethods class provides various methods, such as `insertEmployee()`, `updateEmployeeByPrimaryKey()`, `populateEmployeeDBObjFromReq()`, and `getRecordByPrimaryKey()` to manipulate the records of the database directly. The `insertEmployee(EmployeeDBObj)` method inserts a new record in the `PEOPLE_EMPLOYEE` table. Similarly, the `updateEmployeeByPrimaryKey(EmployeeDBObj)` method updates the table with new information set with the EmployeeDBObj object passed to the method as an argument. Other methods are used to populate the `EmployeeDBObj` object with the data either fetched from the table (`getRecordByPrimaryKey()` method) or sent with the request (`populateEmployeeDBObjFromReq()` method).

Listing 23.11 shows the code of the `EmployeeDBMethods.java` file (save the `EmployeeDBMethods.java` file in the `people-mgmt\WEB-INF\src\com\Employee` folder):

Listing 23.11: Showing the Code of the EmployeeDBMethods.java File

```
package com.Employee;
import java.sql.*;
import javax.servlet.*;
import javax.servlet.http.*;
import java.io.*;
import java.util.*;
import java.util.ArrayList;
```

```
import com.Employee.EmployeeDBObj;

public class EmployeeDBMethods
{
   public String DBUser;
   public String DBPswd;
   public String DBUrl;

   public EmployeeDBMethods(){ }
   public EmployeeDBMethods(String inDBUser, String inDBPswd, String inDBUrl )
   {
         DBUser = inDBUser ;
         DBPswd = inDBPswd;
         DBUrl  = inDBUrl;
   }
   public void initializeEmployeeDBObj(EmployeeDBObj inEmployeeDBObj )
   {
         inEmployeeDBObj.emp_id =  "";
         inEmployeeDBObj.emp_f_name = "";
         inEmployeeDBObj.emp_m_name = "";
         inEmployeeDBObj.emp_l_name = "";
         inEmployeeDBObj.org_id = "";
         inEmployeeDBObj.level_id = "";
         inEmployeeDBObj.dept_id= "";
         inEmployeeDBObj.dob= "";
         inEmployeeDBObj.dojoin= "";
         inEmployeeDBObj.address_1= "";
         inEmployeeDBObj.address_2= "";
         inEmployeeDBObj.city= "";
         inEmployeeDBObj.state= "";
         inEmployeeDBObj.nationality= "";
   }
   public EmployeeDBObj getRecordByPrimaryKey(String inEmpId, String inEmpFName)
   {
         EmployeeDBObj  employeeDBObj = new EmployeeDBObj();
         java.sql.Date date;
         try
         {
                System.out.println("DBUser=="+DBUser+",DBPswd=="+DBPswd+",
                DBUrl=="+DBUrl);
                DriverManager.registerDriver(new
                oracle.jdbc.driver.OracleDriver());
                Connection conn= DriverManager.getConnection
                (DBUrl,DBUser,DBPswd);
                Statement stmt = conn.createStatement();
                String lSqlString =     "select * from PEOPLE_EMPLOYEE ";
                lSqlString = lSqlString + "where emp_id='"+inEmpId+"' ";
                if( inEmpFName != null && inEmpFName.length() > 0)
                lSqlString = lSqlString + "and emp_f_name='"+inEmpFName+"' ";
                ResultSet rs  = null;
                rs  = stmt.executeQuery(lSqlString);
                System.out.println("lSqlString====trtrt==within
                      getRecordByPrimaryKey== "+lSqlString);
                if( rs.next())
                {
                employeeDBObj.emp_id =  rs.getString("emp_id");
                employeeDBObj.emp_f_name = rs.getString("emp_f_name");
                employeeDBObj.emp_m_name = rs.getString("emp_m_name");
                employeeDBObj.emp_l_name = rs.getString("emp_l_name");
                employeeDBObj.org_id = rs.getString("org_id");
                employeeDBObj.level_id = rs.getString("level_id");
                employeeDBObj.dept_id = rs.getString("dept_id");
                date=rs.getDate("dob");
                employeeDBObj.dob = date.toString();
                date=rs.getDate("dojoin");
                employeeDBObj.dojoin = date.toString();
```

```
                employeeDBObj.address_1 = rs.getString("address_1");
                employeeDBObj.address_2 = rs.getString("address_2");
                employeeDBObj.city = rs.getString("city");
                employeeDBObj.state = rs.getString("state");
                employeeDBObj.nationality = rs.getString("nationality");
                System.out.println("fffff==="+rs.getString("emp_id"));
                }
                else
                {
                        initializeEmployeeDBObj(employeeDBObj);
                }
                System.out.println("fffff====="+employeeDBObj.emp_id);
        }
        catch(SQLException  ex)
        {
                ex.printStackTrace();
        }
        return employeeDBObj;
}
public int updateEmployeeByPrimaryKey(EmployeeDBObj inEmployeeDBObj)
{
        int recupd = 0;
        String lQuery = "";
        lQuery = lQuery +"update PEOPLE_EMPLOYEE set
                emp_m_name='"+inEmployeeDBObj.emp_m_name+"'  ";
        lQuery = lQuery +" , emp_l_name='"+inEmployeeDBObj.emp_l_name+"' ";
        lQuery = lQuery +" , org_id='"+inEmployeeDBObj.org_id+"' ";
        lQuery = lQuery +" , level_id='"+inEmployeeDBObj.level_id+"' ";
        lQuery = lQuery +" , dept_id='"+inEmployeeDBObj.dept_id+"' ";
        lQuery = lQuery +" , dob=to_date('"+inEmployeeDBObj.dob+"', 'yyyy-mm-dd') ";
lQuery = lQuery +" , dojoin=to_date('"+inEmployeeDBObj.dojoin+"', 'yyyy-mm-dd') ";
        lQuery = lQuery +" , address_1='"+inEmployeeDBObj.address_1+"' ";
        lQuery = lQuery +" , address_2='"+inEmployeeDBObj.address_2+"' ";
        lQuery = lQuery +" , city='"+inEmployeeDBObj.city+"' ";
        lQuery = lQuery +" , state='"+inEmployeeDBObj.state+"' ";
        lQuery = lQuery +" , nationality='"+inEmployeeDBObj
        .nationality+"' ";
        lQuery = lQuery + "where emp_id='"+inEmployeeDBObj.emp_id+"' ";
        lQuery = lQuery + "and emp_f_name='"+inEmployeeDBObj
        .emp_f_name+"  ";
        System.out.println("lSqlString===:"+lQuery);
        try
        {
        DriverManager.registerDriver(new oracle.jdbc.driver.OracleDriver());
        Connection conn= DriverManager.getConnection(DBUrl,DBUser,DBPswd);
                Statement stmt = conn.createStatement();
                recupd  = stmt.executeUpdate(lQuery);
        }
        catch(SQLException  ex)
        {
                ex.printStackTrace();
        }
        return recupd;
}
public EmployeeDBObj populateEmployeeDBObjFromReq(HttpServletRequest inReq)
{
        EmployeeDBObj  employeeDBObj = new EmployeeDBObj();
        employeeDBObj.emp_id   =  (String)inReq.getParameter("emp_id");
        employeeDBObj.emp_f_name = (String)inReq.getParameter("emp_f_name");
        employeeDBObj.emp_m_name  = (String)inReq.getParameter("emp_m_name");
        employeeDBObj.emp_l_name  = (String)inReq.getParameter("emp_l_name");
        employeeDBObj.org_id = (String)inReq.getParameter("org_id");
        employeeDBObj.level_id = (String)inReq.getParameter("level_id");
        employeeDBObj.dept_id = (String)inReq.getParameter("dept_id");
        employeeDBObj.dob = (String)inReq.getParameter("dob");
        employeeDBObj.dojoin = (String)inReq.getParameter("dojoin");
```

```
        employeeDBObj.address_1 = (String)inReq.getParameter("address_1");
        employeeDBObj.address_2 = (String)inReq.getParameter("address_2");
        employeeDBObj.city = (String)inReq.getParameter("city");
        employeeDBObj.state = (String)inReq.getParameter("state");
        employeeDBObj.nationality = (String)inReq.getParameter("nationality");
        return employeeDBObj;
    }

    public int insertEmployee(EmployeeDBObj inEmployeeDBObj){
        int recupd = 0;
        String lQuery = "";
        lQuery = lQuery +"insert into PEOPLE_EMPLOYEE values ( ";
        lQuery = lQuery +" '"+inEmployeeDBObj.emp_id+"'  ";
        lQuery = lQuery +" , '"+inEmployeeDBObj.emp_f_name+"'  ";
        lQuery = lQuery +" , '"+inEmployeeDBObj.emp_m_name+"'  ";
        lQuery = lQuery +" , '"+inEmployeeDBObj.emp_l_name+"' ";
        lQuery = lQuery +" , '"+inEmployeeDBObj.org_id+"' ";
        lQuery = lQuery +" , '"+inEmployeeDBObj.level_id+"' ";
        lQuery = lQuery +" , '"+inEmployeeDBObj.dept_id+"' ";
        lQuery = lQuery +" , to_date('"+inEmployeeDBObj.dob+"',
        'yyyy-mm-dd')";
        lQuery = lQuery +" , to_date('"+inEmployeeDBObj.dojoin+"',
        'yyyy-mm-dd')";
        lQuery = lQuery +" , '"+inEmployeeDBObj.address_1+"' ";
        lQuery = lQuery +" , '"+inEmployeeDBObj.address_2+"' ";
        lQuery = lQuery +" , '"+inEmployeeDBObj.city+"' ";
        lQuery = lQuery +" , '"+inEmployeeDBObj.state+"' ";
        lQuery = lQuery +" , '"+inEmployeeDBObj.nationality+"' ";
        lQuery = lQuery + " )";
        System.out.println("lSqlString===:"+lQuery);

        try
        {
                DriverManager.registerDriver(new
                oracle.jdbc.driver.OracleDriver());
                Connection conn= DriverManager.getConnection(DBUrl,DBUser,DBPswd);
                Statement stmt = conn.createStatement();
                recupd  = stmt.executeUpdate(lQuery);
        }

        catch(SQLException  ex)
        {
                ex.printStackTrace();
        }
        return recupd;
    }
}
```

In Listing 23.11, there are several methods for adding, updating, and deleting profiles of people. These methods are then used in the `people_employee` servlet. The description of the `GenerateId` class is provided in the next subsection.

Creating the GenerateId Class

The `GenerateId` class is developed for the purpose of auto-generation of `Employee Id`, which is the primary key in the database. As you know that a primary key in the database should be unique; however, a user can enter duplicate `Employee Id` that causes an error or exception. This is because a record with duplicate primary key cannot be added into a database. To avoid this situation, the `GenerateId` class is designed, which automatically generates the value of the `Employee Id` field.

Listing 23.12 shows the code for the `GenerateId.java` file (save the `GenerateId.java` file in the `people-mgmt\WEB-INF\src\com\Employee` folder):

Listing 23.12: Showing the Code of the GenerateId.java File

```
package com.Employee;
import java.sql.*;
import javax.sql.*;
public class GenerateId
{
    public int generateEmployeeId(){
    int emp_id=0;
    try{
      Class.forName("oracle.jdbc.driver.OracleDriver");
      Connection conn=
DriverManager.getConnection("jdbc:oracle:thin:@192.168.1.123:1521:"+"XE","scott","
tiger");
           Statement stmt = conn.createStatement();
      String query="select max(emp_id) as emp_id from PEOPLE_EMPLOYEE";
      ResultSet rs = null;
      rs = stmt.executeQuery(query);
      if(rs.next()){
          String id = rs.getString("emp_id");
          emp_id=Integer.parseInt(id);
      }
      emp_id = emp_id + 1;
      }
      catch(SQLException  ex){
          ex.printStackTrace();
      }
      catch(Exception e) {
          e.printStackTrace();
      }
   return emp_id;
}
}
```

The Employee Id or the value of the `emp_id` column is automatically generated for the record of a new employee because the query executed in Listing 23.12 returns the maximum value of the `emp_id` coulmn and then the value is incremented by 1.

Creating Views

There are three interfaces designed as view components in this module. The first interface (`employee_list`) is used to display the complete list of employees whose records are maintained in the database, and the other interface (`employee_search`) provides the fields on the basis of which the records of employees are searched. The third interface (`employee_edit`) is used to edit the details of an employee. These three interfaces are created by three JSP pages, namely `employee_insert`, `employee_edit`, and `employee_search`. The code for these JSP pages is discussed under the following sections.

Creating the employee_insert JSP Page

The `employee_insert` JSP page provides a form to be filled with the details of a new employee. The profile of the employee is normally created at the joining time of the employee. This form includes various fields, such as `Employee Id`, `First Name`, `Middle Name`, `Last Name`, `Department`, `Date of Birth`, `Join Date`, `Address1`, `Address2`, `City`, `State`, and `Nationality`. The client-side validation is used to specify the mandatory fields that must be filled by a user. If the user leaves any mandatory field as blank, a message is displayed to fill that field. The user can also view the employee_insert JSP page by clicking the Create Profile hyperlink, which calls the `people_employee` servlet. After clicking the hyperlink, the user's request is redirected to the employee_insert JSP page, which displays all the fields that are to be filled by the user.

Listing 23.13 shows the code of the `employee_insert.jsp` file (save the `employee_insert.jsp` file in the `people-mgmt\jsp` folder):

Listing 23.13: Showing the Code of the employee_insert.jsp File

```
<%@ page language="java" %>
<%@ page session="true" %>
<%@ page  import="com.Employee.*" %>
<%  GenerateId gen=new GenerateId();
    int emp_id=gen.generateEmployeeId();
%>
<html>
<head>
<title>www.peoplemanagementsolutions.com/Create Profile</title>
<link rel="stylesheet" href="../css/mystyle.css" type="text/css" />
<script language="javascript">
  function validateForm() {
   var myName=document.form1.emp_f_name.value;
   if (myName =="") {
      alert ("First name cannot be blank");
      document.form1.emp_f_name.focus();
      return false;
   }
   myName=document.form1.emp_l_name.value;
   if (myName =="") {
      alert ("Last name cannot be blank");
      document.form1.emp_l_name.focus();
      return false;
   }
   myName=document.form1.dob.value;
   if (myName =="") {
      alert ("Date Of Birth cannot be blank");
      document.form1.dob.focus();
      return false;
   }
   myName=document.form1.address_1.value;
   if (myName =="") {
     alert ("Address1 cannot be blank");
     document.form1.address_1.focus();
     return false;
   }
   myName=document.form1.city.value;
   if (myName =="") {
     alert ("City cannot be blank");
     document.form1.city.focus();
     return false;
   }
   myName=document.form1.state.value;
   if (myName =="") {
     alert ("State cannot be blank");
     document.form1.state.focus();
     return false;
   }
   myName=document.form1.level_id.value;
   if (myName =="Select Designation") {
     alert ("You Should select a Designation");
     document.form1.level_id.focus();
     return false;
   }
   myName=document.form1.dept_id.value;
   if (myName =="Select Department") {
     alert ("You Should select a Department");
     document.form1.dept_id.focus();
     return false;
   }
   myName=document.form1.dojoin.value;
   if (myName =="") {
      alert ("Date of Join field cannot be blank");
      document.form1.dojoin.focus();
      return false;
   }
   myName=document.form1.nationality.value;
   if (myName =="Select Nationality") {
     alert ("You Should select a Nationality");
     document.form1.nationality.focus();
```

```
        return false;
    }
    form1.submit();
  }
  </script>
  </head>
  <body>
  <table width="900" border="0" align="center">
  <tr>
  <td colspan="2"><%@ include file="../jsp/people_header.jsp" %></td>
  </tr>
  <tr>
  <td width="900">
  <%@ include file="../jsp/people_default_menu.jsp" %>
  </td>
  </tr><tr>
  <td width ="750" valign="top" align = "center">
  <p> </p>
  Enter Profile Detail for New Employee.
  <hr width=100% color=#AAAAAA/>
  <table  border="0" align="top" width=100% >
  <form name="form1" method="post">
  <input type='hidden'  name='emp_id' id='emp_id 'size ='10' value='<%=emp_id%>'/>
  <tr>
  <td>Employee Id</td>
  <td align='left'><input type='text' disabled='disabled' name='emp_id' id='emp_id
  'size ='10' value='<%=emp_id%>'/></td>
  <td> </td>
  <td align='left'> </td>
  </tr>
  <tr>
  <td>First Name<sup>*</sup></td>
  <td><input type='text' name='emp_f_name' id='emp_f_name 'size ='10'
  value=''/></td>
  <td>
  Middle Name</td><td><input type='text' name='emp_m_name' id='emp_m_name' size
  ='10' value=''/></td>
  <td>Last Name<sup>*</sup></td><td><input type='text' name='emp_l_name'
  id='emp_l_name' size ='10' value=''/>
  </td>
  </tr>
  <tr>
  <td>Org Id</td><input type='hidden' name='org_id' id='org_id' size ='10'
  value="KLSI"/>
  <td align='left'><input type='text' name='org_id_dup' id='org_id_dup'
  disabled='disabled' size ='10' value="KLSI"/>
  </td>
  <td>Designation<sup>*</sup></td>
  <td align='left'><select name="level_id" id="level_id">
  <option value='select Designation' selected> Select Designation
  <option value='CW'> Content Writer
  <option value='TS'> Tester
  <option value='HR'> Human Resource Manager
  <option value='AC'> Accountant
  <option value='AM'> Admin Manager
  <option value='EM'> Event Manager
  <option value='TL'> Team Leader
  <option value='PM'> Project Manager
  <option value='TR'> Trainer
  </select></td></td>
  </tr>
  <tr>
  <td>Department<sup>*</sup></td>
  <td align='left'><select id='dept_id' name='dept_id'>
  <option value='select Department' selected> Select Department
  <option value='CS'> Content Solutions
  <option value='TS'> Testing
  <option value='HR'> Human Resource
  <option value='AC'> Accounts
  <option value='AD'> Administration
  <option value='EM'> Event Management
  </select></td>
```

```
<td>DOB<sup>*</sup></td>
<td align='left'><input type='text' name='dob' id='dob' size ='10' value=''/>
(yyyy-mm-dd)</td>
</tr>
<tr>
<td>JoinDate<sup>*</sup></td>
<td align='left' colspan='2'><input type='text' name='dojoin' id='dojoin' size
='10' value=''/>(yyyy-mm-dd)</td>
<td> </td>
<td> </td>
</tr>
<tr>
<td>Address1<sup>*</sup></td>
<td align='left' colspan='2'><input type='text' name='address_1' id='address_1'
size ='40' value=''/> </td>
<td> </td>
<td> </td>
</tr>
<tr>
<td>Address2</td>
<td align='left' colspan='2'><input type='text' name='address_2' id='address_2'
size ='40' value=''/> </td>
<td> </td>
<td> </td>
</tr>
<tr>
<td>City<sup>*</sup></td>
<td align='left'><input type='text' name='city' id='city' size ='10' value=''/>
</td>
<td> </td>
<td> </td>
</tr>
<tr>
<td>State <sup>*</sup></td>
<td align='left'><input type='text' name='state' id='state' size ='10' value=''/>
</td>
<td>Nationality<sup>*</sup></td>
<td align='left'>
<select name='nationality' id='nationality'>
<option selected>Select Nationality
<option value='IN'> Indian
<option value='RS'> Russian
<option value='PK'> Pakistani
<option value='AM'> American
<option value='BR'> British
<option value='SR'> Srilankan
</select></td>
</tr>
<tr>
<td> All the ( <sup>*</sup>) marked are mandatory</td></tr><tr>
<td align='center' colspan='4'>
<input type="submit" name="submit" id="submit" size ="10" value="Submit"
onClick="return validateForm()"/>
<input type='hidden' name='action_submit' id='action_submit' size ='10'
value='people_employee_insert_submit'/>
</td>
</tr>
</table>
<hr width=100% color=#AAAAAA>
</td>
</tr>
<tr>
<td colspan="2"><%@include file="../jsp/people_footer.jsp"%></td>
</tr>
</table>
</body>
</html>
```

When you click the `Create Profile` submenu from the `Employee` menu, the `employee_insert` JSP page is displayed, as shown in Figure 23.5:

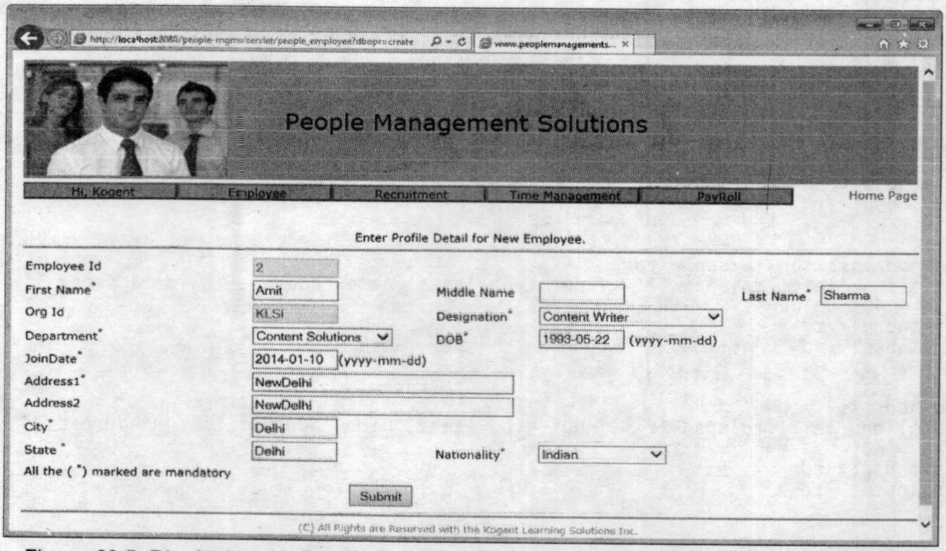

Figure 23.5: Displaying the Details for a New Employee in the employee_insert JSP Page

After filling up and submitting the employee_insert JSP page, the request is forwarded to the `people_employee` servlet. The value of the `dbopr` parameter in the query string is set as `create`, which invokes the `insertEmployee()` method of the `EmployeeDBMethods` Java class, resulting in the insertion of a new record to the PEOPLE_EMPLOYEE table after checking the existence of such an employee. No two employees in the table can have the same `Employee Id`.

Creating the employee_search JSP Page

The employee_search JSP page is designed to search a particular record of an employee on the basis of the `employee id` and `first name` of the employee entered in the page. When this JSP page is submitted, the `people_employee` servlet sets the action attribute and then calls the `getRecordByPrimaryKey(lEmpId, lEmpFName)` method on the object of the `EmployeeDBMethods` Java class. The `EmployeeDBObj` object returned by this method is set as a session attribute that can be used in the next JSP page (`employee_edit`) to display information corresponding to a particular employee.

Listing 23.14 shows the code of the `employee_search.jsp` file (save the `employee_search.jsp` file in the `people-mgmt\jsp` folder):

Listing 23.14: Showing the Code of the employee_search.jsp File

```
<%@ page language="java" %>
<%@ page session="true" %>
<html>
<head>
<title>www.peoplemanagementsolutions.com/Search</title>
<link rel="stylesheet" href="../css/mystyle.css" type="text/css" />
</head>
<body>
<table width="900" border="0" align="center">
<tr>
<td colspan="2">
   <%@ include file="../jsp/people_header.jsp" %>
</td>
</tr>
<tr>
<td width="900">
   <%@ include file="../jsp/people_default_menu.jsp" %>
</td></tr><tr>
<td width ="750" valign="top" align = "center">
<p> </p>
<div align=center>Enter Employee Id & First Name</div>
```

```
<hr bgcolor="#AAAAAA" width=500>
<table  border="0" align="top" width=50% align="right">
<form name="form1" method="post">
<tr>
<td>Employee Id</td>
<td align='left'><input type='text' name='emp_id' id='emp_id 'size ='10'
value=''/></td>
</tr>
<tr>
<td>First Name</td>
<td align='left'><input type='text' name='emp_f_name' id='emp_f_name 'size ='10'
value='' /></td>
</tr>
<tr>
<td align='center'colspan='2' >
<input type='submit' name='submit' id='submit' size ='10' value='Submit'/>
</td>
</tr>
<input type='hidden' name='action_submit' id='action_submit' size ='10'
value='people_employee_search_submit'/>
</form>
</table>
<hr bgcolor="#AAAAAA" width=500>
</td>
</tr>
<tr>
<td colspan="2"><%@include file="../jsp/people_footer.jsp"%></td>
</tr>
</table>
</body>
</html>
```

Click the `Edit Employee` link from the navigation bar; a search page appears containing two fields—`Employee Id` and `First Name`. You need to provide the employee id and first name of the employee whose details need to be searched, as shown in Figure 23.6:

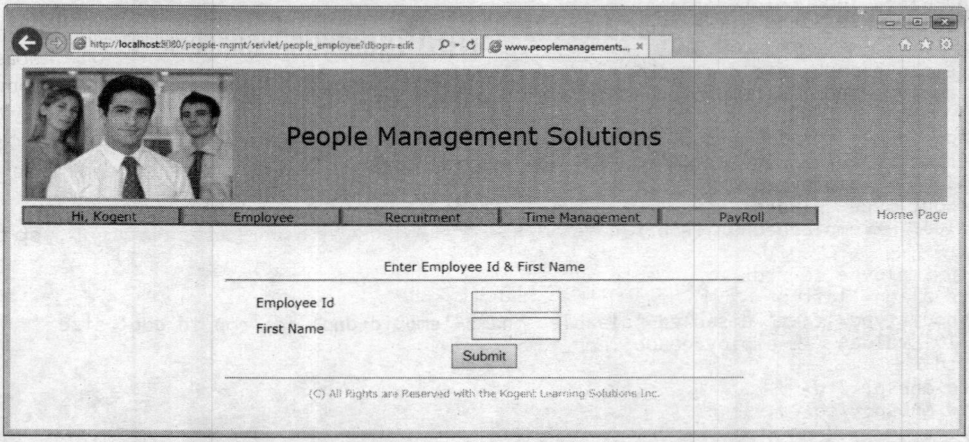

Figure 23.6: Displaying the employee_search JSP Page to Search an Employee

Figure 23.6 displays the `employee_search` JSP page with two fields, `Employee Id` and `First Name`, to be entered by a user. On the basis of the values entered in these fields, an employee record is searched and displayed for editing. If the record is found in the database, the employee id is forwarded to the `employee_edit` JSP page; otherwise, it is forwarded to the home page with the Employee does not exist error message.

The next section discusses about the `employee_edit` JSP page.

Creating the employee_edit JSP Page

The `employee_edit` JSP page is similar to the `employee_create` JSP page; except that the two fields, `Employee Id` and `First Name`, are disabled in the `employee_edit` JSP page. A user can enter the updated data in all other fields of the `employee_edit` page on the basis of which the record in the database is updated for new values. The code for the employee_edit JSP page is provided in Listing 23.15 in which the `EmployeeDBObj` object is used to retrieve the values set by the `people_employee` servlet.

Listing 23.15 shows the code of the `employee_edit.jsp` file (save the `employee_edit.jsp` file in the `people-mgmt\jsp` folder):

Listing 23.15: Showing the Code of the employee_edit.jsp File

```
<%@ page language="java" %>
<%@ page session="true" %>
<%@ page  import="com.Employee.*" %>
<html>
<head>
<title>www.peoplemanagementsolutions.com/Edit Employee</title>
<link rel="stylesheet" href="../css/mystyle.css" type="text/css" />
</head>
<body>
<table width="900" border="0" align="center">
<tr>
<td colspan="2"><%@ include file="../jsp/people_header.jsp" %></td>
</tr>
<tr>
<td width="900">
  <%@ include file="../jsp/people_default_menu.jsp" %></td> </tr><tr>
<td width ="750" valign="top" align = "center">
<p> </p>
Employee Detail
<hr width=100% color=#AAAAAA>
<table  border="0" align="top" width=100% >
<%
  EmployeeDBObj employeeDBObj = new EmployeeDBObj();
  employeeDBObj = (EmployeeDBObj)session.getAttribute("employeeDBObj");
%>
<form name="form1" method="post">
<input type='hidden' name='emp_id' id='emp_id' size ='10'
value="<%=employeeDBObj.emp_id%>"/>
<input type='hidden' name='emp_f_name' id='emp_f_name 'size ='10'
value="<%=employeeDBObj.emp_f_name%>"/>
<tr>
<td>Employee Id</td>
<td align='left'>
<input type='text' disabled='disabled' name='emp_id_dup' id='emp_id_dup' size
='10' value= "<%=employeeDBObj.emp_id%>"/>
</td>
<td> </td>
<td> </td>
</tr>
<tr>
<td>First Name</td>
<td align='left'>
<input type='text' disabled='disabled' name='emp_f_name_dup' id='emp_f_name_dup'
size ='10' value="<%=employeeDBObj.emp_f_name%>"/>
</td>
<td colspan=2>
Middle Name   
<input type='text' name='emp_m_name' id='emp_m_name' size ='10'
value="<%=employeeDBObj.emp_m_name%>"/>
   Last Name   
<input type='text' name='emp_l_name' id='emp_l_name' size ='10'
value="<%=employeeDBObj.emp_l_name%>"/>
</td>
```

```
</tr>
<tr>
<td>Org Id</td>
<td align='left'>
<input type='text' name='org_id' id='org_id' size ='10'
value="<%=employeeDBObj.org_id%>"/>
</td>
<td>Designation</td>
<td align='left'>
<input type='text' name='level_id' id='level_id' size ='10'
value="<%=employeeDBObj.level_id%>"/>
</td>
</tr>
<tr>
<td>Dept</td>
<td align='left'>
<input type='text' name='dept_id' id='dept_id' size ='10'
value="<%=employeeDBObj.dept_id%>"/>
</td>
<td>DOB</td>
<td align='left'><input type='text' name='dob' id='dob' size ='10'
value="<%=employeeDBObj.dob%>"/>
(yyyy-mm-dd)</td>
</tr>
<tr>
<td>Join Date</td>
<td align='left'>
<input type='text' name='dojoin' id='dojoin' size ='10'
value="<%=employeeDBObj.dojoin%>"/>
(yyyy-mm-dd)</td>
<td> </td>
<td> </td>
</tr>
<tr>
<td>Address1</td>
<td align='left' colspan='2'>
<input type='text' name='address_1' id='address_1' size ='40'
value="<%=employeeDBObj.address_1%>"/></td>
<td> </td>
<td> </td>
</tr>
<tr>
<td>Address2</td>
<td align='left' colspan='2'>
<input type='text' name='address_2' id='address_2' size ='40'
value="<%=employeeDBObj.address_2%>"/>
</td>
<td> </td>
<td> </td>
</tr>
<tr>
<td>City</td>
<td align='left'>
<input type='text' name='city' id='city' size ='10'
value="<%=employeeDBObj.city%>"/>
</td>
<td> </td>
<td> </td>
</tr>
<tr>
<td>State</td>
<td align='left'>
<input type='text' name='state' id='state' size ='10'
value="<%=employeeDBObj.state%>"/>
</td>
```

```
<td>Nationality</td>
<td align='left'>
<input type='text' name='nationality' id='nationality' size ='10'
value="<%=employeeDBObj.nationality%>"/>
</td>
</tr>
<tr>
<td align='center' colspan='4'>
<input type='submit' name='submit' id='submit' size ='10' value='Edit'/>
</td>
<input type='hidden' name='action_edit' id='action_edit' size ='10'
value='people_employee_edit_submit'/>
</td>
</tr>
</table>
<hr width=100% color=#AAAAAA>
</td>
</tr>
<tr>
<td colspan="2"><%@include file="../jsp/people_footer.jsp"%></td>
</tr>
</table>
</body>
</html>
```

In Listing 23.15, the code is provided to disable the fields that are automatically generated using the GenerateId class.

Figure 23.7 shows the employee_edit form for updating a record of an employee with two disabled fields:

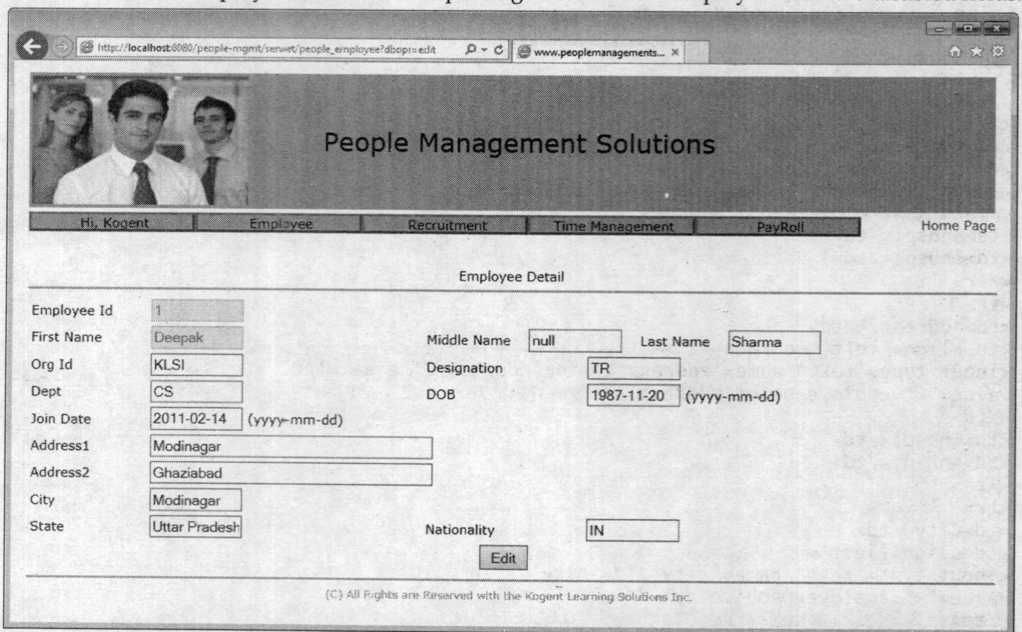

Figure 23.7: Displaying the employee_edit JSP Page for Editing an Employee Record

After filling the updated values in the `employee_edit` JSP page (Figure 23.7), click the Edit button, which submits the values of the hidden attributes, such as `emp_id` and `emp_f_name`, to a servlet. Then, the servlet determines the execution path on the basis of the hidden attribute; and accordingly sets the value for the action attribute.

In this section, you have learned how to develop the Profile Management module that handles profile of all the employees. The module helps you to create the profile of a new employee and edit the profile of an existing one, to incorporate the changes in the database. The entire module is composed of one servlet (people_employee), its two helper classes (EmployeeDBObj and EmployeeDBMethods), and three JSP pages, employee_insert, employee_search, and employee_edit.

Creating the employee_list JSP Page

The employee_list JSP page is designed to display the details of all the employees of the organization. This JSP page displays various fields, such as Employee Id, First Name, Last Name, Designation, and DOB. The page also provides the Edit, Delete, and Detail links for each employee record that is retrieved with the help of the people_employee servlet class.

Listing 23.16 shows the code of the employee_list.jsp file (save the employee_list.jsp file in the people-mgmt\jsp folder):

Listing 23.16: Showing the Code of the employee_list.jsp File

```
<%@ page language="java" %>
<%@ page session="true" %>
<%@ page import="com.Employee.*" %>
<%@ page import="java.io.*" %>
<%@ page import="java.util.*" %>
<html>
<head>
<title>www.peoplemanagementsolutions.com/Employee List</title>
<link rel="stylesheet" href="../css/mystyle.css" type="text/css" />
</head>
<body>
<table width="900" border="0" align="center">
<tr>
<td colspan="2"><%@ include file="../jsp/people_header.jsp" %></td>
</tr>
<tr>
<td width="900"><%@ include file="../jsp/people_default_menu.jsp" %></td>
</tr><tr>
<td width ="750" valign="top">
<div align=center class=boldblack>List of Employees</div>
<hr bgcolor="#AAAAAA">
<table  border="0"  width=100% >
<%!
  EmployeeDBObj employeeDBObj;
  ArrayList employeeList; // = new ArrayList();
%>
<%
   String dbopr = "";
   dbopr = (String)session.getAttribute("dbopr");
%>
<tr class="whitetext" height=20>
<td bgcolor ='#AAAAAA'>Emp Id</td>
<td bgcolor ='#AAAAAA'>F Name</td>
<td bgcolor ='#AAAAAA'>L Name</td>
<td bgcolor ='#AAAAAA'>Designation</td>
<td bgcolor ='#AAAAAA'> DOB</td>
<td bgcolor ='#AAAAAA' align='center' >Edit</td>
<td bgcolor ='#AAAAAA' align='center' >Delete</td>
<td bgcolor ='#AAAAAA' align='center' >Detail</td>
</tr>
<%
  employeeList = new ArrayList();
     employeeList = (ArrayList)session.getAttribute("EmployeeList");
  if ( employeeList != null && employeeList.size() > 0 ){
  for ( int size = 1; size <= employeeList.size() ; size++ ){
  employeeDBObj = new EmployeeDBObj();
  employeeDBObj = (EmployeeDBObj)employeeList.get(size-1);
%>
<form name="form1" method="post">
<tr bgcolor ='#AAAAAA' height=18>
<td align='left'><%=employeeDBObj.emp_id%></td>
<td align='left'><%=employeeDBObj.emp_f_name%></td>
<td align='left' ><%=employeeDBObj.emp_l_name%></td>
```

```
<td align='left'  ><%=employeeDBObj.level_id%></td>
<td align='left' ><%=employeeDBObj.dob%></td>
<td align='center' bgcolor="#AAAAAA">
<a href='http://localhost:8080/people-mgmt/servlet/people_employee?dbopr=edit'
class="yellowlink">Edit </a>
</td >
<td align='center' bgcolor="#AAAAAA">
<a href='http://localhost:8080/people-
mgmt/servlet/people_employee?dbopr=detail&&emp_id=<%=employeeDBObj.emp_id%>&&emp_f
_name=<%=employeeDBObj.emp_f_name%>' class="yellowlink">Detail </a>
</td >
<td align='center' bgcolor="#AAAAAA">
<a href='http://localhost:8080/people-
mgmt/servlet/people_employee?dbopr=delete&&emp_id=<%=employeeDBObj.emp_id%>'
class="yellowlink">Delete </a>
</td >
<%} }
%>
</tr>
</td>
</table>
</tr>
<tr>
<td colspan="2"><%@include file="../jsp/people_footer.jsp"%></td>
</tr>
</table></body></html>
```

The `Edit` link is used to forward the request of a user to search a page where the user has to fill the details of an employee. The user can delete an employee record from the database by using the `Delete` link, and can view the details of the employee by clicking the `Detail` link in the `employee_list` JSP page.

Figure 23.8 shows the `employee_list` JSP page:

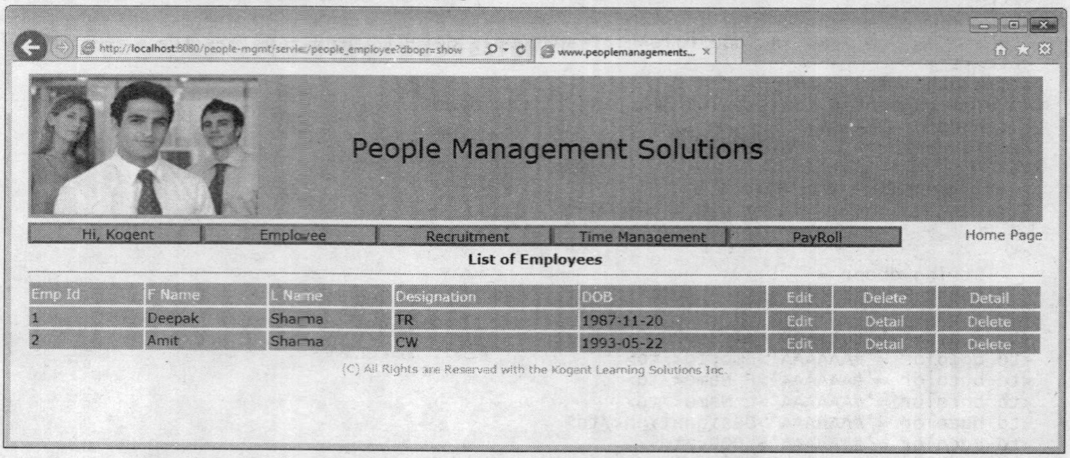

Figure 23.8: Displaying the List of Employees in the employee_list JSP Page

The records of all the employees added in this application are shown in Figure 23.8.

The next subsection describes the `employee_profile JSP` page.

Creating the employee_profile JSP Page

The `employee_profile` JSP page is designed to display the complete information of a particular employee. This JSP page contains all the fields that are used in the `employee_insert` JSP page. However, in the `employee_profile` JSP page all the fields are disabled. The employee records are retrieved on the basis of the values of the `Employee Id` and `First Name` fields.

Listing 23.17 shows the code of the `employee_profile.jsp` file (save the `employee_profile.jsp` file in the `people-mgmt\jsp` folder)

Listing 23.17: Showing the Code of the employee_profile JSP Page

```
<%@ page language="java" %>
<%@ page session="true" %>
<%@ page  import="com.Employee.*" %>
<html>
<head>
<title>www.peoplemanagementsolutions.com/Employee Detail</title>
<link rel="stylesheet" href="../css/mystyle.css" type="text/css" />
</head>
<body>
<table width="900" border="0" align="center">
<tr>
<td colspan="2"><%@ include file="../jsp/people_header.jsp" %></td>
</tr>
<tr>
<td width="900">
  <%@ include file="../jsp/people_default_menu.jsp" %></td>
</tr><tr>
<td width ="750" valign="top" align = "center">
<p> </p>
Employee Detail
<hr width=100% color=#AAAAAA>
<table  border="0" align="top" width=100% >
<%
  EmployeeDBObj employeeDBObj = new EmployeeDBObj();
  employeeDBObj = (EmployeeDBObj)session.getAttribute("employeeDBObj");
%>
<input type='hidden' name='emp_id' id='emp_id' size ='10'
value="<%=employeeDBObj.emp_id%>"/>
<input type='hidden' name='emp_f_name' id='emp_f_name 'size ='10'
value="<%=employeeDBObj.emp_f_name%>"/>
<input type='hidden' name='emp_m_name' id='emp_m_name' size ='10'
value="<%=employeeDBObj.emp_m_name%>"/>
<input type='hidden' name='emp_l_name' id='emp_l_name' size ='10'
value="<%=employeeDBObj.emp_l_name%>"/>
<input type='hidden' name='org_id' id='org_id' size ='10'
value="<%=employeeDBObj.org_id%>"/>
<input type='hidden' name='level_id' id='level_id' size ='10'
value="<%=employeeDBObj.level_id%>"/>
<input type='hidden' name='dept_id' id='dept_id' size ='10'
value="<%=employeeDBObj.dept_id%>"/>
<input type='hidden' name='dob' id='dob' size ='10'
value="<%=employeeDBObj.dob%>"/>
<input type='hidden' name='dojoin' id='dojoin' size ='10'
value="<%=employeeDBObj.dojoin%>"/>
<input type='hidden' name='address_1' id='address_1' size ='40'
value="<%=employeeDBObj.address_1%>"/>
<input type='hidden' name='address_2' id='address_2' size ='40'
value="<%=employeeDBObj.address_2%>"/>
<input type='hidden' name='city' id='city' size ='10'
value="<%=employeeDBObj.city%>"/>
<input type='hidden' name='state' id='state' size ='10'
value="<%=employeeDBObj.state%>"/>
<input type='hidden' name='nationality' id='nationality' size ='10'
value="<%=employeeDBObj.nationality%>"/>
<tr>
```

```
<td>Employee Id</td>
<td align='left'>
<input type='text' disabled='disabled' name='emp_id_dup' id='emp_id_dup' size
='10' value= "<%=employeeDBObj.emp_id%>"/>
</td>
<td> </td>
<td> </td>
</tr>
<tr>
<td>First Name</td>
<td align='left'>
<input type='text' disabled='disabled' name='emp_f_name_dup' id='emp_f_name_dup'
size ='10' value="<%=employeeDBObj.emp_f_name%>"/>
</td>
<td colspan=2>
Middle Name   
<input type='text' disabled='disabled' name='dup_emp_m_name' id='emp_m_name' size
='10' value="<%=employeeDBObj.emp_m_name%>"/>
   Last Name   
<input type='text' disabled='disabled' name='dup_emp_l_name' id='dup_emp_l_name'
size ='10' value="<%=employeeDBObj.emp_l_name%>"/>
</td>
</tr>
<tr>
<td>Org Id</td>
<td align='left'>
<input type='text' disabled='disabled' name='dup_org_id' id='dup_org_id' size
='10' value="<%=employeeDBObj.org_id%>"/>
</td>
<td>Designation</td>
<td align='left'>
<input type='text' disabled='disabled' name='dup_level_id' id='dup_level_id' size
='10' value="<%=employeeDBObj.level_id%>"/>
</td>
</tr>
<tr>
<td>Dept</td>
<td align='left'>
<input type='text' disabled='disabled' name='dup_dept_id' id='dup_dept_id' size
='10' value="<%=employeeDBObj.dept_id%>"/>
</td>
<td>DOB</td>
<td align='left'><input type='text' disabled='disabled' name='dup_dob'
id='dup_dob' size ='10' value="<%=employeeDBObj.dob%>"/>
(yyyy-mm-dd)</td>
</tr>
<tr>
<td>Join Date</td>
<td align='left'>
<input type='text' disabled='disabled' name='dup_dojoin' id='dup_dojoin' size
='10' value="<%=employeeDBObj.dojoin%>"/>
(yyyy-mm-dd)</td>
<td> </td>
<td> </td>
</tr>
<tr>
```

```
<td>Address1</td>
<td align='left' colspan='2'>
<input type='text' name='dup_address_1' id='dup_address_1' disabled='disabled'
size ='40' value="<%=employeeDBObj.address_1%>"/>
</td>
<td> </td>
<td> </td>
</tr>
<tr>
<td>Address2</td>
<td align='left' colspan='2'>
<input type='text' disabled='disabled' name='dup_address_2' id='dup_address_2'
size ='40' value="<%=employeeDBObj.address_2%>"/>
</td>
<td> </td>
<td> </td>
</tr>
<tr>
<td>City</td>
<td align='left'>
<input type='text' disabled='disabled' name='dup_city' id='dup_city' size ='10'
value="<%=employeeDBObj.city%>"/>
</td>
<td> </td>
<td> </td>
</tr>
<tr>
<td>State</td>
<td align='left'>
<input type='text' disabled='disabled' name='dup_state' id='dup_state' size ='10'
value="<%=employeeDBObj.state%>"/>
</td>
<td>Nationality</td>
<td align='left'>
<input type='text' disabled='disabled' name='dup_nationality' id='dup_nationality'
size ='10' value="<%=employeeDBObj.nationality%>"/>
</td>
</tr>
</table>
<hr width=100% color=#AAAAAA>
</td>
</tr>
<tr>
<td colspan="2"><%@include file="../jsp/people_footer.jsp"%></td>
</tr>
</table>
</body>
</html>
```

Listing 23.17 specifies the code of the `employee_profile` JSP page that would be displayed after clicking the `Detail` link of the `employee_list` JSP page. In employee_profile.jsp file all the fields are disabled to prevent the profile from any modification. Figure 23.9 shows the `employee_profile` JSP page:

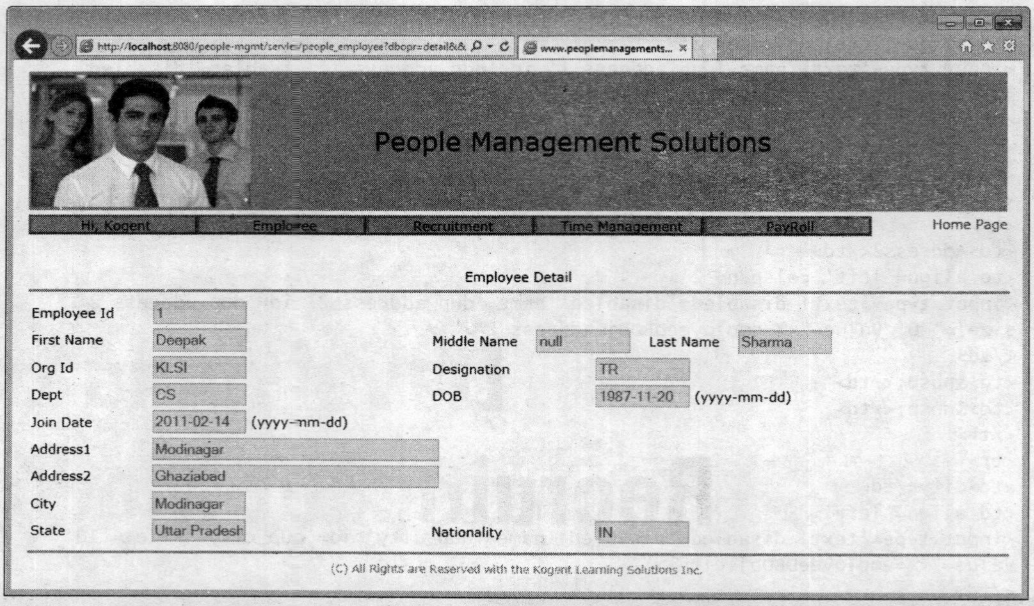

Figure 23.9: Displaying Complete Profile of a Selected Employee in the employee_profile JSP Page

Figure 23.9 shows the complete profile of an employee.

In the next section, you learn how to develop the Recruitment module, which deals with the recruitment process of a new candidate in an organization. The work of this module starts with registering a new candidate and updating the number of test details for different rounds.

Section C

Developing the Recruitment Module

Recruitment of a new employee is a process in which an organization tests the skills of an applicant on the basis of various tests and finally selects the appropriate applicant for the vacancy. The process starts with the registration of the applicants and calling the short listed candidates for written test. Next, the results of all the candidates are updated on the basis of the marks obtained by them. The candidates who clear the written test are called for the next round, in our case, technical round. This process continues till the final selection of the candidate happens. Let's now learn to develop the Recruitment module that provides various interfaces to handle the recruitment process of the new applicants.

Registering a New Applicant

The recruitment process starts with the registration of the applicants whose profiles have been searched or who have sent their resumes for consideration for a particular job opening in an organization. Any new candidate is registered by entering the necessary details, for which you need to design the the `applicant_register` interface and update the respective data in the `PEOPLE_APPLICANT` table. Further, you can see the list of registered candidates in the `applicant_list` JSP page and can also modify or delete a particular candidate's information.

Let's now create the following files for the recruitment module:

- people_applicant.java
- ApplicantDBObj.java
- ApplicantDBMethods.java
- GenerateId.java

In addition to these Java classes, you also need to create the following JSP pages:

- applicant_register.jsp
- applicant_edit.jsp
- applicant_list.jsp

The next subsection discusses about the `people_applicant` servlet class.

Creating the people_applicant Servlet

The `people_applicant` servlet handles the process of registering an applicant with the help of the `ApplicantDBObj` object and the methods of the `ApplicantDBMethods` class. This servlet forwards the request of a user to the JSP page according to the action that has been set with the request. The object of the `ApplicantDBObj` class is used as a Data Transfer Object (DTO) for this module, and its values are initialized by using the methods of the `ApplicantDBMethods` class.

Listing 23.18 shows the code of the `people_applicant` servlet (save the `people_applicant.java` file in the `people-mgmt\WEB-INF\src` folder):

Listing 23.18: Showing the Code of the people_applicant.java File

```
import javax.servlet.*;
import javax.servlet.http.*;
import java.util.ArrayList;
import java.io.*;
import java.util.*;
import java.sql.*;
import com.Applicant.*;
import javax.servlet.annotation.*;
import javax.servlet.annotation.WebServlet;

@WebServlet(name="people_applicant", urlPatterns="/servlet/people_applicant")
public class people_applicant extends HttpServlet{
   String lDBUser  = "";
   String lDBPswd  = "";
   String lDBUrl   = "";

/**Initialize global variables*/
   @Override
```

```
    public void init(ServletConfig config) throws ServletException{
          System.out.println("initializing controller servlet.");
          ServletContext context = config.getServletContext();
          lDBUser = "scott";
          lDBPswd = "tiger";
          lDBUrl  = "jdbc:oracle:thin:@192.168.1.123:1521:"+"XE";
          super.init(config);
    }
  /**Process the HTTP Get request*/
    @Override
    public void doGet(HttpServletRequest request, HttpServletResponse response)
        throws ServletException, IOException{
          doPost(request, response);
    }
  /**Process the HTTP Post request*/
    @Override
    public void doPost(HttpServletRequest request, HttpServletResponse response)
        throws ServletException, IOException{
          response.setContentType("text/html");
          PrintWriter out = response.getWriter();
          HttpSession session = request.getSession();
          session.setAttribute("lErrorMsg",null);
          String target = "";
          String action = request.getParameter("action");
          String lDBOpr = "";
          lDBOpr = (String)request.getParameter("dbopr");
          session.setAttribute("dbopr",lDBOpr);
          if( (lDBOpr != null && lDBOpr.length() > 0) &&
              (lDBOpr.equals("register")) ){
                 target = "/jsp/applicant_register.jsp";
          }
          else
          if( (lDBOpr != null && lDBOpr.length() > 0) &&
              (lDBOpr.equals("edit")) ){
                 action = "people_applicant_edit";
          }
          else
          if( (lDBOpr != null && lDBOpr.length() > 0) &&
              (lDBOpr.equals("delete")) ){
                 action = "people_applicant_delete";
          }
          else
          if( (lDBOpr != null && lDBOpr.length() > 0) &&
              (lDBOpr.equals("detail")) ){
                 action = "people_applicant_detail";
          }
          else{
                 action = "people_applicant_select";
          }
          String action_submit = request.getParameter("action_submit");
          String action_edit = request.getParameter("action_edit");
          System.out.println("action_submit=="+action_submit);
          if ( action_submit != null || action_edit != null ){
                 if ( request.getParameter("submit").equals("Submit") ){
                        System.out.println("in the  Submit");
          if ( action_submit.equals("people_applicant_register_submit") ){
            System.out.println("in the people_applicant_register_submit ");
            action = "people_applicant_register_submit";
          }
          else
          if (action_submit.equals("people_applicant_search_submit")){
                 action = "people_applicant_search_submit";
          }
    }
    else
```

```
    if ( request.getParameter("submit").equals("Update") ){
           if ( action_edit.equals("people_applicant_edit_submit") )
                 action = "people_applicant_edit_submit";
           }
    }
    if (action!=null){
           System.out.println("in the  "+action);
         if (action.equals("people_change_pswd_submit")){
                 target = "/jsp/people_user_login_pswd_change.jsp";
         }
         else
         if (action.equals("people_applicant_register_submit")){
              ApplicantDBObj popApplicantDBObj = new ApplicantDBObj();
                   ApplicantDBMethods applicantDBMethods = new ApplicantDBMethods
                   (lDBUser, lDBPswd, lDBUrl);
              popApplicantDBObj = (ApplicantDBObj) applicantDBMethods.
                   populateApplicantDBObjFromReq(request);
              ApplicantDBObj applicantDBObj = new ApplicantDBObj();
              applicantDBObj = (ApplicantDBObj)applicantDBMethods.
                   getRecordByPrimaryKey(popApplicantDBObj.applicant_id);
          if ( ( (popApplicantDBObj.applicant_id) != null &&
              (applicantDBObj.applicant_id) != null) &&
              (popApplicantDBObj.applicant_id).equals(applicantDBObj.applicant_id) ){
                 String lErrorMsg = "Applicant Already Exist!!";
                 session.setAttribute("lErrorMsg",lErrorMsg);
                 target = "/jsp/applicant_register.jsp";
           }
           else{
           int rval =  applicantDBMethods.insertApplicant(popApplicantDBObj);
           ArrayList ApplicantList = new ArrayList();
           String criteria = "";
               ApplicantList = (ArrayList)applicantDBMethods.
                               selectApplicantByCriteria (criteria);
           session.setAttribute("ApplicantList",ApplicantList);
           target = "/jsp/applicant_list.jsp";
    }
  }
  else
  if (action.equals("people_applicant_select")){
  ApplicantDBMethods applicantDBMethods = new ApplicantDBMethods(lDBUser,
                                            lDBPswd,lDBUrl);
  ArrayList ApplicantList = new ArrayList();
  String criteria = "";
      ApplicantList =
      (ArrayList)applicantDBMethods.selectApplicantByCriteria(criteria);
      session.setAttribute("ApplicantList",ApplicantList);
      target = "/jsp/applicant_list.jsp";
  }
  else
  if (action.equals("people_applicant_edit")){
    String lApplicantId= "";
    lApplicantId = (String)request.getParameter("applicant_id");
    ApplicantDBMethods applicantDBMethods = new ApplicantDBMethods(lDBUser,
                                                  lDBPswd,lDBUrl);
    ApplicantDBObj applicantDBObj = new ApplicantDBObj();
    applicantDBObj =
           (ApplicantDBObj)applicantDBMethods.getRecordByPrimaryKey(lApplicantId);
    if ( applicantDBObj != null && ( applicantDBObj.applicant_id != null &&
          applicantDBObj.applicant_id.length() > 0 ) ){
           session.setAttribute("applicantDBObj",applicantDBObj);
           target = "/jsp/applicant_edit.jsp";
    }
    else{
           target = "/jsp/applicant_list.jsp";
    }
```

```
    }
    else
    if (action.equals("people_applicant_edit_submit")){
       ApplicantDBObj popApplicantDBObj = new ApplicantDBObj();
       ApplicantDBMethods applicantDBMethods = new
                        ApplicantDBMethods(lDBUser,lDBPswd,lDBUrl);
       popApplicantDBObj = (ApplicantDBObj)applicantDBMethods.
                              populateApplicantDBObjFromReq(request);
       ApplicantDBObj applicantDBObj = new ApplicantDBObj();
       int rval =  applicantDBMethods.updateApplicant(popApplicantDBObj);
       applicantDBObj = (ApplicantDBObj)applicantDBMethods.getRecordByPrimaryKey(
                           popApplicantDBObj.applicant_id);
       session.setAttribute("applicantDBObj",applicantDBObj);
       String criteria = "";
       ArrayList ApplicantList = new ArrayList();
       ApplicantList = (ArrayList)applicantDBMethods.
                          selectApplicantByCriteria(criteria);
       session.setAttribute("ApplicantList",ApplicantList);
       target = "/jsp/applicant_list.jsp";
    }
    else
    if (action.equals("people_applicant_delete")){
       String lApplicationId = "";
          lApplicationId = (String)request.getParameter("applicant_id");
       ApplicantDBMethods applicantDBMethods = new ApplicantDBMethods(lDBUser,
                                                   lDBPswd,lDBUrl);
       applicantDBMethods.deleteApplicant(lApplicationId);
       ArrayList ApplicantList = new ArrayList();
       String criteria = "";
       ApplicantList = (ArrayList)applicantDBMethods. selectApplicantByCriteria(
          criteria);
       session.setAttribute("ApplicantList",ApplicantList);
       target = "/jsp/applicant_list.jsp";
    }else
    if (action.equals("people_applicant_detail")){
       String lApplicationId = "";
       lApplicationId = (String)request.getParameter("applicant_id");
       ApplicantDBMethods applicantDBMethods = new ApplicantDBMethods(lDBUser,
          lDBPswd,lDBUrl);
       ApplicantDBObj applicantDBObj = new ApplicantDBObj();
       applicantDBObj = (ApplicantDBObj)applicantDBMethods.
                          getRecordByPrimaryKey(lApplicationId);
       session.setAttribute("applicantDBObj",applicantDBObj);
       target = "/jsp/applicant_edit.jsp";
    }
    }
       /* forwarding the request/response to the targeted view */
       RequestDispatcher requestDispatcher = getServletContext().
                                      getRequestDispatcher(target);
                requestDispatcher.forward(request, response);
       } // doPost closed
    }// class closed
```

In Listing 23.18, the @`WebServlet` annotation is used for servlet mapping, which eliminates the need to define servlet mapping in the `web.xml` file. The @`Override` annotation used in Listing 23.18 specifies that a method is overridden in the current class.

The next subsection describes the ApplicantDBObj class, which is used as a DTO.

Creating the ApplicantDBObj Class

The `ApplicantDBObj` class contains member variables matching with the columns of the PEOPLE_APPLICANT table. The methods of the `ApplicantDBMethods` class use the `ApplicantDBObj` object to manipulate database with the data set being represented by the `ApplicantDBObj` object.

Listing 23.19 provides the code of the `ApplicantDBObj.java` file (save the `ApplicantDBObj.java` file in the `people-mgmt\WEB-INF\src\com\Applicant` folder):

Listing 23.19: Showing the Code of the ApplicantDBObj.java File

```
package com.Applicant;
public class ApplicantDBObj
{
   public String applicant_id;
   public String applicant_name;
   public String address_1;
   public String address_2;
   public String current_location;
   public String email;
   public long phone;
   public long mobile;
   public String dob;
   public String gender
   public String nationality;
   public long work_exp
   public String skill;
   public String industry;
   public String category;
   public String roles;
   public String current_employer;
   public double current_sal;
   public String highest_degree;
   public String second_highest_degree;
   public String domain
}
```

Listing 23.19 provides code of the ApplicantDBObj class that contains all the variables with respect to the PEOPLE_APPLICANT table.

The next subsection discusses about the `ApplicantDBMethods` class.

Creating the ApplicantDBMethods Class

The `ApplicantDBMethods` class provides methods that are used to make the required changes in the details of an applicant, which is stored in the database. This implies that the methods and variables defined in the `ApplicantDBMethods` class are used to interact with the database. In the PeopleMgmt project, these methods separate the code responsible for the real interaction with the database. This class contains various methods that are used within other methods to perform various processes, such as:

- The insertApplicant() method: Inserts the details of a new applicant
- The updateApplicant() method: Updates the details of an existing applicant
- The deleteApplicant() method: Deletes the record of an applicant from the database
- The populateApplicantDBObjFromReq() method: Populates the ApplicantDBObj object with the values passed along with a request

Listing 23.20 provides the code of the `ApplicantDBMethods.java` file (save the `ApplicantDBMethods.java` file in the `people-mgmt\WEB-INF\src\com\Applicant` folder):

Listing 23.20: Showing the Code of the ApplicantDBMethods.java File

```
package com.Applicant;
import java.sql.*;
import javax.servlet.*;
import javax.servlet.http.*;
import java.io.*;
import java.util.*;
import java.util.ArrayList;
import com.Applicant.ApplicantDBObj;
public class ApplicantDBMethods
{
   public String DBUser;
   public String DBPswd;
```

```
    public String DBUrl ;
    public ApplicantDBMethods(){ }
    public ApplicantDBMethods(String inDBUser, String inDBPswd, String inDBUrl )
    {
         DBUser = inDBUser ;
         DBPswd = inDBPswd;
         DBUrl  = inDBUrl;
    }
    public void initializeApplicantDBObj(ApplicantDBObj inApplicantDBObj )
    {
         inApplicantDBObj.applicant_id =  "";
         inApplicantDBObj.applicant_name = "";
         inApplicantDBObj.address_1= "";
         inApplicantDBObj.address_2= "";
         inApplicantDBObj.current_location= "";
         inApplicantDBObj.email = "";
         inApplicantDBObj.phone = 0;
         inApplicantDBObj.mobile = 0;
         inApplicantDBObj.dob= "";
         inApplicantDBObj.gender = "";
         inApplicantDBObj.nationality= "";
         inApplicantDBObj.work_exp= 0;
         inApplicantDBObj.skill= "";
         inApplicantDBObj.industry= "";
         inApplicantDBObj.category= "";
         inApplicantDBObj.roles= "";
         inApplicantDBObj.current_employer= "";
         inApplicantDBObj.current_sal= 0;
         inApplicantDBObj.highest_degree= "";
         inApplicantDBObj.second_highest_degree= "";
         inApplicantDBObj.domain= "";
    }
    public ApplicantDBObj getRecordByPrimaryKey(String inApplicantId)
    {
         .. .. .. ..
         .. .. .. ..
    }
    public ArrayList selectApplicantByCriteria(String inCriteria)
    {
         .. .. .. ..
         .. .. .. ..
    }

    public int updateApplicant(ApplicantDBObj inApplicantDBObj)
    {
         .. .. .. ..
         .. .. .. ..
    }

  public ApplicantDBObj populateApplicantDBObjFromReq(HttpServletRequest inReq)
    {
         .. .. .. ..
         .. .. .. ..
    }
    public int insertApplicant(ApplicantDBObj inApplicantDBObj)
    {
         .. .. .. ..
         .. .. .. ..
    }
    public void deleteApplicant(String inApplicantId)
    {
         .. .. .. ..
         .. .. .. ..
    }
  }
```

Listing 23.20 defines the prototypes of each method depicting what a method accepts as an argument and what is being returned by the method.

Let's now discuss the code of each method.

The `getRecordByPrimaryKey()` method accepts a String as an argument, i.e. an applicant id of the applicant whose record from the PEOPLE_APPLICANT table is to be retrieved. This method executes a select query statement and the retrieved `ResultSet` object is saved to the `ApplicantDBObj` object. This object is then returned to the resultant JSP page.

Listing 23.21 provides the code of the `getRecordByPrimaryKey()` method:

Listing 23.21: Showing the Code of the getRecordByPrimaryKey() Method of the ApplicantDBMethods.java File

```
public ApplicantDBObj getRecordByPrimaryKey(String inApplicantId){
   ApplicantDBObj  applicantDBObj = new ApplicantDBObj();
   java.sql.Date date;
   try{
        DriverManager.registerDriver(new oracle.jdbc.driver.OracleDriver());
        Connection conn= DriverManager.getConnection(DBUrl,DBUser,DBPswd);
        Statement stmt = conn.createStatement();
        String lSqlString =      "select * from PEOPLE_APPLICANT ";
        lSqlString = lSqlString + "where applicant_id='"+inApplicantId+"' ";
        ResultSet rs  = null;
        rs  = stmt.executeQuery(lSqlString);
        System.out.println("lSqlString====trtrt==within getRecordByPrimaryKey==
                         "+lSqlString);
            if( rs.next()){
          applicantDBObj.applicant_id =  rs.getString("applicant_id");
          applicantDBObj.applicant_name = rs.getString("applicant_name");
          applicantDBObj.address_1 = rs.getString("address_1");
          applicantDBObj.address_2 = rs.getString("address_2");
          applicantDBObj.current_location = rs.getString("current_location");
          applicantDBObj.email = rs.getString("email");
          applicantDBObj.phone = rs.getLong("phone");
          applicantDBObj.mobile = rs.getLong("mobile");
          date=rs.getDate("dob");
          applicantDBObj.dob = date.toString();
          applicantDBObj.gender = rs.getString("gender");
          applicantDBObj.nationality = rs.getString("nationality");
          applicantDBObj.work_exp = rs.getLong("work_exp");
          applicantDBObj.skill = rs.getString("skill");
          applicantDBObj.industry = rs.getString("industry");
          applicantDBObj.category = rs.getString("category");
          applicantDBObj.roles = rs.getString("roles");
          applicantDBObj.current_employer = rs.getString("current_employer");
          applicantDBObj.current_sal = rs.getDouble("current_sal");
          applicantDBObj.highest_degree = rs.getString("highest_degree");
          applicantDBObj.second_highest_degree =
               rs.getString("second_highest_degree");
          applicantDBObj.domain = rs.getString("domain");
          System.out.println("fffff==="+rs.getString("applicant_id"));
        }
        else{
             initializeApplicantDBObj(applicantDBObj);
       }
          System.out.println("fffff====="+applicantDBObj.applicant_id);
       }
       catch(SQLException  ex){
          ex.printStackTrace();
          }
   return applicantDBObj;
}
```

The getRecordByPrimaryKey() method defined in Listing 23.21 returns the ApplicantDBObj object, as it searches the applicant on the basis of a primary key. Similarly, the `selectApplicantByCriteria()` method takes the inCriteria String variable containing the select query with the where clause used to obtain the desired result. The result may contain a list of the `ApplicantDBObj` objects; thereby, returning an object of the `ArrayList` class.

Listing 23.22 provides the code of the selectApplicantByCriteria() method:

Listing 23.22: Showing the Code of the selectApplicantByCriteria() Method of the ApplicantDBMethods.java File

```
public ArrayList selectApplicantByCriteria(String inCriteria){
  ArrayList ApplicantList = new ArrayList();
  java.sql.Date date;
  try{
        DriverManager.registerDriver(new oracle.jdbc.driver.OracleDriver());
        Connection conn= DriverManager.getConnection(DBUrl,DBUser,DBPswd);
        Statement stmt = conn.createStatement();
        String lSqlString =     "select * from PEOPLE_APPLICANT ";
        if( inCriteria != null && inCriteria.length() > 0 ){
              lSqlString = lSqlString +" "+inCriteria+"" ;
        }
        lSqlString = lSqlString +" order by applicant_id" ;
  System.out.println("Criteria===== "+inCriteria+" and query="+lSqlString);
  ResultSet rs  = null;
  rs  = stmt.executeQuery(lSqlString);
  while( rs.next()){
        ApplicantDBObj  applicantDBObj = new ApplicantDBObj();
        applicantDBObj.applicant_id =  rs.getString("applicant_id");
        applicantDBObj.applicant_name = rs.getString("applicant_name");
        applicantDBObj.address_1 = rs.getString("address_1");
        applicantDBObj.address_2 = rs.getString("address_2");
        applicantDBObj.current_location = rs.getString("current_location");
        applicantDBObj.email = rs.getString("email");
        applicantDBObj.phone = rs.getLong("phone");
        applicantDBObj.mobile = rs.getLong("mobile");
        date=rs.getDate("dob");
        applicantDBObj.dob = date.toString();
        applicantDBObj.gender = rs.getString("gender");
        applicantDBObj.nationality = rs.getString("nationality");
        applicantDBObj.work_exp = rs.getLong("work_exp");
        applicantDBObj.skill = rs.getString("skill");
        applicantDBObj.industry = rs.getString("industry");
        applicantDBObj.category = rs.getString("category");
        applicantDBObj.roles = rs.getString("roles");
        applicantDBObj.current_employer = rs.getString("current_employer");
        applicantDBObj.current_sal = rs.getDouble("current_sal");
        applicantDBObj.highest_degree = rs.getString("highest_degree");
        applicantDBObj.second_highest_degree =
                                 rs.getString("second_highest_degree");
        applicantDBObj.domain = rs.getString("domain");
        ApplicantList.add(applicantDBObj);
  }
}
catch(SQLException  ex){
  ex.printStackTrace();
}
return ApplicantList;
}
```

The code of Listing 23.22 is used to retrieve an applicant record on some `criteria`, such as `applicant_id` and the `test status`. The other important methods are `updateApplicant()`, `insertApplicant()`, and `deleteApplicant()`. These methods are used for updating, inserting, and deleting an applicant from the database.

Listing 23.23: Showing the Code of the updateApplicant(), insertApplicant(), deleteApplicant() Methods of the ApplicantDBMethods.java File

```
public int updateApplicant(ApplicantDBObj inApplicantDBObj){
  int recupd = 0;
```

```
    String lQuery = "";
    lQuery = lQuery +"update PEOPLE_APPLICANT set
                    email='"+inApplicantDBObj.email+"'  ";
    lQuery = lQuery +" , applicant_name='"+inApplicantDBObj.applicant_name+"' ";
    lQuery = lQuery +" , address_1='"+inApplicantDBObj.address_1+"' ";
    lQuery = lQuery +" , address_2='"+inApplicantDBObj.address_2+"' ";
       lQuery = lQuery +" ,
                   current_location='"+inApplicantDBObj.current_location+"' ";
    lQuery = lQuery +" , phone="+inApplicantDBObj.phone+" ";
    lQuery = lQuery +" , mobile="+inApplicantDBObj.mobile+" ";
    lQuery = lQuery +" , dob=to_date('"+inApplicantDBObj.dob+"','yyyy-mm-dd') ";
    lQuery = lQuery +" , gender='"+inApplicantDBObj.gender+"' ";
    lQuery = lQuery +" , nationality='"+inApplicantDBObj.nationality+"' ";
    lQuery = lQuery +" , work_exp="+inApplicantDBObj.work_exp+" ";
    lQuery = lQuery +" , skill='"+inApplicantDBObj.skill+"' ";
    lQuery = lQuery +" , industry='"+inApplicantDBObj.industry+"' ";
    lQuery = lQuery +" , category='"+inApplicantDBObj.category+"' ";
    lQuery = lQuery +" , roles='"+inApplicantDBObj.roles+"' ";
    lQuery = lQuery +" ,
                   current_employer='"+inApplicantDBObj.current_employer+"' ";
    lQuery = lQuery +" , current_sal="+inApplicantDBObj.current_sal+" ";
    lQuery = lQuery +" , highest_degree='"+inApplicantDBObj.highest_degree+"' ";
    lQuery = lQuery +" ,
          second_highest_degree='"+inApplicantDBObj.second_highest_degree+"' ";
    lQuery = lQuery +" , domain='"+inApplicantDBObj.domain+"' ";
    lQuery = lQuery +" where applicant_id='"+inApplicantDBObj.applicant_id+"' ";
    System.out.println("lSqlString===:"+lQuery);
    try{
          DriverManager.registerDriver(new oracle.jdbc.driver.OracleDriver());
          Connection conn= DriverManager.getConnection(DBUrl,DBUser,DBPswd);
          Statement stmt = conn.createStatement();
          recupd  = stmt.executeUpdate(lQuery);
    }
    catch(SQLException  ex){
          ex.printStackTrace();
    }
    return recupd;
  }
  public int insertApplicant(ApplicantDBObj inApplicantDBObj){
    int recupd = 0;
    String lQuery = "";
    lQuery = lQuery +"insert into PEOPLE_APPLICANT values ( ";
    lQuery = lQuery +" '"+inApplicantDBObj.applicant_id+"'  ";
    lQuery = lQuery +" , '"+inApplicantDBObj.applicant_name+"'  ";
    lQuery = lQuery +" , '"+inApplicantDBObj.address_1+"' ";
    lQuery = lQuery +" , '"+inApplicantDBObj.address_2+"' ";
    lQuery = lQuery +"   '"+inApplicantDBObj.email+"'  ";
    lQuery = lQuery +"   "+inApplicantDBObj.phone+" ";
    lQuery = lQuery +"   "+inApplicantDBObj.mobile+" ";
    lQuery = lQuery +"   to_date('"+inApplicantDBObj.dob+"','yyyy-mm-dd')";
    lQuery = lQuery +"   '"+inApplicantDBObj.gender+"' ";
    lQuery = lQuery +"   '"+inApplicantDBObj.nationality+"' ";
    lQuery = lQuery +"   "+inApplicantDBObj.work_exp+" ";
    lQuery = lQuery +"   '"+inApplicantDBObj.skill+"' ";
    lQuery = lQuery +"   '"+inApplicantDBObj.industry+"' ";
    lQuery = lQuery +"   '"+inApplicantDBObj.category+"' ";
    lQuery = lQuery +"   '"+inApplicantDBObj.roles+"' ";
    lQuery = lQuery +" , '"+inApplicantDBObj.current_employer+"' ";
    lQuery = lQuery +" , "+inApplicantDBObj.current_sal+" ";
    lQuery = lQuery +" , '"+inApplicantDBObj.highest_degree+"' ";
    lQuery = lQuery +" , '"+inApplicantDBObj.second_highest_degree+"' ";
    lQuery = lQuery +" , '"+inApplicantDBObj.domain+"' ";
    lQuery = lQuery +" , '"+inApplicantDBObj.current_location+"' ";
    lQuery = lQuery + " )";
    System.out.println("lSqlString===:"+lQuery);
```

```
        try{
              DriverManager.registerDriver(new oracle.jdbc.driver.OracleDriver());
              Connection conn= DriverManager.getConnection(DBUrl,DBUser,DBPswd);
              Statement stmt = conn.createStatement();
              recupd  = stmt.executeUpdate(lQuery);
        }
        catch(SQLException  ex){
              ex.printStackTrace();
        }
        return recupd;
    }
    public void deleteApplicant(String inApplicantId){
        try{
              DriverManager.registerDriver(new oracle.jdbc.driver.OracleDriver());
              Connection conn= DriverManager.getConnection(DBUrl,DBUser,DBPswd);
              Statement stmt = conn.createStatement();
              String lQuery = "";
              lQuery = lQuery +"delete from PEOPLE_APPLICANT ";
              lQuery = lQuery +" where applicant_id='"+inApplicantId+"' ";
              System.out.println("lSqlString===:"+lQuery);
              stmt.executeQuery(lQuery);
        }
        catch(SQLException  ex){
              ex.printStackTrace();
        }
    }
```

In Listing 23.23, the `insertApplicant()` method inserts the details of an applicant; whereas, the `updateApplicant()` method updates the applicant profile, if edited. The `deleteApplicant()` method deletes an applicant profile. The last method, `populateApplicantDBObjFromReq()`, accepts the `HttpServletRequest` object as an argument and populates an object of the `ApplicantDBObj` class with the values fetched using the `request.getParameter()` method, and finally returns that object.

Listing 23.24 provides the code of the `populateApplicantDBObjFromReq()` method:

Listing 23.24: Showing the Code of the populateApplicantDBObjFromReq() Method of the ApplicantDBMethods.java File

```
    public ApplicantDBObj populateApplicantDBObjFromReq(HttpServletRequest inReq){
       ApplicantDBObj  applicantDBObj = new ApplicantDBObj();
       applicantDBObj.applicant_id   =  (String)inReq.getParameter("applicant_id");
       applicantDBObj.applicant_name =
                                  (String)inReq.getParameter("applicant_name");
       applicantDBObj.address_1 = (String)inReq.getParameter("address_1");
       applicantDBObj.address_2 = (String)inReq.getParameter("address_2");
       applicantDBObj.current_location =
                                 (String)inReq.getParameter("current_location");
       applicantDBObj.email  = (String)inReq.getParameter("email");
       applicantDBObj.phone  = Long.parseLong((String)inReq.getParameter("phone"));
       applicantDBObj.mobile =
                             Long.parseLong((String)inReq.getParameter("mobile"));
       applicantDBObj.dob = (String)inReq.getParameter("dob");
       applicantDBObj.gender = (String)inReq.getParameter("gender");
       applicantDBObj.nationality = (String)inReq.getParameter("nationality");
       applicantDBObj.work_exp =
                            Long.parseLong((String)inReq.getParameter("work_exp"));
       applicantDBObj.skill = (String)inReq.getParameter("skill");
       applicantDBObj.industry = (String)inReq.getParameter("industry");
       applicantDBObj.category = (String)inReq.getParameter("category");
       applicantDBObj.roles = (String)inReq.getParameter("roles");
       applicantDBObj.current_employer =
                                 (String)inReq.getParameter("current_employer");
       applicantDBObj.current_sal =
                      Double.parseDouble((String)inReq.getParameter("current_sal"));
       applicantDBObj.highest_degree =
                                  (String)inReq.getParameter("highest_degree");
       applicantDBObj.second_highest_degree =
```

```
                        (String)inReq.getParameter("second_highest_degree");
    applicantDBObj.domain = (String)inReq.getParameter("domain");
    return applicantDBObj;
}
```

The code given in Listing 23.24 is used to populate the applicant details from the request page by using the object of the `HttpServletRequest` interface. Compile the Java files to get class files and place them in the `WEB-INF/classes` folder.

Creating the GenerateId Class

The `GenerateId` class is developed for the purpose of auto-generation of the `applicant_id`.

Listing 23.25 shows the code for the `GenerateId.java` file (save the `GenerateId.java` file in the `people-mgmt\WEB-INF\src\com\Applicant` folder):

Listing 23.25: Showing the Code of the GenerateId.java File

```
package com.Applicant;
import java.sql.*;
import javax.sql.*;
public class GenerateId
{
   public int generateApplicantId(){
   int applicant_id=0;
   try{
      Class.forName("oracle.jdbc.driver.OracleDriver");
      Connection conn=
      DriverManager.getConnection("jdbc:oracle:thin:@192.168.1.123:1521:"+
                                  "XE","scott","      tiger");
         Statement stmt = conn.createStatement();
      String query="select max(applicant_id) as applicant_id from
                            PEOPLE_APPLICANT ";
      ResultSet rs = null;
      rs = stmt.executeQuery(query);
      if(rs.next()){
         String id = rs getString("applicant_id");
         applicant_id=Integer.parseInt(id);
      }
      applicant_id = applicant_id + 1;
      }
      catch(SQLException ex){
         ex.printStackTrace();
      }
      catch(Exception e) {
         e.printStackTrace();
      }
   return applicant_id;
}
```

Listing 23.25 contains the code for auto-generation of the `applicant_id` field.

Let's now learn how to create the user interfaces in the next subsections.

Creating an Interface for Applicant Registration

After creating the required Java source files, let's now create all the required JSP pages of the recruitment module. There are three view pages designed for this module, namely, `applicant_register`, `applicant_edit`, and `applicant_list`. These JSP pages provide forms for entering details of the new applicants and display the details of all applicants in a tabular form.

Let's now discuss all these JSPs with their functionalities and codes.

Creating the applicant_register JSP Page

The recruitment process begins by registering a new applicant. The form required for a new registration is provided by the `applicant_register` JSP page. This page includes a form with fields, such as `Applicant`

Id, Name, Address1, Address2, City, Date of Birth (DOB), and Professional & Educational Details.

Listing 23.26 shows the code of the applicant_register JSP page, which creates a form with all the previously stated fields (save the applicant_register.jsp file in the people-mgmt\jsp folder):

Listing 23.26: Showing the Code of the applicant_register.jsp File

```
<%@ page language="java" %>
<%@ page session="true" %>
<%@ page  import="com.Applicant.*" %>
<%  GenerateId gen=new GenerateId();
    int applicant_id=gen.generateApplicantId();
%>
<html>
<head>
<title>www.peoplemanagementsolutions.com/Register New Applicant</title>
<link rel="stylesheet" href="../css/mystyle.css" type="text/css"/>
<script language="javascript">
   function validateForm() {
     var myName=document.form1.applicant_name.value;
      if (myName =="") {
         alert ("Applicant name cannot be blank");
         document.form1.applicant_name.focus();
   return false;

      }
      myName=document.form1.address_1.value;
      if (myName =="") {
         alert ("Address1 cannot be blank");
   document.form1.address_1.focus();
         return false;
      }
      myName=document.form1.current_location.value;
      if (myName =="") {
         alert ("Current Location cannot be blank");
   document.form1.current_location.focus();
         return false;
      }

      myName=document.form1.email.value;
      if (myName =="") {
         alert ("Email cannot be blank");
   document.form1.email.focus();
         return false;
      }
      myName=document.form1.phone.value;
      if (myName =="") {
         alert ("Phone Field cannot be blank");
   document.form1.phone.focus();
         return false;
      }
      myName=document.form1.mobile.value;
      if (myName =="") {
         alert ("Mobile cannot be blank");
   document.form1.mobile.focus();
         return false;
      }
      myName=document.form1.dob.value;
      if (myName =="") {
         alert ("You Should Provide Date of Birth");
   document.form1.dob.focus();
         return false;
      }
      myName=document.form1.skill.value;
      if (myName =="") {
```

```
            alert ("You should provide the Skills, you know");
        document.form1.dept_id.focus();
            return false
        }
        myName=document.form1.highest_degree.value;
        if (myName =="") {
         alert ("Provide Highest Qualification");
    document.form1.dojoin.focus();
         return false;
        }
        myName=document.form1.second_highest_degree.value;
        if (myName =="") {
         alert ("Provide your Second highest Qualification");
    document.form1.second_highest_degree.focus();
         return false;
        }
        myName=document.form1.domain.value;
        if (myName =="") {
         alert ("Provide the domain on which you can work");
    document.form1.domain.focus();
         return false;
        }
   form1.submit();
   }
</script>
</head>
<body>
<table width="900" border="0" align="center">
<tr>
<td colspan="2" >
<%@ include file="../jsp/people_header.jsp" %>
</td>
</tr>
<tr>
<td width="900" valign="top">
   <%@ include file=". /jsp/people_default_menu.jsp" %>
</td>
</tr>
<tr>
<td width ="750">
<table  border="0" align="top" width=100%>
<form name="form1" method="post">
<input type='hidden' name='applicant_id' id='applicant_id 'size ='10' value='<%=
                                  applicant_id %>'/>
<tr>
<td bgcolor ='#AAAAAA' colspan='4' align=center height=20><b>Contact
                                  Information</b></td>
</tr>
<tr><td width=150 >Applicant Id</td>
<td align='left' ><input type='text' disabled='disabled' name='dup_applicant_id'
         id='dup_applicant_id 'size ='10' value='<%= applicant_id %>'/></td>
<td> </td><td> </td>
</tr>
<tr>
<td>Name<sup>*</sup></td><td>
<input type='text' name='applicant_name' id='applicant_name 'size ='40' value=''
                                                            /></td>
<td> </td><td> </td>
</tr>
<tr><td>Address1<sup>*</sup></td>
<td><input type='text' name='address_1' id='address_1' size ='40' value=''/></td>
<td> </td><td> </td>
</tr>
<tr><td>Address2</td>
<td><input type='text' name='address_2' id='address_2' size ='40' value=''/></td>
```

```
<td> </td><td> </td>
</tr>
<tr><td>Current Location<sup>*</sup></td>
<td>
<input type='text' name='current_location' id='current_location' size ='15'
                                        value=''/>
</td><td>Email<sup>*</sup></td>
<td><input type='text' name='email' id='email' size ='25' value=''/></td>
</tr>
<tr><td>Phone<sup>*</sup></td>
<td><input type='text' name='phone' id='phone' size ='15' maxLength="8"
                                  value=''/></td>
<td>Mobile<sup>*</sup></td>
<td><input type='text' name='mobile' id='mobile' maxLength="10" size ='15'
                            value=''/></td>
</tr>
<tr>
<td bgcolor ='#AAAAAA' colspan='4' align=center height=20><b>Personal
                                  Information</b></td>
</tr>
<tr><td colspan='4'><br>
DOB<sup>*</sup><input type='text' name='dob' id='dob' size ='10' value=''/>(yyyy-
       mm-dd)   
Gender   <input type='radio' name='gender' id='gender' size ='10'
value='Male'/> Male    <input type='radio' name='gender' id='gender'
                                  size='10' value='Female'> Female
   Nationality   
<select name='nationality' id='nationality'>
<option selected>Select Nationality
<option value='IN'> Indian
<option value='RS'> Russian
<option value='PK'> Pakistani
<option value='AM'> American
<option value='BR'> British
<option value='SR'> Srilankan
</select><br></td>
<tr>
<td bgcolor ='#AAAAAA' colspan='4' align=center height=20><b>Professionals &
                                  Educational Details</b><td>
</tr>
<tr><td>Work Exp</td>
<td><input type='text' name='work_exp' id='work_exp' size ='10' value=''/></td>
<td> </td><td> </td>
</tr>
<tr><td>Skills<sup>*</sup></td>
<td><input type='text' name='skill' id='skill' size ='30' value=''/></td>
<td> </td><td> </td>
</tr>
<tr><td>Industry</td>
<td><input type='text' name='industry' id='industry' size ='30' value=''/></td>
<td> </td><td> </td>
</tr>
<tr>
<td>Category</td>
<td><input type='text' name='category' id='category' size ='10' value=''/></td>
<td> </td><td> </td>
</tr>
<tr><td>Roles</td>
<td><input type='text' name='roles' id='roles' size ='10' value=''/></td>
<td> </td><td> </td>
</tr>
<tr><td>Current Employer</td>
<td><input type='text' name='current_employer' id='current_employer' size ='30'
                                                  value=''/></td>
<td >Current Salary </td>
```

```
<td ><input type='text' name='current_sal' id='current_sal' size ='10'
                                                    value=''/></td>
</tr>
<tr><td>Highest Degree<sup>*</sup></td>
<td><input type='text' name='highest_degree' id='highest_degree' size ='10'
                                            value=''/></td>
<td colspan=2 align=right>Second Highest Degree<sup>*</sup>
    
<input type='text' name='second_highest_degree' id='second_highest_degree' size
                                                        ='10' value=''/>
</td></tr>
<tr><td bgcolor ='#AAAAAA' colspan='6' align=center height=20><b>Domain
                                    Knowledge<sup>*</sup></b></td>
</tr>
<tr><td>Domain<sup>*</sup></td>
<td><input type='text' name='domain' id='domain' size ='10' value=''/></td>
<td> </td><td> </td>
</tr>
<tr><td> All the ( <sup>*</sup>) marked are mandatory</td></tr><tr>
<td colspan=4 align=center><input type='submit' name='submit' id='submit' size
                ='10' value='Submit' onClick="return validateForm()"/></td>
</tr>
<input type='hidden' name='action_submit' id='action_submit' size ='10'
                    value='people_applicant_register_submit'/> </table>
</td>
</tr>
<tr>
<td colspan="2"><%@include file="../jsp/people_footer.jsp"%></td>
</tr>
</table></body></html>
```

In Listing 23.26, the value of the `Applicant Id` field is automatically generated and filled by the `generatApplicantId()` method of the `GenerateId` class. Due to this, the `Applicant Id` field is disabled. The client side validation is used for some fields, such as `Name`, `Address1`, `Email`, `Phone`, `DOB`, `Mobile`, and `Skills` to ensure that the user does not leave those fields blank.

Figure 23.10 shows the output of the `applicant_register` JSP page, in which the details of a new applicant are filled:

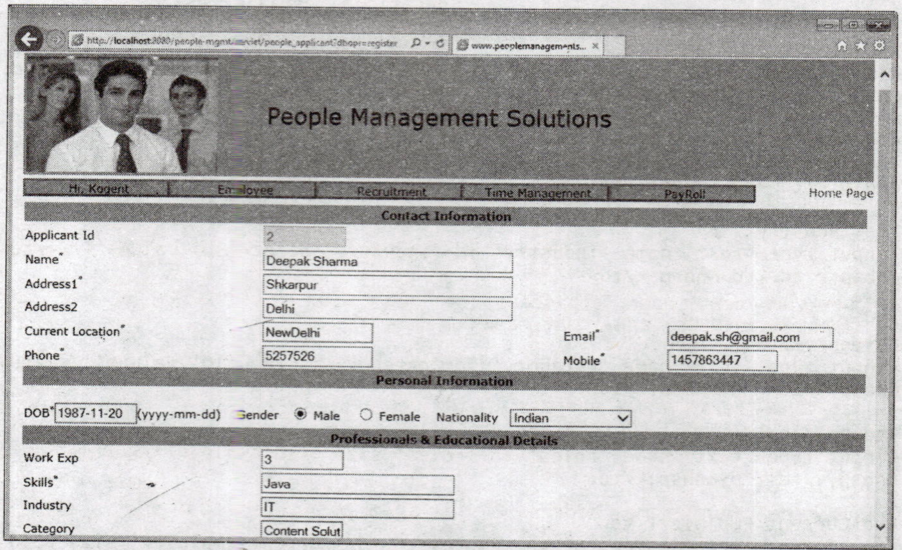

Figure 23.10: Displaying the Candidate Registration Form as the applicant_register JSP Page

Figure 23.10 shows the applicant registration form that needs to be filled up for all the applicants.

Creating the applicant_edit JSP Page

The `applicant_edit` JSP page allows you to edit the details of an applicant. You can update all the enabled fields with new values and submit the page to update the record for that applicant in the database.

The code of the applicant_edit JSP page has been shown in Listing 23.27 (save the `applicant_edit.jsp` file in the `people-mgmt\jsp` folder):

Listing 23.27: Showing the Code of the applicant_edit.jsp File

```
<%@ page language="java" %>
<%@ page session="true" %>
<%@ page  import="com.Applicant.*" %>
<html>
<head>
<title>www.peoplemanagementsolutions.com/Edit Applicant</title>
<link rel="stylesheet" href="../css/mystyle.css" type="text/css" />
</head>
<body>
<table width="900" border="0" align="center">
<tr>
<td colspan="2">
  <%@ include file="../jsp/people_header.jsp" %>
</td>
</tr>
<tr>
<td width="900" valign="top"><%@ include file="../jsp/people_default_menu.jsp"
%></td>
</tr>
<tr>
<td width ="750">
<table  border="0" align="top" width=100% >
<%
  String dbopr = "";
  dbopr = (String)session.getAttribute("dbopr");
  ApplicantDBObj applicantDBObj = new ApplicantDBObj();
  applicantDBObj = (ApplicantDBObj)session.getAttribute("applicantDBObj");
%>
<form name="form1" method="post">
<tr>
<td bgcolor ='#AAAAAA' colspan='4' align=center height=20><b>Contact
Information</b></td>
</tr>
<tr>
<td width=150 >Applicant Id</td>
<td align='left' >
<input type='text' disabled='disabled 'name='applicant_id_dup'
id='applicant_id_dup 'size ='10' value='<%=applicantDBObj.applicant_id%>'/>
</td>
<td>
<input type='hidden' name='applicant_id' id='applicant_id 'size ='20'
value='<%=applicantDBObj.applicant_id%>'/>
</td>
<td> </td>
</tr>
<tr><td>Name</td>
<td><input type='text' name='applicant_name' id='applicant_name 'size ='40'
value='<%=applicantDBObj.applicant_name%>' /></td>
<td> </td><td> </td>
</tr>
<tr><td>Address1</td>
<td><input type='text' name='address_1' id='address_1' size ='40'
value='<%=applicantDBObj.address_1%>'/></td>
<td> </td><td> </td>
</tr>
<tr><td>Address2</td>
<td><input type='text' name='address_2' id='address_2' size ='40'
value='<%=applicantDBObj.address_2%>'/></td>
<td> </td><td> </td>
</tr>
<tr><td>Current Location</td>
```

```
<td><input type='text' name='current_location' id='current_location' size ='10'
value='<%=applicantDBObj.current_location%>'/>
</td>
<td>Email</td>
<td><input type='text' name='email' id='email' size ='25'
value='<%=applicantDBObj.email%>'/></td>
</tr>
<tr><td>Phone</td>
<td><input type='text' name='phone' id='phone' size ='15' maxLength="8"
value='<%=applicantDBObj.phone%>'/></td>
<td>Mobile</td><td><input type='text' name='mobile' id='mobile' size ='15'
maxLength="10" value='<%=applicantDBObj.mobile%>'/></td>
</tr>
<tr>
<td bgcolor ='#AAAAAA' colspan='4' align=center height=20><b>Personal
Information</b></td>
</tr>
<tr><td colspan='4'><br>
DOB   <input type='text' name='dob' id='dob' size ='10'
value='<%=applicantDBObj.dob%>'/>
 (yyyy-mm-dd)   Gender   <input type='text'
name='gender' id='gender' size ='10' value='<%=applicantDBObj.gender%>'/>
   Nationality   <input type='text'
name='nationality' id='nationality' size ='10'
value='<%=applicantDBObj.nationality%>'/><br>.
</td>
<tr>
<tr>
<td bgcolor ='#AAAAAA' colspan='4' align=center height=20><b>Professionals &
Educational Details</b><td>
</tr>
<tr><td>Work Exp</td>
<td><input type='text' name='work_exp' id='work_exp' size ='10'
value='<%=applicantDBObj.work_exp%>'/></td>
<td> </td><td> </td>
</tr>
<tr><td>Skills</td>
<td><input type='text' name='skill' id='skill' size ='30'
value='<%=applicantDBObj.skill%>'/></td>
<td> </td><td> </td>
</tr>
<tr><td>Industry</td>
<td><input type='text' name='industry' id='industry' size ='30'
value='<%=applicantDBObj.industry%>'/></td>
<td> </td><td> </td>
</tr>
<tr><td>Catecory</td>
<td><input type='text' name='category' id='category' size ='10'
value='<%=applicantDBObj.category%>'/></td>
<td> </td><td> </td>
</tr>
<tr><td>Roles</td>
<td><input type='text' name='roles' id='roles' size ='10'
value='<%=applicantDBObj.roles%>'/></td>
<td> </td><td> </td>
</tr>
<tr><td>Current employer</td>
<td><input type='text' name='current_employer' id='current_employer' size ='30'
value='<%=applicantDBObj.current_employer%>'/></td>
<td >Current Salary </td>
<td ><input type='text' name='current_sal' id='current_sal' size ='10'
value='<%=applicantDBObj.current_sal%>'/></td>
</tr>
<tr><td>Highest Degree</td>
<td><input type='text' name='highest_degree' id='highest_degree' size ='10'
```

```
value='<%=applicantDBObj.highest_degree%>'/></td>
<td colspan=2 align=right>Second Highest Degree    
<input type='text' name='second_highest_degree' id='second_highest_degree' size
='10' value='<%=applicantDBObj.second_highest_degree%>'/>
</td>
</tr>
<tr>
<td bgcolor ='#AAAAAA' colspan='6' align=center height=20><b>Domain
Knowledge</b></td>
</tr>
<tr><td>Domain</td>
<td><input type='text' name='domain' id='domain' size ='10'
value='<%=applicantDBObj.domain%>'/></td>
<td> </td><td> </td>
</tr>
<%   if (dbopr != null && !dbopr.equals("detail")) { %>
 <tr>
 <td align='center' colspan='6'>
 <input type='submit' name='submit' id='submit' size ='10' value='Update'/> </td>
 <input type='hidden' name='action_edit' id='action_edit' size ='10'
value='people_applicant_edit_submit'/> </td>
 </tr>
<% } %>
</table>
</td>
</tr>
<tr>
   <td colspan="2"><%@include file="../jsp/people_footer.jsp"%></td>
</tr>
</table></form></body></html>
```

The `applicant_edit JSP page` (Listing 23.27) contains the fields similar to those defined in the `applicant_register JSP page`. The only difference is that some fields, such as `Applicant_Id` and `Name`, are disabled in the `applicant_edit JSP page`. In Figure 23.11, you can see that the `Applicant Id` field is disabled and all the other fields can be filled up with the new values to be updated in the database.

Figure 23.11 shows the applicant_edit JSP page:

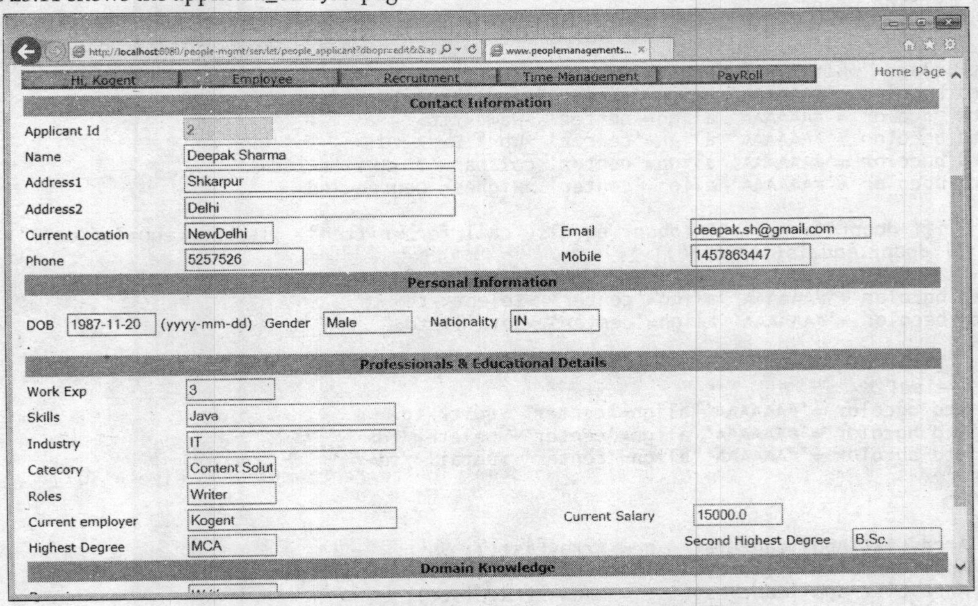

Figure 23.11: Displaying the Edit Page of an Applicant

In Figure 23.11, the details of a new applicant are displayed in the `applicant_edit JSP page`.

The next subsection describes the `applicant_list.jsp` file.

Creating the applicant_list JSP Page

The result of the `applicant_list` JSP page displays the details of all the registered applicants that can be deleted or edited, along with the list of applicants that have been shortlisted for the written round.

Listing 23.28 shows the code of the `applicant_list.jsp` file (save the `applicant_list.jsp` file in the `people-mgmt\jsp` folder):

Listing 23.28: Showing the Code of the applicant_list.jsp File

```
<%@ page language="java" %>
<%@ page session="true" %>
<%@ page  import="com.Applicant.*" %>
<%@ page  import="java.io.*" %>
<%@ page  import="java.util.*" %>
<html>
<head>
<title>www.peoplemanagementsolutions.com/Applicant List</title>
<link rel="stylesheet" href="../css/mystyle.css" type="text/css" />
</head>
<body>
<table width="900" border="0" align="center">
<tr>
<td colspan="2"><%@ include file="../jsp/people_header.jsp" %></td>
</tr>
<tr>
<td width="900"><%@ include file="../jsp/people_default_menu.jsp" %></td>
</tr>
<tr>
<td width ="750" valign="top">
<div align=center class=boldblack>List of Applicants</div>
<hr bgcolor="#AAAAAA">
<table  border="0"  width=100% >
<%
    String dbopr = "";
    dbopr = (String)session.getAttribute("dbopr");
%>
<tr class="whitetext" height=20>
<td bgcolor ='#AAAAAA' align='center' >Applicant Id</td>
<td bgcolor ='#AAAAAA' align='center' >Name</td>
<td bgcolor ='#AAAAAA' align='center' >Work Exp</td>
<td bgcolor ='#AAAAAA' align='center' colspan='2'>Skills</td>
<td bgcolor ='#AAAAAA' align='center' >Highest Degree</td>
<%
    if( dbopr != null && (dbopr.equals("call_for_written") || dbopr.equals("call")
  || dbopr.equals("remove")) ){
%>
<td bgcolor ='#AAAAAA' align='center' >Select</td>
<td bgcolor ='#AAAAAA' align='center' >Detail</td>
<%
    }
    else{ %>
  <td bgcolor ='#AAAAAA' align='center' >Edit</td>
  <td bgcolor ='#AAAAAA' align='center' >Delete</td>
  <td bgcolor ='#AAAAAA' align='center' >Detail</td>
<% }%>
</tr>
<%
  ArrayList ApplicantList = new ArrayList();
  ApplicantList = (ArrayList)session.getAttribute("ApplicantList");
  ArrayList applicantTestList =  new ArrayList();
  applicantTestList = (ArrayList)session.getAttribute("applicantTestList");
  if ( ApplicantList != null && ApplicantList.size() > 0 ){
```

```
        for ( int size = 1; size <= ApplicantList.size() ; size++ ){
                ApplicantDBObj applicantDBObj = new ApplicantDBObj();
                applicantDBObj = (ApplicantDBObj)ApplicantList.get(size-1);
%>
<form name="form1" method="post">
<tr bgcolor ='#AAAAAA' height=18>
<td align='center'  ><%=applicantDBObj.applicant_id%></td>
<td align='left'  ><%=applicantDBObj.applicant_name%> </td>
<td align='center' ><%=applicantDBObj.work_exp%></td>
<td align='left' colspan='2' ><%=applicantDBObj.skill%></td>
<td align='center' ><%=applicantDBObj.highest_degree%></td>
<%
  if( dbopr != null && ( dbopr.equals("call_for_written") ||
  dbopr.equals("call") || dbopr.equals("remove") )){
%>
<td align='center' bgcolor="#AAAAAA">
<a href='http://localhost:8080/people-
  mgmt/servlet/applicant_test_dtl?dbopr=call&&applicant_id=<%=applicantDBObj.a
        pplicant_id%>' class=yellowlink>Select</a></td >
<td align='center' bgcolor="#AAAAAA">
<a href='http://localhost:8080/people-
  mgmt/servlet/people_applicant?dbopr=detail&&applicant_id=<%=applicantDBObj.a
  pplicant_id%>' class=yellowlink>Detail </a></td >
<%
  }
  else{
%>
<td align='center' bgcolor="#AAAAAA">
<a href='http://localhost:8080/people-mgmt/servlet/people_applicant?
dbopr=edit&&applicant_id=<%=applicantDBObj.applicant_id%>' class="yellowlink">Edit
</a>
</td >
<td align='center' bgcolor="#AAAAAA">
<a href='http://localhost:8080/people-mgmt/servlet/people_applicant?
dbopr=delete&&applicant_id=<%=applicantDBObj.applicant_id%>'
class="yellowlink">Delete </a></td >
<td align='center' bgcolor="#AAAAAA">
<a href='http://localhost:8080/people-mgmt/servlet/people_applicant?
dbopr=detail&&applicant_id=<%=applicantDBObj.applicant_id%>'
class="yellowlink">Detail </a></td >
<%  } %>
</tr>
<% }
  if( applicantTestList != null && applicantTestList.size() > 0){
%>
<th bgcolor ='#AAAAAA' align='center' colspan='8'><font color=white>The Selected
  Applicant</font></th>
<%
  for ( int size = 1; size <= applicantTestList.size() ; size++ ){
  ApplicantDBObj applicantDBObj = new ApplicantDBObj();
  applicantDBObj = (ApplicantDBObj)applicantTestList.get(size-1);
%>
<tr bgcolor ='#AAAAAA'>
<td align='center'  ><%=applicantDBObj.applicant_id%></td>
<td align='left'  ><%=applicantDBObj.applicant_name%></td>
<td align='center' ><%=applicantDBObj.work_exp%></td>
<td align='left' colspan='2' ><%=applicantDBObj.skill%></td>
<td align='center' ><%=applicantDBObj.highest_degree%></td>
<%
  if( dbopr != null && ( dbopr.equals("call_for_written") ||
        dbopr.equals("call") || dbopr.equals("remove") )){
%>
<td align='center' colspan='2' bgcolor="#AAAAAA">
<a href='http://localhost:8080/people-mgmt/servlet/applicant_test_dtl?
        dbopr=remove&&applicant_id=<%=applicantDBObj.applicant_id%>'
```

```
        class=yellowlink>Remove </a></td >
<%} %>
</tr>
<% }%>
<% }
    if( dbopr != null && ( dbopr.equals("call") || dbopr.equals("remove") || (
        applicantTestList != null && applicantTestList.size() > 0) )){
%><tr>
<td align='center' colspan='8'><input type='submit' name='submit' id='submit' size
                ='10' value='Enter Test Detail'/> </td>
<input type='hidden' name='action_select' id='action_select' size ='10'
                value='applicant_call_for_wrtn_test_submit'/>
</tr>
<%  }
  }
  else{
   out.print("Applicant does not exist!!!");
} %>
</table>
</td>
</tr>
<tr>
<td colspan="2"><%@include file="../jsp/people_footer.jsp"%></td>
</tr>
</table></body></html>
```

The applicant_list JSP page shows the details of all the candidates in the form of a list, along with the Edit, Delete, and Detail links for all the applicants. The Edit and Delete links are used to edit or delete a registered applicant profile, respectively. The third link, `Detail`, is used to display the complete profile (non-editable) of an applicant.

Figure 23.12 shows the `applicant_list JSP page` containing the list of candidates:

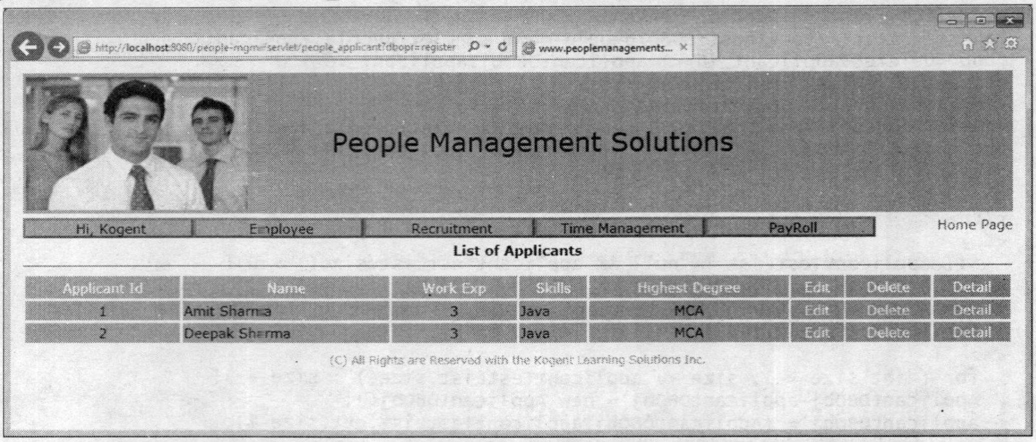

Figure 23.12: Displaying the List of Candidates in the applicant_list JSP Page

After registering all the details of the applicants, let's now provide the code to create the pages used to handle the details of different rounds of test during an interview, update the test result of each round, and select applicants for the next round.

Conducting Rounds of Test

After registering a new applicant, the shortlisted candidates are called for various rounds of test, which include written test, technical round, and finally the HR round. The Recruitment module deals with the process of shortlisting the selected candidates for further rounds; calling candidates for written test, technical round, and HR round by setting the test id, time, and date on which the test is to be conducted; and updating the results of the tests in each round. The process ends up with the issuing of the offer letter to the selected candidates.

The whole recruitment process is handled by a single servlet, applicant_test_dtl, which acts as a main controller servlet of the module. Let's now create the applicant_test_dtl servlet.

Creating the applicant_test_dtl Servlet

The applicant_test_dtl servlet is the most complex servlet, as it handles lots of requests and performs the desired task according to the request.

NOTE

As the code file for the applicant_test_dtl.java file is very large in size, we are not providing the full code in the section. You can find the complete code in the people-mgmt\WEB-INF\src folder online.

When the `people_applicant` servlet is invoked, a parameter named `dbopr` is passed with the query string, which is used to select the required path of execution by the servlet.

Listing 23.29 shows the code for the `applicant_test_dtl.java` file (save the `applicant_test_dtl.java` file in the `people-mgmt\WEB-INF\src` folder):

Listing 23.29: Showing the Code of the applicant_test_dtl.java File

```
import javax.servlet.*;
import javax.servlet.http.*;
import java.util.ArrayList;
import java.io.*;
import java.util.*;
import java.sql.*;
import com.Applicant.*;
import javax.servlet.annotation.*;
import javax.servlet.annotation.WebServlet;

@WebServlet(name="applicant_test_dtl", urlPatterns="/servlet/applicant_test_dtl")
public class applicant_test_dtl extends HttpServlet{
  String lDBUser  = "";
  String lDBPswd  = "";
  String lDBUrl   = "";
  /**Initialize global variables*/

  @Override
  public void init(ServletConfig config) throws ServletException{
        System.out.println("initializing controller servlet.");
        ServletContext context = config.getServletContext();
        lDBUser = "scott";
        lDBPswd = "tiger";
        lDBUrl  = "jdbc:oracle:thin:@192.168.1.123:1521:"+"XE";
        super.init(config);
  }
  /**Process the HTTP Get request*/

  @Override
  public void doGet(HttpServletRequest request, HttpServletResponse response)
  throws ServletException, IOException {
        doPost(request, response);
  }
  /**Process the HTTP Post request*/

  @Override
  public void doPost(HttpServletRequest request, HttpServletResponse response)
  throws ServletException, IOException {
        response.setContentType("text/html");
        PrintWriter out = response.getWriter();
        HttpSession session = request.getSession();
        session.setAttribute("lErrorMsg",null);
        String target = "";
        String action = request.getParameter("action");
        String lDBOpr = "";
        lDBOpr = (String)request.getParameter("dbopr");
```

```
        session.setAttribute("dbopr",lDBOpr);
        if( (lDBOpr != null && lDBOpr.length() > 0) &&
        (lDBOpr.equals("call_for_written")) ){ //call_for_written
                action = "people_applicant_select";
        }
        else if( (lDBOpr != null && lDBOpr.length() > 0) &&
                (lDBOpr.equals("call")) ){ //call
                action = "people_applicant_call";
        }
        else    if( (lDBOpr != null && lDBOpr.length() > 0) &&
                        (lDBOpr.equals("remove")) ){
                        action = "people_applicant_remove";
        }
        else    if( (lDBOpr != null && lDBOpr.length() > 0) &&
                        (lDBOpr.equals("detail")) ){
                        action = "people_applicant_detail";
        }
        else    if( (lDBOpr != null && lDBOpr.length() > 0) &&
                        (lDBOpr.equals("upd_wrtn_performance"))){
                        action = "upd_applicant_wrtn_performance";
        }
        else    if( (lDBOpr != null && lDBOpr.length() > 0) &&
                        (lDBOpr.equals("upd_tech_performance"))){
                        action = "upd_applicant_tech_performance";
        }
        else    if( (lDBOpr != null && lDBOpr.length() > 0) &&
                        (lDBOpr.equals("upd_hr_performance"))){
                        action = "upd_applicant_hr_performance";
        }
        else    if( (lDBOpr != null && lDBOpr.length() > 0) &&
                        (lDBOpr.equals("upd_wrtn_record"))){
                        action = "upd_wrtn_record";
    }
    else  if( (lDBOpr != null && lDBOpr.length() > 0) &&
                (lDBOpr.equals("upd_tech_record"))){
                action = "upd_tech_record";
    }
    else  if( (lDBOpr != null && lDBOpr.length() > 0) &&
                (lDBOpr.equals("upd_hr_record"))){
                action = "upd_hr_record";
    }
    else  if( (lDBOpr != null && lDBOpr.length() > 0) &&
                (lDBOpr.equals("shortlist_after_wrtn"))){
                action = "shortlist_after_wrtn";
        }
    if( (lDBOpr != null && lDBOpr.length() > 0) &&
                (lDBOpr.equals("shortlist_after_tech"))){
                action = "shortlist_after_tech";
    }
    if( (lDBOpr != null && lDBOpr.length() > 0) &&
                (lDBOpr.equals("shortlist_after_hr"))){
                action = "shortlist_after_hr";
    }
    else  if( (lDBOpr != null && lDBOpr.length() > 0) &&
          (lDBOpr.equals("applicant_call_for_tech"))){
                action = "applicant_call_for_tech";
    }
    else  if( (lDBOpr != null && lDBOpr.length() > 0) &&
                (lDBOpr.equals("applicant_call_for_hr"))){
                action = "applicant_call_for_hr";
    }
    else  if( (lDBOpr != null && lDBOpr.length() > 0) &&
          (lDBOpr.equals("applicant_call_for_final"))){
                action = "applicant_call_for_final";
    }
```

```
    else  if( (lDBOpr != null && lDBOpr.length() > 0) &&
                (lDBOpr.equals("delete")) ){
                action = "applicant_remove_for_tech";
    }
    else  if( (lDBOpr != null && lDBOpr.length() > 0) &&
          (lDBOpr.equals("discard")) ){
                action = "applicant_remove_for_hr";
    }
    else  if( (lDBOpr != null && lDBOpr.length() > 0) &&
                (lDBOpr.equals("discard_for_final")) ){
                action = "applicant_remove_for_final";
    }
    else  if( (lDBOpr != null && lDBOpr.length() > 0) &&
                (lDBOpr.equals("final_selected")) ){
                action = "applicant_final_selected";
    }
    String action_submit = request.getParameter("action_submit");
    String action_wrtn_dtl_submit = request.getParameter("action_wrtn_dtl_ submit ");
    String action_edit = request.getParameter("action_edit");
    String action_select = request.getParameter("action_select");
  ...................
  .......................
  ........................
    } // end of doPost
  } // end of class
```

In Listing 23.29, two annotations, `@WebServlet` and `@Override`, are used. The use of the `@WebServlet` annotation has eliminated the need to define the servlet mapping in the web.xml file and the `@Override` annotation is used to depict that the method is overridden. All the further actions taken by the servlet depend upon the various checks applied on the value set for the action variable. Various if-else blocks are used in the code to test numerous combinations of conditions resulting in an execution of different lines of code.

The servlet and other JSP pages in this document are highly reusable by nature, i.e. the same code file can be used in a number of ways for different purposes. The other important variable, named `criteria`, is set throughout the code with different string values, as shown in Listing 23.26. The same variable is being used multiple times specifying the criteria being concatenated to the query executed by the methods of the `ApplicantTestDtlDBMethods` class. The following code snippet shows how to set a value for `criteria` to execute different types of queries:

```
  .. .. .. ..
  .. .. .. ..
  .. .. .. ..

  if(dbopr != null && dbopr.equals("upd_wrtn_record"))
  criteria = "where test_status='W'";
  else
  if(dbopr != null && dbopr.equals("upd_tech_record"))
   criteria = "where test_status='T' and applicant_id not in (select applicant_id
     from APPLICANT_TEST_DETAIL where test_status in ('HR','confirm'))";
  else
  if(dbopr != null && dbopr.equals("upd_hr_record"))
   criteria = "where test_status='HR' and applicant_id not in (select applicant_id
     from APPLICANT_TEST_DETAIL where test_status in ('confirm'))";
  .. .. .. ..
  .. .. .. ..
  .. .. .. .
```

To view the full code of the servlet, you can get the file `applicant_test_dtl.java` from `people-mgmt\WEB-INF\src` folder placed online on the Dreamtech website.

The next subsection discusses the `ApplicantTestDtlDBObj.java` file.

Creating the ApplicantTestDtlDBObj Class

The `ApplicantTestDtlDBObj` class is similar to other data access objects that define attributes corresponding to the columns of the APPLICANT_TEST_DETAIL table. The object of this class is used to retrieve data from the APPLICANT_TEST_DETAIL table and make the data available to the programmer.

Listing 23.30 shows the code of the `ApplicantTestDtlDBObj.java` file (save the `ApplicantTestDtlDBObj.java` file in the `people-mgmt\WEB-INF\src\com\Applicant` folder):

Listing 23.30: Showing the Code of the ApplicantTestDtlDBObj.java File

```
package com.Applicant;
public class ApplicantTestDtlDBObj
{
   public String test_id;
   public String test_name;
   public String applicant_id;
   public String applicant_name;
   public String test_date;
   public String test_time;
   public String present_status;
   public long   total_marks;
   public long   marks_gained;
   public String test_status;
   public String pass_fail;
   public String next_round;
}
```

Creating the ApplicantTestDtlDBMethods Class

As the name suggests, the `ApplicantTestDtlDBMethods` class contains methods that are used by the `applicant_test_dtl` servlet to interact with the database and manipulate the data of the APPLICANT_TEST_DETAIL table

Listing 23.31 shows various methods for the `ApplicantTestDtlDBMethods` class (save the `ApplicantTestDtlDBMethods.java` file in the `people-mgmt\WEB-INF\src\com\Applicant` folder):

Listing 23.31: Showing the Code of the ApplicantTestDtlDBMethods.java File

```
package com.Applicant;
import java.sql.*;
import javax.servlet.*;
import javax.servlet.http.*;
import java.io.*;
import java.util.*;
import java.util.ArrayList;
import com.Applicant.*;
public class ApplicantTestDtlDBMethods
{
   public String DBUser;
   public String DBPswd;
   public String DBUrl ;
   public ApplicantTestDtlDBMethods(){ }

   public ApplicantTestDtlDBMethods(String inDBUser, String inDBPswd, String
          inDBUrl )
   {
          DBUser = inDBUser ;
          DBPswd = inDBPswd;
          DBUrl  = inDBUrl;
   }
   public void initializeApplicantTestDtlDBObj(ApplicantTestDtlDBObj
   inApplicantTestDtlDBObj )
   {
          .. .. .. ..
          .. .. .. ..
          .. .. .. ..
   }
```

```
public ApplicantTestDtlDBObj getRecordByPrimaryKey(String inApplicantId)
{
    .. .. .. ..
    .. .. .. ..
    .. .. .. ..
}
public int updateApplicantTestDtl(ApplicantTestDtlDBObj
    inApplicantTestDtlDBObj)
{
    .. .. .. ..
    .. .. .. ..
    .. .. .. ..
}
public ApplicantTestDtlDBObj populateApplicantTestDtlDBObjFromReq
(HttpServletRequest inReq)
{
    .. .. .. ..
    .. .. .. ..
    .. .. .. ..
}

public int insertApplicantTestDtl(ApplicantTestDtlDBObj
    inApplicantTestDtlDBObj)
{
    .. .. .. ..
    .. .. .. ..
    .. .. .. ..
}

public void deleteApplicant(String inApplicantId)
{
    .. .. .. ..
    .. .. .. ..
    .. .. .. ..
}
}
```

The ApplicantTestDtlDBMethods class contains various methods similar to the methods of the `xxxxxMethods` classes developed earlier in the project. For example, the `insertApplicantTestDtl()` method is used to insert a new record, the `updateApplicantTestDtl()` method is used to update an existing record, and the `deleteApplicant()` method is used to delete a record from the APPLICANT_TEST_DETAIL table.

Let's now discuss the different JSP pages that are used for view.

Designing JSP Views

In this project, the servlets are created to process and control the flow of the requests; whereas, other classes are used to implement other functionalities, such insert, edit, or delete records from the database. To implement the defined functionalities, you need to create user interfaces by using JSP pages.

Let's start the discussion with the `applicant_test_dtl_create` JSP page.

Creating the applicant_test_dtl_create JSP Page

The `applicant_test_dtl_create` JSP page is designed to provide the details of a new test. This JSP page contains various fields, such as `Test Id`, `Test Name`, `Test Date (yyyy-mm-dd)`, `Test Time (hh:mm)`, and `Total Marks`. The code of the `applicant_test_dtl_create` JSP page has been given in Listing 23.32 (save the `applicant_test_dtl_create.jsp` file in the `people-mgmt\jsp` folder):

Listing 23.32: Showing the Code of the `applicant_test_dtl_create.jsp` File

```
<%@ page language="java" %>
<%@ page session="true" %>
<html>
<head>
  <title>www.peoplemanagementsolutions.com</title>
  <link rel="stylesheet" href="../css/mystyle.css" type="text/css" />
```

```
</head>
<body>
<table width="900" border="0" align="center">
<tr>
  <td colspan="2" ><%@ include file="../jsp/people_header.jsp" %></td>
</tr>
<tr>
<td width="900" valign="top"><%@ include file="../jsp/people_default_menu.jsp"   %></td>
</tr>
<tr>
<td width ="750" valign="top">
<p> </p>
<hr width=500 color="#AAAAAA">
<table  border="0"  width=500 align=center>
<form name="form1" method="post">
<tr>
<td bgcolor ='#AAAAAA' colspan='4' align=center class=whitetext><b>Test
              Detail</b></td>
</tr>
<tr>
<td >Test Id</td>
<td align='left'><input type='text' name='test_id' id='test_id 'size ='10'
          value=''/></td>
<td>Test Name</td>
<td align='left'><input type='text' name='test_name' id='test_name' size ='10'
      value=''/></td>
</tr>
<tr>
<td>Test Date(yyyy-mm-dd)</td>
<td align='left'><input type='text' name='test_date' id='test_date 'size ='10'
           value='' /> </td>
<td>Test Time(hh:mm)</td>
<td align='left'><input type='text' name='test_time' id='test_time' size ='10'
         value=''/> </td>
</tr>
<tr>
<td>Total Marks </td>
<td align='left' ><input type='text' name='total_marks' id='total_marks' size
          ='10' value=''/></td>
<td> </td>
<td> </td>
</tr>
<tr>
<td align='center' colspan=4>
<input type='submit' name='submit' id='submit' size ='10' value='Submit Detail'/>
<input type='hidden' name='action_submit' id='action_submit' size ='10'
  value='people_applicant_wrtn_test_dtl_submit'/>
</td>
</tr>
</table>
<hr width=500 color="#AAAAAA">
</td>
</tr>
<tr>
<td colspan="2"><%@include file="../jsp/people_footer.jsp"%></td>
</tr>
</table></body></html>
```

In Listing 23.32, a hidden field is used to submit the test details. Figure 23.13 displays the output of the `applicant_test_dtl_create` JSP page:

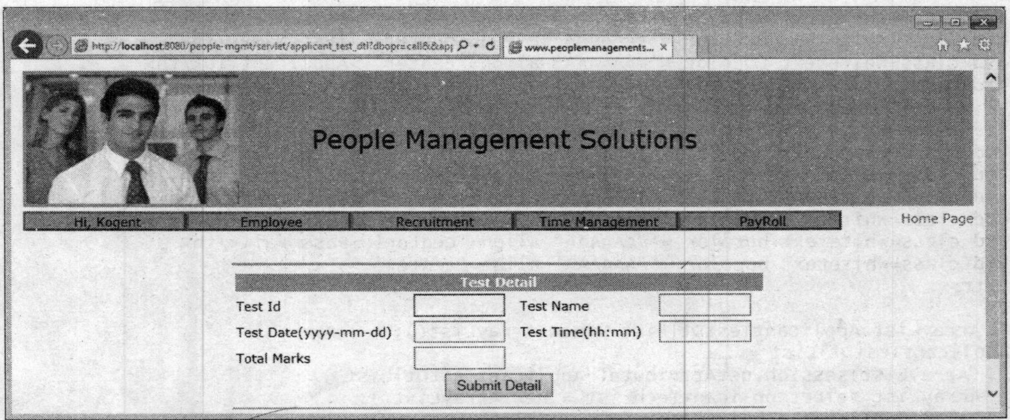

Figure 23.13: Displaying the applicant_test_dtl_create JSP Page to Add Test Details

In the `applicant_test_dtl_create` JSP page, you need to enter various details, such as `Test Id`, `Test Name`, `Test Date`, `Test Time`, and `Total Marks`.

Let's now discuss the other view page, the `applicant_test_dtl_list` JSP page.

Creating the applicant_test_dtl_list JSP Page

The `applicant_test_dtl_list` JSP page is used to provide a list of all the tests and their results. On the basis of the parameters that are passed with the query string, the details of an applicant for a round are displayed on the `applicant_test_dtl_list` JSP page. Listing 23.33 shows the use of the `dbopr` parameter to find out the proper if-block to be executed according to the specific round (`written round`, `technical round`, and `HR round`).

Listing 23.33 shows the code of the applicant_test_dtl_list.jsp file (save the `applicant_test_dtl_list.jsp` file in the `people-mgmt\jsp` folder):

Listing 23.33: Showing the Code of the applicant_test_dtl_list.jsp File

```
<%@ page language="java" %>
<%@ page session="true" %>
<%@ page  import="com.Applicant.*" %>
<%@ page  import="java.io.*" %>
<%@ page  import="java.util.*" %>
<html>
<head>
<title>www.peoplemanagementsolutions.com/Applicant Test Detail List</title>
<link rel="stylesheet" href="../css/mystyle.css" type="text/css" />
</head>
<body>
<table width="900" border="0" align="center">
<tr>
<td colspan="2"><%@ include file="../jsp/people_header.jsp" %></td>
</tr>
<tr>
<td width="900">
  <%@ include file="../jsp/people_default_menu.jsp" %>
</td>
</tr>
<tr>
<td width ="750" valign="top">
<table  border="0"  width=100% >
<%
  String dbopr = "";
        dbopr = (String)session.getAttribute("dbopr");
%>
<tr>
```

```
<td class=whitetext bgcolor ='#AAAAAA' align='center' >Test Id</th>
<td class=whitetext bgcolor ='#AAAAAA' align='center' >Test Name</th>
<td class=whitetext bgcolor ='#AAAAAA' align='center' >Applicant Id</th>
<td class=whitetext bgcolor ='#AAAAAA' align='center' colspan='2' >Applicant
        Name</th>
<td class=whitetext bgcolor ='#AAAAAA' align='center' >Test Date</th>
<td class=whitetext bgcolor ='#AAAAAA' align='center' >Test Time</th>
<td class=whitetext bgcolor ='#AAAAAA' align='center' >Present Status</th>
<td class=whitetext bgcolor ='#AAAAAA' align='center' >Total Marks</th>
<td class=whitetext bgcolor ='#AAAAAA' align='center' >Marks Gained</th>
<td class=whitetext bgcolor ='#AAAAAA' align='center' >Pass Fail</th>
<td class=whitetext bgcolor ='#AAAAAA' align='center' >--</th>
</tr>
<%
  ArrayList ApplicantTestDtlList = new ArrayList();
ApplicantTestDtlList =
  (ArrayList)session.getAttribute("ApplicantTestDtlList");
  ArrayList selectApplicantTechList = new ArrayList();
  selectApplicantTechList =
        (ArrayList)session.getAttribute("selectApplicantTechList");
  if ( ApplicantTestDtlList != null && ApplicantTestDtlList.size() > 0 ){
        for ( int size = 1; size <= ApplicantTestDtlList.size() ; size++ ){
        ApplicantTestDtlDBObj applicantTestDtlDBObj = new
                        ApplicantTestDtlDBObj();
        applicantTestDtlDBObj =
                (ApplicantTestDtlDBObj)ApplicantTestDtlList.get(size-
                        1);
%>
<form name="form1" method="post">
<tr bgcolor ='#AAAAAA'>
<td align='center'  ><%=applicantTestDtlDBObj.test_id%>
<input type='hidden' name='test_id' id='test_id' size ='20'
        value='<%=applicantTestDtlDBObj.test_id%>'/>
</td>
<td align='left'  ><%=applicantTestDtlDBObj.test_name%>
<input type='hidden' name='test_name' id='test_name' size ='20'
  value='<%=applicantTestDtlDBObj.test_name%>'/>
</td>
<td align='center'  ><%=applicantTestDtlDBObj.applicant_id%>
<input type='hidden' name='aplicant_id' id='aplicant_id' size ='20'
  value='<%=applicantTestDtlDBObj.applicant_id%>'/>
</td>
<td align='left' colspan='2' ><%=applicantTestDtlDBObj.applicant_name%>
<input type='hidden' name='applicant_name' id='applicant_name' size ='20'
  value='<%=applicantTestDtlDBObj.applicant_name%>'/>
</td>
<td align='center' ><%=applicantTestDtlDBObj.test_date%>
<input type='hidden' name='test_date' id='test_date' size ='20'
        value='<%=applicantTestDtlDBObj.test_date%>'/></td>
<td align='center' ><%=applicantTestDtlDBObj.test_time%>
<input type='hidden' name='test_time' id='test_time' size ='20'
        value='<%=applicantTestDtlDBObj.test_time%>'/>
</td>
<%
    if( applicantTestDtlDBObj.present_status != null )
   out.println("<td align='center'><input type='text' disabled='disabled'
 name='present_status' id='present_status 'size ='5' value='"
        +applicantTestDtlDBObj.present_status+"' /> </td>");
    else{
   out.println("<td align='center'  ><input type='text' disabled='disabled'
    name='present_status' id='present_status 'size ='5' value='' /></td>");
  }
%>
<td align='center'><%=applicantTestDtlDBObj.total_marks%>
<input type='hidden' name='total_marks' id='total_marks' size ='20'
```

```
    value='<%=applicantTestDtlDBObj.total_marks%>'/>
  </td>
  <td align='center'>
  <input type='text' disabled='disabled' name='marks_gained' id='marks_gained' size=
    '5' value = '<%=applicantTestDtlDBObj.marks_gained%>' />
  </td>
  <%
      if( applicantTestDtlDBObj.pass_fail != null )
    out.println("<td align='center'><input type='text' disabled='disabled'
    name='pass_fail' id='pass_fail 'size ='5' value='"
         +applicantTestDtlDBObj.pass_fail+"' /> </td>");
      else{
    out.println("<td align='center'><input type='text' disabled='disabled'
    name='pass_fail' id='pass_fail 'size ='5' value='' /> </td>");
    }
    if( dbopr != null && ( dbopr.equals("shortlist_after_wrtn") ||
    dbopr.equals("applicant_call_for_tech") || dbopr.equals("delete")) ){
    out.println("<td align='center' bgcolor ='#AAAAAA'>");
    out.println("<a href='http://localhost:8080/people-mgmt/servlet
    /applicant_test_dtl?dbopr=applicant_call_for_tech&&applicant_id="+applicantT
         estDtlDBObj.applicant_id+"' class=yellowlink>Select For Tech </a>");
       out.println("</td >");
    }
    else
    if( dbopr != null && ( dbopr.equals("shortlist_after_tech") ||
    dbopr.equals("applicant_call_for_hr") || dbopr.equals("discard")) )
    {
      out.println("<td align='center' bgcolor ='#AAAAAA'>");
    out.println("<a href='http://localhost:8080/people-
    mgmt/servlet/applicant_test_dtl?dbopr=applicant_call_for_hr&&applicant_id
    = "+applicantTestDtlDBObj.applicant_id+"' class=yellowlink>Select For HR
    </a>");
      out.println("</td >");
  }
  else
    if( dbopr != null && ( dbopr.equals("shortlist_after_hr") ||
          dbopr.equals("applicant_call_for_final") ||
                      dbopr.equals("discard_for_final")) )
    {
      out.println("<td align='center' bgcolor ='#AAAAAA'>");
      out.println("<a href='http://localhost:8080/people-
          mgmt/servlet/applicant_test_dtl?dbopr=applicant_call_for_final&&
          applicant_id="+applicantTestDtlDBObj.applicant_id+"' class=
                yellowlink>Select For FInal </a>");
      out.println("</td >");
    }
    else
    if( dbopr != null && ( dbopr.equals("upd_wrtn_performance") ||
          dbopr.equals("upd_wrtn_record")) )
    {
      out.println("<td align='center' bgcolor ='#AAAAAA'>");
      out.println("<a href='http://localhost:8080/people-
          mgmt/servlet/applicant_test_dtl?dbopr=upd_wrtn_record&&
          applicantid="+applicantTestDtlDBObj.applicant_id+" ' class=
                yellowlink>Edit </a>");
      out.println("</td >");
    }
    else
    if( dbopr != null && ( dbopr.equals("upd_tech_performance") ||
                dbopr.equals("upd_tech_record")) )
    {
      out.println("<td align='center' bgcolor ='#AAAAAA'>");
      out.println("<a href='http://localhost:8080/people-
          mgmt/servlet/applicant_test_dtl?dbopr=upd_tech_record&&
          applicantid="+applicantTestDtlDBObj.applicant_id+" '
```

```
        class=yellowlink>Edit </a>");
      out.println("</td >");
    }
    else
    if( dbopr != null && ( dbopr.equals("upd_hr_performance") ||
                 dbopr.equals("upd_hr_record")) )
    {
      out.println("<td align='center' bgcolor ='#AAAAAA'>");
      out.println("<a href='http://localhost:8080/people-
        mgmt/servlet/applicant_test_dtl?dbopr=upd_hr_record&&
        applicantid='+applicantTestDtlDBObj.applicant_id+" ' class=
        yellowlink>Edit </a>");
      out.println("</td >");
    }
    }
  }
  else{
    out.println("Applicant does not exist!!!");
  }
  if( selectApplicantTechList != null && selectApplicantTechList.size() > 0)
  {
  out.println("<tr>");
  out.println("<td class=whitetext bgcolor ='#AAAAAA' align='center'
    colspan='13'>The Selected Applicant</th>");
  out.println("</tr>");
  for ( int size = 1; size <= selectApplicantTechList.size() ; size++ ){
    ApplicantTestDtlDBObj applicantTestDtlDBObj = new ApplicantTestDtlDBObj();
    applicantTestDtlDBObj =
                (ApplicantTestDtlDBObj)selectApplicantTechList.get(size-1);
    out.println("<tr bgcolor ='#AAAAAA'>");
    out.println("<td align='center'  >"+applicantTestDtlDBObj.test_id+"</td>");
    out.println("<td align='center'  >"+applicantTestDtlDBObj.test_name+"
        </td>");
    out.println("<td align='center' >"+applicantTestDtlDBObj.applicant_id+
                "</td>");
    out.println("<td align='center' colspan='2' >"+applicantTestDtlDBObj.
                applicant_name+ "</td>");
    out.println("<td align='center' >"+applicantTestDtlDBObj.test_date+"</td>");
    out.println("<td align='center' >"+applicantTestDtlDBObj.test_time+"</td>");
    out.println("<td align='center'>"+applicantTestDtlDBObj.present_status
                    +"</td>");
    out.println("<td align='center' >"+applicantTestDtlDBObj.total_marks
                    +"</td>");
    out.println("<td align='center' >"+applicantTestDtlDBObj.marks_gained
                    +"</td>");
    out.println("<td align='center' >"+applicantTestDtlDBObj.pass_fail+"</td>");
  if( dbopr != null && ( dbopr.equals("shortlist_after_wrtn") ||
    dbopr.equals("shortlist_after_tech") || dbopr.equals
          ("applicant_call_for_tech") || dbopr.equals("delete") )){
    out.println("<td align='center' colspan='2' bgcolor ='#AAAAAA'>");
    out.println("<a href='http://localhost:8080/people-mgmt/servlet/
    applicant_test_dtl?dbopr=delete&&applicant_id="+applicantTestDtlDBObj.
          applicant_id+" ' class=yellowlink>Delete</a>");
    out.println("</td >");
  }
  else
  if( dbopr != null && ( dbopr.equals("shortlist_after_tech") ||
    dbopr.equals("applicant_call_for_hr") || dbopr.equals("discard") )){
    out.println("<td align='center' colspan='2' bgcolor ='#AAAAAA'>");
  out.println("<a href='http://localhost:8080/people-mgmt/servlet
  /applicant_test_dtl?dbopr=discard&&applicant_id="+applicantTestDtlDBObj
    .applicant_id+" ' class=yellowlink>Discard</a>");
    out.println("</td >");
  }
  else
```

```
if( dbopr != null && ( dbopr.equals("shortlist_after_hr") || dbopr.equals
("discard_for_final") || dbopr.equals("applicant_call_for_final")  )){
   out.println("<td align='center' colspan='2' bgcolor ='#AAAAAA'>");
   out.println("<a href='http://localhost:8080/people-mgmt/servlet/
        applicant_test_dtl?dbopr=discard_for_final&&applicant_id="+
        applicantTestDtlDBObj.applicant_id+" ' class=yellowlink
              >Remove</a>");
   out.println("</td >");
   }
   out.println("</tr>");
}
if( dbopr != null && (  dbopr.equals("delete") || dbopr.
              equals("applicant_call_for_tech") )){
   out.println("<tr>");
   out.println("<td align='center' colspan='13'><input type='submit'
   name='submit' id='submit' size ='10' value='Call For Tech'/> </td>");
   out.println("<input type='hidden' name='action_submit' id='action_submit'
        size ='10' value='applicant_call_tech_dtl_submit'/> ");
   out.println("</tr>");
}
else
if( dbopr != null && (  dbopr.equals("discard") || dbopr.equals
        ("applicant_call_for_hr") )){
   out.println("<tr>");
   out.println("<td align='center' colspan='13'><input type='submit'
   name='submit' id='submit' size ='10' value='Call For HR'/> </td>");
   out.println("<input type='hidden' name='action_submit' id='action_submit'
              size ='10' value='applicant_call_hr_dtl_submit'/> ");
   out.println("</tr>");
}
else
if( dbopr != null && (  dbopr.equals("discard_for_final") || dbopr.equals
        ("applicant_call_for_final") )){
   out.println("<tr>");
   out.println("<td align='center' colspan='13'><input type='submit'
   name='submit' id='submit' size ='10' value='Select Final'/> </td>");
   out.println("<input type='hidden' name='action_submit' id='action_submit'
        size ='10' value='applicant_select_for_final_submit'/> ");
   out.println("</tr>");
}
}
out.println("</tr>");
%>
</table>
</td>
</tr>
<tr>
    <td colspan="2"><%@include file="../jsp/people_footer.jsp"%></td>
</tr>
</table>
</body>
</html>
```

The `applicant_test_dtl_list` JSP page shows different rounds of results on the basis of the value of the `dbopr` variable, and can be executed by clicking the `Update Result` hyperlink provided for different rounds, such as written, technical, and HR.

Figure 23.14 displays the output of the `applicant_test_dtl_list` JSP page, showing the list of applicants to be updated for the written round:

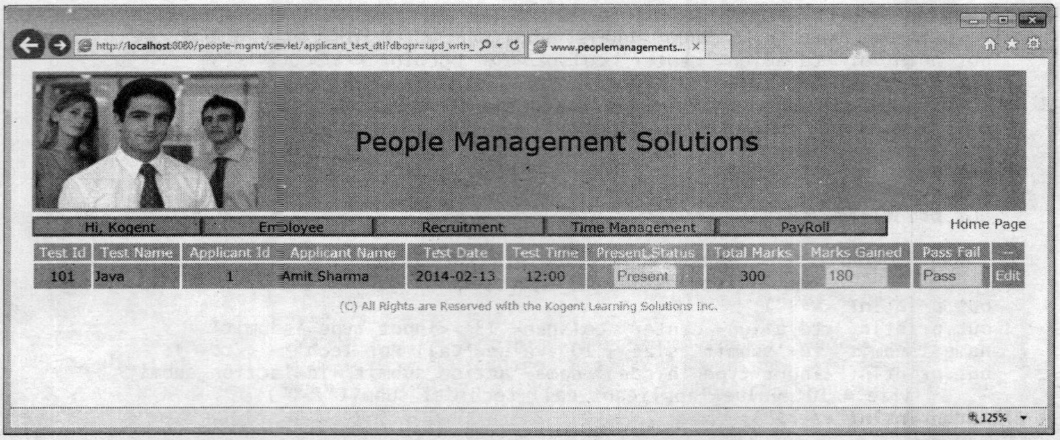

Figure 23.14: Displaying the Test Details for Written Round in the applicant_test_dtl_list JSP Page

The applicant_test_dtl_list JSP page is used to show the test details for all rounds and allows you to edit the test details by clicking the `Edit` link. This results in the invocation of the `applicant_test_dtl_update JSP page`.

Creating the applicant_test_dtl_update JSP Page

The `applicant_test_dtl_update` JSP page provides a form to update a test result. The same JSP page is used to update the results of all rounds of tests. Listing 23.34 shows the code of the `applicant_test_dtl_update.jsp` file (save the `applicant_test_dtl_update.jsp` file in the `people-mgmt\jsp` folder):

Listing 23.34: Showing the Code of the applicant_test_dtl_update.jsp File

```
<%@ page language="java" %>
<%@ page session="true" %>
<%@ page  import="com.Applicant.*" %>
<%@ page  import="java.io.*" %>
<%@ page  import="java.util.*" %>
<html>
<head>
<title>www.peoplemanagementsolutions.com/Test Detail Update</title>
<link rel="stylesheet" href="../css/mystyle.css" type="text/css" />
</head>
<body>
<table width="900" border="0" align="center">
<tr>
  <td colspan="2" ><%@ include file="../jsp/people_header.jsp" %></td>
</tr>
<tr>
<td width="900"  valign="top"><%@ include file="../jsp/people_default_menu.jsp" %></td>
</tr>
<tr>
<td width ="750" valign="top">
<p> </p>
<div align=center class=boldblack>Update Result</div>
<hr width=500 color=#AAAAAA>
<table  border="0"  width=300 align=center >
<form name="form1" method="post">
<%
  ApplicantTestDtlDBObj applicantTestDtlDBObj = new ApplicantTestDtlDBObj();
  applicantTestDtlDBObj =
  (ApplicantTestDtlDBObj)session.getAttribute("applicantTestDtlDBObj");

%>
```

```
    <input type='hidden' name='applicant_id' id='applicant_id' size ='20'
    value='<%=applicantTestDtlDBObj.applicant_id%>' />
    <input type='hidden' name='test_id' id='test_id' size ='20'
    value='<%=applicantTestDtlDBObj.test_id%>' />
    <input type='hidden' name='test_name' id='test_name' size ='20'
    value='<%=applicantTestDtlDBObj.test_name%>' />
    <tr><td>Status in Test</td>
    <td>
    <select name='present_status'>
    <option value=Absent >Absent</option>
    <option value=Present selected>Present</option>
    </select>
    </td></tr>
    <tr><td>Total Marks</td>
    <td>
    <input type='hidden' name='total_marks' id='total_marks' size ='20'
                  value='"+applicantTestDtlDBObj.total_marks+"'/>
    <%=applicantTestDtlDBObj.total_marks%>
    </td></tr>
    <tr>
    <td> Marks Gained</td>
    <td><%
    if( applicantTestDtlDBObj.marks_gained != 0 )
        out.println("<input type='text' name='marks_gained' id='marks_gained'
             size= '5' value = '"+applicantTestDtlDBObj.marks_gained+"' />");
    else
        out.println("<input type='text' name='marks_gained' id='marks_gained'
                          size= '5' value = '0' />");
      %>
    </td></tr>
    <tr><td>Result</td>
    <td>
    <%
    if( applicantTestDtlDBObj.pass_fail != null )
          out.println("<input type='text' name='pass_fail' id='pass_fail' size
                  ='5' value='"+applicantTestDtlDBObj.pass_fail+"' />");
    else{
          out.println("<SELECT name='pass_fail' ><option value=></option>
                          <option value=Pass>Pass</option><option value=Fail>
                                  Fail</option></SELECT></td>");
    }
    %>
    </td></tr>
    <tr><td colospan=2 align=center>
    <input type='hidden' name='action_submit' id='action_submit' size ='10'
                  value='people_applicant_wrtn_test_dtl_upd_submit'/>
    <input type='submit' name='submit' id='submit' value='Update Detail'/>
    </td></tr>
  </table></td>
  </tr>
  <tr>
    <td colspan="2"><%@include file="../jsp/people_footer.jsp"%></td>
  </tr>
  </table></body></html>
```

The code given in Listing 23.34 is used to update the results of an applicant. Figure 23.15 shows the output of the `applicant_test_dtl_update` JSP page:

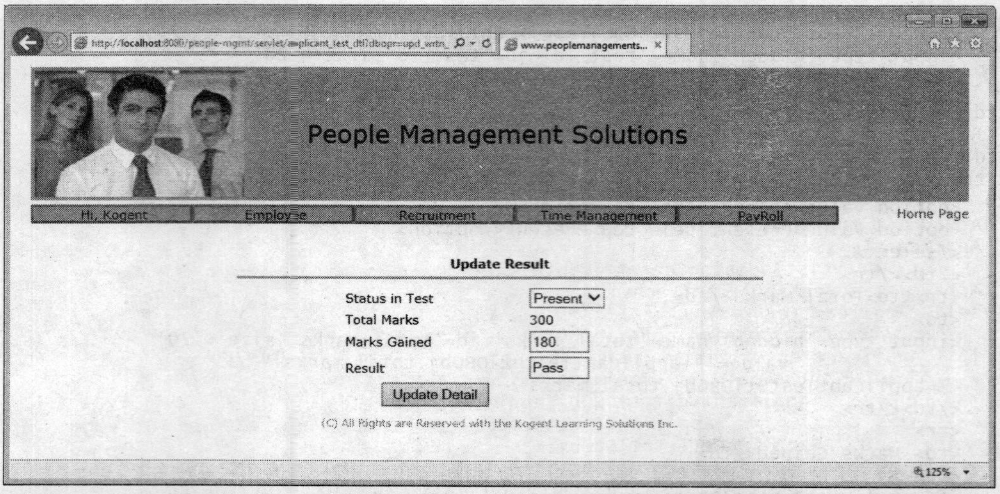

Figure 23.15: Displaying the Update Result Form as the Output of the applicant_test_dtl_update JSP Page

The `applicant_test_dtl_update` JSP page is used to update the results of the applicants.

Let's now discuss the `applicant_final_selected_list` JSP page.

Creating the applicant_final_selected_list JSP Page

The `applicant_final_selected_list` JSP page shows the list of finally selected candidates. In this page, the `ApplicantTestDtlList` ArrayList is used as a container to store the details of all selected candidates who have passed all the tests and cleared all the rounds.

Listing 23.35 shows the code of the `applicant_final_selected_list.jsp` file (save the `applicant_final_selected_list.jsp` file in the `people-mgmt\jsp` folder):

Listing 23.35: Showing the Code of the applicant_final_selected_list.jsp File

```
<%@ page language="java" %>
<%@ page session="true" %>
<%@ page  import="com.Applicant.*" %>
<%@ page  import="java.io.*" %>
<%@ page  import="java.util.*" %>
<html>
<head>
<title>www.peoplemanagementsolutions.com/Selected Candidates</title>
<link rel="stylesheet" href="../css/mystyle.css" type="text/css" />
</head>
<body>
<table width="900" border="0" align="center">
<tr>
   <td colspan="2"><%@ include file="../jsp/people_header.jsp" %></td>
</tr>
<tr>
<td width="900"><%@ include file="../jsp/people_default_menu.jsp" %></td>
</tr>
<tr>
<td width ="750" valign='top">
<p> </p>
<div align=center class=boldblack>List of Selected Candidates to be
         Appointed.</div>
<hr width=400 color=#AAAAAA>
<table  border="0"  width=100% >
<%
    String dbopr = "";
    dbopr = (String)session.getAttribute("dbopr");
```

```
%>
<tr height=20>
<td class=whitetext bgcolor ='#AAAAAA' align='center' colspan='2'>Applicant
  Id</td>
<td class=whitetext bgcolor ='#AAAAAA' align='center' colspan='2' >Applicant
  Name</td>
<td class=whitetext bgcolor ='#AAAAAA' align='center' colspan='2'></td>
</tr>
<%
  ArrayList ApplicantTestDtlList = new ArrayList();
  ApplicantTestDtlList =
        (ArrayList)session.getAttribute("ApplicantTestDtlList");
  ArrayList selectApplicantTechList = new ArrayList();
  selectApplicantTechList =
        (ArrayList)session.getAttribute("selectApplicantTechList");
  if ( ApplicantTestDtlList != null && ApplicantTestDtlList.size() > 0 ){
        for ( int size = 1; size <= ApplicantTestDtlList.size() ; size++ ){
                ApplicantTestDtlDBObj applicantTestDtlDBObj = new
                        ApplicantTestDtlDBObj();
                applicantTestDtlDBObj =
                (ApplicantTestDtlDBObj)ApplicantTestDtlList.get(size-1);
        %>
<form name="form1" method="post">
<tr bgcolor ='#AAAAAA'>
<input type='hidden' name='test_id' id='test_id' size ='20'
                value='<%=applicantTestDtlDBObj.test_id%>'/>
<input type='hidden' name='test_name' id='test_name' size ='20'
                value='<%=applicantTestDtlDBObj.test_name%>'/>
<input type='hidden' name='aplicant_id' id='aplicant_id' size ='20'
                value='<%=applicantTestDtlDBObj.applicant_id%>'/>
<td align='center' colspan='2' ><%=applicantTestDtlDBObj.applicant_id%></td>
<input type='hidden' name='applicant_name' id='applicant_name' size ='20'
        value='<%=applicantTestDtlDBObj.applicant_name%>'/>
<td align='center' colspan='2' ><%=applicantTestDtlDBObj.applicant_name%></td>
<input type='hidden' name='test_date' id='test_date' size ='20'
        value='<%=applicantTestDtlDBObj.test_date%>'/>
<input type='hidden' name='test_time' id='test_time' size ='20'
        value='<%=applicantTestDtlDBObj.test_time%>'/>
<td align='center' bgcolor="#AAAAAA">
<a href='../jsp/selected_applicant_dtls.jsp' class=yellowlink>Detail </a>
</td >
<td align='center' bgcolor="#AAAAAA">
<a href='../jsp/offerletter.jsp' class=yellowlink>Issue Joining Letter </a>
</td >
<%
  }
}
  out.println("</tr>");
%>
</table>
</td></tr>
<tr>
   <td colspan="2"><%@include file="../jsp/people_footer.jsp"%></td>
</tr></table></body></html>
```

The output of the code provided in Listing 23.35 for the `applicant_final_selected_list JSP page` is shown in Figure 23.16:

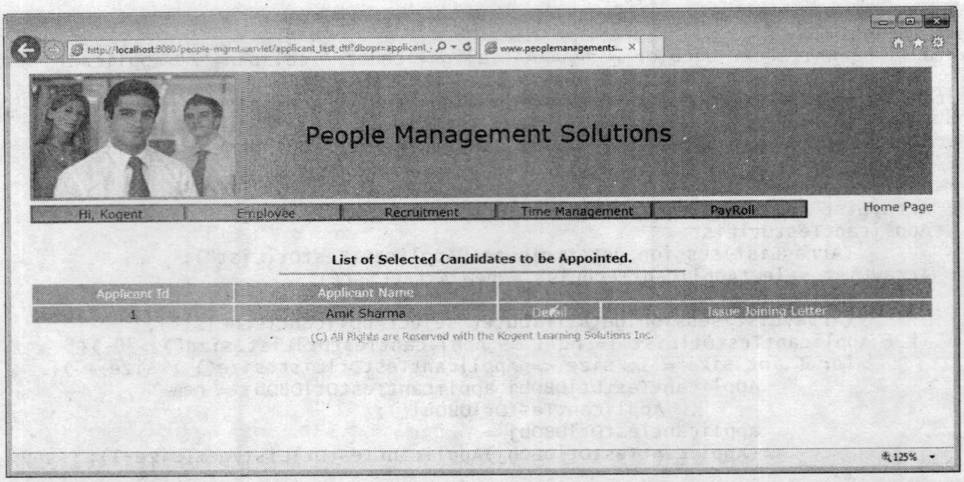

Figure 23.16: Displaying the List of Selected Candidates in the applicant_final_selected_list JSP Page

Figure 23.16 shows the list of all the selected candidates.

Let's now discuss the functioning of the recruitment module.

Working of the Recruitment Module

The recruitment process starts with the registration of new applicants. To register a new applicant, you need to click the `New Applicant` submenu from the `Recruitment` menu, and fill all the details of the applicant, such as name, address, qualifications in the relevant fields.

The `applicant_list` JSP page, shown in Figure 23.12, also contains the `Update Applicant` link that allows you to view the details of an applicant, delete an applicant, and update the details of the applicant. To find the list of all the candidates who can be called for the written test, click the `Call for Test` link under the `Written Round` section. The `applicant_list` JSP page appears, from where you can click the `Select` link to select an applicant for the written test, as shown in Figure 23.17:

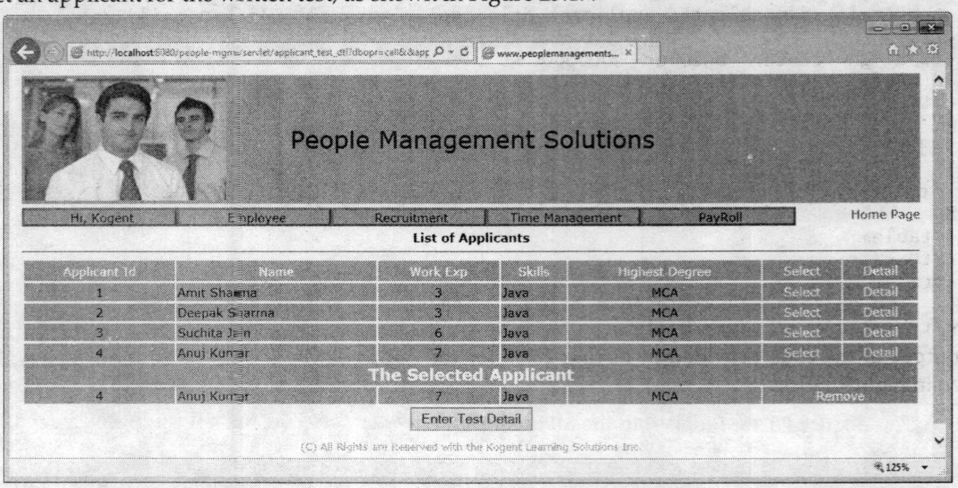

Figure 23.17: Displaying the Applicants Available for Written Test in the applicant_list JSP Page

When you click the `Enter Test Detail` button, the request is forwarded to the `applicant_test_dtl_create JSP page`, where you need to enter the details for a new test, such as `Test Id`, `Test Name`, `Test Date (yy-mm-dd)`, `Test Time (hh:mm)`, and `Total Marks`, as shown in Figure 23.13. The names of the applicants who have cleared the written round are displayed for the technical round, as shown in Figure 23.18:

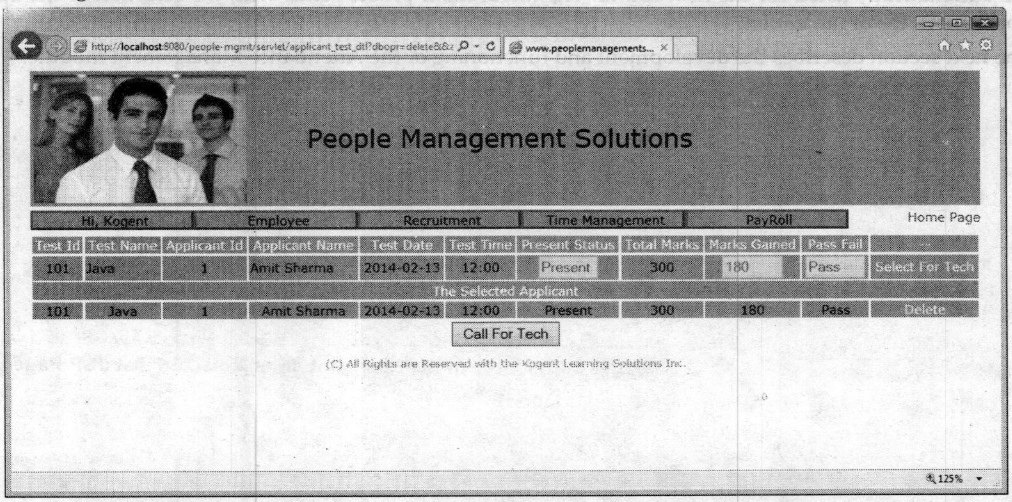

Figure 23.18: Displaying the List of Applicants Selected for the Technical Round

After the applicants clear the technical round, they are called for the HR round. The list of the applicants selected for the HR round is displayed by clicking the `Shortlist for HR Round` link under the `HR Round` section.

Figure 23.19 shows the list of the applicants shortlisted for the HR round:

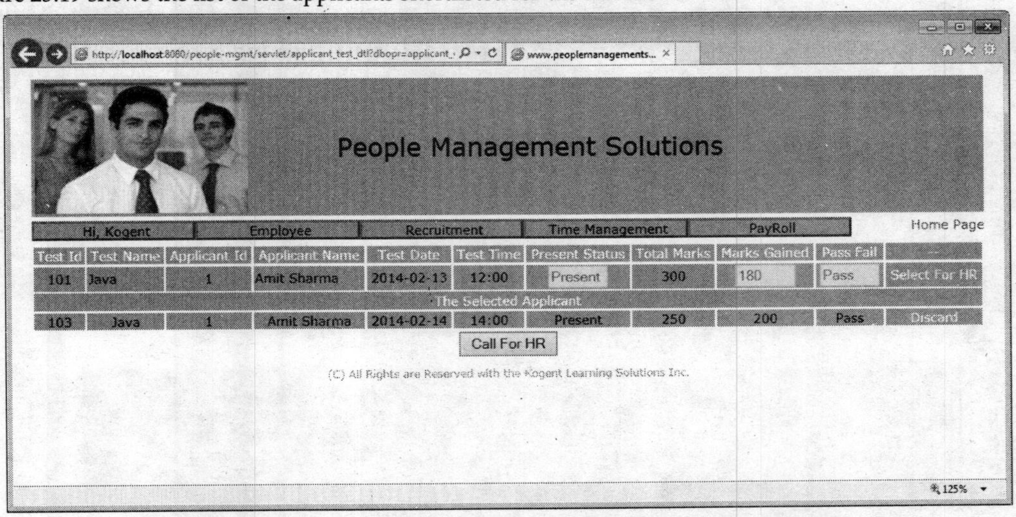

Figure 23.19: Displaying the List of Candidates Selected for the HR Round

The appropriate applicant is finally selected on the basis of the tests conducted in the HR round. You can check the list of selected candidates by clicking the `Selected Candidate` link under the `HR Round` section.

The recruitment module described in this section handles the registration of a new applicant and maintains tests details of the shortlisted applicants. The test results can be updated and the applicants who have cleared a round are automatically listed for the next round. The recruitment process ends with the selection of the appropriate applicant in the organization.

The next section describes the development and functioning of the Attendance Management module.

Section D

Developing the Attendance Management Module

The Attendance Management module is designed for handling the daily attendance details of every employee; for example, time of entering and leaving the office and number of leaves taken in a month. These details help the HR department in deciding the number of working hours of an employee. This module has been developed using the MVC pattern, similar to the earlier modules.

The following code files need to be created for developing the Attendance Management module:

- time_management.java
- DateYearMonthDayDBObj.java
- EmpDailyAttendanceDBObj.java
- TimeManagementDBMethods.java
- employee_daily_attendance.jsp
- employee_daily_attendance_summary.jsp

Let's start the discussion with the time_management servlet.

Creating the time_management Servlet

The `time_management` servlet class is invoked when any one of the two links—`Enter/Update Attendance` or `Daily Attendance Summary` is clicked. This servlet sets the values for the action and target variables and forwards a user request to a specific JSP page.

Listing 23.36 shows the code of the `time_management.java` file (save the `time_managment.java` file in the `people-mgmt\WEB-INF\src` folder):

Listing 23.36: Showing the Code of the `time_management.java File`

```
import javax.servlet.*;
import javax.servlet.http.*;
import java.util.ArrayList;
import java.io.*;
import javax.servlet.annotation.WebServlet;
import com.Employee.EmployeeDBMethods;
import com.Employee.EmployeeDBObj;
import com.TimeManagement.*;

@WebServlet(name="time_management", urlPatterns="/servlet/time_management")

public class time_management extends HttpServlet{
   String lDBUser   = "";
   String lDBPswd   = "";
   String lDBUrl    = "";

/**Initialize global variables*/
   @Override
public void init(ServletConfig config) throws ServletException{
   System.out.println("initializing controller servlet.");
   ServletContext context = config.getServletContext();
   lDBUser = "scott";
   lDBPswd = "tiger";
   lDBUrl  = "jdbc:oracle:thin:@192.168.1.123:1521:"+"XE";
   super.init(config);
}
/**Process the HTTP Get request*/
   @Override
public void doGet(HttpServletRequest request, HttpServletResponse response)
   throws ServletException, IOException{
   doPost(request, response);
}
/**Process the HTTP Post request*/
   @Override
public void doPost(HttpServletRequest request, HttpServletResponse response)
   throws ServletException, IOException{
   response.setContentType("text/html");
```

```
PrintWriter out = response.getWriter();
HttpSession session = request.getSession();
session.setAttribute("lErrorMsg",null);
String target = "";
String action = request.getParameter("action");
String lDBOpr = "";
lDBOpr = (String)request.getParameter("dbopr");
if( (lDBOpr != null && lDBOpr.length() > 0) &&
     (lDBOpr.equals("daily_attendance_entry")) ){
     target = "/jsp/employee_search.jsp";
}
else
if( (lDBOpr != null && lDBOpr.length() > 0) && (lDBOpr.equals
            ("daily_attendance_summary")) ){
     action = "daily_attendance_summary";
}
else
if( (lDBOpr != null && lDBOpr.length() > 0) &&
     (lDBOpr.equals("edit")) ){
     action = "daily_attendance_summary_edit";
}
String action_submit = request.getParameter("action_submit");
String action_edit = request.getParameter("action_edit");
System.out.println("action_submit=="+action_submit);
if ( action_submit != null || action_edit != null ){
if ( request.getParameter("submit").equals("Submit") ){
     System.out.println("in the  Submit");
     if ( action_submit.equals("people_employee_search_submit") ){
             System.out.println("in the people_employee_insert_submit ");
             action = "people_employee_search_submit";
     }
}
else
if ( request.getParameter("submit").equals("Submit Detail") ){
     if ( action_submit.equals("emp_daily_att_dtl_submit") )
             action = "emp_daily_att_dtl_submit";
     }
}
if (action!=null){
     System.out.println("in the  "+action);
     if (action.equals("people_employee_search_submit")){
     String lEmpId = "";
     String lEmpFName = "";
     lEmpId = (String)request.getParameter("emp_id");
     lEmpFName = (String)request.getParameter("emp_f_name");
     TimeManagementDBMethods timeManagementDBMethods  = new
             TimeManagementDBMethods(lDBUser,lDBPswd,lDBUrl);
     DateYearMonthDayDBObj dateYearMonthDayDBObj = new
                     DateYearMonthDayDBObj();
     dateYearMonthDayDBObj = (DateYearMonthDayDBObj)timeManagement
             DBMethods.getCurDateYearMonthDayDBObj();
     session.setAttribute("dateYearMonthDayDBObj",dateYearMonth
                             DayDBObj);
     EmployeeDBObj employeeDBObj = new EmployeeDBObj();
     EmployeeDBMethods employeeDBMethods = new EmployeeDBMethods(
                             lDBUser,lDBPswd,lDBUrl);
     employeeDBObj = (EmployeeDBObj)employeeDBMethods.getRecord
             ByPrimaryKey(lEmpId,lEmpFName);
     EmpDailyAttendanceDBObj empDailyAttendanceDBObj = new
                     EmpDailyAttendanceDBObj();
     empDailyAttendanceDBObj = (EmpDailyAttendanceDBObj)time
             ManagementDBMethods.getRecordByPrimaryKey(lEmpId,dateYear
             MonthDayDBObj.today_date);
     if ( (employeeDBObj.emp_id != null &&
     employeeDBObj.emp_f_name.equals(lEmpFName)  ) ){
```

```
        session.setAttribute("empDailyAttendanceDBObj",
                        empDailyAttendanceDBObj);
        session.setAttribute("employeeDBObj",employeeDBObj);
        target = "/jsp/employee_daily_attendance.jsp";
        }
        else{
                String lErrorMsg = "Employee doesn't Exist";
                session setAttribute("lErrorMsg",lErrorMsg);
                target = "/jsp/people_default.jsp";
        }
        }
        else
        if (action.equals("daily_attendance_summary_edit")){
                String lEmpId = "";
                String lTodayDate = "";
                String lEmpFName = "";
                lEmpId = (String)request.getParameter("emp_id");
                lTodayDate = (String)request.getParameter
                                ("today_date");
                TimeManagementDBMethods timeManagementDBMethods  =
                new TimeManagementDBMethods (lDBUser,lDBPswd,lDBUrl);
                DateYearMonthDayDBObj dateYearMonthDayDBObj = new
                                DateYearMonthDayDBObj();
                dateYearMonthDayDBObj = (DateYearMonthDayDBObj)time
                ManagementDBMethods.getCurDateYearMonthDayDBObj();
                EmployeeDBObj employeeDBObj = new EmployeeDBObj();
                EmployeeDBMethods employeeDBMethods = new
                        EmployeeDBMethods(lDBUser,lDBPswd,lDBUrl);
                employeeDBObj = (EmployeeDBObj)employeeDBMethods.get
                        RecordByPrimaryKey(lEmpId,lEmpFName);
                EmpDailyAttendanceDBObj empDailyAttendanceDBObj = new
                                        EmpDailyAttendanceDBObj();
                empDailyAttendanceDBObj = (EmpDailyAttendanceDBObj)
                timeManagementDBMethods.getRecordByPrimaryKey
                        (lEmpId,lTodayDate);
                session.setAttribute("empDailyAttendanceDBObj",
                                empDailyAttendanceDBObj);
                session.setAttribute("employeeDBObj",employeeDBObj);
                session.setAttribute("dateYearMonthDayDBObj",
                                        dateYearMonthDayDBObj);
                target = "/jsp/employee_daily_attendance.jsp";
        }
        else
        if (action.equals("daily_attendance_summary")){
        TimeManagementDBMethods timeManagementDBMethods  =
        new TimeManagementDBMethods(lDBUser,lDBPswd,lDBUrl);
        DateYearMonthDayDBObj dateYearMonthDayDBObj = new
                                DateYearMonthDayDBObj();
        dateYearMonthDayDBObj = (DateYearMonthDayDBObj)timeManagement
        DBMethods.getCurDateYearMonthDayDBObj();
        session.setAttribute("dateYearMonthDayDBObj"
                                ,dateYearMonthDayDBObj);
        ArrayList empDailyAttendanceList = new ArrayList();
        String criteria = "";
        criteria = " where today_date='"+dateYear
                                MonthDayDBObj.today_date+"'";
        empDailyAttendanceList = ( ArrayList)timeManagement    DBMethods.
                selectEmpDailyAttendanceByCriteria(criteria);
        session.setAttribute("empDailyAttendanceList"
                                        ,empDailyAttendanceList);
        target = "/jsp/employee_daily_attendance_summary.jsp";
        }
        else
        if (action.equals("emp_daily_att_dtl_submit")){
                EmpDailyAttendanceDBObj  popEmpDailyAttendanceDBObj =
```

```
                    new EmpDailyAttendanceDBObj();
            TimeManagementDBMethods timeManagementDBMethods  =
            new TimeManagementDBMethods(lDBUser,lDBPswd,lDBUrl);
        popEmpDailyAttendanceDBObj = ( EmpDailyAttendanceDBObj)timeMana
        gementDBMethods.populateEmpDailyAttendanceDBObjFromReq(request);
        EmpDailyAttendanceDBObj  empDailyAttendanceDBObj =
                            new EmpDailyAttendanceDBObj();
        empDailyAttendanceDBObj = (EmpDailyAttendanceDBObj)    timeManagement
        DBMethods.getRecordByPrimaryKey(popEmpDailyAttendanceDBObj.emp_id,
                            popEmpDailyAttendanceDBObj.today_date);
        if ( ( empDailyAttendanceDBObj.emp_id != null &&
        (popEmpDailyAttendanceDBObj.emp_id).equals(empDailyAttendanceDBObj
        .emp_id)) && (popEmpDailyAttendanceDBObj.today_date).equals(
                            empDailyAttendanceDBObj.today_date) ){
        int rval=timeManagementDBMethods.updateEmpDaily
            AttendanceDBObjByPrimaryKey(popEmpDailyAttendanceDBObj);
        empDailyAttendanceDBObj = (EmpDailyAttendanceDBObj)timeManagement
        DBMethods.getRecordByPrimaryKey(popEmpDailyAttendanceDBObj.emp_id,
            popEmpDailyAttendanceDBObj.today_date);
        session.setAttribute("empDailyAttendanceDBObj",
                                    empDailyAttendanceDBObj);
        }
        else{
          int rval =  timeManagementDBMethods.insertEmp
                        DailyAttendanceDBObj(popEmpDailyAttendanceDBObj);
      empDailyAttendanceDBObj= (EmpDailyAttendanceDBObj)timeManage
          mentDBMethods.getRecordByPrimaryKey(popEmpDa ilyAttendanceDBObj.
                            emp_id,popEmpDailyAttendanceDBObj.today_date);
          session.setAttribute("empDailyAttendanceDBObj"
                            ,empDailyAttendanceDBObj);
        }
        DateYearMonthDayDBObj dateYearMonthDayDBObj = new
                            DateYearMonthDayDBObj();
        dateYearMonthDayDBObj = (DateYearMonthDayDBObj)
                  timeManagementDBMethods.getCurDateYearMonthDayDBObj();
        session.setAttribute("dateYearMonthDayDBObj",dateYearMonthDayDBObj);
        ArrayList empDailyAttendanceList = new ArrayList();
        String criteria = "";
        criteria = " where today_date='"+dateYearMonthDayDBObj
            .today_date+"'";
        empDailyAttendanceList = ( ArrayList)timeManagementDBMethods.
        selectEmpDailyAttendanceByCriteria(criteria);
         session.setAttribute("empDailyAttendanceList",
            empDailyAttendanceList);
        target = "/jsp/employee_daily_attendance_summary.jsp";
        }
    }
    /* forwarding the request/response to the targeted view */
    RequestDispatcher requestDispatcher = getServletContext().getRequest
            Dispatcher(target);
    requestDispatcher.forward(request, response);
    }// doPost closed
  }// class closed
```

In Listing 23.36, the @WebServlet annotation is used to provide the servlet mapping in the `time_management` servlet.

Let's now create the classes in the `com.TimeManagement` package.

Creating the Classes in the com.TimeManagement Package

The `com.TimeManagement` package contains three classes, namely `DateYearMonthDayDBObj`, `EmpDailyAttendanceDBObj`, and `TimeManagementDBMethods`. These classes support the `time_management` servlet to complete the entire process of attendance management.

Creating the DateYearMonthDayDBObj Class

The `DateYearMonthDayDBObj` is a simple Java class that contains various member variables, such as today_date, month, day, and year to store attendance-related information of an employee.

Listing 23.37 shows the code of the `DateYearMonthDayDBObj.java` file (save the `DateYearMonthDayDBObj.java` file in the `people-mgmt\WEB-INF\src\com\TimeManagement` folder):

Listing 23.37: Showing the Code of the `DateYearMonthDayDBObj.java` File

```
package com.TimeManagement;
public class DateYearMonthDayDBObj {
   public String today_date ;
   public String month ;
   public String day ;
   public long year ;
}
```

Creating the EmpDailyAttendanceDBObj Class

The `EmpDailyAttendanceDBObj` class is used as a DAO. The member variables of this class are used to store information to be added in the `EMPLOYEE_DAILY_ATTENDANCE` table, which is used to maintain the attendance records. An attendance record consists of the `emp_id`, `emp_name`, `today_date`, `month`, `day`, `year`, `in_time`, `out_time`, and `remark fields`.

Listing 23.38 shows the code of the `EmpDailyAttendanceDBObj.java` file (save the `EmpDailyAttendanceDBObj.java` file in the `people-mgmt\WEB-INF\src\com\TimeManagement` folder):

Listing 23.38: Showing the Code of the `EmpDailyAttendanceDBObj.java` File

```
package com.TimeManagement;
public class EmpDailyAttendanceDBObj {
   public String emp_id ;
   public String emp_name ;
   public String today_date ;
   public String month ;
   public String day ;
   public long year ;
   public String in_time ;
   public String out_time ;
   public String remark ;
}
```

Creating the TimeManagementDBMethods Class

The `TimeManagementDBMethods` class defines various methods, such as `getCurDateYearMonthDayDBObj()`, `initializeEmpDailyAttendanceDBObj()`, and `getRecordByPrimaryKey()`, which are used to retrieve the desired result from the `EMPLOYEE_DAILY_ATTENDANCE table`. An object of the `EmpDailyAttendanceDBObj class` is used either as an argument type or as a return type.

Listing 23.39 shows the code of the `TimeManagementDBMethods.java` file (save the `TimeManagementDBMethods.java` file in the `people-mgmt\WEB-INF\src\com\TimeManagement` folder):

Listing 23.39: Showing the Code of the `TimeManagementDBMethods.java` File

```
package com.TimeManagement;
import java.sql.*;
import javax.servlet.http.*;
import java.util.*;
import java.util.ArrayList;

public class TimeManagementDBMethods{
   public String DBUser;
   public String DBPswd;
   public String DBUrl ;
   public TimeManagementDBMethods(){ }
```

```
public TimeManagementDBMethods(String inDBUser, String inDBPswd, String
      inDBUrl ){
      DBUser = inDBUser;
      DBPswd = inDBPswd;
      DBUrl  = inDBUrl;
}
public DateYearMonthDayDBObj getCurDateYearMonthDayDBObj(){
      DateYearMonthDayDBObj dateYearMonthDayDBObj = new
            DateYearMonthDayDBObj();
      GregorianCalendar calendar = new GregorianCalendar();
      String month = Integer.toString((calendar.get(Calendar.MONTH) + 1));
      String day   = Integer.toString(calendar.get(Calendar.DATE));
      String year  = Integer.toString(calendar.get(Calendar.YEAR));
      if( month != null && month.length() < 2 ) month = "0"+month;
      if( day != null && day.length() < 2 ) day = "0"+day;
      String date = year+"-"+month+"-"+day;
      dateYearMonthDayDBObj.today_date = date;
      dateYearMonthDayDBObj.month = getMonth(calendar.get
                  (Calendar.MONTH));
      dateYearMonthDayDBObj.day = getDay(calendar.get(Calendar
                  .DAY_OF_WEEK));
      dateYearMonthDayDBObj.year = calendar.get(Calendar.YEAR);
      System.out.println("YEAR: " + calendar.get(Calendar.YEAR));
      System.out.println("MONTH: " + calendar.get(Calendar.MONTH));
      System.out.println("DATE: " + calendar.get(Calendar.DATE));
      System.out.println("DAY_OF_WEEK: " +
                        calendar.get(Calendar.DAY_OF_WEEK));
      return dateYearMonthDayDBObj;
}
public String getDay( int day ){
      String strDay= "";
      if(day == 1) strDay = "SUN";
      else if(day == 2) strDay = "MON";
      else if(day == 3) strDay = "TUS";
      else if(day == 4) strDay = "WED";
      else if(day == 5) strDay = "THU";
      else if(day == 6) strDay = "FRI";
      else if(day == 7) strDay = "SAT";
      return strDay;
}
public String getMonth( int month ){
      String strMonth = "";
      if(month == 0) strMonth = "JAN";
      else if(month == 1) strMonth = "FEB";
      else if(month == 2 ) strMonth = "MAR";
      else if(month == 3) strMonth = "APR";
      else if(month == 4) strMonth = "MAY";
      else if(month == 5) strMonth = "JUN";
      else if(month == 6) strMonth = "JUL";
      else if(month == 7) strMonth = "AUG";
      else if(month == 8) strMonth = "SEP";
      else if(month == 9) strMonth = "OCT";
      else if(month == 10) strMonth = "NOV";
      else if(month == 11) strMonth = "DEC";
      return strMonth;
}
public void initializeEmpDailyAttendanceDBObj(EmpDailyAttendanceDBObj
            inEmpDailyAttendanceDBObj ){
      inEmpDailyAttendanceDBObj.emp_id   = "";
      inEmpDailyAttendanceDBObj.emp_name = "";
      inEmpDailyAttendanceDBObj.today_date  = "";
      inEmpDailyAttendanceDBObj.month  = "";
      inEmpDailyAttendanceDBObj.day = "";
      inEmpDailyAttendanceDBObj.year = 0;
      inEmpDailyAttendanceDBObj.in_time = "";
      inEmpDailyAttendanceDBObj.out_time = "";
      inEmpDailyAttendanceDBObj.remark = "";
}
public EmpDailyAttendanceDBObj getRecordByPrimaryKey(String inEmpId, String
                  inTodayDate){
      EmpDailyAttendanceDBObj  empDailyAttendanceDBObj = new EmpDaily
                  AttendanceDBObj();
```

```
try{
    DriverManager.registerDriver(new oracle.jdbc.driver.OracleDriver());
    Connection conn= DriverManager.getConnection(DBUrl,DBUser,DBPswd);
    Statement stmt = conn.createStatement();
    String lSqlString =     "select * from EMPLOYEE_DAILY_ATTENDANCE ";
    lSqlString = lSqlString + "where emp_id='"+inEmpId+"' ";
    lSqlString = lSqlString + "and today_date='"+inTodayDate+"' ";
    ResultSet rs  = null;
    rs  = stmt.executeQuery(lSqlString);
    System.out.println("lSqlString====trtrt==within
            getRecordByPrimaryKey== "+lSqlString);
    if( rs.next()){
            empDailyAttendanceDBObj.emp_id = (String)rs.getString("emp_id");
            empDailyAttendanceDBObj.emp_name = (String)rs.getString("emp_name");
            empDailyAttendanceDBObj.today_date = (String)rs.getString("today_date");
            empDailyAttendanceDBObj.month = (String)rs.getString("month");
            empDailyAttendanceDBObj.day = (String)rs.getString("day");
            empDailyAttendanceDBObj.year = rs.getLong("year");
            String intime=rs.getString("in_time");
            if(intime!=null)
            empDailyAttendanceDBObj.in_time = intime.substring(11,16);
            String outtime=rs.getString("out_time");
            if(outtime!=null)
            empDailyAttendanceDBObj.out_time = outtime.substring(11,16);
            empDailyAttendanceDBObj.remark =
                                    (String)rs.getString("remark");
            System.out.println("fffff==="+rs.getString("emp_id"));
            }
            else{
            initializeEmpDailyAttendanceDBObj(empDailyAttendanceDBObj);
            }
    System.out.println("fffff====="+empDailyAttendanceDBObj.emp_id);
    }
    catch(SQLException  ex){
            ex.printStackTrace();
    }
    return empDailyAttendanceDBObj;
}
public ArrayList selectEmpDailyAttendanceByCriteria(String inCriteria){
    ArrayList EmpDailyAttendanceList = new ArrayList();
    try{
    DriverManager.registerDriver(new oracle.jdbc.driver.OracleDriver());
    Connection conn= DriverManager.getConnection(DBUrl,DBUser,DBPswd);
    Statement stmt = conn.createStatement();
    String lSqlString =     "select * from EMPLOYEE_DAILY_ATTENDANCE  ";
    if( inCriteria != null && inCriteria.length() > 0 ){
            lSqlString = lSqlString +" "+inCriteria+"" ;
    }
    System.out.println("Criteria===== "+inCriteria+" and query="+lSqlString);
    ResultSet rs  = null;
    rs  = stmt.executeQuery(lSqlString);
    while( rs.next()){
    EmpDailyAttendanceDBObj  empDailyAttendanceDBObj = new
                    EmpDailyAttendanceDBObj();
    empDailyAttendanceDBObj.emp_id   =  (String)rs.getString("emp_id");
    empDailyAttendanceDBObj.emp_name = (String)rs.getString("emp_name");
    empDailyAttendanceDBObj.today_date  = (String)rs.getString
                            ("today_date");
    empDailyAttendanceDBObj.month  = (String)rs.getString("month");
    empDailyAttendanceDBObj.day = (String)rs.getString("day");
    empDailyAttendanceDBObj.year = rs.getLong("year");
    String intime=rs.getString("in_time");
    if(intime!=null)
            empDailyAttendanceDBObj.in_time = intime.substring(11,16);
            String outtime=rs.getString("out_time");
            if(outtime!=null)
            empDailyAttendanceDBObj.out_time = outtime.substring(11,16);
            empDailyAttendanceDBObj.remark = (String)rs.getString
                                    ("remark");
            EmpDailyAttendanceList.add(empDailyAttendanceDBObj);
    }
}
```

```
    catch(SQLException  ex){
          ex.printStackTrace();
    }
    return EmpDailyAttendanceList;
  }
    public int updateEmpDailyAttendanceDBObjByPrimaryKey(EmpDailyAttendanceDBObj
              inEmpDailyAttendanceDBObj){
          int recupd = 0;
          String lQuery = "";
          lQuery = lQuery +"update EMPLOYEE_DAILY_ATTENDANCE set
                      emp_name='"+inEmpDailyAttendanceDBObj.emp_name+"'  ";
          lQuery = lQuery +" , month='"+inEmpDailyAttendanceDBObj.month+"' ";
          lQuery = lQuery +" , day='"+inEmpDailyAttendanceDBObj.day+"' ";
          lQuery = lQuery +" , year="+inEmpDailyAttendanceDBObj.year+" ";
          lQuery = lQuery +" , in_time=to_date('"+inEmpDailyAttendanceDBObj .today_date+"
          "+inEmpDailyAttendanceDBObj.in_time+"','yyyy -mm-dd HH24:MI') ";
          lQuery = lQuery +" , out_time=to_date('"+inEmpDailyAttendanceDBObj
          .today_date+" "+inEmpDailyAttendanceDBObj.out_time+"','yyyy-mm- dd
                HH24:MI') ";
          lQuery = lQuery +" , remark='"+inEmpDailyAttendanceDBObj.remark+"'
                ";
          lQuery = lQuery + "where emp_id='"+inEmpDailyAttendanceDBObj
                      .emp_id+"' ";
          lQuery = lQuery + "and today_date='"+inEmpDailyAttendanceDBObj
                      .today_date+"' ";
          System.out.println("lSqlString===:"+lQuery);
          try{
          DriverManager.registerDriver(new oracle.jdbc.driver.OracleDriver());
          Connection conn= DriverManager.getConnection(DBUrl,DBUser,DBPswd);
          Statement stmt = conn.createStatement();
          recupd  = stmt.executeUpdate(lQuery);
          }
          catch(SQLException  ex){
                ex.printStackTrace();
          }
          return recupd;
    }
    public EmpDailyAttendanceDBObj populateEmpDailyAttendanceDBObjFromReq
              (HttpServletRequest inReq){
          EmpDailyAttendanceDBObj  empDailyAttendanceDBObj = new
                      EmpDailyAttendanceDBObj();
          empDailyAttendanceDBObj.emp_id    =  (String)inReq.getParameter
                ("emp_id");
          empDailyAttendanceDBObj.emp_name = (String)inReq.getParameter
                      ("emp_name");
          empDailyAttendanceDBObj.today_date  = (String)inReq.getParameter
                      ("today_date");
          empDailyAttendanceDBObj.month  = (String)inReq.getParameter
                ("month");
          empDailyAttendanceDBObj.day = (String)inReq.getParameter("day");
          empDailyAttendanceDBObj.year = Long.parseLong((String)inReq.
                      getParameter("year"));
          empDailyAttendanceDBObj.in_time = (String)inReq.getParameter
                      ("in_time");
          empDailyAttendanceDBObj.out_time = (String)inReq.getParameter
                ("out_time");
          empDailyAttendanceDBObj.remark = (String)inReq.getParameter
                      ("remark");
          return empDailyAttendanceDBObj;
    }
    public int insertEmpDailyAttendanceDBObj(EmpDailyAttendanceDBObj
              inEmpDailyAttendanceDBObj){
          int recupd = 0;
          String lQuery = "";
          lQuery = lQuery +"insert into EMPLOYEE_DAILY_ATTENDANCE  values ( ";
          lQuery = lQuery +" '"+inEmpDailyAttendanceDBObj.emp_id+"'  ";
          lQuery = lQuery +" , '"+inEmpDailyAttendanceDBObj.emp_name+"'  ";
          lQuery = lQuery +" , '"+inEmpDailyAttendanceDBObj.today_date+"'  ";
          lQuery = lQuery +" , '"+inEmpDailyAttendanceDBObj.month+"' ";
          lQuery = lQuery +" , '"+inEmpDailyAttendanceDBObj.day+"' ";
          lQuery = lQuery +" , "+inEmpDailyAttendanceDBObj.year+" ";
```

```
            lQuery = lQuery +" , to_date('"+inEmpDailyAttendanceDBObj
            .today_date+" "+inEmpDailyAttendanceDBObj.in_time+"','yyyy-mm-dd
                HH24:MI')";
            lQuery = lQuery +" , to_date('"+inEmpDailyAttendanceDBObj
            .today_date+" "+inEmpDailyAttendanceDBObj.out_time+"','yyyy-mm-dd
                    HH24:MI') ";
            lQuery = lQuery +" , '"+inEmpDailyAttendanceDBObj.remark+"' ";
            lQuery = lQuery + " )";
            System.out.println("lSqlString===:"+lQuery);
            try{
            DriverManager.registerDriver(new oracle.jdbc.driver.OracleDriver());
            Connection conn= DriverManager.getConnection(DBUrl,DBUser,DBPswd);
            Statement stmt = conn.createStatement();
            recupd  = stmt.executeUpdate(lQuery);
            }
            catch(SQLException  ex){
                ex.printStackTrace();
            }
            return recupd;
    }
}
```

The TimeManagementDBMethods.java file contains the methods that are used to insert, update, and delete records from the database.

Let's now create the view pages for the Attendance Management module.

Creating JSP Views

In the Attendance Management module, the two JSP pages required to update and monitor daily attendance records are employee_daily_attendance and employee_daily_attendance_summary. The employee_daily_attendance JSP page allows the employees to provide various details, such as the incoming time and outgoing time on a particular day; whereas, the employee_daily_attendance_summary page displays the details of the attendance of all the employees in a summarized format.

Creating the employee_daily_attendance JSP Page

To mark daily attendance, an employee needs to click the Enter/Update Attendance link in the Time Management menu. This displays the employee_search JSP page, in which an employee needs to enter his Employee Id and First Name. On submitting the details entered in the employee_search JSP page, the employee_daily_attendance JSP page is displayed, where the employee needs to enter the In Time and Out Time for the current date. Listing 23.40 shows the code of the employee_daily_attendance JSP page (save the employee_daily_attendance.jsp file in the people-mgmt\jsp folder):

Listing 23.40: Showing the Code of the employee_daily_attendance.jsp File

```
<%@ page language="java" %>
<%@ page session="true" %>
<%@ page  import="com.Employee.*" %>
<%@ page  import="com.TimeManagement.*" %>
<html>
<head>
<title>www.peoplemanagementsolutions.com/Attendance</title>
<link rel="stylesheet" href="../css/mystyle.css" type="text/css" />
</head>
<body>
<table width="900" border="0" align="center">
<tr>
  <td colspan="2" ><%@ include file="../jsp/people_header.jsp" %></td>
</tr>
<tr>
<td width="900" valign="top"><%@ include file="../jsp/people_default_menu.jsp"
  %></td>
</tr><tr>
<td width ="750" valign="top">
<table  border="0"  width=100% >
<p> </p>
<hr width=100% color=#AAAAAA>
<%
```

```
    String dbopr = "";
    dbopr = (String)session.getAttribute("dbopr");
    EmployeeDBObj employeeDBObj = new EmployeeDBObj();
    employeeDBObj = (EmployeeDBObj)session.getAttribute("employeeDBObj");
    DateYearMonthDayDBObj dateYearMonthDayDBObj = new DateYearMonthDayDBObj();
    dateYearMonthDayDBObj = (DateYearMonthDayDBObj)session.getAttribute
          ("dateYearMonthDayDBObj");
    EmpDailyAttendanceDBObj empDailyAttendanceDBObj = new EmpDailyAttendanceDBObj();
    empDailyAttendanceDBObj = (EmpDailyAttendanceDBObj)session.getAttribute
                ("empDailyAttendanceDBObj");
%>
<form name="form1" method="post">
<tr>
<td bgcolor ='#AAAAAA' colspan='4' class=whitetext height=20 align=center><b>Enter
        In/Out Time</b></td>
</tr>
<tr>
<td>Employee Id</td>
<td>
<%=employeeDBObj.emp_id%>
<input type='hidden' name='emp_id' id='emp_id 'size ='10' value='<%=employeeDBObj
        .emp_id%>'/>
</td>
<td>Date</td>
<td>
<%=dateYearMonthDayDBObj.today_date%>
<input type='hidden' name='today_date' id='today_date 'size ='10' value='<%=date
        YearMonthDayDBObj.today_date%>' />
</td>
</tr>
<tr>
<td>Employee Name</td>
<td><input type='hidden' name='emp_name' id='emp_name' size ='10' value='<%=employ
eeDBObj.emp_f_name%> <%=employeeDBObj.emp_m_name%> <%=employeeDBObj.emp_l_name%>/>
<%=employeeDBObj.emp_f_name%>
<%
  if(employeeDBObj.emp_m_name!=null)
  out.print(employeeDBObj.emp_m_name);
%>
<%=employeeDBObj.emp_l_name%>
</td>
<td>Day</td>
<td>
<%=dateYearMonthDayDBObj.day%>
<input type='hidden' name='day' id='day' size ='10' value='<%=dateYearMonthDay
                DBObj.day%>'/>
</td>
</tr>
<tr><td>Department</td><td><%=employeeDBObj.dept_id%></td>
<td>Month</td>
<td><input type='hidden' name='month' id='month' size ='10' value='<%=dateYearM
                onthDayDBObj.month%>'/>
<%=dateYearMonthDayDBObj.month%>
</td></tr>
<tr>
<td> </td><td> </td><td>Year</td>
<td><%=dateYearMonthDayDBObj.year%>
<input type='hidden' name='year' id='year' size ='10' value='<%=dateYearMon
        thDayDBObj.year%>'/>
</td></tr>
<tr><td>In Time</td>
<%
  if( empDailyAttendanceDBObj.in_time != null )
  out.print("<td><input type='text' name='in_time' id='in_time' size ='10'
        value='"+empDailyAttendanceDBObj.in_time+"'/>(HH:MM) </td>");
  else
  out.print("<td align='left' ><input type='text' name='in_time' id='in_time'
                size ='10' value=''/>(HH:MM) </td>");
%>
<td>Out Time</td>
<%
  if( empDailyAttendanceDBObj.out_time != null )
```

```
    out.print("<td><input type='text' name='out_time' id='out_time' size ='10'
         value='"+empDailyAttendanceDBObj.out_time+"'/>(HH:MM)</td>");
   else
    out.print("<td><input type='text' name='out_time' id='out_time' size ='10'
               value=''/>(HH:MM) </td>");
%>
</tr>
<tr><td>Remark</td>
<td colspan=3><input type='text' name='remark' id='remark' size ='85'
       value=''/></td></tr>
<tr><td colspan=4 align=center>
<input type='submit' name='submit' id='submit' size ='10' value='Submit Detail'/>
<input type='hidden' name='action_submit' id='action_submit' size ='10' value=
      'emp_daily_att_dtl_submit'/>
</td>
</tr>
</table>
<p> </p>
<hr width=100% color=#AAAAAA>
</td>
</tr>
<tr>
<td colspan="2"><%@include file="../jsp/people_footer.jsp"%></td>
</tr>
</table>
</body>
</html>
```

Figure 23.20 shows the `employee_daily_attendance` JSP page:

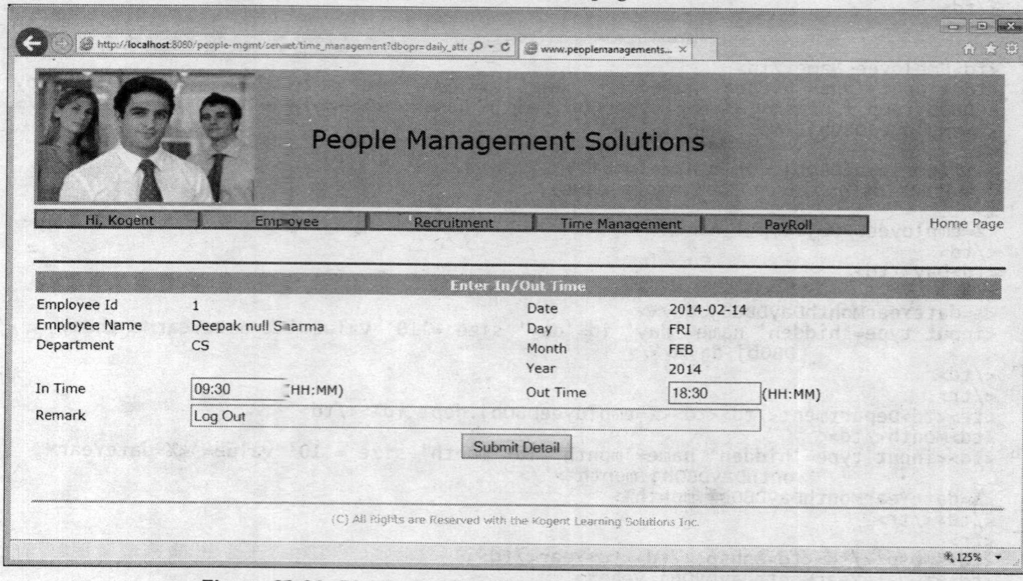

Figure 23.20: Displaying the Attendance Form of an Employee

Let's now create the `employee_daily_attendance_summary` JSP page.

Creating the employee_daily_attendance_summary JSP Page

The `employee_daily_attendance_summary` JSP page shows the daily attendance records of all the employees of an organization. The details displayed in the `employee_daily_attendance_summary` JSP page include various fields, such as Employee Id, Employee Name, In Time, Out Time, and Remark.

Listing 23.41 shows the code for the `employee_daily_attendance_summary` JSP page (save the `employee_daily_attendance_summary.jsp` file in the `people-mgmt\jsp` folder):

Listing 23.41: Showing the Code of the `employee_daily_attendance_summary.jsp` File

```
<%@ page language="java" %>
<%@ page session="true" %>
<%@ page  import="com.TimeManagement.*" %>
<%@ page  import="java.io.*" %>
<%@ page  import="java.util.*" %>
<html>
<head>
<title>www.peoplemanagementsolutions.com/Attendance Summary...</title>
<link rel="stylesheet" href="../css/mystyle.css" type="text/css" />
</head>
<body>
<table width="900" border="0" align="center">
<tr>
<td colspan="2"><%@ include file="../jsp/people_header.jsp" %></td>
</tr>
<tr>
<td><%@ include file="../jsp/people_default_menu.jsp" %></td>
</tr><tr>
<td width ="750" valign="top">
<p> </p>
<div align=center class=boldblack>Daily Attendance Summary</div>
<hr width=100% color=#AAAAAA>
<table  border="0"  width=100% >
<%
   String dbopr = "";
   dbopr = (String)session.getAttribute("dbopr");
%>
<tr>
<td bgcolor ='#AAAAAA' align='center' class=whitetext>Employee Id</td>
<td bgcolor ='#AAAAAA' align='center' class=whitetext>Employee Name</td>
<td bgcolor ='#AAAAAA' align='center' class=whitetext>In Time</td>
<td bgcolor ='#AAAAAA' align='center' class=whitetext>Out Time</td>
<td bgcolor ='#AAAAAA' align='center' class=whitetext>Remark</td>
<td bgcolor ='#AAAAAA' align='center' class=whitetext>Opr</td>
</tr>
<%
    ArrayList empDailyAttendanceList = new ArrayList();
    empDailyAttendanceList = (ArrayList)session.getAttribute("empDailyAttend
         anceList");
         if ( empDailyAttendanceList != null && empDailyAttendanceList.size() > 0 ){
         for ( int size = 1; size <= empDailyAttendanceList.size() ; size++ ){
      EmpDailyAttendanceDBObj  empDailyAttendanceDBObj = new EmpDailyAttendan
                ceDBObj();
      empDailyAttendanceDBObj = (EmpDailyAttendanceDBObj)empDailyAttendanceLis
                t.get(size-1);
%>
<form name="form1" method="post">
<tr bgcolor ='#AAAAAA'>
<td align='center'><%=empDailyAttendanceDBObj.emp_id%></td>
<td align='center' ><%=empDailyAttendanceDBObj.emp_name%> </td>
<td align='center' ><%=empDailyAttendanceDBObj.in_time%></td>
<td align='center' ><%=empDailyAttendanceDBObj.out_time%></td>
<td align='center' >
<%
  if(empDailyAttendanceDBObj.remark!=null)
     out.print(empDailyAttendanceDBObj.remark);
  else
     out.print("--");
%>
<td align='center' bgcolor=#AAAAAA >
<a href='http://localhost:8080/people-mgmt/servlet/time_management?dbopr=edit&&
emp_id=<%=empDailyAttendanceDBObj.emp_id%>&&today_date=<%=empDailyAttendanceDBObj.
today_date%>' class=yellowlink>Edit</a></td >
</tr>
<%
    }
   }
   else{
     out.println("Employee does not exist!!!");
   }
```

```
%>
</table>
</tr>
</td>
<tr>
<td colspan="2"><%@include file="../jsp/people_footer.jsp"%></td>
</tr>
</table>
</body>
</html>
```

In Listing 23.41, the `ArrayList` class is used to fetch the data from the database and show the attendance of all the employees for the current day. The employee_daily_attendance_summary JSP page also contains a link, named `Edit,` to edit the attendance record.

Figure 23.21 shows the daily attendance record of all employees for the current date:

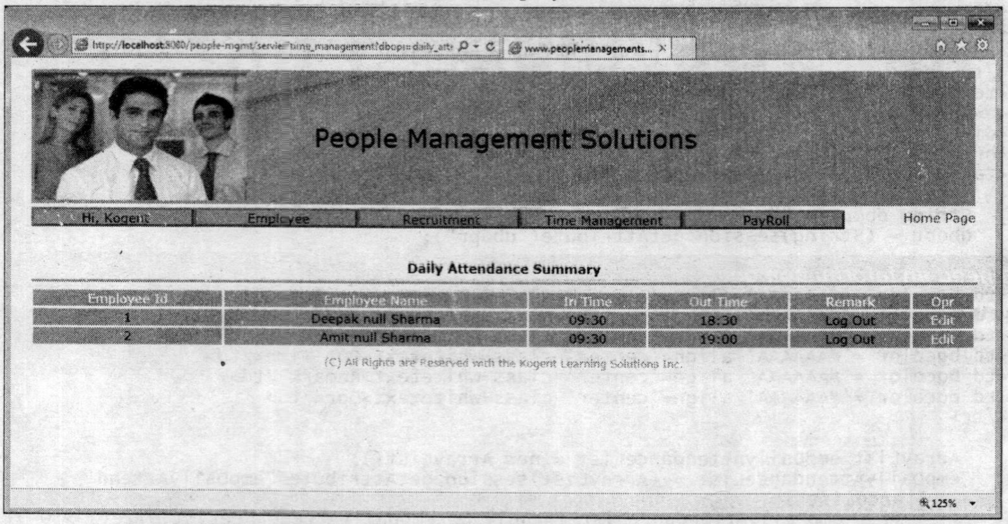

Figure 23.21: Displaying the employee_daily_attendance_summary JSP Page Containing Employees Attendance List

In this section, the Attendance Management module has been designed to handle attendance details of employees of an organization. You have also developed several Java classes as well as servlets used to make this module functional. In addition, this module contains two JSP pages, one for entering in and out time and another for showing daily attendance records of all employees.

The next section deals with the development of the Leave Management module.

Section E

Developing the Leave Management Module

Every organization needs to keep a record of the leaves taken by its employees. The responsibility of granting and managing leaves comes in the purview of the HR department. The HR department can approve or reject the leave of an employee on the basis of reason for leave, projects assigned to the employee, and number of leaves available. In this section, let's develop the Leave Management module to facilitate the HR management in managing the leaves of the employees. This module provides an interface to fill the leave request details and submitting the details for approval. In addition, this module provides another interface, displaying the leave requests approved by the HR management in a summarized format.

The following Java source files are to be created in this module:

- `leave_management.java`
- `LeaveRequest.java`
- `LeaveMgmtBeanMethods.java`
- `GenerateId.java`

In addition to these Java classes, the following JSP files are needed:

- `leave_request.jsp`
- `leave_request_edit.jsp`
- `leave_request_reject.jsp`
- `leave_request_list.jsp`

Let's now create the `leave_management` servlet.

Creating the leave_management Servlet

The leave_management servlet is the controller servlet for this module. Any request for the interaction with the Leave Management module is handled by this servlet, which guides the user to the required JSP page after executing appropriate segments of code. This servlet class uses three other Java classes, i.e. `LeaveRequest`, `GenerateId`, and `LeaveMgmtBeanMethods`, which are discussed later in this section.

Listing 23.42 shows the code of the `leave_management.java` file (save the `leave_management.java` file in the `people-mgmt\WEB-INF\src` folder):

Listing 23.42: Showing the Code of the leave_management.java File

```
import javax.servlet.*;
import javax.servlet.http.*;
import java.util.ArrayList;
import java.io.*;
import java.util.*;
import java.sql.*;
import javax.servlet.annotation.*;
import javax.servlet.annotation.WebServlet;
import com.LeaveManagement.LeaveMgmtBeanMethods;
import com.LeaveManagement.LeaveRequest;
@WebServlet(name="leave_management", urlPatterns="/servlet/leave_management")
public class leave_management extends HttpServlet{
   String dbuser  = ""
   String dbpswd  = ""
   String dburl   = ""
/**Initialize global variables*/
   @Override
public void init(ServletConfig config) throws ServletException{
   System.out.println("initializing controller servlet.");
   ServletContext context = config.getServletContext();
   dbuser = "scott";
   dbpswd = "tiger";
   dburl  = "jdbc:oracle:thin:@192.168.1.123:1521:"+"XE";
   super.init(config);
}
/**Process the HTTP Get request*/
   @Override
public void doGet(HttpServletRequest request, HttpServletResponse response) throws
ServletException, IOException {
```

```
    doPost(request, response);
  }
  /**Process the HTTP Post request*/
    @Override
  public void doPost(HttpServletRequest request, HttpServletResponse response) throws
  ServletException, IOException {
          response.setContentType("text/html");
          PrintWriter out = response.getWriter();
          HttpSession session = request.getSession();
          session.setAttribute("lErrorMsg",null);
          String target = "";
          String action = request.getParameter("action");
          String dbopr = "";
          dbopr = (String)request.getParameter("dbopr");
          session.setAttribute("dbopr",dbopr);
          if( (dbopr != null && dbopr.length() > 0) && (dbopr.equals("leave_request")) ){
                  target = "/jsp/leave_request.jsp";
          }
          else
          if( (dbopr != null && dbopr.length() > 0) && (dbopr.equals("leave_approve")) ){
                  action = "select_leave_request";
          }
          else
          if( (dbopr != null && dbopr.length() > 0) && (dbopr.equals("approve")) ){
                  action = "leave_request_approve";
          }
          else
          if( (dbopr != null && dbopr.length() > 0) && (dbopr.equals("approved_leave")) ){
                  action = "approved_leave_request";
          }
                  else
                      if((dbopr != null && dbopr.length() > 0) &&
  (dbopr.equals("leave_reject")))
                      {
                          action="select_request_request";
                      }
                  else
          if( (dbopr != null && dbopr.length() > 0) && (dbopr.equals("reject")) ){
                  action = "leave_request_reject";
          }
                  else
          if( (dbopr != null && dbopr.length() > 0) && (dbopr.equals("rejected_leave")) ){
                  action = "rejected_leave_request";
          }
          String action_submit = request.getParameter("action_submit");
          System.out.println("action_submit=="+action_submit);
          if ( action_submit != null ){
                  if ( request.getParameter("submit").equals("Submit") ){
                          System.out.println("in the  Submit");
                          if ( action_submit.equals("employee_leave_req_submit") ){
                                  System.out.println("in the employee_leave_req_submit ");
                                  action = "employee_leave_req_submit";
                          }
                  }
                  else
                  if ( request.getParameter("submit").equals("Approve") ){
                          if ( action_submit.equals("employee_leave_req_edit_submit") )
                                  action = "employee_leave_req_edit_submit";
                  }
                          else
                  if ( request.getParameter("submit").equals("Reject") ){
                          if ( action_submit.equals("employee_leave_req_reject_submit") )
                                  action = "employee_leave_req_reject_submit";
                  }
          }
```

```
            if (action!=null){
                    System.out.println("in the  "+action);
                    if (action.equals("leave_request_approve")){
                    String reqId = "";
                    reqId = (String)request.getParameter("req_id");
                    String empId = "";
                    empId = (String)request.getParameter("emp_id");
                    LeaveMgmtBeanMethods leaveMgmtBeanMethods = new
    LeaveMgmtBeanMethods(dbuser,dbpswd,dburl);
                    LeaveRequest leaveRequest = new LeaveRequest();
                    leaveRequest =
    (LeaveRequest)leaveMgmtBeanMethods.getRecordByPrimaryKey(reqId,empId);
                    session.setAttribute("leaveRequest",leaveRequest);
                    target = "/jsp/leave_request_edit.jsp";
            }
                            else
                    if (action.equals("leave_request_reject")){
                    String reqId = "";
                    reqId = (String)request.getParameter("req_id");
                    String empId = "";
                    empId = (String)request.getParameter("emp_id");
                    LeaveMgmtBeanMethods leaveMgmtBeanMethods = new
    LeaveMgmtBeanMethods(dbuser,dbpswd,dburl);
                    LeaveRequest leaveRequest = new LeaveRequest();
                    leaveRequest =
    (LeaveRequest)leaveMgmtBeanMethods.getRecordByPrimaryKey(reqId,empId);
                    session.setAttribute("leaveRequest",leaveRequest);
                    target = "/jsp/leave_request_reject.jsp";
            }
            else
            if (action.equals("select_leave_request") ||
    action.equals("approved_leave_request")){
                    LeaveMgmtBeanMethods leaveMgmtBeanMethods  = new
    LeaveMgmtBeanMethods(dbuser,dbpswd,dburl);
                    ArrayList leaveRequestList = new ArrayList();
                    String criteria = "";
                    if( action.equals("select_leave_request") )
                            criteria = " where leave_status='Req' ";
                    else
                            criteria = " where leave_status='Aprv' ";

                    leaveRequestList = (
ArrayList)leaveMgmtBeanMethods.selectLeaveRequestByCriteria(criteria);
                    session.setAttribute("leaveRequestList",leaveRequestList);
                    System.out.println("leaveRequestList.size()"+leaveRequestList.size());
                    target = "/jsp/leave_request_list.jsp";
            }
            else
            if (action.equals("employee_leave_req_submit")){
                    LeaveRequest popLeaveRequest = new LeaveRequest();
                    LeaveMgmtBeanMethods leaveMgmtBeanMethods = new
    LeaveMgmtBeanMethods(dbuser,dbpswd,dburl);
                    popLeaveRequest =
    (LeaveRequest)leaveMgmtBeanMethods.populateLeaveRequestFromReq(request);
                    popLeaveRequest.leave_status = "Req";
                    LeaveRequest leaveRequest = new LeaveRequest();
                    leaveRequest =
    (LeaveRequest)leaveMgmtBeanMethods.getRecordByPrimaryKey(popLeaveRequest.req_id,popLeaveRe
    quest.emp_id);
    // Qouted Today
                    //if ( (popLeaveRequest.emp_id).equals(leaveRequest.emp_id) &&
    (popLeaveRequest.req_id).equals(leaveRequest.req_id) ){
                    //      String lErrorMsg = "Employee Already Exist";
                    //      session.setAttribute("lErrorMsg",lErrorMsg);
                    //      target = "/jsp/leave_request.jsp";
                    //}
```

```
                //else{
                        int rval =
leaveMgmtBeanMethods.insertLeaveRequest(popLeaveRequest);
                        LeaveRequest sLeaveRequest = new LeaveRequest();
                        sLeaveRequest =
(LeaveRequest)leaveMgmtBeanMethods.getRecordByPrimaryKey(popLeaveRequest.req_id,popLeaveRe
quest.emp_id);
                        session.setAttribute("leaveRequest",sLeaveRequest);
// Inserted Today
                        if ( rval > 0 ){
                        LeaveRequest leaveRequest1 = new LeaveRequest();
                        leaveRequest1 =
(LeaveRequest)leaveMgmtBeanMethods.getRecordByPrimaryKey(popLeaveRequest.req_id,popLeaveRe
quest.emp_id);
                        session.setAttribute("LeaveRequest",leaveRequest1);
                        ArrayList leaveRequestList = new ArrayList();
                        String criteria = "";
                        criteria = " where leave_status='Req' ";
                        leaveRequestList = (
ArrayList)leaveMgmtBeanMethods.selectLeaveRequestByCriteria(criteria);
                        session.setAttribute("leaveRequestList",leaveRequestList);

   System.out.println("leaveRequestList.size()"+leaveRequestList.size());
                        target = "/jsp/leave_request_list.jsp";
                        }
                        // target = "/jsp/leave_request_edit.jsp";
                //}
        }
        else
        if (action.equals("employee_leave_req_edit_submit")){
                LeaveRequest popLeaveRequest = new LeaveRequest();
                LeaveMgmtBeanMethods leaveMgmtBeanMethods = new
LeaveMgmtBeanMethods(dbuser,dbpswd,dburl);
                String ldbopr = (String)session.getAttribute("dbopr");
                System.out.println("dbopr????????????????//"+ldbopr);
                popLeaveRequest =
(LeaveRequest)leaveMgmtBeanMethods.populateLeaveRequestFromReq(request);
                if(ldbopr != null && ldbopr.equals("approve"))
                        popLeaveRequest.leave_status = "Aprv";
                else
                        popLeaveRequest.leave_status = "Req";

   System.out.println("dbopr????????????????//"+popLeaveRequest.leave_status);
                int rval = leaveMgmtBeanMethods
.updateLeaveRequestByPrimaryKey(popLeaveRequest);
                if ( rval > 0 ){
                        LeaveRequest LeaveRequest = new LeaveRequest();
                        LeaveRequest =
(LeaveRequest)leaveMgmtBeanMethods.getRecordByPrimaryKey(popLeaveRequest.req_id,popLeaveRe
quest.emp_id);
                        session.setAttribute("LeaveRequest",LeaveRequest);
                        ArrayList leaveRequestList = new ArrayList();
                        String criteria = "";
                        criteria = " where leave_status='Aprv' ";  // changed from Req
                        leaveRequestList = (
ArrayList)leaveMgmtBeanMethods.selectLeaveRequestByCriteria(criteria);
                        session.setAttribute("leaveRequestList",leaveRequestList);

   System.out.println("leaveRequestList.size()"+leaveRequestList.size());
                        session.setAttribute("dbopr","approved_leave");
 //added today
                        target = "/jsp/leave_request_list.jsp";
                }
                else{
                        target = "/jsp/employee_edit.jsp";
                }
```

```
        }else
                    if (action.equals("employee_leave_req_reject_submit")){
                LeaveRequest popLeaveRequest = new LeaveRequest();
                LeaveMgmtBeanMethods leaveMgmtBeanMethods = new
LeaveMgmtBeanMethods(dbuser,dbpswd,dburl);
                String ldbopr = (String)session.getAttribute("dbopr");
                System.out.println("dbopr????????????????//"+ldbopr);
                popLeaveRequest =
(LeaveRequest)leaveMgmtBeanMethods.populateLeaveRequestFromReq(request);
                if(ldbopr != null && ldbopr.equals("reject"))
                        popLeaveRequest.leave_status = "Rej";
                else
                        popLeaveRequest.leave_status = "Req";

   System.out.println("dbopr????????????????//"+popLeaveRequest.leave_status);
                int rval = leaveMgmtBeanMethods
.updateLeaveRequestByPrimaryKey(popLeaveRequest);
                if ( rval > 0 ){
                        LeaveRequest LeaveRequest = new LeaveRequest();
                        LeaveRequest =
(LeaveRequest)leaveMgmtBeanMethods.getRecordByPrimaryKey(popLeaveRequest.req_id,popLeaveRe
quest.emp_id);
                        session.setAttribute("LeaveRequest",LeaveRequest);
                        ArrayList leaveRequestList = new ArrayList();
                        String criteria = "";
                        criteria = " where leave_status='Rej' ";  // changed from Req
                        leaveRequestList = (
ArrayList)leaveMgmtBeanMethods.selectLeaveRequestByCriteria(criteria);
                        session.setAttribute("leaveRequestList",leaveRequestList);

   System.out.println("leaveRequestList.size()"+leaveRequestList.size());
                        session.setAttribute("dbopr","rejected_leave");
//added today
                        target = "/jsp/leave_request_list.jsp";
                }
                else{
                        target = "/jsp/employee_edit.jsp";
                }
        }
        } // (action== null )
        /* forwarding the request/response to the targeted view */
        RequestDispatcher requestDispatcher =
getServletContext().getRequestDispatcher(target);
        requestDispatcher.forward(request, response);
  } // doPost closed
}// class closed
```

In Listing 23.42, the servlet uses objects of the `LeaveRequest` and `LeaveMgmtBeanMethods` classes to perform the operations according to the parameter passed and the values of the `action` and `target` variables. The methods defined in the `LeaveMgmtBeanMethods` class perform the actual database interaction on behalf of the servlet and return the object of the `LeaveRequest` class. This object is used as a carrier of data from one method to another.

Creating the LeaveRequest Class

The member attributes of the `LeaveRequest` class are set with the information associated with a leave request, including whether it has been approved or not. This information is updated in the `LEAVE_REQUEST` table. The `LeaveRequest` class has member variables matching with the table attributes. In other words, these member variables are being used as form beans without any setter and getter methods, and data is being set and fetched from the corresponding object manually.

Listing 23.43 shows the code for the `LeaveRequest.java file` (save the `LeaveRequest.java` file in the `people-mgmt\WEB-INF\src\com\LeaveManagement` folder):

Listing 23.43: Showing the Code of the LeaveRequest.java File

```
package com.LeaveManagement;
public class LeaveRequest {
  public String req_id;
  public String emp_id;
  public String emp_name;
  public String today_date;
  public String level_id;
  public String dept_id;
  public String from_date;
  public String to_date;
  public int days;
  public String reason;
  public String leave_type;
  public String activity_1;
  public String activity_2;
  public String activity_3;
  public String person_1;
  public String person_2;
  public String person_3;
  public String detail_1;
  public String detail_2;
  public String detail_3;
  public String leave_status;
  public String remark;
  public String address;
}
```

In Listing 23.43, the attributes of the `LeaveRequest` class are same as those of the leave request form. The object of this class is used to store the data related to the leaves of employees in the database.

Let's now create the `LeaveMgmtBeanMethods` class in the next subsection.

Creating the LeaveMgmtBeanMethods Class

The `LeaveMgmtBeanMethods` class defines various methods, such as `updateLeaveRequestByPrimaryKey()` `insertLeaveRequest()`, and `populateLeaveRequestFromReq()`, which are used to insert, retrieve, and update data in the LEAVE_REQUEST table. All these methods are used to execute one or another SQL query to interact with the database and perform the particular operation.

Listing 23.44 shows the code of the `LeaveMgmtBeanMethods.java` file (save the `LeaveMgmtBeanMethods.java` file in the `people-mgmt\WEB-INF\src\com\LeaveManagement` folder):

Listing 23.44: Showing the Code of the LeaveMgmtBeanMethods.java File

```
package com.LeaveManagement;
import java.sql.*;
import javax.servlet.http.*;
import java.util.ArrayList;

public class LeaveMgmtBeanMethods{
  public String DBUser;
  public String DBPswd;
  public String DBUrl ;
  public LeaveMgmtBeanMethods(){ }
public LeaveMgmtBeanMethods(String inDBUser, String inDBPswd, String inDBUrl ){
      DBUser = inDBUser ;
      DBPswd = inDBPswd;
      DBUrl  = inDBUrl;
}
public void initializeLeaveRequest(LeaveRequest inLeaveRequest ){
  inLeaveRequest.req_id ="";
  inLeaveRequest.emp_id ="";
  inLeaveRequest.emp_name ="";
  inLeaveRequest.today_date="";
  inLeaveRequest.level_id="";
  inLeaveRequest.dept_id="";
  inLeaveRequest.from_date="";
```

```
      inLeaveRequest.to_date="";
      inLeaveRequest.days= 0;
      inLeaveRequest.reason="";
      inLeaveRequest.leave_type="";
      inLeaveRequest.activity_1="";
      inLeaveRequest.activity_2="";
      inLeaveRequest.activity_3="";
      inLeaveRequest.person_1="";
      inLeaveRequest.person_2="";
      inLeaveRequest.person_3="";
      inLeaveRequest.detail_1="";
      inLeaveRequest.detail_2="";
      inLeaveRequest.detail_3="";
      inLeaveRequest.leave_status="";
      inLeaveRequest.remark="";
      inLeaveRequest.address="";
   }
   public LeaveRequest getRecordByPrimaryKey(String inReqId, String inEmpId){
      LeaveRequest  leaveRequest = new LeaveRequest();
      java.sql.Date date;
      try{
         DriverManager.registerDriver(new oracle.jdbc.driver.OracleDriver());
         Connection conn= DriverManager.getConnection(DBUrl,DBUser,DBPswd);
         Statement stmt = conn.createStatement();
         String lSqlString ="select * from LEAVE_REQUEST ";
         lSqlString = lSqlString + "where req_id='"+inReqId+"' ";
         lSqlString = lSqlString + "and emp_id='"+inEmpId+"' ";
         ResultSet rs  = null;
         rs  = stmt.executeQuery(lSqlString);
         if( rs.next()){
            leaveRequest.req_id   =  (String)rs.getString("req_id");
            leaveRequest.emp_id   =  (String)rs.getString("emp_id");
            leaveRequest.emp_name = (String)rs.getString("emp_name");
            date=rs.getDate("today_date");
            leaveRequest.today_date  = date.toString();
            date=rs.getDate("from_date");
            leaveRequest.from_date  = date.toString();
            date=rs.getDate("to_date");
            leaveRequest.to_date = date.toString();
            leaveRequest.level_id = (String)rs.getString("level_id");
            leaveRequest.dept_id = (String)rs.getString("dept_id");
            leaveRequest.days =    rs.getInt("days");
            leaveRequest.reason = (String)rs.getString("reason");
            leaveRequest.leave_type = (String)rs.getString("leave_type");
            leaveRequest.activity_1 = (String)rs.getString("activity_1");
            leaveRequest.activity_2 = (String)rs.getString("activity_2");
            leaveRequest.activity_3 = (String)rs.getString("activity_3");
            leaveRequest.person_1 = (String)rs.getString("person_1");
            leaveRequest.person_2 = (String)rs.getString("person_2");
            leaveRequest.person_3 = (String)rs.getString("person_3");
            leaveRequest.detail_1 = (String)rs.getString("detail_1");
            leaveRequest.detail_2 = (String)rs.getString("detail_2");
            leaveRequest.detail_3 = (String)rs.getString("detail_3");
            leaveRequest.leave_status = (String)rs.getString("leave_status");
            leaveRequest.address = (String)rs.getString("address");
            leaveRequest.remark = (String)rs.getString("remark");
            System.out.println("fffff==="+rs.getString("emp_id"));
      }
      else{
            initializeLeaveRequest(leaveRequest);
      }
      System.out.println("fffff====="+leaveRequest.emp_id);
   }
      catch(SQLException  ex){
            ex.printStackTrace();
```

```
    }
    return leaveRequest;
  }
  public ArrayList selectLeaveRequestByCriteria(String inCriteria) {
    ArrayList LeaveRequestList = new ArrayList();
    java.sql.Date date;
    try{
          DriverManager.registerDriver(new oracle.jdbc.driver.OracleDriver());
          Connection conn= DriverManager.getConnection(DBUrl,DBUser,DBPswd);
          Statement stmt = conn.createStatement();
          String lSqlString =     "select * from LEAVE_REQUEST ";
          if( inCriteria != null && inCriteria.length() > 0 ){
                lSqlString = lSqlString +" "+inCriteria+"" ;
          }
          lSqlString = lSqlString +" order by req_id" ;
          System.out.println("Criteria===== "+inCriteria+" and
                query="+lSqlString);
          ResultSet rs  = null;
          rs  = stmt.executeQuery(lSqlString);
          while( rs.next()){
                LeaveRequest  leaveRequest = new LeaveRequest();
                leaveRequest.req_id   =  (String)rs.getString("req_id");
                leaveRequest.emp_id   =  (String)rs.getString("emp_id");
                leaveRequest.emp_name = (String)rs.getString("emp_name");
                date=rs.getDate("today_date");
                leaveRequest.today_date  = date.toString();
                date=rs.getDate("from_date");
                leaveRequest.from_date  = date.toString();
                date=rs.getDate("to_date");
                leaveRequest.to_date = date.toString();
                leaveRequest.level_id = (String)rs.getString("level_id");
                leaveRequest.dept_id = (String)rs.getString("dept_id");
                leaveRequest.days =    rs.getInt("days");
                leaveRequest.reason = (String)rs.getString("reason");
                leaveRequest.leave_type = (String)rs.getString("leave_type");
                leaveRequest.activity_1 = (String)rs.getString("activity_1");
                leaveRequest.activity_2 = (String)rs.getString("activity_2");
                leaveRequest.activity_3 = (String)rs.getString("activity_3");
                leaveRequest.person_1 = (String)rs.getString("person_1");
                leaveRequest.person_2 = (String)rs.getString("person_2");
                leaveRequest.person_3 = (String)rs.getString("person_3");
                leaveRequest.detail_1 = (String)rs.getString("detail_1");
                leaveRequest.detail_2 = (String)rs.getString("detail_2");
                leaveRequest.detail_3 = (String)rs.getString("detail_3");
                leaveRequest.leave_status = (String)rs.getString("leave_status");
                leaveRequest.address = (String)rs.getString("address");
                leaveRequest.remark = (String)rs.getString("remark");
                LeaveRequestList.add(leaveRequest);
          }
    }
    catch(SQLException  ex){
          ex.printStackTrace();
    }
    return LeaveRequestList;
  }
  public int updateLeaveRequestByPrimaryKey(LeaveRequest inLeaveRequest){
    int recupd = 0;
    String lQuery = "";
    lQuery = lQuery +"update LEAVE_REQUEST set emp_name='"+inLeaveRequest.emp_name+"'  ";
    lQuery = lQuery +" , today_date=to_date('"+inLeaveRequest
          .today_date+"','yyyy-mm-dd') ";
    lQuery = lQuery +" , level_id='"+inLeaveRequest.level_id+"' ";
    lQuery = lQuery +" , dept_id='"+inLeaveRequest.dept_id+"' ";
    lQuery = lQuery +" , from_date=to_date('"+inLeaveRequest.from_date+"', 'yyyy-mm-dd') ";
    lQuery = lQuery +" , to_date=to_date('"+inLeaveRequest.to_date+"', 'yyyy-mm-dd') ";
```

```
    lQuery = lQuery +" , days='"+inLeaveRequest.days+"' ";
    lQuery = lQuery +" , reason='"+inLeaveRequest.reason+"' ";
    lQuery = lQuery +" , leave_type='"+inLeaveRequest.leave_type+"' ";
    lQuery = lQuery +" , activity_1='"+inLeaveRequest.activity_1+"' ";
    lQuery = lQuery +" , activity_2='"+inLeaveRequest.activity_2+"' ";
    lQuery = lQuery +" , activity_3='"+inLeaveRequest.activity_3+"' ";
    lQuery = lQuery +" , person_1='"+inLeaveRequest.person_1+"' ";
    lQuery = lQuery +" , person_2='"+inLeaveRequest.person_2+"' ";
    lQuery = lQuery +" , person_3='"+inLeaveRequest.person_3+"' ";
    lQuery = lQuery +" , detail_1='"+inLeaveRequest.detail_1+"' ";
    lQuery = lQuery +" , detail_2='"+inLeaveRequest.detail_2+"' ";
    lQuery = lQuery +" , detail_3='"+inLeaveRequest.detail_3+"' ";
    lQuery = lQuery +" , address='"+inLeaveRequest.address+"' ";
    lQuery = lQuery +" , remark='"+inLeaveRequest.remark+"' ";
    lQuery = lQuery +" , leave_status='"+inLeaveRequest.leave_status+"' ";
    lQuery = lQuery + "where req_id='"+inLeaveRequest.req_id+"' ";
    lQuery = lQuery + "and emp_id='"+inLeaveRequest.emp_id+"' ";
    System.out.println("lSqlString===:"+lQuery);
    try{
          DriverManager.registerDriver(new oracle.jdbc.driver.OracleDriver());
          Connection conn= DriverManager.getConnection(DBUrl,DBUser,DBPswd);
          Statement stmt = conn.createStatement();
          recupd  = stmt.executeUpdate(lQuery);
    }
    catch(SQLException  ex){
          ex.printStackTrace();
    }
    return recupd;
 }
 public LeaveRequest populateLeaveRequestFromReq(HttpServletRequest inReq){
    LeaveRequest  leaveRequest = new LeaveRequest();
    leaveRequest.req_id   =  (String)inReq.getParameter("req_id");
    leaveRequest.emp_id   =  (String)inReq.getParameter("emp_id");
    leaveRequest.emp_name = (String)inReq.getParameter("emp_name");
    leaveRequest.today_date  = (String)inReq.getParameter("today_date");
    leaveRequest.from_date  = (String)inReq.getParameter("from_date");
    leaveRequest.to_date = (String)inReq.getParameter("to_date");
    leaveRequest.level_id = (String)inReq.getParameter("level_id");
    leaveRequest.dept_id = (String)inReq.getParameter("dept_id");
    leaveRequest.days = Integer.parseInt((String)inReq.getParameter("days"));
    leaveRequest.reason = (String)inReq.getParameter("reason");
    leaveRequest.leave_type = (String)inReq.getParameter("leave_type");
    leaveRequest.activity_1 = (String)inReq.getParameter("activity_1");
    leaveRequest.activity_2 = (String)inReq.getParameter("activity_2");
    leaveRequest.activity_3 = (String)inReq.getParameter("activity_3");
    leaveRequest.person_1 = (String)inReq.getParameter("person_1");
    leaveRequest.person_2 = (String)inReq.getParameter("person_2");
    leaveRequest.person_3 = (String)inReq.getParameter("person_3");
    leaveRequest.detail_1 = (String)inReq.getParameter("detail_1");
    leaveRequest.detail_2 = (String)inReq.getParameter("detail_2");
    leaveRequest.detail_3 = (String)inReq.getParameter("detail_3");
    leaveRequest.leave_status = (String)inReq.getParameter("leave_status");
    leaveRequest.address = (String)inReq.getParameter("address");
    leaveRequest.remark = (String)inReq.getParameter("remark");
    return leaveRequest;
 }
 public int insertLeaveRequest(LeaveRequest inLeaveRequest){
    int recupd = 0;
    String lQuery = "";
    lQuery = lQuery +"insert into LEAVE_REQUEST  values ( ";
    lQuery = lQuery +" '"+inLeaveRequest.req_id+"'  ";
    lQuery = lQuery +" , '"+inLeaveRequest.emp_id+"'  ";
    lQuery = lQuery +" , '"+inLeaveRequest.emp_name+"'  ";
    lQuery = lQuery +" , to_date('"+inLeaveRequest.today_date+"','yyyy-mm-dd') ";
    lQuery = lQuery +" , '"+inLeaveRequest.level_id+"' ";
    lQuery = lQuery +" , '"+inLeaveRequest.dept_id+"' ";
    lQuery = lQuery +" , to_date('"+inLeaveRequest.from_date+"', 'yyyy-mm-dd') ";
    lQuery = lQuery +" , to_date('"+inLeaveRequest.to_date+"','yyyy-mm-dd') ";
```

```
        lQuery = lQuery +" , "+inLeaveRequest.days+" ";
        lQuery = lQuery +" , '"+inLeaveRequest.reason+"' ";
        lQuery = lQuery +" , '"+inLeaveRequest.leave_type+"' ";
        lQuery = lQuery +" , '"+inLeaveRequest.activity_1+"' ";
        lQuery = lQuery +" , '"+inLeaveRequest.activity_2+"' ";
        lQuery = lQuery +" , '"+inLeaveRequest.activity_3+"' ";
        lQuery = lQuery +" , '"+inLeaveRequest.person_1+"' ";
        lQuery = lQuery +" , '"+inLeaveRequest.person_2+"' ";
        lQuery = lQuery +" , '"+inLeaveRequest.person_3+"' ";
        lQuery = lQuery +" , '"+inLeaveRequest.detail_1+"' ";
        lQuery = lQuery +" , '"+inLeaveRequest.detail_2+"' ";
        lQuery = lQuery +" , '"+inLeaveRequest.detail_3+"' ";
        lQuery = lQuery +" , '"+inLeaveRequest.address+"' ";
        lQuery = lQuery +" , '"+inLeaveRequest.remark+"' ";
        lQuery = lQuery +" , '"+inLeaveRequest.leave_status+"' ";
        lQuery = lQuery + " )";
        System.out.println("lSqlString===:"+lQuery);
        try {
                DriverManager.registerDriver(new oracle.jdbc.driver.OracleDriver());
                Connection conn= DriverManager.getConnection(DBUrl,DBUser,DBPswd);
                Statement stmt = conn.createStatement();
                recupd  = stmt.executeUpdate(lQuery);
        }
        catch(SQLException  ex){
                ex.printStackTrace();
        }
        return recupd;
    }
}
```

In Listing 23.44, the `insertLeaveRequest()` method inserts a leave request in the `LEAVE_REQUEST` table; whereas, the `updateLeaveRequestByPrimaryKey()` method updates the status of the leave request, such as approved or rejected, in the `LEAVE_REQUEST` table.

Creating the GenerateId Class

`The GenerateId` class is developed for the auto-generation of the value of the `req_id field in the database`. Listing 23.45 shows the code for the `GenerateId.java` file (save the `GenerateId.java` file in the `people-mgmt\WEB-INF\src\com\LeaveManagement` folder):

Listing 23.45: Showing the Code of the GenerateId.java File

```
package com.LeaveManagement;
import java.sql.*;
import javax.sql.*;
public class GenerateId
{
    public int generateRequestId(){
    int req_id=0;
    try{
            Class.forName("oracle.jdbc.driver.OracleDriver");
            Connection conn= DriverManager.getConnection("jdbc:oracle:thin:
                    @192.168.1.123:1521:"+"XE","scott","tiger");
            Statement stmt = conn.createStatement();
            String query="select max(req_id) as req_id from LEAVE_REQUEST ";
            ResultSet rs = null;
            rs = stmt.executeQuery(query);
            if(rs.next()){
                    String id = rs.getString("req_id");
                    req_id=Integer.parseInt(id);
            }
            req_id = req_id + 1;
        }
            catch(SQLException  ex){
                    ex.printStackTrace();
            }
            catch(Exception e) {
                    e.printStackTrace();
            }
    return req_id;
    }
}
```

In Listing 23.45, the `req_id` field is generated automatically, as the select query returns the maximum value of the `req_id` coulmn. This maximum value retrieved from the database is incremented by 1 to allocate a unique id for a new leave request.

This ends up the discussion on the creation of the Java files. You should compile all the Java files and save the generated .class files in their respective folders. You do not need to specify servlet-mapping in the `web.xml` file as the @WebServlet annotation has been used to map a servlet to a url-pattern.

Let's now design the JSP pages for this module.

Designing JSP Views

After writing code for servlet and other Java classes, let's design the required JSP pages for user interface. There are three JSP pages designed for this module, i.e. `leave_request`, `leave_request_edit`, and `leave_request_list`. The first JSP page, `leave_request`, provides a form for a leave request; and the second JSP page, `leave_request_edit`, is used to set the status of the leave, i.e. approved or not. The third JSP page, `leave_request_list`, lists all the leave requests of all the employees of the organization.

Creating the leave_request JSP Page

The `leave_request` JSP page provides a form containing the fields required to apply for a leave. The form consists of data entry fields that are categorized into various sections, such as employee details, leave details, and activity details. These details include `employee id`, `name`, `designation`, `department`, the number of days worked, activities the employee is currently responsible for, and the name of the person who will be responsible for the respective activities in the absence of this employee.

Listing 23.46 shows the code for the `leave_request.jsp` file (save the `leave_request.jsp` file in the `people-mgmt\jsp` folder):

Listing 23.46: Showing the Code of the leave_request JSP Page

```
<%@ page language="java"  import="java.util.*, java.text.SimpleDateFormat" %>
<%@ page session="true" %>
<%@ page  import="com.LeaveManagement.*" %>
<%  GenerateId gen=new GenerateId();
    int req_id=gen.generateRequestId();
%>
<html>
<head>
<title>www.peoplemanagementsolutions.com/Leave Request</title>
<link rel="stylesheet" href="../css/mystyle.css" type="text/css" />
<script language="javascript">
   function validateForm() {
     var myName=document.form1.emp_id.value;
      if (myName =="") {
         alert ("Employee Id field cannot be blank");
         document.form1.emp_id.focus();
    return false;
      }
      myName=document.form1.emp_name.value;
      if (myName =="") {
         alert ("Employee Name cannot be blank");
    document.form1.emp_name.focus();
         return false;
      }
      myName=document.form1.from_date.value;
      if (myName =="") {
         alert ("Provide the starting Date of Leave");
    document.form1.from_date.focus();
         return false;
      }
      myName=document.form1.to_date.value;
      if (myName =="") {
         alert ("Provide the date to which Leave applied");
    document.form1.to_date.focus();
```

```
            return false;
        }
        myName=document.form1.reason.value;
        if (myName =="") {
            alert ("Provide the Valid reason for Leave");
     document.form1.reason.focus();
            return false;
        }
        myName=document.form1.address.value;
        if (myName =="") {
          alert ("Address Field cannot be blank");
     document.form1.address.focus();
          return false;
        }
    form1.submit();
    }
</script>
</head>
<body>
<table width="900" border="0" align="center">
<tr>
<td colspan="2"><%@ include file="../jsp/people_header.jsp" %></td>
</tr>
<tr>
<td width="900" ><%@ include file="../jsp/people_default_menu.jsp" %></td>
</tr><tr>
<td width ="750" valign="top" align = "center">
<form name="form1" method="post">
<input type='hidden' name='req_id' id='req_id 'size ='10' value='<%= req_id %>'/>
<table  border="0" align="top" width=600>
<tr>
<td colspan='4' height=20 height=20 bgcolor ='#AAAAAA' class=whitetext
  align=center>Leave Application</td>
</tr>
<tr>
<td >Request ID</td>
<td align='left'><input type='text' disabled='disabled' name='dup_req_id'
  id='dup_req_id 'size ='10' value='<%= req_id %>'/> </td>
<td >Date(YYYY-MM-DD)</td><input type='hidden' name='today_date' id='today_date
'size ='10' value='<%= new SimpleDateFormat("yyyy-MM-dd").format(new Date()) %>'/>
<td align='left'><input type='text' name='dup_today_date' disabled='disabled'
id='dup_today_date 'size ='10' value='<%= new SimpleDateFormat("yyyy-MM-
dd").format(new Date()) %>'/> </td>
</tr>
<tr>
<td>Employee Id<sup>*</sup></td>
<td align='left'><input type='text' name='emp_id' id='emp_id 'size ='10'
  value=''/> </td>
<td>Name<sup>*</sup></td>
<td align='left'><input type='text' name='emp_name' id='emp_name 'size ='20'
value='' /> </td>
</tr>
<tr>
<td>Designation</td>
<td align='left'><select name="level_id" id="level_id">
<option value='Select Designation' selected> Select Designation
<option value='CW'> Content Writer
<option value='TS'> Tester
<option value='HR'> Human Resource Manager
<option value='AC'> Accountant
<option value='AM'> Admin Manager
<option value='EM'> Event Manager
<option value='TL'> Team Leader
<option value='PM'> Project Manager
<option value='TR'> Trainer
```

```
</select></td>
<td>Department</td>
<td align='left'><select id='dept_id' name='dept_id'>
<option value='select Department' selected> Select Department
<option value='CS'> Content Solutions
<option value='TS'> Testing
<option value='HR'> Human Resource
<option value='AC'> Accounts
<option value='AD'> Administration
<option value='EM'> Event Management
</select> </td>
</tr>
<tr>
<td colspan='4' height=20 bgcolor ='#AAAAAA' class=whitetext align=center>Leave
Detail</td>
</tr>
<tr>
<td>From(YYYY-MM-DD)<sup>*</sup></td>  
<td>To(YYYY-MM-DD)<sup>*</sup></td>
<td>Days</td>
<td> </td>
</tr>
<tr>
<td align='left' ><input type='text' name='from_date' id='from_date' size ='10'
value=''/> </td>
<td align='left' ><input type='text' name='to_date' id='to_date' size ='10'
value=''/> </td>
<td align='left'><input type='text' name='days' id='days' size ='5' value=''/>
</td>
<td> </td>
</tr>
<tr>
<td colspan=2>Reason For Leave(100 letters only)<sup>*</sup></td>
<td align='left' colspan=2><textarea name='reason' id='reason' col='80' rows='4'
value=''/></textarea></td>
</tr>
<tr>
<td colspan=2>Type Of Leave Applied For</td>
<td align='left' colspan=2><SELECT name='leave_type' >
<OPTION VALUE=></OPTION>
<OPTION VALUE=CL>CL</OPTION>
<OPTION VALUE=SL>SL</OPTION></SELECT>
</td>
</tr>
<tr>
<td colspan='4' height=20 bgcolor ='#AAAAAA' class=whitetext align=center>Major
Activity to Be Handled During The Leave Applied</td>
</td>
</tr>
<tr>
<td align=right>S.No.</td>
<td>Activity Details</td>
<td>Name Of the Person Responsible</td>
<td>Details</td>
</tr>
<tr>
<td align=right>1.</td>
<td align='left'><input type='text' name='activity_1' id='activity_1' size ='20'
value=''/> </td>
<td align='left'><input type='text' name='person_1' id='person_1' size ='20'
value=''/> </td>
<td align='left'><input type='text' name='detail_1' id='detail_1' size ='20'
value=''/> </td>
</tr><tr>
<td align=right>2.</td>
```

```
<td align='left'><input type='text' name='activity_2' id='activity_2' size ='20'
value=''/> </td>
<td align='left'><input type='text' name='person_2' id='person_2' size ='20'
value=''/> </td>
<td align='left'><input type='text' name='detail_2' id='detail_2' size ='20'
value=''/> </td>
</tr>
<tr>
<td align=right>3.</td>
<td align='left'><input type='text' name='activity_3' id='activity_3' size ='20'
value=''/> </td>
<td align='left'><input type='text' name='person_3' id='person_3' size ='20'
value=''/> </td>
<td align='left'><input type='text' name='detail_3' id='detail_3' size ='20'
value=''/> </td>
</tr>
<tr>
<td colspan='4' height=20 bgcolor ='#AAAAAA' class=whitetext align=center>Contact
Details of the applicant during the leave period</td>
</tr>
<tr>
<td>Address<sup>*</sup></td>
<td align='left' colspan='2'><input type='text' name='address' id='address' size
='20' value=''/></td>
<td></td>
</tr>
<tr>
<td>Remark</td>
<td align='left' colspan='2'><input type='text' name='remark' id='remark' size
='20' value=''/> </td>
<td></td>
</tr>
<tr><td> All the ( <sup>*</sup>) marked are mandatory</td></tr><tr>
<td align='center' colspan='4'>
<input type='submit' name='submit' id='submit' size ='10'
value='Submit'onClick="return validateForm()"/>
<input type='hidden' name='action_submit' id='action_submit' size ='10'
value='employee_leave_req_submit'/>
</td>
</tr>
</table>
</td>
</tr>
<tr>
<td colspan="2"><%@include file="../jsp/people_footer.jsp"%></td>
</tr>
</table>
</body>
</html>
```

In Listing 23.46, the `req_id` field is disabled because it is generated automatically with the help of the `GenerateId` class. The validations are imposed on some fields, such as name, designation, and department, as these fields cannot be left blank. When you click the `Leave Apply` link under the `Leave Management` section, the `leave_management` servlet redirects you to the leave_request JSP page, showing various fields to be filled to apply for a leave.

Figure 23.22 shows the leave request form:

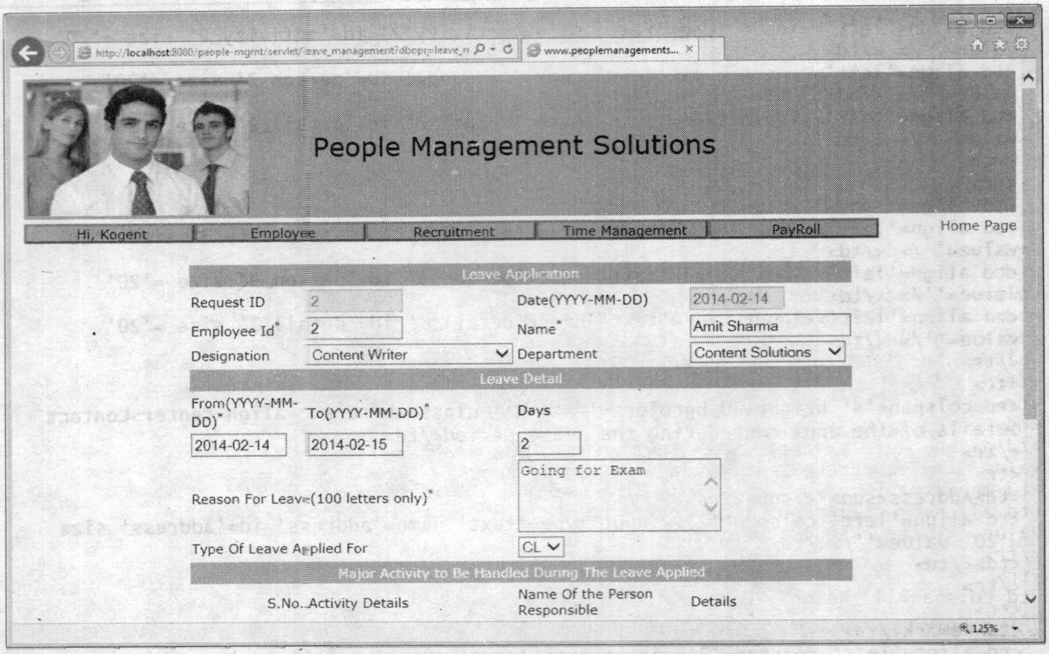

Figure 23.22: Displaying the leave_request JSP Page

Creating the leave_request_edit JSP Page

The `leave_request_edit JSP` page is similar to the `leave_request JSP page`, except that all the fields provided in the `leave_request_edit` JSP page are already filled with the leave details. The fields can be updated for new values and submitted to the servlet for performing the update operations in the table.

Listing 23.47 shows the code of the `leave_request_edit.jsp` file (save the `leave_request_edit.jsp` file in the `people-mgmt\jsp` folder):

Listing 23.47: Showing the Code of the leave_request_edit.jsp File

```
<%@ page language="java" %>
<%@ page session="true" %>
<%@ page  import="com.LeaveManagement.*" %>
<html>
<head>
<title>www.peoplemanagementsolutions.com/Leave Request</title>
<link rel="stylesheet" href="../css/mystyle.css" type="text/css" />
</head>
<body>
<table width="900" border="0" align="center">
<tr>
<td colspan="2"><%@ include file="../jsp/people_header.jsp" %></td>
</tr>
<tr>
<td width="900"><%@ include file="../jsp/people_default_menu.jsp" %></td>
</tr><tr>
<td width ="730" valign="top" align = "center">
<table  border="0" align="top" width=600 >
<%
  LeaveRequest leaveRequest = new LeaveRequest();
  leaveRequest = (LeaveRequest)session.getAttribute("leaveRequest");
%>
<form name="form1" method="post">
<tr>
<td colspan='4' height=20 height=20 bgcolor ='#AAAAAA' class=whitetext
```

```
align=center>Leave Application</td>
</tr>
<tr>
<td >Request ID</td>
<td align='left'><input type='text' name='req_id' id='req_id 'size ='10'
value='<%=leaveRequest.req_id%>'/> </td>
<td >Date(YYYY-MM-DD)</td>
<td align='left'><input type='text' name='today_date' id='today_date 'size ='10'
value='<%=leaveRequest.today_date%>'/> </td>
<tr>
<tr>
<td>Employee Id</td>
<td align='left'><input type='text' name='emp_id' id='emp_id 'size ='10'
value='<%=leaveRequest.emp_id%>'/> </td>
<td> Name</td>
<td align='left'><input type='text' name='emp_name' id='emp_name 'size ='20'
value='<%=leaveRequest.emp_name%>' /> </td>
</tr>
<tr>
<td>Designation</td>
<td align='left'><input type='text' name='level_id' id='level_id' size ='10'
value='<%=leaveRequest.level_id%>'/> </td>
<td>Department</td>
<td align='left'><input type='text' name='dept_id' id='dept_id' size ='10'
value='<%=leaveRequest.dept_id%>'/> </td>
</tr>
<tr>
<td colspan='4' height=20 bgcolor ='#AAAAAA' class=whitetext align=center>Leave
Detail</td>
</tr>
<tr>
<td>From<br>(YYYY-MM-DD)</td>
<td>To(YYYY-MM-DD)</td>
<td>Days</td>
</tr>
<tr>
<td align='left' >
<input type='text' name='from_date' id='from_date' size ='10'value=
'<%=leaveRequest.from_date%>'/> </td>
<td align='left' ><input type='text' name='to_date' id='to_date' size ='10'
value='<%=leaveRequest.to_date%>'/> </td>
<td align='left'><input type='text' name='days' id='days' size ='5'
value='<%=leaveRequest.days%>'/> </td>
</tr>
<tr>
<td colspan='2'>Reason For Leave(100 letters only)</td>
<td align='left' colspan='2'><input type='text' name='reason' id='reason'
col='80' rows='4' value='<%=leaveRequest.reason%>'/>
</textarea>
</td>
</tr>
<tr>
<td colspan='2'>Type Of Leave Applied For</td>
<%
  if( leaveRequest.reason != null )
    out.print("<td align='left'><input type='text' name='leave_type'
id='leave_type' size ='10' value='"+leaveRequest.leave_type+"'/></td>");
  else
    out.print("<td align='left'><SELECT name='leave_type' > <OPTION
   VALUE=></OPTION> <OPTION VALUE=CL>CL</OPTION>
   <OPTION VALUE=SL>SL</OPTION></SELECT></td>");
%>
</tr>
<tr>
<td colspan='4' height=20 bgcolor ='#AAAAAA' class=whitetext align=center>Major
Activity to Be Handled During The Leave Applied</td>
</td>
</tr>
```

```
<tr>
<td>S.NO</td>
<td>Activity Details</td>
<td>Name Of the Person Responsible</td>
<td>Details</td>
</tr>
<tr>
<td>1.</td>
<td align='left'><input type='text' name='activity_1' id='activity_1' size ='20'
value='<%=leaveRequest.activity_1%>'/> </td>
<td align='left'><input type='text' name='person_1' id='person_1' size ='20'
value='<%=leaveRequest.person_1%>'/> </td>
<td align='left'><input type='text' name='detail_1' id='detail_1' size ='20'
value='<%=leaveRequest.detail_1%>'/> </td>
</tr>
<tr>
<td>2.</td>
<td align='left'><input type='text' name='activity_2' id='activity_2' size ='20'
value='<%=leaveRequest.activity_2%>'/> </td>
<td align='left'><input type='text' name='person_2' id='person_2' size ='20'
value='<%=leaveRequest.person_2%>'/> </td>
<td align='left'><input type='text' name='detail_2' id='detail_2' size ='20'
value='<%=leaveRequest.detail_2%>'/> </td>
</tr>
<tr>
<td>3.</td>
<td align='left'><input type='text' name='activity_3' id='activity_3' size ='20'
value='<%=leaveRequest.activity_3%>'/> </td>
<td align='left'><input type='text' name='person_3' id='person_3' size ='20'
value='<%=leaveRequest.person_3%>'/> </td>
<td align='left'><input type='text' name='detail_3' id='detail_3' size ='20'
value='<%=leaveRequest.detail_3%>'/> </td>
</tr>
<tr>
<td colspan='4' height=20 bgcolor ='#AAAAAA' class=whitetext align=center>Contact
Details of the applicant during the leave period</td>
</tr>
<tr>
<td>Address</td>
<td align='left' colspan='3'><input type='text' name='address' id='address' size
='20' value='<%=leaveRequest.address%>'/> </td>
</tr>
<tr>
<td>Remark</td>
<td align='left' colspan='3'><input type='text' name='remark' id='remark' size
='20' value='<%=leaveRequest.remark%>'/> </td>
</tr>
<tr>
<th colspan='4' bgcolor ='#AAAAAA'></th>
</tr>
<tr>
<td align='center' colspan='4'><input type='submit' name='submit' id='submit' size
='10' value='Approve'/> </td>
<input type='hidden' name='action_submit' id='action_submit' size ='10'
value='employee_leave_req_edit_submit'/> </td>
</tr>
</table>
</td></tr>
<tr>
<td colspan="2"><%@include file="../jsp/people_footer.jsp"%></td>
</tr>
</table>
</body>
</html>
```

In Listing 23.47, a hidden input field, submit, is used to differentiate between the leave requests submitted by the employees, and those approved or rejected by the HR department.

Let's now create the `leave_request_reject` JSP page.

Creating the leave_request_reject JSP Page

The `leave_request_reject JSP` page is similar to the `leave_request_edit JSP page`, except that this page has the submit button with value `Reject`. Listing 23.48 shows the code of the `leave_request_reject.jsp` file (save the `leave_request_reject.jsp` file in the `people-mgmt\jsp` folder):

Listing 23.48: Showing the Code of the leave_request_reject.jsp File

```
<%@ page language="java" %>
<%@ page session="true" %>
<%@ page  import="com.LeaveManagement.*" %>
<html>
<head>
<title>www.peoplemanagementsolutions.com/Leave Request</title>
<link rel="stylesheet" href="../css/mystyle.css" type="text/css" />
</head>
<body>
<table width="900" border="0" align="center">
<tr>
  <td colspan="2"><%@ include file="../jsp/people_header.jsp" %></td>
</tr>
<tr>
<td width="900"><%@ include file="../jsp/people_default_menu.jsp" %></td>
</tr><tr>
<td width ="730" valign="top" align = "center">
<table  border="0" align="top" width=600 >
<%
  LeaveRequest leaveRequest = new LeaveRequest();
  leaveRequest = (LeaveRequest)session.getAttribute("leaveRequest");
%>
  <form name="form1" method="post">
  <tr>
  <td colspan='4' height=20 height=20 bgcolor ='#AAAAAA' class=whitetext
  align=center>Leave Application</td>
  </tr>
  <tr>
  <td >Request ID</td>
  <td align='left'><input type='text' name='req_id' id='req_id 'size ='10'
  value='<%=leaveRequest.req_id%>'/> </td>
  <td >Date(YYYY-MM-DD)</td>
  <td align='left'><input type='text' name='today_date' id='today_date 'size ='10'
  value='<%=leaveRequest.today_date%>'/> </td>
  <tr>
  <tr>
  <td>Employee Id</td>
  <td align='left'><input type='text' name='emp_id' id='emp_id 'size ='10'
  value='<%=leaveRequest.emp_id%>'/> </td>
  <td> Name</td>
  <td align='left'><input type='text' name='emp_name' id='emp_name 'size ='20'
  value='<%=leaveRequest.emp_name%>' /> </td>
  </tr>
  <tr>
  <td>Designation</td>
  <td align='left'><input type='text' name='level_id' id='level_id' size ='10'
  value='<%=leaveRequest.level_id%>'/> </td>
  <td>Department</td>
  <td align='left'><input type='text' name='dept_id' id='dept_id' size ='10'
  value='<%=leaveRequest.dept_id%>'/> </td>
  </tr>
  <tr>
  <td colspan='4' height=20 bgcolor ='#AAAAAA' class=whitetext align=center>Leave
  Detail</td>
  </tr>
  <tr>
  <td>From<br>(YYYY-MM-DD)</td>
  <td>To(YYYY-MM-DD)</td>
  <td>Days</td>
```

```
</tr>
<tr>
<td align='left' >
<input type='text' name='from_date' id='from_date' size ='10'
value='<%=leaveRequest.from_date%>'/> </td>
<td align='left' ><input type='text' name='to_date' id='to_date' size ='10'
value='<%=leaveRequest.to_date%>'/> </td>
<td align='left'><input type='text' name='days' id='days' size ='5'
value='<%=leaveRequest.days%>'/> </td>
</tr>
<tr>
<td colspan='2'>Reason For Leave(100 letters only)</td>
<td align='left' colspan='2'><input type='text' name='reason' id='reason'  col='80'
rows='4' value='<%=leaveRequest.reason%>'/>
</textarea>
</td>
</tr>
<tr>
<td colspan='2'>Type Of Leave Applied For</td>
<%
if( leaveRequest.reason != null )
  out.print("<td align='left'><input type='text' name='leave_type' id='leave_type' size
='10' value='"+leaveRequest.leave_type+"'/></td>");
else
  out.print("<td align='left'><SELECT name='leave_type' > <OPTION VALUE=></OPTION>
<OPTION VALUE=CL>CL</OPTION><OPTION VALUE=SL>SL</OPTION></SELECT></td>");
%>
</tr>
<tr>
<td colspan='4' height=20 bgcolor ='#AAAAAA' class=whitetext align=center>Major Activity
to Be Handled During The Leave Applied</td>
</td>
</tr>
<tr>
<td>S.NO</td>
<td>Activity Details</td>
<td>Name Of the Person Responsible</td>
<td>Details</td>
</tr>
<tr>
<td>1.</td>
<td align='left'><input type='text' name='activity_1' id='activity_1' size ='20'
value='<%=leaveRequest.activity_1%>'/> </td>
<td align='left'><input type='text' name='person_1' id='person_1' size ='20'
value='<%=leaveRequest.person_1%>'/> </td>
<td align='left'><input type='text' name='detail_1' id='detail_1' size ='20'
value='<%=leaveRequest.detail_1%>'/> </td>
</tr>
<tr>
<td>2.</td>
<td align='left'><input type='text' name='activity_2' id='activity_2' size ='20'
value='<%=leaveRequest.activity_2%>'/> </td>
<td align='left'><input type='text' name='person_2' id='person_2' size ='20'
value='<%=leaveRequest.person_2%>'/> </td>
<td align='left'><input type='text' name='detail_2' id='detail_2' size ='20'
value='<%=leaveRequest.detail_2%>'/> </td>
</tr>
<tr>
<td>3.</td>
<td align='left'><input type='text' name='activity_3' id='activity_3' size ='20'
value='<%=leaveRequest.activity_3%>'/> </td>
<td align='left'><input type='text' name='person_3' id='person_3' size ='20'
value='<%=leaveRequest.person_3%>'/> </td>
<td align='left'><input type='text' name='detail_3' id='detail_3' size ='20'
value='<%=leaveRequest.detail_3%>'/> </td>
</tr>
<tr>
<td colspan='4' height=20 bgcolor ='#AAAAAA' class=whitetext align=center>Contact
Details of the applicant during the leave period</td>
```

```
    </tr>
    <tr>
    <td>Address</td>
    <td align='left' colspan='3'><input type='text' name='address' id='address' size ='20'
     value='<%=leaveRequest.address%>'/> </td>
    </tr>
    <tr>
    <td>Remark</td>
    <td align='left' colspan='3'><input type='text' name='remark' id='remark' size ='20'
     value='<%=leaveRequest.remark%>'/> </td>
    </tr>
    <tr>
    <th colspan='4' bgcolor ='#AAAAAA'></th>
    </tr>
    <tr>
    <td align='center' colspan='4'><input type='submit' name='submit' id='submit' size ='10'
     value='Reject'/>
    <input type='hidden' name='action_submit' id='action_submit' size ='10'
     value='employee_leave_req_reject_submit'/>
    </td>
    </tr>
  </table>
  </td></tr>
  <tr>
      <td colspan="2"><%@include file="../jsp/people_footer.jsp"%></td>
  </tr>
  </table></body></html>
```

In Listing 23.48, a hidden input field, submit, is used to differentiate between the leave requests submitted by the employees, and those rejected by the HR department.

Let's now create the `leave_request_list` JSP page.

Creating the leave_request_list JSP Page

The `leave_request_list` JSP page displays the names of employees who have requested for leave in a list format. The code for the `leave_request_list` JSP page has been shown in Listing 23.48 (save the `leave_request_list.jsp` file in the `people-mgmt\jsp` folder):

Listing 23.49: Showing the Code of the leave_request_list.jsp File

```
<%@ page language="java" %>
<%@ page session="true" %>
<%@ page  import="com.LeaveManagement.*" %>
<%@ page  import="java.io.*" %>
<%@ page  import="java.util.*" %>
<html>
<head>
<title>www.peoplemanagementsolutions.com/Leave Request List</title>
<link rel="stylesheet" href="../css/mystyle.css" type="text/css" />
</head>
<body>
<table width="900" border="0" align="center">
<tr>
  <td colspan="2"><%@ include file="../jsp/people_header.jsp" %></td>
</tr>
<tr>
<td width="900"><%@ include file="../jsp/people_default_menu.jsp" %></td>
</tr><tr>
<td width ="750" valign="top">
<p> </p>
<%
    String dbopr = "";
    dbopr = (String)session.getAttribute("dbopr");
%>
<%
  if(dbopr != null && !dbopr.equals("rejected_leave")){
%>
<div align=center class=boldblack>List of Approved Leave Requests</div>
<% } else { %>
```

```
<div align=center class=boldblack>List of Rejected Leave Requests</div>
<% } %>
<hr width=100% color=#AAAAAA>
<table  border="0" width=600 align=center>
  <tr>
  <td class=whitetext bgcolor ='#AAAAAA' align='center' >Request Id</td>
  <td class=whitetext bgcolor ='#AAAAAA' align='center' >Employee Id</td>
  <td class=whitetext bgcolor ='#AAAAAA' align='center' >Employee Name</td>
  <td class=whitetext bgcolor ='#AAAAAA' align='center' >Request Date</td>
  <td class=whitetext bgcolor ='#AAAAAA' align='center' >From Date </td>
  <td class=whitetext bgcolor ='#AAAAAA' align='center' >To Date </td>
  <td class=whitetext bgcolor ='#AAAAAA' align='center' >Days</td>
  <%
  if(dbopr != null && !dbopr.equals("approved_leave") && !dbopr.equals("rejected_leave"))
  out.println("<td class=whitetext colspan='3' bgcolor ='#AAAAAA' align='center'
  >Approve/Reject</td>");
  %>
    </tr>
  <%
  ArrayList leaveRequestList = new ArrayList();
  leaveRequestList = (ArrayList)session.getAttribute("leaveRequestList");
  if ( leaveRequestList != null && leaveRequestList.size() > 0 ){
        for ( int size = 1; size <= leaveRequestList.size() ; size++ ){
                LeaveRequest  leaveRequest = new LeaveRequest();
                leaveRequest = (LeaveRequest)leaveRequestList.get(size-1);
                %>
                <form name="form1" method="post">
                <tr bgcolor ='#AAAAAA'>
                <td align='center'><%=leaveRequest.req_id%></td>
                <td align='center'><%=leaveRequest.emp_id%></td>
                <td align='center' ><%=leaveRequest.emp_name%> </td>
                <td align='center' ><%=leaveRequest.today_date%> </td>
                <td align='center' ><%=leaveRequest.from_date%></td>
                <td align='center' ><%=leaveRequest.to_date%></td>
                <td align='center' ><%=leaveRequest.days%></td>
                <%
                if(dbopr != null && !dbopr.equals("approved_leave") &&
                !dbopr.equals("rejected_leave") ){
                out.println("");
                %>
<td align='center' bgcolor='#AAAAAA'><a href='http://localhost:8080/people-
mgmt/servlet/leave_management?dbopr=approve&&req_id=<%=leaveRequest.req_id%>&&emp_id=<%=le
aveRequest.emp_id%> ' class=yellowlink>Approve</a></td>
<td align='center' bgcolor='#AAAAAA'><a href='http://localhost:8080/people-
mgmt/servlet/leave_management?dbopr=reject&&req_id=<%=leaveRequest.req_id%>&&emp_id=<%=lea
veRequest.emp_id%> ' class=yellowlink>Reject</a>
                </td>
                <%}%>
                </tr>
  <%
        }
  }
  else{
        out.println("Request does not exist!!!");
  }
%>
</table>
<hr width=100% color=#AAAAAA>
</td>
</tr>
<tr>
    <td colspan="2"><%@include file="../jsp/people_footer.jsp"%></td>
</tr>
</table>
</body>
</html>
```

In Listing 23.48, the `Approve` and `Reject` link is provided beside the name of every leave request. The HR department can approve the leave by just clicking `Approve` link or can reject the leave by clicking `Reject` link.

Figure 23.23 shows all the leave requests that are not yet approved or rejected by the HR department:

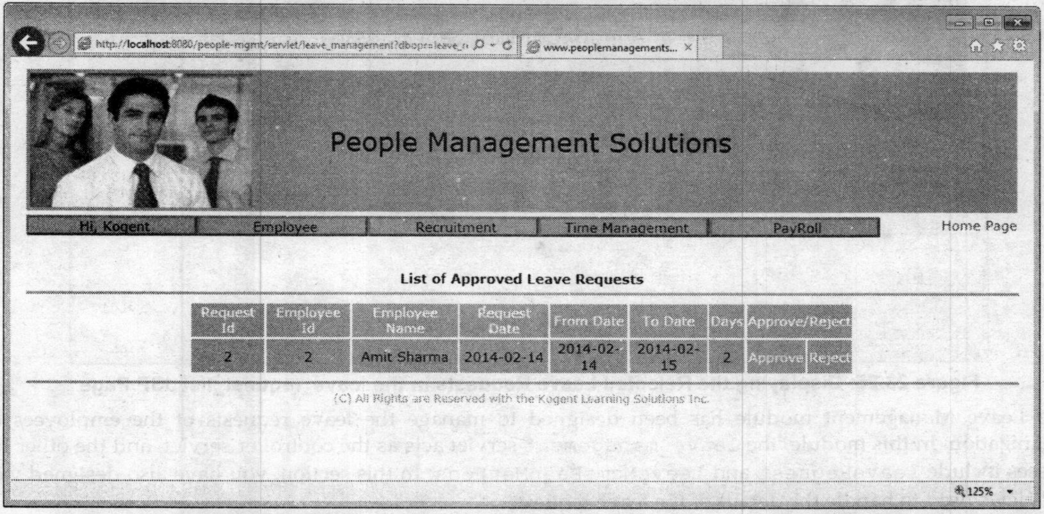

Figure 23.23: Displaying the List of Leave Requests in the leave_request_list JSP Page

When you click on `Approve` link shown in Figure 23.23, then after approving the leave request a Web page of approved leave requests is displayed. Figure 23.24 displays approved leave requests in the `leave_request_list` JSP page:

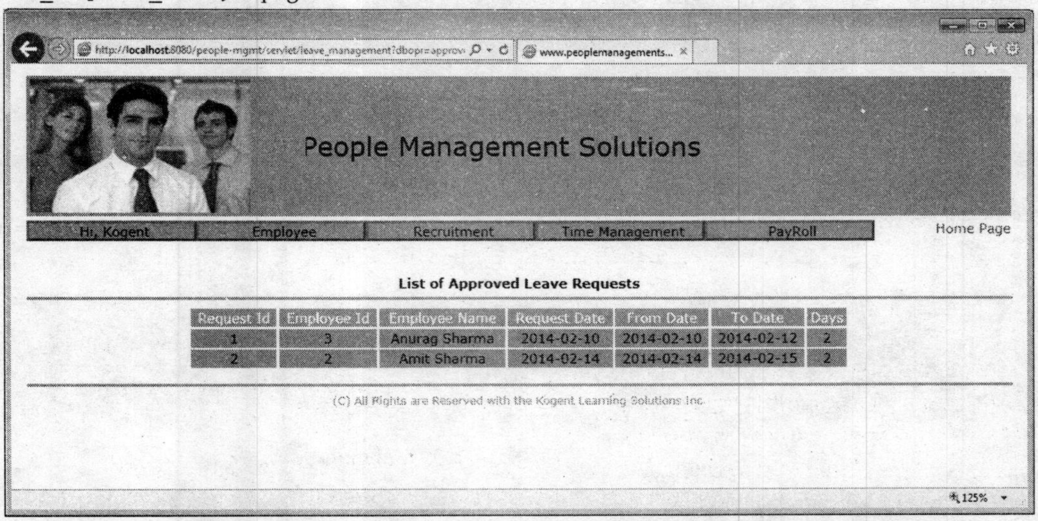

Figure 23.24: Displaying the Approved Leave Requests in the leave_request_list JSP Page

When you click on `Reject` link (Figure 23.23), then after rejecting the leave request a list of rejected leave requests is displayed. Figure 23.25 displays rejected leave requests in the `leave_request_list` JSP page:

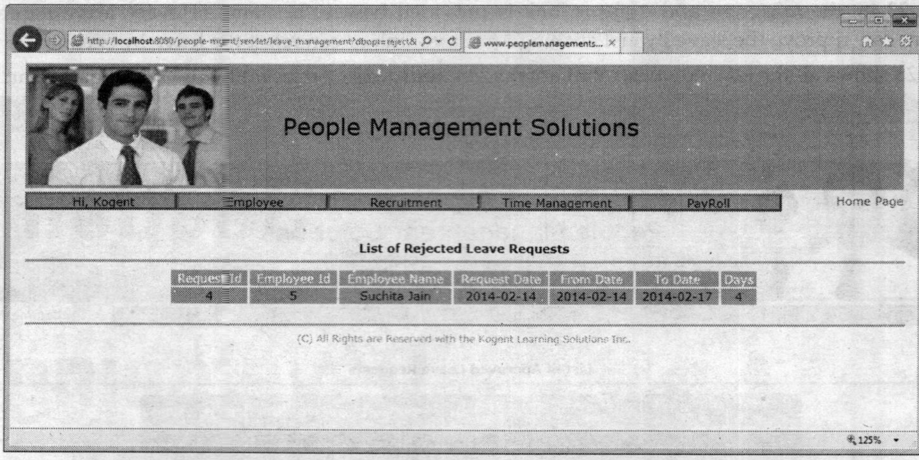

Figure 23.25: Displaying the Rejected Leave Requests in the leave_request_list JSP Page

The Leave Management module has been designed to manage the leave requests of the employees of an organization. In this module, the `leave_management` servlet acts as the controller servlet, and the other helper classes include `LeaveRequest` and `LeaveMgmtBeanMethods`. In this section, you have also designed various JSP views used to handle the details of the leave requests.

In the next section, we discuss the development of another module, the payroll module.

Section F

Developing the Payroll Module

Disbursing salaries on time and generating pay slips after calculating the monthly salaries of all employees of an organization is one of the most complex functions of the HR department. There are a number of things that need to be considered while generating monthly salary of an employee, such as leave balance, attendance, and salary package. Every employee has a salary package that is divided into many allowance types, such as basic salary, House Rent Allowance (HRA), Dearness Allowance (DA), Transportation Allowance (TA), and Provident Fund (PF). In this module, you learn to create applications to update the salary statement and calculate the salary of employees for every month.

Similar to other modules, this module also implements the MVC architecture with a servlet, Java classes, and JSP pages. The list of Java source code files to be created for this module is as follows:

- people_payroll.java
- EmpSal.java
- EmployeeAgreement.java
- PayrollBeanMethods.java

The following JSP pages also need to be created in this module:

- salary_search.jsp
- employee_agreement.jsp
- employee_agreement_edit.jsp
- salary_slip.jsp

The next section discusses how to update salary statement of an employee.

Updating Salary Statement

Salary statement can be described as the information containing the details of the salary package of an employee that includes different heads and the amount being paid under that head, such as basic salary and other allowances. A new statement is made for every new employee who joins the organization. This statement gets updated on every salary revision (increment/decrement) of the employee. This employee statement is used to calculate monthly salary of a particular employee.

Let's now create the `people_payroll` servlet.

Creating people_payroll Servlet

The people_payroll servlet plays the role of the controller servlet for this module. This implies that all the requests for payroll-related functions are handled by this servlet. This servlet is similar to other servlets developed in this project, and forwards the request to the appropriate JSP view after performing the required operations. This servlet can be used in various ways by going through different execution paths. Different parts of the servlet can be executed according to the values passed by the `dbopr` and `action` parameters to the servlet.

Listing 23.49 shows the code of the `people_payroll.java` file (save the `people_payroll.java` file in the `people-mgmt\WEB-INF\src` folder):

Listing 23.49: Showing the Code of the people_payroll.java File

```
import javax.servlet.*;
import javax.servlet.http.*;
import java.util.ArrayList;
import java.io.*;
import java.util.*;
import java.sql.*;
import javax.servlet.annotation.*;
import javax.servlet.annotation.WebServlet;
import com.Employee.*;
import com.Payroll.*;
import com.LeaveManagement.*;
import com.TimeManagement.*;
@WebServlet(name="people_payroll", urlPatterns="/servlet/people_payroll")
public class people_payroll extends HttpServlet{
```

```
    String dbuser  = "";
    String dbpswd  = "";
    String dburl   = "";
  /**Initialize global variables*/
      @Override
  public void init(ServletConfig config) throws ServletException{
    System.out.println("initializing controller servlet.");
    ServletContext context = config.getServletContext();
    dbuser = "scott";
    dbpswd = "tiger";
    dburl  = "jdbc:oracle:thin:@192.168.1.123:1521:"+"XE";
    super.init(config);
  }
  /**Process the HTTP Get request*/
       @Override
  public void doGet(HttpServletRequest request, HttpServletResponse response) throws
  ServletException, IOException{
    doPost(request, response);
  }
  /**Process the HTTP Post request*/
       @Override
  public void doPost(HttpServletRequest request, HttpServletResponse response)
  throws ServletException, IOException{
    response.setContentType("text/html");
    PrintWriter out = response.getWriter();
    HttpSession session = request.getSession();
    session.setAttribute("lErrorMsg",null);
    String target = "";
    String action = request.getParameter("action");
    String dbopr = "";
    dbopr = (String)request.getParameter("dbopr");
    session.setAttribute("dbopr",dbopr);
    if( (dbopr != null && dbopr.length() > 0) && (dbopr.equals
          ("employee_agreement")) ){
          target = "/jsp/employee_search.jsp";
    }
    else
    if( (dbopr != null && dbopr.length() > 0) && (dbopr.equals("edit_head")) ){
          action = "edit_sal_head";
    }
    else
    if( (dbopr != null && dbopr.length() > 0) && (dbopr.equals("delete_head"))
    ){
          action = "employee_sal_head_delete";
    }
    else
    if( (dbopr != null && dbopr.length() > 0) && (dbopr.equals
          ("calc_employee_salary")) ){
          target= "/jsp/salary_search.jsp";
    }
    String action_submit = request.getParameter("action_submit");
    System.out.println("action_submit=="+action_submit);
    if ( action_submit != null ){
          if ( request.getParameter("submit").equals("Submit") ){
                System.out.println("in the  Submit");
          if ( action_submit.equals("people_employee_search_submit") ){
                System.out.println("in the people_employee_search_submit ");
                action = "people_employee_search_submit";
          }
          }
    else
    if ( request.getParameter("submit").equals("Edit") ){
    if ( action_submit.equals("employee_sal_head_edit_submit") )
          action = "employee_sal_head_edit_submit";
    }
```

```
else
if ( request.getParameter("submit").equals("Submit Detail") ){
if ( action_submit.equals("emp_agreement_dtl_submit") )
        action = "emp_agreement_dtl_submit";
}
else
if ( request.getParameter("submit").equals("Calc") ){
if ( action_submit.equals("salary_calc_submit") )
        action = "salary_calc_submit";
}
}
if (action!=null){
        System.out.println("in the  "+action);
if (action.equals("people_employee_search_submit")){
        String lEmpId = "";
        String lEmpFName = "";
        lEmpId = (String)request.getParameter("emp_id");
        lEmpFName = (String)request.getParameter("emp_f_name");
        EmployeeDBObj employeeDBObj = new EmployeeDBObj();
        EmployeeDBMethods employeeDBMethods = new
        EmployeeDBMethods(dbuser,dbpswd,dburl);
        employeeDBObj = (EmployeeDBObj)employeeDBMethods.
        getRecordByPrimaryKey(lEmpId,lEmpFName);
        System.out.println("iiiii="+employeeDBObj.emp_id+"ffff=
        "+employeeDBObj.emp_f_name);
if ( (employeeDBObj.emp_id != null && employeeDBObj.emp_f_name != null) ){
        session.setAttribute("employeeDBObj",employeeDBObj);
        PayrollBeanMethods payrollBeanMethods = new PayrollBeanMethods
        (dbuser,dbpswd,dburl);
        ArrayList employeeAgreementList = new ArrayList();
        String criteria = "";
        criteria = " where emp_id='"+employeeDBObj.emp_id+"'";
        employeeAgreementList = (
        ArrayList)payrollBeanMethods.selectEmployee
        AgreementByCriteria(criteria);
        session.setAttribute("employeeAgreementList"
        ,employeeAgreementList);
        target = "/jsp/employee_agreement.jsp";
}
else{
        String lErrorMsg = "Employee doesn't Exist";
        session.setAttribute("lErrorMsg",lErrorMsg);
        target = "/jsp/people_default.jsp";
}
}
else
if (action.equals("edit_sal_head")){
        String empId = "";
        String allowanceName = "";
        empId = (String)request.getParameter("emp_id");
        allowanceName = (String)request.getParameter("allowance_name");
        PayrollBeanMethods payrollBeanMethods  = new PayrollBeanMethods
        (dbuser,dbpswd,dburl);
        EmployeeAgreement employeeAgreement = new EmployeeAgreement();
        employeeAgreement =(EmployeeAgreement)payrollBeanMethods.getEmployee
        AgreementRecord(empId,allowanceName);
        session.setAttribute("employeeAgreement",employeeAgreement);
        target = "/jsp/employee_agreement_edit.jsp";
}
else
if (action.equals("salary_calc_submit")){
        PayrollBeanMethods payrollBeanMethods  = new PayrollBeanMethods
        (dbuser,dbpswd,dburl);
        String empId = (String)request.getParameter("emp_id");
        int year = Integer.parseInt((String)request.getParameter("year"));
```

```
int month = Integer.parseInt((String)request.getParameter("month"));
String lEmpFName = "";
EmployeeDBObj employeeDBObj = new EmployeeDBObj();
EmployeeDBMethods employeeDBMethods = new EmployeeDBMethods
(dbuser,dbpswd,dburl);
employeeDBObj = (EmployeeDBObj)employeeDBMethods.getRecord
ByPrimaryKey(empId,lEmpFName);
int totalAttendance = 0;
totalAttendance = getTotalAttendance(empId,year,month);
System.out.println("totalAttendance======"+totalAttendance);
session.setAttribute("totalAttendance",Integer.toString
(totalAttendance));
int totalLeave = 0;
totalLeave = getTotalLeave(empId,year,month);
System.out.println("totalLeave======"+totalLeave);
session.setAttribute("totalLeave",Integer.toString(totalLeave));
session.setAttribute("employeeDBObj",employeeDBObj);
session.setAttribute("year",Integer.toString(year));
session.setAttribute("month",Integer.toString(month));
ArrayList empSalExist = new ArrayList();
String criteria = "";
criteria = " where emp_id='"+empId+"' and year='"+year+"' and
month='"+month+"' ";
empSalExist = ( ArrayList)payrollBeanMethods.select
EmpSalByCriteria(criteria);
if ( empSalExist != null && empSalExist.size() > 0 ){
        ArrayList empSalList = new ArrayList();
        criteria = "";
        criteria = " where emp_id='"+empId+"' and year='"+year+"' and
        month='"+month+"' ";
        empSalList = ( ArrayList)payrollBeanMethods.selectEmpSal
        ByCriteria(criteria);
        session.setAttribute("empSalList",empSalList);
        System.out.println("empSalList.size()======"
        +empSalList.size());
}
else
if( totalAttendance > 0 ){
        ArrayList employeeAgreementList = new ArrayList();
        criteria = "";
        criteria = " where emp_id='"+empId+"'";
        employeeAgreementList = ( ArrayList)payrollBeanMethods.select
        EmployeeAgreementByCriteria(criteria);
        for (int rec =1; rec <= employeeAgreementList.size() ; rec++
        ){
        EmployeeAgreement employeeAgreement = new
                EmployeeAgreement();
        EmpSal empSal =  new EmpSal();
        employeeAgreement = (EmployeeAgreement)employeeAgree
        mentList.get(rec-1);
        empSal.emp_id =  employeeAgreement.emp_id;
        empSal.year = year ;
        empSal.month = month;
        empSal.allowance_name =  employeeAgreement.allowance_name;
        empSal.allowance_type =  employeeAgreement.allowance_type;
        empSal.amt =  employeeAgreement.amt;
        empSal.taxable =  employeeAgreement.taxable;
        empSal.percentage =  employeeAgreement.percentage;
        payrollBeanMethods.insertEmpSal(empSal);
 }
 ArrayList empSalList = new ArrayList();
 criteria = "";
 criteria = " where emp_id='"+empId+"' and year='"+year+"' and
 month='"+month+"' ";
 empSalList = ( ArrayList)payrollBeanMethods.selectEmpSalByCriteria
```

```
                    (criteria);
session.setAttribute("empSalList",empSalList);
System.out.println("empSalList.size()======"+empSalList.size());
}
else{
        String lErrorMsg = "your criteria is not correct .. salary is
                    not prepared!!!";
        session.setAttribute("lErrorMsg",lErrorMsg);
if(session.getAttribute("empSalList")!=null)
        session.removeAttribute("empSalList");
}
target = "/jsp/salary_slip.jsp";
}
else
if (action.equals("emp_agreement_dtl_submit")){
        EmployeeAgreement popEmployeeAgreement = new
                    EmployeeAgreement();
        PayrollBeanMethods payrollBeanMethods = new
        PayrollBeanMethods(dbuser,dbpswd,dburl);
        popEmployeeAgreement = (EmployeeAgreement)payrollBeanMethods.
                populateEmployeeAgreementFromReq(request);
        EmployeeAgreement employeeAgreement = new
                EmployeeAgreement();
        employeeAgreement = (EmployeeAgreement)payrollBeanMethods.get
                EmployeeAgreementRecord(popEmployeeAgreement.
                emp_id,popEmployeeAgreement.allowance_name);
if ( (popEmployeeAgreement.emp_id).equals(employeeAgreement.emp_id)
&& (popEmployeeAgreement.allowance_name).equals(employee
Agreement.allowance_name) ){
        String lErrorMsg = "Allowance Already Exist";
        session.setAttribute("lErrorMsg",lErrorMsg);
        target = "/jsp/employee_agreement.jsp";
}
else{
        int rval =  payrollBeanMethods.insertEmployeeAgreement
        (popEmployeeAgreement);
        EmployeeAgreement sEmployeeAgreement = new
        EmployeeAgreement();
        sEmployeeAgreement = EmployeeAgreement)payrollBeanMethods.get
                EmployeeAgreementRecord(popEmployeeAgreement.emp_id
                ,popEmployeeAgreement.allowance_name);
        ArrayList employeeAgreementList = new ArrayList();
        String criteria = "";
        criteria = " where emp_id='"+popEmployeeAgreement.emp_id+"'";
        employeeAgreementList = ( ArrayList)payrollBeanMethods.
        selectEmployeeAgreementByCriteria(criteria);
        session.setAttribute("employeeAgreementList",
        employeeAgreementList);
        session.setAttribute("employeeAgreement",sEmployeeAgreement);
        target = "/jsp/employee_agreement.jsp";
}
}
else
if (action.equals("employee_sal_head_edit_submit")){
    EmployeeAgreement popEmployeeAgreement = new EmployeeAgreement();
    PayrollBeanMethods payrollBeanMethods = new  PayrollBeanMethods
    (dbuser,dbpswd,dburl);
    popEmployeeAgreement = (EmployeeAgreement)payrollBeanMethods.
    populateEmployeeAgreementFromReq(request);
    int rval = payrollBeanMethods.updateEmployeeAgreement
    ByPrimaryKey(popEmployeeAgreement);
    if ( rval > 0 ){
        ArrayList employeeAgreementList = new ArrayList();
        String criteria = "";
        criteria = " where emp_id='"+popEmployeeAgreement.emp_id;
```

```
                employeeAgreementList = ( ArrayList)payrollBeanMethods.select
                EmployeeAgreementByCriteria(criteria);
                session.setAttribute("employeeAgreementList",
                employeeAgreementList);
                target = "/jsp/employee_agreement.jsp";
            }
            else{
                target = "/jsp/employee_agreement_edit.jsp";
        }
        }
        else
        if (action.equals("employee_sal_head_delete")){
                String empId = "";
                String allowanceName = "";
                empId = (String)request.getParameter("emp_id");
                allowanceName = (String)request.getParameter
                ("allowance_name");
                PayrollBeanMethods payrollBeanMethods = new
                PayrollBeanMethods(dbuser,dbpswd,dburl);
                payrollBeanMethods.deleteEmployeeAgreement
                (empId,allowanceName);
                ArrayList employeeAgreementList = new ArrayList();
                String criteria = "";
                criteria = " where emp_id='"+empId+"' ";
                employeeAgreementList = ( ArrayList)payrollBeanMethods.select
                EmployeeAgreementByCriteria(criteria);
                session.setAttribute("employeeAgreementList",employee
                AgreementList);
                target = "/jsp/employee_agreement.jsp";
        }
        }
/* forwarding the request/response to the targeted view */
RequestDispatcher requestDispatcher = getServletContext().getRequest
Dispatcher(target);
requestDispatcher.forward(request, response);
} // doPost closed
public int getTotalAttendance( String inEmpId, int inYear,int inMonth ){
  ...................
  ...................
  ...................
  ...................
}
public int getTotalLeave( String inEmpId, int inYear,int inMonth ){
  ...................
  ...................
  ...................
  ...................
}
public String getMonth( int month ){
  String strMonth = "";
  if(month == 0) strMonth = "JAN";
  else if(month == 1) strMonth = "FEB";
  else if(month == 2 ) strMonth = "MAR";
  else if(month == 3) strMonth = "APR";
  else if(month == 4) strMonth = "MAY";
  else if(month == 5) strMonth = "JUN";
  else if(month == 6) strMonth = "JUL";
  else if(month == 7) strMonth = "AUG";
  else if(month == 8) strMonth = "SEP";
  else if(month == 9) strMonth = "OCT";
  else if(month == 10) strMonth = "NOV";
  else if(month == 11) strMonth = "DEC";
  return strMonth;
}
}// class closed
```

In Listing 23.49, four packages, such as com.Employee, com.Payroll, com.LeaveManagement, and com.TimeManagement are imported, as some of the classes from these packages are used to implement an operation. Apart from the standard init(), doGet(), and doPost() methods, this servlet has two more methods—getTotalAttendance() and getTotalLeave(), which help in calculating the salary of an employee by providing the details of the total attendance and the number of leaves taken in a month.

The getTotalAttendance() method described in Listing 23.50 returns total attendance of a particular employee for a specific month of a given year. The people_payroll.java file defines the selectEmpDailyAttendanceByCriteria() method of the TimeManagementDBMethods class, as shown in Listing 23.50:

Listing 23.50: Showing the Code of the getTotalAttendance() Method in the people_payroll.java File

```
public int getTotalAttendance( String inEmpId, int inYear,int inMonth )
{
   TimeManagementDBMethods timeManagementDBMethods = new
         TimeManagementDBMethods(dbuser,dbpswd,dburl);
   int totalAttendance = 0;
   ArrayList attendanceList = new ArrayList();
   String criteria = "where emp_id ='"+inEmpId+"' and year='"+inYear+"' and
         month='"+timeManagementDBMethods.getMonth(inMonth-1)+"' ";
   attendanceList =
         (ArrayList)timeManagementDBMethods.selectEmpDailyAttendanceBy
         Criteria(criteria);
   if( attendanceList != null && attendanceList.size() > 0)
   totalAttendance = attendanceList.size();
   return totalAttendance;
}
```

The getTotalAttendance () method provided in Listing 23.50 returns the total attendance of an employee. This method invokes the selectEmployeeAttendanceByCriteria() method of the com.TimeManagement.TimeManagementDBMethods class that returns total attendance of the employee. Similarly, the getTotalLeave() method returns the total number of leaves of an employee in a given month of a given year by using the selectLeaveRequestByCriteria() method of the LeaveMgmtBeanMethods class.

Listing 23.51 provides the code for the getTotalLeave() method:

Listing 23.51: Showing the Code of the getTotalLeave() Method in the people_payroll.java File

```
public int getTotalLeave( String inEmpId, int inYear,int inMonth )
{
   LeaveMgmtBeanMethods leaveMgmtBeanMethods = new
         LeaveMgmtBeanMethods(dbuser,dbpswd,dburl);
   int totalLeave = 0;
   ArrayList leaveList = new ArrayList();
   String strtdate = ""
   String enddate = "";
   strtdate = "01/"+inMonth+"/"+inYear+"";
   enddate  = "31/"+inMonth+"/"+inYear+"";
   String criteria = "where emp_id ='"+inEmpId+"' and leave_status='Aprv' and
   from_date >='"+strtdate+"' and to_date <='"+enddate+"'  ";
   leaveList = (ArrayList)leaveMgmtBeanMethods.
   selectLeaveRequestByCriteria(criteria);
   if( leaveList != null && leaveList.size() > 0)
   {
         for (int i = 1;i<=leaveList.size() ;i++ )
         {
               LeaveRequest leaveRequest  = new LeaveRequest();
               leaveRequest = (LeaveRequest)leaveList.get(i-1);
               totalLeave = totalLeave + leaveRequest.days;
         }
   }
   return totalLeave;
}
```

You should note that the people_payroll.java file uses the @WebServlet annotation for servlet-mapping. The use of the @WebServlet annotation removes the need of specifying the servlet-mapping in the web.xml file.

Let's now create the EmpSal class.

Creating the EmpSal Class

The `EmpSal` class is a simple java class having a set of member variables matching the `EMP_SAL` table. An object of this class is used to represent the salary of an employee for a month. The details include `emp_id`, `year`, `month`, and `amt`.

Listing 23.52 provides the code of the `EmpSal.java` file (save the `EmpSal.java` file in the `people-mgmt\WEB-INF\src\com\Payroll` folder):

Listing 23.52: Showing the Code of the EmpSal.java File

```
package com.Payroll;
public class EmpSal
{
   public String emp_id ;
   public int year;
   public int month;
   public String allowance_type;
   public String allowance_name;
   public double amt;
   public String taxable;
   public double percentage;
}
```

In Listing 23.52, the datafields are specified corresponding to the `EMP_SAL` table.

Creating the EmployeeAgreement Class

The `EmployeeAgreement` class represents a salary statement showing details of the entire salary package of an employee. An object of this class represents the details of the allowance given to an employee, such as the head name and amount.

Listing 23.53 provides the code of the `EmployeeAgreement.java` file (save the `EmployeeAgreement.java` file in the `people-mgmt\WEB-INF\src\com\Payroll` folder):

Listing 23.53: Showing the Code of the EmployeeAgreement.java File

```
package com.Payroll;
public class EmployeeAgreement
{
   public String emp_id;
   public String emp_name;
   public String level_id;
   public String allowance_type;
   public String allowance_name;
   public double amt;
   public String taxable;
   public double percentage;
   public String agreement_date;
}
```

Listing 23.53 represents an entity corresponding to the fields of the `employee_agreement` JSP page.

Let's now create the `PayrollBeanMethods` class.

Creating the PayrollBeanMethods Class

The `PayrollBeanMethods` class contains the methods that directly interact with different tables to perform various functions, such as fetching and updating records. This class uses the fields that are specified in the `EmpSal` and `EmployeeAgreement` classes with the `EMP_SAL` and `EMPLOYEE_AGREEMENT` tables, respectively.

Listing 23.54 provides the code of the `PayrollBeanMethods.java` file (save the `PayrollBeanMethods.java` file in the `people-mgmt\WEB-INF\src\com\Payroll` folder):

Listing 23.54: Showing the Code of the PayrollBeanMethods.java File

```
package com.Payroll;
import java.sql.*;
import javax.servlet.*;
import javax.servlet.http.*;
import java.io.*;
import java.util.*;
import java.util.ArrayList;
import com.Payroll.EmployeeAgreement;
public class PayrollBeanMethods
{
  public String DBUser;
  public String DBPswd;
  public String DBUrl ;
  public PayrollBeanMethods(){ }

  public PayrollBeanMethods(String inDBUser, String inDBPswd, String inDBUrl )
  {
        DBUser = inDBUser ;
        DBPswd = inDBPswd;
        DBUrl  = inDBUrl;
  }
public void initializeEmployeeAgreement(EmployeeAgreement inEmployeeAgreement)
  {
        inEmployeeAgreement.emp_id = "";
        inEmployeeAgreement.emp_name = "";
        inEmployeeAgreement.level_id = "";
        inEmployeeAgreement.allowance_type ="" ;
        inEmployeeAgreement.allowance_name ="";
        inEmployeeAgreement.amt  = 0;
        inEmployeeAgreement.taxable  ="";
        inEmployeeAgreement.percentage =  0;
        inEmployeeAgreement.agreement_date = "";
  }
  public EmployeeAgreement getEmployeeAgreementRecord(String inEmpId, String
        inAllowanceName)
  {
        EmployeeAgreement  employeeAgreement = new EmployeeAgreement();
        java.sql.Date date;
        try
        {
DriverManager.registerDriver(new oracle.jdbc.driver.OracleDriver());
Connection conn= DriverManager.getConnection(DBUrl,DBUser,DBPswd);
              Statement stmt = conn.createStatement();
              String lSqlString =     "select * from EMPLOYEE_AGREEMENT ";
              lSqlString = lSqlString + "where emp_id='"+inEmpId+"' ";
              lSqlString = lSqlString + "and allowance_name='"+
              inAllowanceName+"' ";
              ResultSet rs  = null;
              rs  = stmt.executeQuery(lSqlString);
              System.out.println("lSqlString====trtrt==within
                    getRecordByPrimaryKey== "+lSqlString);
              if( rs.next())
              {
              employeeAgreement.emp_id   =
                    (String)rs.getString("emp_id");
              employeeAgreement.emp_name =
                    (String)rs.getString("emp_name");
              employeeAgreement.level_id =
                    (String)rs.getString("level_id");
              employeeAgreement.allowance_type =
                    (String)rs.getString("allowance_type");
              employeeAgreement.allowance_name =
                    rs.getString("allowance_name");
              employeeAgreement.amt = rs.getDouble("amt");
```

```
            employeeAgreement.taxable =
                    (String)rs.getString("taxable");
            employeeAgreement.percentage = rs.getDouble("percentage");
            date=rs.getDate("agreement_date");
            if(date!=null)
            employeeAgreement.agreement_date = date.toString();
            System.out.println("fffff==="+rs.getString("emp_id"));
            }
            else
            {
                    initializeEmployeeAgreement(employeeAgreement);
            }
            System.out.println("fffff====="+employeeAgreement.emp_id);
            if(rs != null)
            rs.close();
            if( conn != null)
            conn.close();
        }
        catch(SQLException  ex)
        {
            ex.printStackTrace();
        }
        return employeeAgreement;
    }

    public ArrayList selectEmployeeAgreementByCriteria(String inCriteria)
    {
        ArrayList EmployeeAgreementList = new ArrayList();
        java.sql.Date date;
        try
        {
            DriverManager.registerDriver(new
            oracle.jdbc.driver.OracleDriver());
            Connection conn= DriverManager.getConnection(DBUrl,DBUser,DBPswd);
            Statement stmt = conn.createStatement();
            String lSqlString =     "select * from EMPLOYEE_AGREEMENT ";
            if( inCriteria != null && inCriteria.length() > 0 )
            {
                    lSqlString = lSqlString +" "+inCriteria+"" ;
            }
            System.out.println("Criteria===== "+inCriteria+" and
                    query="+lSqlString);
            ResultSet rs  = null;
            rs  = stmt.executeQuery(lSqlString);
            while( rs.next())
            {
                    EmployeeAgreement  employeeAgreement = new
                            EmployeeAgreement();
                    employeeAgreement.emp_id   =
                            (String)rs.getString("emp_id");
                    employeeAgreement.emp_name =
                            (String)rs.getString("emp_name");
                    employeeAgreement.level_id =
                            (String)rs.getString("level_id");
                    employeeAgreement.allowance_type =
                            (String)rs.getString("allowance_type");
                    employeeAgreement.allowance_name =
                            rs.getString("allowance_name");
                    employeeAgreement.amt = rs.getDouble("amt");
                    employeeAgreement.taxable =
                            (String)rs.getString("taxable");
                    employeeAgreement.percentage = rs.getDouble("percentage");
                    date=rs.getDate("agreement_date");
                    if(date!=null)
                    employeeAgreement.agreement_date = date.toString();
                    EmployeeAgreementList.add(employeeAgreement);
            }
```

```
                if(rs != null)
                rs.close();
                if( conn != null)
                conn.close();
        }
        catch(SQLException  ex)
        {
                ex.printStackTrace();
        }
        return EmployeeAgreementList;
}

public int updateEmployeeAgreementByPrimaryKey(EmployeeAgreement
        inEmployeeAgreement)
{
        int recupd = 0;
        String lQuery = "";
        lQuery = lQuery +"update EMPLOYEE_AGREEMENT set
                emp_name='"+inEmployeeAgreement.emp_name+"'  ";
        lQuery = lQuery +" , level_id='"+inEmployeeAgreement.level_id+"' ";
        lQuery = lQuery +" ,
                allowance_type='"+inEmployeeAgreement.allowance_type+"' ";
        lQuery = lQuery +" , amt="+inEmployeeAgreement.amt+" ";
        lQuery = lQuery +" , taxable='"+inEmployeeAgreement.taxable+"' ";
        lQuery = lQuery +" , percentage="+inEmployeeAgreement.percentage+" ";
        lQuery = lQuery +" ,
        agreement_date=to_date('"+inEmployeeAgreement.agreement_date+"', 'yyyy-mm-dd') ";
        lQuery = lQuery + "where emp_id='"+inEmployeeAgreement.emp_id+"' ";
        lQuery = lQuery + "and
                allowance_name='"+inEmployeeAgreement.allowance_name+"' ";
        System.out.println("lSqlString===:"+lQuery);
        try
        {
                DriverManager.registerDriver(new
                        oracle.jdbc.driver.OracleDriver());
                Connection conn= DriverManager.getConnection(DBUrl,DBUser,DBPswd);
                Statement stmt = conn.createStatement();
                recupd  = stmt.executeUpdate(lQuery);
                if( conn != null)
                conn.close();
        }
        catch(SQLException  ex)
        {
                ex.printStackTrace();
        }
        return recupd;
}

public EmployeeAgreement populateEmployeeAgreementFromReq(HttpServletRequest
        inReq)
{
        EmployeeAgreement  employeeAgreement = new EmployeeAgreement();
        employeeAgreement.emp_id   =  (String)inReq.getParameter("emp_id");
        employeeAgreement.emp_name = (String)inReq.getParameter("emp_name");
        employeeAgreement.level_id = (String)inReq.getParameter("level_id");
        employeeAgreement.allowance_type =
                (String)inReq.getParameter("allowance_type");
        employeeAgreement.allowance_name =
                inReq.getParameter("allowance_name");
        if( (String)inReq.getParameter("amt") != null &&
                ((String)inReq.getParameter("amt")).length() > 0 )
        employeeAgreement.amt =
                Double.parseDouble((String)inReq.getParameter("amt")) ;
        else
        employeeAgreement.amt = 0;
        employeeAgreement.taxable = (String)inReq.getParameter("taxable");
```

```
        if( (String)inReq.getParameter("percentage") != null &&
              ((String)inReq.getParameter("percentage")).length() > 0)
        employeeAgreement.percentage =
              Double.parseDouble((String)inReq.getParameter("percentage"));
        else
        employeeAgreement.percentage = 0;
        employeeAgreement.agreement_date =
              (String)inReq.getParameter("agreement_date");
        return employeeAgreement;
    }
    public int insertEmployeeAgreement(EmployeeAgreement inEmployeeAgreement)
    {
        .. .. ..
        .. .. ..
    }

    public int insertEmpSal(EmpSal inEmpSal)
    {
        .. .. ..
        .. .. ..
    }

    public ArrayList selectEmpSalByCriteria(String inCriteria)
    {
        .. .. ..
        .. .. ..
    }

    public void deleteEmployeeAgreement(String inEmpId , String inAllowanceName)
    {
        .. .. ..
        .. .. ..
    }
}
```

In Listing 23.54, the `getEmployeeAgreementRecord()` method returns the `EmployeeAgreement` object. Other methods, such as `selectEmployeeAgreementByCriteria()` and `updateEmployeeAgreementByPrimaryKey()`, are used to retrieve and update an employee's salary, respectively. The `selectEmployeeAgreementByCriteria()` method returns the salary of an employee in the form of the elements of the ArrayList object. The `updateEmployeeAgreementByPrimaryKey()` method returns an `int` value on the basis of the number of records updated in the database. The PayrollBeanMethods class also provides methods to insert or delete a record from the table. All these methods accept arguments to create queries and return an object containing the result of the query. For example, the `insertEmpSal()` method takes an object of the `EmpSal` class and inserts a new record in the `EMP_SAL` table. This method returns an int value, depending upon the number of records updated by the execution of the insert query. In our case, the 1 value is returned by the `insertEmpSal()` method.

Listing 23.55 provides the code of the `insertEmpSal()` method of the `PayrollBeanMethods` class:

Listing 23.55: Showing the Code of the insertEmpSal() Method of the PayrollBeanMethods Class

```
public int insertEmpSal(EmpSal inEmpSal)
{
   int recupd = 0;
   String lQuery = "";
   lQuery = lQuery +"insert into EMP_SAL  values ( ";
   lQuery = lQuery +" '"+inEmpSal.emp_id+"'  ";
   lQuery = lQuery +" , "+inEmpSal.year+"  ";
   lQuery = lQuery +" , "+inEmpSal.month+" ";
   lQuery = lQuery +" , '"+inEmpSal.allowance_type+"' ";
   lQuery = lQuery +" , '"+inEmpSal.allowance_name+"' ";
   lQuery = lQuery +" , "+inEmpSal.amt+" ";
   lQuery = lQuery +" , '"+inEmpSal.taxable+"' ";
   lQuery = lQuery +" , "+inEmpSal.percentage+" ";
   lQuery = lQuery + " )";
   System.out.println("lSqlString===:"+lQuery);
```

```
        try
        {
                DriverManager.registerDriver(new
                        oracle.jdbc.driver.OracleDriver());
                Connection conn= DriverManager.getConnection(DBUrl,DBUser,DBPswd);
                Statement stmt = conn.createStatement();
                recupd  = stmt.executeUpdate(lQuery);
                if( conn != null)
                conn.close();
        }
        catch(SQLException  ex)
        {
                ex.printStackTrace();
        }
        return recupd;
    }
```

The code provided in Listing 23.55 is used to insert the salary of an employee in the `EMP_SAL` table. The other method named `selectEmpSalByCriteria()` accepts a string as an argument to execute the query to find salary details of an employee. The passed string is used as a criteria and contains the `where` clause. The method returns an ArrayList containing objects of the `EmpSal` type. Each object in that ArrayList represents the details of allowances given to a particular employee.

The code for the selectEmpSalByCriteria() method of the PayrollBeanMethods class is shown in Listing 23.56:

Listing 23.56: Showing the Code of the selectEmpSalByCriteria() Method of the PayrollBeanMethods Class

```
    public ArrayList selectEmpSalByCriteria(String inCriteria)
    {
        ArrayList EmpSalList = new ArrayList();
        try
        {
                DriverManager.registerDriver(new oracle.jdbc.driver.OracleDriver());
                Connection conn= DriverManager.getConnection(DBUrl,DBUser,DBPswd);
                Statement stmt = conn.createStatement();
                String lSqlString ="select * from EMP_SAL  ";
                if( inCriteria != null && inCriteria.length() > 0 )
                {
                        lSqlString = lSqlString +" "+inCriteria+"" ;
                }
                        System.out.println("Criteria===== "+inCriteria+" and
                                query="+lSqlString);
                        ResultSet rs  = null;
                        rs  = stmt.executeQuery(lSqlString);
                        while( rs.next())
                        {
                                EmpSal  empSal = new EmpSal();
                                empSal.emp_id   =  (String)rs.getString("emp_id");
                                empSal.year = rs.getInt("year");
                                empSal.month = rs.getInt("month");
                                empSal.allowance_type =
                                        (String)rs.getString("allowance_type");
                                empSal.allowance_name =    rs.getString("allowance_name");
                                empSal.amt = rs.getDouble("amt");
                                empSal.taxable = (String)rs.getString("taxable");
                                empSal.percentage = rs.getDouble("percentage");
                                EmpSalList.add(empSal);
                        }
                        if(rs != null)
                        rs.close();
                        if( conn != null)
                        conn.close();
                }
                catch(SQLException  ex)
                {
                        ex.printStackTrace();
                }
                return EmpSalList;
    }
```

The `selectEmpSalByCriteria()` method provided in Listing 23.56 returns the salary of an employee as an object of the ArrayList class. The `insertEmployeeAgreement()` method takes an object of the `EmployeeAgreement` type and inserts the details of the salary statement in the `EMPLOYEE_AGREEMENT` table. The values to be inserted are obtained from the passed object.

Listing 23.57 provides the code of the `insertEmployeeAgreement()` method of the `PayrollBeanMethods` class:

Listing 23.57: Showing the Code of the insertEmployeeAgreement() Method of the PayrollBeanMethods Class

```
public int insertEmployeeAgreement(EmployeeAgreement inEmployeeAgreement)
{
   int recupd = 0;
   String lQuery = "";
   lQuery = lQuery +"insert into EMPLOYEE_AGREEMENT  values ( ";
   lQuery = lQuery +" '"+inEmployeeAgreement.emp_id+"'  ";
   lQuery = lQuery +" , '"+inEmployeeAgreement.emp_name+"'  ";
   lQuery = lQuery +" , '"+inEmployeeAgreement.level_id+"' ";
   lQuery = lQuery +" , '"+inEmployeeAgreement.allowance_type+"' ";
   lQuery = lQuery +" , '"+inEmployeeAgreement.allowance_name+"' ";
   lQuery = lQuery +" , "+inEmployeeAgreement.amt+" ";
   lQuery = lQuery +" , '"+inEmployeeAgreement.taxable+"' ";
   lQuery = lQuery +" , "+inEmployeeAgreement.percentage+" ";
   lQuery = lQuery +" , '"+inEmployeeAgreement.agreement_date+"' ";
   lQuery = lQuery + " )";
   System.out.println("lSqlString===:"+lQuery);
   try
   {
         DriverManager.registerDriver(new oracle.jdbc.driver.OracleDriver());
         Connection conn= DriverManager.getConnection(DBUrl,DBUser,DBPswd);
         Statement stmt = conn.createStatement();
         recupd  = stmt.executeUpdate(lQuery);
         if( conn != null)
         conn.close();
   }
   catch(SQLException  ex)
   {
         ex.printStackTrace();
   }
   return recupd;
}
```

The `insertEmployeeAgreement()` method described in Listing 23.57 takes the `EmployeeAgreement` object as an argument and inserts employee details in the `EMP_SAL` table. The other method, `deleteEmployeeAgreement()`, deletes a salary statement record from the EMPLOYEE_AGREEMENT table. Listing 23.58 provides the code of the `deleteEmployeeAgreement()` method of the `PayrollBeanMethods` class:

Listing 23.58: Showing the Code of the deleteEmployeeAgreement() Method of the PayrollBeanMethods Class

```
public void deleteEmployeeAgreement(String inEmpId , String inAllowanceName)
{
   try
   {
         DriverManager.registerDriver(new
                oracle.jdbc.driver.OracleDriver());
         Connection conn= DriverManager.getConnection(DBUrl,DBUser,DBPswd);
         Statement stmt = conn.createStatement();
         String lQuery = "";
         lQuery = lQuery +"delete from EMPLOYEE_AGREEMENT ";
         lQuery = lQuery +" where emp_id='"+inEmpId+"' and
                allowance_name='"+inAllowanceName+"' ";
         System.out.println("lSqlString===:"+lQuery);
         stmt.executeQuery(lQuery);
         if( conn != null)
         conn.close();
   }
```

```
        catch(SQLException  ex)
        {
                ex.printStackTrace();
        }
    }
```

The deleteEmployeeAgreement() method, specified in Listing 23.58, deletes the salary details of a specific employee from the `EMP_SAL` table.

After creating the required Java source files, you need to compile all the .java files and place their .class files in the `WEB-INF/classes` folder along with their package directory.

Let's now design the JSP views for the Payroll module.

Designing JSP Views

In this section, let's design the JSP pages for the Payroll module. These JSP pages provide forms to enter the details related to the salary of the employees, such as salary statement of a particular employee and allowances granted to an employee. In this module, you need to create the employee_agreement, employee_agreement_edit, salary_search, and salary_slip JSP pages. Let's first create the `employee_agreement JSP page`.

Creating the employee_agreement JSP Page

The `employee_agreement` JSP page displays the values of various fields, such as `employee id`, `employee name`, `department`, and the `designation` of the employee. In addition, this page allows you to enter the values in the `Allowance Name` and `Allowance Type fields`. You also need to specify whether the salary lies in the taxable slab or not; if the tax needs to be deducted from the salary, you need to specify the percentage for the same.

Listing 23.59 provides the code of the `employee_agreement.jsp` file (save the `employee_agreement.jsp` file in the `people-mgmt\jsp` folder):

Listing 23.59: Showing the Code of the employee_agreement.jsp File

```
<%@ page language="java" %>
<%@ page session="true" %>
<%@ page  import="com.Employee.*" %>
<%@ page  import="com.Payroll.*" %>
<%@ page  import="java util.*" %>
<html>
<head>
<title>www.peoplemanagementsolutions.com/BreakUp of Salary</title>
<link rel="stylesheet" href="../css/mystyle.css" type="text/css" />
</head>
<body>
<table width="900" border="0" align="center">
<tr>
<td colspan="2" ><%@ include file="../jsp/people_header.jsp" %></td>
</tr>
<tr>
<td width="900" valign="top"><%@ include file="../jsp/people_default_menu.jsp"
%></td>
</tr>
<tr>
<td width ="750" valign="top">
<p> </p>
<table  border="0" width=100% align=center>
<%
   String dbopr = "";
   dbopr = (String)session.getAttribute("dbopr");
   EmployeeDBObj employeeDBObj = new EmployeeDBObj();
   employeeDBObj = (EmployeeDBObj)session.getAttribute("employeeDBObj");
%>
<tr>
<td bgcolor ='#AAAAAA' class=whitetext align=center height=20><b>Salary Heads
Distribution</b></td>
```

```
</tr>
<form name="form1" method="post">
<%
  if(dbopr != null && ( dbopr.equals("employee_agreement") ||
  dbopr.equals("edit_head") || dbopr.equals("delete_head") ) ){
%>
<tr>
<td>
<table  border='0'width=400 align=center>
<tr><td >Employee Id</td>
<td align='left' >
<%=employeeDBObj.emp_id%>
<input type='hidden' name='emp_id' id='emp_id 'size ='10' value=
'<%=employeeDBObj.emp_id%>'/>
</td></tr>
<tr><td>Employee Name</td>
<td align='left'>
<input type='hidden' name='emp_name' id='emp_name' size ='10' value='<%=employee
DBObj.emp_f_name%> <%=employeeDBObj.emp_m_name%> <%=employeeDBObj.emp_l_name%>'/>
<%=employeeDBObj.emp_f_name%> <%=employeeDBObj.emp_m_name%> <%=employee
DBObj.emp_l_name%>
</td></tr>
<tr><td>Department</td>
<td align='left'><%=employeeDBObj.dept_id%></td></tr>
<tr><td>Designation</td>
<td align='left'><%=employeeDBObj.level_id%>
<input type='hidden' name='level_id' id='level_id 'size ='10' value='<%=employee
DBObj.level_id%>'/>
</td></tr>
<tr><td>Agreement Date</td>
<td align='left'> <input type='hidden' name='agreement_date' id='agreement_date'
size ='10' value='<%=employeeDBObj.dojoin%>'/>
<input type='text' disabled='disabled' name='d_agreement_date' id='d_agreement_
date' size ='10' value='<%=employeeDBObj.dojoin%>'/> (yyyy-mm-dd)</td></tr>
<tr><td colspan=2>
<table border=0>
<tr>
<td>Allowance Name</td>
<td align='left'>
<SELECT name='allowance_name' >
<OPTION VALUE=></OPTION>
<OPTION VALUE=Basic>Basic</OPTION>
<OPTION VALUE=HRA>HRA</OPTION>
<OPTION VALUE=PF>PF</OPTION>
<OPTION VALUE=SPLAL>SPLAL</OPTION>
<OPTION VALUE=DA>DA</OPTION>
</SELECT>
</td>
<td>Allowance Type</td>
<td align='left'>
<SELECT name='allowance_type' >
<OPTION VALUE=></OPTION>
<OPTION VALUE=Income>Income</OPTION><OPTION VALUE=Deduction>Deduction</OPTION>
</SELECT>
</td>
</tr>
<tr>
<td>Amount</td>
<td align='left'><input type='text' name='amt' id='amt' size ='10' value=''/></td>
<td>Taxable</td>
<td align='left'>
<SELECT name='taxable' >
<OPTION VALUE=></OPTION>
<OPTION VALUE=Yes>Yes</OPTION><OPTION VALUE=No>No</OPTION>
</SELECT>
```

```
</td>
</tr>
<tr>
<td>Percentage</td>
<td align='left'><input type='text' name='percentage' id='percentage' size ='10'
value=''/></td>
<td></td>
<td></td>
</tr>
</table>
</td>
</tr>
<tr>
<td>
<input type='submit' name='submit' id='submit' size ='10' value='Submit Detail'/>
<input type='hidden' name='action_submit' id='action_submit' size ='10'
value='emp_agreement_dtl_submit'/>
</td>
</tr>
</table>
</td></tr><tr><td>
<%
}
   ArrayList employeeAgreementList  = new ArrayList();
   employeeAgreementList = (ArrayList)session.getAttribute("employeeAgree
   mentList");
   if ( employeeAgreementList != null && employeeAgreementList.size() > 0){
   out.println("<table border=0 align=center>");
   out.println("<tr bgcolor='#AAAAAA'>");
   if(dbopr != null && !( dbopr.equals("employee_agreement") ||
   dbopr.equals("edit_head") || dbopr.equals("delete_head")) ){
        out.println("<td class=whitetext align=center>Employee Id</td>");
        out.println("<td class=whitetext >Employee Name</td>");
    }
%>
<td class=whitetext align=center>Allowance Type</td>
<td class=whitetext align=center>Allowance Name</td>
<td class=whitetext align=center>Amount</td>
<td class=whitetext align=center>Taxable</td>
<td class=whitetext align=center>Percentage</td>
<td class=whitetext align=center>Opr</td>
<td class=whitetext align=center>Opr</td>
</tr>
<%
    double totalSalary = 0;
    for ( int rec = 1; rec <= employeeAgreementList.size(); rec++ ){
         EmployeeAgreement employeeAgreement = new EmployeeAgreement();
         employeeAgreement = (EmployeeAgreement)employeeAgreementList.
         get(rec-1);
         out.println("<tr bgcolor ='#AAAAAA'>");
         if(dbopr != null && !( dbopr.equals("employee_agreement") ||
         dbopr.equals("edit_head") || dbopr.equals("delete_head") ) ){
         out.println("<td align='center'>"+employeeAgreement.emp_id+"</td>");
         out.println("<tdalign='center'>"+employeeAgreement.emp_name+</td>");
         }
%>
<td align='center' ><%=employeeAgreement.allowance_name%> </td>
<td align='center' ><%=employeeAgreement.allowance_type%> </td>
<td align='center' ><%=employeeAgreement.amt%></td>
<%
  if ( employeeAgreement.allowance_type.equals("Income") ){
        totalSalary     =   totalSalary + employeeAgreement.amt;
  }
%>
<td align='center' ><%=employeeAgreement.taxable%></td>
<td align='center' ><%=employeeAgreement.percentage%></td>
```

```
<td align='center' bgcolor="#AAAAAA">
<a href='http://localhost:8080/people-mgmt/servlet/people_payroll?dbopr=edit_head
&&emp_id=<%=employeeAgreement.emp_id%>&&allowance_name=<%=employeeAgreement.allowa
nce_name%>' class=yellowlink>Edit</a>
</td >
<td align='center' bgcolor="#AAAAAA">
<a href='http://localhost:8080/people-mgmt/servlet/people_payroll?dbopr=delete_he
ad&&emp_id=<%=employeeAgreement.emp_id%>&&allowance_name=<%=employeeAgreement.allo
wance_name%>' class=yellowlink>Delete</a>
</td >
</tr>
<% } %>
</table>
</td>
</tr>
<tr>
<td align=center class=boldblack>Gross Salary:<%=totalSalary%></td>
</tr>
<% } %>
</table>
<hr bgcolor="#AAAAAA">
</td>
</tr>
<tr>
<td colspan="2"><%@include file="../jsp/people_footer.jsp"%></td>
</tr>
</table>
</body>
</html>
```

The code provided in Listing 23.59 is used to design a salary slip for an employee. All employees have their own salary statements according to which their salary is calculated. To enter a new salary statement, click the `Employee Agreement` submenu under the Payroll menu. The `employee_agreement` JSP page is displayed, in which you need to enter values for various fields, such as Basic, HRA, Provident Fund, and Medical.

Figure 23.24 shows the output form of the `employee_agreement` JSP page:

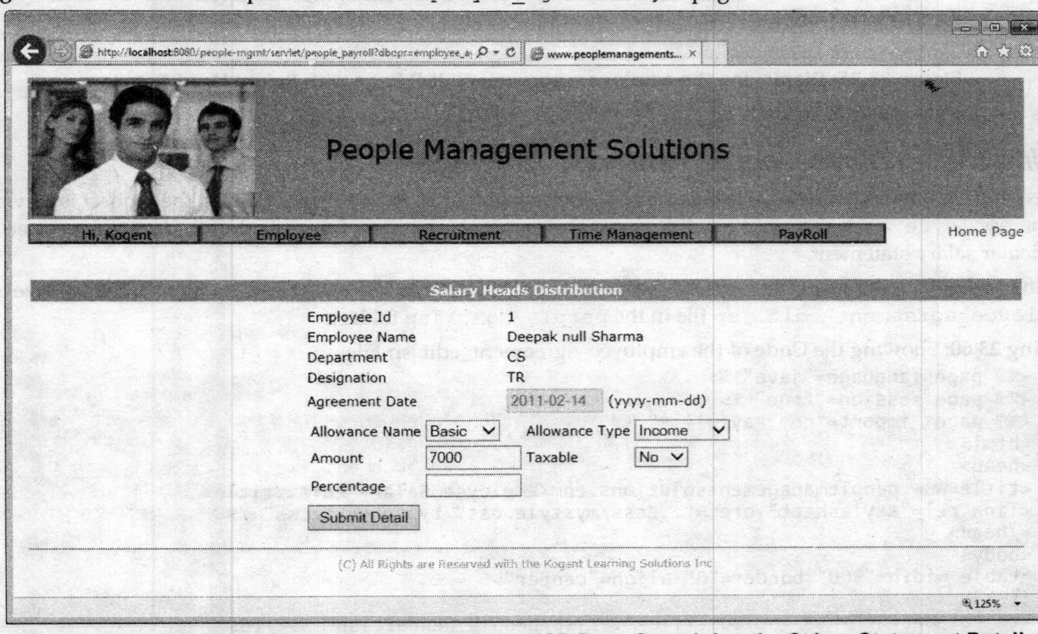

Figure 23.24: Displaying the employee_agreement JSP Page Containing the Salary Statement Details

In the `employee_agreement` JSP page, you need to enter the respective details and click the Submit Detail button. As a result, the `people_payroll` servlet re-executes and updates the data in the database. Further, the user is redirected to the `employee_agreement` JSP page that shows salary details.

Figure 23.25 shows the two salary heads that have been added for a particular employee:

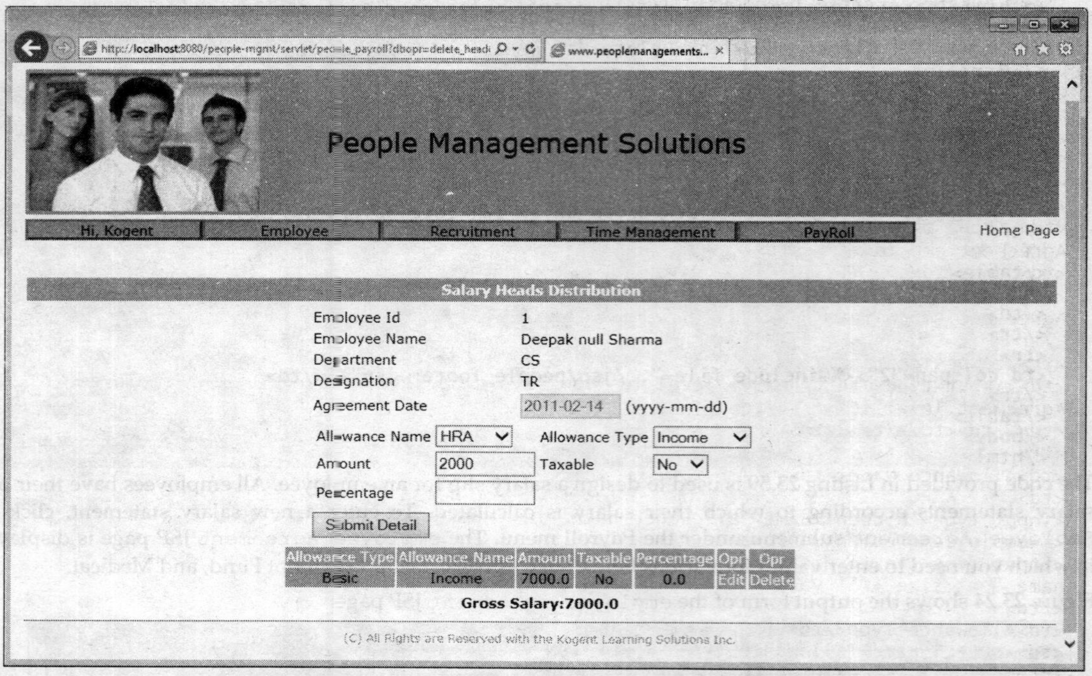

Figure 23.25: Displaying the employee_agreement JSP Page with Salary Head Details

Let's now create the `employee_agreement_edit JSP` page.

Creating the employee_agreement_edit JSP Page

When you click the `Edit` link in the `employee_agreement JSP page` (Figure 23.25), the request is forwarded to the `employee_agreeemnt_edit` JSP page. This page appears as a form filled with data to be edited for a particular salary statement.

Listing 23.60 shows the code of the `employee_agreement_edit.jsp` file (save the `employee_agreement_edit.jsp` file in the `people-mgmt\jsp` folder):

Listing 23.60: Showing the Code of the employee_agreement_edit.jsp File

```
<%@ page language="java" %>
<%@ page session="true" %>
<%@ page  import="com.Payroll.*" %>
<html>
<head>
<title>www.peoplemanagementsolutions.com/Employee Salary Edit</title>
<link rel="stylesheet" href="../css/mystyle.css" type="text/css" />
</head>
<body>
<table width="900" border="0" align="center">
<tr>
<td colspan="2"><%@ include file="../jsp/people_header.jsp" %></td>
</tr>
<tr>
<td width="900"><%@ include file="../jsp/people_default_menu.jsp" %></td>
</tr>
```

```
<tr>
<td width ="730" valign="top" align = "center">
<table  border="0" align="top" width=100%>
<%
  EmployeeAgreement employeeAgreement = new EmployeeAgreement();
  employeeAgreement = (EmployeeAgreement)session.getAttribute("employeeAgreement")
%>
<form name="form1" method="post">
<p> </p>
<table align=center>
<tr>
<td colspan=4 bgcolor=#AAAAAA class=whitetext align=center height=20><b>Employee
Salary BreakUp</b></td>
</tr>
<tr><td>Employee Id</td>
<td><input type='text' name='emp_id' id='emp_id 'size ='10' value='<%=employee
Agreement.emp_id%>'/></td>
<td>Name</td>
<td><input type='text' name='emp_name' id='emp_name 'size ='30' value='<%=employee
Agreement.emp_name%>' /></td>
</tr>
<tr><td>Designation</td>
<td><input type='text' name='level_id' id='level_id' size ='10' value='<%=employee
Agreement.level_id%>'/></td>
<td></td><td></td></tr>
<tr>
<td>Allowance Name</td>
<td>
<input type='hidden' name='allowance_name' id='allowance_name' size ='5' value='
<%=employeeAgreement.allowance_name%>'/>
<input type='text' disabled='disabled' name='allowance_name_dup' id='allowance_
name_dup' size ='5' value='<%=employeeAgreement.allowance_name%>'/>
</td>
<td>Allowance Type</td>
<td><SELECT name='allowance_type' > <OPTION VALUE=></OPTION> <OPTION VALUE=Income>
Income</OPTION><OPTION VALUE=Deduction>Deduction</OPTION></SELECT></td>
</tr>
<tr>
<td>Amount</td>
<td><input type='text' name='amt' id='amt' size ='5' value='<%=employee
Agreement.amt%>'/></td>
<td>Taxable</td>
<td><SELECT name='taxable'> <OPTION VALUE=></OPTION> <OPTION VALUE=Yes>Yes
</OPTION><OPTION VALUE=No>No</OPTION></SELECT></td>
</tr>
<tr>
<td>Percentage</td>
<td><input type='text' name='percentage' id='percentage' size ='5' value='
<%=employeeAgreement.percentage%>'/></td>
<td>Date</td>
<td><input type='text' name='agreement_date' id='agreement_date' size ='10'
value='<%=employeeAgreement.agreement_date%>'/> (yyyy-mm-dd)</td>
</tr>
<tr>
<td colspan=4><input type='submit' name='submit' id='submit' size ='10' value=
'Edit'/>
<input type='hidden' name='action_submit' id='action_submit' size ='10' value=
'employee_sal_head_edit_submit'/> </td>
</tr>
</table>
</td></tr>
<tr>
<td colspan="2"><%@include file="../jsp/people_footer.jsp"%></td>
</tr>
</table></body></html>
```

Figure 23.26 displays the output of the `employee_agreement_edit` JSP page for a particular employee:

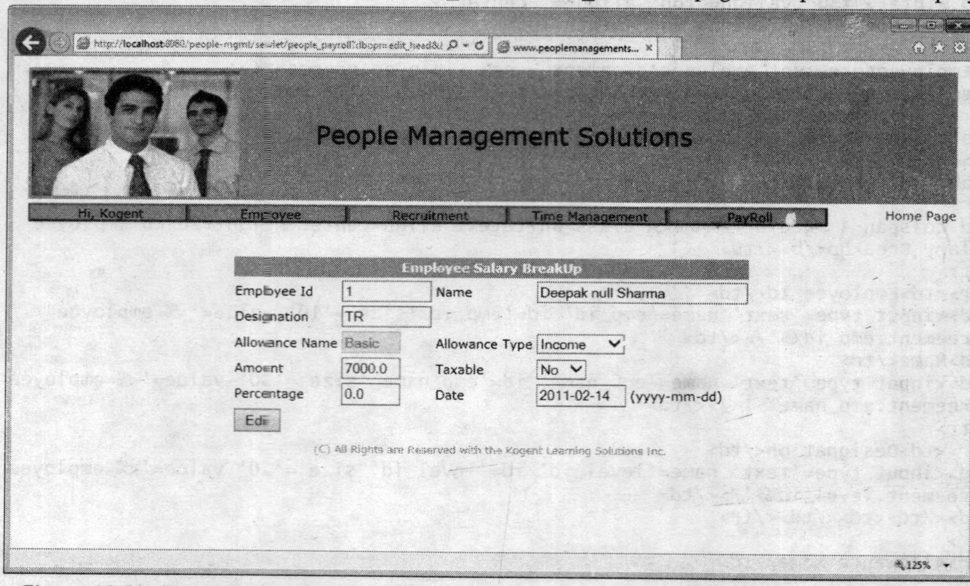

Figure 23.26: Displaying the employee_agreement_edit JSP Page to Edit Salary Head Details

Figure 23.26 shows the salary details of an employee whose `Employee Id is 1`.

Let's now create the `salary_search JSP` page.

Creating the salary_search.jsp File

The `salary_search` JSP page displays a search form used to search the salary details of a particular employee. The form submission consequently generates a salary slip of that employee for a given month, showing all the salary details.

Listing 23.61 provides the code for the `salary_search.jsp` file (save the `salary_search.jsp` file in the `people-mgmt\jsp` folder):

Listing 23.61: Showing the Code of the salary_search.jsp File

```
<%@ page language="java" %>
<%@ page session="true" %>
<html>
<head>
<title>www.peoplemanagementsolutions.com/Salary</title>
<link rel="stylesheet" href="../css/mystyle.css" type="text/css" />
</head>
<body>
<table width="900" border="0" align="center">
<tr>
<td colspan="2"><%@ include file="../jsp/people_header.jsp" %></td>
</tr>
<tr>
<td width="900"><%@ include file="../jsp/people_default_menu.jsp" %></td>
</tr><tr>
<td width ="750" valign="top" align = "center">
<p> </p>
<div align=center class=boldblack>Calculate Salary</div>
<hr width=400 color=#AAAAAA>
<table  border="0" align="top" width=200 align="right">
<form name="form1" method="post">
<tr><td>Employee Id</td>
<td align='left'><input type='text' name='emp_id' id=emp_id size=10 value=''/>
</td></tr>
<tr><td>Year</td>
```

```
<td align='left'><select name='year' >
<option value=></option>
<%
  for(int i=2014;i>2000;i--)
  out.println("<option value="+i+">"+i+"</option>");
%>
</select></td></tr>
<tr><td>Month</td>
<td align='left'><SELECT name='month'>
<option value=></option>
<%
  for(int i=12;i>0;i--)
  out.println("<option value="+i+">"+i+"</option>");
%>
</SELECT></td></tr>
<tr><td align='center'colspan='2' >
<input type='submit' name='submit' id='submit' size ='10' value='Calc'/>
<input type='hidden' name='action_submit' id='action_submit' size ='10' value='
salary_calc_submit'/>
</td></tr>
</table><hr width=400 color=#AAAAAA>
</td>
</tr>
<tr>
<td colspan="2"><%@include file="../jsp/people_footer.jsp"%></td>
</tr>
</table></body></html>
```

In Listing 23.61, the `salary_search` JSP page is designed, which contains three fields, `Employee Id`, `Year`, and `Month`. When the user fills these fields and clicks the `Calc` button, the data is retrieved from the EMPLOYEE_AGREEMENT table.

Figure 23.27 displays the `salary_search` JSP page:

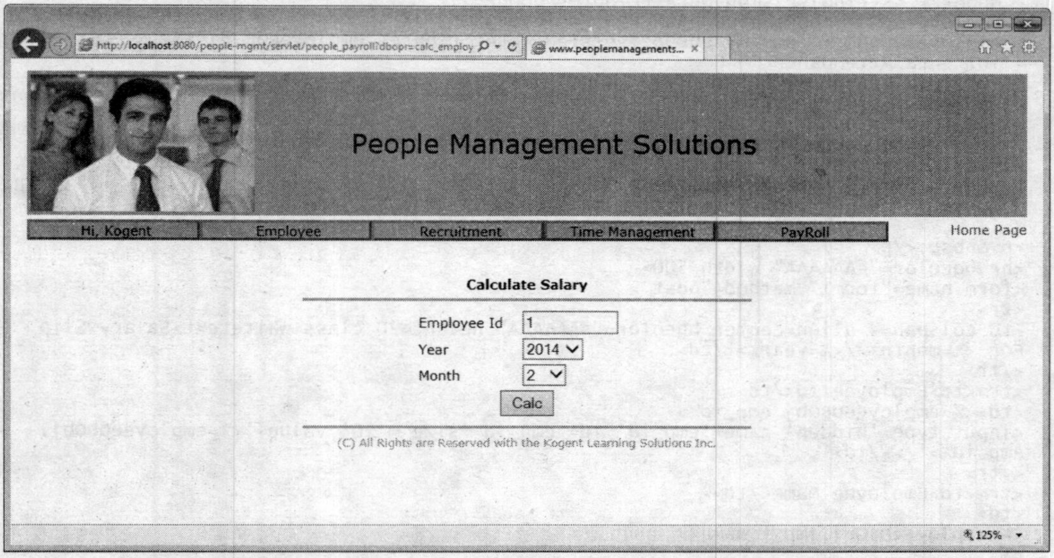

Figure 23.27: Displaying the salary_search JSP Page with Fields for Salary Slip Detail

Figure 23.27 shows the `salary_search` JSP page used to find the salary details of the employee having the `Employee Id`,1.

Let's now create the `salary_slip` JSP page.

Creating the salary_slip JSP Page

The `salary_slip` JSP page displays a salary slip of the employee whose details have been provided in the `salary_search JSP` page. In addition to the `employee id`, `employee name`, `department`, and designation, the generated salary slip shows various allowances given to the employee, amount of each allowance, total attendance of the employee, total number of leaves taken by the employee in that month, and the total salary for that particular month.

Listing 23.62 provides the code for the salary_slip.jsp file (save the salary_slip.jsp file in the people-mgmt\jsp folder):

Listing 23.62: Showing the Code of the salary_slip.jsp File

```
<%@ page language="java' %>
<%@ page session="true" %>
<%@ page  import="com.Employee.*" %>
<%@ page  import="com.Payroll.*" %>
<%@ page  import="java.util.*" %>
<%@ page  import="java.text.DecimalFormat" %>
<html>
<head>
<title>www.peoplemanagementsolutions.com/Salary Slip</title>
<link rel="stylesheet" href="../css/mystyle.css" type="text/css" />
</head>
<body>
<table width="900" border="0" align="center">
<tr>
<td colspan="2" ><%@ include file="../jsp/people_header.jsp" %></td>
</tr>
<tr>
<td width="900" valign='top"><%@ include file="../jsp/people_default_menu.jsp"
%></td></tr><tr>
<td width ="750" valign="top">
<table  border="0"  width=500 align=center>
<%
  String dbopr = "";
  dbopr = (String)session.getAttribute("dbopr");
  EmployeeDBObj employeeDBObj = new EmployeeDBObj();
  employeeDBObj = (EmployeeDBObj)session.getAttribute("employeeDBObj");
  int totalAttendance  = 0;
  int totalLeave       = 0;
  int year  = 0;
  int month = 0;
  totalAttendance= Integer.parseInt((String)session.getAttribute(totalAttendance);
  totalLeave = Integer.parseInt((String)session.getAttribute("totalLeave"));
  year = Integer.parseInt((String)session.getAttribute("year"));
  month = Integer.parseInt((String)session.getAttribute("month"));
%>
<p> </p>
<hr bgcolor="#AAAAAA" width=500>
<form name="form1" method="post">
<tr>
<td colspan=4 align=center bgcolor="#AAAAAA" height=20 class=whitetext>Salary Slip
For <%=month%>/<%=year%></td>
</tr>
<tr><td>Employee Id</td>
<td><%=employeeDBObj.emp_id%>
<input type='hidden' name='emp_id' id='emp_id 'size ='10' value='<%=employeeDBObj.
emp_id%>'/></td>
</tr>
<tr><td>Employee Name</td>
<td>
<%=employeeDBObj.emp_f_name%>
<%
  if(!"null".equals(employeeDBObj.emp_m_name))
  out.print(employeeDBObj.emp_m_name);
%>
<%=employeeDBObj.emp_l_name%>
<input type='hidden' name='emp_name' id='emp_name' size ='10' value=
'<%=employeeDBObj.emp_f_name%>
<%=employeeDBObj.emp_m_name%> <%=employeeDBObj.emp_l_name%>'/></td>
</tr>
<tr><td>Department</td><td><%=employeeDBObj.dept_id%></td></tr>
<tr><td>Desination</td><td>
<%=employeeDBObj.level_id%>
<input type='hidden' name='level_id' id='level_id 'size ='10' value=
```

```
'<%=employeeDBObj.level_id%>'/></td>
</tr>
</table>
<%
  ArrayList empSalList  = new ArrayList();
  empSalList = (ArrayList)session.getAttribute("empSalList");
  if ( empSalList != null && empSalList.size() > 0){
%>
<table align=center width=500>
<tr bgcolor ='#AAAAAA' align=center>
<td class=whitetext>Allowance Name</td>
<td class=whitetext>Amount(Rs.)</td>
</tr>
<%
  double totalSalary = 0;
  double taxAmt  = 0 ;
  for ( int rec = 1; rec <= empSalList.size(); rec++ ){
        EmpSal empSal = new EmpSal();
        empSal = (EmpSal)empSalList.get(rec-1);
        out.println("<tr bgcolor ='#AAAAAA'>");
        out.println("<td align='center' >"+empSal.allowance_name+"</td>");
        if ( empSal.allowance_type.equals("Income") ){
                out.println("<td align='center' >(+)"+empSal.amt+"</td>");
                totalSalary     =   totalSalary + empSal.amt;
        }
        else
        if ( empSal.allowance_type.equals("Deduction") ){
                out.println("<td align='center' >(-)"+empSal.amt+"</td>");
                totalSalary     =   totalSalary - empSal.amt;
        }
        if ( empSal.taxable.equals("Yes") ){
                taxAmt = taxAmt + (empSal.amt * empSal.percentage/100);
        }
        out.println("</tr>");
  }
%>
<tr>
<td class=boldblack>Total Present: <%=totalAttendance%></td>
<td class=boldblack>Total Leave: <%=totalLeave%></td>
</tr>
<tr>
<td class=boldblack>Total Salary: <%=totalSalary%></td>
<td class=boldblack>Tax: <%=taxAmt%></td>
<% double monthSalary=0.0;
   double deduction=0.0;
   String output="";
   String monthsalary="";
   if(totalLeave > 0) {
            deduction = totalSalary/30;
       deduction = deduction*totalLeave;
       monthSalary = totalSalary - deduction;


  }
   else
   {
        deduction = 0.0;
        monthSalary=totalSalary;
   }
DecimalFormat myFormatter = new DecimalFormat("#######.##");
       monthsalary=myFormatter.format(monthSalary);
       output = myFormatter.format(deduction);
%>
</tr>
<tr>
<td class=boldblack>Deduction     : <%=output%> Rs.</td>
<td class=boldblack>Month's Salary: <%=monthsalary%> Rs.</td>
</tr>
</table>
<%}
  String lErrorMsg="";
```

```
    lErrorMsg = (String)session.getAttribute("lErrorMsg");
    out.println("<div align=center class=boldred"+lErrorMsg+"</div>");
  %>
  </table>
  </td></tr>
  <tr>
  <td colspan="2">
  <%@include file="../jsp/people_footer.jsp"%>
  </td>
  </tr></table></body>
  </html>
```

Listing 23.62 shows the code to design the salary slip of the specified employee.

Figure 23.28 displays the salary_slip JSP page:

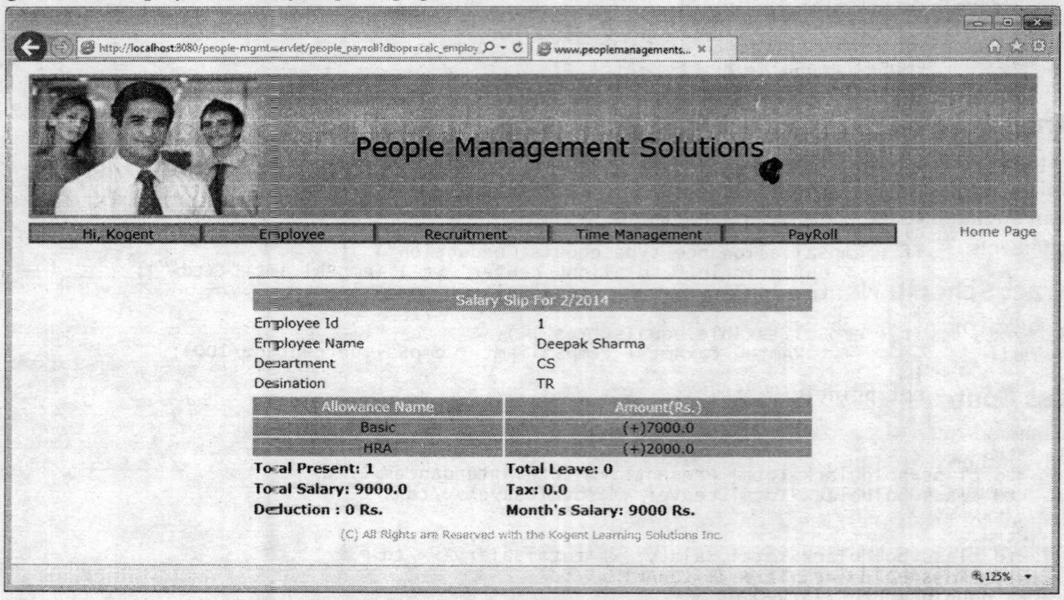

Figure 23.28: Displaying the salary_slip JSP Page

Figure 23.28 displays the salary slip of an employee for the 2nd `Month` of the 2014 year.

This section has explained the logic behind the development of the Payroll module that can be used to handle salary statements of all employees of an organization. This module generates salary slips of all the employees for a given month by considering number of leaves and number of attendances.

As all modules of the ProjectMgmt project are designed in similar manner; therefore, a reader can go through a single module to understand the implementation logic of the MVC architecture. Every module of this project has its own controller servlet, helper Java classes, and the JSP pages that are used as user interfaces. The model part has been implemented using data transfer objects that are being populated manually using ResultSet. The JSP pages have been used as View in the architecture. You should note that the project is designed to maintain the reusability of the code throughout the modules. In other words, all servlets and almost all JSPs are being reused in some way; thereby, decreasing the number of files created in the project.

Glossary

Abstract Schema
A part of the Deployment Descriptor for an entity bean. An abstract schema defines the bean's relationships, persistent fields, or query statements.

Abstract Schema Name
A logical name that is referenced in EJB QL queries.

Access Control
A method to restrict access to resources so that only authorized entities are allowed to access and interact with them. These resources are limited to groups of users or programs for implementing integrity, confidentiality, or availability constraints.

ACID
The properties of a transaction, i.e. atomicity, consistency, isolation, and durability are collectively known as ACID property.

Activation
The process of associating a bean instance with an EJB object to service a request.

Activatable Remote Object
Activatable remote objects are remote objects that require persistent access over time and that can be activated by the application

Advice
Advice defines both the purpose of an aspect and when to perform that purpose. The advice can be applied either before or after method invocation.

AJAX
AJAX stands for Asynchronous JavaScript and XML. Its primary components are JavaScript and XML. AJAX is a technique that describes how other technologies such as JavaScript, DOM (Document Object Model), and XML can be used together to create interactive Web applications.

Anonymous Access
Accessing resources without authentication.

AOP proxy
It is an object that has been advised to the target object. It is created by the AOP framework. In Spring, there are two types of AOP proxies, JDK dynamic proxy and CGLIB proxy.

Applet
A small Java application program, which can be retrieved from a Web server and executed in a Web browser.

Applet Container
A container supporting the applet programming model.

Application Assembler
The person responsible for assembling the JAVA EE components and other modules into a single deployable unit.

Application Client
A JAVA EE client component that executes in its very own JVM and has access to JAVA EE platform APIs.

Application Client Container
The container supporting application client components.

Application Client Module
A module containing the application client's Deployment Descriptor and some associated classes.

Application Component Provider
A vendor who provides classes implementing components' methods and some Deployment Descriptors.

Application Configuration Resource File
A file used to configure resources for a JSF application. It is used to define converters, validators, listeners, renderers, navigation rules, and components for the application.

Archiving
The process of taking backup of the state of selected objects, which can be restored later when needed.

Asant
A Java-based building tool that can be extended using Java classes. It uses configuration files, which are XML-based, for building an application.

Aspect
An aspect combines both advice and pointcuts. In other words, aspect consists of information such as what the job of the aspect is, where to apply the aspect, and when to apply the aspect.

Attribute
A qualifier on an HTML or XML tag that provides additional information about either of these tags.

Authentication
Authentication is a process of setting and verifying identities usually with the help of a username and password.

Authorization
A process to determine whether a user has proper access control rights to perform a requested action. Authorization mechanisms are required to limit the access to code according to the identity property of the user.

Authorization Constraint
A rule to determine who is authorized to access a resource collection.

B2B
B2B is a business-to-business communication between two organizations.

Backing Bean
Backing beans are specific JavaBeans that can handle or store data between the business model and the UI component at the intermediate stage. In other words, backing beans handle the interaction between views and models. Backing beans are normal JavaBeans that contain properties and event handler methods for storing and manipulating user data.

Basic Authentication
In HTTP Basic Authentication mechanism, the caller is authenticated using a username and password obtained by a client using a browser-provided dialog box.

Bean-Managed Persistence
In bean-managed persistence, all persistence logic is explicitly written in the bean class, giving more flexibility to manage the state between the bean instance and the database.

Bean-Managed Transaction
In bean-managed transaction, the EJB code itself manages the transaction including start, stop, commit and rollback of the transaction.

Binding (JavaServer Faces Technology)
Binding of UI components to back-end data sources, such as backing bean properties.

Binding (XML)
Generating the code needed to process a well-defined portion of XML data.

Build File
A simple XML file containing an application and at least a target. A target is a set of tasks you want to execute. In case there is no target, the default target is executed.

Business Logic

This is the code implementing functionality of an application. Business logic is specific to an application.

Business Method

Method of an EJB that contains the code implementing the business logic of an application.

Business Process Management

A well-defined set of tasks developed by users or software systems providing well-defined rules about when tasks should be performed and who should perform them.

Callback Methods

The component methods to notify the components for the events in their life cycle. The callback methods are called by the Java EE container.

Caller Principal

The Principal identifying the invoker of the enterprise bean method.

Cascade Delete

A deletion that triggers another deletion in database. This can be specified for a container-managed persistence bean.

Certificate Authority

A trusted organization that issues public key certificates and provides identification to the bearer as a security mechanism for JavaEE Web applications. These certificates are cryptographically signed by their owners and are difficult for anyone else to forge.

Common Gateway Interface (CGI)

An open standard abstraction between an HTTP adapter (Web server) and an external application written using any of the programming language such as C, and C++.

Client-certificate Authentication

An authentication mechanism using HTTP over SSL in which the server, and sometimes, the clients also authenticate each other with a public key certificate.

Component Contract

A contract between a JavaEE component and its container. This includes managing the lifecyclelifecycle of the component, a context interface and a list of services that every container must provide for its components.

Common Client Interface (CCI)

CCI provides function call APIs for Java EE application servers and their components via a JCA resource-adapter to create and manage connections with an EIS resource, to execute an operation with an EIS resource, and to manage data object/records as input, output, or return values.

Connector

A connector provides connectivity to Enterprise Information System (EIS). A connector consists of a Resource adapter and tools for EIS connectivity.

Connector Architecture

The architecture integrating JavaEE products with different Enterprise Information Systems (EIS). This architecture has two parts: a Resource adapter provided by an EIS vendor and the JAVA EE product allowing this Resource adapter to plug in.

Container

Provides lifecyclelifecycle management, security, and deployment and runtime services to JAVA EE components. Different types of containers for different types of components provide component-specific services.

Context Attribute

Any object bound to a context associated with a Servlet.

Context Root

The name that is mapped to the document root of a Web application.

Conversational State

The set of field values of the Session bean.

Cookie

Information sent by a Web server to a Web client, saved on the client side for the given domain and path.

CORBA

An acronym for Common Object Request Broker Architecture, CORBA is a language-independent distributed object model.

Credentials

The information describing the security attributes of any security principal.

Declarative Security

The security implemented and expressed in a declarative syntax in a Deployment Descriptor.

Deployer

Person responsible for installing JAVA EE modules and applications into an operational environment.

Deployment

The process of installing software into an operational environment.

Deployment Descriptor

A configuration file with the xml extension provided with each module and a JavaEE application that describes how these modules and applications should be deployed. A Deployment Descriptor instructs a deployment tool how to deploy a module or application with a specific container.

Dependency Injection

A technique that allows a component to obtain a reference of another component by injecting a container to the other component by using the setter method or an instantiate variable.

Dependency Bijection

A technique that assembles the stateful components from different contexts in the Seam framework. The values from the context variables are injected to the components and can be outjected from the components back to the respective Seam context.

Deserialization

The process of converting byte streams into Java objects.

Design Pattern

Design patterns provide standardization and simplicity to enterprise applications. Software developers should have a set of ideas and strategies in mind when they develop applications. These set of ideas came from problems faced by a group of software developers in developing an enterprise application.

A design pattern in general should include the following:

- The definition of the problem
- The context of the problem
- The most suitable solution to the problem
- Implementation issues and the consequences involved in using the pattern

Directory Service

A service that provides operations for creating, adding, removing, and modifying the attributes associated with objects in a directory. NDS or Novell Directory Service, ADS or Active Directory Service and NIS (Network Information Service) are the popular directory services used by organizations.

Digest Authentication

It is an authentication mechanism in which a Web application is authenticated to a Web server by sending a message digest with an HTTP request to the server. The digest is much smaller than the HTTP request and does not contain the password.

Distributed Application

An application consisting of a collection of different components running on different runtime environments or platforms connected through a network. They may be based on the 2-tier, 3-tire, or n-tier architecture.

Document Object Model

Document Object Model (DOM) provides a platform and language independent interface that can be used by programs to dynamically access and modify content in an XML document.

DTD

Short for Document Type Definition, DTD is a set of instructions that provides constraints on the structure of an XML document.

EAR File

Short for Enterprise Archive file. It is a JAR archive that represents a JavaEE application, which can be deployed on an application server.

An EAR file may contain a Web module, EJB module, client module and some additional JAR files.

ebXML

Short for Electronic Business XML, ebXML is a specification used by enterprises to conduct business through the exchange of XML-based messages. Enterprises of any size and from any geographical location can conduct business using XML-based messaging over the Internet with ebXML.

EJB Container

A container that manages the runtime environment for Enterprise beans including security, concurrency, lifecyclelifecycle management, transactions, deployment, naming and other services.

EJB Container Provider

A vendor providing an EJB container.

EJB Context

An EJB context is used by enterprise bean to call services provided by the EJB container and to fetch information about the caller of a client-invoked method.

EJB Endpoint

The WSEE 1.2 specification allows a stateless session bean to implement a Web service deployed in an EJB container. This stateless session bean is also known as an EJB endpoint.

EJB Home Object

An EJB home object provides all lifecycle operations such as creating, finding, and removing an enterprise bean. All EJB home objects implement the EJBHome interface. JNDI is used to locate an EJB home object and a reference of the EJB home object is used to perform lifecycle operations by a client.

EJB JAR File

JAR archives file containing an EJB module.

EJB Module

A module with one or more enterprise beans and an EJB Deployment Descriptor.

EJB Server

A software providing services to an EJB container. For example, the transaction manager, which is a part of EJB server, helps in managing transactions within the EJB container.

EJB Server Provider

A vendor providing an EJB server.

Enterprise Information System

Enterprise Information System (EIS is an organized information system for an enterprise. A new application may require to be integrated with these EIS's. EIS is also known as legacy system.

EJB Invocation Model

EJB Invocation model tells us how to invoke Session and Entity beans from a Resource adapter.

Enterprise JavaBeans (EJB)

A JAVA EE component that implements a business entity and is hosted by an EJB container. EJB is used to develop object oriented, distributed, transactional, secure and scalable enterprise-level applications. They are of three types—Session, Entity, and Message-driven.

Enterprise JavaBeans Query Language (EJB QL)

Used to define queries for finder and select methods of an entity bean with CMP. EJB QL is portable across various containers and persistence managers.

Entity

An individual but distinct item that can be included in an XML document by referencing it. An entity reference may be a reference to an entire document, an external entity or a collection of DTD definitions.

Entity Bean

An Enterprise Java Bean (EJB) that represents persistent data maintained in a database. An Entity is a real-world object and an Entity Bean may correspond to any business object in the persistent state. In other words, an Entity is a table in a database and an instance of an Entity Bean represents a single row in the table.

External Entity

An entity residing in an external XML file and included in an XML document using an entity reference.

Event Handling

In Java, events are generated by objects, and when an event is fired, a specific method of the object (to be notified) is called. This method is then notified about the event and the event object is passed as parameter to that method. These methods are known as event handlers. The process of handling events is known as event handling.

Filter

A component that is invoked when a client requests a resource that the filter is mapped to, such as a URL pattern or a Servlet name. Normally, a filter is used to wrap and manipulate request, response, or header values before or after the execution of the original request target and does not itself return any response to the client.

FilterChain

An interface with one method, void doFilter (ServletRequest, ServletResponse). We can use this method for passing a request to the next component in the chain, which could be either another file or a chain.

Finder Method

A finder method is called through the CMP Entity Bean's Home interface. All finder methods are declared inside the Home interface of the Entity bean and they return a reference of the Entity bean matching an EJB QL query. All finder methods must declare that they throw FinderException.

Form-based Authentication

An authentication mechanism in which we can customize the user interface presented by the HTTP browser. This type of authentication is simple but not secure, as content is sent in the form of plain text and therefore exposes user names and passwords as a security threat. This authentication is not based on SSL.

Group

A set of users grouped together according to some common traits. All members of a group inherit all the roles assigned to that group.

Handle

An object used to identify an Enterprise bean. A client can serialize or de-serialize a handle and to get an Enterprise bean reference.

Handler Mapping

It is used for mapping incoming requests to the appropriate handlers.

Hibernate

A powerful, high-performance object/relational persistence and query service. Hibernate lets you develop persistent classes following the object-oriented standards of association, inheritance, polymorphism, composition, and collections.

HQL

Hibernate provides a very powerful language based on the relational object model. Hibernate Query Language (HQL) is an object-oriented extension to SQL. This bridges the gap between object-oriented systems and relational data sources.

HTML

HTML stands for Hypertext Markup Language. It is a markup language for hypertext documents hosted on the Internet. HTML enables the embedding of images, sounds, video streams, form fields, references to other objects with URLs, and basic text formatting.

HTTP

Stands for Hypertext Transfer Protocol. It is an Internet protocol used to send and receive hypertext object from a client to a server and vice versa.

HttpServletRequest

An HttpServletRequest object always represents a client's HTTP request. The HttpServletRequest object is primarily used to get request headers, parameters, and files or data sent by a client.

HttpServletResponse

The HttpServletResponse object helps set the content type of the response. It may also redirect an HTTP request to another URL.

HTTPHeaders

The HTTP headers are set by a client to give information to a server about the software that the client is using and how the client wants the server to send back the requested information.

HTTP Tunneling

A technique used by RMI system to get across firewalls by encapsulating RMI calls within an HTTP POST request.

HTTPS

HTTPS (Hypertext Transport Protocol Secure) is a protocol used for accessing a secure Web server.

IDL

Stands for Interface Definition Language. It is used to define interfaces to remote CORBA objects, which are platform and programming language independent.

IIOP

Stands for Internet Inter-ORB Protocol. It is a protocol used to communicate between CORBA object request brokers.

Impersonation

An act in which an entity assumes the identity and privileges of another entity. Impersonation can be defined as a case of simple delegation.

Implementing Web Services Specification (WSEE)

The WSEE specification introduces service architecture, packaging and deployment to make Web services portable on different Java EE application server implementations.

Introduction

An important concept by which you can add methods or fields to an existing object of an Advice class.

Initialization Parameter

A parameter that initializes the context associated with a Servlet.

Internationalization

The process of enabling a Web application to present different country and region specific formats without making any changes in the code or recompiling the application. The term is generally abbreviated as i18n, since there are 18 characters between the letters "i" and "n".

Inversion of Control (IoC) Container

The IoC container uses the dependency injection pattern or an inversion of the control pattern to handle the configuration management of application objects by using an assembler code.

Java EE

Java Platform, Enterprise Edition (Java EE) is a component-based technology, which simplifies enterprise application development and deployment. The JAVA EE platform consists of a set of services, application-programming interfaces (APIs) and protocols providing all the necessary functionality for developing multi-tiered, web-based applications.

Java EE Application

A Java EE application is a collection of Java EE modules. These modules can be for Web components (Servlets and JSPs), EJBs, connectors and other application clients. All these modules are combined to form an integrated enterprise application. A single archive file with the .ear extension represents a JavaEE application.

Java EE Component

A self-contained functional software unit supported by a container and configured at deployment time. The Java EE specification defines number of Java EE components such as application clients, applets, Java Servlets, JavaServer Pages (JSP) and Enterprise Java Beans (EJB). All Java EE components are written in Java programming language and assembled into a Java EE application.

Java EE Connector Architecture (JCA)

A Java-based technology solution for connecting Application servers and Enterprise Information System (EIS) as part of Enterprise Application Integration (EAI) solutions.

Java EE Product Provider

A vendor who supplies a JAVA EE product.

Java EE 5 SDK

A Java EE 5 SDK is a software development kit, required for running the Java EE 5 applications.

Java EE Server

The runtime environment required by a Java EE product is provided by the Java EE server. A Java EE server provides EJB or Web containers or both.

J2ME

An acronym for Java 2 Micro Edition (J2ME), J2ME is used to build applications for micro devices such as mobile phones pagers and digital set-top boxes.

J2SE

Acronym for Java 2 Standard Edition, J2SE is a set of APIs used for developing a variety of applications including standalone applications, applets and client applications.

JAR

Short for Java Archive, JAR is a platform-independent file format that permits many files to be aggregated into one file.

Java/XML Binding

The Java/XML binding defined by using JAXB 2.0 annotations in Java classes. Each Java class maps to a unique XML schema component depending on annotations of these Java classes.

Java API for XML Binding

The JAXB 2.0 specification helps to bind XML instances with Java classes.

Java API for XML based Web Services (JAX-WS)

A Java Web services specification that is used for deploying and invoking Web services. JAX-WS 2.0 server side facilities helps us deploy a Web service partially and JAX-WS 2.0 on the client side helps us in building a SOA-based client to consume or invoke a Web service.

Java API for XML Processing (JAXP)

JAXP enables applications to parse and transform XML documents using an API that is independent of a particular XML processor implementation. JAXP also provides a pluggability feature that enables applications to easily switch between XML processor implementations. JAXP facilitates the use of XML on the Java platform.

Java API for XML Registries (JAXR)

The Java API for XML Registries (JAXR) API provides a uniform and standard Java API for accessing different kinds of XML Registries.

JAXR Client

A client program accessing registry through the JAXR provider.

JAXR Provider

JAXR Provider is an implementation of JAXR API, which is used to access registeries such as UDDI or ebXML registry by the JAXR client.

Java/XML Type Mapping

Java/XML type mappings are implemented between an existing Java application and existing XML schema definitions of the developed application. This mapping is done by using user defined mappings between XML and Java. In this process, there is no generation of machine generated artifacts at runtime.

Java API for XML-based RPC (JAX-RPC)

The Java API for XML-based RPC (JAX-RPC) enables Java technology developers to build Web applications and Web services incorporating XML-based RPC functionality according to the SOAP (Simple Object Access Protocol) 1.1 specification.

Java Mail API

The Java Mail API provides a framework to build mail and messaging applications. This framework is both platform- and protocol- independent. All API classes and interfaces have been organized in the javax.mail package and its sub packages.

Java Mail Protocol

Mail protocols can be defined as a set of some rules, formats, and functions for exchanging messages between the components of a messaging system. The following are the five types of mail protocols:

- Simple Mail Transfer Protocol (SMTP)
- Post Office Protocol version 3 (POP3)
- Internet Message Access Protocol (IMAP3)
- Multipurpose Internet Mail Extensions (MIME)
- News Network Transport Protocol (NNTP)

Java Message Service (JMS)

An API used to invoke operations on enterprise messaging systems.

Java Persistence API (JPA)

JPA provides the POJO (Plain Old Java Objects) standard and Object Relational Mapping (ORM) for persistent data among the applications. The persistence deals with storing and retrieving the application data. A developer can program persistence using the Java Persistence API introduced in EJB 3.0.

Java Persistence Query Language (JPQL)

JPQL is the extended version of the EJB Query Language (EJB-QL), which operates on classes and objects (entities) available in the Java workspace.

Java Transaction API

The Java Transaction API (JTA) specifies standard Java interfaces between a transaction manager and the components involved in a distributed transaction system, such as the Resource manager and Resource adapter.

Java Transaction Service

Also known JTS, it is an implementation of transaction manager that supports JTA and implements Java mapping of the Object Management Group Object Transaction Service 1.1 specification.

Java Web Service

Web services present a model by which tasks of e-business processes are distributed widely through Internet. This model is not restricted to a specific business model. Web services are not graphical user interfaces but they can be used in software meant for user interaction.

JavaServer Faces

JavaServer Faces is a specification given by Java Community Process (JCP) in an attempt to standardize the way we develop Java Web applications and provide a set of rich and ready to use UI (User Interface) components.

JavaServer Faces UI Component

A user interface control that outputs data to a client or allows a user to input data to a JavaServer Faces application.

JavaServer Faces UI Component Class

A JavaServer Faces class that defines the behavior and properties of a JavaServer Faces UI component.

Java Server Faces HTML Tag Library

The JSF HTML tag library contains JavaServer Faces component tags for all UIComponent and HTML RenderKit Renderer combinations defined in the JavaServer Faces specification

JavaServer Faces Core Tag Library

The JSF core tag library contains tags for different JSF custom actions that are independent of the particular render kit. The JSF core tags can be categorized according to their usage in an application. For example, we have core tags to support event handling, to implement standard JSF validators and converters, and to create item(s) in a list.

JavaServer Faces Input Validation

JSF being a UI framework equips all input component classes and corresponding tags to handle validation of their values.

JavaServer Faces Type Conversion

JSF provides its own set of standard converters, to convert String values to Java types such as Integer, Boolean, Short and Double. These standard convertors can be registered with input as well as output UI components.

JavaServer Faces Page Navigation

A Web application is a collection of Web pages linked together in a particular sequence to solve a particular purpose, such as shopping. Clients need to go through these pages to perform a desired task and the Web developer has to implement the navigation logic to do so. JSF provides a simple way to configure all navigation rules declaratively in a single location that is in the faces-config.xml file.

JavaServer Pages (JSP)

A technology that combines the HTML/XML markup languages and elements of the Java programming language to return dynamic content to a Web client.

JavaServer Pages Standard Tag Library (JSTL)

A tag library that encapsulates core functionality common to many JSP applications. JSTL has support for common, structural tasks such as iteration and conditionals, tags for manipulating XML documents, internationalization and locale-specific formatting tags, SQL tags, and functions.

jBPM

jBPM is a business process management engine for the Java environment, which manages business processes by representing the process or the user interaction as nodes of the Seam application. The nodes represent the wait states, decisions, tasks, and Web pages.

JBoss Seam

JBoss Seam is an application framework for developing Java-based applications. This framework is used to create Web 2.0 applications by integrating technologies such as Java Server Faces (JSF) and Enterprise JavaBeans (EJB 3).

JDBC

JDBC stands for Java Database Connectivity. It is an API for connecting Java programs with different databases.

JNDI

JNDI stands for Java Naming and Directory Interface. JNDI provides a standard unified interface to different naming and directory services for Java applications.

Joinpoint

A point where an aspect describing information such as what the job of an aspect is, where to apply the aspect, and when to apply the aspect to be plugged in.

JSP Action

JSP actions are commands given to the JSP engine. They direct the engine to perform certain tasks during the execution of a page. These commands are: jsp:include, jsp:forward, jsp:useBean, jsp:setProperty, jsp:getProperty, jsp:plugin.

JSP Container

A container that provides the same services as a Servlet container and an engine that interprets and processes JSP pages into a Servlet.

JSP Declaration

A JSP scripting element used to declare methods and variables in a JSP page.

JSP Directive

JSP directive provides general information about a JSP page to the JSP engine. There are three types of directives, i.e. page, include and taglib.

JSP Element

A portion of a JSP page that is recognized by a JSP translator. JSP elements include directive, action, or a scripting element.

JSP Expression

A JSP expression tag contains a scripting language expression that is evaluated and converted to a String, and inserted where the expression appears in a JSP file. Because the value of an expression is converted to a String, you can use an expression within a text in a JSP file.

JSP Expression Language

The language used to write expressions to access the properties of JavaBeans components.

JSP Fragment

JSP fragments are portions of JSP code in an object represented by the JspFragment class that can be invoked as many times as needed. JSP fragments are configured either by specifying the <jsp:attribute> standard action in a tag file as a fragment type or as a body- content of a simple tag.

JSP Implicit Objects

JSP provides implicit objects encapsulating the functionality of classes such as HttpServletRequest, HttpServletResponse, and HttpSession that are often required in a JSP page.

JSP Model I Architecture

In JSP Model I architecture, the Web browser directly accesses the JSP pages of a Web container. The JSP pages interact with the JavaBeans of the Web container, which represent the application model.

JSP Model II Architecture

The JSP Model II architecture uses Servlets, which are positioned between the Web browser and JSP pages. The Servlets act as a controller to dispatch requests to the next JSP view, such as the URL, based on the client request and input parameters. The controller also decides which JSP page needs to be forwarded as a response, based on the client request. The JavaBean invokes the database server if data is needed from a database server.

JSP Page

A document having static text and JSP elements that describes how to process an incoming request and how to generate a response. A JSP page is translated into a Servlet and it handles requests as a Servlet.

JSP Scripting Element

The JSP scripting element enables us to insert Java code into a JSP page. Scripting elements are classified as Expressions, Scriptlets, and Declarations.

JSP Scriptlet

A JSP scripting element that contains a Java code fragment valid in the scripting language used in a JSP page.

JSP Tag File

Sources file containing a reusable fragment of JSP code that is translated into a tag handler when a JSP page is translated into a Servlet.

JSP Tag Library

A collection of custom tags described through a tag library descriptor and Java classes.

Keystore

A file that contains keys and certificates used for authentication.

LDAP

Short for Lightweight Directory Access Protocol, LDAP is a lightweight protocol for accessing directory services, specifically X.500-based directory services. LDAP runs over TCP/IP or other connection oriented transfer services and can play a vital role in networks of all sizes.

LDAP Server

The LDAP server is a directory server. There are varieties of LDAP servers such as the openLDAP server and Eudora's free LDAP server for Windows. The most popular LDAP server today is iPlanet's Directory server.

Lifecycle Management Model

The Lifecycle Management model comprises interfaces for managing the lifecycle of a resource adapter instance.

Message

In Java messaging, serving a message can be an asynchronous request, a report or an event that is created, sent and consumed by an enterprise application.

Message Consumer

An object that is created by a JMS session. It is used for receiving messages sent to a destination.

Message Producer

An object created by a JMS session. It is used for sending messages to a destination.

Message-driven Bean

Also known as MDB, it is an Enterprise Java Bean (EJB). Introduced in EJB 2.0, MDBs have been designed to handle asynchronous JMS messages, i.e. they behave as asynchronous message consumers. A message bean can be accessed by sending a message to the destination for which the bean is a message listener.

Method Permission

An authorization rule that determines who is permitted to execute one or more enterprise bean methods.

Mutual Authentication

An authentication mechanism employed by two parties for proving the identity of each other to one another.

NetBeans IDE

A rich-client architecture that provides various tools to develop different applications, such as the Web, Enterprise, Plug-in modules, and mobile applications in different languages including Java, C/C++ and Ruby. The NetBeans IDE is platform-independent and is compatible with Windows, Linux, UNIX and Solaris.

Namespace

A specification that lets you specify a unique label for the set of element names defined by a DTD.

Naming Service

The Naming Service enables you to create standard names for a given set of data. It is a software application that integrates a name and the location of information or services, which means that the software would use objects irrespective of where they are located. These objects need not necessarily lie in the local machine on which software is written, but they can be on any neighboring machine on the network.

Naming Context

A set of relation between unique, small, people-friendly identifiers and objects.

Notation

A mechanism for defining a data format for a non-XML document referenced as an unparsed entity and makes it easier to build a program to process XML data.

Object Relational Mapping (ORM)

ORM is a programming technique that is used for converting data between incompatible type systems in databases and Object-oriented programming languages. It is also known as O/RM, ORM, and O/R mapping. ORM involves mapping of an Object-oriented data to relational data.

Packaging

Packaging is the process of assembling components into modules, and modules into Enterprise or Web applications. The Java EE Web application is packaged in a WAR file and the Java EE Enterprise application is packaged in an EAR file. The WAR or EAR file is a compressed file containing code and configuration of an application. These files contain Java EE modules, which are deployed on an application server.

Parameter Entity

An entity that consists of DTD specifications, as distinct from a general entity. A parameter entity lets you reuse parts of a DTD in multiple places of an XLM file.

Parsed Entity

A general entity that contains XML and, therefore, is parsed when inserted into the XML document, as opposed to an unparsed entity.

Parser

Parser is a module that reads XML data from an input source and breaks it into chunks so that your program knows when the parser is working with a tag, an attribute, or element data. A non-validating parser ensures that the XML data is well-formed but does not verify its validity.

Passivation

The process of disassociating an instance of a stateful bean from the Objects related to an EJB.

Persistence

The protocol for transferring the state of an entity bean between its instance variables and an underlying database.

Pointcut

Many joinpoints are grouped together to make a pointcut where an advice may be executed. We know that in Spring, a joinpoint is always a method invocation. Therefore, we can say that a pointcut is a set of methods.

Port Component

The WSEE specification defines a port component as a component that is packaged and deployed on a container to implement a Web service.

Privilege

A security attribute that does not have the property of uniqueness and that can be shared by many security principals.

Prolog

The part of an XML document that precedes the XML data and contains a declaration that identifies the document as an XML document.

XML Processing Instruction

Processing instructions in an XML file gives commands or information to an application that is processing the XML data. Processing instructions are application-specific and are not meant for the XML parser. The parser acts as a medium to pass these instructions to the application.

Query String

A component of an HTTP request URL that contains a set of parameters and values that affect the handling of a request.

RAR

Stands for Resource Adapter Archive. It is a JAR archive that contains a Resource adapter module.

Realm

Realm is a database of users and groups used to identify valid users of a Web application.

Registry

Registry is a shared resource among number of different businesses to make B2B interaction possible in a flexible way and in the form of a Web-based service. In Web service architecture, registry plays a key role in publishing, finding and utilizing Web services.

Relationship Field

A virtual field of an entity bean having container-managed persistence. It identifies a related entity bean.

Remote Object

An implementation class that is placed out of the reach of a client. The RMI system helps clients to invoke the functionality of a remote object on the client side.

Remote Object Activation

With the introduction of Remote Object Activation, remote objects remain in the active state as long as they are used. When they are not required, they switch into the passive state.

Remove Method

This method is declared in the Home interface and it is called to destroy a bean.

Render Kit

A set of renderers that render output to a particular client. The JavaServer Faces implementation provides a standard HTML render kit, which is composed of renderers that can render HMTL markup.

Renderer

A Java class that can render the output for a set of JavaServer Faces UI components.

Resource Adapter

A Java EE component that is used to implement the connector architecture for a specific type of EIS. A resource adaptor enhances the communication between the Java EE application and the EIS used in the application. A resource adaptor is usually stored in a RAR file and it can also be deployed on any Java EE application server.

Resource Bundle

The ResourceBundle class provides the mechanism to separate user interface (UI) elements and other locale-sensitive data from the application logic. The ResourceBundle class is used to segregate localizable elements such as buttons, labels, error messages, and headings from the rest of the application. These localizable elements are bundled into a .properties file, known as resource bundle.

Resource Manager

The resource manager manages a group of EIS resources that are sharable. The resource manager may be transactional and participate in transactions. In connector architecture, a resource manager may have two types of clients—a client tier application or a middle-tier application server. The resource manager and clients are located on different machines.

ResultSet Object

This is an interface packaged in the `java.sql` package provided by the JDBC core API. The java.sql.ResultSet interface is used to represent the data in tabular form, which is generated by executing an SQL query. It implies that a ResultSet object is a table of data returned by executing an SQL query. A ResultSet object encapsulates the resultant tabular data obtained when a query is executed. A ResultSet object holds zero or more objects where each object represents one row that may span over one or more table columns.

RowSet Object

The RowSet interface contains JavaBean properties, which allow a RowSet object to be configured and connected to the JDBC data source. Each RowSet object inherits the ResultSet interface and therefore has its capabilities. Therefore, RowSet objects contain a set of rows from a ResultSet or some other tabular data source, such as file or spreadsheet.

Seam Component

Seam components are POJO components used in the Seam framework. The components are simply JavaBeans or Enterprise JavaBeans (EJB 3).

Seam Context

Seam context holds the association between EJBs with Seam components and provides a naming convention context for developing a stateful Web application.

RMI

Acronym for Remote Method Invocation, RMI can be used to invoke methods on remote Java objects.

RMI-IIOP

The new version of RMI for IIOP (Internet Inter-ORB Protocol) that combines RMI's easy programming features with CORBA's interoperability.

Rollback

The point in a transaction when all updates to any resources involved in the transaction are reversed.

Root

The outermost element in an XML document. It is the element that contains all other sub elements.

Secure Socket Layer (SSL)

A technology that provides secure Internet communications for Web browsers and Web servers.

Security Role

An abstract name associated with the resources in an application. This name is used to access user-specific resources in an application. The roles defined in an application server are generally referred to as keys used to open locks.

Servlet

A simple Java program, which is executed on the server and generates dynamic content using Java technology. The dynamic content is normally HTML, though it may also be XML. A Java Servlet is capable of maintaining a state among server transactions. A Web container in a Web server is responsible for managing the lifecycle of the Servlet.

Serialization

Serialization enables Java objects to be transmitted between address spaces by converting the objects into byte streams.

Servlet Container

A part of a Web server that provides all the necessary services to a Servlet and manages the lifecycle of the Servlet.

Servlet Context

A Servlet context provides information about the environment of a Servlet where it is running. Using the context, a Servlet can log events, obtain URL references to resources, and set and store attributes, which other Servlets in the context can use.

Servlet Collaboration

Communication between Servlets usually by sharing some information.

Servlet Endpoint

The Service implementation bean, which when implemented as a servlet class, is known as servlet endpoint.

Servlet Events

Servlet events are events describing the lifecycle of Servlets. These events can be of different types, such as request, session, or application level events.

Service Oriented Architecture (SOA)

SOA is an architecture for distributed/parallel computing, which depends on the request-response design model of synchronous and asynchronous applications.

Service Endpoint Interface (SEI)

SEI is a key artifact in a port component deployed on an application server.

Service Implementation Bean (SIB)

WS-Metadata 2.0 specifies some conditions on Java class to deploy it as a Web service. The Java class that satisfies these conditions is known as SIB.

Servlet Mapping

Defines the association between a URL pattern and a Servlet. This type of mapping is used to map requests to Servlets.

Session

An uninterrupted series of request-response interactions between a client and a server. A session is used to track a user's interaction with a Web application across multiple HTTP requests.

Session Bean

An enterprise bean created by a client and usually exists only for the duration of a single client server session. A session bean performs operations, such as calculations or database access, for the client.

SGML

Acronym for Standard Generalized Markup Language—the parent of both HTML and XML.

Simple API for XML

Simple API for XML (SAX) is an alternative to DOM, and can be used to parse XML documents. SAX is based on the streaming model.

Skeleton

The RMI system generates a skeleton instance (helper class) to communicate between a Java object and a stub instance via the RMI protocol. The skeleton instance reads the arguments of a method call, makes a method call to the remote service implementation class, accepts the return value, and finally writes the return value on the stub instance.

SOAP

Stands for Simple Object Access Protocol. It is a lightweight protocol intended for exchanging structured information in a decentralized, distributed environment. It defines, using XML technologies, an extensible messaging framework containing a message construct that can be exchanged over a variety of underlying protocols.

SOAP with Attachments API for Java (SAAJ)

The basic package for SOAP messaging. SAAJ contains an Attachment API for creating and populating a SOAP message.

SOAP Fault

If you send a message which is not up to SOAP standards, you will get a response message having the SOAPFault element. The SOAPFault element gives details about the problem. There should be only one SOAP fault element per message. A SOAPFault object may consist of four elements: Fault code, Fault string, Fault actor, and Detail object.

SOCKS Protocol

A networking proxy protocol that allows working with any Internet service through a chain of SOCKS or HTTP proxies to hide the real IP address.

Spring

A layered Java/JAVA EE-based framework that introduces a simple approach to develop an application easily, with reduced testing cost and improved quality. Spring supports IoC and AOP features that ease the application development.

Spring Core Module

The Spring Core module is the most fundamental functionality of the Spring framework that provides an IoC container.

Spring AOP Module

A module that allows us to implement concerns or aspects in a Spring application. These concerns are transaction management, logging and failure monitoring.

Spring DAO Module

The Spring Data Access Object (DAO) package in the Spring framework provides excellent DAO support. It is achieved by using technologies such as JDBC, Hibernate or JDO. DAO provides a JDBC abstraction layer that removes the need of tedious JDBC coding and the JDBC package provides programmatic as well as declarative transaction management classes. The Spring DAO package supports heterogeneous Java Database Connectivity and O/R mapping that makes it easier for Spring to work with several data access technologies such as JDBC and Hibernate.

Spring Web MVC Module

Spring's MVC module provides a Model-View-Controller (MVC) implementation for constructing Web applications. It provides a clean separation between Model code and Web forms (or view) code. In Spring MVC implementation, a request goes through many components, such as the DispatcherServlet class, handler mappings, controllers, ModelAndView object, ViewResolver objects and views (Web pages).

Spring Web Flow Module

The Spring Web Flow module is an extension of the Spring Web MVC module. The Spring Web MVC framework provides form controllers such as the SimpleFormController and AbstractWizardFormController classes to implement a predefined workflow. Spring Web Flow helps in defining an XML file or a Java class that manages the workflow between different pages of a Web application similar to a wizard.

Stateful Session Bean

A Session bean with a conversational state.

Stateless Session Bean

A Session bean with no conversational state. All instances of a stateless Session bean are identical.

System Contracts

System contracts enable the Resource adapter to link services to manage connections, transactions, and security with the application server

Streaming API for XML (StAX)

The StAX 1.0 specification is a joint effort of BEA and Sun Microsystems. The StAX API allows programmers to perform iterative and event-based processing of XML documents.

Stub

The Stub class resides on the server and is transmitted to a client whenever a reference to a remotely accessible object is established. This is the actual object that the client interacts with. The stub object delegates all method calls across the network to their corresponding skeleton objects on the server.

Tag

A piece of text that describes a unit of data or an element in XML documents. The tag is distinguishable as a markup, as opposed to data, because it is surrounded by angle brackets (< and >). To treat such markup syntax as data, you use an entity reference or a CDATA section.

Tag Handler

A tag handler is a Java class where a custom tag is defined. The Web container invokes the tag handler object to evaluate a custom tag during the execution of a JSP page.

Classic Tag Handler

A classic tag handler is a Java class that implements the Tag, IterationTag, or BodyTag interface, and is a mechanism to evaluate custom tags. The JSP page implementation class instantiates a tag handler object, or reuses an existing tag handler object for each action in the JSP page. The handler object is responsible for the interaction between the JSP page and additional server-side objects.

Simple Tag Handler

A simple tag handler is a Java class that implements the SimpleTag interface. A simple tag handler should have a no-argument constructor.

Tag Library Descriptor (TLD)

An XML document that describes a tag library.

Target object

The object that is being advised is called the target object. The target may be referred as an object you write or a third-party object that you want to add for providing a custom behavior.

Transaction

A small unit of work that modifies data. A transaction encloses one or more program statements, all of which either complete or roll back. Transactions enable multiple users to access the same data concurrently.

Transaction Attribute

A value specified in an Enterprise bean's Deployment Descriptor that is used by the EJB container to control the transaction scope when the enterprise bean's methods are invoked. A transaction attribute can have the following values: Required, RequiresNew, Supports, NotSupported, Mandatory, or Never.

Transaction Isolation Level

The degree to which the intermediate state of the data being modified by a transaction is visible to other concurrent transactions and the data being modified by other transactions is visible to it.

Transaction Manager

Provides the services and management functions required to support transaction demarcation, transactional resource management, synchronization, and transaction context propagation.

Tool Provider

Provides tools for developing, assembling and deploying Web applications through component providers, assemblers, and deployers.

UML

Stands for Unified Modeling Language. It is used for graphical representation of a set of elements related to an application.

UML Symbols

UML uses diagrams to represent Object-Oriented systems. There are particular shapes and symbols that represent different states and roles in a software system.

UML Diagrams

A UML diagram lets developers and customers view a software system from a different perspective and in varying degrees of abstraction.

URI

Stands for Uniform Resource Identifier. It is a string that identifies any resources. It is a super set of URL and URN.

URL

Stands for Uniform Resource Locator. These are the common Internet protocols, such as HTTP and FTP.

URN

Stands for Uniform Resource Name. It is a unique identifier that identifies a resource but does not specify how to access the resource.

View Resolver

ViewResolver is an interface used for resolving views by name. It is used for providing a mapping of actual views and view names. The state of view cannot be changed during the running of an application. In Spring, views are addressed by a view name and resolved by a view resolver.

WAR File

Stands for Web Application Archive file. A WAR file is a JAR archive that contains a Web module.

Weaving

Weaving is a process that applies aspects to a target object to create AOP proxy objects. This process can be performed at compile time, load time, and the runtime stage of the target object.

Web Application

An application developed for the Internet that includes JSP, Servlet, CGI, and Perl.

Web Component

A component that provides services in response to requests; can be either a Servlet or a JSP page.

Web Container

A container that manages the execution of JSP pages and Servlets. It serves as a runtime environment for a Web application. JSP and Servlets are known as Web components.

Web Container Provider

A vendor that supplies a Web container.

Web Module

A deployable unit that consists of one or more Web components, other resources, and a Web application Deployment Descriptor contained in a hierarchy of directories and files in a standard Web application format.

Web Service

A Web service can be described as a collection of various standards and sets of protocols that are used for transferring data from one application to another. A Web service can be used by any application running on any platform and developed in any language. In other words, it is a software component that may be described in WSDL and can be accessed using a standard protocol.

Workflow Management Model

In the Workflow Management model, the Resource adapter can do work by submitting Work instances to an Application server for execution. This is done by Workflow management, which specifies a contract between an Application server and a Resource adapter.

Web Service Description Language (WSDL)

WSDL is an IDL on the basis of which SOA components can easily communicate with each other. It is a standard language to write guidelines for communicating with a component.

Web Services Metadata (WS-MetaData)

The WS-Metadata 2.0 API provides annotations that are used to develop and deploy Web services on Java SE 6 and Java EE 5 platforms. This API simplifies the development, deployment, and invocation of Web services.

XHTML

XHTML is Extensible Hypertext Mark-up Language and a hybrid of XML and HTML. XHTML can be parsed by any language with an XML parser.

XML

Short for Extensible Markup Language, XML is a universal syntax for describing and structuring data independent from the application logic. XML can be used to define unlimited languages for specific industries and applications.

XML Schema

XML schema is nothing but Metadata. The XML schema holds all the information of the XML file, including tags that are exchanged to and from other XML files.

XSLT

XSLT stands for XSL Transformations. XSLT is yet another popular W3C specification that defines XML-based syntax used to transform XML documents to any other text format, such as HTML or XML.

Index

@

P

Q

R

S

T

X